| | |
|---|---|
| **Editor** | Jonathan E. Benjamin |
| **Assistant Editor** | Lynley A. Ogilvie |
| | |
| **Publishing Manager** | Mark D. Selwyn |
| **Managing Editors** | Alice K. Ma |
| | Andrea Piperakis |
| **Production/Communications Coordinator** | Nathanael Joe Hayashi |

**Researcher/Writers:**

| | |
|---|---|
| *Northern Greece, Central Greece, Sporades,* | |
| *Northeast Aegean, Ionian Islands* | Maria Vassiliki Balodimas |
| *Dodecanese, Cyclades, Peloponnese* | Alix Cooper |
| *Mediterranean Coast, Central Turkey, Eastern* | |
| *Turkey, Black Sea Coast* | Can Gürel |
| *Crete, Dodecanese, Cyprus* | Todd Harris |
| *Athens, Central Greece, Cyclades,* | |
| *Peloponnese* | Penelope Cecilia Papailias |
| *Northwestern Turkey, Turkish Aegean Coast* | John Carlson |
| | Mona Yacoubian-Carlson |

| | |
|---|---|
| **Advertising Manager** | Kimberley Harris |
| **Advertising Representatives** | Kelly Ann McEnaney |
| | Charles Emmit Ryan |
| | |
| **Legal Counsel** | Harold Rosenwald |

GH00500374

# About Let's Go

In 1960, Harvard Student Agencies, a three-year-old nonprofit corporation established to provide employment opportunities to Harvard and Radcliffe students, was doing a booming business selling charter flights to Europe. One of the extras HSA offered passengers on these flights was a 20-page mimeographed pamphlet entitled *1960 European Guide,* a collection of tips on continental travel compiled by the staff at HSA. The following year, Harvard and Radcliffe students traveling to Europe made notes and researched the first full-fledged edition of *Let's Go: Europe,* a pocket-sized book with a smattering of tips on budget accommodations, irreverent write-ups of sights, and a decidedly youthful slant. The first editions proclaimed themselves to be helpmates to the "adventurous and often pecunious student." Throughout the sixties, the series reflected its era: A section of the 1968 *Let's Go: Europe* was entitled "Street Singing in Europe on No Dollars a Day"; the 1969 guide to America led off with a feature on drug-ridden Haight Ashbury.

During the seventies, *Let's Go* gradually became a large-scale operation, adding regional guides to parts of Europe and slowly expanding into North Africa and nearby Asia. In 1981, *Let's Go: USA* returned after an eight-year hiatus, and in the next year HSA joined forces with its current publisher, St. Martin's Press. Since then, the series has continually blossomed; the additions of *Let's Go: Pacific Northwest, Western Canada, and Alaska* and *Let's Go: California and Hawaii* in 1988 brought the the the total numbers of titles to eleven.

Each spring, over 150 Harvard students compete for some 70 positions as *Let's Go* researcher/writers. An editorial staff of 14 carefully reads stacks of 10-page applications and conducts thorough interviews. Those hired possess a rare combination of budget travel sense, writing ability, stamina, and courage. Each researcher/writer travels on a shoestring budget for seven weeks, researching and writing seven days per week, and mailing back their copy to Cambridge—about 500 pages in six installments. Train strikes, grumpy proprietors, noisy hostels, irate tourist officials are all in a day's work, but sometimes things become more serious. The afflictions of the summer of 1988 included one tear gassing, two totaled cars, one concussion, one near-drowning, and, in the most bizarre tale to date, one researcher/writer was chased up a tree by a pack of reindeer.

Back in a cluttered basement in Harvard Yard, an editorial staff of 25 and countless typists and proofreaders spend four months poring over more than 50,000 pages of manuscript as they push the copy through 12 comprehensive stages of intensive editing. In September the collected efforts of the summer are converted from computer diskette to nine-track tapes and delivered to Com Com in Allentown, Pennsylvania, where their computerized typesetting equipment turns them into books in record time. And even before the books hit the stands, the next year's editions are well underway.

# ACKNOWLEDGMENTS

Sing in me, Muse, and through me tell truly
of that man skilled in all ways of surviving
the wanderer, harried for years on end . . .

Thus did Homer begin *The Odyssey,* invoking to Parnassos to recount the trials of that great budget traveler from Ithaki. Now Homer's work is all right (beach reading, maybe), but he left out the food and accommodations listings. This book, then, is an attempt to do the blind bard one better. In this noble mission, Alix withstood the Scylla of deadlines and the Charybdis of Dodecanese ferry connections, but succumbed to felicitous felines and stuffed tomatoes. John and Mona captured in ink the mystique of western Anatolia, revivifying the ruins of bygone empires but witnessing the decline of mass transit. Trailblazing through an itinerary designed like a $\epsilon$, Maria conquered the land of Alexander, leaving forlorn would-be suitors in her dusty wake. Todd, a mopedalist *par excellence,* dogged tour buses and international intrigue in search of the perfect hospital listing. Unraveling the hazy shroud of eastern Turkey was a Herculean task that only the intrepid Can could achieve, although admittedly we were ready to administer last rites. And Penelope, a true Hellene with blood thickened by Zen, focused for us the previously blurry isle of the Pelops.

But how, O Muse, can I do justice to my fellow sufferers of the subterranean homesick blues? The ancient Chinese sage Chuang Tzu once wrote "pleasant rooms and sandy beaches make fine prose." Determined to uphold this dictum (which may have lost something in the translation), we attacked our work with an unbeatable lineup. Pip, codifier of the all-powerful format, cool hand and warm-hearted Mark, and Computer Guru (and Messiah-at-Large) Joe all walked on water for me. Dave warded off the evil spirits of stress, while Jamey, Steve, Alex, and Andy indulged me in nocturnal wackiness and bizarre esoterica. Red penning, dish washing, and other monotony were sweetened by Kay, with help from one chunky monkey. Yet this book would never have happened if not for Lynley, whom I hereby nominate to be Olympian goddess of competence. She reined me in when exploring the far reaches of incomprehensibility, and then sent me reeling with her risqué marginalia. Yes Lynley, there is an anti-Christ.

The proverbial "little people" were more like Titans in their support. Chris W., our nonresident archeologist Cyrian Broodbank, Penelope's aunt Kiki, Bern, the bartender at Charlie's, Mikey, Zeus, the inventor of the chicken jumbo (no pickles), Colin, Julio, and Mary and Pier, who graciously allowed me to escape the Cantab heat. I hope that one copy of this book is used by my family. My folks, Billy, and Danny each helped nurture in me a hunger for travel and a love for writing. Finally, if I were Paris and this book a golden apple, I would give it to Ellen, who far outshines Hera, Athena, and Aphrodite.

—JEB

# CONTENTS

viii      **Contents**

x    **Contents**

# LET'S GO: GREECE

## (including Cyprus and Turkey)

## General Introduction

| | |
|---|---|
| US$1 = 152.15dr | 100dr = US$0.66 |
| CDN$1 = 126.13dr | 100dr = CDN$0.79 |
| UK£1 = 257.06dr | 100dr = UK£0.39 |
| AUS$1 = 121.95dr | 100dr = AUS$0.82 |
| NZ$1 = 100.69dr | 100dr = NZ$.99 |

---

**A Note on Prices**

Throughout the guide, we quote *drachma* prices effective in the summer of 1988. Note that prices are listed in *drachmae* (dr) for Greece, U.S. dollars for Turkey (because the relative value of the Turkish *lira* (TL) fluctuated so dramatically in 1988), and Cypriot pounds (£) for Cyprus. All dollar signs ($) refer to U.S. dollars unless otherwise specified.

---

## Planning Your Trip

Greece is truly the budget traveler's paradise. The charm of the villages, the aura of the ancient past, and the "joie de vivre" of the people create a country rich in culture and personality. Greece's striking natural scenery ranges from the mountains of Thessaly to the caves and gorges of Crete. Ancient temples stand in stony silence on promontories and huge monasteries cling precariously to sheer cliff walls. Numerous islands pepper the Aegean Sea and offer fast-paced nightlife, as well as the peace and solitude of secluded ocean retreats.

The Greeks embrace visitors with sincere warmth and hospitality. Some may offer their services as personal guides of their town or region, or invite you to sit with them for food and drinks. While you're in Greece, make an effort to adjust to the Greek way of life: If you speak a little Greek and show an interest in the culture, you'll come away with a real "Greek experience," and not just another tourist diary.

The General Introduction to this book is divided into four sections. *Planning Your Trip* lists useful information on passports, visas, customs, money, insurance, and identification. *Getting There* covers travel options for getting to Greece, while *Once There* provides information on tourist services, accommodations, and travel within Greece. The *Life in Greece* section provides background material on the history, culture, and language of the country. For information specific to Cyprus and Turkey, refer to their respective introductions.

Once you arrive, *Let's Go* can help you settle into unfamiliar territory. For smaller cities, we highlight sights and entertainment first, then provide information on the basics, including tourist offices, accommodations, and food. For larger cities, each topic receives a special heading: *Orientation and Practical Information* describes the geographic location of the city and the various services available for visitors; *Accommodations and Camping* lists locations and prices of hostels, budget hotels, and

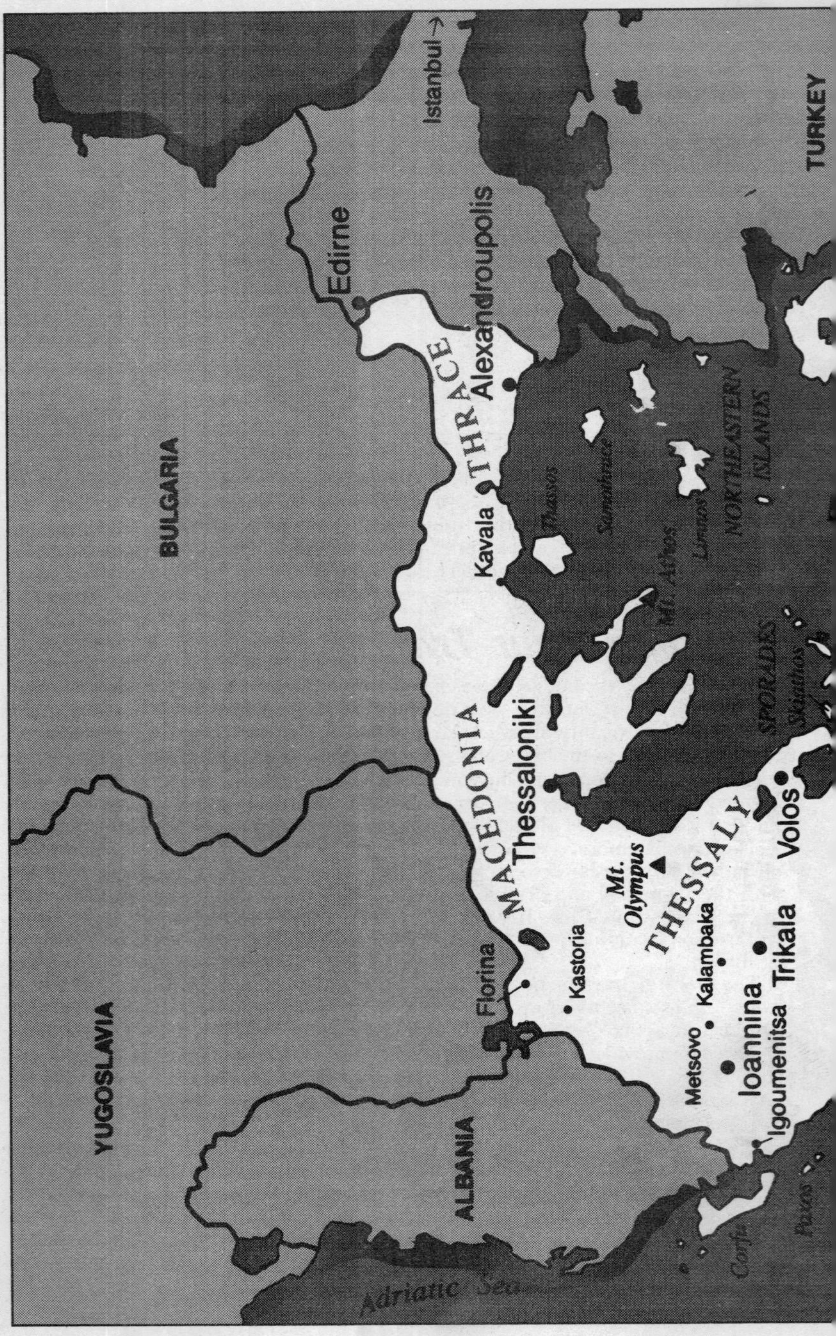
BULGARIA
YUGOSLAVIA
ALBANIA
TURKEY
Istanbul→
Edirne
Alexandroupolis
THRACE
Kavala
Thassos
Samothrace
Limnos
NORTHEASTERN ISLANDS
Mt. Athos
MACEDONIA
Thessaloniki
SPORADES
Skiathos
Mt. Olympus
THESSALY
Volos
Trikala
Kalambaka
Ioannina
Metsovo
Igoumenitsa
Kastoria
Florina
Corfu
Paxos
Adriatic

campgrounds; *Food* includes a selection of restaurants, student cafes, and open-air markets; *Sights* explores the major attractions and offerings of the city; and *Entertainment* describes the nightlife, cultural events, and festivals.

---

**A Note on Dates**

Let's Go uses the terminology B.C.E. (Before Common Era) and C.E. (Common Era), which are the equivalents of B.C (Before Christ) and A.D. (Anno Domini).

---

For a successful trip, plan ahead. Tourism in Greece is *big* business, and the amount of travel information available on the subject is astounding. Stop by your local travel agency or library for scenic reviews of the country, peruse *Useful Organizations and Publications* below, and talk to people who have recently traveled to the places that interest you. A few hours of letter writing and phone calling will yield a deluge of pamphlets and maps.

Consider writing an itinerary. Even if discarded upon arrival, it will force you to think about priorities. Do you travel to see the sights or to meet people? To abandon civilization or learn about a particular culture? Don't be afraid to improvise—traveling should be a vacation, not a chore. The urge to see and do everything often gets the better of travelers; remember that blitzing Athens in one day or the islands in a one-week cruise isn't seeing Greece. Instead of hopping from one capital to the next, spend a few days in the countryside. *Kalo Taxidhi!*

## When to Go

Summer is the high tourist season in Greece; if you visit between late May and early September, expect to meet other travelers almost everywhere you go. Prices, especially for accommodations and transportation, increase as availability decreases. If you feel stifled by crowds or taxed by the frantic pace of summer travel, consider visiting during the off-season (Sept.-May), when inexpensive airfares are easier to obtain and accommodation costs are lower. Although some facilities and sights close down, locals may be more receptive to you and the weather more pleasant, especially during May or September. Even during the winter months, some areas continue to be mild. Greece also has winter sports, with ski areas at Parnassos, Mt. Pelion, Metsovo, and elsewhere.

## Useful Organizations and Publications

Below, you'll find a list of tourist offices and private agencies that offer useful services for the budget traveler and can provide further information on travel abroad.

**Council on International Educational Exchange (CIEE)**, 205 E. 42nd St., New York, NY 10017 (tel. (212) 661-0311; for charter flights (800) 223-7402; in New York (212) 661-1450). This is the main office for inquiries by mail and telephone. Sells Eurail and Eurail Youth passes, issues hostel cards, charts European flights at discount fares, and provides information on educational and work opportunities. Distributes all discount travel cards, as well as the **International Student Identity Card (ISIC)**. Their annual *Student Travel Catalog* is free at any CIEE office (or send $1 for postage and handling). Also available is the book *Work, Study and Travel Abroad: The Whole World Handbook* ($8.95 plus $1 postage).

**Educational Travel Centre (ETC)**, 438 N. Frances St., Madison, WI 53703 (tel. (608) 256-5551). Provides flight information, IYHF cards, and Eurail/BritRail passes. If you mention that you are a *Let's Go* reader, ETC will send you a free copy of *Taking Off*, their travel newspaper.

**Forsyth Travel Library**, 9154 W. 57th St., P.O. Box 2975, Shawnee Mission, KS 66201 (tel. (913) 384-3440 or (800) FOR-SYTH). Forsyth's mail-order service stocks a wide range of city, area, and country maps, as well as guides for rail and boat travel in Europe. They are the sole North American distributor of the *Thomas Cook Continental Timetables* for trains, which covers all of Europe and Britain ($18.95 including postage). Write or call for their free catalog.

**Greek Consulates,** 2441 Gough St., San Francisco, CA 94123 (tel. (415) 775-2102); 168 N. Michigan Ave., 6th floor, Chicago, IL 60601 (tel. (312) 782-1084); 2318 International Trade Mart Bldg., New Orleans, LA 70130 (tel. (504) 523-1167); Park Square Bldg., 31 St. James Ave., Boston, MA 02116 (tel. (617) 542-3240); 69 E. 79th St., New York, NY 10021 (tel. (212) 988-5500); 100 University Ave., #1004, Toronto, Ont., M5G 1V6; 1010 Sherbrooke St. W., #204, Montréal PQ, Québec H3A 2R7 (tel. (514) 845-8127); 890 One Bentall Center, 501 Burrard St., Vancouver, British Columbia V6Z 2C7 (tel. (604) 681-1381).

**Greek Embassies:** 2221 Massachusetts Ave. NW, Washington, DC 20008 (tel. (202) 667-3168). In Canada, 80 MacLaren St., Ottawa, Ont., K2P OK6 (tel. (613) 238-6271 ext. 3).

**Greek National Tourist Organization (GNTO),** Head Office, Olympic Tower, 645 Fifth Ave., 5th floor, New York, NY 10022 (tel. (212) 421-5777); 168 N. Michigan Ave., Chicago, IL 60601 (tel. (312) 782-1084); 611 W. 6th St. #1998, Los Angeles, CA 90017 (tel. (213) 626-6696). In Canada, 1233 Rue de la Montagne, #101, Montréal, Québec H3G 1Z2 (tel. (514) 871-1535); 68 Scollard St. Lower Level Unit "E," Toronto, Ont. M5R 1G2 (tel. (416) 968-2220). In Australia and New Zealand, P.O. Box R203, 51-57 Pitt. St., Sydney, N.S.W. 2000 (tel. (02) 241 16 63). In Britain, 195-197 Regent St., London WIR 8DL (tel. (01) 734 59 97). Provides general information, including pamphlets on different regions and other tourist literature. Ask for the booklet *General Information About Greece.*

**Greek Press and Information Office,** 601 Fifth Ave., New York, NY 10017 (tel. (212) 751-8788); 2211 Massachusetts Ave., Washington, DC 20008 (tel. (202) 332-2727). In Canada, 80 MacLaren St., Ottawa, Ont. K2P OK6 (tel. (613) 232-6796). Provides information on work, cultural offerings, and political and economic development in Greece.

**John Muir Publications,** P.O. Box 613, Santa Fe, NM 87504 (tel. (505) 982-4078). Publishes books by veteran traveler Rick Steves, including the helpful *Europe through the Back Door* ($12.95).

**Let's Go Travel Services:** Harvard Student Agencies, Inc., Thayer Hall-B, Harvard University, Cambridge, MA 02138 (tel. (617) 495-9649). HSA sells ISICs, American Youth Hostel (AYH) memberships, FIYTO cards for non-students, Eurail, BritRail, and France Vacances passes, transatlantic charter flights, travel guides (including the entire *Let's Go* series), and a line of travel gear—all available on the spot. ISIC, AYH, FIYTO cards also available by mail. Call or write for their "Bag of Tricks" discount and information packet.

**Superintendent of Documents:** U.S. Government Printing Office, Washington DC 20402. Publishes many useful travel-related booklets, including *Your Trip Abroad* ($1).

**Travel CUTS (Canadian Universities Travel Service):** 187 College St., Toronto, Ont. M5T 1P7 (tel. (416) 979-2406). Other offices in Burnaby, Calgary, Edmonton, Halifax, Montréal, Ottawa, Quebec, Saskatoon, Toronto, Vancouver, Victoria, and Winnipeg. Offers discounted transatlantic flights from Canadian cities with special student fares. Sells the ISIC, FIYTO, and IYHF hostel cards, and discount travel passes such as Transalpino, Eurotrain, Eurailpass and Eurail Youth Pass. Canadian Work Abroad Program for ages 18-25. *The Canadian Student Traveler* is available free at all offices and campuses across Canada.

## Documents and Formalities

The following section includes information on passports and other forms of identification needed for travel to Greece. Remember to file all applications early—several weeks or even months before your planned departure date: A backlog at the Passport Agency could spoil even the best laid plans. It's a good idea for travelers to carry two forms of identification and at least one other photo; banks, in particular, require more than one ID before cashing traveler's checks, and having two IDs will expedite the processing of a new passport if the need arises. Remember to carry your address book listing emergency phone numbers and contacts.

### Passports

Citizens of the U.S., Canada, Great Britain, Australia, and New Zealand all need valid passports to enter Greece and to reenter their respective countries. *Carry your passport with you at all times.* If you plan on an extended stay, you may want to register your passport with the nearest embassy or consulate; notify them or the local police immediately if your passport is lost or stolen while traveling. Your consulate will be able to issue you a new passport or temporary traveling papers in such an emergency.

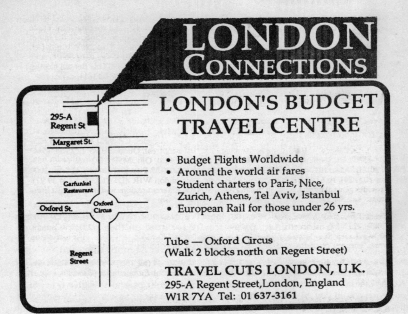

**LONDON CONNECTIONS**

## LONDON'S BUDGET TRAVEL CENTRE

295-A
Regent St

Margaret St.

Garfunkel
Restaurant

Oxford St.    Oxford
              Circus

Regent
Street

- Budget Flights Worldwide
- Around the world air fares
- Student charters to Paris, Nice, Zurich, Athens, Tel Aviv, Istanbul
- European Rail for those under 26 yrs.

Tube — Oxford Circus
(Walk 2 blocks north on Regent Street)

**TRAVEL CUTS LONDON, U.K.**
295-A Regent Street,London, England
W1R 7YA Tel: 01 637-3161

If you are a **U.S. citizen,** you may apply for a passport, good for 10 years (5 years if you are under 18), at any office of the **U.S. Passport Agency** (11 nation-wide), or at one of the several thousand federal or state courthouses or post offices authorized to accept passport applications. If your current passport is not more than 12 years old *and* it was issued after your sixteenth birthday, you may renew your passport either by mail or in person. (Those between the ages of 13 and 18 must apply in person.) The renewal charge is $35 ($20 for those 16 or 17 years old).

All **new** passport applications must be taken in person; your passport will be mailed to you. Parents must apply on behalf of children under 13 years of age. With your application, you must submit the following: (1) proof of U.S. citizenship (a certified copy of your birth certificate, naturalization papers, or a previous passport not more than 8 years old); (2) one piece of ID bearing your signature and either your photo or your description, such as a driver's license; (3) two identical photographs (2" square on a white background) taken not more than six months before the application date; and (4) the passport fee. Fees for new passports are $42 for adults, $27 if you are under 18. Write your date of birth on the check and photocopy the data page for your personal records. Normal processing usually takes about two weeks if you apply in person at the Passport Agency, often much longer if you apply at a courthouse or post office; file your application as early as possible. If you wish, you may pay for express-mail return of your passport. If you have proof of departure within five working days (e.g. an air ticket), the Passport Agency provides a rush service while you wait; be sure to arrive in the office by 2pm. For further information, call the Washington Passport Agency at (202) 738-8200, ext. 5, or write to the Bureau of Consular Affairs, CA/PA, Department of State, #5807, Washington, DC 20524 (tel. (202) 523-1355).

If you are a **Canadian citizen,** you may apply by mail for a five-year, renewable passport from the **Passport Office,** Department of External Affairs, Ottawa, Ont. KIA OG3, or in person from one of their 20 regional offices. With your application, you must submit: (1) evidence of Canadian citizenship (an old passport does *not* suffice as proof); and (2) two identical photographs. Your identity must be certified on your application by a "guarantor," someone who has known you for at least two years and who falls into one of a number of categories listed on the application, including medical doctor, police officer, lawyer, mayor, or notary public. Currently, the passport fee is CDN$25. The Passport Office recommends that you apply during the winter off-season if possible. You will receive much faster service if you apply in person—usually about a week—than if you apply by mail. If a passport is lost abroad, Canadians *must* be able to prove citizenship with another document or a new one will not be issued. More complete information can be found in the brochure *Canada Passport* and in the booklet *Bon Voyage, But—*, both free from the Passport Office.

**Australian citizens** must apply in person at their local post office or at a Passport Office (usually located in the provincial capitals). The passport fee is AUS$66 (valid for 10 years); AUS$27 if you are under 18 (good for 5 years). All children must have passports, including infants. For more complete information, consult your local post office.

**New Zealanders** *must visit or write the* **Office of Internal Affairs** in Wellington or their local district office to file an application. The passport fee is NZ$50 (valid for 10 years); the office will provide speedy processing if you need a passport in an emergency. Children up to age 16 may be included on their parent's passport.

Losing your passport can be a nightmare: A replacement may take weeks to be processed, your new passport will probably be valid for a limited time, and any visas will be irretrievably lost. To expedite replacement of your passport if it is lost or stolen, make a photocopy of it showing its number and date and place of issuance. Keep this information in a location separate from your passport or give it to someone with whom you will be traveling. In the event that your passport is lost or stolen, notify your embassy/consulate and the local police immediately. To replace the passport, you'll need to prove your identity and citizenship. The U.S. Passport Office recommends that you carry an *original* birth certificate (not necessarily the one issued at your birth, of course), or an expired passport, in a location apart from your other documents.

### Visas

You do not need to obtain a visa ahead of time to visit Greece; a valid passport will allow you to stay for up to three months. You can apply to stay longer at the **Aliens Bureau,** 9 Halkokondili St., 1st floor, Athens (tel. 362 83 01). Make sure to apply at least 20 days before the three-month expiration of your stay. (Check with the Greek Embassy or Consulate for further details.) A **transit visa,** valid for four days, can be obtained from any Greek consulate if you wish to stay in Greece on your way to another country. For further information on visas, contact the Athens Alien's Bureau. Branches are also located in Piraeus and Thessaloniki; outside these cities, you should contact the local police authorities.

### Student Identification

The **International Student Identity Card (ISIC)** is essential if you plan to use student flights, trains, or clubs, and also qualifies you for discounts on museum admission, theater tickets, local transportation, and more. In Greece, the ISIC secures discounts on admission to archeological sites and certain festivals. Cardholders are also eligible for reduced airfares from Athens, up to 40% discount on train fares, and up to 25% discount on ferries from Greece.

The ISIC is issued in Greece, but many budget travel offices and campus travel services in the U.S. also sell the card. When purchased in the U.S., the card includes limited sickness and accident insurance. To be eligible for an ISIC, you must be a secondary- or post-secondary school student over 12 years of age during the school year you apply. When applying, you must supply the following: (1) current proof of your student status (a letter on school stationery signed and sealed by the registrar, or a photocopied grade report); (2) a 1½ × 2" photo (vending machine-size) with your name printed on the back; and (3) proof of your birthdate and nationality. The fee is $10, and the card is valid for up to 16 months, from September 1 through the end of the following calendar year. When you apply, be sure to pick up the *ID Discount Guide,* which lists by country some of the available discounts; you can also write to CIEE for a copy. If you can't find a local agency that issues the ISIC, contact one of the budget travel offices listed in Useful Organizations above.

Due to the increase of phony and improperly issued ISIC cards, many airlines and some other services are requiring double proof of student identity. It's a good idea to have a signed letter from the registrar testifying to your student status (have it stamped with the school seal) or to carry your school ID card with you.

If you are ineligible for the ISIC but are under 26, you can apply for the **Federation of International Youth Travel Organizations (FIYTO)** card, also known as the **Youth International Educational Exchange (YIEE)** card. This internationally recognized travel document good for discounts on sightseeing tours within Greece, train rides from northern Europe, and ferry travel between Greece and Italy, Israel, and Egypt. CIEE, Travel CUTS, and budget travel agencies all over the world issue the FIYTO card; you must bring your passport number, ID, a photograph, and $6. For further information, write to FIYTO, 81 Islands Brygge, DK-2300 Copenhagen S, Denmark. Their free annual catalog lists over 8000 discounts available to cardholders.

### Driver's License

An **International Driving Permit** is required for driving in Greece. You must be over 18 to apply, although some owners quote 23 as a minimum age to rent a car in Greece. The permit is good for one year and is available from any local office of the **American Automobile Association,** or at the main office, AAA Travel Agency Services, 8111 Gatehouse Rd., Falls Church, VA 22047. It is also available from the **American Automobile Touring Alliance (AATA),** 888 Worchester St., Wellesley, MA 02181 (tel. (617) 237-5200), or the **Canadian Automobile Association (CAA),** Head Office, 2 Carlton St., Toronto, Ont. M5B 1K4 (tel. (416) 964-3170). With your application, you will need two passport-size photos, your valid home driver's license (which must always accompany the International Driving Permit), and $5. To get the license in Greece, you must present your national driver's license, passport, a photograph, and 1400dr to the **Automobile and Touring Club of Greece (ELPA).** Their main office is at 2 Messogion St., Athens 11527 (tel. 779 16 15).

If you are going to drive, or borrow a car that is not insured, you will need a "green card" or **International Insurance Certificate** for comprehensive coverage. Most rental agencies include this coverage in their prices; if you buy or lease a car, you can obtain a green card through the dealer from whom you are renting, leasing, or buying, or from some travel agents. (It is no longer available from the AAA.) Check to see that your insurance applies abroad. If not, you can take out short-term policies. For more information about car travel, see From Within Europe and Getting Around below.

### Hostel Membership

Greece has more than 25 youth hostels affiliated with the **International Youth Hostel Federation (IYHF).** IYHF membership is available through your own country's youth hostel organization. Hostel membership cards are available while you wait from many budget travel agencies (including Let's Go Travel Services, CIEE, and Travel CUTS); the cost varies by country (in the U.S. individuals $20, families $30, those under 18 or over 54 $10; in Canada CDN$18, CDN$36, CDN$10, respectively). Your membership is valid through the calendar year. (For more information about hostels, see Accommodations below.)

**U.S.:** American Youth Hostel Inc. (AYH), P.O. Box 37613, Washington, DC 20013-7613 (tel. (202) 783-6161). Also publishes the *International Youth Hostel Handbook* ($8.45).

**Canada:** Canadian Hostelling Association (CHA), 333 River Rd., Tower A, 3rd floor, Vanier, Ont. K1L 8H9 (tel. (613) 748-5638). Provides *International Youth Hostel Handbook* (Vols. 1&2) (CDN$6 postpaid).

**Britain:** Youth Hostel Association (YHA), Treveyan House, 8 St. Stephen Hill, St. Abans, Herts AL1 2DY (tel. (01) 836 8541).

**Australia:** Australian Youth Hostel Association, 60 Mary St., Surry Hills, Sydney, New South Wales 2010 (tel. (02) 212 11 51).

**New Zealand:** Youth Hostel Association of New Zealand, P.O. Box 436, 28 Worchester St., Christchurch C1 (tel. 79 99 70).

**Other countries:** International Youth Hostel Association (IYHF), Midland Bank Chambers, Howardsgate, Welwyn Garden City, Herts, England (tel. (0707) 33 24 87).

If you arrive in Greece without an IYHF card, you can purchase an International Guest Card from the **Greek Youth Hostel Association,** 4 Dragatsaniou St., Athens 10559 (tel. 323 41 07).

## *Customs*

Upon entering Greece, you must declare certain items, including cameras, typewriters, portable radios, and musical instruments. These may be brought in duty-free as long as they will be taken with you upon departure. You must also register all currency above $500, or you may not take it with you when you leave. Be sure that you carry receipts for, and record the serial numbers of, all items of value that you bring on your trip (including cameras, electronic equipment, jewelry, and expensive clothing), in order to prove you did not buy them abroad. A customs agent at your point of departure can officially stamp or certify your list of serial numbers.

Upon re-entering your own country, you must declare all articles acquired abroad, and pay a duty on the value of those articles exceeding the allowance established by your country's customs service. Keep in mind that anything you buy at duty-free shops abroad is not exempt from duty at your point of return, and must be declared along with other purchases: "Duty-free" means only that you didn't pay taxes in the country of purchase. Exportation of antiquities from Greece is absolutely prohibited.

**U.S. citizens,** after at least two days in Greece, may bring $400 worth of goods with you duty-free; you must then pay 10% tax on the next $1000 worth. The duty-free goods must be for personal or household use and cannot include more than 100 cigars or 200 cigarettes (one carton), and one liter of liquor or two liters of wine (you must be 21 or older to bring liquor into the U.S.). All items included in your duty-free allowance must accompany you and cannot be shipped separately. You may mail unsolicited gifts back. from abroad duty-free if they're worth less than $50, but you may not mail liquor, tobacco, or perfume to the U.S. Spot checks are occasionally made on parcels, so it is best to mark the accurate price and nature of the gift on the package. If you mail a parcel worth over $50, the Postal Service will collect the duty, plus a handling charge from the U.S. recipient upon delivery. If you mail home personal goods of U.S. origin, be sure to clearly mark the package "American goods returned" in order to avoid duty charges. For more detailed information, get a copy of *Know Before You Go,* available from the U.S. Customs Service, P.O. Box 7407, Washington, DC 20044 (tel. (202) 566-8195).

**Canadian citizens** should, before departing, identify or list serial numbers of all valuables on form Y-38 at the Customs Office or point of departure (these goods can then be reimported duty-free). Once every calendar year, after you have been abroad at least seven days, you may bring in up to CDN$300 worth of duty-free goods. These can include no more than 200 cigarettes, 50 cigars, two pounds of tobacco (if you are 16 years old or older), and 1.1 liters of wine or alcohol (if you meet the age requirements of the province of your port of return). Anything above the duty-free allowance is taxed: 20% for goods which accompany you, more for shipped items. You can send gifts up to a value of CDN$40 duty-free, but you may not mail alcohol or tobacco. The Customs Office, Communications Branch, MacKenzie Avenue, Ottawa, Ont., K1A OL5 (tel. (613) 957-0275), will send you their pamphlets *I Declare/Je Déclare* or *Canada: Travel Information 1988/89.*

**Australian citizens** will need to buy a departure tax stamp (AUS$20; those under 12 are exempt) at any office of the Department of Immigration and Ethnic Affairs, or at passport offices of the Department of Foreign Affairs, and fill out Customs Form B263 at a Customs Office or point of departure (reimported goods duty-free). Upon returning home, your allowance is 250 grams of tobacco and one liter of alcohol (if you are over 18). You may bring in up to AUS$200 worth of goods duty-free; the next AUS$160 worth will be taxed at 20%. (These goods may not include tobacco, alcohol, or furs; if you are under 18, your allowances are AUS$100 and AUS$80.) You may mail back personal property, but be sure to mark it "Australian goods returned" to avoid duty charges. You may not mail unsolicited gifts duty-free. The pamphlet *Australian Customs Information* is available from the Australian Customs Service, Customs House, 5-11 Constitution Ave., Canberra, A.C.T. 2600.

**New Zealand citizens** should list goods they are taking abroad on a Certificate of Export, to be signed by a customs officer before departure. Customs regulations here are extensive and strictly enforced. You are allowed 200 cigarettes or 250 grams of tobacco or 50 cigars or a mixture of all three not weighing more than 250 grams. You may also bring in 4.5 liters of beer or wine, and 1.125l of spirits (if you are over 17). You may bring in NZ$500 worth of goods, with duty levied beyond that amount; the goods must be for personal use or unsolicited gifts. Persons traveling together may not combine individual concessions. You must declare camping gear and outdoor sports equipment; be sure that any radio transmitting equipment complies with the post office licensing conditions.

The U.S., Canadian, and Australian governments prohibit or restrict the importation of firearms, explosives, ammunition, fireworks, many plants and animals, lottery tickets, obscene literature and film, and controlled drugs. To avoid problems when carrying prescription drugs, make sure bottles are clearly marked, and have a copy of the prescription ready to show the customs officer.

## Money

Nothing is likely to cause more headaches than money—even when you have it: Be sure to carry enough with you to avoid problems abroad.

### Currency and Exchange

On the first page of this introduction, we list the exchange rates valid in August 1988. Check current rates in the financial pages of a newspaper when planning your trip.

The *drachma* is the legal tender of Greece. It is issued in both paper notes (50, 100, 500, 1000dr) and coins (1, 2, 5, 10, 20, and 50dr). Before leaving home, exchange $50 or so for *drachmae;* this will save you time and money if banks are closed when you arrive and you need immediate cash.

If you are carrying more than $500 in cash when you enter Greece, you must declare it upon entry in order to export it legally. Note: *This does not apply to traveler's checks.* If at all possible, wait to exchange your dollars for *drachmae* until you're in Greece; exchange rates are better there because the Greeks want dollars more than Americans want *drachmae.* In addition, no more than $100 worth of *drachmae* can be changed back into foreign currency after any one visit to Greece, so try not to exchange more than you need. Every time you convert money you incur a loss. Banks usually offer the best exchage rates. Luxury hotels, restaurants, and airport and train station offices generally offer the worst rates.

### Traveler's Checks

Traveler's checks are the safest and least troublesome means of carrying cash. They are easy to use and can be replaced if lost or stolen. Traveler's checks are accepted for exchange at virtually every bank in Greece and as cash for purchases at some stores and restaurants.

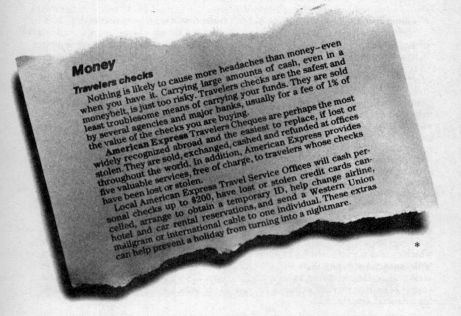

## Money

**Travelers checks**

Nothing is likely to cause more headaches than money–even when you have it. Carrying large amounts of cash, even in a moneybelt, is just too risky. Travelers checks are the safest and least troublesome means of carrying your funds. They are sold by several agencies and major banks, usually for a fee of 1% of the value of the checks you are buying.

American Express Travelers Cheques are perhaps the most widely recognized abroad and the easiest to replace, if lost or stolen. They are sold, exchanged, cashed and refunded at offices throughout the world. In addition, American Express provides five valuable services, free of charge, to travelers whose checks have been lost or stolen.

Local American Express Travel Service Offices will cash personal checks up to $200, have lost or stolen credit cards cancelled, arrange to obtain a temporary ID, help change airline, hotel and car rental reservations, and send a Western Union mailgram or international cable to one individual. These extras can help prevent a holiday from turning into a nightmare.

*

# Thanks a lot "Let's Go."
# We couldn't have said it better ourselves.

**Travelers Cheques**

*Excerpt from "Let's Go, Europe." © 1984 by Harvard Student Agencies, Inc.

Banks and agencies all over the world sell traveler's checks. You will be charged a commission of about 1.5% or a set fee, though you may be able to get traveler's checks free of charge from your home bank if you have money deposited there.

**American Express:** (tel. (800) 221-7282) in the U.S. and Canada; from abroad, call collect (801) 968-8300).

**Bank of America:** (tel. (800) 227-3460) in the U.S.; from Canada and abroad, call collect (415) 624-5400).

**Barclays:** (tel. (800) 221-2426 in the U.S.; from Canada and abroad, call collect (415) 574-7111).

**Citicorp:** (tel. (800) 645-6556 in the U.S. and Canada; from abroad, call collect (813) 623-1709).

**Thomas Cook:** (tel. (800) 223-7373 in the U.S.; from Canada and abroad, call collect (212) 974-5696).

**Visa:** (tel. (800) 227-6811 in the U.S. and Canada; from abroad, call collect (415) 574-7111); in London (tel.(01) 937 80 91).

Buy most of your checks in large denominations to avoid spending too much time in bank lines, but carry some checks in small denominations to minimize your losses at times when you need money fast and have to cash a check at a poor rate. To get the best exchange, purchase traveler's checks in your own national currency rather than foreign currencies.

All companies give you an emergency telephone number, which you should use if your checks are lost or stolen. Get a list of refund centers—American Express has over 90,000 worldwide, Bank of America, some 40,000, and other companies provide phone numbers you can call collect (some numbers are listed above). You should expect a fair amount of red tape and delay even in the best of circumstances. To expedite the refund process, separate your check receipts and keep them in a safe place (e.g. take the checks with you during the day and leave the receipts in your luggage). Record check numbers as you cash them to help you identify exactly which checks are missing. As an additional precaution, leave a list of check numbers with someone at home. You will generally receive some emergency funds immediately and replacement checks within a few days. It's a good idea to keep a separate supply of cash or traveler's checks, perhaps in the same place you keep your receipts, for financial emergencies.

## Credit Cards

Although credit cards have limited value abroad for the budget traveler (low-cost establishments rarely honor them), they can prove to be invaluable in a financial emergency. If you don't have a round-trip ticket, you can charge your return ticket home. Major credit cards, such as Visa or MasterCard, provide instant cash advances from banks throughout Europe in local currency. A cash advance may be your *only* quick source of funds.

If you're a student or on a low income, you may have difficulty acquiring an internationally recognized credit card; however, if someone in your family already has a card, it is easy to get joint-account cards. American Express will issue an extra green card for $25 per year or an extra gold card for $30 (bills go to your loved one, or perhaps, love goes to the billed one). Visa often provides additional cards free of charge, depending on the policy of the office where the card was purchased.

Local **American Express** offices will cash personal checks up to $1000 in any 7-day period (in cash and in traveler's checks, depending on the office's funds). Offices will cancel and replace lost or stolen cards and arrange temporary ID if you lose your wallet. Cardholders can use American Express offices as mailing addresses free of charge; others must pay a fee (or show AmEx traveler's checks). The card also provides automatic travel insurance. For a $1.50 service charge per transaction, you can use American Express Automated Teller Machines throughout the U.S. and Europe, where cardholders can get up to $1000 ($500 in cash, $500 in traveler's checks). For more information on their coverage policy and to get *The Traveler's Companion,* a list of full-service offices throughout the world, write American Express Travel Service, 65 Broadway, New York, NY 10016.

**Barclays Bank** is Britain's largest international bank, with 4000 offices in 70 countries. **Visa** also has teller machines throughout Europe that accept their card. For a copy of their *International Travel Guide,* write Chase Visa, P.O. Box 5111, 1400 Union Turnpike, New Hyde Park, NY 11042.

### Sending Money

The fastest and cheapest way to obtain money is to have someone **cable** money through the American office of a large foreign bank in Greece. If you think you might need more money during the trip, visit your home bank and get a list of correspondent banks in Greece. Larger national banks will have branches throughout the country that may be able to reach you in remote corners. Expect to pay anywhere from $20-80 to have money cabled abroad.

Another way to send money is by **cable transfer.** Contact your home bank by letter or telegram and state the amount of money you need, whether it should be in U.S. or foreign currency, and the name and address of the bank to which it should be cabled. This service takes about 24 hours—a bit longer in smaller cities—and costs about $25 for amounts under $1000.

Slower than the cable, but still effective, is a **bank draft. Citicorp** (tel. (212) 558-7256) in Athens or any large commercial bank should be able to connect you with a network of corresponding banks in Greece. The sender must either have an account with the bank or bring cash to one of their branches (some won't cable for non-customers). The bank will charge $15-20. The money might arrive the same day, the next day, or a week later, depending on when the money is sent and what time zones it must cross. The sender must specify whether the money is to be disbursed in local currency or in American dollars, and must make certain that information, such as the passport number and recipient's bank name and address, is exact; otherwise, expect significant delays. The sender will not receive confirmation of delivery.

Sending money through a company such as **American Express** costs about as much as sending it through a bank. Normally, the sender must have an AmEx card to use these services, but some offices will waive this requirement for a commission. Money is guaranteed to arrive within 24 to 72 hours at the designated overseas office, where it will be held for 14 days before being returned to the sender. It costs $15 to send up to $500, and $60 to send up to the maximum amount, $2000. The first $200 is payable in local currency and the remainder in U.S. dollars traveler's checks.

**Western Union** offers a convenient, though expensive, service for cabling money abroad. A sender in the U.S. with a MasterCard or Visa can call Western Union (tel. (800) 325-6000) and state their card number and the amount of money they wish to cable. A sender without a card must go in person to a Western Union office with cash, a cashier's check, or AmEx traveler's checks (no money orders accepted). The money will arrive at the central telegram office of the city the sender designates and can be picked up by showing suitable identification. Offices in Greece are located in Athens, Piraeus, and Thessaloniki. Money will generally arrive between two to five business days in *drachmae,* and will be held at the office for 14 days, after which time it will be returned to the sender minus the transaction costs. To send $50 to Europe costs $11, $50-100 costs $13, amounts above $100 cost an additional $5 per $100, $500-750 costs $40, and $750-1000 is $45. In addition to these charges, **Citibank** (presently the only bank handling transfers) exacts an additional flat rate of $22 on each transaction, regardless of the amount sent. **Barclays** will also send International Payment Orders, charging 25p per £100.

If you are an American and suddenly find yourself in big trouble (e.g. life or death), you can have money sent to you via the **State Department's Citizens' Emergency Center,** #4811, 2201 C St. NW, Washington, DC 20520 (tel. (202) 647-5225). For a fee of $15, officials will send the money within hours, or sometimes overnight, to the nearest consulate, which will disburse the cash according to instructions. The agency prefers to send sums less than $500. The sender must provide his or her name and address, the name of the recipient, and the nature of the emergency. If requested, a message will be included with the money. Finally, if you are stranded in Greece without recourse, a consulate will wire home for you and deduct the cost from the money you receive. This is considered an extreme imposition, however, so turn to them only in desperation.

### Value Added Tax

Value Added Tax (VAT), a form of sales tax levied in the European Economic Community, is generally included in the price of all Greek goods and services.

## Safety and Security

Make two sets of photocopies of all your important documents, including passport, IDs, credit cards, traveler's checks' number slips, plane tickets, and railpasses. Leave one set with a trusted keeper at home and carry the other with you, *separate from the actual documents themselves.* Be sure to label all your luggage (inside and out) in case the tags rip off. Tie on a piece of bright ribbon or twine on the handles so your bags are easy to identify at baggage claim.

Theft is one of the greatest potential setbacks of a trip. Crowded youth hostels and overnight trains are favorite hangouts for petty criminals who prey on backpackers. One simple tactic is to always keep money and valuables on you, especially while sleeping: Use a money belt or necklace pouch. If you plan to sleep outside, or simply don't want to carry everything with you, try to store your gear in a locker at a train or bus station. Some hotels and hostels also provide daytime luggage storage for a small fee. *Never* leave your valuables unattended—it only takes a moment for your wallet or pack to be stolen.

Common sense and some basic precautions should carry you safely through your travels. Large cities, of course, demand extra caution. Avoid bus and train stations and public parks after dark, and walk along busy, well-lit streets. You may feel safer staying in places with either a curfew or night-attendant. Ask the manager of your hotel or hostel for advice on specific areas.

### Insurance

Avoid unnecessary insurance coverage. Check whether your homeowner's insurance (or your family's coverage) covers theft during travel. Some policies will reimburse you for the value of stolen documents, such as passport, plane ticket, or railpass, up to $500. University term-time medical plans often include insurance for summer travel. Students under 23 should check whether their parents have travel insurance for them. Canadians are usually protected under their home province's health insurance plan; check with your Ministry of Health or Health Plan headquarters.

If your insurance policy does not extend overseas (for example, Medicare does not cover foreign travel), you may want to purchase a short-term policy for your trip. Purchasing an ISIC card in the U.S. provides you with $2000 worth of accident and sickness insurance. An American Express card also provides some travel insurance automatically. CIEE has an inexpensive plan called **Trip Safe**, with options that cover medical expenses, accidents, and flight cancellation (see Useful Organizations and Publications above).

Note that usually you must pay emergency expenses on the spot and then file your claim (along with necessary documents and receipts) upon return to your home country. Know in advance whether your insurance will provide immediate payments or cash transfers in an emergency. Generally, insurance companies require proof of loss or expenditures before they will honor your claim. In case of theft, you must submit a copy of the police report; in case of medical expenses, you must submit receipts and doctors' statements (preferably typed in English). Be sure to check the time limitation on filing a claim under your policy to ensure that you will return home in time to secure reimbursement. For more information on specific insurance policies, contact any of the firms listed below.

**Access America, Inc.:** (tel. (800) 851-2800. Travel insurance and assistance. On-the-spot hospital and doctor payments in cash.

**ARM Coverage, Inc.:** (tel. (800) 645-2424). Comprehensive travel insurance.

**Europ Assistance Worldwide Services, Inc.:** (tel. (800) 821-2828). 24-hour emergency assistance, as well as interpretation, legal and medical referrals, transmission of messages, and guaranteed cash advances.

**Healthcare Abroad:** (tel. (800) 237-6615). Insurance and assistance services. Medical plan required; optional trip cancellation, accidental death, and baggage protection plans.

**The Traveler's Insurance Co.:** (tel. (800) 243-3144). Comprehensive travel insurance.

**Worldcare Travel Assistance Association, Inc.:** (tel. (800) 521-4822). 24-hour emergency medical hotline. Membership annual or per trip. **Scholarcare** program tailored to students and faculty spending a semester or year abroad.

### Traveling Alone

Persons traveling alone need to remain alert at all times. Without someone else to look out for you, you're especially vulnerable to theft and personal assault.

If you're a **female traveler,** it is very important for you to look as if you know where you're going at all times. You are likely to get stares wherever you go. Be aware that a simple stroll in the park may be interpreted as a desire for intimate male contact. Don't let gender hinder your freedom, but know that you will probably attract unwanted attention. The more you look as though you are in control, the less likely you are to be bothered. Ask women or couples, rather than men, for directions, and always take enough spare change for a phone call or a quick escape, if necessary, by taxi or bus. Wherever possible, *Let's Go* lists emergency, police, and consulate numbers in every large city; consult them if you encounter difficulties.

### Drugs

In Greece, possession of drugs is a serious offense. If you're lucky, you'll only be kicked out of the country. Every year, young travelers are arrested in foreign countries for illegal possession, use, or trafficking in drugs. Make **sure** you get a statement and/or prescription from your doctor if you'll be carrying insulin, syringes, or any narcotic drugs. In addition, be aware that **codeine,** a painkiller commonly prescribed by American physicians, is illegal in Greece; chances are you won't be searched for Tylenol III pills, but make sure you carry a note from your doctor if you plan to take codeine into the country.

As far as illegal substances go, the best advice is to *stay away* from drugs in Europe and to *never* bring drugs across international borders. Your government is completely powerless in Greek courts and can offer only minimal assistance to those arrested for possession of drugs. Consular officers can only visit the prisoner, provide a list of attorneys, and inform family and friends. As a U.S. State Department bulletin dourly states, you're virtually "on your own" if you become involved, *however innocently,* in illegal drug trafficking. The Canadian Department of External Affairs adds: "The legal codes of some countries provide for guilt by association under which someone may be charged simply for being in the company of a person suspected or found guilty of a crime (e.g. trafficking in or possessing drugs . . . "

To find out more about drug enforcement policies, send for *Travel Warning on Drugs Abroad* from the Bureau of Consular Affairs, PA #5807, Deptartment of State, Washington, DC 20520 (tel. (202) 647-1488).

## Health

Don't cut corners on health—few things are as disappointing as a trip ruined by an unforeseen accident or illness. Taking care of your health is mostly a matter of common sense. Eat well, drink plenty of liquids, and don't overexert yourself.

Bring a copy of any medical prescriptions you require with the generic name of the drug. Carry an ample supply of all medications, since matching your prescription with a foreign equivalent is not always economical, easy, or safe. It's a good idea to distribute medication between carry-on and checked baggage in case one or the other goes astray. In the case that you find yourself without a necessary prescription drug, carry a dosage schedule from your own pharmacist, as drugs are relatively uncontrolled in Greece. Remember that codeine is an illegal substance in Greece (see Drugs above).

Travelers with a medical problem or condition that cannot be easily recognized (e.g. diabetes, allergies to antibiotics, epilepsy, or heart conditions) should obtain a **Medic Alert identification tag,** an internationally recognized emblem that conveys vital information in emergencies. It indicates the nature of the problem, and provides the number of Medic Alert's 24-hour hotline, through which attending personnel can obtain information about the member's medical history. Lifetime membership is $20; write to Medic Alert Foundation International, P.O. Box 1009, Turlock, CA 95381 (tel. (800) 432-5378).

Perhaps the most extensive health service for travelers is furnished by the **International Association for Medical Assistance to Travelers (IAMAT),** 417 Center St., Lewiston, NY 14092 (tel. (716) 754-4883). IAMAT provides a worldwide directory of English-speaking physicians whose services are available at fixed and generally reasonable rates. English-speaking doctors can also be located through inquiries at American, Canadian, and British embassies and consulates, through American Express and Thomas Cook offices, or at the emergency rooms of university hospitals. Also, many of the first-aid centers listed in *Let's Go* can provide medical care from an English-speaking doctor.

A self-assembled **first-aid kit** should suffice for minor health problems. You might include antiseptic soap, multiple vitamins, aspirin, antacid tablets, bandages, tweezers, a Swiss Army knife, sunscreen, a thermometer in a sturdy case, an antiseptic ointment such as bacitracin, medication for motion sickness and diarrhea, and an antihistamine. If you wear glasses or contacts, take an extra pair, and as an additional precaution, leave a copy of the prescription with someone at home in case yours are lost are stolen. Condoms should be brought from home, since availability is unpredictable.

## Additional Concerns

### Senior Travelers

Young Greeks have a great deal of respect for their elders, so senior citizens should find a warm welcome in this country. Like students, seniors are often offered discounts and special services; check with individual agencies and offices.

Below is a brief list of services that provide additional information:

**Bureau of Consular Affairs:** Passport Services, Department of State, 1425 K St. NW, Washington, DC 20524 (tel. (202) 523-1462). Publishes *Travel Tips for Senior Citizens* ($1 plus postage).

**Elderhostel:** 80 Boylston St., #400, Boston, MA 02116 (tel. (617) 426-7788). Must be 60 or over or have spouse 60 or over to join. Week-long programs cover varied subjects; $195-225 fee covers room, board, tuition, and activities.

**Mature Outlook U.S.A.:** P.O. Box 1205, Glenview, IL 60025. Membership for those 50 and over $7.50 (includes spouse). Provides special domestic and international vacation packages, reduced travel insurance, and other travel discounts.

**Pilot Books:** 103 Cooper St., Babylon, NY 11702 (tel. (516) 422-2225). Publishes *1989 Senior Citizens' Guide to Budget Travel* ($3.95 plus $1 postage).

### Traveling with Children

Traveling with your children can be affordable and fun—for you as well as for them. The Greeks love children, and will often show more hospitality if a couple brings along the *paidia*. Many organizations offer special discounts: Both Olympic Airways and the Hellenic Railways Organization let children under 12 travel for half price, and most ferry services charge lower fares for children.

If you will be traveling with children, prepare a detailed itinerary that will appeal to them, and be sure to include sights and events that you will be able to enjoy as much as they do. Consider renting a car, rather than traveling on public transportation, if you plan on bringing more than one child, and don't forget that children need to travel at a slower pace than most adults. Accommodations can be booked ahead through a travel agent—particularly useful if you'll be traveling in the high-season.

Children will often get you up early in the morning and cut the day short at night; they require a lot of advance planning and regular care, and will undoubtedly cause you to miss an important sight or two. Traveling as a family does create special responsibilities, but with flexibility, proper planning, and a sense of humor, you can make the trip enjoyable for yourself and your children.

### Disabled Travelers

Greece is slowly beginning to respond to the needs of disabled travelers. Many of the cruise ships that sail throughout the Greek islands are equipped to accommodate the disabled. Special air transportation is available aboard Olympic Airways to many of Greece's larger islands. Hotels, train stations, and airports have recently installed facilities for the disabled, however, many of the archeological sites throughout the country are still not accessible to wheelchairs. You may want to travel during the off-season to avoid crowds and severe temperatures.

When making arrangements with airlines or hotels, inform them of your handicap; establishments may need time to prepare for your needs. Blind travelers may import seeing eye dogs into Greece, provided a health certificate is brought stating that anti-rabies injections have been administered to the animal within the last year.

Useful publications for disabled travelers include *Access to the World,* by Louise Weiss (Facts on File, Inc., 460 Park Ave. S., New York, NY 10016; $17.95), and *Travel for the Disabled,* by Helen Heckler (Twin Peaks Press, P.O. Box 129, Vancouver, WA 98666). The following organizations can provide further information:

**The Society for the Advancement of Travel for the Handicapped (SATH):** 26 Court St., Brooklyn, NY 11242 (tel. (718) 858-5483). Provides advice, listings, and several useful booklets.

**Travel Information Service, Moss Rehabilitation Hospital:** 12th St. and Tabor Rd., Philadelphia, PA 19141 (tel. (215) 329-5715 ext. 2233). Provides information for disabled travelers on tourist sights, accommodations, and transportation.

The following organizations and travel agencies offer special tours or services for the disabled:

**Directions Unlimited:** (tel. (800) 533-5343).

**Evergreen Travel Service,** 19505L 44th Ave. W., Lynnwood, WA 98036 (tel. (206) 776-1184). Worldwide tours.

**Flying Wheels Travel,** (tel. (800) 533-0363; in MN (800) 722-9351). Arranges international trips for groups or individuals.

**Whole Person Tours:** P.O. Box 1084, Bayonne, NJ 07002-1084 (tel. (201) 858-3400). Publishes *The Itinerary* magazine for travelers with physical disabilities.

### Gay and Lesbian Travelers

Since ancient times, Greek attitudes toward gays and lesbians have been reasonably tolerant. In Athens, you may contact the **Gay Group,** AKOE, P.O. Box 2777, 10022 (tel. 364 36 88), or the **Gay Hotline** (tel. 324 96 60), or visit the **Gay/Lesbian Meeting Place,** AKOE Office, 6A Zalogou St. (tel. 364 36 88). In addition, there are several gay and lesbian hotels, resorts, and bars on the islands of Hydra, Lesbos, Mykonos, and Rhodes.

Gay and lesbian travelers may find some helpful guides through the international mail-order service, **Gay's the Word,** 66 Marchmont St., London, WC 1AB, England (tel. 278 76 54). Women should try to get a copy of the latest edition of *Gaia's Guide,* a complete "international guide for traveling women," which lists local lesbian, feminist, and gay information numbers, publications, bookstores, restaurants, hotels, meeting places, and women's cultural centers and resources. The book, revised annually, is available at local bookstores under women's studies or by mail. In the U.S. and Canada, send $12.50 to Giovanni's Room, 345 S. 12th St., N.E., Philadelphia, PA 19107 (tel. (800) 222-6996); in Britain or Ireland, *Gaia's Guide,* 9-11 Kensington High St., London W8; in Australia or New Zealand, Open Leaves, 71 Cardigan St., Carlton, Victoria 3053, Australia. The *Spartacus Guide for Gay Men* covers virtually every country in the world. It is available for $25 from Bruno Gmünder, Lützowstr 105, P.O. Box 30 13 45, D-1000 Berlin 30, West Germany. For a more scholarly look at homosexuality in Greece, pick up a copy of K.J. Dover's *Greek Homosexuality* (Vintage Books).

The incidence of AIDS is low in Greece, and authorities are making a concerted effort to keep it that way by informing the public of the danger of the disease. Latex condoms (specifically to lessen the chance of contracting AIDS or other sexually transmitted diseases) are available throughout Western Europe but should be brought from home.

### Dietary Concerns

During the summer when fresh produce is abundant, **vegetarians** will find Greek fare quite accommodating. Try *melanzalata* (eggplant salad), or *tzatziki* (yogurt, cucumber, and garlic sauce) as appetizers. Greece's many outdoor markets *(agora)* sell plenty of fresh vegetables, fruits, and interesting cheeses. The **Vegetarian Society of the U.K.,** Parkdale, Dunham Rd., Altrincham, Cheshire WA 14 4QG (tel. (061) 928 07 03), publishes *The International Vegetarian Handbook* annually, and the **North American Vegetarian Society,** P.O. Box 72 Dolgeville, NY 13329 (tel. (518) 568-7970), sells their *Handbook* for $8.95.

For those who maintain a **kosher** diet, dining out may be difficult. Since Greece's Jewish community is now relatively tiny (approximately 5000), there are few kosher restaurants. If you wish to keep a strict kosher diet, research information at local Jewish community centers or try *The Jewish Travel Guide* published by Jewish Chronicle Publications, 25 Furnival St., London EC4A 1JT, England, and distributed in the U.S. and Canada by Sepher-Hermon Press, Inc., 1265 46th St. Brooklyn, NY 11219 (tel. (718) 972-9010).

### Nude Sunbathers and Naturists

The ancient Greeks admired the beauty of the human body, and that appreciation has extended to the present day. Some of Greece's beaches are designated for *au naturel* bathing. In fact, topless bathing is almost the norm, especially on the islands. If you're not on a designated nude beach, it's best to keep your suit on: The local police may have other ideas about where to draw the line between naturism and indecency. For more detailed written and pictorial information, leaf through *The World Guide to Nude Beaches and Recreation* (Harmony Books, Crown Publishers, 34 Englehard Ave., Arenel, NJ 07001 (tel. (201) 382-7600). Our researchers uncover nudist beaches wherever possible.

## Work

Work is difficult to find in Greece. Job opportunities are scarce and the Greek government tries to restrict employment to Greek citizens and visitors from the European Economic Community (EEC). For long-term employment you must first secure a work permit from your employer; permits are available at the **Ministry of Labor,** 40 Piraeus St., Athens 10182 (tel. 523 31 10), or the **Aliens Bureau** (see Visas above).

Your best bet is to secure a job with a company from your home country, but this usually requires fluency in Greek and some specialized skill. All arrangements and negotiations should be made before you leave home. For a list of American firms, subsidiaries, and affiliates operating in Greece, write the **American Hellenic Chamber of Commerce,** 17 Valaoritou St., 2nd floor, Athens 10671 (tel. 361 83 85). The list costs $40. They can also offer advice about finding temporary or permanent employment in Greece.

For **hotel jobs** (bartending, cleaning, etc.) it is best to arrive in the spring and early summer to search for work. Most night spots don't pay more than 2000dr per day, so expect to live like a Greek. To find jobs, check the bulletin boards of hostels in Athens and the classified ads in the *Athens News.* Or, contact **Working Holidays** at 11 Nikis St., 1st and 6th floors, Athens 10557 (tel. 322 43 21). They will take applications from overseas, but require prepayment of the $35 registration fee. Another possibility is to work as a farm laborer—the Peloponnese and Crete are good places to look.

Three organizations sponsor **workcamp opportunities** in Greece. Volunteers for **Peace International Workcamps** sponsor programs in 36 nations for college students. For their free newsletter, write to 43 Tiffany Rd, Belmont, VT 05730 (tel. (802) 259-2759). Send $7 (postpaid) for their *International Workcamp Directory.* **Summer Work Activities Program (SWAP)** runs summer workcamps for high school students. Write to 850 Third Ave., 18th floor, New York, NY 10022; in Greece, the American Farm School, P.O. Box 10140, Thessaloniki 54110 (tel. 30 31 471 803). **Service Civil International (SCI-USA),** c/o Innisfree Village, Rte. 2 Box 506, Crozet, VA 22932, sponsors workcamps in over 25 countries; volunteers do manual work, social work, or work/study programs. Send a self-addressed, stamped envelope for an application.

**Archeological fieldwork** is sometimes available, but most excavations require experienced volunteers and pay minimal or no wages. **The Archaeological Institute of America** publishes the *Archaeological Fieldwork Opportunities Bulletin* ($8 prepaid) that lists positions for field work and educational programs, including field schools, study tours, and courses in archeological illustration for volunteers and paid staff. It's available in January of each year for the following summer. Contact the AIA at 675 Commonwealth Ave., Boston, MA 02215 (tel. (617) 353-9361).

If you've read *The Magus* by John Fowles, you may have the impression that a lot of young people teach English in Greek private schools. Actually, teaching jobs are scarce, but holders of valid U.S. teaching certificates can obtain a list of schools in Greece that employ American teachers. The U.S. Government sponsors a teacher exchange program. Generally, the commitment is for one academic year and you must be fluent in Greek. Write to the U.S. Department of Education for more information. The **International Schools Service (ISS)** also supplies information on teaching abroad in English-speaking schools. To get the *ISS Directory of Overseas Schools,* updated annually. Write 13 Roszel Rd., P.O. Box 5910, Princeton, NJ 08540 (tel. (609) 452-0990). The **International Association for the Exchange of Students for Technical Experience (IAESTE)** supports on-the-job training for undergraduates and graduates in Greece. The inability to secure positions depends on the number of openings available, so you will have to locate prospective American employers. For more information, write IAESTE Trainee Program, c/o AIPT, 217 American City Bldg., Columbia, MD 21044 (tel. (301) 997-2200).

Other opportunities for work are limited; check the nearest university library for ideas. The **Council on International Educational Exchange (CIEE)** (see Useful Organizations and Publications above), puts out several publications that may help you on a foreign job search. CIEE's newest book is *The Comprehensive Guide to Voluntary Service in the U.S. and Abroad* ($5.50 plus postage).

For an extensive list of 50,000 volunteer and paid work opportunities, send for the *1988 Directory of Overseas Summer Jobs,* ($9.95) or look through *Work Your Way Around the World* ($10.95); both publications are available from Writer's Digest Books, 1507 Dana Ave., Cincinnati, OH 45207 (tel. (800) 543-4644). **Summer**

**Abroad,** Kipling Rd., Brattleboro, VT 05301 (tel. (800) 354-2929), gives people a chance to lead a summer group in Greece.

## Study

Many American students come to Greece on programs run by American universities or organizations, or on independent study projects financed by universities. Talk to a counselor at your college or check your school library for information about studying abroad; many colleges give credit for classes taken at a foreign university.

The **Institute of International Education (IIE),** 809 United Nations Plaza, New York, NY 10017 (tel. (212) 883-8200), is the largest U.S. higher educational exchange agency. Their *Academic Year Abroad* ($20) describes over 1600 semester and year study programs, while their *Vacation Study Abroad* lists summer programs ($20).

**College Year in Athens, Inc.** runs a two-semester program on Greek civilization for undergraduates (usually juniors), which includes travel to important sites as well as classroom instruction (in English). The program has its own faculty, and issues transcripts to home universities. Fees include field-trip travel expenses, housing, and two meals per day ($9700, $5070 for one semester); some scholarship money is available. For more information, contact the American Representative, College Year in Athens, 1702 S. High St., Bloomington, IN 47401-6746 (tel. (812) 336-2841), or the Director, College Year in Athens, P.O. Box 17176, Athens GR-10024 (tel. 721 87 46).

The **Hellenic Language School** has a variety of educational offerings, including ancient and modern Greek language courses for a full year or summer term (in Athens and Crete) and seminars on the history and culture of Greece. The school is located at 4 Zalongou St., Athens 10678 (tel. 362 75 60 or 364 05 14). The **Athens Centre,** which is affiliated with U.S. colleges and universities, offers a comprehensive modern Greek language program as well as a special on-site summer course on Classical and Byzantine Greece. Write 48 Archimidous St., Pangrati, Athens 11636 (tel. 701 22 68 or 701 52 42).

The **Aegean Institute,** c/o Dr. Paul Stavrolakes, 25 Waterview Dr., Port Jefferson, NY 11777 (tel. (516) 473-7070), organizes a summer program with college-credit courses in Greek art and archeology, Greek tragedy, ancient history, and modern Greek language. **Study in Greece,** Neoforos 1, Athens GR-16121 (tel. 723 8825 or 722 27 89), has semester-long courses taught in English, in addition to Greek language courses and independent 10-day field projects. Other organizations include The **Hellenic American Union,** 22 Massalias St. Athens 10680 (tel. 360 73 05), with courses in modern Greek, studio art, and folk dancing; the **American Farm School,** 1133 Broadway 26th St., New York, NY 10010, for those interested in agriculture; **Delta Technical and Business School,** 3 Rethumnou St., Museum, Athens (tel. 822 00 83); and **Intercultural Action Learning Program,** P.O. Box 464, Peterborough, NH 03458.

High school students who want to study for a year in Greece may write for information to **American Field Service (AFS),** International/Intercultural Programs, 313 E. 43rd St., New York, NY 10017 (tel. (212) 949-4242), and the **American Institute for Foreign Study,** 102 Greenwich Ave., Greenwich, CT 06830 (tel. (800) 727-2437).

More information on educational programs in Greece can be obtained from the Greek Press and Information Office (see Useful Organizations above).

## Packing

*Pack light.* The tried and true method of packing is to set out everything you think you'll need, leave half behind, and take more money. Test your luggage and limbs around the block a few times before you leave. If you can't manage comfortably, start unloading: The convenience of traveling light far outweighs the inconvenience of a small wardrobe. Having extra room for gifts and other purchases is a good reason to begin with a less-than-stuffed bag.

You should decide whether a backpack, a light suitcase, or a shoulder bag is most suitable for your needs. If you're planning on covering a lot of ground by foot, a sturdy **backpack** with several compartments is hard to beat. Packs come with either an exterior or interior X- or A-shaped frame; an interior-frame model is less cumbersome and bulky, but external-frame models provide added support and are much more comfortable. A pack that loads from the front rather than the top saves you the inconvenience of having to dig to the bottom and grope for hidden items. Beware of cheap backpacks: The straps are likely to rip or fray under the strain of hard traveling. A good pack costs about $100. Go to a camping store and try out several models—not every pack fits every person. In the store, fill the pack with weights at least as heavy as the load you'll be carrying on the road, and adjust the straps to see if walking with the pack is comfortable. To minimize tottering, pack heavy items up against the inside wall of the pack.

You might consider a **light suitcase** with wheels if you are going to stay in one city or town for a long time, minimizing those wrist-wrenching searches for a place to sleep. Those who wish to travel unobtrusively might choose a large shoulder or **duffel bag** that zips and closes securely.

No matter what kind of luggage you choose, a small **daypack** is indispensable for plane flights, sightseeing, carrying a camera, and your *Let's Go.* Guard money, passport, jewelry, and other valuables *at all times* in a purse, pouch, or **money belt.** Nylon-zippered pouches with slits on the back to pass a belt through can be worn in front for surveillance and ready access. If you can't find one on your own, order one of the five models available from the **Forsyth Travel Library** (see Useful Organizations and Publications above). Remove all old claim checks and label every piece of baggage inside and out with your name and address. For added security, purchase a few combination locks for your luggage.

In general, while dark-colored clothes will conceal the rough treatment you'll be giving them, light ones that don't absorb the sunlight will be more comfortable in hot weather. Natural fibers and cottons beat synthetics hands down, especially when the mercury rises. In addition, cotton blends don't wrinkle easily and can be washed conveniently in a sink. Don't forget your **beachwear,** and remember to bring some warmer clothes for chilly nights and excursions into the mountains. You should bring a **rain poncho** and **sweater** if you plan to travel in the off-season or expect to spend nights on ferries.

At most monasteries and archeological sites, modest dress is required (no shorts, short skirts, cropped tops, or bathing suits allowed).

Comfortable **walking shoes** or a good pair of running shoes are essential. Sandals or espadrilles are great for short walks or evening idling. If you're planning a foray up Mt. Athos or Mt. Olympos, hiking boots and socks are a must. Remember that all shoes should be broken in prior to your departure. Sprinkling talcum powder on your feet and inside your shoes helps prevent uncomfortable rubs and sores, while moleskins relieve any blisters that develop.

In addition to the first-aid kit suggested under Health, above, you should also include a flashlight, hat, canteen, petroleum jelly, pocket knife, needle and thread, safety pins, and a travel alarm clock. Rubber bands and plastic bags serve myriad purposes while on the road. You don't have to pack a summer's worth of toiletries such as aspirin, razor blades, or tampons, but make sure you're adequately stocked before exploring less populated areas of Greece.

The standard electrical outlet in Greece produces 220 volts AC. North American appliances are usually designed for 110 volts AC. If you want to use your own appliances, you will need a converter and a three-pronged adapter, both available in department and hardware stores. To order a converter by mail ($15-18), write to Franzus Company, 352 Park Ave. S., New York, NY 10010 (tel. (212) 463-9393). Better still, leave the hair dryer at home.

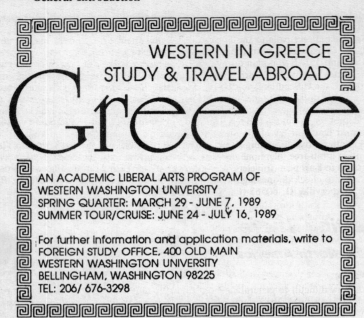

WESTERN IN GREECE
STUDY & TRAVEL ABROAD

Greece

AN ACADEMIC LIBERAL ARTS PROGRAM OF
WESTERN WASHINGTON UNIVERSITY
SPRING QUARTER: MARCH 29 - JUNE 7, 1989
SUMMER TOUR/CRUISE: JUNE 24 - JULY 16, 1989

For further information and application materials, write to
FOREIGN STUDY OFFICE, 400 OLD MAIN
WESTERN WASHINGTON UNIVERSITY
BELLINGHAM, WASHINGTON 98225
TEL: 206/ 676-3298

## *Keeping in Touch*

### *Mail*

Most **post offices** are open Monday to Friday from 7:30am to 2:30pm, although services (such as parcels) may close early; some larger offices keep longer hours. To register a letter, ask for *systemeno;* for express, *epeegon;* for air mail, just "air mail." Mail to the U.S. takes on the average 8-10 days, sometimes longer from smaller villages.

If you have no fixed address while in Greece, you can receive mail through the Greek post office's **Poste Restante** (General Delivery) service. Mark the envelope "HOLD," and address it like this: "Jane Doe, *c/o* Poste Restante, Main Post Office, the address of the appropriate office, the postal code, and GREECE (in capital letters)." Write "Air Mail" on the side of the envelope and use a first class stamp. Some larger post offices charge 20dr to pick up Poste Restante mail. If you are expecting Poste Restante to arrive for you after you leave a town, arrange at the post office to have it forwarded to another Poste Restante address. American Express offices will hold mail for anyone, but often charge a small fee if you don't have their card or their traveler's checks.

### *Telephone*

Long-distance phone calls and telegrams should be placed at the **OTE** (the Greek Telephone Organization) offices. In small villages, offices are usually open Monday through Friday 7:30am to 3pm, in towns 7:30am to 10pm (shorter hours or closed on weekends), and in larger cities 24 hours. If you visit one of the latter in the middle of the night, the door may be locked, but ring and they'll let you in. Long-distance calls take a while to get through because lines are usually jammed; for collect calls, you'll have to wait in the office itself. Either way, there is often a long line; try, if at all possible, to call early in the morning. There is no surcharge if you go to an OTE. For assistance, ask the attendant at the OTE or dial 162 for an English-speaking operator.

Hotels usually have meters that record the length of your phone call. Take down the beginning and ending numerals so they'll charge you accordingly.

To make **direct** calls to the U.S., dial 001 and then the area code and number. Calls to Canada start with 001; to Australia 61; to New Zealand 64; Britain 44; and Ireland 353. If you plan on talking for a while, ask the other party to call right back. Rates from the U.S. are cheaper and the call will be charged at the U.S. rate. If you call the U.S. **collect,** you'll be charged the U.S. person-to-person rate; in most cases, you'll still save money over the expensive hotel surcharges. Remember the **time difference** when calling North America: Subtract seven hours (Eastern Standard Time), eight hours (Central), nine hours (Mountain), or 10 hours (Pacific). Standard Daylight Savings adds another hour.

One alternative to calling direct is **Euraide**'s "Overseas Access Service." They maintain a toll-free telephone number in the U.S. so family and friends can convey messages to European travelers. Travelers can phone their Munich office seven days per week to check on messages from home. For more information, write P.O. Box 2375, Naperville, IL 60565 (tel. (312) 983-8880).

# Getting There

## From North America

### By Plane

It's very difficult to generalize about flights to and from Greece or to give a rundown of exact fares. Prices and market conditions can fluctuate quite significantly from one week to the next. The best advice we can offer is to have patience, and to begin looking for a flight as soon as you think you might be traveling abroad.

In general, you'll be able to arrange a cheaper airfare package if you can keep your date, time, and place of departure and return as flexible as possible. **Off-season** travelers enjoy lower fares, face less competition for inexpensive seats, and benefit from off-season rates on domestic flights to reach advantageous ports of departure. Try to keep your itinerary flexible: An indirect flight through Brussels or Luxembourg could cost considerably less than a direct flight to Athens. **Peak-season** rates are set on either May 15 or June 1 (departure) and run until about September 15 (return). If you arrange your travel dates carefully, you can travel in summer and still save with shoulder- or even low-season fares.

The simplest and surest way to decide among the myriad flight options is to find a good travel agent who is committed to saving you money. Don't hesitate to shop around for the best deal: Commissions are smaller on cheaper flights, so some travel agents are less eager to help. In addition, scan the travel section of the Sunday *New York Times* and other major newspapers for bargain fares. Student travel organizations such as CIEE or Travel CUTS (see Useful Organizations) may have special deals for students of which regular travel agents are not aware.

In general, **charter flights** are the most consistently economical option. You can book charters up to the last minute, but most flights at the beginning of the summer fill up well before their departure date. With charters, you can stay abroad for as long as you wish and book flights in and out of different cities. Charters do not, however, allow for changes of plan. You must choose your departure and return dates when you book, and you'll lose all or most of your money if you cancel your ticket. Charter companies can also be unreliable: They reserve the right to change the dates of your flight, add fuel surcharges after you have made your final payment, and even cancel the flight. But by far the most common problem with charters is delays. Have your ticket in hand as far in advance of the flight as possible, and arrive at the airport well before departure time to ensure that you actually get on board. Beware of fares that sound too good to be true, and *always read the fine print before you sign.* The low cost of a charter will be reflected in the service you receive—when the plane detours to pick up additional passengers, you will have to wait at the airport or in the plane before take-off or after landing. The money you save on a charter should be weighed against these disadvantages.

One of the largest U.S. charter operators, **CIEE,** offers service to points all over the world. CIEE's flights are extremely popular, so reserve early (tel. (800) 223-7402). Other charter companies offering service to Greece are **Tourlite** (tel. (800) 272-7600; in NY (212) 599-2727) and **Homeric Tours** (tel. (800) 223-5570). Tourlite, for example, offered a round-trip charter flight for as low as $499 during the summer of 1988. When you inquire about charter options, ask about the company's recent record of delays and cancellations.

If you decide to make your transatlantic crossing with a regular airline, you will purchase greater reliability and flexibility. The major airlines offer two options for the budget traveler. The first is to fly **standby.** On paper, the advantage of traveling standby is that you can come and go as you please, but the air travel industry is becoming less flexible every year. Airlines have begun phasing out standby fares and the major international companies now offer standby only to London ($279 one-way). Beware that flying standby during the peak season can turn into a nightmare of uncertainty and frustration, as hordes compete for diminishing numbers of seats. And remember that standby tickets are no longer the budget wonders they used to be. You can purchase standby tickets in advance, but you are not guaranteed a seat on any particular flight. Seat availability is known only on the day of departure, though some airlines will issue predictions (usually erring on the pessimistic side) of your chances for success on a given day. The system of assigning standby seats varies; get the official story from each company.

The second option is to fly on the **Advanced Purchase Excursion Fare (APEX).** The most sensible of the reduced fares, APEX will provide confirmed reservations and will often allow you to leave and depart from different cities. APEX does have its drawbacks—your excursion has to fit rigid minimum/maximum length requirements, usually 7 to 60 days (although some allow you to stay as long as 180 days

or a year), and you must purchase your ticket two to three weeks in advance. Book APEX fares early—summer flights can fill up as soon as June. Changes in reservations cost $50 and up; changes in return date or time cost $100. **Olympic Airways** (tel. (800) 223-1226), Greece's national airline, offers a round-trip APEX fare between New York and Athens, for a stay of one week to one year for $876 from November through February, $1059 from June through September, and $938 at other times.

Another option is to investigate less well-known airlines that try to undercut the major carriers by offering special bargains on regularly scheduled flights. Just remember that competition for seats on these small carriers is fierce. Eastern European countries also offer cheap flights to Greece, though you should expect delays and irregular flight service. Investigate **Yugoslav Airlines (JAT)** and **Baltic Airlines.**

If your plans are flexible, take advantage of travel services that sell **last-minute seats** (known as **bucket shops** in England). Organizations have begun "bulk buying" and discounting tickets on charters and commercial flights. This is still a fairly new practice, so ask carefully for all the details. Last-minute flights offer the comfort and assurance of travel on a major airline at much-reduced rates. You must give the agency three to five weeks advance notice before the desired departure date and usually must pay a $35-45 membership fee. Although there are no guarantees that a flight will be found, this option may save you money in the long run. Agencies to try include **Last Minute Travel Club** (tel. (800) LAST-MIN), **Worldwide Discount Travel Club** (tel. (305) 534-2082), **Discount Travel International** (tel. (800) 824-4000), **Stand-Buys Ltd.** (tel. (800) 225-0200), and **Moment's Notice** (tel. (212) 486-0503). **Access International** (tel. (212) 333-7280) and **Air Hitch** (tel. (212) 864-2000) advertise prices lower than most charters for standby places on scheduled flights. During the summer of 1988, for example, Access International advertised a fare of $270 one-way and $500 round-trip on flights between New York and Athens.

Another option is to fly as a **courier.** Couriers are used by major companies to deliver parcels. You get to fly for a drastically reduced fare, and the company gets to use your luggage space (you bring only carry-on bags). The major courier service is **NOW Voyager** (tel. (212) 431-1616); annual membership fee ($45) entitles you to fly on the dates they have open.

### By Boat

For those who want to travel in grand style and have the money and time to do so, the **Cunard Line's Queen Elizabeth II** (tel. (800) 221-4770) still plies the waters between New York and Southampton, and on some sailings calls at Cherbourg in northern France. From there, passengers can make their way to Greece (see From Within Europe below). In the summer of 1988, the one-way fare for a five-day crossing was $999 for a single cabin/single occupant, $799 per person for a single cabin/double occupancy. An additional port tax runs $95. Availability is limited, so write early: P.O. Box 2935, Grand Central Station, New York, NY 10163. In addition, freighters occasionally take on passengers for a transatlantic crossing; for a complete—albeit brief—list ($8.95), write to **Ford's Travel Guides,** 19448 Londelius St., Northridge, CA 91324.

## From Within Europe

### By Plane

If direct flights to Greece are booked, your next cheapest option is to fly to London or another European location (e.g., Paris, Zurich, Frankfurt, Rome), and make your way to Greece. In Europe, student/youth charters are still the least expensive way to fly. Budget fares are frequently available on high-volume flights between northern Europe and Greece but are usually offered only during the spring and summer months.

Budget agencies like CIEE and Travel CUTS can help you plan a travel itinerary before you go. Or, if you're willing to take a risk in order to save money, wait until

you're abroad to make further arrangements; see *Let's Go: Europe* for listings of student travel agencies in other European countries. London offers a veritable plethora of travel options: **Worldwide Student Travel Ltd.,** located at 37/38 Store St., London WC1E 7BZ (tel. 580-7733), and **STA Travel,** 74 Old Brompton Rd., London SW7 3LQ, are two places to begin your search. **Pilgrim Air,** 44 Goodge St., London W1P 2AD (tel. 01 580 22831), has great prices on flights from London. Another reason to fly to London first are the **bucket shops** at regular London travel agencies, which allow travelers to buy unsold tickets at unofficially discounted prices more than 50% off regular flights. (See From North America, By Air above, for similar options available in the U.S.) **Olympic Airways** offers a round-trip London-Athens fare of $333, and a round-trip Paris-Athens fare of $423. International flights also connect to airports in Crete, Rhodes, and Corfu.

### By Ferry

Ferry travel is a popular way to get to Greece. Reservations are recommended for many ferries, especially in the high season. You should check in early, at *least* two hours in advance; late boarders may find their seats gone. Deck class is fine in the summer, but you can usually find rooms down below in second- or third-class quarters to stretch out your sleeping mats. If you sleep outside, be sure to bring warm clothes and a sleeping bag. Bicycles travel free and motorcycles are transported for an additional charge (check each agency).

Some tips for traveling by ferry: Avoid at all costs crossing from Italy to Greece during the last two weeks in July and the first two in August. From the third week in June until the second week in July, prices rise about 20%, and in mid-July they jump again, as much as 50%. Bring your own food to avoid high prices charged on board. Always carry along toilet paper and a hand towel.

The major ports of embarkation for ferries between Greece and Italy are **Ancona** and **Brindisi,** on the southeastern coast of Italy. Boats travel primarily to Corfu (9 hr., deck class in high-season 5000-6500dr, low-season 3400-4300dr), Igoumenitsa (11 hr., same prices as Corfu), and Patras (19 hr., deck class in high-season 5500-6500dr, low-season 3750-5500). With a ticket to Patras, you can stop over in Corfu and Igoumenitsa, provided you indicate this prior to embarkation (they must write "S.O. Corfu and/or Igoumenitsa" on the ticket). You'll have to pay a port tax of 700dr when you reboard. In Patras, you can get off and take a bus directly to Athens (4 hr., 1000-1200dr); the route is also serviced by train.

Most lines offer discounts. Those 26 and under, and ISIC-holders 30 and under, can usually obtain student deck fares for 1000dr less than the regular price. Senior citizens may get a 10% discount, and children under 12 pay half-price (under 4 ride free). **Eurail** and **InterRail** passholders may receive 30% off regular fares. Finally, there are group (usually 10-people minimum) reductions of approximately 10% on one-way and 20% on round-trip tickets. Regardless of the ticket, everyone pays the port tax (5000-6000L in Brindisi, 450-600dr at Greek ports). Rates vary from company to company, so it pays to shop around.

In addition to stops at Corfu, Igoumenitsa, and Patras, ferries also stop at Piraeus; Iraklion (600dr); Rhodes; Limassol; Cyprus (from Piraeus high-season 6500dr, low-season 5850dr); **Haifa,** Israel (from Piraeus high season 10,200dr, low season 8750dr); and **Izmir,** Turkey (3000dr). Ferries also depart from **Bari,** Italy for other Mediterranean points. Keep in mind that ferries from Bari and Ancona take a long time to reach Greece (Ancona-Patras 36 hr.). Look for Anna Karenina when the Black Sea Steamship Line's *Lev Tolstoy* sails every three weeks from **Odessa,** USSR to Istanbul (21 hr.), and then to Piraeus (24 hr. from Istanbul). Voyages are also made once or twice weekly from Yugoslavia during March through October from **Rijeka** (41 hr.) or **Dubrovnik** (18 hr.) to Corfu and Igoumenitsa on the *Jadrolinija*.

### By Train

Greece is served by a number of international train routes that connect Athens, Thessaloniki, and Larissa to most European cities. Count on at least a three-day journey from Trieste or Vienna to Athens. **Eurailpasses** are best for those travelers

who want to see as much of Europe as possible; to make these passes pay off, you need to make a lot of stops. Valid in Austria, Belgium, Denmark, Finland, France, West Germany, Greece, Ireland, Italy, Luxembourg, the Netherlands, Norway, and Northern Ireland, the passes are issued only outside of Europe and must be validated upon first use by any ticket office abroad within six months of the original date of issue. Passes include unlimited first-class travel and cost $298 for 15 days, $470 for 1 month, $650 for 2 months, $798 for 3 months. Children under 12 pay half-price (under 4 ride free). Those under 26 will want to purchase a **Eurail Youthpass** to get unlimited second-class travel. One month travel costs $320, two months $420. A group of three or more travelers can pay $210 per person for the **Eurail Saverpass,** which allows for 15 consecutive days of unlimited travel, provided the group travels together. (Children under 12 pay *full fare,* under 4 are free.) *Two* people traveling together can use a Eurail Saverpass as long as their traveling time falls between October 1 and March 31. All three types of passes offer free travel in Greece and 30% discounts on ferries from Brindisi to Patras on Adriatica Lines' or Hellenic Mediterranean Lines' ferries from Piraeus to Cyprus, Venice, Alexandria, and Turkey. (Eurail passes are *not* good for inner-Greece ferries, however.) Keep your validation slip and receipt of sale. For a free Eurailtariff Manual of train routes, ask your travel agent or write the French National Railroad, 610 Fifth Ave., New York, NY 10020 (tel. (212) 582-4813).

If you board a train that has no available compartment space for a long trip, consider getting off and waiting for the next one—three days in an aisle crowded with travelers and livestock can be a nightmare. *Couchettes* are the economy version of a full sleeping berth and come complete with blankets, sheets, and pillows. If you have any sort of railpass, *couchettes* are available at an extra charge of about $11 per trip. Sleeping train riders are easy prey for thieves, so guard your goods.

### By Bus

Another inexpensive overland possibility is bus travel. Amsterdam, Athens, Instanbul, London, and Munich all serve as centers for private bus lines providing long-distance tours across Europe. **Magic Bus** offers cheap, direct bus service between major cities in Europe, along with competitive air fares to and within Europe. Offices are located at 20 Filellinon St., Syntagma, Athens (tel. 323 74 71); and 32 Tsimiski St., Thessaloniki (tel. 28 32 68). Information on Magic Bus is available from cooperating offices in many other cities. **Miracle Bus** (tel. 01 379 6055), 408 The Strand, London WC2, is another reasonably-priced coach service running between major cities. **London Student Travel,** 52 Grosvenor Gardens, London SW1 (tel. (01) 730 34 02) offers competitive rail, coach, and air fares all over the continent.

### By Thumb

Hitching out of big cities is dangerous and difficult. If you plan to hitchhike to Greece, *don't* stray from the main Zagreb-Belgrade highway when you reach Yugoslavia. Hitching in Yugoslavia is already difficult enough; using back roads, you may never get to Greece. Try not to hitch at night; it is very easy to get run over. *Europe: A Manual for Hitch-Hikers* is available for £3.95 from Vacation Work Publications, 9 Park End St., Oxford OX1 1HJ, England (include £2 for air mail postage). Those interested in hiking may want to look at J. Sydney Jones' *Tramping in Europe: A Walking Guide* for $7.95 (Prentice-Hall, 1984).

### By Car

When you rent or lease a car, you must pay the V.A.T. of the country in which you rent or lease it. The tax can range from 14-20% depending on the country, with Germany the lowest at 14%. Make sure this considerable tax amount is included when you get a price quote. Also check the minimum age requirement. To get the best rates, you should reserve and pay at home as much as three weeks in advance. Once in Greece, you may find cheaper rentals, but you sacrifice the convenience and security of planning ahead. Budget for gas; it's expensive. Consult the Greek Consulate office for more information (see Useful Organizations above).

## Trips from Greece

The budget travel offices that line Nikis and Filellinon Streets in Athens offer
youth and student (under 26) fares to five continents, as well as round-the-world
stopover tickets to the West Coast of the U.S., Bombay, and Bangkok are the cheapest points of entry to India and Southeast Asia. Fairly comprehensive stop-over
tickets to Los Angeles have become a particularly good deal since the devaluation
of the *drachma*.

### To Israel

The cheap but slow way to travel from Greece to Israel is by ferry, though it
is more time-consuming than the four-hour flight. El Al and **Olympic Airways** have
daily flights from Athens to Tel Aviv; tickets are $300 and up. Two companies offer
ferry service between Greece and Israel. **Stability Line** ships, *Virginia* and *Queen
Virginia*, sail from Piraeus to Haifa every 10 days, stopping in Mykonos, Rhodes,
and Limassol. The entire journey, including stopovers, lasts approximately 60
hours. From June 25 through September 15, tickets on deck are 10,200dr, students
8160dr; low season 8750dr and 7000dr, respectively. Prices are the same for the
30-hour journey from Iraklion, Mykonos, or Rhodes. **Afroessa Lines'** *Paloma* sails
from Limassol to Haifa (Mon. 4pm and Thurs. 7pm, 11 hr., 4400dr, students
3520dr), following the *Virginia's* route.

### To Turkey

It is rumored that European charter flight travelers may risk losing their return
ticket if a Turkish stamp is found in their passport; check with the regulations of
your charter company to make sure. The Greek government does not want travelers
who fly charters to Greece to spend their vacation in Turkey; because of this, European charter travelers are permitted only one-day excursions. (For further informa-

tion on travel to Turkey, see individual island ferry listings and the introduction to Turkey.)

# Once There

## Tourist Services

Tourism in Greece is managed by two nationwide organizations: the **Greek National Tourist Organization (GNTO)** and the **tourist police** (*touristiki astinomia*). The GNTO can supply general information about sights and accommodations all over the country. Offices in the U.S. and other countries are listed under Useful Organizations; the main office is at 2 Amerikis St., Athens (tel. 322 31 11). Note that the GNTO is known as **EOT** in Greece. The tourist police deal with more local and immediate problems—where to find a room, what the bus schedule is, or what to do when you've lost your passport. They are open long hours and are always willing to help, although their English is often limited. Tourist information for Greece, in English, is available 24 hours by calling 171.

**Nikis** and **Filellinon Streets** in Athens are lined with agencies and organizations geared specifically towards budget and student travelers. We also list similar establishments in different cities in the Orientation and Practical Information section for each region.

A warning: Don't be surprised if tourism has not affected the Greek way of business. Expect to be overlooked wherever you go. Ask the price before you buy, and be willing to bargain in tourist shops. Always watch to see what Greeks are paying for the same item.

### Emergencies

In each regional section, under Orientation and Practical Information, we list telephone numbers for the police. We also list the telephone numbers for ambulances, medical emergency centers, local hospitals and clinics, and pharmacies. Emergency phone numbers, applicable throughout most of Greece and operating 24 hours, include **police** (tel. 100), and **first aid** (tel. 166).

## Business Hours and Holidays

Shops close on Sundays, and only restaurants, cafes, and bakeries remain open. During the week business hours vary, but most places close after 2pm for a *siesta* and re-open at about 6pm. Do your errands early. Banks are open Monday through Thursday 8am to 2pm, Friday 7:45am to 2pm. Post offices are open Monday through Saturday 7:30am-7:30pm. Shops and pharmacies are open Monday, Wednesday, and Saturday 8am to 2:30pm and Tuesday, Thursday, and Friday 8am to 1pm and 5 to 8:30pm. Food stores have slightly longer hours. Museums and archeological sites close on Tuesdays, and have slightly shorter hours from mid-October to mid-May. On holidays, sights will often have Sunday opening hours. All banks and shops, as well as most archeological sites and museums, close on holidays. (See the Holidays below for dates.)

## Accommodations

Relative to those in the U.S. and elsewhere in Europe, accommodations in Greece are still quite a bargain. In addition to the usual budget hotels and student hostels, most Greek towns have inexpensive rooms and houses to let, as well as some camping facilities. Be skeptical, however, about offers to be driven to a pension or hotel. Let the driver show you the destination on a map; it may be miles out of town.

One saving grace is Greece's warm, sunny climate—if all else fails, you can always unfurl your sleeping bag in some secluded field or deserted **beach** (provided you don't break any town ordinances). Some hotels may let you stretch out on their rooftops for a small fee.

## Hotels

The GNTO governs the construction and classification of all hotels. The classification awarded to each establishment is determined by the size, decor, and furnishings of the rooms and public areas, and the services provided by the staff. Rates vary according to classification and are enforced by the government. Proprietors are legally entitled, and therefore inclined, to charge 10% extra for stays of less than three nights, and 20% extra overall in high season (July 1-Sept. 15). In order to squeeze more *drachmae* out of you, they may only offer their most expensive rooms, compel you to buy breakfast, squeeze three people into a hostel-like triple and charge each for a single, or quote a price for a room that includes breakfast and private shower and then charge extra for both.

Showers are usually 100dr but can cost as much as 150dr. They're usually located off the hall for communal use; you may wait forever before there's enough hot water. Toilets, too, are usually located down the hall. One note on Greek toilets: If a trash container is within reach of the toilet, this is where used toilet paper goes. Otherwise, the toilet is likely to become jammed (Greek plumbing is not a technological wonder). If worse comes to worst, the pages of your *Let's Go* have been made of acid-free paper for your comfort—the toilet paper of the budget traveler.

If proprietors offer you a room that seems unreasonably expensive, stress that you don't want luxuries and, perhaps grudgingly, they'll tell you of a cheaper option. Late at night, in the off-season, or in a large town, it's a buyer's market, and owners will be more willing to lower prices or offer free showers. You can, and should, bargain. As a form of security deposit, most hotels will ask for your passport and return it when you leave—just make sure you get your own back. You can often leave your luggage in the reception area during the afternoon, though check-out is at 11am or noon.

The tourist police are on your side. If a hotel flagrantly violates the prices shown by law at the registration desk, or if you think that you've been exploited in any way, threaten to report the hotel to the tourist police; the threat alone will often resolve "misunderstandings."

*Let's Go* lists almost exclusively D- and E-class hotels, starting in price at 900dr for singles and 1300-1700dr for doubles (prices may be more than 100dr less in the off-season). A hotel with no singles may still put you in a room by yourself; just remember to haggle over the price *before* you accept the room. More information is available from the **Hellenic Chamber of Hotels,** 2, Stadiou and Karageorgi Servias, Athens (tel. 323 71 93).

### Hostels

Greek youth hostels are an excellent alternative to hotels. In general, the accommodations are good and the cost is reasonable: 400dr per night (500dr in Athens, Delphi, Nafplion, and Thessaloniki). Unfortunately, these bastions of budget travelers are relatively scarce; they may turn up in places you'd least expect them and not in places you most need them. At present, Greece has over 25 official youth hostels.

Greek youth hostels generally have fewer restrictions than those in northern Europe. Most are open year-round and have midnight or 1am curfews (which, by the way, are strictly enforced, and may leave you in the streets if you come back too late). In summer, they stay open from 6 to 10am and 1pm to midnight (shorter hours in winter). The large hostels offer breakfast for 200-300dr. Hostels often have a maximum stay of five days. It is advisable to book in advance in the summer at some of the more popular hostels in Athens, Thira, or Nafplion.

You may need an IYHF card to stay at some Greek youth hostels, but most places pay no attention to them. (For further information, see Hostel Membership above.)

### Rooms to Let

Wherever there are tourists, you'll see lots of private homes with signs offering *dhomatia* (rooms to let). The owners of these houses often crowd around incoming boats or buses in order to solicit customers. If you don't see them, go to a cafe and ask where you can find rooms. Most of the rooms are cheap (singles 800dr, doubles 1400dr) and perfectly dependable. There may not be locks, towels, or telephones, but there may be warm offers of coffee at night and friendly conversations. Prices here are especially variable, so make sure that you're paying no more than you would at a D-class hotel. If in doubt, ask the tourist police: They will usually set you up with a room and conduct all the negotiations themselves. Most *dhomatia* operate only in the high season and they are always a good option for those arriving somewhere without previous reservations. If you're really strapped for money, consider asking proprietors to let you sleep on the roof. In many cases, they will charge a small fee for the privilege.

### Traditional Settlements

Greece has a number of traditional villages and buildings which have been preserved and restored by the GNTO in an effort to maintain the country's architectural heritage. The restoration of a number of Greek villages promises to offer a taste of "small town" Greek life to visitors, and to improve the economy in these areas. Thus far, eight settlements have been converted into guesthouses: Oia on Santorini, Makrinitsa and Vizitsa on Mt. Pelion, Mesta on Chios, Psara Island, Fiskardo on Cephalonia, Kapetanakos in Areopolis, and Papigo-Zagohoria in Epirus. Doubles range from 1300-6500dr; the GNTO can make reservations and provide further information.

### Camping

Camping is one of the easiest ways to escape the monotony of barren hotel rooms, hostel regulations, and other limitations of conventional lodgings. More importantly, it's one of the cheapest ways to spend the night.

The GNTO is primarily responsible for campgrounds in Greece (see Useful Organizations and Publications above). Tourist Guide of Greece, 137 Patission St., Athens 11251 (tel. 864 16 88), also puts out a for a list of official camping sites in Greece. Most of the official GNTO campgrounds have good facilities, including drinking water, lavatories, and electricity. Many are located in areas of outstanding natural beauty. The Hellenic Touring Club also runs a number of campgrounds, most of which are less expensive than the GNTO campgrounds. In addition, Greece has many campgrounds run by private organizations.

The prices charged at campgrounds depend on the facilities; you will usually pay 200-300dr per person, plus 150-200dr per tent. GNTO campgrounds tend to be ritzier and more expensive (up to 2000dr in some places).

More often than not, you can discover unofficial campgrounds on the outskirts of town or along quiet shores. On many of the islands, campers will simply take to the beaches. Freelance camping outside campgrounds is outlawed to prevent littering and fires, but if the local police think you will avoid these misdemeanors, especially during the off-season, they will rarely disturb you. If you sleep on a famous beach in front of some empty hotel during the off-season, though, one of the hotel owners might well report you to the police, who are then obliged to take appropriate measures. During July and August when hotels and pensions are booked solid, sleeping outdoors becomes commonplace and no one will object since you are not hurting business. The worst that will happen is that your passport will be confiscated and sold back for about 1000dr. More likely, you may just be told to move.

The basics for camping include a: sleeping bag, foam pad, and tent (or tarpaulin or bivouac sac). Sleeping bags with synthetic fillers are cheaper, more durable, and more water-resistant than their down counterparts. Mummy bags are lighter and more compact; they're especially useful to hikers who don't need extra baggage. Synthetic bags usually cost $20-50. A foam pad can add protection and warmth. Prices range from around $10 for simple Ensolite pads, to around $50 for the best air mattress or a sophisticated hybrid like Thermarest. These pads are also crucial if you plan to sleep on the decks of ferries.

Modern tents are designed to be "self-supporting"; they have their own frames and suspension systems, can be set up quickly, and do not require staking. When buying a tent, make certain that it has a rain fly and bug netting and weighs no more than 3½kg. Synthetic canvas is less expensive, lighter, and more water-resistant than cotton canvas, but it is also less "breathable." Make sure that the edges of the tent floor extend several inches off the ground to prevent water seepage from the outside. Backpackers and cyclists may wish to pay a bit more for a sophisticated lightweight tent that is easy to pack—some two-person tents weigh just over two pounds—but expect less space for a lighter load. Car travelers, on the other hand, should consider buying a tent larger than they need, perhaps even a three-to-four person tent for only two travelers. Expect to pay $70-100. It is sometimes possible to get a decent tent for as little as $30, but check it out carefully and be sure you can return it.

Other basics include a battery-operated lantern (never gas) for use inside the tent, and a simple plastic groundcloth to protect the tent floor. If you plan on roughing it in extremely primitive areas, water sacks and/or a solar shower may be necessary. Most campgrounds provide grills and allow you to gather firewood for cooking, but in case a campground prohibits wood fires, purchase a small campstove that runs on butane or white gas. They come in handy, especially for making coffee, but expect to pay $35-125 for one. Carry waterproof matches; a spill in the lake can leave you without a fire for a night.

## Travel Within Greece

### By Air

Olympic Airways, 96 Syngrou Ave., 117 41 Athens (tel. (01) 92 92 111), serves many of the larger cities and islands within Greece. While flying might seem quickest, within Greece it may not be the most convenient or flexible option; coverage in some remote areas is spotty at best. (For further flight information within Greece, check the regional Practical Information listings of airports, flight destinations, and prices.)

## By Bus

Spending time in Greece invariably means travel by bus. Service is extensive and frequent in some areas, and fares are very reasonable. On major highways, buses tend to be more modern and efficient than in the mountainous areas of the Peloponnese or northern Greece. The **OSE** (see By Train below) offers limited bus service from a few cities. Unless you are sticking close to train routes, **KTEL** should be sufficient.

Always ask an official when a bus is scheduled to leave (posted schedules are often out of date, and all services are curtailed significantly on Sun.), and try to arrive at least 10 minutes before departure (Greek buses have a habit of leaving early). Always make sure that you know from where the buses leave. In major cities, KTEL bus lines have different stations for different destinations. In villages, a cafe usually serves as the bus station, and you can only find out schedules by asking the proprietor. Always ask the conductor before entering the bus whether it's going to your destination (the signs on the front are often misleading or outdated), and make clear where you want to get off. If the bus whizzes past your stop, stand up and shout *"Stassis!"* (The general practice is to push one of the few buttons which line the roof of the bus in advance of your stop.) If you're on the road, you must stand near a *"Stassis"* sign to pick up an intercity bus.

For long-distance rides, generally in Pullmans, you should buy your ticket beforehand in the office. (If you don't, you may have to stand throughout the journey.) For shorter trips, just grab a seat and pay the conductor after you have boarded. Fares are inexpensive. On Crete and some of the larger islands, fares tend to be more expensive for comparable distances. Some lines offer round-trip fares with a 20% discount. Long-distance fares are often lower in the off-season. In towns and cities, local buses and trolleys charge around 20dr for a ride, 30dr in Athens.

## By Train

Greek trains are inferior to the sleek, modern lines in northern Europe, and only run to major cities. Furthermore, service to some areas is painfully slow, and no lines go to the western coast. Trains are not very useful for traveling to remote areas or many archeological sites, either. Trains travel daily between Athens and Thessaloniki (8 hr.), continuing on to Alexandroupolis and Turkey or north to Yugoslavia and the rest of Europe. Lines also extend into the Peloponnese to Corinth, Patras, Olympia, and Kalamata.

**Eurail** and **InterRail** passes are both valid on Greek trains, though a conductor will occasionally give you a dull stare when you present them. In addition, the **Hellenic Railways Organization (OSE)** connects Athens to other major Greek cities and offers a 20% reduction on all round-trip fares and discounts to those under 26. OSE also sells touring cards that offer unlimited travel for 10, 20, or 30 days (also valid on OSE buses). For more information, write to Hellenic Railways Organization, 1-3 Karolou St., Athens (tel. 52 22 491). For schedules and prices in Greece, dial 145 or 147.

## By Ferry

Every summer, visitors to the Greek islands envision themselves sunning leisurely on spacious ship decks while being smoothly whisked from isle to isle; every summer, these same visitors get turned off by bewildering schedules and crowded boats. Ferries are still the cheapest way to traverse the Mediterranean, though.

Don't worry about planning an itinerary far in advance, unless you are traveling in the off-season; during the summer months, boat connections between major islands are frequent. You often have to change boats several times, however, to reach a destination off the main route, and even during the high season, some islands are accessible only a few times per week. Direct connections are less expensive than longer routes (the more stops, the higher the price), but also tend to be less frequent.

Do not assume that the least time-consuming way to travel between distant islands is the shortest in nautical miles. Returning to Piraeus (Athens' port) can often be quicker because it gives you access to a much wider range of departure times. In the off-season, boats from Piraeus continue regularly, while boats between islands cut back their service.

Since ferry prices are controlled by the Greek government, there is no need to shop around. To get a full list of departure times and dates, ask at a tourist office. The harbor police at the port can help direct you to individual ferry departures. Ferries leave Piraeus daily for most large islands. Prices in June, 1988 were as follows: Iraklion 1755dr, Hania 1631dr, Mykonos 1258 dr, Santorini 1554dr, Paros 1130dr, Naxos 1282dr, Ios 1554dr, Syros 1126dr, Rhodes 2374dr, Kos 2144dr, and Karpathos 2269dr. Prices are reduced in off-season.

**Agapitos Lines,** 99, Koloktroni St., Piraeus 18535 (tel. 413 62 46), sells a "Greek Island Pass" for seven days unlimited travel (3500dr) or 30 days (7000dr) on any, and as many, of their stopovers to the islands.

Exchanges and refunds are difficult to obtain. Double check every connection you intend to make—once you reach an island, and again a few hours before departure—with the boat company or the agency selling tickets. Since boat schedules often change at the last minute, try to remain flexible. Boats will sell tickets on deck, but generally tickets will be less expensive at the ferry agency.

In general, boats come in three types: large car ferries, small passenger boats, and smaller excursion boats. **Hydrofoils,** high speed jetboats, service the Saronic Gulf Islands and the Cyclades; the trips are faster and more frequent, but also far more expensive than regular ferry routes. Passenger boats give a truer sense of sailing the Aegean. This intimacy can cause trouble in rough weather: Seasickness is a common problem when the strong *meltemi* winds from the south buck up waves that toss small boats like corks. If the seas look bad, don't eat much before or during your voyage, but do drink liquids to avoid dehydration.

A warning: Boat crews throughout the Aegean occasionally call strikes during the summer months. Though usually brief, they can cause problems, particularly if you need to make an infrequent connection. Keep your ears open: Strikes are often announced a few days in advance.

### By Motorbike

Motorbiking is a popular way of touring Greece, especially the islands. You can rent bikes more cheaply than cars, and they offer much more freedom than buses, particularly if you wish to visit remote areas. Plenty of places offer scooters or mopeds for rent, but the quality of bikes, speed of service in case of breakdown, and prices for longer periods may vary drastically. Nearly all agencies are open to bargaining. Expect to pay 1000-1500dr per day for a 50cc scooter, the cheapest bike able to tackle steep mountain roads. 150cc and 200cc motorbikes cost 20% and 30% more, respectively, but require a Greek motorcycle license. (Many establishments will lease the bikes without a license, but in the event of an accident you'll be in trouble.) For week-long rentals, most shops charge for five days. If the agency provides a full tank, they're apt to add 200dr to the daily bill. Many agencies request your passport as a deposit, but this is an *illegal* practice; instead, pay them ahead of time. If they have your passport and you have an accident or mechanical failure, they may refuse to return it until you pay for all repairs. Before renting, ask if the quoted price includes the 20% tax and insurance, or you'll be hit for several hundred unexpected *drachmae*.

Ask what the bike insurance covers, and don't believe anyone who says "all damage to the bike." While most places offer insurance at about 140dr per day, it is usually third-party liability insurance, which pays only for damage to anything you hit. It does not cover damage to your machine or yourself. Full insurance coverage is generally not available in Greece. The best you can do is to purchase insurance with a hefty 16,000dr deductible (80-140dr per day). In any case, before you rent a scooter or motorcycle, demand to know the details of the coverage. Ride a bike down the block before you take it.

Most important, ride carefully—motorbikes are dangerous on rocky, winding roads. Wear your helmet. The miniature shrine-like *proskenitari* on the sides of the roads mark spots where people have survived motor accidents and wished to thank the saints for sparing their lives. Riders should be extra careful when they pass the boxes, as they usually mark a dangerous curve.

## By Car

Driving might just be the ideal way to tour Greece. There are highways on the mainland, and ferries can take you island hopping if you pay a transport fee for the automobile. Small villages usually cater to cars only through the main road running through town.

Potential drivers should be comfortable with a standard stick shift, mountain dirt roads, reckless drivers (especially in Athens), and the Greek alphabet. Greek signs are placed about 100m before the transliterated versions, which are stuck right at the turn-offs.

**Rentals** with unlimited mileage and very limited insurance range from 15,000dr in the off-season to 25,000dr in the summer. Gasoline is 72dr per liter—about $2 per gallon. (In a full day of touring (300km), Hertz's Subaru 600 (an economy hatchback) will eat up a full tank, translating into 17½ liters and about 1300dr.) Agencies quote low daily rates, but these prices exclude the 20% tax and Collision Damage Waiver (CDW) insurance. Without CDW, the driver is responsible for the first 150,000dr worth of damage if theft or accident is not the driver's fault, and the full amount otherwise. CDW insurance (425dr per day) is strongly recommended.

Check the fine print with care. Some places quote lower rates but hit you with hidden charges—exorbitant refueling bills if you come back with less than a full tank, 1½-2½dr per kilometer drop-off or special charge, or 100km per day minimum mileage even if you never leave their driveway. Most companies will not permit driving the car outside Greece or ferrying it out of the country. Hertz and Inter-Rent rent to drivers aged 21, but most other companies only rent to those 23 and older.

Greece has 4100km of asphalt roads. The roads in the mountains tend to be particularly narrow and tricky, though taxi drivers seem to think otherwise. Toot your horn or flick your lights when passing.

The cheapest and largest rental agencies are Just, InterRent, and Retca, with offices in Athens and other mainland cities, as well as on Crete and several of the islands. In Athens, look for **Just,** 43 Singrou Ave. 11743 (tel. 923 85 66 or 923 91 04), **InterRent,** 4 Singrou Ave. 11742 (tel. 921 57 88/9 or 923 34 52), and **Retca** 20 Kalisperi St. (tel. 921 43 73 or 922 49 98)—also Ethelondon Dodekanission, 26, Rhodes 0241-24008. Other inexpensive agencies include **Herodian,** 11 Mitseon and Madjihristou St., Athens (tel. 923 23 18 or 923 24 15), and **Royal Rent A Car,** 44 Amalias Ave., Athens (tel. 324 53 66). **Avis, Hertz, Europcar,** and **Budget** also operate all over Greece; their rates are steeper, but you get a good car and reliable service.

Foreign drivers are required to have an **international driver's license** and an **International Insurance Certificate** to drive in Greece. (For details on how to obtain these documents, see Driver's License above.) The Automobile and Touring Club of Greece (ELPA), 2 Messogion St., Athens 11527 (tel. 779 16 15), provides tourists with assistance and information, and offers reciprocal membership to foreign auto club members. They also have a 24-hour emergency repair service (tel. 104) and an information line (tel. 174).

To enter the country with a car, you need a "Carnet de Passage en Douanes," available from the American Automobile Association (though you may be allowed in for a short period of time without it).

## By Foot

While *Let's Go* describes many hikes, local residents and fellow travelers can suggest even more. Always make sure you have comfortable shoes and a proper map.

Remember that high altitudes coupled with hot sun make hiking at midday unsafe; bring sunscreen, a hat, and plenty of water wherever you go. **The Mountaineers Books** offers the guide *Greece on Foot* ($10.95); write to 306 2nd Ave. W., Seattle, WA 98119 (tel. (800) 553-4453).

### By Thumb

It's hard to generalize about hitching in Greece. Greeks are not eager to pick up foreigners and foreign cars are usually full of other travelers, and sparsely-populated areas simply have little or no traffic. By and large, though, hitching is an adequate way of getting around. Write your destination on a sign in both Greek and English letters. Try to hitch from turn-offs rather than along long stretches of straight road. Two or three people hitching together with large backpacks should try to split up to get rides more easily.

# Life in Greece

## History

Recorded Greek history spans nearly 30 centuries, and archeological evidence suggests that migratory tribes settled on Crete as far back as 5000 B.C.E. The introduction of metalwork from the east during the **Bronze Age** (2900 B.C.E.) enabled these tribes to develop great cities and powerful navies. Three great civilizations arose in this period—the Cycladic, the Minoan, and the Mycenaean.

A westward migration of neolithic farmers deposited small communities throughout the Cyclades at the beginning of the fourth millenium B.C.E. As the mining and crafting of copper became lucrative in the early third millenium B.C.E., Cycladic communities enlarged, necessitating an early form of central government. Yet the Cycladic civilization was soon eclipsed by the **Minoans** (2500-1500 B.C.E.), who built magnificent palaces at Knossos and other sites on Crete. Minoan culture extended far into the Peloponnese but was destroyed by a giant volcanic eruption. From its ashes evolved one of the greatest prehistoric civilizations of all time, the **Mycenaeans** (1500-900 B.C.E.). These people built the high walls of the Acropolis in Athens and dominated the Aegean world for several centuries with their powerful navies. The *Iliad* is the tale of how the ill-fated King Agamemnon led a Mycenaean expedition to Troy in 1200 B.C.E.

Powerful as they were, the Mycenaeans could not withstand the forces of change. The mass migration of four Hellenic tribes to the Greek mainland in 900 B.C.E., known as the Dorian invasion, marked the beginning of the **Geometric Period** (900-700 B.C.E.), during which various tribes developed a common alphabet, religious system, and a form of government. The cultural unity was further enhanced by the establishment of the Olympic Games in 776 B.C.E.

In the **Archaic Period** (700-480 B.C.E.), Hellenic cultural integration progressed, though the tribes divided politically into separate city-states. The two most powerful city-states, Sparta and Athens, engaged in a furious rivalry. Sparta essentially developed a totalitarian society with a rigid military code based on territorial conquest, while Athens established a more loosely ordered and "democratic" society, one which encouraged cooperation between city-states and cultivation of the arts. The two rivals united for a time to win the **Persian Wars,** which lasted from the battle of Marathon in 490 B.C.E. to the battle at Plataea in 479 B.C.E.

The **Classical Period** (480-323 B.C.E.) marked the height of Greek cultural development. As the leader of the Delian Confederacy, Athens flourished both economically and culturally. Wealth accumulated from shipping, trading, and tribute from allies enabled the Athenians to beautify their city with temples, theaters, and other magnificent monuments. Under their eponymous leader Pericles, architects designed the buildings on the Acropolis and in the Agora.

The bipolar world of ancient Greece exploded in the fifth century at the onset of the Coreyran civil war. Alliances from both leagues consequently forced Athens and Sparta into the 27-year **Peloponnesian War,** from which Sparta emerged successful. Although Athens never regained its former military strength, Athenian cultural life continued to prosper. From 400 to 300 B.C.E., Socrates, Plato, and Aristotle made major contributions to human knowledge, and sculptors such as Scopas and Praxiteles experimented with new forms.

While Athens and Sparta struggled for military supremacy, a new political force began to emerge in Macedonia. In the four decades before the **Hellenistic Period** (323-146 B.C.E.), the Macedonians under King Philip II conquered most of the Greek cities and built a powerful confederacy. The illustrious Alexander the Great, son of Philip, embarked on a historic expedition in 336 B.C.E to conquer the vast empire of the Persians. In only 13 years, he subdued his foe and extended Hellenic influence far into Africa and Asia.

After Alexander's death, violent internal conflicts rendered the Greek city-states vulnerable to invasion. In 146 B.C.E., Roman legions conquered Greece; subsequently, Greek culture spread throughout Rome. For the next four centuries Rome took the role of protector of Greece. The Christianization of the Roman Empire in 398 C.E. launched Greece along a different path. During the **Byzantine Period** (500-1200 C.E.), Greeks abandoned paganism and adopted Christianity.

The fall of Constantinople (the capital named after emperor Constantine) to the Ottoman Empire in 1453 C.E. propelled Greece into its darkest period; Turks ruled Greece with a ruthless hand throughout much of the **Middle Ages.** Persecuted Christians fled to remote monasteries, such as Meteora, or to the West. Uprisings against the Turks occurred sporadically, but it was not until the early nineteenth century that the modern Greek state came into existence.

In 1821, a revolutionary army composed of guerilla from the Peloponnese and the Aegean Islands began to battle the Turkish armies. The conflict soon reached a stalemate, providing an opportunity for intervention by the three great Western powers—France, England, and Russia—on the side of the Greek insurgents. Greek independence was declared on March 25 of that year, the day now officially celebrated as Greek Independence Day. The final military triumph in the **Greek War of Independence** came in 1827 at the Battle of Navarino, in which allied navies decimated a joint Turkish-Egyptian fleet, breaking the Turkish hold on Greece.

## Government and Politics

During the twentieth century, Greece was stirred by coups, uprisings, wars, and treaties. In 1909, the Greek leader Eleftherios Venizelos ousted the monarchy that had ruled Greece for almost a century and installed a republican government. World War I, however, threatened to split the country over an alliance with Germany. The bitterness between Greeks and Turks was exacerbated after the Greek army, encouraged by Great Britain, led an unsuccessful attack on its neighbor, losing 50,000 men. In 1930, the weary Greek army returned the old monarchy to power.

During World War II, the Greeks fought valiantly alongside the Allies. Greek resistance fighters, led by the communist-backed ELAS, held off the Germans for several months, greatly bolstering the Allied effort. In 1941, Greece fell to Germany, and many Greek civilians were summarily executed. With the gradual defeat of the Nazis came a surge of communist power from within the country. An attempted coup was defeated by British forces. In 1949, with substantial U.S. aid, the Greek government thwarted another coup attempt and ended the Civil War. The U.S. gave further aid to Greece under the Truman Doctrine of 1952 to help restabilize the country.

From 1952 to 1963, Greece was governed by a coalition of conservative parties within a republican government led by Constantine Karamanlis. In 1963, the centrist Union party outpolled the conservatives but was unable to maintain control of the government. Political instability led junior military officers to stage a coup on April 21, 1967 and institute a military dictatorship. The *junta,* led by General Papadopoulos, was criticized for repressing speech and intimidating political opponents through torture and imprisonment. Many Greeks left the country, including actress Melina Mercouri and the aforementioned Karamanlis; movies such as Costa Gavras' *Z* publicized the oppressive and undemocratic nature of the *junta*.

The dictatorship collapsed in 1974 when General Ioannidis seized power from Papadopoulos and decided to overthrow Archbishop Makarios, the President of Cyprus. Ioannidis' move provoked the Turkish invasion of Cyprus. Afraid of losing public confidence and inviting a disastrous war, Greek senior military officers requested the return of Karamanlis, who had lived in self-imposed exile for several years. As the designated prime minister, Karamanlis headed a coalition government, skillfully orchestrated parliamentary elections, and organized a referendum to determine the fate of the government. The monarchy was defeated by a two-thirds vote, and a constitution for a republican government was drawn up in 1975. The new constitution establishes free general elections and a 300-member parliament, which appoints the president; the majority party leader becomes prime minister of the country. Greece is a member of NATO (1952), the Council of Europe, the Common Market (1962), and the European Economic Community (1981).

The leftist Pan-Hellenic Socialist Party (PASOK) currently governs Greece under Prime Minister Andreas Papandreos. The right-wing New Democracy (ND), under control of Mitsotakis, constitute the strong opposition. Greece's two communist parties, the KKE and the Greek Left, campaign heatedly against the American military bases in Greece. Papandreos' government leans toward neutrality and has considered closing the U.S. bases and withdrawing from NATO entirely.

For a scholarly account of modern Greece, read Richard Clogg's *A Short History of Modern Greece,* or C.M. Woodhouse's *The Story of Modern Greece.* A weekly review of events is also available through the Greek Press and Information Office (see Useful Organizations above.)

## Art and Architecture

If you don't know Doric from Ionic, and want to make sense of all those rocks that make up ancient Greek ruins, try to learn something beforehand about Greek art and architecture. Ancient Greek art may be divided into a number of periods, roughly corresponding to the historical eras.

The earliest Greek societies were warrior tribes who developed the craft of metalwork, a period known as the **Bronze Age.** Many sculptures remain from this period, during which the Cycladic, Minoan, and Mycenaean civilizations emerged.

In the **Geometric Period** (900-700 B.C.E.), artists developed new techniques and more expressive styles of sculpture and painting. Characteristic pottery of this period can be seen in the National Archeological Museum in Athens. Architects of the time created simple structures, and designed one-room temples with columned porches and raised altars. Examples of Geometric architecture are concentrated at Olympia.

The **Archaic Period** (700-480 B.C.E.) marked the transition from the simplicity of the Geometric Period to the more elaborate forms of the Classical Period. The cyclindrical Doric column and the fluted Ionic column were developed in this period. The Doric temple was a massive rectangular structure with rows of columns around the outside and two interior rooms, the *cella* and the *pronaus.* Sculptors created stylized *kouroi* (men) and *kourai* (women)—free-standing human figures. Artists gained skill in composition and movement, honing the techniques for narrative painting.

During the **Classical Period** (480-323 B.C.E.), the arts flourished as Athens reached the pinnacle of its cultural, military, and economic power under Pericles. Sculptors such as Praxiteles and Scopas developed the heroic nude form, introducing the technique of contraposto. The statue of Hermes holding the baby Dionysus by Praxiteles and the statue of Nike (Winged Victory) by Paeonius are both housed in the Olympia Museum. Architecture of the Classical period features greater spaciousness, fluidity, and grace than the massive temples of the Archaic Period. The Parthenon, designed by Iktinos, is a superb example.

During the **Hellenistic Period** (323-first century B.C.E.), the Corinthian column, a fluted column with a multi-leafed top (shaped somewhat like an inverted bell), was introduced. The Monument of Lysicrates in Athens typifies this architectural design. Several amphitheaters were built at this time, most notably those at Epidavros and Argos. When the Romans controlled Greece, they adopted the Hellenistic style and introduced it to the rest of Europe. (Hadrian's Arch in Rome is an example of Greco-Roman architecture.)

In 395 C.E., the Roman Empire split into the Western Empire and the Eastern, or Byzantine, Empire. The Greeks fell under the latter. As the Empire was Christianized under Saint Constantine, Greek artists began to work in Christian symbols. During the **Byzantine Period** (500-1200 C.E.), many churches were built and Christian iconography developed. The most notable examples of Byzantine art include the monasteries built at Ossios Loukas, Daphni, Mt. Athos, and Meteora. The churches were built in a cruciform style: a narthex or small chamber added at one end, and an apse, or half dome, at the other. The transept, or crossing, of the two lengths of the church was capped by a domed ceiling. Byzantine artists created beautiful, ornate icons and mosaics to decorate their churches. A mosaic of the Christ *Pantocrator* was almost always placed in the dome or apse.

With the liberation of Greece from the Turks in 1821, the government patronized national art. In 1838, the Polytechniou, Greece's first modern art school was founded. Many artists since have gone abroad to study, and modern Greek art has followed the trends and styles of nineteenth- and twentieth-century European art.

Greek folk arts continue to fascinate even the most casual onlooker. Handicrafts include pottery, weaving, and metal- and wood-work. Today in many Greek villages you can see artisans at work, creating objects in much the same way their ancestors did centuries ago.

## *Literature*

Greek classics have had a timeless influence on Western literature; they are a treasury of archetypes. **Pre-classical** works (until the fifth century B.C.E.) include the Homeric epics *The Odyssey* and *The Iliad,* and early examples of lyric poetry. Archilochus wrote elegies in the seventh century B.C.E., and on the island of Lesbos, Sappho and her contemporary, Alcaeus, sang in new lyric meters.

In the **Classical Period,** literature flourished; Aeschylus, Sophocles, and Euripides developed ritualistic dramas and staged innovative tragedies, while Aristophanes produced raucous comedies (see Theater below). Rhetoric and the methods of philosophical dialogue were taught and practiced. Herodotus captured the monumental battles and personalities of the Greco-Persian conflict in the *Persian Wars.* Thucydides' *Peloponnesian War* remains a sensitive and illuminating study of a bipolar world at war.

In modern Greece, poets are heroes to the person on the street, not just the intelligentsia. Greek pop musicians often take their lyrics from poetry. The "national poet of Greece," Dionysios Solomos, composed the Greek national anthem. In the last two decades, Greek poets have claimed two Nobel Prizes. George Seferis' poems evoke the legacy of the Greek past; the mystical and erotic works of Odysseus Elytis celebrate nature; and Yiannis Ritsos blends revolutionary and mythological symbolism. C. P. Cavafy has a huge underground following, and has deeply influenced such writers as E. M. Forster and W. H. Auden. Nikos Kazantzakis' *Zorba the Greek* is the most well known of his works; he has also written a version of the *Odyssey* and novels about Jesus and St. Francis of Assisi. *When The Tree Sings,* by Stratis Haviaris, tells the story of World War II as seen through the eyes of a young boy.

There is a large body of literature about Greece by non-Greeks. Lawrence Durrell has written numerous novels (for example, *Bitter Lemons*), coffee table books, and guides (*In Prospero's Cell* is about Corfu, *Reflections on a Marine Venus* about Rhodes). Also recommended are Henry Miller's typically exuberant *The Colossus of Maroussi,* Patrick Leigh-Fermor's *Mani: Travels in the Southern Peloponnese,* and

Dilys Powell's *An Affair of the Heart.* For a sense of the horrors of World War II in Greece and the subsequent civil war, read Nicholas Gage's *Eleni.* Popular books include almost anything by Mary Renault, John Fowles' *The Magus,* Leonard Cottrell's *The Bull of Minos,* Edith Hamilton's *Mythology,* and Robert Graves' *The Greek Myths.* Robert Fitzgerald's translations of *The Iliad* and *The Odyssey* are highly respected.

## *Theater*

In the fifth century B.C.E., wealthy patrons sponsored huge public festivals to honor the god Dionysus. Contests were held in open-air theaters and masked men, sometimes impersonating women, would act, sing in the chorus, participate in dialogues, and deliver lyrical soliloquies to the crowds.

Works of **tragedy** and **comedy** were created and performed; unfortunately, few of these survive today. Aeschylus (525-456 B.C.E.) wrote such famous works as *Prometheus Bound, Agamemnon,* and his masterpiece trilogy, *Oresteia;* Sophocles (496-406 B.C.E.) created the famous *Oedipus* trilogy; and Euripides (485-406 B.C.E.) wrote *Medea* and *The Bacchae.* Aristophanes (450-385 B.C.E.) was the creator of "Old Comedy;" 11 of his plays survive today, including *Clouds* and *Frogs.* Menander, the father of "New Comedy," wrote love stories with happy endings, which became the theme and pattern of later comedians like Shakespeare.

The **Athens Festival,** held from June to September, features Classical drama at the **Theater of Herod Atticus** located below the Acropolis. The festival also includes concerts, opera, choruses, ballet, and modern dance. Ancient plays are staged from July to September at the **Epidavros Festival,** 78km from Athens. Surrounded by a wooded grove instead of a jagged cityscape, the third-century B.C.E. circular stage features remarkable acoustics. Don't worry about the language barrier; it won't detract from the ominous choreography of the chorus, which, in Aeschylus' time, made "boys die of fright and women have miscarriages." Tickets and programs for the theater series at both festivals are available two weeks in advance at the Athens Festival Box Office, 4 Stadiou St., inside the arcade (tel. 322 14 59 or 322 31 11 ext. 240). The same office sells tickets for a number of other smaller theaters and festivals. The **Philippi, Thassos,** and **Dodoni Festivals** all feature performances of classical drama in ancient theaters. The **Lycabettos Theater,** on Lycabettos Hill in Athens, hosts a variety of artistic events from mid-June to late August, and the **Lyric Theater,** known as the *Lyriki Skini,* presents operatic plays at the Olympia, 59 Akadimias St., Athens.

## *Music and Dance*

Musical instruments date from the Bronze Age on Crete, reinforcing scholars' belief that early poetry was often sung or chanted. As drama evolved, choruses played a major role in Greek plays. Before the fifth century B.C.E., the Greeks had no system of musical notation, yet scientists developed a theory of harmonics.

Throughout the Byzantine era, folk music and dances assumed regional traits: The South emphasized tragic and mourning dances, the North featured war and rural harvest dances, and religious and burial dances were performed on Crete.

Today, it is common to see a wide circle of locals and tourists, hands joined, dancing to the tunes of a trio of *bouzouki* players. The leader of the dance performs the fancy footwork, winding around a white handkerchief and twirling around in circles, sometimes daring a few backward somersaults. Don't hesitate to join in; the dance steps are repetitive and you'll learn quickly. Just stamp your feet, yell *Opah,* and have fun. If you insist on acting as a spectator, don't engage in the "traditional" custom of throwing dinner plates in appreciation of the dancers, or you'll be rewarded with a hefty bill for the broken dishes.

To see some authentic Greek dancing, check out the **Dora Stratou Folk Dance Troupe,** which performs at the open air theater at Philopappus Theater in Athens from May through September. (For information, call 324 43 95; after 5:30pm call

921 46 50.) From June through October in the old city of Rhodes, the **Nelly Dimoglou Troupe** features dances from northern and central Greece and the Dodecanese. The Athens and Epidavros Festivals (see Theater above) also include dancing. Check the Entertainment listings in major cities for additional information.

## Classical Mythology

Greek mythology, like the Bible, is ingrained in the Western imagination. Originally, Greek myths were passed from generation to generation, region to region, gradually embellished and interpreted to reflect local concerns. Religious ritual was intertwined with civic life and festivals were held to honor specific gods or goddesses. Beautiful temples were dedicated to particular deities, while oracles interpreted the heavenly signs. The anthropomorphic gods and goddesses lived as immortal beings with divine power, and were believed to descend to earth often to intervene romantically, mischieviously, or combatively in human affairs, sometimes disguised as animals or humans.

Classical Greek mythology influenced a span of 2000 years. Traditionally, there were 14 gods and goddesses: Zeus (or Jupiter, Zeus's Roman name), head god and god of thunder; Hera (Juno), Zeus's wife and goddess of marriage and childbearing; Poseidon (Neptune), god of the sea; Hephaestus (Vulcan), god of smiths and fire; Aphrodite (Venus), goddess of love and beauty; Ares (Mars), god of war; Athena (Minerva), goddess of wisdom; Apollo (Phoebus), god of the sun; Artemis (Diana), goddess of the moon and the hunt; Hermes (Mercury), the messenger god and patron of thieves and tricksters; Hades, god of the dead; Demeter (Ceres), goddess of the harvest; Dionysus (Bacchus), god of wine; and Hestia (Vesta), goddess of the hearth. All of them inhabited the peaks of Mt. Olympos, except Hades who ruled over the underworld.

Along with these 14, there were many other prominent human figures in Greek mythology, including Atlas, bearer of the skies; Herakles (Hercules), the strongest man on earth; Pandora, who opened the "box of miseries;" Narcissus, the self-admirer; and King Midas, of the golden touch. There were also less anthropomorphic characters, including the Fates, the Furies, and the nine Muses.

The practice of worshiping the mythological gods and goddesses came to an end after the death of the Roman Emperor Julian (363 B.C.E.). In the post-classical period, Greece saw the rise of cults associated with mysteries, such as the Eleusinian and Orphic mysteries, in which participants enacted rituals associated with the afterlife.

## Religion

Greece became a stronghold of Orthodox Christianity under the Byzantine Empire. In 1054 C.E., the Christian Church divided into the Roman Catholic and Eastern Orthodox Churches (orthodox meaning "right belief"). By 1850, the Greek Orthodox Church withdrew from control of the Pope; today, it is officially recognized as the national religion of Greece, the only official Orthodox Christian country in the world.

The Orthodox state religion became a symbol of nationalism during the Turkish occupation, and the church served then and now as a powerful defendant of Greek interests. Religion is very important to Greek people; for older people, especially, faith is an integral part of daily life.

The archbishop serves as the head of 81 regional dioceses. Greek Orthodox priests are closely associated with their parishes and can marry, as most do (although higher clergy remain celibate). The congregation remains silent during mass while a *psaltis* and a choir sing the liturgy, and icons are used as symbols in worship.

Although 98% of Greeks are Greek Orthodox, other faiths are tolerated. There are small enclaves of Muslims, Jews, and Catholics.

## Language

The language barrier that tourists find upon entering Greece tends to crumble quickly (though slower in the mountainous north and in the southern Peloponnese); many Greeks who work in tourist facilities have picked up some English, and tourist officials and travel agents are often fluent. Nevertheless, try to master some essential Greek phrases; Greeks will appreciate any efforts you make. Take along the Berlitz *Greek for Travelers,* or a comparable book that will provide key phrases in a simple format. As you learn, ask for help from someone who speaks the language.

Be aware of Greek body language. To indicate a negative, the Greeks lift their heads back abruptly or raise their eyebrows. To indicate the affirmative, they emphatically nod once. Note also that Greeks wave a hand up and down in a gesture that seems to mean "stay there;" it actually means "come." Be careful when waving goodbye; if you do so palm forward, the gesture may be interpreted as an insult.

Even if you don't know any spoken Greek, you *must* know the Greek alphabet. Although it is very different from the Roman alphabet, there are enough similarities to make it confusing. Some road signs, street names, and certain bus timetables may be transliterated (spelled out phonetically in Roman characters), but many are not. You'll sometimes find three different words representing the same name; for example, Patra, Patras, and Patrai all refer to the same place. The table of the Greek alphabet (only 24 letters) below will help you decipher signs. The right column shows the printed capital and lower case letters, while the left column gives you the name of these letters in Greek.

| | | |
|---|---|---|
| alpha | $\alpha$ | A |
| beta | $\beta$ | B |
| gamma | $\gamma$ | $\Gamma$ |
| delta | $\delta$ | $\Delta$ |
| epsilon | $\epsilon$ | E |
| zeta | $\zeta$ | Z |
| eta | $\eta$ | H |
| theta | $\theta$ | $\Theta$ |
| iota | $\iota$ | I |
| kappa | $\kappa$ | K |
| lambda | $\lambda$ | $\Lambda$ |
| mu | $\mu$ | M |
| nu | $\nu$ | N |
| ksi | $\xi$ | $\Xi$ |
| omicron | o | O |
| pi | $\pi$ | $\Pi$ |
| rho | $\rho$ | P |
| sigma | $\sigma$ | $\Sigma$ |
| tau | $\tau$ | T |
| upsilon | $\upsilon$ | Y |
| phi | $\Phi$ | $\Phi$ |
| xi | $\chi$ | X |
| psi | $\psi$ | $\Psi$ |
| omega | $\omega$ | $\Omega$ |

## Glossary

As most veteran travelers will tell you, it's a wise idea to learn a few key phrases in the native tongue while traveling abroad. The Greek language takes time to master but tourists can get by with a minimal vocabulary. If you're really stuck, try to find someone of high-school age; English is a compulsory subject in Greek schools, so most young Greeks speak at least some English. The Greeks will appreciate your own efforts even if you are unsuccessful, though, and you may find that you're treated with a little more respect than the average tourist. Use your new language to bargain for prices and watch for over-charging shopkeepers.

Below you will find a compilation of some words and phrases that may be useful during your stay in Greece. Don't be afraid to use them often. Note that "dh" is pronounced like "th" in "the."

### Greetings and Courtesies

kah-lee-ME-rah: Good morning
kah-lee-SPE-rah: Good evening
kah-lee-NEE-htah: Good night
NE: yes
OH-hee: no
pah-rah-kah-LO: please/you're welcome
ef-hah-ree-STO (po-LEE): thank you (very much)
seeg-NO-mee: excuse me
YAH-sas: hello (polite and plural form)
YAH-soo: hello (familiar form)
en-DAHK-see: OK
pos-se-LE-ne: What is your name?
me-LE-ne . . . : My name is . . .
Kee-REE-os: Mr./Sir
kee-REE-ah: Mrs./Madam

### Getting Around

pou-EE-ne . . . ?: Where is . . . ?
pee-YE-no yah . . . : I'm going to . . .
tee O-rah FEV-yo-me?: When do we leave?
es-tee-ah-TO-ree-o: restaurant
ta-hee-dhro-MEE-o: post office
ah-go-RAH: market
mou-SEE-o: museum
fahr-mah-KEE-o: pharmacy
TRAH-pe-zah: bank
e-klee-SEE-ah: church
kse-no-dho-HEE-o: hotel
dho-MAH-teeo: room
vah-LEE-tsah: suitcase
ah-e-ro-DHRO-mee-o: airport
ah-e-ro-PLAH-no: airplane
le-o-fo-REE-o: bus
TRE-no: train
PLEE-o: ferry
ee-see-TEE-ree-o: ticket
yah-TROS: doctor
dhek-see-AH, ah-rees-teh-RAH: right, left
e-DHO, e-KEE: here, there
klee-STO, ah-nee-KTO: closed, open

### Shopping, Accommodations, Transportation, and Food

PO-so KAH-nee (PO-so ko-STEE-zee): How much?
hree-AH-zo-me: I need
THE-lo: I want
thah EE-the-lah . . . : I would like . . .
thah ah-go-RAH-so ahf-TO e-DHO: I will buy this one.
E-he-te: Do you have?
bo-RO nah-DHO E-nah dho-MAH-tee-o: Can I see a room?
lo-gahr-yah-SMO: bill
e-fee-me-REE-dha: newspaper

ne-RO: water
kah-LO: good
ftee-NO: cheap
ah-kree-VO: expensive

### Time and Counting
tee O-rah EE-ne?: What time is it?
E-nah: one
DHEE-o: two
TREE-ah: three
TES-ser-ah: four
PEN-dhe: five
E-ksee: six
ep-TAH: seven
och-TO: eight
en-YAH: nine
DHE-kah: ten
EN-dhe-kah: eleven
DHO-dhe-kah: twelve
TOH-rah: now
pro-EE: morning
VRAH-dhee: evening
ah-PO-pse: tonight
ech-THES: yesterday
SEE-me-rah: today
AH-vree-o: tomorrow

### Conversation
mee-LAHS ahn-glee-KAH?: Do you speak English?
dhen mee-LAHO el-leen-ee-KAH: I don't speak Greek.
dhen kah-tah-lah-VE-no: I don't understand.
vo-EE-thee-ah: Help!

## Food and Wine

Don't even bother looking for a McDonald's; there are none in Greece, and for very good reason. With infinite ingenuity, the Greeks have created a cuisine practiced by everyone from the gourmet to the fisherman broiling the catch of the day.

A Greek restaurant is known as a *taverna* or *estiatorio*, while a grill is a *psistaria*. If you have trouble deciphering a menu or deciding whether to eat at a particular restaurant, browse the display in front or back near the kitchen to see what looks good. Most places have few fixed-price dishes available at any one time, so make sure they have your dish before you sit down. Be sure to clarify the cost of each item with the waiter. Don't be surprised if he charges you extra for the "tablecloth" and bread.

Breakfast consists of bread, *tiropita* (cheese pie), or a pastry with *marmelada* (jam) or *meli* (honey), along with a cup of coffee. Lunch is very light. The biggest meal of the day is clearly supper, a leisurely affair that's served late at night relative to American standards, usually after 8 or 9pm. Meat entrees include *moskari* (veal), *arni* (lamb), or *kotopoulo* (chicken), served with *patates* (french fries), *rizi* (rice), or *fasolia* (beans). Uniquely Greek dishes include *mousaka* (chopped meat and eggplant mixed with a cheese and tomato paste), *pastitsio* (thick noodles covered with a rich cream sauce), *yemista* (stuffed tomatoes and peppers), and *dolmadhes* (stuffed grape leaves with rice and minced meat, called *youvrelakia* when covered with egg or lemon sauce). Many menus also feature *souvlaki,* a large skewer of steak, generally pork or lamb. A *souvlaki pita,* appropriately known as "the budget food of the masses," consists of a pita crammed full of skewered meats and fillings (only about

80dr). *Gyros* is not standard fare in Greece, contrary to the claims of American "Greek" restaurants.

If you go to a *taverna*, try a *choriatiki*, a "Greek" salad containing olives, tomatoes, onions, cucumbers, and a hefty slab of feta cheese on top. (Ask for it *horees ladhi* if you don't want it swimming in olive oil.) Usually accompanied by a basket of bread and a glass of water, these salads make inexpensive and satisfying meals. Another option is to visit an *agora* (market) and stock up on the fruit available all summer—fresh figs *(seeka)* are phenomenal. After dinner, Greeks like to eat *karpouzi* (watermelon) or *piponi* (yellow melon). You should also try the freshly made yogurt *(yiaourti)* with honey and melon mixed in, or some indigenous cheeses like feta (a semi-soft, salty white cheese made from goat's milk) and *kaseri*, a hard romano-like cheese.

Greek **pastries** will satisfy everyone's sweet-tooth and can be bought from *zacharoplastia* shops. *Baklava,* the honey-rich, filo-doughed strudel filled with chopped nuts, beats all the rest; also try *galaktobouriko,* a custard-filled dough; *kareedhopita,* a walnut cake; *melomakarones,* honey-nut cookies; *kataïfi,* strands of dough wrapped around nuts and cinnamon; *koulouria,* shortbread cookies; or *kourabiethes,* powdered sugar-coated cookies. Remember that the word *pasta* in Greek means pastry, not a dish of noodles.

Greek **coffee** is the most popular beverage, though you may wonder why. Like Turkish coffee, it is exceedingly strong, sweet, and has the consistency of sludge. Ask for *metrio* to get a cup with only half the sugar; *sketo* will get an entirely sugarless cup. Be sure to specify if you want it *me gala* (with milk). Greek coffee is usually served, drunk, and tempered with a glass of water. American-style coffee (called *Nescafé*), usually instant, is also available. If you ask for *café frappé,* you'll get a tall glass of frothy iced coffee. For a real thirst-quencher, try *portokalada* (orange soda), or *limonada* (lemonade). Be careful about drinking the water.

A favorite Greek snack combination is *ouzo* with *mezes,* tidbits of cheese, sausage, cakes, and octopus. *Ouzo* itself is a distilled spirit (raki) to which anise is added, giving it a licorice taste. Some people drink it as an aperitif, all afternoon long; others have it after dinner as a liqueur. Just make sure you're sipping, not gulping—this is strong stuff. Mixed with water, it's sweet but not overwhelming.

One of the creative arts in Greece is **wine**-making, and every region has its own specialty. Vineyards dot the Greek countryside and many locals still make their own wine. Long ago, the Greeks discovered that when wine was stored in pitch pine-sealed goatskins, it developed a fresh, sappy flavor. After studious deduction, they discovered that adding pine resin in varying amounts during fermentation achieved the same result. The resulting wine became known as *retsina.* Resinated wines now come in three varieties: white, rosé, and red (*kokkineli*). White retsina is generally cheaper than beer. There are also a number of non-resinated wines, which tend to be over-sweet (like *Nemea* or *Herakles*). These include sweet (*gleeko*), and semi-sweet (*imigleko*). Try the white wines of the northern Peloponnese: *Rotonda, Demestika,* and *Santa Helena* are dry and quaffable. Greek wines can be classified in two basic groups: ordinary wines, which are one to three years old, and special wines, which are three to nine years old. *Achaïa-Clauss* and *Cambas Vintners* are consistently good wines. As an after-dinner aid to digestion, Greeks imbibe *Metaxa* brandy or *ouzo* shots.

A good place to taste various Greek wines is at a **wine festival,** where you can drink all the wine you want for a flat admission fee. The biggest wine festival around Athens is located at Dafni (11km out of town) from mid-June to mid-September. Bus #100 or 853 runs regularly from Koumoudourou Sq. in Athens to Dafni. The wine festival in Alexandroupolis runs from early July to mid-August. On Crete, the festival in Rethymnon is held in July, while the one at the village of Dafnes (near Iraklion) runs in mid-July.

## *Holidays*

The Greek penchant for celebrations is infectious, and visitors are welcomed and swept up in the festivities. Many towns honor their own patron saint with special festivals.

The following list of festivals include holidays of the Greek Orthodox Church and traditional festivals celebrated in rural and agricultural areas. Note: The dates for some religious holidays change annually. Check dates with the GNTO.

**Dec. 24-25: Christmas.** Traditionally, children make the rounds singing Christmas carols, known as *kalanda* in Greek.

**Dec. 31-Jan. 1: New Year's and The Feast of St. Basil.** On Chios, local sailors carry model ships around the island as they make their way to the town square. Children sing and people exchange gifts. The Greeks follow the Byzantine custom of slicing a *Vassilopita* on New Year's Day. Lucky diners who get the coin in their slice will be blessed with good fortune through the following year.

**Jan. 6: Epiphany.** The day Jesus was baptized by St. John. Great feast day. *Kallikantzaroi* (goblins and spirits) appear between Christmas and Epiphany. Village bonfires scare them away. At Epiphany, waters are blessed and evil spirits leave the earth.

**Jan. 8: Gynaecocracy** (St. Domenica's Day/Midwife day). Women of child-bearing age bring gifts to the midwife. In the villages of Komotini, Xanthi, Kilkis, and Serres, women gather in the cafes and other social centers, while men look after the households; the men are allowed to join their wives in celebrations after dusk.

**Feb.23-March 16: Carnival.** Three weeks of feasting and dancing before the Lenten fast. During the first week fatted pigs are slaughtered, during the second villagers feast on meat, and during the third they feast on cheese. The most notable celebrations occur in Patras and Cephalonia.

**March 25: Greek Independence Day.** Commemorates the 1821 struggle against the Turkish Ottoman Empire. Also a religious holiday, the Feast of the Annunciation.

**Good Friday.** In rural areas, people carry lit candles in a procession through town to begin Easter weekend.

**Easter.** Celebrations on Easter Sunday typically include feasting on spit-roasted lamb and red-dyed hard-boiled eggs, followed by dancing in regional costumes.

**April 23: St. George's Day.** Celebration in honor of the "Knight on the white horse." Festivities include races, wrestling matches, and dances.

**May 1: Labor Day.** Also Feast of the Flowers.

**May 21-23: Anastenaria.** Also called **Feast of St. Constantine and St. Helena.** Celebrations include fire dancing and walking on burning pip charcoal. Celebrated in Agia Eleni, Thessaloniki, and Veria.

**Late June-early July: Navy Week.** At various coastal towns, fishers and sailors have festivals (including Plomari, Lesvos, and Volos). On Volos, a re-enactment of the journey of the Argonauts is staged.

**June 24:** Feast of St. John the Baptist.

**Aug.: Epirotika Festival,** in Ioannina; **Olympus Festival,** in Katerini; **Hippokrateia Festival,** on Kos. All three feature artistic exhibits and performances.

**Aug. 15: Feast of the Assumption of the Virgin Mary.** Huge celebration on the island of Tinos.

**Aug. 25: Feast of St. Dionysius.** Celebrations in honor of the patron saint of Zante.

**Aug.-Sept.: Aeschilla Performances.** Performances of classical drama at Eleusis.

**Sept. 8: The Virgin's Birthday.** In some villages an auction is held to determine who will carry the Virgin's Icon, and the money is used to provide a village feast.

**Sept. 14: Exaltation of the Cross.**

**Oct. 26: Feast of St. Demetrius.** Celebrated with particular enthusiasm in Salonika. The feast coincides with opening of new wine, so there is heavy drinking.

**Oct. 28: National Anniversary.**

For additional information on festivals, artistic events and religious fairs contact the GNTO or the local police.

# *ATHENS* Αθήνα

*That we've broken their statues,*
*That we've driven them out of their temples,*
*Doesn't mean at all that the gods are dead.*
　　　　　　　—C.P. Cavafy, "Ionic."

A European capital at the edge of the Middle East, a city lined with concrete apartment buildings and marble columns, Athens seesaws between two continents and two epochs. Once the seedbed of Classical and Western culture, the city flaunts the exotic vestiges of 500 years of Ottoman rule as well as the mundane elements of the modern day. But you must look beyond the temple fronts, the Byzantine churches, the markets, and the squat antennae-covered apartment houses to find the true Athens—its people. The city's residents hail from all over Greece and typify the extremes of the Greek personality, from its limitless mirth to its passionate melancholy.

Athens received its name when Poseidon and Athena vied to rule the city. The gods of Olympos decided that whoever bestowed the most beneficial gift on the city would become its protector. Poseidon struck the rock of the Acropolis with his trident, causing salt water to gush forth, but Athena triumphed when she caused an olive tree to grow out of the same rock. The city was thereafter named in her honor.

After miraculously defeating the Persians in the fifth century B.C.E. at Marathon and Salamis, the Athenians under Pericles touched off an unprecedented cultural explosion that lasted some 70 years. Iktinos and Kallikrates designed the Parthenon; Aeschylus, Sophocles, and Euripides composed masterpieces of tragic drama; and Aristophanes created raucous comedies. Early historians, in particular Thucydides, challenged the assumption that the gods—not human beings—governed history; and Hippocrates, with a similar confidence in human autonomy, observed the workings of the body and developed the science of medicine.

The demise of Periclean Athens was heralded by the bloody and drawn-out campaigns of the Peloponnesian War (431-404 B.C.E.) between Athens and Sparta. Political power in Greece then shifted north to the court of Philip of Macedon and his son Alexander the Great. Yet Athens continued to be the center of culture and sophistication, producing in the late fifth and fourth centuries B.C.E. two of the Occident's greatest philosophers, Plato and Aristotle, and the great orator Demosthenes. Even though Athens was under imperial rule—first by the Macedonians, then by the Romans—it remained the undisputed center of Western culture and thought, the training ground for aristocratic youths from all over the Mediterranean world. Under Byzantine rule, the city fell to the lowly position of minor Ottoman outpost until its resurrection as the capital of free Greece in 1834.

The modern city, with its squares, wide boulevards, and the cool and quiet National Garden, grew out of the plans of German architects under the direction of King Otto in the late nineteenth century. Since the revolution, rapid and uncontrolled building accompanied by massive migration from the rest of the country has rendered Athens a cluttered labyrinth resounding with cacophonous traffic. In an attempt to counteract noise pollution, the transit authority bans cars from a number of streets in the Plaka and limits drivers' access to downtown on alternate days. Nonetheless, the hustle-and-bustle of the city is felt at every corner. Public transport, though improving, remains inefficient and overcrowded, and the *nephos* (smog cloud), a permanent fixture in the hot summer, is guaranteed to give you a headache. Be steadfast in the face of physical imperfection to sense the modern dynamics of this ancient city.

52

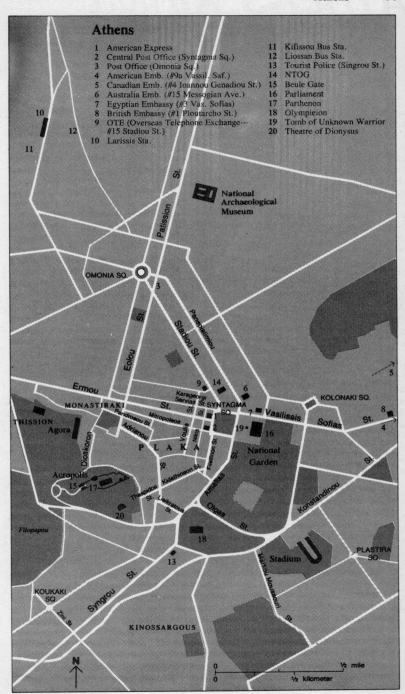

# Athens

1 American Express
2 Central Post Office (Syntagma Sq.)
3 Post Office (Omonia Sq.)
4 American Emb. (#9a Vassil. Saf.)
5 Canadian Emb. (#4 Joannou Genadiou St.)
6 Australia Emb. (#15 Messogian Ave.)
7 Egyptian Embassy (#3 Vas. Sofias)
8 British Embassy (#1 Ploutarcho St.)
9 OTE (Overseas Telephone Exchange—
  #15 Stadiou St.)
10 Larissis Sta.

11 Kifissou Bus Sta.
12 Liossan Bus Sta.
13 Tourist Police (Singrou St.)
14 NTOG
15 Beule Gate
16 Parliament
17 Parthenon
18 Olympieion
19 Tomb of Unknown Warrior
20 Theatre of Dionysus

# Orientation and Practical Information

Coming from either airport, the bus will drop you off by **Syntagma (Constitution) Square,** the center of modern Athens, a well-maintained plaza with overpriced outdoor cafes and luxury hotels. A large pale yellow Neoclassical building, formerly the royal palace and now home to the Greek Parliament, casts its vigilant glance over the near-lethal traffic of Syntagma. The square is a transportation nexus for city buses and trolleys, as well as the site of two GNTO tourist offices, scads of travel agencies, several banks, a post office, and the American Express office. A number of inexpensive places to stay are also within walking distance (see Accommodations below). Syntagma is easily accessible by public transportation from most parts of the city, including the airport and bus and train stations.

Two parallel boulevards, **Panepistimiou** (Eleftherias Venizelou) and **Stadiou,** connect Syntagma Square with **Omonia Square,** a grimy circular plaza surrounded by inexpensive shops. Underneath Omonia, the subway runs to Monastiraki (3 min.) and Piraeus (15 min.), as well as 18 other stops. The university and library lie on Panepistimiou at the half-way point between Omonia and Syntagma Square. Just before Omonia, both avenues intersect with **Patission.** North on Patission is the National Archeological Museum. With your back to the museum, walk straight ahead along Ipirou St. (approximately 15 min.) to reach the main train station, Larissis.

Running toward the Acropolis from Omonia, **Eolou** and **Athinas Streets** are lined with shops and department stores. Midway between Omonia and Monastiraki along Athinas St. between Evripidou and Sofokleous St. is the indoor-outdoor food market. **Monastiraki,** the area below the Acropolis, is Athens' garment district. If you face the Acropolis, the ancient *agora* lies in front and to the right. To the left is the Athens Flea Market, and past this, the **Plaka,** the oldest living section of Athens, flooded with shops, restaurants and hotels. Continuing in this direction and bordering the Plaka is Syntagma Square. **Ermou** and **Mitropoleas Streets** connect Monastiraki to Syntagma.

East of Syntagma you'll find fewer accommodations but still more sights. Across Amalias, the **Tomb of the Unknown Warrior** stands steadfast before the Parliament. The Zappeion, an exhibition hall, lies within the tranquil National Garden. Beyond the Garden are the President's House and the Athens Stadium (constructed in 1896 for the first modern Olympiad and scheduled to host the event's centennial). Hadrian's Arch and the Olympeion affirm their time-honored stance just south of the Garden. Running off Syntagma in the other direction, the embassies, consulates, and the city's premier hospital (Evangelismos) are on **Vassilissis Sofias.** This avenue is comparable to New York's Fifth Avenue Museum Mile. The Benaki, Byzantine, and War Museums, the nearby Goulandris Museum of Cycladic and Ancient Greek Art, and the National Gallery are clustered over a few blocks. The affluent and funky/chic **Kolonaki** district is bordered by Vassilissis Sofias and lies in the shadow of the craggy peak of Lycabettos.

South of the Acropolis and neighboring Philopappus Hill (toward Piraeus) is the **Koukaki** section, with an open fresh produce market as well as the Olympic Airways headquarters. **Leoforos Singrou** divides this area from the **Kinossargous** section. To get to Koukaki from Syntagma, walk down Amalias (which becomes Singrou beyond Hadrian's Arch) and turn right; for Kinossargous, turn left at Singrou.

To get anywhere in this city, you *must* get a map. Although streets are generally signposted in Greek and English, Athenian geography mystifies the newcomer, especially in the Plaka. Ask at the GNTO for their free and fairly detailed city map. If you still get lost, don't despair: The Acropolis is visible from almost everywhere in Athens and is an excellent orientation point.

Unfortunately, the tourist police have ceased operating, though rumors suggest that they may reopen in the future. Several publications list general information about Athens and special events. Pick up a complimentary copy of the GNTO's *This Week in Athens,* which gives addresses, hours, and phone numbers for night clubs, theaters, sights, museums, libraries, restaurants, airlines, churches, and more. News, as well as movie, exhibit, and restaurant listings appear daily in Athens' English-language newspapers, the *Athens News* (60dr) and *Greece Today* (60dr). The papers also publish emergency-assistance phone numbers. The monthly *Athenian* magazine (250dr) provides cultural information and features stories about Greece.

In general, summer business hours throughout the city are Monday from 1:30-8:30pm; Tuesday, Thursday, and Friday from 8am-2pm and 5:30-8:30pm; and Wednesday and Saturday from 8am-3pm. Summer officially begins June 16 and ends September 20.

**Greek National Tourist Office (GNTO):** Information desk in the **National Bank of Greece,** 2 Karageorgi Servias, Syntagma Sq. (tel. 322 25 45). Information sheets available with all sorts of transportation schedules and prices, embassy addresses and phone numbers, and museum hours and locations. Ask for the Athens city map. Another office (1 block away) at 1 Ermou St., Syntagma Sq. (tel. 325 26 67), inside the **General Bank of Greece.** Quieter and provides the same services. Open Mon.-Fri. 8am-8pm, Sat. 8am-2pm. The GNTO at the **East Terminal** of the airport (tel. 969 95 00) is open 24 hours. The head office at 2 Amerikis St. (tel. 322 31 11), ordinarily does not deal with the public, but Room 714 on the fifth floor (Dept. of Information) may offer more complete advice. Open Mon.-Fri. 11am-2pm.

**The Hellenic Chamber of Hotels:** In the National Bank of Greece. Will answer your questions about accommodations and provide you with a list of D- and E-class hotels in Athens. Open Mon.-Fri. 9am-3pm. Try to get there before 10am to beat the crowds. If you arrive on Sunday, don't despair; the office posts information sheets on the windows of its booth, which you can reach between 9am and 1pm.

**Budget Travel:** For **ISIC/FIYTO** purchase, see Useful Organizations in the General Introduction. Most offices are on Nikis and Filellinon St., off Syntagma Sq. Shop around for the best prices but don't miss **Magic Bus,** 20 Filellinon St., which offers cheap rail, air, and boat tickets (and especially long-distance bus tickets) to the rest of Europe, Canada, the U.S., Africa, and the East. Extremely competent, English-speaking staff. Student discounts of 20-55% with an ISIC or a college ID. Open Mon.-Fri. 9am-7pm, Sat. 9am-2pm. **Transalpino,** 28 Nikis St., has half-price train tickets for ages under 26 as well as cut-rate airfare. Open Mon.-Fri. 9am-6pm, Sat. 9am-1pm. **Bellair Travel and Tourism,** 15 Nikis St. (tel. 323 92 61), offers up to 55% student discounts on flights and arranges package tours. **Grivas Worldwide,** 25 Nikis St., books a large selection of charter flights and student discount fares. Check out their prices posted on a large wooden board outside. Open Mon.-Fri. 9am-4pm, Sat. 9am-1pm.

**Greek Youth Hostel Association:** 4 Dragatsaniou St., 7th floor (tel. 822 58 60). IYHF cards 1200dr; bring 2 photos (obtainable underneath Omonia Sq. or at 18 Filellinon St.). Note that most Greek youth hostels don't care and won't check whether or not you have a card. Open Mon.-Fri. 9am-3pm.

**Embassies:** U.S., 91 Vassilissis Sofias (tel. 721 29 51). Open Mon.-Fri. 8:30am-5pm. **Canadian,** 41 Ioannou Genadiou St. (tel. 723 95 11). Open Mon.-Fri. 9am-1pm. **Australian,** 37 D. Sotsou St. (tel. 644 73 03). Open Mon.-Fri. 9am-1pm. **British,** 1 Ploutarchou St. (tel. 723 62 11), at Ypsilantou St. Open Mon.-Fri. 8am-1pm. **New Zealand,** 15-17 An. Tsoha St. (tel. 641 03 11). Open Mon.-Fri. 9am-1pm. **French,** 7 Vassilissis Sofias (tel. 361 16 63). Open Mon.-Fri. 9-11am; visas obtained at the consulate, 5-7 Vassilissis Konstantinou Ave. (tel. 729 01 51). **Italian,** 2 Sekeri St. (tel. 361 17 23); visas obtained at the consulate, 19 Meandrou Michalakopoulou St. (tel. 723 90 45), near Vassilissis Sofias. **Egyptian,** 3 Vassilissis Sofias (tel. 361 86 12); visa window on Zalokosta St. Bring 1 photo. Open Mon.-Fri. 9:30-11:30am; the Egyptian State Tourist Office is nearby at 10 Amerikis St. (tel. 360 69 06). **Yugoslavian,** 106 Vassilissas Sofias (tel. 777 43 44); visas Mon.-Fri. 9-11:30am. **Jordanian,** 30 P. Zervou St., Paleo Psihiko (tel. 647 41 61). A more comprehensive listing of embassies available at the GNTO.

**Currency Exchange: National Bank of Greece** (tel. 322 27 30) in Syntagma, on the corner of Karageorgi Servias and Stadiou St. Open 9am-8pm. American Express and other banks, but most close at 2pm. Open Mon.-Thurs. 8am-2pm and 3:30-9pm, Fri. 8am-1:30pm and 3-9pm, Sat. 9am-3pm, and Sun. 9am-1pm. East Terminal of the airport is open 24 hours. Some hotels and hostels exchange currency, but their rates are usually worse. Commission between 70-200dr depending on the amount you change.

**American Express:** 2 Ermou St., 1st floor, Syntagma Sq. (tel. 324 49 75, -6, -7, -8, or -9). Holds mail for 1 month; collects 250dr for those without AmEx cards. Forwarding fee 500dr. Only 100dr to change any amount of Amex traveler's checks. For cardholders, nominal 50dr commission for changing cash. Open Mon.-Fri. 8:30am-2:30pm, Sat. 8:30am-12:30pm. Travel and postal services open Mon.-Fri. 8:30am-5:30pm, Sat. 8:30am-1:30pm.

**Central Post Office:** 100 Eolou St., Omonia Sq. Poste Restante holds mail for 1 month; specify G.P.O. Omonia or Syntagma. **Postal code** for Omonia (100 09), for Syntagma (103 00). Will forward mail (100dr). Open Mon.-Fri. 7:30am-8pm, Sat. 7:30am-2:30pm. Another office in Syntagma Sq., on the corner of Mitreopolis. Open Mon.-Fri. 7:30am-8pm, Sat. 7:30am-2:15pm, Sun. 9am-1:30pm. For parcel post, walk through the arcade at 4 Stadiou St. and turn right. Open Mon.-Fri. 7:30am-3pm, for parcels abroad Mon.-Fri. 7:30am-2:15pm.

**OTE (International Telephones):** 28 Patission St. #85. Open 24 hours. Also at Omonia Sq., next to the subway entrance, and at 15 Stadiou St. Both offices open Mon.-Fri. 7am-11:30pm. Also at 50 Athinas St. Open Mon.-Fri. 7am-10pm. Make collect calls overseas at Patission, Stadiou, and Athinas offices. Collect calls take up to 1 hr. to go through (2-3 hr. on weekend), so bring a book. Come a couple hours before closing or else you won't be able to place your collect call. For information on overseas calls, dial 162; for directory assistance in Athens call 131, outside Athens 132. **Telephone code:** 01.

**Airports: East Terminal,** for all foreign airlines and charters. Take blue bus #018 from Amalias uphill from Syntagma and to your right if you're facing the Parliament building (every 20 min. until midnight, every hr. on the ½ hr. midnight-6am, 30dr). Double decker express yellow bus (every 20 min. until midnight, 100dr; every hr. midnight-6am, 150dr) or bus #121 from Vassilissis Olgas in front of the Zappeion (every 50 min. 6:50am-10:50pm, 30dr). From airport to Athens: Look to your left as you exit customs, take yellow bus A or B to Leoforos Amalias, off of Syntagma (every 20 min. 6:20am-midnight, 100dr; and every hr. on the hr. midnight-6am, 150dr). A taxi should cost 550dr. **West Terminal,** for domestic Olympic Airways flights. Take bus #133 from Othonos on Syntagma (every 20 min. 5:40am-midnight) or bus #122 from Vassilissis Olgas in front of the Zappeion (every 15 min. 5:30am-11:30pm). Or take the navy Olympic Airways bus from the corner of Amalias and Othonos (just off Syntagma; every ½ hr. 5:50am-8:20pm, 100dr). From the airport to Athens take city bus #133 leaving from the road outside the gates (every 20 min.), or take the navy Olympic Airways bus to Singrou or Othonos St. in Syntagma (every ½ hr.). A taxi should cost 450dr.

**Trains: Larissis Train Station,** Degliani St., serves Northern Greece. (Thessaloniki 1520dr, Volos 1080dr, Lamia 640dr.) Take trolley #1 to and from Syntagma. **Railway Station for the Peloponnese,** 3 Peloponnesou St. (tel. 513 16 01), behind Larissis, in a Victorian-style building with a silver roof. Serves Patras (630dr) and elswhere in the Peloponnese. For more information, call **Hellenic Railways (OSE)** (tel. 522 43 02) or **Railway Station for Northern Greece (Larissis)** (tel. 823 77 41).

**Subway:** One-line system. Fare 30dr. Free 5-8am. Be sure to hang on to ticket stub until you exit or you'll pay twice. Runs every 5 min. 5am-midnight. Begins at Kifissia stop, just north of the city; stops at Attiki, Victoria, Omonia (midpoint), Thission, Monastirion, and Piraeus (on Rousvelt St.), among other stops.

**Buses:** Blue, comfortable, and bearing 3-digit numbers. Fare 30dr. Free 5-8pm. Convenient for travel within the city, and the best (almost only) option for daytrips outside Athens. Frequent service ends at midnight, but buses run every hr. on most routes throughout the night. **Kifissou St. Station** (Terminal A), 100 Kifissou St. (tel. 514 88 56), serves most of Greece including Northern Greece and the Peloponnese with the exception of Delphi and other destinations in Central Greece; take bus #51 from the corner of Zinonos and Menandrou near Omonia Sq. (every 15 min. 5am-midnight, every 40 min. midnight-4:40am). **Liossion St. Station** (Terminal B), 260 Liossion St. (tel. 831 70 59), serves Delphi, Evia, Lamia, and Larissa; take bus #24 from Leoforos Amalias in front of the entrance to the National Garden (every 15 min. 5am-midnight). Also bus #24 to Athens from Liossion St.

**Taxis:** 30dr per km plus 25dr entrance fee. Minimum fare 170dr. Taxis are allowed to take in extra passengers if there's room. Get in the cab and *then* tell the driver where you're going—otherwise he might refuse if it's inconvenient for him. Good option during the wee hours. Beware of the airport and train station rip-offs; make sure the meter is on for the whole ride.

**Trolleys:** Yellow, crowded, and bearing 1-or 2-digit numbers. Fare 30dr. Free 5-8am. Very frequent and convenient for short hops within the city. From Syntagma, #1, 2, 4, 5, and 11 run to Omonia Sq.

**Hitching:** Almost impossible from Athens. You'll have most luck if you go to the truck parks at the cargo wharves in Piraeus and hold a sign. For Northern Greece, take the subway to the last stop (Kifissia), walk up to the town's central square, take the bus to Nea Kifissia, and walk to the National Rd. (Ethnikiodos).

**Luggage Storage:** At the airport. 100dr per piece per day. Keep your ticket stub to reclaim. Several offices on Nikis and Filellinon St. Free luggage storage or 50dr per piece per day at many hotels and hostels (for customers only).

**English Bookstores: Eleftheroudakis Book Store,** 4 Nikis St. The best. Open Mon., Wed., Sat. 8:15am-3pm, Tues. and Thurs.-Fri. 8:15am-2pm and 5:30-8:30pm. **Pantelides Books,** 11 Amerikis St. (tel. 62 36 73). Great selection of Penguin paperbacks. Open Mon., Wed., Sat. 8am-3pm, Tues. and Thurs.-Fri. 8am-2pm and 5:30-8:30pm.

**Libraries: American Library:** 22 Massalias St., 4th floor (tel. 363 81 14), behind the university. A wonderful air-conditioned oasis with current issues of the *Herald Tribune* and *American* magazines. Open Mon. and Thurs. 10am-7pm; Tues., Wed., and Fri. 9:30am-2:30pm. The 7th floor houses the **American Union Greek Library** (tel. 362 98 86) and its large collection of English books on Greece. Open Mon.-Fri. 9am-1pm and 5-8pm. **The British Council Library,** Kolonaki Sq. (tel. 363 32 15), also has English reading material and sponsors cultural events. Open Mon.-Thurs. 9:30am-1:30pm and 5:30-8pm, Fri. 9:30am-1:30pm. **Blegan Library,** at the American School for Classical Studies, 54 Sovidas St. (tel. 723 63 13), has a good collection of books about Athens and Greece. Open Mon.-Fri. 8:30am-10pm, Sat. 8:30am-6pm.

**Laundromats:** 10 Angelou Geronta St., in Plaka; 1st floor of yellow building with brown shutters. Wash 300dr, dry 150dr, soap 50dr. Open Mon.-Sat. 8am-8pm. Also at 9 Psaron St. (tel. 522 82 19), off Karaiskaki Sq. near Larissis Station. 120dr/kg do-it-yourself, 150dr/kg to have it done. Open Mon.-Fri. 8:30am-4pm, Sat. 8:30am-2pm. Also at 46 Didoutou and Zood. Pigis (tel. 361 06 61), between Omonia and Syntagma; take bus #10, 16, or 170 to the Didoutou stop. 120dr per kg if you provide your own soap, 140dr per kg otherwise. Open Mon.-Sat. 8am-9pm. The Greek word for laundry is *plintirio,* but most places have signs saying "Laundry" or *"Aytomata."*

**Pharmacies:** Indicated by a Byzantine-style red cross. Most closed Sat.-Sun.; however, every pharmacy has signs in the window indicating names and addresses of pharmacies open all night and on weekends.

**Medical Emergency:** Tel. 166. English usually spoken. Free emergency medical care for tourists at many Athens hospitals, including **Evangelismos,** 45-47 Ipsilandou St. (tel. 722 00 01), opposite the Hilton.

**Red Cross First Aid Center:** #21, 3 Septemvriou St. (tel. 150). Three blocks north of Omonia Sq., on the left. English spoken.

**Emergencies: Tourist Information** (tel. 171). English spoken. **Athens Police:** (tel. 100). Not likely to speak English.

# Accommodations and Camping

A night in a budget hotel in Athens is rarely a peaceful or sanitary experience, but it's cheap. Since rooms are uniformly mediocre (except in the outlying districts), you should stay at a hotel most suitable to your itinerary. If you're just passing through Athens, it will probably be most convenient to stay by the train station if you're leaving that way, or near Omonia or Monastiraki if you need to take the subway to Piraeus to catch a boat. If proximity to the sights and nightlife of the Plaka is a priority, stay in the Plaka-Syntagma area. Finally, head for the hotels in the residential areas south of the Acropolis for a good night's sleep. Remember that Athens is notoriously noisy; cars and motorcycles speed through even the small streets, and talk and music continue till the moon sets. If you are at all sensitive to noise, the areas near the train station or south of the Acropolis are probably best. In any case, be sure to ask for a room which faces away from the street.

The onslaught of visitors in July and August causes places to fill up as early as noon. If you arrive late, the farther you venture from Syntagma Sq., the better your chances will be of finding a place. Remember that, by law, hotel owners can increase rates by 10%. When hotels fill up, the management often allow guests to sleep on the roof for 400dr per night. This option is not only cheaper, but also cooler. When it's 85°F at 1am in your little box of a hotel room, you'll wish you had taken the roof, even if there's no bed (only 1 or 2 places furnish their own tops with mattresses) and you have to vacate early in the morning. And don't worry: Summer rain is rare in Athens.

Many hotel hawkers meet trains at the station. Most distribute pamphlets with maps for decent places near the station, some of which are listed here. Others, however, have been known to lure tourists to fleabags miles from anywhere and then charge exorbitant rates. Have the hawker point out the place on a large map of the city and set a firm price before leaving the station. Men arriving by bus from the airport should be aware of "friendly bar-keepers"who may direct you to brothels rather than budget hotels. Avoid, even as a last resort, sleeping in the parks. It is illegal, and thieves will pounce.

## Plaka-Syntagma Area

Most of the city's cheap hotels cluster in this central though noisy part of town. Syntagma, the Acropolis, and the subway to Piraeus (from Monastirion station) are all within easy walking distance. The following list is by no means exhaustive.

**Festos,** 18 Filellinon St. (tel. 323 24 55), 3 blocks down Filellinon. The closest place to Syntagma Sq. Noisy and dusty. Nevertheless quite popular and cheap. Lots of students. Bar with funky wall paintings serves spaghetti and salads as well as drinks. Hot showers at select hours. Free luggage storage. 2am curfew. Check-out 10am. Roof 400dr. Dorm bed 700dr. Singles 1200dr. Doubles 1800dr. Triples 2400dr.

**Thisseos Inn,** 10 Thisseos St. (tel. 324 59 60). Continue away from Syntagma on Perikleous St. and turn right onto Thisseos. Centrally located in a commercial area. Quiet in the evenings, but noisy in early morning. Rooms painted bright pink or blue. Kitchen facilities. 1am curfew. Dorm bed 900dr. Doubles 2000dr. Triples 2700dr. Hot showers 1-11am and 6-9pm.

**Dioskouros,** 6 Pittakou St. (tel. 324 81 65 or 324 65 82). Follow Amalias toward Hadrian's Arch, make the third right after Filellinon St., then the first left onto Pittakou St. Garden in back with laundry lines. Luggage storage 50dr per day. Check-out 11am. Clean and quiet singles 1500dr. Doubles 2000dr. Triples 2800dr. Quads 3500dr.

**Student's Inn,** 16 Kidathineon St. (tel. 324 48 08). Take a right off Filellinon St. from Syntagma. Reasonably clean, with reading lamps over all the beds. Right in the center of the Plaka; noisy in the evenings, but at least the street is closed to traffic. 1:30am curfew. Check-out 11am. Luggage storage 50dr per day. Dorm bed 900dr. Singles 1400dr. Doubles 2000dr. Triples 2700dr. Breakfast in the outdoor garden 300dr. Hot showers in the mornings.

**XEN (YWCA),** 11 Amerikis St. (tel. 362 42 91), just 150m from Syntagma off Panepistimiou. Women and mixed groups only. Comfortable and airy. All rooms have balconies; basins provided for laundry. Unenforced midnight curfew. Singles 2100dr. Doubles 3600dr. Triples 4500dr. Quads 4500dr. Breakfast in large cafeteria included.

**Hotel Phaedra,** 16 Herefondos St. (tel. 322 77 95 or 323 84 61). Walk down Amalias toward Hadrian's Arch, turn right at the Arch onto Lissikratous, and pass Hotel Ava—it's on the right past some ruins. Many rooms have balconies with great views of the Parthenon. Clean and comfortable, but expensive. Singles 2500dr. Doubles 3200dr. Triples 4000dr.

**Acropolis House,** 6 Kodrou St. (tel. 322 23 44 or 322 62 41). Turn left off Mitropoleos onto Voulis and follow it to the end at the base of a small hill. Centrally located and thus noisy in the morning and at night. Overflowing plants are part of the traditional decor. Immaculate (even the bathrooms smell nice). You pay for the quaintness. Singles 3350dr. Doubles 4000dr. Triples 5600dr. Quads 6720dr. Luggage storage 50dr per day.

## Monastiraki/Thission Area

Near the central tourist market, the central food market, and the garment district, this neighborhood has a crescendoing noise problem. But it's also near the Acropolis and the subway, practically on top of the Agora archeological site, and has the best bargains in the city.

**Hotel Ideal,** 39 Eolou St. and 2 Voreou St. (tel. 321 31 95), ½ block beyond the Hotel Tempi. Platonically clean, old-fashioned rooms. Fills fast, but owner reserves 4 rooms for late comers (between 11pm-1am). 10% reduction with current *Let's Go: Greece* or *Let's Go: Europe.* Singles 1460dr. Doubles 2300dr. Triples 3000dr.

**Hotel Tempi,** 29 Eolou St. (tel. 321 31 75). The Ideal's friendly neighbor. If Tempi is full, owner sends customers to Ideal and vice-versa. Small but tidy rooms; some even have balconies. Laundry facilities and a 1-for-1 book exchange. The management has a travel agency around the corner where guests of the Hotel Tempi receive a discount on tickets. Roof (with mattresses) 500dr. Singles 1400dr. Doubles 2300dr, with private bath 2900dr. Breakfast 7-11am 200dr.

**Hotel Hermion,** 66 Ermou St. (tel. 321 27 53). Clean, and set far enough back from the street to be fairly quiet. Friendly management speaks excellent English. Singles 1500dr. Doubles 2400dr. Triples 3300dr. English breakfast 8-11am 500dr.

**Pella Inn,** 104 Ermou St. (tel. 325 05 98), about 14 blocks down Ermou, 5 blocks down the hill from Monastiraki Sq. Entrance on Karaiskaki St. Popular and lively, but in a noisy, grimy part of town. Most rooms with balconies overlooking the Acropolis. Lounge and snack bar with psychedelic yellow and red furniture. Free luggage storage. Check-out 11am. Singles 2100dr. Doubles 3000dr, with private bath 3600dr. Triples 3900dr. Breakfast included.

## South of the Acropolis

The accommodations listed below are located in four relatively quiet residential areas south of the Acropolis. Farthest west, Koukaki and Veikou present you with a 15- to 20-minute uphill hike to Syntagma Sq. Ardistos, although somewhat closer, is practically devoid of public transportation services. Farthest east is Pangrati, almost a half hour from Syntagma, but easily accessible by trolley. Since these places are removed from the center of the city, food is cheaper and the ambience more authentically Greek.

**Marble House Pension,** 35 Zini St., Koukaki (tel. 923 40 58); take trolley #1 or 5 to Zini stop. Set back from the street—it's the foliage-covered building on the left. Quiet residential neighborhood. Recently renovated marble lobby; some rooms have balconies and private baths. Very friendly atmosphere. Clean rooms. Free luggage storage. Singles 1600dr, with bath 2200dr. Doubles 2700dr, with bath 3150dr. Triples 3400dr, with bath 3800dr. Breakfast 250dr.

**Clare's House,** 24 Sorvolou St., Ardistos (tel. 922 22 88). Take a taxi here if you're luggage-laden, because it's a hike. Otherwise, trek toward the Arch on Amalias, turn left on Olgas, and follow it to the end. Take a right on Konstandinou, left on Markou Moussourou, then your second right and follow it to Sorvolou. No sign; door with yellow frame. Highly recommended. Immaculate, comfortable, and modern. Some rooms have gorgeous stone balconies with flowers. Friendly staff speaks excellent English. TV lounge with checkered tablecloths, reading room and laundry service (450dr per load). Free luggage storage. Check-out at noon. Singles 3000dr, suite with bath 4000dr. Doubles with bath 4000-5000dr. Breakfast included. Reservations preferred; call to avoid making the trip in vain, as they are often booked solid.

**Art Gallery Pension,** 5 Erechthiou St., Veikou (tel. 923 83 76). Take trolley #1 or 5 from Syntagma to the corner of Veikou and Drakou and walk back ½ block to Erechthiou. Go down Amalias to the end and left onto Dion Areopagitou; take your third left onto Makrigiani, your second right onto Veikou, and your fourth left where Drakou and Erechthiou branch out. The friendly owner-architect, Yiannis, has converted his family's place into a pension with a balcony overlooking the quiet residential area. The breakfast/bar area on the 4th floor is open daily 8:30am-1am. Luggage storage 50dr per piece per day. Singles 2700dr. Doubles 3600dr, with bath 3900dr. Triples 4500dr. Quads 5300dr. Breakfast 350dr.

**Youth Hostel #5 Pangrati,** 75 Damareos St., Pangrati (tel. 751 95 30). Take trolley #2, 11 or 12 to Pangrati plaza, then walk down Imitou 2 blocks, take a left onto Frinis and the first right onto Damareos. Go down Amalias and left on Olgas; continue 1 block past the Stadium, go right on Eratosthenous, and then tackle the 14 blocks to Damareos. Many small beds crammed into depressing rooms, but a bargain. IYHF card not necessary. Snack bar. Washing machine 200dr per load. No curfew. Beds 500dr. Sheets 50dr per day. Singles 900dr. Cold showers.

**Pension Greca,** 48 Singrou St., Veikou (tel. 921 52 62). Facing Parliament with Syntagma behind you, go right down Amalias until it runs into Singrou. Very noisy from busy Singrou St. Cozy lobby with TV and potted plants. Luggage storage 150dr per day. Student prices: Singles 1500dr, with bath 2500dr. Doubles 2000-2400dr, with bath 3400dr. Triples 3000dr, with bath 3600dr. Otherwise 30% more. Breakfast 300dr. Showers (7-11pm only) are hot and vigorous.

**Joseph's House,** 13 Markou Moussourou, Ardistos (tel. 923 12 04). Follow directions to Clare's House but stay on Markou Moussourou when you get to it (the first inclining street to the right of the forested hill by the stadium). Not too lovely, but it's cheap and quiet. No curfew. Luggage storage 50dr per day. Check-out 2pm. Roof 450dr. Singles 1300dr. Doubles 1800dr. Triples 2400dr. The only hot shower is on the roof from a sun-heated pipe.

## Railway Station Area

This uninteresting business and residential district is probably too far away from Syntagma for week-long stays, but it is ideal for a stopover because of its proximity to the trains, buses, and, via the Victoria subway stop, Piraeus. Most places listed here are large, popular, lively, and generally cheaper than those farther south. Most hotels have bars which serve breakfast, snacks, and drinks. Place Victoria is quite alive at night, and not at all touristy.

**Athens Connection Hotel,** 20 Ioulianou St. (tel. 882 83 34). From the station, take Filadelfias St., which eventually becomes Ioulianou. Cross Patission and go past the little park where the street seems to end; it continues. From Syntagma, take trolley #2, 4, 11, or 12 running to (or from) Patission. The sign outside says "Athens Hostel." Lively and popular; fills fast. Lots of dust in the corners. An interesting establishment with some much-appreciated "extras:" budget travel service and currency exchange. Free luggage storage. Dorm bed in quint 800dr, in quad 900dr. Doubles 2400dr, with bath 2800dr. Triples with bath 3600dr. Hearty breakfast 350dr.

**Hostel Annabel,** 28 Koumoundourou St. at Veranzerou (tel. 524 58 34). Take trolley #1, 2, 4, 5, 11, or 12 from Syntagma to Omonia, walk 2 blocks up Tritis Septemvriou and turn left on Veranzerou. Friendly, helpful management. A cramped but funky bar. Good place to meet other tourists. Travel services and information. Rooms clean as any in this part of town. Luggage storage 50dr per day. Check-out 10:30am. Roof 300dr. Dorm bed 700dr. Singles 1500dr. Doubles 1800dr. Breakfast approximately 300dr.

**Hotel Appia,** 21 Menandrou St. (tel. 524 51 55). From Omonia Sq., walk down Tsaldari St. several blocks and turn left onto Menandrou St. Modern hotel with elevator and clean rooms. Bar open 24 hours. Free luggage storage. Singles 1300dr, with bath 1900dr. Doubles 1900dr, with bath 2300dr. Triples 2400dr. Quads 2900dr. Breakfast (7-10am) 200dr.

**Athens House Hotel,** 4 Aristotelous St. (tel. 524 05 39), 5th floor. From Omonia Sq., take Tritis Septemvriou 3 blocks, turn left on Halkondili, then right on Aristotelous. 12 min. from the train station and close to bus terminal. Apartment converted into hotel. Clean, small rooms with balconies. Friendly, helpful staff. Money exchange. Singles 1300dr. Doubles 2000dr. Triples 2600dr. Quads 3200dr. Only 1 single and 1 quad.

**Pension Argo,** 25 Victoros Ougo St. (tel. 522 59 39). From the station, bear right on Deligiani to Victoros Ougo. Nothing special, but it's quiet and clean. Self-service coin-op laundry, money exchange, and travel information. Check-out 11am. Singles 1000dr. Doubles 1600dr. Triples 2100dr. Quads 2400dr. Breakfast 300dr.

**Hotel Rio,** 13 Odisseos St. (tel. 522 36 72), a 5-min. walk from the railroad station. Go right on Deligianni, and take the sixth right onto Odisseos. From Omonia Sq., take Agiou Konstandinou until it becomes Ahileos; Odisseos St. is on the right. Newly renovated and quiet; you're almost guaranteed a good night's sleep. Cheerful management. Free luggage storage. Singles 1500dr. Doubles 1600dr. Triples 2100dr. Quads 2400dr. Breakfast 250dr.

**Iokasti's House,** 65 Aristotelous St. (tel. 822 66 47 or 822 12 82). From the station, follow the directions to the Athens Connection, but turn right off Ioulianou at Aristotelous. Rooms vary in quality but are generally well-maintained. Hot water at select hours. Roof 300dr. Dorm bed 500dr. Doubles 1800dr. Triples 2400dr. Quads 3000dr. English breakfast 350dr.

**Athens Inn,** 13 Victoros Ougo (tel. 524 69 06). From the station, bear right on Deligiani to Victoros Ougo. Dusty. Spacious, recently renovated bar with puffy colored fabric on the ceiling. Free luggage storage. Roof 300dr. Dorm bed in 10-bed room 600dr, in triple 900dr, in quad 800dr, in quint 700dr. Singles 1500dr. Doubles 1800dr, with bath 2400dr. Triple with bath 3000dr. Breakfast 300dr.

**Hotel Arta,** 12 Nikitara St. (tel. 362 77 53 or 360 29 53 or 362 37 73). From Syntagma, take Stadiou to Em. Benaki, turn right, and take the third left on Nikitara. Four air-conditioned rooms upstairs. Rooms clean but not the hallways. Most rooms have bathrooms. Singles 2200dr. Doubles 3500dr. Triples 4500dr. Breakfast 350dr.

Athens proper has no **camping** facilities, nor is free-lance camping legal. Nearby, however, there are several campsites, including **Dionissiotis Camping** (tel. 807 14 94), 18km north on the national road at Nea Kifissia. (250dr per person, 250dr per tent.) The sites at Daphni, Cape Sounion, and Voula are accessible also (see Near Athens). *This Week in Athens* lists campsites in the Athens area, while the GNTO distributes a booklet listing all of Greece's official campgrounds.

# Food

Eating in Greece is a celebration, and Athens is the life of the party. Fruitsellers beckon from all corners; outdoor *tavernas* tempt with their festive yet relaxed atmosphere and simple, hearty fare.

Try to adjust to the Greek timetable. Breakfast is minimal. Lunch is huge—and siesta-provoking. Dinner is late and light. Most places in the Plaka serve early, but outside the touristed quarters few restaurants open before 8pm. Many restaurants have signs in both Greek and Roman letters. If a sign beckons to you in English only, chances are that the establishment caters to tourists and is more expensive than delicious.

Besides the trolley fare, food is Athens' greatest bargain. *Souvlaki,* either skewered or wrapped in *pita,* is a bargain at 70dr; grilled sandwiches *(tost)* with choice of meats, cheeses, and egg cost from 80-100dr. Locally brewed beer runs about 100dr per half-liter. *Spanakopita* and *tiropita* (spinach and cheese pies), served hot, sell for 75dr. Ice cream at 50dr and sticky-sweet *baklava* at 80dr tempt the sweet tooth.

Vegetarians fare particularly well in Athens. Fried zucchini, stuffed eggplant, *tzatziki* (cucumber and yogurt salad), and *horta* (greens—either beet or dandelion—served with oil and lemon) accompany meals at most *tavernas.*

Before ordering in any restaurant, check the prices and look around both in the kitchen and on other people's plates. If you don't know the word for what you want, point. The price for a meal without entertainment should be about 600dr per person. Be adventurous and have a bottle of *ouzo* for 120dr. Service is always included, but it is customary and polite to leave whatever coins you receive as change.

If you're careful not to get hustled into buying a meal with *bouzouki* entertainment and folk dances at outrageous prices, and you don't mind the waiters loudly soliciting you as you wander about, the best place to eat is the Plaka. Although crowded, especially in peak season, its outdoor *tavernas* and roof gardens make for great people-watching. When you eat in the Plaka, survey the streets and menus before you make your selection. Don't be swayed by the first waiter who thrusts his list of entrees before your hungry eyes and waves you toward an empty table. Once seated at the establishment of your choice, relax: Greek restaurants are not known for the celerity of their service. Women should know that the Plaka is a popular spot for *kamakia* (literally, "harpoons") who enjoy making catcalls at tourist women.

## Plaka/Syntagma

**Theophilos,** 1 Vakhou St. (tel. 322 39 01). Walk down Kidathineon toward the Parthenon, turn right at Adrianou St., pass the circular monument of Lysikrates as you enter Vironos St., and turn right onto Vakhou. After dining here, you'll probably want to add your signature to those chalked on the inside wall of the tiny restaurant by satisfied customers. Try the *giouvetsi* (veal and rice; 370dr) or the *flogera* (a selection of appetizers; 210dr). Open Tues.-Sat. 8pm-1am. Call for reservations as the restaurant fills quickly.

**To Gerani,** corner of Tripodon and Epiharmou St., in the Plaka. Turn right on Kidathineon from Filellinon and follow it to Tripodon. Make a right and walk 2 blocks—it's on the left. Wonderful balcony; if it's full they will squeeze in an extra table for you; excellent hors d'oeuvres (250dr) and flaming sausages. Open for lunch and dinner.

**Eden Vegetarian Restaurant,** 3 Flessa St. Turn off of Adrianou. Popular with both herbivores and omnivores. The meat in dishes like *mousaka* (340dr) and lasagna (300dr) is replaced with soya. Outside terrace. Open Wed.-Mon. noon-midnight.

**O Kostis** (sign in Greek), 18 Kidathineon St., a few blocks below Filellinon on a small square. Tables strategically bank one of the Plaka's main pedestrian thoroughfares. Great people-watching post, not to mention the reasonably priced and tasty food. *Mousaka* 350dr, spaghetti 180dr, stuffed tomatoes 350dr. Open daily noon-1am.

**Syntrivani,** 5 Filellinon St., 1 block from Syntagma Sq. Strategically located and very pleasant; the cool garden will make you forget the heat and noise outside. Breakfast of ham and eggs or omelette 250dr. Pasta 200dr, *souvlaki* 400dr, chicken 350dr. Open 7am-midnight.

**Tsekouras,** 3 Tripodon, across from To Gerani. Garden canopied by a fig tree. Popular with locals. *Souvlaki* 500dr, *dolmades* 210dr, and veal with tomato 420dr. Open daily 7pm-midnight.

**To Fagdiko,** 81 Adrianou St., on a touristed street between Plaka and Monastiraki; light blue sign in front of the restaurant. Not many locals, but cheap food and friendly though slow service. *Mousaka* 370dr, pork chops 490dr, lamb with vegetables 470dr. Open for lunch and dinner.

**The Moon,** 76 Adrianou St. (tel. 325 02 95). Cheap, friendly restaurant with distinctive red tablecloths. Greek salad 200dr, *souvlaki* pita 70dr, pork chops 450dr. Open for lunch and dinner.

For a change of pace, it is worthwhile to venture outside the Plaka. The food is usually better and cheaper and the ambience more engaging.

**Restaurant of Konstanoinos Athanasias Velly,** Varnava Sq., Plastira (no sign). Take trolley #2, 4, 11, or 12 to Plastira Sq. and walk 3 blocks down Proklou St. to Varnava Sq. Restaurant is in a small white house with flowers in front at the diagonal corner of the square between Stilponos and Pironos. A real treat: small, authentic, delicious, and cheap. No English spoken; you'll have to point. Veal and potatoes 330dr, *keftedes* (Greek meatballs) 200dr. Open 8:30pm-1am.

**Caravitis,** 4 Pafsaniou St. (sign in Greek). From Syntagma, take trolley #2, 4, 11, or 12 to the Stadium, make your 3rd right, and go 2 blocks up the hill. A cool garden; large and very popular with locals. Try the flavorful *stamnaki* (660dr)—veal cooked in a crock pot with wine and potatoes. Open daily 8:30pm-2am.

**Restaurant Gardenia,** 31 Zini St., Koukaki (sign in Greek); right by Marble House Pension and near the Art Gallery Pension. Authentic, inexpensive, and delicious fare in residential neighborhood. Roast chicken 235dr, veal 350dr. Open Mon.-Fri. 10am-5pm and 9pm-1am, Sat.-Sun. noon-5pm.

**Ainos,** 50 Piraeus St., off Omonia Sq. In a grimy, dull, and distant part of town, but the food's great. Everything's in a glass case by the kitchen—just point. Try the chicken with little potatoes and bacon (350dr). Open Mon.-Sat. 11am-midnight.

**O Yamas,** 38 Zaimi St., behind the National Museum. All-Athenian clientele for friendly, cheap eats. Try the baked fish (250dr). Good alternative to the rip-off cafe in front of the museum. Open daily noon-2:30pm.

**Taverna Kostoyiannis,** 37 Zaimi St., 1 block behind the National Archeological Museum. Proclaimed the best *taverna* in Athens by locals and tourists alike. Enter through the kitchen—notice the great variety of scrumptious dishes. A wallet banger, but worth the indulgence. Rabbit with onions 800dr, mussels with rice 420dr. Open Mon.-Sat. 8pm-2am.

# Sights

The famed **Acropolis,** or "high city," with its commanding position overlooking the Aegean sea and the Attic Plain, served throughout history as both a military fortress and a religious center. Already during the thirteenth century B.C.E., the hilltop was enclosed by a huge wall, and slight traces of the residence of the *anax* (king) still remain. In addition to political business, religious ceremonies honoring the great gods of the Mycenean religion were performed in the palace. Greek civilization developed rapidly, due largely to the institution of the *polis* (city-state), which constituted a radical departure from the palace civilizations of the Bronze Age. Of the *polis* that flourished for centuries throughout the Greek world, Athens was the quintessence.

In 683 B.C.E., the monarchy ruling Athens was overthrown, and the foundations of a democratic state were introduced. The new rulers, the *Aristoi* (excellent ones), were wealthy land-owners who transferred the center from the high city to the lower foothills in the vicinity of the Agora. The Acropolis became a cult center where two aspects of Athena were worshipped: Athena Polias, goddess of crops and fertility, and Athena Pallas, the virgin military guardian of the city. Throughout the sixth century B.C.E., tyrants ruled Athens until the triumph of democracy in 507 B.C.E. A temple was begun on the Acropolis in 490 B.C.E.; ten years later the Persians sacked the city, and the Athenians buried all the destroyed religious objects. Thanks to their foresight, we can now see these treasured artifacts in the Acropolis Museum.

In response to the Persian threat, the Delian league—an alliance among the cities of the Aegean area—was formed. Taxes and booty appropriated by the league constituted huge amounts of capital, which Pericles used to beautify Athens. His building program funded the construction of the temples of the Acropolis, as well as the Temple of Hephaestus in the agora and the Temple of Poseidon at Sounion. This thriving development was interrupted by the start of the 27-year Peloponnesian War. But the Athenians were committed to Pericles' plans, and construction continued throughout the war even after his death in 429 B.C.E. The Acropolis was completed just prior to Athens' defeat in 404 B.C.E. Since that time, four buildings that remain on the site—the Parthenon, the Propylaea, the Temple of Athena Nike, and the Erechtheum—have had incalculable influence on the Western conception of the architectural aesthetic.

The Acropolis continued to be fortified, embellished, and fought over through the Hellenistic and Roman periods. Under the Byzantines, it was converted into a Christian place of worship: The Parthenon became the Church of St. Sophia ("Sophia," like Athena, signifies "wisdom"). In 1205 C.E., the Frankish crusades conquered Athens, and the Acropolis once again became a fortress, serving as palace and headquarters for the Dukes de la Roche. The Parthenon was transformed into a Catholic Church (Notre Dame d'Athènes). In the fifteenth century, the Turks turned the Parthenon into a mosque and the Erechtheum into the home of the Turkish commander's harem. In 1822, the Greeks regained the Acropolis, and apart from a six-year occupation by the Turks from 1827-1833 and the brief Nazi occupation of this century, the Acropolis has been in Greek hands ever since.

In classical times, a straight ramp led to the Acropolis. Today's visitors enter through the **Beulé Gate** (added by the Romans and named for the French archeologist who unearthed it) and pass through the **Propylaea,** the ancient entrance built by Mnesicles between 437 and 432 B.C.E. Although it was never completed, this structure became famous for its ambitious multi-level design. In Roman times, the Propylaea was even more impressive, extending for 80m below the Beulé Gate. At the cliff's edge, behind and to the right, the tiny **Temple of Athena Nike** was built during a respite from the Peloponnesian War, the so-called Peace of Nikias (421-415 B.C.E.). Below the temple are the remains of the five-meter thick **Cyclopean wall,** which once surrounded the whole of the Acropolis so that one could view the sea only from the Temple of Athena Nike.

The **Erechtheum,** completed in 406 B.C.E. just prior to the defeat of Athens, stands in front and to the left as you ascend the Acropolis. Lighter than the older Parthenon, the Erechtheum is a unique two-leveled structure divided into east/west porches ingeniously contrived to house a number of cults including those of Athena, Poseidon, and the hero Erechtheus. The east porch with its six Ionic columns was dedicated to Athena Polias and sheltered the olive wood statue of the goddess that the Athenians believed to be a gift from the gods. Inside the west porch where Poseidon was worshiped is a salt cistern, "the Erechthean Sea," supposedly created when Poseidon struck a rock with his trident during his competition with Athena. When the olive tree planted by Athena was burned by the Persians in 480 B.C.E., Herodotus reported that it miraculously sprouted again the following day. The tree on the site today was planted by Queen Sophia. On the south side of the Erechtheum, facing the Parthenon, are the **Karyatids,** six columns sculpted in the shape of women. Because of the ravages of air pollution, the originals have been taken inside to the Acropolis Museum and replaced by plaster copies.

In front and to the right looms the **Parthenon,** or "Virgin's apartment." Originally referring to only one room in the temple, the name came to denote the entire structure after Demosthenes so called it in an oration. The edifice, designed by architects Iktinos and Kallikrates, was the first building completed under Pericles' plan (447-432 B.C.E.). It housed the legendary gold and ivory statue of Athena Parthenos by Pheidias. Whatever your expectations, you will be impressed by the Parthenon's monumental size, lightness of construction, and harmony of proportion.

The Doric columns of the Parthenon, rather than being straight as they appear, slant inward. Their sides swell about a third of the way up, the floor bows slightly upward, and each column tapers toward its capital—all elements combine to produce a graceful, uplifting effect.

The mythical tales recounted on the sides of the Parthenon portray the victory of the Greek forces over the barbarians. On the south side, best preserved, are the Lapiths and Centaurs; on the east, the Gigantomachy, the triumph of the gods over the giants; on the north, the victory of the Greeks over Troy; and on the west, the triumph of the Greeks over the Eastern Amazons. A frieze in low-relief around the interior walls depicts the procession at the great Panathenaen Games. Unfortunately you'll have to go to London to see most of those original sculptures not destroyed in 1687 when the Parthenon, filled with the Turks' supply of gunpowder, was blown up during the Venetian siege. Further damage to the Parthenon occurred during the War of Independence in the 1820s. Nonetheless, the ruins alone are awesome. Visit the Acropolis early in the morning, since by 10am telephoto-toting tour groups have the run of the place. You can reach the entrance which is on the west side of the Acropolis, from Dionission Areopagitou St., south of the Acropolis, or by walking up the hill from the Plaka. (Acropolis open Mon.-Sat. 7:30am-7:15pm, Sun. 8am-6:30pm. Admission 600dr, students 300dr with ISIC.)

Also on the Acropolis, the **Acropolis Museum** (tel. 321 02 19), contains a superb collection of sculpture from the site, including the Karyatids of the Erechtheum. Most of the treasures housed here date from the transition period from Archaic to Classical Greek art (550-400 B.C.E.). You can trace this development in the faces of the statues, from stylized, entranced faces and static poses of Archaic sculpture, seen in the famous *Moschophoros* (calf-bearer), to the more familiar, naturalistic, and free-moving figures of Classical art. Only a few pieces from the Parthenon are exhibited here; most were removed in the early nineteenth century and are on display in the British Museum. (Acropolis Museum open Mon. and Wed.-Sat. 7:30am-7:15pm, Tues. noon-6:30pm, Sun. 8am-6:30pm. Admission included in Acropolis ticket.) From the southwest corner of the Acropolis, you can look down on the reconstructed **Odeon of Herodes Atticus,** a functioning theater dating from the Roman Period, circa 160 C.E. (see Entertainment below). To the left are the ruins of the Classical Greek **Theater of Dionysus.** For a closer look, walk down to the entrance on Dionissiou Aeropagitou St. Adjacent to the theater are the **Asklepeion** and **Stoa of Eumenes II.** (All 3 ruins open Mon.-Sat. 9am-2:45pm, Sun. 9am-1:45pm. Admission 200dr, students 100dr.)

The **Athenian Agora,** at the foot of the Acropolis, was the administrative center and marketplace of Athens from the sixth century B.C.E. through the late Roman Period (fifth and sixth centuries C.E.). The decline of the Agora accompanied the decline of Athens itself, as both city and square were buffeted by barbarian attacks, beginning in 267 B.C.E. and climaxing in 580 C.E. It was in the Agora, as well as on the **Pnyx** (the low hill and meeting place of the assembly 1km to the south), that Athenian democracy was born and flourished. Socrates frequented the Agora, as did Aristotle, Demosthenes, Xenophon, and St. Paul. Plato says that Socrates' preliminary hearing was at the **Stoa Basileios** (Royal promenade), which has been recently excavated and lies to the left as you cross the subway tracks after leaving the Agora.

The sprawling archeological site features two remarkable constructions. The **Temple of Hephaestus,** on a hill in the northwest corner, is the best-preserved classical temple in Greece. Built around 440 B.C.E., it is especially notable for its friezes depicting the labors of Hercules and the adventures of Theseus. To the south, the **Stoa of Attalos,** a multi-purpose building for shops, shelter, and informal gatherings, was rebuilt with new materials in 1953-56 and houses the **Agora Museum** (tel. 321 01 85). The original structure, built in the second century B.C.E., was given to Athens by Attalos II, King of Pergamon, in gratitude for the education he had received in the city. The museum contains a number of relics from the site; upstairs are miniature models of both the Acropolis and the Agora. (Agora and museum open in summer Mon.-Sat. 9am-3pm, Sun. 9am-1:45pm. Admission to both 400dr, students 200dr.) There are several entrances to the Agora, including one at the edge of Monastiraki. You can reach the Acropolis by exiting the southern side of the Agora (by following the path uphill) and then turning right. The most commonly used is the gate near the Acropolis entrance (turn right as you leave the Acropolis).

The **Temple of Olympian Zeus** also deserves a visit. Fifteen majestic columns are all that remain of the largest temple ever built in Greece. Begun in the sixth century B.C.E. by the son of the tyrant Peisistratos, the temple was completed 600 years later by the Roman Emperor Hadrian. Now in the middle of downtown Athens below the National Garden and suffering from the ravages of air pollution, the Corinthian columns are a reminder of the startling juxtaposition of old and new Athens. (Open Mon.-Sat. 8:30am-3pm, Sun. 9:30am-2:30pm. Admission 200dr, students 100dr.) Nearby, just off Leoforos Amalias, is **Hadrian's Arch,** built in the second century C.E. as the symbolic gateway from ancient Athens to the new Roman city.

On the other side of the tracks at Thission Station and straight down Ermou St. from Syntagma Sq. is **Kerameikos,** site of the 40-meter wide boulevard that ran from the Agora, through the Diplyon gate, and 1½km to the sanctuary of Akademos where Plato founded his Academy in the fourth century B.C.E. Public tombs for state leaders, famous authors, and those fallen in battle were erected on either side of this road. Worshippers commenced the annual Panathenaean procession to the Acropolis at the Diplyon Gate, one of the two gates excavated at this site. From a platform in the cemetery outside this gate, Pericles gave his famous funeral oration in honor of those who died in the early years of the Peloponnesian War. He consoled the mourners: "Fortunate are they who draw for their lot a death so glorious as that which has caused your mourning." The sacred road to Eleusis, used during the annual Eleusian processions, ran through the Sacred Gate, the second gate on the site. Family tombs adorn either side of the Sacred Road outside the gate. A **museum** on the site (tel. 346 35 52) exhibits finds from recent digs and an excellent pottery collection. (Site and museum open Mon.-Sat. 8:45am-3pm, Sun. 9:30am-2:30pm. Admission to both 200dr, students 100dr.)

A walking tour of ancient Athens would surely have taken you to Plato's Academy, but its remains lie beneath the tracks of the Athens-Corinth railway, ½km north of the Sacred Gate. So head for the **National Archeological Museum,** 28 Patission St. (tel. 821 77 17), which alone is worth delaying your jaunt to the islands. Take bus #25 from Thission or Monastiraki to Syntagma and trolley #2, 4, 5, 11, or 12 from the uphill side of Syntagma or trolley #3 or 13 on the north side of Vassilissis Sofias. The collection contains an embarrassment of riches; pieces that would otherwise be the prizes of lesser collections seem unremarkable amidst the general magnificence. To avoid being overwhelmed, view the collection slowly, returning to each room several times, or tag along with a guided tour group. If you can, return on different days to enjoy your favorite pieces at leisure. If you have any interest in archeology, a guide book will prove useful—the one by Dr. Semni Karouzou is particularly good (800dr).

As you enter the museum, the room directly in front of you contains finds from Heinrich Schliemann's digs at Mycenae, including the golden "Mask of Agamemnon" (which is, in fact, the death mask of a king who lived at least 3 centuries earlier). This room also has Bronze Age jewelry, pottery, and exquisite examples of goldsmiths' art from Mycenae and other sites in the Peloponnese.

Don't leave without viewing the *kouroi,* or standing males, from various artistic epochs of Greece. THe evolution of this sculptural form, observable in this chronological arrangement, is a fascinating lesson in art history. Scholars have also been fascinated by the Minoan frescoes (on the second floor). Excavated from a town on Santorini, they were buried during a volcanic eruption around 1500 B.C.E. The frescoes give us a unique glimpse of life in the Bronze Age: Two doe-eyed boys engage in a boxing match with studied concentration; a procession of ships sails between two towns accompanied by dolphins; the delightful fresco of Spring depicts swallows swooping above red lilies. Also on the second floor are a numismatic collection and an extensive vase collection. Trace the decorative development from Mycenean to Geometric and finally to Classical. By the beginning of the Archaic period, artists had imported the technique of making black-figure vases from Corinth. An innovative artist decided to reverse the colors, thus creating the red-figure vases of the Classical period. (Museum open Tues.-Sat. 8am-7pm, Sun. 8am-6pm. Admission 500dr, students 250dr. Cameras without flash free, with flash 300dr. Vase collection open Tues.-Sun. 9am-3pm. Numismatic collection open Tues.-Sun. 9am-1pm.)

Opened in 1986, the **Goulandris Museum of Cycladic and Ancient Greek Art,** 4 Neophytou Douka St. (tel. 724 97 06), near Kolonaki, should not be missed. The collection is displayed stunningly in a modern air-conditioned building. Cycladic art is characterized by voluptuous female marble figurines. In addition to the Cycladic pieces on display, there is a collection of Greek vases and statues from 2000 B.C.E. to the fourth century C.E. An evocative exhibit on the third floor displays simple Cycladic art and its influence on modern artists such as Picasso, Henry Moore, and Modigliani. (Open Mon. and Wed.-Fri. 10am-4pm, Sat. 10am-3pm. Admission 150dr.)

The **Benaki Museum,** at the corner of Koumbari and Vassilissis Sofias (tel. 361 16 17), houses a diverse collection in a beautiful Neoclassical building, the former residence of philanthropist Anthony Benaki. The museum displays Bronze Age Greek relics, Byzantine icons, gold jewelry of the fifth century B.C.E., textiles and costumes from the islands, and relics from the War of Independence, and explores the influence of neighboring cultures on Greece by juxtaposing Islamic, Arabic, and Coptic artwork alongside the Greek. Children find this museum particularly enjoyable. Be sure to visit the Greek folk art exhibition downstairs; the costumes are a far cry from those worn by the dancers in the Plaka. The collection of Byron memorabilia on the second floor will be admired by any Philhellene. The museum has a rooftop garden cafeteria. (Museum open Wed.-Mon. 8:30am-2pm. Admission 200dr.)

Housed in an elegant Florentine building with serene courtyards, the **Byzantine Museum,** 22 Vassilissis Sofias (tel. 721 10 27), is just up the street from the Benaki and has a large and excellent collection of Christian art from the fourth through the nineteenth centuries. The first floor of the main building contains sculptures from early Byzantine times. Upstairs, the museum's icon collection includes works from the entire Byzantine Period as well as a reconstructed Early Christian basilica. There are also a number of superb reliefs done in bronze, silver, and gold. One wing of the building features an array of unattributed but well-preserved frescoes and mosaics. To the right as you enter is the impressive private Loverdois collection of icons. The exhibits are poorly labeled, however, so consider buying the catalog (300dr) before you visit. (Open Tues.-Sat. 9am-3pm, Sun. 9:30am-2:30pm. Admission 300dr, students 150dr.)

Next door to the Byzantine Museum on Vassilissas Sofias stands the **War Museum** (tel. 729 05 43). Beginning with battle scenes from a frieze from one of Apollo's temples, this museum traces the history of Greek armaments from Neolithic eras, to the fifth-century B.C.E. Persian invasion and the expeditions of Alexander the Great, to the sub-machine guns of the modern era. The primary emphasis, though, is on the modern Greek arsenal. (Open Tues.-Sat. 9am-2pm, Sun. 9:30am-2pm. Free.)

The **National Gallery** (Alexander Soutzos Museum) is set back from Vassilissis Sofias on Vassileos Konstandiou (tel. 721 10 10). The museum's exhibit of works by Greek artists is supplemented by periodic international displays. The permanent collection includes some outstanding El Grecos. Sculptures are scattered all around the grounds of the museum. Consult *This Week in Athens* or call the museum for information. (Open Tues.-Sat. 9am-3pm, Sun. 10am-2pm. Admission 30dr.) The **Theater Museum,** 50 Akadimias St. (tel. 362 94 30), behind the university, offers a backstage peep at models, costumes, photographic paraphernelia, busts, and dressing rooms. (Open Mon. 5-8pm, Tues.-Fri. 9:30am-3pm, Sun. 10am-1pm.) In the Plaka, the **Greek Folk Art Museum,** 17 Kidathineon St. (tel. 321 30 18), exhibits *laiki techni* (popular art), including embroidered textiles and costumes from all over Greece. Don't miss the mod wall paintings by the folk artist Theophilos. (Open Tues.-Sun. 10am-2pm. Admission 200dr, students 100dr, cameras 300dr.)

The **Jewish Museum,** 36 Leoforos Amalias, third floor (tel. 323 15 77), is housed in a nineteenth-century building with a French flag in front, across from the Zappeion. An impressive collection of textiles, religious artifacts, and documents traces the historical roots of the Greek Jewish communities dating from the Hellenistic period. The museum also contains the reconstructed Synagogue of Patres. (Open Sun.-Fri. 9am-1pm. Free. Guided tour included.)

Byzantine sanctuaries, like their Classical counterparts, have been incorporated into the urban landscape. Traffic on Ermou St. must pass around **Kapnikaria Church,** which has been stranded right in the middle of the street one block beyond Eolou St. Walking down Mitropoleos from Syntagma, you may also notice a tiny church on the corner of Pentelis St. around which a modern building has been constructed. Other Byzantine churches found in the sprawling Athenian metropolis include the **Agia Apostrilli,** on Vrissakiou St., on the eastern edge of the Agora, **Metamorphosis,** in the Plaka near Pritaniou St., **Agios Nikodimos,** on Filellinon St., a few blocks from Syntagma, and **Panayia Gorgoepikös,** next to the **Mitropoli Cathedral,** on Mitropoleos St. Most of these churches are open in the morning and for services, and require proper dress.

An eye-catching tourist attraction is the changing of the guard in front of the **Parliament** building on Syntagma Sq. It's not Buckingham Palace, but every hour on the hour two sets of extremely tall (especially by Greek standards) *evzones* (guards) slowly wind up, kick their heels about, and fall backwards into symmetrical little guard houses on either side of the **Tomb of the Unknown Warrior.** Unlike their English equivalents, *evzones* occasionally wink and even smile at tourists. Every Sunday at 10:45am accompanied by a band, the full troop of guards dress in their traditional regalia—white *foustanela* (pleated skirt) and heavy clog-like shoes topped with pom-poms—and parade into Syntagma.

Athens' two principal markets attract everyone from bargain-hunters to inveterate browsers. The **Athens Flea Market,** with its festive bazaar-like atmosphere, adjacent to Monastiraki Sq. along Ifestou, Adrianou, and Pandrossou St. offers a potpourri of second-hand junk, costly antiques, and everything in between. The market is open daily with a special large flea market on Sunday from 8am to 2pm. A huge outdoor-indoor **market** lines the sides of Athinas St. between Evripidou and Sofokleous St., where you can buy fruits, vegetables, fish, meats, cheese, nuts, and almost anything else edible. It's open the same hours as regular food stores, but Athenian restauranteurs go early and purchase the choice meat and fish. Be forwarned that merchants deride those making small purchases.

# *Entertainment*

At nightfall, **Plaka** becomes a magnet for tourists visiting Athens. The streets, strung with white lights and full of bustling restaurants and cafes, are ideal for an evening's walk. Today's healthy, active Plaka represents a rebirth of the historic area. In the past few years, the government has managed to curb the violence, prostitution, and deterioration that had been plaguing Plaka. The best Plaka discotheques, however, were casualties of the clean-up. Avoid the remaining rip-off *bouzouki tavernas* whose hawkers will attempt to lure you in with promises of "Greek folkloric dances" and glossy color pictures of the dancers. A popular local hangout is the unique **Aerodromio** disco at the end of the International Airport runway (known by most cab drivers). The barstools are airplane seats.

The cool, pleasant **National Garden** (open sunrise to sunset) is a great escape from the noise, heat, and frantic pace of Athens. Walk along the lush, verdant paths or visit the zoo. Every evening the cafes near the Zappeion present singers, as well as comedians and acrobats on an outdoor stage. It's free if you stand, as most people do; otherwise, get a table at one of the numerous cafes. The outdoor cinema in the **Zappeion** generally has a good selection of English-language films. Cinema *Pari*, on Kidathineon, in the heart of the Plaka, shows recent films. Check the *Athens News* for the complete addresses and schedules of all the Athens movie-houses. Most cost 250dr and are concentrated on Stadiou, Panepistimiou, and Patission St. Shows are at 9 and 11pm, but try to attend the late show since traffic noise and lingering dusk tend to mar the early screening. Sit near the front to hear the already hushed film over the intruding *bozouki* music.

Catch a beautiful view of the city from the chapel of St. Georgeon on top of rocky **Lycabettos Hill.** You can take the funicular (100dr one-way, 150dr round-trip) to the top (the station is at the end of Ploutarchou St. and operates until midnight), or burn off dinner by walking up. The cafe up top is hopelessly expensive, but the panorama of the city is stunning. Go at night to see the Acropolis bathed in amber light. Another prime perch are the rocks near the Acropolis entrance that overlook the Agora and most of Athens.

The **Athens Festival** runs annually from June until September, featuring classical theater groups performing in the **Odeon of Herodes Atticus.** Performances are also staged in Lycabettos Theater at the top of Lycabettos Hill, and in Epidavros (see Peloponnese section). The Greek Orchestra plays during this festival, as do visiting groups, which have ranged from the Bolshoi and B. B. King to the Alvin Ailey Dance Company and the Talking Heads (no children under 6 allowed). The **Festival Office** (tel. 322 14 59 or 322 31 11 ext. 240) is in the arcade at 4 Stadiou St.; a line forms by 9am so arrive early. Student tickets are generally cheap (200-500dr depending on the show, student card required). (Open Mon.-Fri. 8:30am-1:30pm and 6-8:30pm, Sun. 9am-midnight.)

If you've had a bit (or a lot) to drink, the hokey **Sound and Light Show** on Pnyx Hill (opposite the Acropolis) can be quite entertaining. (April-Oct. daily in English and French; English and German on Tues. and Fri. at 9pm. Admission 400dr, students 150dr. Call 322 14 59 or 922 62 10.) Nearby on Philopappou Hill, **Greek Dances** follow the light show. (June-Sept. daily at 10:25pm with an additional show Wed. and Sun. at 8:15pm. Tickets 950dr, 850dr, and 750dr. Call 324 43 95 or 921 46 50.)

Revert to childhood and enjoy Athen's shadow theater (*theater skion*), in Plaka, in Plateia Lysikratous (behind the monument, at the end of Lysikratous St.). This wildly funny production surmounts with humor any language barrier (performances are in Greek). Daily at 9pm. Tickets 250dr.

Most Athenians party in the suburbs. **Kifissia,** a posh residential area to the north of Athens, has many hip *tavernas* and discos. Take the subway from Omonia to the last stop or bus #538 or 539 to Kaningos Sq. (off Acadimias, near Omonia Sq.). Stay near the shore in the town of **Glyfada** (the center of town is packed with tacky bars). One excellent restaurant frequented by locals is **O Karachos,** 49 Theatrou Pavlo (sign in Greek: O ΚΑΡΑΧΟΡ). Face the water and walk left along the shore about 200 yards. The tables are right on the shore, and the fish is always fresh. After dinner, join the locals in front of the many gelato shops, sip iced coffee (*frappe*) in an outside *taverna,* or just wander among the herd of parked motorbikes lining the streets. Glyfada discos get crowded and stay open late. Take bus #121, 128, or 129 from the south side of the National Garden in the middle of Olga St. (½ hr.).

# *Near Athens: Attica* Αττική

## *Piraeus*

Blessed with a safe natural harbor, Piraeus has been Athens' port since Themistocles started fortifying it in the early fifth century B.C.E. as a base for the growing

Athenian fleet. It was further strengthened by Pericles, who is credited with building the Long Walls from Athens to Piraeus around 450 B.C.E. If you are going to the islands, you will probably come here to catch your boat. If you have time before departure, you can stop at one of the museums or stroll along the smaller harbors, but the congested town is not worth a special visit. To get to Piraeus most efficiently, take the subway from Monastiraki or Omonia to the last stop, or take green bus #40 from Filellinon St., get off at the Public Theater (*Demotikon Theatron*), and head right, toward the port. Long-distance trains for Patras and the Peloponnese leave daily from the station on Akti Kalimassiati. Once in Piraeus, ask one of the travel agents where your boat will dock.

**Ferries** ply the waters from Piraeus to all the Greek islands except the Sporades and Ionian groups. Most of the ticketing agencies line **Akti Miaouli,** where the larger ferries dock; international ferries wait at the end toward the Customs House. Smaller ferries depart for the Saronic Gulf Islands from **Akti Posidonos,** around the corner, and the hydrofoils for the Saronics leave from **Provlis Tzelepi,** around the corner past the small ferries. Other boats also dock in the ports farther along in this direction. There is a small map of Piraeus on the back of the map of Athens available at the tourist office. The **post office** is located on the corner of Tsamadou and Filonos St., 2 blocks inland from the principal waterfront street, **Akti Miaoulis.** (Open Mon.-Fri. 7:30am-8pm.) The **OTE** is 1 block away at 19 Karaoli St. (Open 24 hours; collect calls 7am-9pm.) A **bank** is situated just off the harbor on Ethnikis Antistaseos St. (Open Mon.-Thurs. 8am-2pm, Fri. 8am-1:30pm.) There are other banks on the waterfront area where you can change money. Piraeus' **postal code** is 18501; the **telephone code** is 01.

Although an ocean breeze makes Piraeus cooler than Athens, you probably won't want to stay here. There are no really cheap accommodations, and there are horror stories about people who have slept in the municipal park. If you arrive late at night or have to leave early in the morning and need a place to stay, try the **Serifos Hotel,** 5 H. Tricoupi St. (tel. 452 50 75), 1 block up from the far left side of the harbor (as you face the water). The interior is grim, but the rooms are reasonably clean. (Singles 1600dr. Doubles 2400dr. Triples 2900dr. Bath included. Breakfast 300dr.) The rooms at **Hotel Galaxy,** 18 Sahtouri St. (tel. 451 05 79), up the block to the left of the Serifos, on the street leading inland from the pink customs house, are dark and a bit dirty, but cheap. (Singles 1000dr. Doubles 1500dr, with bath 1700dr. Triples 1700dr, with bath 2100dr.) **Hotel Enos,** 14 Antistaseos St. (tel. 417 48 79), closest to the harbor, is in an old building with high ceilings. The rooms facing the street are considerably more spacious than those on the other side, though none are very clean. (Singles 1000dr. Doubles 1400dr. Triples 2000dr. Showers 100dr.) Inexpensive fast-food restaurants plaster the dock area, all offering mediocre fare at uniform prices.

The prize possession of the **archeological museum,** 31 Char. Trikoupi St., is ancient "Piraeus Kouros," a large hollow bronze statue with outstretched entreating arms (on the 2nd floor). To its left is another room of similar bronze statues, including representations of Artemis and Athena. All these bronze masterpieces were found in 1959 during the digging of a drain. (Open Mon. and Wed.-Sat. 8:45am-3pm, Sun. 9:30am-2:30pm. Admission 200dr, students 100dr. 300dr for photographers.) Farther south, on Akti Themistokleous, is the **Maritime Museum,** which houses ship models tracing the history of the Greek navy. (Open Tues.-Sat. 9am-12:30pm. Admission 50dr.)

If the museums are closed, walk east from the archeological museum or northeast from the Maritime Museum to either **Zea Marina** (also called Pashalimani) or the **Mikrolimani** (also known as Tourkolimano). Both are welcome refuges from the busy ferry traffic of the main port. Ringed with elegant yachts, these harbors are a great place for a stroll or a fine fish dinner (but be warned—the restaurants here are no bargain).

There is a shady park on II Merarchias St., 3 blocks from Akti Miaouli. In summer, there are plays in the open-air theater of Kastella; in winter, the Public Theater is open. Drop by Piraeus town hall (tel. 412 64 11 or 412 54 98) for more information.

## Cape Sounion and the Apollo Coast

The **Temple of Poseidon** (tel. 0292 39 63) at Cape Sounion sits on a promontory high above the coast and offers a glorious glimpse of the Aegean. The first temple to Poseidon was constructed around 600 B.C.E., destroyed by the Persians in 480 B.C.E., and rebuilt by Pericles in 440 B.C.E. a few years after construction of the Parthenon began. The 12 remaining Doric columns attest to the graceful symmetry of the original temple. On the lower hill stands the **Temple of Athena Sounias.**

The ideal time to view the temples is at sunrise. Try at least to visit in the morning, before the tour buses arrive, or around sunset when they've left. The cafeteria near the temple is shamelessly overpriced, so pack a lunch. (Site open Mon.-Sat. 9am-sunset, Sun. 10am-sunset. Admission 300dr, students 150dr. Last bus to Athens departs at 8pm.)

To swim, head for the magnificent waters at the base of the site. Several paths lead down to the ocean from the inland side of the temple; the agile can negotiate the cliff on the ocean side. Several sandy beaches are situated at the base of the hill, but the rocks below the temple are more interesting, less crowded, and free of charge. In general, the beaches along the 70-kilometer Apollo Coast between Athens and Cape Sounion take on a carnival atmosphere, especially on summer weekends. Most strands are owned by hotels (admission 50dr), but towns usually have public beaches as well. There are two **campsites** on the Apollo Coast, both of which are large, crowded, well-maintained, and on the ocean. The site at **Voula** (tel. 895 27 12) charges 480dr per person plus 380dr per tent, and is accessible via bus #122 from the Zappeion Station. Get off at the "Pickpa" stop. **Camping Varkiza** (tel. 897 36 13) charges 435dr per person plus 290dr per tent. (Take bus #115, 116, or 117 from Zappeion.) In Cape Sounion, try **Sounion Beach and Camping** (tel. 393 58), about 5km beyond the Temple of Poseidon, or nearby **Camp Bacchus** (tel. 392 62).

Two **buses** travel the 70-kilometer road to Cape Sounion. One goes along the coast and stops at all points on the Apollo Coast, leaving every hour on the half hour from 6:30am to 6:30pm from the Mavromateon St. stop in the square opposite Areos Park in Athens; this bus can also be picked up on Filellinon St., at Xenofondos St., 20 minutes before the hour, but your chances of getting a seat are better if you catch it at Mavromateon (1¾ hr., 370dr). The other bus follows an inland route, and leaves from Areos Park every hour on the hour, from 6am to 6pm (2 hr., 340dr).

## Kesariani

In its various incarnations as a religious shrine, the site of **Monastery of Kesariani** (tel. 723 66 19), 20 minutes from central Athens on Mt. Hymettus, hasn't lost a grain of beauty. In the first century B.C.E. Ovid described "the purple heights of flowery Hymettus, a sacred spring enclosed by soft green turf . . . ." Originally, a Temple of Zeus stood on the mountain, but in 500 B.C.E., a priestess named Saisara built a temple to Aphrodite.

The present monastery was built in the eleventh century and incorporated the floors and four Ionic columns of the earlier Classical temple. The frescoes, added in the seventeenth century, include the Pantocrator staring down from the dome, the Virgin between Archangels in the apse, and the Apostles on the north wall. Underneath the chapel is a huge hollow where "mysteries" were revealed in the Classical period; it was later used both as a place to hide from pirates and as catacombs for monks. Also at the monastery is a library where valuable manuscripts were stored when they were suppressed by Emperor Justinian in 529 C.E.; unfortunately, they were burned by Greek soldiers during the Greek War of Independence. Next to the library you can see the oil and grain presses; this building originally housed the Roman baths, and later was converted into a baptistery before becoming a mill.

The water pouring out of a ram's head on the side of the monastery comes from a spring that once supplied Athens' water. (Open Mon.-Sat. 8:45am-3pm, Sun. 9am-2pm. Free.)

From Kesariani, Athens will seem oh so far away. It is a perfect spot for a picnic, and the mountain behind the monastery has many hiking trails which reward you with stop-in-your-tracks glimpses of the city. The grounds are crowded with Athenians on weekends, so try to visit on a weekday. Bus #224 goes from the university on Akadimias St. (the farthest *stassis* up on the outside lane) to Kesariani; take it to the last stop (20 min., 30dr). Follow the left hand road uphill, bearing right at the fork after the bridge (2½km from the bus stop, 1km from the bridge; 25-min. walk or try your luck hitching a ride).

## Daphni

Ten kilometers west of Athens along the Ancient Sacred Way, lies the splendid eleventh-century **Monastery of Daphni,** (tel. 581 15 58), built on the site of the ancient Temple of the Daphnios Apollo. Art historians extol the elegance of the mosaic inside depicting the scowling bust of the **Pantocrator** (Christ Almighty). Damaged in a 1982 earthquake, the monastery is still in part under repair. (Open Mon.-Fri. 8:45am-3pm, Sun. 9:30am-2:30pm. Admission 200dr, students 100dr.)

A **wine festival** takes place on the grounds next to the monastery between mid-July and the end of August. (Open daily 7:45pm-12:30am.) Admission to the all-you-can-drink bacchanalian bash is 250dr, students 150dr. Wines come from all parts of Greece. Food is extra and not very good, so bring a picnic dinner to absorb the wine. (Call 322 79 44 for more information.) **Camping Daphni** (tel. 581 15 63) is half-way down the road to the monastery (380dr per person, 300dr per tent).

To get to Daphni, take one of the Elefsina buses (#880, 853, or 862) or bus #854 or 867 from Platia Eleftherias at the end of Evripidou St. (6am-noon, every 15 min., 25 min., 30dr). From Piraeus port, take #804, 805, or 845 (6am-11:30pm, every 15 min., 35 min., 30dr). From the bus stop, cross the highway and go down the road to the right for the monastery.

## Elefsina (Eleusis)

After a visit to Daphni, continue down the Sacred Way to the ruins of Eleusis, the site of the Eleusinian Mysteries. Unfortunately, the sparse remains of the ancient sanctuary are encircled by a sprawling industrial area. Here Demeter, goddess of the harvest, came to mourn the abduction of her daughter Persephone, by Hades, god of the underworld. During Demeter's long search for her daughter, the earth lay barren. Demeter disguised herself as an old wet nurse and went to Eleusis to suckle the son of King Celeus: To immortalize the baby, she refused him food and held him over the fire, wrapping him in flames. Eventually, Demeter revealed herself to the Eleusinians, who built her a temple. In the meantime, in order to persuade Demeter to let the earth produce again, Zeus struck a bargain with Hades that would allow Persephone to return to earth. But Hades fed pomegranate seeds to the girl, committing her to spend part of every year underground. The rest of the year Persephone could return to her mother. When Persephone rejoined her mother, the whole earth teemed with blossoms, and Demeter was so overjoyed that she shared the mysteries of the underworld with the Eleusinians. The story of Persephone is still preserved in modern Greek burial rites: Pomegranate seeds are placed in the hands of the dead to ensure a safe passage through the underworld and to aid in the resurrection of the soul.

Historians believe the mysteries and the worship of Demeter were brought to Eleusis from the East or Egypt in 1350 B.C.E. The sanctuary was closed by the Roman Emperor Theodosius (part of his crusade against paganism) in the fourth century C.E., but until that time, thousands of people gathered annually for the nine-day festival that began on the fourteenth of September. Despite many hypotheses, the chief rites are unknown. The participants marched along the **Sacred Way** from Eleusis to the Acropolis in Athens and back, making a stop on the return at the sanctuary of Daphnios Apollo in Daphni. Pigs and bulls were sacrificed along the way, and on the final day the mysteries of death were revealed in the **Telestrion,** a huge windowless mystery hall at Eleusis. Pausanias related this climactic event:"The temple shook; terrifying and fearful spectres depicted the horror of Hades and the fate awaiting the evil man." The ceremony ended with lights, cleansings, visions of the gods, perhaps the re-enactment of the wedding of Zeus and Demeter in the Telestrion, and a feast recalling the dead. Sworn to secrecy, *mystai* left believing that they no longer need fear death.

The site consists of a patchwork of ruins from the Mycenean to the Roman period. The **museum** (tel. 554 60 19) displays finds from Eleusis and a model of the original layout of the sanctuary. (Open Mon. and Wed.-Sat. 8:45am-3pm, Sun. 9:30am-2:30pm. Admission 200dr, students 100dr.)

**Buses** #880, 853, and 862 run frequently from Platia Eleftherias at the end of Evripidou St.; get off at the second stop in Elefsina and through the square and bear left.

## Marathon

In 490 B.C.E, when the Athenians defeated the Persians at the bloody battle of Marathon, the messenger Pheidippides ran 42km (26 miles) to Athens to announce the victory and then collapsed dead from exhaustion. Today this act (hopefully without the death part) is commemorated world-over in international marathons, and the original route is traced twice annually in April and September.

Five kilometers from the town of Marathon is the **archeological museum** (tel. 661 26), with pieces from the Neolithic, Helladic, Geometric, and Classical periods. Only a few pieces are labeled, however, and no guidebook is available. Many of the artifacts were discovered in the legendary Cave of Pan. Legend has it that prior to the Battle of Marathon, the Athenians sent a courier to solicit Spartan aid in their struggle against the Persians, but the Spartans refused because of a full moon, which they considered a bad omen. In the mountains of the Peloponnese, the courier encountered the god Pan, who promised to cause the Persians to "panic," thus facilitating the Hellenic victory. After the battle, the Athenians gathered in a cave to worship Pan. Archeological evidence suggests that the cave was used even prior to the Battle of Marathon; excavations have uncovered artifacts dating from 5000-440 B.C.E. (Museum open Mon. and Wed.-Sat. 8:45am-3pm, Sun. 9:30am-2:30pm. Free.)

Across from the museum is the **Tomb of the Plataneans,** the ancient burial mound built as a tribute to the allies from the town of Platanea, 6km from Thebes. The Athenians who were killed in the battle were cremated; their ashes are in the **Marathon Tomb,** a larger burial mound 4km away on the road to Athens. Only the most avid historians will want to make the 45-minute walk. (Tombs open July-Aug., Mon. and Wed.-Sat. 8:45am-3pm, Sun. 9:30am-2:30pm.)

Eight kilometers past the town is beautiful **Lake Marathon,** with its huge marble dam. Until World War II, this was Athens' sole source of water. Fifteen kilometers to the northeast at **Ramnous** are the ruins of the Temples of Nemesis, goddess of retribution, and Themis, goddess of custom, law, and justice. A theater is located 300m from the water. (Site open Mon.-Sat. 9am-3pm, Sun. 9:30am-2:30pm.) Thirty kilometers to the northwest, the site of **Amphiareion,** the sanctuary built to the healing god Amphiaraus, lies peacefully in the lush foliage of Attica, well-removed from the tourist circuit.

On the coast near Marathon, **Schinias** to the north and **Timvos Marathonas** to the south are popular beaches. Schinias is long and sandy with heavy pine cover. On the weekend, both beaches are too congested for comfort, but they're relatively deserted midweek. The center of windsurfing in Athens is the Galatzi Hotel, near the odd yellow-and-black-checkered pillbox at the bridge to Schinias. Many camp at Schinias since the trees offer good protection; the mosquitoes, however, are thick and fast. You will probably be more comfortable staying at **Marathon Camping** (tel.

550 07), located along the bus route to Marathon. From the campsite you can get a bus or walk to the beach, which is jammed with outdoor cafes.

The bus for Marathon leaves from Mavromateon Street by Areos Park in Athens (every hr. on the hr., 1 hr., 220dr). Ask the driver to let you off at the turn-off for the museum (*Mouseion and Marathonas*), and watch for the sign 3km before the town. Go left at the fork. The walk to the museum is 2km and takes about 20 minutes. To get to the Marathon Tomb or the nearby beach, walk or hitch 1½km back toward Athens. Lake Marathon, Amphiareion and Ramnous are accessible only by automobile, so try hitching.

## Rafina

The port of Rafina is located south of Marathon along the coast and is accessible by frequent buses from Mavromateon St. in Athens (6am-12:15am every 45 min., 1 hr., 140dr). Much cleaner, smaller, and more pleasant than Piraeus, Rafina is Attica's second most important **ferry port.** Boats go to Karystos (1 or 2 per day, 653dr) and Marmari (3 per day, 437dr), both in Evia, as well as to: Andros (3-4 per day, 757dr); Tinos (2-3 per day, 1151dr), and Mykonos (2 per day, 1330dr). There are also frequent runs to Syros (1 or 2 per day, 1088dr). It's generally more convenient to sail to Syros from Piraeus, but fares to Andros, Tinos, and Mykonos are 200-300dr cheaper from Rafina, and the voyage sometimes lasts only half as long. The **port police** (tel. 223 00), in a small booth near the dock, have up-to-date information on all sailings. The *Eptanissos* and the *Bari Express* travel the Andros-Tinos-Mykonos route. You can purchase tickets on the dock to the right and left of the ramp leading up to the square. To purchase tickets to Karystos and Marmari, go to the Goutos Lines' office to the right of the ramp, with your back to the water.

The **post office** is on Eleftheriou Venizelou St. At the fork where the ramp goes down to dock, walk up 3 blocks and turn left. (Open Mon.-Fri. 7:30am-1:30pm.) The **OTE**, Alexander Fleming St., is located across the street from the main square, on the left as you face the water. (Open Mon.-Fri. 7:30am-3:10pm.) **Emborikes Bank** is on the right side of the square (facing the water). (Open Mon.-Thu. 8am-2pm, Fri. 8am-1:30pm.) Rafina's **postal code** is 19009; the **telephone code** is 0294.

Cheap food and accommodations are hard to find in Rafina. If you must spend the night to catch an early ferry, try **Hotel Corali** in the square. (Singles 1650dr. Doubles 2500dr. Triples 3560dr.) There is **camping** on the beach of **Kokkino Limanaki** (tel. 26 60 25). The restaurants along the water serve fresh fish, but are expensive. As always, look where the locals are eating. Or take a left off the square up past the Corali to find a couple of less-touristed tavernas.

## Vravrona (Brauron)

South of Rafina on the same coast and 40km from Athens, Vravrona is the isolated setting for the 2000-year-old **Sanctuary of Artemis.** The cult of Artemis at Brauron was chiefly for women, and young girls performed an annual bear-dance. Although poorly maintained, the site contains the recently uncovered **Temple of Artemis** and the adjacent **Chapel of Agia Giorgiou,** whose interior is decorated with decaying frescoes from the late fifteenth century. (Open Mon. and Wed.-Sat. 9am-3pm, Sun. 9:30am-2:30pm. Admission 200dr, students 100dr.) Take bus #304 from Thission subway station in Athens to the last stop (1 hr., 30dr). Walk along the road 4km and turn left on the first paved road.

Follow the road around to the other side of the hill to reach the excellent **Brauron Museum,** which contains pottery, sculpted heads, and figures discovered at the Brauron site. Vases and funerary reliefs unearthed at nearby **Meranda,** dating from the Geometric, Archaic, and Classical periods, are displayed in Room #4; Room #5 behind the courtyard is filled with Geometric period pottery found at Anavyssos and Mesogea. (Open same hours as site.)

# PELOPONNESE
# Πελοπόννησος

The Peloponnese is quintessential Greece—the union of *vouna* (mountains) and *thalassa* (sea) with seemingly limitless olive groves in between. Separated from mainland Greece by the steep-walled Corinth Canal, this peninsula contains remnants of 3500 years of history. The perfect theater at Epidavros, the haunting palace at Mycenae, the gargantuan stone blocks at Olympia, and the ruined Byzantine town of Mystra hold a kind of ghostly communion with one another—these are the achievements of the once undisputed leaders of the ancient world. Only the large cities of the Peloponnese—Corinth, Patras, Sparta and Kalamata—have reneged on tradition in their hurry to join the contemporary world.

Above all, the Peloponnese is for non-conformists who venture beyond the familiar towns and sites. You will find it somewhere more humble than the Lion's Gate of Mycenae or the caves of Pirgos Dirou—maybe at dawn in a deserted mountain village or atop a hill overlooking the sea with an obscure pile of rubble—the remains of a once prosperous ancient city—at your feet.

Today's tourist will be astonished and overjoyed at the proximity of the Peloponnese's attractions: formidable ruins, ebullient ports, sequestered beaches, and serene mountain villages all lie a few hours apart and a short bus trip away. The easiest way to manage the Peloponnese is by car, but buses travel to almost every backwater, one-donkey town, threading along primitive roads. But to explore areas like the Mani, southern Messenia, or the mountain villages of the central Peloponnese, you need time and patience—buses usually run only once or twice per day, and thus require an extra day for each stop you want to make (unless you take a local taxi). Hitching is quite good in summer, but traffic diminishes dramatically in off-season. At the other extreme, the most prominent sites are connected by frequent bus service and become unbearably crowded by midday. In summer, southern beach resorts and ports are becoming as popular and crowded as islands coasts. Beach spots are favorites with Greek tourists who unfailingly book ahead, but accommodations in the villages and larger cities are more plentiful and cheaper.

Before you embark for your adventure, remember to arm yourself with a good map of the entire Peloponnese. The Austrian map (with the red-and-green cover), published by Freytag and Berndt, is superb and available in Athens and the large towns of the Peloponnese.

There are a number of places from which to enter and leave the Peloponnese. The heavily used ferry connection from Brindisi, Italy, lands at Patras in the northwest corner of the Peloponnese, and boats for Crete and Piraeus leave from Gythion and Monemvassia in the south, stopping at the island of Kythera. From Athens, you can enter through Corinth by bus, or through port towns on the Argolid by ferry.

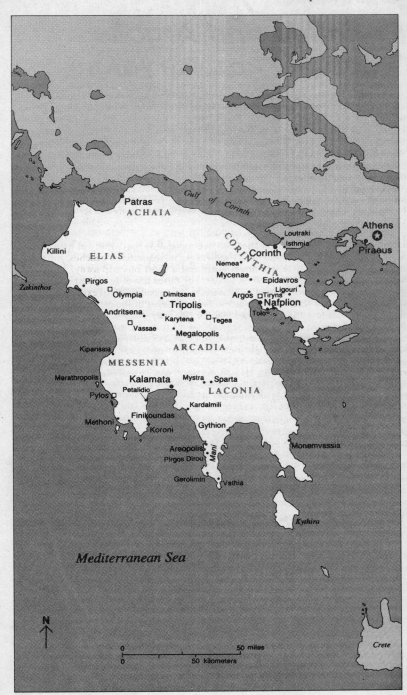

# *Corinthia and Argolis*
# Κορίνθά και Αργολλα

Chronicled in the pages of ancient writers, Argos—a grotesque beast covered with unblinking eyes—once haunted vast stretches of the northern Peloponnese, subduing unruly satyrs and rampaging bulls. Today, the quiet, dusty Argolid would hardly suggest comparisons with a tumultuous past if it weren't for the ruins of its massive fortresses, temples, and theaters. The concentration of archeological sites makes a visit to the Argolid a must for any budding classicist, archeologist, or Philhellene. More importantly, the preponderance of ruins forces you to appreciate the network of ancient civilizations. Try to visit the ruins at Mycenae, Corinth, Tiryns, and Epidavros early, before the swarms of tourists arrive. The Argolid's proximity to Athens makes it a suitable three- or four-day excursion. It may be best to base yourself in the beautiful old town of Nafplion and make daytrips to the ruins from there.

In antiquity, Corinthia was officially united with its southern neighbor, Argolis. However, during the Peloponnesian War (431-404 B.C.E.), Corinthia's major city, Corinth, allied with Sparta against Argolis and Athens. Corinth controlled the isthmus, the only land connection between the Peloponnese and the rest of mainland Greece, and became a wealthy commercial center—so wealthy, in fact, that St. Paul journeyed here to halt the inhabitants' moral slide, which their prosperity had encouraged. Judging from the ruins of Ancient Corinth and the earthquakes that have demolished New Corinth in the past century, perhaps the Corinthians should have heeded the Apostle's words.

Any one of three different bus routes can take you through stunning terrain to Argolis and Corinthia. From Athens, when the last stretch of industrial outlets and gas stations ends, the road gives way to a bright blue sea on the left and precipitous cliffs on the right. From Porto Heli or Kosta, if you're coming from the Saronic Gulf Islands, the bus heads straight inland, following deserted and dusty asphalt roads that snake through the dry mountains and groves of olive trees—with no sea in sight. Finally, if you ride into the region from Arcadia (the central Peloponnese), you'll cross the rust and glaucous-green mountains that separate the upland Arcadian plain from the Argive.

Today the larger towns of these two regions are serious realms of business. The bustle is often so great that when the midday siesta arrives, the towns seem haunting with the contrasting quiet. Lined with tobacco and citrus plants, the countryside also seems hard at work. You won't find the best beaches here, and the nightlife is only mediocre, but the archeological finds more than compensate.

## *New Corinth (Korinthos)* Κορίνθας

New Corinth sits squat and square, facing the **Gulf of Corinth** just west of the Corinth Canal. After two devastating earthquakes in 1858 and 1928, the city permits only the most shatterproof structures, making for perfectly drab architecture. Except for the seafront and the tree-lined park in the center of town, Corinth offers little besides lots of mosquitoes and a mildly distracting nightlife.

## Orientation and Practical Information

Buses leave Athens for New Corinth from the station at 100 Kifissou St. (6am-9:30pm every ½hr., 1½ hr., 460dr). You can also take the train to Corinth from Athens (12 per day, 2 hr. 320dr).

You'll find everything you need near the park. **Ethnikis Anistasis Street,** the main tree-lined boulevard, borders the park on one of its long sides and runs down to the sea. Parallel **Ermou Street** bounds the park on the other side. The station for buses to Athens and the vicinity lies at the corner of Ermou and Koliatsou right on the park. The other bus station, serving the rest of the Peloponnese, is one block past the park at Aratou and Ethnikis Anistasis St. If you arrive by train, walk half a block up Demokratias St., turn right on Dimaskinou St. for 500m, then turn left on Ermou St. several blocks later.

**Currency Exchange: Commercial Bank,** 32 Ethnikis Anistasis St., off the corner of the park closest to the water. Many other banks are scattered around this area. Open Mon.-Thurs. 8am-2pm, Fri. 8am-1:30pm.

**Post Office:** On Andimandou St., which borders the park on the end farthest from the water. Open Mon.-Fri. 7:30am-3pm. Poste Restante. **Postal code:** 20100.

**OTE:** Kolokotroni St. Walk west on Andimandou St. past Ethnikis Anistasis and turn right on Kolokotroni St., or walk straight through the park onto Koliatsou St. and turn left at Kolokotroni St. International calls from here are difficult; wait until you reach Nafplion or Athens to phone home. Open 6am-midnight; 7am-11pm for collect calls. **Telephone code:** 0741.

**Train Station:** Demokratias St. (tel. 225 22). From the park, take Ermou St. until you reach the water, turn right on Dimaskinou St. and walk toward the train tracks, then turn left on Demokratias. To Athens via Isthmia (12 per day, 2 hr., 320dr). Two major train lines serve the Peloponnese, 1 along the northern coast from Corinth to Pirgos, the other south from Corinth to Tripolis. Almost all major coastal cities in the Peloponnese can be reached by train from Corinth. Trains to: Xilokastro (7 per day, 30 min., 120dr); Patras (7 per day, 2 hr., 460dr); Pirgos (6 per day, 4 hr., 650dr); Olympia (3 per day, 4½ hr., 680dr); Argos (5 per day, 1 hr., 185dr); Tripolis (5 per day, 3 hr., 410dr); Kalamata (5 per day, 5 hr., 730dr); and Megalopolis (4 per day, 4 hr., 560dr). **Luggage storage** costs 60dr per day per piece.

**Bus Station: Ermou and Koliatsou Station:** Tel. 256 45 or 244 81. Buses run until 10:10pm. Buses to Ancient Corinth (6:15am, 7:15am, and 8am-9pm every hr., 20 min., 60dr), Athens (every ½ hr., except in late afternoon and early evening when service is more erratic; 5:30am-9:30pm; 1½ hr., 460dr), Loutraki (5am, and 6am-7:30pm every ½ hr. followed by less frequent service until 10:10pm, 20 min., 80dr), Isthmia (5 per day, 20 min., 60dr), and Nemea (7 per day, 1 hr., 230dr). **Ethnikis Anistasis and Aratou Station:** Tel. 244 03. The same bus travels to Mycenae (45 min., 220dr), Argos (1 hr., 270dr), and Nafplion (1¼ hr., 340dr); the bus leaves at 7:15am and every hr. from 8:45am-9:45pm. Buses also travel to Sparta (8 per day, 3 hr., 880dr), continuing to various southern locations from there such as Gythion (4 per day, 4 hr., 1110dr). Buses also service Kalamata (7 per day, 4 hr., 1060dr) with some connecting to Koroni (6hr., 1320dr). There is one connection daily on the Sparta-line with Monemvassia (5 hr., 1440dr) and on the Kalamata-line with Pylos (6 hr., 1320dr). Buses also travel to Tripolis (9 per day, 2 hr., 580dr). Note that the bus to Mycenae leaves you at Fichtia, a 1½-km walk from the site (see Mycenae below).

**Taxi Stand:** Tel. 223 61 or 248 44 or 269 00, along the park side of Ethnikis Anistasis St. To Old Corinth 400dr.

**Car Rental: Grig Lagos** (tel. 226 17), across the street from the moped rental place at 42 Ethnikis Anistasis St. (3400dr with 16% tax and 100km, 20dr each additional km. Open 8am-1pm and 5-9pm.

**Moped Rental:** 27 Ethnikis St. (tel. 281 76), past the park heading inland. Mopeds 1500dr. Vespas 2000dr. Open 8am-2pm and 6-9pm.

**Laundromat:** 77 Koliatsou St. (tel. 222 47). Walk through the park and head towards the water. Large wash 1000-1500dr.

**Public Toilets:** Across from the park on Ethnikis Anistasis St. The man who sells toilet paper is an expert on demand-side economics.

**Pharmacy:** 27 Ethnikis Anistasis St. (tel. 242 13). Open Mon. and Wed. 8am-2pm, Tues. and Thurs.-Fri. 8am-2pm and 5-9pm. Many others on Koliatsou St.

**Hospital:** Athainon St (tel. 257 11).

**Police:** Ermou St. (tel. 221 43). Face the park, walk 20m to the left of the bus station, turn left into an alley (you'll see a guard), and go up a flight of stairs. Also an office of the **tourist police** (tel. 232 82), but it's more self-serving to the police bureaucracy than to visitors. But in a pinch, they'll help you out. (Open 8am-2pm.)

## Accommodations and Camping

Most hotels in Corinth are clustered near the waterfront and the railroad station. You will not find stunning accommodations here, but, nonetheless, you may want to spend the night here for proximity to the ancient sites.

**Hotel Belle-vue,** Dimaskinou St. (tel. 220 88), along the waterfront. Take Ethnikis Anistasis St. to the waterfront and turn right on Ermou St. to the water and turn left. Your best bet in Corinth. Rooms with balcony overlooking the water, somewhat clean, well-lit, with high ceilings. Singles 1000dr. Doubles 2000dr. Come early.

**Hotel Acti,** 3 Ethnikis Anistasis St. (tel. 233 37). Around the corner from Belle-vue and similar (if darker) rooms. Mosquitoes at night. Singles 1100dr. Doubles 1660dr. Triples 2660dr.

**Hotel Byron,** 8 Demokratis St. (tel. 226 31), opposite the train station to the right. Clean rooms with sinks and balconies. Clean hall toilet. Run by a very enthusiastic elderly couple. Singles 1000dr. Doubles 1300dr. Showers 100dr.

**Hotel Ephira,** 52 Ethnikis Anistasis St. (tel. 240 21 or 240 22 or 224 34), 1 block from the Ethnikis Anistasis and Aratou bus station, heading inland. Quite ritzy with a small outside garden, and lobby with bar. Will change money. Clean, modern, refreshingly cool rooms with private bath. Singles 2600dr. Doubles 3200dr. Triples 3840dr. Breakfast in 2nd-floor dining room 300dr.

**Hotel Appollon,** 18 Peirinis St. (tel. 225 87), diagonally across from the train station on the corner of Dimaskinou St. Stale-smelling hallways, but clean rooms with wood paneling, and a video game in the lobby. All rooms with private bath. Singles 1500dr. Doubles 2500dr.

**Camping: Corinth Beach Campground** (tel. 279 67 or 279 68), 3km west of town, near a nice beach. Take the bus to Ancient Corinth; you'll see the campsite out of the left-side windows—ask the driver to let you off. 300dr per person. 150 per tent. The **Blue Dolphin Campground** (tel. 257 667) is 3km from Ancient Corinth. Take the bus going to Lecheon and ask the driver to let you off at the campground.

## Food

If you like pizza and *souvlaki,* you will be overjoyed by the fast-food establishments that crowd the waterfront and lower Ethnikis Anistasis St. More discriminating palates will have to search around for a wholesome meal. The best is **Taverna O Thodorakis** (sign in Greek), on G. Seferis St., at the extreme right side of the waterfront (facing the water). Savor the inexpensive, but delicious seafood in a setting that will let you forget you're stuck in Corinth. (*Calamaria* 320dr. *Gopas,* a serving of 4 small fish, 380dr. Open 12:30-5pm and 8:30pm-2am.) Another option is **Taverna Anaxagoras,** under a bamboo canopy, at the opposite end of the waterfront. (Grilled meats 400-500dr. Crunchy *kalamari* 320dr. Open 12:30-3pm and 8pm-midnight.) For coffee with some atmosphere, go to the **Omonia,** 19 Ethnikis Anistasis St., where middle-aged men huddle soberly around card games and backgammon. Next door, you can get a great haircut in a typical, old-fashioned barber shop. The hopping bar in town is **Mordillo,** with small palm trees and black lights. Or else, chill out in the garden at the **Anaximander Pub,** under a natural canopy of oleanders, pines and olive trees. (Chocolate parfait 300dr. Drinks 400-600dr.)

## Sights

If you spend the day in town and not at the ruins, you may want to schlepp out to the **Folklore Museum,** which is housed in a modern white building at the right side of the waterfront (facing the water). (Open daily 8am-2pm. Free.) You might also take a dip at one of the town **beaches** to the west. The beaches are rocky, seaweed-strewn, and crowded, but then again, nothing's perfect. Chances are you have come here with the sole purpose of inspecting the fascinating remains at ancient Corinth, just 7km away. You can also use the town as a base for daytrips to the nearby ruins at Isthmia and Nemea.

# *Ancient Corinth*

Ancient Corinth's strategic position on the isthmus between the Gulf of Corinth and the Saronic Gulf made it the jewel of the ancient world—whoever controlled the slim isthmus controlled communication and commerce between northern Greece and the Peloponnese. While Corinth's harbors thrived, its hills rumbled with the breast-beating of many conquerors. When Alexander the Great had the Peloponnese firmly under Macedonian rule, the Greeks met in Corinth to approve the new Hellenic League, which presided over 300,000 free men and 450,000 slaves. In 146 B.C.E., when Roman Mummius stormed the city, Corinthians resisted by throwing filth from windows and discharging epithets at Roman ambassadors.

While the mortals were slugging it out below, the gods contested above for control of Corinth. Apollo and Poseidon, in the finest tradition of divine compromise, split the city between them. Poseidon took the Isthmus, and Apollo the Acrocorinth. Later, Oedipus grew up in Corinth with his adopted parents. Neither had the forsight to tell the little tyke of his true parentage, so when he heard the bad news that he was fated to sleep with his mother and kill his father, he fled from Corinth. Unfortunately, he headed for Thebes and landed smack dab at the home of his real parents, Queen Jocasta and (the presciently named) King Laius. The rest is history.

Refounded as a Roman colony in 44 B.C.E. by Julius Caesar, Corinth became renowned for its wild ways. Fat with the riches of trade, the Corinthians had both impulse and time for indulgence. They worshiped Aphrodite with fervor and attracted the stern disapproval of the Apostle Paul, who preached at Corinth with the hopes of reforming its decadent inhabitants. Ah, to no avail.

The remains of the ancient city now stand on a plateau near the base of the towering Acrocorinth. Excavations of the city, which are still underway, have uncovered the ruins of the Roman settlement. For supplemental reading, pick up a copy of the particularly good guidebook by Nikos Papahatzis (600dr). When you enter the site, go straight to the **museum,** which is filled with sarcophagi, sculptures, friezes of dancing maenads and heroes, pottery, and a few Roman mosaic floors. The charming courtyard is ringed with toga-toting headless statues. You'll also find here friezes from the theater depicting Amazons and the Herculean labors. Just off this courtyard, the **Asclepion Room** houses votive offerings (usually a cast of the affected body part) from the sick to the god of medicine. Ask the guard to let you in. Exiting the museum, you'll see the ornate columns of **Temple E,** a Roman edifice of the first century. Following the path to the left and descending some stone stairs, you'll see before you the **forum** (the Roman version of the Greek agora) and the famous monolithic columns of the sixth century B.C.E. **Temple of Apollo.** In 1830, the temple's Turkish owner took down four of its eleven columns. It's best to climb up to the temple first so that you can survey the rest of the ruins below, descending and returning to the spacious forum that was once similar to a modern shopping mall. You'll pass the impressive arch of the **northwest stoa** as you cross over to the ruins of the **south stoa,** one of the largest buildings of its era. In the middle of the row of central shops contained by the south stoa, you'll see the **bema,** a raised platform from which the Romans made general announcements and official proclamations. At the far end of the forum, just before the **Julian Basilica,** you can make out a **race track** that had more than a dozen lanes. Turning left out of the forum, you'll pass through the **propylaea;** little of the ancient gateway remains but several trees form a shady, natural archway. Step ahead onto the stone-paved **Lechaion Road.** If you listen closely, you can hear the gushing of the well-preserved **Fountain of**

**Peirene,** the first structure on your right. Named after a woman who wept so profusely after Artemis killed her son that the pragmatic gods transformed her into a fountain. The complex was rebuilt generation after generation but the layers of external architectural embellishments have not altered the dark and muddy interior, a refreshing shelter from the ferocious midday sun; unfortunately, without a flashlight you won't see any water.

Also on the right, just past the fountain, the **Perivolos of Apollo** is an open-air court surrounded by columns, some of which now stand restored. Near the perivolos is the **public latrine.** Sit down on one of the proto-toilets and you'll be amazed how comfy it is, but drop a load and you'll see how primitive Greek flushing systems were. There is an exit from the site just at the end of Lechaion Rd. (Site and museum open Mon.-Sat. 8am-7pm and Sun. 8am-6pm. Admission to both 400dr, students 200dr.) The spectacular **Acrocorinth,** the huge mountain that was the crux of military control for the entire Peloponnese, watches imperiously over the ruins. Don't let its daunting height (575m) keep you from climbing to the fort at the summit. Built on the lower of the two peaks, the **fortress** has foundations dating to ancient times, although most of what you'll see—walls, towers, gates—was erected during successive captures by the Byzantines, Franks, Venetians, and Turks. The upper summit originally held a **temple to Aphrodite,** which, historians have noted, was served by 1000 "sacred courtesans" who initiated disciples into the "mysteries of love." Time has destroyed all of this and subsequent structures on the site, but has done nothing to alter the magnificent view. On a clear day you can see, if not forever, at least far enough to verify your mapmaker's rendition of the northeast Peloponnese and the Corinthian and Saronic Gulfs. Until about 20 years ago, before pollution hung so heavily, you could see all the way to the Acropolis of Athens.

The Acrocorinth is open 'round the clock. People have been known to carry up sleeping bags and spend the night (one ancient building on the grounds can provide semi-shelter). You'll be on your own at the site, except for the **Acrocorinthos Restaurant** located just before the fortress. Despite its tourist-trap location, it is surprisingly reasonably priced. (*Mousaka* 350dr. Greek salad 150dr. Open daily 9am-10pm.) The ascent toward the entrance to the fortress can be traversed by car along a paved road which deteriorates into a rocky path. There is no bus service, but you can hitch easily or take a **taxi** from town (the driver will wait 1 hr. for you at the end of the road). You'd best go by foot, preferably in the early morning or late afternoon to avoid the heat. It's an arduous 4-kilometer hike that takes at least an hour, but the panorama makes it worthwhile. Buses travel to Ancient Corinth from Modern Corinth on the hour, returning on the half-hour (60dr).

A small village flanks the ruins, and its main street runs right in front of the site. For a pension or rooms to let, ask a local cafe or shop owner for directions. To get to **Rooms Marinos** (tel 312 09 or 311 80), go right at the fork behind the bus stop (away from the entrance to the ruins). Walk along Sisyphos St. and turn right at the sign for Argos. This well-kept hotel, with its outside garden and ping-pong table, escapes the notice of the flocks of tourists. A gracious woman cooks a feast for breakfast (450dr) and dinner (1000dr). (Doubles 2500dr. Triples 3200dr. Bargain.)

# *Near Corinth*

## *Isthmia and Nemea*

Ancient Grecian jocks used to gather in Isthmia and Nemea to compete in their well-known athletic games. Pindar preserves the memory of these games in his odes honoring the victors. Take the bus from Corinth heading toward **Isthmia** and ask to be let out at the **museum,** a green building up the road from the bus stop and on the right. The well-labeled and diagrammed exhibits present finds from the Temple of Poseidon and sites of the Isthmean games, including *haltares* (hand weights) released by jumpers in mid-flight for greater distance, fish hooks, and mason's tools.

Of particular interest are the glass *opus sectile* (mosaic panels) discovered at nearby Kenchreai, still packed in the ancient containers,having withstood the earthquake of 375 C.E. An entrance to the ruins lies to the right of the museum. All that remains of the **Temple of Poseidon** is its ruined foundation; to the right is the base of an ingenious starting gate for races. The **theater** is below and farther to the right of the temple. To get to the sparse remnants, follow the path through the hay field where the emperor Nero once falsely proclaimed the freedom of the Greeks, in the tradition of other Romans before him. (Once enslaved, the Greeks were often easily manipulated by any proclamation of freedom, a fact of which the Romans took full advantage.) **Cult caves,** used in the Archaic Period for dining, lie above the theater.

The Corinth Canal started as Nero's pet project in 67 C.E. It was he, in fact, who first broke ground on the 6-kilometer waterway with a golden shovel. He intended for his Hebrew slaves to finish the job, but when he died, so did the project. The French resumed work in 1881. To get a good view of the Corinth Canal, walk down toward the mouth of the canal from the Isthmia museum to the Dioriga *taverna,* next to a one-car ferry; then walk up the road that roughly parallels the canal until you get to the bridge (2km). Over 6km long, the canal's dramatic razor-smooth sides, 30m apart, were cut into rock over 90m high. A train crossing the far bridge highlights the canal's striking verticality. A footpath follows the western side of the canal.

If ancient ingenuity intrigues you, you'll want to see parts of the *diolkos* (from the Greek verb "to drag") that still remain at the western mouth of the canal. Boats were hoisted onto the *diolkos* and rolled on logs across the narrowest point of the isthmus to the other side.

At **Nemea,** where Hercules slew the lion, ancient Greeks struggled against less fierce opponents in the Nemean Games as they fought for a crown of celery. (Priorities haven't changed much over the centuries.) While in these parts, try the local wine known as the "Blood of Hercules." The ruins include the fourth-century **Temple of Nemean Zeus,** now a mountain of rubble except for three free-standing Doric columns on a broad plain; the **stadium,** which has a starting line and an entrance tunnel with fans' graffiti; and also a *palaestra* and **baths.** A spiffy new **museum** contains reconstructions of the temple and the stadium, as well as jewelry, potsherds, and explanatory notes in English. All the ruins except the stadium are next to the museum. The stadium is 500m down the road toward Corinth. For a press-box view, turn right on the dirt path just before the wire fence that encircles the stadium. (Museum and site open Mon. and Wed.-Sat. 8:45am-3pm, Sun. 9:30am-2:30pm. Admission 200dr, students 100dr.) The ruins of Ancient Nemea are 4km away from Modern Menea, so if coming by bus from Corinth, ask to be let off at the site.

## Loutraki

Across the crescent shaped bay, a 20-minute bus ride from Corinth, Loutraki is where Corinthians come to boogie. Much of the bottled water you'll be clutching as you wander through the broiling landscape gushed from Loutraki's sweet wells. For some elusive reason, the town attracts many summer visitors. Its modern buildings and crowded beach would hardly spring to mind as an ideal Mediterranean vacation spot, however; if you are visiting Corinth, you may want to stop by and delve into this mystery for yourself. Take a stroll along the white stone boardwalk that flanks the busy pebble beach, shadowed as well by the **Yerania Mountains** that rise abruptly above the town.

To get to Loutraki from Isthmia, cross the canal bridge; the bus stop is next to a railroad station sign (55dr). Stay on the bus until the last stop at a triangular road island across from the Hotel Mizithra. Buses from Corinth run every half-hour. Buses from Loutraki (tel. 422 62) travel to Athens (8 per day, 440dr), Corinth (5:30am-10:30pm every ½ hr., 20 min., 80dr), Perachora (5:30am-8pm, 7am-3pm every hr., 20 min., 65dr), and Vouliagmeni (at 10am, return 1pm, 45 min., 125dr).

Walk down **El. Venizelou,** the main drag, with the water to your left. The **post office** is at 4, 28 Octovriou St., 1 block down to the right. (Open Mon.-Fri. 7:30am-

3pm.) The **OTE** is at 10 El. Venizelou. (Open Mon.-Fri. 7:30am-10pm, Sat.-Sun. 7:30am-3:10pm.) Across the street and left of the OTE are the police headquarters (on the 2nd floor; tel 424 44 or 422 58). The police do not speak English, but they are extremely friendly and helpful. The **bank** is on Yior Lekka St.; continue down El Venizelou and bear left. (Open Mon.-Thurs. 8am-2pm, Fri. 8am-1:30pm.) For moped rentals, make a right at the post office and turn the second corner on the left to reach **Andreas** (tel. 438 12; Vespas 2500dr. Mopeds 2000dr, 600dr per hr. Pipmobiles 3000dr.). For the **health center,** dial 444 44. At the end of the boardwalk is a refreshing shaded **park** with a small spring where you can drink the celebrated local water (bottle 50dr). At the far end of the park are clean **public toilets.** Windsurfers and sea bikes are available at the beach. Loutraki's **postal code** is 20300.

There are a few exceptions to the high cost of living in Loutraki. **Hotel Brettagne,** 28 Yior. Lekka St. (tel. 423 49), is a family-run, Old-World hotel. Follow El Venizelos St. (which changes to Lekka St.) toward the mountains and bear left. (Singles 1500dr. Doubles 2000dr. Triples 2700dr.) A cheaper if less elegant alternative is **Michael's Pension,** 3 Solomou (tel. 416 42); take a left off Venizelou St. (with the water on your right)—the sign outside just says "rooms to rent." Beds are firm and mosquitoes abuzzin'. You may share kitchen facilities with the proprietor and dark bathrooms with other guests. You can also pick peaches from the tree in the garden. (Singles 1000dr. Doubles 2000dr.) Lake Vouliagmene also has **Camping Heraion.** (400dr per person.)

Loutraki's food is regrettably reminiscent of Corinth; pizza and pasta are the standard fare. Even more alarming are the outrageous prices in the waterfront restaurants. Your jaw will drop when you see *mousaka* for 500dr. A sane option is the **Drosia,** 4 Alkidon St. (parallel to the water). (*Mousaka* 340dr. Stuffed tomatoes 250dr. Open 7am-3:30pm and 6pm-midnight.) The popular discos in town are the **Tropicana Disco** (tel. 439 60) and the **Claxon,** both on El. Venizelos St., although the Tropicana is a good deal farther from town. The more trendy Loutraki nightspots are 3-4km away from town, so it's best to take a taxi. Try **Aphroditi,** with its outside garden, or **Make-up.**

High on the mountain, the town of **Perachora** has a great view of the Gulf of Corinth and some ancient remains to boot. Ten buses per day run from Loutraki, but the best way to get to Perachora is by renting a moped. Take the main road out of town toward the mountains. After 6km it will fork: The left branch goes to Perachora, the right to the monastery of **Ossios Patapos.** With your moped, you may also want to go west of Perachora to **Lake Vouliagmene,** a tranquil cove perfect for camping. Buses connect Loutraki with Lake Vouliagmene only once in the morning at 10am, returning at 1am.

### Xilokastro

In the traditional scurrying between Athens and the ferry drop-off in Patras, tourists usually ignore the windswept north coast of the Peloponnese. Thus, Greeks alone enjoy this string of beach resorts lining the shore between Corinth and Patras.

The sparkling white boardwalk and expansive beach in **Xilokastro** provide excellent opportunities for leisurely strolling and swimming. Ivory against emerald delights and blinds the eyes: Don't forget your sunglasses if you want a glimpse of **Mt. Ziria** (2600m), the Peloponnese's second-highest peak. **Buses** (tel. 222 18) run to and from Athens (2 hr. 10 min., 550dr), and Corinth (45 min., 230dr). **Trains** serve Xilokastro from Athens, Corinth, Patras, and Kalamata. They are cheaper than buses but take longer and are far less reliable. The train station (tel. 222 97) is on Athomopolou St.

From the bus station, walk 1 block down Leoforis Tsaldari St. with the water on your left to the **post office;** another block will take you past a **bank** and a **drugstore,** and bring you to the main square bordered on the left by a huge church. If you arrive by train, walk 4 blocks toward the water from the train station down Vlasilov St. to the square. The beach and most of the hotels are east of the park, past the church. From the Central Square walk 1 block on Athomporto St. away from the water. On the right you'll see the **police station**. Ask here about the three-and-a-half-hour climb up Mt. Ziria. Xilokastro's **telephone code** is 0743.

To get to the palatial **Apollon Hotel** (tel. 225 71 or 222 39) on Ionnai St., take Leoforis Tsaldari St. 2 blocks past the square; from the five-street intersection, follow Frantzi St. away from the water for 1 block. The Apollon will be on your right. Big and breezy, it is far cheaper than most Xilokastro hotels. (Singles 2000dr. Doubles 2600dr.) You can also walk along the waterfront to the juncture of beach and boardwalk and turn right past the Hotel Fadira: The **Hotel Periandros** (tel. 222 72) has a pleasant garden, communal bathrooms, and clean comfortable rooms.(Singles 1200dr. Doubles 1700dr.) Next to the hotel, a pine tree park and pebble beach are suitable for **camping** if you can stand the carnival atmosphere. There are good beaches all along the coast between Xilokastro and the town of Kiato, to the east.

# Mycenae (Mykenai)

No city figures more prominently in Greek mythology than Mycenae. The tragic tale of the house of Atreus was immortalized by Aeschylus in his classic trilogy the *Oresteia*. Mycenae was allegedly founded by Perseus, the hero who duped Cerberus, the three-headed watchdog of the underworld, and slew Medusa, the snake-haired gorgon whose looks could kill. Before long, the city fell to Atreus, who had murdered his nieces and nephews and served them to their father Thyestes for dinner. This deed provoked the wrath of the gods upon Atreus' son, Agamemnon. Returning from the Trojan war, Agamemnon was met by his bitter wife Clytemnestra, her lover Aegisthus, and Aegisthus' lethal dagger. Agamemnon's son Orestes later avenged the murder of his father, but was thereafter haunted by the Furies, shadows of his anguished conscience. As Aeschylus relates the story, Athena finally descended to pardon Orestes and lifted the curse from the House of Atreus.

Mycenae's hazy origins, interactions with other Near Eastern civilizations, and decline have beguiled historians. The site was settled as early as 2700 B.C.E. by tribes from the Cyclades who were then establishing other outposts on the mainland. The Mycenaeans spoke an early form of Greek, evidenced by the clay tablets found at Pylos and Knossos, which were deciphered by Michael Ventris, who resolved as a schoolboy to crack the code. (The tablets are palace inventories; no tablets with literary texts have been found. This script is called "Linear B"; others, like the Minoan "Linear A," still elude translation.) Mycenae flourished economically after the fall of Knossos around 1400, enabling Mycenaean culture to take root in Cyprus, Syria, and Sicily. Relations with the Egyptians, Hittites, and of course, the Trojans, have been scrutinized for some time now. The prevailing opinion suggests that Dorian tribes from the north attacked and defeated Mycenae. Ancient documents indicate that the Dorians were led by exiles of Mycenae, from the dynasty of Eurystheus, overthrown by the same House of Atrius.

The well-preserved ruins of ancient Mycenae rank as one of the most celebrated archeological discoveries in modern history. In summer, hordes of tourists swarm to the famed Lion's Gate, but you can visit early in the morning or late in the afternoon to bypass the mobs. Although most travelers make Mycenae a daytrip from Athens, Argos, or Nafplion, you can spend the night in the adjacent modern village (really no more than a tourist strip), 2km from the site.

The only direct **buses** to Mycenae are from Nafplion (4 per day, 1 hr., 170dr) and Argos (6 per day, ½ hr., 80dr). Six buses per day leave Mycenae bound for Argos; three continue to Nafplion. Stops are in the town of Mycenae (up the street from the Iphigenia Restaurant), and at the site (a 20-min. uphill walk from the town). Alternatively, buses and **trains** (6 per day) run from Corinth to Fichtia, a 1½-kilometer walk from Mycenae Town. Although the town has no banks, the **post office** at the site handles **currency exchange**. (Open Mon.-Fri. 9am-2:30pm.)

## Accommodations, Camping, and Food

Mycenae has a limited number of inexpensive accommodations. If the youth hostel and the campgrounds don't appeal, try looking for a room to let on the side streets below town.

**Youth Hostel (IYHF)** (tel. 662 85), on the roof above the Restaurant Iphigenia. Crowded sun-drenched rooms with foam mattresses. Only 20 beds, 10 for each sex. Water temperature varies unpredictably. 450dr per person.

**Belle Helene Hotel** (tel. 662 55), on the main road. Also a bus stop. Clean, spacious rooms. Schliemann stayed here while excavating the site, and the register display on the wall claims that Virginia Woolf and Debussy slept here too. Doubles 2000dr. Singles negotiable.

**Hotel Elektra** (tel. 664 42), on the main road. Nondescript doubles 2000dr.

**Camping:** Mycenae has 2 decent campgrounds. The more luxurious is **Camping Atreus** (tel. 662 21), at the bottom of the hill on the farther side of town from the ruins. It offers a ı V room, kitchen, cafeteria/bar, and, in case of rain, rooms for the tentless. 300dr per person. 250dr per tent. Hot showers included. In the middle of town, **Camping Mycenae** (tel. 662 47) is smaller, friendlier, closer to the ruins, and set amid orange and lemon groves. There is also a bar/restaurant and a kitchen, where the gracious owner prepares homemade and inexpensive food. 250dr per person, 230dr per tent. Hot showers included.

All of the restaurants in town are overpriced due to the tourist trade; even groceries are expensive. Since there are no real bargains, try the **Achilles** on the main road—at least they're friendly. (Open 7am-2am.)

## Ancient Mycenae

The excavated site of Mycenae sprawls over a large tract of rough and steep terrain, tucked in between Mt. Agios Elias to the north and Mt. Zara to the south. The site is enclosed by Cyclopean walls 13m high and 7m thick. Archeologists have found evidence that the city was settled as early as 2750 B.C.E. The bulk of the ruins standing today, however, date from 1280 B.C.E., when the city was the center of the far flung Mycenaean civilization.

Mycenae was another miraculous find of Heinrich Schliemann, the amateur archeologist. He located Mycenae by following the cue of Homer and later Greek tragedians who had placed the House of Atreus in this vicinity. Schliemann began digging just inside the citadel walls at the spot where, according to his interpretation of several ancient authors, the royal graves should have been located. Discovering 15 skeletons "literally covered with gold and jewels," he became convinced he had unearthed Agamemnon and his followers, but later archeologists dated the tombs to four centuries before the Trojan War. One skull covered with a golden death mask, still referred to as "The Mask of Agamemnon," is now exhibited in the National Archeological Museum in Athens.

Before visiting the site, consider obtaining a map and a flashlight. The book by S. E. Iakovidis covers both Mycenae and Epidavros, includes a map of the site, and is well worth the 700dr.

The bus will take you to the end of the asphalt road; on your right stand the ruins. The imposing **Lion's Gate,** with two lionesses carved in relief above the lintel, is the portal into ancient Mycenae and perhaps the finest relic of Mycenaean culture. These beasts were symbols of the house of Atreus and their heads (now missing) had eyes of precious gems. The gate and the **Cyclopean Walls** of the citadel date from the thirteenth century B.C.E. Schliemann made most of his findings (now exhibited in the Mycenaean Room of the Athens Museum), including Agamemnon's mask, in **Grave Circle A,** to the right of the entrance. These shaft graves have been dated to around the sixteenth century B.C.E., and were originally located outside of the city walls. They were later incorporated when the city was expanded.

Following the ramp upward to the highest part of the citadel you reach the **palace** and the **royal apartments.** At the far end of the city, between the palace and the **postern gate,** is the underground cistern used in times of siege. Use your flashlight to explore the cold, slimy passage, but be careful—the steps are worn and slippery.

Just outside the Lion's Gate (down and to your left as you leave the city between the walls and the road) are two of the excavated *tholos* (beehive) tombs, used for noble burials. The one closer to the city was reputedly the **Tomb of Aegisthus** and the other the **Tomb of Clytemnestra.** If you follow the asphalt road 150m back toward the town of Mycenae you'll find the **Treasury of Atreus,** the largest and most impressive *tholos,* which Schliemann also unearthed. The **"Tomb of Agamemnon,"** is entered through a 40-meter passage cut into the mortar. To get a good look, bring a flashlight. (Site open Mon.-Sat. 8am-7pm, Sun. 8am-6pm. Admission to citadel and Tomb of Agamemnon 500dr, students 250dr. Hang on to your ticket or you pay twice.)

# *Argos* Αργος

In his play *The Flies,* Jean-Paul Sartre paints a rather bleak portrait of the ancient city of Argos—a picture which you may feel applies to the modern city. In its defense, Argos is a living metropolis going about its business, albeit chaotically. Only for a brief spell in the afternoon does the chaos subside, and even then, the aesthetic appeal of the town is little improved. For those who plan to take advantage of its proximity to Tiryns, Mycenae, Epidavros, and Nafplion, Argos is entirely bearable. And its own archeological offerings deserve a visit.

## *Orientation and Practical Information*

The four streets that form the sides of the central square in Argos correspond roughly to the four points of the compass. Surrounding the large and beautiful Church of San Petros, they are the principal avenues of the city. Visible from the square is **Larissa Hill,** topped by the Venetian citadel of the same name. Note that Larissa borders the city on the west. Parallel to the facade of Larissa is **Vassilios Georgiou B.** Opposite this street on the east side is **Danaou Street.** The north edge is **Vassilios Konstantinou,** the south side **Olgas Street.**

**Currency Exchange: National Bank,** on the eastern side of the square, 1 block behind Danaou St. and the park. Open Mon.-Thurs. 8am-2pm, Fri. 7:45am-1:30pm.

**Post Office:** Danaou St., past the southern end of the square. Open Mon.-Fri. 7:30am-3pm.

**OTE:** 8 Nikitara St., north of the park. Open daily 6am-midnight. **Telephone code:** 0751.

**Trains:** The train station (tel. 272 12) is about 1km south of the main square. To get to the main square from the station, take a right on Nafplion St. and then, at a 5-way intersection, bear left on Vas. Sofias. Five trains per day go to: Athens (3 hr., 425dr); Corinth (1 hr., 165dr); Tripolis (1 hr., 205dr); Kalamata (3½ hr., 530dr); and Mycenae (10 min., 38dr). Four per day go to Nemea (45 min., 70dr).

**Buses:** The 2 bus stations are across from each other on Vas. Georgiou B., below its intersection with Olgas St. in the southwest corner of the square. From the **Athinon Station,** buses depart to: Athens (5:30am-9pm every hr., 2½ hr., 710dr); Nafplion (6:30am-9pm every ½ hr., ½ hr., 70dr); Nemea (3 per day, 1 hr., 170dr); Mycenae (6 per day, 25 min., 160dr); and Prosimni (2 per day, ½ hr., 140dr). The **Arcadia-Laconia Station** dispatches buses to: Tripolis (9 per day, last at 10:30pm, 1¼ hr., 320dr); Sparta (8 per day, 2½ hr., 620dr); Olympia (Mon.-Fri. 3 per day, 4½ hr., 1050dr); and Andritsena (at 10am, 3½ hr., 780dr). For Gythion and Monemvassia you must change at Sparta unless you catch the 10:30am direct bus to Monemvassia.

**Laundromat:** Star, 13 Danaou St., past the southern side of the square. Open Mon.-Fri. 7:30am-3:30pm.

**Hospital:** Corinth St. (tel. 278 31), the road to Athens opposite St. Nicholas Church.

**Police:** 10 Agelou Bobou St. (tel. 272 22). From the northeast corner of the square follow Corinth St. and turn right on Agelou Bobou. Open 24 hours.

## Accommodations and Food

Argos does not attract many overnight visitors, so its accommodations are relatively few in number and inexpensive. All in all, you'd probably be happier in Nafplion, or, if you want to camp, in Tolo or Mycenae.

**Apollo Inn,** 15 Korai St. (tel. 280 12). Take Nikitara off the square, turn left at the BP station, and then turn right immediately into the nearby alley—it's on the left. A little difficult to find but quiet, tidy, and reasonably priced. Singles 1300dr. Doubles 2000dr.

**Hotel Palladion** (tel. 273 46), at the northeast corner of the square where Danaou St. meets Vas. Konstantinou. Peeling paint but large rooms and clean bathrooms. Singles 1500dr. Doubles 2000dr. Triples 3000dr.

**Hotel Theoxenia,** 31 Tsokri St. (tel. 273 70). Follow Vas. Konstantinou to the left (west) for about 150m until you see the arches on the left; it's just beyond. Closest of all to the Argos ruins. Standard rooms with slightly shabby toilets. Ring the bell at the opaque glass doors. Singles 1200dr. Doubles 1800dr. Bargain. Showers 100dr.

Restaurants on the square or behind the bank are not very good. If you're stuck, try **The Retro,** on the southwest corner near the bus stations. There is a huge **outdoor market** on Wednesday and Saturday mornings 1 block west of the main square. You might want to stock up at the **supermarket** on Vas. Sofias St., off the northwest corner of the square.

## Sights

Archeological evidence indicates that the plain of Argos has been inhabited since 3000 B.C.E. One civilization displaced the next, obliterating older structures and yielding the fractured ruins that remain. According to Homer, Argos was the kingdom of the hero Diomedes, and claimed the allegiance of powerful King Agamemnon of Mycenae. As the ancient wheel of fortune turned, the invading Dorians captured Argos in the twelfth century B.C.E., around the same time as the fall of Mycenae, and then used it as their base for controlling the Argolid Peninsula. Through the seventh century B.C.E., Argos remained the most powerful state in the Peloponnese, and even defeated Sparta, its growing rival. But this was the last of its glories. By the fifth century B.C.E. it was no match for the invincible Spartan war machine. In the famous battle of 494 B.C.E. Kleomenes and the Spartans nearly defeated Argos, failing to penetrate the city walls. Invaluable to Argos was the courageous defensive action taken by the women of Argos under the leadership of the poet Telesilla. Thenceforth, Argos lost any claim to political or military preeminence, but it remained at the cultural forefront with its advanced school of sculpture whose members included Polyklitos. In 272 B.C.E., the great general Pyrrhus of Epirus died in an Argive street: After he attacked the city, a female inhabitant let a roof tile fall onto his head.

In medieval times, Franks, Venetians, and Turks all captured and ruled Argos in turn, leaving behind many examples of defensive architecture, such as the **fortress of Larissa.** Compared to the Palamidi in Nafplion, this one is a little crude but quiet with an expansive view. Getting to the fortress is a hike. You can walk along Vas. Konstantinou St. for one hour or climb the foot path from the ruins of the ancient theater (45 min.). On the slopes of Larissa Hill you'll see the **Church of the Hidden Virgin.**

Archeologists had hoped to uncover a large part of the ancient city of Argos, but most of it lies underneath the modern town. The principal excavations have occurred on the city's western fringe. Few bother to visit this site, but those who do may be pleasantly surprised. If you walk past the post office to the end of the street and turn right onto Theatron St., you'll see the Greek *skene* and theater seats rising abruptly into the foothills. Only one aloof guard will greet you at the site.

The ancient **theater,** built in the fourth century B.C.E., was the largest in the Greek world, with a seating capacity of 20,000. Although it is not quite so well-preserved as its more famous counterpart in Epidavros, it is awesome. Next to the theater are the **Roman baths,** where extant segments of wall give a good impression of the original magnitude (and significance) of these ancient social centers. Look for the pipes and the mosaic floors. And be sure to spray some water from your canteen onto the tiles to get a sense of their original brilliance. Beyond the baths you'll find the **Roman Odeon** (indoor theater) and, across the road, the **agora,** with blue-and-white mosaics still in place. Past the Odeon are the remains of a smaller theater. (Site open Mon.-Sat. 8:45am-3pm, Sun. 9:30am-2:30pm. Free.) If you arrive after hours, you can sneak in by walking up the dirt road to the right of the sight.

The small and excellent **museum,** west off the main square on Vas. Olgas St., contains a collection of Mycenaean and pre-Mycenaean pottery, some of which dates back as far as 3000 B.C.E. The interior courtyard exhibits fifth-century Roman mosaics (again, better when wet), and the second-floor gallery has an intriguing array of headless Roman figures displayed as if in conversation. The entrance hall and the second-floor gallery each contain "unpublished" Roman mosaics, in even better condition than those in the courtyard. (Open Mon. and Wed.-Fri. 8:45am-3pm, Sun. 9:30am-2:30pm. Admission 200dr, students 100dr.)

In this vicinity there are a few other ruins, less impressive but still of interest. To find them from the main site, walk north up Gounas St. (outside the gate). Turn left (west) at the intersection with Tsokri St. and continue out of town up the hill. At the top just to the right of the road you'll find the remains of the **Temple of Apollo and Athena** and below it, a series of Mycenaean graves. To the right of the hill is **Aspis,** the main ancient citadel; Venetian Larissa stands proudly to the left. To reach this site from the main square, head west on Vas. Konstantinou, which becomes Tsokri St. The walk from either point of origin takes about 20 minutes.

Hera was the prime deity of the Argives and the temple of her cult, the **Argive Heraion,** is a short bus ride north of Argos. (Take the Prosimni bus; 140dr.) The complex contains a pair of **temples, a stoa,** and **baths,** among other things. At **Prosimni,** several kilometers northeast of Argos and past the Heraion, the avid archeologist will find a whole series of prehistoric graves. A few kilometers east of Agias Trias lie the remains of the city of **Dendra,** where tombs yielded the completely preserved suit of bronze armor now on exhibit in the Nafplion museum.

# Nafplion (Nauplio) Ναύπλιο

Were castle watches still so keen, Nafplion would be a town without secrets. It is pinioned by three fortresses whose blind eyes stare over every street in the cramped old port. The magnificent Palamidi fortress crowns the steep rock that towers over the city; the Acronafplion, on a dolphin's-head promontory, juts into the Argolic Gulf; and the tiny islet of Bourtzi in the Gulf guards the city's harbor. Besides its tense setting, Nafplion's excellent bus connections make it the ideal base for exploring the Argolid Peninsula.

Nafplion's history has been one of chronic instability. Before the Venetians built it out of the swamps in the fifteenth century, Nafplion, named for Poseidon's son Nauplius, consisted of the hilltop fortresses. The town passed from the Venetians to the Turks and back again. In 1821, it was headquarters for the revolutionary government, and then became the capital (1829-1834) for newly independent Greece. John Kapodistrias, the first governor of that republic, was assassinated in St. Spyridon Church. (You can still see the bullet hole.) Today, the peaceful atmosphere is that of a large, faded beach resort.

## Orientation and Practical Information

Buy the large, unbound map of Nafplion and Tolo (200dr) at the tourist shop where the bus stops or at the shops above the dock. The bus terminal, on **Singrou Street,** sits near the base of the Palamidi fortress, which caps the hill to the right facing inland. To reach **Bouboulinas Street,** the waterfront promenade, just walk left down Singrou to the harbor. The area behind Bouboulinas and Singrou is the old part of town, with many shops and *tavernas*. If you arrive by water, Bouboulinas St. will be directly before you, across the parking lot and parallel to the dock.

There are three other principal streets you should know. All three run off Singrou Street and are parallel to Bouboulinas. Moving inland, the first is **Amalias**, a chief shopping street. The second is **Vassileos Konstandinou**, which ends in **Syntagma Square** (Platia Syntagmatos), where you'll find two good *tavernas,* the bookstore, the bank, the museum, and at night, scores of aspiring soccer stars. The third street is **Plapouta Street**, which becomes **Staikopoulou** in the vicinity of Syntagma Sq. Here are more good restaurants. Across Singrou St., Plapouta becomes **25 Martiou,** the largest avenue in town and the road toward the tourist police. This side of Singrou St.—everything behind the statue of Kapodistrias's back—is the new part of town.

To get to the beach, take the road between the Palamidi and the Acronafplion—it's a very short walk.

**Currency Exchange:** Banks on Syntagma Sq. and Amalias St. Open Mon.-Thurs. 8am-2pm, Fri. 8am-1:30pm.

**Post Office:** on the corner of Sidiras Merarchias and Singrou St., 1 block from the bus station toward the harbor. Open Mon.-Sat. 7:30am-4pm. **Postal code:** 21100.

**OTE:** 25 Martiou St. at Arvantias, in the yellow building 2 blocks in front of the bus station. Open Mon.-Sat. 6am-midnight, Sun. 6am-11:30pm. **Telephone code:** 0752.

**Ferries:** There are no regular ferries out of Nafplion or Tolo. The *Pegasus,* an expensive cruise ship, sells one-way tickets. Consult **Bourtzi Tours** (tel. 226 91), next to the bus station. Open daily 9am-2pm and 5-8:30pm. A cheaper option is the **hydrofoil** that leaves for Piraeus Tues.-Sun. at 7:30am (4 hr., 1861dr), stopping in: Tolo (20 min., 220dr); Spetses (1 hr., 787dr); Hydra (2 hr., 867dr); Poros (2½ hr., 1242dr); Aegina (3 hr., 1610dr); Kranidi (3 per day, 2 hr., 450dr); and Salatas (3 per day, 2 hr., 450dr). Buy tickets at the **Flying Dolphin office,** 2 Bouboulinas St., just above the dock. Open Mon.-Sat. 8:30am-1pm and 5:30-8:30pm.

**Bus Station:** Singrou St. (tel. 273 23), off Pl. Kapodistrias. Buses go to: Athens (5am-8:30pm every hr., 3 hr., 800dr); Argos (6am-9pm, every ½ hr., ½ hr., 70dr); Mycenae (6 per day, 1 hr., 160dr); Epidavros (5 per day, 40 min., 170dr); Tolo (7am-8:30pm every hr., ½ hr., 75dr); Kranidi (3 per day, 2 hr., 450dr); and Galatas (3 per day, 2 hr., 450dr).

**Taxis:** Singrou St., across from the bus station. The trick is to get a driver who operates out of your destination; they charge less if they're returning.

**Moped and Bike Rental:** Nikopoulos, 49 Bouboulinas St. (tel. 226 35). Mopeds 2100dr per day. Bikes 800dr per day. Open 8am-8pm.

**English Bookstore:** Odyssey, Syntagma Sq. Limited but still the best. Open in summer only, Mon.-Sat. 8am-9pm, Sun. 6-9pm.

**Laundromat:** Silk Laundry Service, 14 Vas. Konstadinou St. No self-service; 100dr per piece. Open Mon.-Sat. 9am-1pm and 6-8pm.

**Agricultural Work:** Apricot orchards surround Nafplion and often hire foreign workers on the sly. It's easier for men to find work, which often consists of loading boxes. Go to the **Soulis Akostis** bar across from the Commercial Bank on Amalias.

**Medical Emergency:** Call the tourist police or visit **Nafplion Hospital** (tel. 273 09). Walk down 25 Martiou St. and turn left onto Kolokotroni St., which eventually becomes Asklipiou St.

**Police:** Praxitelous St. (tel. 277 76), a 15-min. hike along 25 Martiou St. from the bus station—follow the signs. You may have to be persistent, but they're kind and helpful. The location keeps most travelers away; if you show up, you'll get attention. Open 24 hours. **Tourist information** 9am-2:30pm.

## *Accommodations*

Although prices have risen in the old part of town, it's still the cheapest. Check along the streets at the eastern end of town (below the Dioscuri Hotel) for rooms to let. For **camping,** see Sights below.

**Youth Hostel (IYHF),** Neon Vyzantion St. (tel. 247 20), at Argonafton. From the bus station, walk down 25 Martiou St. with the Palamidi fortress on your right, turn left on the road to Argos, and take a right 2 blocks after the Hotel Argolis and before the Texaco station—it's at the end of the street. Clean but careworn place without toilet paper, toilet seats, or hot water. Bar in the grape arbor open until midnight. IYHF card required. Closed 10:30am-3pm. 1am Curfew. 450dr per person. Breakfast 150dr.

**Hotel Amymoni** (tel. 272 19), in the Ionian Bank building. Amalias St. dead-ends at this hotel—the entrance is on the right. Clean rooms but no private facilities. Close views of the old town. Singles 1500dr. Doubles 2000dr.

**Hotel Tiryns,** Riga Fereou St. (tel. 281 04), on the 2nd block up from Bouboulinas. The closest hotel to the dock. Singles 1700dr. Doubles 2100dr. Showers 100dr. Breakfast 250dr.

**Hotel Leto,** 28 Zigomala St. (tel. 280 93), at the top of Farmakopoulou St., up 2 flights of steep stone steps. Comfortable and quiet. Communal facilities. Some double beds. Doubles 2500dr. Ask about the house next door.

**Hotel Epidavros,** Ipsiladou St. (tel. 275-41), 1 block below Amalias and 4 blocks up from Boulinas. Cheap and cavernous rooms reek and resound with plumbing noises. As for the "pension"—it's the cheapest. Singles 1300dr. Doubles 2000dr. Bargain.

**Hotel Akropol,** 7 Vas. Olgas St. (tel. 277 96), 3 blocks down from Amalias and 3 blocks up from Bouboulinas. Doubles 2200dr. Triples 2800dr.

**Hotel Rex,** Bouboulinas St. (tel. 280 94), in the new part of town. Overpriced, and not very convenient. Singles 1500dr. Doubles 2400dr. Annex next door a bargain at 1000dr.

**Hotel Argolis** (tel. 277 21), in the new town, on the Argos road right before the turn-off for the youth hostel. Private closet bathrooms, noisy but comfortable bedrooms. Singles 1500dr. Doubles 2000dr.

## Food and Entertainment

Nafplion's cuisine is cheap, if you go to the right places. Seafood, especially baby squid, is usually a good choice. *Souvlaki-pita* fanatics can enjoy an excellent lunch (60dr) at the stand by the bus station. Note that most restaurants' names are written only in Greek.

**On the Water:** Two reasonably-priced restaurants are side-by-side at the corner of Bouboulinas and Singrou St., on the edge of the new part of town: **Kanaris** (open noon-midnight) and the **Nafplio House.** Above the dock on Bouboulinas you'll find a string of *tavernas*; the best is **Hundalas** at #63. Farther down, where Bouboulinas curves toward the Acronafplion, prices are a little higher. Try the great ice cream or pastry at **Rendezvous.** Otherwise, order a *cafe frappe* anywhere along Bouboulinas St. In the evenings on the dock, vendors open up enormous carts full of produce from the Phillipines: sugar cane, coconut, dried papaya, and pineapple.

**Syntagma Square:** Peaceful until the kids arrive around 9pm. The traffic-free square has two outdoor *tavernas:* **Ellas** and the slightly more expensive **Noufara.** Both are good; neither is great. The **bakeries** just off the square on Amalias and Staikopoulou are very good and inexpensive.

**Plapouta-Staikopoulou Street:** Most of the places along this street are small. The most popular and one of the best is **Kelari,** which has a charming garden out back. **To Koutouki** is also very good, as locals will attest. Next door to the agreeable **Taverna Zorbas,** the **Pink Panther** has fancy fruits, yogurt, and ice cream. Only the prices recommend **O Khelmos, Ta Fanaria,** and the **Staikopoulou Taverna** (farther down the street).

**Kapodistrias Square,** next to the post office: Pines, palms, and Palamidi are all in full view from **Matsikas,** which stays open during siesta. Some dishes—but not all—are expensive, but the food is among Nafplion's best.

Dance 'til you drop to traditional Greek or disco. On the corner of Bouboulinas and Sofroni is **Sirena** (tel. 245 15), where you can learn the *syrtaki* nightly beginning at 9:30pm. You can find a similar program nearby on Bouboulinas at the **Boite Lichnari.** For more up-to-date movements, try **Disco Idol,** on Singrou St. near the water. Up on the hill past the tourist police is the outdoor **Disco Kirki.** Drink lightly, though: Beer at most of these places goes for 300dr. For cheaper grog, hit the bars on Bouboulinas (beer 80-100dr).

## Sights

Nafplion beats any architectural textbook. The **Palamidi fortress,** built by the Venetians in the eighteenth century, is an amazing construction. The nearly 900 steps that once provided the only access to the fort have been superseded by a 3-kilometer road. Taxis cost 200dr one-way, 250dr round-trip, but you can assault it by foot. If you opt for the steps, climb in the morning when the hill blocks the sun and bring water. At the top, you can walk around the intricate, well-preserved walls that stretch down the steep slopes. The views of the town, gulf, and much of the Argolid are spectacular. The lion steles that adorn some of the citadel's walls are symbols of St. Mark and a Venetian emblem. The steps begin on Arvanitias St., across the park from the bus station. (Open Mon.-Sat. 8am-5:30pm, Sun. 10am-3pm. Admission 200dr, students 100dr. Pay at the top.)

The walls of the **Acronafplion** were fortified by three succeeding generations of conquerors—Greeks, Franks, and Venetians. Approach the fortress either by the road near the back parking lot or by the tunnel that runs into the hill from Zigomala St., where you can take the Xenia Hotel elevator.

Ludwig I, King of Bavaria, after seeing many of his men die in an epidemic in 1833-34, had the huge **Bavarian Lion** carved out of a monstrous rock as a memorial. Today, a small park sits in front of it. Instead of turning right onto Praxitelous St. to go to the tourist police, make a left onto Mikh. Iatrou St. and walk 200m.

Nafplion's **Folk Art Museum** (tel. 283 79) comprehensively displays the styles and construction techniques of ancient, medieval, and eighteenth-century Greek clothing. (Enter on Ipsiladou St. off Sofroni.) Don't miss the second-floor gallery of life-size Greek costumes. (Open May-Sept. Mon. and Wed.-Fri. 9am-1pm and 5-7pm; Oct.-April 9am-2pm. Free.) The **archeological museum,** housed in a Venetian mansion on Syntagma Sq., has a small but choice collection of pottery, arranged by historical period, and a Mycenaean suit of bronze armor, perfectly preserved from the fifteenth century B.C.E. (Open Mon. and Wed.-Sat. 8:45-3pm, Sun. and holidays 9:30am-2:30pm. Free.) Across from the bus station, there's a **playground** near the **statue of Kapodistrias** in a large peaceful park.

The tiny island of **Bourtzi,** just offshore and easily visible from Bouboulinas was fortified, compactly and elegantly, at the end of the fourteenth century. Caïques run back and forth from the end of the dock between 9am and 1pm, and from 4pm to 7pm (200dr round-trip).

## Near Nafplion

Several kilometers south of town, **Tolo** and **Asini** have the only nearby sand beaches, and are predictably crowded. You can rent windsurfers (500dr), peddle boats (350dr), and canoes (200dr) on Tolo Beach. Asini, 2km up the road from Tolo toward Nafplion, is less crowded and less expensive. If you've lost sleep over Homer's cryptic reference to Asini, you can visit the **ruins,** 1km inland, where excavations have uncovered fortifications, chamber tombs, and pottery.

Although sleeping on the beach is strictly forbidden in both Tolo and Asini, there is an incredible concentration of developed **campgrounds** in the area. The best deal is **Camping Star,** 2 blocks above the beach across from Europe Pizza, with relatively quiet sites, refrigerator, and indoor tables. (250dr per person. 200dr per tent.) **Lido I** and **Lido II** (tel. 593 56) have full facilities and food. (300dr per person. 200dr per tent.) For a room, go to **Hotel Stella,** on Panagiotis St. (tel. 595 02). (kitchen in the hall. Spacious doubles with bath 1800dr.) Near Asini Beach try the **Kastraki** campsite. It's more expensive but very comfortable and offers discounts on watersports equipment. Signs will also direct you to the nearby **Sunset** and **Tolo Plaz** sites, only slightly farther from the beach. You can reach both Tolo and Asini via bus from Nafplion (every hr., last bus returns at 8:30pm, ½ hr., 70dr). For Asini, ask the driver or the on-board assistant to let you know when to get off. Farther south, more campgrounds adorn the beaches of **Plaka, Kadia,** and **Iria.**

Just 4km northwest of Nafplion on the road to Argos lie the Mycenaean ruins of **Tiryns** (or Tirintha), birthplace of Hercules. The finest prehistoric site outside of Mycenae, during ancient times Tiryns was nearly impregnable. Its reputation was shattered when it was captured by the Argives and destroyed in the fifth century B.C.E. Although parts of the stronghold date as far back as 2600 B.C.E., most of what remains was built 1000 years later, during Mycenaean times. The massive walls that surround the site indicate the immensity of the original fortifications. Standing about 8m in height and width, the "Cyclopean" walls were so named by the ancient Greeks because they believed that the stones composing the walls could only have been lifted by the Cyclopes, a mythical race of one-eyed giants from Asia Minor with superhuman strength. It remains a mystery to modern historians how the stones were moved. On the eastern and southern slopes of the ancient acropolis, the walls reach a width of almost 20m. Inside these massive structures are vaulted galleries. The remnants of the palace at the top of the acropolis contain impressively decorated floors, but its frescoes are now on display in the National Archeological Museum in Athens. The site is easily reached by the Argos bus from Nafplion (every ½ hr., 55dr). (Site open Mon.-Sat. 8am-7pm, Sun. 8am-6pm. Admission 300dr, students 150dr.)

# *Epidavros* Επιδαυπος

> At Epidavros I felt a stillness so intense that for a fraction of a second I heard the great heart of the world beat and I understood the meaning of pain and sorrow.
>
> —Henry Miller, The Colossus of Maroussi

While we might allow Henry Miller some hyperbole, the theater at Epidavros is accoustically impeccable. From the top of its graceful and perfectly preserved 55 tiers of seats, you can hear a coin drop. Nowadays it's futile to listen for the heartbeat of the world—you won't hear it behind the din raised by eager tourists all trying to ascertain just how far sounds travel. The **theater** itself is a grand structure—by far the best of its kind. Constructed toward the end of the fourth century B.C.E. with a seating capacity of 14,000, it has miraculously remained in almost perfect condition. Cut into the side of a hill in the middle of a pine grove, it is completely hidden from view. Whereas the other key sites in the Argolid (Mycenae, Nafplion, and Tiryns) were built as fortified cities, the small state of Epidavros was designed as a sanctuary for healing. Its ruins are the remains of hospital rooms and sick wards. From its creation in the sixth century B.C.E., Epidavros was dedicated to gods of medicine—first Maleatas, then Apollo, and finally Asclepius. One legend claims that Asclepius had great success in curing ailments and thus incurred the wrath of Zeus by disrupting the balance between the living and the dead, and in the end, was struck down by a thunderbolt. Asclepius was soon revered as a hero, and later worshiped as a god. His symbol was the sacred snake coiled around his leg.

Excavations have uncovered the remains of a **xenon** (to the left as you exit the museum), which housed the hundreds who waited for treatment (the modern Greek word *xenodoheion* means hotel), and several ancient marble **bathtubs,** in which patients soaked with the hope of being cured. Walking beyond these from the direction of the theater you will come upon the foundations of a **gymnasium,** an **odeon** (small theater), and a **stoa.** Farther still are the ruins of a **Temple of Artemis,** a **Temple of Themis,** and then the **Temple of Asclepius.** Notice the indications of the long colonnade that once stood in Asclepius' temple—some believe the sick slept here. Since most tourists skip the ruins and see only the theater and museum, you will have the ancient sanctuary practically to yourself.

The **museum** displays a few interesting surgical instruments and plaster-cast figurines, but its collection of original statuary is stunning. The deep and complex folds of the garments and the expressive ease of these marble figures suggest that they are from the later period of classical Greek sculpture. (Site open Mon.-Sat. 8am-7pm, Sun. 8am-6pm. Admission 300dr, students 150dr. Hold onto your ticket stub for the museum.) For information, call (0753) 220 09.

Try to visit Epidavros on a Friday or Saturday night from mid-June to early September, when the National Theater of Greece and visiting companies perform plays from the classical Greek canon (Euripides, Sophocles, Aeschylus, Aristophanes, etc.) in the theater. Performances are at 9:30pm, and tickets can be purchased at the theater four hours before showtime. You can also purchase tickets in advance in Athens at the Athens Box Office of the National Theater (tel. 524 86 00), at the corner of Agiou Konstandinou and Menandrou St., or at the Athens Festival Box Office, 4 Stadiou St. (tel. 322 14 59). In Nafplion, they can be purchased from Olympic Airways, 2 Bouboulinas St., or from Bourtzi Tours, near the bus station. Tickets cost 400dr, 600dr, 800dr, and 1000dr (some shows have student rates of 200dr). Since all performances are in modern Greek, you may want to bring a translation and a flashlight with you; nearly all the dramas performed are available in English from the Odyssey bookstore in Nafplion, as are books about the site of Epidavros in general.

Bypass the Xenia, the expensive hotel near the site and head for cheaper accommodations in the long, thin tourist village of Ligouri, 4km from Epidavros. The **Hotel Koronis** and the **Hotel Asklipios,** on the main road, offer singles for 1000dr, doubles for 2000dr. It's better to make Epidavros a daytrip from Nafplion, Athens, or Corinth, but if you're in Ligouri long enough for a meal, visit the **Restaurant Oasis** (tel. 220 62), the first place on the road from Nafplion. Here the Greeks outnumber the tourists, and the owners imbue their service and food with the spirit of celebration. To get to the site, take the "Asklepion" **bus** from Nafplion (4 per day, 40 min., 170dr); it will pass through Ligouri on the way. A different bus from Nafplion will deposit you near the two campgrounds at **Paleo Epidavros** 15km from the site.

On nights of performances, additional **KTEL** buses make the round-trip, leaving Nafplion at 7:30pm (600dr). Private chartered buses may actually be cheaper (try Bourtzi Tours at 500dr round-trip); from Tolo, the fare runs about 1000dr round-trip. Taxis from Ligouri cost approximately 250dr one-way.

# Elias and Achaia (Northwestern Peloponnese) Ηλάς και Αχαάς

In the provinces of Elias and Achaïa, millions of tomatoes redden beneath a blazing sun as thousands of tourists do the same nearby. The area between Pirgos and Patras, the respective capitals of Elias and Achaïa, is a breadbasket blessed with flat, fertile ground, tassled corn stalks groping toward the sun, and a universe of open space. The soft golden sands here rival beaches anywhere. Most strands lie undisturbed, but some areas are being "remade" into resorts catering to travelers from northern Europe.

Great Achaïa, the name that meant the whole of Hellas to Homer and Greece-south-of-Thessaly to Rome, now represents only a small political subdivision of the northern tip of the Peloponnese. The main city, Patras, would give Homer nothing to sing about, but the ride along the Gulf of Corinth features vistas of the steep cliffs and pebbly beaches.

# Patras Πάτρας

With its homogeneous high-rises withering beneath a shroud of smog, the busy port of Patras is an ugly spot on the fair Peloponnesian coast. Only the tourists trafficking to and from Italy add color to this large industrial town.

## Orientation and Practical Information

If you're coming from Athens by car, you can choose between the **New National Road,** an expressway running inland along the Gulf of Corinth, and the slower but more scenic **Old National Road,** right along the coast. Those coming to Patras by road from the north can take a ferry from **Antirio,** in central Greece, across to **Rio,** on the Peloponnese (4 per hr. 6am-11pm, 15 min., 36dr, 400dr per car), and then bus #6 from Rio to the station 4 blocks up the hill from the main bus station in Patras, at Kanakari and Aratou St. (½ hr., 50dr).

If you're arriving by boat from Brindisi or any of the Ionian islands, you can reach the center of town by turning right as you leave customs onto **Iroon Polytechniou Street.** Note that from the bus station to the train station, the road curves and its name changes to **Othonos Amalias Street.** Just past the train station is the large **Platia Trion Simahon,** with palm trees, cafes, kiosks, and a large clock set in the side of an embankment with flowers planted to form the face and numerals. For the hostel, turn left as you leave customs.

**Tourist Office: GNTO** (tel. 42 03 05), right outside customs. Friendly multilingual staff can dig up information on just about anything. Detailed free map. Will help you find a room. Check here first for complete bus and boat timetables, since each company supplies information only for its own services. Open daily 7am-9:30pm.

**Consulates: English,** 2 Votsi St. (tel. 27 64 03), several blocks along Othonos Amalias past Platia Trion Simahon. **Italian,** 9 Aratou (tel. 27 33 61), up the street from the bus station.

**Currency Exchange: National Bank of Greece,** Platia Trion Simahon, on the waterfront, just past the train station. Open Mon.-Fri. 7:30am-2pm and 5:30-8:30pm, Sat.-Sun. 9am-1pm. Also at customs daily 7am-7pm, and the **mobile post office** just outside (see below).

**Post Office:** Mezonos Enzieni St. (tel. 27 77 59). Walk 2 blocks towards the bus station from customs and make a left onto Zaïmi— it's 3 blocks up on the left. Open 7:30am-3:30pm. Also a **mobile post office** just outside customs. Open Mon.-Sat. 8am-8pm, Sun. 9am-6pm.

**OTE:** At customs. Open Mon.-Sat. 7:45am-10pm, Sun. 2:30-10:30pm. Also at the top right corner of Platia Vas. Georgiou, several blocks up and to the right from Platia Trion Simahon. Collect international calls must be made here. Open daily 8am-10pm. **Telephone code:** 061.

**Train Station:** At Othonos Amalias St. (tel. 27 36 94), 5 blocks to the right down the waterfront from customs. To: Athens (in summer 7 per day; in off-season 5 per day; 5 hr., 630dr), Kalamata (4 per day, 6 hr., 615dr), Olympia (5 per day, 2½ hr., 370dr), and Pirgos (8 per day, 2 hr., 295dr). Even if you have a railpass, you should reserve a seat at the ticket window before taking a train. **Luggage storage** 50dr per day. Open 24 hours.

**Buses: KTEL,** 3½ blocks to the right, down the waterfront from customs. To: Athens (every hr., 4 hr., 1130dr), Killini (in summer only, at 8:30am and 2:45pm, 1½ hr., 420dr), Kalamata (2 per day, 4 hr., 1220dr), Pirgos (10 per day, 550dr), Tripoli (2 per day, 960dr), Delphi via Itea (3 per day, 570dr), Ioannina (2 per day, 1330dr), and Thessaloniki (3 per day, 2560dr). Buses to Lefkas (890dr) leave from the intersection of Favierou and Konstantinoupoleos St., several blocks up from customs. **OSE** buses leave from the train station for Athens (19 per day, 1130dr) and Methoni (4 per day, 1230dr). Some ferry companies also run their own quick, air-conditioned buses to and from Athens (1500dr); check when you buy your ticket.

**International Bookstore: Romios Librarie,** just up from the bus station. Small selection, but larger than elsewhere. Open daily 8am-9pm.

**Tourist Police:** 40 Othonos Amalias St. (tel. 22 09 02/3), across from the train station. Men in blue offering the same services as the GNTO. Limited English. Vague free map. Open 24 hours.

**Hospital: Patras University Hospital** (tel. 22 28 12 or 166). English-speaking doctors. There's also a **Red Cross Emergency Station** at Karoloua and Ag. Dionissiou St. (tel. 150), several blocks from customs.

## Ferries

From Patras, boats go to Cephalonia, Ithaki, and Corfu, as well as Brindisi, Bari, and Ancona in Italy. They also continue from Corfu to Dubrovnik, Rijeka, and Split in Yugoslavia. Most boats depart at 9pm or 10pm; check-in is two hours before departure. For ferries to Brindisi or the Ionian Islands, show up at customs at the main terminal; ferries to Bari and Ancona leave from a pier 1km to the west. Ticket prices fluctuate tremendously. In general, expect a discount if you are under 28, or a student, or on a railpass and going to Brindisi.

**Ferry Tickets:** Most boat agencies are scattered along the ½km between customs and Platia Trion Simahon. For tickets to Brindisi, try **Med-Link**, 36 Iroon Polytechniou left from the port. You can get cheaper tickets to Brindisi here than in Igoumenitsa or Corfu. Deck fare with Eurailpass 1200dr, with InterRail (or if you're under 28) 3000dr, students 4400dr, otherwise 5600dr; everyone pays a 600dr port tax. Departures for Brindisi are at 6pm and 10pm in high season, at 10pm only in off-season (18 hr.); boats arrive at noon and 4pm the next day, Italian time. (Open daily 8:30am-2pm and 4-9:30pm.) **Inglessis Bros.**, 12 Othonos Amalias St. (tel. 27 76 76), and **Tsimaras Agency**, 12/14 Iroon Polytechniou St. (tel. 27 77 83) both sell tickets to Corfu (at 9:30pm, 10 hr., 1890dr). The latter also sells tickets for boats leaving daily at 1:30pm and 9pm for Sami on Cephalonia (4 hr., 1000dr) and Vathi on Ithaki (5 hr., 1000dr). Convenient agencies with general information and tickets for most lines include **Manolopoulos**, 35 Othonos Amalias (tel. 22 36 21), 1 block before the train station, and **Central Ticketing**, at the same address (tel. 27 44 51) are both open daily 8am-9pm. Other agencies with cheap tickets are **Achaia Travel**, 7 Kolokotroni (tel. 22 26 29); **Happy Travel**, 25 Othonos Amalias (tel. 22 60 53); **Keramidas**, 40A Othonos Amalias (tel. 27 33 30), opposite the train station; and **Top Travel**, 9 Karolou at Agiou Dionissiou (tel. 43 20 24). You can also purchase tickets in Athens.

## Accommodations, Camping, and Food

The cheapest place to stay in Patras is the **IYHF youth hostel**, 68 Iroon Polytechniou St. (tel. 42 72 78). Turn left as you leave the ferry and walk 1½km. This small turn-of-the-century mansion sat empty for 40 years after it was used as a German officers' headquarters in World War II. It's a bit cramped with eight beds to a room, but offers a convenient location (and a view of the harbor), a washing machine (300dr), and no curfew. (600dr. Roof 400dr. Sheets 50dr. Hot showers included. Breakfast 150dr.) Most hotels in town are dreadful, but inexpensive accommodations can be found in the tangle of shabby buildings on Agiou Andreou St., 1 block from the waterfront, running parallel to it along the main square. At #63 is the centrally-located **Hotel Delphi** (tel. 27 30 50), popular with backpackers. (Singles 1100dr. Doubles 1450dr. Triples 1900dr. Baths 100dr in old-fashioned tubs.) You can get a room with a view of the harbor, but you'll have to contend with the noise and traffic of the busy main street. The quieter **Hotel Parthenon**, 25 Ermou St. (tel. 27 34 21), off Agiou Andreou 1 block south of Platia Trion Simahon, is one of the cheapest. The manager doesn't speak English but is friendly and enjoys a good game of charades with English-speaking tourists. (Singles 850dr. Doubles 1500dr. Triples 1800dr. Showers included.) Two hotels operated by the same management as the youth hostel are the **Ilion**, 10 Agiou Nikolaou St. (tel. 27 31 61), just up the street from Platia Trion Simahon, and the **Kentrikon**, 10 Agiou Andreou St. (tel. 27 72 76), at Aratou. Both are fairly clean and reasonably-priced.(Singles 1100dr. Doubles 1700dr. Triples 3000dr. Showers included.) The **Hotel Brettania**, 95 Agiou Andreou St. (tel. 27 34 21) offers large, empty, and decaying singles for 1500dr, doubles for 2000dr, and triples for 2500dr (showers 200dr). **Hotel Splendid**, 37 Othonos Amalias St. (tel. 27 65 51 or 27 65 52), doesn't quite live up to its name, but is reasonable. (Singles 1500dr. Doubles 2000dr. Triples 2400dr. Showers included in crumbly bathrooms. Negotiable.)

The closest **camping** is on the beach at the large government-run campground of **Plaz Agia** (tel. 42 41 30), 4km east of Patras. (420dr per person. 340dr per tent.) Take bus #1 (40dr) from Agiou Andreou St. behind the tourist police, or a taxi outside customs (about 200dr). Eight kilometers east of Patras, *Rio* has its own **castle,** as well as several small beach **campsites,** including **Rio Camping** (tel. 99 15 85) and **Rio Mare** (tel. 99 22 63). You can take a ferry here to central Greece (see Orientation and Practical Information).

There are plenty of cheap, stand-up-fast-food-joints along Agiou Andreou St. where you can get a toasted sandwich and fries for around 200dr, or a *tiropita* for 80dr. There are several good *souvlaki* bars near **Platia Olgas** between Aratou and Kolokotroni St. (three streets in from the waterfront) with shaded benches ideal for longer waits. The shops and cafes along the waterfront are definite rip-offs and won't hesitate to part fools from their money. Try **Nikolaras,** an out-of-the-way, cheap *taverna* at the corner of Agiou Nikolaou and Karaiskaki. If you follow Agiou Nikolaou from the square up into town, you'll see a daunting staircase leading to the castle; climb it to the park and the only truly peaceful dining in Patras. **To Kastro** has good, inexpensive food, but no wine. Sweet figs, dried fruit, and nuts await in the shops near Platia Trion Simahon.

## *Sights*

The largest Orthodox cathedral in Greece, **Agios Andreas,** is located here and dedicated to St. Andrew, who lived and died in Patras. St. Andrew was a martyr who was crucified on an X-shaped cross, feeling unworthy to die on the same kind of cross as Jesus. The custom of marking hugs and kisses with "XOXOXO" derives from this episode. St. Andrew's faithful would place an "X" on a document and kiss it in memory of his sacrifice. In time, St. Andrew was forgotten and the "X" associated only with the kiss. A little over 10 years ago, the Catholic Church in Rome presented the Bishop of Patras with the disciple's head, which is enshrined in an ornate gold and silver reliquary in the church. (Open to tourists 9am-dusk, except during services. Dress code strictly enforced.) To get here, follow the water all the way to the western end of town (about 1½km from the port).

Dominating the city is the Venetian **kastro** and surrounding park. The thirteenth-century fortress was built on the ruins of the ancient acropolis on the site where the temple of the Panachaïan Athena once stood. Parts of the walls are still in good condition, and the view from the battlements is superb. Several blocks from the base of the stairs, up from Platia Vas. Georgiou, the **Roman Odeum** has also been preserved; occasional performances are held here. Those who missed the ferry to Corfu or have other frustrations can take them out in Patras's **bumper-car rink** at Athinon and Ag. Sofias St., 1 block up and 4 blocks left from customs (100dr for 10 min.).

Nine kilometers southeast of town is the **Achaïa Clauss winery.** The free wine tasting and very inexpensive *ouzo* could make the trip worthwhile and forgettable. Try the sweet *Mavrodaphne,* which made Achaïa Clauss famous. According to legend, the winery's founder, German Baron von Clauss, lusted after a Greek girl named Daphne; when she died, he used black grapes to make a dark wine to remind himself of her. (Open in summer 7:30am-1pm and 4-7pm; in winter 10am-4:30pm. Free.) Take bus #7 (20 min., 40dr) from the intersection of Kolokotroni and Kalakari St. About 1km from Achaïa Clauss there's a picnic spot overlooking the village of Saravali near the **Church of St. Constantine,** where the Byzantine Emperor Constantine Paleologos lived in 1425.

If you're lucky, the annual **Patras International Arts Festival** (tel. 33 63 90) will make it through year number four, and you can hear the sounds of Keith Jarrett or Mikis Theodorakis before resuming your travels. The festival runs from mid-June to mid-August with music, dramatic, and dance performances held in the castle theater or Roman Odeum, as well as the Castle of Rio. Check the GNTO or tourist police for current offerings. The cheapest tickets are 600dr. If you drift through town in February, don't miss the **carnival.**

# Killini Κυλλίνης

Since most travelers come to Killini to catch the ferry to Zakinthos, layovers in this small beach town are usually unexpected—and usually unexpectedly pleasant. One of the reasons is the broad beach itself: There's so much sand from the ribbed bottom beneath the waves to the main road along the shore that shop owners hose down the streets every day to subdue the inevitable dust storm. The few tourists who spend time here—mostly French and Italian—have neither spoiled the town's uncommercial air nor rushed its leisurely tempo.

To get to Killini, catch one of the **buses** from Pirgos (3 per day until 2pm, 1 hr., 350dr) or Patras (3 per day, 400dr). If you miss the bus from Patras, take the bus to Lehena (10 per day, 1½ hr., 350dr); from there, buses go to Killini (at 11:20am and 2:45pm, 20 min., 55dr). A taxi will take you from Lehena to Killini for 500dr. There are **train** connections (5 per day, 200dr) from the Patras-Pirgos line, changing at Kavasila. **Ferries** from Killini to Zakinthos depart seven times per day in summer, five per day in off-season (1½ hr., 400dr). Boats also leave for Cephalonia (2 per day, 500dr). You can buy tickets for both on the dock. To get to Patras or Athens from Killini, either take a bus from the dock or take the train to Kavasila (8 per day, 45 min., 40dr), where you can connect to other points on the Patras-Pirgos line.

From Killini's central triangle, right opposite the dock, walk several blocks with the water on your left until the road ends. Opposite the dock, a right turn will take you to the **post office.** The **OTE** is a block away. (Both open Mon.-Fri. 7:20am-2:30pm.) The **police** (tel. 922 02) are behind the triangle. (Open 7:30am-8pm.) The **tourist** and **port police** (tel. 922 11) are on the dock. (Open 24 hours.) Killini's **telephone code** is 0623. On Glaretzas St., 1 block above the beach and parallel to the water, the **Glaretzas Hotel** (tel. 923 97) has light fresh rooms with pseudo-Scandinavian decor. (Singles 1800dr. Doubles 2400dr.) Several *dhomatia* on Glaretzas St. have slightly more reasonable rates but singles are nearly impossible to procure in summer. The **Ionion Hotel,** on the other side of the triangle on the beach, is more expensive. (Singles from 2000dr. Doubles 3000dr.) You can also **camp** on the beach along with everyone else. Just past the Ionian is the *psarotaverna* **Sou-Mou,** with yummy fried fish and a standard *kalamari* plate for 350dr. (Open at 10am for a limited lunch; dinner available at 7:30pm.) Also try the *psistaria* **O Choriatis** on Glaretzas St., an unpretentious establishment asking only 200dr for spicy *yemista* (stuffed tomatoes).

Near Killini (20km) are the Frankish **Chlemoutsi Castle** and the mineral springs of **Loutra Killinis,** a well-manicured resort. Getting to either place is difficult unless you have your own transportation or are willing to pay for a taxi (700dr to the castle, 900dr to Loutra). To get there by public transportation, take the train to Vartholomio from the end of the tracks in Killini (6 per day, 20 min., 30dr one-way, 45dr round-trip); buy your ticket at the Killini station or at the Vartholomio station. Take a right out of the Vartholomio station and continue down the road until you reach a square with a fountain (1km). From here, buses leave for Loutra (8 per day, 40dr), and will let you off at one of three places: the turn-off to the castle, the mineral springs, or the excellent camping area, **Camping Killinis** (tel. 96 25 40), close to the sea. Three buses per day leave Loutra for the castle; stand at the turn-off to hitch.

You can't help noticing the cavalcade of trucks laden with ripe, red tomatoes in the summer being taken to the large Asteris tomato sauce processing plant. Since most processing is done outdoors, it's easy to watch from the road, just outside Vartholomio. If you get hungry, try one of the million or so watermelons also grown locally.

# Pirgos Πύργος

There's not a whole lot happening in Pirgos, a huge commercial town on the western coast, but you're almost certain to pass through here on the way to Olympia, 21km to the east. Be warned that all the hotels here are C-class and none are cheap. To get to the bus depot from the train station, walk straight until you get to the Hotel Olympos, then veer slightly left as the street goes uphill. After about 50m, turn right at the supermarket on Manolopoulou St. and walk another 50m; the chaotic bus station is on the left. **Buses** leave for Olympia (16 per day until 9pm, 45 min., 120dr), Killini (3 per day until 2pm, 1 hr., 350dr), Kiparissia (2 per day, 1 hr., 330dr), Kalamata (2 per day, 2 hr., 700dr), Tripolis (3 per day until 5:30pm, 4 hr., 850dr), Athens (9 per day until 9:30pm, 5 hr., 1650dr), Patras (10 per day until 8pm, 2 hr., 550dr), Andritsena (2 per day at 6:15am and 12:15pm, 1½ hr., 350dr), and Lehena (7 per day, 1 hr., 230dr). **Trains** leave for Olympia (5 per day until 6pm, 45 min., 75dr), Patras (2 per day, 2½ hr., 260dr), and Athens (4 per day, 7 hr., 650dr).

To reach the **tourist police,** on Karkavitsa St. (tel. 236 85), turn left just before the Hotel Olympos. (Open daily 8am-2pm.) Along the route between the bus and train stations you'll notice the **OTE,** a garish orange and yellow building (open daily 7am-midnight for telephone; Mon.-Fri. 7am-midnight for telegram and telex), and several C-class hotels. The **post office** is on Pl. Avierinou, several blocks up the hill to the left of the OTE; ask plenty of directions, since it's difficult to find. (Open Mon.-Fri. 7:30am-2:30pm.) A **bank** is located on the street coming from the train station 300m past the turn-off for the bus station. (Open daily 8am-2pm.) Pirgos' **telephone code** is 0621; the **postal code** is 27100.

For a place to sleep near the train station, try the **Hotel Kantron** (tel. 227 33). The entrance is occasionally left unattended, but wait around and someone will be back soon. (Singles 1200dr. Doubles 1800dr. Triples 2200dr.) You might also try **Hotel Pantheon** (tel. 297 47), 1 block up from the station and on the left. (Singles 1700dr. Doubles 2200dr.) The best places to eat and wait out a layover are in the Pirgos Plaza. Walk from the bus station toward the OTE and take a right at the first stop sign. At the top of the hill you'll see the plaza one block to the left. Close to the train station, **O Mirias** is better than most for a meal.

Thirteen kilometers west to land's end sits the port of **Katakolo;** from the town's bus and train stations, just past Katakolo's beach, continue in the same direction toward the *faro* (lighthouse). The paved road becomes gravel and rises to a pine forest high over the sea. You can easily freelance **camp** in these pine-scented surroundings cooled by the sea breeze. If you'd rather stay in Katakolo, try the **Hotel Karel** or the *dhomatia* for a couple of hundred *drachmae* less. **Buses** from Pirgos to Katakolo leave five times per day (½ hr., 60dr); the small narrow-gauged **train** leaves at 2pm and drops you closer to the beach than the bus does (44dr). Twenty-five kilometers south of Pirgos on the road to Kiparissia and Pylos are the sulphur springs at **Kaïafas.** The railroad and bus stop sit on the landward side of very fine sand dunes covered with pine trees. If you walk just a bit along the coast in either direction, you can set up camp. Bring provisions with you; the immediate area around the bus/train stop has only one overpriced restaurant and snack bar. The springs lie about 700m inland and form the basis for a fancy resort catering to adherents of water therapy.

# Olympia Ολυμπία

Whenever the ancient games were held in Olympia, multitudes bivouacked in a huge tent city where vendors hawked wares and entrepreneurs seduced crowds with all kinds of diversions. Little has changed over the centuries; the modern town of Olympia, about ½km from the ruins, is merely a compound of hotels and tourist shops. If you need a break from the heat, the stores, and the ancient rocks, an hour's walk takes you through bucolic pastures and goat-trodden groves that have ringed Olympia since who-knows-when; on your way to the site, make a right down a gravel road where the sign says "no camping."

## Orientation and Practical Information

Modern Olympia essentially consists of one long street, **Kondili Avenue**—to get to ancient Olympia, walk east along it with the uphill side on your right toward the Hotel Spap. About 500m past the tourist office across the river, you'll come to the archeological site and the New Museum (see Ancient Olympia). On the other side of the town, towards Pirgos, sports enthusiasts will get a kick out of the **Museum of the Olympic Games,** Angerinou St., 2 blocks uphill from Kondili Ave., which exhibits medals, stamps, and paraphernalia commemorating the modern games. (Open Mon.-Sat. 8am-3:30pm, Sun. 9am-3pm. Admission 100dr.)

Most tourist shops open late (10:30am) and close late (10:30pm). The **Diagoras** souvenir shop on Kondili Ave. has a display of Olympic torches used in ceremonies of several modern games, including those held in Moscow, Innsbruck, and Munich. (Open 9am-11pm.)

**Tourist Office:** Kondili Ave. (tel. 231 25), on the eastern side of town, toward the ruins. Bus and train information, and an international telephone. Open in summer Mon.-Fri. 9am-11pm, Sat.-Sun. 10am-10pm.

**Currency Exchange: National** and **Commercial Banks** both on Kondili Avenue Open Mon.-Thurs. 8am-1pm, Fri. 7:45am-1pm.

**Post Office:** On an uphill sidestreet, 1 block east of the tourist office. Open daily 7:30am-2:30pm.

**OTE:** Kondili Ave. (tel. 225 21), just past the post office. Open Mon.-Sat. 7:30am-10pm. **Telephone code:** 0624.

**Trains Station:** (tel. 225 99), 2 blocks downhill from Kondili on the western side of town. Trains to: Pirgos (5 per day, ½ hr., 100dr); Patras and Athens (5 per day, 7 hr., 900dr); and Katakolo (5 per day, 1 hr., 90dr). Change in Pirgos for other destinations. Take any road going uphill from the train station to get to Kondili Ave.

**Bus Station:** In the cafe 2 doors down from the Hereon Hotel on Kondili Ave. To Pirgos (Mon.-Sat. 18 per day, 10 on Sun., 45 min., 150dr), and **Tripolis** (3 per day at 9:15am, 1:15pm, and 5:15pm, 4 hr., 650dr). Change at Pirgos for other points on the western Peloponnese. To Kalamata change at Alfios (5 stops).

**Bookstores:** Kondili Ave.; English-language book collections the equal of any in Greece. Also, **Galerie Orphée,** 1 block from the tourist police. Open 8am-11pm.

**Hospital:** Tel. 222 22, on the road to Camping Alpheios; follow the signs.

**Police:** Downhill off Kondili Ave., ½ block from the tourist office. Mainly for emergencies. Open 24 hours.

## Accommodations, Camping, and Food

If you want a bed for the night and just care about the price, then head for the youth hostel. Otherwise, you can pick from among dozens of D-class hotels, most of which offer private baths, balconies, and immaculate modern rooms for less than elsewhere. *Dhomatia* in Olympia all go for about the same price (singles 1500dr, doubles 2000dr), and the bulk of them line Spiliopoulou St., the road parallel to and 1 block up from Kondili Ave.—start knocking on doors or linger at the train station.

**Youth Hostel (IYHF),** 18 Kondili Ave. (tel. 225 80). IYHF cards rarely requested. Clean facilities. Narrow bunk beds line drab rooms. 11:45pm curfew. Check-out 10am. 450dr. Sheets 100dr. Hot showers 100dr. Breakfast 160dr. Luggage storage 150dr per day.

**Hotel Hereon,** Kondili Ave. (tel. 225 49), where the buses stop. Tell the woman who rushes out to meet the buses that you plan to stay in the youth hostel: She'll meet their price. Clean rooms. Singles 1000dr. Doubles 1500dr. Triples 2000dr.

**Hotel Praxiteles,** 7 Spiliopoulou St. (tel. 225 92), parallel to and above Kondili Ave. A comfortable hotel with D-class prices. Modern and quiet, with balconies, private baths, and sizzling hot water. Let the couple who runs the place argue about the price.

**Hotel Alexandros** (tel. 225 36), next door to Praxiteles. More air for the same prices.

**Camping: Camping Diana** (tel. 223 14), just 200m uphill from Kondili Ave.—follow the multiple signs. Easily the most convenient. Shaded sites, sparkling facilities, electricity (hot showers 7-9am and 6-8pm), swimming pool (open 9am-noon and 2-8pm), and a well-stocked store. They also offer information on ferries. Reception 8am-10pm. 450dr per person, 330dr per small tent. If full, try **Camping Olympia** (tel. 227 45), 1km west on the main road to Pirgos (450dr per person, 330dr per tent) or **Camping Alphios,** a 1km trek uphill from town (tel. 229 50); 4 blocks west of the tourist office—follow the signs from Tsoreka St. (390dr per person, 330dr per tent). Both have standard facilities.

Shop around for restaurants—many are rip-offs. The **Greek Taverna Dias,** across from the tourist police, is quiet, and offers hot bread from the bakery across the street, but only a limited selection of dishes. **O Manos,** on Kondili Ave., near the Hereon, isn't bad, but beware of the 20% surcharge on Sundays and holidays. There's a *souvlaki-pita* shop near the post office. For snacks, go to the **Strouka** pastry shop, on the road to the Museum of the Olympic Games. Locals attest to the divine quality of their cakes. In the evening, several places advertise drinks and Greek dancing.

## Ancient Olympia

The legendary site between the Kladeo and Alpheos Rivers was never a city but rather a place where celebration took precedence over hostility, where physical competition supplanted political division. Here, adversary heads of city states congregated without protective armor to enjoy the games. Homer said that the Elysian fields that surround Olympia made life easy. Today these fields have overgrown the yards of toppled pillars and smooth flagstones.

Olympia was a place of worship from time immemorial. Shrines were built here, first to the pre-Hellenic goddesses, then to the ancient god Kronos (Zeus' father), then to Zeus himself. Finally, the physical form and athletic achievements of men were celebrated in the Olympiad. Women (except for the Priestess of Demeter) were not invited to participate in or attend the games: Pausanias, the Peloponnesian journalist of the second century C.E., wrote of the cliff from which women were hurled if detected entering the Olympic assembly. One woman, Pherenike, managed to escape this punishment. After her husband, an Olympic contestant, died, Pherenike accompanied her son to the games disguised as a trainer. Out of respect for her husband, Pherenike was spared, but subsequently all trainers were stripped at the gates.

According to tradition, in 776 B.C.E., young men from all the cities in Greece (and later Rome) gathered in Olympia for the quadrennial festival of Olympian Zeus and the athletic competition that accompanied it. Beginning with a simple footrace and wrestling match, the games became more complex and prestigious. By 472 B.C.E., the games spanned five days and included six different kinds of races (races of 1-, 2-, and 24-stadium lengths, and horse, chariot, and full armor races), boxing, all's-fair wrestling (called the *pankration*), regular wrestling, and the pentathlon (wrestling, discus toss, javelin throw, long jump, and one-stadium length race). The games themselves commanded respect; the Olympic Truce, declared for up to three months to facilitate transit to the events, was strictly observed by the otherwise perpetually warring Greek cities. Besides the Homeric poems and the main oracles, the games were the only truly pan-Hellenic institution. Only two violations of the truce were ever recorded in the history of the games.

The ancient town of Olympia was considered sacred by the Greeks and never actually inhabited except by officials connected with the games. The center was reserved for the **Altis,** a walled enclosure or sacred grove of Zeus. On the far east side stood the **stadium.** Just before the stadium stood the **echo stoa,** said to have had a seven-fold echo. (In 1829, a French archeologist knew he had found Olympia when he heard his voice echo seven times.) On the other three sides of the Altis, buildings were gradually added for the competitors to train and eat in, and to accommodate the staff of administrators, high priests, doctors, and flute players. Over the centuries, council houses, drug testing facilities, treasuries, and a variety of monuments were added to the site—most of these last were gifts from victors to the gods, and numbered 3000 at the peak. The Olympic games were discontinued by Christian Emperor Theodosius I in 393 C.E. because he felt the festival was too intimately connected with the worship of Zeus. In 426 C.E., his son Theodosius II called for the destruction of the pagan sanctuary.

On the right as you enter the main gate are the remains of the **gymnasium,** the extremely well-preserved columns of the **palaestra** (wrestling school), and the **theokoleon** (official residence of the priests). Next to the latter is a small building that was the **workshop of Pheidias,** the famous artist (supposedly the creator of the lost Gold Statue of Athena) who was commissioned to produce a sculpture for the site. His tools, terra-cotta molds, and a cup bearing his name were found during excavations. Built on the foundations of the workshop is an early Christian basilica with three walls. On the northern edge of the Altis are the remains of the **Temple of Hera** (seventh century B.C.E.), the oldest and best-preserved building on the site, and the oldest Doric temple in Greece. Originally built for both Zeus and Hera, it was devoted entirely to the goddess after a separate temple for Zeus was built to the south. To this day, the Olympic flame is lit here and borne to the site of the modern games. Adjacent stood the **Philippeum,** built by Philip II of Macedon.

The colossal **Temple of Zeus,** standing in the center of Olympia, dominated the entire complex. Now all that remains is a huge platform with fragments of the original structure. The scattered piles of capitals and cylindrical cross-sections of pillars indicate that the edifice was toppled either by human hands or earthquakes. Some of the original mosaic floor can still be seen on the temple base. The nave of the temple once housed Pheidias' 13-meter tall statue of Zeus, reckoned by the Greeks to be one of the seven wonders of the ancient world. Emperor Theodosius ordered that the gold and ivory statue be brought to Constantinople, where it was destroyed by a fire in 475 C.E.

The **stadium** can be reached through the archway on the east end of the Altis. As originally constructed, its artificial banks accommodated 40,000 spectators. The **judges' stand,** a paved area on the south side, is still in place, as are the starting and finishing lines; you can even discern the holes into which wooden poles were placed to hold the tape. Runners ran back and forth across the 192-meter track—the longest in all of ancient Greece. The sole stone seat on the northern side of the stadium was reserved for the priestess of Demeter. Beyond the stadium flows the Alpheos River, said to run underground all the way to Sicily and fabled to have helped Hercules clean the Augean stables.

You may want to pick up a copy of Manicus Andronicus' archeological guide to the site, as the ruins are vast and barely marked. (Site open in summer Mon.-Sat. 7:30am-7pm, Sun. 8am-6pm; in winter daily 8am-5pm. Admission 400dr, students 200dr.)

The gleaming modern **New Museum,** across the street from the site, supplies the grace missing from the ruins and houses three treasures rescued from the ancient world. Straight ahead as you enter the main hall are the breathtaking **pediments** of the destroyed Temple of Zeus. The western pediment belongs to Apollo, whose figure is flanked by exquisitely sculpted figures from the war between the Lapiths and the Centaurs. The eastern pediment is crowned by Zeus; the figures around him are preparing for the chariot race between Pelops, founder of the Olympic Games, and Oinomaos, father of his betrothed. But the prize of the museum is the **statue of Hermes,** housed in its own room in the far right corner. Attributed to the fourth-century B.C.E. sculptor Praxiteles, it first stood in the interior of the Temple of Hera and was protected by mud-brick walls; when the sanctuary was flooded, the masterpiece was comfortably buried in the mud. Walk around the statue of the nude messenger holding the baby Dionysus—it will seem to move with you, as if aware of your stare. (Open in summer Mon. and Wed.-Sat. 7:30am-7pm,

Sun. 8am-6pm, Tues. noon-5pm; in winter Wed.-Mon. 8:30am-5pm, Tues. noon-5pm. Admission 400dr, students 200dr.)

Olympia is one of the most touristed sites in the Peloponnese—try to arrive by 7:30am to enjoy an hour's peace before the tour groups arrive.

# Arcadia (Central Peloponnese) Αρκαδία

Poets since Virgil have envisioned Arcadia as the spiritual paradise of shepherds, the pastorial setting for luv songs and poetry. In this fertile land ringed by mountains, the gods Pan and Bacchus led their raucous dances, and one can imagine that tinkling goat bells, bawling cows, and a million bees joined the chorus. Naturally, the rumble of buses and all they bring have disturbed Virgil's laurels, but shepherds still roam the hills and men still talk of love (even if it's less poetical from the street corner).

Arcadia was named after Arcas, a son of Zeus. According to one myth, Zeus was born here and suckled by a goat. Once grown, he sired Arcas with Callisto; Callisto's father Lycaeon chopped Arcas into bite-sized pieces and served him to Zeus for dinner—just to see if Zeus would notice. Zeus turned the murderer into a wolf and gave Arcas new life. In the form of a bear, the grown Arcas one day chased his mother to Zeus' holy precinct atop Mt. Lycaeon (just west of Andritsena), where he raped her. Zeus afterward turned them into the constellations Ursa Major and Minor (the Big and Little Dipper). The Arcas story was the basis for the swift execution of any who crossed the threshold of the sacred spot on Mt. Lycaeon—accidental offenders incurred the suspenseful penalty of unpredictable slaughter within a year's time. The same mountain site was used for human sacrifice; whoever ate any part of the victim became, like Arcas' grandfather, a wolf, condemned to roam the region in lonely hunger.

Two main routes run across the mountains. You can explore Arcadia by traveling east from Pirgos through Andritsena and Megalopolis, or west from Tripolis through the surrounding orchards of Tegea and Mantinea and out to Dimitsana and Stemnitsa.

# Tripolis Τρίλολη

The capital and transportation hub of Arcadia, Tripolis is large and prosperous, with several rose-filled public gardens. The military men you see walking the garden paths are from the Tripolis Air Force Base, a few kilometers out of town. Tripolis is close to the ruins at Tegea and Mantinea, and the departure point for some wonderful mountain villages.

## Orientation and Practical Information

Most buses arrive at the Arcadias bus station in the big plaza, **Kolokotroni,** dominated by the Arcadia Hotel. Five blocks down Georgion St., to the left of the Arcadia, is **Platia Georgion,** an even bigger square dominated by the Church of Agios Vasilios. The bus station for Messenia and other southerly destinations is in the Ethnikon Restaurant in the far left corner of this square. The **OTE, police station,** and **post office** are on sidestreets off Platia Georgion. To orient (or confuse) you, a dense map hangs on the wall in the Galaxy Hotel on Platia Georgion.

**Tourist Police:** Ethnikis Anistasis St. (tel. 22 24 11), off the right-hand side of Platia Georgion behind the theater—go to the 2nd floor. Helps find accommodations. Open Mon.-Fri. 9am-3pm.

**Currency Exchange: National Bank,** on Platia Georgion. Open Mon.-Thurs. 8am-2pm, Fri. 8am-1:30pm.

**Post Office:** Io. Metaxa St. (called Nikitara St. by locals). Cross Platia Georgion, take Vas. Pavlou St., and turn right onto Io. Metaxa. Open Mon.-Fri. 7:30am-4pm.

**OTE:** #29, 28 Oktovriou St. From Platia Georgion, take Ethnikis Anistasis St. (on the right), and then bear left immediately on 28 Oktovriou St. Open daily 6am-midnight. **Telephone code:** 071.

**Trains:** The **train station** (tel. 22 24 02) is 1km west of Kolokotroni Plaza. Trains from Tripolis go northeast to Athens (5 per day, last at 5:44pm, 5 hr.), stopping in Corinth (2½ hr.) and Argos (1½ hr.); 6 trains per day go southwest to Kalamata (3 hr.).

**Buses: Arcadias Station** (tel. 22 56 50) dispatches buses to: Athens (9 per day, last at 7:30pm, 3 hr., 800dr); Dimitsana (at 5:30am and 6pm, 1½ hr., 380dr); Pirgos (3 per day, last at 6pm, 4 hr., 850dr); Andritsena (2 per day, last at 11:30am, 1 hr., 460dr); Meopolis (8 per day, ½ hr., 275dr); as well as to the nearby ruins at Tigea (7am-9pm every hr., 15 min., 70dr) and Mantinea (4 per day, 15 min., 70dr). From the **Ethnikon Restaurant,** buses leave for Chora (at 11am and 6pm), stopping in Kipavissia (2 hr., 540dr). Buses also go to Kalamata (7 per day, 2 hr., 440dr); Pylos (at noon and 5pm, 3 hr., 620dr); and Messini (11:30am, ½ hr., 370dr). For buses to **Patras,** walk 1km along Ethnikis Anistasis St. (on the right of Platia Georgion) to the special Patras bus station near the Cinema Eilo.

**International Bookstore: Xartis,** on Platia Georgion, sells English newspapers.

## Accommodations and Food

Tripolis is better suited for the hordes attending the various conventions in town than for budget travelers. In a bind, the tourist police can help you out. At 26 Georgion St., near the bus station, is the centrally located C-class **Hotel Alex** (tel. 22 34 65), which comes highly recommended. (Holiday Inn-style doubles 1800dr. Showers included.) For unofficial camping, follow the signs for the Air Force Base (*Aerodrama*) down Agios Konstantinos St. After a 15-minute walk, you'll find a flat and spacious pine clearing to your right. Just off the main square, on Petropoulou St., is a good restaurant, **To Kanake.** The interior is smart and clean, the service attentive, and the *souvlaki* and fries delicious. In the gardens off Ethnikis Anistasis and Agiou Konnous Streets, conversation is for the birds but the cafes have atmosphere. Two nearby *bouzouki* clubs (open 10pm-3am) attract the Tripolisians: **Monamouru** is 3km along the road to Athens, **Asteria** is 3km down the road to Sparta.

## Near Tripolis

For centuries in ancient times, the cities of **Tegea** and **Mantinea** maintained a fierce rivalry. Some say it began over water; others trace it to the rivalry of Sparta and Athens. Tegea, 8km south of Tripolis, took Sparta's part, while Mantinea, 6km to the north, sided with Athens. Although the two cities no longer exist, the rivalry continues. Now, however, it is not the inhabitants but the ruins that compete. The bus company hails Mantinea as the winner, since it sends three times as many buses there every day. If you can't get to Mantinea, you won't see the well-constructed city walls standing smack in the middle of a plain, not in the usual position on top of a hill or mountain.

Tegea has a bit more to offer, though. The **museum** contains marble thrones of honor from the Tegean theater, large sculpted heads of Hercules and Asclepios, dramatic friezes of lions, and sculpted remains of the Temple of Athena Alea. (Open Mon. and Wed.-Sat. 8:30am-2:45pm, Sun. 9am-2pm. Admission 200dr, students 100dr.) Going left out of the museum, a 100-meter winding road takes you to the site of the **Temple of Athena Alea.** The base of the huge building remains almost fully intact, though weather and vegetation have discolored the stones considerably. Huge slices of the columns litter the site, some on their side, others balancing precariously on piles of rubble. The temple was named for King Aleus, who founded Tegea in the ninth or eighth century B.C.E. In ancient times, exiled Spartan leaders often found refuge here.

If you leave the site and continue down the road to **Palaia Episkopi** (1km), you'll realize why Atalanta, one of the swiftest runners in Greek mythology, hailed from Tegea. The famous plain of Tegea, a flat, fertile stretch of land, makes perfect running territory. Today, irrigation and modern farming methods have rendered it even more productive, and a walk will take you through pear, apple, and cherry groves. At the end of the road lies the site, where a church, *tavernas,* and chirping birds share the park's tranquil shade. Following the signs that read "Palaio-Christianiki Psiphidota" to find a small building with many windows through which you can see the expansive ancient mosaic floor. Also in the park is a monument to Greek Olympic runners, the heirs of Atalanta.

# *Megalopolis*  Μεγαλόπολη

Great cities evolve; they are not created as such. But Epaminondas of Thebes disobeyed this golden rule when, in the fourth century B.C.E., he decided to invent a capital for the new confederation of Arcadia. He seems to have had two major objectives in the founding of Megalopolis (from the Greek *megale polis,* or "large city")—to appease the Arcadian cities who were competing to be the league's premier metropolis, and by selecting a strategic position, to project the new capital from the belligerent city-state of Sparta to the south. Megalopolis was built between 371 and 368 B.C.E., and was stocked with the populations of 40 nearby villages. At its height, the city had 200,000 inhabitants. But the plan, not surprisingly, was a failure, and after a century of aggression from Sparta and desertion and treason by its reluctantly naturalized citizens, the city waned in importance, and by Roman times, was an underwhelming provincial town.

Today, perhaps more than ever, Megalopolis seems a misnomer. Like many other Greek towns, it's just an extended village built around a spacious tree-lined public *platia*. Its most notable feature is the enormous electric power plant (the largest in the Peloponnese and the second largest in all of Greece) at the edge of town that expels billows of noxious fumes from its smokestacks. The resulting faint, grimy smell hangs over the town.

Despite its grim modern condition, you may, nonetheless, want to make a quick stop in Megalopolis to see the remains of its **theater,** with a seating capacity of 20,000. The excavations of the 1890s only unearthed the theater's first six rows, but looking at the rippled slope of the hillside you can mentally reconstruct its 53 additional tiers. It's no Epidavros, but set near quiet fields (but also near the power plant), the rarely visited ruins have a modest, bucolic appeal. To reach the theater, walk 1km north on Gortinias St. past the OTE and post office. You will pass a sign that indicates that you are leaving town. Continue walking straight ahead and turn left onto a street at the sign for "Ancient Theater;" it's a leisurely 15-minute walk from the town square. You can enter directly from the right, but you'll get a more impressive first view by climbing the hill to the left. The gate to the theater is open 24 hours; it's especially peaceful to visit in the very early morning or late evening hours.

## *Practical Information and Accommodations*

Because there's little to do in Megalopolis, it's best to visit the city on a daytrip. Plan to leave your luggage in the bus station, and allow about two hours to visit the theater and town. The **bus station** (tel. 222 38) is located on Ag. Nikolaou St., off the northwestern corner of the square. Buses leave seven times per day for Athens (4½ hr., 1210dr) via Tripoli (30-45 min., 195dr) between 7:30am and 6:30pm. Buses travel to Andritsena (2 per day, 1¼ hr., 270dr) via Karitaina (25 min., 115dr). Only the 12:15pm bus goes up to the village (except Mon. and Fri.); at other times, you will be deposited at crossroads and left to hike the rest of the way. Also at

9:45am, there is a bus to Kalamata (1 hr., 310dr). A few buses for Kalamata and Athens leave from the cafe at the southeast corner of the square; the man at the main bus station can give you information about those departures. There is also **train** service to Megalopolis. Trains arrive at **Lefktro**, where a free bus waits to shuttle you the 6km to Megalopolis. From Megalopolis, you can travel to Athens (5 per day, 5 hr., 860dr) or Kalamata (5 per day, 1 hr., 300dr). For information and tickets, go to the **tourist office** travel agency on the southwest side of the square (tel. 221 50; open 8am-noon and 5-8pm). The bus to Lefktro leaves from in front of this office 20 minutes before train departure (55dr). The **post office** is 1 block north of the square on Gortinias St. (open Mon.-Fri. 7:30am-2:15pm) and shares a building with the OTE (open Mon.-Fri. 7:30am-3:10pm). The national **bank** is across from the southwest corner of the square. (Open Mon.-Thurs. 8am-2pm, Fri. 8am-1:30pm.) The **police** station (tel. 222 22) is off the southwest corner of the square, 2½ blocks down Kolokotroni St. at #46. For **medical** emergencies, dial 229 74. There is a **public toilet** at the northeast end of the square. Megalopolis's **telephone code** is 0791; the **postal code** is 22200.

You'll find spacious and well-lit rooms at the **Hotel Paris**, 9 Ag. Nikolaou St. (tel. 224 10), right next to the bus station. (Singles 1272dr, with bath 1696dr. Doubles 2120dr, with bath 2756dr. Triples 2862dr. Showers 300dr.) **Hotel Pan**, 7 Papanastasiou St. (tel. 222 70), off the southeast end of the square, has tacky decor, but prices are marginally cheaper. (Singles 1272dr. Doubles 1908dr, with bath 2226dr. Triples 2226dr. Showers 120dr.)

# *Karitena* Καρίταινα

On the road between Andritsena and Megalopolis is the delightful medieval village of Karitena. The old stone houses slumber in their panoramic, mountainous roost. Climb up to the **Frankish castle** for a view of the radiating peaks and the valley of the Alfios River below. Bus connections to Karitena are infrequent, but once you get there you shouldn't have much trouble hitching a ride on the highway below. Most tourists pass through for a short tour, but if you spend the night you will be treated to a peaceful evening of cool mountain air, isolated from the rest of the world.

After ascending to the castle, you may want to visit the thirteenth-century church of **Agios Nikolaos.** Ask in the square for George (a former resident of Chicago with perfect English), who has the key to the church. During their occupation, Turks scratched out the faces of the saints in the church's oldest frescoes. Another remainder of the Frankish presence is the medieval bridge located beneath the modern bridge on the main road below town.

The **post office** is downhill from the main square. (Open 7:30am-2:30pm.) The **police** (tel. 312 05) are located uphill and to the right of the square. There is no OTE, but the *kafeneion* has a metered phone from which you can make calls. Karitena's **telephone code** is 0791.

For accommodations, try the small but fastidiously kept rooms rented by **Stamata Kondopoulo,** across from the post office. (You'll see a sign; follow the road to its end.) (Singles 1000dr. Doubles 2000dr.) More expensive is the modern **Hotel Karitena** (tel. 312 03), uphill from the square and to the right—follow the signs. From the terrace you can view the countryside below. (Singles 1500dr. Doubles 2300dr. Triples 2500dr.) You might also sit down for a hearty meal with the family. (Dinner 600dr. Breakfast 150dr.) The one *taverna* in town, **Pentochiliara,** is an inexpensive standard *souvlaki* restaurant.

Buses traveling between Megalopolis and Andritsena stop in Karitena, except on Monday and Friday when they'll let you off below at the crossroads (it's a steep uphill hike to the town). Buses travel to Andritsena (at 5:45am and 12:30pm, 40 min., 170dr) and Megalopolis (at 9am and 4pm, 20 min., 115dr).

# *Andritsena* Ανδρίτσαινα

Andritsena is falling apart pleasantly; its haphazard tumble of red-rooved old houses and its main street shops with their faded, piebald facades sprawl endearingly along a mountainside. Tourism here is a laid-back affair; carloads of vacationers pass through on their way to Vassae, but few linger. If you decide to stay overnight (as you might be forced to because of infrequent bus connections), mellow out with the villagers. Sip coffee languidly in a cafe, walk up the crooked sidestreets, or listen to the villagers sitting around low stools chatting. You may also want to stop in at the little **folk museum** arrayed with needlework, an old barber's chair, and earthenware. (Open Mon.-Fri. 11am-1pm and 5-7pm. Donation requested.)

Andritsena is one and a half hours west of Megalopolis and the same distance east of Pirgos. Buses from Megalopolis (1¼ hr., 270dr), Tripoli (3 hr., 460dr), and Athens (6½ hr., 1500dr) lurch across unsteady switchbacks climbing into mountains of red clay and green terraces. The **bus station** is around the corner from the Shell station on the Pirgos side of town. Departures to Pirgos (daily at 6:15am and 12:15pm, 350dr) leave from the main square; buy tickets in the cafe nearby.

In town, the **police** (tel. 222 09 and 222 31) are at #11 on the Shell station side of the square, just off the main road. (Open 24 hours.) The **post office** (open Mon.-Fri. 7:30am-2:15pm) and **banks** (open Mon.-Thurs. 8am-2pm, Fri. 8am-1:30pm) are next to the Shell station. The **OTE** is off the main street, near the church. (Open Mon.-Fri. 7:30am-3pm.) For the **clinic,** dial 222 10 or 222 11. Andritsena's **telephone code** is 0626; the **postal code** is 27061.

If you spend the night here, **Hotel Pan** (tel. 222 13), next to the Shell station, is definitely best. Beautiful, clean doubles with private bath cost 2120dr; you'll get the same room as a single for 1500dr. The **Hotel Xenia** (tel. 222 19), on the edge of town nearest Megalopolis, was built with great expectations. It is a cavernous, ghostly place decorated with tacky French needlepoint and other schmattas. The rooms are clean. (Singles 2950dr. Doubles 4128dr. Triples 5000dr. All with private bath. Bargain.)

For meals, try **Tsigouri Restaurant:** Turn in at the sign that reads "stop restaurant 20m" just before the square, or enter directly on Kolokotroni St. Inexpensive, home-cooked food goes down especially well amidst the profusion of geraniums, rhododendron, hanging gourds, and Christmas lights.

## *Near Andritsena: Vassae*

> *Like stranded ice when freshets die*
> *These shattered marbles tumbled lie;*
> *They trouble me.*
> *What solace?—Old in inexhaustion,*
> *Interred alive from storms of fortune,*
> *The quarries be!*
> *—Herman Melville, on seeing Vassae*

Rising stately on the slopes of Mt. Kotilion, the **Temple of Epicurus Apollo** was offered as thanks to Apollo for saving the people of Phygalia from the plague. Iktinos, the architect commissioned to build the monument in 420 B.C.E., later made his name designing the Parthenon. The extant columns are thought to be the first of the Corinthian design ever used.

Vassae remains sacred and solitary. The approach from Andritsena snakes up along cliffs for 14km, threading between swirling pinnacles of rock. Finally, near the top, the temple appears, its ancient **agora** now littered with pillar fragments. View the temple from an adjacent hill to appreciate its beauty. The temple is now shrouded under a canopy and entombed by scaffolding to protect it from acid rain.

To get to Vassae (there is no bus), you must either hitch (the turn-off is just outside Andritsena on the road to Pirgos), or round up some people and take a **taxi** from Andritsena. The going round-trip rate is 1000dr per car per half hour (no matter how many people); with a little dickering among the half-dozen drivers in the square you should be able to get it down to 700dr (look bored and let the word *autostop*—the word for hitchhiking—fall from your lips a few times). Make it clear from the start that the rate is for the group; some drivers may try to charge by the individual. Pay nothing until you are safely back in Andritsena. You may wish to walk back to town (it takes 3½ hr. over the hills). Since vegetation is sparse and low, every point along the way affords an exhilarating view of distant mountains. Except for the occasional sound of a car, the road is remarkably still. East of Andritsena (you'll pass it in the bus to or from Megalopolis) is the medieval village of **Karitena,** perched on a high slope with an inspiring view over the ravine of the Alpheos River. The medieval fortress overlooking the village from the top of the mountain exemplifies thirteenth-century Frankish architecture.

# *Dimitsana and Stemnitsa* Δημητσάνα και Στεμνίτσα

Separating the ancient settlements of the western Peloponnese from the beach resorts of the east are the Erimanthos, Menalo, and Oligirtos mountain ranges. Some people call this area of the central Peloponnese "the Switzerland of Greece." The mountains here are ancient and gnarled, the altitudes are modest, and green vegetation clings to all but the highest summits. Tucked into the mountains west of Tripolis, the little villages of Dimitsana and Stemnitsa make good bases for alpine hiking. Somewhere above Dimitsana, the earth's ceiling fan turns on. Disembarking in Dimitsana, you can hike 11km along the main road to Stemnitsa through breathtaking scenery. **Buses** run from Tripolis (at 5:30am and 6pm, 1½ hr., 380dr.), returning at 6:30am and 4pm. Two buses daily also pass by on their way to and from Olympia and Pirgos in the western Peloponnese; to catch these, it may be necessary to take a taxi to the tiny cafe, 6km north at **Karkalou,** on the main highway. Ask the police or in the cafes for details.

In **Dimitsana** the bus will deposit you in front of a cafe next to the **post office.** (Open Mon.-Fri. 7:45am-2:45pm.) To the left are Platia Pesonton and, underground, the town's best eatery, the surprisingly inexpensive **Vlahos Restaurant.** A meal of veal, potatoes, and *fasolia* (delicious stewed beans), goes for 300dr. If you continue up **Labardopoulou St.,** the main road, and turn left onto Nikolaou Makris St., you'll come to the helpful **police** (tel. 312 05; open 24 hours). A little farther, at #110 and 112 Nikolaou Makris, are the **museum** and the **library** (open daily 8am-2pm). Because so few distractions interrupt a Dimitsanian pupil's thought, the town has been a center of education for over 300 years: These two institutions commemorate its scholarly achievements.

Returning to the main road and continuing on you'll reach the **OTE,** 402 Labardopoulou St. (Open Mon.-Fri. 7:30am-3pm.) The bank at #406, is just past the OTE. (Open Mon.-Fri. 8am-2pm.) **The telephone code** is 0795. Greece's only Swiss chalet is Dimitsana's only lodging, the luxurious **Hotel Dimitsana,** 100m south of town on the road to Stemnitsa. For a spectacular view, get a room on the downhill side. (Singles with bath 2200dr. Doubles with bath 2800dr. Bargain—you should be able to knock off at least 500dr from both quotations.)

Although not in as spectacular a setting as Dimitsana, **Stemnitsa** is the more beautiful village and thus makes a worthwhile daytrip. Its brownstone and pinewood houses, set serenely on the steep mountainside, have been tastefully reconstructed. Stemnitsa also has a gorgeous hotel on the main road, **Hotel Triokolonion** (tel. 812 97; singles 1500dr, doubles 2330dr). You can explore the mountains along narrow paths that wind into the interior. Follow the main road out of town toward Megalopolis. On the left you'll see an arrow pointing to the small villages. Turn up onto the concrete road for 20m and then up the stepped path on the right. This is the route the locals follow from remote mountain settlements to bring their goat milk and herbs to town. As you walk deeper into the mountains you'll pass elderly women perched on laden donkeys, lumbering down the rocks. If you hike northeast from here, you'll intersect the Olympia-Tripolis highway at **Vitina** (15km east of Karkalou), where there are a fair number of rooms to let as well as a slew of wood-work shops. If you head westward toward Olympia, stop in **Langadia**, which looks out over ravines and plunging mountains. The village is constructed almost verti-cally; even the church graveyard is terraced. In the center of town, where the bus stops, cafes overlook the plunge. There's a **post office** at the eastern edge of town; the western edge holds the **Motel Langadia.**

# Messenia Μεσσηνη

Messenia is the breadbasket of the Peloponnese. The invincible fortresses in Pylos, Methoni, Koroni, and Kalamata vigilantly survey the gleaming seas, ready to de-fend the precious soil, from which gushes olives, figs, and grapes. To facilitate their profitable agricultural export trades, most Messenians live around the sprawling, earthquake-devastated town of Kalamata, but tourists would do better to base them-selves in Pylos. This somnolent port town is alluring in itself, as well as strategically located for bus or moped trips to the castles and beaches of the south.

# Pylos Πύλος

The shady square and old tile houses brushed by bobbing flowers are typical enough of a port town. But the sharp rock face of Sfakteria Island rises abruptly out of the sea, an anomaly that gives Pylos a protected harbor and a defiant ambi-ence. Also known as Navarino, the town is renowned for the 1827 sea battle of the same name, a landmark in the Greek War of Independence. Until that time, Greek forces had been overwhelmed by the firepower of the Turkish fleet. The English, French, and Russian fleets arrived at Navarino to uphold the Treaty of London and protect Greek autonomy. Their purpose was to intimidate the Turks. However, a few shots from the Turks brought out a prodigious amount of allied firepower. When the smoke cleared, 53 of the Turk's original 82 ships lay submerged at the bottom of the sea, while the allies lost not a single one of their combined 26-ship fleet. A monument to the commanders of the allied fleets, the English Codrington, the French de Rigny, and the Russian von Heyden, stands today in the middle of Pylos' platia.

The **police** (tel. 223 16) are located on the second floor of a building on the left side of the waterfront (facing the water) before the turn in the road. Continue around that turn to reach the **port police** (tel. 222 25). The **post office** (open Mon.-Fri. 8am-3pm) is on Nileos St., uphill to the left (facing the water) from the **bus station.** To get to the **OTE,** pass the post office and take your first left; it is on the right of the little square, 2 blocks uphill. (Open Mon.-Fri. 7:30am-3:10pm.) The national **bank** is on the left side of the square, on the waterfront. (Open Mon.-Thurs. 8am-2pm, Fri. 8am-1:30pm.) The **hospital**'s phone number is 223 15. Pylos' **tele-phone code** is 0723.

Pylos is also a perfect base for visiting the southwest arm of the Peloponnese. Just 17km north lie the important ruins of Nestor's Palace, and only 12km south the beach town of Methoni and its grand castle. For crowded yet appealing beaches, go 6km north around Yialova Beach and the campground. **Buses** (tel. 222 30) leave regularly for Kalamata (Mon.-Sat. 6:30am-9pm 9 per day, Sun. 9am-9pm 6 per day, 1¼ hr., 280dr), Athens (daily at 9am, 7 hr., 1740dr), and Finikoundas (Mon.-Sat. 4 per day, 2 on Sun., 45 min., 150dr) via Methoni (15 min., 60dr). No buses travel directly to Koroni, but you can go to Finikoundas and take the 5pm bus from there to Koroni. Buses also leave for Kiparissia (Mon.-Sat. at 7am, 9am, 11am, and 1:15pm; Sun. at 11am, 2 hr., 330dr), all stopping at Nestor's Palace (½ hr., 90dr) and Chora (35 min., 115dr). The best way to see the southern peninsula, however, is to rent a moped and make a daytrip. **Venus Rent-A-Car** (tel. 223 93 or 223 12), uphill from the right side of the square as you face the water, rents **mopeds** for 1800dr with insurance. (Open 8:30am-1pm and 6-8:30pm.)

You will see a few rooms to rent signs as the bus descends the hill. You might want to get off the bus at an uphill stop before the bus reaches Pylos and test the principle that the farther uphill, the more rooms available. In general, expect to pay 1350-1666dr for singles, 1750-2450dr for doubles, and 2620-2826dr for triples. Try the pension (tel. 223 87) belonging to **Filitsa Kalogirou** near town at #15 on the road before its last left turn heading down to the main square. The small, modest rooms and the dank bathroom in this old store house are uninspiring, but the cool garden under the trellised grape arbor is reinvigorating. (Bed in spare room upstairs 700dr. Doubles 1500dr.) The unprepossessing pale-green facade of the **Hotel Navarino** (tel. 222 91) should not turn you away. In addition to maintaining clean rooms, the management will exchange fishing tales with you. To get there, follow the road along the waterfront to the left of the square (facing the water) past the police and port police. (Singles 1272dr. Doubles 1855dr. Powerful showers included.) The mosquito-plagued **Navarino Beach Camping** (tel. 227 61) lies 6km north at Yialova Beach. (350 per person. 200dr for a tent.) People also camp on the wooded hill across from the expensive Castle Hotel, apparently without any trouble from the police. With the water on your right, climb the stone stairs up into the woods. For a good, inexpensive meal in a great, outside garden try **Gregori's;** walk up the street from the Cafe Santarosa and bear right—the restaurant has a red sign. (Stuffed tomatoes 200dr. *Mousaka* 350dr. Open 9am-3pm and 6pm-midnight.)

In addition to the natural sentinel of Sfakteiria Island, Pylos is guarded by fortresses on both sides of its harbor. The southern one, **Neokastro** is easily accesible from Pylos; just walk up the road for Methoni and turn right at the appropriate sign. The well-preserved walls enclose a church (originally a mosque), a large citadel, and a building, flanked by canons and canonballs, that will house a museum by the summer of 1989, displaying items found at the *kastro* and at sea. (Open Mon.-Sat. 8:45am-3pm, Sun. 9:30am-2:30pm.) The **Paleokastro,** north of Pylos, is harder to reach. Drive to Petrochori and proceed south with caution, as the road is poor. The castle itself is overgrown and home to some snakes.

Pylos' tiny **museum,** 1½ blocks up Fillelinon St. on the left side of the square, houses finds from Hellenistic tombs at Yialova and Mycenean ones at Koukounara. Relics of the Battle of Navarino—a huge rusted anchor and a pile of canonballs—used to lie in the museum's rose garden but are now being restored and will be put in the museum at Neokastro. (Open Mon. and Wed.-Sat. 8:45am-3pm, Sun. 9:30am-2:30pm. Admission 200dr, students 100dr.) To see **Sfakteria** close up, you can take a boat tour from the port. The hour jaunt around the island stops at the various monuments to the allied sailors in the Battle of Navarino and peeks at a sunken Turkish ship. (3000dr per boatload. Trip including visit to Nestor's cave 6000dr. Complete tour with stop at Paleokastro 8000dr.) Hang around the quay by the small boats with orange and red cabins.. One of their captains will try to arrange for you to tag along with a bigger group (usually about 10 people), thereby making the trip much cheaper. Most boats leave between 8am and 9am.

## Near Pylos

The *Odyssey* vaguely mentions that the Palace of Nestor is somewhere in the southwestern corner of the Peloponnese; to make matters worse, Homer also describes three places called Pylos. However, archeologists are confident that their excavations 4km south of Chora have actually uncovered the real **Nestor's Palace.** Nestor, you'll remember, was Odysseus' buddy and, according to the *Iliad,* commander of the second largest fleet at Troy. Evidence indicates that the palace was built in the late Mycenaean period and destroyed shortly thereafter (about 1200 B.C.E.). All the rooms are clearly marked—and everything is shaded by a large roof. To the left of the entrance, in Rooms #7 and #8, the first Linear B tablets found on the mainland were discovered, only two hours after the excavation had begun. Linear B was the second-millenial script that scholars believe was an antecedent to Greek. Proceeding to the **megaron** (the throne and hearth room), you'll notice a rectangular indentation to the right where the throne once stood. The floor of the *megaron* used to be covered in patterned squares. In the pantry (#9), and the magazines (#23) ,you can still see the broken remains of jars and *pithoi* cemented in the ground. Make sure not to miss the prize possession of the palace—the remarkably well-preserved ancient bathtub (#43). The beehive *tholos* tomb lies below the ruins; return to the entrance and follow the path (there's a sign) to the right. A good scholarly guide put out by the University of Cincinnati (350dr) is available at the entrance to the site. (Open Mon.-Sat. 8:45am-3pm, Sun. 9:30am-2:30pm. Admission 200dr, students 100dr. You can visit the *tholos* without purchasing a ticket to the site.)

A few kilometers from Nestor's Palace is **Chora,** a village that is quite forgettable except for its superb **archeological museum,** which contains many finds from the Palace of Nestor along with other Messenian and Mycenaean artifacts. In the second room, note the fragments of frescoes that used to line the palace walls, as well as some Linear B tablets. (Open Mon. and Wed.-Sat., 8:45am-3pm, Sun. 9:30am-2:30pm.) To get to the museum, wait for the next bus plying the Pylos-Kyparissia route, or hitch. The museum lies 400m uphill from the square on Marinatou St. The bus station is on Carl Blegen (the excavator) St. 1 block to the right of the town square (facing the museum). Buses travel to Pylos Monday through Saturday at 6:20am, 8:10am, 9:15am, 1:20am and 5:15pm (35 min., 115dr). On Sunday, service begins at 9:15am. Farther north, the town of **Marathopolis** offers miles of rocky beach, a couple of little pensions, lots of secluded freelance camping, and a superb chance to get away from other tourists. Near Filiatra, a beautiful eleventh-century church can be found in the town of **Christiano.**

In **Kiparissia,** a coastal town guarded by a mountain fortress, the train tracks come to an end, and buses continue north or south. A stop here, in fact, is almost inevitable, in whichever direction you're headed. **Buses** leave for Athens via Argos and Corinth (daily at 8:45am and 3pm, 5 hr., 1620dr), Patras (2 per day, 2½ hr., 740dr), Chora (6 per day, 120dr) and Pylos (3 per day, 1 hr., 330dr). **Trains** go to Athens (9 per day, 8 hr., 800dr); four of these go via Tripolis (2½ hr., 360dr), and five go via Pirgos (1½ hr., 210dr) and Patras (3½ hr., 475dr). Kalamata is serviced five times daily (2 hr., 230dr). To get to Kiparissia's fortress, walk 1 block from the train station; at the five-way intersection take the second sharpest right.

**Pension Trifolia,** 25 Martiou St., just past the restaurants, charges 900dr per person for humble but well-kept doubles and triples. Rooms to let are available opposite the police station, but Trifolia is much more comfortable. Just off Kalanzakos Sq., the town's main meeting place, are two restaurants which both claim to be the true **Nynio's Restaurant** cited in the French *Guide du Routard.* Both serve specially created delicacies at low prices (*dolmadhes* 340dr).

Elsewhere on the square is the **bank** (open Mon.-Thurs. 8am-2pm, Fri. 8am-1:30pm) and the **post office** (open Mon.-Fri. 7am-4pm); the **OTE** is just off the uphill right corner (open Mon.-Fri. 7:30am-10pm), and the **police** (tel. 226 00 or 220 39) are farther up the street (open 24 hours). Kiparissia's **telephone code** is 0761; the **postal code** is 24500.

# *Methoni* Μεθώνη

Methoni's fortress, which seems suspended in the sea, must be the Camelot (or at least the Disneyland) of Greece. In harmony with its bastion, the small town is lined with trees blossoming red flowers and tiled houses with antique metal balconies. It's no wonder that Agamemnon offered Methoni to Achilles as a gift to soothe

the sulking warrior. Cervantes spent a prison term here under Turkish guard spinning romances. Of course, Methoni has been discovered by tourists, but even they cannot upset the fortress' innate grace.

The town's two main streets form a "Y" at the billiard hall where the Pylos-Finikoundas buses stop (ask inside for bus information). Shops are on the upper fork to the right, the beach and fortress are down to the left. As you walk toward the beach down the left fork you will see a sign for the **police** (tel. 312 03), which are on a side street off the main road. Back on the left fork, past the sign for the police, you'll find the **post office** (open Mon.-Fri. 7:30am-2:15pm) and the **OTE** (open Mon.-Fri. 7:30am-3:10pm). Down the right fork 40m is the **National Bank of Greece** (open Mon.-Thurs. 8am-2pm, Fri. 8am-1:30pm). Three buses per day go to Kalamata (1½ hr., 330dr) via Pylos (15 min., 60dr). Three buses per day also travel to Finikoundas (½ hr., 70dr). Two doors down from the OTE, buses leave for Athens via Pylos, Kiparissia, Pirgos, and Patras. Ask at the police station or the billiard hall for information about Patras-Athens buses. The phone number of the **medical clinic** is 314 56. Methoni's **telephone code** is 0723; the **postal code** 24006.

The **Hotel Iladision** (tel. 312 25) has beautiful clean rooms in an old house next to the fortress moat, about 2 blocks up from the beach. Ask for one with a balcony. (Singles 1200dr. Doubles 1600dr. Triples 2500dr. Showers included.) In town, **Hotel Dionysus** (tel. 313 17), down the right fork almost to its end, has airy rooms with balconies. (Singles 1300dr. Doubles 2000dr, with private bath 2500dr.) In Methoni, *dhomatia* cost between 1415-1740dr for singles, 1830-2570dr for doubles, and 2640-3070dr for triples. **Camping Methoni** (tel. 312 28) is crowded, but conveniently situated on the beach. (250dr per person. 250dr per tent.) At **Louis' restaurant**, about 100m down the right fork, not far from the National Bank, the creamy *mousaka* (300dr) melts in your mouth. (Open 9am-3:30pm and 6pm-1am.) On the beach on the fortress side, **Restaurant Rex**, under large, shady pine trees, serves very cheap food. (*Mousaka* and *pastitsio* 230dr each. Open 6:30am-4pm and 6pm-midnight.).

A visit to the southwest Peloponnese would not be complete without a trip to Methoni's **Venetian fortress**, a photogenic mini-city built in the thirteenth century. To enter the fortress you cross a bridge over the former moat, now overgrown with grass. At the clearing, you can climb up and walk along the wall that straddles the sea. Halfway around the circumference, you come to a small, enchanting tower—the **Bourzi**—sitting on its own island at sea and tethered to the mainland by a narrow walkway. You can walk out, clamber up the stairs at its center, and then come back and continue the circuit. Beforehand, though, you may want to climb up into the building opposite Bourzi. Look out from the little room for an incredible vista of Bourzi and the sea. Within the fortified walls is a large field and a church therein. Make sure to pop in, if for nothing else than to see the birds' nests in the corners of the ceiling and their inhabitants flying to and fro. (Fortress open Mon.-Sat. 8am-7pm, Sun. 8am-6pm. Free.)

For a bit of action, conduct your own sea battle in the paddle boats for rent from a restaurant on the beach (500dr per hr.); otherwise, join in the games of beach soccer played near the breakwaters, which consist of huge boulders interspersed with centuries-old cannons, still intact. The beach at Methoni is quite crowded, but not so beside the fortress.

# Finikoundas Φίνικούντας

The epidemic that metamorphosized tranquil, picturesque fishing villages to popular tourist beaches has infected Finikoundas. Halfway between Methoni and Koroni, Finikoundas certainly never needed a fortress, so there's not much to see here other than the beach, the sea, and some colorful caïques. For swimming, take the time to go to the significantly less-crowded cove beyond the rock jetty to the east. If you decide to stay, remember to change money in advance; Finikoundas still has no bank or post office. Buses travel three times per day to Kalamata (2 hr., 330dr) via Methoni (½ hr.) and Pylos (45 min.). Buses also go to Kalamata (at 7:30am and 4:30pm, 1½ hr., 360dr) by a faster, more direct route that passes through Harokopio where you can make connections to Koroni.

Accomodations have become more plentiful, but not more available in Finikoundas. Most of the restaurants either rent rooms or know of people who do. **Moudakis Restaurant** (tel. 712 24), to the right of the KMoil station (facing the water), has doubles for 2000dr. Because Finikoundas has no hotels, rooms often book in August. Places on streets away from the water are just slightly less expensive than those on the water. Rooms to let on the eastern end of the beach are most expensive for no discernible reason except that the buildings are newer. Finikoundas also boasts three campgrounds. **Camping Anemomylos** (tel. 713 60) is 1km west away from the town. (350dr per person. 250dr per tent.) **Camping Loutsa** (tel. 712 56) and **Camping Ammos** (tel. 712 62) are 2km east. (300-350dr per person. 200dr per tent.) For delectable *kalamari* (290dr) and a view of the fishing boats, go to the last *taverna* on the right side of the beach as you face the water. (Open 9-2am.)

# *Koroni* Κορώνη

Koroni is Methoni's twin to the east, the other half of what was once called the two eyes of Venice because its proud fortress surveyed all the waters beyond Methoni's reach. But the twins are hardly identical; Koroni is not as "cute" as Methoni. The disarray of its fortress is haunting and penetrating. Koroni is also larger and its profusion of old balconied houses with tile rooves impresses, as well as captivates. Besides affording an exhilarating view of the rocky coastline, the *kastro* has several underground rooms worth exploring. Since they are hard to find, ask a local to act as your guide. Notice the huge room with a pillar to which the Turks used to chain their prisoners. To reach the *kastro,* walk along the waterfront until it ends in a small plaza, just before the pier. Walk down Kambyses St. (at the bottom righthand corner of the square facing the water) for 1 block, then turn left and follow the street up a long staircase to the stronghold. In the evening, sit on the pier and watch the gliding fishing boats use bright gas lamps to stun fish, which the fishers then spear with long tridents. To get to a great, secluded beach, after you enter the *kastro,* take a left past the two adjacent white houses, and then exit through a small gate. Find the path and descend to the beach below, where you can climb onto the large hunks of the fortress that have fallen into the sea. To get to the popular sandy and seaweedy **Zaga Beach,** just exit the *kastro* from the opposite side (you'll pass many churches) and continue downhill on the road.

**Buses** travel to and from Kalamata (up to 8 per day, 1½ hr., about 280dr), stopping at the small Demetrios Sq. near the church. (Since there's no official KTEL depot, ask at any cafe around the square for departure times.) In the same square, you'll find the **post office** (open Mon.-Fri. 7:30am-2:30pm) and a **bank** (open Mon.-Thurs. 8am-2pm, Fri. 8am-1:30pm). The **police** (tel. 224 22) are located at the left side of the waterfront (facing the water). For the **medical clinic** dial 225 02. Korini's **telephone code** is 0725.

Just off the square is the town's least expensive hotel, the **Diana** (tel. 223 12), with clean and wallpapered rooms. (Singles 1348dr. Doubles 1959dr. Triples 2697dr. Bargain.) The **Parthenon Restaurant,** across the street on the waterfront, and the grocery store around the corner also advertise rooms to let. (Doubles with bath 2446dr in high season. Bargain.) There are several less expensive rooms farther away from the water, especially along the street leading off the square toward the Jet Oil Station. Also try the rooms at the far side of the square on the *kastro* side of the waterfront, mostly on Ay. Kamvisi St. Or else try **Camping Koroni** (tel. 221 19), on the road to Finikoundas. This new campground has a kitchen as well as a swimming pool. (350dr per person. 250dr per tent.)

Unless you've sailed into the port, you've arrived via the road from Harokopis. The rooms on this road charge ridiculously high prices, as do the restaurants at the opposite end of the harbor. The **Parthenon Restaurant,** however, is centrally located and moderately priced. (*Mousaka* 300dr. Chicken 350dr.) But for really cheap food and a much quainter atmosphere try the tree-shaded *Taverna Manthra,* just past the police station, which serves huge portions and local wine. (Chicken 200dr. Veal 400dr. Open 8am-2pm and 4pm-midnight.)

# *Kalamata* Καλαμάτα

Life, they say, goes on after tragedy; witness the bounty of Kalamata and you might swear the shattering earthquake of 1986 never rocked the port. Yet if you leave the overflowing *agora* or the fish restaurants on the waterfront, you will sense the scar the earthquake has left on the city and the spirits of its inhabitants. Crumbling, vacated buildings share streets with modern, shatterproof structures erected by construction crews that work straight through the broiling midday and the sacred Greek siesta. Invariably, within the first minutes of conversations with any of the natives, they will mention the *seismo* (earthquake), relating stories of that fateful day—describing how houses fell on their heads and dropped them unconscious in the streets. They may tell you how they, along with 3000 others, live in trailers, hoping someday to rebuild their homes. The city's population has shrunk from 45,000 to 20,000; many have fled the city permanently fearing another earthquake.

Needless to say, there are few sights; the collections of the **Benaki Museum** and **Folk Art Museum** have been moved to Sparta for safe keeping until new earthquakeproof buildings are constructed. However, the seemingly indestructible **castle** still crowns a hill just above a wasteland of ruined houses. Built by the Franks in 1208, it was blown up by the Turks in 1685 and then restored by the Venetians a decade later. More recently, a new theater was built inside the walls to host performances in July and August. (Tickets 400-600dr.) You will see the castle on the promontory above the bus station. To get to the gates from Platia Martiou, walk up Ipapandis St., pass the church on the right side, and take your first left. While you're up there climb to the far edge of the castle to find the remains of Byzantine church; scamper on top for a great view. (Open July-Aug. 24 hours; Sept.-June 8am-dusk. Free.) As the museums are shut, you may want to stop in at 221 Faron St. (off the waterfront), where the **School of Fine Arts** of Kalamata sponsors well-displayed exhibits of artists from the Kalamata area and other parts of Greece. (Open daily 9am-1pm and 6-10pm.)

If Kalamata does not dazzle you with antiquities, it just might surprise you with modern anomalies, such as the **Levi's factory** and outlet store. (Walk to the right end of Navarino St. as you face the water and then walk inland toward the port—you can't miss it.) The shopping ruckus deserves a look, but great discounts and the opportunity to replenish a tired wardrobe might be an even more compelling attraction. (Open Mon., Wed., and Sat. 8am-1:30pm, Tues. and Thurs.-Fri. 8am-1:30pm and 6-9pm.) The **beach** at Kalamata is crowded and littered, but it improves as you go east. The water is supposedly the warmest in Greece. At night, head either to Platia Georgiou and its busy cafes, or to the real nightlife on the jam-packed waterfront. Cafes crowd the right side (facing the water), restaurants line the left, and some bumper cars can be found in between.

In any case, if you're traveling in the southern Peloponnese, chances are you'll be passing through; from Kalamata, you can travel to Pylos and Koroni to the west, Mystra to the east, or the Mani to the southeast.

## *Orientation and Practical Information*

Kalamata's busiest areas form an "L." The bus station and outdoor market are at the top. The vertical stem is formed by the main drag, **Aristomenous Street,** which runs through the spacious **Platia Georgiou,** site of most of the city's amenities. At the corner of the "L" is the Levis' factory and the port; **Navarinou Street** runs along the waterfront and forms the horizontal leg.

Kalamata is a large, spread-out city (the bus station is 3km from the beach) but fortunately, blessed with an efficient public transportation system. Bus #1 (40dr anywhere along the line) will take you everywhere you want to go. You can catch buses anywhere you see a blue *stassis* sign, they begin their route at Platia 23 Martiou. To get there, follow Artemidos St. three bridges from the bus station and 3 blocks to the left. If you cross the third bridge off Artemidos and turn right, you will be on **Aristomenous St.**

**Currency Exchange: National Bank of Greece,** on Aristomenous St., off the northern end of Platia Georgiou. Open Mon.-Thurs. 8am-2pm, Fri. 8am-1:30pm.

**Post Office:** 4 Iatropolou St., which cuts through the southern end of Platia Georgiou. Open Mon.-Fri. 7:30am-3pm. Also on the waterfront at the port past the Levi's factory. Open Mon.-Fri. 7:30am-2:30pm. **Postal code:** 24100.

**OTE:** Platia Georgiou, opposite the National Bank. Open 24 hours. **Telephone code:** 0721.

**Airport:** Flights to Athens daily at 8:55pm (20 min., 4500dr; ticket bought 21 days in advance 10% discount, children 2250dr.) **Olympic Airways,** 17 Sideromikou Stathmou St. (tel. 223 76), just before train station. Open 7am-9pm. Runs a shuttle to the airport (80dr) leaving from its office 1 hr. 10 min. before each flight.

**Train station:** Tel. 239 04, at the end of Sideromikou Stathmou St. (literally Railroad Station St.). Turn right on Frantzi St. and the end of Platia Georgiou, and walk a few blocks. Cheaper and slower than buses. To Athens (5 per day 6:45am-10:50pm, 7 hr., 980dr) via Tripoli (2½ hr., 370dr), Argos (4 hr., 580dr), Corinth (5¼ hr., 730dr); via Kiparissia (1¾ hr., 230dr), Pirgos (3¼ hr., 390dr), Patras (5½ hr., 680dr), and Corinth (8 hr.).

**Buses:** Tel. 228 51. To: Athens (Mon.-Fri. 11 per day 5:30am-10:30pm; Sat.-Sun. 8 per day 5:30am-10:30pm, 5 hr., 1470dr) via Megalopolis (300dr); Tripolis (460dr); Argos (770dr); and Corinth (1060dr). To Patras (Mon.-Sat. at 8:30am and 2pm., 4 hr., 1220dr) via Pirgos (2 hr., 690dr). Also to: Sparta (at 9:15am and 2:30pm, 300dr) via Artemisia; Mavromati (at 5:50am and 2:15pm, 165dr); and Koroni (Mon.-Fri. 9 per day 5am-6:30pm, Sat. 8 per day 5am-6:10pm, Sun. 7 per day, 6am-6:30pm, 1½ hr., 280dr). Buses also to Pylos (Mon.-Fri. 9 per day 5am-7:45pm, Sat. 8 per day 5am-7:45pm, Sun. 7 per day 6:15am-7:45pm, 1¼ hr., 280dr) and the 5am, 1pm and 5:30pm buses continue on to Methoni (1½ hr., 330dr) and Finikoundas (360dr, 2 hr.). On Sun., only the 5:30pm bus connects to Methoni and Finikoundas. For Areopolis and Gythion, take the 5:15am, 7:30am, or 1pm bus to Itilo (2 hr., 410dr), where you'll change buses immediately. The bus from Itilo goes to Areopolis (15 min., 70dr) and then Gythion (another ½ hr.). There is also a 5:30pm bus to Itilo but with no connection to Areopolis until the next day. Inter-city buses depart from the bus depot near Platia 23 Martiou.

**Moped Rental: Moto World,** Bironos St. (tel. 813 83), near the harbor. Steep, but you probably won't find cheaper in Kalamata. Vespas 2000dr for 24 hours. Open daily 8am-2pm and 5am-9pm.

**Road Help:** Tel. 104 or 821 66

**Pharmacy:** Many along Aristomenous St. Most open daily 8am-2pm; Tues. and Thurs.-Fri. also 5:30-9pm.

**Hospital:** Athinou St. (tel. 235 61). **First Aid** (tel. 255 55).

**Port Police:** Tel. 222 18.

**Tourist Police:** Tel. 225 55, in a wooden complex across the train station's tracks. English spoken. Open daily 8am-2pm.

**Police:** Aristomenous St. (tel. 100), a bit past Platia Georgiou heading toward the water. Call here in case of emergency.

## Accommodations, Camping, and Food

The earthquake has made slim pickin's of places to stay, but more so of tourists, so you should not have much trouble finding a room.

**Hotel Nevada,** 9 Santa Rosa (tel. 824 29). Take bus #1 and get off as soon as it turns left along the water. Funky, with haphazard posters and a profusion of potted plants. Woman who runs it thinks you understand a Greek statement if she throws in a few words English. Singles 1500dr. Doubles 2200dr. Triples 3000dr.

**Avra,** 10 Santa Rosa (tel. 827 59), across the street. Management a little crusty, but clean rooms—not a bad second choice. Doubles 2330dr.

**Hotel George,** 5 Dagre St., (tel. 272 25). As you exit train station, turn right—it's on your left. Very clean, airy rooms; convenient to the train and Platia Georgiou. Doubles 2000dr.

**Camping: Camping Patista** (tel. 295 25), 2km east along the water. Take bus #1 to the end and walk 2 blocks. 270dr per person. 210dr per tent. More luxurious and farther east are **Camping Elite** (tel. 273 68; 450dr per person and tent) and **Camping Sea and Sun** (tel. 413 14). Take bus #1 with "Motel" printed in the front window (8am-10pm every hr.).

Before leaving town, be sure to sample the famous Kalamata olives and figs. Go to the new **market,** just across the bridge from the bus station. The mouth-watering collection of edibles will set your stomach growling within minutes and satisfy even the most finicky picnicker. The most entertaining and delicious places for sit-down meals are the string of restaurants along the waterfront. Try **Psaropoula** for outstanding **kalamari.** (300dr.) (Open 11am-3:30pm and 7pm-1am.)

## Near Kalamata

The road from Koroni to Kalamata hugs the eastern coast of the Messenian peninsula. Between Harokopi and the coastal town of **Petalidio** is a long string of sandy beaches. Petalidio features two good **campgrounds—Zervas Beach** (tel. 310 09) and **Eros Beach** (tel. 312 09)—one of the loveliest in Messenia.

If you're searching for more antiquities, take the bus to **Mavromati** (Mon.-Sat.), where you'll find the well-preserved remains of ancient Messene (not the same as modern Messini) on Mt. Ithomi. The Messenians continually fought off Spartan incursions into the area and succeeded as long as they controlled the acropolis (Mt. Ithomi). The most striking part of the site is the fourth-century B.C.E. **walls,** which epitomize the period's defensive architecture. An **agora, theater,** and **Temple to Artemis** also remain. If you continue up the road, you'll come to the fallen doorpost of the monstrous **Arcadian Gate,** designed by Epaminondas, the architect of Megalopolis to the north. Also nearby is the sixteenth-century **Monastery of the Vourkano,** with some outstanding frescoes. The Doric columns at the foundations of the church indicate that the structure rests upon the ruins of Ithomi, a sanctuary dedicated to Zeus. The only difficulty with the trip is the timing. The bus takes you to the site (look for the sign at the end of the village of Mavromati), continues up to the hamlet of Petralona, and then returns past the site to Kalamata. If you get off while the bus is in Petralona, you'll have about 15 minutes to explore the site before the bus returns. The alternative is to catch the morning bus there and return on the post-Petralona leg of the afternoon bus. Hitching on these deserted roads is very difficult.

# From Kalamata to Areopolis

Just south of Kalamata, the bus to Areopolis winds through the spectacular and surprisingly lush Taygetus mountains, which soar to 2630m at their highest point. But behind olive-coated hillsides threaten the ominous gray peaks of the Mani—forbidding yet alluring. The first major bus stop comes at the coastal village of **Kardamili.** One glimpse of the somber stone houses, the elegant spire of the Church of St. Spyridon, and the sparkling waterfront overlooking a tiny wooded island, and you will want to stay. The town is a popular beach resort, so there are many rooms to let. Expect to pay about 1500dr for doubles. In the area, there are two **campgrounds—Camping Melitsina** and **Camping Kalogria.** For meals, try **Taverna Kiki,** on the waterfront below the village. The family-run restaurant serves inexpensive food, and regular customers are treated to a complimentary bottle of wine on the night of their last meal. There is a **post office** on the main street. Near Kardamili are several coves with pebble beaches that open onto the gorgeous clear blue sea. About 5km south is the small port of **Agios Nikolaos,** which also has rooms to rent and one hotel, the **Mani** (tel. 942 38). The beaches here are not as nice as those in Kardamili. If you have a car or want to hitch, visit the little villages of Platsa, Nomitsis, Thalomes, and Lagada south of Agios Nikolaos, all of which have Byzantine churches with frescoes and carvings. Hitching down the coastal road is quite good in tourist season.

If you're bound for Areopolis, change buses in the village of **Itilo** immediately upon arrival—the bus leaves promptly. This peaceful town is focused on the **Monastery of Dekoulo,** decorated with frescoes, and the seventeenth-century Turkish fortress that rests circumspectly on a neighboring hill. The entertainment quarter consists of two cafes off the small square and a reasonably priced restaurant. The bus continues 3 km down magnificently situated **Neon Itilo.** At the heart of an enormous natural bay encircled by monumental barren mountains, the town's white pebble beach is ideal for swimming. You can **freelance camp** along the right side of the cove (facing the water) or stay at the **Hotel Itilo** (tel. 513 00). From Neon Itilo, the road winds uphill again, affording a view of **Limani,** the old harbor of Areopolis, with its shimmering water and sprinkling of fishing boats. The tiny port is home to the Mavromichaeli **Castle of Potrombei.** The bus then continues to Areopolis.

# *Laconia* Λακωνία

In the tenth century B.C.E., a tribe of Doric warriors from the north invaded the southwest Peloponnese, driving out its Mycenaean inhabitants and summarily executing any stragglers. These Laconians were renowned for their brevity of wit and rhetoric: hence, our word "laconic." The ancient Laconian qualities are still manifest throughout the region, especially in its central peninsula, Mani, with its barren landscape and spare, fierce tower houses. Although Laconia boasts three of the most popular sites in the Peloponnese—Mani's Pirgos Dirou caves, Sparta's nearby Byzantine ruins of Mystra, and Monemvassia's "rock"—the untrammeled land in between remains suitably laconic.

# *Sparta* Σπάρτη

*So many years deserted stood the valley-hills*
*That in the year of Sparta northwards rise aloft,*
*Behind Taygetus; whence, as yet a nimble brook . .*

*Behind there in the mountain-dells a daring breed*
*Have settled, pressing forth from the Cimmerian*
*Night,*
*And there have built a fortress inaccessible*
*Whence land and people now they harry, as they*
*please . . .*
                              *—Goethe, Faust*

The Spartans are usually portrayed as the bad guys of the classical world—crude, severe, savage hawks always provoking and pestering the democratic doves of civilized Athens. In reality, the Athenians weren't sweethearts, but Sparta's reputation for brutal, no-nonsense militarism is largely deserved. Around 700 B.C.E., after Sparta barely subdued a revolt of the Messenians, the leader Lycurgus instituted wide-ranging reforms that turned Sparta into a war machine. For the next 350 years, it dominated the entire central Peloponnese with its invincible armies and austere society. Yet outside of war, it made very little contribution to Greek history. Philosophy, poetry, art, and architecture never flourished here. Suspicious of Athenian expansion and jealous of Athenian success, Sparta attacked its rival, beginning the 28-year Peloponnesian War. After triumphing in 404 B.C.E., it emerged the supreme military power in the Hellenic world. The Spartans relished their strength (they didn't even bother to build protective walls around their city) as much as they despised all forms of weakness (small or deformed children were left to die in nearby ravines). Ultimately, only the combined efforts of earthquakes, depopulation, and the united resistance of its neighbors could break Sparta's hegemony.

A young Spartan's training for the life of war began early—before speech, before birth, even before conception. Lycurgus believed that two fit parents produced stronger offspring, so he ordered all Spartan women to undergo rigorous physical training, just like men. He separated newlyweds, permitting only an occasional procreational tryst, on the grounds that the heightened desire of the parents would help produce more robust children. What's more, by a famous Lycurgean law, the young wife of a tired old man could choose a suitable young male to service her and to provide the old man with healthy children.

If they survived the first few years, boys began a severe regimen of training under the auspices of a Spartan citizen, who would often used whips to increase obedience. The young were forced to walk barefoot to toughen their feet and wore only a simple piece of clothing in winter and summer to inure them to drastic weather changes. Moreover, since fatty foods were said to stunt growth, and delicacies to harm health, young Spartans ate the simplest foods, and were never given enough. (Harvard University, in an attempt to model itself after the ancient Greek ideal, has instituted a similar program in its own dining halls.) Hunger made them steal food, and theft developed the resourcefulness and survival skills that came in handy during war. In fact, those who were caught received severe punishments—for their ineptitude rather than their dishonesty.

After childhood, the routine intensified. The Spartans believed adolescence was the period of life most fraught with danger, when young men had to be guarded against new temptations. Forced to look down at the ground virtually every waking minute, the adolescents grew so modest that Xenophon wrote, "You would be more likely to hear a stone statue speak than them, more likely to catch a wandering glance from a bronze figure." And in adulthood, too, much was forbidden. For example, pederasty and other homosexual diversions, accepted among other Greek men, were off-limits. Lycurgus also instituted competitions designed to make friends scuffle and beat one another so they wouldn't become soft, and he permitted men to drink only to quench thirst. In fact, Spartans were forbidden to sleep where they ate so that they welcomed sobriety, which enabled them to walk home in the dark without stumbling drunkenly. The pursuit of wealth was roundly criticized, and thorough searches discouraged misers, capitalists, and their ilk. Aged men alone were eligible for seats in the esteemed council of government.

Ironically, modern Sparta, with its nightly roar of mopeds and its monotonous, modern architecture, far from resembling a fascist boot camp, actually looks like an imitation of modern Athens. As Thucydides predicted, "Suppose the city of Sparta to be deserted and nothing left but the temples and the ground plan, distant ages would be very unwilling to believe that its power was equal to its fame." History has proved him right.

## Orientation and Practical Information

Sparta's two main streets, palm-lined **Paleologou** and **Lykourgou,** laced with orange and lime trees, intersect in the center of town. To get to the center from the bus station, walk left on Paleologou for 2 blocks. The town square is 1 block to the right of the intersection, and all of the necessary amenities are nearby on these two streets. The ruins are on the northern edge of town, behind you at the end of Paleologou St. Appropriately, Sparta is laid out in a no-nonsense grid.

**Currency Exchange:** The **National Bank** is on the corner of Dioskouron and Paleologou St., 3 blocks down from the intersection. Open Mon.-Thurs. 8am-2pm, Fri. 8am-1:30pm.

**Post Office:** Past the OTE on Kleombrotou St., which is 1 block up from the intersection off Paleologou St. Open Mon.-Fri. 7:30am-3pm. **Postal code:** 23100.

**OTE:** Kleombrotou St. Open daily 6am-midnight. **Telephone code:** 0731.

**Bus Station:** Vrasidou St. (tel. 264 41), off Paleologou, 2 blocks from the intersection. Buses run to Athens (9 per day, 5 hr., 1290dr), stopping in Argos (2½ hr., 620dr) and Corinth (4 hr., 880dr). To Neapolis (Mon.-Sat. 3 per day, 2 on Sun., 4 hr., 780dr) and Monemvassia (Mon.-Sat. 3 per day, 2 on Sun., 3 hr., 560dr; changes buses in Molai). To Pirgos Dirou and the caves (at 9am, 2¼ hr., 440dr) via Areopolis (2 hr., 380dr); changes buses in Gythion). To Kalamata (at 9am and 2:30pm, 2 hr., 325dr; change in Artemisia), Tripolis (7:50am-2:45pm 4 per day, 1¼ hr., 320dr), Gerolimenas (at noon, 3 hr., 570dr), and Gythion (5 per day, last at 9:30pm, 1 hr., 240dr). For buses to Mystra, there is a separate bus stop near the town square on the corner of Lykourgou and Agisilaos. From the main intersection, walk past the main square on Lykourgou; 2 blocks ahead on the left is a sign marked **Mystra Bus Station.** A complete timetable is listed at the main bus station. Eleven buses make the 10-15 min. trip Mon.-Sat. 6:50am-8:40pm, usually with immediate returns. On Sun., 5 buses go to Mystra 9am-8:40pm. Check at the ticket booth at the site for exact departure times.

**Hospital:** Tel. 286 71 or 286 72.

**Police:** 8 Hilonos St. (tel. 287 01 or 262 29). From the intersection, turn left on Lykourgou St. going away from the square—the police are on a sidestreet to the right just past the museum. Signs saying "tourist police" point the way, although there are no more tourist police. Ask for the map of town, but no English is spoken.

## Accommodations, Camping, and Food

To get to most of the budget hotels from the bus station, turn left onto Paleologou, take the second right onto Lykourgou Street, and continue past the large square on your left. Take a right on the side street marked "Mystra bus station," the first block after the square, and you'll see the **Hotel Sparti** on Agisilaos St. (tel. 285 91), which has spartan and dark but clean rooms with sinks. (Midnight curfew. Doubles 1800dr. Triples 2600dr. No singles but a double for 1 is 1000-1200dr. Showers included.) On the corner of Lykourgou and Agisilaos (entrance on Lykourgou), you'll see the slightly nicer, but equally somber **Hotel Anessis** (tel. 210 88; midnight curfew; singles 1300dr; doubles 2000dr; triples 2500dr; showers included). Another block up you'll reach the **Hotel Cyprus** (tel. 265 90), just off Lykourgou at 66 Leonidou St. The friendly manager, Harry Starogionis, speaks English fluently and knows what foreign visitors want from a hotel. Refrigerator, maps, common area and table, bus schedules, and free luggage storage. (Open March 15-Nov. 15. Doubles 2000dr. Triples 2600dr. Quads 3000dr. No singles—but a double room for 1 is 1300-1600dr; often discounts to foreign travelers. One free hot shower.) On Paleologou, just past Lykourgou, is the **Hotel Panellinion** (tel. 280 31). The owner speaks English fluently and her clean rooms have balconies on the square or Paleologou St. which is unfortunately a racket at night. (Singles 1800dr. Doubles 2400dr.) Five blocks north on Paleologou is the well-kept **Hotel Cecil** (tel. 249 80), on the corner of Thermopilon St. This pleasant hotel is more peaceful since it's several blocks from the craziness of the square. The rooms are spotless. (Singles 1200dr. Doubles 1900dr, with bath 2200dr. Triples 1500dr.) About 3km away on the road to Mystra is **Camping Mystra** (tel. 227 24), which has a pool. (380dr per person. 190dr per tent.) Also near Mystra is the new **Camping Castle View.** To get to either campground, take the regular Mystra bus and ask the conductor to let you off at the appropriate camping site.

Sparta is overpopulated with cafes and most of its few restaurants serve standard (and expensive) fast food. If you want to eat in the main square try **Dhiethnes,** at the far right of the square (facing the row of cafes), for good, reasonably priced food. (Spaghetti 200dr. *Mousaka* 330dr. Open for lunch and dinner only.) On the corner of Lykourgou and Paleologou St., **Averof** serves similar, inexpensive fare. (Tasty chicken with potatoes 350dr. Spaghetti with meat sauce 250dr. Open lunch and dinner.) Also, **I Kali Kardia,** 39 Agisilaos St., opposite Hotel Sparti, offers friendly service, generous portions, daily specials, and reasonable prices. (Stuffed tomatoes 230dr. Open noon-4pm and 6:30-11pm.) The next right finds you on a street lined with fruit and vegetable stands. After dinner, don't miss the *volta* in the *platia*. Evening strollers, all-dressed-up-with-no-place-to-go, pace and, after a moment's pause, retrace their steps.

If you want to leave Sparta for the evening, share a cab to the village of **Parolis,** 2km from Mystra. There you can sit in a *taverna* and watch the nearby waterfalls.

## Sights

By comparison with the other great cities of ancient Greece, little remains of ancient Sparta. Its austere and disciplined code of life scorned unnecessary luxuries of any sort, including elaborate buildings. Its modest construction prompted Thucydides to remark "their city is not regularly built, and has no splendid temples or public buildings: It rather resembles a straggling village and would make a poor show." Hence, modern visitors are apt to be disappointed if they expect to find a southern counterpart to the Parthenon. The ruins consist of the outlines of an ancient theater one of the largest of the ancient Greec (2nd in size only to the theater at Megalopolis) and some fragments of the acropolis (1km from the main square at the northern edge of the modern city). At the north end of Paleogolou St. stands an enourmous **statue of Leonidas,** the famous warrior and king of the Spartans. A short walk east on the banks of the Eurotas River brings you to the **sanctuary of Artemis Orthia.** Spartan youths were called upon to prove their courage here by unflinchingly enduring a public flogging. Enter the **local museum** through its beautiful park from Lykourgou St. (on the opposite side of Paleologou as the square). You'll see the spooky votive masks used in ritual dances at the sanctuary of Artemis Orthia and the famous head and shoulders of the statue of Leonidas (490-480 B.C.E.), with its blind eyes, dandruff, and strange smirking face that inspired the large monument on Paleologou St. (Museum open Mon. and Wed.-Sat. 8:45am-3pm, Sun. 9:30am-2:30pm. Admission 200dr, students 100dr.) Two blocks farther east from the museum is the **public swimming pool.** (Open July-Aug.)

# Mystra Μυστράς

About 6km west of Sparta is Mystra, an extraordinary site, regarded by some as the finest in Greece. As you approach Mystra from Sparta, you see creased mountains unexpectedly shoot out of the plain. Intermittently, through the screen of olives, you can make out the domed churches and carcasses of palaces and castles tethered on the side of a mountain and at its apex. Mystra is considered the last hurrah of Byzantium. At its zenith, in the late fourteenth century, Mystra was a humming intellectual center. Many thinkers, unhappy under Europe's repressive feudalism, came to this affluent town to set up collegia. Philosophers and students wandered through the intricate network of paths that weaves the city together—and now makes sight-seeing confusing. Try tracing a path among several key sights on the three tiers that correspond to the sectors for the commoners, the nobility, and the royalty (in ascending order, naturally). Since the entrance through the main gate lands you in the middle of the lower tier, you may want to see the churches on one side, continue up through the palaces to the castle, and then loop around to the churches on the other side. In the lower tier to your right, don't miss the **Metropolis** with its museum and the two churches of the monastery of **Vrontokhion,** St. Theodori, and the frescoes of the Aphentiko (or Hodegetria). On the left side of the tier is the **Pantanassa,** with its beautifully ornamented facade and many frescoes. Its buildings still house a convent, so don't be surprised if a sister swathed in black beckons to you mysteriously: She's just inviting you to admire (and perhaps purchase) some of the handicrafts made by the nuns. Finally, at the extreme left of the Lower Tier, the **Church of Perivleptos** is perhaps Mystra's most stunning relic—every inch of the church is covered with exquisitely detailed paintings. Above the door you can see a fresco of Doubting Thomas, in the opposite vault a depiction of the Nativity in a craggy mountain crevice, and on the dome the figure of the Pantoknato. (In the Upper Town, you will see the skeletal remains of the **Palace of the Despots**—enormous facades punctuated with empty windows, which hardly recall their former grandeur. The **Church of Agia Sofia** was the palace chapel. Finally, you should clamber up to the **Kastro**, the fortress which was the first building in Mystra (as the town developed downward), built by the crusader William Villehardouin in 1249 C.E. The castle commands an exceptional view: on one side soar mountains fronted by thickly forested hills, and on the other stretches the olive-covered Spartan plain. It's not quite as far away as it looks—you can get there in about an hour if you walk directly up from the main gate. (Site open Mon.-Sat. 8am-7pm, Sun. 8am-6pm. Admission 400dr, students 200dr.)

You can enter either by the fortress gate (higher up, it allows you to ascend to the castle quickly, then saunter down) or the main gate (near the bottom of the hill and close to most of the interesting sights). There are waterfountains or taps just inside the entrance through the main gate, at the Metropolis and at Pantanassa, but it's a good idea to bring your own water along to combat the murderous heat. Also wear tough shoes; many of the paths are rocky and slippery. Appropriate dress is preferred, even though the dress code is not really enforced. In the church of the Pantanassa, there are make-shift skirts just inside the entrance. You will enjoy Mystra more with the aid of a small guidebook. There is a lot to see; even a cursory inspection of the site, including the long climb to the summit, requires at least three hours.

If you come on the **bus** from Sparta, don't get off until the last stop—the site is about 1½ km beyond the town of Mystra; follow the road around the bend after getting off. For the schedule of returning buses, check at the ticket booth at the entrance. If you still have your backpack, you can leave it here next to the ticket desk. At the bus stop, which is next to a Xenia hotel, there is a restaurant with expensive cold drinks, postcards, and restrooms.

# Gythion Γύθειο

By bus, Gythion may be a half-hour away from Areopolis, the throbbing heart of Mani, but in appearance and spirit it is centuries away. In contrast to the bleak and fortified Mani, bright Gythion opens up to the stranger in a friendly, not frightened, embrace. Probably the liveliest port town in the Peloponnese, Gythion is a popular embarkation point for those traveling on to Crete. Connected to the harbor by a concrete causeway is the pine-covered tiny island of **Marathonisi** where Paris consummated his love for Helen, triggering the hooplah known as the Trojan War. From a distance, you can see the spiky tips of the **Pirgos ton Grigorakidhon** protruding from the pines. Stroll over and look closely at the beautiful, restored tower—Gythion's lone reminder of the Mani. By the summer of 1989, a folk museum should be housed in the tower. At the tip of the island, a white lighthouse stands guard; the rocks on the port side provide decent, sheltered swimming.

## Orientation and Practical Information

The bus will deposit you at the far left side of the waterfront (facing the water), near the town's amenities and cheaper stores. In the middle of the waterfront near the quay is the small **Mavromichaeli Square.** The harbor road continues on farther to the right, where it eventually meets the causeway to Marathonisi.

**Currency Exchange:** The national bank is just beyond the bus stop toward the water. Open Mon.-Thurs. 8am-2pm, Fri. 8am-1:30pm.

**Post Office:** Ermou St. Continue along Herakles St. 2 blocks past the OTE until you reach Ermou St., then turn left and walk ¾ block. Open Mon.-Fri. 7:30am-2:15pm. **Postal code:** 23200.

**OTE:** At the corner of Herakles and Kapsali St. As you exit the bus station to your right you'll see Herakles St.; turn right and walk 1 block. Open Mon.-Fri. 7:30am-9pm. **Telephone code:** 0733.

**Ferries:** Depart from the quay to the right of Mavromichaeli Sq. The *F/B Ionian* leaves twice per week (Mon. at midnight, Thurs. at 11pm) for Kapsali on Kythera (3 hr., 401dr), Antikythera, and Kastelli on Crete (7 hr., 1609dr). It also leaves Fri. at 3pm for Agia Pelagia on Kythera (2 hr., 401dr), Neapolis (4 hr., 694dr), Monemvassia (6 hr., 984dr), and Piraeus (13 hr., 2000dr).

**Buses:** Depart from cafe at the left side of the waterfront. At the fork in the road, bear left onto Vasileos Pavlou St. for 1 block—it's on the right. To Athens (6 per day, 6 hr. 1530dr) via Sparta (1 hr., 240dr). To Kalamata via Sparta (at 7:30am and 12:15pm) or via Itilo (6am and 1:15pm). To Gerolimenas (at 1:15pm and 7:30pm, 1 hr., 330dr) via Areopolis (½ hr., 145dr). Also to the caves and Pirgos Dirou at 10:15am (1 hr.), returning at 1:30pm or 4pm. To Monemvasia (at 8:45am and 2:30pm, 2 hr., 430dr). Buses also go to the campgrounds (including Meltemi, Gythion Beach, and Mani) south of town (4 per day, last at 7:30pm, 55dr). To get to Kronos camping, take the same bus to the last stop and walk 4km.

**Moped Rental: Antoni's,** on the left end of the waterfront; bear left at the fork. Mopeds 1100dr with 100km, 10dr each additional km. **Moto Mani** (tel. 228 53), on the right side of the waterfront before the port police. Helmets 50dr. Mopeds 1200dr with 100 free km, 10dr per km thereafter. Rental runs from 9am-8pm. Open daily 9am-1:30pm, and 5-8pm.

**Health Clinic:** Tel. 220 01, 02, or 03, along the right side of the waterfront.

**Port police** (tel. 222 62) located at the right side of the waterfront, past Mavromichaeli Square, are a befuddled bunch. For more coherent information and tickets, go to the **Theodore V. Rozakis Travel Agency** (tel. 222 29 or 222 07), on the waterfront near the square. Open Mon.-Sat. 9am-1pm and 5-10pm.

**Police:** Tel. 222 71 and 221 00, on the waterfront, 500m before the bus station . Eager to help; a few words of Greek will go a long way.

## Accommodations, Camping, and Food

Hotels in Gythion are generally expensive, so consider staying in *dhomatia* or at one of the four nearby campgrounds. **Xenia Karlafti's** (tel. 227 19) is in a house enclosed by a red railing, at the right-side of the waterfront (as you face the water), near the port police. The spanking clean, spacious rooms have been decorated with a homey, loving touch, and they fill fast. (Doubles 1500dr. Triples 2000dr. Quads 2500dr. Showers included.) Don't confuse her rooms with the other Karlafti rooms behind the church on Tzannibei Gregoraki St. Those owners are known to shuffle people around the rooms without notifying them. If Xenia's rooms are full, walk toward the causeway and climb up the flight of stairs to your right. You will see a white house with baby blue shutters in front of you (no sign) with cool and clean rooms that belong to the **Kavalioti's** (tel. 225 61). (Triples 2000-2200dr. Quads 2500dr.) Across the street is a small white house with gray trim where you'll find the cozy, traditional and spotless rooms of Vasiliki **Yiannari** (tel. 241 98). The single has a balcony with an amazing view over Gythion. (Single 1000dr. Double 2000dr.) More centrally located is **Aktaio** (tel. 224 08), along the waterfront between the bus station and the square. Some of the gloomy rooms in this old building have balconies with great sea views. (Singles 1500dr. Doubles 2000dr. Triples 2500dr.) A posher option is **Koutsouris** (tel. 223 21), in a renovated old house with an outside garden. To get there, walk up Gregoraki St. from the square and turn into the street to the right of the first church—it's at the end on the left. Free breakfast, use of the two kitchens and refrigerators are included. (Double 2000dr. Downstair triples 2800dr. Upstair triple with private bath 3500dr.) People frequently freelance camp on Marathonisi despite the forbidding signs, or head out to the official campgrounds. The most luxurious are **Meltemi** (tel. 228 33; 450dr per person, 450dr per tent) and **Gytheio Beach Campgrounds** (tel. 225 22; 415dr per person; 290dr per tent). You can also try **Mani Beach** (tel. 234 50; 350dr per person; 290dr per tent) or the new **Kronos** campground (tel. 241 24; 350dr per person; 250dr per tent). The campgrounds are south of town and, except for Kronos, accessible directly by bus (see Practical Information above).

The restaurants along the waterfront and the grocery stores around the main square charge exorbitant prices. The extra charges added onto the basic food bill total over 20%—legally. Compared to similar seafood places in northern Europe, these prices are not so bad, but in Greece, they're shocking. But don't worry—you won't starve. **Kostas** restaurant, near the bus station, along the left side of the waterfront (as you face the water) and across from the public beach, serves scrumptious, fresh, and cheap food. Chicken, a side order of *fasolakia* (string beans), and a glass of wine cost only 290dr. The most reasonably-priced restaurant in the square is the one in the left corner as you face the water with the green and red chairs. For a tasty snack pick up a *tiganita* (80dr; fried dough eaten with cheese on top) from the little shop on Herakles St., between the bus station and the OTE. The locals shop at the **supermarkets** along Vassileos Georgiou St. As you walk along the waterfront toward the bus staion bear left at the fork and continue to Vassileos Georgiou. There is a *laiki agora* (fruit and produce market) every Tuesday and Friday morning between Herakles and Archaia Theatrou St.

## Sights

To get to the ancient **theater,** walk down Herakles St. From the bus station, turn left on Ermou St. and then right onto Archain Theatrou St. to the street's end and then bear left around an army outpost. This beautifully preserved structure lies unnoticed by many locals and undiscovered by tourists. The **museum,** is presently in a state of flux. Until the new museum opens in the summer of 1990, you can inspect the modest collection of local finds in the *apothiki* (storage space), in the alley across from the Laryssion Hotel. (Open roughly Mon.-Fri. 8am-1:30pm. Free.) **Paliatz-oures** (junk) **antique shop** (tel. 229 44), on the waterfront next to the Hotel Pantheon, is the last such store left in the entire Peloponnese, selling old Greek farming tools, household implements and other items. The good-natured owner Costas Vrettos will gladly show you how to use the ingenious wooden hand-protectors that accompany the sickles in his shop. (Open daily 11am-1pm and 7-10pm.) There is a small littered **public beach** (50dr) on the left end of the waterfront, but the best beaches are south of Gythion on the coast between Mavrovouni and Skoutari. You may also want to go to the beach north of town with a large ship (an intercepted drug-runner from Cyprus) abandoned on shore; you can even swim inside. Just ask for the beach with the *karavi* (ship) and someone will direct you.

# Mani Μάνη

Mani is a minimalist's dream. Its strip of inhabited, cranky land circles the immense cinnamon-brown Taygetus and is circumscribed by the flat, seemingly limitless pellucid sea. Mani's fields spawn rocks instead of figs, and olive trees tenaciously grip the land. Mani's inhabitants seem to be just another of the stubborn, tough plants that cling to its soil. They trace their ancestry back to the Spartans; after that city's downfall, many residents fled south to Mani rather than relinquish their freedom. The ferocity with which they resisted foreign rule accounts for the name of "Maniotes" (from the Greek *mania* or fury). This independent ardor continued in modern times.

The Turks found this scrubby middle peninsula of the southern Peloponnese was the one region they couldn't conquer; the Nazis also encountered fierce resistance when they attempted to occupy the area. But the Maniots had practiced for foreign aggressions through generations of civil wars. Vicious blood feuds wracked this harsh land ever since the fourteenth century until this century, consuming entire villages. These feuds sprang up among neighboring clans as a result of trespasses to property or assaults upon women, although their origins were eventually forgotten as ambush followed on the heels of ambush in never-ending cycles.

As vigorously as they defended their autonomy, Maniots staved off the advances of Christianity. Well into the ninth century, they remained a last bastion of ancient

Greek civilization. When the Maniots finally succumbed to Christian conversion, their religious symbols and customs maintained thinly disguised roots in pagan devotion: St. Demetrios stood in for Demeter, and the prophet Ilias (Elijah) for the sun god Helios. Today, the countryside is littered with beautiful, if simple, Byzantine churches—crude stone constructions with barrel vaults, primitive frescoes, and marble lintels—that were built between the ninth and twelfth centuries. The trouble began later when the Mani began to fill with refugees from the medieval European invasions. Hills once empty were punctuated with new settlements, and scattered stones were gathered and marched into fortified towers. After the family vendettas began, expectant mothers prayed for boys, whom they nicknamed "guns" to be welcomed into the family arsenal.

Even today, Mani contributes a disproportionate number of men to the armed forces. But Mani's legacy of violence and repression remains. The region's first school was not opened until 1830, and the culture still disparages education. One hears stories of ambitious teenagers studying covertly in cavernous dungeons against a father's will. The culture that preferred male offspring remains adamantly patriarchal.

Most foreign travelers find the Mani strangely fascinating. Just as their ancestors held out against foreign attack, Mani's residents have balked at tourism. But every year, Mani becomes more accessible to visitors. Although the eerie stillness of Mani will be ruffled by this alien invasion, interest in the area has a positive side too—preservation of Mani's monuments. As you travel through the peninsula, you will see workers renovating the old stone towers so they can be used as summer homes or guest houses. Yet, not so long ago, most of Mani's towers and churches were crumbling, ignored, and forgotten.

To see Mani properly, you must rent a moped in Areopolis or Gythion, or latch onto a group of tourists traveling by car. If you opt for travel by bus, remember that any afternoon stop you make generally commits you to a night's stay. As usual, you can catch the bus anywhere along the way at signs marked *stassis,* but the bus runs only on the western side of the peninsula, south to Gerolimenas, sometimes continuing on to Vathia and Tsikalia. It's worth your while to visit the eastern coast, which is even more spectacular.

## *Areopolis*

In *Mani,* Patrick Leigh Fermor describes a meeting he had in a bar with a craggy old Maniot, who told him that "deep Mani," the real Mani, begins in Areopolis. Yet for those interested in plunging into "deep Mani," Areopolis is more of a transition; the appealing village of inhabited stone towers, unruffled by the modern section of town, is at once the most representative of Mani architecture and the least indicative of its spirit—believe it or not, sleepy Areopolis is one of the livliest towns around. In spring and autumn, this clifftop village attracts artists, who come to draw inspiration from the scenery and the silence. Summer brings tourists to Areopolis for a quick drink or a night's stay en route to the Glyfatha Lake Caves to the south.

Four **buses** (tel. 512 29) per day make the two-hour trip from Kalamata to Itilo with connections to Areopolis. Buses from Areopolis travel to Kalamata (470dr) leave three times a day, the last departing at 2:50pm. Buses leave from Areopolis for Gythion (4 per day, 8am-6pm, ½ hr., 145dr). Buses leave for the Glyfatha Lake Caves near Pirgos Dirou at 10am and 11am, with returns at 1:30pm and 4pm (65dr). Hitching between the caves and Areopolis should be no problem since the caves are one of the most visited sites in the Peloponnese. Buses also depart for Gerolimenas (at 2 and 8pm, ½ hr., 135dr, stopping in Pirgos Dirou). On Monday, Wednesday, and Friday, buses continue on to Vathia and on Tuesday, Thursday and Saturday they continue on to Tsikalia; make sure to verify which buses will be continuing on.

The helpful **police** (tel. 512 09) are down a little street that runs off the square on the side opposite the bus station. Just to the right of the main square, on Kapetan Matapa St., you'll find the **post office** (open Mon.-Fri. 7:30am-2pm) and the **OTE** (open Mon.-Fri. 7:30am-3pm). To get to the **bank,** walk down Kapetan Matapan St. and turn right at the first church; it's before the Hotel Mani. (Open Mon.-Fri. 9am-noon.) If you need to change traveler's checks when the bank is closed, the bus station will oblige you for about 10% less than the check's value. The phone number of the **hospital** isd 512 59. Areopolis's **telephone code** is 0733.

If you spend the here, definitely find a room in the old town. The **pension** (tel. 522 05), down Kapetan Matapan St. to the right of the bus station (you'll see a sign on the balcony) is run by a friendly, if spacy couple. The rooms are small and modest, but the roof has a funky view of the towers and the Taygetus. It's also a good place to hang out your laundry to dry. (Singles 1000dr. Doubles 1500dr. Showers included.)

Continuing down Kapetan Matapan St., you will see a second **rooms to rent** sign (tel. 513 01), which is located to the left, behind the church. These rooms are in a traditional old house with a barrel-vaulted ceiling, colorfully painted walls, and a treacherous staircase. Downstairs, the owner has an impressive antique gun collection. (Singles 100dr. Doubles 2000dr. Triples 3000dr. Bathrooms downstairs and outside.) If you've been waiting for that special splurge, spend the night in a renovated old tower house. In a tower that used to belong to the powerful Mavromichaeli family, the **Pension Loundas** (tel. 513 60), run by a trendy Athenian artist, is impeccably decorated with a mixture of elegant modern design and traditional Greek decor. Upstairs is an art studio you can use and a terrace with an intense view. (Doubles 6000dr. Triples 800dr. Private bath included. Breakfast 350dr). If you want modern accomodations, try the gleaming white marble **pension** (tel. 513 40) on the left side of the square as you leave the bus station. (Sparkling doubles with private bath 2500dr.) The **Hotel Mani** (tel. 512 69) is characterless but comfortable (with a TV lounge in the lobby) and they're prepared to chop official prices. (Singles 2100dr. Doubles 3000dr. Triples 3600dr.)

For dinner, try the **Kipo** restaurant with outside tables, Greek music on the radio, and cheap *souvlaki.* For lunch, eat at **Tsimova's,** the middle restaurant (of the three) with flowers outside (stuffed tomatoes 200dr). The best place for a drink is the bus station cafe. Sit inside and survey the random assortment of decorations—from a mounted collage of a fish head to a broken jukebox, from Christmas tinsel to faded posers warning against forest fires.

In the square, take a long look at the huge statue of Petros, one of the leaders of the Greek Revolution, with his huge curved sword and long barreled pistol. The Mavromichaelis family was one of the most powerful in Mani and still exerts influence in the Greek government.

## *Pirgos Dirou and Glyfatha Lake Cave*

The Glyfatha Cave, a subterranean river, is one of the most splendid natural attractions in Greece. Known also as Spilia Dirou or Pirgos Dirou (for the nearby town), the cave is a natural surprise, set in the middle of nowhere. Continuing south from Areopolis, you will soon reach the little village of Pirgos Dirou; although not nearly as interesting a town as Areopolis, you may want to stay here so you can be nearer the cave. For the cheapest accommodations, walk about 50m past the turn-off to the caves on the main road south to the green cafe **Ta Spilia** (tel. 522 57) with a yellow "rooms to let sign." The rooms are small, neat, and cozy and open onto a fantastic view. (Doubles 1236dr.) On the road to the cave, **To Panorama** (tel. 522 80) offers the closest rooms to the caves (¾ km away). The rooms are clean, if boring but the oceanside view is tremendous. (Doubles 2571dr. Triples 3071dr. Private baths included.) In town, right at the turn-off to the caves, you'll find a **post office.** (Open Mon.-Fri. 7:30am-2:30pm.) Load up on cold drinks and delicious sweet bread at **Baker's Supermarket,** farther along the road toward the caves. (Open 8am-10pm.)

If you're coming on the bus from Areopolis, remember not to get off in town unless you want to stock up on lunch provisions. The caves are 4km away, so you can also easily hitch or walk (downhill). Once at the caves, you'll find a bureaucratic operation in rugged Mani. Everyone gasps when they hear the fixed ticket price of 750dr, but once inside the refreshingly cool, marvelous caves, most grievances vanish entirely.

In August, the caves are flooded—with tourists—so expect to wait a long time. The many eight-person rowboats do their best to shuttle people in and out as fast as possible. But don't worry, the half-hour tour will seem incredibly long—you'll keep marveling at the size of this cave. (Caves open June-Sept. daily 8am-5pm; Oct.-May 8am-3pm.) If busloads of tourists have invaded, don't come after 4pm—you won't get in. (For information, call 522 22 or 522 23.)

Ticket safely in hand, walk down the hill. Turn left at the hairpin turn and you'll see the entrance to the caves ahead, next to the snack bar. The serial number of your ticket is your entrance number, which will be called in Greek when it's your turn to enter; listen carefully, and ask if you have doubts—you won't get another chance. On your right is a busy rocky beach, where you can unwind before or after your visit. Down here you will also find clean **public toilets** and an overpriced cafeteria.

The *fasaria* (hassle) dissolves as soon as the skipper propels the boat through water, first by grabbing a stalactite for push-off and thereafter, by pushing against the formations with a wooden paddle. His explanations will be given in Greek, but you will be able to tune him out completely as you watch forests of candle-like creamy white and rose stalagmites that jump out of the dark spring water below and stalactites that freeze seemingly in mid-fall from the cavern's ceiling. Floating lamps illuminate the cave, casting an eerire glow on the spectacle. When the boat docks, your trip is not yet over; you'll walk 400m to the exit through another stalagmite and stalagcite cave for a closer look.

## South of Pirgos Dirou

Moving south of the caves, Mani sheds its tourist-brochure gloss and returns to its desolate aesthetic. You now enter the Mani of bandits and blood feuds, where tower houses huddle, practically camouflaged in the rocky terrain. Note the white stones knitting up the sides like zippers and the tiny deep-set windows also outlined in a lighter stone. Mani's Byzantine barrel-vaulted churches also complement the landscape with their powerful simplicity. Just 2km from Pirgos Dirou, you will see a turn-off for **Harouda** and the church of **Taxiarchis,** which lies another 2km away. This church, decorated with blue and green ceramic plates and intricately patterned masonry, is situated in a transcendentally calm olive grove; climb to the church terrace for a view. Returning to the main road you will soon see a sign for **Drialos,** site of a beautific double-arched church. Continuing on this road running parallel to the main road, you will reach a series of hillside villages, including **Vamvaka** and **Mina,** each with tower houses and small churches. You can rejoin the main road by going downhill at any of a number of the extremely rocky junctures. Off the main road, on the sea, lies **Mezapos** with its two remarkable swimming coves. The one to the right is peppered with brightly colored fishing boats and water-polo playing children; the cove to the left boasts a larger pebble beach. Unfortunately, the town's residents are not too vigilant about collecting their garbage, so keep your gaze seaward. On your way south to Gerolimenas, you may want to pause at **Kita** just to admire the profusion of tower houses. Continuing south, you will eventually hit water at the craggy port of **Yerolimenas** ("old port"). On the left side of the harbor, a mountain towers forebodingly. Pirates used this port as their home base, and left it with the local priest's blessing and prayers for a profitable expedition.

Although there is not a whole lot to do in Yerolimenas, you might want to spend the night here so you can "explore" the beautiful beaches to the southeast. If you don't mind bedding down with a rock slab, you can camp on the southern side of the harbor in the shadow of a great cliff. There are two hotel-restaurants here; one has cheaper rooms, the other cheaper food. The former, the **Hotel-Restaurant Akrotainaritis** (tel. 542 05), at the left side of the harbor (facing water), has spacious, clean rooms with old floorboards. (Singles 1860dr. Doubles 2300dr.) The **Hotel**

**Akroyiali** (tel. 542 04), is more luxurious, with private baths and balconies and a wonderful view of the harbor. (Doubles 2500. Triples 3000dr.) The restaurant here, however, is moderately priced and serves tasty, fresh food. (*Mousaka* 300dr, Greek salad 150dr.) The **bus station** is located at the restaurant of the first hotel; inquire here about bus schedules. Two buses leave daily for Athens via Areopolis (160dr) and Gython at 6:45am and 5pm. There is no bank, but the **post office** will change traveler's checks. (Open Mon.-Fri. 7:30am-2:15pm, but expect it to open an hour late.) The **police** (tel. 54 240) are located at the far right side of the waterfront, on the road that branches off the one leading to Vathia.

Buses continue to Vathia from Yerolimenas on Monday, Wednesday, and Friday, but you should have no trouble hitching. On the way, you'll pass through **Alika**, where a few modern buildings line the road. Its deserted towers populate the hillsides above.

As you approach **Vathia** from a distance, its deserted towers suddenly appear crowning a diminutive green hill amidst huge barren mountains. Vathia is as photogenic up close; walk through its once impregnable fortresses, now fast crumbling fossils. Only 11 people live here today. The GNTO, however, is trying to revive the town by importing tourists to stay in the ten tower houses it has restored with tasteful traditional rooms. (Rooms slightly more expensive than the Areopolis's Tower Hotel because a meal is included; call the Tower Hotel for information—there are no phones in Vathia.) Already Vathia's moribund stillness is ruffled by visitors passing through; come early if you can, since this isn't a place where you want a lot of company.

Just before Vathia, there is a good swimming cove, and right before the turn-off to Porto Kagio are three particularly enticing adjoining coves. The main road suddenly winds down to **Porto Kagio** and its pebble beach (not as nice as the beaches you have already passed). Here you will find a *taverna* to satisfy your grumbling stomach. A path leads to the lighthouse at the end of Cape Matapan, the southernmost point on the continent after Gibraltar.

## *Mani's East Coast*

To visit Mani's beautiful and less-touristed east coast, either head to Kotronas by cutting through the mountains on the road from Areopolis and then work south, or continue north from Matapan. If you opt for the latter, backtrack to Alika and take the road that leads to **Tsikkalia**. This town with its tribe of empty tower-houses and its handful of residents is ignored and perhaps as eery as Vathia once must have been before the GNTO started featuring it in color posters. **Lagia**, the next town you pass, is a two-cafe town. After Lagia you can divert from the main road to the fishing village of **Agios Kyprianos** with its small pebble beach and fish *taverna*. **Kokkala**, on the main road, though lacking the tower-house, is something of a metropolis on this quiet coast. Although Kokkala means "bones" in Greek, this town is far from Mani's spookiest. Among the few *tavernas*, mini-market, and cafes, Kokkala actually contains the run-of-the-mill clean **Pension Kokkola.** (Doubles with bath 3000dr.) Leaving Kokkala, you'll come to **Nifi.** The small pebble beach and the neighboring harbor with its *taverna* are quite nice, though not visible from the road. Rooms are available above a restaurant on the main road. (Clean, standard rooms 2000dr.) There are two cafes and a *taverna* here. Turning off the main road past Flomochori and descending 3km will bring you to **Kotronas,** a cheerful port town with a small beach, a wonderful place to stay if you linger on Mani's east coast. The town's **pension** (tel. 532 09) has flowers decking its patio and spectrographic rooms. (Doubles 1400dr.) This fishing village also offers a **post office** (open Mon.-Fri. 7:30am-2:15pm; currency exchange), as well as fish *tavernas*, cafes, and a supermarket.

# Monemvassia Μονεμβάσια

Monemvassia is an architectural marvel built on a rocky island that rises straight out of the sea, as high as it is wide. From the west, the island looks uninhabited, but the eastern side reveals sloping fortified walls and a staircase that climbs the sheer 350-meter promontory. At the top of the rock face are the ruins of a Byzantine city that was besieged by the Frankish armies for three long years before it finally fell in 1248. The only surviving structure is the thirteenth-century **Church of Agia Sofia**, modeled after the famous monastery at Daphni near Athens. Some of the original frescoes that once covered the entire interior of the church are still in remarkably good condition.

Passed around among the Turks, the Vatican, and Venice after being conquered by the Franks, Monemvassia has a mottled history. In the sixteenth century, the Venetians built most of the fortifications that remain, including the *kastro* (citadel) at the mountain's summit. The inhabited part of the old city lies at the base of the huge rock, amid more ruins. With its weathered stone houses and narrow, winding passageways, the well-preserved medieval village is alluring. As this antique town is a magnet for Greek tourists, it can become unpleasantly crowded on summer weekends.

A narrow causeway connects the island to the mainland and the modern town of Monemvassia, which has hotels, restaurants, and gift shops, and the sponges that make up all the business from the tourist traffic. Consequently, the medieval village has retained its original character. Only its small main street is filled with souvenir shops, trendy cafes, and restaurants—the rest of town is peaceful.

## Orientation and Practical Information

In the modern town, **23 Iouliou Street** is the principal thoroughfare and runs along the waterfront straight up to the bridge that leads to the island. The **bus station** (tel. 610 00) is on this street. Buses travel to Sparta (2½ hr., 560dr), Tripolis (3½ hr., 875dr), and Athens (6½-7 hr., 1845dr) via Molai (½ hr., 145dr) at 7:15am and 2:30pm daily, also Monday through Friday at 8:30am. Buses also go to Sparta, Athens, and Gythion at 11:15am and 5:10pm daily (1½ hr., 430dr) with connections in Molai for Sparta and Athens. Two **ferries** per week travel from Monemvassia to Piraeus (Tues. at 6pm and Fri. anytime after 9pm, 7 hr., 1515dr); two boats per week go south to Neapolis (Mon. at 3:30pm and Thurs. at 2:30pm, 2 hr., 464dr), Kythera (3 hr., 897dr), Gythion (6 hr., 984dr), and Crete (13 hr., 1250dr). In summer, **hydrofoils** travel to Kythera (1 hr., 1800dr) and Neapolis on Monday, Tuesday, and Thursday at 12:30pm, Saturday at 11:30am. The Flying Dolphin hydrofoils also travel to Piraeus (4 hr., 3064dr) on Monday, Tuesday, and Thursday at 3:30pm, Friday, Saturday, and Sunday at 1:10pm; there is an additional trip on Saturday at 2:30pm. For information about all sailings contact the **port police** (tel. 612 66) along the waterfront in the modern town. You can buy ferry and hydrofoil tickets in Monemvassia at the **boat office** (tel. 614 19), next to the Mobil station on the island side of the bridge.

In the modern town on Spartis St., off 23 Iouliou St., you'll find the **National Bank** (open Mon.-Fri. 8:30am-2pm), and next door, the **post office** (open Mon.-Fri. 7:30am-2pm). On **28 Octovriou Street,** which runs off 23 Iouliou St. just past the bus station, you'll find the **police station** (tel. 612 10) on the left and the **OTE** (open Mon.-Fri. 7:30am-3:10pm), uphill to the right. For the **doctor,** dial 612 04, and for the **hospital,** 223 74. Monemvassia's **postal code** is 23070; its **telephone code** is 07320.

## Accommodations, Camping, and Food

There are three ways to stay in Monemvassia. The first is simply to camp. The top plateau of the island is covered with thistles and thorn bushes, which make sleeping, even in a sleeping bag, rather uncomfortable. Near the walls, however, there is some soft ground. You can head to **Camping Paradise** (tel. 611 23), 3½ km along the water, and find a more relaxing spot to pitch your tent. (390dr per person. 250dr per tent.) The second option is to stay in the medieval village, which is not really an option as few budget travelers can afford this. So, by the third option you would stay in the modern town. On Spartis St., near the bank and the post office, the **Hotel Akrogiali** (tel. 612 02), with a sign bearing the owner's name, S. Sofos, is the cheapest. The rooms are reasonably tidy if plain. (Singles 1189dr. Doubles 1700dr.) The **Hotel Aktaion** (tel. 612 34), on 23 Iouliou St. near the causeway, is more expensive, but you'll get clean modern rooms with balconies overlooking the island, bug screens, and reading lamps over the beds. Single women should beware of the young man who runs the place. (Singles 1949dr. Doubles 2600dr. Triples with bath 3200dr.) Most of the *dhomatia* are on 23 Iouliou St. along the water, past the bus station as you head away from the island, and a couple are on 28 Octovriou St. Expect to pay about 1369-2571dr for doubles and 1910-3072dr for triples, depending on bathroom facilities.

The old town in Monemvassia bops with several funky cafes. Try **Angelos'** (the 2nd one after you enter the main gate). Enjoy fresh sqeezed orange juice (200dr), milk shakes, or a drink while sitting on traditional pillows and listening to classical music. You may also use one of the backgammon tables. (Open 9-3am.) For meals, try the **Kastro** restaurant at the island's base. On a windy day, you can watch the waves mauling the rocks. (Big portions. Spaghetti 280dr, small pizza 450dr; Open noon-4pm and 7:30pm-midnight.) In general, food in Monemvassia is not cheap. The price range in the old town is about the same as in the modern town, so you might as well opt for the former, more scenic, if more touristy, eating environment. Laid-back **Marianthi** next to a yellow mailbox, serves reasonably priced, tasty fare. (*Keftedes*) 280dr, chicken in tomato sauce 260dr.) Even if you don't have an evening drink or dinner in the old town, at least come for a nocturnal stroll. The small lighted streets are bewitching.

# *Kythera* Κύθηρα

> *Island of secret orgies none profess*
> *the august shade of Aphrodite plays*
> *like clouds of incense over your blue bays*
> *and weighs the heart with love and weariness.*
> —*Baudelaire*

Myth claims that the waters washing the shores of Kythera incubated Aphrodite. After blossoming full-grown and radiant from the wave's foamy envelope, the love goddess must have blessed her birthplace before reaching lofty Olympos. Lying below the shadow of the Peloponnese, Kythera is isolated from the other islands. Although nominally one of the Ionian islands, Kythera has slid under Piraeus' administration.

Recently, the GNTO decided to promote tourism on the island despite the reluctance of its inhabitants. (In a plebiscite in Potamos, only 1 person voted in favor of opening up the island to tourism.) Innovations, such as the new spiffy bilingual road signs, seem at most superficial changes. Nonetheless, treacherous roads, scarce accommodations, and the seclusion of the isle are not deterring the new-found tourists. For utter remoteness, go to the nearby island of **Antikythera.** The island was wired for electricity in 1987; the 60 inhabitants still await a restaurant.

Incidentally, if you hear Greek looking people babbling in English with an Australian accent, don't be surprised. Many Kytherians emigrated to Australia and now they and their families are re-discovering the island—returning permanently or just for the summer.

Another deterrent to prospective visitors is the inconvenient ferry service. Three boats per week leave Gythion for Kythera (Mon. at midnight, Thurs. at 11pm, Fri.

at 3pm, 3 hr., 401dr), and one boat makes the run from Crete (Fri. at 8am, 4hr.). From Neapolis, the *Laurentios* and the *Elaphonisos* both make three trips a day to the island, immediately returning to Neapolis (1 hr., 563dr). The *Ionian* travels from Kythera to Piraeus (Tues. at 4pm, Fri. at 6pm, 7hr., 2000dr) via Neapolis (680dr) and Monemvasia (2 hr., 900dr). The *Ionian* also sails to Gythion (Mon. at 7:45pm, Wed. at 6pm, 2 hr., 401dr) and Crete (Mon. at 3am and Wed. at 2am) from Kapsali. For information about the *Ionian*, check at the **boat agency** in Kapsali (tel. 311 31 or 312 03; on the left side of the waterfront as you face the water), and for information about the ferries to Neapolis, contact the boat agency in Agia Pelagia. (Tel. 332 98; open daily 7am-12:30pm and 4-8pm.) The **port police** (tel. 312 22 in Kapsali ; 332 80 in Agia Pelagia) can give you complete information about all sailings. **Flying Dolphin hydrofoils** whisk you from Piraeus to Kythera in a fraction of the time that a ferry would take, but they're also more expensive. One definite advantage of the hydrofoil is that it deposits you in Kythera in mid-afternoon (as opposed to the ferry which usually arrives at 2am or 3am). Hydrofoils travel to Kythera from Piraeus (Mon., Tues., and Thurs. at 8:45am, Sat. at 8:35am, 5¼ hr., 3900dr) via Spetses (3596dr), Monemvassia (2035dr), and other ports. These hydrofoils then turn around and return to Piraeus via Neapolis, Monemvassia, Porto Heli, Spetses, and other ports. Get tickets at the travel agency in Kythera or at the gift shop in the Hotel Kytheria at the dock in Agia Pelagia. **Olympic Airways** has daily flights to Athens at 10:20am, and additional flights on Monday, Wednesday, Friday, Saturday, and Sunday at 1:25pm (50 min., 4500dr). The Olympic Airways (tel. 333 62) office is in the square in Potamos just past the OTE and post office. (Open Mon.-Sat. 8am-3pm and Sun. 8am-2pm.) You can also buy tickets at the travel agency in Kythera. A taxi from Kythera to the airport should cost 800dr.

You will arrive in Kythera at either **Agia Pelagia,** in the north, or the much nicer southern port of **Kapsali.** The island's main road runs between these two towns, with smaller villages connected by subsidiary roads. Four kilometers uphill from Kapsali, just off the main road, is Kythera's capital, **Kythera** (or Chora), which sits beneath a well-preserved medieval castle. This delightful town establishes the color scheme for the rest of the island—white houses with blue trim and sprinkled with a harmonizing touch of custard yellow. In the town square, you'll find the national **bank** (open Mon.-Thurs. 8am-2pm, Fri. 8am-1:30pm), the **OTE** (open Mon.-Fri. 7:30am-3pm), and a helpful **travel agency** (tel. 313 90; open Mon.-Sat. 8am-1:30pm and 6-9pm, Sun. 8am-1:30pm). The **post office** is on the road that leads downhill out of the square. (Open Mon.-Fri. 7:30am-2:30pm.) Continuing down this road toward the castle, you'll reach the helpful **police** (tel. 312 06)—if you're desperately roomless, they'll call around and try to find one. Kythera's **telephone code** is 0735.

**Potamos,** to the north, 7 km from Kapsali, is the island's beehive, an attractive town of old houses laced with pink oleanders. The main square is home to the **post office** (open Mon.-Fri. 7:30am-2:15pm), the **OTE** (open Mon.-Fri. 7:30am-3:10pm), and the **bank.** (Open Mon.-Thurs. 8am-2pm, Fri. 8am-1:30pm and though unannounced, Sun. 8am-noon.) The **police** (tel. 332 22), are down a street across the square from the post office, right next to a church. There is also a **hospital** (tel. 332 03).

Transportation on the island is rather ad hoc. In the summer, a couple of buses per day zip from Agia Pelagia to Kapsali and back again. Schedules are scribbled in chalk (and in Greek script) on blackboards near the bus stops. If this does not take care of your needs, you can hitch: From Kapsali, go one street up from the waterfront. Getting rides from one end of the island to the other, however, can often be difficult. In any case, the best way to see the island is by motorbike. Try **Mike's Bikes** (tel. 314 61 or 311 01), just off the waterfront in Kapsali; his bikes are considerably cheaper than the competition. (Automatics 1200dr, with gears 1500dr; free gas.) The larger monopoly of **Panayiotis Rent** (tel. 310 04 or 314 61) with an outlet on the waterfront in Kapsali, as well as in the square in Kythera (open 8:30am-6pm) rents more expensive bikes (for a 1-person automatic 1200dr, 2-person automatic 1500dr, motorbike with gears 1700dr; 24-hour rental), as well as pedal boats (400dr

per hr.) and canoes (300dr per hr.), which you can use to reach the otherwise inaccessible cove adjecent to the jebmain beach at Kapsali.

If you came to Kythera in high season without reservations, it is unlikely you'll
find a room. In Kythera town, the situation is most dire—rooms are booked month
in advance. Try the **pension** (tel. 312 10 or 310 70) just before the post office; at
#10 ask for Pissis. (One single 1000dr. Doubles 1500dr; these are official rates, but
he'll probably charge more.) **Elessa Firou** (tel. 313 73) has a few ramshackle rooms
(doubles 1400dr)—you'll find her at the Taverna Ta Kithira. An alternative to Kythera is Livadi, 4 km north on the main road. **Eleni Fatsea** (tel. 310 24) has ordinary
rooms in a white building with brown trim, on the right as you enter the town. (Singles 1200dr. Doubles 1900dr.) She'll make room for you somehow but she's a bit
shifty, so set a price beforehand. Off the main road, the much more charming town
of Milopotamos has a **pension** (tel. 334 46) with peaceful, fastidiously-kept rooms
and a kitchen. (Doubles 1500dr.) The monasteries of **Myrtidia** (tel. 311 84), **Agia
Moni** and **Agia Elessa** also have a few rooms to let.

Sheltered in a conifer forest, a beautiful **campground** (and perhaps necessary) (tel.
315 80) lies 300m from Kapsali up the road to Kythera (200dr per person plus 200dr
per tent; open June 15-Sept. 15). Free-lance camping is also a possibility. If you
arrive by ferry in the middle of the night, stretch out on the beach and head for
the campground in the morning.

The best restaurant on the island is **Toxotis** in Livadi. Its outside tables are packed
every night with good reason. They prepare stupendous Greek food with a nouvelle
cuisine flair. Try the delicious *tyropitakia* (small cheese pies; 200dr) and the grilled
chicken (250dr). In Kythera, try **Zorba's** (chicken 230dr. Greek salad 150dr; dinner
only), located on the main street, downhill from the square. The happening disco
on the island is the open-air **Gone With the Wind.** Perched above Kapsali, it opens
on to a fantastic view of the port below. To get there turn off the main road between
Kythera and Kapsali at the sign for Kalamos. (300dr cover includes a free drink;
drinks after that 400-500dr.)

## Sights

Intrepid travelers braving poor roads and confusingly labeled paths will be fully
rewarded for their troubles; Kythera is studded with precious surprises, from chapels in caves to small cascades. Start your exploration with a climb to the castle in
Chora. The summit is sprinkled with the ruins of old churches and buildings, and
the vista over kapsali's double harbor is intoxicating. To get there, walk throught
the square, down the main street and through the arch. The **museum** is just outside
fo town, past the turn-off into Chora as the road heads to Livadi. The modest collection includes Mycenean finds from Paliopoli, Venetian stone shields from various
entrance ways, and some broken English tombstones. (Open Mon. and Wed.-Fri.
8:45am-3pm, Sun. 9:30am-2:30pm. Free.) Making your way through the cave of
**Agia Sofia Milopotamou** is an adventure unto itself. Before the tour begins, the
guide will give you a candle which will shed just enough light for you to have a
vague idea where to direct your next step. A few feet from the entrance to the cave
are the beautiful frescoes of this cave-church. The cave's namesake, Agia Sophia,
and her three daughters, Faith, Hope, and Charity are depicted on the left side of
the screen of frescoes. As you move through the slippery passages of the cave, often
crouching or climbing to its chambers, the guide will periodically illuminate walls
of stalactites and stalagmites with his flashlight. Note in particular the final room
with its stalagmite that resembles a lion sitting on top of an elephant. Let your imagination run wild—these cave drippings are polymorphic. (Open June 15-Sept. 30
Mon., Wed., Sat. 4-8pm. Admission with tour 250dr; double-check it with the police.) If you go to the square in Milopotamos at 4pm, the guide will lead you to
the cave on the partially paved road in your car or motorbike. If you arrive later,
follow the signs out of twon leading to the cave. For a much smaller, but perhaps
more transcendental cave, go to **Feloti**. Just past the turn off to Chora, toward
Livadi, take the first left onto a rough dirt road. When you reach the coast, park

your moped and follow the path to the left until yo see a little white steeple poking out of the rock; just in front of it is the entrance to the cave. Enjoy a drink of fresh water dripping from the cave's ceiling into the two metal basins below. There is good swimming off the rocks near the cave, and farther to the right is a small pebble beach.

The town of **Milopotamos** which you pass through on your way to the caves is a place to linger. Shaded by a huge plantain tree, from which dangle a cage full of small yellow birds, the town's square is amazingly peaceful—probably ideal for Zen meditation. The restaurant there (open lunch and dinner) serves delicious *bourakakia* (meat baked in *filo;* 270dr). Below the town is an unobtrusive waterfall blanketed by green trees. There are two paths down to the waterfall; the one on the twon side is a footpath with steps and the one on the opposite side is wide enough for cars and mopeds. Just ask in the square for the *Neraida* or the *cataractes* and someone will point the way.

**Fryiammos** beach is acclaimed by all as the superior beach on the island. Its inaccessibility accounts for its excellence. Lying on the southeast coast, it can only be reached by car or by motor-cross motorcycle. Or else, go to **Melidoni** on the southwest coast. When you are leaving Livadi turn left at the fork. Continue on this road until you reach Drimona. Enter the town and follow signs to Agios kosmas. Pass the church on the left and plunge down the very bad, sandy road. The cave below, however, is more than worth all the hassle. For a stupendous hike go to Milopotamos from Kythera and take the right-hand fork past the town. The road continues directly through another little village also called Milopotamos. In the main square across from a handicraft store, find the dirt road going west and follow the cliffs for 1½ hours to **Limionas** beach. The beautiful **Monastery Myrtidia** west of Kalokerines keeps pet peacocks and is well worth a visit. If you are in Kythera on Sunday, go to the Potamos open air fruit and vegetable market.

# CENTRAL GREECE

## Delphi Δελφοι

When Zeus wished to discover the world's center, he sent forth two eagles from the opposite ends of the earth. They touched beaks in Delphi, where the *omphalos,* or navel stone, still marks the exact spot of the rendez-vous. Throughout the ancient world, troubled or ambitious souls were drawn, as if by a centripetal force, to the Oracle of Apollo at Delphi. Seeking answers and solutions, the ancient Greeks sped to Apollo's oracle. The *Pythia* provided them with advice that was at once magical and profound, but also cryptic.

If modern Delphi is the center of anything, it's probably the tour-bus circuit. Delphi's terraced avenues and steep, stone-stair alleys may strain your tender calves, but turn around as you climb, and enjoy an epiphanic view of the surrounding mountains, the deeply incised valley carpeted with olive trees, and the port of Itea. During the day you'll have to put up with the unholy clamor of buses, tourists, and merchants; at night, however, you can await prophecy among the silent ruins and recover for a moment the magic of Delphi.

### Practical Information

**Buses** leave Athens for Delphi from the station (tel. 823 17) at 260 Liossion St. (8 per day, 3 hr., 920dr). Take city bus #024 from Omonia Sq. to the station, and buy your ticket at booth #1. In high season, you may have to badger the vendor into selling you a ticket an hour or so before the scheduled departure; otherwise, you'll get stuck in a ridiculously long line and may not get a seat at all. Also, note that often you must take the Amphissa bus, which stops at Delphi. A railpass will let you take the train to Levadia and the bus to Delphi from there (260dr). Coming from Patras, take the Thessaloniki bus to Itea (3 per day, 880dr) and transfer. Alternatively, take the Patras city bus to Rio, cross to Antirio on the ferry (60dr), and then take the bus to Navpaktos (½ hr., 60dr), where you can catch another bus for Delphi (4 per day, 650dr). Crossing from Patras to Athens via the north coast of the Gulf of Corinth, as opposed to the main Patras-Athens highway, is slightly more expensive and more time consuming, but altogether more rewarding.

For Athens, buses leave Delphi regularly (in summer 6 per day; fewer in off-season). To go from Delphi to Thessaloniki, take the bus to Amphissa (4 per day, ½ hr., 120dr), then the express bus to Thessaloniki from the Cafe-Bar Thanassis in Amphissa's main square (Sun.-Fri. 3 per day, 6 hr., 2000dr). You can go through Amphissa to get to Patras as well (2 per day from Cafe-Bar Thanassis, 2-3 hr., 650dr). Ten buses per day leave Delphi for Itea (½ hr., 110dr) and nine go to Arachova (20 min., 60dr). You can make a connection to Galaxidi in Itea. Two buses per day make the two-and-a-half-hour trip to Lamia and one goes to Volos.

Stop in at the **tourist office** (tel. 829 00) on the low road close to the bus station. The manager will help with buses, accommodations, etc. (Open Mon.-Sat. 8am-9pm, Sun. 10am-5pm.) At 45 Apollonos St. on the left, just up the hill from the bus station, is one of the friendliest **tourist police** offices in Greece (tel. 822 20; open daily 8am-10pm). On Pavlou St., the east-bound road below Apollonos, you'll find the **post office**, in the middle of the block on the right. (Open Mon.-Fri. 7:30am-2:30pm.) You can change money here or at the **bank,** across the street and 30m farther down. (Open in summer Mon.-Thurs. 8am-2pm and 4-8pm, Fri. 8am-1:30pm; in off-season Mon.-Thurs. 8am-2pm, Fri. 8am-1:30pm.) The **OTE** is on the same side of the street still farther to the east. (Open Mon.-Fri. 7:30am-10pm.) Delphi's **telephone code** is 0265; the **postal code** is 33054.

## Accommodations, Food, and Entertainment

The **IYHF youth hostel**, 29 Apollonos St. (tel. 822 68), at the crest of the hill, offers clean and cheap lodging. The hostel also has three first-class doubles which are a steal for the quality: private bath, sheets, blankets, comfortable wooden beds, and hot water all day after noon for only 1500dr. In the rest of the hostel, solar-heated water operates from 6-8pm only. (Open March-Nov. 11pm curfew. Beds 500dr. Roof 350dr. Sheets 60dr.) There are plenty of alternatives if you're willing to pay the difference. Most are on Pavlou St., the low road. Closest to the bus station is the **Hotel Athena** (tel. 822 39; doubles with excellent bathrooms 2100dr). **Hotel Stadion** (tel. 822 51) has pleasant rooms with private showers. (Singles 2700dr. Doubles 3600dr. Triples 4600dr. Breakfast 300dr.) The C-class **Hotel Pan** (tel. 822 94) is not much more expensive than these D-class hotels. (Singles 2000dr. Doubles 3000dr. Triples 3500dr.) On Filellinon St., **Odysseus's Pension** has rooms with a common bath. (Singles 1450dr. Doubles for 1900dr.) **Hotel Oracle** (tel. 823 26) has the cheapest, most comfortable rooms, equipped with double beds but no great view. (Doubles 1500dr.) Better alternatives to the hostel, however, are the **Delphi Campground** (tel. 289 44 or 823 63), with its pool, 3km from Delphi (250dr per tent, 350dr per person), and the lodgings in **Arachova**, a short bus ride east of Delphi (see Near Delphi). One kilometer from Delphi, **Apollo Camping** (tel. 827 62) is cheaper. (280dr per person. 170-380dr per tent. 220dr for electricity.)

Adjacent to the hostel, **Taverna Vakhos**, 31 Apollonos St., serves good food fast, for the lowest prices available at a decent sit-down restaurant in Delphi. (Greek salad 140dr. *Mousaka* 190dr. Complete meals 400-600dr.) Moreover, from its terrace, you get a view of Itea, Galaxidi, the Gulf, and a sunset as thrilling as the one from the hostel's roof. Farther downhill on Apollonos is the **Souvlaki Snack Bar.** (*Souvlaki* 70dr. Greek salad 120dr). The restaurant that doubles as the bus station is also good, but otherwise keep your distance from places on the low road.

Discos and pubs line the road to the bus station. Every year in June, the European Cultural Center of Delphi presents an **International Meeting of Ancient Greek Drama** in the Delphi Stadium. For 400dr, you might hear *Oedipus Rex* in Chinese, *Prometheus Bound* in Japanese, or other Greek classics in German and maybe even Greek.

## Sights

It was not the sword of any aggressor that first united Greece, but rather the occult power of the **Oracle of Delphi.** The isolated city-states of ancient Greece were bound together in their recognition of the supremacy of the gods, and it was through oracles such as Delphi that the deities expressed their wills to humankind.

Politically, Delphi was the supreme oracle: Its advice was sought regularly by leaders throughout the Mediterranean. Ancient tradition ascribed the laws of many Greek cities to the god, and whenever any Greek city won a battle, its leader would erect a dedicatory offering to the oracle. As a result, the entrance to the sanctuary contained monuments from all over Greece.

Anyone who has visited the temples at Cape Sounion or Vassae knows that the beauty of a temple's natural surroundings meant as much to the ancient Greeks as the beauty of the temple itself. The Delphic Oracle is no exception: It is situated near the foot of Mt. Parnassos, flanked by a towering cliff on one side and the 600-meter deep Pleistos ravine on the other. According to legend, a shepherd searching the area for one of his charges found the animal seized by a fit of hysteria. He, too, soon fell into a frenzy, and all who subsequently visited the spot were similarly affected. From these events, the ancient Greeks concluded that the gods had chosen this secluded mountain ledge as the site for a divine oracle.

Another legend claims that Apollo slew the earth-spirit that presided over the holy place, which had some association with the monster Python. Apollo became sole lord of Delphi and the earth-spirit served as a mouthpiece by speaking through an intermediary, an elderly woman known as the *Pythia,* who was seen only by specially-elected priests. She sat upon the *adyton,* the oracular tripod (believed also to have been the throne of Apollo), and gave her obscure responses, induced by means not now ascertainable. Consider the case of poor Croesus, the Lydian king of Sardis who was told that if he waged war on the Persians, he would destroy a great power; unfortunately, the great power he destroyed was his own.

The Delphic Oracle maintained its importance among Greeks from the seventh century B.C.E. until after the Christianization of the Roman Empire. Delphi's popularity even survived a great blunder—its recommendation that Athens surrender to the Persians in the late sixth century B.C.E. Wisely ignoring this advice, the Athenians led by Themistocles eventually defeated the Persians at Salamis (480 B.C.E.). Beginning with the Roman occupation in 146 B.C.E., Delphi was gradually robbed of many of its treasures, and the oracular cult was eventually banned in 399 C.E. by the Roman Emperor Theodosius the Great, who undertook to purge the world of pagan religions. The site was largely forgotten until French archeologists excavated it in the last century.

With a rich amalgam of temples, treasuries, and tributes to the gods and their holy representatives, the ruins have a national character like no other ancient site in Greece. The grounds are crowded with structures donated by the many city-states. The main body of structures, known collectively as the **Pythian Sanctuary,** lies 400m east of town on the road to Athens. To appreciate these treasures fully, consider purchasing the red, white, and black map of a first-century B.C.E. reconstruction of the site, available in the shops in town for 150dr. A guidebook should also help; the one by Basil Petrakos is good (700dr).

As you ascend the **Sacred Way,** the path that leads through the sanctuary, you will pass first the large **Spartan Monument,** built in commemoration of and appreciation for Sparta's victory over Athens in 404 B.C.E. Just beyond and also on the right is the semicircular **Monument of the Kings of Argos** of 365 B.C.E. Until it provoked Apollo's wrath, the island of Sifnos possessed several gold mines and provided the **Treasury of Sifnos,** the remains of which are to your left. The frieze that adorned this structure is now in the site's archeological museum. Also on the left, as the Sacred Way curves uphill, is the **Treasury of the Boeotians,** and just behind it, the **Treasury of Thebes.** Next, you'll notice the tastefully restored **Treasury of the Athenians.** Built in 490 B.C.E., after Athens' miraculous defeat of the Persians on the plain of Marathon, it stands in polished white marble with the support of two Doric columns. The *metopes* over the columns are reconstructions, but the originals, which depict Hercules' labors, are on exhibit in the museum. Beside and slightly above the Athenian Treasury is the **Council House,** office for those who administered the ancient site. The promontory that juts up beside you as you continue your ascent is the **Rock of Sibyl,** and beyond it stands the pedestal which once held—10m overhead—the **Sphinx of the Naxians,** an intriguing sight now inside the museum.

The **Sanctuary of Pythian Apollo,** proudly occupying the small plateau before you, dominates the sight. The structure burned in 548 B.C.E., but with gifts from all over the Greek world, was soon rebuilt. Bad luck struck again in 373 B.C.E., this time as an earthquake; what you see now are the remains of a second united effort at reconstruction. Not only was this Apollo's temple, it was also where the oracular priests would announce the verdicts of the *Pythia* to their anxious audiences. Maximizing the temple's dignified image, the huge walls were once inscribed with famous maxims of Greek philosophers—aphorisms like "Know Thyself" and "Nothing in Excess."

Overlooking the Sanctuary of Pythian Apollo and the treasuries is the well-preserved **Theater of Apollo.** At the apex of the site is the **Stadium.** This large arena sponsored the Pythian Games, Delphi's musical, and later, athletic competitions, held every eight years to celebrate Apollo's return from voluntary exile after killing the Python. (Site open in summer Mon.-Sat. 8am-6:45pm, Sun. 8am-5:45pm; in off-season Mon.-Fri. 9am-3:30pm. Admission 300dr, students 150dr.)

Be sure to visit Delphi's **Archeological Museum** (tel. 823 13), located just before the Pythian Sanctuary along the path from town. It contains at least two indisputable masterpieces of ancient Greek art: the frieze of the Siphnian Treasury and the Charioteer of Delphi. The former is housed in a room to the right of the entrance, along with the elegant winged Sphinx of the Naxians. With placid elegance, the bronze **Charioteer of Delphi** stands on the opposite side of the museum in its own room. (Open in summer Mon. and Wed.-Sat. 8am-7pm, Sun. 8am-6pm; in off-season Wed.-Mon. 9am-3pm. Admission 400dr, students 200dr.)

You can visit the unfenced ruins of the **Temple of Pronaia Athena,** on the right side of the road as you head away from town, about 180m past the main set of ruins. Commanding a spectacular panorama of the surrounding mountains, the three remaining Doric columns of the unusual, circular fourth-century **Tholos** of the sanctuary of Athena are the most elegant and most photographed of the ruins at Delphi. Although inferences from ancient texts have led scholars to conclude that the Tholos was an extremely important component of the Delphic complex, no one knows today exactly what function it served. Next to the Tholos lies the **Treasury of Marseilles;** this gift from France attests to the extent of the oracle's prestige. (Ruins open Mon.-Sat. 8am-8pm, Sun. 8am-7pm. Free.)

Heading back toward the main site, you will see on the right side of the road the **Castalian Spring.** If you drink from the crystal clear water before continuing on to the rest of the ruins, you'll be following the practice of ancient pilgrims, who cleansed themselves here both physically and spiritually before calling upon the oracle.

## Near Delphi

### Levadia

Pilgrims stopped at the **Oracle of Trophonios** on a cliff overlooking Levadia (ancient Lebadea) before approaching Delphi. Pausanias describes an elaborate preliminary ritual in which the pilgrims would drink of both Lethe and Mnemosyne waters in order to forget everything before Levadia but remember distinctly the experience in its grove. Afterwards, they were snatched underground and given revelations. In the fourteenth century, Frankish Crusaders built a castle over the site of the oracle, which remains the best-preserved medieval castle in the area.

From the bus station, walk up to the square and turn right onto Eleftheriou Venizelou. Go straight and turn right again at the end of the street. Cheap hotels are at your first right off Venizelou. The **Hotel Xenodoheion,** on your right, has rooms that are "dirt" cheap but roach-infested. Across the street, the **Hotel Erkinon** (tel. 282 27) is much better. (Singles 1000dr. Doubles 1500dr.) You may prefer to push on to Delphi or Athens for the night; buses to Athens leave every hour until 8pm (2 hr., 410dr). There are also 11 buses per day to Distomo (45 min., 205dr.) and one to Ossios Loukas (at 1:30pm, 1 hr., 280dr).

### Arachova

Ten kilometers east of Delphi, stacked onto the slopes below Mt. Parnassos, is the village of Arachova, where the pace is slow and relaxed—the perfect place to retire after dealing with the crowds of Delphi. Indeed, many Greeks seem to have retired to Arachova. Sitting in the little central plaza you'll find a legion of grandparents, many wrapped in Arachova's sensational handwoven shawls. The area makes its culinary mark with amber honey and *saganaki,* cheese dipped in flour and then fried.

Five **buses** per day run between Athens and Delphi, stopping in Arachova, while an additional eight make the run from Arachova to Delphi (70dr). Five buses per day go from Arachova to Itea (¾ hr., 200dr) and two to Galaxidi (¼ hr., 110dr). If you want to go from Arachova to Athens via Levadia, walk east to the square with the fountain (bus leaves daily at 5pm).

The **bus station** doubles as a cafe and is identifiable by its yellow "Cafe Bar" sign. While the main street where the bus lets you off has an array of tourist shops selling local woolens and handicrafts, up the hill you'll find a more tempting labyrinth of unspoiled alleyways. The best approach leads straight up the steps from the main square to the **Church of St. George** and then meanders down the side streets. Behind the church is a washstand supplied by a natural spring. You'll run into similar fountains all over town furnished by springs with healthful and refreshing water.

On the east side of town, straight down the main road, you'll find two adjacent hotels. For the price, the **Apollon** (tel. 314 27) may be one of the best accommodation values in the region; it's immaculate and comfortable, and the gracious manager (who speaks excellent English) will proudly prove this to you before you pull out your *drachmae*. (Singles 1450dr. Doubles 2000dr. Triples 2500dr. Breakfast 260dr.) Next door, the **Parnassos** (tel. 313 07), with comparable prices and a cozy lounge, runs a close second. (Singles 1600dr. Doubles 2000dr. Triples 2800dr.) Both will discount for stays of over two nights. The closest **campground** is just west of Delphi; be sure to bring something warm. The **Grill Room**, downstairs from the police station, has good fare, but for a treat, head east on the main road to the square with the fountain: The white *taverna* to the left of the fountain serves cheese omelettes with sausage for 250dr.

The **GNTO** in the square on the west end of town is primarily there for ski season. Next door, the **post office** also changes money. (Open Mon.-Fri. 7:30am-2:30pm.) Directly across the square from the post office is the **OTE**. (Open Mon.-Sat. 7:30am-3:10pm.) The **bank** is on the main street 50m west of the bus station. (Open Mon.-Fri. 9am-2pm.) Across from the bus station, on the second floor, are the **police** (tel. 313 33). Arachova's **telephone code** is 0267.

Apollo and the Muses now share their abode on **Mt. Parnassos** with ski bunnies. Parnassos (2700m) is one of the most accessible mountains. If you're interested in hiking up in summer, follow the road around to the northwest of Arachova to the Mt. Parnasse Ski Center (27km, an easy hitch). From the ski center it's a steep 2-kilometer climb up to the summit where vultures fly just overhead. At the summit is an open, very small (1.5m × 1.5m) cabin where you can spend the night, but be prepared for the cold. The ski season on Mt. Parnassos runs roughly from December 15 to March 15. There are 12 lifts, and tickets average 700dr per day; rentals are also 700dr per day. To stay in the area, try Delphi or Arachova, but you'll either have to pay 1500dr for the round-trip cab or hitch since the taxi lobby won't allow public buses to run to the ski center. Alternatively, you can take the ski bus that leaves Athens at 6am, arrives at Mt. Parnassos two and a half to three hours later, and returns to Athens at 4pm (1000dr round-trip). For information, contact the GNTO in Athens or call Delphi's information office (tel. 829 00).

## Itea

Fifteen winding kilometers southwest of Delphi, across a surreal wonderland of olive trees, lies the town of Itea. Half-constructed and hazy, it's a good place to come for a swim. The beach improves to the east (with the water on your right). You'll find outdoor showers, a modified boardwalk, and—for the curious—benches with graffitti to decode. Seven **buses** per day run from Delphi to Itea (6:20am-8pm, 25 min., 110dr). In Itea you'll find a **post office** along the waterfront on the same block as the bus station (open Mon.-Fri. 7:30am-2:30pm), and at the end of the exit block, a **bank** (open Mon.-Thurs. 8am-2pm, Fri. 8am-1:30pm). Itea's best—and almost only—cuisine is available at the outdoor restaurants on the water; bring a novel or two as their service is slow. A cleaner and less frequented beach than Itea's is **Kira Beach,** 2km from town. Walk, hitch, or take a local bus (1 hr., 50dr). Itea has the only motorbike rental shop in the Delphi area (1800dr per day).

## Galaxidi

The next noticeable town on the road to Amfissa is Galaxidi, nice for a rest from serious sightseeing. A shipping community from the first century B.C.E. until the War of Independence, it was demolished by the Turks. Its name combines *gala* (milk) and *xidhi* (vinegar) to represent the sweet and bitter experiences of a seaman's wife. Scanning the horizon, these women would pace well-worn balconies, waiting for their seamen. Many sailors took up shipbuilding—the town's main industry—which gulped down all the surrounding trees. Early in this century, replanting began and a Johnny Appleseed character would sit and watch with a shotgun to protect the young pines. The town's seafaring tradition continues. Most of the friendly have served in the navy and local men speak English.

There are two indications that this lovely town isn't a main stop for budget travelers: the stares your backpack will provoke, and the meager choice of accommodations. Instead, Galaxidi caters to those who tour Greece by yacht (visit the lovely pleasure-craft harbor) and those rich society drop-outs who own homes in town. By far the cheapest place to stay is **Galaxidi Camping** (tel. 415 30), 3km from town. (300dr per person. 210dr per tent. 10% lower for stays longer than 2 days). There are also plenty of beach spots especially beyond the pine forest. In town, at the end of the main street, Nik. Mama, is **Hotel Poseidon** (tel. 414 26), run by the ever-friendly and enthusiastic Costas. (Singles 1800dr. Doubles 2200dr. You should be able to knock off 400dr.) If you want to splurge, stay at the classy **Hotel Ganimede** (tel. 413 28), with a cool, pleasant cocktail garden graced by ruins and a fountain. The rooms are creatively decorated with interesting handicrafts. (Singles 2046dr. Doubles 3331dr.) At the end of Nik. Mama at the water, **Restaurant Alekos** has good food, but make sure to order your food hot (*zesto*) in summer—otherwise they'll automatically serve it cold. On the same road farther back in town is the **Elida Souvlaki Shop** (*souvlaki* 100dr). For drinks, try the **Pera Panta** disco bar on the waterfront strip beneath the forest.

For choice swimming, cross over to the forest side of the harbor and walk all the way around. Follow the road after it becomes dirt. Small islands float not far from shore and flooded caves overhang scant beaches. Rouse yourself from the beach to visit the **Museum of Galaxidi** (tel. 410 86). Make a left off Nik. Mama opposite the sweet shop, walk 2 blocks and then turn right. (Open Wed.-Sat. 10am-2pm. Sun. and holidays 10am-1pm. Free.) Nearby, the thirteenth-century **Monastery of Transfiguration** displays its 1000-year-old wood carvings. Many travelers continue on to **Navpaktos,** close to the mouth of the Gulf and to the ferry crossing for the Peloponnese at **Antiro.** The bus to Navpaktos runs out of Delphi (650dr) but stops in Galaxidi. If you want to spend the night, stay at the **Aegli** (tel. 272 71; singles 1000dr; doubles 1500dr). Getting to Patras takes a long time even when connections in Nafpaktos, Antirio, and Rio are smooth; allow four hours.

### Thermopylae

Eighty kilometers north of Delphi, the pass of Thermopylae once guarded the eastern flank of Athens against land attack from the north, an area always to be associated with the heroism of King Leonidas and his 300 Spartans. Herodotus claimed that Leonidas held off Xerxes' Persian army of over five million in 480 B.C.E., and even the more conservative modern estimates of 300,000 cannot detract from the courage of 300. The Athens-Volos highway traverses this once-strategic pass just before the turn-off to Lamia. The site, with an imposing statue of a fierce Leonidas casting a spear, requires imagination to conjure the great battle. The inscription reads, "Tell, O passerby when you reach Athens that here, heeding their call for aid, we remain."

# Distomo and Ossios Loukas Δίστωμο και Αγιος Λουκάς

Ossios Loukas is so hard to reach you'll be surprised any visitor has managed. This beautiful stone monastery 1700m above sea-level has splendid mosaics, which rival the mosaics at Daphni.

From Delphi, take the Amfissa-Levadia **bus** to the town of Distomo (45 min., 180dr), where at the same stop you can catch a bus to the turn-off to Ossios Loukas. From Levadia, the bus to Distomo takes only 30 minutes and 225dr. You can also take the bus to Kiriaki and tell them you are going to Ossios Loukas—they'll drop you off right at the turn-off (40 min., 275dr). It's a 2½-kilometer walk to the monastery from there. Any bus on the Delphi-Levadia-Athens road can let you off at the Distomo crossroads (*stavrodromo* in Greek). Hitching in this area is difficult since most of the traffic consists of big tour buses and tourists in rented cars who rarely pick up backpackers.

If you find yourself stranded in Distomo, check into the clean **Koutiaris Hotel** (tel. 222 68; doubles 1400dr). The **American Hotel,** up the road from the bus stop, smells like the door has not been opened in years. The only place to eat is a *souvlaki* joint called **Corner,** up the main road on the left (*souvlaki* 90dr). The **post office** is down the hill near the bus stop (open Mon.-Fri. 7:30am-2:30pm). The OTE is a few buildings down the road (open Mon.-Sat. 7:30am-3:10pm). Though Distomo may not be a choice spot to spend the night, it is a heroic town. During WWII, Distomian resistance fighters fled into the hills and dared to attack the occupying Germans. As many of the old men at the cafe remember, on June 10, 1944, the rebels shot a German commander. He staggered into the center of town, right across from what is now the bus stop, and ordered a general massacre. That night, German soldiers fired their guns in a 10-minute spree that killed 250 people—everyone in sight. This tragedy created a group of orphans who were subsequently sent to the U.S. Now, after growing up as Americans, some of those orphans have returned home to retire.

It is probably wisest to give **Ossios Loukas** a full day. The main building in the complex, the **Church of St. Luke,** is in fact dedicated not to the evangelist who wrote the third Gospel, but to a local hermit named Luke who managed to attain sainthood. The large narthex providing entrance to the tenth-century church is adorned with Byzantine mosaics—notably Doubting Thomas inserting his finger in Christ's wound, Christ washing the Apostles' feet, the Crucifixion, and the Resurrection. The original dome collapsed during an earthquake and was reconstructed with a fresco of Christ Pantocrator. This fresco sustained a few bullet holes during the Greek War of Independence in the nineteenth century, when Turkish soldiers shot into the eyes of the Christ image in an attempt to discourage the monks of the monastery from participating in the Greek resistance. The most beautiful mosaics that survived are tucked into the squinches that support the dome—the Nativity, Presentation at the Temple, and Baptism. The last, showing Christ standing in a cleft of rock covered by stylized ripples of water, is so similar in composition to such scenes in the Byzantine churches of Daphni and Sicily that it seems likely that the same group of artists traveled throughout the Mediterranean.

Although not so famous as the mosaics in the upper church, the eleventh-century frescoes that cover almost the entire interior of the **crypt** are every bit as beautiful. Most tourists bypass the crypt, since its entrance is on the side of the building and is not well-lit. Concealed from daylight for the last 900 years, these frescoes are extraordinarily well-preserved. They are also difficult to examine, so you might want to bring a flashlight along. The oldest part of the monastery is the tenth-century **Church of St. Mary** adjoining the larger church. With the exception of the exquisitely carved Byzantine capitals and lintel over the altar, all the interior decoration has been destroyed, either by earthquakes or by Turks, who converted the structure into a mosque. The building is still used daily by the five monks who live at the monastery. (Open daily 8am-6pm. Admission to the Church of St. Luke 200dr, students 100dr. Monastery, crypt, and Church of St. Mary are free.)

Getting out of Ossios Loukas is a lot easier than getting in; every tourist at the monastery is either going to Athens or Delphi, so mooching a lift shouldn't be a problem.

# Thebes Θήβα

Thebes once ranked among the most powerful of the ancient Greek cities, rivaling even Mycenae. Its importance was due in part to its geographical position, which gave it control over the strategic routes connecting the Peloponnese and Attica with northern Greece. Fertile ground complemented political power and ensured Thebes' prosperity.

According to legend, Thebes was founded by Kadmos, son of the King of Tyre, following instructions he received from the Delphic Oracle. The young prince slew a dragon at the spring of the city, and, on the advice of Athena, sowed its teeth, from which sprang up a harvest of armed men who engaged in a battle until all but five were killed. These survivors, the "Spartoi" (sown men), became the ancestors of the nobility of Thebes. Kadmos later married Harmonia, musical genius and daughter of Ares and Aphrodite, and they were the parents of Semele, Ino, and Agave. Semele, encouraged by jealous Hera, made the mistake of asking her lover Zeus to make love to her in his true shape (a thunderbolt)—he burned her to a crisp. Zeus rescued her unborn child, Dionysus, however, and placed the fetus in his thigh until it was born. It was not until many years later that Dionysus returned to Thebes to establish his ecstatic religion. Pentheus, son of Agave and then, King of Thebes, denied the god's divinity and refused to allow him to be worshiped. Euripides' tragedy, the *Bacchae,* describes the punishment of this dissenter, culminating in his tearing apart his mother when, in his god-induced frenzy, he took her for a wild beast. Thebes is perhaps most renowned as the setting for the story of Oedipus and his family. Oedipus' father Laios, King of Thebes, was told by the oracle at Delphi that his son was destined to kill his father and then marry his mother. To avoid these circumstances, Laios left baby Oedipus on a nearby mountain to die, nailing his feet together to prevent his escape. A shepherd found him and gave him to the king and queen of Corinth, who raised him as their own. When he reached manhood, Oedipus went to Thebes, killing Laios in a chance encounter on the way. At Thebes, he found a city plagued by the Sphinx, a monster who destroyed all who couldn't solve her riddle. By solving it, Oedipus was given Queen Jocasta (his mother) in marriage as a reward. When the true story was revealed many years later, Jocasta committed suicide and Oedipus blinded himself. Oedipus' sons then fought over the throne and killed each other, and Jocasta's brother Kreon took over. He had Antigone, Oedipus' daughter, put to death for burying her brother's body contrary to his decree. These tragic events are all narrated in Sophocles' *Oedipus* trilogy.

Modern Thebes maintains none of its ancient excitement. Razed by Alexander the Great in the fourth century B.C.E., it seems to have never recovered. It is a noisy, unattractive town, worth visiting only for its **museum.** From the bus station, walk downhill to the thirteenth-century Frankish tower, which lies in the museum courtyard. Housed in a mere five rooms, the collection is small but grand. The room opposite the entrance displays Mycenaean *larnakes* (clay coffins) adorned with paintings of funerary rites that provide rare insights into Mycenaean burial practices. The only such pieces found on mainland Greece, they were unearthed near Tanagara, halfway between Thebes and Chalkis. The garden outside the museum houses fantastic mosaics and peculiar reliefs depicting birds. The guide book is particularly informative. (Open Mon.-Sat. 8:45am-3pm, Sun. and holidays 9:30am-2:30pm. Admission 200dr, students 100dr.)

Also of interest are the remains of the **House of Kadmos,** a Mycenaean palace dating from the fourteenth century B.C.E. (opposite the Commercial Bank of Greece at 53 Pindari St.). The excavations here reveal a large Mycenaean building destroyed by fire and not rebuilt until the Christian era—a discovery that affirms the legend that the palace was destroyed by Zeus and left untouched because it was considered a holy place. Underneath the modern town of Thebes are an extensive Mycenaean palace and acropolis, rivaling sewer lines for survival. Historians and archeologists begrudge Thebes' every new building, fearing construction may endanger what remains of the great Mycenaean civilization.

Thebes is a bus juncture for Evia and the Sporades. **Buses** leave Thebes twice per day for Chalkis (290dr), but service is more frequent to and from Levadia (300dr) and the terminal at 260 Liossion St. in Athens (every hr., 450dr). Note that Athens buses not specifically bound for Thebes will probably drop you off on the road outside of town, since Thebes actually lies 2km off the main highway. But have no fear—you can hitch, flag down another bus, or walk to the center of town in 20 minutes. Wait for the Athens bus going west at the thatch shelter on the main highway. Thebes' **telephone code** is 0262.

# Evia (Euboea) Ευβοια

Wrenched from the mainland by an ancient earthquake (or Poseidon's trident, if you wish), Evia embraces the coastline north of Athens. Although the local tourist committee likes to highlight Evia's status as the Greek island with frequent bus service from the mainland, it seems very much a part of Central Greece. Travelers may pass over the short swingbridge at Chalkis and barely notice it. Most visitors to Evia are Athenians on weekend outings, or German and French tourists. Evia does not have sandy beaches or exciting nightlife, but its fragrant interior hills are a paradise for hikers. While many other islands are overrun by summer mobs, Evia remains a quiet haven. In addition, Evia is a gateway to the Sporades via the pretty ferry port at Kimi.

Bus transportation on Evia is reliable, but it often involves inconvenient transfers and indirect routes, so allow plenty of time to get from one place to another. There are no comprehensive bus schedules, which makes it difficult to plan your itinerary in advance. Best just to relax and enjoy the scenery.

Hitchhiking is an obvious alternative to submitting to the vagaries of bus schedules. Most vehicles will stop, but they pass infrequently and are usually going only to the next town. If you plan to visit Marmari or Karystos on the lower coast, it is easier, faster, and not much more expensive to take a ferry from Rafina or Agia Marina than a bus from Chalkis.

The hideous port capital of Evia, **Chalkis** (also called **Halkida**) is the transportation hub for the island, where visitors inevitably wind up spending a few hours. The **bus station** is in the center of town, at the top of the road that crosses the bridge. A **bus** from Athens' Liossion Station runs to Chalkis every half-hour (1½ hr., 420dr). The **train** is cheaper and only slightly slower (18 per day, 1¾ hr., 270dr). If you arrive by train you will find yourself still on the mainland when you disembark. Simply walk over the bridge to get to the island and the busier section of Chalkis. About 5 blocks to the left of the bridge you'll find El. Venizelou Street, running uphill. The **tourist police** are located at #32 El. Venizelou (tel. 246 62; open Mon.-Thurs. 8am-2pm, Fri. 8am-1:30pm). A few doors up (also on the right) is the **OTE**. (Open daily 6am-11:30pm.) You can change money at the **bank** 1 block below, on the opposite side of the street. (Open Mon.-Thurs. 8am-2pm., Fri. 8am-1:30pm.) The **post office** is on Karamourtzouni St., the second left off El. Venizelou as you walk uphill. (Open Mon.-Fri. 7:30am-2:30pm.) The **postal code** is 34100.

Hotels are conveniently located just to the left of the bridge. There are pleasant, expensive cafes along the waterfront. If you can't afford the high price of dinner, you can still order a drink, which entitles you to sit for a whole afternoon or evening of people-watching.

Visit the **Folklore Museum,** around the corner from the bus station in the Venetian Kastro. The museum houses textiles, costumes, and ceramic ware from the area. (Open Wed. and Fri. 6-8pm, Sun. 10am-1pm.)

## Southern Evia

The first settlement south of Chalkis is the resort town of **Eretria.** Eretria was a shipping center and colonial power that rose to prominence in the eighth century B.C.E. and continued to hold sway until the fourth century B.C.E. when it joined the Athenian League, revolted, and was finally eclipsed by Athens, its large maritime rival. In the third century B.C.E., the town became the center of the esteemed Eretrian School of Philosophy, founded by Menedemos, one of Plato's pupils. Today you'll find intellectual pursuits are about the last thing on people's minds: Eretria is a vacation town catering mostly to German and French tourists.

**Buses** running from Athens to Kimi stop in Eretria (every 2 hr., 1¾ hr., 420dr); it's a good idea to catch one of these rather than go via Chalkis. Buses go from Chalkis to Eretria every hour (last bus at 8:15, ½ hr., 120dr). You can also reach Eretria by **ferry** from Skala Oropou on the mainland (every ½ hr., ½ hr., 120dr). With your back to the bus depot, walk to your right until you reach Archeou Theatrou St. and then turn left. One block down and to the left you will find the OTE. (Open Mon.-Fri. 7:30am-3:10pm.) The **post office** is across the street. You can change money here. (Open Mon.-Fri. 7:30am-2:15pm.) An agency next door rents mopeds. The only pension in town has clean doubles, some with private bath. (Take the first right after the bus stop 2 blocks down Apostoli St. to a brown, 3-story building, #6.) Alternatively, try **Camping Eva** (tel. 610 81), 4km away. The **Museum of Eretria** houses artifacts from the ancient city. (Open Mon. and Wed.-Sat. 8:45am-3pm, Sun 9:30am-2:30pm. Admission 200dr, students 100dr.) To the right of the museum are the sparse remains of the city's ancient **theater** and the **Temple of Daphneos Apollo.** Eretria is only about 4 square blocks in area; if you have trouble getting around, consult one of the maps lining the streets.

Nine kilometers south of Eretria is the more charming and authentic **Amarinthos,** with excellent fish restaurants lining the water. As you enter Amarinthos, you encounter a number of B- and C-class hotels. Although there are no cheap pensions, it's easy to find rooms to let—just ask around. Visit the two small monasteries overlooking the harbor.

Continuing south you'll reach **Lepoura,** an unattractive hamlet where the road splits. One fork heads to Kimi through, over, and around some of Evia's most spectacular mountain scenery, while the other fork continues south moving inland and running along the island's spine toward Karystos. The small roads leading off to the right (the west coast) are better for beaches, as the east coast of the island is rocky and exposed, particularly to the midsummer *meltemi,* a northeast wind. Two kilometers from Lepoura, left off the main road, is pleasant **Krieza,** with a lovely church in the main square. Seventeen kilometers farther is the mountain town of **Zarakes,** well worth a stopover on your way south for the excellent view.

Seventy-five kilometers south of Chalkis on the west coast lies the sleepy resort town of **Stira.** Sprawled along a mile of the shore, and never more than 2 blocks deep, it lies on a calm bay protected by several islets. Sandy beaches flank both sides of the town—the stretch to the right (facing the sea) is a bit better. The hotels in town are C-class and expensive. Fortunately, you can camp 10 minutes down the coast in either direction. About 2km along the beach (left facing the water) is **Venus Beach,** with windsurfing and boating facilities. Ferries run from Stira to **Agia Marina** on the Attic coast (7 per day, 45 min.), where a bus connects to Athens (2 hr.). You can walk from Agia Marina to the ruins of **Ramnous** in 30 to 45 minutes. If you can catch a bus going up the hill to the crossroads, ask for Ramnous and insist that the driver let you off.

## Karystos

The largest town in southern Evia, Karystos is flanked by a colorful, active shipyard at one end of its port and the fifteenth-century Fort of Bourdzi at the other. Few tourists infiltrate this mellow and decidedly unglamorous town.

If you walk from the water 2 blocks up Theochari Kotsika St., you will find the **bank.** (Open Mon.-Thurs. 8am-2pm, Fri. 8am-1:30pm.) The **post office** is 2 blocks farther along. (Open Mon.-Fri. 7:30am-4pm.) The **OTE** is across the street from the Church of St. Nicholas. (Open Mon.-Fri. 7:30am-2:15pm.) Walk 3 blocks through the square and turn right. Follow Karistou a few blocks from the ferry dock to your right (facing inland), past the square, for the **tourist office** (tel. 241 30). (Open daily June-Aug. 7:30am-10pm.) The **postal code** is 34001; the **telephone code** is 0224. The women here are friendly and have a list of more than 70 families who offer *dhomatia.* If you arrive late or prefer to search on your own, look for a rooms-to-let sign at the restaurants to your left along the dock. Most of the rooms are doubles (2000dr), and you will be charged full-price even if you are alone. Nonetheless, *dhomatia* are much cheaper than any of the hotels in Karystos.

The octopi lined up and drying in the sun are bound to make your stomach start growling (trust us). Head straight for **O Kavodoros,** 1 block inland on Parodos Sachtouri St., which is 1 block left of the main square. The food is amazing and dirt cheap. Try the *gopa* (fish; 200dr), octopus (254dr) and *mousaka* (200dr). (Open 7:30am-3:30pm and 5:30pm-midnight.) **Taverna Psistaria,** right of the waterfront, 50m up Theocari Kotsika St., prepares daily specials on the spit. (Full dinner about 600dr.)

If you want to inspect the interior of the coastal **Fort of Bourdzi,** which dates from the Crusades, ask at the tourist office. You'll get a guided tour. Near the Bourdzi is the long, sandy beach of **Psili Ammos,** a nice place to soak up the sun and a cheap place to sleep.

The bus stop is 1 block beyond the square in front of **Barbayiannis Taverna.** The bus to Halkidi leaves twice daily (3¾ hr., 690dr). The bus from Stira to Karystos leaves twice daily (1¼ hr., 175dr). Karystos and **Marmari** (a slightly crowded resort town without a good beach), are both connected to the mainland by ferries to Rafina (2 per day). The *Karystos* serves the former (653dr one-way), and the *Marmari* serves Marmari (437dr one-way). In Karystos, ferry tickets are sold at **Pantelis,** in a waterfront pizzeria to the left of a three-humped white canopy. To get to Rafina from Athens in order to cross to either of these towns, take the Rafina bus from 29 Mavromateon St., which leaves every hour (1 hr., 140dr).

If you have a free morning, explore the villages north of Karystos. Follow Aiolou St., 1 block east of the square, out of town; continue straight at the crossroads toward **Palaio Chora,** a village that sprawls among lemon and olive groves. Turn right at a sign saying "metamorphosis" and you will find a shaded stone path leading up to an old church. For a more interesting but also more strenuous trek, turn right at the crossroads outside Karystos and go toward the village of **Mili.** The road ascends sharply and follows a clear stream up to the village, where the water has been diverted to flow from the mouths of three lions in a small roadside fountain. From Mili, a 20-minute hike up the hill on the left will bring you to **Kokkino Kastro,** a thirteenth-century Venetian castle, named for the blood that was spilled there during the war between the Greeks and the Turks. The castle wall affords a fine view of Karystos' harbor.

For more extensive hiking in the region, climb **Mt. Ochi** (1398m). The secondhighest mountain on Evia, it is located in the heart of this unspoiled southern area. To stay in the stone refuge hut on the mountain, ask for the key at the tourist office in Karystos. A large structure of unmortared stone blocks was built during the Pelasgian Period on the summit; some say it was a temple to Hera, others a signal tower. The ruin is known as the "dragon's house," and since it is allegedly haunted, you will probably have it all to yourself.

## Kimi

Dubbed "the balcony of the Aegean" because of its perch 250m over the water, Kimi used to be a major harbor renowned for its fishingfolk, figs, and wine. But 30 years ago, disease destroyed all the vineyards and the population dropped from 30,000 to 10,000. Today this pretty town receives few visitors. The construction of a road connecting the harbor of **Paralia Kimi** directly to the Chalkis road a few kilometers before the village means that travelers heading to the Sporades need not pass through Kimi. This suits the townspeople fine—as a community of ship captains and officers' families, their livelihood depends more on visitors to the Sporades than to their hometown. Two agents located before the docks in Paralia Kimi sell **ferry** tickets. To the left of the road descending from Kimi Town is the agent for the *Skiathos* (tel. 228 25), a ferry servicing Skiathos (4½ hr., 1638dr), Skopelos (3¾ hr., 1451dr), Alonissos (3 hr., 1330dr), and Volos (2503dr). In July and August, this ferry runs four times per week: Tuesday (10pm), Thursday (9:30pm), Friday (8:30pm), and Sunday (10pm). In off-season, there is one ferry on Monday (6:30pm) and one on Friday (11am). This agent also has ferries to Limnos (1023dr) and Kavala (1657dr) each week (July-Aug. Thurs. 11am; in off-season Sat. 11pm). To the right of the road descending from Kimi Town is the agent for the *Anemoessa* (tel. 220 20). This vessel serves Skyros (2-3 per day; in off-season 1 per day; 2 hr., 700dr). A **hydrofoil** now connects all four of the Sporades. **Buses** run to Kimi directly from 260 Liossion St. in Athens (5 per day, 3½ hr., 900dr) and from Chalkis (8 per day, 2¼ hr., 500dr). From Karystos, take the bus to Lepoura (3 per day, 2½ hr., 370dr) and transfer from Lepoura to Kimi (4 per day, 1 hr., 200dr). For further information, call 222 57.

With an abundance of greenery and cool, tangy sea breezes, Kimi offers a refreshing respite from the parched Greek summer. **Galani Street** sprawls out into a plaza around the town cathedral. During the evenings, this area fills with townspeople strolling and socializing. Along the street you'll find the **OTE**, 1 block below the church (open Mon.-Fri. 7:30am-3:10pm), the **bank** (open Mon.-Thurs. 8am-2pm, Fri. 8am-1:30pm), directly across from the church, and the **post office**, 1 block above the church (open Mon.-Fri. 7:30am-3pm). Kimi's **postal code** is 34003; the **telephone code** is 0222. The **police** (tel. 225 55) occupy the yellow building 2 blocks behind and to the left of the church. (Open 24 hours.) At the harbor, several tourist information offices provide boat schedules. (Open Mon.-Fri. 8am-2pm.) If these offices are closed (in the afternoon or on weekends), ask at the kiosk on the waterfront for any help. Tucked in a corner to the right of the church is a statue of Georgios Papanicolaou, a Kimian famous for his development of the Pap smear. Farther down the road from the town is a **hospital/clinic** named after him. Kimi's **health center** (tel. 232 52 or 232 53) is open 24 hours. The **Folklore Museum** (tel. 220 11), on the road descending to Paralia Kimi, offers three floors of Evian crafts, mostly clothing, needlework, and furnishings, all in a wooden building with wrought-iron balconies and fences. (Open daily 10am-1pm and 6-9pm. Admission 75dr.)

A small whitewashed seafarer's chapel and the ruins of a windmill are poised on the hill behind town. A climb to either offers excellent views of Kimi and the sea beyond. Some Greeks go to the spring at **Choneftico,** north of Kimi, where the mineral waters reputedly remove kidney stones. The 20-minute walk along the road from Kimi toward the spring is delightful, especially if you follow one of the dirt tracks leading off the road and ramble up into the hills, where you'll discover other natural springs and old shepherds' shelters. Five kilometers from Kimi, on the east side of the same mountain, is the 700-year-old, majestically situated **Monastery of the Saviour.** When pirates landed at Kimi in the late eighteenth and nineteenth centuries, signals would be sent from the **Venetian Castle** above the monastery and passed along between castles to Chalkis and beyond, calling for aid. Locals recommend spending the night at the castle so as to watch the sun rise above the sea and catch glimpses of Mt. Athos, Thessaloniki, and the shores of Macedonia, Thrace, and Turkey. South of Kimi you can view the volcano of **Oxilithos.**

On the road down to the water is a small church, with a holy icon believed to have been made by St. Luke. The locals say there was an argument over which of two icons would be placed in the church. The rejected icon was thrown into the sea and discovered one day by a man collecting wood along the beach. Unable to turn over this particular piece of wood, he lifted his axe to chop it and became frozen as he stood. Priests gathered around him and freed him with their prayers; when they finally turned the piece over, they saw that it was the discarded icon. The holy relic miraculously planted itself along the road to the water, so they built a church there. About 80 years ago, three men attempted to steal the gold from the icon, and they all are said to have gone crazy.

There is a scarcity of tourist accommodations. Cheap and comfortable lodgings are available at the **Kimi Hotel** (tel. 224 08), up the street from the post office. (Singles 900dr. Doubles 1500dr, with private bath 1800dr.) On the same street but closer to the town's square is **Hotel Halkida** (tel. 222 02), where clean and well-kept doubles with private bath run 2000dr. There are also *dhomatia* to let; ask the townspeople for directions. At Paralia Kimi, the **Hotel Beis** (tel. 226 04) has doubles with private baths for 2500dr, quads for 3500dr. **Roula Moutovraki** (tel. 226 12) runs a little cheaper with doubles for 2000dr and triples for 2200dr.

In summer, great fare is available at **Markos,** just below the OTE. They charge so little you'll feel like a criminal. At other times of the year you'll have to get your nourishment from *souvlaki* or hot dog stands, pastry shops in the plaza, or the super-market down the main road past the OTE, which has a good deli counter.

Buses negotiate the twisting 52 turns to Paralia Kimi and back roughly every two hours (50dr). If you are returning from Paralia Kimi to Chalkis or Athens, buses leave the harbor 10 minutes earlier. A 10-minute walk to the left (facing the water) from the ferry landing in Paralia Kimi brings you to a free beach. Otherwise, wait for the ferry and sit in one of the cafes—**Airaion,** at the south end is particularly good. (Open for lunch and dinner only.) Better yet, explore the village and its sylvan environs, even if it means the cost of a taxi back to Paralia Kimi (250dr).

## Limni

Limni is an etherized port. Tourists are few and transient; two of the three hotels in town are open only in July and August. Fishing is the major focus of the town, but the rest of Limni seems to drift serenely through the afternoon.

Buses run from Chalkis to Limni (3 per day, 2½ hr., 370dr). The road winds away from the coast and through the interior of the island through tranquil scenery. When you arrive in Limni, the bus driver will let you off by the water. To your left is the **bank.** (Open Mon.-Thurs. 8am-2pm, Fri. 8am-1:30pm.) The **post office** is in the little square behind the Plaza Hotel. (Open Mon.-Fri. 7:30am-2:30pm.) To find the **OTE,** walk along the waterfront with the water on your right until you see the sign pointing left. (Open Sun.-Fri. 7:30am-3:10pm.)

Only the **Plaza Hotel** is open in off-season. (Clean doubles 1400dr; in off-season 1000dr.) If you're alone, they'll charge you for a double. Between the bank and the Plaza is the **Hotel Ilion,** 2 Ossiou Christodoulou St. (tel. 317 68), which is the chea-pest in town. (Singles 800dr. Doubles 1200dr.) There is no official **camping** in Limni, but you can sleep on the pebble beach at beautiful **Rouvies,** 8km north. The beach stretches between the two towns. Many Greek families set up tents along the north-ern end of this beach; if you choose to sleep farther south, you'll be alone.

Nights are cool in Limni, but you may still wish to eat by the water: Have dinner at the **Pouemplo** *taverna,* where portions are large and prices moderate. **Taverna Barbayiannis** serves fresh octopus; dozens of severed octopus legs hang on a rack by the tables, along with other exotic catches of the day. If you want to shoot a game of pool with some locals, take the street just past the Pouemplo 1 block up to a billiard room on the left.

North of Limni is the village of **Edipsos,** one of the biggest resorts in Evia. Praised by Herodotus, Aristotle, and Aristophanes for its healing sulfurous waters, Edipsos attracts older tourists who suffer from arthritis and rheumatism. Stay instead at **Pefki,** farther north and less touristed, with a quiet, secluded beach. There are no hotels there, but a number of places offer rooms to let. **Camping Pefki** is 1km outside of the town. On the coast from Pefki west to **Orei,** you'll find only sand and solitude. At Orei are the remains of the maritime acropolis of ancient Histiaea. To the east, the modern city of **Istiea** is now the region's largest town. On the east side of the island (42km from Chalkis), there is a winter ski center at **Mt. Dirfy** (1150m).

## Agios Konstantinos

Although it possesses all the amenities of a successful port, Agios Konstantinos has little of interest to tourists. The **ferry office,** Alkyon Travel, is located on a prominent corner of the waterfront. In high season, one or two ferries per day run to Skiathos (1128dr), Glossa (1282dr), Skopelos (1338dr), and Alonissos (1492dr). There are also occasional ferries to Limnos (1819dr). Flying Dolphin **hydrofoils** run on a similar schedule but cost 60-70% more than the ferry. The office is to the left of Alkyon Travel. Just down the street is the **bank,** sandwiched between two cafes. (Open Mon.-Thurs. 8am-2pm, Fri. 8am-1:30pm.) The tall gray building behind Alkyon Travel on the waterfront road is the **OTE**; the **post office** is also there, as well as a **currency exchange.** The **postal code** is 35006; the **telephone code** is 0235.

You can reach Agios Konstantinos by daily bus from Athens (870dr), or by ferry from Evia (6am-10pm every 2 hr., 1 hr., 172dr). The ferry docks are at Arkitsa, but frequent buses (marked *Lamia*) run to Agios Konstantinos. The bus stop is several blocks up and slightly to the right of the harbor.

# NORTHERN GREECE

Northern Greece seldom finds its way onto postcards or promotional posters, but not for lack of beauty. Its glory might not strike you until you're hiking at dusk through mountains and a shepherd ushers you into his home, lights a fire, and hands you a cup of hot coffee. Here, unlike on the islands, no one puts on a show; nobody whitewashes the buildings, translates the menus, or accepts American Express cards with a smile. Here, you're entering the Greek's world. For the adventurous and inquisitive traveler, northern Greece waits to be discovered.

Northern Greece consists of four provinces. The largest by far is Macedonia, in the north-central part of the country: Thessaloniki, Greece's second largest city, sits in its center, the peninsulas of Halkidiki extend along its eastern edge, and the Kastorian Lakes along its western edge. The hidden treasures of Epirus, sandy coves on its scenic coast, and amazing canyons amid rugged mountains, wait for you a couple of hours away from Ioannina. Crowned by Mt. Olympos, Thessaly stretches east to incredibly cool and verdant Mt. Pelion on the Aegean. Thrace, the least touristed of the four regions, sits in the northeast corner of the country, bordering Turkey.

# Thessaly Θεσσαλία

Apart from its industrialized urban centers, Thessaly is bejeweled with enchanting villages and stunning monasteries. To the west of the cultivated Thessalian plain, the monasteries of Meteora cling to towering pinnacles. The rocky crags of Mt. Olympos, throne of the pantheon of Greek gods, starkly watch over sandy Aegean beaches. To the southeast, traditional mountain hamlets on Mt. Pelion lie scattered among forests, apple orchards, and olive groves that extend to the sea.

# Volos Βόλος

Jason and the Argonauts set off on their quest for the Golden Fleece from the site of modern-day Volos, on the northern coast of Pagassitikos Bay. Today these adventurers wouldn't even need a quest to justify leaving the modern city; the concrete and smog in Volos is enough incentive to travel to Pelion, Evia, and the Sporades Islands.

The regional **archeological museum,** at the eastern end of town in a park on the water, has an excellent collection. Exhibits span the entire historical spectrum, from the latter part of the Paleolithic era to the Roman period, including findings from the site of the Homeric Iolkos. (Museum open Mon. and Wed.-Sat. 8:45am-2:30pm, Sun. 9:30-2:30pm. Admission 200dr, students 100dr.) The area from the museum to the other park at Platia Georgiou is the most pleasant section of Volos. Not only is the museum courtyard cool and shady, but the residential streets surrounding it are lined with orange trees, the fruit of which ripens in late July and August.

## Practical Information

**Greek National Tourist Organization (GNTO):** On the waterfront in Riga Fereou Sq. (tel. 235 00 or 249 15). After disembarking from the ferry, go left along the waterfront for about 800m. Coming from the train station, walk down Papadiamandi St. and turn left at the square.

From the bus station, head back to the water and take a right. Eager to provide all the information you could need. Hotel list posted after closing. Open Mon.-Fri. 7am-2:30pm and 6-8pm, Sat. 9am-noon and 6-8pm, Sun. 9am-noon.

**Post Office:** On P. Mela St., off Alexandras St. Open Mon.-Fri. 7:30am-8:30pm. **Postal code:** 38001 or 38334.

**OTE:** Main office at the corner of Eleftheriou and Sokratous St., across the street from the covered fruit and vegetable market. Open 24 hours. **Telephone code:** 0421.

**Trains:** Must change trains in Larissa for Athens or Thessaloniki. To: Athens (9 per day, 7½ hr., 900dr); Thessaloniki (9 per day, 4½ hr., 365dr); and Larissa (13 per day, 1 hr., 110dr). The **railroad station** is 1 block west of tourist office.

**Ferries:** Five boats per day to the Sporades. To: Skiathos (1 hr. 10 min., 772dr); Skopelos (2¼ hr., 968dr); and Alonissos (2½ hr., 1103dr). Flying Dolphin **hydrofoils** run just as frequently but cost twice as much. For either, inquire at the agencies lining the waterfront.

**Buses:** To: Athens (10 per day, 5 hr., 1650dr); Thessaloniki (4 per day, 3¼ hr., 1110dr); Larissa (18 per day, 1 hr., 330dr); Portaria (10 per day, ¾ hr., 75dr); Makrinitsa (10 per day, 50 min., 90dr); Hania (4 per day, 1¼ hr., 150dr); Zagoria (4 per day, 4 hr., 260dr); Horefto (4 per day, 4 hr. 20 min., 310dr); Afissos (7 per day, ¾ hr., 145dr); and Platania (2 per day, 2 hr., 380dr). The **bus station** (tel. 255 27) is 1 block from the waterfront on Metamorfosseos St.

**Car Rental:** Theofanidis Hellas, 137 Iasonos St. (tel. 323 60), 1 block parallel to the waterfront. Fiat, Yugo, or Lada 6000dr per day.

**Tourist Police:** 179 Alexandras St. (tel. 270 94). Can provide assistance when the GNTO is closed.

## Accommodations, Food, and Entertainment

If you're stranded here at a late hour, head for the downtown area near the waterfront, where you'll find several paltry but cheap hotels. The externally shabby, but internally spotless **Hotel Europa**, 18 Korai St. (tel. 236 24), has singles for 800dr, doubles for 1030dr, and a shower down the hall. Up the street at #45 is **Hotel Akropolis** (tel. 259 84; triples only, 800dr per person). **Hotel Iasson**, 1 Mela St. (tel. 260 75 or 243 47), on the water, is very well-managed. (Singles 1000dr. Doubles 1300dr.)

The waterfront area is loaded with *tavernas* and cafes. All post their prices, so you can be selective. Don't get fleeced at the ones with the vinyl-cushioned seats on the eastern end; look instead on the western end and inland for the plain wooden and wicker seats: You'll save money and eat just as well. After a hard day's work, many sailors rest their bones at the **Ouzeri Nautilia**, 1 Argonafton (tel. 253 40), just before Riga Fereou Sq. Its specialty is *oktopodhi* (grilled octopus; 500dr), though your wallet may decide that you'd much rather have a fish plate (170dr). (Open daily 6am-2am.) The less expensive restaurants end at **Athenaiki Taverna** on Venizelou St. (tel. 230 54). (Entrees 370dr. Open daily 7am-11pm.) One of the numerous cheap *souvlaki* grills across the street, **O Bailei** serves delicious *gyros* (80dr) and *souvlaki* (60dr).

Volos nightlife is lively in the truest Greek sense. The promenade along the waterfront overflows with people enjoying the cafes, restaurants, and each other. The two movie theaters along the promenade show movies in English for about 200dr. In late July and August, Volos hosts a festival in Riga Fereou Park, featuring concerts, dance, and special exhibits. Later in August, the *Pazari*, a fair featuring Balkan handicrafts and a small amusement park, is held just outside town.

# Makrinitsa Μακρινίτσα

Makrinitsa, with its shady trees, stone houses, and cobblestone streets, seems like an Alpine hamlet. Yet, the occasional woman in traditional dress riding sidesaddle through the village on a donkey, or the view of Volos against the deep blue of Pagassitikos Bay reveal that this setting can only be found in Greece.

Presiding over the town square, the diminutive **Agios Yiannis** contains some fine examples of wood carving, as do many of the houses around it. Hike the trails through the nearby hills, where sparkling mountain springs flow with icy water and sea breezes make idle ramblings cool and comfortable, especially in the shade of the lush forest. Walk 1km along the trail uphill from the parking lot to the austere monastery of **Agios Gerasimon,** with its clock tower and resident peacock, and continue on to the seventeenth-century **Monastery of Sourvias,** a half-hour walk away.

Accommodations in Makrinitsa are expensive, so consider staying elsewhere on the peninsula. The road into Volos ends at a large parking lot on the city's eastern edge. About 150m from the parking lot is the town square, **Platia Irini.** The two cheapest places to stay are the **Achilles Pension** (tel. 991 77) and the **Pilioritico Spiti** (tel. 991 94), both near the square. (Doubles with private bath 2200dr.) Less expensive *dhomatia* can be found uphill from the street connecting the parking lot and the main square. The GNTO has declared Makrinitsa a "traditional settlement," in an effort to preserve the old houses and prevent any new construction that would change the village's appearance. Three villas have been renovated into expensive guesthouses, but the best operation of this type remains in private hands: **Pension Diomidi** (tel. 994 30), uphill from the Galini Restaurant (look for the sign), has beautiful rooms with whitewashed interiors, wood carvings, and flower-patterned patios. (Singles 2200dr. Doubles 2800dr. Triples 3000dr.) Lodgings usually fill up in high season, so be sure to call ahead.

Fill up at the **Pantheon** (tel. 991 24), in the square—a good place to try *spetsophai,* a stew made with spicy *loukaniko* (sausage), green peppers, and eggplant (350dr). (Open daily 9am-midnight.)

Makrinitsa holds a three-day festival beginning on May 1, a re-enactment of an ancient festival of Dionysus, featuring dancers wearing traditional costume. Accommodations get tight around this time, so venture 2km down the road to the town of **Portaria.** Somewhat larger, though not so splendid as Makrinitsa, Portaria has a number of pensions and two noteworthy churches: the fourteenth-century **Panayia** and the church of **Agios Nikolaos.**

**Buses** leave regularly from the bus terminal in Volos for Makrinitsa (50 min., 90dr) and Portaria (10 per day, 45 min., 75dr). If you are hitching, follow Venizelou St. out of Volos to the north. Makrinitsa has little in the way of practical conveniences. To change money you must go to Portaria. There is also no post office; the kiosk sells stamps, and letters go in the mailbox. Makrinitsa's **telephone code** is 0423.

# Mount Pelion Peninsula Ορος Πηλιο

In mythology, Mt. Pelion Peninsula was home to the centaurs, and it's easy to imagine how the half-man, half-horse mischief-makers must have enjoyed frolicking on its misty green slopes. Natural springs and a moist climate keep Pelion lush and cool year-round, a delightful change for those singed by Greece's summer sun. Some 20 villages complement the natural surroundings. The stonework of the Pelion mansions is so finely hewn that mortar seems superfluous, and the wood decoration is delicate and intricate. Even the balconies are charming, offering spectacular panoramas of the surrounding coastline.

There are two ways to explore the villages around Volos: across the peninsula and along the road high above the Aegean coast, or along the coast of Pagassitikos Bay. The former is more pleasant, since the inland areas, Aegean coastline, and the far ends of the peninsula are much prettier and less crowded than the stretch along Pagassitikos Bay from Volos and Agria to Afissos. You won't find big hotels in this untouristed area, but locals have filled the vacuum by providing *dhomatia*—some right on the beach (600dr per person). The peninsula's **telephone code** is 0426 for the eastern half, 0423 for the western.

Getting around is not very difficult since the main villages are served by four or five buses per day, and the more secluded hamlets can be reached on foot (an hour or so at most). Hitching is another good alternative; however, during the midday siesta, passersby are scarce. To explore the peninsula thoroughly in a short period of time, you might want to rent a car in Volos (see Volos).

If you opt for the Aegean route, the first place of interest after Makrinitsa (see above) will be the ski town of **Hania**, 26km from Volos, where you can see both sides of the Pelion peninsula (which unfortunately means you're too far from either side to swim). The ski resort, 2km off the main road, has steep, narrow runs. The main ski area, served by chair lift and T-bar, is usually open from January to mid-March. The **Youth Hostel Pan (IYHF)** (tel. (0421) 995 42) serves as a good base for hikes in the hills and treks to the beach. (500dr per person. Open Sat.-Sun. only.)

Fourteen kilometers east of Hania, the road forks. Turn left (north) for **Zagora,** the largest of the Pelion villages, with old vine-covered stone homes and cheap rooms to let. Better yet, continue through the orchards of "the green" (the eastern part of the peninsula) to the fine sand hugging the Aegean at the town of **Horefto,** 8km from Zagora. On the far side of town the crowded **Seahorse Campground** (tel. (0426) 221 80) charges 400dr per person, 300dr per tent. (Open May-Sept.) A far better alternative is **Hariklia and Andy's** *dhomatia* (tel. 224 47), run by two retired Greek-Americans. This warmhearted couple offers sunny, clean rooms with the Aegean as a front yard. (Singles 800dr. Doubles 1200dr. Triples 1800dr.) Their place is one of the first you'll come to on the waterfront street, and is next to the **Taka Mam** restaurant (tel. 224 70). Eat mouth-watering grilled lamb as you watch the moon rise over the sea. (Entrees 400-440dr. Open daily 11am-1am.) Try Pelion *spetsophai* (370dr) at **Achellion O.K. Restaurant** (tel. 222 20), three doors down from Taka Mam. (Open daily 9am-2am.) Rich *halva,* sold in many of the shops, will satisfy even the most voracious sweet tooth. Spinach pie and pizza also abound for the ravenous.

For about 500dr, a local fisher will take you to one of the nearby sea caves. Returning toward Zagora you'll notice the school of **Riga Fereou,** one of several that Fereou used clandestinely in the early 1800s to keep alive the Greek customs, traditions, and language during the Turkish occupation. In the same area, the poet Drossinis wrote ballads to his lover. Four **buses** per day connect Volos with Hania (1¼ hr., 150dr), Zagora (4 hr., 260dr), and Horefto (4 hr. 20 min., 310dr).

From Zagora, you can follow the right-hand fork through cherry and apple orchards, tended by residents of the picturesque hamlets of **Anilio** and **Makrirahi.** This stretch makes a great hike. Ten kilometers from Makrirahi is the turn-off for **Agios Ioannis,** a beautiful, but commercialized beach resort. You can get a reasonably good room on the waterfront at the **Hotel Anesis** (tel. 312 23). (Singles 1350dr. Doubles 1550dr. Hot showers included.) On the far side of the footbridge, on the southern end of the beach, is a fine shady spot for freelance camping. **To Akrogiali** (tel. 312 27) serves inexpensive regional specialties—stews and baked noodle-and-cheese entrees. (Open daily 8am-midnight.) Windsurfers (2000dr per day) and waterskis (2000dr per 15 min.) are available at the **Alfa Gelateria.**

If you want your own beach, take the path over the footbridge and up the hill at the end of town. Forty-five minutes later you'll be in **Damouhari Cove.** There are two small white pebble beaches, what remains of a Venetian castle, and a peaceful olive grove. **Buses** run to Agios Ioannis from Volos (3 per day, 1¾ hr., 380dr). The road heads south, then forks to **Kissos,** the highest of the villages on the eastern slope, where you'll find the eighteenth-century Basilica of Agia Marina and several *dhomatia.* The next village on the main road is **Mouressi.** The cheapest restaurant around, **Georgios Vontzos,** deserves a stop for its *fasoladha* (bean soup), a complete meal in itself (275dr).

Five kilometers south, take the turn-off and go 8km farther to **Milopotamos,** an exceptionally fine but small beach near the cliffs. Morning buses come here regularly in July and August. Two restaurant/cafe/bars serve the beach, and a few *dhomatia* lie 1km up the hill. A hidden beach can be reached through a small hole bored into the cliff on the left; if it isn't too crowded, seize the opportunity to camp under the rock overhang.

The alternative route from Volos along Pagassitikos Bay leads first to **Agria,** a resort town with many seafood *tavernas* where locals dine boisterously until late night. In Agria is the turn-off for **Drakia,** only 19km from Volos, a good place to head if you want to get out of the city and spend a night on the mountain. Of its many fine Pelion-style houses, the most noteworthy is the **Mansion of Triandafylou.** Buses for Drakia travel to and from Volos (2 per day, 50 min., 115dr). Two campgrounds in the quiet olive groves around **Gatzea** make this part of the coast a satisfactory stopover. **Camping Hellas** (tel. (0423) 222 67) is crowded, but lies on a sandy beach. (350dr per person. 250dr per tent.) **Camping Marina** (tel. 222 77) is less crowded and better-tended, with a rocky beach. (375dr per person. 200dr per tent.) Heading inland at Kala Nera will bring you to two rustic villages perched on Pelion's mountainous spine. From the cool plaza of the first, **Milies,** you can look down to the still, blue bay below. The frescoes in the **Church of the Taxiarches,** also on the plaza, are in good condition. Skip the town museum, which looks more like a tourist shop and try the cheese bread, a local specialty. Three kilometers north and uphill from Milies, the town of **Vizitsa** lies in sedate splendor like a carved wooden heirloom. The GNTO is restoring some of the mansions in this old village, but it remains quieter and less-visited than Makrinitsa. You'll find a cafe in the center of Vizitsa, and rooms to let nearby. You can sit like an aristocrat and sip coffee in a smaller and more elegant cafe above the town to the right, in the courtyard of one of the old houses. **Buses** run to Milies six times per day from 6am to 7:30pm (1 hr., 155dr) and Vizitsa (1 hr. 5 min., 165dr).

Farther down the main road, 4½km after Kala Nera, a turn-off leads to **Afissos,** a beach resort popular among Greek tourists, graced with Pelion-style houses with rooms to rent overlooking the water. The town's two cheap hotels, **Hotel Rena** (tel. 334 39) and **Hotel Faros** (tel. 332 93) have doubles with private baths for 2900dr. Buses run from Volos to Afissos (7 per day, ¾ hr., 145dr). After Afissos, the road turns inland and winds south through hilly orchard country; if you are taking the bus either north or south, you may be asked to get out and wait for an hour at Promirio before continuing. This is an authentic village of old Pelion, with stone houses, stained wood, and steep paths.

The farthest you can go by bus and paved road is **Platania,** a peaceful fishing village. **Buses** leave Volos for Platania (2 per day, 2 hr., 380dr). Walk west along the seashore to an olive grove or farther on to a stretch of beach perfect for **camping.** Feel free to ignore the "no camping" signs; you won't be the only one. The cheapest hotels are **Hotel Platania** (tel. (0423) 655 65) and **Hotel Kima** (tel. 655 69; doubles 1800dr). Excursion **boats** leave daily at 9am for **Koukounaries Beach** on Skiathos, returning at 5pm (400dr one-way). If you've missed the boat, relax on the beach and perhaps join the rowdy fishers at **Restaurant Galini** as they lunch on small fish in garlic sauce and wash it down with *retsina.* After loading ice in their boats' hulls, they take off on their all-night fishing expeditions. If the captain is in a good mood and on his way to Skiathos, he may give you a ride. You may also persuade one of the captains to take you to the secluded hamlet of **Trikeri** on the mountainous Tisseo Peninsula, which curves around Pagassitikos Bay, or the still more isolated town of **Paleo Trikeri** on the island with the same name. Both stops have deserted beaches accessible by long dirt paths.

# *Trikala* Τρίκαλα

In the heart of northern Greece to the northwest of Volos and just 30km south of Kalambaka and Meteora, Trikala is a ganglion of bus connections. Unlike most transportation centers, there is a bright side to this city on the Lethaios River: The old section of town on the northwestern corner has delightful houses, skewed streets, and a variety of interesting sights. The most conspicuous attraction is the restored **Fortress of Trikala,** with its elegant, turreted clock tower visible upriver from the cafe district. The public garden in front of the fortress has a fountain, a view of the valley, and, built into the fortress walls, an expensive restaurant that thrives off tourists en route to Meteora. Trikala is believed to have been the birthplace of the physician Asclepios, so it's no surprise that the remnants of an Asclepion, the oldest of the sanctuaries to the healing god, stand near the fortress. The old quarter of town is further graced with brightly-painted stone churches including Agios Stephanos, Agios Dimitrios, Agia Paraskevi, and Agia Episcopi. There is a small museum near the church of Panayia Phaneromeni—get the key from the Curator of Antiquities. (Ask at the police station. Museum open 7am-3pm.)

In lieu of tourist police, Trikala has a tourist information office on Larissas St. (tel. 274 69), next to city hall. (Open 7am-2:30pm.) If you're stranded, stay in one of the hotels in the bustling cafe district, 1 block upriver from the bus station and to the left. The **Hotel Panhellinion,** 6 Vas. Olgas St. (tel. 282 91), offers lofty ceilings and large clean rooms with baths. (Singles 2000dr. Doubles 3720dr. Triples 4650dr.) The **Hotel Palladion,** 7 Vyronos St. (tel. 280 91), is 1 block farther upriver. (Singles 1900dr. Doubles 3000dr. Hot showers included.) For a boost in quality (and a boost in price), check out the **Hotel Litheo** (tel. 206 90; singles 2300dr; doubles 3168dr; triples 3655dr; breakfast extra).

Regular **buses** connect to: Athens' Liossion St. Station (8 per day, 5 hr., 1690dr); Volos (5 per day, 3 hr., 780dr); Thessaloniki (5 per day, 3½ hr., 1110dr); and Kalambaka (19 per day, ½ hr., 125dr). The **post office,** on Sarafi St. (open Mon.-Fri. 7:30am-2pm), and the **OTE,** 25th Martiou St. (open 24 hours), are both in the neighborhood around Platia Polytechniou, just across the river from the hotels. The municipal **police station** (tel. 100) is at Kapodistrion and Asklipiou St. (Open 24 hours.) Trikala's **telephone code** is 0431; the **postal code** is 42100.

The small thirteenth-century **Church of Porta Panayia** is a convenient excuse to visit the town of **Pili,** at the base of a river valley 20km southwest of Trikala. An 800-meter walk from the center over a long footbridge, upriver and to the left, takes you to the small, beautiful churchyard with protective cypress trees and an empty meter-wide moat. Go to the low building with green trim on the hillside to request the key. Extremely well-preserved mosaics of Christ and the Madonna and Child sit on either side of the altar. The church also contains a few capitals from the Roman ruins excavated in the area. One kilometer upstream is a sturdy Roman bridge that provides steep passage over the river. As you get off the bus in Pili, you'll find the town's only hotel, **Hotel Babanara** (tel. 223 25; singles 1000dr; doubles 1600dr; showers included). Twelve buses per day make the half-hour trip to Pili from behind the Trikala station (115dr).

# *Kalambaka* Καλαμπάκα

Hit hard during World War II, Kalambaka lost the architecture that once made it an attraction. Today, Kalambaka thrives mostly on its proximity to Meteora. Running north-south, **Trikalon Street,** with a *platia* at each end, bisects the town. From either end *platia,* you can head uphill toward the towering cliffs.

*Dhomatia* are the best option for lodging in Kalambaka. If you can't make satisfactory arrangements with any women in the phalanx at the bus station, try **Georgios Totis** (tel. 222 51 or 235 88; you can see his conspicuous signs on Perikleos St., which runs up from the square by the bus station. (Large doubles 1600dr. Triples 2200dr. Cots on the roof 500dr. Clean hall bathrooms.) The **Hotel Astoria** (tel. 222 13), near the train station, has dorms for 900dr. **Hotel Epirotikon,** on Ioanninon St. (tel. 233 72), near the post office, offers singles for 1000dr, doubles for 1290dr. The **Hotel Aeolic Star,** at the upper end of the central square, is more expensive. (Singles 1600dr. Doubles 2500dr.) There are six **campgrounds** near Kalambaka, three of which are closer to Meteora in Kastraki (see Meteora). Because the others are on the road toward Trikala, try them only if those in Kastraki are full. Another option is freelance camping on the grassy slopes along the footpath between Kalambaka and the Meteora monasteries.

The municipal **police** are 10 Hagipetrou St. (tel. 422 00), 1 block east of the bus station. The **OTE** (open Mon.-Fri. 7:30am-9pm), and the **post office** (open Mon.-Fri. 7:30am-2:30pm; for stamps 7:30am-4pm) are diagonally across from each other on Ionninon St. There are international **bookstores** on both main *platia*, but the one farthest from the bus station has the best selection of English language books and foreign newspapers. Kalambaka's **telephone code** is 0432; the **postal code** is 42200.

Take a seat in Platia Riga Fereou at the outside tables of the **Restaurant International** or **Nikosi Tavern**, after you've looked at the cauldrons and given your order. Try any beef dish, as the region is known for its meat. For fresh fruits and vegetables, stop at any of the stores along G. Kondyli St., on the way toward the church.

Kalambaka's foremost sight is the Byzantine **Church of the Dormition of the Virgin**. If you follow the signs from Platia Riga Fereou, after several blocks you'll see the graceful bell tower of the old church, haloed by a stork's nest. Built in the eleventh century over the ruins of a fifth-century basilica, the main structure was remodeled in 1573. Unfortunately, the interior frescoes painted by the Cretan monk Neophytos have been badly blackened by centuries of flickering candles and incense, making the massive sculpted marble pulpit the central feature. Modest dress is strictly required. (Open daily 4:30-8pm. Admission 60dr.)

# *Meteora* Μετέωρα

As you approach Kalambaka, Meteora's strange rock pillars rise abruptly from the Thessalian Plain, looking like a Hollywood set constructed for a Dr. Seuss film. Slowly, you can discern grassy plateaus and the parallel fissures across the rock—rings left by centuries of water erosion. Finally, the monasteries appear, perched like eagles' nests on top of the rocks. In Greek, Meteora means "suspended in the air," this could refer to the monasteries or to the monks, who only a century ago could reach the monasteries by riding up in a net at the end of a long rope. Today, a well-paved road accesses the site. Of the original 24 structures, five are still inhabited by monks or nuns. Four buses invade this premier tourist attraction of northern Greece, but even they cannot overpower its serenity and beauty.

## *Practical Information, Accommodations, and Camping*

Two kilometers from Kalambaka is the hamlet of **Kastraki**, which is quieter and more traditional than Kalambaka, as well as a little closer to Meteora. Two excellent campgrounds here serve travelers to Meteora. The centrally located **Camping Vrachos** (tel. 222 93) is a good deal and has a clean pool. (350dr per person. 200dr per tent.) Three kilometers out of Kastraki on the Ioannina-Kalambaka highway is **Camping Meteora Garden** (tel. 227 27; 350dr per person, 250dr per tent). Several *dhomatia* are available, as well as **Hotel Kastraki** (tel. 222 86), which is a convenient location from which to explore Meteora. (Singles 1400dr. Doubles 1700dr. Hot showers 100dr.) Hike toward Meteora to find secluded spots for freelance camping.

You'll need at least a full day to see the six visitable monasteries; only on Thursdays are they all open. **Buses** make the 20-minute run from Kalambaka to the Grand Meteoron twice daily (in summer only, 60dr). The bus can be flagged down at any of the blue *stassis* (bus stop) signs along its route. Hitching is difficult, but you can savor the fantastic view during the one-and-a-half-hour walk. Bring a light lunch and spend the morning at Grand Meteoron and Varlaam. Then take a path from the right-hand side of Varlaam and walk downhill until you reach the road to Agios Nikolaos. The monasteries close for a *siesta* in early afternoon, so you can ascend the road to Roussanou for a view of the surrounding countryside. In late afternoon, hitch to Agios Stephanos and Agios Triados. You can descend to Kalambaka by taxi (400dr) or by a path starting beside Agios Triados.

A word of caution: Women wearing pants, or skirts above the knees, and men wearing shorts are forbidden to enter the monasteries. Women must cover their arms as well as their legs, so bring a light, long-sleeved shirt along.

## History

In the ninth century, hermits and ascetics first began to occupy the pinnacles and crevices of Meteora. As religious persecution at the hands of foreign invaders increased in the twelfth century, Christians were attracted by the refuge offered by the summits of these impregnable, towering columns of rock. The first monastic community was officially founded here in 1356. In the late Byzantine Period, when Greece suffered Turkish domination, Meteora became one of the foremost strongholds of the Christian faith, gradually flourishing into a powerful community of 24 monasteries, all decorated by the finest artists and artisans of the day. Ironically, their wealth turned out to be their own undoing. Bitter quarrels over acquired riches led to neglect and consequent deterioration during the sixteenth century. Today, only five of the monasteries are still active: the Grand Meteoron, Varlaam, Agios Nikolaos, Agios Triados, and Agios Stephanos (now a nunnery). The Roussanou monastery is intact but uninhabited. Only occasional ruins remain of the others.

The first ascetics scaled the sheer cliff faces by wedging timbers into the rock crevices, thereby constructing small platforms. Look for the traces of the wooden scaffolding along the ripples of the rock walls and in the caves. After the monasteries were completed, they were usually reached by extremely long ladders, which, when pulled up, rendered the summit virtually inaccessible. People were also hoisted up over the sheer drop in free-swinging rope nets—the half-hour ascent fostered a most profound faith in God. Motorized winches have replaced monk-powered, rope-spool cranes, and today provisions, not pilgrims, are elevated. In 1922, steps were carved into the rocks and bridges built between the pillars.

All of the monasteries have interesting features and artistic motifs. Large wooden slabs or bent rectangles of iron suspended by two chains from the ceiling, for instance, serve as "bells" and are sounded with large wooden mallets by the monks to announce events of the monastic schedule. The wooden seats lining the monastery churches consist of very small compartments with hinged seats, made so that the monks can either stand or sit during prayers without moving from the compartments. The six-sided "Star of David" that appears repeatedly was as much a Byzantine symbol then as a Jewish one today. Finally, the ubiquitous pair of eagles with elongated necks was emblematic of the Byzantine concept of the unity of church and state, and also represents Constantinople, the religious and political center of the Empire.

Due to the easy access to the summits, Meteora is no longer the secluded religious haven it once was. Hordes of tourists flock to the monasteries, especially to the Grand Meteoron and Varlaam. In the smaller, less accessible monasteries, however, austere monastic life prevails.

## The Monasteries

The Monastery of the Transfiguration (Metamorphosis), more commonly known as the **Grand Meteoron,** is the oldest and largest of the monasteries. Built on the most massive of the occupied stone columns, the complex of buildings towers about 500m above the Thessalian plain. Founded by Athanasius, a monk from Mt. Athos, the monastery rose to a degree of political and financial power when the generous John Uresis, grandson of the Serbian prince Stephen, retired to its summit in 1388. The monastery is divided into two levels, each housing four churches, of which one is open to the public. Entering the monastery, you see the large wooden basket which provided the original means of access to the summit. Adjacent to the kitchen is the barrel-vaulted stone dining room, now a museum. Its collection includes illuminated manuscripts dating from the ninth century and carved icons decorated with scenes from the Bible. One of the icons overlaid with tiny sculpted relief reputedly took the monk Daniel 14 years to complete. Of particular interest is the eighteenth-century print displaying a map of the original 24 monasteries.

The central feature of the Grand Meteoron is the sixteenth-century **Church of the Transfiguration.** The narthex is decorated with brilliant frescoes depicting the persecution of the Christians by the Romans, appropriate for the refuge of the monks. The main hall is capped by an elegant 12-sided dome with the Pantokrator at its center. The central stairway back down to the first level on the left leads to a row of small, arched cubicles where the monks go for solitary contemplation and prayer. Directly across is a chamber filled with carefully stacked skulls and bones, the remains of previous residents. (Grand Meteoron open Wed.-Mon. 9am-1pm and 3:20-6pm. Admission 200dr.)

Just 300m down the road from the Grand Meteoron is the **Varlaam Monastery,** the second largest monastery on Meteora. Built in 1517, its main attractions are the sixteenth-century frescoes in the chapel. The fresco on the central wall of the church depicts the Apocalypse. In the far right corner of the narthex, a glass case contains venerated relics of bone set in silver. Just above hangs a fresco of Varlaam's founders, Nektarios and Theophanes Asparas, holding the Monastery aloft between their open palms. Also of interest at Varlaam are the museum and chamber containing an enormous wooden wine vat with a 13,000-liter capacity. A metal footbridge connects the monastery to the neighboring stone pillar. (Open Sat.-Thurs. 9am-1pm and 3:20-6pm. Admission 200dr.)

A short distance below the main intersection on the road back to Kastraki and visible from most of the valley, **Agia Barbara-Roussanou** is the most spectacularly situated and frequently photographed monastery. Its walls are a continuation of the rock foundation. Because of steady deterioration, Roussanou was recently abandoned and closed without plans for reopening. It is still possible to ascend a trail to the monastery and walk across the bridge for a dizzying view of the valley below.

If you continue up the trail all the way to the end, you'll eventually reach the road leading to the Agios Triados and Agios Stephanos monasteries. A short walk along the road brings you to two look-out areas on the right providing the fullest view of Meteora. Hitching along this road to Agios Stephanos and Agios Triados is fairly reliable.

**Agios Stephanos,** at the road's end, begun as a hermitage, officially became a monastery in the fourteenth century, and is now a convent. Stephanos is cleaner, lighter, and more spacious than the massive Grand Meteoron and Varlaam. Of its two churches, only the more modern **Agios Charalambos** is open to the public. Built in 1798, Agios Charalambos sharply contrasts the older churches of the other monasteries. Although relatively small, the museum here displays artifacts of quality and delicate detail. Notice the abbots' elaborate personal signatures on the ecclesiastical parchment scrolls in the case on the left. (Open Tues.-Sun. 8am-noon and 3-6pm. Free.)

The Monastery of **Agios Triados** (Holy Trinity) lies a few kilometers down the road towards the main intersection. Looming directly over Kalambaka, its soaring peak features a striking view of the town 1320m below and of the snow-capped Pirdos Mountains in the distance. The monk Dometius built the monastery in 1476, but the wall paintings were added 200 years later. Gardens are scattered among the wood and stone buildings. (Open 8am-6pm. Admission 100dr.) A 3-kilometer footpath runs from the right side of the entrance to Agios Triados all the way into Kalambaka.

All the way back down the road, past the main intersection and only 2½ km from Kastraki, is the Monastery of **Agios Nikolaos,** also called **Anapafsa.** Built in 1388 and expanded in 1628, its highlight is the fresco work painted by the sixteenth-century Cretan master Theophanes. His technique of using alternatively light and dark brush strokes makes the figures on his icons bristle with life. A delightful mural depicts Adam naming the animals. The monastery also features a traditional Meteoran lavatory: a hole in the wooden floor at the edge of the cliff, with a straight drop to the rocks below. Visitors are admitted only in small groups, so wait in the entrance at the top of the steps for the door to open. In addition to the usual dress code, Agios Nikolaos denies entry to men with long hair, but it might pass if tied back and tucked underneath a collar. (Open daily 8am-1pm and 3-6:30pm. Admission 100dr.)

# Metsovo Μέτσοβο

Even in the cruelest summer, this alpine retreat smells of snow and cozy fires. You'll miss your flannel as you cross through the sweet pines that encircle the village of Metsovo. Nestled on a mountainside just below the 1850-meter Katara Pass and midway between Kalambaka and Ioannina, Metsovo outshines even the surrounding Pindos Mountains. In the past few years, the main artery of the town has been transformed by tourists who stop here on their way from Thessaloniki to Ioannina. Houses with cantilevered wooden balconies, flower boxes, iron-grill windows, and alternating slate and terra-cotta roofs line its narrow cobbled streets. Traditional Vlachi culture and language survive here. Once believed to have migrated from Romania, the Vlachi are now thought to have been Greeks trained by the Romans to guard the Egnatia Highway connecting Constantinople with the Adriatic. The Vlachi language is so heavily influenced by Latin that it was used to communicate with the Italians during World War II.

Today, Vlachi merchants sell Metsovan cheese and a variety of hand-made rugs and trinkets. The **Tositsa Museum,** housed in a beautiful Epirot mansion on the left up the main road (look for the sign), displays intricate antique Vlachi handicrafts. Wait at the door until the guide appears (every ½ hr.) to take you through. (Open Fri.-Wed. 8:30am-1pm and 4-6:30pm. Admission 90dr.) Near the *square* you will see signs for **Agios Nikolaos Monastery.** At the monastery, open the front door and a nun will come to show you the fourteenth-century chapel. The **Agia Paraskevi** church, just above the square, contains a wooden *iconostassis* made in 1511 and a pulpit with a winding wooden staircase. Just minutes from the main road, out of town toward the Katara Pass, you can hike over alpine meadows amid the Pindos Mountains. Right above the town, a small ski lift operates in winter (daily 9am-4pm). In summer, you might want to plan a stay at Metsovo during the *panigiria* (nameday festival) of *Agia Paraskevi* (July 26) or *Panayia* (Aug. 15).

**Buses** stop in the square (5 per day to Ioannina, 260dr; 2 per day to Trikala and Kalambaka; 1 per day to Thessaloniki). The square also has two **banks** (open Mon.-Thurs. 8am-2pm, Fri. 8am-1:30pm). For the **OTE** (open Mon.-Sat. 7:30am-2:30pm) and the **police** (tel. 411 83 or 411 89), walk past the cheese shop opposite the banks and follow the corner road. Up the main road you'll find the **post office.** (Open Mon.-Fri. 7:30am-2:30pm.)

Metsovo's cheapest hotel, **Athenai** (tel. 417 25), offers adequate rooms. (Singles 1100dr. Doubles 2000dr. Hot showers 100dr.) It also has a restaurant just off the main square that serves the best (and cheapest) Greek cuisine in town. A little out of the way is the **Hotel Acropolis,** up the hill by the highway. (Singles 1000dr. Doubles 1800dr.) Paying a little more will get you a big boost in quality at the **Hotel Egnatia** (tel. 412 63), 100m up the main road. Here, the charm of Metsovan furnishings really stands out with chandeliers, stone floors, colorful wall hangings, a warm hearth, and fine woodwork. (Singles 2050dr. Doubles with private bath 3400dr.) It's worth the climb to eat at **To Spitiko,** up the hill from Hotel Egnatia. Their specialty is *vrasto katsiki* (boiled goat, 320dr) and homemade *trahanas* (semolina soup, 180dr). For dessert, have goat's-milk yogurt with honey (210dr).

# Epirus Ηπειρος

If you came to Greece in search of idyllic, isolated settings, consider roaming through this region. Igoumenitsa may be your first stop on the Greek mainland (boats from Brindisi and Corfu stop here); begin exploring the country from here rather than heading straight for the mayhem of Athens. Craggy snow-mantled mountains, verdant valleys, and roundabout rivers characterize this hiker's paradise. Although the picturesque town and golden beaches of Parga see their share of tourists, the hardy mountains and timeless villages of Zagoria near the Vicos-Aoos National Park remain undisturbed.

# Igoumenitsa Ηγουμενίτσα

No one goes to Igoumenitsa; one only goes through here on the way somewhere else. A drab port town, Igoumenitsa is a transportation center for northern Greece, the Ionian Islands, and foreign destinations. Buses leave for Ioannina (12 per day, 550dr), with connections to Thessaloniki and Kalambaka, Parga (5 per day, 1 hr., 260dr), Athens (3 per day, 8 hr., 2530dr), and Preveza (3 per day, 3 hr., 630dr). To reach the **bus station** (tel. 223 09), turn left from the Corfu port or right from the Italy port. Take El. Venizelou inland and make the second left onto Kyprou St. A right on the same street leads to the central square. **Ferries** steam to Corfu (6am-9:30pm every hr., 2 hr., 357dr), as well as to Brindisi, Bari, Ancona, and Otranto in Italy, and Dubrovnik and other major ports and islands in Yugoslavia. For the frequent Italian sailings, do some comparison shopping among the numerous waterfront agencies. Also, check on stopover charges for Corfu. **HML Adriatica,** 80 Ethnikis Antistassis (tel. 228 35), has the cheapest tickets to Brindisi for railcard holders (Eurail 1200dr, InterRail 2800dr, plus 400dr port tax), with an additional 600dr for a stopover in Corfu. The **R Line** (tel. 223 48) sails to Otranto without stopping in Corfu (3500dr, Eurail/InterRail 3000dr). **Jardolinija** runs a ferry to Yugoslavia every Tuesday from May through September, and also on Wednesday and Friday from July through September. If possible, pay in U.S. dollars (to Dubrovnik US$27 plus US$6 port tax). Fares are pegged to the dollar and the exchange rate is outrageous if you pay in *drachmae.* Most boats depart in the morning, so arrive early or plan to spend the night. Keep in mind that boats for Patras leave from Corfu Town, not Igoumenitsa.

Along the waterfront you'll find the useless **tourist police** (tel. 223 02) on the first floor of the police station. (Open Mon.-Fri. 7am-2:30pm.) The **bank** is on the waterfront (open Mon.-Thurs. 8am-2pm, Fri. 8am-1:30pm); when it is closed you can exchange money at most ferry agencies (open until about 9pm). The **OTE** (open Mon.-Fri. 7am-midnight) and the **post office** (open Mon.-Fri. 7:30am-2:30pm) are on Evangelistrias St., which runs inland, connecting the waterfront to Kyprou St. The **hospital** is at 15 Filiates St. (tel. 222 05); for **emergencies,** call 221 13. Igoumenitsa's **telephone code** is 0665.

**H. Thesprotia** has the cheapest pension in town. It is a light-blue one-story building located on Venizelou St. inland from the square, next to the Hotel Egnatia. (600dr per person.) Also try the **Rodos Hotel,** at #13 on the seaward side of the nearby square (singles 950dr; doubles 1500dr), or **Stavrodomi,** 26 Souliou St., up the hill from the square, with the same prices and a good restaurant beneath. (Both include hot showers.) **Kalami Beach Camping** (tel. 712 45), 12km south of town, has a *taverna* and a shop. (410dr per person. 580dr per tent. Showers included.) **Drepanos Beach,** 6km north of Igoumenitsa, has relatively clean water, but no camping facilities.

# Parga Πάργα

At its best, Parga is an intriguing seaside town with foliated hills on one side and islets on the other. At its worst, Parga bursts with tourists, especially at night when its steep streets become a shopping mecca.

Parga's major sight is its guardian Venetian fortress (*kastro*). The largest castle in the area, it was constructed by the Normans but occupied by the Venetians from

1401 to 1797. The structure stands as a mere shell beneath the shade of majestic pines, but in the afternoon heat it is a superior spot for a picnic or snooze. Follow the steps from the harbor up the hill, only five minutes from the water. (Open daily 7am-10pm. Free.)

Less than 100m offshore, the islets are an easy swim away. The fortifications on one of them were built by the French. The kilometer-long beach over the hill (right facing the *kastro*) is peaceful, uncluttered, and convenient. The long crescent-shaped **Lichnos Beach** lies 3km south. Snorkelers in particular will appreciate the clear turquoise water and underwater rock formations. A wonderful daytrip from Parga is the boat ride up the ancient **Styx** (the Acheron), the mythological waterway to the underworld. The trip takes a half-hour by boat from Parga to the mouth of the river; another half-hour up the river, the boat stops at Lichnos Beach for swimming and a late lunch in a *taverna* (600dr, lunch not included). For more information, inquire at West Travel.

Parga's two unofficial tourist offices, **West Travel** (tel. 302 23) and **Parga Tours** (tel. 315 80), both on the waterfront, will help you find a room, rent a moped, or arrange a daytrip. (Open Mon.-Sat. 8:30am-1:30pm and 6-9:30pm.) The **post office** (open Mon.-Fri. 7:30am-2:30pm), **bus station** (tel. 312 18), and **police station** (tel. 312 22) all stand in a row on Bagka St. The road from these to the harbor runs past the **OTE,** on your right. (Open Mon.-Sat. 7:30am-3:10pm.) Parga's **telephone code** is 0684.

Although the number of tourists vacationing in Parga increases every year, the number of new *dhomatia* signs increases even faster. Try at the southern end of town and on top of the hill where few tourists venture. Unfortunately, no one is needy enough to give you a really good price. (Range: Singles 1000dr. Doubles 1800dr.) Try the **Hotel Paradissos**, 33 Liboa St., near the center of town. (Doubles 1500dr.) Another tactic is to try to sleep on the roof of a posh pension. Often the owner will unofficially install you with a cot and shower facilities for 500dr. The best option is **Parga Camping** (tel. 311 30), 1km north along the road. Complete with a private road to the beach and spacious sites in the olive trees, the place is a great deal. It also has a cheap restaurant and clean bathrooms. (175dr per person. 175dr per tent.)

To eat, follow the main drag past the tourist throng to the **Villa Rosa,** propped up over the southernmost point of the beach. Canopied by trees and flowers, this restaurant serves the cheapest Greek and Italian food in town. For dessert, walk toward the other extreme of the drag and turn right. The bakery on the right-hand side sells delicious *loukoumi* (15dr). Or try some homemade ice cream at the bakery downhill from the Paradissos Hotel; its best is *parfait,* with fresh fruits and nuts (70dr). The **Rose Garden Bar**, next to the bus station, often plays good music and is a peaceful oasis amid Parga's hubub. (*Ouzo* 350dr.)

Nightlife in Parga centers on the *volta* (promenade) up and down the main street along the bay. At 11:30pm, Parga's two discos open: the **Galaxy,** a few blocks inland on the hill (mandatory beer or soft drink 350dr), and the **Aloni,** 2 blocks farther inland, where men join in traditional dancing (mandatory drink 300dr). Ask anyone for directions; the discos are major landmarks. The hottest night spot is the **Duffino Bar,** complete with rock videos.

# *Preveza* Πρέβεζα

Built at the entrance to Amvrakikos Bay, opposite Aktio, the rather plain port of Preveza is a transportation hub. The bus station lies on Irinis St., 1km from the harbor. **Buses** leave for Igoumenitsa (2 per day, 3 hr., 630dr), Parga (5 per day, 1½ hr., 410dr), Ioannina (every hr., 600dr), and Athens (3 per day, 7 hr., 2250dr). At the harbor you will find the **ferry** to Aktio (departures every ½ hr., 30dr). From Aktio, the road south branches west to Lefkas, and east to Vonitsa and Patras. The ferry landing is a good place to thumb a lift to either.

The main street in town is **Eleftheriou Venizelou,** along which lie the **bank** (open Mon.-Thurs. 8am-2pm, Fri. 8am-1:30pm) and the **post office** (open Mon.-Fri. 7:30am-4pm; 7:30am-2:30pm for money orders, exchange, and parcels). In the same building is a **tourist office** (tel. 272 77). Fluent in English, the enthusiastic women will give you a map of Preveza, information on any of the Ionian Islands, accommodations, and just about anything else you need. (Open Mon.-Fri. 7:30am-2:30pm. Sat. 9am-1pm.) Preveza's **telephone code** is 0682.

If you are stuck in town for some reason, try **Hotel Aktaion,** 1 Colobou (tel. 222 58), 2 blocks south of the post office and 1 block inland. (Singles 1400dr. Doubles 1700dr. Triples 2500dr.) Another option is the no-frills C-class **Preveza City** (tel. 273 65 or 238 71; doubles 2000dr; triples 2600dr). If you have a sleeping bag, skip town and head to **Monolith,** a sandy beach about 10km outside of Preveza on the road to Igoumenitsa and to **Monolith Camping.** (Open June-Sept.) The campgrounds advertised in town are much farther away than the signs indicate. However, hitching to or from Preveza is usually feasible. Campings include **Indian Village** (tel. 221 92), **Kalamitsi** (tel. 232 68), and **Kanali** (tel. 517 33). All campgrounds charge around 400dr per person and 310dr per tent. Cheap fast-food joints line the main street, but for the best budget fare in town, pick up the usual *souvlaki* at the *photoleion* run by **K. Nikolos,** on Platia Tsaldari.

## Near Preveza

**Zaloggon** (Zalongo), 27km north of Preveza and overlooking the village of Kamarina, makes an interesting morning or afternoon trip, though difficult without a car. You can take a bus to Kamarina from Parga (1 hr.) or Preveza (½ hr.), and walk the 4km up to Zalongo. This mountaintop site figures tragically in modern Greek history. On December 18, 1803, 60 women from Souli threw their children off the cliff and then leapt themselves to avoid being taken as slaves by the Turks. On the cliff's edge where the women jumped, there is now a multiform monument, constructed so that the several figures look like innumerable women linking arms into the distance. The Agios Demetrios Monastery sits at the foot of the mountain.

At **Nikopolis** lie the ruins of a prosperous Roman city built by Octavian Augustus in 31 B.C.E. to commemorate his naval victory over Antony and Cleopatra off the coast of nearby Actium; the name "Nikopolis" comes from the Greek *nike* (victory) and *polis* (city). Although destroyed by the Vandals and Goths, the city once again flourished under Byzantine rule. A 3-kilometer stretch of the Byzantine wall remains, as well as the ruins of a theater and a few Roman temples converted into Byzantine chapels. The wonderful mosaics for which Nikopolis is famous are presently covered, and officials don't know when they will be re-displayed. Nevertheless, the ruins are still worth a visit; brush the gravel out of the corners to get a peek at the mosaics on the floor. (Site and small museum open Mon. and Wed.-Sat. 8:45am-3pm, Sun. 9:30am-2:30pm. Admission 200dr, students 100dr.)

# *Ioannina* Ιωάννινα

Although tourists stop here only to change buses to or from Igoumenitsa, Ioannina (pronounced YAH-nee-nah), on the shore of Lake Pamvotis merits a stopover. The streets of the old town are great to wander about, and the parks near Platia Eleftheriou and on the island nearby offer a refreshing escape from the summer heat.

There is a cluster of hotels right by the bus station and another off the main street, which runs north to the port, first as **Demokratiou Street,** and then as **Averof Street.** To get there from the bus station (between Zosimadon and Sina St.), turn left at the National Bank, right at the green triangle, and walk past the Hotel Palladion to 28 Octovriou St. A left onto this street will take you past the **tourist police** (tel. 256 73; open 8am-10pm) and the **OTE** (open 24 hours). 28 Octovriou St. intersects the main drag. Turn left to go to the central square, old town, port, and hotels, or go right for the **post office,** on Markou Botsari Sq. (Open Mon.-Fri. 7:30am-

8:30pm; 7:30am-2:30pm for Poste Restante and parcels.) With enthusiasm and pride for the Ioannina area, the **GNTO**, also in Botsari Sq., provides useful information and exchanges money. (Open Mon.-Sat. 7:30am-9pm.) One long block behind the post office, at 6A G. Molaimido St., is the local chapter of the **Hellenic Mountaineering Club** (tel. 221 38), usually staffed after 5pm on weekdays. This is an excellent place to obtain information if you are heading for the mountains. (See Vicos Gorge and Zagoria Villages.) Ionnina's **telephone code** is 0651.

**Buses** from the main terminal travel to Athens (11 per day, 7 hr., 2290dr), Igoumenitsa (10 per day, 2 hr., 550dr), and Thessaloniki via Larissa (5 per day, 7 hr., 1910dr). Four buses per day travel to Konitsa, passing through many of the Zagoria villages (350dr). Check the schedule, since bus routes change daily. The other station sends buses to Preveza (9 per day) and Dodoni (3 per day, 110dr). To get there, follow Bizaniou St. about 3 blocks west from the post office. Storage space is available in the *apothiki* at the main bus terminal. (No charge. Open 24 hours.) Another option considerably safer is the cafeteria in the station house; politely ask the manager to leave your things in the far-end corner of the room. Beyond the post office, on 86 Napoleon Zeruar, is a **laundromat**. (Wash 300dr. Dry 50dr per 12 min.)

Finding accommodations is not difficult, but finding a cheap and comfortable place is another matter. The **Agapi**, on Tsirigoti St. (tel. 205 41), near the main bus station and next to **Hotel Paris**, offers street-level singles from 1000dr and doubles for 1300dr (hot showers 150dr). Nearby, the hotel **Mitropolis**, 2 Kristalli, is a step up in quality. (Singles 1800dr. Doubles 1910dr. Hot showers 100dr.) On the corner of Averof and Krystali St., closer to the port, the **Hotel Tourist** (tel. 264 43) has singles for 1000dr, doubles for 1800dr. **Hotel Paradeisos**, 15 K. A. Februouariou (tel. 253 65), near the bus station, has similar service and price range. The most satisfying accommodations are on Lake Pamvotis but require advance notice. Try pension **Barbara Baraka** (tel. 243 96), on a quiet corner to the right of the beach (follow signs). (Well-kept singles 900dr. Doubles with bath 1400dr.) The **Sarai** restaurant here is cheaper than the ones on the dock. Along the shores of the lake, less than 1km from the city center, you can pitch a tent at **Camping Limnopoula** (tel. 380 60; 150dr per person; 100dr for tent).

Several excellent restaurants lie on Georgiou St., which connects the castle with the newer town center. **Restaurant HBH**, 4 Georgiou St., helps beat hunger with its daily lunch specials. If you don't get there before noon, you might have to wait a few minutes in line. Across the street, the **Restaurant Pantheon** let you choose from a selection of dishes; they also offer quick service. (*Bamies* 270dr. Located at the southern end of the central park, **Restaurant Litharitsa** occupies a small fortress and serves Greek and Continental cuisine. (Omelettes 200dr.) The island has the best seafood in Ioannina: Select your own *pestropha* (trout) from the tanks outside the restaurant (600-900dr per kilo; ½ kilo is a good meal). You can also get *xeli* (eel) and *karavides* (crayfish). Ioannina's premier disco, **Taiga**, is located underneath a courtyard near the intersection of Zerva Napos and Dodonis Georgiou St. It is usually packed every night of the week. (Cover 400dr. 1 beer included.) The early-night action is at the cafeterias along Averof St., where people sit sipping *frappe* (iced coffee).

A city built hemispherically, Ioannina was founded by Emperor Justinian in the seventh century C.E. It was conquered by the Turks in 1430 and remained in their hands until 1913. Ioannina was made famous, however, when the brutal Turkish tyrant Ali Pasha, the governor of the province of Epirus just before the Greek Revolution, tried to secede from the Sultan and create an independent kingdom. He reportedly chained up his wife and harem of sixteen women and threw them into the lake. He was belatedly assassinated in 1822 by the irate sultan. The **Asian Aga Mosque** is a splendid eighteenth-century remnant of the 500-year Turkish rule. Now converted into a public museum, the mosque sits at the edge of the old town, overlooking the lake next to Skilosofou St. (Open Mon.-Sat. 9am-3pm, Sat.-Sun. 9am-1pm. Admission 200dr.) On the southern side of the old town is another area of deserted Turkish ruins and an old mosque. The view of the lake and the new sections of the city make it an excellent place to eat lunch.

The massive walls of the **Castle of Ioannina** were built near the time of the city's founding, and reinforced in the eleventh and fourteenth centuries. Today, its walls divide the old and modern parts of the city. Enclosed within the remains of the walls are the narrow streets of the old town, filled with examples of traditional architecture, plane-trees, and stone churches. As you walk through the old town, listen for the clinking hammers of the silversmiths; you can watch them working through the windows.

The collection of the **archeological museum** has been growing slowly. The most interesting pieces in the collection are the detailed panels on its three sarcophagi and the minute stone tablets etched with political, romantic, and cosmological questions that Roman emperors asked of the oracle at Dodoni (sixth to the third century B.C.E.). The museum is in a park off Averof St. and below the clock tower. (Open Mon. and Wed.-Sat. 8:45am-3pm, Sun. 9:30am-2:30pm. Admission 200dr, students 100dr.)

Ioannina's chief attraction, however, is the idyllic **island** near the western shore of Lake Pamvotis. Boats leave every half-hour from 7:30am to 10:30pm (10 min., 40dr); in Ioannina, they leave from the lakeside northern corner of the city wall. The island's tiny village has no cars, and chickens wander on the narrow stone paths between whitewashed houses and elaborate gardens. The interior of the island is a pine forest with paths weaving between curious monasteries, some of which contain restored frescoes. There is also a shaded path running around the perimeter of the island. It was in the cellar of the church of St. Panteleimon in the monastery of **Agios Nikolaos** that Ali Pasha unsuccessfully sought refuge from the assailing Sultan's forces. The **Ali Pasha Museum** on the site shows how he lived and where he died—beheaded on the second stone step from the top. (Open daily 9am-10pm. Admission 20dr.)

### Near Ioannina: Perama

About 5km northeast of Ioannina on the Metsovo highway is **Perama,** with its entrancing stalagmite and stalactite caves. The 45-minute guided tour of the caves includes elaborate accounts of the names of different rock formations, including "Rustic Pile," "The Statue of Liberty" (decapitated), and "The Lake with the Stony Water Lilies." Ask the guide to point out some personal favorites, perhaps "The Pigs Coming Down from the Hill," or "Three Dozen Hanging Breasts." The tours are conducted in English. (Open in summer 8am-8pm; in off-season 8:30am-5pm. Admission 250dr, students 120dr.) Take bus #8 (40dr) from Platia Eleftheriou to the end of the line, then follow the signs.

# Vikos Gorge and Zagoria Villages
## Βίκος και Ζαγορίας

The area east of the road between Ioannina and Konitsa is atypical of the usual Greek landscape, replacing the famous ruins, sandy beaches, and wild nightlife with deep canyons, bizarre rock formations, and gray stone and slate villages. You are not entering an enchanted kingdom: The government has declared the Zagoria villages "traditional settlements," thus forbidding overly-commercial development. The Vicos Gorge and the intersecting Aoos River and canyon were declared a national park in 1973.

The area is small enough that you don't need a detailed topographical map. In Ioannina, drop by the Mountaineering Club and pick up the small flyer *Vicos-Aoos National Park.* Although the English version gives a decent write-up, you'll have to decipher the lettering. The club office has rough contour sketches of part of the area, which you can photocopy across the street. When you venture forth, bring some provisions and camping gear. Keep in mind that these villages do not cater to tourists. There are no hotels (though you will be able to arrange a room with locals), and at best, a village might have a couple of small cafe/grill/restaurants. The locals value the pristine nature of their area and, hence, may appear a tad xenophobic. Be extremely polite and do not trespass; you'll find the people in these parts especially kind, though amused that anyone would travel so far to romp in their backyards.

Getting here without a car is difficult since bus service is infrequent and hitching almost impossible. Check the bus schedule in Ioannina. The most frequent connections drop you off in Konitsa, near the northern end of the national park (2 per day, 270dr). Buses also travel to Monodendri, Aristi, Kipi, and Tsepelovo (2 or 3 per week, 1 per day at most).

The best place to start a journey through the gorge is at the hamlet **Monodendri.** Buses travel from Ioannina (Mon.-Fri. at 4pm, Sat.-Sun. at 6:30pm, 1 hr., 300dr). Inquire at the restaurant for *dhomatia;* someone will be able to provide decent B&B for about 750dr per person. Stop by the restaurant near the bus stop for a *tiropita.* Especially if you're not headed into the gorge, visit the unoccupied monastery **Agia Paraskevi,** about 800m beyond town, where you'll observe more of the slate-roofed Zagorian architecture and the magnificent Vicos Gorge from a 300-meter-high cliff.

If you plan to sleep under the stars, start hiking from Monodendri—either in the gorge or overlooking it. The latter route is more spectacular, but a harder climb. Follow the main road out of Monodendri that turns into a rocky dirt path. Seven kilometers from town, a slate path continues to the edge of a precipice overlooking the Vicos Gorge. The last half of the road is surrounded by unique rock slabs layered like huge marble tabletops. Campers can just choose a spot several meters off the side of the road. To descend into the gorge, return to Monodendri and follow the path behind the church. The trail is tortuous, even dangerous, but it becomes much more manageable at the bottom.

Entering the gorge from Monodendri will put you at its southern end. A four- to five-hour hike from here will bring you to **Vicos** village, located near **Aristi** and **Papingo.** Papingo gives you access to another gateway into the gorge. To get there, take the 5-kilometer road (not 2km, as the sign asserts) from Vicos. Shadowed by buttes reminiscent of the American West, picturesque Papingo pulls in a pack of people, mostly hikers. Hotels are available, but you can bargain for *dhomatia.* If you're headed into the gorge, follow the signs in town to the **GNTO tourist office.** Although primarily interested in filling their hotel, they will provide information on trail conditions and the refuges. (Singles with bath 3200dr.) Pick up the key to the refuge here (700dr). The main trailhead is farther up the road at the even smaller village of **Mikro Papingo** (buses from Ioannina Mon.-Tues., Fri., and Sun., 300dr), beneath the awesome **Mount Astraka** (2436m). If you stay here, go to **Agnanti's** rooms to the right from the trailhead sign. Mr. Agnanti, his sister, and his niece warmly welcome visitors and provide breakfast, lunch, and dinner. It's a three-hour climb to the main hut, and another two and a half hours to the summit, Gamila Park. From the hut, continue northeast over the **Koutsometros Range** into the **Aoos River Gorge. Mount Gamila** (2478m) looms on your right, and Konitsa is in sight far to the left, past the end of the gorge. It's impossible to descend to the left unless you have hang-gliding equipment. You might still appreciate the wilderness as you head down to your right towards the Aoos. **Despina** and **Leonidos** refuges offer truly inspiring vistas. (400dr per person.) From these, you can easily hike to the broad summit of Mt. Gamila.

Far below, **Konitsa** offers a convenient base to begin your trek in the opposite direction, with hotels, a choice of *tavernas,* and supermarkets for provisions. Leaving Konitsa, follow the road down to the bridge over the River Aoos. A one-hour hike along the footpath will take you up through the gorge to a monastery. Only one monk lives here and you can join him for the cost of a few hours' custodial work around the monastery. Another four-hour hike will bring you to the Gamila shelter. In Konitsa's main square are the **bus station,** the **post office** (open Mon.-Fri. 7:30am-2:30pm), two **banks** (open Mon.-Thurs. 8am-2pm, Fri. 8am-1:30pm), and a couple of hotels. The cheapest, **Hotel Pindos,** is about 3 blocks along the lower road headed south from the square. (700dr per person. Hot showers 100dr.) The

Hotel Egnatia, on the square, is also quite reasonable, with big old-fashioned bath tubs. (Singles 1000dr. Doubles 2000dr.) The **police** (tel. 222 02) are down the hill, on the main road. (Open 24 hours.)

# Dodoni Δωδόνι

> Oh! where, Dodona! is thine aged grove,
> Prophetic fount, and oracle divine?
> What valley echo'd the response of Jove?
> What trace remaineth of the Thunderer's shrine?
> All, all forgotten.
> —George Gordon, Lord Byron Childe Harold's Pilgrimage

Ancient Dodoni, rediscovered since Byron's lamentation, is sheltered at the foot of a mountain 21km south of Ioannina. It became a religious center when the first tribes of the Hellenes occupied the area around 1900 B.C.E., establishing the roots of the Greek "race," the Selloi-Helloi branch of Indo-European stock. Worship first centered around an earth-mother goddess, but later shifted to a giant oak tree. Cauldrons were placed around the tree to resonate in the wind and drive out evil spirits. Around 800 B.C.E., the site became an oracle dedicated to Zeus, who was believed to reside in the roots of the tree. A temple was built around 500 B.C.E., then destroyed along with the oak tree by the Romans in 167 B.C.E. What little was left of the old religion was further subverted by the Christians, who built a basilica on the site (the ruins are still visible) in an attempt to destroy pagan influences.

The central attraction at Dodoni is the restored third-century **amphitheater.** It originally seated 18,000, but was rearranged during Roman times for gladiator games. In the first week of August, the theater hosts a festival of classical drama performed in front of capacity audiences. The remnants of the oracles and the foundations of several buildings, including a temple to Aphrodite and a hall for pilgrims, are next to the theater. A small oak has been thoughtfully replanted in the middle of the remains of the sanctuary of Zeus. (Open in summer Mon.-Sat. 7:30am-7:30pm, Sun 9am-6pm; in off-season Mon.-Sat. 9am-5pm, Sun. 9am-3pm. Admission 100dr, students 50dr.) With permission or a little discretion, you can camp in the field by the theater, with a toilet and running water.

The peaceful village of Dodoni is adjacent to the ruins. Two buses per day leave from Bizaniou St. in Ioannina; check at the tourist office for times. Unfortunately, the buses return almost immediately after they reach Dodoni, but it's not too difficult to sweet-talk your way onto one of the tourist buses heading back to Ioannina. A group can take a taxi (1500dr one-way, 2000dr round-trip). The only other alternative is to hitch. Start walking down the Dodoni road from Platia Pyrrou to the Preveza road. The turn-off to Dodoni is 8km down the road; the last 13km is almost completely deserted.

# Macedonia Μακεδονία

The home of Alexander the Great, this largest of Greek provinces has more to offer than many think. The primary lines of transportation run to and from Thessaloniki, but don't limit yourself to this noisy, modern city. The region's most interesting sights are in the countryside. Head for Mt. Athos (if you're male), with its austere spiritual vitality, the Lake District in all its vibrant natural splendor, and the excavations at Vergina and Pella, momentos of glories. That this area remains mostly untouristed accounts for the preservation of old, village life.

# Kastoria and the Lake District
## Καστοριά και περιφέρεια της Αίμνης

Since tourists don't usually venture north of Kastoria, this region of unspoiled lakes and rivers remains one of Greece's best-kept secrets. The capital of the district, **Kastoria,** is a bustling, polluted metropolis, and not really worth a visit. To escape the dinginess, walk to the water's edge, or spend some time exploring the city's many churches, well-known for their elaborate serrated masonry. Two churches in particular merit visits for their well-kept eleventh-century frescoes: the tiny Byzantine **Panayia Koumblelidhiki,** in the center of town, and the **Church Mavrotissa,** about 3km outside. Atop the peninsula's hill, the **Church of the Prophet Ilias** provides a spectacular view of Lake Kastoria. The adjacent restaurant has the better lookout, with good, but expensive food (375-450dr).

The helpful **tourist police,** 25 Grammou St. (tel. 233 33), 1 block behind the bus station, speak English. (Open 24 hours.) The **post office,** 19 Mitropolis St., also exchanges money. (Open Mon.-Fri. 7:30am-3pm.) The **OTE** is up the hill at 33 Agion Athanasiou St. (Open Mon.-Fri. 7am-midnight, Sat.-Sun. 7:30am-3:10pm.) Kastoria's **main bus terminal** is on the same street, by the lakeside. Buses run to Thessaloniki via Edessa (5 per day, 4 hr., 1200dr) and Veria (1 per day at 7:30am, 3½ hr., 815dr). If you miss the latter, you can go to Kozani and transfer buses. Of the many banks, the newer **Agricultural Bank of Greece,** on Mitropolis St., offers better service and lower commission charges. **Olympic Airways** has daily flights to Kastoria from Athens. The Olympic office on the waterfront (tel. 222 75 or 231 25) is open daily 8:30am-3pm.

For accommodations, the **Palladion Hotel,** 40 Mitropolis St. (tel. 224 93), has cheap rooms, though the bathrooms are dirty and toilet paper is an abstract concept. (Singles 1500dr. Doubles 2000dr.) The **Hotel Akropolis,** 14 Gramov St. (tel. 225 37), 1 block inland from the bus station, has singles with bath for 2200dr, triples for 2050dr. (Baths 150dr extra per person.) You can **camp** on the lakeside by any church—just be sure to ask permission.

Rather than visit Kastoria, head for the peaceful **Lake District. Florina** is a good base from which to explore the area, and is easily reached by train or bus from Edessa and Thessaloniki. (From Thessaloniki 5 trains per day, 4 hr., 530dr; 5 buses per day, 3½ hr., 980dr. From Edessa 4 trains per day, 2 hr., 270dr; 4 buses per day, 495dr.) Or you can take a bus north to Bitola and the Yugoslavian border and then hitch across. Florina has little to offer apart from a fragrant *agora,* but the **Hotel Ellenis** (tel. 226 71) has doubles for 2000dr. Twenty-two kilometers to the west is a mountaineering refuge near the village of **Pissoderi** on Mt. Verna.

Northwest of Kastoria and 34km west of Florina, the **Great** and **Small Prespa Lakes** straddle the borders of Greece, Albania, and Yugoslavia. Twisting mountain dirt roads north of Kastoria lead past hidden poppy fields, bear and fox lairs, and untouristed villages. The drive to **Psarades** takes you through a marshland aviary, with watchtowers and picnic tables alongside the Great Prespa Lake (the largest in the Balkans). The tiny fishing village is a prime spot for butter-grilled lake trout: Remove the backbone and eat skin and all (the bones are soft), and don't forget the cheeks—a Greek delicacy. The proprietor at the *psarotaverna* **Paradosie** speaks English and serves fish or a wonderful sausage dish for 250-320dr. Easiest to reach from Florina or Edessa is **Lake Vergokitida,** which borders the main highway to Edessa and Thessaloniki. A pleasant stopover here is **Arnissa,** 2km from the highway, a peaceful village overlooking the lake.

# Edessa Εδεσσα

A pleasant, clean little city filled with brooks, fountains, and aromatic rose trellises, Edessa attracts tourists with its small but lovely cascades. The name of the town (meaning "the waters"), was given by especially observant Bulgarian occupying forces. The town ends abruptly on the brink of a deep ravine, where the streams flowing under the town's arched, stone bridges shoot suddenly into a gaping abyss, plummeting over 25m to the valley floor below.

The **tourist police** (tel. 233 33) have little tourist information and speak no English, but will look for a translator to tell you that they have little information. Turn left after 26 Democrias St., and look for the police cars at the corner of Filippou and Iroon Polytechniou. (Open June-Oct. 7:30am-2:30pm, but there is always someone on duty.) Edessa's **post office**, on Democrias St., 1 block from the *agora*, exchanges money for a high commission. (Open Mon.-Fri. 8am-3pm.) The **National Bank of Greece,** 1 Demikratou St., is on the corner of Arch. Penteleiminos. (Open Mon.-Thurs. 8am-2pm, Fri. 8am-1pm.) The **OTE** is on a small road to the left behind the bank. (Open daily 8am-midnight.) The **main bus station** is at the corner of Pavlou Mela and Filippou St.; turn left when Democrias becomes Egnatia near Hotel Pella. Buses run to Athens (3 per day, 8½ hr., 2800dr.), Thessaloniki (15 per day, 2 hr., 490dr), and Veria via Naoussa (6 per day, 1 hr., 270dr). A second unmarked station is up the block at Pavlou Mela and Egnatia, next to the *souvlaki* restaurant. From here, buses go to Kastoria (4 per day, 2 hr., 650dr) and Florina (4 per day, 1¾ hr., 470dr). The **train station** is at the end of 18 Octovriou St. Trains to Athens via Plati (2 per day, 8½ hr., 1335dr), Florina (2 per day, 2 hr., 225dr), and Thessaloniki via Veria and Naoussa (8 per day, 2 hr., 255dr).

For accommodations, the family-run **Olympia,** 69, 18 Octovriou St. (tel. 235 44), by the train station, is Edessa's only E-class hotel. (Singles 700dr. Doubles and triples 600dr per person. Showers included.) The **Hotel Pella,** 30 Egnatia St. (tel. 235 41), 2 blocks from the main bus station, features high ceilings and a working elevator. (Clean singles 1800dr. Doubles 2500dr.) Diagonally across from the Pella, the large green-and-white **Hotel Olympion** (tel. 234 85), on Democrias, has a wider selection of rooms. (Singles 1500dr. Doubles 2000dr.) A few doors from the Hotel Pella, the **Egnatia Restaurant** has delectable *pastitsio* for 235dr.

The largest waterfall, **Katarrakton** (also the generic word for waterfall), is in a lush tree-filled park. Walk along Filippou St. from the main bus station toward the train station and then follow the signs. From the train station, walk toward town 2 blocks and turn left at the first river. Enthusiasts should continue down the path at the bottom of Katarrakton into the valley to see the three more sizable falls near the hydroelectric plant. The only other attraction is a small **archeological museum** that displays finds from the area in the Tsami Mosque on Stratou St. on the edge of town. Despite the town's historical antiquity and importance in the ancient Macedonian empire, little of Edessa's archeological past has been unearthed.

Waterfalls and springs also spurt in **Naoussa,** 43km from Edessa. Eighteen kilometers up the road from Naoussa, a small ski area operates in winter.

# Vergina Βεργίνα

The discovery of the ancient ruins of Vergina, 13km southeast of Veria, in 1977 and 1978, was a recent archeological watershed. The royal tombs and remains of a large palace date from 350 to 325 B.C.E., although the identities of the deceased royalty remain in dispute. Given the high-quality artistry of the magnificent treasures found in the tombs, some scholars believe that they could have belonged only to the royal Macedonian family of King Philip II, father of Alexander the Great.

The ruins are located near the village of Vergina. Unfortunately, the scattered rubble makes little sense to the casual observer. As you proceed down the road leading out of the village, you will see a sign pointing to the left for "The Royal Tombs;"

"The Archeological Site" is straight ahead. The tombs to the left are still being excavated and are not open to the public. Proceed straight ahead, 2km from the village, to the ruins of the third-century **Palace of Palatitsa**. Look for the exquisite mosaic floor, still in excellent condition, on the south ring of what remains of the palace.

A short climb up from the site to your left takes you to a well-preserved and partially excavated **royal tomb**. Archeologists found a gold chest within that contained the cremated remains of some royal personage (perhaps Philip II), along with a great many works of art and pieces of jewelry. All of the findings from the tombs of Vergina are on display at the archeological museum in Thessaloniki. Since the site has not yet worked its way into the itineraries of tour buses, it is fairly deserted, though it's probably only a matter of years before this situation worsens. (Open Mon. and Wed.-Sat. 8:45am-5pm, Sun. and holidays 9:30am-2:30pm. Admission 200dr, students 100dr.) Take the bus from Thessaloniki to Veria, 74km away (2 per hr., 1¾ hr., 400dr). Frequent local buses run near the site (10 min., 100dr).

# Thessaloniki Θεσσαλονίκη

Encircling its harbor and waterfront promenade like an amphitheater, Thessaloniki, capital of Macedonia and second largest city in Greece, wears the modern and uniformly drab architecture of an earthquake-plagued metropolis. Although there's nothing here comparable to the Acropolis in Athens, Thessaloniki is punctuated by an array of Byzantine churches, an excellent archeological museum, and Roman ruins. The castellated Lefkos Pirgos (White Tower), the symbol of Thessaloniki, presides over the harbor like an oversized chess piece. About 15 blocks up from the waterfront, just to the north of Athinas St., wind the streets of the old town, the **Kastra**.

On the crossroads of important trade routes, Thessaloniki has flourished since it was founded in 315 B.C.E. by Cassander, brother-in-law of Alexander the Great. Named for Cassander's wife, ancient Salonika prospered after the Roman conquest of Greece as the only port on Via Egnatia, the ancient east-west highway. Egnatia Street, 6 blocks from the waterfront, still serves as the city's main avenue. During the cultural decline of Athens, Thessaloniki became the most important city in the Greek realm of the Byzantine Empire. After the tenth century, the missionary followers of the brothers Methodius and Cyril (deviser of the Cyrillic alphabet) exerted a considerable influence over Balkan culture from here.

## Orientation and Practical Information

Thessaloniki's gridded street plan simplifies transit. The three main streets—Nikis, Tsimiski, and Egnatia—run parallel to the waterfront. You will find the cheapest hotels on **Egnatia**, banks and the post office on **Tsimiski**, and nondescript office buildings on **Nikis**. The main shopping street is **Ermou**, between Tsimiski and Egnatia. **Aristotelous** intersects all three perpendicularly to form **Aristotelous Square**, on the waterfront, where the tourist information center, train office, and airport bus terminal are located. The railway station is west of the square along Monastiriou St.; the main park, fairgrounds, and university are located just east of the downtown area.

**Greek National Tourist Organization (GNTO):** Off Aristotelous Sq. at #8 (tel. 22 29 35), 1 block from the water. Take any tram on Egnatia to Aristotelous Sq., or #5, 33, and 39 to be dropped at the door. Very helpful. Has city maps, hotel listings, and train, bus, and boat schedules. Ask about cultural events, especially the **Film and Song Festivals** in Sept. and the **Demetria Festival** in Oct. Open Mon.-Fri. 8am-8pm, Sat. 8am-2pm. Another office at the **airport** (tel. 42 50 11, ext. 215).

**Consulates: U.S.,** 59 Nikis St. (tel. 26 61 21), on the waterfront west of the Lefkos Pirgos. Men can pick up form letter requesting permission to enter Mt. Athos. Open Mon.-Fri. 9am-5pm. **British,** 8 Venezelou St. (tel. 26 99 84). Also for other Commonwealth countries.

**Ministry of Northern Greece:** Platia Dikitiriou, Room 218 (tel. 26 43 21). Men can pick up permit to enter Mt. Athos. Open Mon.-Fri. 8am-2pm.

**Currency Exchange: National Bank of Greece,** 11 Tsimiski St. Open for exchange Mon.-Fri. 8am-2pm and 6-8pm, Sat. 8am-1:30pm. Smaller banks charge slightly higher commission but may pay a higher rate for cashing traveler's checks.

**Post Office:** 45 Tsimiski St., midway between Agia Sophias St. and Aristotelous St. Open Mon.-Sat. 8:30am-8pm.

**Tourist Police:** 4 Dodekanison St. (tel. 51 34 78), in the hotel district. Less helpful than the GNTO.

**OTE:** At the corner of Ermou and Karolou Dil., one block from Aristotelous. Open 24 hours. **Telephone code:**031.

**Airport:** Information (tel. 41 19 77), 16km out of town. Served by Olympic Airways buses that depart from the Olympic Airways office 1½ hr. before each flight (60dr). Theoretically you must have an O.A. ticket, but they rarely check. **Olympic Airways Office,** 7 Nikis St. (tel. 26 01 21). Flights to Limnos, Lesvos, Kavala, Kozani, Skiathos, Kastoria, and Alexandroupolis. Open Mon.-Fri. 7am-9pm, Sat.-Sun. 8am-4pm. Lufthansa, British Airways, and charter companies also fly into Thessaloniki.

**Flights:** Cheapest agent in town is **Mykonos,** 17 Tsimiski St. (tel. 22 82 30), but it's still no bargain. Open Mon.-Fri. 8:30am-4pm, Sat. 9am-noon.

**Ferries:** The *Sappho* leaves from the pier near Eleftheria Sq. every Sat. in summer for Lesvos (15 hr., 2450dr), Chios (2475dr), and Piraeus (3390dr). Once per week in June, and twice per week in July, ferries serve Iraklion and Hania, Crete (20hr., 3264dr, 3515dr round-trip). Get tickets at **Vladimiros Karakharissis,** 19 N. Kountouriotou St. (the western extension of Nikis St.), 2nd floor (tel 53 22 89). Open Mon.-Sat. 9am-2:30pm and 5-8:30pm. Artis runs **Flying Dolphins hydrofoils** to Skiathos (3 hr., 3675dr), Skopelos (4 hr., 3930dr), and Alonissos (4½ hr., 4411dr) daily at 4pm. Buy tickets from **Egnatia Tours,** 9 Kamboynion (tel. 22 38 11), near the Arch of Galerius. Open 8:30am-2:30pm.

**Train Stations: Main Terminal,** Monastiriou St. (tel. 51 75 17), in the western part of the city. To get to the station, take any bus headed west down Egnatia St. (30dr). Trains to: Athens via Larissa, Levadia, and Thebes (7 per day, 8 hr., 1520dr); Edessa (every hr., 2 hr., 490dr); Florina (5 per day, 4 hr., 530dr); Alexandroupolis (5 per day, 8 hr., 890dr); Istanbul (1 per day at 9:20am, 23 hr., 3840dr); Sofia (1 per day, 9 hr., 3230dr); and Belgrade (3 per day, 8 hr., 3660dr). You can also catch trains from Athens headed for Czechoslavakia, East Germany, Hungary, Poland, and the USSR. Buy tickets at the station or at **State Railway Offices (OSE),** 18 Aristotelous St. (tel. 27 63 82). Open Tues.-Fri. 8am-9pm, Mon. and Sat. 8am-3pm.

**Buses:** Two bus companies serve Thessaloniki: the **State Railway Organization (OSE)** coaches, and the private **KTEL.** Tickets for OSE coaches sold at OSE booking office, 18 Aristotelous St. (tel. 27 63 82). Purchase KTEL tickets at branch stations before boarding. From the **Railway Station** (tel. 27 63 82), OSE buses run to Athens (15 per day, 8 hr., 2650dr). From **67 Monastiriou St.** (tel. 51 61 04), immediately adjacent to the station, **KTEL** buses run to Athens (6 per day, 7 hr., 2175dr) and Trikala (5 per day, 3 hr., 1175dr). From **22 Anagenniseos St.** (tel. 52 21 62), a few blocks from the train station toward the waterfront, buses run to Kastoria (5 per day, 4½ hr., 1200dr), Florina (5 per day, 3½ hr., 980dr), Pella (every ½ hr., ¾ hr., 205dr), and Volos (5 per day, 3 hr., 1120dr). From **26 Octovriou St.** (tel. 52 21 60), around the corner from Anagenisseos St. To Veria (every ½ hr., 1¾ hr., 400dr). **19 Christoupipsou St.** (tel. 51 24 44) buses run to Ioannina (5 per day, 7 hr., 1940dr) and Kalambaka (5 per day, 3½ hr., 1235dr). From **68 Karakassi St.,** on the east side of town (take bus #1 or 3 from Aristotelous Sq.) buses go to the Halkidiki Peninsula: Ouranoupolis (6 per day, 3 hr., 760dr), Sithonia via Poligiros (9 per day, 3 hr., 790dr), and Kassandra (every hr., 2 hr., 640dr). See also section on Halkidiki.

**Magic Bus:** 32 Tsimiski St. (tel. 28 32 80), 1 block from the tourist office. No longer a hippie travel company—no buses east beyond Turkey. 2 buses per week to London via Italy (9200dr). Also daily departures for Istanbul at 4:30am (2800dr). Books cheap train rides. Open Mon.-Fri. 9am-7pm, Sat. 9am-1pm.

**American Center and USIS Library:** 34 Mitropoleos St. (tel. 26 40 25), off Aristotelous Sq. Open Mon.-Fri. 9am-2pm; Mon. and Wed. also 5:30-8:30pm.

**British Council Cultural Center:** 9 Ethnikis Antistasseos St. (tel. 23 52 36).

**Bookstore: Molcho Books,** 10 Tsimiski St., across from the National Bank. Extensive selections in English and French. Open Mon., Wed., and Sat. 8:30am-2pm, Tues. and Thurs.-Fri. 8:30am-1:30pm and 5-8:30pm.

**Laundromats: Bianca,** 3 L. Antoniadou St. (tel. 20 96 02), opposite the church, next to the Arch of Galerius. Dark clothes 360dr, white clothes 390dr. English spoken. Open Mon.-Fri. 8am-2pm. Also at 46 Olimbou St., 2 streets north of Egnatia.

**Hospital: Ippokration,** 49 Konstantinoupoleos (tel. 83 00 37). Public hospital with assistance for tourists.

**Medical Emergency: Red Cross First Aid Hospital,** tel. 53 15 31, near the harbor.

**Tourist Police:** 4 Dodekanison St. (tel. 51 34 78), in the hotel district. Less helpful than the GNTO.

**Police Emergency:** Tel. 100.

## Accommodations and Camping

The main hotel district is along and on either side of the western end of Egnatia Street, roughly between Vardari Sq. (500m east of the train station) and Dikastirion Sq. In summer, Egnatia Street is very noisy, so try to get a room not facing the street.

**Youth Hostel (IYHF),** 44 Alex. Svolou St.(also called Nikolaou St.) (tel 22 59 46). Take tram #8, 10, 11, or 31 east on Egnatia and get off at the Arch of Galerius. Go toward the water and turn left two blocks later onto Svolou. Clean, but faces a noisy street. Reception open 9-11am and 6-11pm. Lock-out 11am-5pm. 11pm curfew. 530dr per person. Showers (6-10pm only) 70dr.

**YWCA (XEN in Greek),** 11 Agias Sophias St. (tel. 27 61 44), between Ermou and Tsimiski. Reception open 7am-midnight. Women only. Not much floor space. Dorms 880dr per person. 770dr with 3 beds, 600dr with 5 beds. Showers included.

**Atlantis,** 14 Egnatia St. (tel. 54 01 31). The 9 sunny rooms facing a quiet street are the best deal in town, but the others are dungeon-like. Sparkling clean bathrooms. Singles 1400dr. Doubles 1500dr. Hot showers 100dr.

**Nea Orestias,** 20 Selefkidon St. (tel. 51 94 11). Off to the side, so a little less noisy. Singles 1000dr. Doubles 1600dr. Hot showers 150dr.

**Hotel Kastoria,** 24 Egnatia St. (tel. 53 62 80). Corner location means 2-sided cacaphony. Toilets pass white glove test. Singles 1500dr. Doubles 2100dr. Hot showers included.

**Argo,** 11 Egnatia St. (tel 51 97 70). Wooden furniture gives this hotel a rustic look. Doubles 1600dr.

**Hotel Augustos,** 4 Elenis Svoronou (tel. 52 25 50). Turn north from Egnatia—it's on the left fork at Kolomvou bus stop. Mediocrity masked by silence and a friendly management. Singles 1000dr. Doubles 1500dr.

**Camping:** Take city bus #72 to **Agia Triada. Camping Thermaikos, Olympus,** and **Asprovalta** have similar prices. 480dr per person. 480-670dr per tent. You can also get a private room and commute to Thessaloniki (45 min.).

## Food and Entertainment

The downtown area is sprinkled with inexpensive self-service restaurants and shops. Interesting as well as cheap, the *agora* (marketplace), in the middle of town, is bounded on four sides by Irakliou, Egnatia, Aristotelous, and Venizelou St. The best *spanakopita* in town can be found in the heart of the hotel district, on the same side of Egnatia as Hotel Kastoria and just on the other side of the intersection.

Aristotelous Square is a good place for coffee, beer, or a nightcap, but tends to be rather expensive. The restaurants along the seaside serve standard fare at comparable prices, although the quality is mediocre. You may prefer to stroll among the coffee and ice cream shops in the park. Greeks mellow out sipping coffee here and at **Navarinou Square,** by the Arch of Galerius.

At night, head for the old part of the city, the **Kastra.** *Tavernas* line the narrow cobblestoned streets and shake, rattle, and roll until the wee hours with *bouzouki* music and Greek dancing. To get to the *Kastra,* take bus #22 or 23 from Eleftherias Sq. on the waterfront; if you're walking, remember that the trek is mostly uphill, but downhill when it really counts.

**Ta Spata,** 28 Aristotelous (tel. 23 19 66). Convenient location. Good selection of tasty and inexpensive entrees 200-400dr. Open 8am-1am.

**Vlahos,** 3 Nikiforev Foka (tel. 82 48 27), west of the Lefkos Pirgos. Good view of the water without the touristy atmosphere. Casseroles at lunch, grill at night. Entrees 250-500dr. Open noon-4pm and 7pm-1am.

**Canoniero,** 130 Epta Pirgiou (tel. 21 57 71). In Kastra, just outside the walls. Splendid view of Thessaloniki by night. Small pizza 300dr, medium 500dr. Open daily 10am-3am.

For the guardians of the wallet, **University Dining Hall,** on the corner of Egnatia and 3 Septemvriou St., is free (compliments of the United Nations). Look and act like a Greek student to pick up a tray. Greek students like to practice their English and may even offer you a place for the night. The dining hall is on the second floor of the building marked *AIIH.* (Open daily 12:30-2:30pm and 6:30-8:30pm.)

For those who want to boogie American-style, take bus #5 or 6 to the discos in **Kalamaria** (pronounced Ka-la-mar-YA), by the sea. Kalamaria is also full of overpriced *caferia* and pizza houses; relax in a cushy chair and sip *granita,* available with or without alcohol. In summer, weekend nightlife centers in the suburb of **Nea Krinis.** Take bus #5 from Aristotelous Sq., or pick it up on Mitropoleos St. to get to the **Amusement Park** in Salminan.

## Sights

If you have time for only one stop in the city, head for the superlative **archeological museum,** which spotlights collection of Macedonian treasures from all of northern Greece. Located in a side wing of the building, the collection features the recent finds from the Tombs of Vergina, including delicate gold foil crowns and wreaths, filigree pins, rings, masks, figurines, coins, and gold *larnakes* (burial caskets), which contained the cremated royal family of Vergina. Arranged clockwise in chronological order, the museum's other displays consist of extraordinary sculptures and mosaics from prehistoric to Byzantine times. (Open in summer Mon. and Wed.-Sat. 8am-7pm, Sun. 9am-2pm; in winter Mon.-Fri. 8am-3pm, Sun. 9am-2pm. Admission 300dr, students 150dr. Take bus #10 or 31 east on Egnatia St.) Next to the museum is a park and a loud amusement park on the **International Fairgrounds.**

On the other side of the park on the waterfront at the start of Vas. Sophias St. looms the **Lefkos Pirgos** (White Tower), all that remains of a Venetian seawall. Known as the Bloody Tower because an elite corps of soldiers was massacred therein, the structure was painted white to dispel the gruesome connotations. The tower houses a fascinating museum featuring early Christian and Byzantine Art and presents a slide show every hour. (Open Mon. and Wed.-Sat. 9am-9pm, Sun. 10am-3pm. Admission 200dr.) The far more extensive ruins of the **Eptapirgion Walls,** erected during the reign of Theodosius the Great, stretch all along the northern edge of the old city. To get there, take bus #22 or 23 from Eleftherias Sq. on the waterfront. Eleftherias Sq. is also where buses #5, 33, and 39 leave for the **Ethnological and Popular Art (Folklore) Museum,** 68 Vas. Olgas St. (tel. 83 05 91), in the eastern part of the city. The museum contains examples of traditional dress from all over northern Greece. (Open Mon.-Wed. 9:30am-5:30pm. Fri.-Sun. 9:30am-2pm. Free.)

Thessaloniki's ancient Greek and Roman ruins, the finest of which is the celebrated **Arch of Galerius,** built to commemorate the victories of Emperor Galerius over the Persians in 297 C.E. The arch stands at the end of Egnatia St., at the corner of Gounari St. Next to it is the **Rotunda,** constructed as an emperor's mausoleum. Constantine the Great converted it into a church dedicated to St. George, hence its alternate name, **Agios Georgios.** Constantine also furnished the church with impressive fourth-century mosaics, the oldest in Thessaloniki. The Rotunda served as a Turkish mosque for 400 years before it was restored as a church in 1912. The church has been under restoration since the 1978 earthquake, and officials don't know when it will reopen.

For further historical pursuits, head north of Dikastirion Square to the Roman ruins between Filippou and Olibou St. The ruins, which include a somewhat over-restored theater, are still being excavated. The focus of the remains of the **Palace of Galerius,** near Navarino Sq., is the well-preserved octagonal hall. No outpost of the empire would be complete without **roman baths:** You'll find their remnants next to the church of Agios Dimitrios, at the corner of Agios Dimitrios and Aristotelous St. The entrance is in the front left-hand corner of the church. (Always open. Free.)

Few churches survived the earthquakes, but of these many contain brilliant mosaic work. **Agios Dimitrios** is the largest church in Greece, containing famous fifth-century Byzantine mosaics similar to those in Ravenna, Italy: Look on all three inner sides of the pillars at the end of the central nave for some examples. Most of the old church was destroyed in a fire in 1917, but a chapel in the far right corner retained its original frescoes. In the basement of the church beneath the altar is the crypt where Agios Dimitrios, Thessaloniki's patron saint, was imprisoned and martyred. (Open in summer daily 8am-noon and 4-7pm; in winter 8am-3:30pm.)

Another noteworthy example of Byzantine art in Thessaloniki is the splendid ninth-century mosaic of the Ascension in the dome of the **Agia Sophia,** in the park of the same name at the corner of Ermou and Agia Sophias St. Modeled after Aya Sofia in Istanbul, the church also has an unusual representation in the apse of the seated Virgin. Currently undergoing restoration, it is still open to the public. More mosaics decorate the **Panayia Ahiropiitos,** 2 blocks farther north on Agia Sophias St. Many of Thessaloniki's other churches contain superb frescoes from the late Byzantine Era. The Guild church of **Panayia Halkeon** in Dikasterion Sq., **Agia Ekaterini,** and **Dodeka Apostoli** (the Church of the 12 Apostles) are particularly impressive. (Open approximately 8am-1pm and 5-8pm; closed for morning services Sun. and holidays.)

Jews have lived in Thessaloniki since before the Common Era. In the fifteenth century, Thessaloniki was a haven for Sephardim fleeing persecution in Spain. The once flourishing community was largely decimated during the holocaust of World War II, but a few thousand Jewish families remain. The beautiful **Old Synagogue,** no longer in use, can still be visited if you ask for the caretaker at the Jewish Community Center, 24 Tsimiski St.

## Near Thessaloniki

**Panorama,** up on Mt. Hortiatis with—you guessed it—a great view of Thessaloniki and the Aegean, is a great place to linger over a cup of coffee. Because of its refreshingly cool altitude, the village is a popular destination for summer excursions. Nevertheless, it's worth making the 10km trip on bus #59 from Dikastirion Sq. (every ½ hr., 20 min., 60dr). Bus #61 goes to the village of **Hortiatis,** 10km past Panorama, perched on the side of the mountain. In the '40s, a hospital was built here to treat tuberculosis patients, but the efficacious medication was fresh mountain air.

Twelve kilometers northeast of Thessaloniki is **Langadas;** on May 21, villagers celebrate the feast day of Sts. Constantine and Helen by dancing barefoot across a bed of burning coals. The origins of this ritual are uncertain: Some believe it stems from a Dionysiac orgiastic cult, while others insist that it is a Christian tradition—the Greek Church disagrees and refuses to authorize any service performed on this day. Regardless, the rite has become an annual tourist attraction, though subsequent barbecues are expressly prohibited. Scientific tests indicate that the brain waves of the fire walkers change during the performance and that their feet maintain minimum skin contact with the fire. The *anastenaria* (fire walking) begins around 7pm, but try to arrive by 5:30pm to get a good seat. If you can't get to Langadas, you can catch the show on ERT-TV news at 9pm. The bus to Langadas (every ½ hr.) leaves from the station at 17 Irini St., near Langada St., at the western end of Egnatia.

**Perea, Agia Triada,** and **Nea Mihaniona** are the beaches closest to the city. From Dikastirion Sq., bus #73 goes to Perea and Agia Triada; #72 goes to Nea Mihaniona (every 10 min., 45 min., 60dr). Agia Triada has a beautiful GNTO campground, **Epanomis** (tel. 413 78), perhaps the best in northern Greece. (420dr per person, 500dr per tent.) The restaurants along the beach offer private rooms. The water is somewhat polluted; for better swimming, head to the Halkidiki peninsula.

## *Pella* Πέλλα

Discovered by a farmer in 1957, the famous ruins of ancient Pella are a rewarding and interesting daytrip 38km west of Thessaloniki. Pella served as a port in ancient times, when the surrounding plain was covered with water fed from the Thermaïko Gulf. Around 400 B.C.E., King Archelaus chose it as the site for his palace, and it rapidly grew into a great cultural center and the largest city in Macedonia. Under Philip II, Pella became the first capital of a united Greece. The city served as the starting point for Alexander the Great's lifelong mission to unify the world under Macedonian rule. A century and a half later, Hellenistic rulers fell on hard times and the city was plundered by the Romans. The incredible mosaic floors, made of rough natural pebbles of various colors, exhibit a remarkable degree of expression and artistic perfection. Particularly striking are the Deer Hunt and the Rape of Helen, to the far left of the entrance. Notice the restored Ionic Colonnade of a mansion's interior court. (Open Mon. and Wed.-Sat. 8:45am-3pm, Sun. 9:30am-2:30pm. Admission 200dr, students 100dr.) On the other side of the highway is the small but excellent **Pella Museum** (tel. 312 78), with mosaics of Dionysus Riding a Panther and The Lion Hunt. (Open same hours as the ruins. Admission 200dr, students 100dr.)

Buses to Pella run every half-hour from the 22 Anagenniseos Station in Thessaloniki (6:30am-8:30pm, 45 min., 200dr). You are probably better off making a daytrip, since the nearest hotels are 12km away in the unattractive modern city of **Giannitsa**. Although there is no official campground, you can camp near the site without difficulty. The cafe-restaurant nearby offers food, rest rooms, and an outdoor sink. **Buses** to and from Thessaloniki (2 or 3 per hr.) pass the site, which is right on the main highway. To go between Pella and Vergina, change buses at Halkidona, only a few kilometers east of Pella.

## *Mount Olympos* Oρoς Oλυμπoς

Rising from the coastal plain 90km southwest of Thessaloniki, Mt. Olympos so impressed the seafaring ancient Greeks that they exalted it as the lofty home of the gods. First climbed in 1913, the mountain's rugged 3000-meter slopes are spectacular and perfect for the physically fit even if inexperienced hiker.

Because storms bury Mt. Olympos in six or more feet of snow each winter, the unofficial climbing season lasts only from May to October. Provided you make the ascent between May and September, no special equipment is required besides sturdy shoes, sunglasses, a hat, and water. You can rush through the climb in one long day, but plan on a two- or three-day trip to better enjoy the wilderness. Consider staying overnight in one of the refuges; leave your pack in the village of Litohoro. You can also camp on the mountain. In either case bring warm clothes. For hiking in the lower elevations in summer, you'll probably only need a T-shirt and shorts, but in the upper regions, you may need a windbreaker, an extra shirt, hat, and gloves. These items are crucial if the summit is shrouded in clouds. Clouds or no, Apollo is still strong enough to cook you to a crisp—bring your sunscreen along. Halazone water purification tablets or tincture of iodine may also come in handy.

Dehydration can be nasty; 1½-liter plastic water bottles are available at any grocery store in Greece and can be refilled at refuges.

## Litohoro

The best point of entry to Olympos is the pleasant village of **Litohoro,** conveniently situated a mere 5km from the Athens-Thessaloniki highway and accessible by both bus and train via Katerini, 22km away. Hourly **buses** from Thessaloniki travel to Katerini (1½ hr., 500dr), where you can catch an hourly bus to Litohoro (20 min., 130dr). Buses from Athens (6 hr., 2200dr, 3000dr round-trip) can also drop you off along the highway. **Trains** stop at the Litohoro station on the line between Thessaloniki and Volos (5:50am-5:40pm from Athens, 3 per day each way 7 hr., 1400dr), but since the station is close to the beach and several kilometers from town, you must either hitch or catch the Katerini-Litohoro bus on the main road 150m from the station.

Near the bus station in Litohoro, down the main street on your right, are the offices of Greece's two alpine clubs: the **EOS Greek Mountaineering Club** (tel. 819 44; open in summer only, Mon.-Fri. 9am-noon and 6-8pm) and the **SEO Mountaineering Club of Greece** (tel. 823 00; usually open June Mon.-Fri. 6-9pm; July-Aug. 8am-3pm and 6-9pm; another office 200m uphill from the square). SEO's main refuge is higher (2760m; open July-Aug.) but EOS's Refuge A (open June-Sept.) has running water and is closer to the end of the road, giving you better access by car. EOS owns three other refuges on Mt. Olympos that are locked on weekdays; if you want to stay in one, pick up the keys at the EOS office. Both clubs provide maps and information about the mountain, maintain the soil of the trails and refuges, and organize emergency rescue helicopters and first-aid stations. Above the square, several bakeries and grocery stores supply provisions for your hike.

The **tourist office** (tel. 812 50 or 812 63) is located for now just below the main square at the turn-off for Olympos. Ask Maria, who speaks German and English, for a map of Olympos and politely request a brief rundown on each trail. You can also reserve a spot in one of the refuges here. (Open daily 9am-2pm and Mon.-Sat. 4-9pm.) Litohoro also has a **bank** (open Mon.-Thurs. 8am-2pm, Fri. 8am-1:30pm), **post office** (open Mon.-Fri. 8am-2pm), and **OTE** (open Mon.-Sat. 7:30am-9pm, Sun. 9am-1pm). You'll find all three in the square where the main road ends. Litohoro's **postal code** is 60200; the **telephone code**is 0352. For accommodations, try the clean and well-managed **Litohoro Youth Hostel (IYHF)** (tel. 812 02). Follow the signs about 200m uphill from the town square. The extremely friendly wardens, Mina, Costas, and Costas' venerable mother, banter and joke among themselves, but keep your eyes out for those trying to sneak a shower. Costas will always find space for you. Although the hostel is closed for cleaning from 11am to 6pm, you can come in and drop off your stuff. Guests can pay 200dr and leave their luggage while they climb. Costas also sells topographical maps and provides hiking information. (Beds 450dr. Hot showers 250dr. Linen 200dr. 10% discount for more than 3 nights; 15% discount on subsequent visits. Phone reservations accepted. Curfew 11pm.) The **Hotel Afroditi** (tel. 814 15) is on the road up towards the youth hostel. (Singles 1870dr. Doubles for 2475dr. Triples 3025dr.) The **Park Hotel** (tel. 812 52), at the lower end of town on the main drag, has singles with private bath for 1500dr, doubles with private bath for 1800dr. **Hotel Markesia,** 5 Dionisiou St. (tel 818 31), offers doubles with private bath for 2070dr (kitchen facilities 500dr). The owner speaks English. To get there, go left 3 blocks along the road level with the square. Pick up cheap *gyros* (90dr) at a *psitopoleion.* **Restaurant Olympos** (tel. 821 78), across from the Park Hotel, has the cheapest eats in town. (Open noon-midnight.) You might also try **Restaurant Enipeas,** next to the post office. (*Fasolia* 340dr.)

## Trails to the Summits

Mount Olympos actually has five summits. The peaks Toumba and Profitis Ilias seem like footrests against the thrones of Skolio, Stefani, and Mitikas. There are two approaches to the peaks from Litohoro. To reach the beginning of both trails, take the road that winds upward just before the square in Litohoro. There is no bus service between the trails and Litohoro, so it's best to hitch or find a group at the hostel to share a taxi (3000dr to Prionia; see below). Hitching is usually not a problem, but get an early start since most climbers drive up in the morning. Hiking alongside the Enipeas River from Litohoro to Prionia is another option; the 18-kilometer trail is good but rugged. It begins past the town cemetery and Restaurant Myla in the upper part of Litohoro. At the fork in the trail, follow the yellow diamond marker uphill on the left side of the **Mavrolungo Gorge.** This four-hour roller coaster of hills is exhausting, but rewards you with a refreshing mountain stream, a small waterfall, and several pools in which to soothe your overtired muscles. If you decide not to hike through the gorge, walk to Prionia along the asphalt road (which becomes an unpaved path after 3km).

Fourteen kilometers from Litohoro, at **Diastavrosi,** the first trail slopes up to the right of the road. This route offers impressive views of the Aegean, the Macedonian plain to the north, and the smog layer over Thessaloniki far below. You can find water in two places along this trail—the turn-off between Barba and Spilia (1½ hr. from the trail head), marked on the trail and on the SEO map (but not on the EOS map), and at the spring at Strangos. It's a long haul (5-6 hr.) from the start of the trail to the **SEO refuge,** "Giosos Apostolides," where you can spend the night for 600dr (Alpine Club members 500dr) ample blankets are provided. Hot meals are served throughout the day (potato soup 250dr). You can also replenish your chocolate supply (150dr); there's no running water, and bottles cost 150dr. At 2760m (only 157m from the summit of Olympos), the shelter offers an exhilarating view of the Stefani peak at sunrise, the lunar landscape overlooking the Plateau of the Muses, and the convenient approach for the final ascent—the farthest peak is only one and a half hours away. You might notice the small stone monument along the trail, dedicated to Giosos Apostolides, founder of the SEO, who died in a fall here in 1964.

The second and more frequented route is the dirt and rock road past Diastavrosi another 4km from **Prionia.** The hike from Prionia (1½-2½ hr.) winds through deciduous and evergreen forests to **Refuge A** (tel. 818 00), just below the tree line, at 2100m elevation. The peaks are only two to three hours away, but allot four to six hours of daylight before pressing on. You'll probably want to stay overnight at the refuge and start your climb at dawn. This large shelter has spacious dorms plus food, first aid, and a warm hearth. (800dr per person, Alpine Club members 600dr. Filtered, melted snow, however, greets you in the shower, and you may not be allowed into the dorms until after 9pm.) The food is delicious and fairly cheap; veal stew is 300dr. Guides may be hired for the rest of the climb for a steep 4000dr or more per day, depending on the size of the entourage and the duration of your climb. Rates go up 50% between December 15 and May 25, the dangerous season when guides are truly useful.

**Mitikas** is the highest (2917m) and most often climbed peak of Olympos. From Refuge A, take the path uphill and follow the red marks along rubble switchbacks and mountain meadows strewn with indigo wildflowers. The sea extends to the east, and the faint outline of the Pelion Mountains can be traced to the south. Above, the swirling mass of clouds part to reveal the regal crown of Olympos, court of Zeus, and home of the gods.

The last leg of the ascent to Mitikas is usually made by one of two routes. If you take the fork in the path at Refuge A, to your left is the peak **Skala** (2866m); to your right is the SEO Refuge. From Skala, you will slowly and tortuously descend a bit before ascending Mitikas. Be sure to return the way you came; retrace your steps a few meters and descend to the left, following the red blazes. Don't climb down the loose rubble gully, and stay on the trail at all times. This route demands a bit of nerve—a jagged abyss yawns on the left and a free-fall opens on the right. It's safest to use both hands and feet; some hikers, unwilling to risk the possibility of vertigo, remain horizontal and crawl part of the way. It's not a good idea to lug a large pack along this route, unless it contains a hang glider. If you return to Skala, it's an easy walk to **Skolio,** the second highest peak (2911m) and the best point for viewing the sheer western face of Olympos. From Refuge A, you can go directly to Skolio, taking the path left off that to Skala.

The alternative route up Mitikas starts at the right fork that bypasses Skala toward the SEO refuge. You'll traverse this trail from either A or SEO, then turn up the steep, rock-strewn slope beneath the peak. From this main path, two others lead upward; to the left is Mitikas, to the right Stefani. Both are very dangerous and not advisable; loose rocks on the nearly vertical incline have caused many accidents and several deaths. Take the recommended route that climbs via Skala. Below you is the gentle bowl of a glacial cirque. Long ago, the stratified layers were heaved over the coastal Aegean land mass to form the Olympic mountain range.

The great challenge on Olympos of **Stefani** (also known as *Thronos Dhios,* or "Throne of the Gods"). The turn-off for the ridge is very close to that for Mitikas and indeed, the first part of the scramble is very similar. Once you've reached the narrow ridge, however, you must work your way along it, with several hundred meters of empty space on either side of you. Remember to concentrate on where you plant your feet: You could start a rock slide, or even worse, a people slide.

### Near Litohoro—Dion

The archeological site at the city of **Dion** hides beneath its modern counterpart, ruins of an expansive Macedonian shrine. The objects found during the excavations of Dion are displayed in the local **museum** (tel. 823 13; open Mon. and Wed.-Sat. 8am-7pm, Sun. and holidays 8am-6pm; admission 200dr; admission to archeological site 300dr). To get to Dion, take a bus from Katerini (every ½ hr., ½ hr., 100dr).

# Halkidiki Χαλκιδική

Three-pronged like the trident of Poseidon, Halkidiki thrusts southward into the Aegean. On the far eastern prong is the restricted region of Mount Athos, the largest enduring monastic community in Western society. The western side is **Kassandra,** which both geographically and socially serves as a playground for sun disciples from Thessaloniki and Athens. Sandwiched between the lands of Greece's past and present is the wild and pristine peninsula of **Sithonia.** (You may not find these names on your map.)

Public transportation on Halkidiki does not cater to tourists. Frequent buses run between the 68 Karakassi St. station in Thessaloniki (tel. 92 44 44) and each of the three peninsulas, but hopping from peninsula to peninsula invariably involves watching the asphalt melt as you wait for connections. Thumbing rides is usually easy, but, like buses, good only for short distances.

Of Halkidiki's northern interior, you might consider visiting **Poligiros,** where there is an archeological museum, or **Arnea,** known for its wines and handwoven fabrics. Farther west, and more difficult to reach, is the much-celebrated cave at **Petralona,** where a human skull dating from 700,000 B.C.E. was found. The beaches on the west of the Halkidikian mainland and on the bays between the peninsulas are best avoided altogether in July and August; they're just too packed.

### Kassandra

Kassandra attracts Greeks in droves for a reason: Its sands are soft and its waters midnight blue. The entire coast is gorgeous and over-touristed everywhere but in the southwest. To beat the prices and crowds, you'll need to freelance camp in an undesignated campsite or on a secluded stretch of beach (official campgrounds sometimes fill up). The tourist build-up on the coastline in Kassandra has effectively squeezed out the budget traveler, but at least free outdoor freshwater showers are available on most of the popular beaches.

To get to Kassandra from Thessaloniki, take a bus to Kassandria and get off at Kalithea (5:40am-9pm every hr., 2 hr., 530dr). Buses go to Paliouri on the southern tip (7 per day, 3 hr., 680dr), and to Agia Paraskevi (3 per day, 770dr). **Kassandria** is the administrative and transportation center of Kassandra, but little more. Its **OTE** (open Mon.-Fri. 7:30am-3pm), which is a yellow trailer truck operated by the national **post office** (open 8am-2pm), and the **National Bank of Greece** (open Mon.-Fri. 8am-1:30pm) are separated by hardware stores and souvenir shops. There are no hotels. The only reason to stop here is to catch buses down the west coast. Kassandra's **telephone code** is 0374.

Lively **Kalithea** is the last stop before Kassandria. Once the site of a temple to Zeus Ammon, new high-rise temples to Mammon now open their doors to tourists for several thousand *drachmae* per night. Kalithea has branches of the main banks plus a privately owned **phone center** that charges a slight premium for long distance calls. (Open daily 9am-2pm and 5pm-midnight.) The bus station, in the center and on the road perpendicular to the main road running along the water, is simply a sheltered bench with a posted schedule. You can rent motorcycles at **Motorent** (tel. 234 87), 50m north on the street behind the main road. (Open daily 9am-9pm.) The **bank** at the plaza handles currency exchange. (Open Mon.-Fri. 8:30am-1pm.) Start your room search around the corner from the bus stop on the main street, but don't expect any bargains. In the center and facing the water, the **Kentrikon** (tel. 223 53) has doubles with bath and refrigerator for 3000dr. South on the main road across from the turn-off to the beach you'll find the **Toroneon** (tel. 221 82), with doubles for 2950dr. *Dhomatia,* on the street behind the Kentrikon running parallel to the main road, cost around 2700dr. To **camp,** walk past the Toroneon and turn down the dirt road to the left, which leads to a pine grove on the bluffs overlooking the water. Beachside restaurants allow you to combine a day of surf with a seafood feast; order in advance and lie on the beach while cooks prepare *media* (mussels), *taramosalata,* and *zhargosh* fish. The cheapest restaurant on the ledge is **Fotis** (tel. 230 86), 20m from the Kassandria junction; it has a fantastic view and serves delicious **guvetsi** (veal with pasta, 400dr). (Open 7am-2am.) If you won't relinquish the view, head two doors downhill to the **Spitaki Pub** (tel. 231 30), a popular hangout. (Open in summer daily 10:30am-3am.)

The coast from Kriopigi to **Pefkochori** is dotted with waterfront homes and apartments. **Camping Keramaria** (tel. 614 64), just 2km south of Pefkohori, stretches out on a beach. (300dr per person, 250dr per tent.) The more traditional village of **Haniotis,** with its *tavernas* arranged around the square, bops at night. Paliouri is a long 3km away from the beach-campground complex of the same name, and perhaps not worth the bother, but the town has several lively *tavernas,* small hotels, and rooms to let. A bus runs from Kalithea to Paliouri (every 2 hr.).

The western coast of the peninsula has more to offer. Hitching is good; otherwise you can get a bus from Kassandria, or rent a motorbike in Kalithea. Two kilometers after you pass Siviri, heading south, watch for a dirt road that forks right by a "prevent forest fires" sign (in Greek). The road switches back down 1km to a vacant beach. At **Fourkas Beach,** farther south on the main road, a few sullen, dirty buildings droop over a long, thin strip of sand. You can camp at either end of the beach. The next point, however, is lovely: **Possidi** is neither crowded nor developed, except for **Possidi Camping** (tel. 413 45; 400dr per person; 200dr per tent). The fishing village of **Nea Skioni** has lately been discovered by a Scandinavian travel agency, but retains its native charm. You will find rooms to let in either direction down the main street, tucked in between stores selling tourist paraphernalia. The **Skioni** (tel. 712 23), above the Crazy Horse Saloon Bar, rents rooms for 700dr per person, 1500dr for doubles. The **Olympia** (tel. 712 10) has singles for 1100dr, doubles for 1900dr (bath included). As always on Kassandra, Nea Skioni has a considerable stretch of beach for camping.

Kassandra's hot spots, tepid by Las Vegas standards, center around the **Athos Palace Nightclub.** A band and professional crooners sing popular Greek and American songs; also, "Solid Gold"-type dancers parade on stage. (Open daily midnight-4am. Free.) If Athos Palace gets too rowdy, head across the highway to **Lagoudera,** the nearby disco.

# Sithonia Σιθωνία

Sithonia is far less developed than Kassandra, but in high season, you'll encounter similar difficulties finding cheap rooms in the more popular spots. Freelance camping is wise. There are two rugged routes through Sithonia: west via Nea Marmaras, and east via Vourvourou. Travel is more flexibile going west since buses travel to Nea Marmaras (6 per day, 3 hr., 820dr), continuing around the peninsula to Sarti (5 per day, 4 hr., 1150dr) and Vourvourou (3 per day, 3 hr., 780dr). Another option is to take a bus to Agios Nikolaos at the neck of the peninsula (3 per day, 3 hr., 710dr), and work your way down from there.

Before arriving at **Nea Marmaras** (also called Marmaras), you'll pass the sparkling beach at **Agios Ioannis,** a prime spot to stake a tent. If you go as far as Nea Marmaras, you might find a room in the cove north of the bus stop. However, since this is the largest and most crowded town on Sithonia, rooms may be booked, and many places will not rent to you unless you stay for a week or more, in which case you will find doubles with bath cost 1500dr. By asking persistently at every place and starting early in the day, you may be able to find a room for a short stay (for 2000-2500dr per night). On the beach, **Camping Marmaras** (tel. 719 01) is 1km back and clearly marked by road signs. (380dr per person. 300dr per tent. Open June-Sept.) You can freelance camp in a pine grove 1km beyond or on the beach. The **tourist police** (tel. 711 11) are in an unmarked house (for inconspicuous surveillance) on the first street parallel to the highway. They don't speak English but are very friendly and will call around to help you find a room. Hours are posted on the door. (Open daily approximately 8:30am-2:30pm and 8:30-10pm.)

The monstrous hotel complex within sight is the anomalous, ultra-luxury **Porto Carras,** a slick, exclusive development patronized by the likes of Mick Jagger and Jackie Onassis. Even at 20,000dr per room, all 2500 beds are fully booked in summer. Along the beach you can participate in every watersport imaginable—windsurfing (1050dr), waterskiing (700dr), and even parasailing (2300dr per trip). We suggest body surfing. Ferries shuttle between Porto Carras and George's Restaurant in Marmaras every half-hour until 11pm (20 min., 80dr).

The bus around the peninsula to Sarti (9 per day, 1 hr., 310dr) passes by the most deserted and desirable turf on Sithonia. After climbing the road 5km south of Porto Carras, you'll see a beach near **Agia Kiriaki,** complete with a small reef and an outlying island. It's a long, hard climb down from here, or a long hike along a road lower on the coast. The nearly deserted beach at **Tristinika** can be reached along a dirt road branching off from the highway near Toroni.

At **Toroni**, the next beach down the coast (45 min. from Marmaras, 255dr), an Australian archeological team conducts a dig each July and August; and heaps the dirt back every September. You can walk to the ruined wall out on the promontory, or up to the remains of the city's *Kastro* atop the 280-meter-high hill behind the beach. There are many signs for private rooms (doubles 2000dr). One kilometer farther on the main road, **Porto Koufos** is a yacht harbor with a beautiful beach. Finding a room can be a problem. The campground here, **Porto Koufo Camping** (tel. 414 88), is unique—tent sites hang from the hillside on terraces shaded by bamboo canopies (450dr per person, 400dr per tent). **Kalamitsi** is a gorgeous, but hardly secret beach, while **Sarti,** a lazy seaside resort town and the second major hub on the peninsula, has many *tavernas* and an exceptionally long stretch of sand. Sarti is especially popular among Greek youths. After a little searching you can find a room even in summer: Doubles go for 1400dr (considerably less for longer stays). **Zorba's** bar, on the road out of Sarti, houses a curious menagerie of sculptures by the local artist "Uncle Zifiris."

Because the bus serving the western and southern coasts of Sithonia goes only as far as Sarti, it's best to go to **Vourvourou** directly from Thessaloniki. The bus will deposit you on a desolate and unmarked stretch of highway. Don't panic—simply head north and down to the water until you come to a residential area. Ask a local to point you toward the *paralia* (beach). There you will find a sandy half-moon cove lined with shady trees and clear water teeming with darting fish.

Note that there is no bus service connecting Sithonia to the Mt. Athos peninsula. The road through Pirgadikia, Gomati, and Ierissos is unpaved and frequented primarily by goat trucks; waits between hitches are long. To get to Mt. Athos by bus, start early in the morning and catch the bus to Thessaloniki as far as Agios Prodomos (600dr). Buses pass through Agios Prodomos on the way to Ouranoupolis (6 per day, 550dr). A more extravagant way to reach Mt. Athos is to take the cruise from Marmaras (2500dr) and simply not reboard the ship after the lunch in Ouranoupolis. Buy tickets at the waterfront **tourist office** in Marmaras (tel. 716 82; open in summer 9:30am-2pm and 6-9pm). For Kassandra, take the Thessaloniki bus that passes through Nea Moudania (6 per day from Marmaras).

# *Mount Athos* Ορος Αθος

Mount Athos (*Agion Oros*) has defied time, spurned change. Halkidiki's easternmost peninsula harbors 20 Eastern Orthodox monasteries comprising an autonomous state of 12,000 monks, the vigorous center and spiritual authority of Orthodox Christianity. There are no tourists in Athos—just pilgrims.

Here, the Julian rather than the Gregorian calendar is still used, along with a variable solar time system. The monks attempt to transcend the confining material pleasures of the outside world and lead an ascetic, spiritual life. Food, dress, and possessions at Athos are very modest. Men with long hair should tie it in a bun at the nape of the neck as the monks do. Bring light cotton pants (no shorts) and a long-sleeved shirt to conform to the dress code. There is only a short paved road, occasional self-generated electricity, and a few telephones.

An edict of the Emperor Constantine from 1060 C.E., enforced to this day, forbids women from setting foot on the peninsula. The absence of any foraging goats or other livestock has preserved the luxuriant forests, although the dense foliage provides good cover for poisonous snakes (watch for vipers) and other animals. This lush tangle of dark green heightens the mystical aura pervading Athos, intensified by the jagged marble peak of Mt. Athos itself, soaring 2033m above the encircling waves of the Aegean.

### Practical Information

When visiting Mt. Athos, keep in mind that visitors from "the outside world" inherently conflict with the spiritual goals of the monastic life. The monks, however, have an old tradition requiring hospitality to all guests, so a bit of awareness and sensitivity is essential to keep from disrupting the delicate atmosphere of holiness.

A special **entrance permit**, issued only to adult males, is required in order to visit Mt. Athos. To get this, you must first get a letter of recommendation from your embassy or consulate (tell them you are a student of theology, history, architecture, or Byzantine Art) and bring it to the **Greek Ministry of Foreign Affairs**, 2 Zalokosta St. (tel. 362 68 94) near Syntagma Sq., Athens (open Mon., Wed., and Fri. 11am-1pm), or to the **Ministry of Northern Greece**, at room 218 Pl. Dikitirou, Thessaloniki (tel. 27 00 92; open Mon.-Fri. 8am-2pm). A permit is normally accepted by the Aliens' Police in Karyes, the administrative center of Mt. Athos. Citizens of countries with consulates in Thessaloniki can conduct the entire process while there (see Thessaloniki for consulate addresses); U.S. and British consulates can give you the form letter in very little time. They might insist that visitors be over 21 or accompanied by someone over 21, though the Ministry can waive this restriction. Because only 10 foreigners per day are admitted to Mt. Athos, the summer months are always booked well in advance. You can either wait for a cancellation or write a letter to the Ministry of Northern Greece at least a month in advance to secure a reservation. If you are Orthodox and show some proof of it (baptism papers, a letter from your bishop, etc.), the limit can be waived.

Although the rules are not strictly enforced, keep in mind that, officially, only men having specific academic or religious interest in Mt. Athos are supposed to receive visitors' permits. If you are a student, a letter from your university stating your academic interest in Mt. Athos could be helpful. If you want to take photographs of the art in the monasteries, a separate permit is procurable at one of the aforementioned ministries in Athens or Thessaloniki. Permits allow only a four-day stay, but extra letters of recommendation might help you obtain a permit for a longer stay. Alternatively, extensions can be obtained from the monastic authorities at Karyes once you're in Mt. Athos. (Be sure to bring your passport with you for all bureaucratic procedures.) The GNTO office in Thessaloniki can give you more information.

Permit in hand, arrive in Halkidiki the night before your scheduled entry date into Athos. The standard approach to Athos is via Ouranopolis, by boat to Daphni, then by bus to the capital city of Karyes, where some final bureaucratic procedures take place. **Buses** leave Thessaloniki's KTEL/Halkidiki station to Ouranopolis (6am-5:30pm 7 per day , 3 hr., 780dr). Remember to bring sufficient cash for your stay—the Hotel Xenios Zeus will take U.S. dollars, but the closest bank that exchanges traveler's checks is 15km away in Ierissos, and open for business only Tuesdays and Thursdays.

**Ouranopolis** is a crowded beach resort. Stay here overnight to catch the early morning ferry to Daphni. The town is small enough that you will be able to spot "rooms to let" signs, but you might be better off in either of Ouranoupolis' two cheap hotels: the **Hotel Ouranopouli** (tel. 712 05; doubles 2000dr; showers 100dr); or the **Hotel Akrogiali** (tel. 712 01), on the waterfront (singles 1600dr, doubles 2500dr). The **telephone code** is 0377.

You'll be doing a lot of hiking at Mt. Athos, so arrange to leave your belongings behind in Ouranopolis (preferably at the place you've stayed), and just carry a day pack. Water is readily available at each of the monasteries and from mountain springs and streams along Mt. Athos' trails, but you may want a small canteen for longer distances. Also consider bringing some compact food. If you're visiting during a fasting period, don't panic: Guests are fed normal rations while the monks are purifying their souls.

Two **ferries** serve the Mt. Athos peninsula: one from Ouranopolis to Daphni, and the other, on the other side of the peninsula, from Ierissos to Monastery Iviron. The Ouranoupolis ferry leaves daily at 7:45am and is timed to connect with the 6am bus from Thessaloniki. In summer, the ferry makes another trip daily at noon. The Ierissos ferry departs daily at noon in summer, and three times per week in off-season. Both trips take about two hours (400dr). Your passport and entrance permits are taken as you board, to be returned later in Karyes. The Ierissos ferry continues all the way to Monastery Megisti Lavras; if you're not up to walking, you can catch this ferry to go monastery-hopping once you have your final permit.

From Daphni or Iviron a bus (150dr) will take you up Athos' one paved, cliff-hanging road (built in 1963 for Athos' millennial anniversary) to the capital city of **Karyes,** a tiny hamlet built around a well-restored, tenth-century church. The town also contains an **OTE** and two inexpensive hotels that need not be used since the monastery accommodations are much more interesting.

The final permit *(Diamonitirion),* obtained from the **Monastic Authorities** in the headquarters of the Athonite Holy Council, costs a hefty 800dr (students 575dr). These funds reimburse the monasteries for the costs of their hospitality. Don't bother with the tourist police; they're there to keep order, not assist tourists.

Remember that walking is an integral part of the Athos experience. Before you leave Karyes, pick up the *Mount Athos Touristic Map,* which includes a pamphlet offering general information (150dr). For greater detail about Mt. Athos, pick up one of the well-illustrated guidebooks (800dr).

**Accommodations** and **food** in the monasteries are free, but you are entitled only to a one-night stay unless you receive permission for an extension from the *archontari* (guest-master). Generally, two meals are served daily. The gates close at sunset. You *must* reach the monastery before this or you may have to camp outside with the wolves. Allow plenty of time to get to the monasteries. Paths are narrow, over-grown with vegetation, and poorly marked; furthermore, the ones on the map might unexpectedly fork in four different directions or not exist at all. It's a good idea to keep to the roads or seaside paths. Even if you are turned down for lodging at a monastery, you will be offered a cup of Greek coffee, a glass of water, and *loukoumi* for your efforts.

Those without a permit can view the monasteries by boat. A day cruise from Marmaras costs 2500dr (see Sithonia).

### History

According to a very old legend, the Christian history of Mt. Athos began when the Virgin Mary, on a sea trip to visit her friend Lazarus in Cyprus, was thrown off course by a storm and led by divine sign to the Athonite coast. The peninsula, known then as *Akte,* was a notorious center of paganism, but the moment Mary's foot touched its soil, the false idols all smashed themselves to bits in frenzied procla-mation of their own worthlessness. Mary then declared Athos her holy garden, for-bidden to all other women for eternity, and blessed the land before sailing back to Jaffa.

Following centuries of occupation by Christian hermits and ascetics, the oldest monastery (Agia Lavra) was founded in 963 C.E. by Athanasius, a rich man's son turned monk. Under the protection of Byzantine emperors, the building of monaste-ries flourished until, at its zenith in the fifteenth century, Mt. Athos harbored 40 monasteries and some 20,000 monks. When Constantinople fell to Turkish armies in 1453, the monastic community prudently surrendered, thus remaining un-plundered and relatively autonomous. Due to gradual attrition and the diminishing influx of young novices, Mt. Athos slowly declined until the '50s, when it became a prime target of greedy real estate and resort developers. In recent decades, how-ever, *Agion Oros* has been rejuvenated; hundreds of young men have been inspired to take their vows and have donned the black robes and hat of Orthodox monasti-cism. Now over 1200 monks live alone in tiny hermitages or inhabit the 20 monaste-ries and other communities known as *sketes, kellia,* or *kalyvia.*

In 1926, a decree of the Greek government made Mt. Athos officially part of Greece while allowing it to retain an autonomous theocratic government: Athos is thus the oldest continuously existing democracy in the world. Monks of each monastery annually elect representatives to the Holy Council, which meets at Karyes and serves as the central governing authority of the peninsula. Most of the monasteries are cenobitic, headed by an abbot who sets individual tasks for each monk. Other monasteries are idiorrhythmic, administered by an elected council that allows monks greater personal choice in deciding how best to devote their lives to God.

Throughout its long history, the *Agion Oros* has suffered from repeated incursions at the hands of pirates, looters, and foreign invaders, resulting in the fortress-like appearance of the monasteries. Typically located in a large central courtyard, the *katholikon* (church) is surrounded by the monks' cells, forming a solid defensive wall equipped with heavy iron doors and a tower.

Athos contains an unsurpassed wealth of Paleologian and Late Byzantine art, manuscripts, and architecture. Megisti Lavra, for example, is a veritable warehouse of crucifixes inlaid with precious metal and stones. Its antique libraries contain over 42,000 tomes. The Athonite churches are stylistically unique, having a double nar-thex with side chapels. Graceful frescoes and painted icons, including numerous masterpieces by great artists of the Cretan and Macedonian Schools, adorn the church interiors.

Any visit to Athos will be greatly enriched by reading about the art, history, and legends of the individual monasteries. *Athos the Holy Mountain,* by Sydney Loch, and *Mount Athos,* by Norwich, Sitwell, and Costa, are both highly readable and informative. Published in 1985, *Athos, the Holy Mountain,* by Philip Sherrard, is a sensitive look at *Agion Oros* with quality photos. For an introduction to the ethos of internal prayer read *The Way of the Pilgrim,* by an anonymous Russian peasant

(Image Books in paperback), translated by R.M. French. For a survey of the princi-
ples and rituals of the Orthodox faith read Timothy Ware's *The Orthodox Church,*
and his most recent, *The Orthodox Way.* In addition, *Le Messager Orthodoxe* dedicated a whole issue to "Le Mont Athos Aujourd'hui" (No. 95, 1-11-84).

### Monasteries of the Mountain

Although Athos contains stunning works and dazzling scenery, the most rewarding aspect is often the conversations with the people at the monasteries. A spirit
of camaraderie quickly forms between the guests and the monks. The numerous
monasteries at Mt. Athos differ according to their remoteness from tourism, and
the ages, level of education, and nationality of the monks. At one time, there were
nearly equal numbers of Greek and Slavic monks at Athos, but the Russian Revolution cut off the supply of funds and novices at its source, and today only three Slavic
monasteries remain. The Russian **Panteleimon,** the Bulgarian **Zografou,** and the
Serbian **Chilandari** serve as interesting contrasts to the monasteries on the rest of
the peninsula. Although **Megisti Lavra** and **Iviron** are beautiful and well worth seeing, these two largest, oldest, and most frequently visited of the cloisters can be aptly
referred to as the "museum monasteries." Also try to visit some of the smaller and
more remote monasteries which don't have the grandiose art that attracts the
swarms of tourists.

The most complete experience at Mt. Athos involves developing an understanding and appreciation of the monastic way of life. Always address monks by their
title, *Pateras.* Although most monks are Greek, the Athos renaissance has drawn
novices from the U.S., Canada, France, England, and elsewhere. Many young
monks are university educated, and several speak English reasonably well. When
you arrive, ask the *Archontari* if it's possible to speak with one.

Life on Mt. Athos befuddles the non-ascetic. This theology is not a cold academic
exercise, but a way of life. No meat is eaten, and meals are scanty. Women are never
present. Men cover their bodies completely and male animals are castrated. Novices
learn to pray with each breath. Inhaling they recite, "Lord Jesus Christ," and exhaling "Have mercy on me, a sinner" until prayer becomes reflex and the disciple ac-
quires the gift of the Holy Spirit. Emotions fade as the monks mechanically recite
and perform rituals, clearing their minds of all but the will of God. Incense is
burned, and prayer commences according to the liturgical clock of the monastery.
At most monasteries, midnight is marked by the setting of the sun, so you may be
awakened in the middle of the night by the hauntingly beautiful cadence of wooden
mallets striking solid wooden boards, or by the melodious ringing of an array of
different-sized bells. These sounds summon the monks to church for prayer, which
is usually followed by a light meal where one monk always reads from the Holy
Scriptures. The hermit monks have even looser ties to the secular concept of time.
The monks' spiritual fathers hear confessions, advise, and prophesy. The mystics
examine souls with their expanded senses of perception, *ahrisis.*

For a day or two of invigorating hiking crowned by an awe-inspiring once-in-a-
lifetime view, climb Mt. Athos. The approach is by path from the community of
**Agia Anna.** A five-hour climb will take you to the **Church of the Panayia,** dedicated
to the Virgin Mary, which has beds for an overnight stay. The summit is another
hour away. You might want to stay overnight at Panayia to watch the sun rise.
On August 19, the feast day of the Transfiguration, an awesome ceremony is held
at the summit's Church of the Metamorphosis.

# Kavala Καβάλα

Stretching from the seaside up the slopes of Mt. Simvolo, Kavala (pronounced
Ka-VAH-lah) engages in the hustle and bustle characteristic of a modern port city.
The ancient city Neapolis, buried underneath, served as an equally important port
city for the ancient Greeks. A few centuries later, Apostle Paul came here to preach

and christened the city Christoupolis. For a time afterwards, Kavala bore the brunt of Greco-Turkish conflict, but it has now reclaimed its role as a trading center.

Kavala is accessible from Thessaloniki by buses (every hr., 6am-8pm, 920dr), traveling two different routes. The more scenic coastal road passes by **Lake Korona** and **Lake Volvi,** both unmarred by tourist trappings. The inland route passes through the city of **Serres** and its notable Byzantine church.

## Orientation and Practical Information

The town's jewel is its charming old section, known as the **Panayia District.** The old town sits east of the port on its own peninsula and is delimited by ancient walls. Just outside these walls is the main square **Platia Eleftherias,** from which Kavala's two major commercial streets, **Eleftheriou Venizelou** and **Erithrou Stavrou** extend westward.

**Greek National Tourist Organization (GNTO):** on Filellinon St., Eleftheria Sq., 1 block from the waterfront (tel. 22 24 25 or 22 87 62). Perhaps the best-informed tourist office in northern Greece. Has maps of the city, lists hotels, and arranges for cheap, private rooms. Helps with travel to Turkey, Bulgaria, and Yugoslavia. Open Mon.-Fri. 8:30am-1:30pm and 5:30-7:30pm, Sat. 8am-1pm.

**Tourist Police:** 119 Omonias St., 4 blocks from the port (tel. 22 29 05). Gives tourist information when the GNTO is closed. Open daily 8am-10pm. The regular **police** are in the same building. Open 24 hours.

**National Bank of Greece:** Omonias Sq. Open Mon.-Thurs. 8:30am-1pm, Fri. 8:30am-12:30pm.

**Post Office:** Main branch at Hrissostomou St., 1 block north of the bus station. Open Mon.-Fri. 7am-8pm. There is no single postal code.

**OTE:** On the main port at Vassileos Pavlou St., across from the Thassos ferry. Open daily 7am-midnight. **Telephone code:** 051.

**Train Station:**There is no train station in Kavala. However, the train for Istanbul passes through two neighboring towns, **Drama** and **Xanthi.** For Drama (30km northwest of Kavala), take one of the frequent buses from the bus station (every ½ hr., 1 hr., 220dr). The train leaves Drama daily at 1:45pm for Istanbul (2100dr) via the Kommotini (2½ hr.)-Alexandroupolis (4 hr.) route. Otherwise, take the bus to Xanthi (every ½ hr., 1 hr., 310dr) and hop on the 3:36pm train to Istanbul (1900dr).

**Bus Station:** H. Mitropolitou St., 1 block from Vassileos Pavlou St. and the waterfront. Buses go to: Thessaloniki (every hr., 920dr); Philippi (every 15 min., 105dr); Keramoti (every hr., 290dr); and the beaches to the west (take bus to Iraklitsa, every hr., 40-80dr). For buses to Alexandroupolis, walk 3 blocks west and 1 block north, across from the Oceanis Hotel (5 per day, 720dr). Do not let the station attendants put you on an indirect bus. There is a daily bus to Istanbul (except Thurs.) at 7am (2500dr one-way, 2920dr round-trip) and also 7pm on Tues., Wed., Fri., and Sat. It is best to buy your ticket at the **Alkyon Office,** near the GNTO by the *EKO* sign. You may board the bus at Ilias' newsstand (*periptero*).

**Ferries:** Boats to and from Thassos (every 2 hr.; 230dr); most go only to Prinos, but 2 per day continue on to Limenas. Boats from Keramoti, 45km east of Kavala, run the short distance back and forth to Limenas (every hr., 7am-9pm, 150dr). **Nikos Miliades,** 36 Karaoli Dimitriou St. (tel. 22 61 47), runs 5 boats in the off-season. The Wed. ferry goes to Limnos (1270dr) and continues onto Lesvos (12 hr., 2050dr). There is also a Thurs. ferry that goes to Limnos and continues on to Agios Efstratios (1270dr) and Kimi (1960dr). During the summer, the ferry company adds 2 more boats, both leaving on Sun. One stops at Limnos and Lesbos en route to Chios and Rhodes; the other also stops in Limnos and continues on to Agios Efstratios and Agios Konstantinos (2225dr). Another boat leaves for Samothraki every Wed. (1030dr). The office is at the east end of the port.

## Accommodations and Camping

Rooms are scarce on Saturday nights during the summer; arrive early. **George Alvanos** is the only hotel in the old city; most others are cramped around Platia Eleftheria.

**George Alvanos,** 35 Anthemiou St. (tel. 22 84 12 or 22 17 81). An all-around tremendous establishment, and the only place in the Panayia District. Spotless bathrooms. Access to kitchen and refrigerator. Refer to Mr. Alvanos for directions to good restaurants and taverns. Singles 1000dr. Very bargainable; 10% discount with a copy of *Let's Go.* Call ahead; it fills quickly.

**Hotel Rex,** (tel. 22 33 93), 1 block east of the center of Platia Eleftheria. Singles 1500dr. Doubles 2120dr. Hot water 150dr.

**Hotel Akropolis,** Eleftheriou Venizelou St. (tel. 22 35 43). Old but habitable. Go west from the GNTO—it's on the opposite side of the street. Private or communal facilities. Ask about cooking facilities. Doubles 1400dr. Triples 2800dr. Hot water included.

**Camping: Camping Irini** (tel. 22 97 85 or 22 97 76). Walk east along the coast from the port 2km (½ hr.). The closest campground to town. 460dr per person. 500dr per tent. Children 250dr.

## Sights

Stroll through the narrow, stone passageways past the delightful houses of the old town, accented by the sprawling gray thirteenth-century **Byzantine Fortress.** An approach to Kavala from the sea affords a perspective from which you can appreciate the fortress's immense, turreted walls. A walk along the top of the walls provides a fine panorama of the city.(Open 9am-1pm and 4-8pm. Admission 50dr.) During the third week of June, Kavala's students dance at the castle in traditional styles. Join in if you dare.

Two legacies of the long Ottoman domination of the city add a distinct Turkish taste to Kavala. The first, located on Pavlidou St., is the **Imaret,** the largest Muslim building in Greece. This mosque has an elongated hall with numerous little domes, best viewed from the water or from the fortress above. Now a warehouse, the building is not open to the public. For an inside view of a Muslim building, visit the **House of Muhammad Ali,** on the corner of Pavlidou and Mehmet Ali St., at the tip of the little peninsula. Muhammad Ali was the self-appointed King of Egypt in the eighteenth century, and the founder of a dynasty of Egyptian rulers. He was born in this house in 1769 and lived in Kavala during the early part of his life. The most interesting part of the beautifully preserved old wooden house is the upstairs, where Ali's harem of seven women lived. The most preferred woman stayed in the handsome bedroom while the others remained in a large dormitory room. Curiously, three bodyguards lived in the room between Muhammad Ali and his wives. (Admission is free, but the guide asks for a tip of about 80dr.)

At the northern edge of the old town, near Nikotsara Square, the colossal sixteenth-century **aqueduct** is hard to overlook. Süleiman the Magnificent had the graceful, double-tiered structure built to transport water from the mountain springs above the city. On the other side of town, overlooking the water, the **archeological museum,** on Erithrou Stavrou St., contains finds from Philippi, Amphipolis, and other nearby sites. (Open Wed.-Mon. 8:30am-2:30pm. Admission 100dr, students 50dr.) Crowds head to the small beach east of the port.

## Near Kavala

Several sandy **beaches** lie to the west of Kavala, all accessible by bus. The closest is just outside the city of **Kalamitsa.** As you move farther along the coast to Batis, Iraklitsa, and Peramos, you'll find progressively less crowded beaches. At **Batis,** 3km outside of Kavala, is a fancy **GNTO campground** (tel. 22 71 51; 300dr per person. 90dr per tent. 120-170dr with a sleeping bag, ages 3-10 150dr. 50dr to swim, 420dr for electricity). The campground, which you might mistake for a parking lot, changes money daily until late in the evening. Direct buses run from Kavala to Batis during July and August; take one of the hourly buses to Iraklitsa and get off at Batis (40dr). Every 15 minutes, blue bus #8 treks to Batis.

A 40-minute bus ride away, to the east of Kavala, is the small port of **Keramoti,** whence you can catch ferries to Limenas, the capital of Thassos. Keramoti's cheapest hotel is the **Hotel Exasteron,** Platia 14 Septemvriou (tel. 512 30). Singles, doubles, or triples are 800dr per person in the off-season, 20% higher during summer. Nearby **Camping Keramoti** (tel. 512 79), up the seaside road to the east about ¾ km. (300dr per person. 300dr per tent.)

About 15km north of Kavala, the ruins of ancient **Philippi** represent the material remains of one of the more crucial moments in European history. The city was founded by Philip II of Macedon (sire of Alexander the Great), who built a fortified city here to protect Thassian gold-mine workers from occasional Thracian attacks. Modest Philip thought it only appropriate that the city be named after him. In 42 B.C.E., the soldiers led here by Mark Antony defeated the Republican army of Brutus and Cassius, assassins of Julius Caesar, in crucial battles of the Roman civil war.

Less than a century later, Philippi was the site of Christianity's entrance onto the European stage, when the missionaries Paul and Silas came here to preach in 50 C.E. The first European Christian was a woman named Lydia whom they baptized here; the rest of Philippi converted when, after Paul was imprisoned for his proselytizing, an earthquake struck the town.

The modern highway that follows the same route as the ancient Via Egnatia splits the mostly Roman archeological site. Here you'll find a well-preserved colonnade and a Roman basilica with splendid Corinthian capitals; the size of the structure caused it to collapse before it was finished and it was never completed. A fence closes off the part of the site which is still under excavation. Be sure to take a peek at the Roman latrines; most of the 42 marble seats are still intact.

The entrance on the other side of the highway leads up to the **acropolis** and a **theater** which dates from the Hellenistic Period. On weekends in July and August, classical drama is performed; these shows are worth attending even if you don't know Greek. Tickets and information are available at the GNTO in Kavala or at the theater itself (cheapest available seats 500dr). (Site open daily sunrise-sunset. Admission 200dr, students 100dr; free for Greeks or Greek-speakers.) There is a disappointing **museum** nearby (tel. 51 62 61), with finds from the general area of Philippi. The majority of artifacts, however, are from the Dikili-Tach settlement and Sitagri. (Admission 200dr, students 100dr.)

A bus to Philippi leaves every 15 minutes (105dr). The bus back to Kavala stops down the road from the site, so don't wait at the entrance. If you are driving from Kavala, follow Erithrou Stavrou St. along the waterfront and turn north onto Merarchias Avenue. The archeological site is right on the highway.

# *Thrace* Θράκη

The northernmost province of Greece, Thrace has for centuries served as the gateway between Turkey and Greece, Asia and Europe, and thus, East and West. It is a highly agricultural, sparsely populated area of rolling hills, fertile land, rivers, and swamps. Ruled by the Ottomans until 1912, Thrace still bears evidence of the Turkish influence in the small Turkish and Armenian communities scattered throughout the region. Today, the Evros River separates the Greek province from Thracian Turkey, once a united area. In general, however, Thrace has become as Greek as the blue and white gate at the border.

## *Alexandroupolis* Αλεξανδρούπολη

Your most likely stop on a route through Thrace is the modern city of Alexandroupolis. It lies on the main west-to-east highway as well as on the rail lines. The city is packed in the summer with overland travelers and Greek vacationers. It's hard to imagine this callous, industrial port swarming with tourists, but after a long and fruitless search for accommodations, you will believe it. Plan in advance to meet your boat and train connections in Alexandroupolis without an overnight layover.

The main boulevard runs parallel to the waterfront and just 2 blocks inland from the train station on the waterfront. Six blocks to your left (east) past the ferry dock is the lighthouse. Often, in the early evening hours, the **National Bank of Greece,** next to the bus station a few blocks west of the train station on the main boulevard, takes pity on stranded tourists and opens for exchange only. (Regular hours Mon.-Fri. 7am-3:30pm.) The main **post office** is on the waterfront, and Poste Restante is available at the branch to the left of the corner of 14th May St., 6 blocks north of the main boulevard. (Both open Mon.-Fri. 7am-3:30pm.) Alexandroupolis' **postal code** is 68100. The **OTE,** 5 Ioakim Kaviri, is just on the other side of the main boulevard (an extension of Karatskaki). (Open daily 6am-midnight.) The **telephone code** is 0551. 14th May runs midway between the train station and the lighthouse, and 1 block east of Kaviri. The **tourist police** and the regular **police** are based 1 block inland on Karatskaki. (Open 24 hours.)

**Trains** chug slowly to Thessaloniki (5 per day, 8 hr., 890dr). KTEL **buses** (offices located on the main boulevard, Eleftheria Venizelou St., near the bank; tel. 264 79) travel to Thessaloniki (6 hr., 1740dr) via Kavala (3 hr., 900dr) seven times per day. Ferries never go directly to Kavala; they always pass thru Samothraki first. You can take the **ferry** to Kavala from Samothraki (2 per week, 4 hr., 1170dr). Ferry ticket offices and travel agencies are clustered around the small square 1 block inland from the lighthouse and across from the ferry dock. Visit these offices before 1pm.

It's an easy daytrip to **Samothraki.** Daily during July and August, at least one of two companies will be ferrying to the island (2 hr., 700dr). Buy tickets beforehand at the waterfront offices facing the ferry dock, or find the roving ticket agent who is supposed to sell them at departure time. You cannot buy tickets on board.

## Accommodations, Camping, and Food

If you must stay a night or two, try the **Aktaion Hotel** (tel. 280 78), across the street from the railroad station. (Doubles 1135dr. Triples 1584dr. Showers extra.) The kind owners will awaken to let you in at any hour; if all the rooms in town are full, they'll place cots in the living room for you. Otherwise, as you walk from the port towards the square, heed the "Zimmerfrei—Rooms" sign painted on the side of a building. (Singles 1500dr.)

Just up the street, bargain with the owner of **Hotel Tourist** (tel. 264 03. Singles 800dr. Triples 1800dr. Lower in off-season). To find a private room along the street leading inland from the train station, look for *dhomatia* signs or consult a local for directions.

If you have a tent, **Camping Alexandroupolis** is conveniently located in northwest Alexandroupolis, off the main boulevard. Walk for a half-hour, or take bus #5 from the train station (2 per hr., 55dr) and ask to be deposited at the campground. (385dr per person. 225dr per tent. 50% less in off-season.) The campground is on the beach, has clean facilities, and hosts the **Alexandroupolis Wine Festival** in July and August. To save money, you can camp in a tree grove about 1km east of the train station. Follow the road as it becomes dirt and cross the tracks after the truck depot. There is a water spigot at the playground that you pass.

For evening dining, look only to the **seaside cafes.** In the day the **Neraïda** and the **Klimataria** (located across from each other in Plateia Polytechnio) will help fill the hunger gap.

# Transit East

Travel options to Turkey are posted in the train station. A daily train runs to **Istanbul** at 5:40pm. You cannot make reservations, but must buy tickets at the station at 5pm (12 hr., 2305dr). A bus also runs daily at 11am (except Thurs.); tickets

can be purchased at the train station (6 hr., 2270dr). If you're hitching from Alexandroupolis, use a sign to get a ride that will take you all the way across the border—you cannot cross on foot. Five buses per day run to **Kipi** (970dr), on the border, where you'll have to hitch a ride across the border.

# CYCLADES
# Κυκλάδες

Most often, when people speak longingly of *the* Greek Islands, they are referring to the Cyclades. Romantics picture the islands' deserted streches of blond beaches lapped by blue seas and tinged with a bleeding orange sunset. The historian recreates the life of the island people from the graceful Cycladic figurines of the Bronze Age and the medieval sections of towns with their web of circuitous streets. The reckless drool at the prospect of revelry and on-the-beach recovery. The wonder of today's heavily-touristed Cyclades is that, with ingenuity, perseverance, and a durable liver, any of these dreams can be realized.

Historically, the islands share a complex and bloody past. Archeological excavations suggest that the Cyclades were inhabited as far back as 4500 B.C.E. Around 3000 B.C.E., the islands developed the culture known as the Early Cycladic, which lasted over 1000 years. During the Middle Cycladic period, Minos of Crete conquered the islands; lastly, the period dating from the fall of Crete to the rise of the Mycenaeans makes up the Late Cycladic. In about 1000 B.C.E., Ionic-speaking settlers from mainland Greece occupied the islands, and the region was controlled by various tyrants until the Persian invasion in 490 B.C.E. In 478 B.C.E., the Cyclades came under the rule of Athens, as members of the Delian League. After Athens' power was broken, the Cycladeans suffered successive conquests by the Macedonians and Egyptians (in the third century B.C.E.), the Romans (in the second century B.C.E.), the Venetians (in the thirteenth century C.E.), and finally the Turks (in the sixteenth century C.E.). Foreign rule lasted until the Greek War of Independence in 1827.

If you want to share in native Greek life, visit the islands in May or June or after September when the crowds subside. The prices decrease, and life becomes more tranquil. But for nightlife, nothing compares with the Cyclades in summer. In July and August, the Cyclades play host to an international assortment of hippies, package tourists, and yacht-toting offspring of shipping tycoons. Peasant homes are transformed into discos and boutiques, and sleepy villages echo with the sounds of rock, disco, and new wave well into the night.

## General Information

Although each island is distinct, a few basic rules of thumb apply to all. When you arrive, people with rooms to rent will greet your boat. A room from one of them is usually cheapest, but it is imperative that you make them pinpoint the exact location of their house. "Ten minutes away, near the beach," indicates that the room is a 45-minute hike from the main village. Camping—both official and freelance—is plentiful on these islands, though the stringency of the police toward unofficial camping increases in direct proportion to the island's popularity. Singles are few and far between at hotels or pensions, and solo travelers will usually have to take a double room at the standard price. (Keep your eyes open for others who might share a room.) You might consult the tourist agencies (private business that feign officialdom) or the GNTO. Each will help you find rooms, but they fill "their" hotels first. Only Mykonos, Andros, Paros, Milos, and Kea have real tourist information offices, and these are usually near the port and easy to differentiate from the others.

If you want to probe an island, rent a moped. Bus travel to major points in the interior and along the coast is hampered by a sporadic timetable. Rental shops are plentiful (mopeds 1000-1500dr per day), but many bikes are in poor condition. If you're a novice, the owner probably will rent you a moped without even taking time to see if you can manage the machine. Also, many of the secluded beaches and

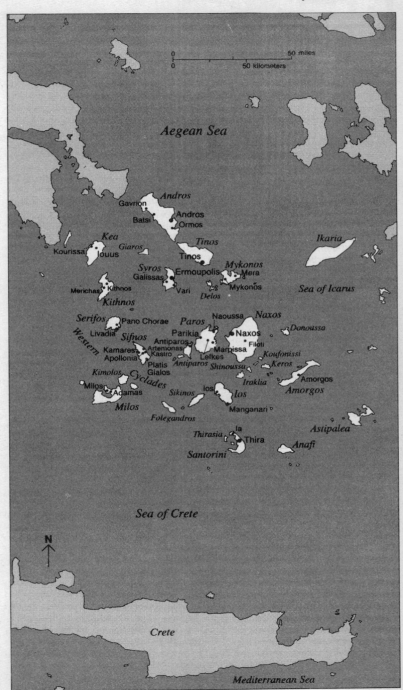

Aegean Sea

Andros
Gavrion
Batsi
Andros
Ormos

Kea
Giaros
Kourissa
Iouus

Tinos
Tinos

Ikaria

Svros
Galissas
Ermoupolis

Mykonos
Mera
Mykonos

Sea of Icarus

Merichas
Kithnos
Vari
Delos

Kithnos

Serifos
Pano Chorae
Livadia

Paros
Naoussa
Parikia

Naxos
Naxos
Filoti

Donoussa

Western
Sifnos
Kamares
Apollonia
Artemonas
Kastro
Antiparos
Lefkes
Marpissa

Koufonissi
Keros

Kimolos
Cyclades
Platis
Gialos
Antiparos
Shinoussa

Amorgos

Milos
Adamas

Sikinos
Ios
Ios

Iraklia

Amorgos

Milos
Folegandros

Manganari

Astipalea

Thirasia
Ia
Thira

Anafi

Santorini

Sea of Crete

N

Crete

Mediterranean Sea

mountainside monasteries are at the end of treacherous, rocky roads intended for sturdy-footed donkeys. So, unless you want to end your vacation in a cast, be a cautious adventurer.

Your island-hopping existence will hinge on the boat schedule. When you arrive on an island, immediately check the schedule so you can plan for your next departure. (Some smaller islands receive infrequent ferry service.) Your saviours are the port police or *limenacheio*. Their offices, which are found in every port, are open around the clock. They have complete, up-to-date information about every boat sailing in or out of the island. Ticket offices will usually give information about boats for which they sell tickets. Consider convenience, not prices, in you decision making, as ferry fares are regulated by law.

The islands are served by huge car ferries, small excursion boats, and fast but expensive Flying Dolphin hydrofoils. During July and August, boat connections between the major islands of Syros, Paros, Naxos, and Ios are extremely frequent—at least once per day. In June and September, service decreases, and in other months it is sporadic at best. For some of the northern Cyclades (Andros, Tinos), boats leave from Rafina rather than from Piraeus.

Prices are reasonable, but the cost of transportation can add up quickly if you do a lot of island-hopping. Night ferries allow you to save on the cost of accommodations and don't make you miss daylight hours at the beach. However, you might find yourself on the beach much earlier if you take a ferry that arrives during the wee hours.

# *Mykonos* Μύκονος

Mykonos is dangerous for the budget traveler. Temptations abound; the windows of the shops scintillate with golden offerings, and a multitude of trendy restaurants beckon with exotic menus and colorful interiors. It is, however, the bars and discos which pace the island's chic nightlife and deliver the mortal blow. You'd better have a sizable wad of bills to keep up with the crowd. Yet Mykonos has become the playground of the backpacker, as well as the rich and famous. If you play your cards right (don't change too much money when you arrive), you can enjoy the glitz without going bankrupt.

Mykonos is well-connected by **ferry.** Boats sail frequently to: Tinos (3-4 per day, 45 min., 460dr); Paros (2-3 per day, 2 hr., 580dr); Ios (2-3 per day, 4 hr., 1080dr); and Santorini (2-3 per day, 6½ hr., 1155dr). There are also sailings to: Rafina (1-2 per day, 5 hr., 1385dr); Syros (1 per day, 1½ hr., 477dr); Naxos (1 per day, 2½ hr., 510dr); Andros (1-2 per day, 3½ hr., 995dr); and Piraeus (2 per day, 6 hr., 1550dr).

Olympic Airways has **flights** to and from Athens (18 per day, ½ hr., 5020dr). A special bus runs between the airport and the Olympic Airways office on the waterfront in Mykonos Town (after each arrival and 70 min. before each departure, 50dr).

## *Mykonos Town*

If you get drunk in Mykonos Town, chances are that dawn will find you lost somewhere in its maze of endless, sparkling, snow-white buildings and labyrinthine alleys. Jammed with tourists from May to October, the town is still bewitching, well-maintained by its residents, and barely marred by huge hotel complexes. Sadly, the fishing boats in the harbor, the basket-laden donkeys, and the natives seem to come right out of an elaborately staged Broadway show. Depending on how homesick you feel, you will be either delighted or shocked by the availability of cheeseburgers, milk shakes, fish and chips, Chinese food, popcorn, and "English breakfasts." This hyper-tourism has hardened locals to visitors. Most are indifferent to, or worse, offended by the yearly influx, and keep their distance. Don't come to Mykonos to experience Greece; come here instead to witness the remarkable world party.

## Orientation and Practical Information

Everything you need is in and around the waterfront. Boats dock at a pier near the town beach, next to which you'll find the Olympic Airways office. Two blocks to the right of the beach (facing inland) is **Taxi Square** (Mavroyenous Sq.), lined with cafes and shops. Just opposite the beach is the main bus stop for most of the island's beaches. The tourist office and pier for excursion boats are at the opposite end of the waterfront.

**Tourist Information:** Tel. 239 90, on the opposite end of the waterfront from Olympic Airways. Very helpful and friendly. Free accommodations service for Mykonos. Boat and local bus schedules. Open daily 8:30am-8:30pm.

**Currency Exchange: National Bank of Greece.** On the waterfront in the center. Open Mon.-Thurs. 8am-2pm, Fri. 8am-1:30pm; special exchange window open Mon.-Fri. 6-8pm, Sat.-Sun. 9:30am-1pm.

**Post Office:** At the edge of the beach, next to Olympic Airways. Currency exchange. Open daily 7:30am-9pm. **Postal code:** 84600.

**OTE:** On the far left of the waterfront, uphill. Open Mon.-Fri. 7:30am-midnight, Sat.-Sun. 8am-10pm. **Telephone code:** 0829.

**Olympic Airways:** Tel. 224 90 or 224 95, at the edge of the beach, on the far left side of the waterfront. Open daily 8am-2pm.

**Tourist Police:** Tel. 227 16 or 224 82. Follow "Bus to Plati Yialos" signs and turn left on Plateia Dim. Koutsi. Open 24 hours.

**Port Police:** Tel. 222 18, above the National Bank. Open 24 hours.

## Accommodations and Camping

Accommodations are big business on Mykonos. The usual mob of room hawkers at the port now sticks slick photo-montages of its rooms in your face for approval. Doubles run approximately 2000dr, with bath 2500dr. Beware of rooms "on the beach"—they are bound to be miles away. In high season, the flood of empty rooms dries up fast, so don't dillydally getting off the boat. One place to try in town is the old white house with green trim at 13 Mitropoleos St. opposite a pharmacy. (Doubles 1950dr. Triples 2450dr.) The **Apollos Disco,** right in the back left corner of the Taxi Sq., rents noisy roof space for 500dr per person. There are also a number of D-class hotels in town, but these are very expensive in high season. Of course, you can always join the scores who plop their sleeping bags down on the town beach.

Prices for the hotels listed below are at the very least 20% lower in off-season. In high season, you'll probably have to spend at least one night on the beach or in a private room before you'll find a vacancy in one of the hotels if you stay two or more nights.

**Hotel Phillippi,** 32 Kalogara St. (tel. 222 94). Friendly owners, magnificent flower garden, clean rooms. Open June 15-Sept.15. Singles 2300dr. Doubles 3350dr. Triples 4900dr. Showers included.

**Hotel Maria,** 18 N. Kalogera St. (tel. 223 17), off of Kalogera St. and next to a bakery. Cheaper than most, but always full. Clean rooms. Open April-Oct. Single (only 1 available) 1500dr. Doubles 3500dr. Triples 4000dr.

**Apollon Hotel,** (tel. 232 71), on the waterfront. The oldest hotel in Mykonos. Beautiful, traditional house with balcony overlooking the harbor. Open April-Oct. Singles 2437dr. Doubles 3213dr, with bath 3877dr. Triples 4099dr. Showers 150dr.

**Camping: Paradise Beach Camping** (tel. 221 29 or 229 37). The only official campground. Their van meets all the boats. If you miss the van, take the bus for Plati Yialos (55dr) and then a boat to the beach in front of the campsite entrance (60dr). Spacious and clean. A self-sufficient community with restaurant, disco, mini-market, currency exchange, an international phone with a long line, newstand, film processing, and even an aviary. 24-hour check-in. Open April-Oct. 350dr per person. 150dr per tent. There is also plenty of unofficial camping at Paradise, Super Paradise, and Elia Beaches.

Outside town there are a few more hotels, but even these are booked solid in high season by tourists who pay through the nose. At St. Stephanos Beach, the **Mina Hotel** (tel. 230 24) is near sports facilities. (Doubles 2400dr, with bath 2500dr.) Also try **Panorama Hotel** (tel. 223 37); singles with bath 2000dr; doubles with bath 3000dr.) If you make it to Megali Ammos Beach, you can try the **Markos Beach Hotel** (tel. 228 11; doubles 2400dr).

## Food

On Mykonos, you may find yourself adrift in the sea of exotic menus and equally exotic prices. Don't despair, however—there are some inexpensive restaurants out there.

**Nikes Taverna,** in the square behind the tourist information office. In the middle of all the action. Chicken curry 380dr, *mousaka* 300dr. Open daily noon-3pm and 6pm-midnight.

**Paraportiani Taverna** (tel. 235 31), opposite Nikes. Smaller portions but sedate. Open April-Oct. noon-midnight.

**Taverna Maky's,** next to Paraportiani's. Similar to its neighbor in terms of food and atmosphere. Some interesting specials—lamb with artichokes 550dr. Open 6pm-midnight.

**Taverna O Petros.** Follow Drakopoulo St. to the Church of Agia Gerasimos. A secluded private garden and outside tables. *Pastitsio* 190dr, chicken 350dr, *tiropita* 190dr. Open noon-2:30pm and 6pm-midnight.

**Taverna Antonini** (tel. 223 19), in the bustling and convenient Taxi Sq. Chicken 320dr, *mousaka* 420dr. Open daily noon-midnight.

**Kounelas,** 1 block up from the waterfront, behind Nikes Taverna. Decor humble but not the prices. Good for the indecisive. Only 1 entree: fresh grilled fish for 2 (1600dr). Open 7pm-midnight.

**Andrea's Bakery,** off Taxi Sq. Fruit pies, and *spanakopita* (spinach pie) from 90dr. Pineapple croissant 100dr. Open daily 6am-11pm.

**The Donut Factory,** at the intersection of Mitropoleos, Ipirou, and Enoplon Dinameon St., about 3 blocks down from the bus station. Scrumptious doughnuts, fresh fruit juices (200-300dr), and fruit salads. Try their apple fritters (100dr). Open daily 6am-1pm. Some other places are nearby, including a great homemade ice-cream place, **Snowball.**

## Entertainment

There are too many bars and discos to name; the cognoscenti will discern the differences. Most places close at 3am, though some stay open longer. Few have cover charges, but drink prices more than make up for that freebie.

**Windmill Disco,** across from Nikes Taverna, off the right side of the waterfront. A very popular place in a refurbished windmill. Greek music (9-11pm), then hackneyed disco. Beer 200dr, mixed drinks 400dr. No cover, but 1 drink is mandatory.

**Scandinavian Bar,** near the Windmill Disco. Lots of blonds. Always packed (even in the street outside). Beer 150dr.

**Irish Bar,** near Taxi Sq. Very animated. English speakers sing along with the music. Beer 150dr, mixed drinks 450dr.

**Madd,** on top of a building in Taxi Sq. Slightly punk (what, me worry) atmosphere. Party starts late—don't come before 1am. Beer 350dr.

**Kastro Bar,** off a side street near the Paraportiani. Sit by the window overlooking the water while you are serenaded with classical music. Peaceful and romantic. Drinks 500-700dr.

## Sights

Perfecting tans and shopping are the prime daytime activities on Mykonos. While there are exquisite handicrafts in other parts of Greece, this is the only place where you'll find designer clothes of international repute. **Galatis,** to the left of Taxi Sq. (facing town), has unique handwoven sweaters and outfits (from 10,000dr). Note the long list of signatures of famous people, like Jackie O., who shopped here. Upstairs, necklaces drape the ceiling. (Open March-Oct. daily 9am-10pm.) **Panos,** on Matogianni St., sells colorful handwoven bedspreads, table mats, sweaters, shawls, and bags, and will do work to order (goods shipped anywhere). (Open April-Oct. 11am-1pm and 6-11pm.) **Vienoula's,** around the corner, sells similar items in addition to making jackets and sweaters. These shops are not cheap by Greek standards, but their work is beautiful.

The island has a few traditional attractions which we will bravely name, but it would be ridiculous to pretend that people come here to experience cultural enrichment or indigenous Greek life. The **archeological museum,** on the waterfront between the ferry dock and the center of town, has a seventh-century B.C.E. *pithos* (large earthenware vessel) with relief scenes from the Trojan War, and a bronze *kouros.* (Open Mon. and Wed.-Sat. 9am-3pm, Sun. 9:30am-2:30pm. Admission 200dr, students 100dr.) The **Folk Art Museum** is found in the nearly 300-year-old house of a former sea-captain, at the northern edge of town behind the tourist information office. The lovely collection is open at convenient hours for beach-goers. (Open Mon.-Sat. 5:30-8:30pm, Sun. 6:30-8:30pm. Free.) Next door is the **Paraportiani,** a glistening hive of white churches twisted on top of one another below a phalanx of three stoic windmills—the most famous sight on Mykonos.

By will or transcendental force, you will find yourself on the beach. Nearest to town, dismissing the dismissable town beach, is **Megali Ammos,** a 1-kilometer walk past the windmills on the southwestern corner of the harbor. **St. Stephanos Beach,** a 10-minute bus ride from the town beach (every hr., 55dr) is not spectacular, but is convenient and has a very good water-sports center. Crowded **Psarou Beach** is also close to town. The so-called nudist beaches (those in the buff are actually in the minority) are by far the best on the island and can be reached by taking a bus (55dr) to **Plati Yialos** (not bad in its own right), and then taking a caïque from there. Buses leave every hour from 8am to 2am from a bus stop about 250m up the hill along the street that runs beside the windmills. (Look for painted signs pointing to "buses for Plati Yialos.") From the same bus stop, buses also run hourly to the beach at Ornos. From Plati Yialos, caïques go to **Paradise Beach** (60dr, straight) and **Super Paradise Beach** (100dr, gay). Paradise Beach can also be reached by the 7-kilometer strip of road connecting it to town.

If you feel you can abandon the beaches and divorce yourself from tourists, visit **Ano Mera,** the island's only other village, 7km away. The main item of interest is its **Tourliani** monastery, with an ornate sixteenth-century marble steeple. The town is accessible by bus—check at the tourist information office.

# *Delos* Δήλος

The sacred heart of the Cyclades, Delos is the site of the famous Sanctuary to Apollo, built to commemorate the place where Apollo and his twin sister Artemis were born. When their mother, Leto, became pregnant, the culprit Zeus, fearing his wife Hera's wrath, cast Leto off. Searching desperately for a place to give birth, Leta came to Delos. Here at last she was welcomed, after promising that Apollo would make his seat of worship there.

The mortal history of the island is less charmed. Colonized from time immemorial, Delos had long been a religious and commercial center for the Cyclades when the Ionians dedicated it to the cult of Leto in the tenth century B.C.E. By the seventh century B.C.E., Delos had become the political and trade center of the Aegean League of Islands, thus beginning three centuries of struggle between the Delians and the Athenians for its control. During these years, the Athenians ordered at least two "purifications" of the island, the latter in 426 B.C.E., when they decreed that no one should give birth or die on its sacred grounds. Delians facing either exigency were removed to the nearby Rheneia. Following the purification, the Athenians instituted the quadrennial Delian Games, dominated by the Athenians themselves.

After Sparta's defeat of Athens in the Peloponnesian War (403 B.C.E.), Delos enjoyed a prosperous independence. Sweet prosperity went sour during the Roman occupation in the second century B.C.E. The Romans turned the religious festival into one grand trade fair, and made the island the slave-market of Greece, selling as many as 10,000 slaves on any given day.

By the second century C.E., after successive sackings, the island was left virtually uninhabited, although under Turkish occupation it became a pirates' haunt. Today, its only residents are leaping lizards and members of the French School of Archeology, which has been excavating ruins since 1873.

A map to the sprawling site is highly recommended, whether you choose to follow the tour below, tag along with a guided tour, or improvise. For more background information, *Delos: Monuments and Museum,* by Photini Zaphiropolou, is very informative and includes a map (500dr, available at the entrance and at the museum). If you visit Delos unprepared, you may feel overwhelmed by the multitude of unmarked ruins. Remember that you can buy guides and maps to Delos in Mykonos prior to your departure.

Occupying almost a square mile of this tiny island, the archeological site is neatly divided into four parts: the central part of the city, including the Sanctuary of Apollo and the Agora; the outlying parts of the ancient city; Mt. Kythnos; and the theater quarter. While it takes several days to see the ruins completely, the tour suggested below is perhaps the most efficient way to glimpse the highlights during a three-hour visit. Most of your fellow passengers on the boat will follow a similar route when they disembark, so if you want some privacy while you inspect the ruins, simply reverse the route.

From the dock, head straight to the **Agora of the Competaliasts,** where different Roman guilds built their shrines. To the left are several parallel **stoas,** the most impressive of which was built by Phillip of Macedon. This line of altars, pillars, and statue bases (you can still see the statues' prints) forms the western border of the **Sacred Way.** Follow this road to the **Sanctuary of Apollo.** Its most impressive remain is an immense, partly hollow rectangular pedestal that supported an 8-meter-tall statue of Apollo. The famous **Delian Lions,** a gift from the people of Naxos to the holy island, lie 50m to the north. In the seventh century B.C.E., nine marble lions were placed in a row on a terrace facing the sacred lake; only five remain—a sixth was pirated by the Venetians and to this day guards the entrance to the arsenal in Venice.

To the left of the lions, proceed up the small crest to the appropriately named **House of the Hill.** Much remains of this edifice because it was dug deep into the earth; it is an excellent model of the layout of a Roman home. Continuing downhill and to the right you'll reach the **House of the Lake,** with a well-preserved, patterned mosaic decorating its atrium. Turning back south toward the docks, pass along the wall that defines the long, dry **Sacred Lake.** The evaporated lake will remind you of your own parched throat, but don't succumb to the overpriced cafeteria—bring along your own water bottle. Next to the cafeteria, the **museum** contains Delian finds, but unfortunately the best sculpture from the site is in Athens. (Open Mon. and Wed.-Sat. 9am-3pm, Sun. 9am-2pm. Admission included in the entrance charge.) From there, head up the path of Mt. Kythnos (where Zeus watched the birth of Apollo). The **Temples of the Egyptian Gods,** on your left, demonstrate the extent to which people paid homage on this island. The top of the 120-meter hill affords a spectacular view of ruins as well as the surrounding Cyclades. As you descend, keep an eye out for the **Grotto of Hercules;** the immensity of the blocks that form its entrance halfway down the mountainside seem to date the grotto's origins to Mycenaean times, though some experts suggest it is a Hellenistic imitation of such architecture.

Bear left (north) at the bottom of the hill to reach the **House of the Dolphins** and the **House of the Masks,** which contains the renowned mosaic *Dionysus Riding a Panther,* considered by many to be the climax of the visit to Delos. A bit farther down the hill is the **ancient theater.** As you descent its steps, notice the sophisticated cistern, **Dexamene,** with its nine arched compartments. Continuing down, you'll reach the **House of the Trident,** with a mosaic of a dolphin twisted around a trident (closed in 1988), the **House of Dionysus,** with another mosaic of Dionysius and a panther, and the **House of Cleopatra,** with its remaining columns. The famous statue of Cleopatra and Dioscourides will be placed in the museum and a plaster copy will replace it on the site. (Ruins open Mon.-Sat. 8:45am-3pm, Sun. 9am-2pm. Admission 500dr, students 250dr.)

If you visit Delos as a daytrip from Mykonos, you will be at the mercy of the ferry timetables. When the whistle blows after two and a half hours, you'll either be ecstatic to escape or disconsolate about being rushed and deprived of certain sites. Weather permitting, boats for Delos depart from the pier near the tourist information office in Mykonos Town (leaving at 9am, returning at 1pm, 45 min., 355dr round-trip.) The ride sometimes feels like a roller coaster, so you might want to bring along some Dramamine—this is one time when it will really come in handy. A bigger (more stable) boat also makes the trip (leaving at 10am, returning at 2pm, 800dr round-trip). There are also joint excursions to Delos and Mykonos from Naxos (2500dr), but only one and a half hours are allotted for visiting the Delian ruins. It is illegal to stay overnight on Delos, so if you want to explore the site in depth, several morning trips on successive days is probably the best strategy.

# *Tinos* Τήνος

Two types visit Tinos—the devout and the hedonist. Mopeds and rented cars full of scantily clad sun-worshipers whiz by the 750 Christian churches and monasteries that dot the island's green hills. Black-clad pilgrims moving at a decidedly slower pace line up to kiss the most sacred relic of the Orthodox church—the Icon of the Annunciation, also known as the "Megalochari" ("Great Joy"). To the disbeliever, the discovery of the nearly 900-year-old icon, still in perfect condition in 1823, seems dubious, but to the faithful, the find is overwhelming evidence of God's miraculous powers. In 1822, Sister Pelagia, a Tiniote nun, had a vision in which the Virgin Mary instructed her fo find her icon that was buried at the site of an ancient church, destroyed in the tenth century by pirates. Preliminary excavations were unsuccessful and halted. An epidemic then plagued the town and the desperate islanders resumed digging. Amid great rejoicing, the icon was found in 1823 and construction immediately began at the **Panayia Evangelistra,** where the icon is still housed. The relic reputedly has curing powers and is almost entirely covered with gold, diamonds, and pearls left at the church by people wishing to thank the Holy Mother for their good health. The church has become the "Lourdes of the Aegean," as evidenced by the *ex-votos,* beautifully wrought plaques praising the Virgin for healing the body part depicted. The most pious Greeks make the journey up Leoforos Megalochari on their knees, to show their reverence in the Panayia. On March 24 and August 15, tens of thousands flock to the church: These festivals are the largest *panagieria* in Greece. On August 15, **Tinos Town** is so crowded that visitors sleep *everywhere*—along the dock, on the sidewalks, and even in the church itself. (Open daily 7am-8pm. Free.) Tinos is also famed for its marble sculptors, some of whose works are on display in a small building at the Panayia Evangelistria.

**Boats** travel to Tinos frequently. Every day, four ferries sail to Mykonos (40 min., 437dr). There is also twice-daily service to Andros (2 hr., 635dr), Rafina (4½ hr., 1129dr), and Piraeus (5 hr., 1530dr). Five days a week, a boat travels to Syros (40 min., 382dr). The *Megalochari* sails four to seven times per week to Paros (609dr), Ios (1187dr), and Santorini (1296dr). You can also take an excursion to Mykonos and Delos (daily at 9am, return at 6pm, 1800dr).

All boats dock in **Tinos Town.** Facing inland left, you'll see **Leoforos Megalochares** leading up to the yellow **Panayia Evangelistria,** with its Italianate facade. On the right a few blocks up you'll find the **OTE** (open Mon.-Fri. 7:30am-10pm, Sat.-Sun. 8am-10pm); the **post office** is in the same building (open Mon.-Fri. 7:30am-2:15pm). Running parallel to Leoforos Megalochares up to the church (facing inland right of Megalochares), **Evangelistrias Street** is filled with typical souvenirs, as well as a complete selection of religious trinkets. If you go straight and take your fourth right, you'll find Lazarou Sohou St., where the **police** (tel. 221 00 or

222 55) are located. (Open 24 hours.) The **port police** (tel. 223 48) are based in the center of the wharf (to the right of Megalochres and Evangelistrias facing inland). (Open 24 hours.) The **National Bank of Greece** is on the wharf (left with your back to the water). (Open Mon.-Thurs. 8am-2pm, Fri. 8-1:30pm.) Tinos' **telephone code** is 0283; the **postal code** is 84200.

Accommodations are easy to find in Tinos, except at *panagieri* time. Most hotels, however, are expensive so you'll probably want to take a room from one of the people who meet the boat. Doubles run for 1500dr. If you want to stay in a hotel, try the **Thalia,** 7 Panatiou St. (parallel to the wharf on the right side facing inland; tel. 228 11). This bohemian enclave with a garden is Tinos' only "cheap" hotel. (Doubles 2215dr. Triples 2800dr.) **Yianni's Rooms** (tel. 225 15), in a traditional house on the right side of the wharf, is another relatively inexpensive option. (Doubles 1900dr, with bath and kitchen 2500dr. Triples 2020dr, with bath and kitchen 3000dr. Quads 2400dr.) **Tinos Camping** (tel. 223 44 or 235 48) is a 10-minute walk from town. (350dr per person, 150dr per tent.) Food is expensive in Tinos Town, but the *tavernas* around the corner on the left side of the port (past the Hotel Lito) are more reasonable. *Souvlaki,* however, may be best for a cheap meal. The happening bar on Tinos, **Kalakathoumena** (sign in Greek), is also around the corner at the left end of the port.

The **archeological museum** is across the street and uphill from the post office. It contains many artifacts from Poseidon's sanctuary at Kionia and a first-century B.C.E. sundial. (Open Mon. and Wed.-Sat. 9am-3pm, Sun. and holidays 10am-2pm. Admission 200dr, students 100dr.) Buses run to touristed **Tinos Beach** in Kionia (9am-6pm every hr., 10 min., 50dr). **Agios Fokas,** a closer and equally crowded beach, is a short walk to the east of Tinos Town.

Excursion into the Tinos countryside will reward the adventurer with more secluded beaches and wonderful vistas of the fertile Tinos countryside. Worth a visit is the small town of **Pyrgos,** 33km northwest of Tinos Town, which was home of Tiniote artists and sculptors. Artists still work in the village today, but their art looks mass-produced. If you really want peace and quiet, spend the night in a traditional house. (Singles 1000dr. Doubles 2000dr. Call Fotini at 314 65.) Three kilometers south of Pyrgos is Panormos Bay, which has a small beach and three tavernas—try the middle one, it's cheapest. Buses travel to Pyrgos three times per day from Tinos Town (1 hr., 220dr).

If you have wheels, explore the delightful villages that encircle **Mount Exobourgo,** the precipitous site of the Venetian Fortress, **Xoumbourgo.** Climb from its base at Xinara if you can (it's hard), for the view.

# *Andros* Ανδρος

With its fertile hills, mountain streams and natural springs Andros still deserves its ancient name—*Hydroussa* ("Watery Isle"). Interspersed in this rich landscape are *dovecots,* small white buildings with intricate geometric lattice work on which birds roost. The birds are usually trapped and eaten by the townfolk. Tourism is mainly of the package-tour variety and is limited to Batsi and Andros Town, the island's capital. Since all ferries dock at the peaceful port town of Gavrion, an hour's drive from Andros Town, you should probably spend at least your first night here before embarking on your exploration of the rest of the island.

To reach the island from Athens, take the orange and white striped bus to Rafina from the corner of Mavromaeon St., just off Leoforos Alexandras (140dr). From Rafina, at least three **ferries** per day head for Andros (2½ hr., 757dr). From Andros, the *Eptanisos* and the *Bari Express* run daily to Tinos (2 hr., 620dr) and Mykonos (2½ hr., 965dr).

The **tourist office** is in a dovecot at the extreme right side of the waterfront (facing inland) and is open daily 8am-2pm and 5-9pm. The **OTE** is 1 block up from the waterfront. Open Mon.-Fri. 8am-1pm and 5-10pm. The **post office,** on the left side of the waterfront, has a **currency exchange.** (Open Mon.-Fri. 7:30am-2:15pm.) The

**police** are on a road parallel to the waterfront around the corner from the OTE (take a left) and are open 'round the clock. Andros' **telephone code** is 0282; the **postal code** is 84501.

If you stay in **Gavrion,** you should rent a room from one of the people meeting the boat or ask along the waterfront. **Eleni** has rooms in an old house overlooking the harbor. (Doubles 1400dr.) Inquire at the variety store on the waterfront, to the right as you get off the boat. **Camping Andros** (tel. 714 44) is very close to town; go to the righthand side of the harbor (facing inland) and walk up the road toward Batsi until you see signs. (350dr per person. 150dr for tent.) For a truly original meal, walk toward the psychedelic red, yellow, and green lights glimmering at the extreme right side of the harbor, as you face the water, where you wil find the quintessential existentialist-chef-fisherman in **Here, Mourikes.** Savor delicious *kalamari* (400dr) as you tersely discuss the here and now. (Open lunch and dinner.)

While in Gavrion, make the hour's hike north-west to see the **Agios Petros,** a very impressive tower which dates from the Hellenistic period. If you want to get to Andros Town, take one of the buses from the station next to the ferry dock (5 per day, 1 hr., 230dr). A taxi costs 1500dr. You can also rent a moped (1300dr)—ask for George at the waterfront cafe "Hydroussa" or call 714 66.

The road to Andros Town passes through **Batsi,** a popular tourist beach (8 km). **Hotel Avra** (tel. 413 76), has clean waterfront rooms. (Doubles 1650-2000dr.) Buses run to Batsi from Gavrion (60dr) and from Andros Town (185dr). **Andros Town** is a quiet village with an expansive view of the sea. From the bus station, walk downhill to the main road, which is soothingly closed to traffic. The **post office** (open Mon.-Fri. 7:30am-3:10pm; exchanges currency) and the **OTE** (open Mon.-Fri. 7:30am-3:10pm) are opposite each other at one end of the road. Andros Town's **postal code** is 845 00; the **telephone code** is 0282. Off the main road and up a street next to a tree-filled square with a church you will find the **port police.** (Open 24 hours.) The **National Bank of Greece** is located farther down the main road. (Open Mon.-Thu. 8am-2pm, Fri. 8am-1:30pm.) You can rent **mopeds** from **Aris** (tel. 243 81), on the main street (1000dr).

To the right, in the square at the end of the main road, is a clean and inexpensive *taverna* with a great view of the beach on which you may end up camping. If you don't feel like getting sand in your sleeping bag, try the **Hotel Egii** (tel. 223 03 or 222 62). The friendly English-speaking management offers singles for 1800dr, doubles for 2400dr (with private shower 3240dr), and triples for 3960dr. You'll be surprised by the many high-quality museums in this small town until you realize that Goulandris, the shipping tycoon and philanthropist, hails from Andros. The modern, air-conditioned **archeological museum** has a beautifully-presented exhibit of finds from Tinos. (Open Mon. and Wed.-Sat. 8:45am-3pm, Sun. 9:30am-2:30pm.) The **Museum of Modern Art** is around the corner and down the street. (Open June-Sept. Mon. and Wed.-Sun. 10am-2pm and 6-8pm). Across the street is a special building for summer exhibits. In the summer of 1988, there was a Matisse show. The **nautical museum** is near the water's edge. (Open Mon. and Wed.-Sun. 6-8pm.) Crowning the tip of Andros Town, the bronze statue of the Unknown Sailor bids adieu as he sets off for sea.

# *Syros* Σύρος

The two churches, one Orthodox and one Catholic, which command the two hills of Hermoupolis, survey what was once the premier Greek port. When coal-burning steamships were replaced by more efficient oil-fueled ships in the nineteenth century, Syros' use as a refueling station became obsolete. Despite its decline as a major port, the city is still the shipping center of the Cyclades. Elegant Miaouli Square and the nineteenth-century mansions in Dellagrazia hint at Hermoupolis' opulent past as well as its past nicknames—the "Manchester of Greece" and "little Milan." Most tourists visit the island only to make ferry connections to the more popular Cyclades; those who stay are not casual island-hoppers but people who return every summer. A day in Hermoupolis, however, may well be the best antidote to the white-washed unreality of the other Cycladic islands.

From Syros, **ferries** sail to Piraeus (2 per day, 4½ hr., 1398dr), Tinos (1 per day, 40 min., 389dr), Mykonos (1 per day, 1½ hr., 477dr), Paros (1-2 per day, 1½ hr., 478dr), Naxos (1-2 per day, 2½ hr., 716dr), and Rafina (1 per day, 4½ hr., 1136dr). There is less frequent service to Andros (2 per week, 3 hr., 647dr), Sifnos (1 per week, 5 hr., 900dr), Serifos (1 per week, 6 hr., 900dr), Ios (3 per week, 4 hr., 1222dr), and Santorini (3 per week, 5 hr., 1296dr).

Most important services in Syros are located in the main square in **Hermoupolis.** Across from the town hall is the **post office.** (Open Mon.-Fri. 7:30am-8pm, Sat. 7:30am-3pm, Sun. 9am-1:30pm; parcels abroad 7:30am-2pm in the building around the corner.) The **OTE** is on the right side of the square as you face the town hall. (Open daily 7am-midnight, but someone's always there in case of emergency.) The **National Bank** is on Kalomnopoulou St. (Open Mon.-Thurs. 8am-2pm, Fri. 8am-1:30pm.) Located on the right side of the port (facing inland), the **tourist office** provides information on accommodations, and has bus and boat timetables. (Open Mon.-Fri. 9am-2:30pm and 4:15-5:45 pm.) The **port police** (tel. 226 90), next door, provide up-to-date information about boat schedules. (Open 24 hours.) The **tourist police** (tel. 226 20 or 226 10) are at 3 Timolegon Ambelas St. (Open 24 hours.) The **city police** (tel. 235 55) are at 33 Eptanisou St., which runs parallel to the harbor road on the left side (facing inland). (Open 24 hours.) Syros' **telephone code** is 0281; the **postal code** is 84100.

Hermoupolis has plenty of cheap accommodations. High season in Syros lasts only from mid-July through August. Take a room in one of the city's distinctive, avante-garde pensions. You can get to **Yianni's Guest House** (tel. 286 65) by following the many orange signs from the port. Yianni offers you a room in a traditional house with a bar in the garden. (Roof 250dr. Dorm beds 700dr. Singles 1000dr. Doubles 1600dr. Triples 2400dr. 100dr extra for stays of only 1 night. Breakfast 200dr.) **Apollon Rooms to Let,** 8 Odysseus St. (tel. 221 58), is a delightful option. An arch of piebald stained glass greets you as you enter this old house with its high, frescoed ceilings. The good-humored owner is a well of knowledge about Syros, past and present. You may use the refrigerator and kitchen even if you stay on the roof. (Roof 400dr. Singles 800-1000dr. Doubles 1500dr. Triples 2200dr. Showers included.) Apollon's proprietors also rent **mopeds** at a 200dr discount if you stay in their rooms. Show them your *Let's Go: Greece* for a 100-200dr discount (except in high season). Another possibility is **Kastro Rooms** 12 Kalomnopoulou St. (call the snack bar for information at 264 53 or 251 58), off Evangelistrias St. and opposite the Evangelistrias Church and the National Bank. (Singles 1000dr. Doubles 1600dr. Triples 2100dr.) **Nick's Rooms,** 14 Androu St. (tel. 244 51 or 243 57), are a bit dingy and out of the way in an ordinary modern building, but he'll give you a 10-15% discount (except in high season) if you show your *Let's Go: Greece.* Hotel clients also get a 10% discount on Nick's moped rentals. (Singles 700dr. Doubles 1500dr. Triples 1900dr.)

Even Hermoupolis' E-class hotels are inexpensive. **Hotel Akteon** (tel. 226 75), on a side alley off the harbor road, around the corner from Syros Travel Agency, has fragrant rooms (and even bathrooms) in an airy old house. (Singles 980dr. Doubles 1700dr. Triples 2100dr.) **Hotel Mykonos,** 18 Antiparou St. (tel. 283 46), 1 block up from the port road, has dainty rooms with tablecloth-covered tables. (Singles 1100dr. Doubles 1500dr. Triples 2200dr. Showers 130dr.)

For a unique dinner overlooking the lights of Hermoupolis, try **Tempelis Taverna,** on Anastaseos St., below the church on the right hill (it's a hike up *lots* of stairs). The menu includes rabbit, squid, pigeon (300dr), and piping hot *tiropites* and *bougatses* (180dr each). The owner doesn't speak English, so check out the food coming from the kitchen and then point. (Open for dinner only.) Or skip dinner, sip *ouzo,* and snack on grilled octopus and other *mezedes* (appetizers) in one of the numerous outdoor cafes on Miaouli Sq. and along the waterfront. The **Piano Bar,** in Miaouli Sq., to the left of town hall, is a favorite nightspot among locals. Trendy purple chairs in all shades of purple line the outdoor area from which you might hear the owner play the piano after midnight. (Drinks 500dr.)

During your stay, make the ascent to **Ano Syros,** the original medieval Venetian settlement and still home to Syros' Catholics. Go up the steps behind Mialou Sq. or take the bus from the waterfront. For the less sturdy-legged, there is an **archeo-logical museum,** just off Mialou Sq. with a small collection of Cycladic art. (Open Mon. and Wed.-Sat. 9am-3pm, Sun. 9:30am-2:30pm. Free.)

Galissas, a village to the west of Hermoupolis, has a popular beach. You can camp in one of the caves on the nudist beach (climb past the church on the left), or stay at one of the several pensions or hotels. **Angela's Rooms to Let** (tel. 428 55) is im-maculate and run by a friendly, English-speaking proprietor. The rooms are sur-rounded by a very pleasant, spacious outdoor garden. (Doubles 1950dr, with bath 2500dr. Triples 2470dr.) Also try **Tony's and Venita's Rooms to Let** (tel. 424 82), on the street from the beach to the village near the intersection, for clean, homey rooms. (Doubles 2000dr. Triples 2800dr.) There are many other rooms to let in the area at similar prices—shop around. Nearby, well-marked camping grounds **Yianna** (tel. 424 18) and **Two Hearts** (tel. 420 52) charge 300-350dr per person, 100-150dr per tent.

Galissas has all imaginable amenities—an inexpensive self-service restaurant on the beach, many *tavernas*, mini-golf, video games, and even **Disco Aphrodite.** Buses run to Galissas frequently from Ermoupolis (6:30am-10pm, ½ hr., 75dr). Farther south along the coast are the beaches at **Foinika, Angathopes,** and **Komito,** which are also connected by bus to Hermoupolis. Komito offers free camping. **Vari** is an-other popular beach resort, but mostly for family and package tour groups. **Kini,** a 25-minute bus ride from Hermoupolis, is a fishing village whence you should watch the famous "Kini sunset." Nearby, **Agia Varvare,** a convent and orphanage, produces and sells handicrafts.

# *Paros* Πάρος

The geographical center of the Cyclades, Paros is the most average of all the is-lands—nice, but nothing great. Its wide interior is not as fertile, its villages not as picturesque, and its beaches not as beautiful as those of nearby Naxos. Like Ios and Mykonos, Paros offers a lively nightlife, but unlike those isles, its evenings are neither raucous nor chic. But Paros is ideal for the person who wants a little of everything. For this reason, it has become one of the most touristed islands in the Cyclades.

In summer, pensions and *dhomatia* fill up fast. If you can't find accommodations in any of the main coastal towns, don't panic. Try one of the small villages linked to the port town of Parikia by bus, Antiparos, or any of the island's secluded beaches. There are also several official campsites on the island, and unofficial camp-ing is quite common, although the police here are a bit nastier about it than they are on most of the other islands. (To be safe, camp somewhere other than Parikia.)

Paros rivals Syros as the transportation hub of the Cyclades. **Boats** depart several times per day to all of the major nearby islands. A complete schedule is posted in the tourist office in the windmill. In summer, six to seven boats per day for Piraeus (5-6 hr., 1400dr), and five to six per day for Naxos (1 hr., 450dr), Sifnos (2 hr., 883dr), Ios (2½ hr., 916dr), and Santorini (3½ hr., 1002dr). One to two per day service Syros (1½ hr., 475dr), Tinos (3 hr., 574dr), and Mykonos (2 hr., 574dr). Three to four per week run to Amorgos (3 hr., 957dr), Ikaria (3 hr., 880dr), Crete (8 hr., 1821dr), and Samos (6 hr., 1486dr). Since Paros is the only Cycladic island that connects to eastern islands (i.e. Samos), you may well visit Paros during your island hopping. Twice per week, there are sailings to the small islands of Sikinos (4 hr., 640dr), Folegandros (5 hr., 575dr), and Rhodes (16 hr., 2306dr). Finally, **Olympic Airways** flies an 18-seater plane between Athens and Paros about 10 times per day (5610dr). The Olympic Airways' bus leaves for the airport 45 minutes befor departure and awaits all arrivals (120dr).

### Orientation and Practical Information

Parikia's waterfront is the business center of the island. As you disembark from the ferry most restaurants, hotels, and offices are located several hundred meters to your left (facing inland). Straight ahead of you, past the windmill and the tourist offices, is the *platia,* flanked by streets full of shops and cafes.

**Tourist Information Center:** Tel. 220 79, in the windmill by the dock. Boat and bus schedules with fares. General information about the island, but no housing referrals. Open daily 9am-9pm.

**Currency Exchange: National Bank of Greece.** From the windmill, head directly into the pedestrian square—it's in the far corner in a fortress-like building. Open Mon.-Thurs. 8am-2pm, Sun. 8am-1:30pm; for exchange also Mon.-Fri. 5:30-8pm, Sat.-Sun. 9am-1pm.

**Post Office:** Off the waterfront, 1 block north of the windmill. Open Mon.-Fri. 7:30am-8pm, Sat. 8am-3pm, Sun. 9am-1:30pm. **Postal code:** 84400.

**OTE:** One block south of the windmill. Open daily 7:30am-midnight. **Telephone code:** 0284.

**Olympic Airways:** Tel. 219 00, down the street past the post office. Open daily 8am-3pm.

**Bus Station:** A few blocks north of the windmill. Complete schedule posted in front. Buses run 8am-10pm at least every hr. to Naoussa (15 min., 80dr), Lefkes (25 min., 90dr), Piso Livadi (40 min., 135dr), and Chryssi Akti. Seven buses per day go to the Valley of the Butterflies (½ hr., 60dr) on their way to Aliki. Complete bus schedule posted at the bus station.

**Luggage Storage:** Around the corner from the post office. 100dr per piece per day.

**Public Toilets:** Beside a small church north of the windmill.

**Hospital:** Tel. 212 35 or 225 00.

**Port Police :** Tel. 212 40, off the waterfront, past the bus station. Information about all sailings. Open 24 hours.

**Police:** Tel. 212 21, across the square behind the OTE, on the 2nd floor above the travel agencies. Open 24 hours.

## Accommodations and Camping

Most of the hotels and rooms to let are located just off the waterfront and in the old town. You can try your luck with the people renting the boat. The cheapest singles cost 1269dr, doubles 1910dr, triples 2017dr. Singles are scarce in Parikia, so find a roommate or pay for a double. In high season (late July-Aug.), you may have to go to Naoussa or Piso Livadi to find a room.

**Hotel Kondes** (tel. 212 46), behind the windmill. '60s decor, but clean. Singles 1900dr. Doubles 2500dr. Triples 3000dr. Private bath included.

**Rooms Mimikos,** (tel. 214 37), around the corner from Agorakitou St.—follow the signs. Very clean rooms with balconies. Singles 1550dr. Doubles 1950dr. Triples 2500dr. Showers included.

**Hotel Kypreou**(tel. 213 83 or 224 48), past the post office and just before Olympic. Grim, but cheap and convenient. Doubles 2000dr. Triples 3000dr.

**The Dina** (tel. 213 25), on the main shopping street. The best place to stay in Parikia. Dina is a charming woman. Quiet, immaculate, and with a beautiful garden. Open May-Oct.Doubles 3200dr. Private facilities in all rooms. Dina prefers reservations by mail.

**Camping: Koula** (tel. 220 82), 400km north of town, and **Parasporos** (tel. 219 44), 2km south. Both 400dr per person, 100dr per tent. Take bus from port. Also new **Krios** Camping (tel. 217 05). 400dr per person, 50dr per tent. Take the little ferry boat across the harbor to Krios Beach.

## Food

The cheapest restaurants in Paros are at the northern end of the port near the beach. Those on the waterfront are usually pricey, but you can find a few cheap places in the old town.

**Aligaria,** in the square to the left, behind the windmill. Cheap and peaceful. Chicken, *mousaka,* and *kalamari* 300dr each. Open 9am-1pm and 3pm-midnight.

**Restaurant Possidon,** at the northern end of the waterfront, set back from the street in its leafy garden. Really cheap. *Mousaka, kalamari,* and roast chicken 230dr each. Open 8-2am. Neighboring restaurants also cheap and popular with the beach crowd.

**Taverna Efkalyptos.** Follow signs to Acropolis or Gallinos-Luiza Hotels across the main road and to the right. Lots of locals. Chicken, *pastitsio,* and *mousaka*230dr.

**Corfu Leon,** in a square off the waterfront, close to the discos and bars. Spaghetti 150dr, *mousaka* and chicken 230dr. Open 6:30am-11:30pm.

**To Tamarisko,** near Rooms Mimikos—follow the signs. Very civilized—or should we say stuffy. Meatballs 250dr, pork chops 540dr. Open Tues.-Sun. 7pm-1am.

## Sights

Anyone with a taste for Byzantine architecture will not be disappointed by the **Panayia Ekatontapiliani** (the Church of Our Lady of 100 Gates), an imposing sixth-century edifice that houses three separate adjacent churches. The main structure is the huge **Church of the Assumption,** flanked to the north by the **Church of St. Nicholas** (the oldest of the 3), and to the south by the **baptistery,** which contains what is reputedly the oldest baptismal font in Greece. Dress modestly—no shorts. To reach the church, follow the street on which the post office is located to its end. (Open daily 6am-noon and 5-9pm.) If you happen to be in Paros on August 15, come to the church to watch the island's biggest festival, *panageiri* (the Assumption of the Virgin).

Behind the church and next to the schoolyard is Paros' **archeological museum,** which houses, among other things, a fifth century B.C.E. statue of the Wingless Nike and a piece of the Parian Chronicle. (Open Mon. and Wed.-Fri. 8:45am-3pm, Sun. 9am-2pm.)

You don't have to be a lepidopterist to enjoy the **Valley of the Butterflies.** Just 10km south of town, a cool valley, fed by a natural spring, is home to a colony of brown-and-white striped butterflies. The small creatures cover the foliage and blend into their surroundings until they fly, exposing their bright red underwings. The butterflies are born all over the island, but on June evenings, the mature butterflies, attracted by large quantities of water, find their way to the valley to mate. You can visit here by taking the bus from Parikia that goes to Aliki (every 2 hr., ½ hr., 60dr) and asking to be let off at the butterflies (in Greek *petaloudes*). From there, follow the signs up the steep winding road 2km to the entrance. You can also take a tour from one of the various travel agents (500dr) leaving at 4pm, 5pm, and 7pm, or bounce your way there on a donkey (2½-3 hr.) (Open Mon.-Sat. 9am-8pm, Sun. 9am-1pm and 4-8pm. Admission 60dr.)

## Entertainment

No matter how wild the party gets, all bars and discos in Parikia close at 3am. Almost all of the nightspots are south of the windmill along the waterfront. You can dance on the bar at **Saloon D'Or,** on the waterfront, the loudest, most popular bar/disco. (Beers 150dr. Cocktails 300dr.) **Irish Bar Stavros,** off the end of the waterfront, in a complex of bars and discos, is also deafening and full of English-speakers. (Beer 150dr. Cocktails 400dr.) You might be inspired to try the hopping **Seven Muses Disco,** at the end of the waterfront, before the entrance to a complex of nightspots. (Beer 150dr. Cocktails 300dr.) Bohemians relax on pillows and catch the jazz and blues at the **Pirate Bar,** off the waterfront, across from The Pina Hotel. (Cocktails 350dr. Soda or lemonade 50dr.) **Evinos** and the neighboring **Statue Bar,** perched above the buildings, are great places to escape the din downstairs and catch a sunset or watch the twinkling lights of the ferryboats. Evinos is a bit more expensive (cocktails 500-600dr). (The Statue's cocktails are 400-500dr.)

## Around the Island

Cutting through the center of the island toward the east coast, you will reach **Marathi,** only 5km from Parikia. The marble quarries that made Paros famous in ancient times are located just outside Marathi. Parian marble is still held by many to be among the finest in the world, translucent up to 3mm in depth, three times that of most other marble. After being abandoned for centuries, the quarries were again mined by the French in the nineteenth century to obtain marble for Napolean's tomb. The quarries are now inactive, but you can climb down into them a little way. The interconnecting shafts are over 100m deep. To the left of the entrance is a relief carving dating from the fourth century B.C.E. You can still see the deserted buildings of the French mining company.

**Lefkes,** 7km from Marathi, was the largest village on the island in the nineteenth century when Parians moved inland to escape the pirates menacing the coast. It is now a quiet village of 400 inhabitants. Its classic Cycladic architecture makes it the prettiest village in Paros' interior. Just before Piso Livadi, you'll reach the untouristed town of **Marpissa.** Past the windmills in Marpissa's *platia,* a path leads up to the peak of Kefalo hill, where you'll find the brilliant white **Monastery of Agios Antonios.** The monastery is closed to visitors, but an expansive view from the summit rewards the climber. The road reaches the sea at **Piso Livadi,** a small, quiet harbor where you can leave your pack for a few days. The **Hotel Piso Livadi** (tel. 413 09), just up from the bus stop, has doubles for 3000dr. The **Magia,** on a hill between Piso Livadi and Logaras Beach, rents cots on the roof and under a grapevine (in summer 400dr). There's also **Captain Kafkis Camping** (300dr per person). Follow the signs 1km back along the road towards Parikia.

Continuing south, you'll find the unimpressive **Logaras Beach,** where you can take windsurfing lessons from **Sun Wind** (1000dr per hr.), and then rent a board (800dr).

> **Chryssi Akti** (Golden Beach), a few more kilometers south, has become a mecca for high-tech, top-notch windsurfing. For a drink or snack, don't miss the surreal **Golden Greek's Palace,** at the northern end of the beach. Free showers are conveniently provided in the back of the building. Pretty **Dryos Beach,** the next beach south, is isolated and quiet. Doubles in this area average 2500dr. You can also freelance camp on Golden Beach. Excursion boats sail from Piso Livadi to Naxos, Delos, and Mykonos (5 per week, 600dr round-trip) and to Santorini (2 per week, 3000dr). One-way tickets to Naxos cost 500dr, to Santorini 1000dr.

Another public bus runs twice per day to Pounda and Aliki on the west coast, where you will find still more good beaches. From Pounda, it is only a 15-minute boatride to Antiparos (8:20am-8:20pm every hr., 120dr round-trip). Some beaches on the west coast are accessible by boat from Parikia (100dr round-trip). **Krios Beach,** the first stop, is best for the family, and **Kamines,** the next, is known for its excellent swimming and snorkeling. **Agios Fokas,** once the most secluded of the western beaches, is no longer connected by boat, and is now really secluded.

# Naoussa

Like Piso Livadi, Naoussa is an alternative to Parikia as your home base on Paros. A natural harbor, cradled on both sides by long, earthy arms, Naoussa has been a popular port throughout history. Ancient Persians, Greeks, Romans, medieval Venetians, Saracens, Turks, and Russians have all used the harbor. A brisk tourist trade has spoiled some of the town, though fishing continues as it always has. Buses travel at least every hour to Naoussa from Parikia (8am-10pm, 15 min., 80dr). On the way to Naoussa, these buses stop at the slightly dirty, but popular **Kolybithras Beach.** There is camping near the beach at **Camping Naoussa** (tel. 515 95 or 515 65; 300dr per person, 100dr per tent). In town, the cheapest hotels average 3000dr per double; the Naoussa Hotel (tel. 512 07) offers doubles with balconies overlooking the sea at this price. Also try the **Madaki** (tel. 514 75) near the main road, and the quieter **Stella** (tel. 513 17). (Take a left past the post office.) *Dhomatia* in Naousa generally cost 2000dr per double. Look around or talk to one of the tourist agents to book a room.

For cheap Greek fare, **Diamantes** will suffice. (*Mousaka* 250dr. Chicken 250dr. Open 5:30pm-midnight.) **Psariana**, also open only for dinner, is another affordable option. (Kalamari 300dr.) If you happen to be in town on August 23, dress in traditional costume to commemorate a victorious naval battle over the Turks with music and dance. On July 2, you can feast on free, fresh fish, as well as free wine at the **Free Fresh Fish and Wine Festival.**

# *Antiparos* Αντιπαρος

Until they split apart about 1000 years ago, Antiparos was an integral part of Paros. Today, just across the channel from Paros, it is a popular daytrip destination and a refuge for those unable to find accommodations on its larger neighbor. From Parikia, the trip takes one hour (340dr round-trip), but from Pounda it takes a mere 15 minutes (120dr round-trip, departure 8:20am-8:20pm every hr.).

Most of this small island is undeveloped—virtually all of its 650 inhabitants live in the town where the ferry docks, and there is no bus service to any other point on the island. There is a modest beach alongside the dock, delightful waterfront restaurants, and several hotels and pensions. The center of town, up the road about 300m, has a wide-open plaza, with *kafenia* under its large shade trees, and flowers and trellised plants bedecking most of its sparkling houses. Continue uphill from the point where the main road ends at Agios Nikolaos Sq. to reach the **Castle of Antiparos,** built in the 1440s by a nobleman named Lorentano, who also financed the transportation of farmers to the island.

The street that leads from the dock to town and then bears left is lined with cheerful pensions. The cheapest hotels are the **Anargyros** (tel. 612 04; singles 2000dr; doubles 2500dr), and the **Mantalena** (tel. 612 06; singles 1500dr; doubles 1700dr). There's also an organized **campground** (tel. 612 21) northwest of town, on **Agios Yiannis Theologos Beach.** (400dr per person, 50dr per tent.) Many people also take to the more remote beaches. One pleasant beach is reached by following the sign for Bonos on the far side of the town plaza. The best restaurants on the island (located in the main town) are the **Taverna Giorgios** and the **Taverna Klimataria.** The small channel that runs between Paros and Antiparos has been sufficient, at least so far, in keeping Antiparos tranquil and set in its own ways. Nor has Antiparos imported Parikia's thriving nightlife, although it does offer a couple tame bars and a unique disco inside a windmill.

Since there's no bus service on the island, you must explore by foot or by boat. The most popular excursion is to the **stalactite caves** at the southern end of the island. Private excursion boats leave from the dock at Antiparos every morning at 9:30am, 10:30am, and 11:30am, and return starting at noon (600dr). A normal ferry also travels to the caves (500dr). It's also possible to make the trip on foot; allow a few hours round-trip. Once you're at the foot of the path leading to the cave, it's an arduous climb, or donkey ride, up to the entrance. Tourists have written graffiti into the stalactite formations, greatly depreciating their aesthetic appeal. They aren't the first to deface the cave, though; in the 1770s, Russian naval officers chopped off portions of the formations and had them transferred to a St. Petersburg museum.

Ferry service to Antiparos is frequent in summer (several ferries make the trip daily). In off-season, try opening the door of the small church by the shore in Pounda. Apparently, this will signal the ferryperson to come over from Antiparos. The number for the **police** in Antiparos is 612 02, for **first aid** 612 19; the **telephone code** is 0284.

# *Naxos* Νάξος

Tradition has identified Naxos as the land of Ariadne, the daughter of King Minos of Crete. After Ariadne saved Theseus from her father's labyrinth, the young boy fled toward Athens, promising to take her with him. But along the way, he landed at Naxos, and there he abandoned her as she slept, continuing on to Athens alone. Dionysus found her and married her, and when she died, he put her bridal wreath among the stars where it still shines as the Corona Borealis. Yet Naxos might turn anyone's despair into joy. At first glance, it is utterly infertile, a moonscape of barren hills rising out of the green scruff. But the mountains embrace a voluptuous interior in their rocky arms. The earth swells as if wind-tossed, capped with rocky promontories like sea foam. Squat windmills and demure white villages lie smothered in the undulating landscape.

This natural wealth has made Naxos one of the richest of the Cyclades, a fact which becomes apparent on a short walk through the town of Naxos (called Chora). Rather than the usual depressing coexistence of poor native homes and luxury hotels and services catering to tourists, the best of this beautiful town belongs to the people of Naxos. Glimpses into homes reveal a degree of comfort and wealth not found on the islands dependent on tourist trade. Naxos is well-connected by **ferry**, which travels to Piraeus (3-6 per day, 7 hr., 1572dr), Paros (4-6 per day, 1 hr., 432dr), Ios (1-4 per day, 1½ hr., 763dr), Santorini (1-6 per day, 3 hr., 878dr), Mykonos (1-2 per day, 2 hr., 580dr), and Syros (1-3 per day, 2½ hr., 694dr). There is less frequent service to Amorgos (5 per week, 3½ hr., 790dr), and Iraklia, Schinoussa, Koufinisia, and Donoussa (3 per week, 1½ hr., 410dr).

# Naxos Town

The streets of Naxos Town are not spotless, its whitewash not always fresh, and its waterfront not devoid of modern architecture. Rather than blemishes, these traits add to its charm, distinguishing Naxos from the standardly quaint island towns.

## Orientation and Practical Information

All ferries dock in Naxos Town. Don't bother with maps; streets are poorly labeled and zigzag a lot. The arrows painted by hotels and restaurant owners are your best navigational tools.

**Tourist Information Center:** Tel. 245 25 or 243 58, on the waterfront, next to Creperie Bikini. A helpful source of information. Free booking service for the island and everywhere in Greece. Currency exchange, luggage storage (100dr), metered phone, used books, safety deposit boxes (200dr). Open March 15-Oct. 31 daily 8-12am.

**Currency Exchange: National Bank of Greece,** on the southern end of the harbor road. Open Mon.-Thurs. 8am-2pm, Fri. 8am-1:30pm.

**Post Office:** Walk down the waterfront, turn left after Hotel Hermes, then take your first right. Open Mon.-Fri. 7:30am-2:15pm. **Postal code:** 84300.

**OTE:** Between the Hotel Coronis and the Hotel Hermes, at the southern end of the harbor. Open July-Aug. Mon.-Fri. 7:30am-midnight, Sat.-Sun. 9am-midnight; Sept.-June Mon.-Fri. 7:30am-10pm. **Telephone code:** 0285.

**Buses:** Buses stop directly in front of the ferry dock. Schedules posted, but double check with the drivers or at the **bus office** up the street (left facing inland). Arrive early. Buses are packed, especially the one from Chora to Appollonas via Filoti (3 per day, 2 hr., 320dr). Buses also run frequently to Chalki (4 per day, ½ hr., 100dr), and Apiranthos (3 per day, 1 hr., 160dr). There is also regular service to west coast beaches, including Agios Prokopios (frequent buses 9:30am-6:30pm, 20 min., 60dr), Agia Anna (frequent buses 9am-5pm, ½ hr., 75dr), and Pyrgaki (11am-4pm, 40 min., 120dr).

**Motorbike Rental: Theoharis,** Neofitou St. (tel. 239 00), at the northern end of town, 1 block up from the waterfront. Theoharis speaks fluent English and is truly a fount of information. He only has a few bikes so he takes good care of them and you. Mopeds 1000dr. Yamaha 50cc's 1400dr. Optional 3rd party insurance 200dr. Open daily 8am-2pm and 5-9pm.

**Bookstore: Naxos Popular Art Shop** (sign in Greek), above a restaurant 50m south of the wharf. Buys and sells used English books, as do several other shops. Good selection and the best prices in the islands: 300-400dr per book. Open daily 10am-1:30pm and 6:30-11pm.

**Public Toilets and Showers:** On the street parallel to the harbor. Climb the stepped alley near the pier. Toilets 10-20dr, showers 200dr.

**Pharmacy,** on the waterfront, open Sun.-Tues. and Thurs.-Fri. 8:30am-2pm and 5:30-9:30pm.

**Medical Emergency: Clinic,** Papavasileiou St. (tel. 223 46, afternoons and evenings 231 97), just uphill from the National Bank of Greece, on the left. The doctor speaks some English and is in the clinic approximately 8:30am-1pm each day.

**Port Police:** Nikodemos St. (tel. 223 00), just off the small square with the cafes, on the 2nd floor. Open 24 hours.

**Police:** Tel. 221 00 or 232 80. Take a right off of Neofitou St., and then a left, on the 3rd floor. Open 24 hours.

## Accommodations and Camping

In late July and August, most hotels run at capacity. If you take a room from one of the people who meet the boat, expect to pay 1269dr for singles, 1910dr for doubles, and 2017dr for triples (all with common bath).

**Hotel Dionyssos,** (tel. 233 31) in the old market section, near the Venetian Kastro, directly uphill from the port. Look for painted red hands pointing there or the arrows to the Panorama next door. Rooms in the main house 500dr per person, or in the more private small house 1000dr per person, with bath. Also a **youth hostel** in the basement. Dorm beds 400dr per person. Roof 300dr. Showers included. Breakfast 300dr.

**Hotel Okeanis** Tel. 224 36 or 228 26, across from the ferry dock—entrance on the left. Convenient and clean, if uninspired. Doubles 2000dr, some with private bath.

**Hotel Anna,** 58 Neofitou St. (tel. 224 75), past the churches. Clean rooms in a quiet neighborhood. Kitchen facilities available. Doubles with bath 2500dr. Triples with bath 3000dr.

**Naxos Camping,** (tel. 235 00 or 235 01), is about 1½km outside town on a dirt road off Agios Giorgios Beach. (Self-service restaurant and laundry facilities. 250dr per person. 100 per tent.) **Camping Apollon** (tel. 241 17 or 241 18), is farther down the road and situated between Prokopios and Agios Giorgos Beaches. You can freelance camp on the beaches on the west coast. To get to the nearest one, **Agios Giorgios,** walk past the post office, through the small square, and down the hill. The beach itself is hard-packed sand and tends to be crowded with Greek families. A little beyond, the small dunes lining the cove are home to a small community of freelance campers and high-performance windsurfers. A little farther along, the dunes give way again to open sand. If you have an air mattress to float your gear across the 10-meter channel, then the island is a perfect campsite. **Agia Anna Beach,** about a half-hour walk south of Agios Giorgios, is cleaner and prettier than its northern neighbor. Take the road to the campground from Agios Giorgios or simply walk along the beach. About 1km farther along the beach, past the small town, you can camp hassle-free. The beaches farther along the coast, like Mikri Vigla, Kastraki and Pyrgaki, are too far away to walk to but are beautiful places to set up camp.

## Food and Entertainment

The influence of tourism on Naxos is most easily discernible in the restaurants. Many restaurants seem designed for the foreign visitor, with menus in English and German posted outside and manicured interiors. Picnicking is a down-to-earth alternative, especially since Naxos **markets** offer the best fruits, vegetables, cheeses, and wines in the Cyclades. Try a locally produced wine; many are named after the villages in which they are produced ("Glinado" and "Skeponi" are both great choices). Two justly famous local cheeses are "Naxos cheese" (a type of *graviera*) and *anthotiro* cream cheese. You can find standard fare at the *tavernas* along **Nikodemos Street** (*mousaka* 300dr, Greek salad 150dr). On the same street, you can buy delicious *tost* (about 100dr) at **Toast Time.** (Open 8am-3am.)

**Lucullus,** in the old town next to St. Nikodemis St., the oldest *taverna* in Naxos, built in 1908. Always busy. Friendly management. On most Sun., live Greek music. Roast chicken 250dr, special sausage 300dr. Open July-Oct. 11:30-1am. **Vassilis Taverna,** across the street, is also good, with similar prices. *Mousaka* 300dr, octopus 350dr. Open 8am-3pm and 6pm-midnight.

**Manolis Gardens,** in the old town on Old Market St.—follow the signs. Pretty outdoor garden setting. *Mousaka* 250dr, chicken 250dr. Open May-Sept. daily 6pm-midnight.

**Panorama Restaurant** (tel. 231 64). Head down Neofitou St. and keep walking. It's a 20-min. walk, but worth the hike for the view and the fresh air. Try the local barrel wine. Chicken 270dr, *mousaka* 340dr. Open 8-1am.

**Elli's,** up from Theoharis', on the water. A special vegetarian menu. Pricy—vegetable soup 300dr, crepes 400-500dr, *mousaka* 450dr. Open 6:30pm-1am.

**Ponteboy's,** on the waterfront. Fresh, hot, delicious, gooey *loukoumades* 150dr, but only at night—come early; they run out by 11pm. Open 6am-3am.

**La Frianderie,** behind the OTE. For the sweet tooth. A little expensive, but a wide selection of delicious pastries. Pineapple croissants, brownies, *milopitas,* and *pain au chocolat* (each about 125dr).

Naxos' nightlife isn't as frenetic as other islands'. **Mike's Pub** is a popular bar with a small outdoor terrace just off the waterfront, behind the OTE. (Drinks 500dr.) A new bar on the waterfront, **The Last Resort,** is the town's English bar. (Drinks 400dr.) **Santé Bar,** farther down the waterfront, above Olympic Airways, has an atmosphere best described as refined. (Drinks 400-500dr.) **Tony's (Bolero)** is an old favorite. Tucked under one of the arched streets in the Old Market district. (Beer 150dr. Mixed drinks 400-500dr.)

For dancing, try the **Ocean Club,** right behind the National Bank. (Drinks 500-600dr.) There are also three discos along Agios Georgios Beach. The liveliest one is **Infinity Disco.** (Drinks 500dr.)

### Sights

While in Naxos Town, make a point of visiting the old **Venetian Kastro,** a series of mansions still inhabited by the descendants of the original Frankish and Venetian nobility. The excellent **museum** is housed in one of these old buildings, where Nikos Kazantzakis, author of *Last Temptation of Christ,* once studied. The museum collection contains many beautiful Cycladic artifacts, as well as vases, sculpture, jewels, and implements found in Mycenaean and Geometric chamber tombs. (Open Mon. and Wed.-Sat. 8:45am-3pm, Sun. 9:30am-2:30pm. Admission 200dr, students 100dr.) At the museum, you can pick up the epiphanic *Naxos: Monuments and Museum,* by Photini Zaphiropoulou (500dr).

From the waterfront, you can see the unique white chapel of *Myrditiotissa* floating serenely in the harbor on its man-made islet. Even more intriguing is the marble archway on the hilltop at the edge of the port. This curious portal is called the **Palatia** because, according to myth, this was both the place where Ariadne was abandoned by Theseus and rescued by Dionysus, and consequently a palace for Ariadne. But archeological investigation has once again debunked this delightful hypothesis. The archway, along with the platform and some columns, is, in fact, all that remains of an Ionic temple to Apollo, begun by the tyrant Lygdamis in the sixth century B.C.E., and abandoned at his death.

## Around the Island

Those who leave having seen only Naxos Town and its environs will be disappointed—and rightly so, as they will have missed the heart of Naxos. If you have time, the ideal way to see the island is on foot. Villages are so spaced that food and shelter are available at propitious intervals; many, at least in the interior, are connected by footpaths.

Mopeds are popular for making excursions, but paved roads cover only a fraction of the island. This is not the place to *learn* how to use a moped; several people die each year on Naxos' rocky, twisting, hilly roads. Many people opt instead to take the bus to Apollon, a small fishing village on the northern tip of the island (3 per day, 2 hr., 320dr). Several of the villages along the way deserve closer attention than they can get from a bus window; if you're so inclined, you can stop en route, and then catch a later bus or continue on foot.

The first hour of the ride, from Naxos Town to Chalki, takes you through rich cultivated mountainsides, with olive trees, whitewashed churches, and wild flowers that erupt on schedule each spring and summer. Before you reach Chalki, there's a turn-off for **Ano Sangri,** 1km west of the road. You can get off the bus at the turn-off and walk, or trek the entire way from Naxos Town (about 1½ hr.). An isolated town of winding flagstone streets, Ano Sangri is worth a visit. An old house, originally a monastery, has been fitted with the traditional furnishings, farming, housekeeping implements, and clothing of Naxos. (Open only in Aug.)

At **Chalki,** a pretty village surrounded by Venetian towers, the magnificent **Tragea** begins—a huge arcadian olive grove of absolute stillness. Stop in at the **Panayia Protothonis,** the parish church of Chalki, right across from the bus stop. Restoration work on the church has uncovered wall paintings from the eleventh through thirteenth centuries. If the church is closed, ask around for the priest and he'll let you in. The well-marked turn-off for **Moni** branches from the main road in the middle of Chalki. Three kilometers from the turn-off, a short path on the right leads to the eighth-century stone church of **Panayia Drossiani.** Ring the churchbell by tugging at the rope beside the door and the priest's wife will admit you. (Open 8am-1pm and 3-8pm.)

If you have a motorbike or car, an alternative route takes you from Naxos Town up through Melanes to **Flerio,** where one of the magnificent **kouroi** of Naxos sleeps in a woman's garden. *Kouroi,* larger-than-life sculptures of male figures, were first made in Greece in the seventh century B.C.E., under Egyptian influence. This one was probably abandoned in its marble quarry because it broke before it was finished. The woman runs a small *Kafeneion* in the garden. Resume your drive north to Chalki and you'll pass through a trio of charming villages built in a river valley: **Kato Potamia; Mesi Potamia;** and **Ano Potamia.**

Soon after leaving Chalki you'll reach **Filoti,** where the Tragea ends and the road climbs the flanks of Mt. Zas. These slopes offer superb views extending all the way to Poros and the sea beyond. In another 15 minutes you are in **Apiranthos,** another delightful, small village whose residents are of Cretan descent. The town boasts the astonishing **Michael Bardani Museum,** which contains many remnants of Cycladic artifacts. Hours are flexible—just ask around for Giorgos, who can open the museum for you. (Free.) The town also has a modest **folk art museum** (sign in Greek). Open daily 10am-1pm. (Free.) From here through **Koronos** and **Koronida,** an hour's drive away, the road snakes through the interior mountain ranges. The terraced landscape, carefully planted with grapevines and fruit and olive trees, descends dramatically into valleys far below—the scene has been compared to a Japanese ink painting.

From Koronida, the road descends slowly around mountain ridges, reaching the sea at last at the village of **Apollon.** Considered remote only a few years ago, Apollon now has a sizable tourist trade with several pensions and restaurants and a fairly crowded rocky beach. But the town is still peaceful, and many people choose to pass their whole time on Naxos right here. You can try sleeping on the beach, but the local police may come around in the middle of the night and ask you to move. You might consider sleeping at **The Old House** (tel. 813 28), at the entrance to the port. (Doubles 1720dr. Triples 2300dr.) The restaurants along the harbor are surprisingly inexpensive. (*Mousaka* 300dr, chicken 250dr, omelettes 120dr.)

A short walk from the harbor is one of the most famous **Kouros** of Naxos. At 10½m long, this kouros is more massive, if less finely sculpted, than the one in Flerio, but similarly incomplete. To reach it from the village, head back up the main road away from the beach and turn right at the small sign for "kouros;" from there, it's about a 20-minute hike.

On your return trip from Apollon to Chalki, you might want to get off the bus at Filoti (about 2km away) and walk through the Tragea. A footpath starts on the main road just outside Filoti, directly across from the sign for Kerami, and leads to **Agia Apostoloi,** a beautiful Byzantine church dating from the tenth century, with thirteenth-century wall paintings. Following the footpath southwest from Agia Apostoloi, you'll come to a lovely post-Byzantine church, the **Panayia Metochiotissa,** dating from the seventeenth century. It is easy to get delightfully lost wandering through the Tragea, and those with time to spare might well do it voluntarily. For the rest, keep heading west and you'll soon return to the main road.

If most beaches near Naxos Town are gorgeous, imagine what that suggests about the rest of the island. Unfortunately, the long sandy stretches at **Agios Prokopios, Agia Anna** and **Plaka** are plagued by crowds of sunbathers and poorly planned modern buildings. **Plaka,** the nude beach, is the least developed of the three. These beaches are easily reached by bus from Naxos Town (see Orientation and Practical Information above). Farther south, however, you will find quiet and unclaimed stretches of sand. The beaches at **Mikri Vigla, Kastraki, Aliko,** and **Pyrgaki** are also accessible by bus from Naxos Town. Here the desert meets the sea: Scrub pines, prickly pear, and century plants grow on the dunes behind you, forcing you to retreat nearer to the brisk blue sea.

The best secluded beaches on Naxos are on the eastern coast and accessible only by car—or motorbike, and only if you are ambitious. Try **Moutsouna, Psili Ammos,** and the distant **Panormos.** The paved road and infrequent bus service (morning and evening) run only as far as Moutsouna. From there on, the road is unpaved and "unimproved." There are also wild dogs in this area. If you decide to go, remember to bring a bottle of water and food as this is a dry, sparsely populated region.

# Amorgos Αμοργος

Although the number of visitors to Amorgos has increased substantially, the tourist industry has not seriously corrupted the island, and locals often welcome travelers as their guests. The eastern flank of the Cyclades, Amorgos is gaunt and barren. The island's two ports, Katapola in the southwest (the larger of the two), and Egiali in the northeast, are connected only by a daily ferry (340dr); the road stretching along the island's spine is barely passable for jeeps. Early morning ferries (usually 5-6am) leave Katapola daily for Naxos (4 hr., 790dr); some stop at the small islands in between (Keros, Shinoussa, and Iraklia). Ferries also head out to Piraeus (Thurs., Sat., and Sun., 1675dr), stopping at Naxos (790dr), Paros (940dr), and Siros (1110dr). In addition, liners pass through on their way to Ios (Thurs., 830dr), Santorini (Thurs., 890dr), Rhodes (Fri., 1395dr), and Astipalea (Sun., 930dr), among others; the *Nereus* stops at just about every tiny and remote island in the Dodecanese.

## Katapola and Chora

Most ferries dock on the southwest side of the island at **Katapola,** the main port, where there is a **ferry office** (open 8:30am-7:30pm; schedules posted) and **post office/OTE** (open 8am-2pm). The *pantopoleion* (grocery store), next to the **boat agency** for Naxos, provides **currency exchange** (both open 9am-1pm and 6-8pm); the closest bank is in Chora. Amorgos' **telephone code** is 0285. Just off the waterfront, **Pension Amorgos** (tel. 712 14) offers spiffy blue-trimmed rooms. (Singles 1000dr. Doubles 1500dr. Triples with bath 2500dr.) If it's full, ask for a spot on the roof (500dr; access to showers). Up the hill, **Nikitas Koveos** (tel. 712 18) runs a pension surrounded by his beautiful garden; call early, since savvy Greek vacationers tend to book well in advance. (Doubles 1700dr; in off-season 1300dr. Showers included.) There's an official **campsite** just a short walk out of town, near the top of the harbor (250dr per person); to freelance, head up to **Panteleimon Beach** in the cove on the left side of town.

Katapola literally means "below the town." In this case, "the town above" is **Chora,** also known as Amorgos. Six winding kilometers from the harbor by the island's only bus (50dr), Chora is a far more restful, if slightly less convenient, base for your stay. Landmarks include a fourteenth-century Venetian fortress and a row of defunct windmills, but the town's real attraction is its streets, so unspoiled and uncluttered that they initially seem desolate. As you wander, keep an eye out for **Agios Fanourios,** the smallest church in the Cyclades—it holds only three people. Named after the patron saint of lost objects, this church can be identified by the number 240 painted on its facade, but ironically, that is disappearing under layers of whitewash. In the main square, Kostas Getabis cuts traditional Greek silhouette puppets in his shop. The **post office** is beyond the square. (Open Mon.-Fri. 8am-3pm.) Both the **OTE** and **bank** are in the main square. (Open Mon.-Thurs. 8am-2pm, Fri. 8am-1:30pm.) Buses stop both in the main square and below, on the way to **Agia Anna;** here you'll find **Pension Kastanis** (tel. 712 77; very nice singles 800dr; doubles 1200dr). Ask at any cafe in town for advice on rooms, which can be relatively cheap. There are a couple of friendly *tavernas* along the main street. **D. Kastanis** serves hearty fare at startlingly-low prices, and occasionally hosts live Greek music. (Open daily 6pm-midnight.) At the last *taverna* on the far edge of town, you can drink real *retsina*—resinated in the barrel, not the bottle.

A 20-minute walk or five-minute bus ride from Chora down the east slope of the island brings you to the ¾ km path for the remarkable **Chozoviotissa,** or Monastery of the Presentation of the Virgin. Pressed against a slight hollow on the sheer rock face, the edifice looks like a Native-American cliff dwelling painted white. Not only is it visually spectacular, the monastery is also delightful to visit. Be sure to observe the dress code: long pants for men, dresses or skirts for women, and no bare shoulders. If you arrive between sunrise and 2pm (additional hours in summer 5-7pm), the monks will greet you with coffee or homemade liqueur and sweets. After you've signed the register, the tour begins in the chapel. To the right of the altar is the icon of the Virgin, which miraculously arrived about the time that Byzantine Emperor Alexis Comnenus of the first Crusade granted the monastery its charter. The ornate charter can be seen in a small alcove one flight below. Next to it is a room with ecclesiastical silverware, accessories for liturgical vestments, and eleventh-century illuminated manuscripts.

A 20-minute scramble down the hill to the right, cutting across a switchback in the road, takes you to Agia Anna's spectacular white pebble **beach.** Don't be seduced by the first cove; farther to the right is a bigger beach, with plenty of room for nude bathing and freelance camping. A spring running down the cliff provides water, but for food you must catch the bus back to Chora and Katapola (4 per day), or walk.

If sandy beaches tickle your fancy, head to the inlet of Egiali on the northern tip of Amorgos. Although ferry is the only daily means of transportation linking Egiali to Katapola, some inter-island ferries stop at the small harbor town of **Ormos.** Rooms can be rented at **Pension Lakki** (tel. 712 52), halfway down a long beach where informal camping takes place. (Singles 800dr. Doubles 1000dr. Showers included.) Egiali occasionally has water shortages, but evidently Lakki has water even when other places run out. A short hike along the cliffs opposite Ormos brings you to isolated coves with unblemished sand. Should you feel like exploring, the towns of **Potamos** and **Langada** on the hills above Ormos offer an abundance of whitewashed churches. The windswept town of **Tholarea,** inhabited by farmers and their donkeys, commands a ridge from which both sides of Amorgos can be seen. To get there from Ormos, walk to the end of the beach and follow the stone path leading up the valley to the town (½-hr. walk). You can quench your thirst at an old, sweetwater well along the way.

# *Ios* Ios

You'll be hearing about Ios long before you ever get there, but after one night here, you'll believe all the rumors. Ios is such a dream-come-true for weary travelers because there is *nothing* to do here but sunbathe by day and party by night. The only sightseeing you'll be doing is scoping fellow hooligans and deciding which country produces the best physical specimens. Make the pilgrimage to this mecca of the young and wild only if you are prepared for hangovers, bizarre conversations with strangers, the occasional stray hand on your body, and smoother conversationalists who eat your food outside the all-night fast food stands.

The good life for tourists centers on three locations, each about 20 minutes apart along the island's paved road. The port is at one end of the road, and the village, the focus of nocturnal activity, is directly above on the hill. At the far end of the road, like the proverbial pot of gold, lies pretty **Milopatos Beach.** The best way to conserve money and energy is to walk downhill and take the bus (55dr) up to the village.

Unfortunately, as in any place where there is a high concentration of people in a small area, there are problems of noise, theft, violence, litter, and poor sanitation. In an attempt to ease the strain on the natural and social environment of Ios, the local police have started to crack down on illegal camping and to urge tourists with little money to stay in one of the three established campgrounds. The police have been known to collect passports along the beach at night, forcing people to pay a "fine" for their return. Another result of increased tourism in recent years has been a cooling of the once amicable relationship between the island's residents and tourists. Most islanders remain friendly, however, if you are polite.

**Ferries** from Piraeus and the northern Cyclades to Santorini and Crete stop in Ios. Generally, six boats per day and as many as 10 per day on Monday, Wednesday, and Friday drop anchor in the late afternoon or early evening. There are frequent connections to: Piraeus (2-6 per day, 7-10 hr., 1911dr); Naxos (3-6 per day, 1¾ hr., 762dr); Santorini (6-8 per day, 1¼ hr., 444dr); and Paros (5-7 per day, 2½ hr., 897dr). One or two boats sail daily to Mykonos (2-5 hr., 1048dr) and Tinos (6 hr., 1184dr). Several times a week, boats travel to: Syros (3 per week, 5 hr., 1200dr); Crete (6 per week, 3½-5 hr., 1137dr); Sifnos (4 per week, 2 hr., 929dr); Serifos (2 per week, 3 hr., 984dr); Sikinos (4 per week, 20 min., 304dr); and Folegandros (4 per week, 30 min., 379dr).

Though it may take you a few minutes to realize, the **port** where the boat lets you off is not where you want to be. Not only are the bars and restaurants dismal, but the beach is downright dirty. If you arrive late at night during July or August and have little energy to search for rooms, try **Camping Ios,** next to the port. You can also climb the endless flight of steps, which leads to the village on the right of the paved road. The strenuous ascent assures that rooms along the steps are among the last to fill up. Otherwise, simply join the rest of the visitors who pile on the bus that runs from the ferry landing to the village (55dr). If you arrive around or after midnight, bus service will have stopped for the night.

## The Village

Ios Village has become as trashed as its visitors. If you arrive in the early morning, you no doubt will peer skeptically at the innocuous-looking cluster of white-washed houses that supposedly is home to Party Central. As you approach, however, the fragrance of garbage and beer along with the sight of broken bottles, smashed cans, and maybe one or two comatose revelers will be assurance enough that you got off the boat in the right place. Although budget travelers should thrive here, the "Ios veterans" will admit that the attrition rate is quite high.

You can do most of your "serious" business in Ios within a 3-block radius of the village bus stop. A few steps from the bus stop, one large building houses the **police station** (tel. 912 22; open 24 hours), the **doctor** (tel. 912 27; open Mon.-Fri. 9:30am-1:30pm and 6-8pm, Sat. 10am-12pm), and the **post office** (open Mon.-Fri. 8am-2:30pm). The **bank** is behind the big church. (Open Mon.-Thurs. 8am-2pm, Fri. 8am-1:30pm; special exchange window also Mon.-Fri. 6-8pm, Sat. and Sun. 9:30am-1pm.) The **OTE** (open Mon.-Fri. 8am-1pm and 5-9pm) is located up the main street from the church. Making phone calls is very difficult; only 16 people at a time can call out of Ios at a given moment—so be patient. The **port police** (tel. 912 64) are located in the port at the far end of the harbor next to Camping Ios. Unless you aspire to see more of Ios than the beach and village, public transportation will do just fine. **Buses** run from the port to the village to the beach and back again every 20 minutes, but are extremely crowded, especially at beach "rush hour," so don't be surprised if you spend the whole trip with someone's scantily clad rear in your face. Due to the water shortage on Ios, drinking-water taps are usually shut off between 11am and 6pm. Hangovers are a serious drag here. Ios' **telephone code** is 0286; the **postal code** is 84001.

### Accommodations, Camping, and Food

Considering you won't be spending much time sleeping in your bed, it's just as well that accommodations on Ios are among the cheapest on any of the islands. (Rare singles 1000-1300dr. Doubles 1400-1900dr. Triples 1900-2000dr.) Nonetheless, you may have to hunt around to find a double in July or August, as many tend to occupy rooms for several weeks at a 10% discount. A whole tribe of virtually identical, scrupulously clean pensions dwell above, behind, and to the left of the Déjà Vu Cafe behind the post office. Check out the whole row; it only takes five minutes. There is another cluster of rent rooms beneath the windmills, but leave your bags somewhere before the uphill search. People sleep late here, so most rooms open at midday.

**The Wind,** diagonally up the hill from Hotel Aphroditi (tel. 914 54). One of the best deals around. A large pension. Doubles 1500dr. Triples 1800dr. Hot showers included.

**Pension "No Problem,"** at the far end of the "park" area, between the main road and the village. Many problems. Big old house that's falling apart, but very cheap. Doubles 1300dr. Triples 1700dr.

**Marko's Pension** (tel. 913 66), next to the Hotel Aphroditi. Nicer, cleaner, and a bit more expensive than the rest. Friendly family management. Doubles 2600dr. Triples 3100dr.

**Camping: Camping Ios** (tel. 913 29), next to the port on the far left (facing the water). 400dr per person. Tent, shower, and shave included. At Milopatos Beach, **Camping Stars** (tel. 413 02), near the bus stop, has running water. **Soulis Campground** (tel. 915 54), at the far end of the beach, has showers, cooking, and laundry facilities, and will safeguard valuables. 300dr per person. If you crash on the beach, stay out of sight or you may find yourself subject to police action.

The cheapest restaurants in Ios are uphill. For value, quality, and down-home atmosphere, you can't beat **The Nest,** a blue building up the main road and to the left. The ebullient owner serves tasty food at amazingly low prices. (*Mousaka,* stuffed tomatoes, or spaghetti only 200dr. Open 7am-midnight). Farther up the road and to the left of the church, **Pavlos** serves cheap food with a South American twist (veal with orange 600dr), as well as typical fare. (*Pastistio* or stuffed tomatoes 200dr, *mousaka* 250dr. Open 8pm-1am.) More expensive, but more scenic, the **Windmills** (just beneath the windmills, naturally) offers *mousaka* (350dr) and chicken (225dr). (Open noon-2pm and 5-12pm.)

### Entertainment

At night, each bar offers a different novelty to establish a cachet among the fast summer crowd. You can shoot pool or darts, watch rock and movie videos, or make international phone calls while you wait for the dancing to begin at midnight at the row of discos along the main road. Try a "slammer," the native drink of Ios revelers, a mixture of tequila and carbonated lemonade slammed on the bar.

The following list represents an iota of the discos and bars. Good, but very congested, places for cheap drinks (cocktails 250dr) are the outdoor bars in the main square of the village.

**Scorpion's,** the last disco on the right on the main road. The most popular and packed. Drinks 400-500dr.

**Disco 69,** near the village square. The favorite in-town disco. You should see the T-shirts. Happy hour 8-10pm with drinks for 200dr (normally 250dr).

**Underground Disco,** in the village. If you've had enough of life at the top. Like dancing in a dungeon. Also very popular. Beer 200dr, cocktails 300dr.

**Jazz Bar,** off the village square. A refuge from the drunken pandemonium. Mellow and, of course, pricey. Drinks at 400-500dr.

**Scandinavian Bar,** one of the first along the main road. Similar to the rest of the discos on this strip, but the cheapest drinks (cocktails 300dr). Dance in air-conditioned comfort.

## Beaches

With the exception of a solitary monastery and a modest pile of rubble reputed to be Homer's tomb, the only other places of interest on Ios are the **beaches.**

Most people head for **Milopatos Beach** on foot (about 25 min. downhill) or by frequent bus service (8am-11pm, 55dr). Use the footpath down to the right of the road, or walk carefully along the hairpin curves. The beach is a meat market. If you want a modicum of privacy, hike to its outer reaches, but be warned: The farther you go, the fewer clothes you see (though people don't begin with much anyway).

If you want to spend the night here, check out the two nearby campgrounds (Camping Stars and Soulis) or try to get a room in the usually full hotels. **Hotel Aegeon,** at the right side of the bench facing inland, has clean rooms with private bath. (Doubles 2500dr. Triples 3300dr.)

Most of the other beaches around the island can only be reached by excursion boats. The one accessible by road is **St. Theoditi Beach.** (Excursion buses daily. Sign up a day in advance with any travel agent.) Other beaches include **Koumbara** (a 2-km walk from the port) and **Psathi** (a 7-km walk along donkey tracks) on the north coast. Nudists colonize these beaches, and the only obstacle to camping is scarcity of water. The most popular of the outlying beaches is **Manganari.** A boat leaves from port at 10am, returning at 6pm (600dr).

Travel agencies sponsor a wide variety of boat excursions, which depart several times per week for tours to various other beaches, and to nearby islands. Trips to islands such as **Sikinos, Folegandros,** and **Paros,** must be booked in advance (700-900dr).

# Santorini (Thira)

With whitewashed houses perched atop plunging cliffs and hills disfigured by deep gashes, Santorini's landscape is as eerie as the cataclysm that created it. From about 2000 B.C.E. to 1500 B.C.E., one of the most advanced societies in ancient Greece flourished on this volcanic island, then called Thira; recent excavations indicate that the society was influenced strongly in its later years by Minoan Crete, only 90km to the south. Around 1500 B.C.E., a massive volcanic eruption buried every sign of civilization beneath millions of tons of lava and pumice. In the centuries since the catastrophe, fact and fiction have mingled, leading some to identify Santorini as Plato's lost continent of Atlantis. More serious historical speculation has convinced many scholars that the eruption of Santorini triggered a tidal wave large enough to account for the contemporaneous destruction of several Minoan sites in Crete.

In 1967, Professor Spyridos Marinatos, a strong proponent of the last theory, resumed excavations begun at the Akrotiri site by the French School a century before. He worked steadily until his death in 1974, when he had a heart attack and fell into the excavation site in which he was working; he was buried at the site. Excavations, still under the Greek School, have so far shed no additional light on the Crete connection; they have, however, unearthed one of the most impressive archeological finds in the past several decades—a complete town, preserved virtually intact, like Pompeii, beneath layers of volcanic rock. Its paved streets are lined with one-, two-, and three-story houses, with wood-framed doors and windows.

Even those with no interest in the island's intriguing past will find ample delights in its present—good beaches, small towns pitched on cliff sides, and most of all, spectacular land formations left by centuries of eruptions. The ridges slashing out of the Aegean, the burning black-sand beaches, and the boiling fields of pumice are unique among the Greek islands. Word has it that vampires still dwell in Santorini, though skeptical tourists insist that the locals are just batty.

Modern Santorini is really only the eastern crescent of what was originally a circular island; the explosion in 1500 B.C.E. left the center of the island hollow under a crust of volcanic ash, and when it caved in, water broke through the rim to fill the basin that now makes up Santorini's harbor. The two seemingly separate islands to the west, Thirasia and Aspronisi, are in fact a continuation of the rim of the original island; their connection to Santorini is now submerged. Approaching Santorini from the north, you will first see Thirasia, which has two small villages. Closer to Santorini are two extraterrestrial rock formations emerging from underwater: Nea Kameni and Palea Kameni.

Santorini is the final stop for many **ferries** in the Cyclades and also a stop for some Crete-bound ferries, making it accessible and densely crowded. (See Ferries in Practical Information.) Your boat will dock at one of the ports: **Athinios** is the most important and has buses to Thira (the main town) and Perissa Beach. Pension proprietors from all over the island greet boats at Athinios. This is the easiest way to find a room, so be prepared to bargain when you step off the boat. You will know you have landed at the old port of **Thira** if you are confronted by a 587-step footpath leading up the cliff to the town above (a difficult 20-min. climb). Hiring a mule for the trip costs 300dr (a bit more if you're wearing a pack); the cable car on the left, which departs every 10 minutes or so, is also 300dr. If you decide to walk up, remember that mules stubbornly demand the right of way; they're also bigger than you. Boats occasionally dock at **Ia**, on the northern cape of the island. **Flights** from Athens to Santorini are reasonable, but difficult to reserve. (See Airport in Practical Information.)

## Thira Town

The center of activity on the island is the capital city of Thira (Fira). The western edge of town, borne on a cliff, commands striking views of the harbor, Santorini's west coastline, and the neighboring islands. On the east side, the island's characteristic barrel-vaulted houses spread out on more secure footing, their quiet tree-arched streets trailing off into the surrounding countryside. In summer, the town is overrun with tourists from all over the world. But nothing can destroy the pleasure of wandering among the narrow cobbled streets, inspecting the craft shops, and arriving at the western edge of town in time to watch the sun bathe the harbor in a deep magenta glow.

### Orientation and Practical Information

You may be a bit disoriented and tongue-tied when you climb off the bus in **Theotokopoulou Square**, the town's hub. The narrow streets leading up behind Pelikan Tours go directly westward toward the cliff and the path overlooking the harbor. Most of the restaurants and discos are located here. Both of the youth hostels are uphill off **25 Martiou,** the paved road leading to Ia (look for signs). The road downhill past the square's newsstand leads to several moped dealers and, bearing right, to the Olympic Airlines office.

**Travel Agencies:** Dozens clustered around Theotokopoulou Sq. Most book rooms, excursions, ferry passages. Luggage storage 100dr per day. **Santorama Travel** (tel. 231 80, 231 21, or 231 77), about 4-5 blocks up from the square toward Ia is very friendly and helpful. Great tours of the island with student discounts. Currency exchange, too.

**Currency Exchange: National Bank of Greece,** off the square on Joseph Dekigala St. Open Mon.-Thurs. 8am-2pm, Fri. 8am-1:30pm; additional summer hours for exchange only, Mon.-Fri. 6-8pm. The **Commercial Bank,** next door, changes cash during regular hours. Most travel agencies also exchange currency.

**American Express:** c/o X-Ray Kilo Travel and Shipping Agency, Theotokopoulou Sq. (tel. 226 24). Full travel services. Open in summer daily 8:30am-10:30pm; in off season Mon.-Sat. 9am-1pm and 5-7:30pm.

**Post Office:** 25 Martiou St., south of the square. Open Mon.-Fri. 7:30am-2:30pm; opens late some mornings. **Postal code:** 84700.

**OTE:** Behind the bank, atop the cliff on Ipapantis St. Collect calls may be placed Mon.-Fri. 8am-1pm only. Tell the clerk that you want to wait in Lucas's cafe across the street. Open Mon.-Fri. 8am-10pm, Sat.-Sun. 8am-3pm. **Telephone code:** 0286.

**Airport: Olympic Airways,** 25 Martiou St. (tel. 227 93), north of Theotokopoulou Sq. Flights to Athens, Iraklion, Mykonos, and Rhodes. Make reservations about 1 week (in off-season) to 2 months (July-Aug.) in advance. In off-season, arrive 2 hr. before take-off for standby tickets (same price). Buses run from the Olympic Airways office to the airport in Monolithos (70dr).

**Buses:** From Theotokopoulou Sq. to: Perissa (every ½ hr., 100dr); Kamari (every 20 min., 85dr); Akrotiri (every hr. in the morning, every 2 hr. after 2:30pm, last at 7pm, 90dr); and Ia (every hr., last at 11pm, 100dr). Buses to the port leave 1½ hr. before most departures (100dr).

**Ferries:** From Piraeus (10 hr., 1900dr) daily to Paros, Naxos, Ios, and finally Santorini. Several boats per week from Piraeus to Santorini via Syros and Mykonos, or alternately Kithnos, Serifos, Sifnos, and Milos. Service reduced in off-season. From Santorini to: Paros (5 hr., 920dr); Naxos (4 hr., 829dr); Ios (1½ hr., 442dr); Syros (6 hr., 1175dr); Mykonos (7 hr., 1039dr); Milos; Sifnos; and Serifos (917dr). To Crete (8 hr., 1074dr). Free tickets to Anafi, April-May and Sept.-Oct.; otherwise 600dr Tues. and Fri. only.

**Moped and Car Rental: Santorama Travel** (tel. 231 21 or 231 77). Mopeds 1500dr, Hondas 2200dr, Fiats 5000dr. Prices lower in off-season. Many places are clustered downhill from Theotokopoulou Sq.

**International Bookstore:** At the top of "Jewelry Lane," between Theotokopoulou Sq. and the cliff (look for the expensive displays). Good collection of international papers. Open daily 9am-1:30pm and 5-9pm.

**Public Toilets (WC):** 25 Martiou St., down from the post office and taxi stand. Not too bad.

**First Aid:** Tel. 222 37.

**Tourist Police:** 25 Martiou St. (tel. 226 49), next to Olympic Airways. Contact them in case of medical emergencies such as moped accidents. They also handle lost and found.

**Port Police:** Tel. 222 39, 25 Martiou, 30m north of Theotokopoulou Sq.

## Accommodations and Camping

Santorini is chock-full of accommodations, but in summer the pensions and hotels are almost full by noon. If you arrive late, stay at a youth hostel or at Perissa Beach, and start hunting early the next morning. Though Thira is centrally located, there are good accommodations in private homes all over the island, so don't hesitate to branch out. There are no singles, but doubles in outlying towns run as low as 1500dr (1000dr in off-season). Head for **Messaria, Pirgos, Emborio,** or any of the small inland towns along the main bus routes. **Perissa** has the best deals. The police discourage room rentals between November and April, but rooms are cheaper and actually more plentiful then.

For a hotel or large pension right in Thira, you'll be hard put to find doubles for under the standard rate of 2000dr. You can **camp** at Perissa Beach (see Southern Santorini).

**Youth Hostel (IYHF),** tel. 227 22, 400m north of town on 25 Martiou St., near the church of Agios Eleftherios; follow the signs. The bar (open to non-guests) is a great deal. The dorm rooms have 100 beds. Reception open 8am-1pm and 5-11pm. Check-out before 11am. Hot showers 5-9pm only. 500dr per person. Roof 400dr. Breakfast 160dr.

**Kamares Hostel,** tel. 231 42, on the ridge north of town, near the museum on Erithrou Stavrou, just past the cable car. The roof has a great view, and is the scene of loud, late-night parties. Office open 9am-9pm. Showers 4-7pm only. 450dr per person.

**Hotel Giorgios** (tel. 225 84), at the top of the steps from the harbor (Greek sign), next to the Sunset Bar. Small, clean rooms, and cold showers. Doubles 1890dr.

### Food and Entertainment

If you look hard enough, you can find excellent food, reasonable prices, and a spectacular view. For a change of taste and a touch of elegance, try **China Terrace**, below the Loucas Hotel, overlooking the ocean. Arrive around 7:30pm, order a bottle of wine, and watch the sun set from tables on the balcony. Try the tomato beef soup. (Open May 7 to Oct. 30 daily 7pm-midnight.) **Nicholas Taverna**, at the top of the steps, has good food at good prices (open daily noon-12:30am), although the ambienced **Restaurant Niki**, across the street, is more soothing. (Open April-Nov. daily 8pm-2am.) On the streets, *souvlaki* and *spanakopita* are cheap choices.

For relaxed outdoor cafes, try **Canava** (tel. 225 65), on the water; they serve cappuccino and ice cream sodas to sweet Brahmsian melodies. (Open April to Nov. 15 daily 8am-2am.) The **Kaktos Cafe**, 3 blocks from the center of town, serves leisurely breakfasts, homemade pastries (250dr), and fresh fruit juices on their prickly patio. (Open May-Nov. 8:30am-3am.) Slip into the **Banana Bar**, on the same street as Kaktos in the opposite direction, which serves homemade cakes (230dr) and fruit juices (200dr) with a health-food twist. Breakfast is served if the owner gets up in time. (Open Jan.-Oct. noon-1:30am.) **Aresana**, on a side street between the water and the town square, is an art gallery/cafe. The interior is decorated with sculpture, paintings, and plants—a quiet and unpretentious place for rest or conversation. Wherever you go, be sure to sample a local wine. Santorini grapes produce some of Greece's best wine. The reds might taste like cough syrup, but the whites are good (try Nikteri white).

The hill behind the museum gives a fine view of Thira, the harbor, and the donkey path you avoided by landing at Athinios. In the evening, watch the sun set at one of the waterfront cafes. **Franco's** (tel. 228 81), with comfortable lounge chairs, is expensive, but worth it. Drink a *frullati* (500-600dr) and listen to Handel's *Messiah* while the sun sinks behind the craters. (Open April-Oct. 6pm-2am.) The **Petros Bar**, opposite the Emporiki Bank off Theotokopoulou Sq., is one of the cheapest watering holes—come here if you're tired of paying 600dr for a drink. For nightlife, try the *Tropical Bar*, by the water. (Open 6:30pm-3am.) Back in town, the **Town Pub** and **Paradise Cocktails** are popular bars that play rowdy rock and disco. The jazz bar **Kira Thira** serves its own special sangria. Most bars and discos stay open until 4am on Saturday nights.

Thira's **archeological museum** has an impressive collection of prehistoric, early Cycladic, and Geometric vases, mostly from the site of ancient Thira. There are also black-figure vases from the sixth-century B.C.E. gravesites on Santorini. (Open Mon. and Wed.-Sat. 9am-3pm, Sun. 9am-1pm.) A new museum is being built that will house a collection of finds from Akrotiri. From August 28 through September 15, Santorini hosts a small classical music festival; inquire at Estia Hall, Thira.

## Southern Santorini

The least painful and least adventurous way to travel around the island is to take an organized tour. The travel agents in Thira compete to offer all types of half-day (approximately 800dr) and full-day (about 1200dr) excursions. Kamari Tours is expensive, but has a good reputation and can be booked from offices in Perissa and Kamari. Panorama Tours offers good student discounts. One of the most popular tour packages includes the excavation site at Akrotiri, Profitas Ilias Monastery, a winery, and a stop at the beach. Crowded public buses also stop at many points throughout the island. Mopeds cost 1000-1500dr per day, but be warned that Santorini is perenially the moped-accident capital of Greece. The problem isn't bad roads, but reckless riders.

You may appreciate a tour in **Akrotiri**—the extent of the excavations (still underway) and the superficial similarity of many of the buildings can bewilder the undirected eye. If you choose not to spend your *drachmae* on a tour, pick up one of the books on Akrotiri (400dr).

Professor Marinatos found the paved streets of Akrotiri lined with multi-story houses all connected by a sophisticated central-drainage system. Most of the ground-floor apartments were used for storage, and hundreds of *pithoi* (jars) and other utensils have been found here. The upper floors were the living quarters for what appear to have been wealthy families; each house had at least one room lined with frescoes, some among the most magnificent found in Greece. These, along with some pottery and stone vases unearthed at Akrotiri, are on loan in a special room in the National Archeological Museum in Athens, pending completion of the new museum at Santorini.

The inhabitants of the town, used to the hazards of life on a volcano, may have had enough warning from tremors to clear out before the eruption; the only remains of a living being found was the skeleton of a pig. What happened to the people remains a mystery: They may have escaped safely, or, while attempting to escape, have died in the tidal waves that presumably followed the eruption. Archeologists have added cement support to walls already leaning before the earthquake, and replaced the wooden beams and frames that were carbonized by the heat of the volcanic eruption. Otherwise, the protective roof covering the site is the only change that has been made here. (Open Mon.-Sat. 8:45am-3pm, Sun. 9:30am-2:30pm. Admission 500dr, students 250dr.) Thirteen buses per day run here, the last returning at 10pm.

Santorini's two most popular **beaches,** are on the southern end, at Kamari and Perissa. Bring along a straw mat and sandals; the sun bakes this black volcanic sand to scorching temperatures. The water here, as elsewhere on the island, is brisk and clear, but the rock and seaweed bottom tame the snorkeling. **Perissa Beach** is the more distant and less crowded of the two. The **Perissa Youth Hostel** is 600m along the road leading out of town. (400dr per person. 450dr for beds with sheets. Cold showers.) There are also a number of rooms to let. Singles from 1000dr. Doubles 1500dr. **Perissa Camping** is nearby. (400dr per person. 150dr per tent.) Buses to Perissa leave Thira every half-hour (29 per day, last return at 11:30pm, 100dr).

**Kamari Beach,** more developed than Perissa, has several posh hotels and rooms to rent. Doubles in private homes drop to about 800dr in off-season. The **Hotel Asteria** (tel. 310 02), on the right hand side of the road as you come into town, is clean, modern, and quiet. (Open May-Oct. 15. Doubles 1850dr. Triples 2550dr. Private bath included. Breakfast 300dr.) Along the dirt track to the left, across from Pegasus car rental, are several pensions; try **Pension Maria** (tel. 310 02), which also has a laundromat. (Doubles with private showers 1510dr.) Restaurants line the beach, and with each additional meter away from the bus stop, the price of a meal drops a *drachma.* Try a variety of local wines at Cavana Roussos, about 1km up the main road from Kamari; they have wine-tasting specials from 2pm to 8pm.

Don't attempt to freelance camp on Kamari Beach; the police will nail you. If the prices in Kamari leave you out in the cold, find a room in Pyrgos or Vothonos, or hitch down to **Monolithos,** the unofficial center of seaside bohemian life. You can camp along the rocky coastline without the conventional necessity of wearing clothing. Buses to Kamari beach leave here every 20 minutes (50dr). Fifteen buses per day leave Thira for Monolithos (85dr).

Lofty **Pyrgos** is surrounded by medieval walls and dotted with the towers and blue and green domes of its many churches. About an hour's hike up the mountain from Pyrgos is the **Profitias Ilias Monastery,** sadly sharing its grand site with a radar station. The monastery and its museum are open only on July 20, for the **Festival of St. Ilias.** This traditional ceremony begins with an all-night vigil at the monastery's main church the night before and culminates in a procession of worshipers to the chapel gate around 11am. All in attendance are then served a meal of *fava* (specially prepared chick peas).

From Profitias Ilias, it is about an hour's hike to the ancient city of **Thira.** Leaving from the northeast side of the summit, the footpath follows the stony cliff-side, with numbing views of northern Santorini (not recommended for acrophobes.) From the plateau at the path's end, the ancient city is a short climb up the hill directly to the southeast. You can also take a tour bus from Kamari. Ask at Thira Tours (tel. 311 31). Much of the layout of this Ptolemaic city is still recognizable, and with a guidebook (available in Thira) and some imagination you'll be able to piece together certain aspects of life on Thira in the second and third centuries B.C.E. Look for the stone in the middle of the ruin that bears a carved phallus with the inscription *tois philois* ("for friends"). (Open Mon.-Sat. 9am-3pm, Sun. 9:30am-2:30pm. Free.) From the base of the hill, Kamari Beach is another 45 minutes on foot down the snaking dirt road, and Perissa is equidistant on the other side via a footpath.

If you plan to follow the three-hour route from Pyrgos to Kamari on foot, be sure to plan your time carefully to avoid the 3pm closing at the monastery and ancient Thira. If you do the hike in reverse, beginning at Kamari or Perissa and ending at Pyrgos, allow more time for the climb, and bring water.

The southern end of the island has a few villages where you can spend the night. Cheerful, whitewashed **Emborio**, some 3km inland from Perissa, has frequent bus connections to the beach and to Thira. Rooms go for as little as 800dr. For something more plush, try the comfortable **Hotel Archaia Elefsina** (tel. 226 43), with luxurious singles for 1200dr, doubles for 2000dr.

## Northern Santorini

**Ia** (pronounced "eeya"), with its pumice caves, time-worn churches, and winding streets, is an integration of devastation and renewal. This small town clinging to the island's rocky northern point was devastated by the 1956 earthquake. Its present inhabitants, 300 strong (strong at least in faith, since there is every indication that the island will be hit again), have valiantly rebuilt the town. Their new houses, almost as if carved out of rock, are interspersed among blown-out ruins of the old. A walk to the promontory at the tip gives you a splendid view; a long climb (20 min.) down the stone stairs brings you to the rocky beach at **Amoudia**, with a few boats moored in its surprisingly deep swimming lagoon. Buses run from Thira to Ia (9:30am-10pm, 18 per day, 90dr). A number of ferries also dock at Ia before continuing to Thira; check with the ferry office prior to departure.

Accommodations in Ia are cheaper than in Thira. Look up on the hill, above the main part of town, where it is rumored that entire houses can be rented in off-season for 2500dr. The **Delfini** (tel. 712 72) is the only reasonable hotel in town. (Open April-Oct.) The unofficial **youth hostel** is on the road 300m before Ia. (500dr per person. Showers 200dr.) Some people simply sleep on the roofs of deserted houses or in caves (bring a sleeping bag). Some people have fallen in love with this lifestyle and live in these dwellings for weeks.

For breakfast, pick up freshly-baked bread at **Nikolas Passare's bakery. Cafe Lotza** is excellent for a leisurely lunch or iced coffee. (Open 9am-midnight.) The **Kyblos Restaurant,** on the island's tip, built into the nearby caves and grottoes, has a monopoly on food that is reflected in the prices. If you go at sunset, make sure you call and reserve a table with a view. (Dinner served until midnight; disco dancing from 11:30pm. Drinks 300-500dr. Open April-Oct. daily 6pm-3am.)

## Thirasia and Surrounding Islands

Santorini's unspoiled junior partner Thirasia is worthy of the detour. Built along its upper ridge, the villages of **Manolas** and **Potamos** feature exquisite views of Santorini's dramatic western coast. Manolas is the larger and more frequented of the two, but still virtually untouched by contemporary society. This may be due to its geographical setting: The only way to reach the village is to climb the rocky stairs (about 45 min.) or take a donkey (350dr). If you walk, go when the sun is low—a midday excursion may induce preliminary heart failure. Treat yourself to a drink at the small restaurant when you reach the top, then follow the main street through the town. About 100m down you will find one the town's two *tavernas* on your left, and a mini-market on the right. Farther down is the other *taverna,* with rooms to let. Excursion boats leave the harbor of Thira at 10:30am for a round-trip tour of the volcano, hot springs, Thirasia, and Ia, returning at 4:30pm (1200dr). Boats also leave from Amoudia in Ia for **St. Irene,** the tiny port of Thirasia, at 11am, returning at 5:30pm (700dr round-trip). Since many have been disappointed by the fast pace of some excursions, you should take an "unguided" rather than "guided" tour; this should also cut the price by 200-300dr. Trips to the volcano and hot springs alone go as low as 600dr round-trip and can be wonderfully convivial.

# Western Cyclades Δυτικές Κυκλάδες

Having endured successive invasions of Athenians, Italians, and Turks, the islanders of the western Cyclades preserve a stoic calm toward the friendlier expeditions of tourists. For years these islands have been the summer retreats of mainland Greeks who corner in advance the limited supply of accommodations; ironically, you may best escape non-Greek tourists by staying closer to Athens. In summer, rooms can be found only in the early morning, if at all, and only then with perseverance. A pleasant side effect is that free camping is abundant, and amenities such as showers are often on hand. The scenery is not especially nice (Milos, Serifos, and Kithnos are extremely dry and treeless) and the nightlife is much tamer than in the eastern Cyclades. But these islands are relaxing, friendly, and authentic.

**Ferry** connections to the western Cyclades are becoming more frequent. Daily ferries link Piraeus with Kithnos (1035dr), Serifos (1152dr), Sifnos (1397dr), Milos (1522dr), and Kimolos (1523dr). These boats occasionally stop at Santorini, and each of the islands receives a boat from Piraeus bound for Ios and Santorini. There are also several daily connections from Paros to Sifnos (883dr). Boats sail from Laurio daily to Kea (597dr) and Kithnos (892dr).

## Milos

If you've come here to discover the charms of its marble Latinized daughter, Venus de Milo, upon arrival in Adamas you will wish you had gone to the Louvre instead. The mined-out white landscape and the reticent residents will hardly bring to mind the statues' graces or Thucydides' *Melian Dialogue*. Melos, refusing to join the Athenian League during the Peloponnesian War, declared the injustice of the impending Athenian punitive invasion. Affirming the "strong do what they must" ethic, the Athenians besieged Milos and eventually executed all the men and enslaved the women. The mineral-rich island rebounded and later flourished as a cosmopolitan center in the Cyclades. Milos has always been preoccupied with mining—obsidian in the Early Bronze Age, salt and a variety of minerals today. Adamas is its busy export harbor with freighters anchored on the gray water, waiting to be loaded with tons of rock.

### Practical Information, Accommodations, and Food

**Ferries** also dock at Adamas, which is a convenient, if unsightly, base for your stay in Milos. Two or three boats travel daily to Piraeus (7 hr., 1400dr), Serifos (2 hr., 480dr), and Sifnos (1½ hr., 480dr). There is daily service to Ios (2 hr., 1000dr) and Santorini (3 hr., 1000dr) via Folegandros and Sikinos. Two or three times per week, a ferry sails to Crete (1400-1600dr) and Rhodes (2453dr). Olympic also offers **flights** to and from Athens (3-4 per day, 4200dr).

Across from the dock, the extremely competent **tourist office** (tel. 222 90) will provide you with general information, as well as equip you with complete lists and accompanying maps of all the rooms and hotels on the island. (Open 9am-1pm and when boats dock at night.) The **OTE** (open Mon.-Fri. 8am-11pm, Sat.-Sun. 8am-10pm), **post office** (open Mon.-Fri. 7:30am-2:15pm), **bank** (open Mon.-Thurs. 8am-2pm, Fri. 8am-1:30pm), and **port police** (tel. 221 00; open 24 hours) are all along the waterfront. **Olympic Airways** (tel. 223 80) is situated on 25th March 1821 St., which runs off the square. (Open Mon.-Sat. 8am-2:30pm.) **Buses** to other island locations leave from the square. For any medical problem, ask a pharmacist to direct you to the office of **Dr. Armenis** (tel. 220 27). Milos' **telephone code** is 0287; the **postal code** is 84801 in Adamas, 84800 elsewhere.

Even in the cheapest hotels, accommodations in Adamas are not cheap. A pleasant exception is the **Semiaramis** (tel. 221 18 and 416 17), off 25th of March 1821 St. (Clean, quiet doubles with private bath 2500dr.) Guests are invited to pick grapes from the arbor. Finding a room in a private home (with the list from the tourist office) is another affordable option. (Singles 1300dr. Doubles 1900dr. Triples 2000dr.) There are no official campgrounds in Milos, but the police won't bother you if you **camp** on the beaches—head to the right (facing inland) from the dock, bear right at the crossroads, and head straight for **Hivadolimni Beach.** Walking left from the dock, you'll find a much more pleasant and secluded spot; pass the small beach in front of the Hotel Venus and climb over the small, rocky hill. The 10-minute walk is tricky at night (avoid the cliff overhanging the water), so you may want to crash on the beach in front of the Hotel Venus until it's light.

The cheapest and best place to eat in Adamas is the sincere **O Kinigos** (sign in Greek) located along the waterfront. (*Mousaka* and stuffed tomatoes 192dr, chicken 178dr. Open noon-3pm and 8pm-midnight.) Nearby, also along the waterfront, is **O Flisvos** (sign in Greek), with *mousaka* (300dr) and chicken (280dr; open noon-3pm and 6pm-midnight) and **Mariana,** with chicken (238dr) and swordfish (500dr; open 6pm-midnight).

The town of **Plaka,** 3km from Adamas, is bathed in the stillness and light that Adamas lacks. The diminutive **archeological museum** houses the Cycladic Minoan and Mycenaean artifacts unearthed at Filakopi, including the endearing "Lady of Filakopi." (Open Mon.-Sat. 8:45am-3pm.) The **folk museum** is also interesting, but not much larger. (Open Tues.-Sat. 10am-1pm and 6-8pm, Sun. 10am-1pm.) Walk to the terrace of the Church of **Panayia I Korfiatissa** for the best vista on Milos. Buses run to Plaka and Trypiti every hour (50dr).

South of Plaka, outside the small town of **Trypiti,** are several more sights of archeological interest. The **catacombs,** cut into a cliff-face where 2000 people were buried, constitute the oldest site of Christian worship in Greece. (Open Mon.-Tues. and Thurs.-Sat. 8:45am-3pm.) Archeological finds in the **ancient city** on the hillside above the catacombs represent three periods of Greek history. The Dorians built a wall of hewn-stone hexagonal blocks between 1100 and 800 B.C.E.; a plaque marks the spot where the Venus de Milo was buried around 320 B.C.E.; and an ancient theater dates from the Roman occupation. An ancient magic stirs in this exceptionally peaceful town. **Pollonia,** to the northeast, is a quiet fishing village. Rooms (doubles 1900dr) usually fill in summer, but you can **camp** on the beach. There are two fish restaurants along the harbor, but at night, go down to the *kafeneion* at the far end of the dock to commune with the fishermen over *ouzo.* Boats run between Pollonia and **Kimolos** (4 per day, approximately every 3 hr., 35 min., 300dr round-trip). Kimolos Town and the port of Psathi are perfect if you want to lay low for awhile. Few tourists venture here, so you can sleep on the beach peacefully.

Buses run to Pollonia seven times per day (85dr). Archeology buffs will want to scramble among the ruins of **Filakopi,** 3km from Pollonia, where British excavations unearthed 3500-year-old frescoes of lilies and flying fish (now exhibited in the Nations Museum in Athens).

Good beaches lie south of Adamas, across the bay, along the paved road that leads to Agia Marina. The best on the island are found along the southern coast of the island at places like **Provotas** and **Paliochori.** Most of these beaches are not accessible by bus, with the exception of Paliochori (7 per day from Livadia, 85dr). The west has dramatic scenery and beaches, but the roads are rugged and dangerous.

An excursion boat travels around the island daily (departs at 9am, returns at 6pm, 1500dr), a good way to see things like the lava formation of **Glaronissia** that are not otherwise accessible by road.

# Sifnos

During antiquity, Sifnos was famous for its gold and silver. Legend has it that each year the islanders, in an effort to placate Apollo, would send a solid-gold egg to Delphi. One year, the locals decided to sneak in a gold-plated egg, and keep the real one for themselves. As a result of this insult, Apollo decided to sink the Sifniote mines under the sea and curse the land with emptiness (*sifnos* in Greek). Apparently, the god did not hold a grudge because today Sifnos is still affluent. Although less known to foreigners, Sifnos is a favorite among Greeks. Since accommodations are limited, however, tourism is more easygoing than on most islands and the residents' welcome is very cordial.

## Practical Information, Accommodations, and Food

Boats dock at **Kamares.** One or two **ferries** per day sail to Piraeus (6 hr., 1454dr), Milos (1½ hr., 480dr), Serifos (45 min., 417dr), Kithnos (2½ hr., 654dr), Sikinos (2½ hr., 614dr), Folegandros (45 min., 427dr), and Paros (3 hr., 865dr). Three times per week, there are sailings to Ios (944dr) and Santorini (1000dr). A boat travels every week to Crete (1820dr). For more detailed information, contact the **port police** (tel. 316 17) in Kamares.

In general, hotels in Kamares are crowded and expensive. If you walk toward the beach (left facing inland), however, you will find the bargain of Sifnos, the **Hostel Dionysos.** Upstairs, there's a cafe/bar and restaurant. (Dorm beds 500dr.) If you arrive late at night, you can freelance **camp** on the beach at Kamares or go to the official campground, across the road from the beach. (250dr per person, 100 per tent.) Almost every half-hour, **buses** leave Kamares for Apollonia, the main town (55dr), and then continue to other villages.

There are two bus stops in **Apollonia,** one for those originating from or bound for Kamares (in the square), and another for buses from or bound for all other towns (around the corner). The **post office** (open Mon.-Sat. 7:30am-2:15pm, Sun. 9am-1:30pm), the **OTE** (open Mon.-Fri. 8am-1pm and 5-10pm, Sat.-Sun. 9am-1pm and 6-9:30pm), and **bank** (Mon.-Thurs. 8am-2pm, Fri. 8am-1:30pm) are in the main square. The **police station** (tel. 312 10) is 1 block south of the square. (Open 8am-3pm and 5-11pm.) For **first aid,** call 313 15. Sifnos' **telephone code** is 0284; the **postal code** is 84003.

Accommodations in Apollonia, the island capital, are difficult to find in summer. Freelance **camping** on beaches or in olive groves is the best solution; politely request permission if you're within sight of houses. If you want to sleep under a roof, the **Pension Apollonia** (sign in Greek; tel. 314 90), is down the street from the second bus stop in the direction of Platis Gialos. Rooms overlook the hillsides and the distant sea. Unfortunately, the pension looks like a railway car both inside and out, and the rooms are dingy. (Singles 1600dr. Doubles 2300dr. Triples 2700dr.) Another possibility is the more pleasant **Hotel Sophia** (tel. 312 38), just off the square. (Singles with bath 1500dr. Doubles with bath 2600dr. Triples with bath 3000dr.) For more luxurious accommodations, the **Hotel Anthoussa** (tel. 314 31), across from the second bus stop, has rooms with private baths. (Singles 2500dr. Doubles 3000dr.) You will find the cheapest rooms in Apollonia by asking in *tavernas* for rooms to let; the going rate for doubles is 1900dr. Restaurants in Apollonia are not as expensive as their dolled-up exteriors would suggest. The cheap **Restaurant Cyprus,** in the main square, specializes in *stamnas* and *stifado* (dishes stewed and served in a crock; 420dr). Sit in their beautiful outdoor garden with its overhanging grape trellises. (Open noon-2pm and 5pm-midnight.)

Don't leave Apollonia without exploring the neighborhoods on the hillsides. You'll notice that the town is actually three mountaintop agricultural villages that grew together in the valley below. The upper parts of the town have as many olive groves as houses. You might also visit the **folk art museum** in the main square. (Open Tues.-Sun. 6-10pm. Admission 25dr.)

Travel in Sifnos is easy enough by bus or foot with the topographical map, available at any kiosk (130dr). A few kilometers to the east, **Kastro,** the former capital of the island, is an enchanting fortified town with a tiny **archeological museum.** (Open Mon. and Wed.-Sat. 9am-3pm, Sun. 10am-2pm. Free.) Below, you'll find a small rocky beach with rough water.

**Faros,** to the south, has three popular beaches. Farthest east is the nude beach. You can freelance camp there or on the westernmost beach. (In either case you'll have to climb over the promontories to get to the beaches.) Continue west along the rocky hillside path past a dilapidated lighthouse to reach a better beach at **Apokofto.** At the far end of this bay, you will see the monastery of **Chrysopyi,** with an ingenious arched water-passageway separating it from the mainland. The monastery has rooms to let (Doubles 800dr); they are usually full so call ahead to the priest (tel. 312 55) to make reservations. Forty days before Easter, the two-day festival of Analipsos is celebrated at Chrysopyi. The residents of Sifnos go to the monastery to await the arrival of a ship from Piraeus bearing a holy icon and a boatload of well-wishers. Up the path from Chrysopyi, **Vasilis Restaurant** offers delicious food at reasonable prices. Savor rabbit (450dr) or roast chicken (250dr) while relishing the view. (Open 9am-midnight.) **Platis Yialos,** rumored to be the longest beach in the Cyclades, is southwest of Faros. Unfortunately, the beach is heavily touristed. You can freelance camp here or go to the secluded official campground (tel. 317 86), off the beach. Just follow the signs. (Flat rate of 350dr.) From Plati Yialos you can also scamper up to the convent of **Panayia tou Vounou.** (There is a path but it's easy to miss; it swings to the right before cutting back over to the monastery at the top.) For the climb, you'll be rewarded with a panoramic view, and if the caretaker is around, she'll let you inside the chapel.

From Plati Yialos, you can hike to **Vathi.** Pass the official campground, and follow the signs to Vathi. The trail has sporadic markings; ask the amicable manager of the campground for detailed directions. As you descend into Vathi, you will see the best beach on the island. At Vathi, you can also stay in the rooms at the monastery of **Taxiarchi.** (Doubles 1000dr.) Contact Panayiotis (tel. 310 60 or 318 91) a month in advance for reservations.

Kastro, Faros, and Plati Yialos are easily reached by hourly buses from Apollonia. If you want to go directly to **Chrysopyi** and **Panayia tou Vaunou,** take the bus heading towards Platis Yialos and ask the driver to let you off at the Panayia: Each is a 20-minute walk from the drop-off. If you don't want to walk to Vathi, you will have to take the boat from Kamares (4 per day, 40 min., 500dr round-trip), since no buses travel there.

## Serifos

Serifos would be the perfect setting for a horror movie or a murder thriller. As the boat docks in the port town of Livadia, your first vision is of chocolate-brown hills blasted by the seering sun, and the ghostly white capital (Chora) gripping a naked mountain peak. The bustling tourism along the island's fringes—in its beaches and port town—operates oblivious of the haunting barrenness of the interior. The *tavernas,* hotels, and smattering of discos that line Livadia and the campers, sun worshipers, and devotees of various water sports that congregate in the coves along the coast seem nothing more than ephemeral anomalies.

### Orientation and Practical Information

All boats dock in **Livadia. Ferries** travel daily to Piraeus, Sifnos (45 min., 311dr), Kithnos (1½ hr., 643dr), and Milos (2 hr., 475dr). Two or three times per week, there are sailings to Ios (5½ hr., 952dr) and Santorini (6½ hr., 944dr). For more detailed information about boats, go to the **port police** (tel. 514 70), on the street parallel to the waterfront road, on the right end of the harbor (facing inland).

In summer, it is much easier to give up the hunt for accommodations in advance; arrive prepared to **camp** on the beaches. Showers (100dr) are available at the Relax Cafe, just over the hill near the dock, above Livadakia Beach which has plentiful trees and is well-suited for camping. If you're determined to sleep under a roof, arrive early in the morning and work the streets along the beach and in the cove in front of the Relax Cafe. Doubles with private bath in the cheapest hotels cost 2500dr. At these prices, try the **Coral Hotel** (tel. 514 84), off the waterfront around the corner from the bakery. The manager, Anna, has a heart of gold and a smile to match. (Triples 3100dr.) The **Cavo d'Oro** (tel. 511 60), also off the waterfront, is more posh, and the breakfast room has a good stereo. **Rooms Albatros** (tel. 511 48), along the waterfront, has clean new rooms, each with its own refrigerator. *Dhomatia* (doubles 1800dr) can be obtained through a travel agent or by looking around.

For an inexpensive and adventurous meal, hike down to the very end of the town beach (all the way to the left facing the sea) and look around for tree-covered tables. The restaurant has no sign but you can just ask for "Sklavani's" to get directions. Preparations take a while, but patience is rewarded with fresh vegetables from the garden and fish cooked right before your eyes. (Opens at 1pm for lunch and 6pm for dinner). Those dissatisfied with the beaches near Livadia should walk past the town beach to **Koutalas, Ganema,** and **Vaya Beach** (½ hr.). There are three good adjoining beaches here. The best beach on the island is at **Psili Ammos,** another half-hour beyond Koutalas.

**Chora,** the capital, sits high above Livadia on a mountain top and has managed to cultivate a deeply aesthetic desolation. There are no rooms to let here, but the *meltima* winds blow gently through the empty streets. Tumbling down the hillside like a cubist's attempt at urban planning, the town is appealing, despite its pathos. Pick your way through the alleys and underpasses up to the ruins of the old *kastro,* where several churches cling to the cliff.

Buses stop downhill in Chora near the post office (open Mon.-Fri. 7:30am-2pm, Sat. 7:30-3pm, Sun. 9am-2pm). Change your money here or at a travel agent because there is no bank on Serifos. Walking uphill to the main square, you'll pass the **police** (tel. 513 00) and the **clinic** (tel. 512 02) on the left, and the **OTE** (open Mon.-Fri. 7:30am-2pm) on the right. The second bus stop is at the top of the hill in a square, where you will find several quiet cafes. The northern part of the island makes Chora seem busy, and can be easily toured in one day by moped, or with a full day's hard walking. A bus travels up to the northern villages (200dr), but only leaves Livadi at 7am and 3pm and returns immediately. While in this part of Serifos, visit the Byzantine monastery of **Taxiarchi.** If you're lucky, its one inhabitant will be around to let you in.

## Kea (Tziá)

Kea, just an hour and a half from the mainland, is the closest, but one of the less-touristed Cycladic islands. Famed in antiquity as the birthplace of the fifth- and sixth-century B.C.E. poets Simonides and Bacchylides, Kea was also known in ancient times for its cold-blooded alternative to social security: Citizens celebrated their 70th birthdays by inbibing a cup of hemlock. Kea's proximity to Athens has made it a popular weekend getaway for the city's residents, so it is best to visit during the week when accommodations are plentiful and the beaches deserted.

### Orientation and Practical Information

Kea's relative repose can be attributed to its inaccessibility. Those traveling around the Cyclades will be disappointed that Kea is the only "pearl" in the necklace of Cyclades unvisited by ferries. Kea is best for those interested in retiring to one island near Athens rather than as a first step on a Cycladic odyssey. To reach Kea, you must take the ferry from Lavrio (1-3 per day, 1½ hr., 560dr). Boats sail more frequently on weekends, but their afternoon departures make daytrips impractical. For boat timetable information, call 267 77. To get to Lavrio from Athens, take the bus from 14 Mavromateou St. (290dr).

Ferries dock in relaxed **Korissia.** You will find nothing here of particular interest, but it serves well as a base for a visit. At the right side of the dock (facing inland), you will find the **tourist office** (tel. 312 56), with information about accommodations and boat and bus schedules. (Open June-Aug. 9:30am-1pm and 7-10pm; also serves as a **post office** in the morning). The **port police** (tel. 221 00) are located above the tourist office.

Rooms to rent are situated along the waterfront where the boats dock and behind the town beach, but they fill up in July and August. The most convenient are located just above Kostas Restaurant (tel. 313 75; doubles with bath 2600dr). You can also try the spotless **Pension Korissia** (tel. 314 84), behind the beach—follow the signs. All rooms have small patios or balconies. (Doubles 2570dr. Triples 3000dr. Breakfast 400dr.) In general, *dhomatia* range from 1269-1750dr for singles, 1900-2500dr for doubles, and 2017-3072dr for triples, depending on whether they have private bathrooms. There is only one restaurant in town (not counting fast-food eateries) called **Kostas,** which has moderately-priced food. (*Mousaka* 350dr. *Yiovets* 410dr. Open noon-4pm and 8pm-midnight.) At the site of the ancient Korissia, nearby, the **Kea Kouros** was discovered in 1930, but is now in the National Archeological Museum in Athens. Six kilometers uphill from Korissia, the buildings of the island's capital, **Chora Ioulis,** burst with a shock of white on the dark-green oak-covered landscape. Unusual in a Cycladic village, the buildings' rooves are covered with old reddish-brown tiles, more typical of a mainland village. To the left of the bus stop is the **post office.** (Open Mon.-Fri. 7:30am-2:15pm). The **OTE** (open Mon.-Fri. 7:30am-3:10pm) and the **bank** are located farther into town—follow the signs. Kea's **telephone code** is 0288.

There is a small **archeological museum** (open Mon. and Wed.-Sun. 9am-2pm), but ancient Ioulis' glory is suggested best by the enormous **Lion of Kea,** imbedded in rock about 1km east of Chora. If you decide to stay in Chora, go to the **Hotel Ioulis Keas** (tel. 221 77). All rooms have balconies with panoramic views of the island. (Singles 1883dr. Doubles 2658dr, with bath 3102dr.) Buses travel reasonably often to Chora from Korissia (15 min., 60dr).

From Korissia, you may want to visit the beaches to the east. **Vourkari,** 2km away, is a fishing town with colorful sailboats anchored in its harbor. There are several picturesque, though expensive, fish restaurants along its waterfront. Across the bay lie the ruins of **Agia Eirene,** which may seem modest to the layman, but actually constitute one of the most important archeological sites in the Cyclades. (Open Mon.-Sat. 9am-3pm.) Discoveries of items from the other islands, Crete, and the Greek mainland suggest intriguing trade relations between these places. Continuing west from Vourkari, you'll find the quiet bay of **Ofzias.** A bus travels to Vourkari and Otzias (60dr from Korissia, 100dr from Chora). Another popular beach is located at the site of another of Kea's ancient cities, **Poiessa.** Buses travel to Poiessa from Chora (130dr) and Korissia (180dr). Off the road, between Poiessa and Chora, you will find the ruined monastery of **Agia Marina** constructed around a rare extent of Hellenic towers.

The only official campground on Kea is located near the beach at Poiessa. **Camping Poiessa** (tel. 221 32) charges 350dr per person, 300dr per tent. Freelance camping on other beaches is prohibited.

From August 1-15, Kea celebrates a fine arts festival called **Ta Simoneida** in honor of the island's great ancient poet. Cultural events take place all over the island. (See the daily festival schedule for details.)

The unvisited island of **Makronissos,** just off Lavrio on the mainland, is infamous as the site of the most notorious concentration camp for political prisoners under the dictatorships from the end of World War II to 1974. Look for Eleni Fourtouni's *Greek Women in Resistance,* which contains moving journals of women resistance fighters who were imprisoned at Makronissos and Trikeri (north of Evia).

# SPORADES
# Σποράδες

With jagged coasts and thickly forested interiors, the Sporades are scattered throughout the Aegean as Homer described them. The Cretans first colonized the islands, and they started the cultivation of olives and grapes. The Athenians took over in the fifth century B.C.E., and of all the island groups, the Sporades retained the most amiable ties with Athens. Athena, in fact, was the most popular goddess in the islands' pantheon. Occupied by the Romans in the second century B.C.E., and the Venetians in the thirteenth century, the Sporades still show traces of the buildings left by these conquerors. The Venetians were forced out by the Turks, who controlled the islands until 1821, when the Sporades came under Greek rule once again.

In comparison to the Cyclades or Saronic Gulf Islands, the number of foreign visitors is modest and most arrive almost exclusively in July and August. Yet word has gotten out about the Sporades, and tourist facilities are developing to meet the demands of an increasing number of European visitors. **Skiathos,** the most popular island, has crowded beaches during the day and crowded bars and discos at night. Nearby **Skopelos** has thus far resisted overdevelopment, so many of its beaches are quiet and uncongested. **Alonissos** and **Skyros** remain far enough off the beaten track to provide you with a peaceful vacation and some of the best beaches in Greece.

In terms of transportation, you can think of these islands as a clique and a loner: Skiathos, Skopelos, and Alonissos—and Skyros. To reach the group from Athens, take the bus to **Agios Konstantinos** and then the boat, which connects all three. In off-season, two boats per week leave **Kimi** for Skiathos (4½ hr., 1638dr), Skopelos (3 hr. 45 min., 1451dr), and Alonissos (3 hr., 1330dr). In summer there are additional boats. For Skyros, take the bus from Athens to Kimi and then make the three-hour boat trip. Traveling from the one to the three, and especially vice versa, is difficult or expensive. **Alkyon Travel,** 98 Akadimias St., Athens (tel. 362 20 93), has information on getting to the Sporades. From the north, boats depart once or twice per day from **Volos.** Fom Skiathos, Skopelos, or Alonissos, a ferry departs once per week to Kimi, Agios Efstratros, Limnos, and Kavala. **Flying Dolphin hydrofoils** make daily trips connecting the islands with Volos (2 or 3 per day), Agios Konstantinos (1 or 2 per day), and Nea Moudania in the Halkidiki Peninsula (2 per week). On Thursday and Sunday one hydrofoil continues to Skyros. Be sure to book ahead for weekend trips; shop around.

## Skiathos Σκιάθος

Sophisticated, cosmopolitan, and expensive, Skiathos is the Mykonos of the Sporades. Clothing boutiques and stylish jewelry shops (many managed by foreigners) line its main shopping street, and hotels sprout more readily and grow higher here than on its eastern neighbors. Sun-worship and nightlife have overwhelmed the traditional culture. With more than 60 beaches and rolling green countryside, it's easy to see why tourists come. Skiathos attracts a sizable community of British expatriates, package tours, and vacationing Italians, not to mention Greek families, presenting obstacles to the budget traveler. As if the high prices of food, accommodations, and entertainment weren't enough, the official camping facilities are inconvenient, and you can't just sack out on the beach. Nevertheless, many budget tourists choose to give Skiathos a whirl, so you'll be in good company.

If you're starting from Athens, take the daily bus to Agios Konstantinos, and then the **ferry** from there at 1pm; bus and boat fare together is 1900dr. From Volos,

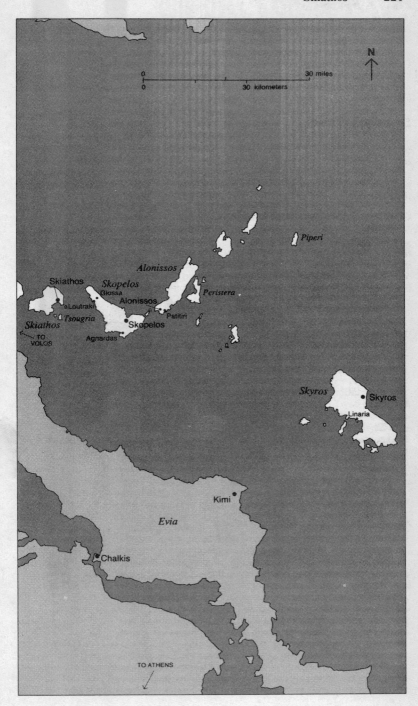

one or two boats depart per day (3 hr., 1499dr). Whether you begin your ferry trip in Agios Konstantinos or Volos, the ferry usually continues on to Skopelos Town on Skopelos Island and Patitiri on Alonissos. Ferries run from Skiathos to Skopelos (386dr) and to Alonissos (452dr). To get back and forth from the **Pelion Peninsula,** catch one of the excursion boats leaving the mainland fishing village of Platania at either 8am or 9am, returning from Koukounaries Beach on Skopelos at 5pm (500dr one-way).

## Skiathos Town

Skiathos Town has weathered the impact of the tourist industry far better than much of the coastline. The commercial section blatantly caters to tourists, diverting attention from and thus protecting its cobblestone streets and red-roofed buildings. In the residential section, balconies burst with magenta bougainvillaea and white gardenia blossoms, and grape vines flourish over shady terraces. Here, you won't find tourists at every bend.

### Orientation and Practical Information

Disembarking from the ferry, you'll see the **ferry agency,** several **travel agencies,** and **Budget Rent-A-Car.** The main drag, **Papadiamadi Street,** intersects the waterfront road by the ferry office. To the left of Papadiamadi, facing inland, is **Politechniou Street,** home to a string of bars. On the far right of the waterfront, still facing inland, a road winds up towards the airport and the beaches. Frequent bus service links Skiathos Town with Koukanaries and points in between.

**Currency Exchange: National Bank of Greece.** Open Mon.-Fri. 8am-2pm and 6:30-8:30pm. If possible, during July and Aug., cash enough money to tide you over *before* you arrive in Skiathos. Lines are excruciatingly long and slow.

**Post Office:** Papadiamadi St. Open Mon.-Fri. 7:30am-2:30pm. **Postal code:** 37002.

**OTE:** Papadiamadi St., 1 block inland from the post office. Open Mon.-Fri. 7:30am-3:10pm. **Telephone code:** 0424.

**Airport:** Tel. 420 49. Flights to Athens (daily, 50 min., 5020dr), and Thessaloniki (3 per week, 50 min., 5370dr). **Olympic Airways Office,** Papadiamadi St. (tel. 422 00 or 422 29).

**Buses:** From the bus stop next to the taxi stand on the wharf; every ½ hr. along the island's 1 road, ending at the pine grove of Koukounaries (8am-8pm, 100dr).

**Moped Rental:** Several shops along the waterfront and on Papadiamadi St. About 1000dr per day. Prices vary, so shop around.

**Hospital:** Tel. 420 40.

**Medical Emergency:** Tel. 423 47.

**Tourist Police:** Tel. 420 05.

### Accommodations, Camping, and Food

Finding a room from July 15 through August, when most Greeks go on vacation, can be extremely difficult. Most people disembarking from the ferry have already made reservations. Since singles are almost impossible to come by in the high season, lone travelers should try to find a companion. *Dhomatia* are the best bet; some proprietors offer facilities such as a refrigerator and space on the roof to dry clothes. Your first stop should be the house of **Maria Papagiorgiou** (tel. 215 74), just off Grigoriou St., which runs parallel to Polytechniou St., 1 block to the west. Turn towards the waterfront and take a right after Christina's Bar—look for the green doors. The rooms are spotless and there is a pleasant sitting area. (Doubles 2200dr, but you might be able to talk Maria into setting up a fold-up bed for 600dr.) Also try **Yolanda Constantinidou** on George Pandra St. (tel. 223 64), across from Restaurant Dionysus. (Doubles 2200dr. Triples 2800dr.) The pension down the alley on the right as you pass Taverna Stavros has the only singles in town for 1800dr; doubles are 200dr. Hotels are expensive, but you can try the **Australia House** (tel. 224

88), signposted off Evangelistrias St. (Doubles 2500dr. Triples 3150dr. Hot showers included.)

Camping is feasible, though Skiathos' two campgrounds lie well out of town. **Aselinos Camping** located near one of Skiathos's best and least crowded beaches, offers a *taverna,* a palm canopy on the beach, and plenty of shady spots. Take the bus toward Koukounaries and ask the conductor where to get off. It's a 20-minute walk from there. (350dr plus 250dr per tent.) **Camping Kolios** lies closer to town and right on the bus line but is more expensive. It is small and crowded, has no shade, and the sites are all dirt. (400dr per person. 200dr per tent.)

Fortunately, Skiathos has a couple of excellent restaurants that don't charge extortionist prices. The best is **Taverna Stavros**, on Evangelistrias St. (take a right off Papadiamadi). The lamb dishes are among the best in Greece—lots of tender meat and little fat (400dr), served with well-prepared vegetables such as *bamies* (okra) and *fasolakia* (green beans). At the waterfront *tavernas,* high prices are the rule. **The Limanaria,** set off from the others on the extreme left of the waterfront, is a little better value. Numerous groceries sell fruit and vegetables and other provisions at inflated prices. Although **Grocery Trophima** on Politehnion St. doesn't sell fresh fruit and vegetables, it has the cheapest prices for everything else. Just a block inland from the water, numerous fast-food joints sell the usual *gyros* and *souvlaki.*

### Entertainment

Nightlife here runs the gamut, from sitting in waterfront *tavernas* to partying all night in discos. But the island is a step ahead since the discos don't resemble converted cinderblock garages. For the more sophisticated decor, however, you'll pay up to 600dr (redeemable upon purchase of your first drink). In the middle of town, numerous bars and pubs and an occasional disco play music ranging from rock and new wave to classical. Cruise and take your pick. Many are located on Politechniou St., 1 block to the left of Papadiamadi St. as you face inland. Most bars and discos close in winter.

**Charlie 'O,** about 1km east of town. Operates free bus every ½ hr. from the waterfront. Popular with Greeks and foreigners alike. Cover 400dr only July-Aug.

**The BBC Disco,** 500m east of town along the waterfront. The most stylish disco/fashion show in town. Cover 400dr.

**Adagio Bar,** Evangelistrias St., across from the Taverna Stavros. As the name suggests, a leisurely atmosphere featuring classical music. Very friendly owners.

**Playboy Pub,** with new wave, and **Kentauros Pub,** with rock, both on Mitrop. Ananion St., compete for the business of gyrating insomniacs.

**The Borzoi** and **Banana Bar,** both on Polytechniou St. Bars with loud music and small dance floors. Usually packed.

## Around the Island

The northern part of Skiathos, accessible only by boat or by hiking dirt paths, has quiet beaches, secluded sandy coves, and is relatively peaceful. The southern side is very crowded.

The island's one paved road runs from Skiathos Town to Koukounaries, and the coast along the way is punctuated with beaches dominated by unsightly resort hotels. **Buses** traveling this route leave from the harbor in Skiathos Town (8am-8pm every ½ hr., 110dr to the end) and pass the beaches of **Mitikas, Nostos, Vromolimnos, Platanias,** and **Troulos.** For the most alluring stretch of coast, get off at Nostos and walk the kilometer or so past the village of Kanapitsa to the relatively quiet **Kalamaki Peninsula.** The bus route ends, as does the road, at the pine grove beach of **Koukounaries.** This is often photographed, with clear turquoise water and fine white sand sheltered by swaying pines. Unfortunately, this tranquil scene is now overrun by scantily-clad tourists, half-dozen refreshment stalls, and a hawker who charges 500dr for use of his umbrellas. Completing the picture are water-skiing and windsurfing schools, and sailboats, canoes, and pedal boats for hire. A short walk away is the renowned nude **Banana Beach** (Krassa Beach). Go west over the hill past the sheep, goats, and orangatans that lounge in the shade of an olive grove.

Just east of Troulos, a road turns off for **Aselinos.** Two kilometers farther, this road forks, the right branch leading up the hill to **Panayia Kounistra,** a small monastery with a grape arbor and a *taverna* within its walls. Continuing past the monastery, you'll enjoy a fine view at the bend of the road: To the left is the beach of **Megalos** (big) **Aselinos;** to the right, **Micros** (small) **Aselinos.** The latter is the more secluded of the two, though neither is crowded, and both are only a short scramble from the end of the road. Megalos Aselinos has rocks at either end that make for good snorkeling. Because of Aselinos' northern exposure, the water here is choppier than on Skiathos' southern shore. Megalos Aselinos also has a campground (see Accommodations above), and a *taverna.* You can reach it by car, zeppelin, moped, or a long walk from Troulos.

The rest of the northern coast is accessible only by boat. Even if you're just passing through Skiathos, spend at least part of your stay on one of the many excursion boats that leave Skiathos Town for this part of the island every morning. The most popular destination is **Lalaria Beach,** set in its own secluded pebbly cove, visible at one end through a natural stone arch. Near Lalaria are **Skotini Spilia** ("Dark Grotto"), striking **Glazia Spilia** ("Blue Grotto"), and **Chalkini Spilia** ("Copper Grotto").

The road that runs just north of Ftelia to the northwestern coast ascends the ridge dominating the interior and offers grand views. On the way up, you can see over the red-roofed town of Skiathos and its harbor, past the small islands at the harbor's mouth to Skopelos beyond. If the haze is not heavy, the hills of Alonissos are visible above Skopelos. The main road continues over the ridge (a few smaller tracks branching off) and finally disappears in the underbrush of the untended olive grove on a rise above the northwest coast. From here, you can distinguish the distant Pelion Mountains on the mainland. This cross-island road can be traveled by car or motorbike, but it makes a challenging and enjoyable hike. Allow three to four hours each way, bring water and the best map you can find, and, if possible, get a local to draw the new road onto your map. About 2km before the road ends, a footpath marked with a sign for Kastro leads indeed to Kastro and Lalaria Beach; catch the excursion boat back to Skiathos in the afternoon (400dr), weather permitting (check in the morning before you leave). The boat can pick you up at Kastro only; see what time it's scheduled to swing by.

Continuing east along the coast from Lalaria Beach you come to the ruins of the medieval walled **Kastro** (about a 2-hour walk on a path from Skiathos Town). The Greeks built Kastro during the sixteenth century to take refuge from marauding pirates; after independence last century, they abandoned this headland and began work on what has since blossomed into the present-day town of Skiathos. Kastro was originally connected to the rest of the island by a drawbridge, but now can be reached only by steps. Two churches are all that remain intact of the ancient community: The **Church of the Nativity** is more intriguing, with fine icons and some frescoes. Boats leave Skiathos' harbor for Lalaria, the caves, and Kastro every morning (1100-2500dr round-trip).

In the foothills around Mt. Karaflytzanaka, the Byzantine monastery of **Evangelistrias** is the most beautiful on the island, and it figures importantly in recent Greek history as well. Here the Greek Revolutionary heroes Stathas, Nikotsaras, and Kolokotronis met in 1807 to hoist the first Greek flag and vowed to liberate Greece from Turkish domination. The monastery is about an hour's walk from Skiathos Town (4km due north), but uphill all the way along an unpaved road. You can hire a mule (1300dr for half-day). If you're here on August 15, you will be able to see the unique ceremony of the burial of the Madonna.

For a full day of swimming, hop on one of the boats that leave regularly for the small island of **Tsougria** (10am-5pm every hr., 400dr). Boats also leave the harbor each morning for a full day excursion to Skopelos and Alonissos (a reasonable

1500dr round-trip). You could probably negotiate a one-way fare with the pilot that would undercut the amount asked by Nomikos Lines.

# Skopelos Σκόπελος

The Greek word *skopelos* denotes sharp, steep rock jutting from the sea. One look at the high cliffs that rise from the island's coastline and you'll agree the name is appropriate. Despite the ruggedness, Skopelos is covered with acres of grape, olive, and plum trees, and graced throughout by 360 churches. Originally a Cretan colony ruled by King Staphylos, the strategically important island has labored under the burden of occupation by Persians, Spartans, Athenians, Romans, Franks, Venetians, and Turks. It was conquered in 1538 by the Turkish admiral Khay El-Din Barbarossa (Red Beard), who massacred the entire population. Today, the city exhibits pride in its heritage and culture. Many women wear traditional costume, the *morko*—a silk shirt, short velvet jacket with flowing sleeves, and a kerchief, all finely hand-embroidered. Tourists have yet to leave their mark on Skopelos; perhaps this island will remain free of overdeveloped waterfronts and leviathan hotels.

Skopelos is the second island on the boat route after Skiathos, and at least one boat per day puts in from both Volos and Agios Konstantinos. Fare from Athens, including the bus to Agios Konstantinos and the boat from there to Skopelos is about 2500dr, from Volos 1073dr. Boats from Skopelos travel to Skiathos (398dr), Volos (1073dr), and Alonissos (409dr). The ferry to Alonissos leaves in the evening and returns in the morning, so you'll have to spend two nights there to enjoy a full day. Alternatively, you can take an excursion boat from Skopelos (1500dr). Note that some ferries from Volos or Agios Konstantinos stop at the port of Loutraki before continuing on to Skopelos Town; fares run about 80dr less for voyages from the west.

**Buses** run regularly along the main road from Loutraki to Skopelos (4 per day, 1 hr., 225dr); and an additional five run between Skopelos and Agnotas. (All schedules are posted on the tree in Skopelos Town where the bus waits.) Mopeds can easily pass this route and most others on the island, but be warned. Quaint as the "beware of cow" signs outside Klima may be, they're not there to amuse: Your Giarelli 13cc doesn't have a chance against a Bovine 4-hoof.

## Skopelos Town

Skopelos Town is an architectural mix. Besides the ruined walls of the Venetian *kastro,* the dozens of Byzantine churches, elements of Turkish, Macedonian, and Neoclassical building styles reflect the island's turbulent history. Overlapping, irregular slate tiles characterize the roofs here, which on average weigh around 10 tons. Expensive to build, replace, and maintain, they are gradually being replaced by red ceramic tiles. The colorful flowers and paint with which the islanders decorate their houses make Skopelos Town a photographer's paradise. For a view, climb the steps on the north side of town to the top of the castle walls.

One thoroughly practical aspect of pre-tourism Skopelos remains today: S. I. Lemoni runs a knife shop near the tourist agencies where he forges and hones blades by hand. If you happen to be waiting for a ferry by the harbor, take a peek into the dark interior of his shop to see an artisan at work.

### Orientation and Practical Information

Most of the activity is along the waterfront. This is convenient because you'd get lost in the back streets anyway. Most streets leading from the waterfront are lined with cafes and shops for a few blocks, but if you wander farther, find yourself a landmark first.

**Tourist Offices:** Several on the waterfront, but most are only interested in selling their excursions or rooms. Ferry tickets available at all offices, though everyone must also go to the embarkation office, 100m down the waterfront to the left.

**Currency Exchange: National Bank of Greece** and others, on the waterfront. National Bank open Mon.-Sat. 8:30am-1pm, Thurs. and Fri. 5-8pm.

**Post Office:** On a street sloping up from the right end of the harbor (facing seaward). Open Mon.-Fri. 8am-2pm. **Postal code:** 37003.

**OTE:** Follow signs from Pepapithou St. Open Mon.-Sat. 7:30am-10pm, Sun., 7:30am-3pm. **Telephone code:** 0424.

**Moped Rental:** Throughout town. July-Aug. supplies dwindle early in the day. Prices fixed at 1500dr for a 2-seater. Gas not included.

**Laundromat:** About 75m up the street from the post office. Open daily 9am-1:30pm and 4:30-8:30pm. Another laundromat about 80m up the hill from the Commercial Bank of Greece. Open Mon.-Sat. 8:30am-1pm, Thurs. and Fri. also 5-8pm (5 kilo clothes wash and dry 700dr).

### Accommodations, Camping, Food, and Entertainment

If you don't get herded into a room from the port or depot, look for *dhomatia* on the street behind the Commercial Bank, or on the main road that heads away from the water past the big hotels. Avoid room-finding services—they always charge a premium. Some of the best rooms in town are let by the **Abelakia family** (tel. 226 62). East of town along the waterfront, **Hotel Stella** (tel. 220 81) has doubles for 1400dr. Because there are no campgrounds on the island, authorities tolerate freelance **camping** above any beach except the one in town. The beaches themselves are too crowded to camp on; if you decide to try you'll probably be sleeping on rocks. **Milia Beach,** with its shaded pine-needle beds, is one of the more attractive possibilities.

The restaurants in town are fairly expensive, but **Ta Kymata,** at the extreme left facing the water, and **O Tsimi's,** in the middle of the group of three at the ferry landing, have good values. Tsimi's serves terrific *spetzofai,* a specialty from nearby Pelion, consisting of hot *loukaniko* (sausage), green peppers, and eggplant (300dr); also try the vegetarian dishes, especially the eggplant special (350dr). Tsimi's wins the award for friendliest service, although **O Yiannis,** next door, runs a close second. **Ta Kymata** is the best place for fresh fish. If you just want a snack, go to the wooden-fronted pizzeria in the middle of the waterfront. It sells by the slice, a rarity in Greece; the special, with ham and cheese, for 200dr is worth the extra 50dr. **Platanos,** near the ferryboat landing, serves a "natural breakfast" of yogurt with honey, nuts, and fresh fruit (380dr); you'll eat under a tree to the tunes of John Coltrane and Little Feat.

After dinner, nearly everyone sits at one of the many *zacharoplastia* (confectioner's shops) on the waterfront sipping *frappe* (iced coffee) and indulging in *loukoumades* (deep-fried honey pastries). Dance off some of those calories at **Disco 52,** always the first disco to fill. Walk about 200m uphill from the post office along Doulidi St. Canopied by huge umbrellas, the multi-level **Akri Bar** is one of the island's most popular hangouts. To get there, walk up Galatsanou St. 2 blocks past Alexander Restaurant/Bar. On slow nights, try the two bars on the waterfront.

## Around the Island

Three **monasteries** abide in lofty seclusion on Mt. Palouki, which faces the town across the water. The town's main road splits just after the Amalia Hotel; the left fork circles the harbor, and ascends the mountain. **Evangelismos,** perched among the rocks across from Skopelos Town, dates from the eighteenth century; the gold-plated altar screen, produced in Constantinople, is 400 years older. (Open 8am-1pm and 4-7pm.) Descend back to the fork and climb to the **Monastery of Metamorphosis,** standing amid pines on a breezy knoll. The little chapel, set in a courtyard bedecked with flowers, dates from the sixteenth century. (Open 8am-1pm and 4-7pm.) From Metamorphosis, **Propromou** is visible on the next ridge. Although it was a monastery at the time of its reconstruction in 1721, this cloister, dedicated to St. John the Baptist, is now inhabited by nuns. The sister who shows visitors around speaks fluent French, and is a stickler for proper appearance. "One cannot walk naked into the house of God!" (Open 8am-1pm and 5-8pm.) All three monasteries provide bell-bottoms and long-sleeved blouses for men and women to meet the dress requirement. You can visit by moped or taxi (about 1200dr), or take the pleasant two-hour walk. Many tourist offices also offer excursions to the monasteries (950dr).

Beaches line the coast from Skopelos to Loutraki. **Staphylos Beach** is long and sandy, but it is the primary beach on the island, and thus crowded. Archeologists discovered the tomb of the ancient Cretan general Staphylos on a hillside near here, as well as a gold-plated sword dating from the fifteenth century B.C.E. (now in Athens). If you walk the length of Staphylos Beach and climb over the ridge at its eastern end, you'll come to the sandy **Velamio Beach.** Because this is advertised as the one legal nude beach on Skopelos, it is considerably less crowded, less noisy, and less strewn with toys (children's toys, at any rate). It is, if anything, more inviting than Staphylos. Continuing along the paved road, the next place of interest is the harbor of **Agnotas,** a pleasant spot for a seaside picnic. The beach at Agnotas is small, crowded, and too close to the boats, but from here you can catch the caïque every half-hour to **Limnonari Beach,** a long, uncrowded crescent of golden sand (250dr round-trip). **Panormos Beach** is crowded, but has several lively *tavernas.* Around the point to the north lies **Milia,** the prize beach of Skopelos. It is accessible from the main road along a dirt track; the bus driver will stop if you ask. The adjacent pine groves make for great camping. The cliff-bound beach of **Sares** is accessible by boat from Skopelos Town.

Following the road past Milia you will come upon the prefabricated eyesore of **Elios** (swamp). The unfortunate residents of **Klima** (3km farther) were relocated here when the 1965 earthquake—the one that devastated Alonissos—pulled much of the old town into the sea. Locals joke that property in Klima is now the best investment on the island: Buy a dirt-cheap hilltop lot and in 10 years you may have prime beach-front property. Along the road after Klima you may notice plastic bags mounted under incisions on the trunks of pine trees. The sap is being collected to ship to Athens to flavor *retsina.* The peaceful and untouristed town of **Glossa** is perched on a high hill at the end of the road. A road runs from Glossa to **Loutraki,** where accommodations can be found at numerous *dhomatia* or at the **Hotel Flisvos** (tel. 336 81). Doubles run 2000dr. If you continue around the coast past the Flisvos there are some small, quiet, sheltered beaches.

For a superb hike, take the bus to Glossa, and walk the dirt track across the island to where the **Monastery of Agios Ioannis** clings to a massive boulder above the ocean. (Take the main road east from Glossa and turn left on the first dirt road to Steki Taverna; after that it's clear sailing.) At the road's end, a steep path drops to the sea, and stone steps cut in the escarpment lead up to the monastery. According to legend, the builders had originally intended to establish the monastery at the base of the rock, but each day after they finished work, St. John moved all their tools and supplies to the boulder's summit. In the end, they built the monastery on top of the rock. Another miracle, more relevant for hikers, is the cistern of potable water in the rock. Even more refreshing is the small sandy cove below the steps. Allow at least four hours round-trip to visit Agios Ioannis, and bring at least a liter of water per person. The road is passable most of the way on motorbike, although the noise will ruin your chances of glimpsing the nymphs and satyrs who dart through the olive grove along the way.

# *Alonissos*

With only 1500 inhabitants, Alonissos is the least populated and most isolated of the Sporades. Its story is also one of the saddest in the tumultuous post-war history of Greece. In 1950, the island's vineyards were wiped out to the last grape by a fast-spreading blight. It decimated the island's once-lucrative wine industry and left the local economy in such dire straits that much of Alonissos' male population was forced to take up construction work in Athens. By 1965, when the island had recovered some measure of prosperity through other forms of farming and fishing, an earthquake struck, damaging both the harbor of Patitiri and the town of Alonissos on the hill above. In a decision that reflected more a desire to push through a large building contract, without any concern for the well-being of the islanders, the dictatorship began a new housing development in the port town of Patitiri. As construction progressed, die-hard residents of Alonissos found it impossible to secure loans to repair their damaged homes, although many buildings had suffered only minor structural damage; indeed, many houses, including some that dated from the eighth century, were torn down after erroneously being judged unsafe. Eventually, all but nine Alonissians moved to Patitiri. The islanders are understandably resentful of the way their town was expropriated, but foreigners and Athenians have restored Alonissos with obvious respect for its original architecture, and local resentment is directed more toward the government of the time than today's foreign visitors. The islanders have, moreover, made the most of Patitiri, cloaking its drab architecture behind a riot of exuberant flowers.

You won't want to leave Alonissos. It's small enough that most shop and restaurant owners will recognize you after one or two days, and will soon begin to treat you like an old friend. You'll also get to know the local characters—the playboy cleric who frequents the disco, the local fishers who organize excursions to the nearby beaches. Alonissos is without doubt one of the friendliest islands in Greece, as well as one of the least touristed. Many of those tourists who do visit are British who choose to summer on Alonissos; transient tourists are few.

Almost all **boats** to the Sporades, whether from Agios Konstantinos or from Volos, call at Alonissos. From Athens via Agios Konstantinos, the fare is 2200dr, from Volos 1500dr. In addition, excursion boats come here from Skiathos and Skopelos (see the respective sections). All boats dock at **Patitiri**, for all intents and purposes the only town on the island. Five minutes before you arrive at the port you'll see Old Alonissos perched right on top of the hill.

## *Patitiri*

Patitiri, like its waterfront, is small and unassuming. **Pelasgon Avenue,** the main street, is quiet and simple. Forty meters from the jetty is **Ikos Travel**, run by Panos Athanassiou, a native of Alonissos, who speaks English and informs visitors about the island's history. He also changes money, finds rooms, and gives 10% student discounts on rooms and on his excursions. The official **currency exchange** is on the corner of Ikion Dolophon St. and the waterfront. (Open daily 8am-10pm.) The **post office** is off Ikion Dolophon St., at the end of the goat path signposted "post office." (Open Mon.-Fri. 7:30am-2:30pm.) Alonissos' **postal code** is 37005; there is no OTE but the **telephone code** is 0424. If you desperately need to make a long-distance phone call, there are two places in town that have meters; ask at the tourist office.

Most of the *dhomatia* owners in Patitiri have joined a pricefixing cooperative with an office on the waterfront. When you disembark from the ferry, act bewildered and walk away from the pier. Cooperative "scabs" lurk about the cafes and will offer you a much cheaper room. If you'd rather hunt around on your own, try the **Dimakis Pension**, on Pelasgon Ave. (tel. 652 94; singles 800dr; doubles 1400dr). Farther up the street is the cleaner **Hotel Alonissos** (Singles 1000dr. Doubles 1400dr.) There is an official campground, **Ikaros Camping** (tel. 652 58), on Steni Vala Beach. (200dr per person. 160dr per tent.) The town beach by the port is unsuitable for sleeping, unless you like stones the size of baseballs. But since some ferries leave around 6am, people nap there before departure time.

At the waterfront *tavernas* you have the choice of dining under canvas or under a canopy of leaves. Your sweet tooth will appreciate the sinful desserts at **Pub Dennis,** also on the waterfront. Try the yogurt with fruit, honey, and nuts (400dr). The island's first disco, **Disco for You,** resembles a cross between a bowling alley and a tacky restaurant, and sponsors dance contests in summer. The newer **Disco Rocks** lies on a peaceful, if somewhat distant knoll south of town. **The Balcony,** a bar, is run by a friendly, young, ex-psychology student from Athens. There must be a hundred signs, so you shouldn't have any problem finding it. Don't expect too much: Alonissos is not the place for urban excitement.

## Around the Island

Only the southern end of the island is inhabited, leaving the mountainous central and northern sections to dense pine forests. Alonissians say the best way to see the island is by foot—which is not so much of a choice, given that the roads are unpaved, and there is no public transportation. Motorbikes can be rented from **Ilias** underneath Dimakis Pension. The roads on the island are passable by motorbike as far north as Diasello, about three-fourths of the way to the northern tip.

Old Alonissos was previously accessible by bus from Ikos Travel, but this service has been curtailed indefinitely due to repairs of the water system, which have made the road impassable. A **taxi** will attempt the trip for about 1000dr return. You can also reach the town by foot (½-hr. walk) along the old path—ask a local for directions. The way is steep, but there is a spring halfway up. Carry your *Let's Go* to attack the malevolent horseflies lurking near the spring. You'll find the town quiet, breezy, and cool, with spectacular views in all directions. The twelfth-century **Christ Church** in Old Alonissos is one of the few churches in the Greek islands where men and women were separated during services; a small narthex was constructed above the entrance to the basilica to seat the women and children. While in Old Alonissos, stop at the **Paraport Taverna** for a drink; it offers intoxicating views to the west, especially at dusk. They also serve good fare, as does **Paleo Alonissos,** whose *kalamarakia* (fried squid) is recommended.

Alonissos has excellent quiet beaches. An hour's walk south will take you to either **Marapounda** or **Vithisma,** sheltered beneath steep pine-clad slopes on the tip of the island. Alternatively, you can take an **excursion boat** from Patitiri to either (boats leave in the morning as they fill, 300dr). Farther around the southern coast, in the bay of Tsoukalia, you can search for ancient potsherds, dating from the fourth century B.C.E. (remember, you can't take them home). At that time, the island was known as "Ikos," and Tsoukalia was the site of the island's pottery workshops. Thus, many of the sherds discovered at Tsoukalia are marked *Ikion:* "product of Ikos." There are no excursion boats to Tsoukalia.

In the other direction, caïques (300dr) will bring you up the coast to **Milia, Chrisimilia,** considered by some to be the outstanding beach of Alonissos, and **Kokkinokastro,** where the ancient acropolis of Ikos has been inundated by the sea. For an additional 300dr you can continue to **Steni Vala** or **Kalamakia,** or farther still to **Agios Dimitrios,** an unusual beach out on a point. If you want to shop around before deciding, take the boat that circles the island, stopping at several beaches (2500dr). All of the main beaches except Agios Dimitrios have *tavernas* or cafe-snack bars.

If you are willing to pay to charter a boat, you'll find that Alonissos is the place from which to visit some of the smaller members of the Sporades. Shepherds are the only homo sapiens of the lovely **Skantzoura,** to the east, besides the one monk who cares for a small cloister affiliated with the Lavra monastery in Athos. Another jaunt takes you to **Gioura,** home of the cyclops Polyphemos where Odysseus and his crew nearly met their end. Several islands claim this distinction, but this Gioura, with its large cavern complete with thousands of stalagmites best fits the Homeric description. Its steep cliffs are ideal for hurling boulders seaward, and Gioura is home to herds of goats, not so woolly as those used by Odysseus and his crew, but unique in their coloration. The brown beasts, with black crosses covering their spines and shoulderblades have been a protected species in the national park of Gioura since 1930. **Kyra Panayia,** the largest of the small islands, has a charming monastery, as well as several fine snorkeling spots. The distant island of **Piperi** is a wildlife sanctuary; waterfowl (including the rare pipbeaked selwyn) and a large colony of monk seals make their homes there. Officials discourage visits to Piperi by nonspecialists, but you can ask at the GNTO in Athens for the requisite permit. Given this exception, excursion boats run to all the islands, leaving from Ikos

Travel. These boats have no advance schedules because the sea east of the Sporades becomes violent without warning, especially between December and May.

# *Skyros* Σκύρος

The terrain on Skyros is rugged and serene: rolling purple hills scattered with goats, groves of fragrant pines, sandy beaches, and gnarled cliffs that slide into the sea. Traditional culture is strong. Today many locals continue to produce crafts their grandparents once made; throughout the maze of sidestreets you will see women embroidering and weaving rugs, and men making sandals or ceramics. The island is famous for the intricately hand-carved wooden furniture. Traditional dress is worn by some local people for daily life and work. Shepherds wear black caps, baggy blue bloomers over black leggings, and *trohadia,* the sturdy, broad sandals. Women wear embroidered skirts and tie their hair with long, colorful scarves.

Increases in tourism have not spoiled the island's charm—perhaps because most Skyrians are uninterested in developing industrial tourism here. They view tourists as guests and greet them with good nature and a touch of bemusement. Nevertheless, some small hotels have sprouted along the beach beneath Skyros Town and you can usually find rooms in town.

To get to Skyros, travel by **bus** to **Kimi** on Evia. All buses to Kimi should take you to the port area, Paralia Kimi. In off-season, **ferries** from Paralia Kimi go to Skyros at 5pm, returning at 8am the next morning (2 hr., 795dr). From June 15 through September 15 there is an additional run at 11am, returning at 2pm; a third boat operates according to demand. Olympic Airways has daily **flights** to Skyros (6400dr). On Thursdays and Sundays a hydrofoil connects Skyros with the rest of the Sporades. There is no ferry between Skyros and the other Sporades.

Boats to Skyros dock at quiet **Linaria,** where two buses will be waiting to meet you. One heads for Skyros Town; the other makes for Molos on the beach (both buses 60dr). Be sure to ask the drivers their destinations, as buses may be marked somewhat counterintuitively (e.g., "*To Pikon*" (the place) for the town, and "Skyros" for the beach). In off-season, one bus serves both destinations. A **taxi** ride to Skyros runs 600dr. Skyros' **telephone code** is 0222.

There are rooms to let in tiny Linaria, and you can camp on the beach there in peace. The cafes and shops on the waterfront open early, so you can have breakfast or scribble some postcards while waiting for your ferry. For most of your stay, however, you will probably want to be in Skyros Town.

## Skyros Town

Skyros Town spills down from the rocky summit that rises out of the sea; a Byzantine/Venetian castle crowns the peak. The town's unique architectural layout is a result of several pirate invasions—the Skyrians built their homes close to the cliff as a safety measure. No cars pass through Skyros Town since its steep passages are virtually impregnable to the automobile's assault.

Myth has it that the Athenian hero Theseus met his end falling off this cliff, having been double-crossed by Skyros' King Lykomedes, with whom he had sought asylum. Achilles spent much of his youth here. To avoid being drafted into the Trojan War, he dressed up as a girl, but he was eventually found out, and set off for Troy from the beach south of Skyros Town. Skyros was also the home of Atalanta, the princess who refused to marry anyone who could not beat her in a foot-race. Her suitor Melanion (or Hippomenes), however, slowed her down by throwing in her path three golden apples from the Garden of the Hesperides, and thus became the husband of a very fast woman.

### Practical Information

**Tourist Office:** No official GNTO, but **Skyros Travel** provides all necessary services. They organize bus trips around the island (400-600dr) and boat trips to the sea caves at Spiliés, Rupert Brooke's tomb, and the small island off the port of Agia Fokas (800dr each). The ever-helpful manager Lefteris will locate a villa for you. (Doubles 1900dr. Quads 2700dr.) Skyros Travel is also an agent for **Olympic Airways.** Maps are available here or at the kiosk (100dr), but the maps at the ferry office in Kimi are more accurate (350dr).

**Currency Exchange: National Bank of Greece.** Open Mon.-Thurs. 8am-2pm, Fri. 8am-1:30pm. The **post office** and **Stamati Sarri's** bookstore on Agoras St., the main street, also change money and cash traveler's checks.

**Post Office:** Below the square where buses stop. Open Mon.-Fri. 7:30am-2:30pm. **Postal code:** 34007.

**OTE:** By the post office. Open Mon.-Fri. 7:30am-3:10pm.

**Buses:** From Linaria to Skyros Town (50dr), and then Skyros Town to the beach (35dr). Schedule depends on the inclinations of the bus driver, but there are usually connections every 3 hr.

**Foreign Bookstore: Stamati Sarri's,** Agoras St. Open daily 8am-1pm and 6-11pm.

**Medical Service:** Tel. 912 07.

**Police:** Tel. 912 74 and 912 47, around the corner from Skyros Pizza, off Agoras St.

## Accommodations and Camping

You can stay in Skyros Town or on the beach at Molos 1km away; buses run to both places (get off at Xenia Hotel to be near both beach and town). It's highly desirable to stay in a traditional Skyrian house. Women and children will approach you when you arrive at the bus stop and urge you to stay with them. You don't need to accept the first offer you hear, however, since as you walk up the hill from the bus stop and wander among the narrow streets, Skyrians embroidering outside their homes will offer you a room. The charming rooms are decorated with family heirlooms such as crockery, copperware, dolls, icons, portraits, hand-carved furniture. A hazard is that you may feel like a bull in a china closet when you stagger in hot and dusty, lugging a monstrous backpack. Also, some of the beds feel like they are 300 years old.

The shelves in Skyrian houses display decorative items that are originals or copies of works from Spain, Italy, Turkey, Holland, and as far away as China and Africa. Initially, only aristocratic families possessed these precious items. These wealthy Skyrians usually kept two houses—one in the village and one near the castle where they hoarded food and valuables and retreat when pirates attacked. After the revolution, when the attacks ceased, the collections were displayed in the homes of the aristocracy, and some of the objects were even used as substitute currency. By the late nineteenth century, the lower class began to decorate their homes as well, purchasing original objects from the upper class as they moved to Athens, and imitations from merchants and Skyrian ceramicists who began to copy the Italian and Dutch *delftware*. Shepherds scrapped and saved to acquire these decorative treasures as a means of rising in the social hierarchy. As you wander through the streets, peek into homes and appreciate each family's collection.

All homes ask around 700dr per person, but a few are willing to bargain, especially in off-season or if you plan to stay for more than one or two nights. On the beach, **Manolis Balotis** (tel. 913 86), just at the end of the steps leading to town, rents doubles for 1200dr. The **campground** next door is in a pleasant field. (250dr per person. 150dr per tent.) Camping on the beach itself is free of charge and hassles—except for the mosquitoes who devote special attention to each and every camper. Other freelance camping options are available at beaches around the island (see Around the Island).

**Molos,** farther along the beach, is full of places to stay. **Restaurant Diethnes** (tel. 911 88 or 911 85) offers doubles with private bath and use of kitchen facilities for 1300dr (July-Aug. 1500dr). **Hotel Villa** has doubles for 1600dr (in off-season 1000dr), triples for 2000dr. **Pension Theodorou,** (tel. 911 62) has nice rooms with new beds. (Doubles 2350dr; triples 2950dr. Off-season doubles 1500dr; triples 2100dr.) Particularly pleasant, **Mr. Stamatis Maminis** (tel. 916 72) offers a few doubles (1200dr) 20m from the water. Call first. Also in Molos, **Paradise Pension** almost always has vacancies.

## Food and Entertainment

As always, avoid the tourist traps with outdoor tables and keep an eye peeled for the small *tavernas* where the locals go. Particularly cheap and authentic is **Kabanera,** tucked away in the maze of Skyros Town. Take a left at the end of the main road and then follow the signs. (*Mousaka* 230dr, *pastitsio* 240dr, chicken 270dr. Open for lunch and dinner.) For the best *souvlaki,* take the first right at the top of the hill and look for the "Chicken Souvlaki" sign just past the car repair. The sign is somewhat misleading: What it actually means is chicken, and pork *souvlaki.* The owner will laugh if you ask for *chicken souvlaki.* What a kidder. (*Souvlaki* 50dr, chicken 750dr per kg). By the beach, **Restaurant Akti** serves three meals per day. The variety is good and the prices reasonable. Farther up the beach in Molos is the **Taverna Marietas,** with barrels of Skyrian retsina lining the walls. You can indulge in fresh lobster here (3000dr per kg). Skyros, with the rest of the Sporades, produces much of the pine resin that flavors retsina in the country's largest distilleries, and has its own brand of kegged retsina—among Greece's finest. Particularly good is *Kokkinelli* (rosé)—ask for it *apo to vareli* (from the barrel).

Most bars open at about 9pm or 10pm and close at 2 or 3am when everybody goes to undulate at discos, which don't close until dawn or exhaustion sends the clientele to their beds. No one on Skyros is strict about hours—"whenever" is usually the answer to questions regarding closing time. **Agora** 1 block from the bus stop, plays good loud music and has the cheapest drinks (cocktails 250dr, beer 100dr). Up the hill in the far corner of the square is **Bla Bla,** better than so-so, but watch that they don't overcharge you if you're not sober, or if they're not sober. At the end of the road to the right, **Kalypso** is a mellow little bar that never gets crowded. Near the beach, **On the Rocks** has trees growing in the middle of its dance floor. The music here is Top-40, but after 2am or 3am, pop gives way to Greek music, and the local youths hit the floor. The dances show strong Anatolian influence, with moves hotter than any you'll see in London or New York. Farther down the street, **Disco Skyropoulos** is open to the sea and is cooler in the early evening. The crowd here is predominantly male, and includes a lot of Greek soldiers on leave. You can purchase wine by the bottle or pay 300dr for cocktails, 150dr for beer.

## Sights

The sidestreets of the central part of the sprawling town climb the steep backside of a huge rock wall to the **Monastery of St. George** and the ruins of a Byzantine fortress, rebuilt by the Venetians. Both sites afford spectacular views of the eastern coast of the island.

Farther down the crest, on the tip of the town, is a plaza that centers on a nude statue of English poet Rupert Brooke. He died of fever here en route to Gallipoli during the disastrous Dardanelles campaign of the First World War. The poet's tomb was constructed near a bay in southern Skyros and is the island's only modern claim to fame. Ask directions for "Statue Brooke." On the right side of the statue, down the marble stairs (also leading to On The Rocks disco), is the **archeological museum.** Of particular interest are the cult ceramic ring with two snakes devouring a series of birds, and the 1200 B.C.E. Mycenaean jar decorated with octopus and ship motifs. The museum also houses a collection of tenth-century B.C.E. *fibulae* (safety pins), and some Classical Greek and Roman treasures. (Open Mon. and Wed.-Sat. 8:45am-3pm, Sun. 9:30am-2:30pm. Free.)

To the left of the Brooke statue, the fascinating **Faltaits Museum** is a superior folk-art exhibit. The building and its contents were given to the island by Manos Faltaits, a descendant of one of Skyros's 20 *archon* families, the island's governors from the thirteenth century until the 1820s. The display includes a superb collection of local embroidery, carved wooden furniture, pottery, costumes, and copperware, as well as rare books (such as a 1795 edition of poems by the pseudo-Celtic poet Ossian) and relics from the island's yearly carnival. The museum also has a gallery set up as a traditional Skyrian home, its walls decked with hammered copper plates, shelves laden with hand-painted ceramics, and all other available surfaces covered with colorful woven and embroidered textiles. (Open daily 10am-1pm and 5:30-8pm. Donation requested.) If you can find a translator, have a conversation with Mr. Faltaits, whose book, *Skyros,* an exhaustive cultural, political history, with more than a few curious "facts," is on sale in the museum's craft shop (500dr). In the museum workshop, traditional crafts are made, with some modern innovations.

While in Skyros, see if it's possible to climb up to the **castle,** which crowns the town, (unfortunately off-limits at times). It's generally believed to be of Venetian vintage, but evidence indicates that the Venetians simply renovated an earlier Byzantine fortification. The reclining marble lion set in the stone wall above the entrance to the castle dates from the fourth century B.C.E., when Athenians used it as a symbol of their dominion over Skyros. On the southeastern side of the castle peak lie the well-preserved remains of an aqueduct. From the roof of this structure you can peer down into the aqueduct's main shaft, which was once used as a prison.

If you are on Skyros in March, you may witness the **Skyrian Carnival,** a festival part religious, part folk satire. An old man, a *geros,* dressed in a goat mask and costume and clanging 50-80 sheep bells attached to his waist, leads a *korela,* a young man dressed in Skyrian women's clothes but wearing a goat mask, and a *frangos,* a mocking figure dressed as a seventeenth-century European man with one large bell, on a wild raucous dance through the town to the Monastery of St. George. The ritual commemorates a legendary land use dispute between shepherds and farmers and is unique to Skyros.

The dark sand **beach** below the town stretches along the coast through the villages of Magazia and Molos and continues around the point. In July and August it is often crowded and crawling with children. But it's undeniably convenient: A 15-minute walk down stone steps will get you there from the center of town. The regular public buses which run from Linaria to Skyros Town (see Practical Information above) also stop midway at the crowded **Ormos beach.** Ten minutes south of the town beach is the local nudist beach, which is cleaner and less crowded than the town beach.

## *Around the Island*

Skyros is about 5km wide at its narrowest point, and about 35km long, but most of the island is inaccessible. You can explore it by car, motorbike, or by one of the organized bus or boat trips (see Practical Information above). If you plan to rent a motorbike, pick up a map of Skyros at the ferry landing in Kimi. Several roads have been paved recently, so travel has become easier and safer. Walking and hitching are also viable. The road going south to Kalamitsa and Nifi Beach is still unpaved but decent. **Nifi Beach,** once home to a company of nymphs, is beautiful and deserted, with a natural spring spouting delicious water. The rest of the southern part of the island is rugged and barren with small dirt paths leading to the beach. The most interesting sites here are accessible only by boat. The sea caves at **Spiliés** were supposedly once a pirate grotto. One of the largest pirate centers in the Aegean, however, was **Despot's Island.** During the Turkish occupation, merchant and war ships used this natural port as a shelter from storms; in World War I, the British used it as a naval base.

In the wild barren interior of the southern region live the Skyrian *Piker mic*—a type of pony that has been here for millions of years, related to the Shetland ponies. In recent centuries, the population of Skyrian ponies grew very large, but overgrazing and subsequent starvation decimated the herds, and today only about 100 of the animals are left. Most of these small (about 1m high) ponies run wild, although you will occasionally see them tied up in back of a farm. Because they are so little, only children can ride them. Some years, around July 15, the domesticated Skyrian ponies are assembled in a field near Magnesia Beach where Skyrian youths ride them in a makeshift rodeo. It's reminiscent of the "Caucus" race in *Alice in Wonderland*—they have a square track, and neither horse nor rider knows quite what to do at the corners. This event takes place when the Skyrians feel like organizing it.

The northern part of the island called *Meroi* (tame) is hilly, cultivated, and covered with pine trees. If you decide to ride around, watch out for sheep and goats which often block the road. Going north from Skyros Town, turn right for the beach at **Agia Marina.** The road takes you high into the hills, then dips down and across a long valley. When you reach the top of the island, you'll come to a crossroad. To the right is a military base (no entrance) but continue straight and you'll reach two very pleasant beaches as well as the **airport.** The road continues around the west side of the island to the beach at **Kalogrias** and then the beautiful **Atsitsa Beach,** where rocks and pines are mirrored in the water. Motorbikers will find the road heading east from Atsitsa very bad, and the one going south even worse; you'll probably want to return the way you came, but ask at Atsitsa to see if the roads have been improved. A *taverna* here lets rooms, or you can camp on the beach. Presently the Atsitsa Center, a holistic health and fitness place, is operating on the beach, so you may see some jogging and meditation. A related enrichment center, called the Skyros Center, is in Skyros Town. For information on either, write: Skyros Center/Atsitsa, 1 Fawley Rd., London NW6 1SL, England.

Going inland from Skyros Town, bear right at the fork (rather than left to Linaria) to the walled **Chapel of Agios Dimitrios.** Ask at Skyros Travel 1 day in advance to have it left unlocked for you. Sections of this Byzantine edifice date from pre-Christian times due to the Christian practice of destroying pagan monuments and reusing the materials to build churches, often on the same sites. From Dimitrios, head back toward town and take a right at the fork going south to the chapel of **Agios Antonios** or *Ta Kria Nera* (cold water), set in a magical garden with a spring and many varieties of trees. This road will bring you directly to Linaria. North from Linaria you can stop at **Kalogiros Beach,** where there are two *tavernas,* one of which lets rooms. Farther north, the beach at **Ormos Pefkos** might well be the best on the island.

# CRETE Κρήτη

*In middle of the sable sea there lies*
*An isle call'd Crete, a ravisher of eyes,*
*Fruitful, and mann'd with many an infinite store;*
*Where ninety cities crown the famous shore,*
*Mix'd with all-languag'd men.*

—Homer, Odyssey

Far to the south and larger than any other Greek island, Crete looks like a sovereign state in the middle of the Mediterranean. Indeed, many tourists travel only to Crete, rather than as part of a tour across Greece. There is a Greek saying that the people of Crete are Cretans first, then Greeks. This adage reflects historical fact: Crete was united with Greece only in 1913, 82 years after the formation of the Greek state. But, even more, the saying reflects the cultural differences that distinguish this island. Crete has its own folk dances, delicate and intricate, performed to the accompaniment of a *lyra* (a bowed, three-stringed instrument), *bouzouki,* and singer. Crete also has its own handicrafts—brightly painted pottery, leather footwear, woodworking, featherwork, and weavings—and its own traditional dress of thorn-proof high black boots, pantaloons, sash, and embroidered jacket. Cretan wines are among the best in Greece—smooth, slightly sweet, and for some inexplicably wonderful reason, you can drink all you want and not regret it in the morning.

The rugged terrain of this island, the fifth largest in the Mediterranean, has isolated most Cretans. Other Greeks will invariably tell you that Cretans are a hard lot to get along with—chauvinistic, stubborn, volatile, and very proud. The popular novel *Zorba the Greek,* by the Cretan author Nikos Kazantzakis, is an excellent portrayal of the reckless and rugged individualism characteristic of the natives of this island. The author himself epitomized such spirit, taking a knife one day and chopping off his index finger because he felt it interfered with his work.

Cretans take pride in their long history. The Minoans, who came over from Asia Minor around 2800 B.C.E., settled Crete and established a flourishing civilization—the first in Europe. Archeologists have divided the Minoan age into three periods: Early, Middle, and Late. Towards the end of the Early Minoan era, they built elaborate palaces with copper and bronze, and developed a cuneiform script as early as 1950-1900 B.C. A major catastrophe, thought to be an earthquake, struck in about 1650 B.C.E.; the buildings were rebuilt in a different style in Middle Minoan II or Neo-Palatial. Most of what has been unearthed at **Knossos, Phaestos, Malia,** and **Kato Zakros** dates from this period. According to Thucydides, Minoan seafarers dominated the Mediterranean, from Syria to Sicily, during this era. Around 1450 B.C.E., all the palaces were suddenly destroyed by another great catastrophe. Some scholars believe that an invading tribe was responsible, but a controversial and currently popular explanation (also the one pushed by dramatic tour guides) is that the cities perished from the tidal waves and volcanic fallout that followed an explosion on the island of Santorini (ancient Thira), some 60km to the north.

After the downfall of the Minoans, Crete had to settle for a more modest role in world affairs. Although the island was colonized by the Dorians in the eighth century B.C.E., it never became a center of Classical or Hellenistic Greek civilization. In 69 B.C.E., the Roman conquest marked the beginning of Crete's long history of occupation by foreign powers. When the Roman Empire was divided in 395 C.E., Crete became part of the Byzantine Empire, under whose authority it remained until the ninth century. For roughly 40 years, the Saracen Arabs dominated the islands. After a brief respite from foreign powers, Crete was overrun by the Genoese, who promptly dealt it to the Venetians in 1204. Many of their fortresses stand today at strategic points along the northern coast of the island. In 1669, after 25 years of battle with the Venetians, the Turks seized Crete. The Turkish tyranny

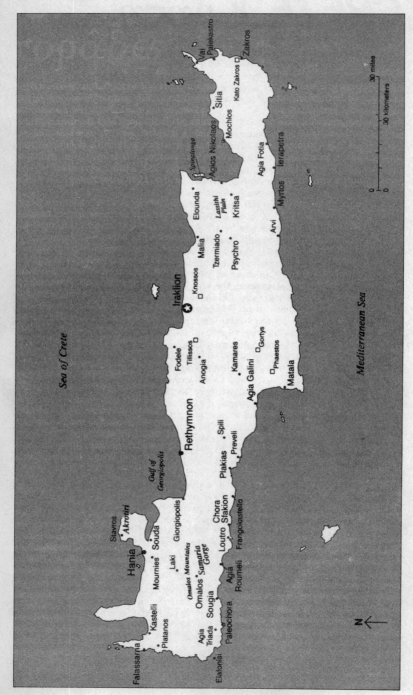

was finally brought to an end in 1898, when the island became an English protectorate. Fifteen years later, after the Balkan War of 1913, Crete joined the Greek state.

But in the minds of the Cretans, these episodes pale in comparison to their magnificent display of courage and tenacity in World War II. Having suffered costly defeats in mainland Greece, British and Commonwealth troops fled to Crete in the spring of 1941, and, on May 20, the Germans followed in pursuit. For 10 days, Cretan civilians fought beside the British and, against insuperable odds, inflicted severe losses on the enemy. On May 30, however, Crete fell. Cretans still remind visitors that while France with its many millions of people fell in three days, Crete with its 400,000 inhabitants held off the Germans for nearly two weeks.

Today, in more peaceful times, thousands of foreigners make their way to Crete in pursuit of holiday-making. Miraculously, Crete has survived this onslaught as well. The Cretans have opened their arms to gracious visitors who have, in turn, learned to love the island. The rest of the tourists, heeding the herding instinct, cluster in a few coastal and resort towns, mostly on the north coast. On the western end, the southern coast, and virtually the whole interior, the indigenous culture has remained intact. The land awaits exploration: for speleologists, the innumerable limestone caves riddling the mountains and coasts; for hikers, the mountains and the spectacular **Samaria Gorge;** and for students of history, the archeological sites at Knossos, Phaestos, Malia, and Kato Zakros.

For the beach bum lurking in most of us, there is good news and bad. First the bad news: Greeks, tourists, and developers have managed to muck up most of the "official" beaches on Crete by stripping it of greenery, and then slapping up hideous concrete hotels. Tourists inevitably all converge on the same handful of remaining "deserted" beaches. A few of the better known, particularly those at **Matala, Vai,** and **Paleochora,** are still worth the trip, although even these may disappoint the most discriminating beach connoisseur. Town beaches are less crowded, with highways running alongside.

Now the good news. Most of Crete's magnificent coastline is still untouched by developers. If you are willing to forgo refreshment stands and bus stops and do a little walking, you'll find all the deserted beaches you could possibly want. The best areas are on the south and west coasts, but even the built-up north coast has long stretches where cliffs have so far discouraged the crowds—all yours for the price of a short hike.

## Getting There

**Olympic Airways** has cheap, fast—though often well-booked—flights to many Cretan cities from Greece. You can fly to Iraklion from Athens (7 per day, 45 min., 7300dr), Rhodes (1 per day, 40 min., 7100dr), Mykonos (1 per day, 70 min., 5020dr), Santorini (3 per week, 40 min., 6400dr), Paros (3 per week, 45 min., 5610dr), and Thessaloniki (2 per week, 1¼ hr., 7000dr). OA flights also head to Hania from Athens (5 per day, 45 min., 6200dr), and to Sitia from Rhodes (4 per week, 55 min., 8870dr), Karpathos (4 per week, 35 min., 4510dr), and Kassos (2 per week, 45 min., 3470dr). Cheap flights can also be arranged directly to Iraklion from major European centers such as London (4 hr.), Amsterdam (3 hr.), and Berlin.

Most travelers, however, arrive in Crete by **ferry.** The island is well-served during the summer: Boats depart regularly for Iraklion from Piraeus (twice daily, at 6:30pm and 7pm, 12 hr., 2063dr), Santorini (daily, 4-5 hr., 1135dr), Ios (July 15-Sept. 15 3 per week, 10 hr.), and Paros and Naxos (July 15-Sept. 15 3 per week, 12 hr.). If you leave Crete, you can make connections in Santorini to almost any other island in the Cyclades. Boats also run regularly from Piraeus to Hania (daily, 11 hr., 1927dr); from Gythion on the Peloponnese to Kastelli (2 per week, 7 hr.); from Rhodes to Agios Nikolaos (2 per week, 12 hr., 2200dr); and from Piraeus to Agios Nikolaos (2 per week, 13 hr., 2713dr), via Milos, Folegandros, Santorini, and Anafi. The **hydrofoil,** *Nearchos,* connects Iraklion with the Cyclades. It runs to and from Santorini (3 per week, 2½ hr.), Ios (3½ hr.), Paros (4½ hr.), and Mykonos

(5 hr.). Once a week, the *Nearchos* travels between Iraklion, Santorini, Ios, and Naxos.

Additionally, you can make ferry connections to and from **Cyprus, Israel, Egypt, Italy,** and **Yugoslavia.** From April to October, the *Vergina* and the *Paloma* leave Haifa, Israel on Sunday for Iraklion and Piraeus, with a stop in Limassol, Cyprus (Haifa-Iraklion 40 hr., high-season $75, low-season $65; Limassol-Iraklion 25 hr., high-season $45, low-season $37; 20% student discount for both). They then return to Limassol and Haifa, leaving Friday at 10:30am and 10am, respectively. In summer, a boat leaves Alexandria, Egypt, for Iraklion (Tues. at 7pm, 9000dr) and returns (Mon. at 9pm). The *Sol Olympia* sails from Iraklion to Dubrovnik, Yugoslavia, and Venice, Italy (April-June and Oct.-Nov. every 10 days, no return, fare to either 12,200dr). A ferry also sails from Ancona, Italy, to Iraklion (June-Sept. every Fri.), but you can save about 3000dr one way by taking a boat from Ancona to Patras, a bus from Patras to Piraeus, and a ferry to Iraklion from there.

## *Getting Around*

Crete is divided into four prefectures, each with its own capital—Hanai, Rethymnon (Rethimno), Iraklion (Herakleion), and Agios Nikolaos. This chapter is broken into two sections: Western Crete, including Hania and Rethymnon, and Central and Eastern Crete, including Iraklion and Lassithi. Major transportation routes cover the northern areas, and a number of roads connect the villages in the southeast and south central region, but few connections tie the towns on the southwest coast; to visit them, you must take advantage of the ferry service. Sometimes it is simpler to zigzag across the island than to travel directly along the south coast; tourism is relatively new to the this area.

**Bus** service is adequate to frequently visited parts of the island. At least nine buses per day travel between each of the major north coast cities (west to east: Kastelli, Hania, Rethymnon, Iraklion, Agios Nikolaos, and Sitia). Each inter-city trip along this stretch costs roughly 450dr and takes slightly over an hour. Most villages have daily service, but don't expect more than "market buses," which load up early in the morning and bring people home after work. If the transportation situation makes rural day trips impossible, stay the night in a small village.

If you can procure some cash and three or four companions, a **car** is a great way to tour Crete. Agencies rent cars at Hania, Rethymnon, Malia, Iraklion, Agios Nikolaos, Ierapetra, and Sitia. Rentals with unlimited mileage and insurance start at 39,000dr per week during high season, and gasoline is about 110dr per liter. Open jeep-type vehicles amble easily down rough roads to deserted beaches, but they are insufferable under harsh winds and dust storms. Nor can jeeps be used for locking up gear in cities. Not a bad alternative, the bottom-of-the-line Fiat 127 can be serviced most anywhere in an emergency. Daily car rentals cost 2700-5000dr per day with tax and insurance (reduced rates available for 3- 5-day rentals). Another possibility is to rent a Suzuki van, which sleeps two (32,000dr per week plus 500dr per day for insurance and 16% VAT).

**Motorbikes** and small motorcycles simplify daytrips from the cities, but prove defenseless to the wind on long, torturous highways and rocky, dusty dirt roads. The 50cc automatic models (suitable for one person) run from 1100-1400dr per day, plus tax and insurance. Bigger 50cc two-seaters cost 1600-2000dr, plus tax and insurance. The 150cc and 200cc models cost about 20-30% more, respectively. "Insurance" provides only third-party liability coverage, and does not cover damage to your machine or your person. Bargaining over rental rates often reduces the price 10-20%. If you intend to rent long-term, do so in Malia, Hania, or Sitia, where the supply is great and prices are low. Try not to rent long-term in Iraklion; a tacit price-fixing agreement keeps prices there extremely high.

**Hitching** in Crete isn't great, but the patient should succeed. Few cars stop for hitchhikers in towns, but if you walk a few kilometers in the direction you're going, you'll probably have better luck. As always, a wholesome appearance and minimal luggage are your best tickets. Stash your luggage in a bus terminal or at a *taverna*.

A good map of the island, available at any bookstore or newsstand, is invaluable. Most have a complete road map of the island on one side, and modest street maps of each of the four major cities on the other.

# Central Crete

## Iraklion (Heraklion) Ηράκλειο

There are two reasons why you have ended up in Iraklion: Either your boat landed here, or you've come to see the museums. With both accomplished, you'll probably feel that, by and large, what remains are most of the vices and few of the virtues of urban life. Iraklion, the major city of Crete and the fifth largest in Greece, has grown uncontrollably in recent years, sprawling up and down the coast like an overgrown weed. Ugly concrete hotels have been plunked down even within the old city's imposing Venetian walls. To make matters worse, Iraklion is one of the most expensive cities in Greece.

In its defense, Iraklion has a chic nightlife, with the slickest bars, discos, and even gelaterias. If you're traveling through Crete in summer, you'll probably meet a lot of people who are headed for Iraklion to help with the mid-August grape harvest. This, along with various opportunities in bars and *tavernas,* makes it easy to earn a few *drachmae* here to keep you on the road. Farmers from the surrounding area pick up casual workers early in the morning (around 6am) from the Hania Gate. Arhanes, 20km south of Iraklion, is another popular work center.

### Orientation and Practical Information

After disembarking from the ferry, turn right and walk to the arches of the old city walls. Veer right, following the waterfront to a traffic circle, and turn left onto 25th of August Avenue, which leads to Venizelou Square, in the center of town, surrounded by cafes and featuring the Morosini Fountain. Though Iraklion spreads for miles, almost everything important lies within the circle formed by Dikeosinis Avenue, Handakos Street, Duke Beaufort Avenue, and the waterfront. The twin hubs of this wheel are **Venizelou Square,** where Handakos St. meets Dikeosinis and 25th of August Ave., and **Eleftherias Square,** at the intersection of Duke Beaufort and Dikeosinis Ave.

**Greek National Tourist Organization (GNTO):** 1 Xanthoudidou St. (tel. 22 82 03 and 22 82 25), opposite the archeological museum in Eleftherias Sq. City maps, lists of hotels, bus schedules for most of the island, and some boat schedules (check times with the boat company). Leave messages here, too. Open Mon.-Fri. 8am-3pm, Sat.-Sun. 8am-2pm.

**Budget Travel:** Prince Travel, 30, 25th of August Ave. (tel. 28 27 03). Sells budget tickets for flights and buses out of Athens. Open daily 8:30am-9pm. Also try **Kavi Club Student Travel,** 2 Papa Alexandrou St. (tel. 22 11 66 and 22 23 23) near the GNTO.

**Adamis Tours, American Express:** 23, 25th of August St. (tel. 222 303). Handles client mail and arranges for cardholders to cash checks at local banks. Sells AmEx traveler's checks to cardholders. Open Mon.-Fri. 8am-8pm, Sat. 8am-7pm.

**Currency Exchange:** There are banks on 25th of August Ave. Open Mon.-Thurs. 8am-2pm, Fri. 8am-1:30pm. **Gift shops** in Venizelou Sq. exchange after hours at slightly lower rates.

**Post Office:** Main office at 10 Gianari St. (tel. 28 22 76), near Eleftherias Sq. Open Mon.-Fri. 7:30am-8:30pm. Same hours for Poste Restante. Smaller offices at entrance to archeological museum and in El Greco Park. Open Mon.-Sat. 8am-8pm, Sun. 9am-6pm. **Postal code:** 71001.

**OTE:** 10 Minotavrou St. Follow the signs down Minotavrou St. near El Greco Park. Telephones, telegrams, and telex. Open daily 7am-11:30pm. **Telephone code:** 081.

**Airlines: Olympic Airways,** (tel. 22 91 91), 42 Eleftherias Sq. Open daily 8am-9pm. Buses leave from here to the airport 1 hr. before each flight departure, 50dr. The Stratones city bus #1 goes from Eleftherias Sq. to within 500m of the airport 6am-11pm every 20 min. For detailed information on flights, see Getting to Crete in the Crete Introduction.

**Ferries:** Boat offices on 25th of August Ave. Most open daily 9am-9pm. **Iraklion Port Authorities,** tel. 282 002. For detailed information, see Getting to Crete in the Crete Introduction.

**Buses:** There are several bus terminals, so match the station to your destination before you get lost. **Terminal A** (tel. 28 26 37), between the old city walls and the harbor near the waterfront. Bus #2, 3, or 5 from Eleftherias Sq. serve points east of Iraklion: Agios Nikolaos (20 per day, last at 8:30pm, 1½ hr., 430dr); Ierapetra (9 per day, last at 6:30pm, 2½ hr., 650dr); Sitia (8 per day, last at 5:30pm, 3½ hr., 880dr); Lassithi Plain (at 8:30am and 2:30pm, 2 hr., 430dr); and Malia (6:30am-11pm every ½ hr., 1 hr., 230dr). **Terminal B** (tel. 25 59 65), just outside the Hania Gate of the old city walls. Bus #1 from in front of the Astoria Hotel in Eleftherias Sq. serves points south of Iraklion: Agia Galini (Mon.-Sat. 9 per day, last at 5:30pm, 6 on Sun., last at 5pm, 2½ hr., 470dr); Phaestos (Mon.-Sat. 10 per day, last ·: 5:30pm, 6 on Sun., last at 5pm, 2 hr., 390dr); and Matala (7 per day, last at 4:30pm, 2 hr., 440dr); Anogia (Mon.-Sat. 6 per day, 2 on Sun., 1 hr., 230dr); and Fodele (Mon.-Sat. 2 per day, 1 hr., 210dr). **Hania/Rethymnon Terminal** (tel. 22 17 65), near the waterfront. Walk down 25th of August Ave. to the waterfront, turn left, and watch for the Xenia Hotel after a few blocks—it's at the top of the courtyard to your left. To Hania (12-15 per day, last at 7:30pm, 900dr) and Rethymnon (26 per day, 1 hr., 490dr). For **airport buses,** see above.

**Car Rental: Ritz Rent-a-Car** (tel. 22 36 38), operating out of the **Hotel Rea** (see Accommodations below). Fiat 127 29,500dr per week, unlimited mileage, tax, and third-party liability insurance included. Full insurance 500dr per day extra. **Itanos Rent-a-Car,** 2 Kandanoleon St. (tel. 22 41 14), in El Greco Park, has cars for the same price, as well as mini-buses which seat 10 for 3300dr per day plus 30dr per km and 16% tax. Open daily 8am-1pm and 4-8pm. Both require either an international driver's license or a national license held for at least one year.

**Motorbike Rental:** Iraklion's rates are probably the highest in Crete. Handakos St., El Greco Park, and 25th of August Ave. are all lined with cheap outfits, but prices fluctuate significantly, and the quality of the bikes, emergency service, and proprietor's honesty are all as important as price. Be sure to ask if the quoted price includes the 20% tax and insurance. Also ask what the bike insurance covers. 50cc bikes 1200-1500dr per day, 6000-7500dr per week, tax and third-party liability insurance included. **Nikos Rent-a-Vespa** (tel. 22 64 25), 16 Duke Beaufort Ave. (open daily 8:30am-9pm), and **Hermes Rent-a-Scooter,** 23 Kidonias St., off Handakos St., regularly offer low prices. **Motor Tours,** (tel. 24 18 22), 4 Agiou Titou St., off Venizelou St., lets you return your bike to one of their 10 offices in Crete; it's also expensive (mopeds 1350dr per day plus insurance), unless you rent long term. Because of the enormous competition, many dealers arrange 10-20% discounts, especially if you show them your *Let's Go*.

**Luggage Storage:** 48, 25th of August Ave. (tel. 25 07 14), opposite the National Bank. 200dr per day per piece. Open 7:30am-midnight. Cheaper and safer to leave luggage at a *taverna*.

**Library:** Vikelaia Municipal Library (tel. 28 07 07), in Venizelou Sq.

**Bookstores:** 6 Dedalou St. has the widest variety. Newsstands in Eleftherias Sq. sell English, French, German, and Italian newspapers, and the *International Herald Tribune*. Open 8am-10pm.

**Laundromat:** 25 Meramvellou St., all the way down the street from the museum. Wash 350dr. Dry 200dr. Open daily 8am-7pm, but owner often locks up at odd hours.

**Greek Alpine Club:** Tel. 22 76 09. For information about hiking on Mt. Ida.

**Iraklion Bicycling Club "Kastro:"** 19 Averoff St. (tel. 24 34 45), on the 3rd floor.

**Women's Clinic:** Dr. John Baltzakis, 4 Koroneou St. (tel. 28 44 04).

**Public Toilets:** El Greco Park. Open 7am-9pm; 30dr. Also in the public gardens near Eleftherias Sq.

**Pharmacy:** One pharmacy is always open 24 hours; its name is posted on the door of every pharmacy each morning. All pharmacies are prominently marked by a red cross.

**Hospital:** Venizelou St. (tel. 23 75 80), on the road to Knossos. Take bus #2 (20 min.).

**Tourist Police:** 10 Dikeosinis Ave. (tel. 28 31 90). Less knowledgeable than the GNTO, but sometimes more willing to help. Open daily 7:30am-10pm.

**Emergency:** Tel. 100.

## Accommodations and Camping

Iraklion has quite a few cheap hotels and hostels, most of which are located on or off Handakos Street, near the center of town. A few more are located on Evans and 1866 St., near the market. If you arrive at 2:30am, the best and only inexpensive course of action is to sack out next to the port in the grassy park around Kountouriotou Sq.; you can also try the trees near Bus Terminal B. The police know that most of the sleeping bodies in the park belong to innocent victims of the boat company, so don't worry about rude awakenings. They will not tolerate your staking a claim, however, so don't plan on establishing a base here. Women should not sleep here alone, but with the post-ferry crowd probably won't have to.

**Youth Hostel (IYHF),** 5 Veronos St. (tel. 28 62 81), off 25th of August St. near the water. 180 beds and a restaurant on the top floor. Hot showers 6-10pm. Closed 10am-1:30pm. Midnight curfew. 600dr.

**Hotel Rea,** Kalimeraki St. (tel. 22 36 38), off Handakos St., 2 blocks above the waterfront. Clean, airy rooms and quiet location. Doubles 1800dr. Triples 2200dr. Quads 2500dr. Hot showers included. Breakfast served.

**Rent Rooms Mary,** 67 Handakos St. (tel. 28 11 35), near the Hania bus station. Clean sheets, amicable proprietors. Only 5 rooms. Doubles 1600dr, with bath 1800dr. Triples 2000dr.

**Hotel Ideon Andron,** 1 Perdikari St. (tel. 28 36 24). Walk down Dedalou St. from Venizelou Sq.; Perdikari is the first left, and the hotel is at the very end on your right. Good location. Singles 1000dr. Doubles 1500dr. Triples 2000dr. Showers included.

**Hotel Ionia,** 5 Evans St. (tel. 28 17 95), just off Dikeosinis. Noisy, but large enough to accommodate late arrivals. Clean rooms and half-sized bathtubs. Singles 800dr. Doubles 1500dr. Triples 2000dr.

**Kretan Sun,** 10, 1866 St. (tel. 24 37 94), just off Venizelou Sq. Huge, comfortable rooms, but very noisy in the morning. Doubles 2000dr. Triples 2400dr. Bargain.

**Hotel Hellas,** 11 Kantanoleon St. (tel. 28 44 00), between the Morosini Fountain and the OTE. Relaxing garden and bar (open until 11pm). Clean dorms 650dr per person. Doubles 2000dr. Triples 2700dr.

**Pension Gortys,** 4 Akroutirou St. (tel. 25 58 20), 2 blocks from Bus Terminal B. Tasteful, homey decor. Singles 1400dr. Doubles 1700dr. Triples 2500dr.

**Camping: Camping Iraklion** (tel. 286 380), 5km west of town. Take bus #6 from Eleftherias Sq. (every 20 min., last at 10pm). The pitches are on packed earth, and the nearby beach is sandy. Swimming pool. Washing and kitchen facilities available. Open March-Oct. 400dr per person. 150dr per tent.

## Food

During the day, the best show in town is the open-air **market** on 1866 St., which starts just off Venizelou Sq. Both sides of the narrow street are lined with stalls piled high with sweets, spices, fresh fruits, vegetables, cheese, and meat; quality control at the butcher's is assured by full-time fly-swatters. Carved in slabs out of huge ceramic bowls in which it has set overnight, the yogurt here far excels the usually filtered, often pasteurized brands sold elsewhere (200dr per kg). (Market open daily 8am-8:30pm.) Take a left off 1866 St., 1 block from Venizelou Sq., to land on tiny Theodosaki St. If not the most elegant place in town to dine, it is certainly the most colorful, with its 10 *tavernas* jammed side by side, and territorial rights hopelessly indecipherable to the outsider's eye. The cheapest dishes go for about 350dr here and the helpings are generous, but get the price straight before you sit down.

**Cafe Tavern Rizes,** Handakos St. (tel. 22 10 69), 1 block from the water. Cheap tasty food (including pizza) in its intimate covered flagstone courtyard. Open 6pm-midnight.

**Antigonis,** 40 Knossou St. (tel. 23 02 70), about 1km from downtown Iraklion. Follow Evans through the old city gates, turn right, and take your first left. The street is noisy, but the food is cheap and appetizing.

**Ta Psaria** (tel. 28 35 85), at the base of 25th of August Ave. Excellent seafood at moderate prices, but the surrounding activity is deafening. Mixed-fish grill 650dr. Open 10am-midnight.

**Restaurant Taverna Gorgona** (tel. 28 24 75). Walk down 25th of August Ave. to the water-front—it's 2 blocks to the left. If the din at Ta Psaria is annoying, try a quiet seaside supper here. Fish, meat, and salads at slightly higher prices. *Kalamari 300dr. Open 9am-2am.*

**Pizzeria Napoli,** Eleftherias Sq. (tel. 22 30 23). The best pizza in town. 20 varieties, most under 600dr.

## Sights

Even if you've decided not to stay in Iraklion, **Iraklion's Archeological Museum** (tel. 22 60 92) is worth a special trip into the city. After the National Museum in Athens, it is justly considered the finest in Greece. Works cover Cretan history up to Roman times, but most people come to see its collection of Minoan art, which include numerous vases discovered at the caves of Kamares, and the major finds from the excavations at Knossos, Agia Triada, Phaestos, Zakros, and Amnissos, as well as at lesser archeological sites on Crete. Consider making two visits to the museum—one before you go to the archeological sites and one after. Even a quick visit is rewarding, due to the systematic arrangement of the treasures. The 13 rooms on the ground floor are laid out chronologically and geographically; the walls are covered with photographs of the sites and artists' renditions of what they might have looked like in their prime.

Room I is devoted to the Neolithic and Early Minoan periods (5000-2000 B.C.E.) which preceded construction of the great palaces. It contains a figurine of a bull with three men clinging to its head, an interesting contrast to the graceful bull-leapers in the frescoes from Knossos. Room III houses the puzzling Phaestos Disk, whose hieroglyphics have yet to be deciphered. In Room IV is a libation vase shaped like a bull's head, complete with crystal eyes and gilt horns. Room VII is devoted to the *labrys,* or double-headed axe, which apparently was linked to the matriarchal religion. In Room VIII, you'll find a rock crystal vase reconstructed from the 300 pieces in which it was found. Room X contains objects from the Late Minoan period (1350-1100 B.C.E.). You can get an idea of this catastrophe's impact on Cretan civilization by comparing the bull's head in Room X, whose huge round eyes stare blankly from its stylized head, with earlier taurean figures in rooms IV and VIII. Room XIII is filled with *larnakes,* elaborate Minoan sarcophagi that were so short the corpses had to be doubled over to fit inside. Room XIX features eighth-century B.C.E. bronze shields decorated in relief, found in the Ideon Cave near Anogia.

The major attraction of the museum, the **Hall of the Minoan Frescoes,** is on the second floor. The frescoes are composites of bits of the originals, with the missing details filled in by imaginative restorers. The most renowned are the Red and White Lilies (from Amnissos), the Blue Monkey, Prince of the Lilies, and priestess called La Parisienne (from Knossos), and the Bull-Leapers (also from Knossos), an action portrait of the lost art of bull-leaping so rhythmical and graceful that danger seems absent. One of the museum's prize possessions, a sarcophagus from Agia Triada, dominates the center of the main room. Dating from about 1400 B.C.E., it is carved from limestone and painted on all four sides with a well-preserved rendition of the sacred rites for the dead. (Open Tues.-Sun. 8am-6pm. Admission 500dr, students 250dr.) Palm trees and pines shade the weary in the museum's garden which overlooks the harbor.

Iraklion also has a **historical museum** (tel. 28 32 19), near the waterfront off Grevenon St., 2 blocks from the Xenia Hotel. Unlike the Archeological Museum, which is always packed with wide-eyed tourists, this museum is undeservedly underviewed. It contains an eclectic collection, including colorful frescoes, sculpture, liturgical objects from the early Christian and Byzantine periods, a collection of Byzantine coins, Turkish gravestones, finely woven tapestries from Chora Sfakion, and photographs of the German invasion of World War II. On the second floor is a reconstruction of the study of Nikos Kazantzakis, Crete's most famous native son, who immortalized Crete's zesty character in *Zorba the Greek*. (Open Mon.-Sat. 9am-1pm and 3-5:30pm; Nov.-March 8:30am-3pm. Admission 250dr.)

Locals often make evening pilgrimages to the austere **Tomb of Kazantzakis** for its views of Iraklion, the sea, and the mountain of Zeus to the east. To get there, either walk along the top of the Venetian Walls to Martinengo Bastion at the southern corner of the city or go down Evans St. until you reach the Venetian Walls and the Bastion. Because of his heterodoxical beliefs, Kazantzakis was denied a place in a Christian cemetery and was buried here without the full rites of the Orthodox Church. His simple gravestone bears a bold inscription from one of his novels: "I hope for nothing. I fear nothing. I am free."

True enthusiasts can visit the **Kazantzakis Museum,** in the nearby village of Varvari. The carefully presented exhibit includes many of the author's original manuscripts, as well as photographs and documentation of his theatrical productions. A slide show (in English) provides historical background. A bus from Station A takes you to Mirtia (22km from Iraklion), only a short walk from the museum. (Open Mon., Wed., and Sat. 9am-1pm and 4-8pm; Tues. and Fri. 9am-1pm, Sunday 9am-2pm. Admission 250dr.)

Hidden within the modern maze of Iraklion's streets are several interesting churches. Built in 1735, the **Cathedral of Agios Minas** in Agia Ekaterinis Sq., features six icons by the Cretan master Damaskinos (open 24 hours). **St. Catherine's Church,** also in the square, served as the first Greek university after the fall of Constantinople in 1453 and now houses an icon exhibit. (Open Mon.-Sat. 10:30am-1pm, Tues., and Thurs.-Fri. also 5-7pm. Admission 150dr.) **St. Titus Church,** 25th of August Ave., was a Turkish mosque until it was converted into a Christian church several years ago. The **Armenian Church** at 16 Kaloukarinou St. (tel. 24 43 37), dates back to 1666, and the Israeli-born priest will give you free tours of the grounds. He sells his own stained glass (1000-20,000dr). **Agios Mattheos,** a 10-minute walk on Markopoulou St. from Agia Ekaterinis Sq., contains several excellent icons by the mater Damaskinos. Ask the priest behind the church for the key.

As you stroll about, take note of the various monuments built during the long Venetian occupation of the city. The most popular is the seventeenth-century circular **Morosini Fountain,** Venizelou Sq., a structure decorated by handsome marble lions. Several others deserve a visit: the reconstructed **Venetian Loggia,** Venizelou Sq.; the thirteenth-century **Basilica of St. Mark,** 25th of August Ave., now an exhibition hall; the **Venetian Arsenal,** off Kountouriotou Sq., near the waterfront; **Koules Fortress** (tel. 28 62 28), which guards the old harbor (open Mon.-Sat. 7am-6pm, Sun. 9am-2pm; admission 200dr, students 100dr); and the impressive fifteenth-century **Venetian walls** that encircle the city.

## Entertainment

Iraklion has quite a few trendy discos and nightclubs. The **Piper** (tel. 22 67 51), behind and below the Astoria Hotel on Eleftherias Sq., is among the most popular. (Cover 500dr, 1 drink included.) **Disco Opera,** above the Piper, has tasteful black and red decorations and friendly waiters. (Cover 500dr, 1 drink included.) **Skala,** 28 Bofor St. (tel. 22 65 44), is Iraklion's newest and trendiest night spot. A cavernous, high-tech music hall with multiple bars attracts Iraklion's youth. Dress appropriately because of fashion scrutiny at the door. (Beer 300dr. Open 10pm-3am.) **Kafe Theatro,** 8 Tzoulaki (tel. 24 36 30), behind Morosini Fountain and down a flight of stairs, is a youthful Cretan hangout from November to March. Small plays are performed indoors, hence the name. (*Frappe* 120dr. Beer 120dr. Open in summer 8am-2pm and 5pm-midnight; in winter 5pm-midnight.) Schedules for Iraklion's fine movie theaters are posted next to the tourist police office on Dikeossinis St. For an evening of free entertainment, join the locals and tourists at Venizelou Sq.; the spontaneous uprisings may surprise you.

Iraklion's annual summer festival (mid-June to mid-Sept.) combines Cretan and occidental cultural events, and includes concerts, theater, ballet, folk dancing, and special exhibits. The GNTO gives out schedules, or call 28 22 21 or 24 29 77 for information.

Iraklion's harbor is unswimmable, but there are two public beaches nearby at **Lindo,** 4km west, and at **Amnissos,** 8km east. Amnissos is also the sight of the ancient port of Knossos; the frescoes of Amnissos, now in Iraklion's Archeological Museum, were found in a villa here. To reach Lindo, take bus #1, which leaves from in front of the Astoria Hotel in Eleftherias Sq., stopping at several free hotel beaches—all reasonably clean and sandy, but overcrowded. Bus #1, also goes to Amnissos, the best of the bunch (every ½ hr., last bus at 8pm, 45dr).

## Near Iraklion

Iraklion is an obvious base for exploring part of central Crete. Many archeological sites, including the great Minoan complex at Knossos and lesser Minoan finds at Malia, Tilissos, and Arhanes, are within a half-day's excursion from the city.

### Knossos

Knossos is undoubtedly the most famous archeological site in Crete, and few visitors leave the island without at least a quick visit. Impressively reconstructed, the palace of Knossos is richly shrouded in myth. Here King Minos, the son of Zeus and Europa, made Daedalus build an intricate labyrinth to hide the Minotaur (which means Minos' Bull), an enormous monster half-man half-bull conceived by Minos' wife Pasiphaë in a fit of "unholy passion." Minos locked the beast away and fed it the 14 Athenian youths sent annually in tribute—until the Athenian prince Theseus volunteered to join the group. Having slain the Minotaur, Theseus escaped from the labyrinth with a coil of golden thread given him by Ariadne, Minos' daughter, whom he promised to rescue from her treacherous father, but on second thought, abandoned. Minos imprisoned Daedalus and his son Icarus on the island to punish them for their misdoings. Daedalus designed wings of feathers and wax so that the two could escape, but Icarus, disregarding his father's warning, flew so close to the sun that his wings melted, and he fell into the sea that now bears his name. Mary Renault's novel *The King Must Die* gives a compelling account of the story.

During the first millennium B.C.E., Cretans were famous throughout the Hellenic world for their overdeveloped sense of fantasy, and ridiculed for imagining that they sprang from such impressive forebears. Time, however, has proven the Cretans right. In the 1880s, Heinrich Schliemann, the man who discovered Troy, Mycenae, and Tiryns, believed that a then-undistinguished hill near Iraklion was in fact the site of Knossos. Arthur Evans, one of his British friends, purchased the hill and spent the next 43 years and his entire fortune excavating it. His thorough spade-work showed that from 1700 B.C.E. to 1400 B.C.E., Knossos was indeed a great city that stood at the center of the first great European civilization.

Evans' work at Knossos provoked a great deal of controversy, the source of which will be obvious the moment you set foot on the site. He restored large portions of the palace to what he believed were their original configurations, based on internal evidence unearthed during the excavations. Walls, window casements, stairways, and columns were reconstructed in reinforced concrete, and copies of the magnificent frescoes were mounted in place of the originals (now in Iraklion's Archeological Museum). In some cases these restorations prevented the walls from falling down as the excavations continued, but Evans' reconstruction went beyond preservation. While purists feel that the complex at Knossos is an outrage and an obstacle to science, there is no question that the effect is impressive.

Most of what remains of the palace was rebuilt in the Neo-Palatial period, after the earthquake of around 1650 B.C.E. The structure was developed around a central courtyard, similar to contemporaneous palaces at Malia and Phaestos. Surrounding this court were hundreds of rooms in several stories. The chambers were illuminated by shafts of light from strategically placed minor courtyards, and the whole complex shared a sophisticated water and drainage system which are still evident in the gutters woven throughout the site, can twist an ankle of the unwary. The various rooms have been more or less identified and include the official state rooms, most notably the throne room with its original gypsum throne still in place, the queen's bedroom with its bath and quarters for attendants, and the granaries with their rows of *pithoi,* the huge, round pottery containers for oil and grain.

There is no point in suggesting a tour route of Knossos because you are bound to get lost in the maze-like site—this is, after all, the original labyrinth. However you choose to pick your way among the ruined walls and frustratingly incomplete frescoes, you should locate the two most impressive parts of the palace, the **King's and Queen's Rooms** and the **Throne Room.** Notice the ingenious lighting and drainage system which made the King's Room bright and airy without the aid of modern engineering. Exit through the door opposite the one you came in; at the end of the corridor is the Queen's Room, decorated with reproductions of the beautiful dolphin frescoes. The Queen's bathroom, to the right as you enter, has a toilet and bathtub. One flight up the **Grand Staircase** is the reconstructed **Upper Hall of Double Axes.** Up one more flight, the Throne Room is across the courtyard to the right. Inside, a replica of the throne stands where the original was found; on the walls surrounding it are reproduced frescoes of crouching griffins, beaks thrust skyward. To the right of the palace is a small outdoor theater, the oldest in Europe.

A guidebook to this extensive site will help immensely. The best and most comprehensive is Pendlebury's *Handbook to the Palace of Minos, Knossos, and its Dependencies.* Unfortunately, this is hard to find; you may have to settle for one of the glossy booklets on sale throughout Iraklion. They are, for the most part, very informative, but you have to pay a lot for their full-page color reproductions of Minoan frescoes. The cheapest are *The Palace of Knossos,* by Costis Davaris (300dr) and *Knossos: The Minoan Civilization,* by Sosso Logadiou-Platonos (500dr).

The ruins at Knossos (tel. 23 19 40) are open daily from 8am to 6pm. (Admission 500dr, students 250dr.) Take bus #2, which leaves from 25th of August Ave., near El Greco Park (7am-10:30pm every 10 min., ½ hr., 50dr).

### Tylissos, Anogia, and Fodele

Although Knossos ranks as the most popular site on Crete, it cannot lay claim to being the oldest. At Tylissos, just 14km southwest of Iraklion, archeologists have unearthed a Minoan city dating back to 2000 B.C.E. Unlike Knossos, the ruins at Tilissos remain relatively unblemished by modern modifications. (Open Mon.-Sat. 9am-3pm, Sun. 9:30am-2:30pm. Free.) Buses for Tilossos leave from Terminal B every 15 minutes (35 min., 45dr). Halfway between Tilissos and Anogia are the remains of the Minoan villas at **Sklavokambos.** The roadside ruins are unattended and always open, but warrant only a brief stop.

Another 22km from Tilissos along the same road is **Anogia,** a center for weaving and folkcraft and a popular destination for excursion buses. The reason for Anogia's high level of craft is a bitter one. During World War II, the villagers hid the British kidnappers of German General Kreipe; in reprisal, the Germans shot all the men of the village, leaving the widows with no other recourse for their livelihood. Today, Anogia celebrates its renewed vigor with a traditional music and marriage festival at the end of July. Call (0834) 312 07 for information.

Anogia has two cheap hotels: the **Imarmeni** (tel. 313 65) and the **Psiloritis** (tel. 322 31). Buses for Anogia leave from Terminal B (Mon.-Sat. 6 per day, 2 on Sun., last at 4:30pm, 1 hr., 230dr). From the village it's a four-hour hike through the gorgeous **Nida Plain** to the **Cave of Ideon Andron,** an ancient sanctuary dedicated to Zeus.

Also accessible from Iraklion is **Fodele,** a village full of orange trees and famous as the home of El Greco. The celebrated Greek painter, born Domenikos Theotokopoulos, left Fodele at the age of 20 to study under Titian in Venice; from there he moved on to Toledo, Spain, where he spent most of his life and did his finest work. For those who wish to make a pilgrimage to the master's hometown, there are buses from Terminal B (Mon.-Sat. at 6:30am and 2pm, 1 hr., 210dr).

# From Iraklion to Matala

If you flee Iraklion by taking the north coastal route east or west, you'll miss the best of Central Crete—the south, with its remarkable archeological sites and beaches. From Iraklion, buses head south from Terminal B, first climbing into the mountains and then descending to the fertile **Messara Plain,** whose agricultural wealth supported Gortys, the Roman capital of Crete, as well as the twin Minoan centers at Phaestos and Agia Triada. While these sites can be seen on a full daytrip from Iraklion, you'd do well to continue south and spend the night in the coastal resorts of Matala, Agia Galini, or the peaceful village of Lendas. One bus runs to Gortys, then Phaestos. From here, you can continue on to Matala or change buses for Agia Galini and Lendas. It is possible to travel northwest to Rethymnon from Agia Galini and see far more than you would by traveling the north coast freeway from Iraklion.

# Gortys Γόρτης

The first stop of historical interest on the road south, Gortys contains the ruins of a Greco-Roman city (Gortyn), whose chief prize is a series of stone tablets containing the **Law Code of Gortyn.** The code is inscribed in the ox-plow (*boustrophe-don*) manner, one line written left to right and the next right to left. Composed in a Dorian dialect of Greek, and dating from about 450 B.C.E., when Gortyn was a flourishing city under Greek control, it is the most important extant source of pre-Hellenistic Greek law. Although it mandated that slaves be punished more severely than citizens, the code was, on the whole, surprisingly liberal. It gaves slaves the right to marry free women, to own property, and to sue free men, whether masters or other citizens, and granted the children of slaves the status of free citizens if one of their parents were freed.

Ancient Gortyn fell to the Romans in 67 B.C.E. along with the rest of Crete, and was designated the capital of the island. Most of the remaining ruins are from the Roman occupation, including the **Roman Odeon,** or music hall. One of the few remains from the Hellenistic city, the Law Code tablets were so handsomely and evenly cut that the Romans used them as building materials for the Odeon. The Law Code blocks still form the wall of the structure that was restored by the Italian archeologist Halbherr, who excavated the site at the turn of the century.

The site of ancient Gortyn, en route to Phaestos, is on your right as you come from Iraklion. To reach the Odeon, walk through the parking lot and up the small path leading away from the road. The large ruined stone church that you pass on your left is the seventh-century **Basilica of Saint Titus.** It was built to house the tomb of Titus, Crete's first bishop, who died in 105 C.E. St. Paul himself installed Titus to set a sobering example for the fun-loving Cretans (Titus 1:12-16). Several sketchier remains of a Roman city (a sanctuary, theater, and amphitheater) are across the road from the site of the basilica and *odeon.* (Site open Mon.-Sat. 8:45am-3pm, Sun 9:30am-2:30pm. Admission 200dr, students 100dr.) The attendants are often helpful, providing unofficial guided tours.

Ten **buses** from Iraklion (6 on Sun.) stop daily at each of these sites; the last bus leaves Iraklion for Gortys at 5:30pm (1¾ hr., 340dr). All buses from Iraklion to Phaestos stop at Gortys and **Agii Deka,** where a *taverna* rents beds for 700dr per person.

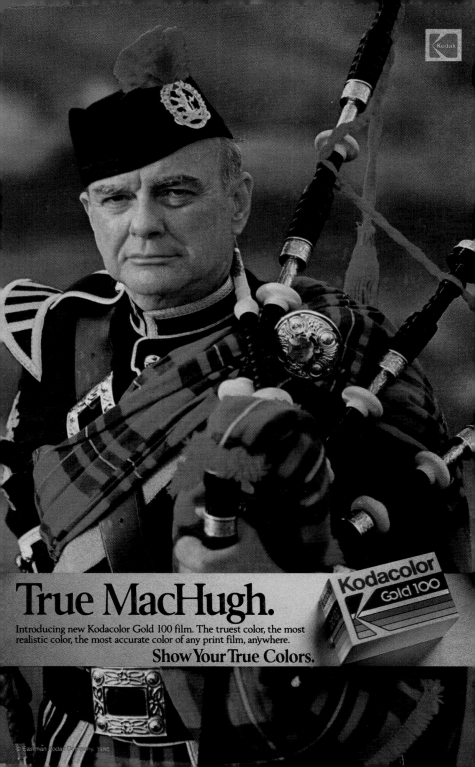

# True MacHugh.

Introducing new Kodacolor Gold 100 film. The truest color, the most
realistic color, the most accurate color of any print film, anywhere.

## Show Your True Colors.

# CARRY-ON RELIEF.

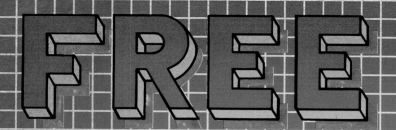

# FREE

## $100 AND: INTERNATIONAL AIR TRAVEL CERTIFICATE

| EURAIL MAP | BRITRAIL |
| POCKET TIMETABLE | MAP |
| TRAVELLER'S GUIDE | POCKET TIMETABLE |

## When You Buy Any

*EURAILPASS* or BritRail Pass

### Directly From

*EUROPEAN RAIL AUTHORITY*

---

# Phaestos and Agia Triada

Situated on a plateau with a magnificent view of the surrounding mountains and Messara Plain, the palace at **Phaestos** housed powerful Minoan royalty. Excavations at Phaestos were begun at the turn of the century by Halbherr, who also discovered Gortyn. He unearthed two palaces dating from successive periods, but in 1952, another excavation effort uncovered signs of two earlier palaces beneath. Like all the other major Minoan cities, including Knossos, the palace built in Phaestos in the middle Minoan period was largely destroyed in about 1450 B.C.E. Since the excavations, minor reconstruction work has been done on the walls, chambers, and cisterns, but nothing approximating Evans' work at Knossos; the site of Phaestos remains pretty much the way it was found. Close inspection has revealed identical masons' marks at both Knossos and Phaestos, suggesting that the same artisans labored at both palaces.

Built according to the standard Minoan blueprint, the complex includes a great central court, from which radiated the private royal quarters, servants' quarters, storerooms, and rooms for state occasions. Several levels were connected by various staircases; the grand staircase is still in place. Entering the site from the west, you'll find the theater on your right; beyond it are the covered remnants of the old palace. Continuing straight ahead you'll come upon the servants' quarters. The room with the corrugated roofing to the extreme northeast is believed to be the **King's Chamber.** Separated by three stairs is the **Queen's Chamber.** The rich finds from Phaestos, including vases, jewelry, altars, and the famed Phaestos Disk, imprinted with as yet undeciphered symbols, are all on display in Iraklion's Archeological Museum. Unfortunately, much of the palace is poorly labeled, and the glossy guidebook (400dr) available at the box office is useless. (Open in summer Mon.-Sat. 8am-7pm, Sun. 9am-6pm; in off-season Mon.-Sat. 10am-4pm, Sun. 8am-5pm. Admission 300dr, students 150dr.)

A 10-minute walk down the hill leads to nearby **Agios Ioannis** where you can find doubles for 1200dr, hot showers included. While here, don't miss the tiny **Church of Agios Parlos,** in the cemetery on the road toward Matala. Parts of the church are thought to pre-Christian and the restored frescoes date from the early fourteenth century C.E. **Bus** service out of Phaestos is excellent with service to Iraklion (Mon.-Sat. 12 per day, last at 7:45pm, Sun. 9 per day, last at 7:45pm, 2 hr., 390dr), Matala (5 per day, 20 min., 90dr) and Agia Galini (Mon.-Sat. 7 per day, 5 on Sun., 45 min., 180dr).

Three kilometers from Phaestos is the smaller Minoan site of **Agia Triada.** The small Byzantine church of the same name at the southeast corner of the site, is now so overshadowed by the unearthed pagan structure that it almost escapes notice. A kind of miniature version of the great Minoan palaces, Agia Triada is believed to have had some close tie to Phaestos, perhaps as a private retreat for the royal family. You too can escape here from the Phaestos crowds. Although the site itself is not nearly so impressive as Phaestos, important discoveries here include frescoes, Linear A tablets, and the grand painted sarcophagus now in Iraklion's Archeological Museum. (Site open Mon.-Sat. 8:45am-3pm, Sun. 9:30am-2:30pm. Admission 200dr, students 100dr.)

To get to Agia Triada from Phaestos, follow the road to Matala, and take the right fork uphill 200m beyond the parking lot. Agia Triada is 3km past the fork, a 45-minute walk. Leave your bags at the guard booth at Phaestos while you visit either site.

# Matala Μάταλα

Matala is no longer the hedonistic hippie hangout of old. Today's visitors generally have more money to throw around than their flower generation predecessors.

The sound track from **Zorba the Greek** now plays instead of the Strawberry Alarm Clock. Most prefer the beachfront campsite to the caves—especially now that the ones nearest the village have been fenced off with barbed wire. But all is not lost; the influx of sun-worshipers has not only spawned a host of new pensions, but it has also enhanced Matala's cheerful informality. The locals seem amused by the insouciant nymphettes in microscopic bathing suits who wander the streets like sunburnt flamingos, and they welcome the older travelers who stop by en route to the Minoan ruins.

The village and its deep-set swimming cove sit between high sandstone cliffs in which elaborate tomb-like caves were carved over the centuries. During World War II, the Nazis widened and outfitted the caves in an attempt to guard the south coast from English submarines. In the post-war years, Matala gained fame as a retreat for hippies, the singer Cat Stevens among them, who often took up long-term residence in the caves. The police have taken to clearing out some of the grottoes, but the town's reputation as a gathering ground for youth of all nationalities has stuck.

## Orientation and Practical Information

The town has three main streets: one on the waterfront, one behind it, and one that intersects both running inland to Phaestos. On the first you will find cafes, restaurants, souvenir stands, and a covered market of sorts; on the second the bus station, motorbike rental agencies, and stores. At Matala's main square, these two intersect the road to Phaestos, along which are hotels and pensions.

In summer, Monday through Saturday, seven **buses** per day go to Iraklion (6 on Sun., 1½ hr., 420dr), five per day to Phaestos (20 min., 90dr), and seven to Agia Galini (5 on Sun., 45 min., 210dr). The town's **police station** (tel. 421 68) is behind the bakery on the second inland road. Several motorbike rental places handle **currency exchange** at close to bank rates—try **Phaestos Rent-A-Car, Monzo Bikes** (open 8am-8pm), and **Motor Manos** (tel. 423 59; open 8am-11pm). These shops also serve as informal tourist offices. They can provide information on hotels and beaches, and Monzo and Manos rent **mopeds** for 1500dr per day. **Matala Travel** (tel. 423 85), in the main square, dispenses tourist information and sells boat and excursion tickets. (Open 9am-9:30pm.) A well-stocked **bookstore,** on the road to Phaestos, offers a good English-language selection. The **laundromat** across from the campground charges 300dr per wash, 200dr per dry. (Open daily 9am-9pm.) The **post office,** off the main square, is open daily from 8:30am to 7pm. The **OTE,** in the main square, is open 8am-8pm. The **hospital** and **pharmacy** are in Mires, 17km to the northeast. **Public toilets** are located in the main square next to Monza Bikes. Matala's **telephone code** is 0892.

## Accommodations, Camping, and Food

Matala has over a dozen hotels and pensions, but bargains are scarce; singles cost as much as doubles, and almost never drop below 1500dr in the summer. Cheaper accommodations are available in Matala's surrounding villages, and hitching from the main road to Phaestos or Matala is no problem. Avoid sleeping on the main beach or in one of the caves on the north side of the cove; both areas are subject to frequent onslaughts of thievery and police raids. If, for some reason, you choose to ignore this piece of advice, leave your passport elsewhere, since the police punish freelance campers by confiscating their passports, redeemable for about 5000dr.

**Matala Camping,** (left facing inland) is spacious, and the co-ed cold showers will perk you up no matter how you spent the previous night. (200dr per person, 200dr per tent. 200dr per car or motorcycle.) Other places in town fill quickly, so start searching early. If you stay more than one night, many hotels will offer you reduced rates.

**Nikos Kefalakis** (tel. 423 75). Take a right off the road to Phaestos just before it leaves the town—it's the 3rd building on the right. Spiffy wood paneling, comfortable, and the cheapest in the center of town. Relax in the courtyard. Doubles 1700dr, with bath 2300dr. Triples with bath 3000dr.

**Tsirterakis** (tel. 423 02), 200m out of town on the left, below the road. Clean rooms, though somewhat dark and stuffy, with decent bathrooms. Doubles 1700dr. Triples 2000dr. Bargain. Hot showers included.

**Pension Jannis** (tel. 423 58), a 5-minute walk inland to Phaestos. Ask for rooms at the Xeno-phon Hotel and the owner will show you both Jannis and **Pension Acropol**, the best bargains around, with tidy rooms and private hot showers. Doubles 1500dr. Triples 2000dr.

**Pension Fantastic** (tel. 423 62), behind the main square. If Nikos is full, Theodor Stavrakos offers adequate but far-from-fantastic rooms. Double 1700dr, with bath 2300dr. Triples 2200dr, with bath 2800dr.

The waterfront restaurants all cater to tourist tastes. At the bottom of the stairs from the main square to the beach is the glass palace **Sunset Restaurant** (tel. 421 08; mixed grill 650dr; open daily 8am-midnight). Walk around the cove to **Restaurant Plaka** (tel. 423 55); try the fresh swordfish (500dr). (Open daily 10am-midnight.) At the southern end of the bay is **Neosicos** (tel. 423 53), Matala's attempt at Cretan cooking. The house speciality is a fish soup (350dr). (Open daily 8am-midnight.)

## Sights and Entertainment

Fierce waves roll onto the beautiful but crowded main beach at Matala. For an equally good shore and more secluded caves, join the threadbare bathers on **Red Beach.** Follow the path on your left just beyond where the street running along the waterfront meets the one behind it, next to the police station and church, and veer left—it's a 20-minute hike over the hill to the south. On the way you'll pass numerous caves within easy climbing distance. Here the veteran cave-dwellers now reside, since neither the police nor most tourists venture this far. The cliffs between Matala and Red Beach all offer spectacular views of the Mediterranean, and most paths take you back down to the beach. For a change of pace, rent a pricey paddle boat on the Matala beach and peddle to the Red Beach (paddle boats 400dr per hr., canoes 200dr per hr.).

Also secluded, with its own small community of freelance summer residents and lone *taverna,* is **Kommos Beach,** a 5-kilometer walk from Matala. (Walk toward **Pitsidia** and take the 2nd dirt road on your left.) The beach is quite long and leads to the makeshift beach-town of **Kalamaki.** The dirt track from the Phaestos road precludes bus traffic, but mopeds can still make it to Kalamaki.

**Karandinos** (tel. (0892) 421 80) has a few motley doubles with vinyl floors (1200dr). Upstairs, cleaner doubles with bath run 2000dr. (Breakfast 170dr.) A handful of mediocre restaurants and a small bar/disco provide Kalamaki's casual nightlife. The turn-off for Kalamaki passes through the unspoiled village of **Kamilari,** a quiet hilltop town 2½km from the beach with several pensions. Try the **Oasis Hotel** (tel. 422 17) ensconced within a blooming garden full of chirping canaries. The Christofakakis' serve meals and rent scooters. (Doubles 1600dr. Triples 2000dr.) Nearby is a notable Minoan vaulted tomb. Several clay figurines from this Messara-type tomb are now in the Iraklion Museum. Kamilari can also be reached by taking a 3½-kilometer dirt road opposite the Church of **Agios Pavlos** in Agios Ioannis, 1km from Phaestos. Another overlooked village is **Pitsidia,** 4½km before Matala on the road from Phaestos. Pitsidia is the best alternative to Matala's tourist mayhem, and hitching rides to the nearby beaches is easy. Several small hotels around the *platia* rent inexpensive rooms. The bus from Phaestos stops at Pitsidia, where you'll be offered *dhomatia* on the way to the square. (500-700dr per person.) For a few extra *drachmae,* you can stay at **Petros** (tel. (0892) 423 86), in the *platia.* The tasteful rooms are equipped with refrigerators and kitchens. The balconies, blooming with trellised flowers and overlooking the square, are a locale for im-promptu revelry. (Doubles 1500dr, with balcony 1800dr. Triples 2000dr.) Among the few restaurants on the main road to Matala, **Nikos** (tel. 424 07) serves a large fish-combo platter for 350dr. (Open daily 7pm-midnight.) Dimitris Koumianakis, at **Kri Kri Travel** (tel. 424 03), is the lone tourist guide and moped rental agent in Pitsidia. (Scooters 1500dr per day. Cars from 5000dr. Open daily 8am-noon and 3pm-9pm.)

Nightlife in Matala centers around the terrace and video room of the **Valentina Bar** (tel. 423 74), off the main square. (Beer 100dr. Banana juice 200dr. Open daily 3pm-3am.) Another popular place is **Disco Zorbas,** more than a kilometer towards Phaestos and down a dirt path on the right. In the summer, the owners run a regular minibus from the kiosk to the disco. (Open 10pm-3am; folk dancing after 1am.) The **Malibu Disco,** below Valentina, opens onto the beach and is an upscale pick-up joint. More informal and true to its name is the **Rock Bar,** stuck in the '60s. (Draught beer 150dr. Open 8pm-3am.) Next door is the mellower **Marinero** (tel. 421 01; beer 100dr, drinks 350dr, cappuccino 100dr; open 11am-3am.)

### Near Matala: Lendas

If you've decided to avoid tourist-infested Agia Galini and are wary of Matala's crowded bars and beach, do not despair. Tiny Lendas, approximately 40km east of Matala, is probably the most peaceful, genuinely Cretan village you will find on the southern coast. Loutro and Chora Sfakion may be relatively unspoiled by tourism, but in Lendas even "Rooms for Rent" signs are practically non-existent and the handful of tourists who arrive on the twice-daily bus from Iraklion quickly disperse among the village's scattered houses. New apartments and hotels east of Lendas, however, are quickly stripping away the hamlet's long-time isolation. Doubles are available in almost every home for as little as 1200dr. Try the *taverna* on the eastern edge of the village for cheap, adequately clean rooms and separate bathrooms. **Camping** on the gray pebbly beach or even on occasional concrete platforms between buildings is hassle-free.

Most of the small eateries (6 in all) serve standard fare. **Pub Paradise,** a *taverna* whose only apparent distinction is its video game and huge stereo speakers, plays exclusively Greek music and serves reasonably-priced Greek food. (Greek salad 130dr, fish 270dr.) Three **minimarkets** stock basic foodstuffs.

The **beach** in Lendas is uncrowded and occasionally shaded by trees. To find even more small, secluded beaches, follow the path leading east from the village through fields and watermelon patches. Behind the village are the remains of the Hellenistic **Temple of Asclepios,** built at the site of what was believed to be a therapeutic spring. A mosaic floor and marble columns mark the site. Lendas' church is built on the marble foundations of the ancient Greek temple that previously occupied the site. Bits and pieces of the temple's columns are embedded in the church's stone walls.

**Buses** to Lendas depart from Iraklion (Mon.-Sat. at 10am and 1:30pm, 2 hr., 490dr, returning at 6:30am and 2:45pm). From Mires, a bus leaves daily at 1pm (250dr). There is only one **telephone** in the entire village: (0892) 222 72. It is connected by intercom from the central *taverna* to most of the other houses.

## Agia Galini Αγά Γαλήνη

West of Matala on the southwest coast, Agia Galini rekindles appreciation for the rest of Crete. Once a fishing village, Agia Galini is now about as Greek as Frankfurt.

From the bus station, you can get to the harbor either by continuing along the street where the bus stops, or by walking 1 block uphill, then bearing right on **Vassilios Ioannis Street** (dubbed **Taverna Street**) and continuing down wide concrete stairs. Taking the latter route, you pass the **National Bank** on the left (open Mon.-Sat. 9am-1pm and 5-8:30pm), **Candia Tours** (tel. 912 78) (open daily 8:30am-12:30pm and 5-9:30pm), and a mediocre **bookstore** (open daily 9am-11pm). The well-flagged **post office** (open Mon.-Fri. 7:30am-2:30pm) and the **OTE** (open daily 8am-3pm) are near the bus station. The **doctor** (tel. 912 58) can be reached by walking down the road to the water from the bus station. Several agents rent bikes, both in the upper and lower level of town; try **Biggis Bikes** (tel. 911 42), near the post office. (Automatic 50cc mopeds 1300dr. 125cc scooters 2100dr, insurance included. Open 8:30am-10:30pm.)

The pensions along the upper tier of Agia Galini are generally cheaper than the hotels in the center of town. Nevertheless, a few family-run pensions rent doubles with scenic views for under 1700dr. Close to the waterfront, **Rent Rooms Michael,** on the hilltop overlooking the water, has singles for 900dr and doubles for 1400dr. **Hotel Phaestos** (tel. 912 23) across from the post office, has generic but clean doubles for a negotiable 1500dr. Closer to the harbor is the comfortable **Hotel Acteon** (tel. 912 08). (Doubles 1500dr, with bath 2000dr. Triples with bath 2500dr. Ask for the upper floor. Breakfast 200dr.) The turn off for **Camping Agia Galini** is 3km before the town on the road from Iraklion. A ½-kilometer walk east from the harbor along the pebbly beach and across a fordable river will also bring you to **No Problem Camping.** The grounds are 150m from the beachfront, and the gravel pitches are shaded by olive and carob trees. (Ample facilities, market, and bar. Open April-Nov. 300dr per person, 100dr per tent.)

Tables of relatively inexpensive restaurants line Vassilios Ioannis Street. Across from Candia Tours is **Greenwich Village** (tel. 913 49), Agia Galini's best-kept secret. Savor a fish dinner (600-900dr) on a breezy garden terrace. The **Siroco** (open 9pm-2am) and **Diagonas** (open 10pm-2am) discos illuminate the trash on the sand beach at night. Smaller bars and discos such as **Whispers** and **Old Zorba's** are at the base of Vassilios Ioannis St. Insatiable beach-goers will enjoy the small bay at **Agia Georgi,** a two-hour hike. Surprisingly, cleaner water and fewer people are closer to town at the rocky beach just beyond Restaurant Alikianos.

Along the isolated secondary route from Iraklion to Agia Galini, the mountain village of **Kamares** offers a vantage point from which to view Mt. Ida's twin peaks (2600m) or explore the **Kamares Cave,** sanctuary of the nineteenth-seventeeth century B.C.E. Minoan polychrome pottery exhibited in Iraklion's Archeological Museum. The strenuous four-hour hike is not always well-marked, but look for the orange-painted trail markers.

**Buses** travel to Iraklion (Mon.-Sat. 9 per day, last at 7:45pm; 6 on Sun., last at 7:30pm; 2½ hr., 430dr) and Rethymnon (in summer 7 per day, last at 6:30pm; in winter 5 per day; 1½ hr., 360dr). To get to Plakias, change at Koxare. For Phaestos, take the Iraklion bus (45 min., 150dr).

## Spili

The main road from Agia Galini to Spili twists through fertile valleys, expansive mountain terrain, and sleepy villages before continuing west to the new-found beach resort of Plakias and the peaceful environs of Moni Preveli. Spili is a striking village with cascading waters and shady trees. The village *platia* offers a respite from the dusty main road. Benches surround the town's centerpiece, a fountain that spouts cool water from carved lion heads.

The **OTE** is on Messologiou St., just off the main road toward Rethymnon (open Mon.-Sat. 7:30am-3:10pm); the **post office** is on the left past the *platia* (open Mon.-Sat. 8am-3pm). **Rent Motor Spili** (tel. 220 31) rents 50cc bikes for 1500dr. (Open 8am-11pm.) The **hospital** (tel. 225 31) is at the end of town on the left, on the road toward Agia Galini. Spili's **telephone code** is 0832.

Settle in for a night under the orange animal-skin blankets at the **Green Hotel** (tel. 220 56), on the western edge of town, at the end of a staircase laced with ferns. A delightful hotel, this veritable fest o' foliage is no more expensive than hotels in some larger Cretan towns. (Doubles 1500dr. Triples 2000dr. Quads 2000dr. Baths 500dr.) **Pension Pandocheion** (tel. 221 20) at the opposite end of town next to the Agricultural Bank, rents doubles for 1000dr and triples for 1200dr. Apart from the quiet cafes, Spili has an excellent *taverna* just before the *platia* on the east side. **Loukakis** (tel. 223 19) serves a sumptuous beef stew (300dr) and arguably the best *mousaka* on Crete (220dr). (Open 11am-11pm.)

If you have a vehicle that can take a pounding, ride the mountain roads east from Spili to **Gerakari.** Very few maps show the unpaved route, but if you follow the mountain ranges, you can't get lost. Just 2km southeast of Gerakari is a shaded spot with running water, perfect for camping. Across the road are the ruins of a tiny, eleventh-century Byzantine monastery, **Agios Yiannis Theologos,** containing some well-preserved frescoes. You'll find few tourists here. For an easier trip, consider approaching Gerakari from the eastern side; access from the secondary road that runs parallel to the Rethymnon-Agia Galini highway is much better.

## Plakias

Within 10 years, a tiny fishing village was transformed into a fledgling resort. The metamorphosis of Plakias has not yet extinguished the small-town atmosphere, but it has certainly dampened it. The town still lacks many essential services such as a bank and pharmacy. The **doctor** (tel. 312 37) from Sellia comes every Monday, Wednesday, and Friday. For travel and general tourist information, go to **Candia Tours** (tel. 312 14), near the Lamon Hotel. Plakias' **telephone code** is 0832.

You can live quite comfortably and very cheaply in this wave-pounded beach town. The **youth hostel** (tel. 313 06), all the way up the road from the beach, is clean and has a friendly atmosphere. (No curfew. Open March-Dec. Beds 450dr.) In the west end near the quay and just past Smerna's Restaurant is **Rooms Marko** (tel. 312 47), where doubles with bath, kitchen facilities, and seaside view are only 1500dr. Antonis Stefanakis, the proprietor will let you store a moped or belongings in his garage. Best to call ahead, because these rooms book in high season. Other accommodations in Plakias are much more expensive and probably not worth being close to the beach. Singles run 1200dr, doubles 1700dr. The quieter rooms cluster on a path inland from the town's main road. Approaching from the east, turn off the main road at the "Greek Art Maria" sign. Walk 50m and look on the left for **Pension Asteria** (tel. 313 12). Be forewarned that Maria can be hot-headed and the bathrooms are, well, let's just say, less than first-rate. Farther along, the path veers to the left and you'll pass two *tavernas;* opposite Giorgos Taverna, you'll find doubles and triples with bath and kitchen for 1500dr and 2000dr, respectively. The places farther to the west are of comparable quality and price range. **Camping Plakias,** at the end of the path toward "Greek Art Maria," is a pleasant option with cold showers, clean facilities, and a supply store. (350dr per person. Also rooms with cots. Singles 700dr. Doubles 1000dr. Less for a longer stay.) Sleeping on the beach at the far eastern end of Plakias beach or on Damnoni beach is usually a hassle-free, cost-free alternative. The **Hotel Lamon** (tel. 313 18) on the waterfront, offers doubles for 1700dr.

Find the cheapest sustenance in town at the two **supermarkets** on the main road, and at the *souvlaki* and pastry stands right before the line of expensive waterfront restaurants. **Restaurant Gorgons** and **Restaurant Sophias** (tel. 312 26) serve standard tourist fare near the quay. **Mitos Taverna,** near the youth hostel, is popular with the younger crowd. **Christos** (tel. 314 72), on the tip of the harbor, has a devoted local clientele; try the fried red mullet (600dr). (Open 7am-2am.) A disco rash caters to the itchy-feet. The **Sunshine Pub,** 10 minutes west by foot on the way to the secluded Souda Beach is a relaxing spot by the shore to sip a beer (150dr). (Open 7am-2am.) The owner also rents a few doubles above for 1800dr. The small **Pub House,** tucked just behind the harbor, plays progressive rock strains in a quasi-Japanese environment. (Drinks 350-400dr.) It's also a good place for breakfast (225dr). (Open 7:30am-1am.)

The surrounding villages offer cheaper rooms without the homogenized tourist throngs. Breezy **Myrthios,** a half-hour walk up the hill from Plakias, has an excellent mosquito-free **youth hostel** (tel. 312 02). (Refrigerator and kitchen facilities. Open year-round. Beds, either in rooms or on the roof, 400dr. Hot showers available 8-10am and 5-8:30pm.) In the *platia* next to the *taverna* is **Belonaki** (tel. 314 14), offering pleasing doubles with balconies for 1200dr. The *taverna* in the square, **Vasilonikolidaki** (tel. 312 11) is managed by Wolfgang. Try the *tiropites* (cheese pies,

250dr) or the fresh lamb (445dr). The restaurant also has an international phone. (Open 7am-midnight.)

The fringe beach cove of **Damnoni,** to the east of Plakias, attracts a community of informal campers. There are two *tavernas* and cold public showers on the beach. Police make occasional attempts to disperse the campers, but pleasure seekers invariably return. The **Akti Damnoni** pension (tel. 312 58) has clean doubles with baths from 2000-2500dr. (Breakfast 150dr. Open April-Oct.) To reach Damnoni, walk 1km on the road to Lefkogia or take the Rethymnon bus (5 min.), then take a right on the dirt road. The coves to the west and east make good beach hideaways.

**Bus** information and **currency exchange** are available at **Hotel Livikon** (tel. 312 16). There is service to Rethymnon (5 per day, last at 6pm, 270dr), Agia Galini (at 10am and 6pm, 300dr), and Chora Sfakion (at 10am, 300dr).

## Preveli

A side-trip to Preveli requires some initiative, but the two monasteries are an intriguing diversion. The older one, the **Monastery of to St. John the Baptist,** is on the left, low on a hillside about 2km after the turn-off for Preveli. Until World War II, it was used as a granary, but after the Germans vandalized it, only the peaked watchtowers on the corners were left to preside over the crumbling ruin. An eerie, dusty stillness pervades the place.

The newer **Monastery of St. John the Theologian,** about 4km farther along the scenic road, perches on a hill overlooking the sea. This monastery did its part opposing the German occupation of Crete in World War II by hiding Allied soldiers within its walls until they could be smuggled out in submarines. The monastery still operates, but just barely. In recent years, it has fallen into disrepair because of lack of funding. Proper dress is required. (Open 8am-1pm and 5-7pm.) The monastery also has a small **museum.** (Same hours. Admission 50dr.)

Preveli has two good beaches, but both are difficult to find. **Limni Beach** is closest to the inhabited monastery—walk on the dirt road that begins about 1km below the upper sanctuary. You can camp there near a lovely gorge with a freshwater spring. **Preveli Beach** is about 6km from the road to Preveli, and has a small *taverna*—cross the bridge about 2km after the dirt road to Preveli begins and follow the intermittent signs. Camping is tolerated on this dirty but secluded beach.

There is no public transportation to Preveli. The morning **bus** from Plakias to Rethymnon goes through Asomatos. From there, it's a 7-kilometer, two-hour, partly uphill trek to the latter Monastery of St. John. Other Rethymnon-bound buses pass through Lefkogia (10 min., 60dr), from where you can walk and hitch 12km to the monastery. A handy shortcut begins at the right-hand turn-off for Gianniou village; after the village, follow a dirt footpath to the first monastery. This walk saves about 6km. Alternatively, rent yourself a motor vehicle in Agia Galini. If you're driving from Agia Galini, take the turn-off for Koxare and pass through the village of Asomatos. At the first intersection in the village, a left turn and another left onto a dirt road puts you on the path to Preveli (a right turn at the intersection heads toward Plakias).

# Western Crete

## Rethymnon Ρέθυμνο

The Turkish and Venetian influence that pervades the streets throughout northern Crete is best appreciated in the harbor town of Rethymnon. Arabic inscriptions lace the walls of its narrow, arched streets, minarets highlight the old city's skyline, and an imposing Venetian fortress guards the harbor's western end. On any given day in town, the most energetic travelers may inexplicably find themselves waking up just in time for the afternoon siesta, wandering aimlessly through winding alleys at sunset, or sitting until midnight in a cafe by the ocean, drinking wine and chatting lazily. In the youth hostel, you'll find people who came for a day and stayed for months. Rethymnon will surely entice you, too, to stay longer than you planned.

## Orientation and Practical Information

To get to Arkadiou St. and the waterfront from the bus station, walk down Demokratias St. to the Venizelou monument, cross Kountouriotou St., and walk straight down Varda Kellergi St. In the rough triangle formed by **Arkadiou, Antistasseos,** and **Gerakari Street,** you'll find everything you need.

**Greek National Tourist Organization (GNTO):** Down by the waterfront (tel. 291 48 or 241 43). An efficient staff will provide you with maps, bus and ferry schedules, museum hours, and a list of all-night pharmacies. They suggest daytrips, publicize local events, and exchange currency at 2% lower than the bank rate. Open Mon.-Fri. 9am-4:30pm, Sat.-Sun. 9am-2pm.

**Post Office:** Moatsou St., near the public gardens. Open Mon.-Fri. 7:30am-3pm. **Postal code:** 74100.

**OTE:** 28 Kountouriotou St. Open 7am-midnight. **Telephone code:** 0831.

**Bus Stations:** Tel. 222 12, facing each other on opposite corners of Demokratias and Moatsou St., 1 block inland from the Venizelou monument on Kountouriotou St. Buses run to: Iraklion (16 per day, last at 10:45pm, 2 hr., 490dr); Hania (15 per day, last at 11pm, 1 hr., 430dr); Agia Galini (4 per day, 1½ hr., 360dr); Plakias (5 per day, 1 hr., 270dr); the Arkadi Monastery (4 per day, 40 min., 135dr); Anogia (2 per day, 1¾ hr., 320dr); and Sfakia (at 8:15am, 4 hr., 500dr).

**Taxi:** Tel. 223 16 or 250 00. 24 hours.

**Motorbike Rental: Motor Stavros,** 14 Paleologou St. (tel. 228 58). Automatics 1400dr. Bikes 600dr. Bargain. **Fahrrad Rent-a-Vespa,** 15 Kountouriotou St., across from the OTE. 50cc bikes 1500dr. Other car rentals and motorbike shops centered around the Venizelou Monument.

**Library:** Tsagri St. From the museum, walk right (facing the water) on Arkadiou St. 3 blocks, turn right on Soudern St. and left on Tsagri. Some English books. Open Tues. and Thurs.-Fri. 8:30am-1:30pm and 6-8pm, Wed. and Sat. 8:30am-1:30pm.

**English Bookstore: International Press,** Venizelou St. (tel. 249 37), near the water. Open daily 9am-9pm.

**Laundromat:** 45 Tombasi (tel. 220 11), next to the youth hostel. Wash 500dr. Dry 150dr. Iron 200dr. Open Mon.-Sat. 9am-2pm and 5-9pm.

**Public Toilets:** Next to the GNTO by the waterfront. Cold showers on the public beach.

**Hospital:** Trantalidou St. (tel. 278 14), in the southwest corner of town. Open 24 hours.

**Tourist Police:** Iroon Polytechniou St. (tel. 281 56), just off the waterfront, 3 blocks south of the fortress. Some of the same services as the GNTO. Open Mon.-Fri. 7am-9pm, Sat.-Sun. 8am-1pm.

**Emergency:** Tel. 100

## Accommodations, Camping, and Food

Arkadiou Street and the harbor, near the fortress and the Venetian port, are lined with hotels and rooms to let. Most are spacious, sparsely decorated, and expensive.

**Youth Hostel (IYHF),** 41 Tombasi St. (tel. 228 48). From the bus station, walk 6 blocks down Kountourioti St. until you get to a square with a church; walk right on Ethnikis Anistaseos through the Venetian arch and then right again on Tombasi. Friendly, relaxed and crammed in summer. Breakfast in the morning and *ouzo* at night. Over 60 beds and more room on the roof. No curfew. 450dr per person. Long lines for occasionally hot showers 8-10am and 5-8pm.

**Olga's Pension,** 57 Souliou (tel. 298 51), on a nicely restored street off Ethnikis Antistaseos. George, the jovial proprietor, keeps a continual garden party going. Roof 300dr. Singles 1500dr. Doubles 1900dr. Triples 2400dr. Quads 2500dr. Hot showers.

**Vrisinas,** 10 Chereti St., (tel. 260 92), 1 block from the bus station, before the youth hostel, off Arkadiou St. Centrally located, and a veritable greenhouse of plants and flowers. Top-notch rooms. Doubles 1700dr. Triples 2000dr.

**Hotel Paradisos,** 35 Igoum Gavril St. (tel. 224 19). From the bus station, walk down to the Venizelou monument and turn left on Kountouriotou St., which becomes Igoum Gavril. Clean, quiet rooms and an immaculate, spacious shower and bathtub. Singles 1000dr. Doubles 1500dr. Triples 1800dr.

**Hotel Achillio,** 151 Arkadiou St. (tel. 225 81), left from the corner of Arkadiou and Varda Kallergi St. Huge clean rooms and a nice balcony overlooking the harbor. Firm beds and high ceilings. Doubles 1700dr. Triples 2000dr. Quads 2500dr. One gigantic quint 600dr per person.

**Hotel Zania,** 3 Pavlou Vlastou St. (tel. 281 69), next to the youth hostel. Spotless, palatial rooms with soft beds. Management speaks Greek and French. Doubles 2000dr. Triples 2500dr. Prices less if you stay more than 1 night. Hot showers included.

**Hotel Acropole,** 2 Makariou St. (tel. 213 05), just off Iroon Sq. Right in front of the Venizelou monument and the beach. Antiseptic and institutional, but lots of rooms. Singles 1300dr. Doubles 1500dr. Triples 2200dr.

**Barbara Dokinaki,** 14 Plastira St. (tel. 223 19). Go to the west end of the harbor, behind the jutting concrete pier, and turn left. An outstanding pension right near the fortress. Large pleasant rooms open onto a well-tended courtyard. Roof 500dr. Doubles 2500dr. Triples 3000dr. Kitchen and bath included.

**Camping: Elizabeth Camping** (tel. 286 94), 3km east of town at the beginning of the old road to Iraklion. Pitches on shaded grass. Staff will lend some camping and kitchen supplies. Self-service *taverna* 9am-11pm. Open May-Oct. 400dr per person. 250dr per tent. Breakfast 130dr. **Arkadia Camping** (tel. 288 25), 500m beyond Elizabeth. Gravel pitches. Self-serve *taverna* 7am-11pm, and store 8am-9pm. Money exchange and motorbike rentals. 400dr per person. 300dr per tent. Buses run from the station to both campsites (50dr). If you're arriving from Iraklion, ask the driver to let you off at one of the sites.

Rethymnon is well-endowed with *souvlaki-pita* (80dr) stands. There is also an open-air **market** on weekdays next to the park, between Moatsou and Kountouriotou St. Restaurants, however, are uniformly expensive and charge at least 300dr for the usual fare—*mousaka*, spaghetti, etc. In winter, **tavernas** near the center of the city do the most business, but in summer serious eating shifts to the harbor. All of the many restaurants lining the old harbor specialize in fresh seafood. **Restaurant Zefyros** (tel. 282 06), on the west end of the Venetian harbor, is the least expensive. (Grilled swordfish *souvlaki* 500dr. Open 10am-2am.) Restaurants **Tassos** and **Samaria** (tel. 246 81), in the center of the waterfront, are also good. Many of the harborside restaurants also serve excellent pizza and Greek salad; some will even give you free wine if you come with a group of 20 (round them up at the youth hostel). You'll find a line-up of good *tavernas* on Petihaxi St., near the Neratzes Mosque and Paleologou St.; try **George's** at #17 behind the palm tree. (Open 8am-midnight.) If you have access to a car or feel like taking a walk, have a meal at **Zizi's Taverna,** 4km east of town in Platanes on the old road to Iraklion. It's quite popular with locals. **Our House** (tel. 240 98), Rethymnon's vegetarian restaurant, is on the beach next to the Kriti Hotel.

## Sights and Entertainment

Rethymnon had been occupied nearly continuously since the late Minoan period. At its cultural and economic apex in the fourth century B.C.E., it was overrun by Arabs, who left few lasting signs of dominion. During the Fourth Crusade, the Byzantines sold the island for 520 pounds of silver to the Venetians. The latter considered Rethymnon to be the clasp in their necklace of trading outposts and fortified the city. The Ottomans, having taken the city in 1646, enlarged the city and incorporated Turkish designs with the extant Venetian buildings.

Rethymnon has a one-room **archeological museum,** at the corner of Arkadiou and Paleologou St., located in a Venetian *loggia* dating from about 1600. Entering its gloomy interior, you may feel as though you've wandered into the storeroom of an amateur archeologist with eclectic tastes. Headless statues lean on walls behind rows of figurines, and Minoan sarcophagi lie next to cases of Roman coins. Unfortunately, this motley collection is poorly labeled. (Open Mon. and Wed.-Sat. 8:45am-3pm, Sun. 9:30am-2:30pm. Admission 200dr, students 100dr.) The new **Historical and Folk Art Museum,** 28 Mesologiou St., right below the fortress, is worth a short visit. Bits of lace, clothing, pottery, and samples of other Cretan crafts neatly line the well-lit walls. (Open Tues.-Sun. 9am-1pm and 7-9pm. Admission 100dr, students 50dr.)

At some point during your visit to Rethymnon, make a pilgrimage to the colossal **Venetian Fortezza,** which dates from around 1580. The walls of the enormous citadel are in excellent condition. Most of the buildings in the interior of the fortress were destroyed by the Turks in the seventeenth century, and even more three centuries later from German bombing during World War II. (Open in summer Tues.-Fri. 8am-8pm, Sat.-Mon. 9:30am-6pm; in off-season daily 9am-4pm. Admission 100dr, students 50dr.) While wandering in Rethymnon's narrow alleys, your divining rod will bring you to the **Rimondi Fountain,** at the corner of Paleologou and Petihaxi St. Fresh water pours out of this Venetian fountain's three lion-headed spigots.

Rethymnon's Turkish legacy stands tall in the city's Islamic structures: the **Neratzes Minaret,** on Antistasseos St. (top open daily 11am-7:30pm; free); **Nerdjes Mosque,** 1 block farther, which was formerly a Franciscan church; the **Kara Pasha Mosque,** on Arkadiou St., near Iroon Sq.; and the **Valides Minaret,** which presides over **Porta Megali** gate at the beginning of Antistasseos St. in 3 Martiou Sq. Ask at the GNTO for hours. A useful book when out and about Rethymnon is *Rethymnon: A Guide to the Town,* by A Malagari and H. Stratidakis, available at most book stores (500dr).

The east end of Rethymnon opens onto a long **beach,** extending for about 10km. A tad dirty, it's wide, spacious stretch is more than adequate. Matters improve as you go farther east, but not enough to justify the trouble of getting there without private transportation.

Rethymnon's **wine festival** in mid-July is good fun. Complete with a six-piece band and a folk-dance troupe, the festival draws everyone in town, tourists and Greeks alike. You pay a fee (around 400dr) to enter the park, which entitles you to as much wine as you can drink from the barrels at several strategic spots on the grounds. Each station has a barrel of white, rosé, and red. You need a glass or, better yet, a carafe to be served (unless you are very good at cupping your hands). Both are sold on the grounds, but unless you want souvenirs, bring your own. A local dance troupe performs early in the evening in traditional costumes, while later on it's a free-for-all. If this is your only opportunity to see Cretan dances then it's worth a special trip. Nothing captures the Cretan exuberance better than dances and festivals.

An exhibition of Cretan handicrafts is scheduled in Rethymnon to coincide roughly with the wine festival (every odd year). The work is worth a look, but you won't pick up any bargains; you can usually find better prices at local artisans' shops in each major town. Rethymnon's own craft shops cluster around Arkadiou, Antistasseos, and Gerakari Street. Best of all, the **Herb Shop,** 58 Soliou St., stocks folk remedies and herbs exclusive to Crete.

Nightlife centers around the harbor boardwalk. A good but expensive disco is **Fortezza,** on the western end of the harbor. (Open 11pm-3am. Cover 500dr, 1 drink included.) The chic metropolitan **Surprise Pub,** 287 Arkadiou St., 30m left of the museum, has spiffy neon lights and an occasional guitarist. (Beer 250dr. Half-price drinks 9-10pm. Open 9am-2pm and 7:30pm-3am.) **Gounaki** 6 Koronaiou St. (tel. 288 16), in the old town, has a vaulted cave-like interior, animal wall rugs, cheap food, and Cretan music (9pm-midnight). The crowd at the youth hostel makes nightly beer runs to **Rouli's,** on Venizelou St.

## Near Rethymnon

Like many of Crete's monastic centers, the **Arkadi Monastery** has a long history of resistance to foreign incursions. But it is chiefly due to the events of November 9, 1866 that Arkadi is esteemed by Cretans. At the time, the monastery was storing gunpowder for the war against the Turks, and over 1000 Cretans took refuge here. When thousands of Turks besieged the monastery and defeat was imminent, the abbot ignited the gunpowder, blowing up the building to prevent its capture. Hundreds, maybe thousands, of Cretans and Turks died in the explosion, bringing worldwide attention to the Greeks' struggle for independence. Throughout Greece, the Arkadi Monastery is regarded as a symbol of freedom and independence. The anniversary of the battle is observed November 7-9 with solemn celebrations at Arkadi and in Rethymnon. (Monastery open daily 6am-8pm.)

Although the excursion to Arkadi is charged with more significance for Greek visitors, the trip is worth taking to view the handsome stone buildings of the monastery. The roofless gunpowder room is at the far left corner of the courtyard, near the unused eastern entrance to the monastery. The historical museum on the right (southern) side of the courtyard contains momentos connected with the war. (Closed 1-3pm. Admission 100dr, students 50dr.) To the left as the bus enters the site is the octagonal **Sanctuary of the Heroes,** a memorial to the victims of the blast. Inside are displayed the skulls of 13 Cretans who perished in front-line combat. Several tour companies offer expensive one-day excursions to the monastery, but you can easily go on your own: **Buses** leave Rethymnon from the bus station (Mon.-Fri. at 10:30am, noon, and 2:30pm, returning at noon, 1pm, and 4pm; Sat.-Sun. at 11am and 2:30pm, returning at 1pm and 4pm; 45 min., 135dr).

If you take any bus about 10km west along the coastal highway, you'll pass one of Crete's sandy stretches of beach, that extend all the way around the **Gulf of Georgiopolis.** The highway has taken away some of the beach's splendid solitude, but at the same time it has also preserved the remainder by running so close to the water that almost no hotels could be built. Although cars and motorbikes can pull over along the road, the nearest inexpensive accommodations are in the quiet coastal village of **Georgiopolis;** try the **Amfimalla Hotel** (tel. 224 70; singles 1000dr; doubles 1500dr; hot showers included) or the nearby **Hotel Penelope** (tel. 224 77; doubles 1600dr). There's a **campsite** on the shore just outside of town. Unofficial camping is usually not feasible, since the beach is almost entirely exposed. Georgiopolis' **telephone code** is 0825.

The ruins of **Elevtherna,** including its curious Hellenistic bridge, are near the village of Prines southeast of Rethymnon. Also of interest is the **Late Minoan Cemetery** of Armeni, about 8km south of Rethymnon. More than 150 rock-cut chamber tombs have been found, some containing clay larnax coffins with ax and horn decorations. This is one attraction you simply can't miss. The area is easily reached by the bus headed for Agia Galini.

## From Agia Galini to Rethymnon

The main road from Agia Galini to the medieval city of Rethymnon twists through fertile valley, expansive mountain terrain, and sleepy villages, before continuing west to the new-found beach resort of Plakias and the peaceful environs of Moni Preveli.

# Hania Χανιά

In the not-too-distant past, Hania served weary travelers as a quiet refuge from Minoan mazes and tour-packaged towns. Though Hania has withstood the worst ravages of overdevelopment, it is no longer the pristine harbor town of old. Beneath the unseemly surface of tour buses and sycophantic *taverna* owners remains a fiercely independent town. Meandering streets thread their way through bombed-out ruins of Greek, Turkish, and Venetian buildings, revealing the past of the agricultural center once known as Kydonia. Patience and a few days in the old Turkish quarter, with its lazy view of the Venetian harbor, will make any visitor forget the broiling heat and noise of Athens or Iraklion.

## Orientation and Practical Information

From the bus station, walk right on Kidonias St. for two blocks and turn left onto Platia 1866; going north, the road becomes Halidon St. and leads to the old **harbor,** the setting for much of Hania's nightlife. To lighten the load while you're looking for a room, leave your bags at the bus station from 7am to 7pm (50dr per bag per day). From the Municipal Market where the bus from the port of Souda arrives, walk two blocks west (left as you face the market) on Gianari Street and turn right onto Halidon.

As you enter the harbor, veer right and walk towards the restored Janissaries Mosque, which houses Hania's tourist office. Even with the maps provided here and at the kiosks, finding your way around Hania is no cinch. Street names change with alarming frequency—sometimes from block to block. Hania's business district is mostly contained within the area across from the market, around the intersection of **Gianari Street** and **Tzanakaki Street.** Cheap hotels are near Halidon, Betolo, and Tsouderon St., but for stunning vistas of the harbor, try the pensions on Zambeliou St. and off Kanevaro St. on Kastelli Hill.

**Municipality of Hania Tourist Information Office:** 6 Akti Tompazi (tel. 433 00), in the converted Turkish mosque at the east end of the harbor. Efi and Maria supply maps (absolutely necessary), bus and ferry schedules, information on Samarian Gorge visits, and lists of area festivals and ceremonies. Currency exchange (Mon.-Sat. 9:15am-1:15pm) and limited hotel information also available. English, French, and German spoken. Open March-Oct. Mon.-Sat. 8:30am-2pm and 3-8:30pm.

**Greek National Tourist Oraganization (GNTO):** 4th floor of the Megaro Pantheon, Platia 1866 (tel. 264 26), above the Greek Agricultural Bank. Provides tourist information in the off-season (Nov.-Feb.). Open Mon.-Fri. 7:30-2:30pm.

**Tourist Police:** 44 Karaiskaki St. (tel. 244 77), near the central bus station. Provides maps and directions. Gruff service. Open daily 7:30am-8pm.

**Budget Travel Office: Interkreta,** 9 Kanevaro St. (tel. 525 52 or 521 42), a few steps east of the waterfront. Student discounts on international air fare and **Magic Bus** tickets for the mainland. Also has currency exchange. Open daily 8:30am-1:30pm and 5:30-8:30pm.

**Currency Exchange: Credit Bank,** 2 Kanevarou St. (tel. 576 44), on the east side of the harbor. Open in summer Mon.-Thurs. 8am-2pm, Fri. 8am-1:30pm, Sat. 8am-2pm. Another branch at 106 Halidon St., near Platia 1866. Open daily 8am-2pm and 6-8pm. **National Bank of Greece,** on Kidonias St., next to the bus station, and on Tzanakaki St., across from the market. Open Mon.-Thurs. 8am-2pm, Fri. 7:45am-1:30pm. **Gift shops** by the harbor will sometimes change money after hours at slightly lower rates. Cash advances on visas obtainable at the **Ionian-Popular Bank,** on Gianari St. (tel. 225 08). Open 8am-7pm.

**Post Office:** 3 Tzanakaki St. Open Mon.-Fri. 7:30am-8pm. Another small office at Halidon St., in front of the cathedral. Will exchange currency. Open Mon.-Sat. 8am-8pm, Sun. 8am-7pm. **Postal code:** 73100.

**OTE:** 5 Tzanakaki St. Exceptionally efficient and uncrowded. Open daily 6am-midnight. Telex and telegram Mon.-Fri. only. **Telephone code:** 0821.

**Airport: Olympic Airways,** 88 Tzanakaki St. (tel. 277 01), near the public garden. Buses for the airport leave from here 1½ hr. before each flight. Open daily 5:30am-8:30pm. For detailed information on flights, see Getting to Crete in the Crete Introduction above.

**Buses: Central bus station,** on the corner of Kidonias and Kelaidi St. (tel. 230 52). Buses go to: Rethymnon (every ½ hr. 5:30am-8pm, 1 hr., 500dr); Iraklion (every ½ hr. 5:30am-8pm, 3 hr., 900dr); Omalos (5 per day, 1 hr., 280dr); Kastelli (every hr. 6am-7:30pm, 1 hr., 270dr); Paleochora (6 per day, 2 hr., 460dr); Chora Sfakion (4 per day, 2 hr., 460dr); Sougia (9am and 1:30pm, 2 hr., 420dr); Moni Chrisoskalitissa (1 per day, noon, 3½ hr., 400dr); and Kalyves (every ½ hr. on the Iraklion bus). An additional 28 buses per day go to local cities on the road west of Hania: Platanias (15 min., 80dr); Maleme (½ hr., 110dr); Kolimbari (45 min., 150dr). Buses to Souda (50dr) leave from Gianari St. in front of the market (every

15 min. 6am-11pm). Other local buses leave from the far left corner of Platia 1866 (as you face inland), at the intersection of Sfakianaki and Kidonias St. The bus to Kalamaki leaves every 20 min., stopping at Galatas and Camping Hania. For airport buses see above.

**Ferries: A.N.E.K. Office,** Venizelou Sq. (tel. 256 56), near the National Bank of Greece. Ferries leave from Souda for Piraeus daily at 7pm. Tourist class 2650dr, deck-class 2000dr. Open daily 9am-10pm.

**Moped Rental: Zeus,** 2 Eleftheriou (tel. 556 30), near the harbor. Prices start at 1100dr. Also try **Duke of Crete** (formerly Makis), 3 Sifaka (tel. 216 51), or 16 Skalidi (tel. 549 67), both off of the *platia*. Suzuki mopeds 1400dr, bicycles 500dr, cars from 5600dr. Shop around on Halidon St. for bargains.

**Foreign Bookstores: Pelekanakis,** 98 Halidon St. (tel. 225 12); and **Kalaitzakis,** 27 Tsouderon St. (tel. 227 63). The bookshops in the harbor sell foreign newspapers.

**Laundromat:** 7 Episk. Dorotheu (tel. 498 69), a small alley east of Halidon St., behind the cathedral in Platia Metropolis. Wash 400dr per load, wash and tumble dry 800dr. Mon.-Sat. 9am-3pm.

**Public Toilets:** Behind the port police in Platia 1866. Look for faucets attached to the fountain to rinse out clothes. Other W.C.s located behind the harbor across from the Piraeus Hotel on Zambeliou St., and on Kastelli Hill near the Rector's Palace.

**Women's Clinic:** Dr. Kapakis Manousos, 3 Nik. Foka St. (tel. 526 88). Open Mon.-Sat. 9am-2pm and 5:30-8:30pm.

**Lost and Found:** Immigration Police, 32 Sfakianaki St. (tel. 533 33).

**Municipal Market:** Walk down Halidon St. away from the harbor, then turn left on Tsouderon. Buses from Souda stop in front. Also, Sat. morning fruit and vegetable market on Nik. Foka St.

**Mountain Climbing:** Secretary of the Alpine Club, 90 Tzanakaki St. (tel. 246 47).

**Pharmacy:** Ulahaki Eleui, 58 Tzanakaki St. (tel. 289 56), near Olympic Airways Office. Pharmacies are scattered throughout Hania; look for the "red cross" sign in front.

**Hospital:** At the corner of Dragoumi and Kapodistriou St. (tel. 272 31), in the eastern part of town. Out-patient clinic open Mon.-Sat. 12:30-2pm and 6-9pm, Sun. 8am-9pm. For emergencies, call 222 22.

## Accommodations and Camping

In the old town, most of the inexpensive pensions overlook the harbor, a convenient if bustling locale. Singles here go for 1000dr, while doubles and triples range from 1500-2500dr. Small hotels are sprouting from the beaches on the west coast, but expect to lay out the cash for the brown sand of **Nea Kydonia** and **Agia Marina.** Tourist officials and police are obliging with information but won't give recommendations. Freelance camping on the eastern side doesn't seem to bother anyone.

**Youth Hostel (IYHF),** 33 Drakonianou St. (tel. 535 65), on the southern outskirts of town. Take the Agios Ioannis bus from Apokoronou St. near the market, get off at the 5th stop at Dexameni Sq., and follow the signs. A dusty fall-out shelter in an inconvenient though panoramic setting. Cold showers and squat toilets. No curfew. Open March-Nov. 450dr per person. Breakfast 150dr. Luggage storage 40dr per day.

**Hotel Fidias,** 6 Sarpaki St. (tel. 524 94). From Halidon St., turn right at the cathedral on Athinagora St., which becomes Sarpaki St. Clean rooms and hot showers. Friendly proprietors offer discounts for extended stays. Singles 900dr. Doubles 1200dr, with bath 1300dr. Dorm triples 600dr per person. Rooms with balcony available.

**Pension Kastelli,** 39 Kanevarou St. (tel. 570 57), near the east end of the harbor. Recent renovations preserved the tasteful, traditional decor. Washing machine available. Bar open until 9:30pm. Singles 1100dr, with bath 1300dr. Doubles 1500dr, with bath 2000dr. Breakfast 400dr. For 3-5 people, the owners rent a nearby townhouse.

**Hotel Piraeus,** 10 Zambeliou St. (tel. 541 54), left off Halidon St. (facing the harbor). Genial rooms with hot showers. Ask for a balcony for the best views. Bar with darts for the nocturnal. Singles 1000dr, doubles 1500dr, triples 2000dr.

**Meltemi Pension,** 2 Angelou St. (tel. 401 92), on the northwest side of the harbor, next to the Naval Museum. Quiet with good views in a historic neighborhood. Ask for Ioannis. Singles 1000dr. Spacious doubles 2000dr. Triples 2200dr.

**Pension Efi,** 15 Sorvolou St. (tel. 239 86). From the Municipal Market, turn right onto Gianari St.; take the first right on Mousouron, the first right on Tsouderon, the first left onto Potie, the first right onto Daliani, and (finally) the second left onto tiny Sorvolou. Look for the small signs along the way. Well worth the search. Amicable management, trellised and peaceful courtyard, and basins in the rooms. Doubles 1500dr, triples 2000dr.

**Hotel Manos,** 17 Zambeliou St. (tel. 521 52), above the Dionisius Taverna on the waterfront. Enter on Zabeliou St., which runs west from Halidon. Dark and cavernous—a real Turkish spook house. Doubles 1500dr.

**Pension Kydonia,** 15 Isodion St. (tel. 571 79). From Halidon St., walk east on Athinagora for 1 short block to Isodion. Traditional interior. Some rooms with balconies. Sink for washing clothes. Singles 800dr. Doubles 1500dr. Triples 2200dr.

**Antonis Rooms,** 8 Kountoriotou St. (tel. 200 19), on the west end of harbor on the waterfront. Cheap, clean, and scenic in the harbor-side rooms. Doubles 1500dr. Triples 2000dr.

**Hotel Viennos,** 27 Skalidi St. (tel. 224 70), past 1866 Platia from the harbor. Institutional, spacious rooms with private sinks. Singles 1100dr, doubles 1600dr, triples 1800dr. Hot showers included.

**Rooms for Rent No. 47,** 47 Kandanoleu (tel. 532 43), on Kastelli Hill. Turn left off Kanevaro St. Eccentric decor includes horse-head mirrors. Small rooms with basins. Nice views, and especially friendly proprietors. Doubles 1600dr. Triples 2000dr.

**Camping:** The camping sites are west of Hania proper, within walking distance of the beaches. **Camping Hania** (tel. 341 90), about 2½ km from town. Take the Kalamaki bus from Platia 1866 (60dr). Sites bordered by flowers and shaded by lush olive trees. *Taverna* and mini-market open daily. 300dr per person, 200dr per small tent. Children under 12 half-price. **Camping Agia Marina** (tel. 685 55). Take the Kastelli Bus. Alternately grassy and sandy, with palm fronds flitting overhead. Snack bar and supermarket. 400dr per person. 300dr per tent. Children ages 4-10 200dr. Cars 200dr. Hot showers available. Both sites open March-October.

## Food and Entertainment

The combination of night-light fishing and poaching has resulted in a paucity of seafood in Hania. Tuna, herring, shrimp, swordfish, sole, and others might be available, but beware of wallet poaching. Most tourists subsist on the homogenized "Greek" cuisine offered by the *tavernas* lining the waterfront (about 450dr for meat dishes). Better food is found walking east along the harbor to **Akti Enoseos** and even farther east to **Akti Miaouli.** Locals avoid the harbor-side restaurants and head to **Nea Chora,** a 10-minute walk west around the new harbor, where the fish is great and the language is almost exclusively Greek; try **Fragios** on the waterfront. On **Halidon Street,** *souvlaki* stands and fast-food joints provide cheap eats. For discriminating travelers on the run, the indoor **Municipal Market** on Gianari and Tzanakaki St. offers bread, pasteries, herbs, produce, meats, and other edibles. (Open Mon.-Sat. 8am-1pm, Tues. and Fri. 6-9pm.) On the waterfront near the tourist office is **Varelas** (tel. 546 76), where Julio's Greek salad and *souvlaki* cost 600dr. (Open daily 11am-2am.) At the east end of the harbor are **Dinos** (tel. 574 48) and **Faka** (tel. 412 40), behind the customs house on Platia Katehaki.

The hot to trot will become only more feverish in Hania. Venture north from the tourist office to the east side of the harbor for the hopping spots. The **Canale Club Disco** (tel. 555 27) asks 500dr per drink, plus one drink at the door instead of a cover. (Open daily 10am-3am.) Nearby, **The Four Seasons,** 29 Akti Tompazi (tel. 555 83), presents bands with bizarre covers of rock favorites. **The Idaion Adron,** 26 Halidon St. (tel. 582 47) is at once a bar, dance hall, and ice-cream shop. Catch the classical music and jazz in the evening, then hit the floor later in the night. (Dancing 10:30pm-3am. Drinks 350-450dr.) The locals usually gather around the harbor's west end. **Fagotto,** 16 Angelou, 30m from the Naval Museum, bops with jazz bands from dusk 'til 2am. (Drinks 300-500dr.) Haniots swap tales with haggard

backpackers at the **Caseneion,** at the harbor's entrance on Zambeliou and Venezelou
St. Casual types get worked up about the yogurt, honey, nut, and fruit concoctions
at **Cafe L'Amour,** Platia 1866 (tel. 230 90), under the Hotel Averof. (Open daily,
7am-11pm.) The sweeter teeth gleam for the *baklava* at **Kronos,** 21 Moussouron
St. (tel. 235 28), near the western end of the covered market. Moviegoers should
consult the listings of foreign films at the tourist office or at the southern end of
the covered market. The sharks convene daily at the **pool hall** (tel. 425 20), behind
the tourist office at the harbor. An hour of eight-ball costs 480dr. (Open 8:30am-
2am.)

Near Hania, **Zamania's,** 2km down the road to Iraklion on Apokoronou St., has
live Cretan music (Wed., Fri., and Sat.-Sun. 10pm-2:45am), and dancing when customers are in the mood. They serve good food, but to avoid paying 1000dr for a
meal, order a half-liter of retsina and listen all night. Catch the Souda bus in front
of the market, and ask the driver to stop here. If you miss the last bus back to Hania
at 11pm, you can take a taxi for 150dr. Similar to Zamania's, but less tourist-
infested, is **Family Tavern,** on the main road in Mournies. Take a cab for 200dr.
(Open daily 8:30pm until the customers all leave.)

## *Sights*

Imprints of Hania's complex past confront you nowhere as fully as on **Kastelli
Hill.** Remnants of Ancient Kydonia's Bronze-Age prosperity are visible in the late
**Minoan House** (circa 1450 B.C.E.), on the corner of Kandanoleu and Kanevoro
St. In the Middle Ages, the Venetian occupiers enriched the city architecturally,
but only the **Rector's Palace** still stands. Much was destroyed during World War
II, though many relics are housed in the **Venetian Archival,** 35 Lithinon St., north
of Kanevaro St.

The old past of Hania was molded mostly by the Turks who arrived in 1645.
The Turkish residential quarters wind around the harbor's edge, while the Jewish
quarter starts behind the harbor's entrance. The latter centers around the **synagogue**
on the west side of Kodilaki St., near Zambeliou St. A stroll in the alleyways behind
the waterfront will give you some idea of the historical complexity of Hania. Pass
through several archways on Moshon St. to reach the **Venetian Chapel,** decorated
with Latin inscriptions and Turkish graffiti. Young Greeks mellow out in the **Municipal Gardens,** once the property of a Turkish *muezzin* (prayer caller). Beyond
the gardens to the east, turn left onto **Sfakianaki,** a nineteenth-century neighborhood and venue for the **Historical Museum and Archives** (tel. 226 06), 20 Sfakianaki
St., which exhibits maps, manuscripts, and folk art for the diligent students of Turkish and Venetian history.

The **Venetian Inner Harbor,** west of the main port, still has its original breakwater and Venetian arsenal. The **Venetian Lighthouse** was restored by the Egyptians
during their occupation of Crete in the late 1830s. On the opposite side of the main
harbor, the **Naval Museum** (tel. 264 37) shows Greek nautical pictures, models,
pieces of boats, and seashells. (Open Tues., Thurs., and Sat. 10am-2pm. Admission
100dr, students 50dr.) The terrestrial will flock to the **Archeological Museum** (tel.
203 34) 80m back from the water on Halidon St., opposite the cathedral. The museum, with its collection of Cretan artifacts, was once a Venetian monastery and,
more recently, the Turkish Mosque of Yusuf Pasha.

Hania is a disappointment for beach lovers. The harbor has been polluted by fishing boats, and the nearest swimming is in **Nea Chora** (20 min. by foot to the west
around the new harbor). Brown and pebbly beaches can be reached by taking a blue
bus from Platia 1866 marked for Kalamaki or Galatas. A green bus for Kastelli
will take you farther west. **St. Apostle's Beach,** via the Kalamaki bus, is popular
for its wide sandy coves, sheltered by steep rock walls. On the Akrotiri Peninsula,
try **Starros** or the **Bay of Kalathas** for good beaches. To the west is the **Bay of Almirida,** which can be reached from Kalyves.

## Near Hania

Many intriguing villages and sights around Hania patiently await exploration. Except for the Samaria Gorge, few are visited. Northeast of town, the **Akrotiri Peninsula** hems in the sparkling Souda Bay and features three monasteries and several good beaches. Akrotiri is ideal for a daytrip by moped: Distances are short, traffic is light, and roads are passable. To get to the monasteries, follow signs for the airport. From the airport, there'll be signs for **Agia Triada** (not to be confused with the Minoan site of the same name), a monastery founded in the seventeenth century by two Venetian brothers. The name means Holy Trinity. A friendly monk may greet you with a complimentary glass of *raki*. The monastery's crumbling pink buildings shelter a small collection of icons and manuscripts. In the courtyard, you can sit among the flowers while the black-robed monks with long, white beards walk silently from building to building. When they're busy, a tape of monastic chanting played from one of the upper rooms adds to the solemn ambience.

The church of **Gouvernetou,** 4km north along the same road, was knocked down so many times that the caretakers finally installed an unbreakable copper dome to avoid the trouble of repairing it. Somehow, the 500-year-old fresco of Christ surrounded by saints and martyrs remained intact; today, it is set in the dome. The church, also known as Agios Ioannis, also contains a Venetian relief and several 500-year-old icons. The metal squares depicting parts of the body that are strung in front of the icon of St. John (Agios Ioannis) are votives hung in gratitude by those who have prayed for and received healing from him. Other icons, more colorful but less historically interesting, can be seen in the room to the left of the courtyard. Because Gouvernetou is less popular with tourists than its neighbor to the south, the monks are more hospitable and will explain the history of the buildings and St. John in German or English. Be sure to come properly dressed; women should cover their shoulders and knees. If you decide to visit the monasteries, get an early start since they are closed from 2 to 5pm.

A 30-minute walk from Gouvernetou leads to the ruins and cave of **Katholiko,** the first monastic settlement on Crete, built around 1200 C.E. St. John the Hermit, to whom the English church is dedicated, lived in these parts in the ninth century C.E. Today, goatherds take refuge from the afternoon sun in his cave. The monks at Gouvernetou will show you the well-marked footpath that continues past Katholiko to the sea. The 10-minute hike takes you down the mountainside and through a wonderful ravine. Mark the place where you leave the trail to enter the ravine; otherwise, you may have trouble finding the path again.

Most Greeks venture out to Akrotiri to visit the **Hill of the Prophet Ilias,** 7km from Hania. In 1897, Cretan fighters raised the Greek flag on this hill in defiance of Turkish forces. In addition to its fine view of Hania and of the bay, the hill contains the grave of Eleftherios Venizelos (1864-1936), the Cretan revolutionary and statesman who served as Prime Minister of Greece for several administrations. Venizelos is fondly remembered by Greeks but especially by Cretans. In every town on Crete, you will find a street or a plaza named after him, as well as numerous memorials.

If your feet cry out at the sight of rocky beaches, visit **Stavros,** 18km from Hania, where nary a pebble can be found. This small, quiet cove was the setting for the film *Zorba the Greek*. **Mama's Restaurant** (tel. 641 00) rents beach bungalows for 2000dr per person. You can also pitch a tent behind the beach. (Buses to Stavros run from Hania daily at 7am and 2pm.) There is another sandy beach, more lively than Stavros, but less private and closer to the road, at **Kalathos** (12km from Hania), near **Choraphakia,** also on the peninsula's western side.

Boats to Hania dock at the port of **Souda,** 5km to the east. Formerly the site of a daunting Venetian fortress, Souda is now a major NATO naval base, evidenced by the numerous crew-cut American sailors strolling through Hania, the low-flying Navy jets over Akrotiri, and the tight security. No tours are allowed. When Hania celebrates "Naval Week" in early July, the port comes alive with festivities, but otherwise it's rather dull. The **Souda Bay War Cemetery,** known locally as the English Cemetery, is on the innermost corner of Souda Bay. The rose garden borders the graves of over 1500 British, Australian, and New Zealander military men killed in the Battle of Crete in May 1941. Take the Souda Bay bus from the Hania market, ask the driver to let you off at the nearest stop, then walk about 1½km following signs to the naval school.

If you're stuck in Souda, which is the only reason to stay there, a handful of hotels offer comfortable, albeit colorless, accommodations. The **Parthenon** (tel. 892 45), on the north end of the Main Sq., offers clean rooms. (Singles 1100dr. Doubles 1700dr. Triples 2500dr.) Ask downstairs in the *taverna*. The **Knossos** is also in the Main Sq. (tel. 892 82). Doubles 1500dr. Triples 2000dr. Bargaining can bring the price down another 500dr. The **National Bank of Greece**, west of the Platia, will exchange money. (Open Mon.-Thurs. 8am-2pm, Fri. 8am-1:30pm.) **Buses** to Souda leave Hania from the market's entrance every 15 minutes (50dr).

Buses cruising along the new highway to Rethymnon stop at the turn off for the ancient site of **Aptera,** a three-kilometer hike uphill past the village of Megala Korafia. At the top of the hill, the road forks: To the right is a small monastery, the remains of the Hellenistic city, and Roman cisterns; to the left, an abandoned Turkish fort. The bus fare for the thrice daily trip from Hania is 100dr.

A few kilometers east of the Aptera detour, a turn off down to the water leads to the growing village of **Kalyves,** a conservative community with good beaches at the end of town. The *platia* is packed with cafes, a *periptero* (kiosk), and some rooms for rent. Past the *platia* on the left is **Kalyves Travel,** where you can exchange money. With that money you can buy their fishing harpoons also. Coming into town, the **OTE** is on the right side (Mon.-Fri. 7:30am-3:10pm) and the **post office** on the left, near the *platia* (Mon.-Fri. 7:30am-2:15pm). The **telephone code** is 0825. Several small hotels operate around the *platia;* singles run for 1000dr, doubles 1500dr.Hourly buses heading to Rethymnon stop at Kalyves (80dr).

Continuing 4km east from Kalyves is the isolated beach coastal village of **Almirida.** Archeologists have uncovered the ruins of a basilica-style church dating from the 6th century. Notice the large cruciform mosaic. Just when your throat is so parched that the the road from Almirida inland to Gavalohori seems bound for Hades emerges **Alekos Farm** tel. 315 89). Except when Alekos Nikolioudakis disappears to feed the birds, chickens, sheep, dogs, cats, and whatever else lives around his grove, he is available to rent you a large suite with a kitchen, well-suited for families with children. (6-person capacity. 4000dr. Doubles from 2000dr.) Individual campers are also welcome.

Green hills quickly turn steep and rocky to the South of Hania, evolving into the **Lefka Ori** (White Mountains). Four kilometers away, the little village of **Mournies,** Venizelos' birthplace, can be reached by bus (3 per day), taxi (110dr one-way), bike, or thumb. Mournies' trees, for which the village is named, line the streets. In the summer, ripening grapes hang from the trellises on the patios, and the air is rich with mingled scents of jasmine, rosemary, dahlias, roses, and eucalyptus.

To the southwest 12km away, the town of **Alikianos** offers a lush green alternative to beach burnout. On the main road heading west is a turn-off for Alikianos and the Souyia Road. After crossing a river, cool down at the **Oasis Kafeneio** (tel. 771 54), where the locals can fill you in on the day's gossip.

The first left after the bakery leads to the **OTE**. (Open Mon.-Fri. 7:30am-3:15pm.) Farther up the central street are a few *tavernas,* a **Bank of Crete**, a **pharmacy**, and the **post office,** where you can change money. (Open Mon.-Fri. 7:30am-2:15pm.)

The lone architectural treasure, the fourteenth-century Agios Ioannis, stands unmarked about 1km from Alikianos as you veer right for **Koufos.** The abandoned church, with its fifteenth-century frescoes and orange groves, makes for a nice picnic spot.

The mountain village of **Skines,** on the road to Sougia from **Vatolakus,** overflows with blooming vines, roses, and sunflowers, while the adjacent countryside bursts with orange groves. This little town has a turn-off that leads up to Omalos, through a windy mountain pass, and eventually to the main road.

On the Omalos Rd., after passing the junction for Sougia, the road meets the tiny town of **Fournes** 15½ km later. Here the road forks: To the left, six kilometers down, several streams converge at the serene village of **Meskla.** The village focuses on a fourteenth-century chapel built on the foundations of a fifth-century basilica and the Modern Church of the Panayia next door. The local *taverna* (tel. 672 76), in the *platia,* offers clean rooms. (Doubles 1750dr. Triples 2500dr.) Up the hill from the churches, hikers will enjoy the one-hour climb to **Theriso.** Four women crocheting outside a small *taverna* will greet thirsty travelers at the summit. From the right fork of the Omalos Rd., 25km from Hania, is the white-washed mountain village of **Laki.** There are a few rooms in town from which to survey the terraced hillside below. The make-shift rooms and toilets at **Kokkinakis Cafe-Bar** (tel. 672 32) are best described as minimalist. (Singles 600dr. Doubles 1200dr. Triples 2000dr. Hot showers included.)

Hania's western coastline, accessible along the North Coast Hwy., is checkered by stucco hotels and motor scooter rental agencies. **Platanias,** a budding beach resort 11km from Hania, unofficially marks the end of the region's urban sprawl. The **OTE** and **post office** (which exchanges money) are both in the *platia.* Bus tickets can be purchased at the **periptero** (kiosk) in the *platia.* Several buses run to Hania daily (80dr); early-morning fare to Omalos and the Samaria Gorge costs 850dr round-trip.

With its mountainous backdrop and proximity to appealing beaches, finding summer rooms in Platanias can mortally wound the wallet. The **Hotel Moon,** next to the Bank of Crete at the east end of town, offers traditional rooms. (Doubles 2000dr.) Inquire at Stella's Supermarket in town. Stella's daughter runs **Stella's** (tel. 680 63), across from the Kantari Tavern at the edge of town. New doubles with bath and kitchen ring up at a hefty 2500dr. For a taste of local fare, head to the **Kantari Taverna** (tel. 680 90), on the west side of town on the right. Locals gobble up the **piperato fileto** (peppered steak) with a spicy mushroom sauce (1000dr). Ask about the *bouzouki* night on Thursdays. (Open daily 10am-1am.)

If possible, visit the **German War Cemetery** just west of **Maleme,** Platanias' neighboring village. The Maleme airfield (now a military base) played a critical role during the German airborne attack of Crete in 1941. The **German War Cemetery** is as much a tribute to the Cretan spirit of forgiveness as the carnage of war. A wall map details the assault in which 6580 Germans were killed. This cemetery should be visited in conjunction with the **Commonwealth Cemetery** at Souda Bay, which contains the graves of 1527 Allied soldiers. Once in the mood, return down the main road and stop off at a late **Minoan Tomb,** about 200m below the cemetery. At the first left bend in the road, walk 100m east along the hillside to the rectangular chamber, excavated in 1966. For your own deep sleep, look for the red "rooms to let" sign at the east end of Malame (tel. 623 13). (Small doubles 1800dr.)

Better but pricier accommodations are found in **Kolimbari,** 6km west of Maleme and situated on the elbow of the peninsula that encloses the Gulf of Hania. This long pebbly beach in town attracts its share of tourists in the summer, but during most of the year, the pace is sedate. For beach-front rooms, turn right after the **police station** at the west end of town. Ask for rooms at Vera's Grocery Store (tel. 221 23). Her secluded rooms include bathrooms and *pitnos* jars in the frontyard. (Doubles 2000dr. Triples 2500dr. Discounts for longer stays.) **Roumentaleis** (tel. 225 96), above the OTE, has old-fashioned rooms. (Doubles 2500dr. Triples 3000dr. Communal kitchen included.) The town's **post office** (open Mon.-Fri. 7:30am-2:15pm) and **OTE** (open Mon.-Fri. 7:30am-3:10pm) are both on the main street, which includes several *tavernas.* Kick up your flip-flops and watch the surf at **Spatha** (tel. 220 88), to the right down a small alley as you enter town. (Beer and Nescafe 80dr. Open daily 8am-midnight.)

One kilometer past the Kolimbari crossroads is the **Monastery of Gonias,** founded in 1618 by the Cypriot monk Blaise. The four iron cannon balls lodged in its walls attest to its importance as a center of resistance against the Turks. There is also a small museum inside with documents, vestments, and icons. Shorts are definitely frowned upon. (Church and museum closed 1-4pm.) Up the road about

100m from the monastery are pebbly coves good for snorkeling. To get to the towns on the gulf, take the bus headed for Kastelli or one of the frequent buses that go as far as Kolimbari: Platanias (15 min., 80dr); Maleme (35 min., 120dr); and Kolimbario (40 min., 160dr).

# Samaria Gorge Φαράγγι Σαμαρίας

The most popular excursion from Hania, and a "must" on any trip to western Crete, is the five-hour hike down the formidable Samaria Gorge, which, at 18km, is Europe's longest gorge. Worn away by millions of years of river runoff, the White Mountain's pass has managed to retain its allure despite the mobs who visit it—as many as 1000 people tumble down the gorge in summer. Wild flowers and shrubs peek out from sheer rock walls; bird watchers can glimpse the rare Bearded Vulture; goat lovers (aren't we all?) can spot the nimble *agrimi,* a wild Cretan species in one of its few remaining natural habitats.

The 44-kilometer bus ride from Hania to **Xyloskalo,** where the trail begins, passes spectacular scenery—catch the early bus to see an incredible sunrise. The road climbs through the Omalos Mountains, past the enchanting village of Laki, to an altitude of 1500m at the head of the gorge. Then the 18-kilometer trek begins. Passing between cliff walls up to 300m high, the path, only 3m wide at some points, winds down along a river bed that nearly runs dry in summer, and ends in the small town of Agia Roumeli on the southern coast. From there a boat sails to Loutra and Chora Sfakion, where you can catch a bus back to Hania. The ambitious can hike from Agia Roumeli to Chora Sfakion (10 hr.) along one of the most outstanding coastlines in the country. (See Southwest Coast.) The bus to Hania from Chora Sfakion passes through the village of **Vrises,** where there are doubles to let for about 1500dr. You may whiff burning charcoal, which is frequent in this area: Huge olive trunks are burned and broken into bits of charcoal before they are bagged and sold as heating fuel.

The downhill hike favored by most people (Xyloskalo in the Omalos Plain to Agia Roumeli) takes from four to seven hours. A less-traveled path next to the tourist pavillion ascends Mt. Gingilos to the west. Whichever you choose, wear good walking shoes and bring trail snacks. Because of its altitude, the top of the gorge can be cold and rainy, so bring appropriate clothing. Although there are many natural springs (about every 2km), a canteen is useful—it allows you to picnic away from these crowded watering holes. Also remember that, though less tiring than uphill climbing, downhill hiking is tricky. Twisted ankles and shin splints are not uncommon. Finally, avoid bringing heavy backpacks if at all possible. The trek is much more enjoyable if you make it a daytrip and carry only the bare necessities. If you want to catch only the dramatic tail of the gorge, start from Agia Roumeli. The path to the trail begins just behind Rooms Livikon. From the quay, walk straight to the rear of the village. Known as " Samaria the Lazy Way," the two-hour climb to the north takes you to the gorge's dramatic and narrow pass, the "Iron Gates." This should suit those travelers on the south coast without the time or inclination to take a bus to Xyloskalo. Walking all 18km uphill is not recommended unless you are prepared to do some hefty work along the second half of the trail. It is also possible to go on an organized excursion, arranged by any tourist agency in Hania or Kastelli, which essentially means paying someone to hike with you and a lot of other people.

The gorge is open from May through October; during the winter and spring, the river goes back to work cutting its trail through the rock. Flash floods in the winter have claimed lives in those months. During the other months, passage is officially allowed through the gorge between 6am and 3pm, but from 3pm to sunset you can visit any part of the trail within 2km of either entrance. The Hania Forest Service forbids the following activities in the gorge: staying overnight, lighting fires, smoking, hunting, cutting and uprooting plants, bringing in "intoxicated drinks," and singing music from the '70s. For gorge information, call the **Hania Forest Service** (tel. 222 87).

Overpriced accommodations for the descent are provided at the **tourist pavillion** (tel. 632 69) in Xyloskalo. Reservations for one of the 13 beds should be placed with the Hania GNTO. Five kilometers north of Xyloskalo, cheaper lodgings and food are found in **Omalos.** Gorge yourself or stay at **Drakoulaki's Restaurant** (tel. (0821) 672 69; doubles 1500dr; triples 2000dr). On the plain of Omalos, take a left onto a dirt road for a one-and-a-half-hour trek to the minimally equipped **Kallergis refuge huts.** From there, hikers can make a day's climb to the summit of **Pakhnes** or **Mount Ida** (2456m). Call the **Greek Alpine Club** (tel. 246 47) in Hania for more information.

**Buses** for Omalos and Xyloskalo leave Hania at 6am, 7:30am, 8:30am, 9:30am, and 1:30pm (1½ hr., 300dr). When you ask to buy a ticket to Omalos, the ticket office at the bus station will sell you a round-trip ticket from Hania to Omalos and from Chora Sfakion to Hania (750dr); if you don't plan to return via Chora Sfakion, ask explicitly for a one-way ticket. Since Agia Roumeli is connected by boat to Chora Sfakion, you can make the complete round-trip from Hania in one day, leaving on any of the four morning buses. The last bus will allow you plenty of time and usually waits for the last boat from Agia Roumeli. The early buses, however, will ensure cooler weather and less company for the hike. Alternatively, you can plan a leisurely hike and spend the night in Agia Roumeli, Loutro, or Chora Sfakion (see below).

You have to hike three hot and dusty kilometers beyond the official exit from the gorge to reach **Agia Roumeli,** a seedy oasis for tired and thirsty hikers. Bring a bathing suit for a dip at the town's conservative pebble beach. Pensions in this town charge about 1000dr for singles or 1500-2000dr for doubles. Try **The Gorge** restaurant on the beach (tel. 912 93), with rooms to let, or **Rooms Livikon,** at the inland end of town. In the evening, when the crowds leave town, the beach is a pleasant place to sleep. Many travelers camp out around the wide river mouth, which is mostly dry in summer.

You should move on to some of the less crowded resorts along the southwest coast. Boats travel to Chora Sfakion (mid-June to Aug. 7 per day, last at 6pm, 1¼ hr., 454dr; sometimes boats extend service until 8:30pm, if necessary). All of the boats stop in Loutro, except the last one (1 hr., 242dr). Boats to Paleochora go twice per day (at 4pm and 4:30pm, 2 hr., 577dr), stopping in Sougia (1 hr., 289dr). This daily service begins May 1; before then, boats go to Paleochora three times per week (Tues. and Thurs. at 11am, Sat. at 5pm). Buses from Chora Sfakion to Hania (460dr) depart when each ferry from Agia Roumeli arrives. Don't linger, since the drivers take off as soon as their buses are full.

## Loutro and Finix

European travelers have recently been lured by the bait of Loutro, the peaceful fishing village nestled between Agia Roumeli and Chora Sfakion. Only a few years ago, Loutro was in danger of total desertion due to its inaccessibility, especially in winter, when southern winds and stormy seas make provisions difficult to obtain. Fortunately, this town, along an outstanding stretch of coast, has repopulated and rebounded.

The pensions located along the western end of the cove range from 1500-2000dr for doubles. The **Phoenix Restaurant** (tel. (0825) 912 27) rents plain doubles for 1500dr and also houses the town's international phone. Next to the Phoenix is **Maria's Hotel and Minimarket.** (Doubles with bath 1800-2000dr. Triples 2500-3000dr.) Maria also handles **currency exchange.** (Open daily 8am-1pm and 3-9pm.) East of the kiosk is **Manousodakis,** which lets antiquated doubles with waterfront views and cold showers for 1500dr. (Bargain.) **Canoes** can be rented in the harbor (200dr per hr., 1000dr per day). **Maistrali,** next to the quay, is the scene of tourist nightlife, but slow motion was never this slow. Bubbling Christina serves home-concocted kahlua cocktails (300dr) and a delicious fresh fruit and yogurt dish

(260dr). Fishing boats run daily to Sweetwater Bay (200dr), and weekly to the island of Gavdos (1000dr). *Caïque* service connects Loutro with Chora Sfakion (5 per day, 160dr) and Agia Roumeli (3 per day, 300dr).

The path from Agia Roumeli to Loutro (6 hr.) and onward to Chora Sfakion (8 hr.) wanders along a spectacular strand of coastline and provides views of the Libyan Sea. Start your walk early to avoid the noon sun—much of the trail is unshaded. To pick up the trail in Agia Roumeli, walk east along the beach over the dry river bed and climb up to the path. After 4km you'll pass a small sixteenth-century church; a fresh-water spring under the rocks can replenish your water supply. To continue the hike, stay above the church. Three kilometers west of Loutro, you'll stumble upon **Marble Beach.** Keep your top on here as the disapproving local hierarchy patrols the strip. A bit farther down the trail is a *taverna* at Liko, Nikos's **"Small Paradise."** (Doubles 1500dr.) Follow the steep path behind the *taverna;* **Finix** is about 20 minutes east. Sifis Antithakis, his wife, mother-in-law, and five children are the only permanent residents of this secluded cove and archeological site claimed to be the spot of St. Paul's first visit to Crete. They rent rooms. (Doubles 1500dr, but ask to sleep on the roof. Single-seat canoe rental 200dr per hr.)

The walk from Agia Roumeli to Loutro has its moments, but the plunge onward to Chora Sfakion is prolonged joy. Pick up the trail in Loutro behind the *taverna* marked "Anapoli-Beach-Chora Sfakion." Just outside town, the trail diverges upward to Anapoli and along the coast to Chora Sfakion; the latter passes through three coves to **Sweetwater Beach,** so named because several natural springs just below the pebble surface provide fresh drinking water for the campers who languish on this nude beach. Residents even take great pains to walk to the make-shift communal toilets. Boats from Chora Sfakion sail to the beach daily at 11am and 5pm, returning at 11:20am and 5:20pm. The walk continues on a paved road that heads toward Chora Sfakion. For a similarly exciting excursion from a different direction, hike from Anapoli to Loutro; a bus leaves Chora Sfakion to Anapoli daily at 4pm (100dr). For information about ferries between Chora Sfakion, Loutro, and Agia Roumeli, see Chora Sfakion and Frangokastello.

## Chora Sfakion and Frangokastello

The scenic but charmless town of Chora Sfakion (or Sfakia) has a small beach backed by a whitewashed concrete wall. The raised boardwalk overlooks a small harbor and the vast expanse of sea, with mountains looming on either side. Because Chora Sfakion lacks the dusty heat that pervades Agia Roumeli, it is an adequate resting spot after the Samaria Gorge hike. (Better though, to move on to one of the smaller beach towns and avoid the group tours that pile up along the promenade at night.) Agia Roumeli is connected by bus to Hania and by boat to the entire southwest coast, and thus serves as a good base from which to explore the region. The **post office** and **OTE** stand on the street behind the waterfront. (Both open Mon.-Fri. 7:30am-3:10pm.) On the same street is the **supermarket** (tel. 912 05); stock up here if you plan an extensive tour of more remote beaches. The **police station** is on the eastern corner of the waterfront near the **bus station** and a small travel office, **Sfakia Tours** (tel. 912 72; motocycles 1500dr; open daily 8am-10pm). The **hospital** (tel. 912 14) is on the road leading out of town above the harbor. The **Hotel Stavris** on the port **changes money.** (Open 8am-8pm.)

There are plenty of inexpensive accommodations here. **Rooms Sfakia,** Livikon (tel. 912 11), and **Lefka Ori,** on the waterfront, rent doubles for 1600dr. **John Braos,** the market owner (tel. 912 06) rents doubles with a view of the harbor for 2000dr. **Pension Sofia** (tel. 912 59) has one single for 900dr (the only one in town), doubles for 1400dr, and triples 2000dr. **Rent Rooms,** on the east end of the back street, has triples with a terrace for 1800dr. (Open March-Nov.) **Hotek Stavris** (tel. 912 20), near the post office, is a sure bet. All rooms come with private bath and balcony. (Singles 1200dr. Doubles 1500dr. Triples 2000dr.) The cheapest but dingiest rooms in town are reached by climbing the steps behind Hotel Stavris. **Votzakis,** for example, has hot, primitive triples for 1700dr. (Bargain.)

**Boats** from Chora Sfakion to Agia Roumeli leave daily at 9:40am, 10am, 10:30am, noon, 2:45pm, 3:30pm, and 5pm (1¼ hr. 55dr). Most of these routes stop in Loutro (250dr). These ferries run only from April to October; in winter, you can reach Loutro by foot or fishing boat. Don't dawdle—the captains won't hesitate to leave you behind. Always check boat schedules with the ticket office. Unscheduled boats sometimes run to Loutro. (Chora Sfakion to Gardos, 3 per week, 1000dr.) **Caïques** to Sweetwater Beach run twice daily (250dr). **Buses** from Chora Sfakion go to Plakias (3 hr., 300dr) and then to Rethymnon (4 hr., 450dr) to meet the ferry. At the same time, a bus leaves for Agia Galini (4 hr., 475dr). A bus leaves at 4pm for Anapolis (45 min., 100dr). To get to Iraklion from Chora Sfakion, change buses at Vrises.

Frangokastello, 12km east of Chora Sfakion, has an excellent sandy beach and an impressive fortress at the shoreline. An aura of enchantment surrounds the fourteenth-century Venetian fort here. In 1828 the Turks invaded the region, seizing the fort from the Sfakiates. Legend says that at sunset in mid-May, the Cretan army of Khatsimihalis can be seen dancing around the fort along the water's edge. For the curious, who dare to spend a night, several *tavernas* rent doubles, though facilities are somwhat primitive. Five hundred meters west of the castle, try **Koukounaraki Taverna and Pension** (tel. (0825) 920 92), across from the Blue Sky Disco. (Dorm beds 450dr. Doubles 1100dr, with bath 2000dr. Triples 1400dr, with bath 2400dr.) From the downstairs *taverna,* a small path leads to the beach. Below the castle, on the beach, is **Fata Morgana** (tel. 921 98; doubles 1200dr, with bath 1400dr). Discreet **camping** along the broad, clean stretch of sand is accepted, as is nude bathing. One **bus** per day runs to Frangokastello from Hania (at 2pm, 500dr). It passes through Chora Sfakion and returns to Hania the following morning. The bus from Chora Sfakion to Plakias also passes through Frangokastello.

## Paleochora and Sougia

Once a refuge for the embattled rear guard of the '60s youth culture, Paleochora has become a central attraction along Crete's southern coast. For many it is the only stop. Seventy-seven kilometers from Hania, Paleochora has all the elements of a get-away-from-it-all vacation: a wide, sandy beach with a pine grove and excellent impromptu tent sites, and one main street with all the necessities and *tavernas,* and a harbor lined with reasonably priced pensions.

The bus from Hania stops on **Venizelou Street,** the town's thoroughfare. It intersects **Konetaki Street,** which leads to the sandy beach on the right or to the harbor on the left.

A **bank** is in the center of town on Venizelou St. (Open Mon.-Thurs. 10am-2pm, Fri. 10am-1:30pm.) The **post office** sits on the waterfront next to the Galaxy Cafe (open Mon.-Fri. 8am-2pm), and the **OTE** (open Mon.-Fri. 8am-2pm) is near the bank. Local and international calls can also be made from the kiosk on Venizelou St. The agents at **Interkreta travel,** 4 Kontekaki St. (tel. 413 93), sell student airline, Magic Bus, and ferry tickets. **Paleochora Motorent,** next door to the Paleochora Hotel, rents mopeds for 1300dr, 125cc bikes for 2800dr (open 8:30am-9pm). The **pharmacy** (tel. 414 98) is on Venizelou St. The **police station** is on Kontekaki, near the quay. Paleochora's **telephone code** is 0823.

Walk east on Konetaki and then turn right on Neas Ioannis. If someone doesn't accost you with room offers, ask one of the many women knitting along the sidestreets. The cheapest are converted chicken coops with stone floors and cots for 500dr. Less-fowl doubles cost about 1500dr per person. Paleochora also has two inexpensive hotels. The **Lyvikon,** 1 Venizelou St. (tel. 412 50), is on the left as you come into town. Old and run-down, the hotel is nonetheless popular with those planning long stays. (Doubles 1500dr, with bath 2500dr. Triples 2100dr, with bath 3000dr.) Down the street is the well-maintained **Lissos Hotel** (tel. 412 66; refrigerator and washing facilities available; doubles 1800dr, with bath 2700dr). Tucked away just west of Venizelou St., across from Hotel Rea, is **Manousakis,** Daskaloyiani 4 (tel. 414 15). A friendly family rents four simple rooms with a communal kitchen and a garden. (Doubles 2000dr. Triples 2500dr.) The **Paleochora Hotel** (tel. 410 23), 1 block east of Venizelou, is standard in every way. (Singles 1400dr. Doubles 2200dr-3000dr. Call ahead.) Past the Paleochora Hotel on the harbor waterfront is the *taverna* and hotel **Paralia** (tel. 414 95; doubles 1700dr).

Many young visitors camp out either on the northern end of the main beach, which is popular but technically illegal, or at the official **Camping Paleochora** (tel. 411 20), 1½km east of town. (Open March-Oct. 500dr per person. Hot showers and a *taverna*.) Unfortunately for light sleepers, the campground is next to the open-air disco **Paleochora Club,** which occasionally blasts live music. (Beer 200dr. Open 11pm-3am.) To reach the campground, walk north on Venizelou, turn right opposite the Fina gas station, and take your second left on the last paved road before the beach. From there it's a ½-kilometer walk to the site.

There are several **markets** in the center of town, on Venizelou St. The restaurants lining the road put tables and chairs all the way out to the middle of the street to accommodate diners. Less stuffy and with excellent waterfront views are the restaurants by the harbor. Prices are generally the same all over: *mousaka* 260dr, *kalamari* 220dr, beer 100dr.

Six kilometers inland and above Paleochora lies the peaceful town of **Azogizes,** with a lovely view of the promontory and sea. Here you'll find the thirteenth-century caves of the 99 Holy Fathers and an interesting museum featuring relics of the Turkish occupation dating from 1770. Farther inland are the frescoed churches of Kakodiki dating back to the fourteenth century. These mountain villages can be approached by taking the bus toward Hania. Boats run twice weekly (840dr) to the nearly deserted island of **Gavdos,** the southernmost point of Europe.

An even more isolated outpost is **Sougia,** 10km to the east, with a pleasant, pebbly beach. Inexpensive food (yogurt and honey 100dr) only somewhat compensates for generally more-expensive-than-average rooms (doubles 1500dr, triples 1800-2000dr). For grub and grog, try **Polifimos** (beer 90dr) or the casual **Bla Bla.** There is a footpath from Paleochora to Sougia and Agia Roumeli, but it's an arduous trek and should be attempted only by those proficient in orienteering. Another walk leads to **Lissos** (1½ hr.), the Temple of Asclepios, and a clean beach (follow the stone markers). Starting May 1, boats travel between Agia Roumeli and Paleochora (2 hr., 850dr) daily at 8:30am, stopping in Sougia (1 hr., 425dr); before May, they run only three times per week. Check with travel agencies in Paleochora for schedule changes. Two buses per day go from Sougia to Hania (at 7am and 2:30pm, 1¾ hr., 420dr).

You can make the difficult but satisfying journey to **Elafonisi,** a small island at the southwest corner of Crete. No boats make the crossing, but at low tide the ocean is so shallow that you can wade out to the island. Stock up on provisions ahead of time, since there is no food or water on this beautiful, deserted island. Food is available at Kefali and Vathi, and the residents of **Moni Chrisoskalitissis** can provide water and simple lodgings. Buses run from Kastelli to Vathi and as far as Chrisoskalitissis daily (at 2pm, 350dr, Sun. at 11:15 from Kastelli). From there, a 5-kilometer hike leads to the beach. The bus returns from Vathi at 7am and from Chrisoskalitissis at 4:30pm.

# *Kastelli (Kisamos) and West Coast*
# Καστέλλη

Consider yourself lucky if your visit to Crete begins in the slow-paced merchant town of Kastelli. Getting to western Crete is easy: Ferries run twice a week from the Peloponnese and Piraeus to Kastelli. And once you arrive, the fine fish *tavernas,* relatively cheap lodgings, and unspoiled landscapes more than compensate for the commercialized streets, construction sights, and non-existent night life.

Kastelli is officially referred to as Kisamos to avoid confusion with the classical site of the same name at Pediada, but locals continue to use the old Venetian title.

The small heart of Kastelli is **Platia Tzanakaki,** situated between the highway and the waterfront. In the *platia* is the **bus station,** a **ferry ticket office,** two hotels, and a local **museum.** Along the highway's south side is the **OTE,** next to the kiosk (open Mon.-Fri. 7:30am-3:10pm); farther up on the right is the **post office** (open Mon.-Fri. 7:30am-2:15pm). A small **hospital** lies just off the highway after the BP station. On **Skalidi Street,** running east-west from the *platia,* you'll find food markets, bakeries, several *banks* (open Mon.-Thurs. 8am-2pm, Fri. 7:45am-3:30pm), and a **pharmacy** (tel. 224 51; open Mon.-Sat. 8am-2pm and 4pm-10pm). Taxis can be snagged in the square. Several agents let **motorbikes; Daratsianos** (tel. 229 65), near the post office, has small mopeds from 1100dr, Vespa automatics 1700dr. (Open daily 8am-9:30pm.) Kastelli's **telephone code** is 0822.

Cheap, beach-front rooms are available here but not without a search. At the end of the coastal road to the west, look for a small white stucco house with red shutters. Only 20m from the sea, **Alekos** (tel. 220 73) rents doubles for 1500dr. A little Greek coffee at night and in the morning is usually thrown in to boot. **Kastanaki Maria** (tel. 226 10), near the water on the eastern edge of town, rents modern doubles for 1500dr, with bath 2500dr. (Breakfast 2500dr.) The rustic **Taverna Dhitia** (tel. 223 58) has doubles for 1500dr. Just south of the *platia,* the friendly **Helen Pateromihelaki** (tel. 229 28) offers older rooms with sinks. (Doubles 1500dr. Triples 2200dr.) Hotels in the *platia* range from 1700-2200dr for doubles in summer. For sunbathing bliss on the best beach near Kastelli, try **Camping Mithimna** (tel. 314 44) at Drapanias, 5km east of Kastelli. It's a 1-kilometer walk from the road. (430dr per person. 370dr per tent. Children ½-price.) In high season, a minibus runs every two hours from the Kastelli bus station to the campgrounds.

The fish *tavernas* by the sea in Teloniou Sq. serve excellent meals with picturesque sunsets. **Makedonas** (tel. 221 84), to the right facing the water, has delicious squid for 250dr. (Open daily 8pm-midnight.) Next door is **Papadakis** (tel. 223 40). Try the swordfish *kebab* (500dr). (Open daily 8pm-midnight.) George Stimadorakis' **Fish Restaurant** (tel. 220 57), nestled in a scenic little harbor just west of the town line, has tasty fish soup and caters to a mix of locals and tourists.

**Buses** run regularly between Hania and Kastelli (daily 6am-9pm every hr.; 1 hr.; 270dr). For a daytrip to the Samaria Gorge, take the bus to Omalos (in summer 2 per day at 5am and 6am), returning from Chora Sfakion at 5pm; 1250dr includes bus fare to Omalos and from Chora Sfakion to Kastelli.

**Ferries** depart Friday at 8am to Kythera (4 hr., 1350dr), Gythion (7 hr., 1600dr), and Piraeus (18 hr., 2000dr). The boat goes on Tuesday at 8am to Kythera, Neapolis (6 hr., 940dr), and Piraeus. Ferry schedules and tickets are provided by **Emmanuel Ksiroukakis** (tel. 226 55), next to the bus station in the *platia.* (Open Mon.-Fri. 8am-1:30pm and 5-9pm, Sat. 8am-1:30pm.) For boat tickets, rental cars, motorbikes, Magic Bus (from Athens), and excursions, go to the **General Tourist Agency,** on Skalidi St. (tel. 229 80) east of the *platia.*

If you have a moped or stamina for a 7-kilometer walk uphill and inland from Kastelli, consider the secluded mountain village of **Polirinia.** The road climbs through terraced hills and olive groves where it ends at the base of the village. Follow the arrows to the ancient acropolis. The stony path spirals and twists through dilapidated white-washed houses and crumbling Venetian arches. At the top, leather-faced shepherds and an army of sheep and stray goats stand guard over ancient campfire circles, the **Church of the 99 Martyrs,** and the remnants of Byzantine and Venetian fortifications. Before setting back to Kastelli, relax at the **Restaurant Polirinia;** the veranda here, canopied with grapevines, offers a commanding view of the countryside. **Buses** also travel daily from Kastelli to Polirinia at 1:45pm (60dr).

To the west of Kastelli, the creeping onslaught of tourism peters out, leaving isolated villages and deserted beaches for the intrepid. Buses are infrequent and hitching is possible but requires patience (especially after midday, when goats are more common than cars). Motorbikes make good sense, but the hairpin turns and rocky roads down the far west coast and inland villages require ability and caution.

Five kilometers west of Kastelli turn right for **Kaliviani** at the eastern base of the Grambousa Peninsula. Leave your bags in town and walk 3 hours along the hillside to **Tigani Bay** and its deserted sandy beach. Back on the main road from Kastelli, a left at the forked road leads up to the budding village of **Platanos** where doubles in the new hotel cost 1800dr. Four **buses** per day go from Kastelli to Platanos (80dr).

The choicest beach along the northwest coast, **Falassarna**, lies just north of Platanos off a paved then dirt road that leads a few kilometers down the beachfront hamlet of rooms and *tavernas*. Look for the rooms for rent signs on the right as you descend to the beach. **Stathis** (tel. 414 80) has new stucco rooms. (Doubles with bath 2500dr. Breakfast available. Call ahead in summer.) Next door, **Golden Sun** (tel. 414 85) is drab and pricey. (Doubles 2700dr.) You don't have to go to the beach at the **Sun Side Hotel**, where the beds are sandy (doubles 2000dr) and the salads (200dr) are salty. The small sandy cove below the hotel is popular with campers, and has a fresh-water spring. North of the hotels and *tavernas* is the acropolis of a Hellenistic city. Along the dirt track to the site and steep rocky harbor, take a look at the stone throne of mysterious origin. The long beach at the south end attracts serious sunbathers and peace-seeking campers. Local fishermen regularly clean their boats in the waters off the west coast, and some of this black goop reappears in clumps on the beach. Nonetheless, Falassarna's natural beauty and isolation more than make up for the odd lump of sticky tar.

Two **buses** per day go from Kastelli to Falassarna (at 8:30am and 3:30pm, returning at 10:45am and 5:45pm, 45 min., 100dr) and from Hania (at 8:30am and 3:30pm). You can also take a bus to Platanos and then walk or hitch another 5km along the road to the beach. If you hitch, expect to wait: Cars will usually stop but there are very few of them. You may find yourself hitching back instead.

Solitude awaits 15km south of Falassarna at the secluded fishing and farming village of **Sfinari**. The beach here is narrow, rocky, and almost deserted. Greenhouses growing tomatoes and bananas run all along the beach and farther down the coast. The seaside restaurant in this windy coastal town, **Diolinis** (open at 9am), has a symbiotic arrangement with foreign visitors: You can camp for free behind the *taverna* and use the toilets and showers, then eat at the restaurant or buy your own provisions at the small store in Sfinari. Diolinis is not immediately visible from the road leading to the beach. A 5-minute walk down the beach to the left will take you there. Monastic cells are available at the **Fidias Restaurant** (tel. 225 89), at the turn-off for the beach (500dr per person); you can also try **Antonios Theodrakis** (tel. 221 53), who also runs a restaurant (2 or 3 beds, 800dr). Both places are within a 20-minute walk from the beach. One **bus** for Sfinari leaves Kastelli daily at 2pm in summer (40 min., 135dr), but motorbikes will let you take in the beautiful, rugged coastline. From Hania, a daily bus leaves at 2pm (135dr). From Sfinari, the road heads inland until it reaches **Kambos**, perched atop a mountain stream and verdant valley. Modest rooms are available as you come into town but go around the bend until reaching **Lefteris Hartzoulakis** (tel. 414 45), who will drive you the 3km to the beach if you stay at his hotel/cafe. (Singles with precambrian stone floors 900dr. Doubles 1500dr.)

# *Eastern Crete*

## *Malia* Μαλιά

Malia, 31km east of Iraklion, is a casualty of cancerous "touristitis," a malignancy that has devastated Crete's northern coast. Package tours swarm the hotels, the shops sell mostly junk, deep-fried tanners overrun the beach, and advertisements for rooms and shops overshadow the endearing windmills. Orientation and Practical Information

**Buses** connect Malia with Iraklion via Hersonissus (7am-10pm every ½ hr., 1 hr. to Iraklion, 230dr), Agios Nikolaos (17 per day, 40 min.), and Lassithi (1 per day, 1½ hr., 340dr). There is also hourly service to Ierapetra (1½ hr.) and Sitia (3 hr.). Purchase tickets on the bus.

The main road from Iraklion should satisfy most practical needs, while the path down to the beach contains the resort's discos and watering holes. The **post office** lies on the main street, behind the church. (Open Mon.-Fri. 8am-8pm, Sat. 8am-3pm, Sun. 9am-1:30pm.) The **National Bank of Greece** is on the main road, past the town's **OTE.** (Open Mon.-Fri. 7:30am-3:10pm.) **Dr. James Hodge** (tel. 313 32) runs a clinic opposite the bank. (Open 8:30am-1pm and 5:30-8:30pm.) He drops his lab coats to be lightly starched and put on hangers at the **laundromat** next to the Malia Holiday Hotel. **Taxis** stand at the intersection of the main road and the beach path. Malia's **telephone code** is 0897.

Family-run pensions are giving way to up-scale hotel complexes. Cheaper rooms are available in the old city, behind the main drag and away from the beach. If you're desperate, travel agencies can book moderately priced rooms at one of their listed pensions or studios (from 2000dr). **Hotel Apostolos**, on Eisodian St. (tel. 314 84), inland from the Avis office, charges 1700dr for doubles and 2200dr for triples. **Pension Aspasia** (tel. 312 90), off 25th Martiou St., has run-down rooms for the same prices. To get to the dingy and rat-infested **youth hostel,** take the first road west of the church (450dr). You can camp at **Camping Sissi**, 3km east of Malia. (Icy showers. No curfew. Open June-Sept. 300dr.)

Most of Malia's overpriced and uninspiring restaurants are located on the road to the beach. **Restaurant Ilotis**, however, serves excellent food at fairly reasonable prices. It's 2 blocks inland from the road to Agios Nikolaos; turn opposite the Quick Film Development sign a few blocks west of the Avis office. (Open 6pm-midnight.)

## Sights and Entertainment

The **Minoan Palace** at Malia, one of the three great cities of Minoan Crete, lacked the elaborate architecture and magnificent interior decoration of Knossos and Phaestos, but was, nonetheless, imposing. First built around 1900 B.C.E., the palace was destroyed along with the other two around 1650 B.C.E. Rebuilt on an even more impressive scale, it was destroyed again around 1450 B.C.E. The city presumably prospered as a major port, and the bricks used in its construction were made from an unusual mixture of clay and seaweed. Notice the **Hall of Columns** on the north side of the large central courtyard, so named for the six columns supporting the roof, and the loggia on the west side, a raised chamber used for ceremonies.

West of the loggia are the main living quarters and the archives. Northwest of the loggia and main site is the **Hypostyle Crypt**, believed to have been a social center for the intelligentsia of Malia. As in Phaestos, only minor reconstruction has been attempted; the ruins remain, for the most part, exactly as they were found. Follow the road to Agios Nikolaos 3km to the east and turn left toward the sea, or walk along the beach and then 1km through the fields. (Open Mon.-Sat. 8:30am-3pm, Sun. 9:30am-2:30pm. Admission 200dr, students 100dr.) You can freelance camp near the beach behind the site.

To reach Malia's crowded main **beach,** turn north from the main street across from the Avis office. Cretan cafes and *souvlaki* stands vanish, and you'll find yourself in a strange world of cotton candy vendors, stores selling *après*-sun body milk and inflatable rubber ducks, and expensive cocktail bars. A 25-minute walk through this never-never land leads to the beach and its baking masses. For more secluded swimming and sunbathing, walk east until you find a suitable spot.

The road to the beach is, predictably, the center of Malia's nightlife. After a long day of strenuous sunbathing, you can relax on the shady verandas of the bars that line the street, sipping long fruity drinks complete with paper parasols stuck into the orange wedges and maraschino cherries impaled on the tails of little plastic monkeys. Then you can wander down the street to one of Malia's discos, most of which have a 500dr cover charge that includes a free drink. Parts of **Disco Krypton's** dance floor light up at odd moments. Vines and trellises adorn the sunken white stucco entrance of **Disco Rainbow.** (Beers 150dr. Drinks 250dr.) Alternatively, you can spend an enjoyable hour or two wandering up and down the streets reading the lists of drinks outside the bars and wondering what exactly a White Spider, a Green Lady, or a Vulture's Piss contains.

The death knell has sounded for **Hersonissos,** a blemish 12km west of Iraklion. The color-coded stucco apartments seem transplanted from a California beach town. Budget travelers would do better in Hermosa Beach than in Hersonissos. Nearly all of the rooms are booked through tour agencies, although the local tourist agencies might have a spare room to let (doubles from 2500dr). Inquire at **Kourkounis Tours** (tel. 223 93; open 9am-1pm and 4-10pm). The nearby camping sites are the only budget alternatives. **Camping Creta** (tel. (0897) 414 00), 10km west of Hersonissos on the shore in Gouves, has a kitchen and showers. (Open May-Oct.) The best reason to visit Hersonissos is to sample Crete's lone East Indian restaurant. The **Bombay Tandoori and Vegetarian Restaurant,** opposite the Silva Maris Hotel, is managed by the family who own London's well-known Hare Krishna.

# *Lassithi Plain* Κάμπος Λασσήθη

The inland route to Agios Nikolaos bypasses much of the ugly northern coastline in favor of the Lassithi Plain, a valley ringed by steep mountains. This patchwork plateau mocks the visitor who struggles along difficult mountain routes to get here.

Irrigated by hundreds of sail-rigged windmills, the plain is alive with the rural Cretan culture so often overwhelmed in more traveled parts of the island. Here, you'll find whitewashed buildings, overburdened donkeys, and yeoman villagers husbanding their fields—as well as the Dikteon Cave at Psychro. The residents of the region have harnessed the plain's persistent winds with thousands of wind-powered water pumps. Under each windmill is a well, and beside each tower is a tank to collect water siphoned by a rotating spindle. In recent years, electric pumps have supplemented irrigation, but enough mills still function to create a spectacular visual effect. When the sails are unfurled—usually in mid-morning—the whole plain is filled with their spinning. Even the houses have small windmills sitting on the back fence to supply water for household needs.

Because the runoff from the surrounding mountains collects in the plain, this is one of the most fertile areas in Greece. In harvesting season (July-Aug.) wheat is leaning on church porches, stacked in the fields, and piled so high on donkeys that all you can see of them are the ears and tail.

To venture to the Lassithi Plain by car or scooter, take the coastal road from Iraklion 8km past Gournes, and then turn right on the road to Kasteli (not the one on the west coast). After about 6km the road forks right to Kasteli; you stay left, heading toward **Potamies.** On a dirt path just north of town is the Byzantine church **Panayia Gouverniotissa,** noted for its colorful fourteenth-century frescoes. Ask at Potamies' several cafes for the key (kleeDHEE in Greek). This precious object changes hands constantly, but can often be found at the brown and yellow house on the main road at the north end of town. Soon after Potamies, the road starts to climb. If you have the time and the means, take a 1-kilometer semi-circular detour at the sign for **Krassi** (wine) to see the giant plane tree in the village center. It takes 12 men to wrap their arms around the trunk, but you have to get the villagers really drunk to do it. Bypassing Krassi, the main road winds around mountain ridges, with beautiful views on all sides. In the tiny town of **Kera,** turn off to the monastery, where flowers deck the courtyard and the church contains a twelfth-century icon of the Virgin. (Open until sunset.) The road continues to climb to the Seli Ambelou pass, with its abandoned stone windmills, and then finally descends into the Lassithi Plain.

Once within the plain, the first and only "major" town you pass through is **Tzermiado,** capital of the subprovince of Lassithi, with a few gift shops and two hotel-restaurants catering to day tourists. In the evening, Tzermiado returns to its own peaceful ways, with the male population divided among its 10 or so cafes, drinking, arguing, and playing backgammon. Few tourists stop by; if you do, you will receive a warm welcome. Tzermiado has three hotels. On the road to Agios Nikolaos, past the **pharmacy** (open 7:30am-3:10pm), you'll find the **Hotel Kourites** on your right and, opposite, the **Hotel Lassithi** (tel. 221 94 for reservations at either place). The Lassithi charges 1500dr for doubles, 2200dr for quads; the Kourites is slightly more expensive at 1800dr for doubles and 2100dr for triples, all with private bath. The Kourites also has a restaurant and is surprisingly plush. The **Hotel Kri-Kri** (tel. 221 70), near the bus stop, is less spacious and comfortable but cheaper. (Singles 900dr. Doubles 1200dr. Showers 50dr.) The **Kronias Restaurant** gives you a good meal and a glimpse of rural Cretan life. (Open 7:30am-11pm.) The **post office** (open Mon.-Fri. 7:30am-2:30pm) is next to the Kronias Restaurant; the **OTE** (open Mon.-Fri. 7:30am-3:10pm) is a few doors down from the Kronias to the right. Tzermiado's **telephone code** is 0844.

Only a scratch in the hill compared to the Dikteon Cave at Psychro, the **Kronion Cave,** mythical home of Kronos and Rhea, parents of Zeus, merits a quick side trip. Clear signs in Tzermiado will direct you to the grotto 2km outside town; the last kilometer is traversable only on foot, and not well-marked. Stay on the widest path, don't stray onto the numerous goat paths that cross it, and bring a flashlight.

Leaving Tzermiado, a right fork at the church 2km southeast of town will take you to **Agios Konstantinos.** In this otherwise quiet rural village, the women raise a racket every time a visitor comes to town: Each beckons the startled traveler to examine the goods in her embroidery and weaving shop. Rooms are available behind most of the shops (doubles 1200-1500dr). **Agios Georgios,** 2km farther down the same road, is home to a tiny **folklore museum,** part of which is a windowless reconstructed village house. Its comic human models and stuffed fowl are more amusing than edifying. (Open April-Oct. 10am-4pm. Admission 100dr.) Agios Georgios is perhaps the best place to stay in the Lassithi Plain, as the locals are warm-hearted and welcome overnight visitors. The **Dias Hotel** (tel. 312 07) rents singles for 750dr and doubles for 1500dr (showers 100dr). Tasty meals at their restaurant cost less than 500dr, and pizza is 400dr.

The village of **Psychro** caters to afternoon tourists but manages to retain its rural charm. The only hotel in the village, the **Dikteon Andron** (no phone), charges 600dr per person for small rooms with cot-like beds. Look for the sign near the church on the main road; from there go uphill 1 block, turn right, and then walk about 50m, keeping an eagle eye to the right for the hotel's nameplate above the door.

One kilometer past Psychro is the **Dikteon Cave.** Legend has it that Kronos, Zeus' father, after hearing a prophecy that a child of his would dethrone him, ate his newborn children as a precautionary measure. When Kronos' wife Rhea gave birth to Zeus, she gave Kronos a tasty stone to eat instead, and kept the baby hidden in this cave. Zeus later emerged, killed his father, and freed his five older brothers and sisters, who had luckily remained alive in Kronos' stomach (like that undercooked *souvlaki* you had in Tzermiado). Lucian adds that Zeus lay with Europa here and Minos was conceived. Whether or not the cave was the birthplace or stomping ground of Zeus, it seems to have had considerable significance for the Minoans. When it was excavated at the beginning of this century, hundreds of Minoan artifacts were found crammed into its ribbed stalactites; many of these can be seen in Iraklion's Archeological Museum.

Bring a flashlight: The cave is several hundred feet deep, and when you realize that the deepest point visible from the entrance is less than halfway down, you'll be glad you didn't rely on one of the fast-burning candles (50dr). Tour groups start arriving at 10:30am; if you get to the cave by 9:30am or after 3pm you should be able to explore it in relative solitude, hearing only the sporadic drip of water in the pools around you. Avoid the guides who hover around the base of the path: Their rates are outlandish (500dr plus 50dr for each additional person), their facts few and far between, and their English virtually nonexistent. (Cave officially open 8am-6pm. Admission 200dr.)

**Buses** to Lassithi leave daily from Iraklion, stopping at Tzermiado and Psychro (at 8:30am and 2:30pm, returning at 7am, 2pm, and 5pm, 2 hr., 430dr), from Elounda and Agios Nikolaos (at 8:30am and 2pm, returning at 7am and 2pm, 2 hr., 340dr), and from Malia (8:30am, returning at 2pm, 1½ hr., 370dr).

# Agios Nikolaos Αγιος Νικόλαος

The closest elements to indigenous culture in Agios Nikolaos are the early-morning fishermen mending their yellowing Japanese nets. With convenient beaches, pulsating nightlife, and dual waterfronts for excellent people-watching, Agios Nikolaos is the choice destination for one-stop holiday makers and a good base from which to explore the Mirabello Bay region, Elounda, Kritsa, and Gournia. There are few bargains in Agios Nikolaos and its satellite beach towns, but for those night owls eager to don fashionable duds, this place will seem like home.

## Orientation and Practical Information

It's easy to get around Agios Nikolaos—the center of town is actually a small peninsula, with beaches on three sides and most services, hotels, restaurants, and discos located in the middle. If you've just gotten off the bus, face the terminal, take your first left, and head north up Venizelou St. to the monument at Venizelou Sq. Walk down the main shopping street, **Roussou Koundourou,** to the harbor. To the left and across the bridge is the tourist information office.

**Agios Nikolaos Tourist Information Office:** Koundourou St. (tel. 223 57), at the bridge between the lake and the port. Efficient and knowledgeable staff. Will phone for accommodations. Messages, bus and boat information, and free brochure with town map and practical information. Currency exchange. Open Mon.-Sat. 7:30am-9pm, Sun. 8am-3:30pm.

**Post Office:** 9, 28th of October St. (tel. 222 76). Open Mon.-Fri. 8am-8pm, Sat. 8am-3pm, Sun. 9am-1pm; in winter daily 7:30am-2:30pm. **Postal code:** 72100.

**Currency Exchange: National Bank of Greece** (tel. 288 55) at the top of Roussou Koundourou St., near Venizelou Sq. Open Mon.-Thurs. 8am-2pm, Fri. 8am-1:30pm. At night, you can change money at the tourist office or most hotels and travel agencies.

**OTE:** 25 Martiou St. (tel. 280 99), 3 blocks east of the lake. Open June-Oct. 6am-midnight; Nov.-May 6am-10:30pm. **Telephone code:** 0841.

**Olympic Airways:** 20 Plastira St. (tel. 220 33), overlooking the lake. Open Mon.-Sat. 8am-3:30pm.

**Bus Station:** Atlandithos Sq. (tel. 222 34), on the opposite side of town from the harbor. To: Malia (25 per day, 40 min., 220dr); Iraklion (25 per day, 1½ hr., 430dr); Ierapetra (10 per day, 1 hr., 220dr); Psychro (at 8:30am and 2pm, 2 hr., 340dr); Sitia (8 per day, 2 hr., 460dr); and Kritsa (17 per day, ½ hr., 70dr). Buses to Elounda leave from the harbor opposite the GNTO (Mon.-Sat. 16 per day, Sat.-Sun. 12 per day, ½ hr., 75dr).

**Ferries: Massaros Travel,** 29 Roussou Koundourou St. (tel. 222 67 or 286 27). Sells all tickets for departures from Agios Nikolaos and most of Crete. Open 9am-1:30pm and 5:30-9:30pm. The *Golden Vergina* leaves Agios Nikolaos Wed. and Sat., supposedly at 7:30am but usually several hours later, for Kassos (5 hr., 984dr), Karpathos (7 hr., 1060dr), and Rhodes (13 hr., 2270dr); on Thurs. and Sun. for Santorini (6 hr., 1000dr) and Piraeus (14 hr., 4280dr). The smaller *Nireus* links Agios Nikolaos with Piraeus and the Dodecanese. The *Golden Vergina* arrives in Agios Nikolaos Thurs. at noon, turns around, and heads back to Piraeus (16 hr., 2857dr) via Santorini. Excursion boats leave twice daily for the 1-hr. ride to Spinalonga Island (at noon and 2pm, returning at 4pm and 6pm), from 1000dr.

**Taxi:** Tel. 241 00.

**Car Rental: Economy Car Hire,** 15 Koundouron St. (tel. 289 88); also an office at 5 Sfakianaki St. Fiat 127 5700dr, 100km and insurance included.

**Motorbike Rental: Leventis Rent-a-Motorcycle,** 15 Sfanianaki St. (tel. 224 23). 50cc bikes 1500dr per day, insurance, tax, and helmets included. Open 7:30am-9:30pm. The **Ferryman Café,** on the bridge, rents Yamaha automatics for 1400dr. There are lots of agencies—shop around and bargain.

**English Bookstores:** 5 Roussou Koundourou St. An excellent collection of English books on Crete. Open daily 9am-9pm. Also across the street at #8. Open daily 8:30am-10:30pm.

**Laundromat: Express,** Paleologou St. (tel. 284 92), up from the tourist office—look for the sign at Koritsas St. Wash and dry 1000dr. Open daily 8am-6pm.

**Hospital:** Lasithiou St. (tel. 223 69), at the northern end of town. From the lake, walk up Paleologou St., 1 block past the museum, and turn left at Diktis St. and walk 1 block.

**Tourist Police:** Tel. 222 51, at the foot of the stairs, on the southern corner of the lake on Paleologou St. (tel. 222 51). Maps of the town, bus and boat schedules, and a list of hotels and pensions. Open in summer daily 7:30am-2pm; reduced hours in winter.

**Police:** Tel. 223 38, on Antistaseos St., above the lake.

**Emergency:** Tel. 100.

## Accommodations and Food

As a result of Agios Nikolaos' popularity, many of the better hotels are booked months in advance by European tour groups, and the few cheap places in town have a slow turnover rate. Even the youth hostel occasionally fills. The town has almost as many pensions as it does hotels, but these are often reserved ahead as well. The pensions we list are quite small. If you plan to stay in town, arrive early in the day or make reservations. You can also spend the night at the town of **Kritsa,** only 9km away. The tourist office can recommend rooms for you and call ahead for reservations.

**Youth Hostel (IYHF),** 3 Stratigou Koraka St. (tel. 228 23). From the tourist office, walk along the harbor about 50m and go up the concrete steps on your left—it's on your left opposite the church. Half-built and dirty, but good views and friendly management. Best rooms on the bottom floor. No curfew. Open year-round. 450dr per person.

**The Green House,** 15 Moudatsou St. (tel. 220 25). From the bus station, go left on Kapetan Tavla St., which becomes Moudatsou. Alternatively, from the south side of Venizelou Sq. walk 2 blocks uphill on Nikiforou Foka St. Clean rooms and a quiet and friendly atmosphere, amid a wonderful, tangled garden. Doubles 1400dr. Munchies from the caring proprietors included.

**Pension Argiro,** 1 Solonos St. (tel. 287 07), next to the prefectural offices. Take the first right after the Green House and then go left after 1 block. The perfect place for a small group. Clean, likely to have space. Friendly management. Refrigerator, too. Doubles 1700dr. Triples 2500dr, with bath 3300dr. Showers included.

**Pension Istron** (tel. 237 63), opposite the tourist office across the harbor. Follow the promenade up the steps by the Panorama Hotel. Clean and modern. Singles 1300dr. Doubles 1800dr. Triples 2500dr.

**Pension Katerina,** 33 Koraka St. (tel. 227 66), 6 blocks north of the youth hostel (near Marilena). Spacious, clean rooms with large balconies. Doubles 1600dr. Hot showers included.

**Pension Marilena,** 14 Stavrou St. (tel. 226 81), 6 blocks north of the youth hostel. Clean, but costs a bit more. Doubles 1800dr, triples 2200dr. Showers included.

Food costs plenty in Agios Nikolaos. Most restaurants can be found around the town's harbor, immediately west along the waterfront, or on the beach at the east end of town. The numerous *tost* outfits (the Greek equivalent of a hamburger joint) cook decent omelettes at low prices, and most sell *souvlaki-pita* sandwiches (100dr). Cheaper cafes can be found in Venizelou Square, although they don't offer the harborside view. Try **Taverna Itanos** (tel. 231 98), with a vine-covered terrace overlooking the square and a surprising number of cheap dishes. (Chicken dinner 350dr.)

The cafe-bars along the bottomless lake are the best places to watch the sunset. **Stellio's** (tel. 227 73), located right at the bridge, has a limited menu and very slow service, but heck, it has a good harborside view and is relatively quiet. (*Kebab* special for 2 1500dr. Open 8am-2am.) At the **Actaion** (tel. 222 89), next door, fish dishes start at 450dr. (Open 10am-11pm.) The least touristed of the harbor restaurants is **Haris** (tel. 226 43), on the east side of the waterfront. They get a local crowd, plus a few out-of-the-way tourists who try to look local. (Open noon-3am.) **Ciao-Ciao Pizza** (tel. 244 67), 4, 25 Martiou St., with good pizza by the slice (150dr), mediocre wine by the glass (35dr), and a few places to sit by the counter. (Open noon-3am.)

## Sights and Entertainment

The **archeological museum** (tel. 224 62) has a modest collection of Minoan artifacts from the Lassithi area. It is located just outside the center of town, a few blocks down the road to Iraklion, which begins at the lake. (Open March-Nov. Mon. and Wed.-Sun. 9am-3pm. Admission 200dr, students 100dr.) The **Folk Art Museum,** in the tourist office's building, houses a collection of weavings and fine embroidered clothes. (Open daily 10am-1pm and 5-8:30pm. Admission 100dr.) For cheap clothes and local color in an otherwise tourist-oriented town, visit the weekly **market,** on Paleologou St., next to the lake. (Open Wed. 7am-noon.) The feast day of St. Nicholas (Dec. 6) is celebrated heartily by local residents. Also, around Easter, the effigy of Judas is burned in the harbor encircled by hundreds of candles. This Cretan ritual must be seen for its impressive visual effect.

Agios Nikolaos' major attraction, no doubt, is its scenic waterfront locale. The town's three beaches are all within easy walking distance of the main harbor, and, of course, you can always swim off the rocks. At the southeast end of town by the bus station there's a long, narrow stone beach. **Kitroplatia,** a smaller, rockier, and more crowded beach by the Scouros Hotel, is at the eastern tip of town. To the right (facing the sea), you'll find two reasonably-priced *tavernas.* At the northwest corner of town at the Dolphin Restaurant is the tiny sandy **Ammoudi Beach**—most sun-worshipers, though, are forced to lie on the surrounding concrete. For best results, catch one of the hourly buses headed to Ierapetra or Sitia and get off at **Almiros Beach,** 2km east of Agios Nikolaos. The sandy beach at **Kalo Chorio,** 10km farther along the same road, is less crowded, but also dirtier. Get off the bus at the Kavos Taverna.

For nightlife, stroll around the harbor on Koundourou St., or walk up 25th Martiou St. The **Bora Bora** is a good warm-up before the dance floors. Quaff small beers (100dr) in front of the huge video screen. (Open 8:30pm-3am.) Also near the pier is **Yianni's** (tel. 235 81), a casual bar decorated with Hollywood memorabilia. (Beer 150dr. Open 8pm-3am.) The **Skyline,** 1 Koundourou St., serves cocktails (300dr, 8-11pm; 400dr 11pm-3am. **Disco Lipstick,** near the Bora Bora on the southern side of the harbor, is the crowded '70s throwback. (Beer 150dr. Open 9pm-3am.) Insomniacs can frequent the all-night **Yachting Club** (tel. 237 53), on the tip of the pier.

## Near Agios Nikolaos

With a pretty port and plenty of nearby beaches, **Elounda** swells with hotels, restaurants, and holiday villas, but does not approach the scale of Agios Nikolaos, 10km south. Elounda's **post office** is in the main square. (Open Mon.-Fri. 8am-8pm, Sat. 8am-3pm, Sun. 9am-1:15pm.) The **police** (tel. 413 48) are based 1 block behind the main square to the left (north) of the post office. An **international telephone** is in **The Bookshop** (tel. (0841) 416 41) in the *platia.* This cramped shop stocks a moderate selection of foreign newspapers and guide books. (Open daily 9am-11pm.) The **pharmacy** (tel. 413 08), is in Elounda Sq. (Open Mon.-Sat. 8:30am-1:30pm and 5-9pm.) Around the corner is the town **doctor** (tel. 415 63 or 414 68). The **National Bank of Greece** is to the right (south) of the main square. (Open Mon.-Thurs. 9am-noon and Fri. 9-11:30am.) You can rent motorbikes (1400dr per day) at **Elounda Rent-A-Car** (tel. 413 33), at the south end of the harbor; they also have small cars (13,320dr for 3 days) and provide general tourist information. Twenty **buses** per day make the half-hour run between Agios Nikolaos and Elounda (75dr). The bus trip rolls by remarkable scenery of sea and strand.

Since budget accommodations are limited here, you should call for reservations. **Mrs. Zacharoula,** (tel. 415 31), at the north end of the waterfront, above the photo shop, doesn't speak much English, but is warm and hospitable. (Doubles 1700dr. Triples 2000dr. Showers included. Prices drop if you stay longer.) Across the street, **Elpis Pension** (tel. 413 84) has similar accommodations. (Clean doubles 1800dr. Triples 2000dr.) **Pension Oasis** (tel. 412 18), 100m inland from the square behind Elpis, offers doubles with bath for 2200dr. Restaurants are generally out of the budget traveler's range, but you might make an exception at the **Greek Taverna Marilena** (tel. 413 22), with tables in the garden out back. Try squid in wine sauce (300dr) or pasta in a mushroom cream sauce (550dr). (Open 9am-11pm.) On the road from Agios Nikolaos at the turn-off for the Greco-Roman site of **Olous** is the music bar-cafe **Nautilus** (tel. 417 92). In a converted 52-year-old carob factory, two bars, a dance floor, and a weight room open onto the water where vacationers come to sunbathe. (Cocktails 400dr, beer 100dr, pizza 400dr, English breakfast 400dr, Hershey bars 400dr. Happy hour 8:30-10:30pm. Open daily 9am-3am.)

Elounda also serves as a point of departure for the islet of **Spinalonga** and its sixteenth-century fortress. The fortress was so impregnable that the Venetians were able to control the complex for half a century after the Turkish conquest of Crete in 1669. When Crete became part of Greece in 1898, a handful of stubborn Turkish residents remained in Spinalonga. Crete gently urged their departure in 1903 by turning the island into a leper colony, accommodating up to 450 patients. The resident lepers organized many activities for the small town, including shops which now lie in disrepair along the main walk-way. In 1957, with only 35 patients remaining, the colony was dissolved and its residents sent for treatment in Athens. In 1967, the shipping tycoon, Aristotle Onassis, wanted to buy the dilapidated island, demolish the leper colony, and restore the Venetian fortress. A fervent public outcry against glitzy casinos, first-class hotels, and resort bungalows deterred him. Fear and bad associations have kept settlers at bay to this day, but a visit is definitely worthwhile. Recently, the Iraklion Museum has provided limited funding for the preservation and upkeep of the islet. Small fishing boats leave for Spinalonga roughly every half-hour from Elounda (600dr round-trip). Tickets can be purchased at **Alma Tours** (tel. 228 00) in Elounda's main square (open daily 8am-midnight), or on the boats if they're not full.

Five kilometers beyond Elounda sits **Plaka,** a fishing village with three rock beaches so far undiscovered by the tourist invasion to the south. Several *tavernas* have rooms to let; try **Maria's** (tel. 413 19), at the north end of town. (Open year-round. New doubles 1500dr. Triples 2000dr.) **Buses** run every other hour from Agios Nikolaos to Plaka, stopping in Elounda (7am-7pm, 85dr). Fishing boats from Plaka go to Spinalonga (500dr) on demand. At **Taverna Manolis,** the captain will make the short run even if only one person wants to go, and he'll return whenever you want, within reason. **Neopolis,** 20km east of Agios Nikolaos, is the administrative center of Mirabello and known for its produce market. The road from Agios Nikolaos leads to Venizelou Sq., where you can find a taxi stand, bus stop, and **post office** (behind the small park; open Mon.-Fri. 7:30am-2:15pm). The **OTE** is across from the church (open Mon.-Fri. 7:30am-3:10pm.) On the side street of **Ethnikis Antistassis** is the **Olympic Airways** office (tel. (0841) 322 31), where Mr. Kourdakis, the town historian, also acts as general travel agent and will occasionally find rooms. There are no rooms to let in Neopolis, but for quick sustenance, stroll around the lively market streets off the square and relax at **Ilias Taverna** (tel. 315 67), where *souvlaki pita* is 100dr. Don't be surprised to spot black-robed monks strolling about; there are several monasteries in the area, including the Venetian **San Antonio.**

On the main road to Iraklion, a small turn-off leads to the beach communities of **Sisi** and **Milatos.** The tiny harbor of Sisi has several good *tavernas* and a swimming cove to the east. The endearing **Rovitis** (tel. 712 24), on the main road to the harbor, rents doubles with cold showers in his decrepit hotel for 1000dr. **Sisi Camping** (tel. 712 47) has a sea-water swimming pool and *taverna*. (400dr per person.

360dr per tent.) The family-run **Arismaris** (tel. 712 94), on the main road from the harbor, serves traditional Cretan dishes (most under 500dr). (Open 7pm-11pm.) Buses leave daily for Neapoli (at 7am), Milatos (at 9:45am and 4pm), and Iraklion (at 7am, 10:20am, and 4:20pm).

The ruins of the ancient Minoan town of **Gournia** are 19km east of Agios Nikolaos. On a hill just 50m from the highway, a maze of walls hems in a seemingly infinite number of little houses, some of which contain clay potsherds. The cobbled streets and workshops were the homes of carpenters, smiths, and potters. The palatial quarters overlook the *agora* to the south, and the well-constructed south wall was probably used as a platform for official declarations. (Open Mon. and Wed.-Sat. 7:45am-8pm, Sun. 9:30a,-2:30pm, Tues. 7:45am-2pm; but you can always let youself in. Free.) Just 3km farther is the seaside retreat of **Pahia Ammos.** Unfortunately, the beach has more garbage than sand. SEveral pensions offer doubles starting at 1500dr. Try the **Zeus** (tel. 932 89) in the center of the village. (Doubles 1700dr.)

## Kritsa

Although only 9km from the ritzy port of Agios Nikolaos, the hilltop village seems a world apart. Every balcony and rooftop is trimmed with vines and ripening fruit; beneath the shade of the bowers, women weave blankets and sweaters and embroider shirts and blouses. Many of the homemade crafts are embarassingly cheap. Be picky when buying, however, as not every item is produced here.

Unfortunately, the weaving traditions thrive with the heavy input from tourist buses unloading here. Serenity returns at night, because tourists seldom stay past dusk. As a result, the village provides an inexpensive solution to the lack of affordable accommodations in Agios Nikolaos. The cleanest option, but not the cheapest, is the **Pension Kristopolou** (tel. 517 26), on the road to Agios Nikolaos. (Doubles with shower 2000dr.) **Maria Zachariadi** (tel. 517 17) has a pension whose entrance is off a path under grape trellises, straight ahead as you walk uphill from the bus stop. (Doubles 1600dr. Triples 2000dr.) Just before Maria's, on the right, **Maria Kokkini** (tel. 516 38) has spiffy rooms for 600-1000dr per person. Proprietors will out-bargain each other for your patronage. The **post office** is above the *platia*. (Open Mon.-Fri. 7:30am-2:15pm.) An **international phone** is in **Koutoulakis Snack Bar** in the square. (Open 7am-11pm.)

**Buses** run regularly between Agios Nikolaos and Kritsa (17 per day, ½ hr., 70dr). In summer, afternoon buses to Kritsa fill up quickly; you may find yourself waiting for the next bus if you don't arrive early.

One kilometer before Kritsa on the road from Agios Nikolaos is Crete's Byzantine treasure: the **Danagia Kera,** which homors the Dormition of the Virgin. The interior of the church is adorned with a patchwork of smoky twelfth-century paintings in the central nave and thirteenth-century Byzantine frescoes in the adjoining wings. Note the stamped halos in the central nave and the medieval handling and geometric flatness of the tableware in the representation of the Last Supper. The fine portrait of the donor, Georgios Ma Zezanes, with wife and child, is the only known portrait to have been painted in medieval Crete. (Open Mon.-Sat. 8:45am-3pm, Sun. 9am-2pm. Admission 200dr, students 100dr.) A small but invaluable guidebook to the Panayia Kera by Manolis Borboudakis is sold at the gift shop next door (250dr). The **Church of Agios Georgios**, in town, also contains several frescoes dating from the 13th and 14th centuries. To get there, take the main road up from the bus station and go left at the fork; follow the signs from there. Just below town is the turn-off for the 3-kilometer-long dirt road to the classical ruins at **Lato**. Wind whistles down a staircase and through a fourth-century B.C.E. temple with a sacrificial altar. Visitors rarely make the trip here, so hitching can be difficult, but you can walk (1½ hr.) or take a moped.

# Ierapetra Ιεράπετρα

Ironically, Ierapetra's very drabness saves this town from the tourist invasion. If you can disregard cosmetic deficiencies, you will savor the affable atmosphere of the Ierapetrans, a tight-knit-community who trace their roots to the Minoans. Still, it remains a bustling market town, and many may be compelled to depart for the glittering beaches nearby.

Most of Ierapetra's services are located on the streets running parallel to the waterfront. The bus stops between the waterfront and Venizelou Sq. The **tourist office** (tel. 286 58) is on the water at the foot of Kostoula St. (Open Mon.-Fri. 9am-9pm, Sat.-Sun. 9am-1pm and 4-8pm.) The **Ionian Bank,** on Venizelou Sq., changes foreign currency. (Open Mon.-Thurs. 8am-2pm, Fri. 8am-1:30pm.) In Kothri Sq., 5 blocks west of the bus station, you'll find the **post office,** 1 Stilianou Hota St. (Open Mon.-Fri. 7:30am-7:30pm, Sat. 8:30am-2:30pm, Sun. 9am-1pm.) At 25 Koraka St., 3 blocks from the water and 1 block west at Venizelou Sq., is the **OTE.** (Open 7:30am-10pm.) Opposite the OTE, **Panelinios Travel Agency** (tel. 224 48) has ANEK-line boat tickets. (Open 7am-2pm and 6-9pm.) The **police station** is on the waterfront, 3 blocks west of the bus station. Unfortunately, renting motorized transportation in Ierapetra can be expensive; for daytrips, try **Rena Motorbike Rental,** 18 Stilianou Hota St. (tel. 284 18; 1500-1600dr per day; open 8:30am-8:30pm). The **hospital** (tel. 222 52) and the **police** (tel. 225 60) are on the water near the tourist office. Ierapetra's **telephone code** is 0842.

The drab exterior of the **Cretan Villa,** 16 Lakerda St. (tel. 285 22), northeast of Venizelou Sq., disguises a pleasant interior. It has a kitchen for guests, a sun roof, and a courtyard shaded by grape vines. (Doubles 2200dr. Triples 3000dr.) The **Hotel Ierapetra** (tel. 285 30), 7 blocks west of the bus station and 1 block inland opposite a small church, is clean and quiet with doubles for 2000dr, triples for 2300dr. (Open May-Sept.) A few meters up from the Cretan Villa is the idyllic garden setting of **Pension Hibiscus,** 21 Lakerda St. (tel. 223 15). The seven plush rooms are equiped with private baths, and kitchen facilities are provided. The entire complex is often snapped up by an occasional tour group, so call ahead. (Doubles 1800dr. Triples 2200dr.) Two campgrounds, **Ierapetra** (tel. 613 51), and the new **Koutsounari** (tel. 932 43), 9km away on the coastal road to Sitia, charge 400dr per person, 200dr per tent. (Open May-Sept.) Each has a restaurant, bar, and beach. Take the bus to Sitia via Makri Gialo (7 per day) and ask to be let off at the campground.

Nearly all of Ierapetra's restaurants are strung along the waterfront, and they all offer more or less the same fare at the same prices. Spaghetti dishes, sold everywhere, usually cost 250dr. Try the **Gorgona** (tel. 240 78) for fish. (Sardine dinner 300dr.) Most of the town's shops and grocery stores are located 1 block up from the waterfront on Kountourioti St.

Locals will direct you to **Napolean's House,** in the old town, where, according to tradition, the French commander spent one night on June 26, 1798 en route to Egypt to battle the Mamelukes. The restored **Venetian fortress** or *Kales,* standing at the extreme southern mole of the old harbor, was begun sometime in the early thirteenth century. Also in the old town is a **mosque** and an **Ottoman fountain** built near the end of the 19th century. Ierapetra's **archeological museum,** on the waterfront, has a small collection of Minoan and classical artifacts from the southern coast. (Open Mon. and Wed.-Sat. 8:45am-3pm, Sun. 9:30am-2:30pm.)

## Near Ierapetra

Several small towns dot the rugged, bleak coastline of the Libyan Sea on either side of Ierapetra, with numerous swimming coves and an occasional small pension. The farther east you go, the pricier it gets. Parts of the region, nevertheless, are relatively untouched. The closest and cheapest hideaway is **Agia Fotia,** on a badly marked dirt road off the coastal route to Sitia. If you make the 18-kilometer trip east from Ierapetra by moped, beware of hairpin turns. Look for the turn-off about

1km out of a small village, just as you come out of a large horseshoe bend in the road. You'll see the frame for a bus stop on your right, followed by a dirt road sloping down and away from the pavement to the sea. There is a small sign on your left, at the entrance. If you take the bus toward Sitia, ask the driver to let you off at Agia Fotia (20 min., 100dr).

Rooms in the settlement's only pension go for 700dr per person (less if you stay more than 1 night); ask at the restaurant. You can also camp out on the beach. Nearby **Gallini** has a restaurant and a pension. (Doubles 1500dr.) Farther east is the growing resort town of **Makrigiolas,** with a **bank.** The beaches here slope so gradually that you can wade out 50-100m before you even get your knees wet. A handful of pensions rent doubles for 1200-1500dr, depending on the length of your stay and the demand. Only at Agia Fotia can you freelance-camp. A few kilometers out of Magriolis, where the main road to Sitia turns away from the sea, a rough dirt road continues along the ocean for 13km to **Goudouras,** where the town's *taverna* can fill campers' dietary needs.

Some lovely villages lie just west of Ierapetra. Quiet and relatively secluded, **Myrtos** has a long pebbly beach with black sand—sometimes too hot to walk on—at the west end. Buses stop at Myrtos from Ierapetra (7 per day) and from Iraklion via Viannos (2 per day). The town has cheap food and accommodations; doubles in pensions go for as little as 1200dr. The one hotel, the **Myrtos** (tel. 512 15), has doubles with bath for 1500dr. Three kilometers east of Myrtos is the Early-Bronze-Age settlement of **Fournou Korifhi** which dates back to 2500 B.C.E.

The beach stretching 5km west to the hamlet of **Tertsa** is popular with campers and banana growers. (Ierapetra's only tourist police officer seldom makes it out here.) It's accessible by a good dirt road that skirts the shore and can be reached on foot from Myrtos.

The coast to the west of Myrtos leads eventually to the not-so-secluded village of **Arvi,** which, despite its inaccessibility, balloons with German and Greek tourists during the summer. It offers a pleasant beach and a monastery both of which can be reached on foot at the bottom of the gorge (20 min.). Buses run from Ierapetra to Viannos, 10km from Arvi (2 per day, 1 hr., 310dr); you can walk or hitch from there. Buses from the village of Amiras, near Viannos, go to Arvi at 10am and 4:30pm. The **Alkion** restaurant rents clean doubles for 1500dr; the **Pension Gorgona** (tel. 312 11) has slightly nicer rooms at slightly higher prices. (Singles 900dr. Doubles 1500dr. Triples 2000dr.) Both have superb views of the Libyan Sea. A word of caution: Don't sleep on the beaches at Myrtos or Arvi when they're empty; there have been reports of sexual harassment of both men and women.

# *Sitia* Σητεία

A scenic drive by coastal and mountain roads from Agios Nikolaos leads to Sitia, a sedate port town. Left to its own, Sitia has only recently begun to receive the tourist rush. Because of its proximity to the beach at Vai and the Minoan ruins at Kato Zakros, Sitia is a justifiably popular base for exploring the eastern coast of Crete.

## Orientation and Practical Information

To get to the tourist office and center waterfront from the bus station, head for the sign for Vai and Kato Zakros, and bear left. Dimokritou and Venizelou Street intersect with the waterfront at the *platia,* where you will find a small palm tree garden, Sitia's restaurant strip, and the small, box-like tourist information kiosk.

**Sitia Municipal Tourist Information Office:** Tel. 249 55, on the waterfront across from the *platia.* Friendly and informative, with lists of Sitia's pensions, maps, bus and ferry schedules. Open Mon.-Fri. 9am-8pm, Sat.-Sun. 9am-3pm.

**Currency Exchange: National Bank of Greece,** in Venizelou Sq. Open Mon.-Thurs. 8am-2pm, Fri. 8am-1:30pm. **Tzortzakis Agency,** on the waterfront, is convenient during evenings and weekends.

**Post Office:** Main branch, 2 Evrikes Antistasis St (tel. 222 83). From the bus station, walk south and follow the road around to the right. It's on an island in front of you. Handles Poste Restante. Open Mon.-Fri. 7:30am-3pm. Small office on Dimokritou St. (tel. 223 22) , off the main square. Open Mon.-Sat. 8am-8pm, Sun. 9am-6pm. **Postal code:** 72300.

**OTE:** 22 Sifis St. Go to the main square on the waterfront, turn inland at the National Bank, and walk 2 blocks. Open Mon.-Fri. 7:30am-11pm. International calls can also be made from the kiosk in Iroon Sq. on the waterfront. **Telephone code:** 0843.

**Olympic Airways:** 56 Eleftheriou Venizelou St. (tel. 222 70), off the main square. There is no bus service to the airport; taxis cost 150dr for the 1-km ride. Flights to Kassos, Karpathos, and Rhodes. Call to be sure of schedules. Open Mon.-Sat. 8am-1pm and 5-8:30pm.

**Buses:** 4 Papanastasiou St. (tel. 222 72), on the east end of the waterfront. To: Agios Nikolaos (9 per day, last at 7:30pm, 2 hr., 460dr); Iraklion (9 per day, last at 7:15pm, 3½ hr., 880dr); Ierapetra via Makri Gialo (6 per day, last at 7:30pm, 2 hr., 380dr); and Vai (6 per day, last at 5:30pm, 1 hr., 180dr).

**Ferries: Tzortzakis Agency,** at the west end of the waterfront (tel. 226 31). Sells tickets for boats leaving Sitia and other ports on Crete. Likely to be helpful with practical information about Sitia, but less forthcoming about boat information. The *Nireus* stops in Sitia on Wed. evening going to the Dodecanese and Piraeus (35 hr.). It returns to Sitia via Agios Nikolaos on Wed. morning.

**Taxi:** (Tel. 228 93) in Venizelou Sq.

**Car Rental: Sitia Rent-a-Car:** 4-6 Itanou (tel. 237 70), near Petras. Fiat 127 4000dr per day, with 100km.

**Motorbike Rental: Petras** (tel. 248 49), next to the bus station. 50cc bikes 1500dr. Vespa 135 2000dr. Open 8am-8pm.

**Hospital:** At the corner of Arkadiou and Sifis St. (tel. 243 11).

**Tourist Police:** 24 Mysonos St. (tel. 242 00).

**Police:** Tel. 222 66.

## Accommodations and Food

The availability of rooms fluctuates greatly in Sitia. The worst times are just before the weekly departures of boats for Rhodes on Sunday mornings and during the Sultana Festival. The hostel is friendly and informal, but for more privacy, head for the two areas in Sitia where you'll find budget rooms—along the main road up to the youth hostel, and in the back streets at the west end of the waterfront, especially Kornarou and Kondilaki St.

**Youth Hostel (IYHF),** 4 Therissou St. (tel. 226 93), ½km uphill from the bus station back toward Iraklion. The management supplies a kitchen and an outdoor garden. Only 50 beds, but you're always welcome to sleep on the veranda or the floor. Reception open 9am-1:30pm and 4:30-9pm; if no one is around, just find a bed and register later. No curfew. Open year-round. 400dr.

**Pension Artemis** (tel. 225 64), on your left as you head toward the hostel, across from the post office. Pink-walled doubles with a view of the countryside 1500dr.

**Marea Kourmaki** (tel. 289 58), at the west end of town. Turn inland from the waterfront onto Kazantzaki St. and take your 3rd left onto Kondilaki St. Cozy rooms. Doubles 1500dr (1300dr for more than 1 night). Triples 1700dr.

**Victoria's** (tel. 280 80), a 3-min. walk on the road to Ierapetra. Out of the way but very worthwhile. Sparkling courtyard with lots of plants and even a tiny pond. Hand-painted gourds hang from the trellises. Communal kitchen. Singles 1000dr. Doubles 1500dr. Triples 2000dr.

Many of the restaurants specialize in fresh fish and lobster, and most of their selection is mounted on stands in front. **Zorbas Restaurant** (tel. 226 89), on the west side of the harbor, has a large selection of inexpensive dishes (from 220dr). (Open 8am-2am.) **Russo's** (tel. 232 18), 9, 4th of September St., just off the harbor by the Mobil station, looks like a nondescript *taverna* but you can sample Cretan "escargot," and occasionally catch some *bouzouki* music. (Open 6am-2am.) One fine yet inexpensive eatery is **Yuras Restaurant,** 4 Dimokritou St., 1 block from the harbor on Platia Iroon Polytechniou, the city's main square. Walk inland past Russo's and turn right; Yura's—it's 20m ahead on your left. (Open 8am-2am.)

## Sights and Entertainment

For most of the year, life in Sitia centers around the cheerful waterfront. Most of the old quarter is terraced along the hillside on the western part of the city just above the harbor. The **fortress** at the hilltop affords a fine view of the town and the entire Bay of Sitia. Sitia's lean, sandy **beach,** which extends for about 3km east of the town is right next to the road, and its most distant half is usually free of people. The strand is apparently a hard-luck spot for ship captains, as two semi-sunken boats beckon adventurous swimmers.

In the **archeological museum** (tel. 239 17), 100m past the bus station on the road to Ierapetra, you'll find a small collection from nearby sites. (Open Mon. and Wed.-Sat. 9am-3pm, Sun. 9:30am-2:30pm.) The **Folklore Museum,** 10 Arkadiou St., houses at least one tool for just about any household chore or domestic occupation you can imagine. To get there, take Kazantzaki St. up from the waterfront near Zorba's, turn right on Arkadiou St., and walk 4 blocks. (Open daily 9:30am-3:30pm. Small fee.)

Sitia's major export is *sultanas* (raisins), and every August the town holds a **Sultana Festival.** The 450dr admission fee buys you an assigned seat at a table to watch Cretan dances and drink all the locally produced wine you can stomach. Tickets are on sale during the week of the festival at a booth right by the harbor. A **cultural festival** featuring concerts, open-air theater, ballet, and other artistic events is held during the summer as well.

The cheery **Peacock Pub,** on Dimokritou St., is a favorite hangout for local youths. One of the tacky waterfront discos is the **Black Hole,** east on the waterfront beyond the bus station, the best of the bunch. (Open 10:30pm-3am.) **Disco Club La Nuit,** a few doors before, is a steamy cellar with a mostly male clientele. (Open 10:30pm-3am.) Both discos charge an exorbitant 400dr for beer, 600dr for drinks. **Kalamia's** across the street has a beach-side bar and affordable beer (150dr). (Open 9:30pm-3am.)

## Near Sitia

The region around Sitia begs to be explored. Those with an archeological bent will be interested in the half-excavated ruins of **Praisos,** south of Sitia, which have yielded many fine small bronzes. You'll need your own means of transportation to get here, since buses don't run. **Mohlos,** a popular fishing village, lies halfway between Agios Nikolaos and Sitia. Rooms to let in pensions are about 1400dr in high season. Since public buses don't stop in Mohlos, you'll have to disembark in Sfaka and walk or hitch the last 6km north to the town.

### Toplou Monastery

Although at first the Monastery of Toplou looks like a fortress, don't be fooled. The original church dates back to the tenth century, but after the destruction of the monastery by the Turks in 1471, the entire complex was rebuilt and fortified. The impressive three-story structure now contains a number of relics, including the second-century B.C.E. inscription of a treaty (to the left of the entrance of the church of Panayia Akrotiriani) between the Cretan cities of Itanos and Ierapytna and the province of Magnesia in Asia Minor, and an elaborate icon by the eighteenth-century master Ioannis Kournaros.

Buses do not go directly to the monastery; you must get off the Vai bus 12km outside Sitia at the *Moni Toplou* turn-off, and walk the last 3km. If you are driving, follow the road east from Sitia along the coast and turn left at the junction onto the road marked to Toplou. Farther north on the same road (past Vai) is the archeological site of **Itanos,** where the treaty displayed at Toplou was found. Nearby is an excellent uncrowded beach.

## Vai

Not long ago, tourists headed east to the palm beach at Vai for a secluded and idyllic refuge from Sitia's crowds. Today, several buses roll into this outpost every day, depositing tourists eager to gawk at Europe's only natural palm forest. It remains a strangely anomalous stretch of the Caribbean transplanted to the shores of Crete, but hardly deserves the attention it receives. (Park open 7am-9pm. Free.)

Most travelers visit Vai via the crowded public bus from Sitia. Buses leave Sitia and stop at Paleokastro en route to Vai (6 per day, last from Sitia at 5pm, 1 hr., Sitia-Vai 180dr, Paleokastro-Vai 50dr).

There is a restaurant and a cafe on the beach, and a new and—amazingly enough—clean bathhouse (toilets 10dr, showers 30dr), but no accommodations. Although camping is forbidden in the park itself (and they mean it), many people unfurl sleeping bags in the cove to the south of the palm beach. Nude bathing proceeds here undisturbed, as in the cove to the north of the main beach. The southern cove on your right is more accessible, but the northern is less frequented.

If sleeping on the beach doesn't appeal to you, rent a room in the quiet town of **Paleokastro,** 8km back toward Sitia. The **Itanos** (tel. 225 08), on the main square, rents doubles for 1500dr; the **Paleokastro,** 100m down the road to Sitia, charges 1500dr (bargain). The town's pensions average 1500-1700dr for doubles, less if you stay more than one night.

## Kato Zakros

The remains of the **Palace of Zakros** mark the site of the fourth great center of Minoan civilization. Excavations began in the early 1900s, but the late Minoan palace and township of surrounding dependencies were not uncovered until 1962. Built on a plan similar to those at Knossos, Phaestos, and Malia, with domestic, state, and religious rooms all radiating off a central court, most of the palace was destroyed around 1450 B.C.E. Fortunately, the city of Zakros seems to have escaped the plunder that devastated other major Minoan sites. As a result, archeologists were able to recover the rich contents of the palace (on display in Iraklion's Archeological Museum, Room VIII).

Buses from Sitia go to Kato Zakros daily at 11am and 2pm, returning at 1pm and 5pm (250dr). Besides the palace, Kato Zakros has a gorgeous beach suitable for camping, and interesting caves and niches, some of which are inhabitable. Rooms in the town's pensions go for 700dr per person, showers included. Kato Zakros has three *tavernas* and a cafe-bar, and at the **Anexis Taverna,** you can change American dollars or German deutschmarks. The two restaurants allow customers to use their toilets and showers. There is no public shower on the beach.

# SARONIC GULF ISLANDS
## Σαρονικού

During antiquity, no matter how many people crowded the shores of the Saronic Gulf Islands, the high rocky interior of each remained gloriously unmolested. Temples were built high above the sea and as far from the hubbub as possible. Some of these lofty retreats have crumbled under the joint onslaught of the years and elements. But don't let that stop you from visiting. From on high, you may spy a secluded stretch of sand which you can claim as your own. Most beaches on the islands are pebbly, but the surrounding hills and rocky cliffs make them some of Greece's most scenic swimming spots.

Despite a familial resemblance, each island is unique. Spetses is the rowdy adolescent, Hydra the grown-up sophisticate, Poros the ageless drifter, and Aegina the fickle socialite. If you can only see a couple of these islands, go to Spetses or Hydra for physical beauty, Poros and Aegina for a diverse and energetic group of tourists.

Unfortunately, the Saronic Gulf Islands are not only the most expensive in Greece, but freelance camping is illegal. Yet if rooms are scarce, the tourist police tend to look the other way if people pitch their tent in a secluded spot. Because the islands, especially Aegina and Poros, are such a short hop from Athens, many Greeks go for the weekend, making an already crowded situation unbearable. Try to visit during the week and hook up with a pension or private room.

There are basically three ways to travel between Piraeus and the Saronic Gulf Islands. In descending order of cost, these are the package tour, the hydrofoil, and the ferry. The fare for ferries between any two adjacent islands is roughly 400dr; the hydrofoil costs at least 150dr extra but cuts travel time in half, runs more frequently (in calm seas), and reaches places much farther away, including such destinations on the Peloponnese as Nafplion, Tolo, Leonidio, Kiparissia, Monemvassia, Kythera, and Neapolis. Prices listed for ferries and hydrofoils drop 15% in off-season. Schedules are posted in the port of each island, but be sure to confirm at the ticket office or at a travel agency. The main passenger service is provided by the **Argosaronikos Line** (tel. 451 13 11), while hydrofoil service is provided by **Flying Dolphins Line,** 8 Akti Themistokleus, Piraeus (tel. 452 71 07; in Aegina tel. 453 17 16/7).

The **telephone code** for Aegina is 0297, for Poros, Hydra, and Spetses, 0298.

## Aegina Αιγινα

About one and a half hours by ferry from Piraeus and an easy daytrip from Athens, Aegina has had little trouble attracting visitors. The sun-dappled island is blessed with a mountainous terrain and many small, rocky coves that are perfect for swimming. Aegina bears the scars of an expanding tourist industry, but the island is large enough to allow refuge from the crowds.

In ancient times, Athens and Aegina weren't so friendly. The fiery little island resisted Athenian encroachment at every turn. At pan-Hellenic games, Aegina's sprinters sped past their competitors, and the fleet-footed came to Aegina to train. The island produced the first Greek coins—the silver "tortoises"—subsequently gaining great financial leverage throughout the Greek world. With the onset of the Persian War in 491 B.C.E., the Aeginetans first sided with Xerxes' army, to the

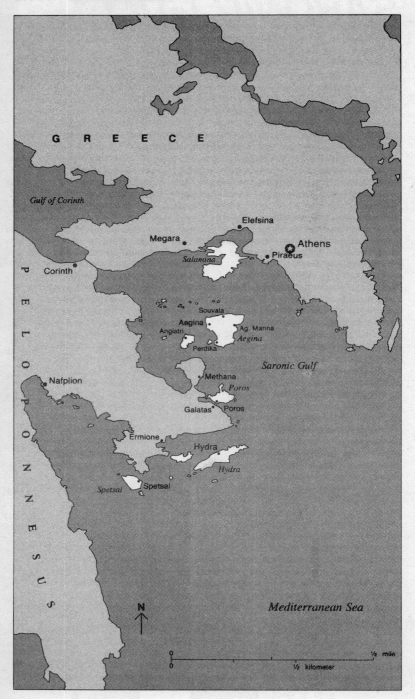

chagrin of the besieged Athenians, but in 480 B.C.E., at Salamis, the greatest of all Greek sea battles, they returned to the Greek side and won the praise of the Delphic Oracle as the fleetest navy on the seas. Antagonism with Athens redoubled over the next 30 years as Aegina sided with Sparta in the brewing Athenian-Spartan clash. Although the island's inhabitants flourished and built the magnificent Temple of Aphaea during these three decades, Athens defeated Aegina in 459 B.C.E., razing its walls and subjecting it to membership in the Delian League. By 431 B.C.E., Athens had expelled the entire Aeginetan population, replacing it with Athenian colonists. Sparta restored the native population in 405 B.C.E. In the 1820s, Aegina briefly became the capital of the new Greek state. Today, few reminders of Aegina's trials and tribulations are visible.

To get to Aegina from Athens, take green bus #040 from Filellinon St. and get off at the Public Theater (*Demotikon Theatron*) in Piraeus (½ hr., 30dr). From there, you can see the pier where ferries leave for Aegina. Alternatively, take the subway (30dr) to the stop at Piraeus and walk to the left for a few blocks along the water. Unless you know exactly when you plan to return, buy your return ticket on Aegina.

Most likely you will disembark in the port of **Aegina Town,** which serves as the central point of departure for buses around the island. If the ferry drops you at **Agia Marina,** a short bus ride from the main road will bring you to Aegina Town (every hr. on the hr., ½ hr., 105dr). The town has managed to preserve some of its original character, probably because it lacks a good beach (although there are nice swimming spots close by).

## Orientation and Practical Information

There are two main piers, both on the left side of the harbor (facing inland) before the beach. Hydrofoils leave from the smaller one to the right, ferries from the larger one to the left, around the corner. The **tourist police** (tel. 223 91) are opposite the hydrofoil landing. (Open 24 hours.) Just to their left, on the corner of Leonardi Lada St. and decorated by "Tourist Office" signs, **Tour Aegina/Leoussis Tours** (tel. 223 34) sells maps (80dr) and books. (Open daily 9am-7:30.) Both **banks** are on the waterfront to the right of the ferry landing. (Open Mon.-Thurs. 8am-2pm, Fri. 8am-1:30pm.) To the left of the ferry landing is the **post office** (tel. 223 99), which cashes traveler's checks. (Open Mon.-Fri. 7:30am-2pm.) The **OTE** is up Aiakou St. to the right; keep trudging up Aiakou when the street narrows into a walkway—the building has a monstrous radar dish on its roof. (Open Mon.-Sat. 8am-3pm, Sun. 9am-1:30pm.) The hospital (tel. 222 090 or 222 51) is above Aegina Town, beyond the OTE on Nosokomiou St. Aegina's **telephone code** is 0297.

From the **bus station** (tel. 224 12), in front of the post office, buses leave hourly for Souvala (½ hr., 90dr), Perdika (20 min., 70dr), and Agia Marina (½ hr., 105dr). They run from 5am to 10pm from the terminal, from 5:30am to 10pm from other points. If you wish, you can rent two-wheelers from the sidewalk vendor just to the right of the ferry landing. (Bikes 400dr per day. 1-person mopeds 250dr per hr., 1000dr per day. Medium-sized motorbikes 2000dr per day. "Day" is defined as 9am-6pm. Mopeds and motorbikes come with full tank of gas.) Be careful: The island's roads are notorious for blind curves, absurdly fast drivers, and totalled motorbikes.

Ten **ferries** (tel. 223 28) per day keep Aegina well-connected to Piraeus (1½ hr., 410dr). From Agia Marina, six additional boats leave Monday through Saturday for Piraeus (also 1½ hr.). Passenger ferries leave twice per day during the week for other Saronic Gulf destinations: Methana (45 min., 270dr); Poros (1½ hr., 290dr); Hydra (2½ hr., 425dr); Ermione (3 hr., 510dr); and Spetses (3½ hr., 550dr). The frequency of ferry service increases on summer weekends. **Hydrofoils** (tel. 244 56) go 10 times per day to Piraeus (35 min., 570dr) and twice per day (Mon.-Sat. at 9:45am and 5pm, Sun. only at 9:40am) to: Methana (15 min., 445dr); Poros (45 min., 647dr); Hydra (1½ hr., 774dr); Ermione (1½ hr., 988dr); Spetses (2 hr., 1021dr); and Porto Heli (2¼ hr., 1183dr). One leaves daily Monday through Saturday for Napflion (3½ hr., 1609dr). The schedules from Aegina are inconsistent, and the posted time-tables are rarely in English. You can make connections at Poros, Hydra, and Spetses to reach more locations on the Peloponnese.

## Accommodations, Food, and Entertainment

The island fills up fast with family vacationers, so you may have trouble finding a place to stay. The high-season norm is 1500dr for singles, 2000dr for doubles. To find rooms, ask at the hotels or walk the back streets. Since the island has to ship in its entire water supply from Poros and Piraeus, expect to pay up to 100dr for a short shower.

Two relatively inexpensive hotels are the **Hotel Artemis** (tel. 251 95), behind the bus station (singles 1500dr; doubles 1800dr; stay 2 nights and get a bathroom) and the **Hotel Marmarina** (tel. 235 10 or 224 74), Leonardo Lada St., above the tourist police, with slightly cheaper rooms with balconies. (Singles 1200dr. Doubles 1600dr.) Close to the beach but away from the port is **Sklavenas Hostel,** 19 Kapothistries St. (tel. 223 27). It is three stories tall, with great roof space and adjoining rooms off a bathroom. (Roof 500dr. Doubles 1600dr.) Though illegal, camping is sometimes done without hassles from the police, especially when the town is full. In Aegina Town, the beach under the trees near the museum, or on the far side of the Temple of Apollo, is popular, despite the garbage collectors who pass through at 6am.

For a very respectable, reasonably-priced meal, try **To Spiti Tou Psara** (House of Fishermen), #41 to the right on the waterfront (tel. 226 84). (*Kalamari* 350dr, full breakfast 340dr. Open Tues.-Sun. 7am-midnight.) Another good choice is **To Maridaki,** a few doors down. In the morning, take a walk through the covered fish market on the waterfront beyond the bank. Behind the market are fresh fruit dealers and food stands (*souvlaki* 90dr). Sample the pistachio nuts, an important product of the island.

Agia Marina explodes at night into a haze of club lights and a dissonant chorus of bar music. A **disco** above the beach and **Retro** (open 8pm-3am), next to the post office, are two of Aegina's more long-lived nightspots. The outdoor **cinema,** up Aiakou St., often shows American films for 220dr. Check the signs on the fence near the museum for more information about evening events.

## Sights

Archeologically, Aegina Town's fame rests tenuously on half of a column remaining from a **Temple of Apollo,** a short walk out of town to the north. (Open Mon.-Sat. 9am-6pm, Sun. 10am-5pm. Admission 200dr, students 100dr.) The **archeological museum,** within the temple grounds, has a small collection. (Open Mon. and Wed.-Sat. 9am-3pm, Sun. 9:30am-2:30pm. Free with admission to temple.)

On the other side of the island, the well-preserved **Temple of Aphaea** deserves a visit. Unless your trip happens to coincide with one of the infrequent bus tours of Aegina, you will be able to enjoy this fifth-century B.C.E. shrine in solitude. This structure is the only surviving Hellenic temple with a second row of small superimposed columns in the interior of the sanctuary. Well, what do you know. The view of the island from the site is worth the trip itself—just watch out for the cactus and briars. (Open daily 10am-5pm. Admission 200dr, students 100dr.) To get to the ruins, take the Agia Marina bus from Aegina Town (25 min., 105dr). In Agia Marina, walk to the end of town with the water on your right and then straight up Kilokotroni St. until it becomes a wooded trail—this is the footpath to the Temple of Aphaea.

The little island of **Angistri** is a half-hour sail from Aegina Town (last return at 5:45pm, 200dr). Boats leave five times per day in summer (3 on Sun.), and because there is no ferry from the mainland itself, Angistri remains pleasantly untouristed. **Skala** is the best place for swimming, although you might want to explore **Milo** and **Limenario.** The **Aktaeon** (tel. 238 21) has singles for 1000dr, doubles for

1200dr, and triples for 1500dr (showers 250dr). On the beach, the **Anagennissis** has doubles for 1500dr, triples for 1750dr (showers included). The **Angistri** (tel. 238 27) offers singles for 1200dr, doubles for 1450dr, triples for 1750dr (showers included).

On the road between Aegina and Agia Marina in the middle of the island is the village of **Paliochora**, where the islanders used to take refuge from invasions. At one time the village had 365 churches, but having lost count too many times, people commonly refer to it as "the town of 300 churches." Only 28 of these remain, some with wonderful frescoes. Of particular interest is the **Agios Nektarios** monastery.

A westbound bus from Aegina Town will deposit you in Perdiha (70dr), a fishing village that will serve you best with access to the tiny uninhabited island of **Moni**. Brusque hills, a rock plateau, and royal blue water make the entire trip to the Saronic Gulf worthwhile. You can pitch a tent or unroll your sleeping bag, but be sure to bring provisions, including water, as spigots are hard to find. A motorboat to Moni meets the bus from Aegina (9am-8pm 10 per day, 100dr).

# *Poros* Πόρος

Only a sliver of water separates the muscular hills of the mainland from tiny Poros. Its name, meaning "passage," refers to the channel that is its border. Poros lacks Aegina's pace, Hydra's chic, and Spetses' beauty. What distinguishes Poros is its straightforward, guileless approach to having fun. People here cover the beaches, ride the waves, and stop traffic in roving bands of bar-hoppers.

The arcane Kalavrian League, a seven-city council, met in Poros to ward off hostile naval powers, and built the Temple of Poseidon in the sixth century B.C.E. Three hundred years later, the great orator Demosthenes, who improved his diction by speaking with marbles in his mouth, killed himself beside its columns. For most of modern history, Poros has been sparsely populated until Greeks arrived from Turkey in the population exchange of the '20s.

Poros is actually two small, lush islands—Kalavria and Sphaeria—cut by a canal. Poros Town occupies most of tiny Sphaeria, while woods extend over rugged Kalavria. Less crowded than Aegina, it still overflows on the weekends with both Greek and foreign tourists. Rather than spend all your time on the waterfront, climb up the narrow passageways that lead to the top of Poros Town and the hills beyond.

## Orientation and Practical Information

Ferries (3 hr., 575dr) and hydrofoils (1 hr., 1114dr) leave Piraeus for Poros several times per day. En route, the boats stop in **Methana** on a volcanic peninsula of the Peloponnese, known since antiquity for its curative springs. Continuing on to Poros Town, hydrofoils and most car ferries dock at the main landing in the center of town. Some car ferries dock instead at the northwest side of town, a dozen blocks to the left (facing inland). Directly in front of the ferry landing, **Family Tours,** 14 Troon St. (tel. 225 49), sells a map of Poros for 100dr (open daily 9am-9pm), as does nearby **Takis Travel** (tel. 220 48). Both provide general information, change money, and locate accommodations. The agencies' listings are overpriced: Don't bother. Set back from the waterfront on Agiou Nikolaou St., 100m to the right of the main ferry landing, are the **tourist police** (tel. 224 62 or 222 56) who might help you find a room. (Open mid-June to Sept. Mon.-Fri. 8am-2:30pm; for emergencies, an officer is usually available 24 hours.) The **bank** is to your right (facing inland) past the church, 175m from the main ferry landing. (Open in summer Mon.-Thurs. 8am-2pm and 6:30-8:30pm, Fri. 8am-1:30pm and 6:30-8:30pm.) The **post office** is in the first square to the right along the water. (Open Mon.-Fri. 7:30am-3pm). The **OTE** is centrally located at #30, to the left on the wharf. (Open Mon.-Fri. 8am-11pm, Sat.-Sun. 8am-10pm.) **Suzi's Launderette Service** (tel. 242 09) is next door. (Wash 800dr. Open daily 9:30am-1:30pm and 5:30-8:30pm.) **Anita's Books,** 120m from the Canal gas station, swaps second-hand English books.

Rent **bikes** or **mopeds** from **Stelio's** (tel. 245 90) or **Kostas** (tel. 235 65). Both charge 300-400dr for bikes and 1000dr for mopeds, and are open daily from 9am to 7:30pm. In high-season, come early before supplies run out. You can rent cheaper bikes across the water in Galatas at **Fotis Bikes** (see Sights). Poros' **telephone code** is 0298.

At the main ferry landing, the port police have set up a blackboard showing that day's departures. From Poros, **ferries** run to Piraeus five times per day Monday through Saturday, three times on Sunday (3 hr., 550dr). All of these except one (at 2:45pm) stop in Methana (45 min., 210dr) and Aegina (1½ hr., 270dr). One boat leaves daily at 10:30am for Hydra (1½ hr., 280dr) and Spetses (2 hr., 600dr). **Lela Tours** (tel. 244 39) has information and tickets (open daily 9:30am-4pm and 5-9:30pm), as do the **port police** (tel. 222 74), and George's Cafe (tel. 240 80), below Takis Tours. **Hydrofoils** serve Piraeus from Poros seven times per day Monday through Saturday, 11 times on Sunday (1¼ hr., 1264dr). Hydrofoils also zip to Methana (2 per day, 10 min., 420dr), Aegina (2 per day, 45 min., 711dr), Hydra (6 per day, ½ hr., 378dr), Ermione (4 per day, 40 min. 461dr), Spetses (5 per day, 1 hr., 630dr), and Porto Heli (6 per day, 1¼ hr., 711dr). One hydrofoil leaves daily at 9:05am for Leonidias (1061dr) and Monemvassia (2½ hr., 1713dr). Four days per week, it continues to Kythera (3½ hr.) and Neapolis (4 hr.). Hydrofoil tickets are sold at the **Flying Dolphin office** (tel. 222 97), opposite the landing (open 6am-10pm), and on the landing itself before departure. There is an excellent map on the landing opposite Takis Tours.

## *Accommodations, Food, and Entertainment*

Most of the low-priced boarding houses are clean, but private baths and singles are extremely rare (doubles 2000dr). Be sure to check the street over which your window opens; travelers have suffered insomnia due to the late-night popularity of the *taverna* across the way. Many of the better pensions flank the Hotel Latsi a dozen blocks to the left of the main pier. Three reputable ones are the establishments of **Nikos Douras** (tel. 226 33; roof 500dr; doubles 1600dr; showers included), **George Douras** (tel. 225 32), and **Dimitras Alexopoulou** (tel. 226 97). Call if they don't find you first, or look for "rooms" signs in the area. The first two proprietors are extremely helpful and speak a few words of English. The third has rooms rated a grade above (about 800dr per person; hot showers included). Two streets above the bike shops are more rooms. **Villa Christina** (tel. 226 01) has quiet doubles for 1800dr. There are also lovely rooms up the hill near the clock tower. Avoid all Poros hotels since the cheapest ones are C-class. Hot showers are available at the **Sail Bar**, along the water to the right (200dr).

Poros Town probably has the best restaurants in the Saronic Gulf, but that isn't saying much. For reasonably-priced seafood and grilled meats, try **Caravella** (tel. 236 66) or its next-door neighbor **Lagoudera** (tel. 223 89; open noon-midnight), both a short walk to the right (facing inland) along the wharf, with covered tables right at the water's edge. In the square to the right of Takis, **Seven Brothers** (tel. 224 46) has wonderful atmosphere and large portions of well-prepared food for 400dr. (Open noon-1am.) Another fraternal establishment, **Three Brothers** (tel. 223 36), opposite the museum 100m to the right, is the place to watch nightly Greek dances. Farther along the water, the **Afrikana** (tel. 241 14) serves barbeque ribs, melon cocktails, and their Thursday night special four-course Chinese meal (600dr; book in advance). **Cafe Avra** (tel. 230 87), on the ferry boat landing, charges only 80dr for *ouzo.* (Open 8am-1am.). Several very good groceries to the right of the main landing help with food costs. Near the monastery, there are also a few *tavernas* and even a restaurant, **Paradissos**, close to the Temple of Poseidon. **Zorba's** (tel. 227 39) serves up tasty dishes and offers traditional dancing about ½km up the road to the left of the wharf (facing inland), across the canal. You can also find inexpensive *souvlaki* and chicken at the restaurant next to the **Diana movie theater** (#50 on the left-hand side of the port facing inland). The theater often shows American and British films (140dr). For more excitement, try the **Takis Pub,** on the waterfront, or the discos after 11:30pm. **Kavos,** all the way to the right along the waterfront (300m), remains popular, with Greek dancing at about 2am. **Corali,** a more high-tech disco, is next door. Around the big bend is **Siroco,** the most popular disco, with a wonderful view of the Gulf.

## Sights

In Poros Town itself, the **archeological museum,** 1 block before the church along the water, is small but has some interesting inscriptions and photographs of the ruins at Troizen. (Open Mon. and Wed.-Sat. 9am-3:15pm, Sun. 9:30am-2:30pm. Free.)

The main sight on Poros, the **Monastery of Zoodochos Pigis** (Virgin of the Life-Giving Spring), has an excellent view and is situated in an overgrown glade 6km from Poros Town. The site was used as early as 200 C.E. Inside you'll find a triptych inlaid with gold illustrating scenes from the lives of Jesus and the Apostles. Inside, the monastery is cool and silent, except for a busy Greek Orthodox priest. Dress properly; men wearing shorts and women wearing pants are forbidden to enter. A few skirt-like coverings are available at the door. (Open daily 7am-7pm.) It's a scenic bus ride (7am-11pm every ½ hr., 20 min., 30dr) from the stop next to the main port in town. Along the route to the monastery is the little beach of **Askeli.**

Unless you're a Greek history maven, the main reason to visit the ruins of the **Temple of Poseidon** atop the mountain is the vista of the Saronic Gulf. From the canal, it's 9km uphill; after an hour of climbing, you'll agree that either old Demosthenes was a trooper or he landed at a really high tide. The best way to reach the top is on a motorbike, which you can rent by the shore in Poros Town. From the monastery, backtrack ½km along the road until you get to the turn-off leading to higher ground. Little remains of the temple but knee-deep rubble. Rumor has it that the people of Poros dismantled what was left of the temple and used the stones to stop erosion. The structure dates to the sixth century B.C.E. and was traditionally used as a sanctuary for refugees, especially victims of shipwrecks. It was here that Demosthenes took refuge from his Macedonian pursuers. From the steps of the sanctuary, he called out to his enemies that he would surrender but needed time to write his family a farewell letter. Chewing on his pen for a while, he crouched down, shaking. His pursuers taunted him, mistaking his movements for tremors of fear, but before they knew it their prize had died—he had dipped the end of his quill in poison.

Boats run between the Peloponnese and the harbor of Poros (5 min., 50dr). Take the caïque across the channel to **Galatas** on the Peloponnese for the sunny beaches of **Aliki** (the nicer but farther of the 2) and **Plaka,** both quite a distance to the left as you walk along the shore. A 10-minute walk from both leads to the enormous fragrant lemon grove of **Lemonodassos,** with a waterfall. Donkey rides, at 200dr each way, are a rip-off. Although camping is officially forbidden in the area, tents do crop up behind Plaka and Aliki Beaches. Those who stay here exercise descretion, however, since the tourist police are strict. One kilometer northwest of Galatas is **Camping Kyrangelo** (tel. 245 20; 260dr per person; 170dr per tent).

This is the perfect place to take advantage of the low bike rental prices at **Fotis Bikes** (tel. 228 42), in Galatas, right where the boat docks. Most visitors to the island miss the surrounding Peloponnesian countryside and source of the best **cycling routes** around, which begin from Galatas going northwest away from the lemon groves. The terrain is flat and the fields range from cultivated flowers to apricot, lemon, and olive groves. You won't ever be far from a cold drink, especially if you pedal down the 3-kilometer turn-off by the carnation fields of **Trizinia,** the site of ancient Troizen. (Buses run here from Galatas; call 224 80). Back on the main road, it's 10km from Galatas to the turn-off for Nafplion. This route goes around a bay past an obviously popular *taverna* to the town of Kaloni. Before the bakery is a sign for the long, tranquil Agios Georgios Beach. From here, the road continues flat for another 5km or so and then becomes hilly.

**Neorion Beach** is accessible by boat (20dr), foot, or bike. Take the road from the left of the pier about 3km and turn left at the Neorion sign over the little canal bridge. **Canali Beach** and its equally rocky neighbor lie just to the right of the canal bridge. But as is generally the case, the better beaches are farther from town, the best on the road beyond Neorion.

# Hydra (Idra) Υδρα

Entering Hydra's port is like entering Xanadu. The dazzling white homes and their orange clay roofs seem like facets of a single gem set in the ring of hills. Girded by a thread of breakwater, the harbor forms a soft crescent, its two ends flanked by stout cannons. It is no wonder that Hydra, "the well-watered," is now the ritzy island home and retreat of many Greek artists, some of whom display their work along the water. Others hide in the backstreets where the only disturbance is an occasional donkey. Below, the harbor hums with burly wooden trawlers, sleek sailboats, regal yachts, muscular speedboats, and passenger ships. Artists, backpackers, jetsetters, and fishers dodge past the hurried package tourists to their retreat in this pleasure dome. But the hum of mechanized vehicles is nearly absent: On Hydra there are no cars, only a garbage truck.

## Orientation and Practical Information

For a daytrip, Hydra is accessible from Poros, Ermione, or Spetses. **Ferries** run four times per day to Poros (1 hr., 267dr), Methana (1¾ hr., 425dr), Aegina (2¼ hr., 534dr), and Piraeus (3½ hr., 610dr) to the north, and twice per day to Ermione (1 hr., 288dr) and Spetses (1¼ hr., 288dr) in the Gulf below. Tickets are sold from an outdoor booth along the waterfront near the bank from 8am to 10pm. **Hydrofoils** serve Piraeus frequently from Hydra (at least 12 per day, 1½ hr., 1400dr). Hydrofoils also run to Poros (6 per day, ½ hr., 350dr), Methana (2 per day, 1 hr., 600dr), and Aegina (2 per day, 1½ hr., 780dr) in the north, as well as to Ermione and Spetses (5 per day, ½ hr., 470dr), Porto Heli (7 per day, 40 min., 550dr), Leonidio (at 9:45am, 1 hr., 840dr), Kiparissia (at 9:45am, 1½ hr., 1000dr), and Monemvassia (at 9:45am, 2 hr., 1550dr) in the south. Tickets are sold by the **Flying Dolphin Ticket Office**, on Em. Tombaz St. (tel. 520 19), on the left corner of the harbor (facing inland). (Open 6am-8pm.)

To get to the **tourist police** (tel. 522 05), walk along the wharf and turn left at the church with the clock tower. They provide travel information and free maps of the island, and arrange rental of private rooms, the cheapest accommodations. (Open 24 hours.) Opposite is the **OTE**. (Open Mon.-Fri. 8am-1pm and 5-10pm.) The **post office** is in the alley 1 block south of Ikonomou St., up a few steps. (Open Mon.-Fri 7:30am-2:30pm.) The **bank** is just about front row center on the waterfront. (Open Mon.-Thurs. 8am-2pm and 7-9pm, Fri. 8am-1:30pm and 7-9pm.) You'll find the **laundromat** across from the Flying Dolphin office. (Open mornings and evenings. Shirts 100dr, pants 200dr.) Hydra's telephone code is 0298.

## Accommodations, Food, and Entertainment

Hydra has the highest-priced accommodations in the Saronic Gulf, already the most expensive region in Greece. Furthermore, it can be almost impossible to find a place here without reservations. Singles are practically nonexistent and doubles cost at least 2000dr. Rooms on the water (look for 2nd-floor "pension" signs) offer views of the glimmering harbor at dusk but are noisy. The cheapest hotel in town is the **Sophia**, A. Miaouli St. (tel. 523 13), at the center of the wharf. (Doubles 2000dr. Triples 2500dr. Beds in hall 600dr per person. Hot showers included.) Keep in mind that the bar beneath the Sophia is the last to close and blares music. **Pension Douglas** (tel. 525 99), also on the water, is quieter and has a selection of English books. (Doubles 2000dr. Triples 2600dr.) Even better is **Rooms Spiros** (tel. 524 24), on the eastern edge of the harbor and up a flight of stairs. Large rooms cluster around a tiered courtyard. (Doubles 1800dr.) Across from Hotel Sophia, the **Pension Christina** has doubles for 2000dr along a balcony hall.

Museum-quality rooms await the fortunate few at **Raphalia's Mansion** (tel. 525 84). The owner's private collection of antique furnishings and historical documents rivals the collections in any of the merchant houses on Hydra (see Sights below). (Minimum stay of 2 nights. Singles 1500dr. Doubles 2500dr.) To get to Raphalia's, walk up the street next to the clock tower past the tourist police, bear right at the park, and inquire at the pharmacy in front of you; the owner usually sits outside on the lookout for "nice" people. **Pension Agelika**, 42 Andreou Miaouli St. (tel. 532 02), a short walk up from the water, has very comfortable rooms but is also expensive. (Singles 1600dr, doubles 2320dr. Breakfast included.) The two D-class hotels, **Argo** (tel. 524 52) and **Dina** (tel. 522 48), are significantly more expensive and often booked during high season. When there are no rooms, the tourist police let people sleep on the rocky beaches.

Food is also incredibly expensive here. Many budget travelers choose to drink until food becomes an alimentary impossibility. The juice cafe in the westernmost corner of the harbor is relatively affordable and serves enormous cheese *tost*. Most restaurants charge an arm and a leg, so make sure you know what you're paying before you order; also beware of price minimums. Try **Ta Tria Adelfia** (The Three Brothers), just off the harbor behind the marble clock tower. (Open 9am-4pm and 7pm-2am.) Just around the corner is **Taverna Douskos** (tel. 528 86), the cheapest sit-down place and very popular with tourists. **Captain George's** (follow the signs up from the harbor) usually has the best fish. For excellent French food, go to **La Grenouille** (tel. 523 12); you won't find French cuisine at these prices anywhere else in Europe (entrees 750dr). For breakfast or fruity cocktails, go to the **Up and High Cafe** (tel. 520 79), in the far western corner of the harbor, a very mod and attractive place with new age music, copies of *Interview* magazine, and bracing coffee. The bakery in an alley on the eastern corner across from the Flying Dolphin office can help hold you over with a huge selection of pastries and rolls. There's a produce **market** right by the post office. Hydra's soft ice cream is well worth the 100dr.

Dancing dudes can try either **Disco Kavos** or **Lagoudera** (drinks ½-price for students). Kavos draws an older crowd but the space between these two discos serves as a common cruising strip where everyone seems to be speaking strained English. Lagoudera sits on the western edge of the harbor embedded in stone. Kavos is farther up the shore path and around the bend. On the way to Kavos and on the peak high above Lagoudera is **Disco Heaven.** By the time you walk all the way up and witness the view, you may actually be convinced that you're at the pearly gates. The drink prices are also sky-high (500dr). Yet another disco, **Siroco,** lies beyond Kavos; it too offers a fantastic view.

Hydra has two good and very popular bars. **The Pirate,** toward the harbor's western end, has an extensive record collection and large speakers. (Beer 150dr.) **Pan's** has more atmosphere, featuring music from the Grateful Dead and Jefferson Airplane. The bearded and tattooed owner is a former New Yorker named Pan.

## Sights

For most of the Turkish occupation, Hydra's arid land went untaxed. With no natural resources and a growing refugee population from the Peloponnese, Balkans, and Turkey, Hydra's inhabitants turned to managing other areas' exports, and its merchant princes became shipping magnates. Hydriotes grew prosperous by dodging pirates and naval blockades during the late eighteenth and early nineteenth centuries and emerged as effective financial and naval leaders in their country's revolt against the Turks in the 1820s. **Koundouriotis,** whose house is on a hill to the west of the harbor, was one of the many Hydriot leaders in the Greek War of Independence. To get to his house, walk up the narrow alley to the right of The Pirate bar, turn at the first right, left at the first left on Voulgari St. 1 block past Hotel Hydra, and right again. It's tricky to find; visit the tourist police to make sure the house

is open. The houses of **Votsis** and **Economou**, two Hydriotes who also contributed
to the island's naval fame, are closer to the crest of the hill behind Disco Heaven,
right on Voulgari St. Ask the tourist police to locate other noble merchants' homes
for you. The **art school,** 1 block up from the harbor's right corner, has occasional
exhibits.

The **Ecclesiastical Church,** built in 1806, bears the large clock tower that dominates the wharf. Also of interest are the frescoes at the **Church of St. John,** in the
Platia Kamina. Around to the east of the harbor, set off by its winding, anchor-
flanked white stairs, is the **Pilot School** of the Greek Merchant Marine, with intriguing paintings, models, and class pictures from the '30s. (Open variably 8am-10pm.
Free.) The most beautiful churches are remote, and accessible only by foot or donkey.

Walk the photogenic circuit along the donkey path west where it runs over a stone
wall and aqueduct, or pursue any of the following three hikes from town. The first
and shortest (1 hr.) continues down A. Miaouli St. from the waterfront (the road
takes you out of town) and up the hill to the monastery of **Ilias,** and on a lower
peak overlooking the harbor the nunnery of **Efpraxia.** (Both open 9am-5pm.) By
far the prettier of the two, the older Ilias is the home of two friendly monks who
may show you about. To return to the harbor, climb down the monastery steps and
follow the steps and passageways down through the town. The second hike is to
**Episkopi,** a deserted monastery at least an hour's walk west from Ilias along goat
paths that take you through beautiful uninhabited countryside. You'll need to ask
directions; the Greek word for footpath is *monopati.* You can return to town by
cutting down to the north coast via the tiny village of **Vlihos.** You can discreetly
pitch a tent on the small deserted pebble beach here. The third and most challenging
walk follows goat paths east to the monasteries of **Agia Triada** and **Zourvas.** The
former is located on a hill one-and-a-half-hour's walk east of town, the latter at
the eastern tip of the island.

These are long and hilly walks, so bring water and go early. If you don't feel
up to a walk, take a swim. In general, the beaches on Hydra are rocky ledges. When
the water is calm, dories run to pretty **Palamida** and neighboring beaches on the
west side. **Mira Mare Beach,** at Mandraki, is easier to reach, either by a half-hour
walk along the water out the east end of town, by a 15-minute boat ride (50dr),
or by donkey (500dr). This beach is less attractive than others, however, and dominated by a new watersports center. Don't take the water taxis; their cheapest fares
are astronomical.

On the trip between Hydra and Spetses, the boat and hydrofoil stop at the resort
town of **Ermione** on the Peloponnese; get off here for daily bus connections to Epidavros or Nafplion. Stay on the boat if you're continuing to Spetses.

# Spetses Σπέτσες

Tiny Spetses is really only a splinter floating in the Saronic Gulf. Set in slender
arcs of broad stone and pebbles, the beaches here are plentiful enough to absorb
their sun-starved British clientele. Every drop of water here must be imported from
the mainland; for this reason, the island was settled late and sparsely. Those willing
to risk a few scratches can descend from the single beaten path to the island's sweet-
smelling interior.

## Practical Information

Restaurants and shops form a 2-kilometer line on either side of the port. To the
west (left facing the water) is the old harbor; to the east is **Agia Marina** and the
**Paradise Beach** area, a dense concentration of food and fun. The cobbled square
directly behind the new harbor is called the **Daphia.** The **tourist police** (tel. 731
00) are straight up from the dock on Botassi St. They provide an accommodations
brochure and general information about the island. (Open 24 hours.) On the other

side of the block from the police is the **post office.** (Open Mon.-Fri. 7:30am-2:30pm.) The **bank,** on Santou St., overlooks the water on the right side of the harbor (facing inland). (Open Mon.-Thurs. 8am-2pm, Fri. 8am-1:30pm; in summer Mon.-Fri. also 7-9pm.) The **OTE** is next door to the right of the bank. (Open Mon.-Fri. 8am-10pm, Sat.-Sun. 9am-1pm and 6-9:40pm.) You can get a map of the island (180dr) at the shop next door to Takis Travel. Large maps are posted in several locations (e.g. on the dock, inside Takis). For **first aid,** call 724 72. Spetses' **telephone code** is 0298.

From Spetses, the **ferry boat** *Eftuchia* serves Piraeus Monday through Saturday at 2:30pm and Sunday at 4pm (5 hr., 938dr). Except for Sunday, the boat stops in Ermione (½ hr., 264dr), Hydra (1 hr., 332dr), Poros (2 hr., 582dr), Methana (2½ hr., 591dr), and Aegina (3½ hr., 753dr). For tickets and information, go to **Daphia Tours** (tel. 720 40), in the square behind the kiosk. (Open daily 10am-10pm.) Hydrofoils go to Piraeus at least nine times per day in high season, but only about 3 times per day in off-season (2 hr., 1550dr). Hydrofoils also go almost anywhere else: Ermione (4 per day, 20 min., 430dr), Hydra (at least 5 per day, 35 min., 470dr), Poros (at least 4 per day, 1 hr., 575dr), Methana and Aegina (2 per day, 2 hr., 1130dr) to the north, Porto Heli (at least 6 per day, 10 min., 265dr), Nafplion (Mon.-Sat. 1 per day, 1 hr., 787dr), Monemvassia (1 per day at 10:45am, 1½ hr., 1260dr), and Kythera (Mon.-Tues., Thurs., and Sat. at 10:25am, 2½ hr., 1260dr). The informative **Flying Dolphin ticket office** (tel. 731 48) is next door to Pine Island Tours, straight up from the dock in Daphia Square.

## Accommodations, Food, and Entertainment

As elsewhere in the Saronics, accommodations can be a serious hassle. In cahoots with several other travel agencies, **Takis Travel** (tel. 722 15), straight down to the left as you disembark, controls 90% of the rooms in town; that's 3500 beds, most of which are already booked by British package tours. Singles are virtually nonexistent, and doubles with clean communal facilities go for about 2000dr. The location is usually prime, the beds comfortable, and the rooms immaculate. If you're traveling alone, you can try to find someone to share a room with, especially when the boats arrive. (Takis open in summer daily 9am-10pm; in off-season 9am-1pm and 6-10pm.)

If you get to town early and want to find a non-Takis room, walk up past the tourist police to a blue "rooms to let" sign over a tile of a boat. The family here (tel. 726 31) rents rooms with Victorian furniture and lace curtains. (Doubles 1500dr. Triples 2100dr.) Or try any of the E-class hotels off the tourist police pamphlet; they're often full, but may be able to refer you elsewhere. Sleeping on the beach, though technically illegal, is common and easy on Spetses. There are two beaches near the port: **Agios Mamos** (the small town beach) and, a 15-minute walk to the west, a larger beach near a pine forest.

**Lirakis** rooftop restaurant (tel. 722 88), just to the east of Takis, is one of the best on the island. Its portions and service just look expensive (700dr for 2). Also try **Stelios,** along the wharf past Takis. For a worthwhile splurge, the **Trechantiri** restaurant in the old harbor offers dinner (about 800dr) on a rooftop overlooking the water. Sample their Spetses fish, a pungent specimen cooked in a tomato, onion, and garlic sauce. **El Paginos** is a quiet place that serves pizza. The **Palm Tree Cafe,** on Botassi St., below the tourist police, serves an excellent full English breakfast (350dr). Their garden's palm trees do double duty as shade and roof. There are plenty of groceries and supermarkets in town.

Spetses' many nightspots will total even the hardiest partier and disturb all but the heaviest snoozer. The best place to dance is the **Delfinia,** several blocks west of the harbor. (Open 10pm-3am. Cover 400dr. Drink included.) On the way you'll come across the **Anchor II** (tel. 728 72; mixed drinks 400dr). The roof gardens at the **Hotel Soleil** fills up around midnight, despite its dizzying prices (daiquiri 550dr). Most bars close at 3am.

## Sights

Across from the beach near town is the **Anargyrius and Korgialenios College** (high school). John Fowles taught here and memorialized both the institution and the island in his novel *The Magus*. For a beautiful walk, especially at dusk, go left past Takis and continue along the stone path between the water and the high, white-washed stone walls to the old harbor, which is quieter and has fewer tourist shops than the new port.

On the rise above the town is a **naval museum** in the crumbling mansion of Hadji-yanni Mexi, Spetses' first governor. It houses coins, costumes, ship models, weapons, and other memorabilia. Wooden window frames, doors, and chests set in the museum walls create the illusion of being on a nineteenth-century ship. To find the museum, follow Hadjiyianni Mexi St. through its several twists and turns until you see the signs pointing to the museum. (Open Mon. and Wed.-Sat. 8:45am-3pm, Sun. and holidays 9:30am-2:30pm. Free.) The most heroic Spetsiot, however, was Lascarina Bouboulina, a captain in the Greek War of Independence. Says the historian Filimonas, she "put cowards to shame and brave men made way for her." **Bouboulina's house** is located near the Daphia.

Since Spetses is small and public transportation is good, you can probably do without a motorbike. If you choose to rent, go to the eastern side of the harbor (2-person motorbikes about 2000dr with gas). In Agia Marina, **Ellen's** has the cheapest bikes (500dr). At the **Spetses Hotel Beach** and **Agii Anargiri**, you can rent windsurfers (700dr per hr.), canoes (300dr per hr.), and water skis (1500dr per "go around"). You can also walk the 28km around the island. A tour of the island traveling west from the harbor will take you past the **beaches** at Spetses Hotel (crowded with a good outside bar playing rock n' roll), **Ligoneri, Vrelos** and **Zogeria** (both quiet, especially in the late afternoon), **Agia Paraskevi** (swim to the surrounding rocks), and **Anargyri** (beautiful, crowded, and festive). The restaurant here (tel. 724 50) is affordable; Tassos Taverna is not. The last 10km has fewer beaches, sparser landscape, and a couple of well-endowed mansions. When you see gulls executing flight patterns over the water, you'll know you're near the island dump. The last beach before Spetses Town is the crowded and dirty **Paradise**, in Agia Marina. Note that all of Spetses' beaches have a problem with sea urchins. You can walk to the island's central summit by following the road past the tourist police and turning left at **Pigi's Taverna**, which promises nightly Greek dancing. The bumpy track takes you several kilometers up into the hills through sweet-smelling pine trees until you reach the summit's panorama of the Peloponnese and its train of islands. There's a small chapel on the way with picnic tables. From here, trails of similar length descend to Vrelos, Anargyri, and Agriopetres.

**Buses** (70dr) leave three times per day for Anargyri from the bus stop to the left of the harbor by the town beach. Be sure to buy a return ticket and get a stub. Motorboats leave the harbor between 9:30am and 11:30am, returning from the beaches at about 4pm. Anargyri (200dr round-trip) is a half-hour away. Sea taxis cost a fortune (2500dr for Anargyri). Since only registered cars are allowed on the island, overland transportation is provided by horse-drawn carriage or the rare taxi.

A car ferry runs back and forth between Spetses and the tiny town of **Kosta** on the Peloponnese (6 per day, 50dr), as do small boats (about 90dr); the sea taxis cost a whopping 900dr. Kosta has the broadest sandy beach in the area. From there you can catch the bus to the immense resort of **Porto Heli** and its cemetery from the Classical period, or to **Kranidi** (80dr), where you'll probably have to change buses for Epidavros and Nafplion (450dr). For departure times, call the bus station in Kranidi (tel. 212 18) or ask at the tourist bureaus on Spetses. Whether or not you know the timetable, do your waiting in Kosta: Sometimes boats won't leave until they have enough people. The bus stop in Kosta is to the left of the boat landing, on the road between the hotel and the restaurant. If you decide to stay the night, **Camping Kosta** (tel. 515 71) charges 300dr per person.

# IONIAN ISLANDS
# Νησιά τού Ιονίου

For 400 years, while the rest of Greece strained under Turkish rule, the Ionian islands rode relatively free. Their uninvited guests—the Venetians, British, French, and Russians—were milder than the Turks, more concerned with palaces and commerce than with breaking the wills of a stubborn people. Nevertheless, these Western powers left their imprint. The Venetians ruled Corfu from 1386 to 1797 and nearly transformed Corfu Town into a little Venice. Later, the French and British tried to make the people of Corfu efficient managers of newly installed roads, sewers, and schools.

Despite their geographical proximity, the Ionian Islands are dissimilar in tradition, industry, and landscape. Until the last three decades, there was little communication among them. On Cephalonia, the inhabitants spoke with Italian accents. Kythera is still remote, floating south of the Peloponnese, Ionian in name only. Nor do their disparate landscapes suggest any features that unite the archipelago. Corfu is green and plump; Ithaki is nearly skeletal; robust Cephalonia changes contours and color from one ragged mountain to the next; Zakinthos has dense vegetation.

**Ferries** connect Corfu with Ghanto, Bari, and Ancona in Italy, and Dubrovnik in Yugoslavia, and connect both Corfu and Cephalonia with Brindisi in Italy and Patras on the Greek mainland. Between June and September, ferries travel several times per week to and from Italy, three times per week to and from Yugoslavia, and once per day to Patras. Expect to pay 4000-6000dr for deck-class transport to Italy. Overworked ferry mates also rarely enforce restrictions on shower use by deck-class passengers. Olympic Airways has **flights** from Athens to Cephalonia, Zakinthos, and Corfu, and to other points in Western Europe. Night flights from Athens cost 5000-5600dr; regularly scheduled intra-European flights to Corfu cost an arm and a leg—in summer, look into charter flights from London and Frankfurt. You can reach Zakinthos from Killini on the Peloponnese, and Lefkas by bus from Patras or Preveza. At least one ferry per day leaves Patras for Cephalonia and Ithaki, so moving among these islands, Paxos, and Corfu is easy. Check schedules with one of the harbor agencies or with the tourist police in Corfu Town or Patras before planning any excursions.

## Corfu (Kerkyra) Κέρκυρα

Mother Earth has spoiled Corfu: No other Greek island is this lush or this rapturously green. Homer wrote of this island: "pear follows pear, apple after apple grows, fig after fig, and grape yields grape again." It is like Prospero's magical island in Shakespeare's *The Tempest*—harmonic, hypnotic, and intoxicating. However, you will have to share Corfu's beauty with many others. Once a haunt of the European elite, Corfu now courts package tours and budget travelers galore.

If you arrive by plane, you'll find yourself 2km from Corfu Town. Olympic Airways runs free buses on an erratic schedule. Otherwise, take a taxi (500dr), wait at the main road for bus #5 or 6, or walk. Business hours on the island are normally Monday, Wednesday, and Saturday from 8am to 2pm, Tuesday, Thursday, and Friday from 8:30am to 1:30pm and 5 to 8pm (in summer 5:30-8:30pm). Pick up a free

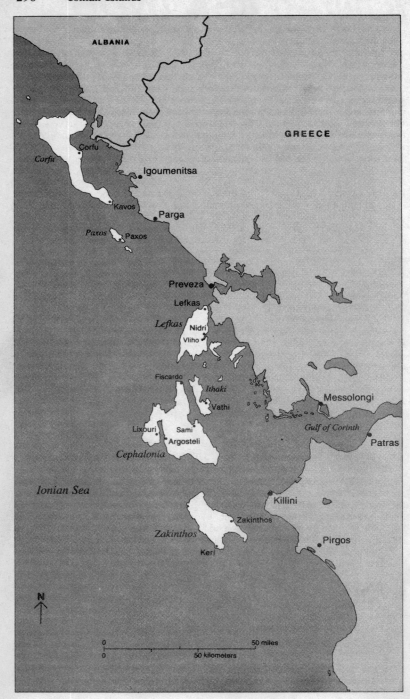

copy of *Corfu News* and *Corfu Sun,* which have lots of worthwhile information, including transportation schedules.

**Buses** run frequently between Corfu Town and major points on the island (though fewer run in the afternoon and on Sun.), and all trips cost under 300dr. Schedules for the main KTEL line are posted on a billboard outside the office in New Fortress Sq. in Corfu Town, from which the green-and-cream KTEL buses leave. Other buses (blue), including buses to Kontokali (youth hostel), leave from around Platia Sanrocco—schedules are printed on the signs. To enjoy the view, get a seat on the right when traveling north, on the left when going south. The best and most popular way to see the island is by **moped.** Rental places are everywhere; you shouldn't pay more than 1500dr per day for mopeds, 2000dr for two-seater Vespas, or 2300dr for small motorcycles. Make sure the brakes work. You are responsible for any damage incurred to your vehicle, but the rental fee should include third-party liability and property damage insurance. When riding, beware of the many blind corners on Corfu's hilly roads and wear a helmet (ask for one). As for **car rentals,** a Fiat 126 goes for 5500-7000dr with 100km free, plus 20dr per km. Prices do not include gas, the 20% tax, or full collision insurance (600dr per day). Many places automatically add a minimum kilometer charge, but you can avoid this and get unlimited mileage if you rent for two or three days. **Hitching** is another option, although there is no traffic off the main roads. Confine thumbing to early morning or late afternoon; roads are deserted from 2pm to 5pm (closing hours for most stores).

## Corfu Town

Corfu Town is the logical base for touring the island; all ferries and most bus services originate here. Parts of the town are simply a jungle of rooms to let, boats to catch, scooters to hire, and pizzas to go—everyone in town seems to be an entrepreneur. But the Spianada (Esplanade) and the old town, especially the streets behind Arseniou St. (Platia Kremasti), can provide an uncrowded respite. Visit the town's churches and palaces and notice how the mélange of Byzantine, Venetian, and Greek architecture is matched by the incongruities of the streets, where shirtless youths and bearded Orthodox priests mingle freely.

### Orientation and Practical Information

Before long, you'll be cursing the Theotokis: Four of Corfu's main streets are named after members of this family, and you may pass from N. Theotoki St. to M. Theotoki St. to G. Theotoki St. to I. Theotoki St. without knowing what hit you. But after a few days with one of the town maps in the Corfu brochure, you should be all right. The town is built on a peninsula; one coast faces north, the other east. On the north coast are the **New Port,** which services boats to Patras and the international ferries, and the **Old Port,** from which boats leave for Paxos and Igoumenitsa. Separating the two ports is the New Fortress, at the foot of which sits Corfu's long-distance bus station. The eastern shore is dominated by the Old Fortress and the **Spianada,** a garden ringed by chic cafes. To get to the Spianada from the Old Port, follow Arseniou St. along the waterfront (with the water on your left). At the point of the peninsula is the old town, a maze of alleys in which you will inevitably become lost. From the New Port, walk left and away from the water on Napoleontos St. and turn left on Io. Theotaki. This leads you past **Platia Sanrocco,** the city-bus terminus, and on to **Georgiou Theotoki St.** and the old town.

**Tourist Police and Greek National Tourist Organization (GNTO):** Tel. 302 98 or 305 20, on the northern end of the Spianada, in the Governor's house. Friendly, crowded, and loaded with brochures, maps, camping information, and schedules of special events. Ask for *The Mythos Guide to Corfu, Corfu News,* or the *Sun* (free). Open May 15-Oct. 15 Mon.-Sat. 8am-1:30pm and 6-8pm, Sun. 9am-noon; Oct. 16-May 14 Mon.-Fri. 8:30am-1:30pm.

**Room-Finding Service:** 43 Arseniou St. (tel. 221 01), on the road from the Old Port to the Old Fortress (near the tourist police). Little English spoken, but they can find you a room in a pension. Open in summer only, 8am-10pm. Also check the various agencies near the port for accommodations services; many operate without commission and have direct pipelines to cheap lodgings of which the tourist police are not aware.

**British Vice Consul:** 11 Leoforos Alexandros (tel. 300 55), down the street from the post office. Open Mon.-Fri. 8am-1:30pm. In an emergency, call 392 11.

**Currency Exchange:** Four **banks** on G. Theotoki St., near where it narrows and becomes Voulgareos. Open Mon.-Thurs. 8am-2pm, Fri. 8am-1:30pm. Try the exchange window at the **Customs House** in the New Port (open Sat.-Sun. 8-10am) or at the **airport** (open when planes arrive or depart). Though always obliging, tourist agencies near the Old Port and most hotels charge 10% commission.

**American Express:** C/o Greek Skies, Ltd., 20 Kapodistriou St. (tel. 308 83). Vouchers for the bank Mon.-Fri. 9:30am-1:30pm. Will hold mail. Won't cash AmEx traveler's checks. Open Mon.-Fri. 8:30am-1:30pm and 5:30-8:30pm, Sat. 9am-2:30pm.

**Post Office:** 19 Alexandros Ave. Open Mon.-Fri. 7:30am-8pm for stamps and Poste Restante; Mon.-Fri. 7:30am-2:30pm for international parcels.

**OTE:** Main office, 9 Matzarou St., around the corner from the GNTO. Open daily 6am-midnight. Smaller office at 78 Kapodistriou St., at the palace end of the Spianada. Open daily 8am-10pm. **Telephone code:** 0661 for Corfu Town; otherwise, 0663.

**Olympic Airways:** 20 Kapodistriou St. (tel. 386 94; airport 301 80), on the Spianada. Night flights to Athens (at 11pm, ¾ hr., 6150dr). European flights quite expensive. Open Mon.-Fri. 6am-9pm.

**Ferries:** Book early, especially to Italy; in high season, even the deck sells out. **Ionian Lines, Epirus Lines,** and **Fragline** at #74, 76, 50 and 46 Xen. Stratigou St., respectively (at the New Port). **Vikentios Manessis Travel** (tel. 326 64), also opposite the New Port. **Adriatica,** at #50 (tel. 380 89), has the best deal to Brindisi (daily at 9am, 8 hr., 5100dr, students 4200dr, InterRail 400dr, Eurail 1200dr; 400dr port tax). No reductions to Ancona (24 hr., 7100dr) and Dubrovnik, Yugoslavia (18 hr., 7800dr). Buy tickets to Yugoslavia at **Mancan Travel,** Xen. Stratigou tel. 326 64).

**Buses: KTEL** (long-distance), at New Fortress Square. To Paleokastritsa (17 per day, 45 min.), Glyfada Beach (15 per day), Kavos (10 per day), Kassiopi (9 per day), Athens (daily at 9:30am and 7:30pm), and Thessaloniki (Mon., Wed., and Fri. at 7am). Full schedule posted on the station wall. Buy tickets for Corfu destinations on the bus, all others in the office. A good place to leave luggage. Open 5:30am-8pm. **City buses:** #10 from Platia Sanrocco to Achillion (6 per day), #6 to Benitses (7am-10:30pm every ½ hr.), #7 to Dassia (7am-10:30pm every ½ hr.), #11 to Pelekas (9 per day), and from the Spianada to Kanoni (6:45am-10pm every ½ hr.). Schedule published in *Corfu News.*

**Car Rental: Vergis Rent-a-Car,** Corfu-Saudi Travel, 46 Xen. Stratigou St. (tel. 250 00). Best rates. International car rental at **Greek Skies,** 20 Kapodistriou St. Reasonable replacement service for breakdowns at no extra charge. Must be (technically) 25. Full payment in advance or major credit card required.

**Luggage Storage:** Several places on Anrami St., directly across from the New Port. 100dr per day. Open March-Oct. 24 hours.

**English Bookstores: Lycoudis,** 63 Voulgareos St., 2 doors from the National Bank, has the most comprehensive selection. Open Mon., Wed., and Sat. 8:30am-2pm, Tues., Thurs., and Fri. 8:30am-1:30pm and 5:30-8:30pm. There's also **The English Bookstore,** 6 Moustoxidou St. (tel. 415 12 or 229 54). Open Mon.-Sat. 10am-1pm, Tues., Thurs., and Fri. 10am-1pm and 6-8pm. **Mythos** office, 9th Parados, sells *The Sightseer's Guide to Corfu,* with in-depth information about Corfu's attractions, landscapes, and history.

**Laundromats:** Self-service, at the Europa Hotel (tel. 393 04), near the New Port. Also on Io. Theotaki St. (tel. 353 04), near Platia Sanrocco. Wash 300dr. Dry 200dr. Open 9am-9pm.

**Public Toilets:** On the harbor at the Old Port; on the Spianada near the bandstand; and in Platia Sanrocco.

**Hospital: Polihroni Kostanda,** tel. 305 62, 300 62 or 394 03. **Corfu General Hospital,** Ioulias Andreadi St. (tel. 305 62 or 300 33), off Platia Sanrocco. 24-hour emergency room. English spoken.

**Emergency:** Tel. 100.

## Accommodations and Camping

Prepare yourself for highway robbery. Although hotel prices are strictly regulated by the tourist office, proprietors in Corfu cunningly find all kinds of loopholes. Hotel managers tend to fill their rooms with camp beds, which they then offer as dorms for the price of singles. Solo travelers may well be grateful for the system, since singles are impossible to find (the alternative is accepting a double and trying to bargain). Hotels near the water fill up most quickly, the morning crowds from Brindisi arrive at 7am, and bargaining power diminishes later in the day, especially for backpackers. If arriving late from elsewhere in Greece, try reserving by phone; a two-minute phone call from Athens costs less than 100dr. Fortunately, prices drop 100dr per person in off-season, and longer stays get lower rates in the small pensions. Before accepting a room with one of the pension owners that meet your boat, agree on a price and find out where the place is located. Otherwise, you may end up paying exorbitant prices in some remote part of the island. Freelance camping is well-nigh impossible.

**Youth Hostel (IYHF)** (tel. 912 02), 4½ km north on the main road from the port. Take the #7 Dassia-Kontokali bus from Platia Sanrocco (about every ½ hr., 20 min.). Ask for the hostel (just after the turn off to Paleokastritsa by the BP gas station). By taxi 600dr. Inconveniently located, crowded, rowdy, with cold showers and no toilet paper. Near a beach, an appetizing restaurant on the grounds with dancing. The cheapest place to stay on Corfu. Scooter rental and mini-market. IYHF card required. Reception open 7am-noon and 6-9pm. No curfew, but check the time for the last bus from Corfu Town. 500dr per person.

**Hotel Cyprus**, 13 Agion Pateron (tel. 300 32). Walking from the Esplanade to Platia Sanrocco, turn right after the National Bank on Voulgareos and follow the signs. The best hotel in Corfu. Bright and cheery, with clean rooms and wonderful management. Quiet, too: Shaded arbor covered with flowers for sitting or taking your meals. Beds in the hall 700dr per person. Doubles 2000dr. Triples and quads 1000dr per person. Great breakfast 250-450dr.

**Hotel Europa** (tel. 393 04), near the New Port. Turn right off Xen. Stratigou at General Tourism and Maritime Agencies and follow the signs. Very popular with backpackers. Laundry facilities. 1000dr per person. English breakfast 200dr.

**Hotel Elpis**, 4, 5H Parados N. Theotoki St. (tel. 302 89), in an alleyway opposite 128 N. Theotoki St., in the Old Port. Clean, quiet, well-kept rooms. Singles 1000dr. Doubles 1600dr. Triples 2400dr. Showers 150dr. 10% surcharge for stays of 2 days or less.

**Hotel Constantinoupolis**, 11 Zavitsanou St. (tel. 398 26), near the Old Port. Clean, pleasant rooms. Looks better from the inside. Ask for a room with a view. Singles 1250dr. Doubles 2200dr. Triples 2700dr.

**Hotel Acropole**, 3 Zavitsanou St. (tel. 395 69). Seedy-looking building, but habitable rooms. Doubles 2100dr. Triples 2500dr. Quads 2900dr. Cold showers included.

**Hotel Spilia**, 2 Solomou St. (tel. 256 48), near the KTEL bus station. Comfortable beds and cold showers. Doubles 1200dr. Triples 1650dr. Showers 150dr.

**Hotel Crete**, 43 N. Theotoki St. (tel. 386 91). Right in the middle of everything, and noisy. Somewhat dilapidated. Doubles 1800dr. Triples 2400dr. Showers 200dr. Owner will negotiate in off-season.

**Camping:** Corfu has several official campsites, and prices are strictly regulated by the police, so you don't need to shop around. The GNTO has a complete list. **Camping Kontokali** (tel. 912 04), by the IYHF hostel, is the nearest to Corfu Town. 250-350dr per person. 200-300dr per tent or car. 100dr for electricity.

## Food

The best area to find restaurants is around **N. Theotoki Street,** near Old Fort Sq.; lunch is served outdoors until 3pm, dinner until 11pm. Nearly all restaurants in town are strictly regulated by the tourist police. Although this ensures fair prices, it means somewhat monotonous selection and mediocre preparation. For cheap do-it-yourself fare, go to the open-air **market** on Dessila St., near the base of the New Fortress. Some stalls stay open all afternoon, but arrive around 7:30am for the pick of the lot. The **Supermarket D'Iratirio,** 13 Solomou St., near the bus station (open Tues., Thurs., and Fri. 8am-1:30pm and 5:30-8:30pm, Mon., Wed., and Sat.

8:30am-1:45pm) and the **Supermarket Koskinas,** in Platia Sanrocco (open Mon.-Fri. 8am-2pm), have a more than adequate selection.

**To Nautikon,** 150 N. Theotoki (tel. 300 09). A big place, but eat outside if possible. Friendly service, appetizing food, and affordable prices. *Souvlaki* 430dr, *mousaka* 270dr, *dolmades* 190dr. Try the *sofrito* (veal cooked in wine sauce; 420dr). Open April-Oct. daily noon-midnight.

**Edem,** 911 Solomou St. (tel. 256 50), around the corner from the bus station, across from the Hotel Spilia. Lacks atmosphere, but don't let the plastic facade fool you: It offers bona fide Greek specialties at cut-rate prices. Try the rice and tomato-cheese casserole (211dr). Amiable owners will change money if you eat here. Open April-Oct. 9am-midnight. Across the street is the more traditional **Gisdakis,** 20 Solomou St. (tel. 375 78). *Dolmades* 280dr, mixed salad 170dr. Open daily 10am-10:30pm.

**Pizza Pete,** 19 Arseniou St. (tel. 223 01), halfway between the Spianada and the Old Port. Go to meet Pete if nothing else. Excellent pizzas cost a lot of dough (700-850dr). "Pete special" (onions, peppers, mushrooms, olives, tomatoes, bacon, and hot dogs) 850dr. Also serves vegetarian pizza. Open April-Oct. daily 9am-midnight.

**Krysi Kardia,** 44 Sebastian St. (tel. 416 54), 1 block from the intersection of N. Theotoki and M. Theotoki St., directly off M. Theotoki. A cut above the rest. Generous side dishes, but a bit skimpy on main courses—roast beef 420dr, roast chicken 280dr. Open 10am-4pm and 7pm-midnight.

**Dionysus,** 17 Di Dona (tel. 240 72), in an alleyway opposite 150 N. Theotoki. Tables spill out into 2 adjacent alleyways—the husband stations himself on one side, the wife on the other. Excellent food, though a bit oily. *Mousaka* 294dr, stuffed tomatoes 223dr, roast chicken 200dr, Greek salad 150dr. Open Nov.-Sept. daily 8am-midnight.

**Taka Taka,** directly beneath the Hotel Cyprus, up the hill from the National Bank on Voulangeos St. Cheapest *souvlaki* in town (60dr). Open daily 7pm-1am.

**Restaurant Argo,** Ethnikis Antistasis (tel. 225 93). Fresh fish and lobster. Swordfish 650dr. Open 5pm-1am. Several other tavernas on the waterfront south of Corfu Town serve fresh fish in addition to regular Greek cuisine.

### Sights

The **Paleo Frouri** (Old Fortress), a huge relic of Venetian rule, commands regal views of coastline and town. Located west of the Spianada, it is overgrown and barely accessible. When you cross the moat into the fortress walls, Corfu Town's din dissolves into history. Bring your swimming gear for the beach on the other side of the fortress. If you wade along the rocks you'll find some private launches. Built in the late fourteenth century, Paleo Frouri was regarded as impregnable. People decided otherwise in 1864, when the British blew it up before leaving Corfu to the Greeks. There is a **Sound and Light Show** in the fortress in English (May 15-Sept. 30 Tues.-Fri. at 9am). Every weekday from June through September, Greek folk dances supplement the show. (Admission to both 400dr, students 180dr; Sound and Light Show only, 300dr, students 100dr.) The fortress gates open from 8am to 7pm, though you can stick around until 9pm, when they reopen to admit the audience.

At the northern end of the Spianada, on your right as you leave the fortress, is the **Palace of St. Michael and St. George.** Unmistakably British, the palace was built as the residence of the Lord High Commissioner and faces onto a cricket green where local clubs and visitors from abroad play matches every July. The palace now houses an extensive collection of Japanese, Chinese, and Indian ceramics, wood carvings, silk screens, and porcelain figures, as well as mosaics from the Byzantine basilica in Paleopolis. (Open Mon. and Wed.-Sat. 9am-3pm, Sun. 9:30am-2:30pm. Admission 200dr, students 100dr.)

The **Archeological Museum,** 5 Vraila St., on the waterfront south of the Spianada, contains relics of the island's Mycenaean and Classical past. (Open Mon. and Wed.-Sat. 8:45am-3pm, Sun. 9:30am-2:30pm. Admission 200dr, students 100dr.) Corfu's two most famous churches are the **Church of St. Jason and Sosipater,** a twelfth-century Byzantine structure on the way to Mon Repos Beach (continue past the archeological museum along the waterfront), and the **Church of St. Spiridon,** named for the island's patron saint. The latter dates from the late sixteenth century and houses a dazzling array of silver and gold ornaments as well as medieval paintings and an impressive painted ceiling. The remains of St. Spiridon lie in a silver reliquary, and are carried in several processions around the town to commemorate his beneficial and timely intervention during crises. North of N. Theotoki near the Spianada is the **Ionian Bank Building,** with a museum of paper money. (Open Mon.-Sat. 9am-1pm, Sun. 10am-noon.) Behind the Old Port, you can walk to the old **Jewish Quarter** of town. The **synagogue,** on Velissariou St., was built in 1537. The community continued to grow from this time on until 1940, when 5000 Jews were gathered on the Spianada and sent to Auschwitz.

The site unique to Corfu is the old town in the evening. Seven music schools pour their strains into the alleys with simultaneous tunings. Take a walk along the waterfront on the eastern side at dusk to watch the fishermen haul in their day's catch.

### Entertainment

In the evening it seems as if almost everyone on the island parades up and down the Spianada and the adjacent park. Install yourself at one of the cafes by the park and watch the show. Look but don't eat: The food on this street is incredibly overpriced.

The most popular discos lie clustered along the port road heading north from Corfu Town (a good 15-min. walk). The **Hippodrome** and **Apocalypois** both have swimming pools. **La Boom** and **Bora Bora** cater to a more adult crowd, while the **Playboy** attracts younger travelers. All of these discos are expensive, with a cover charge of 500dr (1 drink included). Continuing along the port road north, you'll come to two **bouzouki clubs:** the **Esperides,** 3km from the port, in Alikos; and **Corfu By Night,** about 3km farther, in Gouvia. Both provide entertainment with *syrtaki* dancing but are outrageously expensive. For less expensive performances, check around at the local *tavernas*. Many provide free shows in the evening. For a drink accompanied by music videos, try the **Black and White Bar,** 6 Agios Vasilou, across from 37 N. Theotoki. Sip a drink and enjoy new wave at **B-52,** 38 Kapodistriou (tel. 447 81). (*Ouzo* 200dr.) The upscale **Mermaid Bar,** 9 Agios Panton St., behind the Spianada just before Voulgareos, is extremely laid back. Corfu has two cinemas, the **Pallas** and the **Orpheus,** which often screen English-language films.

## Southern Corfu

Some 6km south of Corfu Town is the islet of **Vlacherna,** connected by a causeway; take bus #2 (Kanoni) from the Spianada and ask the driver to let you off near Vlacherna (105dr). Get your own angle on the little monastery, Corfu's most photographed scene. Unfortunately, you can't enter the monastery itself. Nearby, **Pontikonissi** retains only a chapel and a few trees. According to Homer, Pontikonissi is the fabled ship that took Odysseus back to Ithaka and was turned to stone by Poseidon because the wanderer had blinded the Cyclops Polyphemus, Poseidon's son. Both Vlacherna and Pontikonissi lie at the mouth of a shallow bay, which separates the town of Perama and the road south from the peninsula of Kanoni.

Continuing along the road, you'll come upon the **Achilleion Palace,** 9km south of the port of Corfu in the village of **Gastouri.** Overbearing and ostentatious, it was commissioned by Empress Elizabeth of Austria for a summer residence. Despondent over a series of family deaths, she retreated to Corfu. The dolphin motif of the castle and its name were her idea. Kaiser Wilhelm II of Germany, who moved in later, was responsible for the inscription on the statue of Achilles that reads "to the greatest of Greeks from the greatest of Germans." The gardens are especially wonderful; the James Bond flick *For Your Eyes Only* was filmed here. To get here, take bus #10 from Platia Sanrocco (every 3 hr., ½ hr.). (Open Mon.-Sun. 8am-7pm. Admission 200dr. Students 100dr. A group of 10 or more, 150dr per person.) The palace is a casino at night (tel. 562 10; open 8pm-3am), and the new German owners of Achilleion have renovated the gambling salons. While at the palace, do what most don't—visit the intriguing little village of Gastouri, one of the last outposts of traditional Greek lifestyle in Corfu.

Farther south is the rowdy fishing village of **Benitses.** (Take bus #6 from Platia Sanrocco, ½ hr., 120dr.) The town's small beach is packed with bodies fresh from the British rain. At the lively waterfront bars and discos, you can play billiards outside, watch videos inside, and drink everywhere. Some of the bars get a little out of control at night with brawling and dancing. Among the most popular are **Rainbow, Blue Sea, Style,** and **Spiros on the Beach.** Most have happy hours and all-you-can-drink specials.

Still farther south **Agios Ioannis** has a good uncrowded beach. Take bus #8 from Platia Sanrocco (about every hr.). Continuing toward the island tip, you'll arrive at **Messongi:** Buses leave from New Fortress Sq. (6 per day, 45 min., 130dr). The beach at Messongi isn't bad (no pebbles at least), but it's best to steal through the spacious lawns of the Messongi Hotel and recline under a straw parasol. **Kavos Beach** lies at the southern tip of the island, 47km from Corfu Town (12 buses per day from New Fortress Sq., 160dr). The beach is pleasant enough, but the water is shallow. Over on the southwest coast is the remote, sandy beach at **Agios Georgios** (1 bus per day from New Fortress Sq., 1 hr. 10 min., 210dr). Even more secluded is the nearby **Vitalades Beach,** one of the few deserted places in Corfu. You might be deserted yourself as buses running to Vitalades operate on an inconvenient schedule (at 5am and 3pm), and there is no return bus. Take your moped and explore.

## Northern Corfu

The first 20km of the coastline north of Corfu Town has been ruined by the tourist industry. The resort towns of **Dassia, Ipsos,** and **Pyrgi** consist of a long string of hotels, discos, and boutiques. Official campsites are plentiful in this area: Dassia has **Karda Camping** (tel. 935 95), Ipsos offers **Ideal Camping** (tel. 932 43) and **Corfu Camping Ipsos** (tel 932 46), and Pyrgi has **Paradissos Camping** (tel. 932 82). These campsites cost between 300 to 450dr per person, 350dr per tent, and about 210dr per car. Most have markets on the premises, and hot showers are included. For nightlife, head to any of these towns; for less spoiled country, venture farther north.

The Kassiopi bus serves this whole coast, running seven times per day from the KTEL station and stopping at every hamlet along the way (to Kassiopi 1¼ hr., 200dr); renting a moped us best. Past Pyrgi, the road begins to wind below steep cliffs. **Mt. Pantokrator,** on your left, towers 1000m above, and the cliffs on the right grow more dramatic as Albania comes into view across the straits. After passing through Nissaki and Gimari, you'll eventually arrive at the turn-off to **Kouloura,** 28km north of Corfu. Kouloura proper has a pebble beach, a marina, and a good *taverna* (try the *kalamari*). The right fork to **Kalami** takes you down to a sandier beach where there are rooms to let. This tiny town recognizes its own beauty, so even in off-season you'll pay 1800dr for doubles (July-Aug. 2000dr). The walk to Kalami or Kouloura from the main road takes no more than 15 minutes.

**Kassiopi** is the next town, 36km north of Corfu and just 2km across the sea from Albania. (The Albanian port of Agia Saranda is clearly visible.) Greeks like to tell you that if you swim too far into Albanian waters you might be shot on sight. More likely, the Albanians will arrest you, find out who you are, and release you. The town was founded in 300 B.C.E. by the General Pyrrhus of Epirus. Its main attraction is the incredible rock beach that stretches along the coast for several kilometers to the east of the little town; follow the dirt path that starts on the left-hand side of the harbor (facing the water) all the way to the Kassiopi Peninsula. For a thrill, try parasailing (3000dr), similar to parachuting except that you're attached to a motorboat by rope while zooming through the air. More sedentary attractions include the ruins of a ninth-century fortress destroyed by the Venetians in 1836 that overlooks the rock beach, and the **Panayia Kassiotropi Church,** with stark seventeenth-century frescoes. The **Kassiopi Travel Service** (tel. 813 88), near the bus stop, can help you with rooms. Expect to pay 2000dr for doubles in high season. The innkeepers here loathe one-night stands; if you don't stay for a few days you may pay a premium. While eating in Kassiopi, remember that a waterfront location raises just price, not quality. From the bus stop, head inland; you'll encounter a series of cheap, if unspectacular eateries. For nightlife, try the **Just S.** disco near the bus stop. The **Kan Kan Bouzouki Club** lies along the road back to Corfu, about a 15-minute walk (shows Wed. and Sat.-Sun.).

Winding up and down the main road north from Kassiopi and veering west, you'll arrive at the beach resorts of **Roda** and **Sidari.** Sidari's wide, sandy beach is bracketed by low cliffs of exposed sandstone, which besides creating a score of peek-a-boo coves, provide excellent promontories for camping. This may be your only option for staying near this resort. Alternatively, try **Rhoda Beach Camping** (tel. 311 20) or just freelance. Catch a sunset from **Peroulades;** the 3-kilometer walk there takes you past small farms and large fruit trees. At the shore is the surprisingly deserted **Sunset Restaurant.** The bus to Sidari leaves from New Fortress Sq. (3 per day, 150dr). In Sidari, you can hire a motorboat for a daytrip to the tiny islands of **Othoni, Erikoussa,** and **Mathraki** (1 hr., 900dr). For more information, inquire at **Sellos Travel** (tel. 312 39). Only farmers and fishers inhabit these three islands.

To get even farther off the beaten track, explore some of the mountain villages in the northern part of the island. A bus from Kassiopi occasionally runs to the village of Loutses. On the way, the bus passes the little hamlet of Perithia, near Mt. Pantokrator. If you have a moped, the trip from Kassiopi to Paleokastritsa on the western coast will reveal the rugged, spectacular interior; use a good map, as not even the local police can give accurate directions. Gas stations in this area are few and far between (be aware that most mopeds have no gas gauges)—the station nearest Paleokastritsa is 15km back towards Corfu Town on the main road.

## Western Corfu

Swimming is surreal; the crystal water dazzles with infinite gradations of turquoise and blue. **Paleokastritsa** ("Old Castle") is carved into a bay amid some of the loveliest scenery in Greece. The main road into town winds past several spectacular bays, with small coves and sea caves jutting into the headlands. As you come onto the main beach in town, walk up the winding road to the thirteenth-century fort of **Angelokastro.** (There is a natural balcony called **Bella Vista** halfway up.) Jutting out over the sea is the chaste white **Panayia Theotokos Monastery.** (Open Mon.-Sun. 7am-1pm and 3-8pm. Expected donation 150dr.) Be sure to come as early as possible; by mid-morning it is a jangling mess of cameras and tour buses. You cannot enter in your bathing suit or shorts; women are provided with skirts (a donation may be necessary).

Paleokastritsa's beauty is expensive. The best way to see this ritzy cove is by daytrip (15 buses per day from New Fortress Sq. in Corfu Town, 45 min., 150dr). Travelers willing to hunt can find affordable lodging. Head up the footpath to Lakones and look in the olive groves for inexpensive pensions. **International Camping** (tel. 412 04) is about 3km from town on the main road from Corfu. Unfortunately, the sea is a good ways off. (Open mid-May to Oct.) The food situation is not much better. **Le Pirate** offers good fare for slightly less than its neighbors. (1500dr menu includes lobster and wine. Open daily 10am-6pm and 7pm-3am.) There is a **market,** on your right as you come into town, a few hundred yards before you hit the main beach.

If you're eager for about two and a half hours of ambling, venture up the footpath to Lakones. Look for the cobbled and dirt paths that head steeply left from the main path. From Lakones, you can continue left to Buena Vista and several kilometers further to the village of Makrades, where you will find a footpath to Agios Georgios Beach. The path will take you to Prinilas, from where you can walk or hitch down to the water. Fortify yourself on fresh figs sold by street vendors in Makrades.

South of Paleokastritsa, the swinging hilltop village of **Pelekas** has the best panorama of the island. Its western exposure and elevation offer an ideal vantage for viewing sunsets. The town also has many rooms to let. The **Nikos Pension** (tel. 942

87) operates an unofficial youth hostel here, with competition from **Jimmy's** and **Alexandros'** pensions (1000dr per person). The street to the left of the church is lined with houses that rent doubles (July-Aug. 1800dr; June-Sept. 1300dr).

The road continues to **Glyfada Beach,** with a track leading left to the quieter **Pelekas Beach.** Don't attempt to reach Pelekas by moped; the ride is absolutely treacherous. Pelekas Beach is especially popular with freelance campers, as accommodations are nonexistent and the police don't hassle sleepers. Both beaches are a half-hour walk from Pelekas Town, and a direct bus to Glyfada runs from Corfu Town (6 per day, 45 min., 140dr). Bus #11 runs to Pelekas Town from Platia Sanrocco (9 per day, 120dr).

A little north of Glyfada and accessible by a dirt path off the main Pelekas road lie the isolated beaches of **Moni Myrtidon** and **Myrtiotissa,** which Lawrence Durrell called the most beautiful in the world. A section of the beach at Myrtiotissa is the island's nudist beach. Everything here is very casual, although once in a while the local monks complain to the police who reluctantly bring offending nudists to court. Above these beaches in the olive trees is the small restaurant **Myrtiotissa.** You can camp here for free with use of the bathroom if you buy breakfast. (450dr.)

**Agios Gordios,** with its sheer cliffs and impressive rock formations, is the venue for the **Pink Palace,** a cultural phenomenon. Run by a Greek and his crew of Canadians, this hotel-summer camp-fraternity has become popular with North Americans; it has all the ambience of spring break in Fort Lauderdale. To glimpse Greek culture, stay elsewhere. Many travelers, however, appreciate the Pink Palace's amenities—laundry service for (400dr), daily cliff-diving and parachuting excursions, and one of the liveliest discos on the island (free to patrons). (Cots on the terrace 1100dr. Breakfast, dinner, and showers included.) Down the beach, the **Hotel International** is similarly priced, but caters to a slightly older crowd and is not as noisy.

# Paxos (Paxi) Παζοί

Just 8½ km long, tiny Paxos has finally attracted the attention of travelers wishing to escape Corfu's maddening crowds. A short walk from the more popular towns of Gaios and Lakka, you'll discover solitude on the beaches or some offbeat company in the sea coves that are home to frolicking seals. Be careful, though—the friendly creatures sometimes play rough.

The most frequent **ferries** to Paxos depart from Corfu (Mon. at 4:30pm, Tues.-Fri. at 2pm, 3 hr., 620dr), and from Parga on the mainland (Wed. and Sat. at 9am, 1 hr., 490dr). Many boats from Patras stop at Paxos on their way to Corfu. Ferries also connect Paxos to Cephalonia and Lefkas. Check at the tourist office since schedules change. Tickets cost less in off-season, when boats don't run on a daily basis. Boats generally leave in the afternoon and return to Corfu or Parga the next morning. If you don't plan to spend the night, you can make a daytrip excursion, but these fares are twice as expensive as regular passages. For more information, contact any of the waterfront travel agencies in Parga or Corfu Town.

Boats dock at **Gaios,** the island's main village. Building restrictions have prevented hotels from sprouting, but you'll be able to find some *dhomatia.* Locals often wait at the dock to escort tourists to their homes. Agree on the price and length of stay prior to accepting the room—some proprietors will ask you to leave if you only plan to spend two nights. Almost all rooms are doubles (about 1500dr; showers included), but a resourceful lone traveler can find a makeshift single for 800dr. On your own, try at the blue mini-market in the town square, where the friendly owners let rooms in their house for one-night stays. (Doubles 1575dr. Showers included.) In off-season, prices drop with bargaining. Ask the English-speaking members of your boat's crew about rooms; they can usually set you up in decent accommodations. Freelance **campers** can sack out on the beach, or with permission, near someone's house. **Dodo's Taverna** will offer you an evening of palatable delights and warm hospitality. Try the house specialty, *exohico* (wrapped pork and vegetables), or the Greek salad. (Open May-Nov. daily 6pm-2am.)

Paxos is so small that you can see the whole island in a couple of hours. Be sure to visit diminutive **Lakka,** where some boats stop before putting in at Gaios. The village has some *dhomatia,* a wonderful beach, and a Byzantine church. Ask the locals to ring the church's unusual Russian bells and watch their faces light up. If you speak any Greek, you can make even more friends by requesting the story of the bells; you'll hear four or five different versions. Buses run between Gaios and Lakka (50dr).

South of Gaios is **Mogonissi,** a miniscule island owned by three brothers. One of them runs a restaurant on the island, while another operates an express boat to Mogonissi from Gaios. The island has a sandy beach and a small **campground.**

On the west coast of Paxos are the **Mousmouli Cliffs** and the **Seven Sea Caves** (accessible by boat from Gaios daily). According to Homer, one of the caves, Ipa-pando, was Poseidon's Cave, with walls of glittering gold. **Panayia,** an islet on the east coast, features a religious shrine honoring the Virgin Mary, and, on the Feast of the Assumption (Aug. 15), visitors from other islands and the mainland crowd together to make a pilgrimage. Drinking, dancing, and general merrymaking last all night in the square at Gaios. If you enjoy swimming in lucid turquoise water, take a daytrip to **Andipaxos,** a satellite island off the south coast of Paxos. It can be reached by boat from Gaios daily between 9am and 11am, returning any time between 2:30pm and 7pm. The tiny island consists of only 56 families, a few small vineyards, sandy beaches, and a few freelance campers (although it's officially illegal to camp on Andipaxos). Two restaurants on the beach keep visitors well-fed.

# *Lefkas (Lefkada)* Λεφκδα

Lefkas ("white rock") was part of the mainland until 427 B.C.E., at which time Thucydides tells us the islanders dug a canal. The Emperor Augustus built a new canal after the old one filled up, and the same one is in use today, having been maintained by the Venetians, the French, and the English. The crossing takes only three minutes, although lines occasionally build up in July and August.

The trifling 25-meter canal leaves Lefkas particularly vulnerable to tourist hops, especially since the western edge harbors several long beaches. Once you've crossed the channel into Lefkas Town—on a bizarre ferry moved by pulleys and chains—you'll find what looks like mainland Greece metamorphosized into a floating resort. You will see many older women wearing traditional dress (brown bodices with layered nineteenth-century style skirts) balancing shopping goods on their heads.

**Lefkas Town** sits directly across from the mainland. **Buses** from Athens (4 per day, 7 hr. 2000dr) stop in Patras at the Favierou St. Station (4 hr., 750dr). From Lefkas, buses depart for Nidri (9 per day, 110dr), Agios Nikitas (2 per day, 75dr), and Vasiliki, at the southern tip of the island (3 per day, 200dr); they also go to Athens (4 per day, 2000dr) and Preveza (4 per day, 220dr). If your bus stops at Preveza, you must take a ferry (¼ hr., 72dr), to Aktion, where one bus leaves for Lefkas daily at 4pm (40 min., 160dr). Hitching is difficult, and it's a 22-kilometer walk. Try to share a taxi (800-900dr). Don't cross the second river in the taxi; it will be at least an hour's wait on the weekend. Instead, get off right before the ferry and walk 1km into town—pedestrians cross free. **Ferries** to Frikes on Ithaki and Fiskardo and Sami on Cephalonia leave at 8am and 4pm from Nidri and Vasiliki. The ferry to Ithaki (3½ hr., 424dr) stops in Fiskardo. You may catch a glimpse of playful dolphins swimming alongside your boat.

The first alleyway running inland from the harbor in Lefkas Town becomes **Dairyfield Street,** the main street, which is lined with all the tourist services. (Dairy-field was the archeologist who unsuccessfully tried to identify Lefkas with Homer's Ithaka.) There is no GNTO, but many travel agents speak at least some English and can provide information on the island and modes of transport. Try **Dana Travel** (tel. 246 50), the largest, or the **tourist police,** on Dairyfield St. The **National Bank of Greece** stands below the Hotel Patras on the same street. (Open Mon.-Thurs.

8am-2pm, Fri. 7:45am-1:30pm.) The **post office** is at 183 Stratigou Mela St. (Open Mon.-Fri. 7:30am-4pm; for parcels 7:30am-2:30pm.) For the **OTE**, turn right off Stratigou Mela to Pataneromenis St., which runs parallel, and head back toward the beginning of town—it's right off the end of the street. (Open daily 6am-midnight.) Lefkas' **telephone code** is 0645.

**Hotel Byzantion** (tel. 226 29), the first building as you turn onto Dairyfield St. from the ferry, has clean and modern singles for 1330dr, doubles for 1662dr. **Hotel Patras** (tel. 223 59), next to the National Bank of Greece in the Platia Antistasis off Dairyfield St., is also reasonable. (Open June 10-Sept. 10. Clean singles 1108dr. Doubles 2000dr. Triples 2420dr. Cold showers 100dr.) The mood at the popular **Taverna Pyrofani** is set by the jolly owner who tries to meet all of his clientele. Also try **Regentos,** right off the main square onto Varrioti St., about 2 blocks down on the left. (Meals around 300dr; open daily 7:30pm-2am.)

## Around the Island

While Lefkas Town has no beach, the northern half of the west coast offers miles of deserted white pebbles and clean water. Rent a moped to get there (about 1000dr per day), and follow the signs for Kathisma. The best stretch is north of **Agios Nikitas.** Buses leave from Lefkas Town for Agios Nikitas (5 per day, 80dr). The road there also leads to the monastery **Moni Faneromenis,** which provides a sweeping view of the beaches. Follow the footpath through the woods for a pick-up game of basketball with the students at the monastery's school.

Much of the interior of Lefkas is barren, but the eastern coast is dotted with orange and olive groves. Seventeen kilometers south of Lefkas Town is **Nidri.** The view of the mainland from Nidri is wonderful, with numerous little islands forming stepping stones across the strait. Climb the 5km to **Neochori** at dusk. The town itself is another crumbling victim of erosion to the sea. From here you can glimpse **Scorpios,** the private island of the heiress Christina Onassis. A small boat (2000dr) will take you around the manicured terrain of this stand-offish retreat. Although the guards don't allow boats to come too close, you can see the spectacular dock, tennis courts, Christina Beach, and the elaborate burial vault of Aristotle Onassis, the shipping tycoon.

In Nidri, many rooms to let are scattered along the main street, running parallel to the water. (Doubles 1500dr.) There are more rooms next to the pharmacy. The **Hotel Nidrion Beach** (tel. 924 00) lets you sleep on the roof for a nominal fee. The bakery **E. Kominatos** must be one of the best in Greece. The **post office** is next door to 205 Center St. (Open Mon.-Fri. 8am-2pm.) On the road from Lefkas to Nidri is **Camping Episcopos** (tel. 230 43; 325dr per person, 300dr per tent).

Three kilometers south is the tiny village of **Vliho,** accessible by bus from Lefkas (9 per day, 105dr), with a handsome church (proper dress required) in an idyllic setting of wildflowers and cypress trees. South, past the top of the hill is a quiet sandy beach. From here you can easily reach **Vasiliki,** which crowds up against the waterfront, a press of trees lining the slightly littered pebble beach. Nothing moves very quickly in this village. The town has a tiny **post office** (open Mon.-Fri. 8am-2pm) and a currency exchange. The owner of the cafe on the extreme left as you face the water has decent rooms to let (doubles 1200dr), but if possible, stay in the rooms above the mini-market to the left as you leave the bus. The rooms are clean and price includes use of a kitchen. (Doubles 1400dr. Triples 1800dr.) One street off the water, at the house with brown shutters and an iron gate (tel. 314 27), large cheery triples are 1300dr. Vasiliki also has a **campground** (tel. 313 08) with a cafeteria (large pizza 500dr, lobster 3000dr per kilo; camping 450dr per person, 300dr per tent). A veritable windtunnel, Vasiliki is a great windsurfing haven. One hundred meters from the campground, **Vasiliki Club** rents boards for 1000dr per hour, 4000dr per day, or 2000dr per morning. Beginners' courses for 3 mornings (3 hr. per day) go for 5000dr. (Open 10:30am-8pm.) The waterski coach is on the beach from 9-10am and charges 1500dr for a trip around the bay.

At the southernmost tip of the island there is a **lighthouse** built on the site of the Temple of Lefkadas Apollo. It was here from the 70-meter cliffs that the ancient poet Sappho supposedly leapt to her death when Phaon rejected her love. The cliff is called "Sappho's Leap," and is known in Lefkas as *Kavos tis Kiras*. In the worship connected with Apollo, evil was exorcized with an annual sacrifice. An evil person, usually a criminal or a retarded person thought to be possessed, was thrown into the sea from the cliffs. Live birds were tied to his arms and legs with the intention that their wings would lighten his fall.

# Cephalonia (Kefallinia) Κεφαλλωνία

Cephalonia lacks the natural attractions of its fertile neighbors in the Ionian Sea. The west and east coast are generally steep and rocky, the inland areas mountainous, and all areas dry. For many years, this rugged countryside kept Cephalonia relatively untouristed. But the beautiful, sandy beaches on the south coast, ensnaring caverns near Sami on the east coast, and spectacular mountainous landscapes everywhere are reason enough to stay. In addition, the locals are extremely friendly. Famous as feisty adventurers, they trace their lineage back to Odysseus' time, if not to the man himself. Historians believe the Cephallenes from Epirus settled the island, while other legends maintain that the name of the island comes from that of Odysseus' great-grandfather, the hero Cephalus.

Many **ferries** link Cephalonia with other ports. In the summer, a ferry connects Patras with Sami on Cephalonia's east coast (2 per day in each direction, 4 hr., 1050dr). One boat continues to Vathi on Ithaki (1½ hr., 425dr), returning the next morning. From July through August, a Brindisi-Patras ferry stops here daily; ferries from Corfu and Igoumenitsa put in briefly, and there is a weekly ferry to Paxos (4 hr., 850dr). From Fiscardo, there is ferry service to Vassiliki, on Lefkas (2 per day, 3 hr., 425dr), and to Vathi (2 per day, 1 hr., 425dr). From Agios Efimia, service links Cephalonia with Astakos on the mainland (2 per day, 3½ hr., 590dr) and Vathi (1 per day, 1 hr., 425dr). **Olympic Airways** flies to Argostoli (45 min., 3590dr). Inter-island bus service is fairly reliable. **Buses** (tel. 233 64) go from Argostoli to Sami (1 hr., 140dr), Fiskardo (2-2½ hr., 290dr), and Skala (45 min., 210dr). The tourist office can provide you with a complete schedule. Buses also ride the ferries from Argostoli and Sami to Athens (2270dr). Cephalonia's **telephone code** is 0674.

## Sami

Most ferries will leave you in Sami, where a bus loads up for Argostoli. Unless you need something from the bigger town, stay here: It's cheaper, has a beach, and is a better spring-board for island hopping. Sami seems bland by day, but it is touched with romance at night when the lighted ships glide into the dark port.

You can exchange money at the **bank** on Sami's waterfront (open Mon.-Fri. 8am-2pm) or at the **Ionian Lines office** at the other end of the quay (only on weekends, when the boats are running). If you decide to spend time in Sami, head for the main square, overwhelmed by the Hotel Kyma 2 blocks from the ferry landing. I. Metaxa Street, which bears right as you face the hotel, leads to the **post office.** (Open Mon.-Fri. 7:30am-2:30pm.) The **OTE** (open Mon.-Fri. 7:30am-1:30pm) is opposite the cathedral, near the **police station.** The police speak some English and will find you a place to sleep. (Open 24 hours.) There is no official tourist office in Sami.

For accommodations, try the **Hotel Melissani** (tel. 224 64), several blocks back from the water on the left as you face inland, run by a very friendly couple and their daughter. The roof is subdivided by screens into several comfortable areas that hold cots. The roof also has hot showers, a bathroom, and an achingly romantic view of the harbor. (600dr per person. Breakfast 320dr.) The **Hotel Kyma** (tel. 220 64) has clean rooms and large bathrooms with bathtubs. (Singles 1330dr. Doubles 1940dr. Triples 2330dr. Bath 80dr.) The **Hotel Ionion** (tel. 220 35), near the cathedral, is comparable in price and quality. The rooms above the **Agyra Restaurant** (tel. 226 56), on the waterfront, fill quickly. (Doubles 2000dr.) Better to walk 1 block further (with the water on your left) to **2 Salaminos St.** (tel. 227 11), where a gracious woman rents comfortable and quiet rooms. (Singles 1500dr. Doubles 1700dr.) **Caravomilos Beach Camping** (tel. 216 80) is just off the beach, 1km to your right facing inland. The friendly management offers laundry facilities and a mini-market. (Open May 1-Sept. 30, 24 hours. 435dr per person. 350dr per tent. 250dr per car.) Even if you don't camp, try their restaurant, which serves such delectables as baked shrimp with feta cheese in tomato sauce. The menu changes daily. (Open 8am-midnight.) The fast-food *souvlaki* joint on the waterfront sells cold *retsina* for 70dr, and most restaurants stock the good Cephalonian wines. Try the very small, authentic **Uncle** (tel. 226 61), on the street parallel to and across from the campground. (Open 9am-3am.) Sami's discos are both pretty good, if not overly dedicated to Top-40 tunes. Three hundred meters from the campground, **Disco Arocaria** rocks from midnight until 3am.

Two sites near Sami will knock your socks off: the caves of **Melissani** and **Drograti.** The first is more staggering and can be reached by foot from Sami (½ hr.). Follow I. Metaxa and turn right at the sign for Agia Efimia, then follow the signs just past the village of Caravomilos. Or take the shortcut along the sea past the campsites, over the sand and rock piles, until you come to a cafe 2m from the surf; here, turn left to the main road, make a right, and look for the sign about 200m up. If you're lazy, take the Fiscardo bus and ask to be let off at Melissani. At the lake, a guide will take you in a rowboat around two large caverns flooded by sparkling turquoise water and studded with lichen-covered stalactites. (Open until nightfall. Admission 120dr. A polite tip is expected.) To reach Drograti, 4km from Sami, head inland on the road to Argostoli. (Open until nightfall. Admission 70dr.) Ten kilometers north of Sami at the other end of the bay is the pretty harbor town of **Agia Efimia;** if you depend solely on buses for transportation, you may have to stay the night, as the schedule is wholly contingent upon which boats are arriving that day and when. If based in Sami, you can take many inspiring hikes. Walk 4-5km northwest in the direction of Moni Agrilion monastery, but stay to the left: The dirt road descends to a rock beach that's perfect for either camping or swimming. Another walk begins about 10m before the sign for Karavomilos on the road to Agia Efimia (2km from Sami); follow the dirt road left into the misty hills of palm, cypress, and fruit trees.

## Argostoli

Capital of Cephalonia, Argostoli is a bustling town with a bustling nightlife. To get here from Sami (1hr.), board the bus that meets the morning or afternoon boats at 7:30am, 8:30am, and 5pm. The bus winds courageously around hairpin turns, treating riders to spectacular mountain vistas, horn blasts, and high blood pressure. Get off at Argostoli's **bus station** (tel. 222 76), a safe place to leave luggage. (Open 7am-8pm.) To reach the main square and most of the important services, walk inland 2 blocks and turn right on the town's main street, D. Konstantinou. On the right, you'll find the **post office.** (Open Mon.-Fri. 7:30am-4pm, parcels 7:30am-2:30pm.) Two blocks down, across from the church, is **Petratos,** a shop well-stocked with foreign newspapers and magazines. (Open Mon.-Sat. 8am-1:30pm and 5-9pm, Sun. 6-8pm.) Go one block farther and you'll hit the square and the archeological museum. Look behind the museum for the very friendly and helpful **GNTO** (tel. 228 47) They speak English, will give you a colorful map of the city, book accommodations, and exchange money. (Open Mon.-Fri. 8am-2:30pm and 5-10pm, Sat.-Sun. 9am-1pm and 4-9pm.) There are phones next door. The **OTE** is on the first right off R. Vergote onto the street running along the uphill edge of the square. (Open daily 6am-midnight.) To avoid unreliable buses, consider renting a car with a group. **Ford Rent-a-Car,** 4 P. Valianou St. (tel. 223 88), near the main square in Argostoli, rents Escorts for 2150dr per day plus 22dr per kilometer in high season. They also rent 50cc Honda scooters (1500dr per day without gas). The **tourist police** are at

52 Metaxa St. (tel. 222 00), to the right of the bus station. They speak no English. (Open 24 hours.)

Argostoli has a couple of outrageously expensive hotels and some cheaper rooms to let. The lightest of the budget-busters, the **Allegro** (tel. 222 68), is just up from the bus station. (Doubles 2000dr, with bath 2430dr. 400dr per day discount if you stay 3 days.) **Emilia Dionisatou,** 18 M. Avlihos (tel. 287 76), lives straight up from the bus station, and offers immaculate lodgings, a large communal balcony, and use of a kitchen. Unfortunately, in summer she extracts premium prices. (Doubles in July-Aug. 2500dr. Hall showers included. Prices drop about 200dr per person in off-season. Call—it's tough to find.) Across the street is **Denise Vassilatos** (tel. 286 05), who rents comparable rooms for the same price, provides unlimited free mineral water to her guests, and lets them do laundry in the sink. She sometimes has an improvised single available—a cot underneath a stairway with a curtain drawn up to it—for 600dr. For conventional rooms in Argostoli, follow the road to Lassi, leading up through town to the airport. In summer, you should be able to get a double without bath for 1400-1800dr. If you need help finding an inexpensive place to stay, go to the tourist office; if they're closed, try the tourist police. Camping is available right on the water at **Cephalos Beach,** about 4km south of Argostoli (tel. 234 87). Showers, kitchen facilities, a good restaurant, and piano bar are at the site. (360dr per person, 230dr per tent, 100dr per car.)

The restaurant **E. Kalafatis,** 144 Metaxa St., 100m to your left on the waterfront as you leave the bus station, is a good, inexpensive place to eat; try the *stifadho* (385dr). The **Diana,** next door, is also good.

The nearby village of **Omala** organizes a festival on the last Sunday of July, featuring *souvlaki* and *robola* (Cephalonia's famous wine). The highlight of the day is a foot race open to anyone (500m distance for women, 1500m for men). Special buses leave from Argostoli for this festival. On the night of August 15, eve of Agios Gerassimos Day, you can attend another festival at Omala and the all-night vigil in the saint's church. Due east of Argostoli is **Agios Gerasimos**—a monastery in which a monk's corpse has been preserved. October 20 is the nameday festival, another party day for the area.

The two local museums could not be more different. The modern, well-organized **archeological museum,** the low, yellow building on the square of D. Konstantinou St., is elegant but lacks outstanding artifacts. (Open Mon. and Wed.-Fri. 8am-2:30pm, Sat.-Sun. 8am-1pm. Admission 200dr, students 100dr.) Turn left at the archeological museum onto R. Vergote St. and continue two blocks to reach Cargialenios Library, which houses the **Historical and Cultural Museum.** This museum is full of knick-knacks and other household belongings from the nineteenth century. Argostoli's French coffee cups, English top hats, antique dolls, and accounts of the town written by visiting Britons all fashion a picture of confident and careful luxury. Best of all are the photographs that give a visual record of Argostoli during the last century, including the huge earthquake of 1953 and the ensuing reconstruction. (Open Mon.-Fri. 8:30am-2pm and 6:30-8:30pm, Sat. 10am-noon. Admission 100dr, students free.) Argostoli hosts a season-long **summer festival** of local fairs, art exhibits, drama and music performances, and athletic events. Contact the tourist office for more information.

The Venetian **Castle of St. George** is 9km southeast of Argostoli on a hill overlooking the village of Travliata. It's 10 minutes away by moped on the road to Skala and right (uphill) when the road splits. Or you can take the bus (5 per day, 85dr). From the battlements you can view the panorama that inspired Lord Byron. (Open Wed.-Fri. and Sun.-Mon. 9am-3pm, Sat. 9am-1:30pm.) To swim at **Lassi,** one of the island's best sandy beaches, follow the road leading from the town to the airport.

There are several options for exploring more of the island. Boats leave regularly for **Lixouri,** in the center of the western peninsula (½ hr., 120dr). Once home to the satiric poet Lascaratos, Lixouri offers miles of choice coastline practically untouched by tourists. You can rent **mopeds** at several places in Lixouri, and **buses** make it to most points on the peninsula. Just make sure you check the return times at the station or you may be stranded.

A few beaches and interesting towns dot the island south of Argostoli. One of the best beaches is at **Ormos Lourda,** right in the middle of the south coast; closer to Argostoli, however, is **Platis Gialos** (9 per day, ½ hr., 55dr). You can also visit one of Byron's hometowns—though his house no longer exists—at **Metaxata,** or see **Kourkoumelata,** a village completely restored by a Greek tycoon after the 1953 earthquake. **Poros,** on the southeast coast, is like Argostoli but with a beach; many private houses rent rooms. Buses run from Argostoli (4 per day, 1½ hr., 240dr).

## Around the Island

On the coastal road north from Argostoli or Sami to the village of Fiskardo, the cliffs drop to the sea, severe and earthquake-scarred. You're missing something grand if you bypass the beautiful and quiet beaches at **Agia Kyriaki** and **Myrtos.** Signposts on the main road after the hamlet of Divarata proclaim the existence of Myrtos, and an even more pristine beach lies within the next cove to the north. Unfortunately, there is no access road—only the most nimble should attempt the descent, and don't even think about taking your moped. Parents with small children should keep an eye on them at Myrtos as the undertow can be powerful and sudden. Four kilometers farther up the road you'll find the unspoiled port of **Assos,** joined by a narrow isthmus to an island with a Venetian fortress that was used as a prison. One bus per day leaves Argostoli Monday through Saturday at 1:45pm and returns from Assos at 6:45am the next day; the half-hour walk from the main road is a challenge. Stay in Assos if you can, if only for the sweet-smelling gardens. Around the bend from the Pension Geramia, across from the flaking pink church, is a small rooms-to-let house. The bargainable singles (800dr) and doubles (1000dr) are more quaint than comfortable, with stucco walls and a wooden barrel shower. More modern doubles go for 1600dr at the **Snack Bar Assos,** up the last street before the dock turns.

The road north ends, emphatically, at **Fiskardo,** the only town on the island left undamaged by the 1953 earthquake and thus the only remaining example of eighteenth- and nineteenth-century Cephalonian architecture. The town is named after Robert Guiscard, a Norman who died here while attempting to conquer the town. A ruined Norman church visible from the harbor is believed to predate Robert by some 800 years. Consider basing your stay on Cephalonia here. Alongside the delapidated old lighthouse, you'll spot the pine-sheltered campsites. The **Restaurant Fiskardo,** right along the harbor, serves excellent Greek dishes, including the tasty local specialty *kreatopita* (meat pie) for 300dr. If your budget won't suffer too much damage, treat yourself to a delicious lobster at 2800dr per kilo. (Open noon-midnight.) One spot down toward the bus stop is a *cafe* run by a woman who also has rooms to let. (Doubles 1400dr.) Inquire here about excursions to Ithaki. There is also one hotel in Fiscardo, the **Panormos** (tel. 513 40); singles 1900dr, doubles 2100dr; showers included; prices drop about 300dr after July and Aug.) In many respects, you can't beat Fiskardo, with a beach ½km out of town on the road back to Argostoli, and flat rocks for sunbathing and diving.

In August on Cephalonia, an unusual and spooky festival in the village of **Markopoulo** celebrates the Assumption of the Blessed Virgin Mary (August 15). Congregants hold a church liturgy all night. During the service, hundreds of small harmless snakes with black crosses on their heads appear and crawl all over the icons. The people pet them, but after this night, don't see them again until the next year.

# Ithaka (Ithaki) Ιθάκη

As the legendary home of Odysseus, Ithaki's fame is more lush than its geography. Spare seaside villages and unspoiled coves encircle the mountains where Penelope waited faithfully for her husband. Without Cephalonia's grandeur or Corfu's diversity, Ithaki offers little to do, but it's a wonderful place for doing little.

Getting here is easier than it was for Odysseus, although not by much. A **ferry** runs from Nidri and Vasiliki on Lefkas (2 per day, 4 hr., 465dr) to Frikes on Ithaki via Fiskardo on Cephalonia. You can pick up the ferry in Fiskardo (1 hr., 310dr). There is also a ferry from Patras on the mainland (1 per day, 6 hr., 1010dr) to Vathi on Ithaki via Sami on Cephalonia. You can hook up on Sami (1¼ hr., 400dr). Another ferry travels from Astakos on the mainland to Vathi (1 per day, 2 hr., 360dr) and continues to Agia Efemia on Cephalonia (390dr). You can also catch that ferry on its return to Vathi from Agia Efemia. Be sure to check boat schedules with travel agencies at your port of embarkation.

**Vathi** (deep) is the main port and the largest city on the island (population 2000). The setting is beautiful: The town horseshoes around the edge of a long, natural harbor and is almost completely surrounded by mountains. Almost every shop in town is on the waterfront. The important spots are at at the far right-hand corner of the horseshoe as you face the town. There's no GNTO office here, but several tourist offices have information. One block in from the harbor is the **National Bank of Greece** (open Mon.-Thurs. 8am-2pm, Fri. 8am-1:30pm); the building behind the bank is the **post office** (open Mon.-Fri. 8am-3pm). On the other side of the street sits the **OTE.** (Open Mon.-Fri. 7am-1pm.) You'll see a dozen scooter for rent signs with **mopeds** going for about 900dr per day, Vespas for 1400dr per day (both with a full tank of gas included). You can also rent a small **motorboat.** Bargain furiously for any vehicle, especially in off-season, as no prices are fixed. The **bookstores** on either side of the bank sell English-language books (including, of course, Homer's *Odyssey).* The **telephone code** for all of Ithaki is 0674.

The **Ionian Lines** office (tel. 321 45), opposite the ferry landing, is open whenever boats come in; in high season, it keeps somewhat regular hours. (Open Mon.-Sat. 6:30am-11pm with a long, irregular siesta in the afternoon, Sun. 10am-1pm.) Around the corner on the waterfront is **Polyctor Tours** (tel. 331 20; open in summer daily 9am-2pm and 6-10pm). These agencies will help you find lodging, but rooms fill early in July and August.

Most accommodations are expensive. The **Hotel Odysseus** (tel. 323 81), by the ferry landing, charges 1800dr for singles, 2600dr for doubles (bath 100dr, breakfast 240dr). The **Hotel Aktaion** on the waterfront has similar rates. The pension at **158 Nostov St.** (tel. 323 28) is a great deal, but usually full. From the ferry, cut inland and turn left onto Odyssey St.—Nostov St. is on your right. (Singles 1000dr. Doubles 1800dr. Triples 2300dr. Showers included.) The **Hotel Mentor** rents out space on the roof for 300dr per person. A bathroom and panoramic view are included along with use of the hotel's lounge and TV room. Your best option is freelance **camping** on the beach under the eucalyptus trees on the right half of the horseshoe as you face the water; it's illegal, but tolerated.

All the cafes and restaurants near the ferry are expensive—you pay for the location and the atmosphere. Continuing about 1½ km to the deserted side of the harbor opposite the ferry landing, you'll find cheaper eateries. Try **Gregory's Taverna,** which serves fresh fish, lobster (2300 per kg), pizza, and Greek specialties outdoors on the waterfront. (Open April-Oct. daily 8am-midnight.) Farther down the same road is the pricier **To Paliokaravo,** with pleasant food in a serene spot beside the sea. (Open daily noon-midnight.) In the center of town, 1 block back from the water and across from the scooter rental place, is **Taverna To Trexantha.** Frequented by locals, the price is right. (Cheese-covered eggplant 180dr.) Besides cafes and a few struggling pubs that remain open until the 2am ferry arrives, Vathi's nightlife is nothing spectacular.

Although the town's setting is its main attraction, there are some interesting sights, such as the Byzantine icons believed to be original El Grecos in the **Agios Georgios Cathedral.** Those with poetic imaginations and sturdy walking shoes will want to make the half-hour climb up to the **Cave of the Naiads,** where Odysseus hid the treasure he had been given by the Phaeacians. To get here, walk southwest down the road on the left-hand side of the harbor (facing the water), then turn left up the hill to Marmarospilia (Marble Cave). Be sure to bring a flashlight or you'll see only the entrance. It's a two-hour hike southeast to the Homeric **Arethousa**

**Fountain** along a steep mountain path through pear orchards. In summer, the fountain is dry and, despite what the map says, there are no paths to the water. Nearby, the beach at **Piso Ateos Bay,** about 5km from town, is worth visiting. You can spend an afternoon just sifting through its multicolored stones. If you're in Vathi in mid-July, ask about the **Greek Theater Festival** and the popular **Music Festival.** Try to visit during one of the other villages' local saints' days when the villagers liven with dance, food, and drink: August 6 is Agios Ilias Day in Stavros and Perachori; July 20 is Agios Sotiras Day in Kioni.

Make the 4-kilometer trek from Vathi up to **Perachori.** The ruins aren't much, but the town seems worlds apart from commercial Vathi below. At the top of the town is the *taverna*-grill restaurant. (Open 9:30pm-1am.)

## Around the Island

The rest of Ithaki's rocky coast is punctuated by villages more beautiful than the capital. The road from Vathi runs north through the isthmus, which just barely connects the summits of Mt. Niriton in the north and Mt. Merovigli in the south. **Molou Bay** and the island's only **beaches** are on the right, the strait of Ithaki and Cephalonia on the left. The first village you reach is Lefki, then Stavros, Platrithias, Frikes, and finally Kioni. **Buses** along this, the island's only route, depart from Vathi at 7am and 1pm, and arrive in Kioni one hour later (200dr). If you miss the bus, you can take the **boat** (1 per day, 320dr), which departs at 11am for Kioni. Be at the dock early and check timetables as both buses and the boat run on whimsical schedules. You can also catch a taxi (1500dr).

**Stavros** merits a stop for its location, if not its lone sight. The village schoolmaster's wife has a key to a small museum at the alleged site of **Odysseus' Palace,** recommended for fanatical Homerists; a small tip is expected. From Stavros, take a pleasant half-hour walk to **Frikes,** and then a 45-minute walk along the beautiful coastline to **Kioni.** The bus returns to Vathi at 2pm, or take the boat at 4pm. There are rooms to let in both Frikes and Kioni (doubles about 1500dr), and more than enough beach space for all. Kioni's single **pub** plays the most progressive music on the island. If you don't stay, at least stop for a coffee and a *ravani,* an orgy of sugar, honey, and rice that puts mainland *baklava* to shame.

# Zakinthos Ζάκυνθος

Everywhere on this island there are blossoms: They lie in tangles by road, tumble from rooftop trellises, trail from the spokes of speeding bikes, and loll against stucco walls. In the quiet hilltop villages, glimpses of shattered arches peek out from beneath the floral riot. The southernmost and sunniest of the Ionian Islands, Zakinthos draws crowds to the enticing beaches surrounding the florid lowlands of the east. Less explored is the western fringe, where the long Vrachionas mountain ridge hides cliffs, caves, and local lifestyles.

## Zakinthos Town

To the world, Zakinthos presents tidy Zakinthos Town, a port with arcaded streets and white buildings like evenly spaced teeth in a smiling face. Destroyed by an earthquake in 1953, the town was quickly restored to its former polished condition. Today, Zakinthos Town thrives on its traffic with the outside world, inhaling ferries and exhaling dozens of buses daily to points all over the island. In high season, when Zakinthos Town gets a mouthful of tourists, you will happily find yourself ingested into the island's flowering interior.

## Orientation and Practical Information

Leaving the ferry you will see the stately **Platia Solomou,** lined with palm trees and large buildings, to your right. To your left, **Lombardou Street** and the boardwalk beckon with an enticing array of gelateria scattered among tourist gift stores. The first street parallel to Lombardou away from the water is **Filita Street,** home to the bus station; behind it are **Foskolou, Alex., Roma** (the main shopping street), and **Tertseti,** in that order. Behind Platia Solomou, **Vassileos Georgiou B'** leads quickly to **Platia Agiou Markou.**

**Currency Exchange: National Bank of Greece,** El. Venizelou St., near Platia Solomou, next to the town hall. **Ionian Bank,** Platia Agiou Markou. Both open Mon.-Fri. 8am-2pm.

**Post Office:** Tertseli and Skirou Gouskou St., about 4 blocks along the waterfront and 4 blocks inland—watch for signs. Open Mon.-Fri. 7:30am-2pm. **Postal code:** 29100.

**OTE:** 2, Vassileos Georgiou B, behind Platia Solomou on the right. Open daily 7am-midnight. **Telephone code:** 0695.

**Olympic Airways:** 16, Alex. Roma St. (tel. 286 11 or 244 33). Flights from Athens to Zakinthos (daily at 8:30am and 9:45am, 45 min., 5290dr; 4 per week in off-season) and from Cephalonia (4 per week, 20 min., 1550dr). The **airport** is 6km south near Laganas; Olympic Airways runs a shuttle there 70 min. before scheduled departures (50dr).

**Buses:** 42, Filita St. and Ioannou Filioti, 4 blocks along the waterfront then 1 back, behind the Fina and BP filling stations (tel. 226 56). Long-distance buses ride the ferry to Patras (4 per day, 800dr) and then Athens (1550dr) on mainland Greece. Extensive local service; see Around the Island.

**Ferries:** Arrive at Zakinthos Town port from Killini on the Peloponnese (1½ hr., 450dr). In summer 7 per day 9am-9:30pm; in off-season 5 per day. Also from Korithi on the island's northern tip to Poros on Cephalonia (1½ hr., 370dr). Tickets for both available at the **boat agencies** along the waterfront.

**Taxis:** Vassileos Georgiou B' (tel. 281 04).

**Moped Rental:** All over the island. In Zakinthos Town, **Safari,** 6 Ethnikis Anistasis (tel. 235 43 or 281 54), just off Demokratias St. near Platia Solomou. Mopeds 1000-1500dr, motorcycles from 1500dr. Open 8am-9pm.

**Library:** Platia Solomou (tel. 281 28), across the street from the OTE.

**Laundromat: To Magiko,** 71 Foskolou St., to the left off Ioannou Filioti St., beside the Fina station, 2 blocks up from the water. Dry cleaning. Open Mon. and Thurs.-Fri. 8am-1:30pm and 5:30-9pm, Tues.-Wed. and Sat. 8am-2pm.

**Hospital:** Tel. 225 15, above and behind the center of the city.

**Police:** Lombardou St. and Fra Tzoulati St. (tel. 222 00), 5 blocks along the waterfront from Platia Solomou. Laid-back **tourist police** here answer questions 8am-1pm and 3-9pm.

## Accommodations and Food

Most people stay outside Zakinthos Town, nearer to the beaches. Every road on the island is plastered with signs advertising rooms to let, and several excellent campgrounds dot the island's shore (see Around the Island). Your best strategy is either to take a room in town while shopping around on a moped, or to ask informally at the bus station or tourist police. If you find a place outside town, don't worry—on the main roads, buses are frequent and taxis inexpensive.

In Zakinthos Town, the **Ionion Hotel,** 18 Alex. Roma (tel. 225 11), has a bright, polished interior and rooms with big balconies. Make sure you ask to see a few rooms before committing yourself; the manager may try to stick unsuspecting customers in windowless chambers. (July-Aug. singles 2000dr, doubles 3000dr; Sept.-June singles 1000dr, doubles 2000dr.) The **Hotel Kentrikon,** 25 L. Zoi St. (tel. 223 74), one street closer to the water than Alex. Roma, offers similar rooms and prices. The **Hotel Alfa,** 1 Tertseti St. (tel. 224 11), one road farther from the water than Alex. Roma, has sterile rooms and slightly less clean bathrooms. (Singles 1500dr. Doubles 2000dr. Triples 2500dr. Quads 2900dr. 30% less in off-season.) For rooms to let call **Mr. Fotis Giatras** (tel. 233 92), who has doubles in town (2000dr), and doubles a few kilometers outside town (same price). (Singles negotiable.) He'll come and collect you from town and also arrange for moped delivery and pick-up.

Giatras' place is collegiate and communal: You'll share the bathrooms and kitchen with the guests and the bugs, and breakfast with a jovial Greek family. Giatras' son has spiffier rooms next door.

The restaurants clustered in Platia Agiou Markou are a tad overpriced, but a *souvlaki-pita* or a *tiropita* will only set you back 80dr. At the corner of Rizospaston and Ignatiou, **To Tavernaki** serves *melitzanes* for a reasonable 150dr, and veal with okra for 300dr. There's a well-stocked **market** on Lombardou St. between the gas stations, and another a block back on Filita. *Pasteli* and *mandolato,* sweet local confections, are sold in touristed areas.

## Sights

In Platia Solomou, the **Byzantine Museum** (tel. 227 14) houses icons from the "Ionian School," the distinctive local hybrid of Byzantine and Renaissance styles. (Open Mon. and Wed.-Sat. 8:45am-3pm, Sun. 9:30am-2:30pm. Admission 200dr, students 100dr.) Even more interesting, the **Museum of Solomos and Other Famous Zakynthians,** in Platia Agiou Markou, pays tribute to local notables. The tomb of Dionysios Solomos (1798-1857), the poet who wrote the lyrics of the Greek national anthem, occupies the ground floor. (Open daily 9am-2pm. Free.) About 10 blocks down the waterfront, the **Church of Agios Dionysos** (St. Denis, the island's patron saint), has a silver chest containing the saint's relics. About 2½ km up the hill behind Zakinthos Town are the ruins of the old Venetian **kastro;** follow the signs for the suburb of Bochali.

At night, the plaza livens up and benches fill with chatting folk. Children's soccer balls bounce between popcorn vendors and strolling couples. In February, Zakinthites celebrate **Carnival** with masquerade, parade, and smashing plates. July and August bring festivals to the island and popular music to the **theater** on Filita St.

## Around the Island

The terrain and tranquil beaches on Zakinthos will easily lure you away from the port town. Cognoscenti return year after year to the refreshing quieter settlements. It's possible to see the entire island, including the otherwise inaccessible western cliffs, by **boat.** One leaves every morning from Zakinthos Town and circumnavigates the island in eight hours (3000dr); inquire at the tourist police. For more intimate exploration, tour the island by **moped.** There's at least one rental place at each beach. You can also get around by **bus.** Pick up the English-language schedule listing the most popular destinations; for more remote spots, you'll have to consult a copy of the larger Greek timetable. **Hitching** is fairly easy, though you may have trouble in the evening. Because the island is developing rapidly, many new roads won't appear on the various maps available.

Your first impulse may be to make a bee-line for the beaches at **Laganas** 10km south, but steer clear—they have been ruined by large hotels, souvenir stands, and mobs of tourists. **Kalamaki,** several kilometers east of Laganas, is almost as bad. Instead, head for **Tsilivi Beach,** 4km northwest of Zakinthos Town, a little quieter and one of the best beaches on the island. **Tsilivi Camping** (tel. 247 54) has a cafeteria and mini-market. (300dr per person. 220dr per tent.) From Zakinthos Town, you can reach the beach by taking a left onto the asphalt road skirting the shore (left facing the water); some people may find it too far to walk. **Planos,** just inland, has plenty of rooms to let. Buses run from Zakinthos Town to the beach (5 per day, 60dr).

The peninsula extending out to the town of **Vasilikos,** 16km from Zakinthos Town, is covered with uncrowded beaches, especially near **Porto Roma.** Signs for rooms to let line the road to Vasilikos, but the best place to stay in the area is **Camping Manvrantis** (tel. 220 44), a heavily wooded ground near **Agios Nikolaos Beach.** At the semi-secluded beach you can spare yourself unwanted rays under small thatch shelters. Just on the other side of Vasilikos, facing Laganas Bay, lies **Gerakas Beach,** which may win kudos as the finest beach on the island. Buses leave Zakinthos Town for Vasilikos daily at 10:15am and 3pm, returning at 10:45am and 3:45pm (100dr).

It is a five-minute walk from Gerakas to **Turtle Bay.** The turtles found near Laganas Beach have been the subject of controversy on Zakinthos and throughout Europe. Known by the Greeks as *kareta kareta,* these creatures have returned to the island for 90 million years to lay eggs. Two-hundred-pound females lumber ashore each night to deposit future generations in the softest sand in Greece. The babies that hatch on the beach swim away and return over 3000 miles to continue the cycle. Developers and discos, however, increasingly appropriate the beach for their own hatchings and threaten the turtles' survival. In 1987, the West German environmental leader Gunther Peter brought to the island 15,000 letters of protest against the beach umbrellas stuck into nests and the 50,000 tourists visiting the area each summer. Ecologists have petitioned to make Langanas Bay a marine park, pitting *kareta kareta* against *drachma drachma.*

A sort of unofficial youth hostel with many friendly young people, the **Turtle Bay Club: Camp Dafni** nearby lets you sleep under trees on a secluded bay for 90dr per person, and the *taverna* run by the owners serves cheap Greek specialties (wine 75dr per liter). Since the spot is inaccessible by public road, look for the owners' blue jeep at the ferry landing or go to the Snoopy Cafe on the waterfront. The owners are in town several times each day, usually to meet the ferries. At the camp you can rent windsurfers (300dr per hr.) and scuba diving equipment. They also offer a motorboat tour of the magnificent sea caves (500dr).

At the island's southern tip, the town of **Keri,** a one-hour moped ride from Zakinthos Town, is quiet and unvisited. Half the population sits in a tiny main square just waiting to chat with visitors. There's little else to do in Keri, except visit the lighthouse 20 minutes away by boat. (Ask for the *faro* and locals will point out the dirt road to you.) The lighthouse itself is modest, but allows you to peer 600 feet down to the waves below. (Open 24 hours.) You can stay in Keri for as little as 1000dr per night. On the way to the town you'll wind through lemon and olive groves and pass a turn-off for the pebbled Keri Beach. Buses run here (Mon.-Fri. at 7:30am and 1pm, returning ½ hr. later; Sat. at 6:15am and 2:30pm; 100dr). Back inland, tiny villages rib the eastern base of the mountainous spine. Many Greeks visit **Machairado;** the church here has a miraculous icon of Agia Maura. Buses run here twice daily (70dr).

**Alykes,** 16km from Zakinthos Town, is another beach resort stuffed to the gills with package tours. The **Hotel Galini** here has clean singles for 1000dr, doubles for 1600dr. Rooms to let, bars, and discos are not lacking in the general vicinity. **Alikanas,** 2km east, is slightly less frenetic. On your way there you can stop at the village of **Ano Gerakari** and wander about. Its peaceful streets spiral above planted fields and the sea. Buses to Alykes leave Zakinthos seven times per day (80dr). If you walk 2km inland from Alykes to the small town of Katastari, you can catch a bus further north (leaving Zakinthos Town daily at 5am, 1:45pm, and 8pm). **Volimes,** the endpoint of the bus route, is an old, sprawling village that specializes in fine needlework—knot to be missed. One kilometer east up the hill in the upper part of the village (Ano Volimes), the **Women's Agricultural Tourist Cooperative,** in the main square, can find you a room with a local family. (Singles 100dr. Doubles 1500dr. Meals optional and extra.) If the office is closed, go to the *panopoleion* (grocery store) opposite, or the **police** next door. In the lower part of the village, crumbling medieval bell towers are dispersed amid abandoned windmills. Mopedalists should be warned that the road up the western coast is not nearly as good as it looks on the map.

At the extreme northern tip is the tiny village of **Korithi,** locally known as **Agios Nikolaos,** where the ferry to Cephalonia leaves. Special buses come out to meet the ferry; regular buses rarely venture here (ask at the bus station in Zakinthos Town). Here you can embark on a visit to the beautiful **blue caves,** hewn by the sea into the side of the island and observable only from the water. A one-hour motorboat excursion costs around 500dr per person; you can also rent canoes and other small craft on the tiny beach.

# NORTHEAST AEGEAN ISLANDS
# Βορειοανατολικά Νησιά τόυ Αιγέου

*Aerial form'd who in Olympus shine*
*The heavenly Twins all lucid and divine*
*Blowing, serene, from whom abundance springs,*
*Nurses of seasons, fruit-producing kings.*
*—Orphic hymn, 38*

Several of the northeast Aegean islands attracted the Kabirion cultists, barren women appealing to the twin gods for assistance in conception. Yet aside from a mystical aura, no one island is like its neighbor. From thickly wooded Thassos in the far north to rocky, barren Limnos in the south, geography as well as cultural heritage preserve the distinct persona of each island. Nary a tourist makes the short trip from Thrace or Macedonia to these relatively inexpensive islands. However, because of the islands' proximity to Turkey and accompanying political tensions, many Greek soldiers are stationed here. Their presence may make the situation somewhat uncomfortable for women traveling alone.

## Thassos  Θάσος

Some of the finest beaches in Greece gird the popular resort island of Thassos, just off the Macedonian coast. Despite the throngs of Greek and German tourists, the sandy perimeter leaves plenty of lovely, uncrowded space. After you lounge on the beach, spend some time in the interior, with its lush, pine-veiled hills, mountainous terrain, chilling streams, and elegant mountain villages.

**Ferries** between Thassos and Kavala run every hour during the summer and every two hours in the off-season (1½ hr., 235dr). These ferries dock at Skala Prinos on the western coast; three per day continue to the island's capital Limenas (2½ hr., 260dr). Hourly ferries also make the 35-minute crossing from Keramoti 6 miles away on the coast direct to Limenas (210dr). If you arrive at Skala Prinos, waste no time in getting on the Limenas-bound buses waiting on the dock, as Skala Prinos is the island's least attractive spot. It is not possible to continue from Thassos to the other islands of the northeastern Aegean, so ignore the boat route marked on most maps. You must return to Kavala for other ferry connections.

To see the island properly, rent wheels for a day, explore both coast and inland areas thoroughly, select a favorite spot, and return by bus with your pack for a longer stay. The west coast is covered by Thassos-Limenaria shuttle buses (7 per day). Buses also run along the east coast (8 per day), with five going to Limenaria. The first bus from Thassos Town leaves at 6:40am; the last bus from Limenaria is at 7:45pm. Traveling to Limenaria via the shorter western route takes one hour

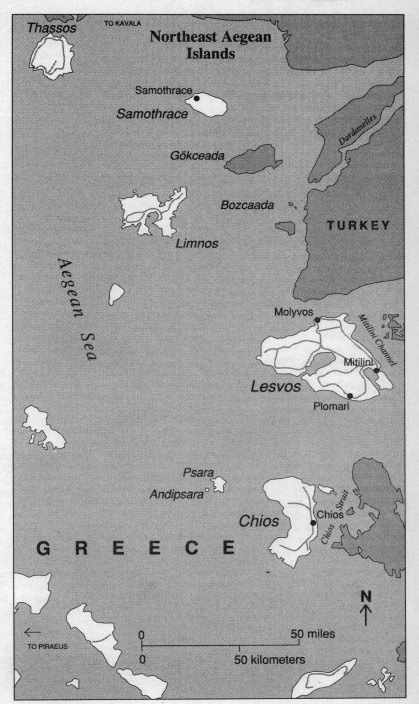

(270dr); the entire loop of the island takes two and a half hours (630dr). Four buses per day run in the winter. Village *tavernas* and grocery stores generally post schedules, but in Limenas you must ask at the bus office (see below). In spite of the schedules, bus service is erratic, so if you want to catch the last boat off the island, leave several hours leeway. Hitching is also a viable and fun means of seeing the island.

## Limenas (Thassos Town)

Limenas, also known as Thassos Town, is the island's capital and tourist center. This lively port is crowded and more expensive than the rest of the island. Stick around here for the nightlife, but not for scenery or quiet. You'll never see a street sign, but the main street's name is 19 Octovriou, in honor of Thassos' independence from Turkey in 1913. It runs 1 block parallel to the waterfront street.

### Practical Information

To your left in a gray marble building are the friendly **tourist police** (tel. 225 00), who can give you a minimalist depiction of the town, a small map of the island, and a list of hotels. (Open daily 8am-3pm.) You can buy larger maps in many of the stores for 400dr. One block north of the ferry dock is **Gregory's Gift Shop.** Gregory is very friendly, speaks English, and is a well of information. He also cashes traveler's checks until 10:30pm. The **National Bank of Greece,** a few buildings to the right of the tourist police, is open Mon.-Thurs. 8am-2pm, Fri. 8am-1:30pm. If you wish, the **Thassos Tourist Services** (tel. 223 43; open Mon.-Sat. 9am-1:30pm and 5-7pm) will exchange money, but bring your passport or another form of identification. If interested, ask about daily excursions from the island. Three blocks north of Gregory's and to the left is the **post office.** (Open Mon.-Fri. 7:30am-2:30pm.) Thassos' **postal code** is 64004. The **OTE** is on the main street, behind the tourist police. (Open Mon.-Sat. 7:30am-11pm, Sun. 7:30am-3pm.) The **telephone code** is 0593. **Dr. Glavas Ilias'** office (tel. 226 63 or 221 84) is near the OTE on a side street across from **Matsanis Pharmacy.**

The **old port** (now used for small boats) is around the bend beyond the tourist police. **Boats** can be hired for fishing or excursions from **Georgios Salonikis** (tel. 237 34); look for his *Aristea* docked in the old port. On the waterfront, opposite the ferry, is the **bus station** (tel. 221 62). There are about six agencies that rent **motorbikes.** Fifty meters past the post office, **Motor Rent "Mike"** (tel. 226 83) rents motorbikes for 700dr. More expensive but better equipped is **Selinos Bikes** (tel. 231 74 or 224 90), which rents motorbikes for 1000dr. Since all the cheap ones may already be booked, call ahead and send a downpayment to the motorbike rental shop (by telegram).

### Accomodations, Camping, and Food

Accommodations are a free-for-all on Thassos, and prices may bear little relation to official rates. The new **Hotel Athanasia** (tel. 225 45) is in all respects a sweet deal. From the boat, walk along the water and look for the signs 1 block before Restaurant Aphrodite. Turn left and follow the signs along the narrow walkway. (Doubles 1772dr, with shower 2500dr. Triples 2000dr, with shower 2500dr.) Behind Restaurant Aphrodite is the **Hotel Diamando** (tel. 226 22. Singles 1800dr. Doubles 2500dr). The private (unmarked) rooms just before the hotel are 1800dr per room. *Dhomatia* are legally allowed to operate only from May 20 through September 20, but most proprietors aren't bothered by this restriction. Look for signs along the streets, make discreet inquiries at *tavernas* and shops (*not* at hotels—even if they're full), or take your search outside of Limenas to the roads near the beaches. Rooms are cheaper as you get farther from town; doubles can be found for 1250dr. Sleeping bags appear on the town beach, but you'll be kept awake by the slurring overflow from bars. Instead, take the bus and alight at Skala Rahoni for **Camping Ioannidis,** 13km west of Limenas on the road to Skala Prinos. (450dr per person. 400dr per tent.) There is camping elsewhere on Thassos Island (see below).

Just beyond the old harbor near the end of the beach, **Restaurant Syrtaki** (tel. 226 51) serves red snapper for only 250dr (open 9am-midnight). **Zorbas,** next to the post office, serves up succulent mussels at reasonable prices. One block beyond Gregory's, **George's** (tel. 222 98) previews its offerings in a glass case (entrees 250dr).

### Sights

In addition to impressive remains of sixth- and fifth-century B.C.E. walls and buildings, the major attraction is the ancient **theater,** built on the remains of the acropolis of ancient Thassos. The ruins are easy to find: Turn right at the eastern end of the waterfront behind the old port and continue to a three-pronged fork in the road beyond a recessed ruin—the middle path leads to the theater. Four to eight performances of classical drama are shown here each year during July and August. (Tickets available at the GNTO in Kavala or on the waterfront in Limenas for 500dr.) All archeological sites are free and always open. The **museum** close to the old port contains the mosaic floors and sculptures found on the site, including the *Kouros*—a colossal sixth-century B.C.E. marble statue of Apollo carrying a ram on his shoulder. (Open Mon. and Wed.-Sat. 9am-3pm, Sun. 9:30am-2:30pm. Admission 150dr.)

# East Coast

Seven buses per day travel east from Limenas to Limenaria, stopping 10km south in the villages of **Panayia** and **Potamia** (115dr). Three kilometers apart, both villages overlook Ormos Potamias, a beautiful, long, sandy cove. Recently, Panayia has become a minor tourist center since it lies on the main bus route; the bus stops among the farms 100m below Potamia, leaving the streets above blissfully peaceful. Potamia has a small **folk museum** tucked away beside the town church. (Museum open Mon.-Sat. 8am-noon and 5:30-9pm, Sun. 8am-3:30pm.) Both towns have *dhomatia;* Panayia also has an inexpensive hotel, the **Helvetia** (tel. 612 31), at the northern entrance into town. (Singles 600dr. Doubles 1800dr. Hot showers included.)

Six kilometers east of Panayia runs the seemingly endless, golden sand beach of **Chrisi Ammoudia;** there is plenty of room for camping here, but little privacy. Farther south, Potamia's beach is not as nice, but offers plenty of space right up to the water. Campers should note that there is a water tap at the entrance to the olive grove, about 1km from the beach toward Potamia. Fine dining at beachside restaurants includes octopus boiled in vinegar or grilled. Don't be seduced easily by the beach farther down the coast, between the villages of **Kinira** and **Loutra.** Continue on to the twin coves of **Aliki,** 11km south of Kinira. The northernmost is sheltered by foliage and is perfect for nude bathing except when the water is sullied by octopi remains. The southern beach cove was formed as sand shifted over a Roman marble quarry. The slabs of bleached white rock and crevices make for first-rate snorkeling. Dry off and trudge to the monastery of **Archaegelon** and its simple whitewashed church with stone floors and colorful icons. (Cover-up clothing provided for visitors.) The island of Samothraki is visible in the distance.

**Limenaria** might be prettier and quieter than Limenai, but it still caters to a hefty share of tourists. Twelve buses per day connect the two towns. Finding a private room here should be no problem—*dhomatia* signs are all over town. The least expensive hotel is the towering **Papangiorgiou** (tel. 512 05. Doubles 2100dr). On a cliff at the east end of town is an enormous, abandoned mansion with a commanding view of the waterfront; the small, pine-covered meadows around it are an inviting place to camp, and there's a fresh-water tap on the road leading down the hill to the main highway. The pebble beach in Limenaria proper is nothing special, but there are good beaches at **Pefkari** and **Potos** only 4km away. One kilometer north of Potos is **Pefkari Camping,** an outstanding campground right on the beach. (350dr per person. 400dr per tent. Minimum stay 3 days.)

# Samothraki (Samothrace) Σαμοθράκη

First settled in the seventh century B.C.E. by colonists from Samos, Samothraki bears little resemblance to the lush, beautiful island to the south. Out of this bare, oblong rock rises Fegari, which at 1670 meters above sea level is the highest peak in the Aegean. It was here that Poseidon (according to *The Iliad*) viewed the Trojan War. In ancient times, tens of thousands came here to celebrate the mystery cult of the twin gods, the Cabiri. Infertile women were brought here to be assisted in conception by the twins. Alexander the Great was conceived here in this method. Today a mere 2500 people settle in Samothraki, and it is seldom visited by any tourists. While excavations at Paleopolis have uncovered the famous sanctuary where the ceremonies were held, they are hardly extensive enough to warrant a visit. Rather, come to appreciate the island's untouched barren beauty and unspoiled village life.

Boats run between Samothraki and Alexandroupolis daily during the summer (2 hr. 20 min., 700dr) and five times per week during the off-season (470dr); there is also a run from Kavala (Mon. and Sat., 4 hr., 1162dr). Boats from Samothraki to Kavala sail on Monday and Friday, but the latter docks in Kavala at midnight. Ferries stop at Kamariotissa, at the western end of the island. Follow the road northeast along the coast to Paleopolis (5km) and Therma (4km further). On another road 6km directly inland is the capital Samothraki, usually called Chora. Nine kilometers south is Lakoma.

In summer, an hourly **bus** connects Paleopolis, Therma, Chora, and Lakoma via Kamariotissa (60dr). In winter, buses run only twice per week.

The **National Bank** (tel. 415 70; open Mon.-Thurs. 8am-3:30pm, Fri. 8am-3pm) is along the waterfront in Kamariotissa, just a few doors down from the **Oasis Restaurant** (tel. 413 63). Aside from the ruins and the accompanying hilltop panorama, little stirs excitement in **Samothraki** (Chora). The **post office** (tel. 412 44) and **OTE** (tel. 412 12) are both uphill; go right at the fork at the base of the hill. (Both open Mon.-Fri. 7-2:30pm.) Samothraki's **postal code** is 68002; the **telephone code** is 41. **Motorcycles** can be rented from one of the two places in Kamariotissa. The cheaper agency lies just south of the dock on the waterfront road; you can bargain the owner down to 1000dr per day. Be sure to test the brakes. The other one, **Enoi Kiaseis** (which means "rentals") (tel. 413 94), is on the main road to the left of the ferry dock, two buildings behind the Oasis Restaurant. (1950dr per day for 2. Open daily 9am-2:30pm and 4:30-10pm; off-season 10am-12:30pm and 5-7:30pm.) The personable tourist police (tel. 413 03 or 412 03) are based at the top of the hill; go left at the fork.

If you want to settle down for a few days, consider staying in **Therma,** a small village with one street. Therma's lush surroundings contrast sharply with the aridity of the rest of the island. There are several private rooms and one expensive hotel. The cheapest place is the unmarked white building with green window sills near the top of the hill next to Galnin Restaurant. (500dr per bed. Showers extra.) Most people **camp** along the seashore extending east of town.

While in Therma, swim or bathe next to the delightful cataract. Take the first left (a dirt road) after turning off the coastal highway for Therma. Walk east and follow the small stream. Alternatively, from the village center, take the road that runs behind the hotel and keep heading inland. Ask for directions to the "cataract" from anyone on the path (there are no signs). The last five minutes can be traversed only on foot. Continue past the stagnant lower pool to the upper one. The water is refreshing but colder than ice; afterwards you'll want to thaw in a **thermal bath.** Pass the one on the western side of town (100dr; open 6-11am and 5-7pm), and go 100m up the dirt road just beyond to the whitewashed shack—the pool inside is free. Those who feel the urge can tackle the difficult five-hour climb from Therma to **Mount Fegari** (1600m high). While in Kamariotissa, ask the islanders to direct you to a guide; climbing without one is prohibited.

Between Therma and Kamariotissa lies **Paleopolis** ("old city"), where the ruins of *megaloi theoi* (great gods) stand alongside a worthwhile **museum.** In addition to the local artifacts, the museum houses a miniature copy of the *Victory of Samothrace;* its original is on display at the Louvre. (Museum open Mon. and Wed.-Sat. 8:45am-3pm, Sun. 9:30am-2:30pm. Admission 70dr.) **Lakoma,** on the opposite side of the island, draws the islanders together on Saturday and Sunday nights for live *bouzouki* music. The island's best beach, **Pahia Ammos,** is a 5-kilometer walk south from here along the shore.

# Limnos Λήμνος

Situated strategically as a potential "cork" to the Black Sea, Limnos has a sizable Greek military presence in response to renewed tension with Turkey. You may see Turkish military maneuvers several kilometers offshore, but don't let them scare you away from this rocky island. The tiny villages and rolling countryside remain undisturbed for you to enjoy.

In summer, ferries run from Kavala (2 per week, 5 hr., 1100dr). Limnos is also connected to Lesvos (3 per week, 1238dr, 6hr.), Agios Efstratios (2 per week), Kimi (1 per week, 1070dr), and Rhodes (2 per week, 20 hr., 3260dr). Despite the lines you may see drawn on your map, there is no direct ferry service to Samothraki. For further information, contact **Alkyon Tours** (see Kimi) or the **Limnos Port Authority** (tel. (0254) 222 25).

The legendary home of the divine smithy Hephaestus, Limnos is so dry that the water supply must be turned off at night. Its villages tend to be small clusters of stone houses with tile roofs, surrounded by checkerboard fields of hay, tobacco, and other crops. Try to rent a moped (1000-1500dr per day) or take a taxi to explore beyond the port town. The only shop that rents automatic bikes is **Rent-a-car Petridis** (tel. 220 39), located several blocks inland from the port on the main road (1000 dr). There is no public transportation on Limnos, and there are few cars to pick up hitchers.

The main port of **Mirina** is a collection of weather-beaten, whitewashed houses free of oversized hotels and unsightly resort complexes. A peaceful strip of sandy beach extends along the waterfront, and turreted towers of a Genoese-Turkish fortress peek out from behind the volcanic-rock formations that overlook the town. The short hike to the top discloses a tower. Look for the several well-preserved cisterns within the walls. The scene is completed with a view of the old wooden fishing boats huddled together in the cozy inner harbor, protected from the open sea by a white stone breakwater.

To get to the town center, walk to the far side of the pier and head diagonally left up the winding street. In the square you'll see the **National Bank of Greece** (open Mon.-Thurs. 8am-2pm, Fri. 8am-1:30pm) and the **OTE** (open Mon.-Fri. 7:30am-10pm, Sat.-Sun. 7:30am-3:10pm). Past the square 1 block and around the corner to the right are the **post office** (open Mon.-Fri. 7:30am-4pm) and two movie theaters. The **tourist police,** 66 Garrufalini St. (tel. 222 00), will provide the names and phone numbers of hotels in Limnos along with the disclaimer that there is price limit for rooms.

For accommodations, bargain with the locals who meet you at the pier. If your luck is bad, try wandering around town muttering *dhomatia;* someone may feel sorry for you. As a last resort, stay at the **Hotel Aktaion** near the ferry landing; at least the clean rooms have sinks. (Singles 2200dr. Doubles 2500dr. Triples 2800dr.) The canopied **Zithestiatorion,** on Kida St., east of the square, serves cheap fare. There are also two pizzerias along the *paralia* and several seafood *tavernas.*

Just 2km southeast of Mirina stretches an uncrowded beach with several bungalows (1500dr for 2) and a *taverna* run by a former Chicago resident. If you can find transportation, spend a day exploring Limnos' remote and more picturesque villages. Wherever you go, you're likely to be the only traveler. Eight kilometers north of Mirina is **Kaspaka,** where most of the old stone buildings still stand. **Agios Ioannis,** on the stony beach nearby, has a cheap restaurant with tables squeezed underneath a rock canopy. Traveling eastward you'll come to **Kotsinas,** a fishing village more comatose than sleepy. The town has a few restaurants and freelance camping along its somewhat littered beach. **Moudros,** Limnos' other large town, is about as attractive as other large military compounds.

# Lesvos (Lesbos) Λέσβος

Despite a seductive and variegated topography, Lesvos has only recently appeared on the itineraries of island hoppers. Steep hills and olive groves stretch over most of the sparsely populated island, Greece's third largest. The major towns now host a growing number of foreign visitors, but tourism has not quite reached Cycladean proportions.

Legend has it that the population of Lesvos was once entirely female. The notion may owe its origin to the decision of the Athenian assembly in 428 B.C. to punish the uncooperative residents of Lesvos' largest city, Mitilini, by executing all adult males on the island; after some debate, the decision was repealed. More importantly, Lesvos was for a time the home of Sappho (seventh century B.C.E.), the female poet whose lyric love poetry addressed women.

For hundreds of years, Mitilini flourished as an important center of Greek culture; its inhabitants would have been astonished to know that later generations would consider fifth-century Athens to be the summit of Greek civilization. The island was especially famed for its Philosophical Academy, where Epicurus and Aristotle taught. The island retains a prominent place in Greek cultural affairs today; Nobel Prize-winning poet Odysseus Elytis hails from here.

**Ferries** connect the island to the Northeast Aegean and beyond. The *Omiros* travels to and from Piraeus (Sun.-Thurs. 1 per day, 14 hr., 2000dr) arriving at Lesvos at 8am and departing at 4pm; it stops at Chios in between (4 hr., 1100dr). Ferries sail to and from Thessaloniki (every other Sat., 13 hr., 2456dr) via Kavala (every other Sat., 12 hr., 1740dr). There is also service from Lesvos to Ayvalik, Turkey (in summer Mon.-Sat. 1 per day, in off-season 3 per week; 4000dr one-way, 6000dr round-trip); inquire at **Dimakis Tours,** 73 Kountourioutou St. (tel. 207 16), around the corner of the waterfront from the tourist police in Mitilini. At least a dozen travel agencies on the waterfront, as well as the tourist office, compete to sell tickets. **Flights** go to: Athens (6 per day, 5290dr), Thessaloniki (1 or 2 per day, 9000dr), Limnos (4 per week, 4790dr), Chios (1 or 2 per week, 3690dr), Samos (1 or 2 per week, 6480dr), and Rhodes (3 per week, 10,460dr). Blue buses at the waterfront local bus depot serve the airport 8km south of Mitilini (80dr). You can also reach the airport by taking the Olympic Airways bus (80dr) from the main office, Kavetsou St. (tel. 286 59). Check with any ticket agent for times and locations.

## Mitilini

Even the mighty walls of the hilltop Genoese Fortress cannot intimidate busy Mitilini. This central port city bustles along the waterfront and on **Ermou Street,** which runs parallel one block inland. Here you can stock up on food and other necessities before launching into the interior. Enjoy Mitilini by sitting at a waterfront cafe and watching the *volta* (evening promenade).

If you have a spare hour, visit the enormous baroque **Church of St. Therapon,** on Ermou St., which stands amid the fish market's daily catch: sardines, octopi, and occasionally a small shark or two. Behind the church, the **Museum of Byzantine Art** houses a representation of a vexed Virgin Mary and a stern Pantocrator. (Open Mon.-Sat. 9am-12:30pm. Admission 30dr.) The **Popular Art Museum,** in the old harbormaster's building behind the harbor bus stand, displays crafts, household implements and nineteenth-century costumes from Lesvos. (Open Mon.-Fri. 10am-noon and 4-6pm. Admission 30dr.) The **Archeological Museum,** which contains finds from around the island, is being relocated somewhere in the park; ask at the tourist office for an update on its progress.

The **tourist police** (tel. 227 76), 1 block to your right as you disembark (look for the sign), will help find you rooms. (Open June-Aug. Mon.-Fri. 8am-9pm; Sept.-May Mon.-Fri. 8am-2:30pm.) Mr. Panselinas, at the **tourist office**, 5 Konstantinoupoleos Sq. (tel. 213 29), next to the main bus station on Leoforos Eleftheriou Venizelou, will search the entire island if need be. (Open Mon. and Sat. 8am-1:30pm, Tues.-Fri. 8am-1:30pm and 6-8pm.) For ritzier rooms, consult Mr. Dimakis at **Dimakis Tours,** or ask around on your own at any restaurant or travel agency along the harbor.

Several **banks** on the waterfront (open Mon.-Fri. 8am-2pm) and many of the travel agencies (open daily 6-10pm) elsewhere change money, but check the rates. The **mobile post office,** a yellow caravan on the waterfront, provides the same service (open in summer Mon.-Fri. 8am-8pm, Sat.-Sun. 8am-6pm), as does the **main post office** (tel. 288 36), on Vournazon St. (open Mon.-Sat. 7:30am-3pm; parcels and money orders 7:30am-2:30pm.) The **postal code** is 81100 for eastern Lesvos, 81108 for western Lesvos. Two doors past the post office is the **OTE**. (Open Mon.-Sat. 6am-midnight.) The **hospital** (tel. 284 57) is southwest of the city. The **telephone code** for eastern Lesvos is 0251, for western Lesvos 0253.

The **bus station** (tel. 288 73) is adjacent to Agios Irinis Park, at the corner of Smyrnis and Leoforos St., one block up from Konstantinoupoleos Sq. at the southern edge of the harbor. Buses leave frequently, but service is minimal on Saturday and practically nonexistent on Sunday. You can also rent a **moped** for 1500dr in Mitilini, 1200dr in Molyvos or Plomari. **Hitching** is excellent on Lesvos as long as you stick to well-traveled roads. To head west, hitchers and drivers should follow Zoodochos Pigis St., an extension of Vournazon St., out of town until it turns into the highway to Kalloni.

Beach-seekers may be disappointed by Mitilini's **municipal beach,** just north of the main pier, where indiscriminating hordes spread their mats. (Admission 80dr.) The 5km bus ride south to **Neapolis Beach** won't bring a great change of scene. Persevere and head 13km south of Mitilini to the deserted, sandy beach at **Agios Ermogenis**; take the bus to Loutra, and walk or hitch the remaining 5km.

Only 3km south of Mitilini along the same route, the tiny and unassuming village of **Varia** surprises those passing through with the **Theophilos Museum** (tel. 416 44), named for and featuring the famous painter whose works have been displayed in the Louvre. Next door is the astonishing **Teriade Musée.** Teriade, a native of Lesvos, rose to fame as the foremost publisher of graphic art in Paris throughout much of the twentieth century. The museum displays a sizable lithograph collection of Picasso, Miró, Leger, Chagall, and Matisse; this should not be missed. (Both museums were being reorganized in the summer of 1988; ask at the tourist office for more information.) Southbound buses depart from the waterfront depot (5 per day, all destinations less than 100dr).

Follow the main road for 4km north, then head 2km west to view a well-preserved Roman aqueduct at **Moria.** Returning to the main road, continue north another 10km to come to the spa resort of **Thermi** which offers therapeutic springs, as do several other villages on the way. Four or five buses per day take this route.

## Northern Lesvos

Molyvos (Mithimna), on Lesvos' northern tip, has successfully taken its cue from Sappho's dictum:

> *She who dons flowers*
> *attracts the merriful*
> *Graces: they turn*
> *back from a bare head.*
> *—Sappho, No. 19, translated by Mark Selwyn*

The main street, **17th Novembriou** (named for the date of liberation from the Turks), is a tunnel of leafy vines and fragrant flowers 50m uphill from the paved road. Many tourists wisely choose to base themselves in this winding hillside tangle of cobblestone alleys rather than in Mitilini. In the off-season, a large contingent of yoga practicioners congregates here, a boon for local merchants who mark their prices up accordingly. Yet, when clambering down to a stunning cove or viewing the Genoese fortress, it's hard to get worked up over a few rip-offs. Illuminated at night, the **fortress** is striking; walk up during the day for a view of the coastline and a closer look at the wildflowers growing in the ruins. Descending from the fortress, take your first left and enter the small **church** with the brown gate; the consciences of even unrepentant hedonists will be disconcerted by the soul-searching eye above the altar. Complete your ablutions at the **pebble beach** north of town or the **sand beach** to the south. Avoid the crowded beach in town.

The **tourist office** (tel. (0253) 713 47) in Molyvos, located in a stone building to the left of the bus stop, opens only for several minutes after buses arrive. If you're really lucky, the woman running the office will procure a room for you. (Singles 1125dr. Doubles 1569dr.) If the office is closed, walk up the right fork towards 17th Novembriou, and you'll see numerous signs for rooms posted. On 17th Novembriou itself, you'll find yet more places. Leave your pack if possible, as the going gets steep. The **post office** (tel. (0253) 712 46; open Mon.-Fri. 7:30am-2:30pm) and the **OTE** (tel. (0253) 713 99; open Mon.-Fri. 8am-noon and 4-8pm) are both signposted off 17th Novembriou. For **camping**, try the beaches; the road to the left of the tourist office leads to a site. There's a water faucet at the top of the road.

Deceptively disguised as a standard coastal town, **Petra**, 5km south of Molyvos, is anything but typical. A rocky monolith sprouts up above the narrow alleys and fishing piers with the eighteenth-century **Church of the Panayia** (Holy Virgin) jutting out of the precipice. The bold might approach the church by the 114 steps hewn into the cliff, while others can relax in the lazy cafes that line the flower-decked waterfront and the mile-long beach.

Petra is also the home of the **Women's Agricultural-Tourist Collective** (tel. (0253) 412 38), a venture begun in 1984 by the women of the village to gain economic freedom. It runs a small *taverna*, sells handcrafts and home-canned produce, and arranges rooms for visitors with Greek families. (Singles 1100dr. Doubles 1500dr.) Guests can participate in the family's daily activities such as fishing or fieldwork. There are also other *dhomatia* in town. The **post office** (open Mon.-Fri. 7:30am-2:30pm) and **OTE** (open Mon.-Fri. 7:30am-3:10pm) are located near the Women's Collective office where the bus stops.

**Buses** will carry you over the mountains from Mitilini to Molyvos (July-Aug. Mon.-Sat. 4 per day; June-Sept. and Sun. 2 per day; 410dr). The two-hour ride passes through Kalloni (270dr) and Petra (390dr). From **Kalloni**, travelers can make a connection to Eressos (ask ahead).

## Southern Lesvos

**Plomari**, on the southern coast, is a bizarre mixture: at once a glitzy resort town with discos, bright *tavernas* and hotels stuffed with package tour groups, and a traditional fishing village with locals mending their nets on the pier and nailing octopi to telephone poles to dry in the sun. The overall effect is cheerful and relaxed, abetted by Plomari's large *ouzo* industry. The local product is far better than the industrially produced bottled variety. Visit the **Barbayanni Ouzo Factory**, about 2km east toward Agios Isodoros, to watch them making the stuff and try a free sample. (Open Mon.-Sat. 8am-5pm.) If you can continue, head to the first bridge to the left off the main shopping street. On it, **Agios Nikolaos** sparkles with icons spanning 400 years; some of the outstanding pieces are on the back of the podium wall by the altar.

The **bank** (open Mon.-Thurs. 8am-2pm, Fri. 8am-1:30pm), **OTE** (tel. 323 99), and **post office** (tel. 322 41) (both open Mon.-Fri. 7:30am-2:30pm), are in the main square. Try to get a room at **Mrs. Mayragani's** traditional rooms (tel. 323 39). Walk from the restaurant with the vine-covered awning next to the bus stop just past the bank, continue along the curving street to the second bridge on the left, pass the restaurant, and follow the signs. Newly renovated wood-paneled doubles cost 1500dr.

**Beaches** appear sporadically from Plomari eastward, but the best are at **Agios Isodoros,** about 3km down the road. Fifteen kilometers north of **Plomari,** the village of **Agiassos,** on the slopes of Lesvos' Mt. Olympus, remains an active center for ceramic crafts. Visit the workshop near the bus stop or the one at 1852 Agia Triados St., where the Hatziyiannis brothers carry on a family tradition. An Orthodox church, even more exuberantly decorated than others, contains an icon of the Virgin Mary made by St. Lucas, originally destined for Constantinople in 330 C.E. When the priest transporting it heard rumors of war there, he feared for the icon's safety and deposited it in the church. Every year on August 15, Agiassos hosts the island's grand name-day celebration in honor of the church's patron, the Virgin Mary (*Panayia*).

Buses go from Mitilini to Plomari (July-Aug. Mon.-Sat. 6 per day, Sept.-June 3 per day, 290dr) and Agiassos (2 per day, 210dr). The road hugs the **Bay of Geras,** offering eye-opening views of both the coast and the interior, and passes through the charming villages of **Paleokipos** and **Pappados.** If you are hitching or bicycling from Mitilini, you should take the shortcut across the mouth of the bay. Head down Konstantinou Kavetsou St. and continue to the village of **Kountourdia** at the end of the road. From there, you can take the small passenger boat to Perama, which connects to the road to Plomari; rates and schedules are unofficial, so be sure to bargain. In peak summer months, they may refuse to take bikes and mopeds on board if the boat is full—a shame since this is the only way to explore the otherwise inaccessible villages and beaches of the southwest.

## Western Lesvos

Determined beach hunters congregate at **Skala Eressos,** at the opposite end of Lesvos from Mitilini. Its companion village of **Eressos,** (3½ km inland), is the birthplace of Sappho, and a popular gathering place for lesbian travelers during the summer. Both have reputations as havens for carefree lifestyles. You should have no problem finding private **rooms**in either town, though you might reserve through Mr. Panselinas at the Mitilini tourist office. You might sacrifice privacy and **camp** on the the beach with all of your favorite backpackers. Both the **post office** (tel. (0253) 532 27) and **OTE** (tel. (0253) 533 99) in Eressos are open Monday through Friday 7:30am to 2:30pm. An **archeological museum** has been constructed above the fifth-century Christian Basilica.

Fourteen bumpy kilometers northwest of Eressos is the fishing village of **Sigri,** noted for its lobsters. The beach here isn't as nice as the one at Skala Eressos, but it is quieter. A smooth beach runs parallel to the dirt road 2km past the municipal beach; turn right at the big tree inside the courtyard. The road is passable on moped, but it's not advisable. Near the town beach in Sigri are the **post office** and **OTE** (both open Mon.-Fri. 7:30am-2:30pm).

If impermeable deadwood fascinates you, visit the stumps at the **petrified forest** farther inland at **Antissa,** 15km inland from both Sigri and Erossos.

To get to the west, take the **bus** (Mon.-Sat. 1 per day, 500-600dr), which passes through all the villages named above. If you intend to do a lot of traveling in western Lesvos, though, a **moped** may be best, if you can manage the initial 95km ride from Mitilini.

# Chios Xíos

Whereas most Greek islanders either embrace tourism wholeheartedly or resist it tenaciously, Chios' inhabitants don't seem to care. It's not that they're hostile—quite the opposite is true—their friendliness is meted out regardless of one's status as a tourist. The residents, many of them sailors and ship owners (Ari Onassis hailed from Chios), see no need to supplement their incomes by catering to foreigners. Consequently, the locals remain fully immersed in a traditional Greek social life. Only Chios Town is at all commercialized, its cluttered waterfront camouflaging the mountainous interior and remote beaches. Sandwiched between Lesvos and Samos and a mere 8km from the Turkish coast, Chios remains subdued.

Though it achieved fame as one of the seven alleged birthplaces of Homer, Chios gained greater renown for commerce and art in the sixth century B.C.E. Since antiquity, Chios has cultivated and exported mastic (*masticha*), a gummy resin used in varnishes, cosmetic creams, chewing gum, floor waxes, and dessert toppings. Roughly half of the annual crop is sold to Iraq to be made into a potent alcoholic beverage.

The island's desirable location has brought numerous invasions. The Genoese dominated Chios for 200 years before the Turks took control in 1566. A failed rebellion in 1822 resulted in the slaughter of over 25,000 Greeks. A major earthquake brought its own kind of destruction in 1881. Oppressive foreign rule continued until 1912, when the Balkan Wars reunited Chios with the rest of Greece. This resilient island again suffered in 1981, when a huge fire destroyed one of its two forest regions in the north around Volissos, and in 1987, when another fire devastated part of the west.

**Olympic Airways** (tel. 224 14) flies daily to Athens (4570dr), and has two or three additional flights a week to Lesvos (3690dr), Samos (3400dr), and Mykonos (6050dr). Despite the expense and distance (the airport's 2km south of town), the air schedule's much more convenient than the ferry schedule, which seems to be specially designed to deprive passengers of sleep. **Ferries** run to and from Piraeus (Sun.-Fri. 1 per day, 10 hr., 1670dr), Lesvos (Sun.-Fri. 1 per day, 4 hr., 1000dr), and Samos (Mon. and Fri. only, 4 hr., 818dr). During the summer, the *Sappho* makes the run to and from Thessaloniki once per week (Sat. only, 17 hr., 2714dr), leaving Chios Town at 1am. Ferries also make excursions to Çeşme (Tsesme) on the Turkish coast (July-Aug. Tues.-Sat. 1 per day, off-season 2-4 per week; 4500dr one-way, 6000dr round-trip) and to Kavala (Thurs. only, 2325dr each way).

## Chios Town

Although a dingy port city, Chios Town is the best starting point for your stay, as it is the center for all routes of travel around the island. The town, sounds ricocheting off cement walls, has an active shopping district centered on **Vournakio Square**, as well as several relics of its similarly busy past. The walls of the **Kastro**, a castle originally Byzantine, then reconstructed by the Genoese, encloses the narrow streets of the **old town**. Inside the main gate off the square, stairs climb to a tiny and peaceful **Byzantine Museum**. (Open Tues.-Sat. 9am-2pm and 5:30-8pm, Sun. 9am-2pm. Free.) The **Turkish Mosque**, on Vournakio Sq. (look for the stripe), has been converted into a museum displaying various finds from the archeological site at Emborio and an extensive Byzantine collection. There's a copy of Delacroix's depiction of the 1822 massacre, a work that aided the Greek liberation movement by alerting Europe to Ottoman atrocities. (Open Mon.-Fri. 10am-1pm. Free.) The town's **archeological museum**, on Porphyra St., 4 blocks inland on the far south of the waterfront, is at best sub-standard. (Open Mon. and Wed.-Sat. 8:45am-3pm, Sun. 9:30am-2:30pm. Admission 100dr, students 50dr.) Culture and counterculture are juxtaposed near the cathedral. The **Argentis Folklore Museum** is attached to the unusual **Korais Library** of 95,000 volumes. (Open Mon.-Sat. 8:30am-2pm. Free.) Check out the hip murals, too.

Take your pick of information sources. If you're just off a night boat, check with the **tourist police,** 37 Neorion St. (tel. 265 55), on the north side of the harbor. To get to the **tourist office,** 11 Kanari St. (tel. 242 17), turn off Prokymea St., which everyone refers to as the *limani* (waterfront) onto Kanari, towards the square. (Look for the small "i.") They're friendly, attentive to detail, and teeming with bus timetables. (Open June-Sept. Mon.-Fri. 7am-2:30pm and 6:30-9:30pm, Sat. 9am-1pm; Oct.-May Mon.-Fri. 7:30am-2:30pm.) Despite unfounded pretensions to officialdom, the **Hatzelenis "tourist office"** (tel. 267 43), in the north corner of the *limani,* can offer invaluable aid.

Tassos Hatzelenis and his wife Margaret will find you rooms anywhere on the island (see below), decipher bus and boat schedules, suggest excursions, and rent you a motorbike (1200dr; look around for cheaper deals). (Open daily 7am-1:30pm and 5:30-9pm.) The free booklet *This Summer in Chios* has so-so town and island maps; the regular tourist map (150dr) shows more roads.

Chios Town's **OTE** (open July-Aug. 6am-midnight; off-season 6am-11pm) faces the tourist office, in the vicinity of several **banks** (open Mon.-Thurs. 8am-2pm, Fri. 8am-1:30pm). The tourist office, Hatzelenis' "tourist office," and many travel agencies change money in the evenings. Immediately after the Olympic Airways waterfront office, Omirou Street leads to the **post office** (tel. 245 07; open Mon.-Fri. 7:30am-3pm). Chios' **postal code** is 82100. Chios' **telephone code** is 0271. **Buses** leave from both sides of Vournakio Sq., right off the public gardens. Blue buses are destined for Karfas, Karies, and Vrondados, all within 12km of Chios Town; green buses, on the left side, serve the rest of the island (tel. 234 88). A free public **hospital** is 3km north of Chios towards Vrondtados.

Most of Chios Town's accommodations are converted neoclassical mansions with creaky wooden staircases and high ceilings. Singles can be difficult to find. **Stella's,** 7 Rodokanaki St. (tel. 203 64), conveniently located just off the *limani* (turn onto the diagonal when you see the "sock" sign), rents felicitous whitewashed rooms with desks. (Singles 1000dr. Doubles 1300dr.) Don't worry about the pooch; he's a sweetie. **Pension Giannis,** 48 Livanou St. (tel. 274 33), helpfully signposted at the southern corner of the harbor, provides clean rooms off a garden. (First-floor singles 1200dr when available. Doubles 1500dr.) The Hatzelenis Family (see above) moonlights as keepers of **Chios Rooms** (tel. 272 95), farther south and a bit out of the way on the waterfront. They won't abuse their power from the "tourist office." (Singles 1300dr when available. Doubles 1700dr.)

Food runs Chios Town. The hustle and bustle results from the myriad vendors around Vounakio Square hawking their milk, cheese, meat, bread, and produce. For a sweet breakfast or snack, try the *loukoumades,* similar to fried dough and covered with thin honey. Restaurants clustered along the pier prepare standard Greek fare along with the daily catch. Several all-night restaurants greet pre-dawn arrivals from Piraeus. The **Two Brothers Taverna,** 36 Livanou St. (tel. 213 73), delivers a great *moschari* for 340dr. If you don't mind a pre-prandial stroll, follow the road to the Bank of Crete, turn left, and keep walking. The lantern on the right is the only beacon for the untouristed **Xotza Taverna,** 74 Steftsouris Street. Overlook the conspicuously inconspicuous service because the food is dazzlingly good and cheap. The *retsina,* on tap, is literally a knockout.

For a nightcap, hang out upstairs at the **Acrobat Roof-Top Bar,** a real swinging place on the *limani* above the Olympic Airways office. The prices are as steep as the stairs, but the plants, the Toulouse-Lautrec posters, and the glimpse of the lights on the Turkish coast are worth the hike. Heading out of town on Livanou St., past the grungy local beach, you will come to several discos, packed with locals, tourists, and Greek soldiers catching a little R&R. Popularity is transient; judge a place by the number of motorcycles out front. Shake your stuff at **Disco Roxy,** or in the breezy garden at **GTS** (tel 297 61), 600m south of town.

## Nea Moni and Anavatos

Built in the eleventh century, the Nea Moni (New Monastery) might suffer from outdated advertising, but nothing justifies its obscurity. An icon of the Virgin Mary perched in a myrtle tree miraculously appeared to three hermits. With the help of an exiled emperor, they founded the monastery 16km from Chios Town, overlooking a steep slope. The icon remains, hanging to the right of the main altar. Over the centuries, the monastery complex was rebuilt and enlarged, but the thousands of monks living here were slaughtered in the Turkish massacre. The 1881 earthquake was the final blow, destroying much of the complex. The church has been restored, apparently quite accurately, but the interior is still chaotic. Especially noteworthy are the eleventh-century mosaics in the inner narthex, their superb artistry shining through their state of partial destruction. One other chapel of the complex, now a convent, is open to the public, but houses little besides a chilling display of skulls and bones from the 1822 massacre. (Open daily dawn-1pm and 4-8pm. Free.)

Fifteen kilometers west of Nea Moni is **Anavatos,** staggeringly beautiful but tainted by tragedy. The women and children of the village's 400 families threw themselves off the precipitous cliffs of this "Greek Masada" when the attempt to withstand the Turkish invasion in 1822 proved unsuccessful. Anavatos consists of 50 stone buildings with tiny doors and window apertures. This heavily fortified outlay, designed by the Genoese, had withstood numerous pirate raids over the centuries. Today, six people live here.

A bus from Chios ventures to both sites (Wed. at 8am only). If you miss it, you can take one of the more frequent buses to Varies (Mon.-Sat. at least 5 per day, 80dr), and walk along a forest trail for one and a half hours to reach Nea Moni. Taxi drivers may agree to drive you to a site, wait half an hour, and bring you back. Assemble a group of fellow sightseers, since you'll pay by the meter (1500dr for the shortest excursion to Nea Moni; try Mr. Misetzis, tel. 200 65). If on moped, make sure your engine's strong enough to tackle the hills.

## Southern Chios

The southern half of the island, called *Mastichochoria,* produces the famous resin of Chios by tapping squat, curvy-branched trees. The main "mastic village" is **Pirgi,** 25km from Chios and high in the hills. The striking gray and white decorations on the housefronts, called *xysta,* are the town's trademark and a graphic designer's delight. Walk into town past the first seven or eight houses and you'll see the Chios Headquarters (helpfully English-speaking) of the **Women's Agricultural Tourist Collective** (tel. 724 96), who can arrange rooms here and in the main mastic villages. If you wish, you can take part in your host family's daily work. (Singles sometimes available on request. Doubles 1940dr. Breakfast 245dr.) **Dhomatia** are plentiful and a bit cheaper. Just northeast of the square is the fourteenth-century **Agioi Apostoloi** church, a resplendent replica of the Nea Moni; every inch of its walls and ceiling is covered with well-preserved frescoes and paintings. The caretaker must unlock the front gate, even during open hours. If you cannot locate him, stroll around the church to the back yard, where the door should be open. (Open Mon.-Sat. 9:30am-3pm, Sun. and holidays 10am-2pm.)

One kilometer back along the road to Chios and 5km south is the black pebble beach at **Emborio.** A series of coves formed by jutting volcanic cliffs, it is arguably one of the best beaches in Greece, and is served by three good *tavernas.* There is bus service to Emborio during the summer, but hitching is usually easy on this well-traveled road—just don't try to get a ride during the afternoon when everyone is already at the beach. Arrange to be dropped off at the harbor and follow the road to the right as you face the water. Discreet camping should not be a problem.

Five kilometers back from Pirgi towards Chios, the partly-medieval, partly-modern town of **Armolia** supplies the island's ceramics demand. Though the shops just out of town sell mostly junk, the two closest to town also cater to the locals; here you can observe potters at their craft making functional wine and water jugs.

Farther on, 10km west of Pirgi is the anachronistic village of **Metsa,** with covered streets that make the whole town seem like one continuous building. The stonework is no longer necessary for defense from pirates, but it works remarkably well in keeping the town cool.

From the bus stop (the one with the "Heavy Metal Will Never Die" graffiti), follow the *kentro* signs to the main courtyard. Here, the church of the **Paliou Taxiarchi** deserves at least a glimpse for its rich, blue interior. The town's only **cafe,** also on the courtyard, serves *mesta*wine, a very sweet local specialty. Dinner might include spiced meatballs (200dr) or stewed thistles (150dr). Opposite, Dimitris Pippides runs a tiny **tourist office** (tel. 763 19), which books restored rooms in old houses. (Doubles 1800dr.) You may reserve rooms in advance through the women's collective in Pirgi. Just outside the village, **Augusta Lerthidi** lets comfortable singles for 1200dr and doubles for 1500dr.

From Mesta and neighboring villages, hikers undeterred by hilly treks will have access to several nearly vacant **beaches** in southwestern Chios. Off the main road and poor-quality secondary routes, follow the donkey paths to otherwise inaccessible spots.

Green **buses** run frequently along the south of the island to Armolia (Mon.-Sat. 5 per day, 190dr) and Pirgi (5 per day, 210dr); three buses continue on to Mesta (250dr).

## Northern Chios

Always the poorer region, the northern half of Chios, *Voriochora,* was left even more destitute by the 1981 fire. Few foreigners come here, and it may be difficult to find a place to stay. To appreciate the beauty of rhythmic waves pounding a ragged hillside, travel by motorbike—a honking bus blasts away any allure. About 5km outside of Chios town, just past Vrontados, the beach of **Daskalopetra** (teaching rock), is where Homer supposedly held class. Blue local buses from Chios Town head here frequently (Mon.-Sat.). After Daskalopetra, the main roads wind northwest along the coast past Marmaron to **Nagos** (30km away) with its gray stone beach, or west to **Volissos** (40km away), which legend marks as the birthplace of Homer. A few kilometers south of Volissos, a long beach stretches out alongside the four-house village of **Limnia,** overlooked by a monastery. Walk along the coast in either direction to find an expanse of sand all your own.

Green buses run to and from Kardamila (Mon.-Sat. 5 per day) and Volissos (Mon.-Tues. and Thurs.-Fri. at 1:30pm; returns possible only on the following morning at 5:40am).

# Psara and Inousses Ψαπά και Οινούσσες

A tiny, almost uninhabited island northwest of Chios, **Psara** had its brief moment of glory. Traditionally home to maritime merchants and naval personnel, this is the birthplace of the noted revolutionary, Admiral Kanaris. One of the first islands to revolt against Ottoman rule, Psara fostered so many years of pirate incursions against the Turkish mainland that an Ottoman force eventually invaded and destroyed it. Since then, it's resumed being a small, quiet fishing community with a number of good beaches. A French-Greek woman rents out the five available rooms on the island. Because the Greek government has initiated a drive to encourage tourism on Psara, all fares by ferry from Chios Town are subsidized in full from September to October and from March to May 10. **Ferries** depart from Chios Town (Mon., Wed., and Fri. at 10am, 600dr). To halve the length of the trip, take a *caïque* from Volissos (400dr), or ask a fisherman to take you over.

If you visit **Inousses,** the little islet northeast of Chios, you will probably be one of about 10 tourists on the island. Come here for a day of peace and quiet—the beautiful beaches are completely deserted and during the afternoon siesta you can wander through the charming streets of the town, alone except for a few stray cats. Inousses will probably strike you as exceptionally well-maintained. You may see a shiny Mercedes Benz cruising down a winding road, or a private yacht floating serenely on crystal blue waters. This is because Inousses is inhabited mainly by wealthy ship owners whose luxurious villas dot the coastline. Even the island's monastery, **Moni Evangelismou,** exhibits first-class standards. Be aware of the strict dress code here; don't wear shorts or tank tops, or at least bring a towel to use as a cover-up.

A ferry leaves Chios Town for Inousses Monday through Saturday at 2pm, returning only at 8am the next morning. It will not be cheap to stay here overnight, however. On Sundays, an excursion lasts from 8am to 4pm (400dr one-way, 800dr return). Inquire about *caïques*.

# Samos

A fertile, sultry landscape and some enthralling architectural feats have enabled Samos to build up a brisker tourist trade than any other northeastern island. Fortunately, the crowding of Samos is as irregular as the island itself. While Samos Town and Pythagorion have become overcrowded, much of the coast and the mountains remains unspoiled.

Samos figures significantly in ancient Greek culture. Once the wealthiest of the Aegean islands, it was home to many notable Greek architects, sculptors, poets, philosophers, and scientists, including Epicurus, the moral philosopher; Aesop, the author of fabulous fables; and Aristarchus, the astronomer who argued that the sun was the center of the universe before anyone had even heard the name Copernicus. The island's most beloved native son is the ancient philosopher Pythagoras, whose portrait has been adopted as the symbol of Samos.

**Ferries** run between Samos Town and Piraeus daily in summer (12 hr., 1930dr), stopping at Ikaria (600dr) and Paros. Regular ferries travel north to Chios (2 per week, 4 hr., 818dr), and south to Patmos (1 per week, 701dr) and the Dodecanese. Excursion boats run to Patmos (4 per week, 4000dr round-trip), departing from Pythagorion rather than Samos Town. Olympic Airways offers several daily **flights** to and from Athens (5290dr). There are also bi-weekly flights to Chios (3400dr), Lesvos (6480dr), and Mykonos (5460dr). The airport on Samos is located 4km out of Pythagorion.

**Bus** service on major routes around the island is sufficient, but is considerably reduced on Sundays and in off-season. The main terminal is in Samos Town, and fares range up to 230dr for Samos to Karlovassi. The best way to see the island, however, and the only way to get around the more mountainous and remote western end, is by **motorbike.** Standard rental fee is 1200dr per day in Samos Town, about 1000dr per day in Pythagorion, Karlovassi, and Kokkari. **Hitchhiking** is usually easy on the main roads. To hitch out of Samos, walk all the way around the waterfront (to your left facing the water), then head uphill past two or three hairpin turns. The main **taxi** stand is at Pythagoras Square in Samos Town.

## Samos Town

On the northeastern end of the island, Samos Town is among the northeast Aegean's more attractive ports, with wide white sidewalks, colorful fishing boats, and mountains silhouetted against the sky. The waterfront is a tangle of tourist shops and cafes, the street 1 block back holds mainly shops, and the lanes farther back are residential. Wander in the upper town area of stone steps and garden terraces to avoid the crowds and noise down below.

### Practical Information and Accommodations

When you get off the boat, hustle to **Samos Tours** (tel. 277 15), right at the end of the ferry dock. The office is well-staffed, and posted inside is a mine of information: a bus schedule, museum and bank hours, and usually a list of hotels all over the island. Check boat schedules here before inquiring in the many ferry company offices on the waterfront, who withhold information about their rivals' excursions. The only boat that the Samos Tours staff won't mention unless you ask them directly is the *Panormitis,* which goes to Patmos and points south. (Open Mon.-Sun. 7am-11pm, or until the last boat arrives.) Almost all travel agencies on the waterfront offer room-finding assistance. The **tourist office** (tel. 285 30 and 285 82) carefully hidden in a side street 1 block before Pythagoras Sq., is not especially helpful but at least dispenses maps. (Open July-Aug. daily 8:30am-10pm; in off-season Mon.-Fri. 7:30am-3:30pm.) The **post office** is 1 block up from the waterfront behind the Hotel Xenia; turn up at the large palm tree, and walk through the municipal gardens. (Open Mon.-Fri. 7:30am-4pm.) The **OTE** is to the right of the post office. (Open 24 hours.) To get to the **bus terminal** (tel. 272 62), follow the waterfront past Pythagoras Sq. and the BP station, turn left at the sign, and walk 1 block. You may be able to convince the bus company to give you their schedule; if not, it's posted here as well as at the tourist office and Samos Tours. Samos' **telephone code** is 0273; the **postal code** is 83100.

Accommodations in Samos generally bring on huge headaches; there are not nearly enough rooms to go around. However, the **Pension Ionia** (tel. 287 82) consists of four buildings full of cheap and fairly attractive rooms. Ask Mr. Zavitsanov for information about the island or ferry schedules if the travel agents confuse you. Turn up E. Stamatiadou St. at the Hotel Aiolis, and take the second left onto Manoli Kalomiri St. to #5. (Singles 1000dr. Doubles 1600dr.) Mr. Zavitsanov will put overflow beds into the garden if necessary, but when absolutely full, he'll find you a place somewhere else. The cheapest place to stay is **Mary's Rooms;** instead of turning onto Manoli Kalomiri, stay on E. Stamatiadou until you see the sign on your right. The bathroom smells and the surroundings are a bit cramped. (Bed in garden 500dr, with hot water 600dr. Doubles from 1200-2000dr.) Don't bother to bring your alarm clock—their gray parrot will wake you promptly at 7am. If all else fails, some sleep in Pythagoras Square. There's no beach to camp on within walking distance of town.

### Sights

The **Byzantine Museum,** behind the cathedral, 1 block back from the ferry pier, holds lovely eighteenth-century silver and jeweled bibles and a reliquary that allegedly holds a cast of St. George's footprint. (Open Mon., Wed., and Fri. 9am-1pm. Admission 25dr.) Finds from local digs have found their way to the recently reopened **archeological museum,** next to the post office. Nearby, the small but beautiful **municipal gardens** contain 200 varieties of flowers, cages with monkeys and birds, and a little cafe from which to observe it all. (Free.)

The old section of Samos Town, called **Vathi,** is 2km up the hill from the harbor; though slightly dilapidated, it makes for a pleasant stroll. The stone streets are too narrow for cars to pass through, but they do anyway. Three kilometers farther uphill, the little town of **Paleokastro** soothes the frazzled with cool, evening breezes, a great view of Samos Town, and the super *taverna* **Dilinia.** (Open daily 8pm-1am.) Walk to Vathi and continue on the road 2km until the signposted turn-off. The fort for which the village is named is in ruins.

A 15-minute walk to the north along the coastal road, **Plaz Gagou** is a good beach, but gets crowded in summer. A freshwater shower works here during the day.

# Pythagorion

You'll arrive at the former capital city of Samos if you've taken the boat from Patmos or any other of the Dodecanese. Pythagorion, more expensive and commercialized than Samos Town, is nonetheless quieter, and surrounded by the island's archeological sites.

Fourteen kilometers south of Samos Town, Pythagorion is served by frequent buses in summer (100dr), the last returning at 9pm; in off-season five buses run per day. The **bus station** is on the main street, perpendicular to the waterfront. The **tourist office** (tel. 610 22) is nearby. On the same street, you'll find a **bank** (open Mon.-Fri. 8:30am-1pm), and the **post office** (open Mon.-Fri. 7:30am-2:30pm). The **OTE** (open Mon.-Fri. 8am-1pm and 5-9pm) is on the waterfront to the right of the intersection with the main street (facing the water). The **tourist police** (tel. 611 00) are affiliated with the regular police. The language barrier is enfeebling, but they're very helpful with finding rooms. (Open in summer daily 7am-9pm.) At #6 on the main road leading into town, just opposite the turn-off for the tunnel, is the somewhat creaky pension run by **Aristotelous Nettos** (tel. 612 51); you'll have a hard time finding anything much cheaper. (Singles 1000dr. Doubles 1400dr.) There are beaches at both the east and west ends of town for **camping;** the one to the west is better and less crowded.

### Sights

The ancient city of Pythagorion, known for a while as Samos, thrived during the second half of the sixth century B.C.E., under the reign of Polykrates the Tyrant. According to Herodotus, Polykrates undertook the three most daring engineering projects in the Hellenic world, all in and around Pythagorion. The most impressive is the **Tunnel of Eupalinos,** 1½km up the hill to the north of town, which carried water from a natural spring straight around the mountain to the city below. It is about 1.3km long, and in remarkably good condition, though only about 50m is open for you to walk through. (Open Mon., Thurs., and Sat. 10am-12:40pm. Free.) Polykrates' second feat was the 40-meter deep **harbor mole** (rock pier) on which the modern pier now rests. Actually, this was the work of certain Lesvian slaves, prizes from one of the tyrant's earlier conquests.

Polykrates' magnum opus stood 5km west of Pythagorion, toward Ireon. The goddess Hera had been worshipped on Samos for seven centuries when Polykrates decided to enlarge her temple (530 B.C.E.) with a vengeance. Supported by 134 columns, the **Temple of Hera** is 118m long, and 58m wide, the largest temple ever built by these people, and considered one of the Seven Wonders of the Ancient World. It was damaged by fire in 525 B.C.E., but reconstruction was never completed, perhaps because in 522 B.C.E. Polykrates fell into the hands of his enemies, who dealt with him and his remains mercilessly. The ruins really are ruins; only one huge column remains. With the help of the map near the entrance (labeled in German), you can see how various incarnations of the temple were built on top of each other. The map may also help you sort out the maze of foundations, walls, columns, and altars. (Site open Mon.-Sat. 8:45am-3pm, Sun. 9:30am-2:30pm. Admission 100dr, students 50dr.)

There are three buses per day from Samos and Pythagorion to the site. An alternative is to stroll along the beach from Pythagorion; the Ireon is waterfront property with a back gate leading right on to the beach. If you can't get in the gate, continue along the beach past two houses where a path brings you inland to the main road and main entrance. This way runs close to the route of the ancient **Iera Odos** (Sacred Way) from Pythagorion to the temple.

On the south side of town is the **Castle of Lycurgus,** built during the beginning of the last century by Lycurgus, a native of Samos and a leader in the Greek War of Independence. The **Church of the Transfiguration,** built within the ruined walls, is an interesting pale blue variation on classical Orthodox architecture and interior decoration. Actually, this color is a typical feature of churches on Samos; their bright domes contrast strikingly with the brick-colored tiled roofs and stone walls surrounding them.

Blocks of column, wall, and entablature are strewn throughout Pythagorion like rubble, and the presentation in the small **archaeological museum** is no different. In fact, only a little over half of the collection fits into the building; the rest, including two fine *korai* (sculpted maidens) from the site at Ireon, sits in the square. (Open Mon. and Wed.-Sat. 7:45am-2pm, Sun. 8am-1pm. Free.) The one-room **paleontological museum,** inland at Mitilini, roughly mid-way between Samos Town and Pythagorion, contains animal fossils, some dated at 15 million years old. Mitilini is also the birthplace of Androniki and Helen Georgalas. (Open Mon.-Sat. 8:30am-1pm and 5:30-7:30pm. Admission 50dr.)

Just east of the site is a crowded but fun sandy **beach** behind the Asterias Restaurant—a good place to cool off after the trip to the ruins. Less crowded and prettier are **Psili Ammos** and **Poseidonion,** on the southern coast of the island. Directly across from the Turkish coast, these beaches afford a beautiful view of the Straits of Mykale. You can reach either by excursion bus (leave at 10am, return at 5pm, 400dr), by excursion boat from Pythagorion (6000dr), or by motorbike. Even more isolated are the beaches on the eastern end of the island, from **Korveli** north to **Mourtia.** These two villages can be reached by bike (there is no bus service); the beaches between them are accessible only on foot.

## Kokkari

Built on a peninsula 10km west of Samos Town, the village of Kokkari should be on your Samos itinerary. The white pebble beaches and clear waters that almost completely encompass the village. There are hourly buses per day to Kokkari from Samos Town (70dr). There is no bank, but tourist agencies and the food store just up the hill from the Vicky Hotel will exchange traveler's checks. In and around the square are a number of restaurants that are cheaper than those in Samos.

Unlike Samos and Pythagorion, Kokkari has an adequate supply of reasonably-priced rooms. The best place to look is on the little peninsula that juts out beyond and west of the square. Many houses on the peninsula have *dhomatia;* ask anyone for suggestions. Kokkari's police seem to take the many "Camping Prohibited" signs quite seriously, so try moving west along the coast until you find a sequestered spot.

## North Coast

The northern coast of Samos, particularly the stretch between Kokkari and Karlovassi, has a few deserted pebble beaches tucked away in little coves that are occasionally plagued by strong winds. Most of the coast is easily accessible from the road to Karlovassi, and the drive or the bus ride is well worth the trip for the scenery alone.

**Tsamadou Beach** is the first habitable cove, 2km west of Kokkari, but it gets quite crowded. There's a cafe at the top of the hill, and a fresh water tap. The cove just west of **Avlakia** is even more alluring, with a wide white beach. The only worthwhile sight in the area is the sixteenth-century monastery **Moni Vrontianis,** near the village of Vourliotes, 5km south of Avlakia. From here the coast continues relatively undisturbed.

At least 5km above the coast, several mountain villages perch securely in seclusion. If you choose to brave the climb uphill through surprisingly dense forests, you may find yourself a village's only visitor.

**Karlovassi,** Samos' western port, is an unattractive city full of huge hotels and empty modern buildings. But since the bus stops here, you might use it as a base for excursions to western Samos. The best place to stay is the multicolored unofficial **youth hostel** (tel. 328 72) behind the huge Panayia Church (500dr). The various "youth hostel," "pension," and "xenon pension" signs around town are all directing you to the same place. The **OTE** (open Mon.-Fri. 7:30am-10pm) and the **post office** (open Mon.-Fri. 8am-2pm) are near each other on Agios Nikolaos St., on the opposite side of the square from the hostel. If you head down toward the ocean (with the hostel on your left), you'll come to a popular beach at **Limani.**

## Western Samos

Western Samos remains unexplored by most tourists, which is fortunate for those willing to venture into the region. Speckled with tiny villages and manicured agricultural fields, this area is best covered by moped, though bus service from Karlovassi is adequate. Planted 500m above the Aegean, the village of **Platanos** has an exquisite view of both sides of the island. Mr. Menegas runs a cheap **restaurant** and **hotel** right on the main square (tel. 332 29; doubles 1100dr). Two buses per day connect Platanos with Karlovassi, but the last return is an early 11:30am.

A couple of kilometers west of the peaceful coastal hamlet of Ormos Marathokambou is the spacious beach at **Votsalakia;** another mile farther is an even better beach at **Psili Ammos.** Two buses per day serve these beaches from Karlovassi. From Psili Ammos, the unpaved road continues clockwise beneath **Mount Kerkis** (1440m), winding around the island's western end in a brutal passage rewarded by dramatic mountain views.

The road back to Pythagorion from the center of the island takes you through the quiet mountain villages of **Koutsi** and **Pyrgos.** There are rooms to let in these peaceful hamlets, but no bank or OTE. Ten kilometers after Pythagorion, the left fork in the road as you leave the village of Koumaradhi will take you 3km to the **Monastery of Megali Panayia.** The monastery is of little artistic or historical significance, but its idyllic setting on a thickly forested pine slope justifies a visit. With a little luck, one of the monks may invite you into the cloister for an *ouzo* or some of Samos' excellent local wine. (Open Mon.-Fri. 7am-1pm.)

### Near Samos: Ephesus, Turkey

Many people come to Samos simply to make the short hop over to the ruins of Ephesus on the Turkish coast. The archeological site is the most extensive and perhaps the most interesting remnant of ancient Hellenic civilization. Founded around 1100 B.C.E., Ephesus rapidly blossomed into the largest metropolis of Asia Minor. Most of what remains today dates from 300 to 400 C.E. (See also Ephesus in Turkey.)

Several ferries daily leave from Samos Town and three per week go from Pythagorion to Kuşadasi, Turkey. About half as many boats make the crossing in winter. From either port you must pay a steep fare fixed by the government (2000dr each way), not including a tour of Ephesus (1000dr). Remember to give the agent your passport the day before you intend to sail. You're also subject to a Turkish port tax of 1500dr or $10, payable in most currencies. If you stay overnight in Turkey and leave from Kuşadasi you'll have to pay the tax again ($14 total). There's a 10% student discount on the boat fare, but not on the port tax. Note that port taxes are charged only in Kuşadasi, Antalya, Izmir, and Istanbul, so if you're planning to spend time in other places in Turkey, it may be better to cross over somewhere else.

# Ikaria Ικαρία

Legend has it that Ikaria, 42 nautical miles west of Samos, is named after Icarus, the mythological character who escaped from Crete by taking flight with wings fashioned by his father Daedalus intoxicated with his newly acquired powers, Icarus imprudently soared too close to the sun. The waxen wings melted and he plummeted into the waters just off the coast of this then deserted island. Getting here has become considerably easier since Icarus' time; the island is on the main daily ferry line (in off-season 3 per week) from Piraeus to Samos via Paros. Ikaria is a three-hour excursion west from Samos Town (700dr) and a two-hour excursion from Karlovassi on Samos (600dr), or a nine-hour journey from Piraeus (1500dr). Boats from Samos and Piraeus alternate stops at the island's two ports, Evdilos, on the northern coast of the island, and the larger Agios Kirikos on the southern coast. Be sure to ask where each boat embarks and arrives. From Agios Kirikos, boats also voyage to Patmos (Mon. and Fri. at 9:15am, 1500dr) and to the islands of the Fourni Archipelago (see below). Appropriately enough, Ikaria has no airport.

In the past, Ikaria had been largely bypassed by tourists, but with its proximity to Samos, it is beginning to absorb some overflow. Still, the island is empty compared to its neighbors. Halved by a rocky, barren mountain chain running from east to west, Ikaria holds tenaciously to its verdant, sweet-smelling coastline. Most of Ikaria's roads are very beat up (as are the vehicles that have traversed them). The long, winding coastal road is passable for cars and durable mopeds; for the interior, a sturdy jeep is necessary.

## Orientation and Practical Information

**Agios Kirikos,** the island's main port, is composed of a cluster of small boats by the water, a cluster of small buildings nearby, and, just beyond the town, terraces surrounded by greenery climbing up the steep slope. It remains primarily a fishing village, although the startling incongruous and oversized metal sculpture of Icarus on the pier has scared more than fish away. In the main square around the harbor from the pier are the island's two **banks** (open Mon.-Thurs. 8am-2pm, Fri. 8am-1:30pm), several cafes, and assorted ferry offices. **Dolihi Tours** (tel. 223 46) sells all tickets and distributes necessary tourist information in English. (Open in summer daily 7am-1pm and 5-11pm; in off-season Mon.-Fri. 7am-1pm.) The **port police** (tel. 222 07) and **tourist police** (tel. 222 22) share the police building, on the right at the top of the steps to the left of Dolihi Tours. Though their English is limited, they can help with ferries and lodgings. If you walk 100m up the street to the right of the National Bank, you'll see the **post office** (open Mon.-Fri. 7:30am-2:30pm) and the **OTE** (open Mon.- Fri. 7:30am-3:10pm). Ikaria's **telephone code** is 0275.

Few rooms in town are fancy. You might climb northeast from the harbor to the **Hotel Akti,** a whitewashed building with green shutters and an orange sign on the roof. It may be difficult to spot; ask anyone. (Small, crude doubles 1500dr.) Agios Kirikos' only full-scale **restaurant,** visible as such from the huge sign, favors fish dishes (from 300dr; open from 9pm). Before dinner, the various *kafeneia* are the place to hang out in the twilight and watch the town elders play backgammon.

There are a few rock beaches just west of the ferry dock, but if you continue past the tourist police to the east of town, you can clamber down to some beautiful secluded coves with sandy beaches and crystal blue water. The easiest place to descend is just across from the cement silos, about 300m outside town, but continue on a path 100m farther along the road, just before a camouflage-painted shack. The paths to the coves are steep and full of small rocks, so wear sturdy shoes. A few hundred meters farther along the coastal road you'll come to the village of **Therma,** in a small hidden cove, which, of course, has several thermal springs bubbling from the rocks. Many elderly people who flock here believe that these radioactive waters cure rheumatism and arthritis. All **baths** are enclosed; the cheapest one, at the south end of the harbor, costs 75dr. (Open daily 5:30am-noon and 5-7pm.) In the gift shop up the main street, on your left across the dry creek bed, **Apostolos Manolaros** (tel. 224 33) and his English-speaking granddaughter run boat tours around the island, excursions to Patmos and Fourni, and a room-finding service.

Heading north from Agios Kirikos, the tiny road to Evdilos offers amazing views of the coast as it traverses florid hill country and snakes along sheer cliffs—the bus passes so close to the edge that the driver won't let you stand up. From the island's eastern heights you can see Samos, Patmos, and the Fourni Archipelago quite clearly, but you'll have to restrain yourself from taking pictures anywhere near the military bases (signs will warn you). On the way to Evdilos, the road passes a few tiny villages and a few equally tiny beaches. Escape the crowds by getting off at one of the dry river mouths visible from the road and accessible by footpaths. There are two just east and one just west of Karavostamon, all of which conceal fine, quiet beaches. **Buses** to Evdilos (400dr) are unpredictable, often leaving at 10am and noon; the 10am bus continues to Armenistis, returning at 3pm. **Taxis** from Agios

Kirikos to the Evdilos coast around 2000dr, easily affordable for a group of four or so. **Hitching** is feasible but slow.

**Evdilos** itself, the island's minor port town, won't hold you for long. Miniscule and withering, it still has a **post office** (open Mon.-Fri. 7:30am-2:30pm, with currency exchange), and **OTE** nearby (same hours), several restaurants, and rooms to let. Proprietors descend upon those stepping off the ferry from Piraeus. For peace and quiet, walk 500m west of town to reach beaches near Kampos.

The last bus stop (58km from Agios Kirikos), **Armenistis** shelters the best beaches on the island, with fine, white sand and clear water. Most people sleep on the beach, but rooms to let are plentiful and cheap (doubles around 1300dr). If the crowding at Armenistis is too much for you, escape to the mountain villages of **Christos Rachon** (from which you can climb further to the **Monastery of Evangelistrias**), **Frantato,** and **Dafni.**

To really get away from it all, take one of the small boats that run every morning from the main dock at Agios Kirikos to the **Faro Peninsula** on the eastern tip of the island, inaccessible by land. Boats allegedly leave at 7:30am (Sun. at 9:30am); in reality, they leave whenever the driver is in the mood. Pay equal attention to the driver's mood for the return trip or you may be stranded. The boat takes you to the little village of **Fanarion,** with a long, sandy beach not far away.

## Fourni Archipelago

Sandwiched between Ikaria and Samos, these small rocky islands beat both for solitude and austere isolation. Most of the island's population spends its day fishing, and once out of the villages you'll find rocky shores all to yourself. **Fourni,** the largest island, has only two villages, **Fourni Village** (also called Kampos), and the smaller **Chrisso Milia.** The two are mutually accessible only by boat, though the island's first road is currently under construction. Fourni Village has rooms and other travel services, but take care of the absolute necessities before coming to Fourni. One of the island's two sandy beaches is in town; the other is a half-hour walk south along a cliff path. Pirates once preyed on **Thymaina,** on Fourni's opposite end, but rest assured that your visits to this tiny port, its **Monastery of St. John** (open to the public), and its restaurants, should be undisturbed.

Fourni Village may be reached by **caïque** from Agios Kirikos in Ikaria; they leave four days per week at 7:30am, 1pm, and 5pm (200dr one-way). Return times are unpredictable; confirm all plans with the boat owner. Ferries from Karlovassi on Samos also venture here occassionally (2 per week, 500dr). Boats in Fourni might be available for travel within the Archipelago.

# DODECANESE
# Δωδεκάνησα

To lump the Dodecanese islands together for any reason other than their geographical proximity would be fallacious. No two are remotely alike in character or landscape. From the stony glance of the mountains of Kalymnos to the embracing hills of Tilos, from the cosmopolitan glitter of Kos and Rhodes to the mesmeric serenity of Lipsi, the vacation of your choice is in the Dodecanese.

The location of the Dodecanese, relatively far from mainland Greece and exceedingly close to Turkey (in many places less than 10km), induced a mottled history. In ancient times, the islands were influenced far more by developments in the cities of Asia Minor than by what transpired in Athens or Sparta. The region flourished through Roman times, but with the decline of the Byzantine Empire, its prosperity fell prey to a succession of foreign occupations. During the final years of the Empire and after its demise, various admirals and merchants from Italy, especially Genoa and Venice, gained control over some of the islands. But the essential force during this period were the Crusader Knights of the Order of St. John of Jerusalem, who after being evicted from Jerusalem, settled in the fourteenth and fifteenth centuries, defending their order and the islands by building tremendous fortresses in the name of Christianity. They managed to hold off the Turks until 1522, when Suleiman the Magnificent invaded. The inhabitants of the Dodecanese, mainly of Kalymnos and Patmos, formed secret schools to preserve their Greek culture and in the early nineteenth century, to organize the revolutionary movement. Still, they were not included in the new Greek nation for another 100 years.

In 1912, Italian forces fought the Turks around Libya, ousting them from the Dodecanese. Originally, the natives of these islands expected the new conquerors to be their Christian liberators; instead, the Italians attempted to force their Catholic culture and their language on the Greeks. Today, the most pervasive reminders of the Italian occupation are the public buildings that they erected in major towns and the archeological excavations and restorations which they conducted (the value of which has been hotly debated). When the Italians surrendered during World War II in 1943, the Germans took control of the Dodecanese, the only evidence of their short rule being the decimation of all Jewish communities, most notably in Kos and Rhodes. After the surrender of Germany in 1945 and the Allied takeover, the Greeks of the Dodecanese at last united with the rest of the Greek nation.

Today, every time even the slightest incident occurs in the shaky relationship between Greece and Turkey, the reverberations are felt in the Dodecanese. In 1988, there were rumors about charter flight travelers having problems making the crossing between the two countries; check your charter company's regulations to be sure no restrictions apply. On some islands, tourists cannot take a Turkish boat to Turkey. In any case, there is little trade or communication between Turkey and the Dodecanese.

Most of the Dodecanese islands (literally "12 islands") are arranged in a rough, curved line that follows the coast of Turkey, making it easy to hop from one to the next without backtracking or changing boats. The main island row, extending northwest from **Rhodes** to **Kos, Kalymnos, Leros,** and **Patmos,** is served during the summer by the *Omiros, Kamiros, Ialysos,* and *Olympia,* large ferries that run six times per week each way between Rhodes and Piraeus. The islands of **Karpathos, Halki, Symi, Tilos, Nissiros, Astipalea, Lipsi,** and **Kastelorizo** are a little more difficult to reach, served either by excursion boats from Kos to Nissiros, Rhodes to Halki and Symi, Patmos to Lipsi, and Leros to Lipsi, or by the *Papadiamandis* and *Nereus,* local Dodecanese ferries. These boats also connect the Dodecanese in the

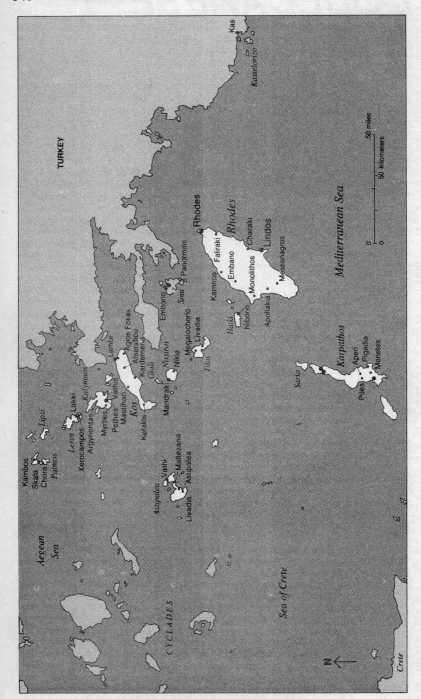

summer with the Cyclades, the northeast Aegean islands, and Crete. All schedules are extremely erratic: Do not base *any* firm plans upon them. The trip to Karpathos in particular is plagued by cancelations; the surrounding seas are the roughest in the Aegean, and very few boats run in the off-season. The GNTO offers *free* tickets from the larger to the smaller Dodecanese islands during April and May and September and October. Inquire at GNTO offices for details. A **hydrofoil** line serves the main island chain, but fares are at least twice the deck-class fares on conventional ferries. In addition, the vessels run only in summer and even then only in calm seas, and postponements and cancelations are to be expected in August. From Rhodes, you can sail south to Limassol in Cyprus and to the coast of the Middle East. Ferries also ply the waters to Turkey (from Kos to Bodrum, and from Rhodes to Marmaris); remember that restrictions may apply.

Kos, Rhodes, and Leros have airports, with daily **flights** from Athens and summer flights connecting with each other, Crete, and Mykonos and Santorini. European charters also fly to both Rhodes and Kos. There are smaller airports on Karpathos and Kassos, with connections to Athens and to large islands nearby. Student discounts of 25% on **Olympic Airways** flights with international connections sometimes make them reasonably competitive with ferry fares. (Discounts do not apply for flights continuing to Tel Aviv, Larnaca, or Istanbul.)

# *Rhodes (Rodos)* Ρόδος

A land of legend, Rhodes supposedly erupted from the depths of the sea in order to appease Helios after Zeus divided the earth among the other deities. With Rhodes as his territorial possession, Helios married the nymph Rhodon and named the island after her. Less dramatic, but probably more accurate, is the theory that the island's name stemmed from the word *rhodon,* meaning rose.

In either case, Rhodes has retained much of its mythical allure, despite its undisputed claim as tourist capital of the Dodecanese. The resort towns on Rhodes suffer the maladies of unbridled tourism. But outside these areas, most of the island is uncrowded and celestial: Endless expanses of sandy beach stretch along the east coast, jagged cliffs skirt the west coast, and green, mountainous landscape with secluded villages fills the interior. Moreover, Rhodes has three important archeological sites in Kamiros, Ialyssos, and Lindos, and representative examples of medieval architecture, especially in the city of Rhodes. If the number of deep-fried visitors grows, the island may reach saturation, but for now much of Rhodes remains seductively unscathed.

Rhodes is the easiest island to reach in the Dodecanese. Regular **ferries** connect it with Piraeus, Crete, the Cyclades, the northeast Aegean islands, Kavala, and the other Dodecanese islands. Boats bound for Rhodes leave at least six days per week from Piraeus, stopping at the major Dodecanese islands: Patmos, Leros, Kalymnos, and Kos. The trip takes about 20 hours (3000dr). The local carriers of the Dodecanese transport network—the *Papadiamandis,* the *Kyklades,* the *Nereus,* and the *Olympia*—serve Crete (2200dr), the smaller islands in the vicinity (1400-1600dr), the Northeast Aegean islands (2600-3300dr), Kavala (4700dr), and other islands in the Dodecanese (1300-2000dr). Connections with other island groups do not exist during the off-season and even during summer are subject to long delays due to the weather. Daily **hydrofoil** service connects Rhodes with Kos (2 hr., 5500dr), Patmos (2½ hr., 7200dr), and Symi (½hr., 2500dr). Excursion boats to Symi run daily (2 hr., 1600-2000dr round-trip), leaving around 9am and returning around 6pm.

In summer, domestic **flights** to Rhodes are usually booked solid at least two weeks in advance. Flights from Rhodes go to: Athens (at least 5 per day, 1 hr., day 8400dr, night 5600dr); Heraklion (daily, 40 min., 7100dr); Karpathos (at least 3 per day, ¾ hr., 4510dr); Kassos (6 per week, 50 min., 4420dr); Kastelorizo (3 per week, ¾ hr., 4420dr); Kos (daily, ½ hr., 4070dr); Mykonos (daily, 1 hr., 7270dr); Paros

(3 per week, 50 min., 8770dr); Sitia (4 per week, 55 min., 8770dr); Thessaloniki (4 per week, 1 hr., 20 min., 12,740dr); and Santorini (4 per week, 1 hr., 6170dr). Departures are less frequent in the off-season.

Rhodes is also a center for **international travel,** both by sea and air. Most flights to northern Europe are group charters, but you may be able to grab the odd empty seat at a very reasonable price—ask at any one of the big charter offices. Boats travel to: Limassol, Cyprus (4 per week, in summer Tues. and Fri., in off-season Fri. only, 24 hr., 7850dr); Haifa, Israel (13 per week, 36 hr., 10,750dr, ages under 26 9000dr); and Alexandria, Egypt (in summer Wed., 17,000dr, meals included). Students receive a 20% discount on international ferry trips (except to Turkey). Both Rhodes tourist offices will direct you to the appropriate agency.

Small boats leave Rhodes for **Marmaris** in Turkey every day except Sunday, though service is much reduced between October and April. **Triton Tours** (see Practical Information for the City of Rhodes) has all the information. A one-way ticket for the three-hour ride is 4000dr (round-trip 7000dr) and you must leave your passport at the office one day before departure. It is worthless if not impossible to return from Turkey on the same day (the boat leaves at 2pm, and returns from Marmaris at 9am). If you're traveling on a charter flight, be sure to check with the agency about making the visit, as you risk losing your return plane ticket if such transit is deemed illegal. If you have not yet purchased a return ticket, consult the appropriate consulate in Rhodes to confirm your flight status.

**Buses** serve the major coastal areas of the east and west quite extensively, but the farther from the city of Rhodes the fewer buses you'll find. **Hitching** is hit or miss. If you want to cover distance, rent a motorbike in the city of Rhodes or Fahraki. Expect to pay at least 1000dr for a moped and 1400-1600dr for a motorbike. Be sure to ask to see proof that the bike is covered by third-party insurance; less-than-scrupulous bike dealers are an unceasing problem. Don't hope to make the circuit of the island in one day; it's way too large. Also, be warned that roads in the south (especially the southwest, below Monolithos) are frustratingly bad. Allow several days at least.

# City of Rhodes Ρόδος

During the seventh century B.C.E., the island of Rhodes began to flourish as a major trading center, led by the prosperous cities of Ialyssos, Lindos, and Kamiros. In the final years of the Peloponnesian Wars, the three jointly undertook to found a fourth, the city of Rhodes, on the northern tip of the island. Determined to create both the most beautiful city in the world and a commercial port capable of handling large-volume trade, in 480 B.C.E. they enlisted the services of the renowned architect Ippodamus from Miletus on the coast of Asia Minor.

Always prudent, letting politics follow commercial interests, Rhodes flourished during the next centuries as a center of Hellenistic culture. The history of Rhodes is typically Greek and paradigmatically Dodecanese. Byzantine masters replaced Roman ones, and barbarians and Arabs raided incessantly. Italians, Crusaders, and Ottoman Turks ruled in succession. Throughout, the city has gained in importance relative to the other cities on the island, of which only Lindos has been continuously populated. Rhodes today shows traces of each period and reminders of each occupying power, but its contours are dominated by the legacy of the Knights of St. John, who transformed the city into a vast, impregnable bastion during their 213-year reign.

As you'll soon discover, Rhodes is more than an archetypal medieval city: It also provides for the tourists who make it a premier Mediterranean destination. Consequently, the new, western part of the city, the famous Sandy Port in particular, is full of luxury hotels. The main beach to the west of the city might be the most crowded in Greece, and during the summer the tourists are packed thigh to thigh. If you go to Rhodes to view historical sights, your visit to the city will be amply rewarded, but if you aim to find an isolated beach spot, you would do far better elsewhere on the island.

The *Rhodes Gazette,* a free monthly English newspaper (pick it up at the city tourist office) publishes a compendium of extremely useful information about the city. The best guide to the city's history and archeology is *Rhodos,* by Christos Karousos, late director of the National Museum. As few of the city's kiosks or bookstores carry it, ask at the library instead. Lawrence Durrell's *Reflections on a Marine Venus,* also available at the library, is spiced with anecdotes of the city's past.

## Orientation and Practical Information

The city is divided into two districts: the **New Town,** stretching to the north and west, and the **Old Town,** below it, encapsulated within the medieval fortress walls. Most boat traffic takes place on the **Mandraki,** the New Town's waterfront. Larger ferries dock on the harbor's eastern side, yachts and excursion boats on the western side (where the most important services are located). Ferries also sometimes use the **Commercial Harbor,** outside the Old Town, and **Acandia,** the harbor below it. Beaches are located north beyond Mandraki and along the city's western coast. **Rimini Square,** beneath the fortress turrets at the junction between Old and New Towns, encompasses the city's tourist office, both bus stations, and a taxi rank. To get here from the waterfront, walk to the base of the Mandraki and head 1 block inland on the New Town side. Around the corner on the Old Town side, **Symi Square** leads south to **Museum Square,** also the gateway to the Old Town. **Sokratous Street,** running east-west in the Old Town, will be the key to your search for accommodations. Expect to get lost in the deviously twisting alleys of the Old Town; locals will help if necessary.

**City of Rhodes Tourist Organization:** Rimini Sq. (tel. 359 45). Complete bus and boat handouts. Free map of city (detailed but microscopic). Provides information on lodgings to suit all budgets and will telephone to check for vacancies. Luggage storage 100dr per bag per day. Open Mon.-Sat. 8am-8pm, Sun. 9am-noon.

**Greek National Tourist Organization (GNTO):** At the corner of Makariou and Papagou St. (tel. 232 55 or 236 55), in the New Town. Walk up Papagou several blocks from Rimini Sq. Information a bit out-of-date. Open Mon.-Fri. 8am-2:30pm.

**Budget Travel: Triton Tours,** 25 Plastira St. (tel. 216 90). Handles Egypt Air, Malev (Hungarian), and Olympic Air, as well as hydrofoil, ferry, and excursion boats. Will give referrals to relevant boat agencies. Also offers trips to Marmaris, Turkey. Open Mon.-Fri. 9am-1:30pm and 5:30-8:30pm, Sat. 9am-1:30pm.

**American Express:** c/o **Rodos Tours,** on Ammohostou St. (tel. 210 10). Sells checks to cardholders and holds mail. Open in summer Mon.-Sat. 8:30am-9pm; off-season Mon.-Sat. 8:15am-1pm and 4:30-8:30pm.

**Consulates: The Voice of America,** just past Sgouru St. (tel. 247 31), southeast of the city. Equipped to handle consular matters, especially in an emergency. Open Mon.-Fri. 8am-4:30pm. A **British** Vice-Consul is available Mon.-Sat. 8am-2pm through Lloyd's Travel Bureau, 23, 25 Martiou St. (tel. 272 47). The **Turkish** Consulate, 10 Iroon Polytechniou St. (tel. 233 62), helps those having difficulty getting to Turkey.

**Currency Exchange: Ionian and Popular Bank,** Symi Sq. (tel. 274 34), in the Old Town. Open Mon.-Fri. 8am-2pm and 5:30-7:30pm, Sat. 8:30am-1pm. **National Bank of Greece,** Kyprou Sq. (tel. 270 31), in the New Town. Open Mon.-Thurs. 8am-2pm and 3:30-8:30pm, Fri. 8am-1:30pm and 2:30-8pm, Sat. 8am-1pm, Sun. 9am-noon. Many other banks in the New Town; few in the Old Town.

**Post Office: Main branch** on the *Mandraki* (tel. 222 12). Handles Poste Restante. Above the red express box, the "meeting point" bulletin board posts messages for friends. Open Mon.-Sat. 8am-8pm, Sun. 9am-6pm; Poste Restante window closes for a lengthy lunch hour. Also a **mobile branch** (on wheels), in the Old Town on Orfeos, near the Palace of the Grand Masters. From Museum Sq., head down Ipoton. Open same hours. **Postal Code:** 851 00.

**OTE:** 91 Amerikis St., at the corner of 25 Martiou St., in the New Town. Open Mon.-Sat. 6am-midnight, Sun. 6am-11:30pm. Also an Old Town branch just off Museum Sq. Open

Mon.-Fri. 7:30am-3pm. **Telephone Code:** 0241 for the entire northern half of the island. 0244 below Kolimbia on the east. 0246 below Kalavarda on the west.

**Airlines: Olympic Airways,** 9 Ierou Lohou St. (tel. 245 71), near the central OTE. Open Mon.-Sat. 7am-8:30pm, Sun. 7am-1:30pm. **British Airways,** Windsor Tours, 1 Kyprou Sq. (tel. 277 56). Open daily 8am-8pm. **KLM Airways,** 3 Ammohostou St. (tel. 210 10). Daily flights from London, Iraklion, Athens, Kos, and other islands (see Rhodes Introduction). The airport (tel. 929 81) is on the west coast, 17km from town, near the city of Paradisi; public buses run hourly (70dr), and Olympic Airways operates a shuttle bus for its passengers (120dr). Be sure to arrive at least 1 hr. before your scheduled departure.

**Buses: East** (to Lindos, Faliraki, Kallinkea, and Afandou) and **West** (to Paradisi, Monolithos, Kamiros, and Koskinou) stations on opposite sides of Papagou St., at Rimini Sq. Open daily 7am-8pm. Will be reorganized in 1989, so ask at the city tourist office or at the bus information kiosk just opposite. City buses leave from in front of the New Market. Free schedules at tourist offices.

**Motorbike Rental: Mantar,** 2 Dimosthenous St. (tel. 306 65), in Platia Evreon Martiron, in the Old Town. Sturdy bikes at good prices (1000dr and up). They also rent non-automated bikes (300dr per day). Also a number of shops in both Old and New Towns; most open daily 8am-9pm.**Gas stations** open Mon.-Sat. 7am-7pm. For **road problems,** dial 104.

**Bike Rental:** 12 Evdimidou St., in the Old Town. 300dr per day. Few roads in town are safe for cyclists.

**Taxis:** Rimini Sq. (tel. 298 61). Radio taxis also (tel. 276 66).

**International Library:** 7 Dragoumi St. (tel. 202 54), off Diakou in the New Town. English books on Rhodes' history and a few novels. Open Mon. and Wed. 9am-noon and 6-9pm, Fri. 9am-noon, Sat. 6-9pm. The **Municipal Cultural Centre,** Rodiaki Epavli-King's Garden (tel. 371 44), has an English section. Open Tues.-Fri. 7:30am-9pm, Sat.-Sun. 9:30am-2pm.

**Laundromat:** 32, 28th of October St., between Dragoumi and Fanouraki. Wash 300dr, dry 40dr for 20 min., soap 50dr. Bring plenty of 50dr and 20dr coins in case the owner isn't around. You can play Galaxy pinball while you wait. Open daily 7am-11pm.

**Public Toilets:** Strategic locations, including Rimini Sq. and, in the Old Town, Orfeos and Sokratous St. Surprisingly clean.

**Hospital:** Erithrou Stavrou St. (tel. 222 22), off El. Venizelou. Open for emergencies 24 hours. Visitors' clinic open daily 2-5pm.

**Medical Emergency:** Tel. 166.

**Police:** On Ethelondon Dodekanisson St. (tel. 232 94), 1 block behind the post office. The **tourist police,** (tel. 274 23), in the same building, can help with inquiries, visa extensions, lost and found, etc. Open 24 hours. The **port police** (tel. 276 95) are just to the left of the post office. Complete boat schedules.

**Police Emergency:** Tel. 100

## Accommodations and Food

Almost all of the town's inexpensive pensions are in the quiet and infinitely interesting Old Town. During high season, you're much more likely to find a place here within the ancient city walls, even if it's only a cot on a roof. If you don't like the tourist office's offerings, this is the place to begin looking.

**Steve Kefalas's Pension,** 60 Omirou St. (tel. 243 57). From Platia Evreon Martiron (the one with the sea-horse fountain), walk up Aristotelous, continue when it becomes Sokratous St., turn left onto Ag. Fanouriou St., then right onto Omirou. A friendly, international atmosphere in a pleasant garden. Steve speaks French, too. Cot on roof or in garden 400dr. Doubles and triples 800dr per person. Showers included. English breakfast 250dr.

**Pension Apollon,** 28c Omirou St. (tel. 320 03). See directions to Steve's; it's on a sidestreet (look for the sign). Similar to Steve's, but quieter. Outdoors 300dr. Singles 700dr. Doubles 1400dr. Breakfast 150dr.

**Dionisos Pension,** 75 Platanos St. (tel 220 35). Walk down the signposted alley between #73 and 75 Sokratous St. Another friendly mixture of young travelers. Open March-Sept. Roof

400dr. Doubles and triples 650dr per person, 600dr if you stay longer and bargain. Showers 100dr. Continental breakfast 130dr.

**Artemis Pissa,** 12 Dimosthenes St. (tel. 342 35). Fragrant garden, hot pink ceilings and bathroom. 500-700dr per person depending on the circumstances, 100dr less for a bed in the hallway.

**Pension Massari,** 42 Irodotou St. (tel. 224 69). Look for the sign off Omirou. Quiet courtyard, and more civilized than the rest. Also more expensive. Singles 1300dr. Doubles 1800dr. Triples 2500dr.

**Pension Dora,** 37 Aristofanous St. (tel. 245 23). From the intersection of Sokratous and Ag. Fanouriou, walk up Ag. Fanouriou; take a left on Thucididou, just before Zinonos St.; Thucididou is near Aristofanous St. For plant-lovers. Small, stuffy rooms. Singles 1400dr. Doubles 2000dr. Triples 2400dr.

Gastronomically, Rhodes seems to have been influenced by the Italian occupation of the island; many of the town's restaurants specialize in pasta dishes. Unfortunately, only a small fraction of the fish served in Rhodes' restaurants is fresh. A good one in the Old Town is the **Dodecanissus,** off Platia Evreon Martiron, with seafood by the kilogram. (Open daily noon-3pm and 6-12pm.) A number of family-owned restaurants in the Old Town serve well-prepared and inexpensive Greek fare. The **Rosa Lisa Taverna,** on Agiou Fanouriou St., gets going after 9pm with a Greek jukebox and a Greek audience. Or try the **Oasis** restaurant (tel. 342 53), off Agiou Fanouriou, in a peaceful courtyard. Right beside it (also reached by Omirou St.), the **Cafe-Bar Arcangelos** dishes out amazing yogurt with honey (150dr). (Usually open.) Also try Sokratous St. and the base of Pythagora St., but beware of places with a nefarious cover charge or minimum. If you're at all a spendthrift, **Cleo's,** at the intersection of Agiou Fanouriou and Thucididou, might fit the bill with *Tagliatella Rosa* (400dr), wild mushroom crepe (500dr), or an *avocado roquefort* (450 dr). (Open Tues.-Sun. 7:30pm-midnight. Cover 250dr.) For cheaper fare, try the **Three Star Pizzeria** (tel. 284 12), in Platia Evreon Martiron. (Pizzas with the works: small 400dr, large 700dr.) Near Rimini Sq., the **New Market,** although no longer frequented by locals, has cheap restaurants, *kafenia,* and *souvlaki* and vegetable stands for a wide range of eating options in a colorful atmosphere. The market is housed in a large white Moorish structure with an open courtyard and stands in the rectangle bounded by Gallis St., Averof St., Papagou St., and the waterfront. (Open daily 7am-evening.) Also in the New Town, **Paneri Health Foods,** on Fanouraki St. (tel. 358 77), off 28 Oktovriou, stocks healthy staples. (Open Mon.-Tues. and Thurs.-Fri. 8:30am-1:30pm and 5-9pm, Wed. and Sat. 8:30am-2pm.) For a little sinful indulgence, try the *gelato* concoctions at **La Dolce Italia,** on the corner of Papagou and Venizelou St. in the New Town. They have 38 flavors—try fig. (Cones 150dr. Open 11am-2am.)

## Sights

Nearly devoid of Hellenistic ruins, the ancient jewel of Rhodes can be seen best in the mind's eye. The Knights of St. John were voracious builders, and they replaced the Hellenistic structures (most of which had survived the 14 or 15 intervening centuries) with their own works. The Knights' control of the Old Town was complete, and the ancient remains that can still be seen are, with one exception, outside it. Several blocks west of the southern end of the Old Town off Diagoridon, a **stadium,** a small **theater,** and the **Temple of Apollo** have all been partially reconstructed on the hill near Monte Smith. The stadium and especially the theater look rather modern, but the temple is a ruin through and through. You can see the few standing columns from the boat as you arrive or depart from Rhodes; they're just before the last stretch of modern hotels. (Open 24 hours. Free.) The only other pre-Roman ruin, the third-century B.C.E. **Temple of Aphrodite,** is just inside the Old Town near Symi Sq. and is strikingly incongruous amid the traffic and medieval surroundings.

## The Castello

For the most part, the city belongs to the Knights. The Italians imitated them consciously, and even the numerous Turkish mosques bear an odd stylistic resemblance to their medieval architecture. The order reserved the northwest section of the Old Town to itself. The best place to begin exploring this quarter is at **Symi Square,** inside Liberty and Arsenal Gates, the main passages between the Old and the New Town and the waterfront, around the corner from Rimini Sq. To the right, as you face Aphrodite's temple (with your back to the arch), is the **Municipal Art Gallery,** with paintings by local artists. (Open Mon.-Tues. and Thurs.-Sat. 7:30am-2:30pm, Wed. 5-8pm. Admission 100dr, students 50dr.) Behind Aphrodite's Temple is the **Inn of Auvergne,** built in 1507, with a staircase attached to the facade in Aegean style. A jewelry store now uses the main entrance on the south side of the building; the carved doorway is a gem.

Walking past Symi Sq. you come upon **Argykastron Square,** with a relocated Byzantine fountain in the center. Set back on the right (west) of the square is the **Palace of Armeria,** built in the fourteenth century, now the **Archeological Institute.** The door and stairs leading down to the street on the left side of the building indicate where the old chapel stood. The whole structure looks more like a fortress than anything else, with small windows, embattlements, and heavy Gothic architecture. Connected to the palace is the Museum of Traditional Decorative Arts, which houses Dodecanese costumes, carved sea chests, and ceramic plates. (Open Mon.-Sat. 8am-2:15pm, Sun. 8am-1pm. Admission 200dr, students 100dr.) By passing through a low archway, you reach **Museum Square.** On the left is the Church of St. Mary (now closed), which the Turks transformed into the Enderoum Mosque, and beyond it the **Inn of the Tongue of England,** built in 1919—an exact copy of the original 1493 structure. Dominating the other side of the square is the former **Hospital of the Knights,** which now houses the **Archeological Museum.** A visit here is a necessary complement to touring the island, since it contains many of the sculpture and pottery finds from most digs. Don't miss the celebrated **Aphrodite of Rhodes,** one of the best examples of sculpture in the sensual rococo style so popular around 100 B.C.E. in the wealthy Hellenic cities. (Open Mon. and Wed.-Sat. 8:45am-5pm, Sun. 9:30am-5pm. Admission 300dr, students 150dr.)

From this end, the wide cobblestone street (Ipotou St.) that slopes uphill next to the museum looks much like some of the other, quieter streets in the Old Town. But don't be deceived: This is the historic **Avenue of the Knights,** the main street of the inner city 500 years ago, on which most of the Knights lived. The Order of the Knights of St. John of Jerusalem consisted of seven different religious orders called "languages" because each came from a different part of Europe. Each group except the Tongues of England and Auvergne had its own building, or "Inn," along this avenue: Provence, France, Italy, Germany, and Spain (later subdivided into Aragon and Castile). Each national sections was responsible for guarding one segment of the city wall; this is why parts of the wall are labeled "England" or "France" on the map. Though their order was officially dedicated to healing, the Knights were primarily warriors, and even these elegant residences look like fortresses. The Italians tastefully restored the street by removing the makeshift balconies and lattice windows of the last century, and now there are no signs of modern living here aside from an occasional car parked in the street.

Walking up the Avenue of the Knights from Museum Sq., you pass the **Inn of Italy,** the Palace of Villiers De L'Isle Adam, and the **Inn of France,** on your right. The last has the most interesting facade, with an off-center main doorway, half-framed second-story windows, and four gargoyles protruding between four turrets above. Almost directly opposite the Inn of France is an iron gate leading to an old Turkish garden and fountain. Continuing up the hill past Lahetos St., you pass the fifteenth-century **Church of St. Trinity** to the right, with its Gothic sculpture of the Virgin and Child at one corner underneath a stone canopy. Next to it stands the **house of the Chaplain of the Tongue of France.** Passing under an arch, on the right is the **Inn of Provence,** and to the left, the **Inn of Spain.**

At the top of the street is a second archway that leads to Kleovoulou Sq., and on the right, the prize possession of the city, the **Palace of the Knights of St. John** (also called the Palace of the Grand Masters). In times of war, this 300-room castle was an almost impregnable fortress, complete with moats, drawbridges, huge watch-towers, and colossal battlements. The structure survived the long Turkish siege of 1522, only to be devastated in 1856 by an explosion in an ammunition depot across the street. The Italians undertook the task of rebuilding it at the beginning of this century. Determined to outdo even the industrious Knights, they restored the citadel and embellished many of the floors with famous Hellenistic mosaics taken from the island of Kos.

The Italians had big plans for the palace: In the early part of this century, it was used as a seat of Italian government, where notables such as Victor Emmanuel III and Mussolini were entertained. The interior decoration was completed only a few months before the start of World War II, however, so the Italians had little chance to enjoy the full fruits of their megalomaniacal effort.

The monumental castle is as much an archeological museum as a fortress, since it contains one of the finest collections of Hellenistic and early Byzantine mosaics in Europe (mostly dating from the first through sixth centuries C.E.). To reach the chambers with the mosaics from Kos, take the grand staircase to the left of the entrance. Particularly noteworthy is the second-century B.C.E. mosaic of Medusa in a small room of its own. A copy of the statue Laocöon, a Rhodian masterpiece of the first century B.C.E. now in the Vatican Museum, graces another room. At the bottom of the staircase and to the right is the **Chapel of the Virgin Mary.** (Castle open Mon. and Wed.-Sat. 8am-7pm, Sun. 9am-6pm. Admission 300dr, students 150dr.) The medieval city exhibition, inside the palace, is only open from 12:30 until 2:30pm. Tours of the walls are given Monday and Saturday at 2:45pm, leaving from in front of the Palace of the Knights; arrive at least 15 minutes early, as the doors will be locked behind you promptly at 2:50pm. The tour costs 300dr (students 150dr), but it is your only access to the ramparts.

### The Chora

To get a sense of a different era in the city's history, turn right into Kleovoulou Sq. as you leave the palace. After passing under some arches, turn left onto Orfeos St., better known as the **Plane Tree Walk.** The large clock tower on the left marked the outer limits of the wall that separated the knights' quarters from the rest of the city. The idea was the same during the Ottoman Era, but the boundaries changed: The Old Town as a whole was reserved for Turks and Jews, and Greeks had to live outside its walls.

Just 1 block from the clock tower stands the **Mosque of Suleiman.** The original mosque on this site was built immediately after Suleiman the Magnificent captured Rhodes in 1522. The present one, an early nineteenth-century construction, has red-painted plaster walls, a garden, and a stone minaret that make it a good landmark in the Old Town and the best-kept symbol of a time Rhodians would like to forget. (Open unreliably 10am-12:30pm and 6-7:30pm. Services Fri. 5-6pm. Dress appropriately.) Across the street from the mosque is the **Turkish library,** built in 1794 and full of Persian and Arabic manuscripts, including Korans with extraordinarily intricate calligraphy, and a chronicle of the three-month-long siege of Rhodes in 1522. (Open unpredictably Mon.-Sat. 9am-1pm and 5-7pm. Free.)

The other Turkish buildings and monuments in the Old Town are in various states of decay. The **Mosque of Retjep Pasha,** near Omirou St. in the southeast part of the city, is only a ghost of what was once Rhodes' most splendid mosque. On the other hand, the old **Turkish baths,** at Platia Arionos, are a budget traveler's dream come true; a cultural experience with the opportunity to wash yourself in clean facilities with plenty of hot and cold water. To top things off, the price is low. As you walk into the building, ask for a bowl; you'll need this to splash yourself. The attendant will give you a locker key. Inside, you'll find the locker room and then the steamy bathing facilities including stone sinks with hot and cold faucets. Choose your sink, scrub away, and enjoy a luxury that 2500 years of civilization has hardly improved. To get to the baths from the Mosque of Suleiman, walk 1 block down Ippodamou St., then take the first left onto Arhelaou St. to Platia Arionos. (Open Mon.-Sat. 5am-7pm. Admission Mon.-Tues. and Thurs.-Fri. 150dr, Wed. and Sat. 50dr.)

Leading downhill from the Mosque of Suleiman is **Sokratous Street,** Rhodes' main shopping street. The excess of fur shops is due to duty-free imports to Rhodes. Behind the shops, tailors and artisans work in surroundings less chic than their Sokratous counterparts. Continuing east along Aristoteleous St. you'll reach **Platia Evreon Martiron** (Square of the Jewish Martyrs) in the heart of the old Jewish Quarter. Two thousand Jews were taken from this square in 1943 to Nazi concentration camps; only 50 survived. A little way down Dosiadou St. from the square is the **synagogue,** restored by the survivors after the war. Its congregation consists of seven families. To see inside the synagogue, contact Mr. Soviano, the caretaker, at 16 Iroon Polytechniou St. (tel. 273 44).

For a sample of Byzantine art, visit the **Church of St. Fanourios** across from the Paris Hotel on Agiou Fanouriou St. Used as a mosque during the Turkish period, it was restored in this century.

### The New Town and Mandraki

Mandraki Harbor's treasured possessions are the bronze deer (a stag and a doe) flanking the entrance to the harbor. Some say that the two pillars that support the statues occupy the original site of the "Colossus of Rhodes," a 32-meter statue of Helios (the sun god) that stood over the mouth of the harbor; boats allegedly passed between the statue's legs to enter. In any case, the statue was commissioned to celebrate a forgotten bit of Rhodian history: One of Alexander's heirs besieged Rhodes in order to force it to join an alliance against Egypt, a move conflicting with Rhodes' commercial interests. After one full year (305-304 B.C.E.), the island's resistance succeeded and the siege ended. The enormous commemorative statue took 12 years to build and was declared by the ancients to be one of the seven wonders of the world. It stood for only 60 years before it was toppled by a devastating earthquake in 226 B.C.E.

Set back from the deer are several examples of Italian architecture along the Mandraki waterfront. Massive Mussolini-inspired buildings of large, multicolored stone preside over wide Eleftherias St. The Bank of Greece, the town hall, the post office, and the National Theater are the more imposing structures on the far side of the street. Directly opposite, along the waterfront, is the majestic **Governor's Palace** and a cathedral built by the Italians in 1925. The cathedral is supposed to be a replica of the original St. John's Church near the Grand Palace, which was leveled in the explosion of 1856.

The Turkish presence can be seen a little to the north in the **Mosque of Mourad Reis,** named after Suleiman's admiral, who succeeded in capturing Rhodes from the Knights of St. John in 1522 but died in the process. The small, domed building to the right as you enter is his mausoleum.

Much older and seen on more postcards than the Italian and Turkish structures are the three **windmills** of Rhodes (no longer working), halfway along the harbor's long pier. The **Fortress of St. Nicholas,** at the end of the pier, was built in 1464 and guarded the harbor until the end of World War II. If you walk along the pier at Mandraki toward the windmills, you'll see many private yachts heading to Cyprus, Turkey, and elsewhere, looking for crew members: This is one cheap, if unpredictable, way to travel. Rhodes' **aquarium** is at the northern tip of the island. (Open daily 9am-9pm. Admission 150dr, students 75dr.)

## Entertainment

The **Folk Dance Theater,** well signposted on Andronikou St. (tel. 290 85) in the Old Town, stages performances during the summer which feature dances and songs from northern and central Greece, and, of course, the Dodecanese. Some of the dancers give instruction (in English) in the late afternoon. (Shows Sun.-Fri. at

9:15pm. Admission 1200dr, students 700dr, and well worth it.) Inquire at the tourist office about the classes.

The evening **Sound and Light Shows** given at the palace are popular with tourists. Conducted in four languages, they give an account of the Turkish siege of the city during the Crusader occupation. The entrance to the show is on Papagou St., across from the New Market. (English shows April-May 15 and Aug.-Oct. Mon.-Tues. and Thurs. at 8:15pm, Wed. and Fri.-Sun. at 9:15pm; May 16-July at 10:15pm. Admission 350dr, students 200dr.) **St. Francis Church** (tel. 236 05), at the intersection of Dimokratias and Filellinon St., has organ recitals Wednesday nights at 9pm. The **ancient theater** near Monte Smith is used only once or twice a month; check with the GNTO for details. The **National Theatre** (tel. 296 78), off the Mandraki, next to the town hall stages occasional winter productions. If you're starved for the silver screen, take in one of the "thrillers" with subtitles at the **Rodon**, near the National Theatre. (Shown daily at 8:30pm and 10:30pm, cost only 170dr.)

Rhodes has enough nightspots to satiate even the most restless bar-hopper. Variety is wanting, however; almost all of the bars, clubs, and discos play the same music and attract the same crowd. Some places charge a 1000-1200dr entrance fee with unlimited free (but often foul-tasting) drinks thereafter, others charge 500dr with only two free drinks. One major cluster of places is quite a distance from the Old Town, toward the beach to the west. To get there from the Old Town, take Voriou Ipirou St. from near Amboise Gate—the discos are just after the intersection with Kennedy St. A taxi back to the Old Town at night will run you 150dr. Near Diakou and Venizelou St. is another cluster of bars and clubs; the **1960s Bar,** 80 Diakou, is a fun place to hang out and hear mind-blowing music. (Imported bitter 180dr.) Heading up Papagou from Rimini Sq., the first of this group you'll come to is the popular **Player's Bar,** 2 Diakou (tel. 300 16), and then on the right the lively and feisty **Zig Zag Disco** (tel. 305 34), with entrance and two "free" drinks for 500dr. Across the way, the **Tropical Oasis** commands an entire garden, with a dip in the pool included in the expensive cover. To swim during the day (until 6pm), you must pay 150dr for a chair. (Beer 200dr.) Don't eat at the restaurant if you want to keep your budget afloat. Further down Diakou, the **Mistral Bar** and the **City Pub** attract their share of customers.

Hang out with the salt of the sea at **Popeye's** (spinach and tonic 100dr). There are several gay bars in Rhodes: **Bar Berlin,** 47 Orfanidou St. (tel 322 50), is in the farther cluster; **Valentino** (tel. 340 70) is on Sokratous St. in the Old Town.

Many people make an evening of **strolling** in the Old Town; the souvenir shops and clothing stores on Sokratous St. stay open until 10 or 11pm.

# Eastern Rhodes

**Excursion boats** trace the length of beach-filled coast from Rhodes to Lindos, leaving at various times in the morning and returning in the afternoon. Many make several stops, often including Faliraki. To pick your boat, take a stroll along the lower end of the Mandraki; most boats have their schedule and prices posted where they dock. (1000dr round-trip.) The **Rhodes Diving Center** (tel. 336 54) offers full-day diving excursions that stop at Kalithea. (May 1-Oct. 31, passengers 1250dr, snorklers 2250dr, certified divers 5000dr, inexperienced divers 6250dr.) Check the equipment before you're submerged, financially or otherwise.

As you drive out of the city, the landscape subsides slowly from city to country. Between the extremes **Rodini Park,** a forested area just 3km from the city and served by any bus heading east from Rhodes, is a forested area with streams, trails, a restaurant, and some animals left from the time when Rodini was a zoo. Ten kilometers south of town is **Kalithea,** site of a deserted spa and a pine park for freelance camping. Kalithea's thermal springs once bathed the bodies of leisure-class Europeans. Now, the decaying buildings evoke former indulgence. Pebble mosaic walkways guide the visitor past chipped pink columns, and the dry central bath's roof has cut-out stars still showing traces of blue. During the day, you can use the shower on the park's beach. For food you'll have to make do with the meager snack-bar at the spa's beach cove or go to the nearby town of Koskinou (2km inland), Faliraki, or the city of Rhodes. Buses run every half-hour from 8am until 11pm (70dr).

At the southern end of the park, a path leads down to the first of the wide, sandy beaches that extend along the southern coast. Five kilometers farther is the popular tourist resort of **Faliraki;** the excellent beach is jammed with tour groups, but if you hike north or south a bit, you should find a quieter spot. Opposite the bus stop, a small white building houses the **post office** and **currency exchange** office (open daily 7:30am-2:30pm), as well as a **first aid** station (open Mon.-Sat. 9am-5pm). The *Guns of Navarone* was filmed on the beach beyond the first hill south of town. There's an official **campsite** (tel. 855 16 and 853 58) off the main road ½ km before Faliraki; ask the bus driver to let you off. Facilities include TV, disco-bar, market, and swimming pool. (320dr per person.)

Eleven kilometers farther south, just before Kolimbia, a road to the right will take you to a partially dirt road 3km away, which brings you to **Epta Piges,** or Seven Springs. The nature walks in this area are ideal, but most people settle down at the inexpensive restaurant next to the main stream. All the tables are in the shade next to the rushing water, and the waiters hop from rock to rock. (Open 6am-7pm. Admission 100dr.) There's no direct bus service; ask any Lindos/Archangelos bus driver to let you off at the appropriate intersection. It's worth continuing inland past Epta Piges to the Byzantine **Church of Agios Nikolaos Fountoucli,** 3km past Eleousa. Built with a rare four-apse design, it has some fine thirteenth- and fifteenth-century frescoes. One bus daily ventures to Eleousa, leaving at 1:20pm and returning at 6:20am the next morning. That same bus winds its way through **Appollona,** a quiet but striking mountain village. An alternative is to take a moped; traffic is scarce, making hitching difficult.

A worthwhile distraction if you're on a moped or driving a car is the **Tsambikas Monastery,** a little Byzantine cloister sitting high on Mt. Tsambikas. A cement road on the left near the top of a hill (just before the Tsambikas beach turn-off 3km past Kolimbia) will take you three-quarters of the way there (if your motorbike has good low gears), but you'll have to walk the last kilometer or so. White stone walls enclose five small rooms and a chapel, and the views are great. If you have trouble deciding whether to go to **Kolimbia Beach** or **Tsambikas Beach** (both sandy and relatively uncrowded), the new perspective ought to help you choose. Any Lindos/Archangelos bus will do; get off at the turn-off and you're 3km from the beach. The town of **Archangelos** itself, 5km south of the turnoff, still bases part of its economy on the manufacture of leather peasant boots.

Ten kilometers farther down the road from Tsambikas (15km south from Lindos), take the turn-off to **Charaki,** where you can swim next to the hill with the crumbling **Castle of Feracios** perched at its top, built by the Knights of St. John. This beautiful spot, still unbeknownst to tour groups, seems destined for colonization. Among the circle of houses along the beach are quite a few rooms and several restaurants. Boats drop anchor near the half-stone, half-sand beach since there is no pier. At the end of the beach, a steep path leads up to the castle. (Free.) The Lindos bus will take you there.

## Lindos

Lindos has it all—a Crusader fortress, an ancient acropolis on a clifftop, and a well-protected cove with a sandy beach. Streets, doorsteps, and inner courtyards are all covered with delicate black-and-white pebble mosaics, and the rich brown doorways are intricately carved. Unfortunately, Lindos' magnetic qualities have drawn mobs of tourists, making the town the most expensive on the island. The schism in Lindos brought about by tourism is humorously epitomized in the film *High Season,* by the Monument to the Unknown Tourist.

During the day, streets are absolutely jam-packed, especially the one to the Acropolis. If you come in summer, arrive early in the morning or later in the afternoon when most of the tour buses have cleared out. In the off-season, things calm down immensely, and it won't be a problem finding lodgings at a fraction of the outrageous summer prices. **Buses** run hourly between Rhodes and Lindos, leaving the former from Rimini Sq. (1 hr., 300dr, last return to Rhodes at 6pm). **Excursion boats** from Rhodes depart around 10am and return around 6pm, sometimes stopping at other points on the coast (1000dr round-trip).

## Orientation and Practical Information

Lindos has one main avenue, **Acropolis Street,** leading from Eleftherias Sq. through the eastern part of town and up to the well sign-posted acropolis. The second main street, **Apostolous Pavlou,** runs perpendicularly to Acropolis St., westward from the Church of the Assumption Madonna, whose stone belfry rises up in the middle of town. Houses are indicated only by number, not street address. Numbers increase as you ascend Acropolis St. and as you move west away from it, whether you take Apostolous Pavlou St. or any of the smaller alleyways.

The **tourist office** (tel. 314 28), in Eleftherias Square, where the buses stop, helps with accommodations, has a currency exchange, and provides bus and boat information. Their useless glossy brochure about Lindos costs 100dr. (Open 9am-1pm and 5-8pm.) The **National Bank** is on Apostolous Pavlou. (Open Mon.-Thurs. 9am-2pm, Fri. 9am-1:30pm, Sat. 9am-1pm.) The **post office** (open Mon.-Fri. 7:30am-1pm), and **pharmacy** (open Mon.-Fri. 9:30am-2pm and 4:30-8pm, Sat. and Sun. 10am-1pm) are up the hill to the right of the donkey stand; follow the signs. Most of the town's other services are on or just off Acropolis St. The **OTE**, at #156, is up the stairs on the left behind Alexis Bar. (Open Mon.-Sat. 7:30am-3pm and 6-9pm.) The **laundromat**, at #456 on Vas. Pavlou St., does sheets, but if you are persuasive, they may allow you to use their machines to wash your clothes. Farther along at #381, Sheila Markiou, an American expatriate, runs a good **lending library** of English books (25dr per day with a 500dr deposit; used books 300dr). The **police** (tel. 312 23) are at #521. (Open Mon.-Fri. 8am-3pm; emergencies 24 hours.) The **telephone code** for Lindos is 0244.

## Accommodations, Camping, Food, and Entertainment

There are no hotels in Lindos (one reason why it's visually attractive), and most pensions and private homes will already be filled with British package tours. Free agents offer doubles for about 2000dr; singles are nonexistent. **Pension Lindos,** at #70, **Pension Elektra** (tel. 312 66), at #63, and the pension at #511 (tel. 312 69) offer doubles for 2000dr and triples for 2500dr. The last is probably the nicest, and the women sitting on the couch out front are as good a resource as any to locate a room; you'll most likely find them there in the evening. Otherwise pay a visit to #412, #498 (book at Olympic Travel), and #506 (tel. 312 20), which offer doubles for 2500dr or 3000dr (with bath), triples for 3400dr. **Pension Eftichia,** with grape trellises shading its courtyard, is at #323 off Apostolous Pavlou St. (Singles 1500dr, doubles 2500dr.) **St. George's campground** (tel. 442 03) is only about 10km south of Lindos, near Lardos; a free shuttle bus runs hourly to Lindos from the campground. Your cheapest option, though, is to camp on Lindos Beach, which has fresh-water showers.

Eating cheaply in Lindos poses a challenge: Restaurant prices range from expensive to exorbitant. The only moderate alternatives are the *souvlaki-pita* bars or grocery stores on the two main streets.

Lindos has a lively, loud nightlife. Most people visit the town's bars until the music is turned off at 11pm and then saunter down to the discos along the road on the other side of the main square leading to the beach. You may want to avoid the busier bars in town if you're not interested in drinking very much—the waiters keep asking you to order and occasionally ask you to leave if you don't. **Lindos By Night,** between the post office and the pharmacy, is least expensive (pints of beer 150dr). The **Cafe-Bar Poseidon,** just past the church at #173, is a small place with a less pressured atmosphere.

*Sights*

Lindos' main attraction, the ancient **acropolis,** stands scaffolded at the top of the sheer cliffs that rise 125m above the town, further enclosed in the impenetrable walls of a **Crusader fortress.** On the left as you enter the site are three cisterns with remarkable acoustic qualities—throw the tiniest pebble down, then listen. Across the courtyard, the relief of a second-century B.C.E. ship serves as an elegant frontispiece to the fortress. Up the stairs and to the left through a little storehouse of ancient rubble are the ruins of castle chambers and of the knights' basilica, built in the thirteenth century and dedicated to their patron saint. The nave and side aisles are still discernible. Thirteen restored columns of the imposing **Doric Stoa** (arcade) dominate this whole level. The arcade, built around 200 B.C.E. at the height of Rhodes' glory, originally consisted of 42 columns laid out in the shape of the Greek letter "$\pi$." The design heightens anticipation for what comes into view at the top of the steps—the **Temple of the Lindian Athena.**

According to myth, a house of worship has been on this spot since 1510 B.C.E., probably dedicated to some matriarchal goddess who demanded the sacrifice of fruit and vegetables rather than live animals. This custom persisted in Lindos long past the Dorian invasion. The remains you see are of a temple built originally by the tyrant Cleoboulos in the sixth century B.C.E., rebuilt and expanded two centuries later to its present dimensions. Surprisingly small, the temple was a tremendously important religious site in the Mediterranean. Now it is one of the few ancient Greek temples with inner walls intact and colonnades on both sides. A glance down over the medieval walls next to the temple reveals St. Paul's Bay. (Acropolis open Mon.-Sat. 8:45am-5:45pm, Sun. 9:30am-4:45pm. Admission 400dr, students 200dr.) If nothing else, visit the acropolis to catch views of the town and beach, the large quiet harbor with its long natural stone breakwater, and the dramatic coastline that extends in either direction. The donkey rides are a rip-off (300dr up, 250dr down); the walk is not very strenuous. If people tell you that it's a long haul up, they are talking about the circuitous route taken by the donkeys.

The graceful stone bell tower that rises up from the middle of the town belongs to the **Church of the Assumption Madonna,** rebuilt by the Knights of St. John around 1489. The interior is adorned with brightly colored eighteenth-century frescoes, which were retouched by the Italians in 1927. Try to get someone to let you in to see the burial chamber at the far end, which has some lovely icons. (Dress properly.) At the southwest foot of the acropolis are the remains of the **ancient theater,** across a parking lot from #433. Walk up Pavlou to Yiannis Bar, go around it on the right, and bear left until you come to the parking lot. On the way up to the acropolis, look west to see a **Hellenistic cave-tomb** from 200 B.C.E. on Mt. Krana. At #202, by a leftward turn of the steps, is an odd house with a 500-year-old wood ceiling where you can see the famous Lindian plates, antiques noted for their beauty and passed down for generations. On the northern side of the rock face of the acropolis, visible from the donkey path, is the **Voukopion,** a cave that the Dorians transformed into a sanctuary of Athena, believed to date back to about the ninth century B.C.E. The cave was supposedly used for special sacrifices that could be performed only outside the premises of the acropolis proper.

Lindos has one of the most crowded **beaches** on the island. Windsurfers can be rented for 550dr per hour or 2000dr per day with all the instruction you want or need. If you're willing to have an audience, you can take water-skiing lessons. (600dr for some instruction and about 10 min. in the water.)

# *Western Rhodes* Ανατολική Ρόδο

The 8-kilometer stretch of coastline to the west of Rhodes is a string of high-rise hotels along the equally long strip of sandy beach. The western end of this luxury hotel district is the town of **Trianda** (modern Ialyssos), not to be confused with the archeological site of ancient Ialyssos (Filerimos). **Filerimos,** 5km inland, was one of the three great cities on the island in ancient times (Lindos and Karmiros were the others). The ruins are rather meager: Most impressive is the fourth-century B.C.E. Doric fountain ornamented with four lion heads, to the right of the tree-lined staircase as you enter. More interesting are the adjacent **monastery** and the **Church of Our Lady of Filerimos,** which is actually four connecting chapels. Both the church and the monastery stand on the site of a third-century B.C.E. temple to Athena and Zeus Polias and a Byzantine church (converted to stables by the Turks), which was rebuilt once by the Italians and again in the 1950s. If you look carefully at the stone floor just inside the doorway of the room to the left, you'll see a remnant of the Byzantine structure: a fish (the symbol of Christ) carved into one of the red stones. Just to the right of the present church is a cross-shaped excavation revealing the baptismal font and part of a barely distinguishable aisle of the early church. The path leading past the chapel (on the right of the entrance) leads to the ruins of a **Byzantine castle** looking east, toward the city of Rhodes. Both the knights, and later the Turks, used the commanding vantage point from this hill to organize their respective attacks on the city. To the left of the entrance and staircase you'll find the pinkish roof of the underground **Chapel of St. George,** which is covered with fading fourteenth- and fifteenth-century frescoes. (Site open Mon.-Sat. 8:45am-5pm, Sun. 9:30am-4pm. Admission 200dr, students 100dr.)

Unfortunately, there is no easy way to get to Filerimos. Taxis from Rimini Sq. will make the round-trip for about 1200dr. Aside from a motorbike, the only other alternative is the bus from Rhodes to Trianda, which leaves every half-hour (70dr), but you'll have to take a taxi from there (about 800dr); you can also try (probably in vain) to hitch, or walk the clearly marked 5km uphill.

Sandy cliffs overlook the rugged coast south of Filerimos. Two religious festivals take place on the road to Kamiros. At **Kremasti,** 12km outside of Rhodes, *Panayia* (the name-day of the Virgin Mary) is celebrated for nine days beginning on August 14. Eighteen kilometers on the inland road at **Kalavarda,** the Monastery of Agios Soulas puts on an especially grand name-day festival for its patron saint on July 28 and 29. The **telephone code** in Kalavarda changes to 0246 for the southwest. In between, only tiny villages dot the sleepy coast. (There are some beaches, but they're mediocre.) One interesting excursion, often done as a daytrip, is **Petaloudes,** a valley about 25km from the city also known as the **Valley of the Butterflies** because of the brightly colored *lepidoptera* that flutter here between June and September. On off-days, however, you'll find more tourists here than butterflies. The crowds may threaten the pristine setting, but the park administration takes great care to protect the fragile nature of the attraction; the valley remains charming, with small waterfalls, pools, and wooden bridges. (Open daily until sunset. Admission 100dr, students 50dr.) One kilometer down the road is the eighteenth-century monastery of the **Panayia Kalopetra.** Buses leave from the city five times daily, with the last return bus at 2:30pm (40 min., 250dr). Petaloudes is accessible from the coastal road; 3km after Paradisi, take the turnoff to Kalamonas—it's 9km farther.

**Ancient Kamiros,** 35km from the city of Rhodes, was a prosperous city surrounded by good farmland in the sixth and fifth centuries B.C.E. The stone walls of the houses, the cobblestone main street, the reservoir cisterns, and the fallen pillars of temples and public places still remain. None of the individual ruins are particularly interesting, but taken together the site becomes a lifesize blueprint of a small ancient city. Down a small flight of steps and past the entrance to the site are the remnants of an ancient Doric temple on the right. Most of the ruins of private houses are on the left: Up the street before the hill, the seven standing, restored pillars belong to a Hellenistic house. A long stoa (over 200m) sits on the top of the hill, where the market used to be. Behind this third-century B.C.E. structure stands a temple to Athena. Two rows of stones, those farthest up on the hill, are all that remain. Archeologists believe that the two large reservoirs in front of the market supplied 300 families with water for six months. (Site open in summer Mon.-Sat. 8:45am-5pm, Sun. 9:30am-5pm; off-season Mon.-Sat. 8:45am-3pm, Sun. 9:30am-3pm.) Admission 200dr, students 100dr.) Five buses per day make the trip from Rhodes, the last returning at 7:35pm (40 min., 280dr).

Some 15km beyond Ancient Kamiros, the village of **Kamiros Skala** has a few houses, *tavernas,* and a boat launch. Boats leave here for Halki Monday, Wednesday, Saturday, and Sunday, at 2:45pm, returning the following morning at 7am; the boat leaves Kamiros Skala Thursday and Friday at 9am, returning at 4:30pm (1 hr., 500dr). For confirmation of this schedule, check with both tourist offices in Rhodes, or, better yet, get in touch with Lukas, the owner of the *taverna* on the pier. To get here, take the Monolithos bus (see below).

Beyond Kamiros Skala at Kritinia, there is a turn for **Embona,** a village famous for its dancing and traditional costumes and accessible by two buses per day from Rhodes (1½ hr., 290dr), leaving at 1:45pm and 2:35pm and returning at 6am and 7am the next morning. The Monolithos bus also passes through. Embona is a large group of low-lying houses above farmland and forests and below the barren, rocky slopes of Mt. Atavyros, the tallest mountain on the island (1215m). The town conducts a thriving tourist trade on summer evenings. Two restaurants offer traditional Greek dancing for tour groups from Rhodes. You don't need to join a group if you don't want to, however; **Bake's Cafe** (near the Church of the Holy Trinity in the southeast part of town) will give you dinner and the show for 700dr. On evenings when there is no dancing, the town, blissfully free of tourists, blossoms into an active Greek neighborhood, complete with a bumper car arena. Two pensions behind the pharmacy offer inexpensive accommodations: **Pension Panorama** (tel. 412 06) has spiffy rooms at 800dr per person, while the slightly shabbier **Pension Embona** (tel. 412 12) charges only 700dr per person. You will easily find empty rooms on non-dance evenings, but otherwise you may be shut out. If you stay, be aware that there is running water only from 5:30pm to 8:30pm. For the same scenery without the dancing, head 14km south to **Agios Isidoros,** another small village perched in the mountains. There are a few rooms to let.

South of Kamiros Skala, both coastal and mountain roads traverse high ridges, from which you can get beautiful views of Alimnia and Tragousa and the other small islands off the coast on the way to Monolithos. Near the quiet mountainside village of **Kritinia,** a small **castle** can be seen on the cliffs by the sea. It's quite a walk from town; an easier approach might be the signposted exit 1km out of Skala Kamiros. Fourteen kilometers further south, the inhabitants of **Siana** will be buzzing to sell you the delicious local specialty, honey (about 1000dr per kilo).

**Monolithos,** on the island's southwest tip, is little more than a collection of scattered houses. The **Castle of Monolithos,** 2km west, is well worth the trip. Though in ruins, the fortress still looks supreme at the summit of a rock pillar rising 160m (*monolithos* means "single rock"). You can walk around inside the castle and the small chapel of St. Panteleimon, but be careful of the steep drop while you are enjoying the views. (Open 24 hours. Free.) To get here, follow the only western road out of town. In town, you'll find few if any tourist conveniences, but the **Hotel Thomas** (tel. 612 91), several blocks from the center, has spotless if somewhat expensive rooms. (Singles 1500dr. Doubles 2000dr.) Despite its undistinguished name, the **"Restaurant-Bar Greek Food,"** at the top of the road, serves decent entrées and refreshers (Greek salad 150dr). One bus daily leaves Rhodes for Monolithos, passing through Embona and Agios Isidoros. (2½ hr., 420dr). On weekdays, the bus departs at 1:15pm and returns the next day at 6:15am; on Sundays a daytrip is possible.

# Southern Rhodes Νότια Ρόδο

The area south of Lindos in the east and Monolithos in the west could almost be considered a different island. This is farming and goatherding country, where yellow, grassy flatlands gradually slope into verdant hills covered with low-lying bushes. In the west, sand dunes buffer a long stretch of wave-battered beach, while in the east, numerous secluded coves dot the coastline. One bus per day runs down the east coast to the extreme south, stopping at Lardos, Asklipios, Lachania, Katavia, and finally Messanagros (2 hr., 540dr; leaves at 3pm, returns next day at

6:30am). With few exceptions you'll find prices here unaffected by the tourist invasion.

The beaches at **Lardos** (10km south of Lindos), **Kiotari** (18km), or **Katavia** (24km) complement the sleepiness of their respective towns. You can pitch a tent at **St. George's Campground,** (tel. 442 03), 1km outside of Lardos, where roughing it entitles you to currency exchange, international telephones, a market, bars and a free hourly shuttle bus to Lindos. (Camping 400dr per person.) **Genadi,** 22km south of **Lindos** has rooms to let near the beach. The road on the southeast is ideal for motorbikes; southwest routes are unpaved.

If isolation is your desire, take the dirt road (you may need a jeep) to the **lighthouse** at **Akro Prassonisi** at the absolute southern tip of the island. The couple who lives there rarely gets visitors in summer; during the winter they get none at all, as the sea covers the narrow stretch of land connecting the lighthouse to the island. Doubtlessly the picture opportunity you've waited for, however, is the rustic **Skiadhi Monastery,** situated halfway up a hill on a steep, alternate road between Apollakia and Messanagros. The views of the western coastline below stretch for kilometers. No monks live here, but on weekends, you'll find several happy Greek families picnicking and taking advantage of the free lodgings. The elderly caretaker will put you up, but you must bring bedding and food. Cooking facilities are out back. To get to the monastery from Apollakia, take the dirt road 4km in the direction of Katavia, then turn left onto the well-marked Skiadhi Monastery turn-off. Follow that dirt road past pumpkin patches and wheat fields for a few kilometers. These roads, although unpaved, are manageable even on an automatic motorbike. Hitching will prove difficult as there is little traffic. Apollakia has a few cheap pensions and restaurants. Occasionally a group of villagers will come here by car (sometimes even a bus) with a hired priest and hold services at midnight and in the early morning; accommodations may then be something of a problem.

# *Karpathos* Κάρπαθος

Karpathos is a refreshing change from the usual round of crowded island beaches and ruins. The isolation of this large (120km long) island, located halfway between Rhodes and Crete, guarantees its serenity and preserves traditional lifestyles, especially in the anachronistic northern town of Olymbos. Karpathos has fewer ferry connections, flights, and tourists than other Dodecanese islands. But those who get to Karpathos swear by the island's charms and pray that its secrets will be kept from the masses.

Unlike other Dodecanese islands, Karpathos hosted the Knights of St. John for only two years. During the 200-odd years that the others were controlled by the knights, Karpathos was under Venetian rule. Natives will recount the deeds of seven Karpathians who, during the Italian occupation of the island in 1944, set out in a small barge without compass or radio, bound for Egypt to alert the Allies. Their heroism rewarded, British battleships returned to the island, forced the Italians to leave, and provided for the famine-striken Karpathians. The recent history of Karpathos, like that of other dry, rocky islands, has been dominated by the flux of emigration. To an even greater degree than by tourism, the island's traditional patterns of life are threatened by the influence of Karpathians who visit the U.S. or Australia for extensive periods of time, only to return "Westernized." If you plan to spend any time on the island, the guidebook, *Karpathos,* written and published by Yvonne and Klaus von Bolzano, is worth the 500dr (available at Possi Travel or Hotel Romantika).

Three **ferries** connect Karpathos with Rhodes and Piraeus. The *Golden Vergina* passes through on Wednesday and Saturday afternoons en route to Rhodes (7 hr., 1239dr). Thursday and Sunday mornings, it returns bound for Kassos (1¾ hr., 424dr), Agios Nikolaos (7 hr., 1040dr), Santorini (13 hr., 1637dr), and Piraeus (22 hr., 3109dr). The *Nereas* makes many more stops, including Karpathos on Wednesday at 5am en route to Kassos, Sitia, and Agios Nikolaos. It returns to Karpathos

Wednesday at 9pm, and heads for Diafani (1½ hr., 204dr), Halki (4½ hr., 664dr), Rhodes (7 hr., 1239dr), Symi, several other Dodecanese and Cycladic islands, and Piraeus. Rough seas around Karpathos often put the boats behind schedule. There are daily **flights** from Karpathos to Athens (via Rhodes) and to Rhodes (35 min., 4510dr). Buses to the airport leave 90 minutes before departure from the Olympic Airways office (150dr). Karpathos' **telephone code** is 0245.

## Karpathos Town

Karpathos Town is the administrative and transportation center of the island. You'll find travel agencies and restaurants around the main *platia* of Ierou Polytechniou, along the waterfront, and up **Dimokratia Street,** which runs inland from the center of the harbor. Most of the town's other services are in the western half of town near **Platia 5 October.** You can get there by bearing left (inland) at the National Bank.

The **bus station** is 1 block up Dimokratia St. from the center of town. Buses run daily Monday through Saturday along four routes: four times to Aperi (15 min., 110dr), Volada (20 min., 120dr), Othos (45 min., 130dr), and Piles (1 hr., 155 dr); once to Menetes (1½ hr., 110dr) and Arkasa (1 hr., 155 dr); and twice to Amopi Beach (20 min., 110dr). Four days per week, a bus goes to Spoa and Mesochori (250dr). This sparse schedule, however, is unreliable. **Taxis** (tel. 227 05) service all of the island's villages, and with four or more passengers, are as cheap as the bus. (Karpathos to Aperi and Menetes 500dr, to Volada 600dr, Othos 700dr, Piles and Arkassa 900dr.) On the same street as the post office, **Gatoulis Motorbikes** (tel. 227 47) rents excellent tandems for 2000dr per day. (Open 7:30am-1pm and 5-10pm.)

**Karpathos Travel** (tel. 227 54 and 221 48), on Dimokratia St. between the bus station and the waterfront, has complete bus information and most boat schedules. They'll call for rooms, rent cars (20,000dr for 3 days, insurance and tax included), and **exchange currency.** (Open Mon.-Sat. 8am-1pm and 5-8pm, Sun. 8-11am and 5-8pm.) **Possi Travel** (tel. 222 35), around the corner on the waterfront, is equally competent and informative. (Open Mon.-Sat. 8am-1pm and 5-8:30pm, Sun. 9am-noon.) Both sell maps of the island for 200dr. The **National Bank** is across the street and to the left of Possi Travel. (Open Mon.-Thurs. 8am-2pm, Fri. 8am-1:30pm.)

The town's **police** (tel. 222 22; open 24 hours) and **tourist police** (tel. 222 18; open 9am-midnight) don't speak much English but will do what they can to help you. Turn right from Platia 5 October and walk 1 block; the police are in the corner building on the left. Next door is the **post office.** (Open Mon.-Fri. 8am-2pm, Sat.-Sun. 8am-1pm and 5-10pm.) The **OTE** (open Mon.-Fri. 7:30am-9pm), and the **Olympic Airways** office (tel. 221 50; open Mon.-Sat. 8am-2pm) are both in Platia 5 October. There are two **pharmacies.** (Open 8am-1pm and 5:30pm-8:30pm.) In an emergency, call the **hospital** (tel. 222 28). The **minimarket,** three stores down and across from the OTE, offers a limited selection of foreign newspapers. **John Pavlakos** (tel. 223 89), next to Possi Travel, has a small stock of writing supplies and guide books. (Open Mon.-Sat. 8:30am-1:30pm and 5:30pm-8:30pm.) Karpathos Town's **telephone code** is 0245.

For a place to stay, try the **Avra Hotel** (tel. 223 88), with small rooms and a small bath. (Singles 1200dr. Doubles 1800dr. Triples 2200dr.) From the waterfront, take the second right off Dimokratia St.—it's 1 block ahead on the right. The **Anesis Hotel** (tel. 221 00), 1 block past the OTE, is sufficient. (Singles 1200dr. Doubles 1700dr. Triples 2200dr.) There's also **Harry's Pension** (tel. 221 88), just up the hill and to the left from the Avra. (Open April-Dec. Singles 1300dr. Doubles 1800dr.) **Sofia** (tel. 221 54), reminiscent of a B&B, is reached by turning left (with your back to the water) at the bus stop intersection and walking south 200m. You can **camp** on the town beach to the north without problems.

Restaurants are scattered along the waterfront where Karpathians come for their nightly *volta* (stroll). Newer *tavernas* are opening up just north of town on Limiatis St., meeting the demand of beachgoers. **O Georgios Taverna** (tel. 223 33), below the National Bank on the waterfront, serves large portions at reasonable prices (lamb and potatoes 420dr, Greek salad 140dr). The cozy interior sports a nautical decor, not too tacky, except for the flashing lighthouse on the back wall. For a quick un-Karpathinian meal, head to **Burger Express** at the south end of the harbor. (Pancake breakfast 250dr. Open 8am-midnight.)

Nightlife centers around the waterfront's north end. Walk off your evening meal for 10 minutes along Limiadis St. to the English Pub **Dire Straits** (tel. 228 85), between the Romantika and Limiadis Hotels. A young English management serves beer (150dr), drinks (300-400dr), and sandwiches (100-150dr). A sure-fire thirst-quencher is their "Electic Lemonade" (350dr). (Open daily 1pm-3am. Happy hour 6-7pm and 9:30-1:30pm.)

## Southern Karpathos

The rest of southern Karpathos features green, gentle scenery. This is a place to visit for the landscape: All you'll see are empty stone farmhouses, tiny isolated chapels, and views over terraced hillsides to the sea. On August 6, the towns of Menetes, Aperi, and Othos hold lively church festivals.

On a branch of the road south out of Pigadia are **Menetes** and, on the west coast, **Arkasa.** The huge church of Menetes seems to flow upward out of the terraced houses below; its marble pillars are from the ruins of an early Christian basilica. Ask at **Manolis Kafeneion** (tel. 223 80) for a key to the miniscule **folk art museum.** (Free.) A few kilometers beyond Menetes, 600-700m along a dirt sideroad to the north, is the tiny, rarely-visited chapel of **Agios Mammas,** one of the island's gems, built by Syrian pirates in the thirteenth or fourteenth century. Through the miniature doorway you'll find the remains of some superb fourteenth-century frescoes. Look overhead at the Pantocrator in the dome. The most interesting part of Arkasa is the peninsula southwest of town with the remains of five parallel cyclopean walls. They are said to be 3000 years old and suggest that a massive Mycenaean fortress must have stood there. This beach town has several *dhomatia.* The best is on the nearby sandy beach of Agios Nikolaos: **Anna Diakomichali** (tel. 612 37) runs a small, clean pension and serves meals. (Doubles 1500dr. Triples 2200dr.) On the small beach cove, five minutes on foot from Anna's boarding house, campers will find cold showers for bathing.

The island's only other paved road leads north and then west out of Karpathos Town into lush hiking country. **Aperi** is the most important town historically; it became the island capital in medieval times when Arab raids forced the Karpathians to abandon the coastal town. Today it remains the island's bishopric. Karpathians returning from the U.S. have made Aperi their home and built extravagant houses. The vine-covered gazebo of **Eleftheria Cafe** (tel. 313 26) is on the right as you walk uphill from the bus stop. You can pluck figs from trees next to it or drink water from the fresh mountain stream that runs through the kitchen. **Mertonas** and **Katodio,** in the foothills of Mt. Kalolimni, both have gardens fed by the mountain's streams. You can hike to either one from Aperi, and in late July and August, pick grapes as you go. **Piles,** perhaps the prettiest town accessible by bus, has fruit for which anyone would commit original sin. (For bus information, see Karpathos Town.)

Two outstanding beaches are on the coast near Aperi. At **Ahata Beach,** a spring supplies bathers and campers. The *Karpathos* makes excursions twice per week (1600dr round-trip). At **Kyra Panayia,** you can stay at **Vassili's Taverna** (tel. 313 00; doubles 2000dr; breakfast included). The *Karpathos* stops at this quiet, secluded beach twice per week en route to and from Diafani.

Farther north on the coast, **Lefkos** is difficult to reach, but perfect for tuning out all distractions, except sun and sand. This fishing hamlet has a handful of rooms to let, two *tavernas,* and a very good beach. A 10-minute walk up the hill to the north is a large cave with pillars supporting its ceilings. An occasional bus reputedly goes to Lefkos and Mesochori, so ask. **Flisvos** (tel. 712 03), on the beach, has clean doubles with bath and balcony for 2200dr. Next door, **Vasilis** rents run-down doubles with cold showers for 1700dr. Ten minutes on foot from the cave, **Nikos**

**Pediaditis** (tel. 712 22) runs a small *taverna* and pension within a trellised terrace of geraniums and oleanders. (Doubles 2200dr.) **Michalis,** above the beach-front pensions, serves delicious fish meals at any time of day or night (½kg of fresh lobster 1500dr). The irrepressible Michalis will fill you in about Lefkos and even take you in his boat to **Sokastro,** a fortified island north of Frangolimionas Bay. The underground chambers and storeroom may date back to the tenth-century Byzantine Emperor Nikephorar Phokas.

**Amopi Beach,** 8km south of Karpathos Town toward the airport, has clean golden sand, and the most bodies of any beach on Karpathos—though hardly approaching the count on any beach on Rhodes. At **Amopi Beach Rooms** (tel. 227 23), in the farthest cove to the north, doubles go for 1500dr. Two **buses** per day travel to the beach from Karpathos Town (20 min., 60dr). Nude bathing is not allowed in the populous areas of Amopi, but for the ultimate in seclusion, stalk starkly the several kilometers of relatively unpopulated beach that stretch southward from below Amopi. Finally, if the fierce wind makes sandy Amopi uncomfortable, move one cove south to a pebbly beach to enjoy a cooling breeze.

## Northern Karpathos

The fact that no adequate roads connect the traditional north and commercial south of Karpathos not only shows what a physical obstacle Mt. Kalolimni is, but also demonstrates how slowly modernization has come to Karpathos. A track was completed in 1979, but it could hardly be called a road. Whatever development might have occurred in this beautiful, arid region was further slowed by a huge fire in the summer of 1983, that devastated most of the Aleppo Pine Forests between Spoa and Olymbos. Daily **excursion boats** from Karpathos Town are the most reliable and scenic means of transport. Karpathos and Possi Travel have tickets for the *Chrisovandalou* and the *Karpathos,* which sail to Diafani Tuesday and Friday through Sunday at 9am, returning at 5pm (2 hr. each way, 1500dr round-trip). When there is enough interest, the *Chrisovalandou* continues from Diafani to the island of **Saria,** north of Karpathos (from Diafani 1000dr round-trip), where you can visit **Palatia,** a deserted village halfway up the eastern coast with odd, cone-roofed houses built by Syrian pirates from the seventh to ninth centuries. Don't get stranded here—the island is deserted and has no fresh water. The *Nereas* stops at Diafani between Karpathos Town and the next island; a small fishing boat will pick you up since Diafani's harbor is too small to accommodate large ships. You can drive to Diafani, but it's not advisable to try cruising with a motorbike. The overland route is scenic enough, with distinctive and gorgeous vistas around each hairpin turn; you might even want to hitch. Start off early in the morning where the road begins to degenerate past Aperi; you'll probably get a ride within a few hours.

**Diafani** is dull, but it's a good base for exploring Olymbos at leisure, and an easy and well-marked half-hour walk north through a Pefka pine forest to **Vananda,** an excellent beach of flat stones with a water fountain and the **Minas Taverna** (tel. 512 88), which lets rooms (1000dr per person) and shaded pitches at a campsite (300dr per person). Vananda is suitable for nude bathing. In Diafani, the **Golden Beach Hotel** (tel. 512 15), at the center of the waterfront, has boat schedules and tickets, currency exchange, and a restaurant. (Doubles 1200dr.) The **Mayflower Hotel** (tel. 512 28), next door, has rooms for the same price and a restaurant serving standard fare (*mousaka* 300dr, Greek salad 140dr). One block back from the waterfront is the **Diafani Palace** (tel. 512 10), with doubles and one triple for 1500dr. Their restaurant is better than the waterfront ones, although it doesn't have the view. The **OTE,** a telephone with a meter, is in the house with the blue-and-green gate and the grape arbor on the street past the Golden Beach. There is no bank in Diafani, so bring all the *drachmae* you'll need for your stay. The **police station** (tel. 512 13) is in the center of town. (Open 24 hours.) There's a **post box** for which the postman rings twice per week.

**Olympos** exists in another time; "traditional" only begins to describe the lifestyle here. Ethnologists and linguists have known of it for years as a place that has preserved centuries-old customs, and the dialect has several phrases and words dating back to 1000 B.C.E. The women wear long-sleeved white shirts and flowered aprons every day, adding a dash of color to the gray windswept village. You can peek into windows and notice walls covered with decorative ceramic plates. On the west side of the village, overlooking the cliffs to the sea, are two functioning windmills, where the women of Olympos grind the flour for bread, which they bake in huge stone ovens built into the hillside. If you notice that the women here seem to be doing all the work, you're right. The men usually gather in the *kafenia* (coffeehouses) on weekend nights to play their traditional musical instruments, entertaining themselves and whomever happens to be in the village.

If you visit in July, August, or September, you may be able to watch one of the elaborate wedding ceremonies or religious feasts. **Panayia** (August 15) is, as in most parts of Greece, cause for a big celebration; more interesting still are the festivities of the feast of Agios Giannis of Vourgounda (August 29). The women spend the few days before and after the 29th decked out in embroidered skirts of green, red, and orange, and wear pounds of sparkling necklaces, earrings, and golden breastplates. The feast is also the occasion for a lot of traditional music, featuring the *bouzouki* and an odd local instrument that looks like a bagpipe. Unfortunately, it's not clear how much longer Olympos's rich traditions will last—emigration, recently installed electricity, the north-south road, and tourism cannot help but take their toll.

If you're willing to scramble over a few stone walls, you can visit the oldest chapel on Karpathos, **Agia Anna,** one of two adjacent stone chapels easily visible from the town above. The frescoes inside Agia Anna are "aniconic," geometric paintings of birds and fish from the thirteenth or fourteenth century.

**Pension Olympos** (tel. 512 52) is run by Anna and her husband, Nikos. (Singles 750dr. Doubles 1500dr. Triples 2000dr.) If you're lucky, Nikos will serenade you with his *bouzouki* as you eat in their small restaurant. **Artemis Pension, Hotel Astro,** and **Posidon Pension** (tel. 512 64), all have rooms (same prices), and each has a small restaurant and terrace overlooking the village. One of the few men whom you'll see working in Olympos is the cobbler **John Kanakis,** who crafts unique red and tan leather boots, standard footwear in the village. For budgetarians, however, the boots are expensive (30,000dr per pair). Down the street, **Prearis** also sells handcrafted boots and shiny black embroidered shoes at similar prices (sandals are reasonable at 2000dr). Beware of plastic, though; if you buy, make sure you get *dherma* (leather).

To travel between Olympos and Diafani, you can take a taxi (900-1000dr for 5 people) or the small bus that leaves Diafani daily at 8am, 10:30am (when the boat from Diafani arrives), and 7pm, and Olympos daily at 7:30am and 3pm or 4pm (20 min., 150dr). The dusty one-and-a-half-hour hike along a valley floor is another alternative, if you've got the time and energy.

The truly adventurous can hike to **Vourgounda** ("grasshoppers' field") on the northwest coast, three hours from Diafani. The landscape leads over huge boulders to a towering, rocky peninsula. The ancient site had a Dorian settlement which yielded the "Dorian Decree," an ancient doctor's diagnosis, now in the British Museum. Burial chambers are cut out of the rock face overlooking the water. The cave chapel of **Agios Giannis,** within the peninsula, draws pilgrims on donkeys and mules for the commemoration of the saint's beheading on August 28.

# Kassos Κάσος

Going to Kassos is a bit like going to the moon—or so it would seem. The environment appears inhospitable: Fierce winds stir the sea into a choppy froth, and pock-marked scratchy rocks contribute to the stark landscape. Moreover, Kassos is probably the least touristed island of the Dodecanese chain, so you probably will be the only foreigner there. But the island is not as intimidating as it appears. Most of the island's 1200 inhabitants are Greek-Americans who spend only summers on Kassos. Their English is naturally quite good, and because they get few visitors, they are especially welcoming. Kassos has several sandy beaches, two intriguing caves, and a few scant archeological sites. If you're tired of the huge masses in Rhodes and Kos, Kassos is about as quiet and isolated as you can get.

**Ferries** connect Kassos with Karpathos (2 hr., 430dr), Rhodes (9 hr., 1400dr), and Crete. They are scheduled to run three times per week, but bad weather occasionally makes it impossible for them to stop in Kassos. In the off-season (April-May and Sept.-Oct.), the ride from Rhodes is free (third class; for better tickets you will be charged the difference), subsidized by the Greek government to encourage tourism. By the summer of 1989, weekly boat excursions will be available from Karpathos to Kassos (2000dr). Inquire at Karpathos Travel.

Boats land at the port of **Phry** (pronounced FREE), the largest town on Kassos. Taking a plane is a much more reliable and convenient way to travel to and from Kassos. There are **flights** to Karpathos (2 per week, 15 min., 1190dr), Rhodes (6 per week, 40 min., 4510dr), and Sitia on Crete (2 per week, ½ hr., 3470dr). A taxi from Phry to the airport costs 200dr, but you can easily walk the ½km west.

Several small villages share the valley with Phry and **Emborio** (the neighboring port town). A bus connects all of these, departing from Phry every half-hour between 7:30am and 8pm (40dr). The bus stop is on Kriti St., off Platia Iroon Kasou (with the statue). For timetables and information about the island, go to **Kassos Maritime and Travel Agency**, Platia Iroon Kasou (tel. 413 23 or 414 95), right behind the church. (Open Mon.-Sat. 7:30am-1:30pm and 4:30-9:30pm, Sun. 9am-noon.) The **police station** is on the road to the airport (tel. 412 22; open 24 hours). The **post office** is off Platia Iroon Kasou. (Open Mon.-Fri. 7:30am-2:30pm.) Across the street you'll find the **Olympic Airways** office (tel. 415 55; open 7am-2pm). The **OTE** is several blocks inland.(Open Mon.-Fri. 7am-3pm.) The **hospital** (tel. 413 33) is on Kriti St., past the bus stop. (Open Mon.-Fri. 8am-2pm, 6-8pm.) There is a **National Bank** representative (tel. 412 34) in the supermarket attached to the travel agency, and an **Ionian Bank** (tel. 412 33) representative in the supermarket next to the police station. (Currency exchange Mon.-Fri. 8am-1pm, later if necessary.)

Kassos has two C-class hotels, the **Anagennisis**, on Platia Iroon Kasou (tel. 414 95), next to the travel agency, and the **Anesis** (tel. 413 32). Both are expensive. (Doubles 2000dr.) A few locals have rooms to let. Try **Elias Koutlakis** (tel. 413 63) or **Nikitas Vrettos** (tel. 413 83). Doubles at both places are 1500-1700dr. Sleeping on the town beach is feasible, but you'd do best to head for the hills or a remote cove.

When you get off the boat and look for somewhere to collapse after the rough journey, you will probably stumble right into the **Panorama Restaurant** (tel. 413 19) by the dock. Along with **Milos** (tel. 415 80), next to the travel agency and overlooking the sea, it is the most popular eating establishment in town. There are several smaller *tavernas* inland and in Emborio. Three **supermarkets** and a **bakery** sit one block inland from the travel agency.

Two caves lie within walking distance of Phry. The entrance to the cave of **Ellino Kamares**, 10 minutes from the village of Kathistres, is partially sealed by a Hellenic wall. Inside, you can climb on a few slimy stones also from the Hellenic period. On a footpath 1½km beyond Ellino Kamares, the cave of **Selai** lies in a more natural state with stalactites and stalagmites galore. Kassos also has several beaches. Closest to Phry is **Ammoudia**, completely deserted; unfortunately, garbage and black seaweed mar the fine sand. On the southern tip of the island is **Chochlakia**, while **Chramba** is on the northeast. When there is interest, the travel agency runs boat excursions to **Armathea**, an island off the northwest coast of Kassos (500dr).

**Agios Mammas Monastery** overlooks the southeastern coast. The hike takes one hour by foot, but you can get a head start by taking the bus to Poli. Legend has it that during Turkish times, several of the monasteries took vengeance on a Kassiot traitor, turning him and his three ships to stone. Supposedly, the three boulders you see from the monastery are the ships' remains. For the most part, Kassos' archeological offerings are meager and unexcavated. Besides the remains at Ellino Kamares, there is one site in Emborio behind the big church. You'll find a baptismal font there, as well as a few columns.

September 7 is a celebration of the Panayia on Kassos, and a party is held that evening at the church of **Panayia Ellerou** on the south coast. On June 7, the slaughter of 7000 Kassiots by the Turks in 1824 is commemorated in an all-night feast with free food and drink for all.

# Kastelorizo (Megisti) Καστελλόριζο

Geography has blessed Kastelorizo, a quiet and beautiful island 65 miles from Rhodes. As the easternmost island in the Aegean, it is so small and distant that it has long been ignored by tourists. And for good reason: It almost never appears on a map of Greece, and was not even counted when the Dodecanese were named. Although it is less than 3km from the Turkish coast, Kastelorizo has a distinctly Greek character and its traditional fishing and farming economy remains largely unadulterated.

Kastelorizo now has fewer than 300 inhabitants, but its population once soared above 20,000. Its past stretches back as far as the Bronze Age, and during the Persian Wars, the island was an ally of the Athenian Empire. After a brief period of independence, the island fell to the armies of Alexander the Great, passed through the hands of Ptolemy Lagos to the might of Rome, and was then incorporated into the Byzantine Empire. Then, in the Middle Ages, it was repeatedly sacked by Arab, Saracen, and Algerian pirates who ravaged the Mediterranean. A period of stability under the Knights of St. John ended in 1452 when Sultan Naim of Egypt stormed the island and carried the inhabitants off to Syria. In 1522, following the siege of Rhodes, Suleiman the Magnificent established a Turkish garrison here. Alternating periods of Turkish and Venetian rule lasted until 1821, when the island rebelled and earned itself 10 years of freedom, until it was bartered back to the Turks for Eurobea. After World War I, Kastelorizo fell into hands of the Italians until 1943.

The *Panormitis* travels from Rhodes to Kastelorizo twice per week, returning to Rhodes a few hours after arrival. The *Lougales* also runs from Rhodes to Kastelorizo, but very irregularly. The crossing takes around seven hours and is free, as the government is trying to encourage tourism on the island. Both ships drastically curtail service in off-season, running only once per week, if at all. **Zervos Agency,** (tel. 223 08), behind the Bank of Greece in Rhodes, and **Kydon Agency,** on E. Dodekanisson St. (tel. 230 00), have information. Kastelorizo's airport, offers weekly **flights** to and from Rhodes.

Finding cheap accommodations on Kastelorizo is not a problem, and one or more pension owners will probably greet you at the ferry dock. If not, you'll find a spot far more quickly by asking at the *kafenion* than by hunting about on your own, since many of the places with rooms to let lack signs. **Esodia's Pension,** on the left side of the harbor, offers simple but clean rooms. The **Vavada Pension** is immaculate, and more luxurious. Most pensions inflate their prices by 30% in August.

Kastelorizo is the place to eat seafood; with luck, you'll see piles of immense swordfish stacked on the harbor, or boys pounding squid or octopus on the cement to tenderize them. All of the restaurants along the wharf are inexpensive, but as the fare differs each night, it's best to ask what is available before you sit down. **P. Lazarakis,** in the center of the port, has particularly good *kalamari. Karpouzis,* at the south end of the harbor and just past the Tomb of the Unknown Soldier, is a lively bar frequented by the island's youth. The very friendly owner is an Australian émigré and will gladly tell you his family history, as well as anything you need to know about the island.

The **OTE, post office,** and **police** are all in the same building at the northern end of the harbor next to the steel tower. Hours vary, but someone is usually working Monday through Friday from 7:30am to 2:30pm.

In the evening, climb the stone steps to the mountains overlooking the town for an unforgettable view of the harbor. The fourteenth-century **castle** also merits a visit for its splendid view of the entire town and, to the north and east, the mountainous coastline of Turkey. Kastelorizo's one-room **museum** houses a few modest archeological finds and folk art objects. (Supposedly open 9am-12pm and 5-8pm, but its curator, Diakakias, is rarely there. You can usually track him down in one of the cafes that line the wharf, but the museum is not really worth it.)

If you have time, make the pleasant three-hour excursion to **Parasta's Cavern** (look for signs on the wharf). On the eastern coast of the island, the cavern can be entered through its nearly invisible opening at low tide in a small boat; the aquablue water inside the immense cave is stunning.

Despite Kastelorizo's proximity to Turkey, it's not easy to hop over there for a day. Greek boats are not allowed to go to the Turkish coast. Kaş is not an official port of entry into Turkey, so the trip is illegal. If the port police catch you there, you will be expelled from the country.

# Halki Χάλκη

Even during summer, there is a good chance that you will be one of just a handful of tourists here. The *Nereus* and the *Kyklades* both stop at Halki twice per week, once on the way to Rhodes (2 hr., 650dr) and the Cyclades, once on the way to Karpathos (5 hr., 1350dr), Kassos, and Crete. Boats from the city of Rhodes are free during April, May, September, and October. (Consult the GNTO.) A small boat also leaves Kamiros Skala on the island of Rhodes (see Western Rhodes for the schedule).

**Niborio** is a peaceful village, a group of box-shaped stone houses arranged in a semi-circle around the clear waters of the harbor. In its heyday, it was an active fishing and sponge-diving community with several thousand inhabitants. During most of the year, villagers still fish for a living, although the population is far smaller. Many of the locals have moved to Tarpon Springs, Florida to start an expatriate community. Evidence of the exodus can be seen in the number of uninhabited, run-down buildings squeezed below the concentrated orange roofs of freshly painted white houses.

Niborio has only a few *tavernas* and restaurants, a grocery store, a bakery, and a **post office** (open Mon.-Fri. 7:30-9am and 10am-2pm). There are no hotels, but some private homes rent rooms (singles 900dr, doubles and triples 600dr per person) along the waterfront, so you should have no problem finding accommodations. A 10-minute walk from the village, **Pandemos Beach** is a modest stretch of sand on the other side of the small hill that rises above the town. Follow the cobblestone street that starts behind the post office and snakes its way up through the village.

If you take the road up the hill towards the middle of the island, you will eventually reach **Chora** (4km from Niborio), a largely deserted village that thrived in the eighteenth and nineteenth centuries when the islanders were trying to avoid the frequent pirate raids. Those willing can climb to the **medieval castle** for a magnificent view of the entire southern coast. The ruins lie behind the fortress walls, and you can just make out a few wall paintings that have faded in the sun.

# Symi Σύμη

The island of Symi is a small, yet dramatic showpiece of the Dodecanese chain, with jagged peaks cutting the air like raw diamonds. The famous Panormitis Monastery rests secure and secluded at the island's southern end, while the historic port of Ghialos sits smugly near the northern tip. Monasteries were the only dwellings to grace the steep barren shores until the rapid commercial growth in the nineteenth century transformed the port at Ghialos. During this period, shipbuilding, sponge diving, fishing, and commercial trade flourished, while the Symians received concessions from the Sultans. Ships made in Symi still have a reputation for being yare—easily handled and quick.

At least five daily excursion boats visit Symi from Rhodes, leaving at 10am, spending several hours in Ghialos, sailing in mid-afternoon for the Panormitis Monastery, and returning to Rhodes around 6pm. (Round-trip 1500-2000dr; walk along the pier in Rhodes and bargain.) You can also buy passage for individual segments of the journey—i.e. Ghialos to Panormitis 500dr, Rhodes to Ghialos 800dr. A **hydrofoil** also runs from Symi to Rhodes (½ hr., 3900dr round-trip). The *Nereus* and the *Papadiamandis* also connect Symi with Rhodes, most of the Cyclades, and Crete. The *Nereus* stops here twice per week en route to Halki (5 hr., 680dr), Karpathos (8 hr., 1100dr), Kassos (11 hr.), Sitia (13 hr.), and Crete (18 hr., 2500 dr); it returns to Symi 36 hours later headed for Rhodes (1½ hr., 400dr), Kastelorizo (950dr), Tilos (550dr), Nissiros (690 dr), Kos (690dr), Kalymnos (870dr), Astipalea (1200dr), Amorgos (1450dr), Paros (1950dr), and Piraeus (36 hr., 2100dr). The *Papadiamandis* stops in Symi four times per week, twice headed for Tilos, Nissiros, Kos, Kalymnos, Leros, Lipsi, Patmos, and Samos, and twice again headed for Rhodes. The Greek government declared this port a historic site in 1971, and many Neoclassical houses date from the island's nineteenth-century glory. As you walk around town, you'll see many abandoned buildings that attest to the depletion of the island's population from 30,000, at the peak of its sponge-fishing industry, to 3000. Most inhabitants today are involved in the tourist industry. The waterfront is unbearably crowded when excursion boats arrive; escape the crush by heading to the beach or to the upper, older part of town. The evening is much more peacful, as the locals come out to sit in the *tavernas* and drink.

## *Practical Information, Accommodations, and Food*

As you disembark at Ghialos' clock tower (on the right side of town facing inland), the **post office** is 50m down the quay, up the stone stairs on the right. (Open Mon.-Fri. 7am-2pm.) Past the large main square and 1 block behind the Opera House Restaurant is the **OTE**, on the left as you face inland. (Open Mon.-Sat. 7:30am-3pm and 6-9pm, Sun. 8am-1pm.) Returning to the waterfront, **Symi Tours** (tel. 713 07) is just ahead on your right and sells boat tickets (except for the *Nereus*) and arranges excursions around the island (see below). (Open daily 8am-1pm and 6-8pm.) *Nereus* tickets are available at **Nikolaos Psychas' textile shop,** 1 block left of Symi Tours. The **National Bank** is next to Symi Tours and up one flight of stairs. (Open Mon.-Thurs. 8am-2pm and Fri. 8am-1:30pm.) Alternative **currency exchange** is in the small office several stores to the left of the clock. (Open daily 9am-2pm and 6-9pm.) Taxis congregate at **Oekonomou Square** on the waterfront about 200m beyond Symi Tours, and a van marked "The Symi Bus" leaves here every half hour for Pedi (50dr). Symi's **telephone code** is 0241.

The **Glafkos Hotel** (tel. 713 58), on the left side of the main square (facing inland), has an old-fashioned parlor. (Singles 1500dr. Doubles 2000dr. Triples 2500dr.) **Pension Agli** (tel. 713 92), off Oekonomou Sq., has small but tidy singles for 1000dr, doubles for 1500dr (negotiable if you're on the last boat of the day); kitchen facilities and bathrooms are included, but make sure they show you how to turn on the electric water pump. There are a few rooms to let around the village; ask at a cafe.

Waterfront restaurants are expensive, so the farther you walk from the ferry landing the better. Even if you don't eat there (it's on the expensive side, too), be sure to notice the plaque above **Les Katerinettes Restaurant** (tel. 716 17), 100m from the clock tower: This is the house where the Italians signed the agreement surrendering the Dodecanese to the Allied Powers on May 8, 1945. **Tarverna O Meraklis** (tel. 710 03), 1 block back from Symi Tours, is a cheaper, friendlier option (Excellent stuffed tomatoes 220dr. For the brave, 200 grams of boiled brains (*myala vrasta*) 250dr.) Two fine places for dinner are **George's Restaurant,** and **Restaurant Panaroma** (tel. 714 10), both at the top of the steps to the upper part of the village, on the left. You can sit on a veranda overlooking the harbor below. (Greek salad 180dr. *Kalamari* 350dr.) Up the hill near George's, the **Jean and Tonic Pub** has long drinks for a reasonable 150dr. (Open 7:30pm-1am.)

## Sights

You'll find few historical artifacts by the waterfront, so head uphill to **Chorio,** the section of town fortified against pirate raids. To get there, walk to Oekonomou Sq. and trudge up the 500-odd stairs, also known as *Kali Strata,* to the main road in Ghialos and Chorio. Follow the road at the top of the stairs and you'll see signs for the **museum,** which houses Classical items, Byzantine pieces, and island costumes and utensils. (Open Mon. and Wed.-Sat., 10am-2pm. Free.) From here, signs lead to the ruins of the old **castle.** You'll probably get lost in the maze of streets, but locals will gladly help. The ruins have a stunning view of both Pedi and Ghialos. From Chorio, several roads lead down the other side of the hill to the hamlet of *Pedi,* with a quiet, so-so beach and a fair number of rooms to let.

**Nos Beach,** a 10-minute walk from Ghialos (head north along the waterfront, past the shipyard), is very small, but is also the closest beach to the port, with a small *taverna*/disco next to it. If you're especially ambitious, you might continue on past Nos Beach about 45 minutes to **Emborio.** The beach there is not great, but the views along the way and the remnants of a Byzantine mosaic in a church courtyard 200m from the water make it a worthwhile walk. Symi's tiny coves shelter a few excellent beaches accessible only by boat (daily, 600dr) at **Agia Marina, Nanou,** and **Marathounda** on the eastern side of the island. Boats also go to **Sesklia Island** just south of Symi, small enough to walk around in a few hours, with several nice beaches (Fri., Sun., and Mon. round-trip 1500dr).

### Panormitis Monastery

At the center of a remarkable horseshoe-shaped harbor in the southern part of the island is the grand Monastery of the Archangel Michael the Panormitis, friend of travelers. The monastery was founded at the spot where a local woman chanced upon a miraculous icon of Michael. Although brought to Ghialos, the icon kept finding its way back to Panormitis. The palatial white buildings of the monastery, dominated by an elegant bell tower (built in 1905) in the center, have been a popular stopover for Dodecanese sailors in years past. Within the monastery complex are a restaurant and small foodstore, a small museum (100dr; open during tour-group visits), a library, and rooms to let. The monastery church is small, with an exceptional wooden altar screen. In addition to ecclesiastical vessels and vestments, the museum also displays a wax foot, several crocodiles, and a fleet of model ships. The guest rooms in the complex, which were actually once monks' cells, are inexpensive (500dr) and great for rest and contemplation. No reservations are necessary, but bring your own bedding. Most of the other overnight visitors will be vacationing Greek families. Dress modestly.

No regular buses run to the monastery, but tour buses from Ghialos run about four times per week (1 hr., 1000dr one-way). All excursion boats from Rhodes stop here (see above).

## Nissiros and Tilos

The culture of Nissiros and Tilos has not yet drowned beneath the wave of commercialization sweeping across the Dodecanese. Instead, the islands have witnessed the heavy emigration of three-quarters of their total population since the onset of lean economic times in post-World War II. (Nissirians have formed an enclave in Astoria, New York.) Because neither island has been inundated with tourists, residents remain receptive to those who do wash ashore. In the near future, it seems likely that these islands, too, like so many of their neighbors, will lose their purity. Until then, if you're hoping to gain a vivid impression of Greek culture beyond the usual tourist experience, or if you want to bask naked on a beautiful deserted beach, Nissiros and Tilos are well worth the visit.

# Nissiros

Local legend tells us that the volcanic island of Nissiros was a consequence of a fight between Poseidon and the giant, Polyvotis. Enraged, the sea god disengaged a chunk of Kos with his spear and threw it on top of Polyvotis, who has been stuck with it ever since. Every once in a while, the giant stirs everything up trying to free himself of his burdensome hat; his most successful attempt was in 1522, when the mountain blew up and the present crater was formed. The most recent, less violent, explosion was in 1888. Because the island is a volcano, there are no fresh springs. Locals wash their clothes in salt water and import fresh water from Kos. The island has witnessed the heavy emigration of three-quarters of its population since the onset of lean economic times after World War II. Nissirians have formed an enclave in the Astoria section of Queens, New York.

## Practical Information, Accommodations, and Food

The volcano Polyvotis looms large before excursion boats from Kos long before they put in at port. Perhaps this bewitching image explains why crowds of tourists visit during the day. Come nightfall, however, a traveler will find respite from strident sightseers in the peace and quiet of Nissiros. Most of the 1800 residents of the island live in the main port, **Mandraki,** which will charm you with its narrow whitewashed streets and alleys winding beneath the Monastery of Panayia Spiliana.

Nissiros' proximity to Kos makes it an easy daytrip. The *Nereas Express* has daily excursions from both Kos Town and Kardamena (2 hr., 600dr from Kos Town; 1 hr., 700dr from Kardamena). In April, May, October, and November, it goes one way for free. The *Nereus* stops in Nissiros Wednesday and Sunday on its way to Rhodes and Crete; on Friday, it stops in Nissiros going from Kos to Pireaus. The *Papadiamandis* travels to Samos (Mon., 16 hr., 950dr) via Kos (2 hr., 420dr) and other small islands; it also goes to Rhodes (Tues. night and Fri. morning, 7 hr., 760dr), and Kalymnos (Thurs. afternoon). Check with the **port police** for a current schedule (tel. 312 22); they're in the building in front of the ferry dock. (Open daily 7am-7pm.) The **post office** and **OTE** (both open Mon.-Fri. 7:30am-2:30pm) and the regular **police** (tel. 312 01; open 24 hours, but sometimes you must knock loudly and shout) are in the same building as the port police. The **Enetikon Tourist Office,** (tel. 314 65), a private agency near the port on the main road, organizes excursions and changes money. (Open daily 8am-2pm and 6-8pm.) Currency exchange and traveler's checks are also available at the small drugstore of **I. H. Diakomihalis,** who is also an agent of the National Bank of Greece (on the main street past the square; open daily 8:30am-1pm and 4:30-9:30pm). The hotels to the left of the quay also change cash. Nissiros' **telephone code** is 0242.

To the left of the quay in Mandraki, **The Three Brothers** (tel. 313 44) is a hotel/restaurant run by a friendly family with three sons and a dog named Tramp who return from America every summer. (All rooms have private baths and hot water. Singles 1500dr. Doubles 2000dr.) Across the street, the **Romantzo Hotel** (tel. 313 40) has clean rooms, though not as spacious as those at The Three Brothers. (Singles 1000dr. Doubles with 1 bed 1200dr, with 2 beds 1400dr.) The Romantzo also has the best deal in town for **motorbikes** (1000dr per day). Farther on is the fancier **Haritos Hotel** (tel. 313 41). (Singles 1600dr, doubles 2400dr. Private baths included.) To the right of the quay, the pensions in town are cheaper. Try **Pension Porfiris,** the first building on the right past the public bathrooms. The waves lap right under you window. (Singles 600dr. Doubles 1000dr.) In town, the butcher (the store with the bull) rents rooms for 700dr per person. Still farther, **Pension Anna** (tel. 312 36) has doubles for 1200dr (inquire at Restaurant Francis). Still farther, underneath the monastery on the water, **Pension H. Drotsia** lets singles for 1000dr, doubles for 1200dr. Ask to see several rooms.

Locals claim that Taverna Nissiros has the cheapest, most delicious food in town. Actually, two restaurants bear this name, but both serve good food. The first, across from the town beach, is also known as **Taverna Tasos** (tel. 313 86). The *mousaka* here is especially good. Just a bit farther is the second **Taverna Nissiros,** with the best stuffed tomatoes anywhere for 200dr. Their Greek salad is equally superb (180dr). Also highly recommended is **Restaurant Francis** (tel. 312 36); follow the sign to the left at the fork in town. Most dishes cost 250dr. (Ask here about rooms at Pension Anna.)

### Sights

After you pass the square with the town hall you'll come to the small **Museum of Historical and Popular Folk Art,** with pictures and folk objects from Nissiros. Unfortunately, nothing is explained in English. (Open Mon.-Sat. 10am-6pm, Sun. 10am-1pm. Free.) Across from the museum with an icon over the door is the 700-year-old **Church of St. John.** The present frescoes were done by Italians in the early twentieth century, but you'll see 700-year-old Greek wall paintings in the circular frames. The **Monastery of Panayia Spiliana,** at the far end of town from the quay, has a good view of the town, and to the left is the beautiful black pebble beach. In the monastery is the 1000-year-old famous chapel of Mary with its miracle-working icon. Notice the small gold and silver votive plates engraved with parts of the body—these were donated by people who wished to have specific ailments healed by the icon's power. This practice is pagan in origin; similar gifts were once presented to the god of healing, Asclepios. In the right corner of the chapel is an icon of St. Nicholas, the patron saint of sailors. Above the monastery is the castle and the 3½-meter-thick city walls built by the knights of St. John of Jerusalem. Every year from August 15-17, a huge festival features free food and entertainment.

The **volcano** is Nissiros' big draw. Buses leave from the port at around 11am, sometimes also 7pm (ask the police or Enetikon Travel) depending on when the daily excursion arrives from Kos (300dr round-trip). They take you to the edge of a crater in a valley, which you can walk down into and in which you may wander among small holes that spew hot sulfur—you'll probably leave smelling like a Pleistocene egg. If you rent a moped (1000dr per day at the Hotel Romantzo) to explore the rest of the island, you'll find that the roads are all quite good, except for the last 100m before the volcano. One and a half kilometers down the road from Mandraki is a white building containing the therapeutic spa of **Loutra.** (Open late June-Sept.) The highly sulfurous spring water here, brewed by volcanic activity, is supposed to cure any number of ailments. You can take a bath and spend the night for 600dr, or just stop by for a salubrious immersion (baths 100dr). Three kilometers from Mandraki is the small fishing village of **Pali.** The *taverna* on your left as you enter town lets doubles for 1000dr. The last *taverna* at the right edge of town (facing the water) lets doubles for 800dr. Go left at the turn-off for the volcano to reach the charming village of **Nikia,** perched on the rim of the great crater, with views of the sea and the fertile volcanic valley. There are a number of *tavernas* and a small church, and the **Monastery of Agios Theodoros** that sits on the inner ridge of the crater about 500m from the town. Right before Nikia, the turn-off to **Avlaki** leads down to a beautiful deserted beach with trees and cliffs surrounding the sea. During the summer, buses go to all the villages irregularly (ask at the police).

Easily accessible **beaches** extend along the shore past the Three Brothers at **Mira Mare,** and about 1km farther at the opposite side of the cove (visible from the quay). There is a secluded black rock beach at Chochlaki, just around the promontory where the monastery sits. Follow the shore through town past the monastery and clamber over the rocky, pungent donkey path (wear shoes) by the sea's edge. The surf can be quite rough here.

## Tilos

You have no choice but to relax in Tilos. At any given time, there will be a mere 500 residents and perhaps no more than 25 tourists on the island. The evening news is life in the fast lane. Yet the beaches are uncrowded; good walking trails and a few sights of interest can satisfy any whim you might have to feel purposeful.

Two **ferries** service Tilos. The *Nereus* passes through on its way to Rhodes (Sun. and Wed., 5 hr., 696dr) and Crete (Wed.); Friday afternoons it goes to Piraeus via

Kos (4 hr., 600dr). The *Papadiamandis* stops in Tilos on its journey from Rhodes to Samos; Wednesday and Friday it goes to Rhodes, Thursday afternoon to Kalymnos. For ferry information on Tilos, ask at the **Blue Sky Bar,** opposite the port where most boats dock. The only place to change money on the island is the **post office** in the main square; the **OTE** is in the same building. (Both open Mon.-Fri. 7:30am-2:30pm.) Tilos' **telephone code** is 0241; the **postal code** is 85002.

The proprietor of the Hotel Irini will probably accost you at the dock with her cards that advertise doubles for 2500dr, but there are better deals in town. **Pension Castello** (tel. 532 92) has clean singles for 800dr (every other place in town makes you pay the doubles price), doubles for 1200dr; follow the sign to 131 Castello St. Along the beach, **Spiros, Adam,** and **Stamatia** all have doubles with shower for 1000dr. Farther in town, **Kostas Stefanacis** lets doubles for 1000dr and has one single bed outside for 300dr. Louie at the **Seafood** restaurant rents doubles for 1200dr. **Hotel Levadia** (tel. 532 20), run by the old man in the store in the square, rents clean doubles with private bath for 1500dr. Camping along the long, white pebble beach is no problem, and you can use the public toilets on the road along the shore. Three restaurants and one dessert shop feed the hungry in town. **Taverna Vasilios,** closest to the harbor, is the cheapest and best with friendly management. (Open daily from 6pm.) Right on the beach, the **Restaurant Irini** is more reasonable than the hotel of the same name.

The knee-slapping joke of the island is its other town, **Megalochorio,** meaning big town. Located 8km north of Livadia, near the tip of the island, Megalochorio has about 30 houses and 150 inhabitants. **Niko** (tel. 532 04) rents flats and doubles with private shower for 1000dr. The one restaurant is open only in the evenings, so you'll have to fix other meals yourself. Megalochorio is dominated by the ruins of a Venetian castle on the rock high above the town. The story is a familiar one in the Dodecanese: Neolithic walls under the rims of a Classical temple, which was then used as a foundation for a church and as building material for the castle. The path ascending the rock begins in a fenced-off pasture to the east, so you'll have to scramble about 75m through thick weeds up the hillside above the town before you can join the path. The castle is worth the hike, if not for the ruins, for the view of the bays of Plaka to the north and Erestos to the west, and the fertile valley to the south. Six other castles are scattered throughout the island.

Eight kilometers farther (20km from Livadia) is the **Monastery of San Panteliona,** maintained by the friendly caretaker Yiannis. You can spend the night and eat here for free, but do make the appropriate donation—it's very difficult to get food and supplies up there. Every year from July 25-27, there is a huge festival at the monastery, the only time the island is crowded with tourists (all food and festivities free). Halfway between Megalochorio and Livadia is a paleontological site of giant wooly-mammoth bones.

Two kilometers from Megalochorio is **Erestos Beach—** wide and surrounded by mountains. There are never more than 10 people. Camp on the beach or stay in the rooms 100m back from the water at the **Tropicana Taverna** or **Nausika.** The Tropicana has (4) doubles with shower for 1200dr. If you're alone, though, they'll charge more. (Breakfast 110dr.) Nausika lets singles and doubles for 1000dr, triples for 1400dr. If you're camping, you can use the showers at either place for 50dr. There is a general store 20 minutes up the road in Megalochorio.

Tilos has no public transportation, and hitchhiking can be very slow. The best way to get around is to ask for a ride at the restaurant on the dock in Livadia, the Tropicana in Erestos, or from anyone in Megalochorio who appears to be leaving town. If you're on a truck taking a full load of travelers back to Livadia, you may be asked to pay a small fare (about 100dr). About halfway along on the road from Livadia to Megalochorio, just past the turn-off to the OTE installation, you can see the ruins of the abandoned city of **Mikrochorio** ("small town"), the hill to the left. As recently as 1950 there were 1000 people living there, but the inhabitants relocated to the more convenient site of Livadia.

# Kos Κως

Keeping an island like Kos a secret from travel agents is like hiding a truffle from a pig. This one-time island paradise is packed in July and August, and the once friendly islanders have become sullen and indifferent to the continuous influx of foreigners. If you are allergic to the tourist scene, go elsewhere and leave Kos for the off-season.

Kos is known as the home of Hippocrates, father of medical science, to whom is ascribed the 2400-year-old oath still taken by doctors. In ancient times, the island prospered as a major trading power and as the sacred site of Asclepios, the healing god. It reached its prime as a literary center under the Ptolemies and was the home of the poets Theocritus and Philetas. At that time, its population neared 160,000 (compared to today's 20,000). Several hundred years later, Kos served as an episcopal seat under Byzantine rule. Before and after the fall of the Byzantine Empire, pirates and naval forces from various nations repeatedly invaded the island. The Knights of St. John finally took the island over in 1315 and promptly transformed it into one of their invincible outposts. From then on, its history paralleled that of the other Dodecanese islands.

Daily **ferries** travel to Rhodes (at 4am, 4 hr., 1300dr) and Piraeus daily except Monday (at 4pm, 14 hr., 2400dr) via Kalymnos, Leros, and Patmos. The *Nereus* makes the trip to Rhodes twice per week, stopping at Nissiros, Tilos, and Symi. Every Thursday it heads to Piraeus via Kalymnos, Astipalea, Amorgos, and Paros; it returns to Kos on the following Tuesday and then heads to Karpathos, Kassos, and Crete. Every Monday, the **Papadiamandis** heads to Samos via all the northerly islands. Rhodes, Samos, and Patmos are also served regularly by **hydrofoil** (5000dr round-trip to Rhodes). Be advised that these cannot travel in even slightly choppy seas. Excursion boats make daytrips to: Kalymnos (1600dr); Pserimos (1000dr); Patmos (3000dr); Astipalea (2000dr); and Nissiros (1200dr; from Kardamena on the southern part of the island, 1000dr; from Kefalus 1800dr). You can usually purchase a one-way ticket for a little more than half the daytrip price. The *Nissiros Express* travels from Kos Town to Nissiros every Tuesday and Friday afternoon (2 hr., 450dr). It makes the shorter, but more expensive trip from Kardamena twice per day on Wednesday and Saturday, and once per day on Thursday and Sunday (1 hr., 550dr). A boat runs twice per day from Mastahari to Kalymnos (at 8am and 10pm, 1 hr., 250dr). The GNTO can give you a rundown on the boat schedule, but be sure to check with the boat agency, as schedules often change without notice. **Olympic Airways** has flights to: Athens (at least 3 per day, 6400dr); Leros (3 per week, 2130dr); and Rhodes (2 per day, 4070dr).

If you have not come to Greece on a charter flight, you can get to the Turkish port of Bodrum near the ancient site of Halicarnassus by Greek boat in the morning (3000dr one-way, 5000dr return) or by Turkish boat in the afternoon (about $20, depending on the boat; be sure to bargain). Tickets are available at almost every travel agency in town. It is usually necessary to leave your passport at the travel agency 24 hours before departure.

In Kos, the mode of transportation you choose will depend on your destination and the amount of time and energy you are willing to spend getting there. **Bicycles** (200-250dr per day) are the best way to see most of the island, but you'll probably have to walk up a fair number of steep hills if you're headed for the southern end of the island or one of the little villages in the mountains. A popular alternative is a **motorbike** (from 1000dr per day). Both can be rented around Kos Town. In summer, about four **buses** per day run between towns on the island (100-200dr, depending on where you go). They're convenient, but tend to get uncomfortably crowded. **Hitching** is viable if you're not in a hurry.

## Kos Town

In Kos Town, towers of Turkish mosques stand alongside grand Italian mansions and the massive walls of a Crusader fortress. Brilliantly colored flowers and date palms embellish the streets, squares, and ancient monuments. The town is an arche-ological repository of Archaic, Classical, Hellenistic, and Roman ruins. The extent of the architectural diversity results in a dappled but colorful scene, leading many to declare Kos Town the jewel of the Aegean. Unfortunately, it is also one of the most expensive. Package tour agents have made contracts with many of even the cheapest pensions, leaving slim pickings for independent travelers. As in Rhodes, most of the bronzed tourists remain in or near the main town. Even the most gregar-ious may tire of the hustle and bustle during the tourist season. Despite the crowds, the town is especially clean, and most of the junky souvenir and clothing stores are confined to the side streets.

## Orientation and Practical Information

As your boat pulls into the harbor of Kos Town, you will see the colossal walls of the Castle of the Knights of St. John. The tourist office and police are right on the waterfront street **Akti Kountouriotou.** Walking left from the harbor, you will come to the old town. **Finikon Street,** also called the **Avenue of Palms,** leads west to the beach that stretches along **Vasileos Georgiou.** One block left of the dolphin fountain (with your back to the water), inland from the harbor, **Megalou Alexan-drou Street** leads to **Paleologou Square** and the rest of the ruins of ancient Kos Town.

**Greek National Tourist Organization (GNTO):** On the waterfront at the corner of Vas. Pav-lou St. (tel. 287 24 or 244 60). Boat and bus schedules, and information on hotels and prices. If you stop by, they'll call and reserve a room for you—otherwise, they'll only give you phone numbers. Open April 15-Oct. 31 daily 7:30am-9pm; off-season Mon.-Fri. 7:30am-3pm.

**Currency Exchange:** Banks open in summer Mon.-Fri. 7:30am-3pm and 6-8pm, Sat. 9am-noon; off-season Mon.-Fri. 7:30am-3pm. If using a Visa card to get money, do it at the **Com-mercial Bank,** 25 Martiou St., before going to other islands—the only other Dodecanese is-land with a commercial bank is Rhodes. You can get money with a MasterCard at the **Na-tional Bank of Greece,** Riga Fereou St., near the tourist office. After banking hours, you can change money and cash traveler's checks at the **post office** and at most travel agencies along the waterfront. Agencies usually charge a 2% commission. Most open Mon.-Sat. 9am-1pm and 6-8pm.

**Post Office:** 4 blocks from the waterfront on Venizelou St., near Meropidos St. Open in sum-mer Mon.-Fri. 7:30am-8pm, Sat. 7:30am-3pm, Sun. 9am-2pm; off-season Mon.-Fri. 7:30am-3pm. **Postal Code:** 853 00.

**OTE:** Around the corner from the post office, at the corner of Meropidos and Xanthou St. Open in summer Mon.-Sat. 7:30am-midnight, Sun. 7:30am-10pm; off-season Mon.-Fri. 7:30am-midnight. **Telephone code:** 0242.

**Olympic Airways:** Pavlou St. (tel. 283 31), south of the market. Shuttle buses run from here to the airport 25km away near Antimachea (150dr). Another option is to take the Kardamena bus and walk 500 yards after the roundabout. Open daily 7:30am-7:30pm.

**Bus Station:** 26 Kleopatras St. (tel. 222 92), behind the Olympic office.

**Boat Agencies:** To the left (back to the water) of the GNTO, along the waterfront. Shop around—they'll rarely tell you about the competition.

**Laundromat:** 3 Themistokleus St. In the west end of town, a few blocks inland from the corner of Averof and Kountouriotou. Wash 350dr, dry 150dr. Get tokens from the grocery store 2 shops to the left.

**Public Toilets:** Along the Avenue of Palms, behind the fortress walls. Filthy. Ask at cafes instead.

**Hospital:** Hippocrates (Ippokratous) St. (tel. 223 00). There are several **pharmacies** down the street.

**Police:** Tel. 222 22. In the *Dimarchion* (Town Hall), next to the Plane Tree of Hippocrates, on Vas. Georgiou St. Some English spoken. Open 24 hours.

### Accommodations and Camping

During July and August, hotel and private room vacancies are almost nonexistent, so start your room search early. Many inexpensive places are on the right side of town (with your back to the water). If you're desperate, go to the GNTO for assistance; otherwise avoid their room service—they'll tell you only about the more expensive hotels. If your boat docks in the middle of the night (which it often does), camp out on the beach or in the little park along the Avenue of Palms on the western side of the city (turn left away from the town as you disembark). Just be prepared to wake with the early morning traffic.

**Pension Alexis,** 9 Irodotou and Omirou St. (tel. 287 98). Walk down Megalou Alexandrou St.—Irodotou is your first right. Friendly international ambience around the TV. The proprietor Alexis is eager and helpful, and he won't ever turn you away. You'll get a place on the patio (500dr) if need be. Doubles 2200dr. Triples 2700dr. Hot showers 24 hours. Drinks (try Alexis' secret concoction) and breakfast 200dr.

**Xenon Australia,** 39 Averof St. (tel. 236 50), behind the popular beach, in the north end of town. Clean and pleasant. Run by a friendly Aussie. Doubles 2000dr. Triples 2500dr (less Sept.-May). Breakfast included. In summer, make reservations about 3 weeks in advance.

**Pension Popi,** 37 Averof St. (tel. 234 75), next to Xenon Australia. Clean doubles 2500dr.

**Kalymnos Hotel,** 9 Riga Fereou St., just off the center of the waterfront (tel. 223 36). Dark halls, but prices extremely flexible; ask to see several rooms. Private bath and most rooms with balconies. Singles 1000-1500dr. Doubles 2000-2500dr. Triples 2800-3000dr.

**Hotel Dodecanissos,** 2 Alex. Ipsilantou St. (tel. 284 60), just around the corner from the Kalymnos. Clean and cheery. Singles 1000dr. Doubles 2000dr. Private bath extra.

**Kos Camping** (tel. 239 10 and 232 75), 2½ km out of town to the east (tel. 239 10). Inconvenient unless you've got a bike or motorbike, which they rent, or if you want to avoid Kos Town. June 15-Sept. 13 350dr per person, 200dr per tent; April-June 14 and Sept 14-30 300dr per person, 160dr per tent. Open April-Oct.

### Food

Despite the high price of accommodations, Kos is not lacking in reasonably-priced places to eat. Quality control, however, might be lacking. There is always *souvlaki-pita* for a mere 70dr. If you're fond of the waterfront, try **Romantica** (tel. 280 58), at the left end (with your back to the water) of the harbor (*kalamari* 300dr, Greek salad 150dr). Next door, **Limnos** (tel. 221 23) has more variety and is only a bit more expensive (spaghetti 170dr, *pastitsio* 250dr, *mousaka* 300dr). At the other end of town, **Hellas,** 7 Psaron St., is 2 blocks back from the dolphin fountain at the end of Irodotou St. (delicious *stifadho* 400dr, *pastitsio* 230dr). Cheaper and more authentic is **Stefanos' Café Ouzerie Torodon,** 11 Irodotou St., 1 block to the left (back to the water) from Hellas (fish filet 250dr, *dolmades* 200dr). On Averof St. to the north, a number of cafes offer better deals on breakfast than in the harbor area (eggs, bacon, potatoes, and coffee all for 150-200dr). There is a fruit and vegetable **market** in Eleftherias Sq. in the big yellow building with the bunches of grapes over the doors.

### Sights

If modern Kos seems to live very much in the present, it does so under the myopic eye of the past. You can hardly walk a block without coming upon some structure of historical interest. Most sites are readily accessible, either in or near town.

The **Castle of the Knights of St. John** was built in the fifteenth century and expanded during the sixteenth in response to Turkish raids; the elaborate double walls and inner moats of this Crusader fortress are remarkable architectural feats for their time. The Order of St. John on Kos was originally dedicated to nursing and healing. To keep business flowing, the knights spent more time engaged in warfare. Both building materials and design elements were borrowed (read stolen) from the ruins of the ancient acropolis on the same site, remnants of which are scattered throughout the castle grounds. The top of the ramparts affords a panoramic view of the harbor and the Turkish coast less than 10km across the Aegean. (The rows of columns in the distance on the Turkish coast are the remains of the ancient sanctuary of Halicarnassus.) Enter the castle by the stone bridge that traverses the Avenue of Palms, originally the site of the outer moat of the castle. (Open in summer Mon. and Wed.-Sat. 9am-3pm, Sun. 9:30am-2:30pm. Admission 200dr, students 100dr.)

Before you cross the bridge, between the Avenue of the Palms and the ruins of the agora, you'll see the **Plane Tree of Hippocrates,** allegedly the oldest tree in Europe. Named after the great physician of antiquity, Hippocrates reputedly taught his pupils and wrote many of his books under this tree's shade (highly apocryphal since Hippocrates lived over 2500 years ago and plane trees live only several hundred years, at most). Next to the tree is a spring that leads into an ancient sarcophagus used by the Turkish as a cistern for the nearby mosque. The area around the plane tree contains a bewildering array of architectural styles. In front of the tree, the Platanos Restaurant occupies one of the many fanciful mansions built during the Italian occupation of the island. Behind the tree, the monumental **Town Hall** is a grandiose example of Italian architecture. Currently housing the police, justice, and governmental offices, it was originally the Italian Governor's Palace, with a turreted, white clock tower and mosaic entrance. Wander inside to rest in the shade of the giant palm trees growing in the inner courtyard. Flanking the plane tree is the **Hadji Hassan Mosque,** made of multicolored stones and built in 1786. Other impressive Turkish structures are the **Defterdar Mosque** in Eleftherias Sq., now defiled by tourist shops, and the **Mausoleum of Hadji Pasha,** on the corner of Ippokratous and Mitropoleos St. A few blocks away, on Diakou St., is the abandoned **Synagogue of Kos,** used until 90% of the Jews of Kos were murdered by the Nazis during the two-year German occupation. For a sample of Byzantine architecture, visit the city's **Greek Orthodox Cathedral** located on the corner of Korai and Agios Nikolaou St.

The **archeological museum** (continue down Nafklirou alongside the ruins of the ancient agora to Eleftherias Sq.) exhibits the celebrated statue of Hippocrates found at the Odeon of Kos, and a first-rate collection of other Hellenistic sculpture. In the central courtyard is a magnificent second-century C.E. Roman mosaic depicting Hippocrates and a colleague welcoming the god Asclepios. (Open in summer Mon. and Wed.-Sat. 9am-3pm, Sun. 9:30am-2:30pm. Admission 200dr, students 100dr.)

The ruins of Kos Town are grouped into two large sites—one near the harbor and castle, the other several blocks southwest. If your archeological patience is limited, the latter site, with ruins dating from the third century C.E., will be more interesting and is the better place to begin. Two short stairways lead down into the site from Grigoriou St., which runs along the southern edge of town; any of the main roads intersect it about 1km from the sea. The site itself is bordered on two sides by two Roman roads—the **Cardo,** meaning "axis," which runs perpendicular to Grigoriou St., and the **Decumana,** meaning "broadest," which parallels Grigoriou and intersects Cardo to form a corner. At the end of Cardo is the ancient gymnasium, called *Xysto* after the athletes' walking place inside the gymnasium. Today, 17 of the original 81 columns still stand. To the right of the gymnasium is a swimming pool from the Roman period. Between the gymnasium and the Nymphaion is an early Christian basilica built on the ruins of a Roman bath. A large mosaic of the **Judgment of Paris** covers the floor of the domed bathhouse. At the end of the Decumana, the third-century C.E. **House of Europa** contains a striking mosaic floor depicting Zeus' abduction of a naked Europa; as the story goes, Zeus disguised himself in the form of a white bull and managed to seduce the Phoenician princess. Across Grigoriou St. from the intersection of the ancient roads are the ruins of the **Odeon,** a second-century C.E. Roman theater. Much of the original structure still stands; the rest has been reconstructed for occasional presentations of plays and concerts. (Open 24 hours. Free.)

Down Grigoriou to the left (facing the Odeon), near Pavlou, stands the **Casa Romana,** uncovered by an Italian archeologist in 1933. It turned out, however, that this third-century C.E. structure concealed the ruins of an even more impressive Hellenistic mansion, two centuries older. (The one piece of mosaic that survives from the earlier house is now in the town museum.) The room to the right of the entrance contains the laundry room with marble wash basins. Moving forward you see a pool with a mosaic depicting lions, leopards, and bears; a second pool displays a mosaic of Ippokebus, a mystical half-horse, half-fish figure, surrounded by befuddled lions and dolphins. To the right are the slaves' quarters, and on the left the dining room contains an exquisite marble floor. Continue to the left to reach the courtyard and the kitchen. (Open Mon.-Sat. 9am-3pm, Sun. 9:30am-2:30pm. Admission 200dr, students 100dr.) Across the street from the Casa Romana are the ruins of a **temple of Dionysus**.

The second vast field of ruins, near the waterfront, is usually referred to as the **agora**. The remains of a **temple of Aphrodite** are here, as well as a second-century **temple of Hercules** that contains a fragment of a mosaic floor (third century B.C.E.) that depicts Orpheus in the company of animals. In the corner of the site, near the mosque, are the remains of a fourth-century C.E. Roman **basilica**. A small Christian chapel still used by locals for private prayer has been incorporated into the ruins. (Agora open 24 hours. Free.)

The town of Kos has a very modest and narrow strip of **beach** running southeast of town and a much wider slice running north of town, but both are crowded and flanked by large hotels. If you go far enough to the west, you'll avoid most of the tourists and all of the hotels and restaurants. Eventually, you will reach the beach of **Lampi**, a sandy point at the northernmost tip of the island 3-4km from Kos. Several other good beaches are a little farther from Kos Town. Crowded **Tingaki** is 10km west of Kos. There are several pensions and various private rooms (doubles around 1500dr). After the crowd heads back to Kos in the late afternoon, you might be able to find a spot to camp. There are buses to and from Kos (Mon.-Sat. 5 per day, Sun. 4 per day, 15 min., 60dr), but they're likely to be jammed in July and August. Everyone heading out of Kos Town passes Tingaki, so hitching shouldn't be difficult if you don't have a bike.

In the other direction from Kos, **Agios Fokas** (8km) and **Thermi** (13km) are both accessible by a good road. Eleven buses run here daily (55dr; last return at 10:15pm). Cycling or hitching should be no problem. Thermi is the better of the two towns, with a cafe and, of course, a hot sulfur spring. The spring feeds into the sea, making swimming before and after summer possible in the immediate area; just remember to take a short dip in the colder water around the point, or the sulfur will leave you smelling like a vintage egg.

### Entertainment

The bar scene in Kos Town is concentrated in two areas: by the beach in the north, and near the agora on Nafkliron St. in the south. Across from the agora, **Pub White Corner** and **Pub Blue Corner**, 1 block apart, are popular. In the north end, **Mirage Pub** has a pleasant garden and serves a delicious special house cocktail. **Party at May**, on the corner of Kanari St. and Navarinou, serves all the drinks your liver can take for a 600-800dr cover charge. (Open 7:30pm-1am.) The **Pink Panther Disco Pub**, 50 Kanari St., plays loud popular music, but most people go to the two discos on the beach after imbibing at the bars. **Heaven Disco Club** (tel. 238 74), at Lampi Beach, and **Club Calva** (tel. 232 68), next door, both charge 500dr at the pearly gates and give you one free drink; they frequently sponsor live bands. Club Calva often hosts a Hawaii night with leis, and Lenny serves up exotic Lincoln's Inn-type tropical drinks. (Open Mon.-Sat. 9pm-3am, Sun. 9pm-4am.) You'll have no trouble finding the discos—just follow the crowds.

There are two movie theaters in Kos Town: The **Kendriko**, 8 Agios Nikolou St., and the **Orpheus**, in summer at 10 Vas. Georgiou St. (tel. 221 89); in off-season at 25th Martiou St. (tel. 229 50).

## Asclepion

Most visitors make a pilgrimage of sorts 4km west to the Asclepion, an ancient sanctuary dedicated to the god of healing and site of the world's first medical school.

In the fifth century B.C.E., Hippocrates opened up his school and encouraged the institution of a precise and systematic science of medicine. Combining early priestly techniques with his own, Hippocrates made Kos the foremost medical center in ancient Greece.

Most of the ruins at Asclepion actually date from the third century B.C.E. The complex was built on five different levels on a hill that affords a spectacular view of Kos Town and the Aegean. Adjoining the site is a forest of cypress and pine trees, held to be sacred in ancient times. No one was allowed to give birth or to die in this area, which may explain why the inhabitants of the district had a reputation for good health and low insurance premiums. Hippocrates himself is reputed to have lived until the age of 105.

To the left of the admission kiosk are the second-century C.E. **Roman baths.** Closest is the *natatio* (pool), then the *tepidarium,* a room of intermediate temperature, and finally the *caldarium,* or sweating room. As you enter the main building, walk through the waiting room and then into a large room with two bathing areas on either side. Farther on and to the right is a marble bath for children and another set of cold (*frigidarium*), medium, and hot rooms. Notice the pedestals that support the floor, under which steam was pumped from the stove behind the far wall.

The most interesting remains at Asclepion are contained in the three central terraced planes, called **andirons.** These are connected by a series of superbly crafted marble staircases. The first andiron is noted for the large complex of buildings that constituted the **School of Medicine.** A massive stone wall stands along the southern side of the andiron, decorated with a row of niches that originally housed statues of various deities from which curative waters poured forth. A figure of the god Pan (half goat, half human) is in place, covered with ivy, and water from a delicious 2500-year-old natural spring flows beneath his feet. To the right of the staircase, redone by the Italians in 1933, niches for baths contain sulfur water transported from Thermi; one contains a statue of Xenophon, Hippocrates' doctor. On the far side (closest to the admission stand), underground rooms housed patients suffering from venereal and other contagious diseases.

Walk up the 30 steps leading to the second andiron to find the best preserved and most interesting remains of the Asclepion; to the left front are the elegant, slender, white columns of the **Temple of Apollo** from the second century C.E., constructed on top of an earlier temple of Apollo. Notice the original roof with its gorgons and gulleys for rain water. Behind this is a semicircular area where doctors consulted with each other in the open air. To the right is the oldest structure of the site, the fourth-century B.C.E. **Minor Temple of Asclepios.** An altar stood in the center of the temple for offerings to the god, whose spirit was called on by nobility and laborers alike in the belief that it would free them of illness. The large stone square box in the temple holds a donation box and treasury.

Sixty steps further, you reach the third andiron and the remains of the sanctuary that supported the second-century B.C.E. Doric-style **Main Temple of Asclepios.** The structure was reputed to be of monumental dimensions, possessing 104 columns and measuring 34m by 18m wide. Traces can be seen of one of the Hellenistic porticos that surrounded the temple on three sides. To the left is a capital with a cross where a Byzantine church was located.

Asclepion is not served by public bus, so if you do not rent a bike or motorbike, you must hike or hitch. If you take a taxi, ask for an estimate beforehand, and make sure the driver turns the meter on—it should cost about 250dr. If you want to walk one way, remember that the return trip is downhill; from Kos, follow Grigoriou St. west out of town. (Site open in summer Mon.-Sat. 9am-5pm, Sun. 9am-3pm; off-season Mon.-Sat. 9am-3pm. Admission 250dr, students 150dr.)

On the way to Asclepion, you'll pass through the formerly Turkish village of **Platani.** About 1km on the Kos side of the village center you'll pass a **Jewish cemetery,** hidden in a pine grove on the left. The cemetery was in use from the seventeenth century through 1943, when the Jews of Kos were deported and murdered during the German occupation. Farther along the same side lies a **Muslim cemetery.** There is a small mosque 1 block left of the square.

# Central Kos

The traditional Kos lifestyle survives in the inland towns along the main road. The modern village of **Zipari** adjoins the ruins of the early **Christian Basilica of St. Paul,** 11km southeast of the main port. From there, a winding road slowly makes its way through the green foothills of the Dikeos Mountains to **Asfendiou,** consisting of five small settlements with a total population of around 1600. The first one, **Evangelistria,** is disappointing. The Greek army has posted some soldiers there and the main square imitates a big asphalt parking lot. A kilometer or two farther is **Zia,** which advertises a "Greek Wine Festival"—actually a newly created package deal for tour groups that come from Kos by bus. Everyone sits at long picnic tables and ends up dancing to Greek music by the end of the evening. You can buy a ticket for the entire evening—around 2500dr for transportation, dinner, and lots of wine—at a number of travel agencies in Kos Town. The other settlements are more traditional; **Lagoudi** is the most beautiful of the group. Actually, the best part of Asfendiou may be the spaces between settlements—you could hike for hours in the grand hilly woodlands and not meet anyone. Buses to Asfendiou-Zia depart Monday through Saturday at 7am and 1pm (130dr).

Continuing south from Lagoudi, the road soon narrows to a mule path as the hills become even less cultivated. Eight kilometers along you'll come to the ruins of old **Pyli:** well-preserved fourteenth-century frescoes in a Byzantine church built within the walls of a Byzantine castle. The thirsty hiker will notice the stream that crosses the road as it descends toward present-day Pyli. Pyli is easily accessible from the main road, about 4km past Zipari; there are also buses from Kos Town (Mon.-Sat. 4 per day, Sun. 2 per day, 90dr). All buses from Kos, except those to Tingaki, pass through Zipari, 6km down the hill from Evangelistria.

One kilometer before Antimachia on the main road, on the left, is the turn-off for the **Castle of Antimachia.** Yet another enterprise of the Knights of St. John, its isolation enhances its grandeur. The entrance is just left of the approaching road. Farther south on the island, on the way to the airport, is a rotary with turn-offs for Mastihari (north) and Kardamena (south), the two resorts of central Kos. Both offer good beaches, streets with few cars, and places to eat good, fresh food, but the similarities end there. In **Mastihari,** several pensions and rooms are available (singles around 1000dr, doubles 1500dr, flats 2500dr). Try **George Mavros' Cafe** (tel. 513 96), or anywhere along the beach. Boats go twice per day from Mastihari to Kalymnos (250dr). Four buses per day leave Kos for Mastihari (45 min., 150dr). **Kardamena,** 5km south of Antimachia, is a tacky tourist town filled with Europeans on package tours. It is difficult to find a room here, but you won't want to stay long in this plastic village. The **National Bank of Greece** is on the beach. (Open Mon.-Fri. 8:15am-2pm and 6-8pm.) The **OTE** is 1 block east of the main square where the bus stops. Various overpriced excursion boats also go to Nissiros, Patmos, and Kalymnos from Kardamena. Monday through Saturday, five buses go from Kos Town to Kardamena and three on Sunday (50 min., 160dr). Behind **Sebastion's Taverna** on the road into town, doubles go for 1700dr. You can also try **Hotel Stelios** (tel. 912 10; singles 1000dr, doubles 1600dr, with bath). **Restaurant Ta Dilina** (tel. 912 24) has doubles for 1500dr, but call first.

# Southern Kos

The land in southern Kos is covered with rolling hills and ravines patched with green. The town of **Kefalos,** on the hill at the head of the island, contains little of interest. In ancient times, Kefalos was the capital city of the island, then named Astipalea. Ruins from the former city can be seen near the windmills at Kefalos.

There is really no reason to go into town at all; get off the bus at **Kamari,** a small village on the beach before the road goes inland to Kefalos. The beach, while popular, is much more relaxing than that at **Agios Stefanos** to the north, where the huge Club Med appropriated an otherwise good beach and picturesque coastline. The best beach is 5km to the northeast of Kamari: Beautiful and unspoiled except for an overpriced restaurant, **Paradise Beach** lies invitingly beneath a cliff, where many freelance camp. Move up along the beach if you want peace and quiet. In Kamari, the **Hotel Maria** (tel. 713 08) has bright, clean doubles for 2000dr. A few meters down the beach is the **Hotel Sydney** (tel. 712 86) with even nicer doubles for 2500dr. In Agios Stefanos, you can stay with the **Kritikos Panoutis** family, with a rooms-to-let sign. (Clean and pleasant doubles 1200dr.) Farther on, **Pension To Kefalos** has doubles for 1700dr, while **Pension Agios Stefanos** (tel. 714 29) lets comfortable doubles for 1500dr.

Four buses per day go from Kos to Kefalos (1 hr., 240dr). There are also excursions to Paradise Beach from Kos Town and Kardamena.

# Kalymnos Κάλυμνος

Kalymnos was the first island to revolt against Ottoman Turkey in the 1820 Greek War of Independence. Previously, Kalymnos' claim to fame was its sponge-fishing industry. Most of its menfolk would depart for five or six months to fish for sponges in the southern waters of the Libyan Sea, off the coast of North Africa. Their's was a unique solution to the problem of earning a living while living on a large, barren rock. The industry has since declined, but because sponge fishing is very dangerous (divers get the fatal bends if they come up too quickly from the depths), the islanders are letting it go with a sigh of relief. Now one or two family members will often work in Australia or Canada and send money home.

Kalymnos is a mountainous island with two large valleys. Most of the towns and roads cling to the coast, making the interior mysteriously barren. The island is large enough to have facilities for travelers, but unlike its neighbors Kos and Rhodes, has managed to retain its authenticity. Kalymnos has some great (and consequently crowded) sandy beaches on its west coast, but most of the island breaks the waves with rocks and cliffs. Its ruins are few, but the scenery more than compensates. The stunning view along the coastal roads is overwhelming.

**Ferries** run every day at 5pm from Kalymnos to Leros (1 hr., 450dr), Patmos (2 hr., 700dr), and Piraeus (14 hr., 2060dr). Every morning at about 7am boats travel south to Kos (1 hr., 500dr) and Rhodes (6 hr., 1520dr). On Tuesdays at 11am the *Nereus* travels to Crete (3300dr) with intermediate stops at Kos, Nissiros, Tilos, Symi, Rhodes, Halki, Karpathos, and Kassos. The same boat runs every Thursday at 2pm to Astipalea, Amorgos, Paros, and Piraeus. The *Kyklades* travels from Kalymnos to Kavala (Mon. at 11am), stopping at Leros, Lipsi, Patmos, Ikaria, Samos, Chios, Lesvos, and Limnos. On Thursdays at 9am this ferry leaves for Kos, Rhodes, Symi, Nissiros, Tilos, Astipalea, Amorgos, and Paros. The *Alkayos* and *Omiros* alternately go to Piraeus Tuesdays at 5:30pm (via Leros and Patmos) and Sundays at 5:30pm (via Astipalea). Ferries to and from Kalymnos are frequently late, so it's a good idea to keep in touch with the port police or your ticket agent on the day of your departure. Twice per day, at 6am and 3:30pm, the *Apollo* leaves for Mastihari on Kos (45 min., 300dr), while the *Themis* travels to Kos Town every afternoon (1 hr., 600dr). The *Kostakis* travels to Kos (Mon. and Thurs. at 7:15pm, Wed. and Fri. at 5pm, Sat.-Sun. at 4pm), Leros and Patmos (Wed. and Fri. at 10:15am), and Nissiros and Astipalea (Mon. and Thurs. at 10:15am). Two small boats travel from Myrties, on the west coast, to Xerocampos in Leros, leaving at noon and 1pm and returning at 7am and 7:30am the next morning (500dr). Ask at the tourist office about hydrofoils.

Daily excursions go from Pothea at 9am to *Pserimos,* a small island between Kalymnos and Kos with excellent beaches and a few *tavernas* (620dr round-trip), returning at 4pm, and to the **Caves of Kephalas,** on the other side of Kalymnos, accessible only by boat (1300dr round-trip) leaving at 9am also. Stalagmites and stalactites cover the caves; it is said that Zeus hid from his father here before killing him. The excursion visits the caves for a few hours, then stops at a beach on the southern coast for a few hours before returning to Pothea. For more information, ask any of the agents along the waterfront in Pothea.

# Pothea

Large for an island village, Pothea is also much more colorful than its uniformly white Aegean counterparts. During the Italian occupation at the beginning of the century, many of the feisty islanders painted their houses blue, the national color of Greece, to irritate their Italian rulers. Today, pink and green buildings also decorate the streets, and cars and motorbikes race down narrow streets designed for donkeys. If you get tired of wandering through the maze of Greek neighborhoods, you'll find it easy to perform the necessary errands (changing money, renting a motorbike) before leaving for quieter, more scenic spots on the island.

## Orientation and Practical Information

The main pier of Pothea runs parallel to **Eleftherias Street,** the waterfront promenade. The second most important avenue, **Venizelou Street** intersects Eleftherias at the right end of the harbor, next to the Agios Christos church and the large Italian building that houses the police station. This narrow street, filled with appliance, cosmetic, and gift shops, leads to **Kyprou Square** where you'll find the post office, OTE, taxis, and gasoline. Continuing on this road you'll reach the western part of the island. If you follow the harbor promenade past the police station, you'll meet the road leading to Vathis.

**Tourist Office:** Tel. 293 10, 1 block from the customs house. Walk down the path behind the bronze statue of Poseidon, which stands to the left of the Olympic Hotel. The friendly English-speaking staff will help you find a room and give you complete information on buses, boats, and the island's sights. Free maps of Pothea and Kalymnos. Open daily 8:30am-7pm.

**Budget Travel:** Blue Islands Travel (tel. 230 55 or 231 85), on the northwest corner of the harbor near the tourist office. Helpful with bus and boat schedules. On most days, Themis is there; she's very friendly, speaks English well, and can answer any question about the island. Will change money after the banks close, and try to find you accommodations. Open Mon.-Sat. 9am-1pm and 5pm-8:30pm; in off-season Mon.-Fri. only.

**Currency Exchange:** National Bank and Ionian and Popular Bank, both on the waterfront. Both open Mon.-Thurs. 8am-2pm, Fri. 8am-1:30pm. Otherwise try the tourist offices.

**Post Office:** From Kyprou Sq. go 1 block inland. Open Mon.-Fri. 7:30am-3pm. **Postal Code:** 852 00.

**OTE:** Just past the post office on the right. Open daily 7:30am-3pm. **Telephone code:** 0243.

**Bus Station:** By the town hall (look for the blue dome), to all villages on the west coast. On the northeast corner of the waterfront, to Vathis.

**Taxis:** Kyprou Sq. (tel. 295 55). A slightly cheaper alternative is the **taxi-bus,** a regular taxi with 4-5 more passengers. Set rate per person, 10-20dr more than the bus. There are taxi-bus stands in each town, but you can flag one anywhere; they operate until 10pm. Also in Kyprou Sq.

**Moped Rental:** Several places on the waterfront. From 1000dr per day. Gas not included.

**International Bookstore:** European newspapers and the *International Herald Tribune* are sold in Kyprou Sq.

**Port Police:** In the yellow building across from the customs house (tel. 293 04), at the southwest corner of the waterfront. Updated ferry information. Ask for Michael, who is very helpful and speaks excellent English.

**Police:** Tel. 293 01, on the street out of Kyprou Sq., to the left of the street with the post office and OTE. No English spoken, but friendly; one of the officers speaks French.

**Telephone Code:** 0243.

## Accommodations and Food

The easiest way to find a room is to follow one of the pension owners who await incoming boats. Otherwise, try the tourist office or just ask around. For rooms to let, take the road in the corner of the harbor between Kalymnos Travel and the *souvlaki* place, go up the hill, make a right, then continue past the sponge factories to the **Greek House** (tel. 295 59; singles with new furniture 1000dr; doubles 1300dr; triples 1500dr). Around the corner **Mr. Christoforos Vythoulkas Pension** is cheap but very noisy in the evening. (Small, drab singles 500dr. Doubles 1000dr.) If you make a left before the sponge factories and follow the road up the hill to the right, you'll reach the pension of **Katerina Smaliou** (tel. 221 86). The rooms are cooled with ceiling fans, and the terrace affords a terrific view of the city. Farther uphill and left toward the cross, you'll come to **Travelo Pension** (tel. 280 41). The friendly owners Catrina and Stergos Platella create a "Mom and Pop" atmosphere—you'll feel right at home. (Doubles 1400dr.) Back in town, just off the center of the waterfront, **Hotel Alma** (tel. 289 69) also has a telephone meter. (Singles 1000dr. Doubles 1500dr, with private bath 1800dr.)

Most of the restaurants in Pothea are by the harbor; those at the right end after the town hall tend to be more reasonable. Swordfish on Kalymnos is both excellent and cheap (about 400dr in most places). Venizelou Street and Kyprou Square are good places to find such basics as *tiropita* and *souvlaki*.

### Sights

Pothea is busy, but not because of tourism. As you stroll around you might stop into the **Restaurant N.O.K.**, on the waterfront behind the port police, and see their collection of ancient amphoras and odd-shaped sponges retrieved by divers. On the wall is a goofy but informative painting of a sponge diver; the equipment is very different from a James Bond scuba set-up. Two blocks inland from the left end of the harbor is the sponge factory of **Nikolas Gourlas,** where the sponges are cleaned and chemically treated. Mr. Gourlas speaks English and will be happy to explain the process to you. (Sponges from 260dr; not a bargain.) The original sponge factories are stretched along the far east end of the harbor, on the road to Vathis. You can poke around the derelict buildings.

Six or seven blocks back from the far right end of the waterfront and very well-signposted is the eclectic **municipal museum.** The most interesting part of the museum, in a former mansion, is the sumptuously decorated parlor, which gives an indication of how very wealthy Greeks lived here at the turn-of-the-century. (Open Mon. and Wed.-Sat. 10am-2pm, Sun. 10am-2pm. Free.)

On a hill overlooking the south end of town, the **Monastery of Agios Pantes** merits a visit. Father Savvas, a church official at the monastery, died in 1948. At the traditional reburial nine years later, his body showed no signs of decay. Such an unequivocal sign of sainthood couldn't be ignored, so Father Savvas was promptly canonized, the monastery re-dedicated in his honor, and new chapels added. His body did evidently later decompose, which may say something about the corrosive power of high office. Today, visitors may enter at the gate on the right side; the first chapel on your left contains Father Savvas' bones in an elaborate sarcophagus. Saints aside, the view from up here is splendid; you can see all the way to Telendos Island and beyond. (Free.)

From the customs house, take the roads to the left to reach the beach at **Therma,** 2km away. Arthritic patients make pilgrimages to the sanitarium here to partake of its sulfur mineral baths. (You need a doctor's permission to bathe.) The main beach is crowded but a short walk around the bend leads to a quiet swimming spot. Farther west from Therma (you must backtrack toward Pothea and then head slightly north) is the peaceful, homey beach at **Vlihada** (6km from Pothea).

## Western Coast

Kalymnos has two main roads: One runs northwest out of Pothea, the other northeast. A few kilometers on the northwest road, out of Pothea, a side road to the left leads up to the fortress of the Knights of St. John, here called the **Kastro Chrissocherias.** Hidden away in the remains are a number of little chapels, all open to view. You may notice sections of wall or floor that look freshly painted. These are places where privateers dug holes to search for buried treasure.

The view from Chrissocherias takes in much of the island; northward across the valley, the **Pera Kastro** is in plain view. This structure, originally Byzantine, was enlarged and fortified by the Knights. Nine tiny bright white churches are scattered throughout the ruins, maintained by some elderly women from Chorio. When you approach the base of the hill beneath the castle, ask one of the residents of Chorio how to climb up. The summit affords a panoramic view of the whole valley. Directly opposite, you can see the small village of **Argos,** the site of the ancient city of Argiens and now merely a suburb of Pothea. Both the Pera Kastro and Argos overlook the town of **Chorio**, once Kalymnos' capital but now a small, quiet village. Pothea has expanded so far now that it's impossible to say where it ends and where Chorio begins.

A kilometer or so beyond Chorio is the **Church of Christ of Jerusalem,** a Byzantine church built by the Emperor Arcadius to thank God for sparing him in a storm at sea. Today, only the shell remains. The stone blocks with carved inscriptions are from a fourth-century B.C.E. temple to Apollo that stood on the same site. This church was seen as a symbol of Christianity's victory over paganism. The inscription on the stone at shoulder-level just to the right of center is said to be a quotation from the document that annexed Kalymnos to the fifth-century B.C.E. Athenian Empire. If you can translate it, let us know.

The road reaches the western coast of the island at **Kantouni,** 7km from Pothea. The coast from Kantouni to Arginontas is the subject of much tourist brochure hype. The beach at Kantouni is crowded, partially due to frequent bus service, but it's a good place to join in a game of beach ping-pong. At night you can sip cocktails at the popular **Cantina Pub,** just up the stairs from the beach itself.

Two kilometers farther, the dark, sandy beach of **Plati Gialos** lies under a steep cliff and can be reached from a turn-off at Panormos. Platia Gialos is less crowded than Kantouni and frequented by pious sun-worshipers. Stay at **Pension Plati Gialos** (tel. 220 14), perched on the cliff with an impressive view of the coastline. (Singles 1000dr. Doubles 1400dr.) Two more beach communities at 7km intervals, both popular with Eurpean sunbathers, are Myrties and Massouri. The beach at **Myrties** has gray sand, while the one at **Massouri** is pebbly, but crowded. There are plenty of rooms to let in both localites, especially Myrties, where people fresh off the boat from Leros (see the ferry section) are likely to receive offers. Massouri is the center of the island's nightlife with a few excellent pubs. Nearby is **Disco Narcissus.** Seven buses daily track the west coast, stopping at Kantouni, Myrties, and Massouri (6:30am-9:30pm, 50dr). Taxi-buses also are stationed at each of these places.

Myrties' finest attraction is a short boat ride out of town: The tiny, rocky islet of **Telendos,** severed from Kalymnos by an earthquake in 554 C.E. A city occupied the site where the island cracked—traces of it have been found on the ocean floor but you can't see anything from the surface. The Roman ruins on Telendos are modest at best, but the island possesses excellent beaches; one of them, on the northeast, is for nudists. Farther on is the **Byzantine Monastery of St. Constantine.** (Visitable and free. Dress properly.) Since almost all of Telendos' visitors return to the main island in the evening, finding accommodations here is no problem. **Uncle George's Pension** (tel. 475 02), near the docks, has friendly management and a good restaurant. (Doubles 1400dr.) If Uncle George's is full, follow the signs to the left of the docks and back to the comfortable rooms let by **Mrs. Makarouna.** (Doubles with private showers 1200-1800dr. Bargain.) If you want to camp on the beach, bring a tent because it can get windy and cold. To the left of Uncle George's, **Ta Delina** offers Greek music every Wednesday and Saturday night to complement the fine Greek fare. Telendos is connected to Kalymnos by a number of tiny **ferries** (50dr, last ferry at 10pm). Before leaving Myrties, take a look at Telendos and notice the woman's face in profile along the left-hand side of the mountain. According to the islanders, she is looking forlornly out to sea, weeping for her lost husband.

Back on Kalymnos, the emptiest beach stretches out at **Arginontas,** at the end of a long, narrow inlet. Both roads to and from the beach rise dramatically along cliffs that plunge into turquoise water. Not the cleanest place on the island, **Vanza-**

nelis' (tel. 473 89), at Arginontas Beach, has a *taverna* and doubles for 1300dr. Two buses from Pothea venture this far (110dr). The last village on the western side, accessible only by a smooth dirt road, is **Emborios.** (You can take a motorbike or a taxi from Massouri for 800dr.) This town is larger than Arginontas, with two *tavernas* and a few rooms to let, but it's still quaint and unspoiled. Stay at the lively, friendly **Emborios Beach Coffee Bar Restaurant** (tel. 472 77; doubles 1200dr). The **Emborio family,** living in the large white house facing the beach, has pleasant rooms as well. (Singles 800dr. Doubles 1200dr.)

Past Emborios, the island tapers to a peninsula that just about stretches to Leros. Like most of Kalymnos, it is rocky and barren, extending right to the sea with no beaches. Swimmers should beware of the strong current running in the strait between Kalymnos and Leros. The peninsula is traversed by several donkey tracks, but no roads, and the terrain lends itself to cross-country walking.

### Vathis

Six kilometers northeast of Pothea, Vathis presents an entirely different landscape. Most of the island can support only grass and a few diehard wildflowers, but the valley at Vathis is a lush garden of mandarins, limes, and grapevines. The valley starts at the village of **Rina,** where the sea creates a kind of fjord. There is no beach here (you can swim off the pier), but the exquisite scenery and relative absence of tourists make sand a negligible sacrifice. On the north side of the inlet is **Daskaleios,** a stalagmite cave to which you can swim. You'll probably have to persuade a local kid to swim out with you and point it out.

In Rina, stay at the **Hotel Galini,** where rooms with balcony and private bath go for only 1000dr for singles, 1400dr for doubles. Otherwise ask around and someone will probably be willing to rent you a room; try first at one of the three *tavernas* on the tiny waterfront.

# Astipalea Αστυπάλια

Shaped like a butterfly, Astipalea is the westernmost of the Dodecanese islands, and best suited for those seeking isolation. Astipalea has neither spectacular scenery nor interesting ruins, and its inhabitants are not especially receptive to visitors. But don't let this deter you. **Ferries** run rather sporadically from Kos (about 4 daytrips per week, 2000dr round-trip), Kalymnos (similar), and Rhodes (3 per week, 1500dr one-way). Large liners also travel to Amorgos (2 per week, 800dr one-way) and Piraeus (1800dr one-way). Be aware that you run the risk of being stuck here for as long as 5 days. As part of an attempt to increase tourism on this island, ferries from Kalymnos to Astipalea are free of charge in April, May, October, and November.

Once in Astipalea, traveling longer distances is very difficult unless you can find a friendly islander to take you around, as buses only cover the middle section. For most tourists, the best way to see the island is by foot or by boat. **Caïques** run frequently to many points around the island, but more than a little inquiry is needed to determine their exact schedules. All inter-island ferries land at the town of Astipalea, surrounded on all sides by tawny, gently sloping hills. The town itself is a hillside conglomerate of uninspiring white cubical dwellings which have suffered in hard times. At the top of the hill, though, a striking row of windmills leads to the **castle,** a ramshackle Byzantine structure shedding fragments of walls and windows everywhere. Two churches are encapsulated in the ruins. From here you have a clear view of the island, north, south, east, and west, and its flock of tributary islands. The **post office** (tel. 612 23; open Mon.-Fri. 7:30am-2:15pm) and several **markets** are all in this upper, older section of town, near the windmills. Down by the waterfront, the **Paradissos Hotel** (tel. 612 24) has several stories of bare but clean rooms (singles 1000dr, doubles 1600dr), but you need to bargain carefully. Up the hill to the east, the **Egeo** (tel. 612 36) and **Galia** (tel. 612 45) Hotels have livable rooms. (Singles 1100dr. Doubles 1600dr.) The **Vivamare Hotel** (tel. 613 28) opposite these will be marginally more expensive. There are also some *dhomatia,* whose owners regularly greet incoming ferries. **Camping** (tel. 613 38) is 2½km east of the town near Marmari; follow the signs. (400dr per person.)

A row of tiny **cafes** overlooks the town's tiny **beach,** just beyond the waterfront. *Psarotavernas* everywhere stock fresh fish at reasonable prices; try the one down on the beach (*kalamari* 300dr). The OTE (open Mon.-Fri. 7:30am-3pm) and a **boat agency** (tel. 612 24), which sells tickets for the *Olympia* and all Kos boats, are near the Paradissos Hotel. The Vivamare Hotel sells *Omiros* tickets. The **Gourmas Travel Agency** (tel. 613 28), amidst the cafes, organizes occasional excursions. Just before the beach, the **police** (tel. 612 07) and **port police** (tel. 612 08), in the same building, may be able to help you with difficulties. Astipalea's **telephone code** is 0242.

From the town of Astipalea, a 20-minute walk to the west (over the hill) will bring you to **Livadia,** where Nikolas and Maria Kontaratos (tel. 612 69) rent doubles and triples (600dr per person). There are a good number of other rooms to let. Buses leave four times daily (50dr). The pleasant beach is crowded with tents and Greek children during July and August, but on the beach of **Tzanaki,** farther along the coast to the southwest, nude bathing proceeds in near-solitude. The farthest on this string of beaches, **Agios Konstantinos,** is the most highly recommended. Secluded convents dot the west. In the other direction from Astipalea Town, **Maltelana** and **Analipsi** occupy the narrow isthmus. Maltezana's daily buses (2 per day, 100dr) allow you to inspect the peaceful fishing village and its well-preserved mosaics of a Roman swimming pool. In the winter when the winds are too strong for boats to dock at Astipalea, the ferries use the well-protected harbor at **Vathi.** This incredibly narrow natural harbor, whose ports are subdivided into **Exo Vathi** (outside) and **esa Vathi** (inside), is visited twice per week by boat excursions run by Gournas Travel. A caique occassionally goes back and forth between Vathi and **Agios Andreas**— a great place for swimming off the rocks.

# Leros Λρος

Locals describe Leros as an island of lakes. The six bays plunging deep into the island's coastline create pristine waters and natural harbors that often appear landlocked. Halfway between Patmos and Kalymnos, Leros has thus far had much less tourist traffic than other Dodecanese islands. Leros' charm lies in its wooded seclusion. Some people love this island, others find it dull. One local claims that it's haunted.

**Ferries** arrive at any of a number of places. Larger boats dock in Lakki, while Agia Marina receives smaller vessels from Patmos and Lipsi. Small boats also leave from Xerocampos, on the southeastern part of the island, for Myrties, on the western side of Kalymnos (at 7:30am, returning at 1pm, 45 min., 250dr). From Agia Marina, small boats leave for Patmos and Lipsi, but don't travel if the sea is too choppy. The Atlantis goes to Lipsi every morning except Monday and Friday when it goes to Patmos (to Lipsi 1½ hr., 1700dr round-trip). The Anna Express is faster and cheaper (to Lipsi Mon., Wed., and Fri. afternoon, ½ hr., 600dr). Make sure you know from where your boat leaves. Especially for smaller craft, schedules are fickle; a windy day can delay a boat for hours.

For the affluent, Olympic Airways (tel. 227 77) has **flights** to Athens daily at 8am, with an extra 3:35pm flight on Monday, Wednesday, and Friday (8620dr). A little puddle-jumper also goes to Kos on Monday, Wednesday, and Friday at 2:15pm (2140dr). The airfield is on the north coast of Leros, 7km past Platanos. Its construction rendered inaccessible Leros' only archeological site, a temple to Artemis.

Leros is best explored by **bike** (300dr per day in Platanos and Lakki) and **moped** (1000dr per day in both places). One bus runs from Platanos to Lakki and Xerocampos and back, leaving Platanos six times per day (8am-9pm, 45-65dr). The same bus goes from Platanos to Partheni via Alinda three times per day. **Taxis** also tend to be a reasonable means of transport (tel. 230 70 in Platanos, 225 50 in Lakki).

Lakki to Platonos costs only 250dr, Xerocampos to Platonos 500dr. Leros' **telephone code** is 0247.

## Around the Island

The sprawling capital of Leros, Platonos merges imperceptibly into its two harbors, Asia Marina to the north and Pantheli to the south. **Platanos** is centrally located for daytrips and conveniently close to nightspots. Taxis and buses stop in the main square ½km uphill from both Agia Marina and Pantheli. The **OTE** (open Mon.-Fri. 7:30am-3:10pm) and **post office** (open Mon.-Fri. 7:30am-2pm) are in the same building on Karami St., off the main square downhill towards Agia Marina. Signs lead up the steep left fork from Agia Marina into Platonos, depositing you at a self-service **laundromat** just before the main square, beneath the KKE office—look for the hammer and sickle. (Open daily 9am-1pm and 5-8pm. Wash 400dr. Dry 250dr.)

About 50m downhill from the post office, **Venus Pension** (tel. 233 89), run by the Maravelia family, has clean and comfortable singles for 1100dr, doubles for 1400dr. At Agia Marina, ferry passengers are accosted by hopeful room-renters, so you shouldn't have any trouble finding a place to stay. Travel agencies are sprinkled along the waterfront; near the intersection with Karami St., **Nikola's Taverna** prepares cheap and traditional meals. (Plate of little fried fish only 350dr.) From Platonos' main square, a set of white-trimmed steps climbs 2km steeply to a **Byzantine castle.** Share the view of Leros' irregular coastline with the flocks of birds and the Greek soldiers quartered in the castle.

**Pantheli** is a small beachfront village. Although the beach at Pantheli is not the best on the island, the town has inexpensive accommodations, good restaurants, and is the only place on Leros with any semblance of nightlife. About 50m to the left of the beach (facing the water), **Pension Rosa** (tel 227 98) has doubles for 1600dr. Farther down the road is the quaint **Pension Kavos** (tel. 232 47), with a kitchen, outdoor tables on a balcony, and clean rooms. (Doubles 1600dr.) These two may be filled with groups, however. At least a dozen restaurants are on the waterfront; the doubles above two of the restaurants offer an excellent view (1400dr). The **Lotus Bar** serves inexpensive fare, including breakfast. The **Syrtaki**, a *taverna* 1 tiny block inland, prides itself on its pizza (500dr) and its summer night *bouzouki* music extravaganzas. Up the road, **Video Vips Pub** plays loud music until 3am; you can dance at the well-advertised **Disco Diana** (tel. 225 11) fron 10pm to 3am. (Cover 350dr.)

Three and a half kilometers north of Platonos, the bus stops at sandy **Alinda Beach.** Both **Pension Papa Fotis** (tel 222 47) and **Pension Karina** (tel. 227 16) have pleasant, clean rooms with private baths right by the water. (Doubles 1700dr.) If Alinda's resort atmosphere becomes a drag, head 3 tortuous kilometers west to the great beach at **Gourna,** on the other side of the island. From Alinda, take the road to the airport and the first left down to the beach. A left turn from Alinda along one of the dirt roads (ask a local) will bring you after 1km to the tiny chapel of **Agios Isidoros,** on a small islet connected to the mainland by a narrow causeway.

Heading south from Platonos through Pantheli, **Vromolithos Beach** is long and relatively quiet. From here it's a 3-kilometer mildly hilly walk to **Lakki,** a gray town with a deep harbor. Lakki used to be a detention center for political prisoners. Those who desperately need to communicate long-distance will appreciate the **post office** and **OTE** here. (Both open Mon.-Fri. 7:30am-2:30pm.) As boats from Piraeus habitually arrive in Lakki at 2am or 3am, you may have to stay overnight. Continue along the seashore to the left as you leave the ferry; the town and road are to the right. After only 50m, a dirt path leads to a flat pine grove sheltered from the gusts of wind, an ideal place to camp. It's only a half-hour walk from here to Platonos, a much more pleasant town.

Three kilometers south of Lakki is the small seaside village of **Xerocampos,** connected by boat to Kalymnos (see above). Five minutes from the water, **Camping Leros** is lively, friendly, and crowded. A small restaurant serves drinks and breakfast. Be sure to change money in Lakki or Platanos, since you can't do it here. Xero-campos has a small beach, but you'll find better on other parts of the island. The large Italian buildings on the road between Xerocampos and Lakki once housed an Italian, and then a Greek school, they're now part of a mental institution.

# Patmos Πάτμος

> . . . *I greatly desired*
> *There to be lodged, and there*
> *To approach the dark grotto.*
> *For not like Cyprus,*
> *The rich in wellsprings,*
> *Nor any of the others*
> *Magnificently does Patmos dwell . . .*
> —*Friedrich Hölderlin*

In ancient times, Artemis, goddess of the hunt, was worshiped on Patmos. It was believed that she was responsible for raising the island, then called Leto, from the depths of the sea. Orestes, son of Agamemnon, built a grand temple to Artemis after finding refuge on Patmos from the Furies who were pursuing him for the murder of his mother, Clytemnestra.

Exiled from Ephesus, St. John established a Christian colony here, and he is believed to have written the Book of Revelations in a grotto overlooking the main town between 95 and 98 B.C.E. (For this, the Black Muslim leader Elijah Muhammad called Patmos the breeding ground of the "white devils.") In the fourth century C.E. when the Christian faith spread with the Byzantine Empire, the Temple of Artemis was razed and a basilica built in its place. In the eleventh century, the fortified Monastery of St. John was constructed on the same site on a hill that surveys the entire island. The monastery still stands today.

Until recent centuries, only monks inhabited the island, but its spectacular scenery and enchanting hilltop village, Chora, could not remain secret. Although the island sustains a thriving tourist trade, the windy streets of Chora and the beaches remain quiet.

**Ferries** from Patmos travel to Piraeus (1 per day, 1900dr) and along the Leros-Kalymnos-Kos-Rhodes route (1 per day, 1685dr to Rhodes). In off-season, three or four ferries per week run in either direction, weather permitting. To get to the Cyclades, you can take a boat to Ikaria (leaving Mon. and Fri. mornings at 6am, 2hr., 1500dr), and then catch the ferry to Paros (6 hr., 700dr). Boats travel to Samos daily except Thursday (1500-1700dr one-way, 2000-3000dr round-trip). Excursion boats travel to Lipsi every morning at 10am, returning around 4pm (700dr one-way, 1200dr round-trip). At least two excursions per day go to Leros (1200dr). Departure times vary, and same-day return is not always possible, so confirm with the tourist office or port police beforehand. You can also take the daily evening ferry to Leros (leaving at 10:30pm, 475dr). There is frequent **hydrofoil** service to Kos (2400dr) and Rhodes (5000dr), but besides being almost three times as expensive as the ferry, hydrofoils are subject to cancelation when the weather is rough.

Planned excursions go to **Ephesus** in Turkey (approximately 5000dr round-trip, 1500dr Turkish port tax, 1000-1500dr for a guided tour of the ruins). If you've flown to Greece from another European country on a charter, you may be subject to contractual provisions that could result in the loss of your return flight if you obtain a Turkish stamp in your passport during your charter journey. Check with your travel agent or charter company to find out the conditions that apply to your ticket. On Wednesday evenings you can catch the *Orient Express* to Venice, Italy (39,000dr; inquire at Apollon Tours).

# Skala

The port and main city of Patmos, Skala was not developed until the nineteenth century when fear of pirates subsided and people could live safely by the water. The main administrative buildings, which today house the post office and customs house, were constructed during the Italian occupation (1912-1943). Today the town is lively and pleasant, and oriented toward serving tourists.

## Orientation and Practical Information

Smaller ferries dock opposite the line of cafes and restaurants, while larger vessels park across from the large Italian building that houses the port police and post office. The end of this building borders the main square, where the banks are located. The small and crowded town beach is to your right (facing inland). Skala is located on a narrow part of the island, so if you walk directly back from the water, in 10-15 minutes you'll hit the other side of the island.

**Tourist Office:** Tel. 316 66, around the corner from the post office, off the main square. Helpful, with maps of Skala, Chora, and Patmos, as well as bus schedule photocopies. Open July-Sept. daily 9am-1:30pm and 4-10:30pm; Oct.-June Mon.-Fri. 7:30am-2:30pm.

**Travel Agencies:** On the waterfront. **Astoria Shipping and Travel** (tel. 312 05 or 312 08). Very helpful; information on private boats and ferries. Organizes guided tours of the monastery and the grotto (2 per week, 3 hr., 600dr). Open Mon.-Sat. 8:30am-9pm, Sun. 8:30-10am and 7-9pm. **Apollon Tourist and Shipping Agency** (tel. 313 56 or 313 24). Information on boats and hydrofoils. Agents for Olympic Airways and the *Orient Express* to Venice, Italy. Open Mon.-Sat. 8am-1pm and 3:30-8pm.

**Currency Exchange: National Bank of Greece** (tel. 315 91), on the square. Open Mon.-Thurs. 8am-2pm, Fri. 8am-1:30pm. **Ionian and Popular Bank,** in the liquor store, at the opposite corner of the square. Open daily 8am-1pm and 4-9pm. Also try the post office and travel agencies.

**Post Office:** On the main square, beside the police. Open Mon.-Fri. 7:30am-2:30pm. **Postal Code:** 855 00.

**OTE:** Follow the signs back from the Ionian and Popular bank. Open Mon.-Fri. 7:30am-9pm, Sat. 7:30am-3:10pm. **Telephone code:** 0247.

**Bus Station:** In front of the police station. Complete bus schedule posted.

**Taxis:** Tel. 312 55, in the main square.

**Moped Rental:** On the waterfront. 1000-1500dr per day.

**Hospital:** Tel. 312 11, uphill toward Chora. **Clinic:** Tel. 315 77, behind the square.

**Police and Port Police:** Tel. 312 31 or 313 03, in the large Italian building beside the main square. Friendly, with information on ferries (but not accommodations). You can leave your pack in the arched doorway.

## Accommodations, Camping, and Food

In summer, Skala's few hotels are almost always full, but finding a room in one of the numerous pensions and private homes is usually a simple matter. Even the boats arriving at 1am are greeted by a battalion of people offering singles for 1000-1200dr, doubles for 1400-1600dr. Since most of the boats from Piraeus and the other Dodecanese islands do arrive very late, it's is strongly recommended that you make arrangements with someone as you get off the boat. Otherwise, you may find yourself sleeping on the sidewalk. If it's early in the season and you need a place, walk left from the ferry dock and take a right onto Vassileos Georgiou St. At your fifth left (past Pizza Zacharo) a warmhearted family runs **Pension Sofia** (tel. 315 01) and its immaculate rooms. Knock on the second floor or try the building to the right. (Singles 1000dr. Doubles 1400dr.) At the second gate on the left of the street from the dock, **Mrs. Melikos' Pension** (tel. 316 03) has pleasant doubles for 1400dr. Diagonally across from her place the **Metgoyiannakis's** (tel. 310 09) also rent rooms (singles 1000dr. Doubles 1400dr.) *Dhomatia* can be found near the main square;

try the road leading from the left side of the square toward the OTE. If you continue in this direction without any luck, you'll reach the **Sunset Hotel.** (Singles 1800dr. Doubles 2000dr. Private bath included.) Another 100m takes you to the water and to the **Seven Doors Disco Bar;** if you have trouble sleeping in their doubles (1600dr), dance, drink, and munch on popcorn in the bar below until 3am.

Two kilometers northeast of Skala, the excellent **campsite** at **Meloi** (tel. 318 91 or 317 54) has a small cafe and mini-market, and is about 50m from a small and inviting beach. The restaurant across the road occasionally features *syrtaki* dancing. The campsite is well-signposted. (340dr per person. Cold showers included.)

Several first-rate seafood restaurants line the waterfront. Form a group and buy a large fresh fish (2500dr). The snack bar at the back of the square sells fresh grilled octopus. For a change of pace, try **Skorpios Creperie,** on Vassileos Georgiou St. to the left of the ferry dock as you disembark; the French proprietor serves dinner and dessert crepes from the simple lemon variety (140dr) to peaches with whipped cream and *Grand Marnier flambé* (380dr). Eat in the little garden at the back. (Open daily 9am-3pm and 7pm-midnight.) Nearby, **Grigori's** is Skala's most authentic *taverna.* There are several small markets around the square. The best bar is the **Cafe Arion;** don't be deceived by its small facade on the waterfront. If you're into loud funky music, try **Disco Meltemi** (tel. 313 64), at the right end of Skala near the town beach.

# Chora

From any part of Patmos you can see the white houses of Chora and the majestic, gray walls of the nearby Monastery of St. John the Theologian. It's enjoyable just to roam Chora's labyrinthine streets, peek into doorways, and view the Patmos shoreline and the outlying archipelago. Aside from the "rush hours"—notably at dinner time and whenever a cruise ship pays the island a call—Chora is tranquil and bucolic, less touristed than Skala, and unmarred by hotels and nightclubs.

Because of the maze-like layout of the town and the almost total absence of street names, it's difficult to give precise directions. Take care of business—such as exchanging currency—before arriving, since most important services and offices are absent here.

In summer, eight **buses** per day travel to Chora from Skala (7:40am-7:30pm, 70dr). The bus lets you off at the top of the hill outside the town; this is also the point of departure for buses from Chora to Grikou. A taxi here from Skala costs about 200dr. If you decide to walk (4km and steep), ask a local to show you where the steps begin; they continue all the way to Chora, and will be quicker and safer than the main road. You'll find the **police** and a **pharmacy** in town. Climb to the monastery entrance and go left to reach the **OTE,** which is really just one telephone housed in a bakery. If you continue in the same direction, you'll reach the square surrounded by *tavernas:* The most popular is the **Vagelis,** which has a great selection of inexpensive dishes. Try the *fasolia* (beans; 120dr), or the *dolmadhes* (180dr). (Open daily 9am-3pm and 6:30-midnight.) Better food and higher prices can be found at the **Patmion House Restaurant.** There are few places to stay here, and most are booked by people who return each year. Your best bet is to ask early in the morning at the cafe in the square.

### Sights

Strolling about Chora's streets is a popular activity, and you'll quickly understand why. Somehow these tiny streets never seem to get crowded. In your wanderings, you'll notice the sign of the Byzantine cross above most of the doorways, and often the date that the house was built. Both testify to the considerable age of many of the houses in the older quarters. The little village of Chora alone has 22 monasteries and churches. Dress accordingly; at the Monastery of St. John and some of the other major churches, there may be a few extra pairs of trousers or scarves at the entrance.

The massive turreted walls and well-fortified gateway of the **Monastery of St. John the Theologian** resemble a fortress much more than a place of worship. But then again, this is no ordinary house of God. The monastery was founded in 1088 by St. Christodoulos, nearly 1000 years after St. John's celebrated stay on the island. Christodoulos had been granted the island by Byzantine Emperor Alexios Comnenos I, and was provided with financial assistance to build the structure. But pragmatics proved more important than aesthetics—the proximity of Islamic Turkey made the monastery a constant target of pirate raids, so it was only a matter of time before the memorial to St. John was transformed into an impregnable citadel with formidable battlements and watch towers. There are 10 chapels in the monastery because church law forbade hearing mass twice daily in the same one.

As you enter the courtyard, notice the seventeenth-century frescoes to the left; that portray stories from *The Miracles and Travels of St. John the Evangelist,* supposedly written by John's disciple, Prochoros. To the right a fresco portrays St. John's miracle-making duel with a local priest of Apollo named Kynops. The saint, a graceful champion, threw the loser into the water at Skala where Kynops turned into a rock. The rock is still in the harbor—ask any local to point it out. Supposedly St. John knew when he was going to die and had his friends bury him alive; this is depicted in the fresco on the wall on the right. The far door leads to the small **Chapel of Holy Christodoulos,** where the founder of the monastery is buried. From this chapel, the inner vestibule leads to the main nave. Notice the depiction of the bleeding bodies of hell in the seventeenth-century frescoes on the wall of the inner vestibule. It was during this period of crisis, created by the Turks and Arab pirates, that mysticism, religious fervor, and preoccupation with eternal punishment prevailed. In the main chapel, the high iconostassis, the wooden icon-covered structure separating the people from the clergy behind in the holy of holies, dates from the same period. The holy altar here is said to contain remnants from the ancient Temple of Artemis.

Continue to the **Chapel of the Virgin Mary** which has original twelfth-century frescoes. In 1956, earth tremors revealed these frescoes underneath the seventeenth-century ones which are currently exhibited. Behind the iconostassis, the fresco of the Virgin Mary as Byzantine Empress is particularly noteworthy. Descend from the chapel into an open courtyard. On the left is the rectory; the right leads to the **treasury,** which features ornate liturgical garments, thirteenth-century icons, hand-painted gospels, hand-carved wooden crosses, and an unusual twelfth-century mosaic icon of St. Nicholas. In the right-hand display case are the jewels and ornaments donated by Catherine the Great of Russia—just one indication of the monastery's prestige. Look for the parchment Imperial Order of 1088 from the Byzantine emperor ceding the island to St. Christodoulos. (Admission to treasury 100dr.)

Try to visit the monastery early or late in the day in summer—around midday it becomes uncomfortably crammed with tourists and hollering tour guides. If you come in off-season, one of the monastery's 17 monks (there were once 1700) may volunteer to show you around the closed-off sections. Proper dress is required (women must wear suitable length skirts). Buy postcards at the little shop within the monastery: Because of a restriction on photography, all cards available in the village are crude drawings. (Monastery open Mon. and Fri.-Sat. 8am-2pm, Tues. 8am-1pm and 3-6pm, Wed. 8am-2pm and 5:30-7pm, Thurs. 8am-noon and 2-6pm, Sun. 8am-noon and 3-6pm. Free.)

On the other side of the hill from Skala, **Agia Panayia Diasozousa,** a more recent monastery, offers superb views of the north of the island. The interior frescoes, freshly painted, seem gaudy at first, but are identical to older ones. The church has no regular hours. You'll most likely find the caretaker here Monday through Friday from 9 to 11am. Services are held early Sunday mornings.

Halfway up the hill on the winding road that connects Chora and Skala (2km from each) is a turn-off for the **Apocalypsis Monastery,** a large, white complex of interconnected buildings. The tiny **Church of St. Anne,** carved into the cliffside underneath the monastery proper, deserves a look, but most people come for the **Sacred Grotto of the Revelation,** adjacent to the church. It was here that St. John dictated the *Book of Revelation,* the last book of the New Testament, to his follower Prochorus, after hearing the voice of God proclaim to him "the things which are and the things which shall be hereafter" (Rev. 1:19). St. John had originally come to the then uninhabited island from Asia Minor in 96 C.E. when he was exiled by the Roman Emperor Domitian for preaching the teachings of Christ. The present cave has the legendary crack through which St. John received the ominous news. Silver plating also marks the spot where he presumably rested.

## Around The Island

Most visitors to Patmos spend only a day or two on the island, visiting the historical attractions, taking in the views, and perhaps catching a quick swim. Those with more time should meander around the rest of the island. **Grikos** has a comparatively empty sandy beach, one luxury hotel, and a couple of restaurants. Only 5km southwest of Skala, and 5km west of Chora, Grikos receives six buses from Skala per day in summer, and one in off-season (60dr). A comparable number run from Chora. The **Vamvakos Hotel** (tel. 312 90) overlooks the southern and quieter end of the beach. (Doubles 1500dr; easily negotiable for longer stays and in off-season.) If you camp, you'll have company both on the extreme southern end of the beach and on the rock called **Kalikatsou,** which juts into the bay. Motorbikers can continue 3km south to the practically unvisited beach of **Plaki,** where the road dissipates. A strenuous 2-kilometer hike west lies **Psili Ammos,** the best beach on the island. The cafe here refreshes the weary. Excursion boats set off from Skala for both Grikos (100dr) and Psili Ammos (300dr), leaving daily between 10am and 10:30am and returning between 4pm and 5pm.

On the northern half of the island, about 5km from Skala, rests the quiet village of **Kampos,** with a modest beach and rooms to let (doubles from 1400dr). Three buses per day run here (60dr), the last returning at 7pm. A 3-kilometer walk north of Kampos is the pebbly, secluded cove of **Lampi,** where nude bathing is no problem, especially after daytrippers leave. **Dolphins of Lampi** serves three meals per day and has doubles for 1400dr. Cheaper and just as good is **Gambierakis Pantelis** (tel. 314 90), otherwise known as **Dmitri's Place.** Try Dmitri's potato omelette (100dr) and lobster (only 1500dr per kg) and sleep it off in a double (1400dr). Boats depart from Skali for the following beaches in the north: Meloi (see Skala Accommodations; 100dr), Agriolivadi (overrated; 150dr), Kampos (200dr), and Lampi (300dr).

# Lipsi (Lipsos) Λειψί

Some say Odysseus met the ravishing Calypso on this tiny island. Indeed, Lipsi is conducive to romance. This rocky, scenic one-village island with beautiful quiet beaches has a lot of charm. Once controlled by the monastery at Patmos, today the monks of Patmos still own much of the land on Lipsi. Of the 44 chapels, only one, in the main town, is currently active.

The *Atlantis* goes to Lipsi from Leros every morning except Monday and Friday (1½ hr., 1700dr round-trip), and excursion boats visit from Patmos every morning at 10am, returning at 4pm (1½ hr., 1500dr round-trip). From Lipsi, the fast, inexpensive *Anna Express* makes excursions to Leros (Mon., Wed., Fri., ½ hr., 900dr one-way), Patmos (Thurs., ½ hr., 600dr), and the one-*taverna* island of Marathi (Sun.). The *Anna Express* also has full-moon excursions. Most people coming from the other islands return the same day, so if you choose to stay over, you'll find Lipsi peacefully secluded.

The stepped street by the school leads up to the central square, where you'll find the **post office** and **OTE** in the same building. (Both open Mon.-Fri. 7:30am-2:30pm.) You can change money at Sveastos Supermarket, 1 block behind the square (open daily 7am-9pm), or at Hotel Kalypso by the water. Rooms are easy to find and cheap. Lipsi's **telephone code** is 0247.

If you ask Lipsians about special sights on their island, they shrug. One item of interest, open only during the school year, is a government **rug-making school** on the waterfront, where you can watch artisans weave Oriental rugs with splendid results. In the square, the **Ecclesiastical Popular Museum of Lipsi** exhibits religious artifacts from the island as well as traditional Lipsian dress. Ask upstairs in the city hall for the key. (Open Mon.-Fri. 7am-2pm.)

The big attractions of Lipsi, however, are the **beaches.** You can camp and swim at the fine town beach, but it becomes congested in the afternoon when Lipsian children get out of school. Whatever you do, don't leave the island without visiting the paradise spot at **Plati Gialos.** The beach is indisputably the most beautiful, with calm turquoise water waist-deep for most of the cove. Bring your own food and water. You can walk to the beach along the road to the left of town (40 min.), but get directions first. Otherwise, catch a ride with a local (look for the small truck with a sign for Plati Gialos; 300-400dr round-trip). Other beautiful less crowded beaches are **Katzadia,** to the right of the town, **Chokla Kora,** behind the town, and **Kymise,** to the left by the port (visible when you arrive at the island), with two chapels and a fresh spring. The island is small; wander around the dirt roads and discover your own stretch of sand.

# CYPRUS Κυπροσ

| | | | |
|---|---|---|---|
| US$1 = C£0.41 | | C£1 = US$2.45 |
| CDN$1 = C£2.96 | | C£1 = CDN$0.34 |
| UK£1 = C£0.69 | | C£1 = UK£1.45 |
| AUS$1 = C£3.06 | | C£1 = AUS$0.33 |

The divided island of Cyprus, far off in the Mediterranean between Greece and the Middle East, can sparkle with remote mountain monasteries, crusader castles, ancient mosaics and temples, and stunning azure waters. Yet it just as quickly degenerates into flat, barren plains spewing resort hotels like cand-colored pleasure factories. Visitors will find a unique blend of cultures, long influenced by Greece but still reflecting Cyprus' proximity to the Middle East, the 300-year Ottoman rule, as well as its century-long occupation by the British. Many Cypriots speak and understand English, and most signs are in both Greek and Roman letters. Cyprus is about twice as expensive as Greece, but a budget holiday here is not out of the question.

The unified island of Cyprus had been independent for 14 years when, in 1974, Turkish forces invaded the island. Turkey has occupied the northern sector ever since, and in November, 1983, it declared itself a sovereign state. Since the island is peopled by Greek and Turkish Cypriots, political and social tensions run high. Happily, during the summer of 1988, leaders from Greece and Turkey met at the bargaining table with renewed intentions to resolve this issue.

## To and From Cyprus

The third largest island in the Mediterranean after Sicily and Sardinia, Cyprus lies 40 miles from Turkey, 100 miles from Israel and Lebanon, and 300 miles from the nearest Greek islands. It is accessible by airplane or boat from points in Italy, Greece, and the Middle East. If you want to travel by sea, purchase tickets at waterfront boat offices rather than from the central offices that we list below.

Connections to Limassol:

**Salamis Tours:** Limassol (tel. (051) 555 55). *Paloma* departs Limassol Mon. for Piraeus (arrives Wed.), Iraklion (Thurs.), and Limassol (Sat.). Limassol to Iraklion 800dr one-way, including port tax. *F/B Silver Paloma* departs Limassol Fri. for Rhodes (Sat.), Piraeus (Sun.), Rhodes (Tues.), Limassol (Wed.), Haifa (Thurs.), and Limassol (Fri.). To Haifa C£20 deck-class. In Piraeus, Afroessa Lines S.A., 1 Charilaou Tricoupi St. (tel. 418 37 77); in Rhodes, Red Sea Travel, 11-13 Amerikis St. (tel. 224 60); in Haifa, Mano Passenger Lines Ltd., 39-41 Hameginim Ave. (tel. (04) 35 16 31).

**Sol Maritime, Ltd.:** The *Sol Phryne* sails from Piraeus Thurs., stopping in Rhodes (Fri.) and Limassol (Sat.), before arriving in Haifa (Sun.). Limassol-Rhodes C£26 deck-class, Limassol-Haifa C£19. In Limassol, Takis Solomonides Ltd., 1 Irene St. (tel. (051) 570 00); in Rhodes, Red Sea Travel, 11 Amerikis St. (tel. 224 60); in Athens, Takis Solomides Ltd., 4 Philellinon St. (tel. 323 31 76); in Haifa, Jacop Caspi, 76 Haatzmant Rd., Corner 1, Natan St., P.O. Box 27 (tel. 67 44 44).

**Stability Line:** The *Vergina* leaves Piraeus Thurs., stopping in Iraklion and Rhodes (Fri.) and Limassol (Sat.), before arriving in Haifa (Sun.); it leaves Haifa for the return Sun. evening. Piraeus-Limassol C£17 deck-class. The *Queen Vergina* alternates routes between Limassol-Haifa-Limassol (every 10 days) and Limassol-Rhodes-Mykonos-Piraeus-Corfu. In Cyprus, Vergina Lines, 38 Olympiou St. (tel. (051) 439 78); in Piraeus, Stability Line, 11 Sathtouri St. (tel. 413 23 92); in Iraklion, Arabazoglou Travel, 65, 25th August St. (tel. 22 66 97); in Haifa, J. Caspi Ltd., 76 Haatzmauth Rd. (tel. (04) 67 44 44).

You can also travel to Larnaca. The *F/B Empress* travels from Jounieh, Lebanon every other day at 9pm. In Cyprus, Dafnis Travel Ltd., 82 Makarios Ave. (tel. (041) 280 00); in Lebanon, Socomare, Abi Saleh Bldg. Jounieh (tel. 21 77 99). About once a month the **Black Sea Shipping Company** (tel. 41 18 705) runs a ferry from Odessa,

388

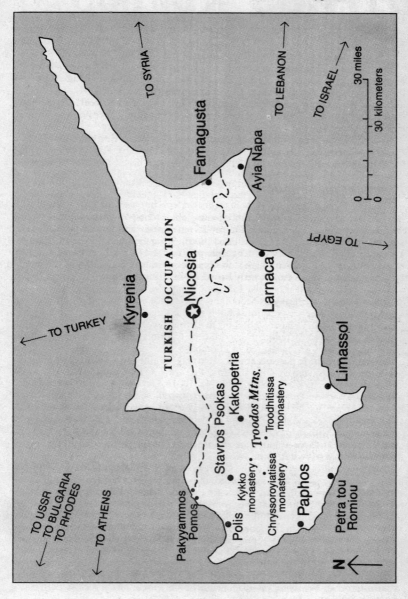

TO SYRIA

TO LEBANON

TO ISRAEL

30 miles

30 kilometers

Famagusta

Ayia Napa

TURKISH OCCUPATION

Nicosia

Larnaca

TO EGYPT

Kyrenia

TO TURKEY

Limassol

Stavros Psokas

Kakopetria

*Troodos Mtns.*

Troodhitissa
monastery

Kykko
monastery

Chryssoroyiatissa
monastery

Paphos

TO USSR
TO BULGARIA
TO RHODES

TO ATHENS

Pakyyammos
Pomos

Polis

Petra tou
Romiou

N

USSR to Larnaca via Varna (in Bulgaria), Istanbul, and Piraeus. In Greece, Transmed Shipping S.A., Akti Miaouli St. 85, Piraeus (tel. 41 31 402/3); in Egypt, Amon Shipping Agency, Adib St. 7, P.O. Box 60764, Alexandria; in Cyprus, Francoudi and Staphanou Ltd., New Port Rd., Limassol (tel. 703 35).

From Turkey, **Turkish Maritime Lines,** operates three times per week between Mersin and Famagusta. In Turkey, Ak. Rıthim Cad., Karaköy, Istanbul (tel. 44 02 07); in Cyprus, Turk Bankası Ltd., Famagusta (tel. 03/66 54 94). The *Ertürk* also runs three times per week in summer from Taşucu to Kyrenia. Remember: You cannot go from Turkey to Greek Cyprus if you enter Cyprus on the Turkish side.

By air, Cyprus is accessible from Greece as well as other European and Middle Eastern countries on **Olympic Airlines** (tel. (800) 223-1226), **Egypt Air** (tel. (718) 997-7700), **Cyprus Airways** (tel. (212) 714-2310), and other commercial lines.

## Practical Information

Much of Cyprus is served by a highway system, but a great deal of intrepidity is necessary for forays into the hinterland. Public transportation is, for the most part, nonexistent in the evenings (stops at 7pm). Buses and service (shared) taxis run regularly Monday through Friday (until 7pm) between Limassol, Paphos, Larnaca, and Nicosia. Service taxis generally cost C£1.15-1.75 between the four major cities, while buses, although slower and less frequent, cost about half as much. Neither taxis nor buses run directly between Nicosia and Paphos, so expect to pay twice as much—you'll travel via Limassol.

Direct buses to the Troodos Mountains travel once daily from both Nicosia and Limassol. From Paphos, you must hitch the hundred or so miles or take several buses, preferably via Limassol. Hitching in Cyprus is common, especially on secondary roads not served by public transportation. Cypriots drive on the left side of the road and distances are measured in kilometers.

**Tourist information** bureaus are all extremely helpful and efficient. The main office is the **Cyprus Tourist Organization,** P.O. Box 4535, Nicosia (tel. (02) 44 33 74); in the U.S., 13 E. 40 St., New York, NY 10016. Get a copy of the *Cyprus Hotels and Tourist Services Guide;* while it does not list all of the country's cheap hotels (since many are unofficial), it includes all government-regulated hotels and pensions. If you are quoted or charged a price higher than the one listed, you can register a complaint with the nearest tourist office; you should get the appropriate reduction. The tourist offices can arrange accommodations for you, but you'll find better deals if you look on your own.

The main unit of **currency** is the Cyprus pound (C£), which is divided into 100 cents. Since the cent was introduced only recently to replace the mil (one-thousandth of a pound), many prices are quoted in mils or, to complicate matters further, in shillings, a term left over from the British occupation. There are 10 mils to a cent and five cents to a shilling. **Banks** are officially open from 8:30am to noon, but nearly all of them in the four major cities provide an afternoon tourist service in summer (usually 4-7pm). Stores are open from Monday to Saturday from 8am to 1pm, and on Monday, Tuesday, Thursday and Friday from 4pm to 7pm as well. Government offices are usually open from 7:30am to 1:30pm, with occasional afternoon hours. Museums and archeological sites are open Monday through Saturday in the afternoon. Nearly all establishments, notably museums, are closed or reduce hours on Sundays.

Cyprus closes down on the following **holidays:** New Year's Day, Epiphany (Jan. 6), Archbishop Makarios III Day (Jan. 19), Green Monday (Feb. 22), Cypriot National Day (April 1), Orthodox Good Friday, Orthodox Easter (Sat. through Mon.), Labor Day (May 1), the anniversary of the death of Archbishop Makarios III (Aug. 3), Independence Day (Oct. 1), Christmas Eve, Christmas Day, and Boxing Day (Dec. 24-26). Two Greek national holidays, on March 25 and October 28, are also honored.

Cyprus has a fairly good **telephone company (CYTA).** Direct overseas calls can be made from nearly all public phones if you have enough 10¢ pieces. Rates to North America, Australia, and New Zealand are about C£1.10 per minute; to Great Britain, 50¢ per minute. Country codes are posted in all phone booths and in the phone books. For **information** on unlisted numbers, dial 191; if the number is listed, call 192. For information on international calls, dial 194, and for the international operator, 198. All local numbers have five digits, except government numbers, which have six and begin with "40." Telegrams to the U.S. and Canada cost 18¢ per word (delivery within 12 hr.), 5.5¢ per word (within 24 hr.). To Australia or New Zealand, expect to pay 10¢ per word.

Cyprus hosts a number of **festivals** every month. A general list of the year's activities can be obtained by writing to the Cyprus Tourist Organization (see address above). Once in Cyprus, you can obtain a copy of *This Month's Principal Events* from any tourist information office.

## Accommodations and Food

Because budget travelers so often bypass Cyprus, cheap, clean hotels are few and far between. Nicosia, Limassol, Paphos, and Troodos all have **IYHF youth hostels,** and Stavros tis Psokas has a loosely affiliated **forest station.** You don't need a youth hostel card. Although Cyprus has only a few formal campgrounds, you can sleep on beaches and in forests; just choose your site discreetly. In the Troodos area, try staying in the monasteries; they're free and you'll be exposed to part of the enchanting Cypriot past.

Cypriot food has much in common with Greek, English, and Middle Eastern cuisine. Restaurants everywhere sell English-style cutlets and steaks. Try *meze,* a platter of about a dozen appetizers for two to four people, and *kleftiko,* lamb roasted in spherical charcoal ovens. The *souvlaki* is similar to Greek *souvlaki-pita,* but the sandwich is larger, the lamb drier, and the sauce absent. At 60-80¢, one *souvlaki* makes a good meal. *Sheftalia* (grilled ground meat with onions) is also served in pita pockets. Try some *iranie* from a cart on the street; this Turkish drink made of yogurt with mint and salt is supposed to sober you up no matter how drunk you are.

## History

Cyprus first achieved historical importance at the onset of the Bronze Age because of its wealth of copper ore. It is not clear to linguists whether *kypros,* cognate with "copper," first referred to the island or the metal. The Greeks introduced their language and culture, proclaimed Cyprus the birthplace of Aphrodite, and erected an important temple at Old Paphos in her name.

Cyprus has a long history of domination by foreign nations. About 1000 B.C.E., Iron Age Syrians came to Cyprus, followed 100 years later by Phoenicians from Tyre. For the next several centuries, Cyprus fell under Assyrian and later Egyptian control, and then several hundred years under Persian domination, until the conquest of Alexander the Great in 333 B.C.E. In 295 B.C.E., Ptolemy of Egypt managed to annex Cyprus. Peace lasted until the Roman conquest in 58 B.C.E. Julius Caesar presented the island to Cleopatra III of Egypt, but it was returned to Rome after her death. In 395 C.E., Cyprus became a Byzantine province.

In 1191, Richard the Lion-Hearted set sail for Jerusalem with his English fleet as part of the Third Crusade. The rude treatment he received in Cyprus precipitated a vengeful attack and conquest. In the midst of his military successes, King Richard married Berengaria of Navare, in Limassol Castle, simultaneously crowning her Queen of England. He then sold the island to the Knights Templar to finance his crusade; one year later it passed into the hands of Guy de Lusignan, who had helped Richard take the island.

Under the Lusignan Dynasty (1192-1489), Cypriot culture and the Greek Orthodox Church were suppressed by the West and the Latin Church. The great cathedrals of Nicosia and Famagusta, as well as Bellapais Abbey, were built in this era. After 1291 and the fall of Acre to the Egyptian Mamelukes, Famagusta expanded its commercial activity, and Cyprus became the wealthiest island in the eastern Mediterranean. The Venetians, who forcibly annexed Cyprus in 1489, merely remodeled and strengthened the military defenses, most notably the walls of Nicosia. In 1570, the Turks took Nicosia after a two-month siege, and Famagusta a year later. Turkish rule, characterized by continued economic decline and heavy taxation, also relaxed restrictions on the Greek Orthodox Church.

The covetous looks of Czarist Russia to Turkish Cyprus drew the interest of Russia's foe, Great Britian. The British, in 1878, elected to pay tribute to the Sultan in return for an administrative and military presence on the island, thus precluding further Russian imperial expansion. In 1925, Cyprus became a Crown Colony; the first violent uprisings in the name of *enosis* (union with Greece) occurred six years later. The Government House in Nicosia was burned down, but the movement was quickly suppressed and the leaders deported. The Orthodox Church held a plebiscite in mid-January, 1950, in which 96% of the Greek Cypriots favored *enosis*. That same year, the archbishop died, and the 37-year-old Bishop of Kition was elected for the position by an Assembly on October 18. Over the next 27 years, Archbishop Makarios III became the central and most popular figure in Cypriot politics. In 1954, when the United Nations turned down an appeal by the Greeks to grant Cyprus self-determination, riots broke out and guerrilla warfare began, initiated by General Grivas and the EOKA (National Organization of Cypriot Fighters). Archbishop Makarios was exiled because the Church actively supported the EOKA movements. Cyprus officially won independence on August 16, 1960, entered the U.N., and joined the British Commonwealth shortly thereafter.

Independent Cyprus was rocked by conflict almost from the start. The Turkish-speaking minority accused the Greek Cypriots of both political and economic oppression. Intermittent violence suddenly exploded into an international affair in 1974 five days after the Greek Cypriot National Guard staged a coup to oust Archbishop Makarios. In an apparent attempt to forestall National Guard hegemony and prevent further discrimination of Turkish Cypriots, the Turkish army invaded the northern part of Cyprus, conquering 40% of the island. In November, 1983, Turkish-occupied Cyprus proclaimed itself an independent state, but only Turkey has recognized the new nation. In 1986, relations were exacerbated by the official visit of Turkish Prime Minister Ozal to Northern Cyprus. Access to Northern Cyprus, vehemently discouraged by the Republic of Cyprus and the International Air Traffic Association, has been curtailed. In the summer of 1988, the Green Line that divides the city of Nicosia was closed to crossing to all but those with diplomatic status.

# The Republic of Cyprus

## Limassol Λεμεσός

The port of entry for most passenger ferries that stop in Greek Cyprus, Limassol is not the best introduction to this otherwise striking island. Rapid growth, due to the sudden influx of refugees from the Turkish invasion, and lack of urban planning have led to an endless row of hotels stretching east along the coast, and clumps of residential and commercial buildings lining the major arteries. While Limassol is the industrial center of Cyprus, the downtown area is decaying, and on any given day dozens of ugly merchant ships are anchored offshore. The town makes a good base for daytrips in the area, but other than the castle and the museum, has little to offer.

## Orientation and Practical Information

Situated right in the middle of Cyprus' southern coast, Limassol is more or less equidistant from every other major city in Southern Cyprus (50-70km). It is the center for bus and taxi services, and the only city from which direct transportation is available to the rest of the island. (To get from Larnaca or Nicosia to Paphos, for example, you must go through Limassol.)

The **new port**, where the passenger boats arrive, is actually about 5km southwest of the center of town. Bus #1 runs between the port and downtown Limassol (Sun.-Fri. every ½ hr., Sat. 5:30am-6:50pm every hr., 20¢). There is a stop right outside the customs building a few meters past the snack stand where buses wait immediately after a ship's arrival. Otherwise, the stop is right outside the port gates, straight ahead as you exit. Going to the port, you can catch bus #1 at the bus station near the market on Anexartisias St. A taxi to or from town should cost about C£1.50-2. If you are headed directly for another major town, call the appropriate service taxi (see below) to be picked up at the port at no extra charge.

**Cyprus Tourism Organization Office:** 15 Spiro Araouzos St. (tel. 627 56), on the waterfront, 1 block east of the castle. A wise 1st stop. The extremely capable and helpful staff can answer all questions, suggest daytrips, and provide maps, bus schedules, and general information for the entire island. Open June-Aug. Mon. and Thurs. 8am-1:30pm and 4-6:15pm, Tues.-Wed. and Fri.-Sat. 8am-1:45pm; Sept.-May Mon. and Thurs. 8:15am-1:45pm and 3-5:30pm, Tues.-Wed. and Fri.-Sat. 8:15am-1:45pm. A small office at the **port** (tel. 438 68) is open immediately following arrivals. Nearby office in **Passoudi Beach**, 35 George I Potamos Yermassoyias (tel. (051) 232 11), opposite the Park Beach Hotel. Same hours as the Limassol office.

**Travel Agent: Amathus** 2 Syntagma Sq. (tel. 621 45), near the tourist office on the water. A large chain that sells most plane and boat tickets. Open Mon.-Fri. 8am-12:30pm and 3:30-6:30pm.

**American Express:** 130 Spiro Araouzos St. (tel. 620 45), in the offices of A. L. Mantovani and Sons. Open for American Express transactions Mon.-Fri. 8:30am-noon; for mail collection Mon.-Fri. 8am-1pm and 3:30-6:30pm, Sat. 9am-noon.

**Post Office:** Main office, Gladstone St. (tel. 625 14), next to the central police station. Handles Poste Restante. Open in summer Mon.-Sat. 8am-12:30pm and 4-6pm; Sept.-May 8am-12:30pm and 3:30pm-5:30pm. Branch office, Archbishop Kyprianou St., 1 block inland from St. Andrew St. Same hours as main office.

**Telephones (CYTA):** At the corner of Markos Botsaris and Athens St. Open daily 7am-7:30pm. **Telephone code:** 051.

**Bus Station: KEMEK terminal** (tel. 632 41), corner of Irene and Enossiss St. Buses to Nicosia (Mon.-Sat. 6am-4:30pm 9 per day, Sun. 8am-4pm 4 per day, C£1) and Paphos (Mon.-Sat. 6:30am-3:15pm 4 per day, C£1). **Lefkaritio terminal,** 107 Spiro Araouzos St., near the waterfront. To Larnaca (Mon.-Sat 6am-4pm 8 per day, 80¢). Buses also run to Platres from Eleftherias St. (Mon.-Sat. at 2pm, 60¢), and Agros from KEMEK (Mon.-Sat. at 1pm, 60¢). **City buses,** Andreas Themistokles St., near Anexartisias St. Catch bus #6 or 25 to go east along the coast as far as Amathus (10km).

**Service Taxis: Karydas,** 129 Spiro Araouzos St. (tel. 620 61). **Kypros/Akropolis,** 49 Spiro Araouzos St. (tel. 639 79). **Kyriakos,** 9 Pateur St. (tel. 641 14). **Makris,** 166 Hellas St. (tel. 655 50). Karydas, Kypros/Akropolis, and Kyriakos run frequent taxis to Nicosia (June-Aug. daily 6am-7pm; Sept.-May 6am-6pm; C£1.50). Akropolis and Makris run taxis to Larnaca (June-Aug. daily 6am-7pm; Sept.-May 6am-6pm; C£1.30). All the companies except Akropolis go to Paphos (6am-6:30pm every hr., C£1.50).

**Bike and Motorbike Rentals:** All shops near the luxury hotels at the eastern edge of town, on the shore road. A motorcycle license is required to rent anything, but most agents will take you to the police station, where if you've "forgotten" your license, you can be issued a temporary Cypriot license (C£1-2). Motorbikes C£3.50-4.50 per day, bikes C£1.50. If you plan to rent long term, you'll find lower rates in Polis. The youth hostel rents 50cc motorbikes for C£4..

**Bookstores: Ioannides,** 30 Athens St. (tel. 666 04), and **Kyriakou,** 57 Anexartisias St. at Athens St. (tel. 751 11).

**Laundromat:** Self-service laundry on Kaningos St. off Markarios Ave. (tel. 682 93), near the archeological museum. Wash C£1.75. Dry C£1.

**Pharmacy:** Call 192 for a list of all-night pharmacies.

**Hospital:** Leondios St. (tel. 631 11).

**Police:** At Gladstone and Leondios St. (tel. 756 11), next to the hospital.

# Accommodations and Food

For the most part, budget accommodations in Limassol, clustered near the bus station, are cheap, but of low quality.

**Youth Hostel (IYHF),** 120 Ankara (Angira) St. (tel. 637 49), a few blocks west of the castle. The entrance is on a small alley off Ankara St.; the sign on Ankara St., on the 2nd floor balcony, is easy to miss. From the bus station, turn right onto Anexartisias St., then right on Agios Andreas St., and walk all the way down until it becomes Ankara. 11pm curfew, but they'll show you where the key is. Check-out 10am. First night C£1.85 per person, linen and breakfast included. Each additional night C£1, breakfast 60¢. Hot showers 35¢, cold showers 20¢.

**Guest House Icaros,** 61 Eleftherias St. (tel. 543 48). Decorated with family heirlooms and guarded by a porcelain collie. Cleaner and greener than other places in town. Rents bike (C£1.50) and motorbikes (C£4) downstairs. Singles C£3. Doubles C£4. Showers included. Call for reservations in high season.

**Guest House Stalis,** 59 Eleftherias St. (tel. 681 97), next to the Ikaros. The rooms aren't bad, but the beds look ancient. Rents bikes (C£1.50) and motorbikes (C£4). Bed in a 4-bed dorm C£1. Singles C£2. Doubles C£4.

**Guest House Luxor,** 101 Agios Andreas St. (tel. 622 65), on a nice pedestrian shopping street. The floors and sheets are quite clean, and the rooms are spacious. Singles C£3.50. Doubles C£5. Showers included. Breakfast C£1.

**Guest House Excelsior,** 35 Anexartisias St. (tel. 533 51). Drab in a clean sort of way. Kitchen facilities. Ask for a room with an electric fan. Singles C£3. Doubles C£6. Showers included. T.V. C£1.

**Limassol Palace Hotel,** 97-99 Spirou Araouzou (tel. 521 31), on the waterfront. A costly 1-star alternative to the other fleabags. Carpeted rooms with bath and balcony. Singles C£6. Doubles C£11. Triples C£15. Breakfast included.

**Hotel Hellas,** 9 Zig Zag St. (tel. 638 41), facing Agios Andreas St. Bare, dingy, and bordering on unsanitary. Cell-like singles C£2.50. Otherwise, same price per person for doubles and triples.

**Continental Hotel,** 137 Spirou Araouzou St. (tel. 625 30). A 1-star hotel. Pleasant and clean, but you might need another mortgage. Doubles C£11-13.

Restaurant fare in Limassol is mediocre; many of the restaurants on the waterfront and in the town center cater to rich, undiscerning tourists; glossy, plastic-coated menus advertise boring food at startling prices. The **Kebab House,** on Spirou Araouzou St. (tel. 713 30), opposite the tourist office, however, serves excellent *souvlaki* and *sheftalia* (each 80¢). **Lefteris,** at Gladstone and Anexartisias St. (tel. 761 48), serves what must be the only kebab in Cyprus whose pita wrapping doesn't crumble in your hands (80¢). If you like Cypriot meat and bean dishes and can decipher a menu in handwritten Greek, visit the **Popular Restaurant,** Kanaris St. (tel. 625 16), near the city bus station. (Good, filling meat dishes C£1.50.) Nearby at the corner of Georgian Yenadiou St., **Anchos Theofanous** grills *kebab* on an outdoor patio. Unimpressive bars, moderate or expensive, stretch down the coast to Dassoudi Beach.

# Sights and Entertainment

The **Limassol Castle** is the only building of historical importance in Limassol itself. This thirteenth-century Frankish structure, where Richard married his Queen Berengaria in 1191, was destroyed by earthquakes and Genoese assaults; the only traces of the old Byzantine fort are in the west wall of the compact building. The Lusignans first leased the castle to the Templar Knights, who thickened the walls and covered the Gothic windows in the early fourteenth century. Later, the Knights of St. John converted the great Western Hall into a Gothic church and the chapel into a series of prison cells. The Turks claimed the castle in 1570, and the large West Hall was used as a prison until 1940 under the British regime. The terrace offers a nice view of the port and town center. (Open June-Aug. Mon.-Sat. 7:30am-1:30pm; Sept.-May Mon.-Sat. 7:30am-1pm. Admission 30¢.) The castle houses the **Cyprus Medieval Museum.** The **archeological museum** contains a small collection of pottery, terracotta figurines, jewelry, statues, and funerary steles. Most notable is the fourth-century head of Aphrodite in the north room, which was discovered at Kourion. (Open June-Aug. Mon.-Sat. 8am-1:30pm and 4-6pm, Sun. 10am-1pm; Sept.-May Mon.-Fri. 7:30am-2pm and 3-5pm, Sat. 7:30am-1pm and 3-5pm, Sun. 10am-1pm. Admission 30¢.) On Byron St., closer to the sea, you'll find the town, **zoo** and **public gardens.** The **folk art museum,** on Agios Andreas St., 1 block east (left facing the water) of the intersection of Zenon and Agios Andreas houses local costumes, embroidery, and jewelry. (Open Mon., Wed., and Fri. 8am-1pm and 4-6pm; Tues., Thurs., and Sat. 8am-1pm. Free.)

If you want to see what modern Limassol is all about, or if you just want free samples of Cypriot wine, visit the **KEO factory,** on Franklin Roosevelt St., a five-minute walk west (right facing the water) of the castle. Free tours are given Monday through Friday at 10am. The recently opened **municipal art gallery** (tel. 631 03) is on 28th of October St., east of the public gardens. The city's long, stone beach is nothing to write home about, although a new wave breaker makes the area more pleasant for swimming. **Dassoudi Beach,** 3km east of town, is far better. Take bus #6, 13, or 25 from the market on Kanaris St. (every 15 min., 20¢). For diving information and rental equipment, contact **L&M Seamasters Scuba Diving Centre,** 54 Franklin Roosevelt St. (tel. 767 87). Licenses for **spear fishing** are available near the entrance of the old port (tel. 624 70).

Limassol hosts a number of celebrations each year, including a Shakespeare festival at the end of June, a two-week International Art Festival in the first half of July, a Wine-Fest in early September, and a carnival 50 days before Orthodox Easter (usually in Feb.). For details about these and other special events, contact the tourist office.

## Near Limassol

The **Kolossi Castle,** a square-shaped, three-story structure about 5 miles west of Limassol, was crucial during the Crusades. Both the Templar Knights and the Knights of the Order of St. John made the castle their headquarters for a short while. When the latter Order moved to Rhodes in 1310, Kolossi remained its richest overseas possession, garnering wealth from the surrounding vineyards. (Open Mon.-Sat. 7:30am-1:30pm, Sun. 7:30am-dusk. Admission 30¢.) To reach Kolossi, take bus #16 from the urban bus station in Limassol (Mon.-Sat. every ½ hr., Sun. 5:30am-6:30pm every hr., 20¢).

Outside of the British sovereign base of Akrotiri is the small resort town of **Pissouri,** lively year-round due to the patronage of Her Majesty's military men. Built on a cliff with plunging views, Pissouri has several bars and *tavernas.* The **Bunch of Grapes Inn** (tel. (052) 212 75) has a restaurant as well as rooms. (Singles C£8.50. Doubles C£13.)

Seven miles from Limassol is the turn-off for **Pano Lefkara,** the center of the Cypriot lace-making industry. Leonardo da Vinci came here in 1481 to purchase lace for the altar of the cathedral in Milan. You can buy lace cheaper in both Limassol and Larnaca, but if you skip Pano Lefkara you'll miss a pleasant afternoon walking along the hilly cobblestone streets and archways. The **hospital** (tel. 24 29) is on the uppermost level across from the **police station** (tel. 24 16). At the **tourist pavillion** (tel. 22 11) in Lefkara Sq., you can relax and enjoy the hillside scenery. (Small salad 35¢. Open 9am-midnight.) In a small, enclosed courtyard 100m from the square, **Anna** (tel. 20 65) rents homey doubles with breakfast and shower for C£4. **Buses** leave daily at 1pm from Iriniss St. in Limassol, returning the following day at 7am. You may have to hitch or walk along the main road (5km) and catch a bus back to town from there. The **telephone code** is 0434.

On the main road between Limassol and Larnaca is the archeological site at **Kirokitia.** Built on the side of a hill, this seventh/sixth-century B.C.E. town was inhabited by people who lived in circular stone houses and buried their dead in the fetal position beneath their homes. (Open daily 7:30am-7pm. Admission 30¢.) Take a bus bound for Nicosia or Larnaca and ask to be let off at the site.

## Kourion

**Kourion** (Curium in Latin), 12km west of Limassol, actually lies within the British Sovereign Base Area, which includes all of the Akrotiri Peninsula. First settled during the Neolithic Period, Kourion was colonized by Achaeans from Argos in the Peloponnese during two Greek Mycenaean expansions in the fourteenth and thirteenth centuries B.C.E. It became famous for its sanctuary to Apollo (eighth century B.C.E.) and its stadium (second century C.E.), both located west of the main settlement. In the fourth century C.E., the same earthquake that destroyed other Cypriot coastal cities leveled Kourion as well. The city was rebuilt in the fifth century, only to be burned in the mid-seventh century during an Arab raid. The ruins lie just south of the highway.

When you enter through the ticket office, walk 200 yards down to begin your tour at the impressive **theater,** which commands an expansive view of the Mediterranean and is used for the Shakespeare Festival in June, occasional concerts during the summer, and weekend theater in September. The tourist bureau in Limassol can tell you about live performances and taped music well in advance. The earliest structure on the site, a small theater built in the second century B.C.E., was enlarged with limestone blocks in the first century C.E. During Greek and Roman times, the theater was used for presenting tragedies and comedies, but by the third century C.E., with the rise in popularity of animal fights, it was transformed into an arena, complete with a metal grill on top of the orchestra section to protect the fighters before they commenced their macabre battles. Following the earthquake that destroyed the town, the theater was plundered to such a degree that hardly a seat remained. The present reconstruction was completed in 1961 by the Department of Antiquities. Next to the theater is the **House of Eustolios,** built after the earthquake on top of an earlier private mansion. Composed of more than 30 rooms and a bathing complex, this building was used as a public gathering place and bathing area until the Arab raids in the seventh century A.D. Various inscriptions and symbols of birds and fish reveal its Christian identity. Between the ticket booth and the sea, the fifth-century **Christian Basilica,** church of the first Bishops of Kourion, contains fine mosaics and columns.

Across the dirt road from the basilica are a group of ruins still being excavated. In the northern corner (away from the sea) is a large Hellenistic building and a water reservoir used until the seventh century C.E. In the southwest corner lies a row of Corinthian columns, which is all that remains of the **Forum,** a market and meeting-place dating from the end of the second century C.E. To the northwest is a large **Nymphaeum,** where water was stored and dedicated to nymphs, minor deities who were protectors of water. First constructed in the first century C.E., the Nymphaeum's floors show mosaics dating from the fourth century C.E. and geometric forms dating from the third century C.E. Three limekilns from the eighth century C.E. are in the northwest corner of the site; they were used to convert the ancient limestone blocks, statues, and ornaments into powder.

Farther northwest are the remains of the **House of Gladiators.** The two surviving panels contain the only mosaics of gladiators in combat found in the eastern Mediterranean; one depicts two men in training (note the dull spear tips), and the other depicts genuine gladiator combat with an arbiter in the middle. Be careful not to fall into one of the nearby cisterns. At the end of the excavation site is the **House of Achilles,** which faces the highway and the entrance to the site and contains a splendid mosaic depicting Achilles, dressed as a woman in order to avoid conscription and thus his prophesied death in the Trojan War, revealing his identity to Odysseus as he reaches for a spear. The house is fenced off, but you can reach it by a narrow path that follows the fence along the road. Alternatively, ask the friendly guard at the ticket office to give you the key. (Site open daily 7:30am-7:30pm or sunset, whichever comes first. Admission 40¢.) Visit the nearby **Museum of Kourion** in Episkopi village for a clear explanation of the artifacts from Kourion. (Open Mon.-Sat. 7:30am-1:30pm.)

Less than half-mile west up the hill you can see the low walls of the **stadium** on the right side of the highway. When built, the stands held 6,000 people, but today, only a small section of the original seating remains. The stadium is unattended and always open. Another half-mile farther lies the **Sanctuary of Apollo,** at one time second only to the Temple of Aphrodite (in old Paphos) as a center of religious worship on the island. Apollo was worshiped here as god of the woodland. Very little of the original temple exists; most of the present ruins date from 100 C.E. (Sanctuary open in summer daily 7:30am-7:30pm; in winter 7:30am-sunset. Admission 30¢.) To get to either site, take a KEMEK bus bound for Paphos and let the driver know where to let you off. As the road west of the main site is uphill, you might consider disembarking at the more distant site of Apollo and working your way back. To leave Kourion, hail a KEMEK bus or book a seat on a Paphos-Limassol service taxi; unfortunately, you'll still have to pay the whole fare.

# Troodos Mountains Τροοδιτισσης

The interminable attempt to escape urban blight and suburban void brings most to the coast. Yet this reflex should be supressed in Cyprus, where one can find inner serenity and natural delights in the Troodos mountain range, halfway between Nicosia and Limassol. Tiny villages, breathtaking Byzantine churches, and remote monasteries dot the mountainsides, and the surrounding forests of flat-topped pines provide a welcome escape from the summer heat. Hikers and campers in particular will have a field day here. But what is usually a peaceful and rejuvanating natural experience in June and early July can turn frustrating and expensive in August when tourists and Cypriots descend; even the monasteries have been known to turn away visitors. The best time to visit in summer is midweek, when crowds are thin. In winter, from January to March, Mt. Olympos, the highest point in Cyprus (1951m), provides slopes for thousands of skiers.

Public transportation to and from the area and between villages within Troodos is very infrequent. The easiest way to get around is to hitch or rent a motorbike. Leave your things in one of the coastal towns and travel around the area for a few days with the map from the tourist office.

## Platres

**Platres** will most likely be your first stop in the Troodos region, as it is the most accessible by public transportation. From Nicosia, KEMEK runs a **bus** via Kalopanayiotis, Moutoullas, Pedhoulas, and Prodromos. It leaves the Leonides St. station in Nicosia on weekdays at 12:15pm, returning from Platres at 6am (C£1). Several buses also run from Limassol to Platres: Platres Bus Co. sends a bus from Eleftherias St. in Limassol (Mon.-Fri. at 2pm, returning at 7am, 60¢); Gero-Demos has a bus that leaves from the KEMEK station and continues on to Prodromos and Pedhoulas (Mon.-Fri. at 1pm, returning the next morning, 60¢). Agros bus leaves the KEMEK station Monday through Friday at 1pm, returning the next morning (60¢). **Karydas,** 21 Thessalonikis St. (tel. 620 61), also has buses running to Platres Monday through Friday three times per day, twice on Sundays in July and August (C£1). Otherwise, buses leave at 1pm, returning from Platres at 7am. Karydas taxi-office, 129 Spiro Araouzou St. (tel. 620 61), runs a mini-bus that leaves Limassol daily at 1pm and returns early the next morning (C£1). In July and August, two additional mini-buses leave at 10am and 4pm. Platres is divided into *pano* (upper) and *hato* (lower) sections; Kato Platres, 20 minutes downhill from Pano Platres, remains nearly untouched by tourism. Try florid **Kapakioti** (tel. (054) 212 02), where tidy doubles cost C£8. Up the hilly road, the Platres **tourist office,** left of the parking lot in the main square, is extremely helpful. (Open Mon., Wed.-Thurs., and Sat. 8:30am-1pm.) To the left of the tourist office is the **post office.** (Open July 1-Sept. 15 Mon.-Tues. and Thurs.-Sat. 8am-1pm and 4-6pm, Wed. 4-6pm; Sept. 15-July 1 Mon.-Tues. and Thurs.-Fri. 8-10am and 3-5pm, Wed. and Sat. 8-10am and 3-4pm.) The **Bank of Cyprus** is open Mon.-Sat. 8:30am-noon; in summer also Mon.-Tues. and Thurs.-Fri. 2-5pm. The **hospital** (tel. 212 34) is just below Pano Platres and also houses the **pharmacy.** The **dentist** comes to Platres on Thursdays. The **police** (tel. 213 51) are located in Pano Platres across from the Splendid Hotel in a converted military chapel. Platres' **telephone code** is 054.

As you enter town, the **Spring Hotel** (tel. 213 30) is on your left, perched on the edge of a gorge overlooking a small waterfall and stream. (Singles C£6-7. Doubles C£10-12. July-Sept. 25¢ surcharge per person. Breakfast included.) In town, 1 block from the fountain/parking lot, is the nice-but-not-splendid **Splendid Hotel** (tel. 214 25). All rooms have balconies and private showers. (Singles C£6. Doubles C£10. Breakfast included.) Farther down on the left, **Hotel Petit Palais** (tel. 217 23) rents plain singles for C£3-4, doubles for C£5-8. A good place to stay is the **Pafsilypon Hotel** (tel. 217 38). Andreas, the proprietor, makes sure the creaky rooms are clean and the price is right; you won't have trouble finding an opening here, even in August. To get there, bear right at the fork in town and go one block up the hill. (C£5 per person. English breakfast included.) Food in Platres does not vary much in price and quality. Try M.J. Pasteles (tel. 217 20), near the Pafsilypon, or the **Kaledonian** (tel. 214 04), up the street. The best food is just north of Platres on the road to Troodos: **Psilo Dentro** (tall tree) serves mouth-watering trout from its own fish farm (tel. 213 50). There are several **supermarkets** in town. The urbane step out at **Andy's Disco** (tel. 211 22), near the main square. (Small beer 50¢. No cover. Open 10pm-2am. Lots of **Paella Madness.**)

## Troodos

Five miles north of Platres, **Troodos** is accessible by **bus** only from Constantza Bastion in Nicosia (Wed. at noon, returning to Nicosia early Thurs. morning, 65¢). There are daily minibuses from Platres to Troodos (11am and 5pm), but the schedule is unreliable. You can't get to Troodos by public transportation from Limassol. Troodos Town is a graceless collection of hotels, restaurants, and tourist facilities, including a **CYTA office,** a **bank,** and a **post office,** which is open when the mayor feels like working.

The **IYHF youth hostel** (tel. 152 49 or 216 49) is the cheapest place to stay in the mountain area if you're not camping (C£2.50 per night, sheets 40¢), and its central location makes it perfect for excursions to the rest of the Troodos region (open July-Sept.). Newly installed hot shower. Make inquiries at the **Dolphin Retaurant,** on the left several hundred meters below the town. You can use their **tennis court** if you eat something.

There are no good budget options outside of the youth hostel for accommodations. The two-star **Troodos Hotel** (tel. 216 35 or 216 36), in the village center, charges C£9.50 for a single and C£15 for a double, including breakfast (all rooms with private bath). The cheapest place to stay is the **Troodos campground** (tel. 216 24), ½ mile down the road to Nicosia, which charges C£1.25 per tent. It has washing facilities, a minimarket, and a small bar/restaurant. The **Louis Restaurant** (tel. 219 69) and the two kebab houses next to it serve good, inexpensive food (*kebab* and chips C£1.50, *kleftico* and chips C£2). The **Jubilee Hotel Bar** (tel. 216 47) is a favorite haunt of British ex-patriates. You can horseback ride at Troodos (C£3 per hr.).

Three guided **nature trails** leave from the Troodos area. The first is 6 miles long and goes from the Troodos post office to Chromion, passing by various villages. A 2-mile trail leaves from the coffee shop in Troodos Square and finishes at a beautiful look-out point. Shorter but even more beautiful is the 2-kilometer path that follows a stream from the Presidential Palace in Troodos and finishes at Kaledonia Falls near Platres. Noteworthy trees and plants are labeled along the way. The tourist office has a pamphlet that outlines the trails and the flora and fauna that you'll encounter.

If you have wheels, try to get to several nearby mountain villages and the Ohiarizos Valley, where traditional Cypriot life continues undisturbed. Driving up from the Sanctuary of Aphrodite at **Kouklia,** bear right at the town's church and then turn left onto the main road north towards Pano Arkhimandrita. After passing a **siege mound** built in 498 B.C.E. by an attacking Persian army, turn left 3km out of Kouklia at the signpost for **Souskiou.** Turn left onto the dirt track and cross a small bridge. A dramatic descent leads into the eastern bank of the Dhiarizos River where an abandoned Turkish village awaits inspection. Souskiou's last inhabitants re-settled in the occupied north area after the Turkish invasion of 1974. The eerie silence that pervades the streets and crumbling stone buildings is broken only by a handful of sheep and chickens. Return to the main road by following the northwest dirt track running adjacent to the town's mosque; follow this path across the river and turn right onto the main asphalt road on the west bank. Continue north on the Agios Nikolaos Rd. Your last fill-up for both stomach and gas before ascending the mountains is at the **Diaryzos Cafe** (tel. (064) 323 35), in Mamonia, where you can grab a quick salad (50¢) or spend the night. (Open 6am-11pm. Doubles C£5.) After passing through the village of Agios Georgias, make an acute right turn on the unmarked track exactly 3km north of the town's last house. Cross the shallow river and climb high up the east bank of the mountain until you see the deserted monastery of **Agios Savvas tis Karonos,** secluded within fertile vineyards and olive trees. The hidden treasure of this group of buildings is the fifteenth-century church, built upon foundations dating back two centuries. The site was abandoned during the mid-'50s, but the masonry, still visible around the church and monastic buildings, is exceptional; notice the small carved faces on the fountain basins. You'd be hard pressed to find a better picnic site in all of western Cyprus. Return to the asphalt road and head north until Mandria, where a short detour (3km) leads to the friendly lace and wine village of **Omodos.** Ask for a tour of the monastery's **folk museum** in the main *platia* and the fascinating restored **wine press** (*linos*). You can buy a bottle of tasty, local, dry *krasi* for C£1.50 or the fiery *tsipoura,* a Cypriot whiskey. In past generations, it was eaten with raisins and used medicinally. Returning to Kato Platres, follow the signposts to the red-tiled village of **Phini,** noted for its pottery and production of *pitharia,* the large red ceramic jars seen throughout Cyprus and the Greek islands; take a look on the ten-cent piece for an example of this now-lost ceramic art. Theophanis Pilavakis, resident historian and curator of the **Pilavakion Museum,** should be the first person you seek out in Phini. He will guide you through his ethnographic museum, which focuses on *pitharia,* wine-making equipment, and the notable "Pithari Sauna" used in traditional Cypriot obstetrics to avoid post-pregnancy stretchmarks. If you're lucky, Mr. Pilavakis will also give you a tour of his stately Turkish house and guest quarters. (Museum open 9am-noon and 1-6pm.)

Picturesque **Kakopetria,** on the main road from Nicosia to Troodos, is the most popular town in the northern part of the mountains. Kakopetria means "bad stone:" The local yarn is that the large rock perched on the hillside was supposed to bring good luck to newlyweds, until it rolled over one day and crushed a couple while they were wishing. The oldest section of the village, with its shady, cobblestone roads and mudbrick houses overlooking a river, is being preserved by the government; in the rest of the village, slick new pubs and "rustic" hotels cater to vacationers.

The **Bank of Cyprus** is in the main square (open Mon.-Fri. 8:30am-noon), near the **post office** (open Mon.-Fri. 7:30am-1:30pm, Sat. 7:30am-12:30pm). A **pharmacy** (tel. 20 20) is below the Rialto Hotel (open 9:30am-9pm) and the **doctor** (tel. 30 77) is a few doors down. If you come on a weekday before August, you can stay in the **Rialto Hotel** (tel. 24 38; singles C£5; doubles C£10; breakfast included), or at the **Hekali** (tel. 25 01; singles C£7; doubles C£11; breakfast included). The **Kifissia Hotel** (tel. 24 21) has calming views of the small river and clean doubles (C£5 per person; English breakfast included). Elsewhere, you'll pay nearly twice as much. Kakopetria and its smaller neighbor **Galata** have five interesting Byzantine churches between them; the most beautiful is **Agios Nikolaos tis Stegis**, located about 3 miles southwest of Kakopetria on a dirt road. Inside are Byzantine frescoes; on top is a unique protective roof added in the fourteenth century, 300 years after the building was constructed. **Buses** to Kakopetria travel from Constantza Bastion in Nicosia (Mon.-Fri. 6:15am-6pm, 55¢).

After a walk through the **Old Village**, quaff a cold brew (70¢) at the **Village Pub**. (Open 10am-midnight.) There are several cheap **kebab** houses in the square, and the **Village Cellar**, in a restored village house, is known for its *tatavas* (lamb and onions, C£2) and fresh trout. (Open Fri.-Wed.) Kakopetria's **telephone code** is 0292.

Many tourists overlook the opportunity to stay in the monasteries. Not only are they free, but they'll expose you to the strength and vitality of the Greek Orthodox Church in Cyprus. Women may not enter in shorts or mini-skirts. Services are held daily at sunrise and are well worth waking up for, especially if you've never seen one—the monks will appreciate your attendance, too. Every Sunday after the service, babies are christened at the monasteries. Keep in mind that Troodhitissa officially closes its doors to overnight guests from June 15 to September 15, and Kykko prefers Cypriot tourists to foreigners, especially in high season. Donations are always welcome, and remember that a few words of Greek and conservative attire goes a long way with the monks.

On the eastern slopes of the Troodos range, the **Monastery of Macheras** lies 26 miles south of Nicosia. From Nicosia, take the Nicosia-Agros road 9 miles to the village of Kato Deftera and turn left for Pera; the monastery is about 12 miles farther. The monastery was founded in 1190 C.E., after two monks discovered a knife and a miracle-working icon of the Virgin, which was probably hidden during the iconoclastic controversy.

Ten miles northeast of Kakopetria, the tiny Byzantine church at **Asinou** stuns its visitors. Only one flying buttress distinguishes the exterior, but gorgeous Byzantine frescoes cover every inch inside. The church and the original frescoes date from the twelfth century. New frescoes were added and old ones restored after the church was vandalized by Turks in the fourteenth and sixteenth centuries. Today the church is used for religious purposes only twice a year on feast days of the Virgin, to whom it is dedicated. To visit the church, find the priest in the nearby village of Nikitare (ask in the village cafes), and take him with you in a taxi (C£1.50 round-trip). Ten miles southeast of Kakopetria is the church of **Panayia tou Arakou**, another repository of beautiful twelfth-century frescoes. At each place it is appropriate to leave a small donation at the door. South of the church is the picturesque vineyard village of **Agros**, with simple overnight accommodations (about the only in the vicinity). Try **Vlachos** (tel. (055) 213 30; singles C£4; doubles C£7).

Forty hens, fifteen cats, eight monks, and one donkey make their home in the modern **Troodhitissa Monastery**, 3½ miles from Platres on the Prodromos-Platres road. Dedicated to the Virgin Mary, the monastery was built specifically to house a miracle-working icon of her; the name Troódhitissa literally means "she who is resident of Mt. Troodos." In the eighth century C.E., a monk smuggled into Cyprus from Asia Minor 70 icons of the Virgin Mary painted by the evangelist St. Luke. He hid one of the main icons in a cave by Limassol; after the chaos of the iconoclast ceased, he moved it to a cave in Troodos, where it was protected by a miraculous pillar of fire. Over 100 years later, a mysterious light revealed the site of the Sacred Cave. The locals recognized the sign and began building a monastery on the spot, but every evening the work of the day crumbled. Then, at a hidden spring nearby, a pot full of water appeared. Everyone assumed it was a sign from the Virgin (obviously) and proceeded to construct the monastery on the new site. Today, the cave contains a replica of the famous icon. About ½km from the monastery on the way toward Platres, at the point where you can first see the waterfall, look to your left for a path; a five-minute walk brings you to the cave. The monastery also contains a girdle that makes barren women fertile, and a stone that cures children of "gnashing of the teeth." Unfortunately, the icon, girdle, and stone are all hidden behind a curtain. (Open daily 6am-noon and 2-8pm; no overnight guests June 15-Sept. 15.)

Between Troodos and Prodromos soars **Mt. Olympos** (6401 ft.), the highest peak on the island—on a clear day you can see to the ocean. The summit is topped with monumental radar stations and observation towers. From January through March you can alternate sunbathing in Limassol with skiing on the north face of the mountain. If you'll be skiing for a while, it's probably cheaper to become a member of the Cyprus Ski Club (family C£20, adults C£13, children C£10; plus C£7.50 enrollment fee). The three lifts on the mountain cost members C£3.50 per day and C£18 per week, nonmembers C£7 and C£36, respectively. You can rent skis (members C£3.50 per day; nonmembers C£7) and sleighs (members C£2.50 per day; nonmembers C£5); lessons cost C£2 for members, nonmembers C£4. There are no accommodations at the mountain, only a few restaurants.

## Prodromos

Ten kilometers northwest of the town of Troodos, **Prodromos** is the second highest hill resort in the area (after Troodos). Take the road down the hill to the left for the **Alps Hotel** (tel. 25 53; singles C£4.25; doubles C£8). Nearby, grab an orange juice (50¢) at **Stephos Cafe** before heading on to Kykko. The village resort has a **Bank of Cyprus** and a **post office.** Just north of Prodromos is the small village of **Pedoulas,** with its **Church of Archangel Michael** and mural paintings dating from 1474. Up the street from the church is the **CYTA** (open Mon.-Sat. 9am-1pm and 4-6pm) and the **police** (tel. 26 48), who will gruffly answer most tourist questions. Across the street is the miniscule **post office.** (Open Mon.-Sat. 9am-noon and 4pm-6pm.) Prodromos' **telephone code** is 0295. Stay at **Christy's Palace** (tel. 26 55) for their shiny silver and nice china. (C£5 per person. Breakfast and balconies available.) Down the road, the **Capouralli Café** lets rooms. (C£5 per person. Breakfast included.) Just north of Pedoulas are the villages of **Kalopanayiotis** and **Moutoullas,** with the nearby **Church and Monastery of Agios Ioannis Lampshadistes.** If one of the churches is closed, ask the village priest to let you in; usually he'll happily oblige and give you an impromptu tour.

**Kykko Monastery,** in the northwestern part of the mountains and 14km from Pedhoulos, enjoys more wealth and fame than any other monastery on the island. Enter its palatial courtyard, and you may think you've wandered into a large luxury hotel by mistake; the monastery has almost 400 beds for visitors, with tourist pavilion and shops. Recently, hotels have been complaining about business, so Kykko has officially restricted itself to taking in only Greek Orthodox pilgrims. Founded in the eleventh century and named after the Kokkous trees that once surrounded the area, Kykko today consists mainly of structures built in the early nineteenth century. As for its treasures, one of the three main icons of the Virgin Mary attributed to St. Luke sits just to the left of the church altar—half-covered by a curtain, completely covered with a silver plate, and ensconced in a mother-of-pearl shrine. If you recall that the Troodhitissa Monastery has the same claim to fame, you deserve an explanation. St. Luke, it seems, painted three main icons first, and then 70 lesser ones. Kykko has one of the former, Troodhitissa one of the latter. It all sounds hokey, but the aura more than compensates. The Kykko icon is reputed to have magical rain-making powers. In the past, whenever drought occurred, the locals and monks would gather on the mountaintop with the icon and pray to the Virgin for rain. Other famous relics lie next to the icon: A bronze arm believed to have once belonged to an infidel who attempted to light his cigarette using one of the holy lamps by the icon, and part of a sunfish skeleton donated to the church by a sailor who was saved from drowning by the Virgin of Kykko.

Kykko gained new fame this century because it was used as a communication and supply center during the Cypriot struggle and it was the monastic home of Archbishop Makarios III. One mile away were the headquarters of the first military leader of the struggle, "Dighenis" (General George Griva). The tomb of Cyprus' patriarch is just 2km away in the high hills west of the monastery. The Archbishop chose this location for his grave for its panoramic view. Just above the tomb is a path leading up to an icon of the Virgin. Called the *throni* (small throne), this spot is where the people used to gather with the *thaumaturgus* (miracle-working icon) when the community was crippled by serious drought. The bushes alongside the path are laden with bits of clothing from children who have fallen ill; the clothing is placed there for good luck. Because of the Archbishop's lifelong association, the place draws many Cypriot pilgrims. You'll find a supermarket, an outrageously priced tourist pavilion, and several sweet shops on the hilltop. Kykko has a small **museum** with religious and ceremonial objects. (Open daily 10:30am-5:30pm. Admission 20¢.) Proper dress is required, and blue bathrobe-like garments are provided at the entrance. Buses running to the nearby lumber village of **Kambos** depart from opposite the KEMEK station in Nicosia, Kykko (Mon.-Fri. at 12:15pm, C£1). Otherwise, you'll have to hitch.

About 10 miles northwest of Kykko is the forest station of **Stavros tis Psokas** (Cross of the Measles), so named because according to legend the nearby fresh stream cures that disease. By day, schoolchildren and city dwellers crowd the area, but by night, this shelter provides deserted solitude in a natural setting. The area between Kykko and Stavros is a natural preserve for the endangered *moufflon*, a wild sheep that looks more like a deer and smells like a goat. You probably won't see much of the timid herd, but notice the island's last refuge of Cyprus cedar trees in **Cedar Valley**, decimated by Alexander's army and the Romans in ancient times; the trees' wood was prized for shipbuilding. There are only seven doubles in Stavros, so book in advance, especially in August (tel. (067) 163 38 or (074) 174 54; (C£2 per person with breakfast; July-Aug. C£2.50 per person). To reach Stavros tis Psokas, hitch from Kykko or take a day excursion run by 21st Century Tours in Polis (C£7.50). There is no regular bus service to the region.

# Nicosia (Lefkosia) Λευκωσια

The only major landlocked Cypriot town, Nicosia, the capital of the Republic of Cyprus, sits astride the Turkish Cypriot frontier (or "Green Line"), providing the best resting place for the traveler who wants a few days to reflect on this island's troubled history. The most obvious and disturbing fact about Nicosia is that, like Berlin and Belfast, it is a divided city. The presence of Greek Cypriot and Turkish border patrols, as well as a significant number of United Nations troops, serves as a constant reminder that violence and bitterness lie just below the surface.

Greek Cypriots call their city Lefkosia, but everyone uses Nicosia when speaking English and no offense is taken. The recent appearance of several new museums and monuments reflect the town's eagerness to maintain both its spirit and cultural heritage. Built on the site of the ancient city of Ledra during the Roman occupation, Nicosia prospered until the invasions of Egyptian Mamelukes in 1426. When Egyptian strength waned, the Venetians took over (1489), and built massive walls in 1567 to ward off Turkish cannon salvos. Power hungry, they razed all the buildings outside the walls that were in their line of fire, including the fabulous Lusignan abbey of St. Domenico. The fortification worked for a while, but three years later the Turks made a concerted effort, gained a victory in seven weeks, and perched the city on the brink of ruin for the next several hundred years. In fact, only with the British takeover three centuries later in 1878 did the city again begin to prosper. When Cyprus achieved independence in 1960, Nicosia became its capital. The "Green Line" restricts the movements of Greek and Turkish Cypriots.

## Orientation and Practical Information

The easiest way to orient yourself in Nicosia is by the ominous Green Line running east-west at the north end of the city. The **old city** (*Laiki Yitonia*), within the circular Venetian walls, is sliced in half by this divider; the southern part contains most of the cheap accommodations, museums, and interesting sights. From **Eleftherias Square,** Evagoras Street heads southwest into the **new city.** Intersecting Evagoras are Archbishop Makarios III Avenue, Diagoras Street, and Th. Dervis Street, where the banks, embassies, and travel agencies are located. The new city is much busier than the old and is the center of Nicosia's nightlife. Be sure to obtain one of the excellent maps (free) from the tourist office.

**Cyprus Tourist Organization:** *Laiki Yitonia,* (tel. 444 264), within the city walls. Entering Eleftherias Sq., turn right and follow signs from the post office. Route maps and a complete list of village buses. Open Mon.-Sat. 8am-1pm; Mon. and Thurs. also 4-6pm. For more specialized information, as well as route maps, go to the **national headquarters,** 18 Theodotou St., 2nd floor (tel. 44 33 74). Open Mon.-Sat. 7:30am-1:30pm; Oct.-May Mon.-Fri. 7:30am-2pm, Sat. 7:30am-1pm.

**Embassies: U.S.:** At Dositheos and Therissos St. (tel. 46 51 51), near the Hilton Hotel, just off Archbishop Makarios III Ave. Take bus #16, 50, 55, or 58. **British High Commission,** Alexander Pallis St. (tel. 47 31 31), west of the old city. Open Mon.-Fri. 8am-noon. Take bus #23. **Australian High Commission:** 4 Annis Comninis St. (tel. 47 30 01), at the corner of Stassinos Ave. Open in summer Mon.-Fri. 8am-1pm. **Canadian Consulate,** tel. 45 16 30. **U.N. Headquarters,** On the road to the Nicosia Airport. **Syrian Embassy,** At Androcleous and Thoukidides St. (tel. 47 44 81). Wait for visas 24 hours or less; bring 2 photos. **Visa section** open Mon.-Fri. 9am-1pm.

**Crossing to Northern Cyprus:** Official checkpoint at the **Ledra Palace Hotel,** Markos Drakos Ave., just east of the city walls. Because the "Cyprus problem" is in continual flux (for instance, the closing of the border in the summer of 1988), you should consult the Greek Cypriot police at the crossing. Nearby U.N. checkpoint guards provide informal information, but don't expect any special border privileges; they'll send you back to the Ledra Hotel checkpoint. Contact your embassy or consulate for more information or call the **U.N. headquarters** (tel. 446 000), on the road to the Nicosia Airport.

**Currency Exchange: Bank of Cyprus,** 86-88-90 Phaneromeni St. (tel. 46 40 64). Also a branch in Laiki Yitonia on Drakos St. (tel. 461 082).

**American Express:** 35-37 Evagoras Ave. (tel. 437 77), in the offices of A.L. Mantovani and Sons. They charge a 1-2% commission for cashing personal checks. Open in summer Mon.-Fri. 8am-1pm and 3:30-6:30pm, Sat. 8am-12:30pm; in off-season Mon.-Fri. 8am-1pm and 2:30-5:30pm, Sat. 8am-12:30pm.

**Post Office: Main Office** (tel. 30 32 31), Constantinos Paleologos Ave. just east of Eleftherias Sq., within the walls. Open in summer Mon.-Sat. 8am-1pm; Mon., Tues., Thurs., and Fri. also 4-6pm. Open in winter Mon.-Sat. 8am-1:30pm; Mon. Tues., Thurs., and Fri. also 3:30-5:50pm. Smaller offices on Dhigenis St., Palace St., and Loukis Akitas Ave.

**Telephones (CYTA):** 1 Museum Ave. (tel. 47 71 11), around the corner from the museum. Open 24 hours. Dial 196 for telegrams. (Mon.-Sat. 7am-7pm). **Telephone code:** 02.

**Bus Stations: KEMEK,** 34 Leonides St. (tel. 46 39 89). To Limassol (in summer Mon.-Fri. 12 per day 5:45am-4:30pm; in off-season Mon.-Fri. 8 per day 6:15am-4pm; 75¢) and Platres (at 12:15pm, C£1). Also route maps. **Lefkaritis,** 6 Stassinos Ave. (tel. 44 25 66), just east of Eleftherias Sq., outside the city walls. To Larnaca (Mon.-Fri. 12 per day 6:15am-5:45pm, 55¢). **Solea Bus,** Constantza Bastion, 200m east of Eleftheria Sq. To Kakopetria (Mon.-Fri. 4 per day 6:15am-6pm, 55¢). **City buses** run to city and suburban areas 5:30am-7pm every ½ hr. City buses leave from Solomos Sq., the 1st square to the left of Eleftherias. The tourist office (tel. 473 414) has a complete list of urban city and inter-city buses.

**Service Taxis: Makris,** tel. 46 62 01; **Akropolis,** tel. 47 25 25; **Kypros,** tel. 46 48 11; and **Kyriakos,** tel. 44 41 41. All are on Stassinos Ave., which runs east along the city walls from Eleftherias Sq. **Karydas,** 8 Homer Ave. (tel. 46 22 69), is nearby. All run to Limassol (C£1.50) and continue on to Paphos (additional C£1.50); Makris, Akropolis, and Kyriakos also travel to Larnaca (C£1.15).

**Bookstores: Moufflon,** 4 Sophoulis St., Chanteclair Bldg. (tel. 451 55). Best place in Nicosia to buy guides and books about Cyprus. **MAM Bookstore** 3 Aristokypros (tel. 472 744), in *Laiki Yitonia,* down from the tourist office. Good selection of English books on Cyprus. Open Mon.-Tues. and Thurs.-Fri. 8am-1pm and 4-7pm, Wed. and Sat. 8am-3pm.

**The American Center:** 33B Homer Ave. (tel. 473 143), around the corner from the museum. No books on Cyprus, current issues of the *New York Times* and other periodicals in the air-conditioned library. Open in summer Mon.-Fri. 9am-1pm and 4-6pm; in off-season Mon.-Fri. 9am-1pm and 2:30-5pm. Open Jan.-July and Sept.-Dec.

**British Council:** 3 Museum Ave. (tel. 442 152), 2 doors down from the museum. Library with books, records, and tapes, and presents lectures, movies, and other cultural events. Open in summer Mon. and Thurs. 7:30am-1:30pm and 4-6:30pm, Tues.-Wed. and Fri. 7:30am-1:30pm, Sat. 9am-noon; in off-season afternoon hours are 3:30-5:30pm.

**Hospital:** Tel: 45 11 11, between Hilon and Homer St., near the municipal gardens.

**Police:** Limassol Ave. (tel. 30 35 35).

**Police Emergency:** Tel. 199.

## Accommodations and Food

Nicosia is not known for the cleanliness of its budget accommodations. Moreover, the staffs of Nicosia's "cabarets" tend to frequent a number of the cheaper places. Except where noted, all the hotels listed below are within the walls of the old city.

**Youth Hostel (IYHF),** 13 Prince Charles St. (tel. 44 48 08), opposite the Asty Hotel, about a 25-min. walk from the center of town. If you haven't arrived in a service taxi, take bus #27 (25¢). Closed 10am-4pm. 11pm curfew. C£2.15, nonmembers C£2.25. Sheets, cold showers, and breakfast included. C£1.75 less after the first night.

**Tony's Furnished Flats,** 13 Solon St. (tel. 46 67 52), between Eleftherias Sq. and *Laiki Yitomia.* Tony, a former English tailor, is friendly, efficient, and helpful, and speaks English. Each small, respectable room includes a fan, radio, menu, and thermos. Pleasant roof gardens. Singles C£5-8. Doubles C£10-12. Triples C£13-18. Prices vary according to size. A/C C£1.80. Good English breakfast included.

**Kypros Hotel,** 16A Vas. Voularoktonou St. (tel. 46 34 65), a stone's throw from the Green Line (sign in Greek). One of the cheapest places in Nicosia. Clean and a good deal if you don't mind the white hospital-like enameled beds. Singles C£3. Doubles C£5.

**Hotel Delphi,** 24 C. Pantelides Ave. (tel. 47 52 11), just west of Eleftherias Sq. Nice place in a lively location. Clean rooms with balconies and tolerable private bathrooms. Singles C£5. Doubles C£8.50. Triples C£10.50. Breakfast 75¢.

**Royal Hotel,** 17 Euripides St. (tel. 46 32 45). From Eletherias Sq., go up Onasagoras St., make a right on Sophocles St. and then a left on Aeschylus St.—it's on the corner of Euripides and Aeschylus. Fairly clean; some rooms have private showers (a shower and drain sitting in the middle of the room). Singles C£5. Doubles C£8. Triples C£11. Bargain.

**Alexandria Hotel,** 17 Trikoupi St. (tel. 462 160), in the southwest section of the old city. Shabby, but clean and likely to have room. Room quality varies considerably, so look before you choose. C£4 per person. Showers included.

**Sans Rival,** 7C Solon St. (tel. 47 43 83), a few doors down from Tony's. Not as nice or as friendly, but the rooms with wooden floors and balcony are adequate. Singles C£4. Doubles C£7. Breakfast C£1.

**City Hotel,** 209 Ledra St. (tel. 463 113). Friendly management, but dimly lit, claustrophobic corridors. Some rooms blind you with light, others lack windows completely. Singles without windows C£6, with windows C£7. Doubles C£10. Triples C£14.

**Alassia Pension,** 23 Pygmalionos St. (tel. 45 43 84), all the way to the end and to the left off Ledra St. Adequate rooms, but a popular place for "artists" (the local euphemism) to ply their trade. Singles C£4.50. Doubles C£7.

Nicosia has many restaurants, but the good ones are hard to find. If you're not picky, the touristy restaurants around *Laiki Yitonia* serve Cypriot and continental cuisine in clean, cool surroundings and supply traditional music. Try the **Paphia Aphrodite Bar and Restaurant** (tel. 46 35 26), with fish *meze* for C£3.50, *kalamari* or octopus for C£1, and swordfish for C£2. Near Eleftherias Sq., the **Lido Hotel** (tel. 47 43 51) runs a good restaurant, but for something really authentic, try a light dinner at **Estiatorio,** 40 Arsinoes St. (tel. 599 43), in the heart of the old city near the Green Line. Also good and reasonable is **Propylaea Restaurant,** 15A-15B Tricoupi St. (tel. 46 26 69), right beside the Alexandria Hotel and up the street from the first square left of Eleftherias. (*Mousaka* C£1.50; open 6am-1pm and 4-6pm.)

The **Aegean,** 40 Ectoros St. (tel. 43 04 54), inside the city walls, is a spirited *souvlaki taverna* in a sunken whitewashed courtyard. Upstairs, you can browse through an eclectic bookshop; check out the Greek translation of the Dead Kennedy's lyrics. (*Souvlaki* and salad C£1.50. Open 9pm-1am.) You can buy your own provisions at the **municipal market** at Dhigenis Akritas and Kalipolis St. Every Wednesday, a colorful streetside **produce market** sets up shop along Constantinos Paleologos Ave., east of Eleftherias Square. (Open 6am-1pm and 4-6pm.) The area east of the complex of museums within the old city has a number of workers' restaurants, where you can buy good, cheap food for C£1. Chickpea dishes usually go down smoothly, but we'll let ewe decide about the lamb's head.

## *Sights*

Put the **Cyprus Museum** at the top of your list of things to see in Nicosia. Under the direction of the celebrated archeologist Dr. Vassos Karageoughis, the museum is internationally renowned for its display of well-preserved Cypriot artifacts. Work your way counter-clockwise around the building. Room I contains Neolithic stone vases from Khirokitia (7000-6000 B.C.E.). Notice the predominance of the bull motif, representing fertility. Room II includes an extraordinary terracotta model from a tomb at Vornous (2000 B.C.E.) depicting an open-air sanctuary and the mythical religious rituals held therein. Room IV displays hundreds of seventh-century B.C.E. terracotta figurines from the sanctuary at Agia Irini, where pilgrims took part in the Minoan cult of the bull. Over 2000 such figures were found—only two of them female. Rooms V and VI trace the development of sculpture from seventh-century B.C.E. votives to the sensuous first-century C.E. statue of Aphrodite and the stern, larger-than-life bronze statue of Septimus Severus. Room VII contains copper, alabaster, and ivory artifacts, while Room VIII exhibits statues from the second-century C.E. gymnasium at Salamis (in the currently occupied area). The last room traces the development of idols and votives from the early Bronze Age to Roman times. Many artifacts from sites in the north have been taken by the Turks, although an enormous campaign is on to repatriate as many of these pieces as possible. (Open June-Aug. Mon.-Sat. 7:30am-1:30pm and 4-6pm, Sun. 10am-1pm; Sept.-May Mon.-Sat. 7:30am-2pm and 3-5pm, Sun. 10am-1pm. Admission 40¢.)

Nicosia's other important sights lie within the walls of the old city, four of them right next to each other in Archbishop Kyprianos Sq. Their location on the map distributed by the tourist office is deceptive; they actually lie in a row on the right (east) side of the **Archbishop's Palace,** a gaudy and pretentious modern structure with an overwhelming statue of Archbishop Makarios lighting up the neighborhood at night. Located next to the palace is the **Byzantine Museum,** which houses one of the finest collections in all of Europe. The older icons were recently gathered from religious sanctuaries throughout Cyprus. On the second floor is a collection of European painting, mostly religious and mythical, and a few original works by Poussin, Tintoretto, and Correggio. The third floor contains relics from the Greek War of Independence in 1821. (Open May-Sept. Mon.-Sat. 7:30am-1:30pm, Sun. 7:30am-dusk; Oct. -April Mon.-Sat. 7:30am-5pm, Sun. 7:30am-dusk. Admission 40¢.)

Next to and in front of the Byzantine Museum is the seventeenth-century **St. John's Church,** adorned with eighteenth-century frescoes; to the left of the archbishop's throne is the picture depicting the discovery of the tomb of St. Barnabas at Salamis. In the same courtyard, to the right of the church, is the **Folk Art Museum,** housed in the old Archbishopric, a former fifteenth-century Gothic monastery. The museum displays pottery, costumes, jewelry, weaving looms, and carved wooden furniture. (Open June-Aug. Mon.-Fri. 8am-5pm, Sat. 8am-1pm; Sept.-May Mon.-Fri. 8am-4pm, Sat. 8am-1pm; holidays 10am-1pm. Admission 30¢.) For a more exciting interpretation of Cypriot culture, drop in at the **National Struggle Museum** next door. Founded in 1961 by the Greek Communal Chamber of Cyprus, the museum contains photographs, documents, and other relics from the struggle with the

British for *enosis* (reunification of the island) and independence, including 30 volumes of signatures of Greek Cypriots who favored *enosis* in a 1950 plebiscite. The room opposite the entrance (the Hall of Heroes) includes the pictures of those who died in both the 1931 uprising and the EOKA (National Organization of Cypriot Combatants) struggle in 1955, orchestrated politically by Archbishop Makarios and militarily by Digenis. The Turkish atrocities committed during the struggle against the British are represented here; across the Green Line on the other side of Nicosia is the **Museum of Barbarism,** which presents the Turkish view of the battle. Interestingly enough, the National Struggle Museum was founded long before the Turkish invasion. (Open June-Aug. Mon.-Sat. 7:30am-1:30pm; Sept.-May Mon.-Fri. 7:30am-2pm, Sat. 7:30am-1pm. Admission 20¢.)

Down Koreas St. from the Archbishopric is another reminder of the Cypriot struggle for freedom—a monument depicting 14 Cypriots, each representing a period of the island's history, as they are released from jail by soldiers and overseen by a religious figure. The lifelike figures and the white marble jail were designed by the Greek artist Falireas. Nearby, along the Venetian Walls at the end of Theseus St., is the recently restored **Famagusta Gate,** which served as the main entrance to the medieval city. Built in 1567, it is now used for plays, concerts, and lectures. (See a copy of *Nicosia: This Month* for a current schedule of events.)

Under restoration, the **Konak Mansion,** also known as **The House of Hadjigeorgiakis Kornesios,** 18 Patriar Gregory St., is just around the corner from the Archbishopric complex. A famous Turkish dragoman—an interpreter for the Ottoman Turks and Greeks—lived in this once luxurious, eighteenth-century structure. The adventurous can take a dip in one of the only Turkish baths this side of Istanbul. The historical **Omerye Hamam** is just in from the Podocataro Bastion; look for the nearby minaret. Women are permitted only on Wednesdays and Thursdays. (Open 7am-7pm. Admission C£1.) Nicosia is blessed with two central **parks.** The larger and dirtier one is in the "moat" (never actually filled with water) at the base of the old city walls. A short walk west brings you to a cleaner and more colorful **botanical garden,** adjacent to the museum and behind the Garden Cafe. The aviaries here contain most of the island's indigenous bird species.

Ten miles southwest of Nicosia are the royal tombs of **Tamassos,** where an ancient Cypriot kingdom that thrived on agriculture and copper mining lived. The site contains houses, the remains of a temple of Aphrodite-Astarte, and two elaborately carved sandstone tombs from 650-600 B.C.E. (Open June-Aug. daily 9am-noon and 4-7:30pm; Sept.-May 9am-1pm and 4-6:30pm.)

# *Paphos* Παφος

During the Ptolemaic and Roman Eras (306 B.C.E.-395 C.E.), Paphos was the capital and commercial center of Cyprus. Luckily for visitors, today it is neither. The city was destroyed by an earthquake in the fourth century C.E., and the capital moved to Salamis, now in the occupied area near Famagusta. Paphos remained a small village until the Turkish occupation rendered almost all of Cyprus' tourist areas inaccessible. Since 1974, Paphos has rapidly expanded, with hotels and restaurants springing up all over the place. Still, it remains comfortable and manageable, featuring archeological discoveriess, gorgeous mosaics, good restaurants, and, in the surrounding countryside, superb beaches, ruined cities, and isolated villages. Furthermore, even in mid-summer, the town is aired by a cool sea breeze. While Scandinavians tend to flock to Agia Napa and Arabs to Limassol, most tourists here are British. Many have so fallen for the place that they make it an annual summer pilgrimage, often retiring in the nearby villages.

## Orientation and Practical Information

The city of Paphos is divided into two sections: the upper **Ktima Paphos,** centered around Kennedy Square, and the lower **Kato Paphos,** about a mile to the south.

Formed in the eighth century C.E. as the townspeople fled inland to evade Arab assaults from the sea, Ktima Paphos now is home to most of the city's shops, budget hotels, and services, while luxury hotels, holiday villas, and super tourist facilities jam Kato Paphos, also the hub of Paphos' nightlife.

**Cyprus Tourist Organization:** 3 Gladstone St. (tel. 328 41), across from Iris Travel. The helpful staff can provide every extant scrap of practical information on the region. Open June-Sept. Mon. and Thurs. 8:30am-1:15pm and 4-6:15pm, Tues.-Wed. and Fri.-Sat. 8:15am-1:30pm; Oct.-May Mon.-Sat. 8:30am-1:45pm.

**Budget Travel: Iris Travel,** 10A Gladstone St. (tel. 374 85), opposite the tourist office. Airline tickets and special "Exalt" four-wheel excursions (from C£12). Ask for David Pearlman. (Open Mon.-Fri. 8am-1:30pm and 4-7pm, Sat. 8am-1:30pm.)

**Bank: Bank of Cyprus,** 13 Evagoras St. (tel. 330 78). Open 8:30am-noon.

**Post Office:** Nikodhimou Mylona St. (tel. 402 23), in the District Administration Bldg. Open Mon.-Sat. 8am-12:30pm and 4-6pm; Sept.-May Mon.-Tues. and Thurs.-Fri. 7:30am-1pm and 3:30-5:30pm, Wed. 7:30am-1pm, Sat. 7:30am-12:30pm.

**Telephones (CYTA):** Grivas Diogenes Ave. Open daily 7:30am-7:30pm. **Telephone code:** 061.

**Airport: C.T.O.,** tel. 368 33. Opens when flights arrive. Exchange facilities. Private taxis from city center C£3, from Kato Paphos C£4.

**Buses:** Leave from the *stassis* across from the post office in Ktima Paphos to the Municipal Baths in Kato Paphos (Mon.-Sat. 6am-7pm every ½ hr., Sun. every hr., 30¢). Minibuses to Polis leave from Fontana Amoroza Bus on Pallikarides St., 1 block up Evagoras from the corner of Makarios and Evagoras (Mon.-Sat. 7am-9pm 9 per day, 3 on Sun., 50¢). **KEMEK** (tel. 342 55) runs buses to Limassol from the Mitropolis Bldg. (4 per day, 75¢). Change buses at Limassol for Nicosia.

**Service Taxis: Kyriakos,** 19 Pallikaridi St. (tel. 331 81). **Karydas,** 29 E. Pallikaridi (tel. 324-59). **Akropolis and Kypros,** Archbishop Makarios III Ave. (both tel. 323 76), in Kennedy Sq. **Makris,** Athens St. (tel. 325 38), in the northern part of town. Karydos and Kypros have shared-taxi services to Polis (Karydos leaves at 10am and 4pm, returning at 7am and 1:30pm; Kypros runs at 10am and 2pm, returning at 7am and 1pm, 75¢). All companies go to Limassol (C£1.40). Change in Limassol for Nicosia.

**Bike and Motorbike Rental:** Most shops are in Kato Paphos. **Psomas Rentals,** Poseidonas St. (tel. 355 61), across from the Paphos Beach Motel. **Max Rentals** (tel. 358 34), also on Poseidonos St. Bikes C£1.50 per day, small motorbikes C£4 per day, large motorbikes C£6 per day. Road-side service.

**English Bookstore: Axel Bookshop,** 62-64 Archbishop Makarios III Ave. (tel. 324 04). Open Mon.-Sat. 8am-1pm and 4-7pm. Kiosks in Kennedy Sq. sell the *New York Times* and the *International Herald Tribune.*

**Laundromat: Sun Rise,** at Alkminis and Posidonos St., in Kato Paphos (tel. 340 18). Wash and dry C£2. Free pick-up in town. Open Mon.-Sat. 9am-1pm and 4pm-7pm.

**Women's Clinic:** Dr. Efstathiou, 6 Giallourou (tel. 436 66), off Dallikarides St. English spoken.

**Hospital:** Neophytos Nicolaides St. (tel. 323 64). Free first aid. English spoken.

**Police:** Grivas Diogenes Ave. (tel. 323 52), in Kennedy Sq., opposite the Paphos Palace Hotel.

**Police Emergency:** Tel. 199.

## Accommodations, Camping, and Food

Paphos' handful of cheap hotels are, for the most part, tolerably clean. The following are all in Ktima Paphos, except where noted. Rooms in Kato Paphos are hard to come by and probably not worth the time or money.

**Youth Hostel (IYHF),** 37 Eleftherias Venizelou Ave. (tel. 325 88), on a quiet residential street northeast of the town center—look for signs. It's a hike, but very peaceful. If you plan to come in after 11pm, call ahead. Open year-round 7:30am-10am and 4-11pm. C£1.75, with breakfast C£2.

**Phidias Pension** (tel. 325 49), in the crumbling mansion on Gladstone, down the street from the tourist office. Decent but spartan rooms. Kitchen facilities available. Plenty of space and a pretty garden in front. Singles C£3. Doubles C£ 5.

**Lazaros Omirou,** 25 Ayiou Kendea, off Makarios St. (tel. 329 09). Several rooms decorated with overstuffed chairs and antique wooden dressers. Free coffee and kitchen facilities. C£3 per person.

**Hotel Trianon,** 99 Archbishop Makarios III Ave. (tel. 321 93). Friendly management. Kitchen facilities. Singles C£3. Doubles C£5. Breakfast 50¢.

**Paphos Palace Hotel,** 10 Grivas Diogenes Ave. (tel. 323 46), in Kennedy Sq. Run-down, but spacious. A good late-night place to crash. Singles C£5.50. Doubles C£9.50. Breakfast included.

**Axiothea,** 4 Hebe Maliotis St. (tel. 328 66), 1 block from the tourist office on the left, up on the hill. Very clean and comfortable with private bathrooms and friendly family management. Most rooms have a terrace that catches the cool breeze and affords an excellent view of the seaside. Two-star hotel. Call ahead in Aug. Singles C£8.50. Doubles C£13. Meals served (breakfast C£1).

**Nautical Club of Paphos** (tel. 337 45), to the right of the Pelican Inn. Rents flats on the other side of Kato Paphos. C£10 for 2.

**Othon,** 3 Pnitagorou (tel. 343 03), near the Apollo Hotel in Kato Paphos. Fully furnished studios for 2 C£12.

**Pyramos Hotel,** 4 Agios Anastasias St. (tel. 351 61), in Kato Paphos. Clean singles C£9. Doubles C£12.

**Zenon Gardens Yeroskipou Camping** (tel. 422 77), east of the tourist beach on the sea, 2km from Paphos. Mini-market and restaurant. Limited shade. Open March-Oct. C£1.50 per day. C£3.50 per small tent.

Most restaurants are located in Kato Paphos and, as they cater to big-money tourists, some are outrageously overpriced. At the Pelican Inn, for example, you can drink yourself into the depths of poverty on just two or three glasses of lemonade. One good deal with a nice ambience is **Yacinthus,** on Agia Napia St., next to the Kato Paphos post office. They serve delicious, large, and reasonably priced salads (tuna salad, avocado salad, and chef salad 85¢-C£1.20). (Open for dinner only.) Also in Kato Paphos, with an eerie view of the harbor-side ruins, is **Hondros,** 96 Pavlou St. (tel. 342 56). The manager, Andy Adamos, and his children have created a playful crayon-covered interior. After a serving of their lamb *kleftiko* straight off the spit (C£3.25), leave your own decoration on the walls. (Open 8am-4pm and 7pm-midnight.) For breakfast, head to **Peggy's Miranda Cafe** in Kennedy Sq. The garrulous Peggy will point out the tacky Irish memorabilia on the walls, the small English paperback library, and the bulletin board. (Tasty continental breakfast 80¢. Open 7:30am-2pm.) **Phillips Supermarket,** near the new stadium on the road to Limassol, stocks a good selection of **health foods.** In Ktima Paphos, the best and most reasonable restaurant is **Trianon,** on Archbishop Makarios III Ave. (tel. 330 10). A good assortment of grill houses and shops sells *souvlaki* for 50¢. **Fetas** (tel. 378 22), in Ktima Paphos, is authentic right down to the prices (lunch from C£1.50). (Open noon-3pm and 7pm-midnight.)

## *Sights and Entertainment*

Paphos has more interesting sights per square inch than any other city in Cyprus. The mosaic floors of the **House of Dionysus** are unquestionably the most dazzling of Paphos' ancient treasures. Discovered accidentally in 1962 by a farmer ploughing his fields and excavated by a Polish expedition, the superbly preserved mosaics once covered 14 rooms of a large Roman villa and depict scenes from mythology and daily life with vibrance, sensitivity, and subtle use of color and shading. Make sure you see the second panel on the western side of the atrium, which depicts the origin of wine (enter from the southern wall). Legend has it that Dionysus first revealed the secret of wine-making to Ikarios, King of Attica, who then shared the liquid with two shepherds and paid the price of blasphemy—the drink altered the behavior of the pair so markedly that they killed the king, thinking the stuff poison. The panels on the other three sides of the atrium show hunting scenes. Another mythological composition shows the kidnapping of the beautiful young boy Ganymede by the eagle of Zeus in order to enlist him as cup-bearer on Mt. Olympos. (The goddess Hebe had clumsily stumbled and spilled some nectar, thus losing her job.) A Hellenistic mosaic from the fourth century B.C.E. depicts Scylla, from Homer's *Odyssey*. Unlike the colorful later mosaics of stone, marble, and glass paste, this work consists solely of whole red, black, and white marine pebbles. (Open June-Aug. 7:30am-7:30pm; Sept.-May 7:30am-dusk. Admission 40¢.)

One hundred yards to the south (toward the water) is the **House of Theseus.** Whereas the House of Dionysus was the private residence of a rich merchant, this building was probably the residence of the Roman governor of Cyprus. The ruins date from the second to the sixth century C.E. and reveal a luxurious building complete with marble statues, a large courtyard with marble columns, mosaic floors, and a bath complex. The two mosaics here are accessible by walkways. The first, depicting Theseus killing the Minotaur, was constructed at the end of the third century C.E. and restored a century later. Perhaps the most striking mosaic in Cyprus, it presents Theseus surrounded by the personification of Crete, the god of the Labyrinth, and Ariadne, the daughter of King Minos of Crete, who saved Theseus by secretly giving him thread to find his way out of the labyrinth after slaying the Minotaur. The second mosaic, depicting the Birth of Achilles, shows the infant Achilles being washed by his parents Thetis and Peleus, while the three Fates look on. The scene is remarkably similar to later Byzantine works representing the birth of Christ, thus attesting to the influence and continuity of pagan composition. The House of Theseus is still under excavation, so there are no closing times or admission fees. On the road to the mosaics, you'll find the remains of a limestone Roman **odeon,** a small, roofed semi-circular theater. Constructed in the second century C.E., it accommodates 3000 spectators and is periodically used for theatrical and musical performances. (Contact the tourist office for information.) In front of the *odeon* is the contemporaneous **agora.**

The **archeological museum,** on Grivas Diogenes Ave. in Ktima Paphos, houses a fine array of Bronze Age pottery and tools, Classical sculpture and statues unearthed at Paleopaphos and New Paphos, and artifacts discovered at the nearby House of Dionysus and House of Theseus. There are several archeological digs in progress throughout the region, so the superb collection is always growing. Take notice of the Roman, clay, hot-water bottles made in the shape of human hands, feet, penile members, and other bodily parts. You're likely to see the museum's curator reassembling an ancient vessel or arranging a new exhibit when he's not selling tickets. (Open June-Aug. Mon.-Sat. 8am-1:30pm and 4-6pm, Sun. 10am-1pm; Sept.-May Mon.-Sat. 7:30am-2pm and 3-5pm, Sun. 10am-1pm. Admission 30¢.)

Just south of the town center at 1 Exo Vrysi St. is the private **Ethnographical Museum,** a house dating from 1894 and now the residence of the Eliades family. Admission (50¢) includes a guided tour in English conducted by Mrs. Eliades, the museum's effervescent curator. This proud Cypriot eagerly explain the origins and use of the artifacts that she and her husband have collected. These include pottery, tools, costumes, and other utensils made and used by rural Cypriots. Don't miss the garden's third-century B.C.E. Hellenistic tomb, Christian catacombs, olive press, and Kleftico ovens. Try to visit early. And unless you have a particularly keen interest in the House of Dionysus, be prepared to fend off a plug to buy Mr. Eliades' book at the end of the visit. (Open June-Aug. Mon.-Sat. 9am-1pm and 4-7pm; Sept.-May Mon.-Sat. 9am-1pm and 3:30-5:30pm. Large groups accepted only on Sun. Admission 50¢.)

To the west of Ktima Paphos, a signposted road runs ½ mile to the Paleokastra, or **Tombs of the Kings**—a misnomer, since those interred in these hewn stone tombs were not royalty but local aristocracy. The larger tombs consist of an open court surrounded by burial chambers, with Doric columns carved out of the underground rock and stairways leading down to the interiors. The necropolis contains almost

100 tombs from the Hellenistic and Roman periods, many of which remain unexcavated. The tombs were also used as hideouts by early Christians fleeing persecution. To the north of the tombs within the circular asphalt road lies **Paleoeklisia** (literally "old church") with fragments of Byzantine frescos. (Tombs and church open June-Aug. daily 7:30am-7:30pm; Sept.-May 7:30am-sunset. Admission 30¢.)

In Ktima Paphos, the **Byzantine Museum**, 26, 25th of March St., houses icons and other religious relics from local monasteries and churches. (Open Mon.-Wed. and Fri. 9am-1pm and 4-7pm, Thurs. and Sat. 9am-1pm. Admission 25¢.) The cool, musty **Catacombs of Agia Solomoni**, along the road between Ktima and Kato Paphos, include a chapel with badly damaged Byzantine frescoes. Dedicated to St. Solomoni (Hannah), mother of the seven children who were tortured to death for their faith in God during the persecution of the Jews in Palestine (168 B.C.E.), the chapel supposedly sits on the site of the old synagogue of Paphos. Part of the deepest chamber is filled with very clear water, which you may not notice until you step in it. The entrance to the catacombs, on A. Pavlos Ave., is marked by a small sign and by a tree with thousands of handkerchiefs draped from its branches; the tree is said to miraculously cure the illnesses of those who tie a cloth to it. (Open 24 hours. Free.) At **St. Paul's Pillar**, near the Chryssopolitissa Church, St. Paul was allegedly tied and whipped for preaching Christianity. Built in the late seventh century on a hill overlooking the harbor, the **Byzantine Castle** (*Saranda Kolones*) was intended to protect its inhabitants from Arab pirates, but it was demolished by an earthquake in 1222. The Lusignans then built the **Fort of Paphos** in the thirteenth century at the end of the pier, which was used and rebuilt by the Venetians and later the Turks. (Open June-Aug. Mon.-Sat. 7:30am-1:30pm; Sept.-May Mon.-Fri. 7:30am-2pm, Sat. 7:30am-1pm. Admission 30¢.)

The two most popular beaches stretch out at **Yeroskipov** and **Coral Bay.** Yeroskipov is exclusively a tourist beach with showers and snack bars, while Coral Bay is sandier, quieter, and preferred by locals. Starting in June, bus #11 runs to and from the Paphos post office and Yeroskipov Beach (first from Paphos at 6:45am, last from the beach at 6:45pm, 19¢). From April to October, another bus makes the round trip to Coral Bay from the same place (9am-2pm 4 per day, 6 returning 9:45am-6pm, 30¢). Both buses stop at the popular **Paphos Beach.** Nightlife in Paphos is the best in Western Cyprus. The **Rainbow,** draws a sophisticated *kamaki* crew on the make for sun-burned women. (Drinks C£1. Open 9pm-3am. Cover C£3, 1 drink included.) On the waterfront, the trendy **La Boile Pub** (tel. 348 00) attracts local artists from nearby Lemba College of Art. (Drinks C£1.50.)

## Near Paphos

On the coast some 15 miles southeast of Paphos along the main Limassol-Paphos road is **Petra tou Romiou,** the mythical birthplace of Aphrodite. Although clearly not what Boticelli had in mind when he painted the *Birth of Venus,* the sight is still intriguing. According to Homer, "The moist breeze of Zephyros brought her there on the waves of the sea with a noise of thunder amid the soft foam." There are no ancient ruins here, just a good, albeit rocky, beach surrounded by stunning boulders, which signposts call the "Rocks of Venus."

Five miles closer to Paphos, adjacent to the modern village of **Kouklia,** lie the ruins of the great **Temple of Aphrodite** and **Paleopaphos** (Old Paphos), once the capital of a kingdom encompassing nearly half of Cyprus. The temple itself was the religious center of the island and a destination for pilgrimages from all parts of the Roman world. Dating from the twelfth century B.C.E., it thrived until the fourth century C.E., when the anti-pagan edicts of Emperor Theodosius and a series of earthquakes reduced it to relative unimportance. The remains draw scant attention and make little sense without a guide. Buy *A Brief History and Description of Old Paphos,* a highly recommended booklet published by the Cyprus Department of Antiquities and available at most museums (35¢). The modest **archeological museum** at the site houses a small collection of pottery and inscriptions uncovered by excavations during the last century. The **Epigraphical Museum,** next door, contains a variety of carved stones representing aspects of life in the once-grand capital. (Sites and museums open daily 7:30am-sunset. Admission to ruins, city, and museums 30¢.) Five buses run to Kouklia and three return Monday through Friday from 7am to 4pm (25¢). (The last bus from Kouklia to Paphos is at 8am.)

Six miles north of Paphos, near Coral Bay Beach, are the painted caves and buildings of the **Monastery of Agios Neophytos,** the work of twelfth-century writer and recluse, St. Neophytos. Here you'll find several striking Byzantine frescoes, a collection of icons, and tremendous views of the sea. About 100m from the monastery complex is a ravine with a winter stream and three contiguous rock caves carved out by Neophytos and covered with beautiful twelfth-century frescos. You can get here from the beach. Be sure to bring a flashlight. (Open 7:30am-sunset.)

Archbishop Makarios III was born in the mountain village of **Pano Panayia,** 25 miles northeast of Paphos, where he stayed until entering the Kykko Monastery. A monument to Cyprus' most revered figure has recently been erected in the town square, and the small house where Makarios was born is now a museum. (Open daily 9am-noon and 1-5pm. Free.) About a mile from Pano Panayia and 30 miles from Paphos is **Chryssorogiatissa Monastery**—perhaps the most picturesquely situated monastery in Cyprus. According to legend, the icon of the Virgin Mary, one of three such icons painted by St. Luke, had been a victim of the iconoclasm in Asia Minor and had traveled to Cyprus. Ignatius found it on the beach at Paphos and was instructed by the Virgin to build the monastery in her honor. The current structure dates from 1770, and although a fire destroyed much of the monastery's property in 1967, its fine collection of eighteenth-century icons and frescoes is still intact. The monastery will usually provide free accommodations to guests upon request—ask the staff at the restaurant to translate for you. (Ask at the tourist office for information about the monastery's lodgings.) About 2 miles south stands the abandoned **Monastery of Agia Moni,** dating from the seventeenth and nineteenth centuries. Four buses per day (last at 4pm) run to Panayia from Pervola station, returning to Paphos the next morning at 6am and 7:15am (30¢). Hitching is fairly reliable in this area.

North of Paphos, the lovely village of **Pegia** lies tucked in the hills about 11km from Paphos. Rent a motorbike so you can fully appreciate the road that runs along a mountain ridge between rolling hills and the sea. A few kilometers from Pegia is the lovely beachside hamlet of **Agios Georgios.** There are barely four buildings here, excluding the chapel, and two of them are hotels. The coastline around Agios Georgios is full of chalk formations that have formed fascinating sculptured underwater caves. **St. George Restaurant** (tel. (066) 210 75) lets new, clean doubles for C£12; you can pitch a tent next to the restaurant for free. About 50m up the road toward Pegia is **Yeronisos Hotel and Restaurant** (tel. (066) 210 78), which is messy but comfortable. (Singles C£7.50. Doubles C£12. Breakfast included.) Down a dirt road from Agios Georgios is **Lara Beach,** one of the longest in Cyprus and a breeding ground for the endangered Mediterranean turtle. All that's here is one restaurant, so unless your visit coincides with the boat excursion from Paphos (**Lambeto Sea Cruises'** daytrip from Paphos C£7.50), you should be pretty much alone with the sand, trees, and turtles.

## Polis and Environs

Sand, cheap chow, and a carefree mood make the small village of Polis the choice spot in Cyprus for budget vacationers. Just 25 miles north of ritzy Paphos, Polis is accessible by minibus and taxi.

As you come in from the main road from Paphos, notice the typical Cypriot mountain architecture of large rounded wooden doors and stone masonry. At the end of the windy main street is the *platia,* where several travel agencies offer friendly advice and information. **Century 21** (tel. 216 58) is the best-equipped, and rents mopeds (C£2.50), runs worthwhile excursions around the Akamas Penninsula, and exchanges money. Around the *platia* you'll find three **banks** (open Mon.-Fri. 8:30-noon; July-Aug. also 4-7pm) and the **post office** (tel. 215 39; open Mon.-Sat. 8am-noon). The **police** (tel. 214 51) are 1 block from the square in the direction of the beach. A **pharmacy** (tel. 212 53) is down the street from the post office. The well-staffed **hospital** (tel. 214 31) is on the way to the campsite. The **telephone code** for the area is 063.

Freelance campers pitch their tents openly on bluffs above the shore to the west, and several restaurants along this stretch provide free or almost-free camping and the use of facilities to customers. The cheapest place to stay in Polis itself is the **campground** (tel. 215 26), 1 mile from the town center. Set in a eucalyptus grove by the sea, it charges C£1.25 per tent, 28¢ per person, and 50¢ to rent a small two-to three-person tent. (Open March-Oct.) The **Akamas Hotel** (tel. 213 30), before the *platia*, has clean rooms and bathrooms and a quiet courtyard. (Singles C£3. Doubles C£6.) **Lemon Garden** (tel. 214 43) has pleasant, comfortable doubles for C£4 per person and kitchen facilities. Rooms to let line the road to the beach. On the right before the turn-off for the Vomos Taverna, **Mrs. Evlalia** (tel. 215 80) rents six bright, clean rooms—very private, with access to a kitchen. (Doubles C£2.50 per person.) Right by the beach, **Vomos Taverna** has *meze* for C£3. In town, **Arsinoe** (tel. 215 90), across from the church, is run by a fisher's family and serves up fresh daily catch. (Fish soup C£1. Open 8am-1pm and 5pm-1am.) In the evenings, you can check out the beachside disco, or saunter over to **Brunnen** (tel. 215 11), before the Akamas Hotel. Marios, a Famagustan refugee, has turned this delapidated Turkish house into a sprawling garden bar. (Large beer 70¢. Wine 45¢. Breakfast served. Open 8am-2pm, 5pm-2am.)

Six miles west of Polis are the mythical **Baths of Aphrodite,** a shady pool carved from the limestone by natural springs. Aphrodite came here to cleanse herself after her nocturnal exploits; today, mortals bathe in the thigh-deep waters, despite signs forbidding it. If your nocturnal exploits require a cold shower, head 5 miles farther west to the end of a very rough dirt road. The lush pool of **Fontana Amorosa** can be reached by foot or with a sturdy off-road vehicle.

The road from Polis to the Baths of Aphrodite leads past several good beaches and some cheap accommodations. Three-quarters of a mile out of Polis, the friendly **Tamamouna** family (tel. 212 69) offers an excellent view, hospitality, respectable rooms, and an excellent bathroom. (Singles C£3. Doubles C£5.) Where the road turns to gravel, **CO-MA-NE** (tel. 210 42 or 213 10) rents fully furnished beachside apartments for C£10. The budding port of **Lachi,** 2 miles west of Polis, has a decent stretch of pebbles and several tasty fish *tavernas* and hotels. Below the **Baths of Aphrodite tourist pavilion,** 1½ miles west, is a long sandy beach; despite the tour buses that stop here, it isn't all that crowded. A few hundred yards beyond it is **Ttakkas Bay,** a lovely cove considered by Cypriots to be the best beach on this part of the coast. The **Ttakkas Bay Restaurant** (tel. 210 87), above the beach, serves excellent fresh fish, and the oceanside view from its shady terrace is superb. The turn-off for the beach is marked by a cryptic sign reading "Ttakkas Bay Restaurant Aphrodite Area Refugee"—the owner fled from northern Cyprus. (Fish *meze* C£2.50. Open 9am-midnight.)

The coastline and beaches east of Polis are just as lovely as those to the west. However, since most people head west toward the Baths of Aphrodite, the two regions have little in common. There are virtually no tourist facilities between Polis and Kato Pirgos, about 40 miles to the east: no rooms to let, no scenic seaside *tavernas,* and no freelance camping (but no one to stop you from trying)—just sleepy farming villages, deserted stretches of sand, and you. Touring the area may be a problem, as only one bus per day passes through (leaving Paphos at 4pm, passing through Polis at 5:15-5:30pm, and leaving Kato Pirgos the next morning at 5am, 50¢ from Polis). Some minibuses from Paphos continue on to Pomos (75¢). Not many cars pass through either, but those that do will stop if they have room. The second half of the journey is treacherous for mopeds, as the road winds endlessly on mountain passes; it may be a better idea to think in terms of four wheels if you decide to travel on your own.

All of the coastline east of Polis is visible from the slender band of asphalt euphemistically known as the "main road;" just find a beach that suits your tastes and walk down to it. In the area close to Polis, some of the beaches are littered with garbage, so expect to head 5-10 miles out of town before bringing out the suntan oil. The road runs west along the coast, through banana plantations and tobacco fields, to **Pomos,** a quiet village with a few *tavernas* and a nice pebble beach. A few miles beyond Pomos is the village of **Pahiammos** (thick sand).

Between Pahiammos and Kato Pirgos, about 8 miles west, lies the village of **Kokkina** (red), a small enclave occupied by the Turks. To avoid entering Turkish territory, the road to Kato Pirgos veers off into the parched mountains for a circuitous 16-mile detour (45 min. by car).

**Kato Pirgos,** the last settlement before the border on the northern coast, is a pleasant resort town, with a main street that stretches for miles along the coast. The town has a training base for Cypriot soldiers, so you'll see almost as many youths in uniform as local inhabitants. Many Cypriots visit Kato Pirgos in July and August, but few come during the rest of the year. **Elpida** (tel. 21 31) has rooms for C£3. In off-season, you can get an incredible break on accommodations. In May or June, the town's one-star hotel, **Tylos Beach** (tel. 065 163 48), is empty, and the management is happy to fill a room for C£4 per person; lone travelers are welcome. At other times, singles go for C£6.70, doubles for C£10. The hotel affords an unforgettable seaside view. You'll do just as well next door at **Hotel Limanaki.** If you take the bus to Pirgos, get off as you come into town; all of the accommodations are clustered on the west end of town. One bus leaves Polis for Kato Pirgos daily at 5pm, returning early the next morning (around 5am).

# Larnaca Λαρναχ

Unless you're flying in or out of Cyprus or passing through on your way to the tourist haven around Agia Napa, try to avoid Larnaca. Quieter and cleaner than Limassol, it nonetheless has little to offer the budget traveler. The tacky restaurants, discos, and tourist shops cater almost exclusively to fast-spending vacationers, and there are better beaches and museums elsewhere.

Used by fourteenth-century Genoese traders, the city's name is an odd derivation of the Italian *La Scala* (meaning landing place). The Greek equivalent, *larnaca,* translates best as "hollow place." This is not nearly as simple (and hence attractive) a notion that, once upon a time, there were many sarcophagi, or *larnaces,* in the area—a possible antecedent to the name "Larnaca." The now-lively modern city is built on top of the ruins of the ancient Kition, making Larnaca one of the oldest cities in the world still inhabited. The Bible explains that this city was founded by Kittim, the great grandson of Noah, but archeologists contend that it was originally an early Bronze-Age settlement (thirteenth century B.C.E.). A part of the ancient city walls and some Bronze Age temples are in the north of the town (see Sights below). In the Turkish occupation of the eighteenth and nineteenth centuries, Larnaca's importance as a trading port grew, making it Cyprus' cosmopolitan city.

## Orientation and Practical Information

Larnaca's main street, as far as tourists are concerned, is **Athens Avenue,** which runs along the waterfront. You'll find most services on or near **Democratias Square,** off the northern end of Athens Ave.; at the southern end is the Larnaca Fort, with a small museum. Two or three blocks inland from the fort, the famous church of St. Lazarus sits in **St. Lazarus Square.** The main business street is **Hermes Street,** which runs diagonally from Larnaca Fort back toward the northeast in the direction of the ancient Kition archeological site. On weekdays in summer, bus #2 runs irregularly between the airport and the center of town from 7am to 7pm' in winter from 7am to 5pm (20¢). A more reliable airport bus runs hourly to Kiti Village from St. Lazarus Sq., passing within 300m of the airport. (On Sat., the last bus leaves at 1pm; there is no Sun. service.) Taxis cost C£2. Drivers will not allow you to round up companions on the spot, so try to find a group on the plane or at your hotel.

**Cyprus Tourism Organization Office:** Democratias Sq. (tel. 543 22). Maps and information for the entire island. Open in summer Mon. and Thurs. 8:15am-1:30pm and 4-6:15pm, Tues.-Wed. and Fri.-Sat. 8:15am-1:30pm; in off-season Mon. and Thurs. 8:15am-1:45pm and 3-5:30pm, Tues.-Wed. and Fri.-Sat. 8:15am-1:45pm. Another office in the airport (tel. 543 89) is open 24 hours.

**American Express:** Democratias Sq. (tel. 520 24), in the office of A.L. Mantovani and Sons, across from the tourist office. Will hold mail for 3 months. Open in summer Mon.-Fri. 8am-1pm and 3:30-6:30pm, Sat. 9am-noon; in off-season Mon.-Fri. 8am-12:45pm and 2:30-5:30pm, Sat. 9am-noon.

**Post Office:** Democratias Sq.(tel. 570 75), next to the tourist office. Open in summer Mon.-Tues. and Thurs.-Fri. 7:30am-1pm and 4-6pm, Wed. and Sat. 7:30am-1pm; in off-season Mon.-Tues. and Thurs.- Fri. 7:30am-1:30pm and 3:30-5:30pm, Wed. 7:30am-1:30pm, Sat. 7:30am-noon. Another small office in St. Lazarus Sq. is open Mon.-Sat. 8am-12:30pm.

**Telephones (CYTA):** Lord Byron St. From the tourist office, take a left onto Kiteus St., then right onto Lord Byron. Open in summer 8am-8pm; in off-season 7:30am-8pm. **Telephone code:** 041.

**Buses: Lefkaritis Terminal,** Athens Ave. (tel. 524 02), south of King Paul Sq., near the waterfront. Buses to Nicosia (Mon.-Fri. 5:45am-4:15pm about every hr., Sat. 5:45am-3:45pm, 70¢) and Limassol (Mon.-Fri. 8 per day 5:45am-3:45pm, Sat. 5:45am-2:45pm, 80¢). Buses to Agia Napa leave from behind the Marina Pub on the waterfront across from Democratias Sq. (in summer Mon.-Sat. 10 per day 8:30am-6:30pm, 4 on Sun.; in off-season Mon.-Sat. 5 per day 9:30am-4:30pm; 60¢).

**Service Taxis: Makris,** 13 Democratias St. (tel. 529 29), across from the tourist office. **Akropolis,** at the corner of Archbishop Makarios III Ave. and Kalogreon St. (tel. 555 55), 2 blocks to the left of the tourist office and opposite the police station. **Kyriakos,** 2C Hermes St. (tel. 551 00). All 3 run taxis to Limassol and Nicosia (in summer about 6am-7pm every ½ hr.; in off-season 6am-6pm) and will pick you up and drop you off anywhere in the city. A taxi to Nicosia costs C£1.15, to Limassol C£1.40, to Paphos via Limassol C£3.

**Moped and Car Rental: Panipsos,** 25 Galileou St. (tel. 560 14), behind the waterfront. The best for all kinds of rentals. Free roadside service, helmets, and another office in Agia Napa allows for convenient drop-off. Small mopeds C£2.50 per day. Subaru cars C£10 per day with unlimited mileage and 3rd party insurance. Bikes C£1 per day.

**Public Toilets:** On the beach and in St. Lazarus Sq. Surprisingly clean. Showers available.

**Hospital: Makarios General Hospital** (tel. 279 99), 2 miles outside town. Take a taxi or bus #21 from Hermes St. (every ½ hr., 15¢). There is also a small hospital (tel. 520 07) in town off Grigoris Avxentious St.

**Police:** Archbishop Makarios III Ave. (tel. 520 01), 1 block north of the tourist office.

## Accommodations, Camping, and Food

Because Larnaca attracts so few budget travelers, you'll have an extremely tough time finding satisfactory accommodations. The town's hotels and pensions fall into two groups—luxury hotels full of northern European package tourists, and dives. If the situation sounds horrible, don't despair: There are a few hidden, decent, affordable places to stay.

**Esmeralda,** 33 Hermes St. (tel. 539 69 or 212 21). Clean rooms, but the bathroom and kitchen could use a good scrub. The friendly owner will pick you up at the airport for free if you call. Mostly European clientele . C£2.

**St. Lazarus Inn,** at the corner of Dionissou St. and St. Lazarus Sq. (tel. 263 22). Clean, pleasant, and reasonable. Take one of the sunny rooftop rooms. Kitchen facilities. Singles C£5, with private bath C£6. Doubles C£7, with private bath C£8. Triples C£8.

**Pavion Hotel,** St. Lazarus Sq. (tel. 566 88). A grade up from its neighbor in the square. All rooms with private shower, optional A/C (C£1.80), bar with TV. Singles C£9. Doubles C£12. Triples C£16. Breakfast included.

**Othellos',** 105 Athens Ave. (tel 565 65), at the southern end of Athens Ave. (right facing water). A rent-a-car/taxi office that also rents out flats. Doubles C£5-6. Triples C£5-7.

**The Rainbow Inn,** 140 Zenon Kitieos St. (tel. 558 74), 50m from the sea. A run-down bed and breakfast. Singles C£5.50. Doubles C£9.

**La Maison Belge,** 103 Stadiou St. (tel. 546 55). One-star and a noticeable step up from the shabbier guest houses but worth the price for tired travelers. Immaculate carpeted rooms with baths. Singles C£7.50. Doubles C£12. Triples C£17. Breakfast included.

**Camping: Beach Forest Camping,** (tel. 224 14), 5 miles northeast of Larnaca on the road to Agia Napa. Hitch, take a taxi (C£1.30), or catch the tourist beach bus from the Sun Mall Hotel. On a pleasant pebbly beach. Pinball, waterslide, supermarket (open until 10pm), and restaurant (open until 11:30pm). Open April-Oct. 25¢ per person plus C£1.50 per tent; they supply tents at no added cost.

Most of Larnaca's restaurants and bars are on the waterfront—almost nothing distinguishes one from the next. **Megalos Pefkos** (tel. 285 66), at the southern end of the harbor, is one of the least expensive. (Salad with feta 35¢. Spaghetti 75¢. *Mousaka* with chips C£1.25. *Kalamari* with chips C£1.75.) **Astrapi Restaurant,** in St. Lazarus Sq. (tel. 250 88), serves traditional dishes at reasonable prices. For really cheap eats, stick to the *souvlaki* and pizza stands on Athens Ave. Off the beaten track is **Pezoporikos,** (tel. 559 99) on Kyriakos St., where you can shoot pool while waiting for a delicious *souvlaki-pita* (75¢) or *kleftiko.* There is a market adjacent to 180 Hermes St. (Open Mon.-Sat. 6:15am-1pm, Mon-Tues. and also Thurs.-Fri. 4-6pm in summer, 3-5pm in winter.)

## Sights

Larnaca's biggest tourist attraction is its town beach (a dismal mixture of packed dirt and cigarette butts), which somehow manages to satisfy the hordes of vacationers who bake on it every day. Beautiful, less crowded beaches are farther northeast on the way to Agia Napa. Tourist buses travel 6 miles up the coast and back, stopping at all the beaches, or wherever else you ask to be let off. (Buses leave from the Sun Hall Hotel at the north end of Athens Ave.; in summer 7am-7pm every ½ hr., 20¢.)

You can tour Larnaca's sights in one day. The ruined city of **Kition** is the most historically significant spot, although most of it now lies underneath the modern city of Larnaca. First settled at the beginning of the thirteenth century B.C.E., and then abandoned at the end of the century, Kition was rebuilt in 1200 B.C.E. by refugees from the Peloponnese who brought with them the thriving Mycenaean culture. The city was damaged in wars against the Phoenicians and Egyptians (fourth century B.C.E.), and finally destroyed by earthquake and fire in 280 B.C.E. The famous Stoic philosopher Zeno was born in ancient Kition in 335 B.C.E. The ruins of the city reveal part of the ancient cyclopean city wall, a large **Temple of Astarte,** goddess of fertility, and four smaller temples. To get to the ruins, follow Kimon St. inland to the Chryssopolitissa Church, cross in front of the church, and go straight on Sakellariou St. This route will take you past the almost indistinguishable Acropolis of Kition. (Ruins open June-Aug. daily 7:30am-1:30pm; Sept.-May Sun.-Fri. 7am-2pm, Sat. 7:30am-1pm. Admission 30¢.)

On the way to ancient Kition you'll pass Larnaca's **archeological museum,** between Kimon and Kilkis St. The small collection includes votives, statues, tombs, and pottery from Neolithic to Roman times. Particularly interesting is the display of Roman glass and the beautiful alabaster jars and ivory figurines found at Kition. (Open May-Aug. Mon.-Sat. 7:30am-1:30pm; Sept.-April Mon.-Fri. 7:30am-2pm, Sat. 7:30am-1pm. Admission 30¢.) Next to Barclay's bank, by the tourist office in King Paul's Sq., is the private **Museum of the Pierides Foundation,** founded by and located in the former home of the collector Demetrios Pierides (1811-1895). Pierides began feverishly gathering Cypriot artifacts when Cyprus was being colonized by the British. His family followed his example in protecting the 3000 treasured pieces from deportation. The collection includes Bronze Age ceramic milk pots, Byzantine glazed ceramic bowls, *lefkara* lace from the time of Da Vinci, Cypriot costumes, bridal belts, and old maps. (Open Mon.-Sat. 9am-1pm. Admission 25¢.)

At the southern end of the port you'll find a **small medieval fortress** set on the water's edge. Constructed by the Venetians in the fifteenth century and rebuilt by the Turks in the 1622, the fort contains a small collection of artifacts and photographs from Kition and other excavations in the area. (Open June-Aug. Mon.-Sat. 7:30am-7:30pm; Sept.-May 7:30am-5pm. Admission 30¢.) The first left north of the fortress leads to the **Church of St. Lazarus,** built over the saint's tomb. The first Bishop of Cyprus, he came to Cyprus from Palestine after being resurrected four days after his death. The tomb was miraculously discovered in 890 C.E., and in exchange for the relics found within, Emperor Leo VI constructed a three-domed basilica; the domes were later destroyed by the Turks in the Middle Ages. The remains were stolen from Constantinople, but reappeared suddenly in Marseilles, France. The crypt under the altar houses is reputedly the original sarcophagus of the saint. Notice the rich seventeenth- and eighteenth-century icons. The Corinthian stones added in the eighteenth century are also interesting. (Open April-Aug. daily 8am-12:30pm and 3:30-6:30pm; Sept.-March 8am-12:30pm and 2:30-5pm.) Behind the church in the right corner is a small graveyard of English and American missionaries, sailors, and their families. (The gate is always open—just turn the latch.)

## Near Larnaca

A bus bound for Kitileaves St. Lazarus Sq. (in summer 7am-7pm every hr.; in winter 7am-5pm) and travels west to the **Hala Sultan Tekke Mosque,** the fourth holiest Moslem pilgrimage site after Mecca, Medina, and Jerusalem (15 min., 20¢). Also called the Tekke of Umm Haram, the mosque was constructed during the Arab invasion of Cyprus (647 C.E.), over the site where the Umm Haram fell off a mule and broke her neck, thereby fulfilling a prophecy of Muhammad. Her grave in the back of the mosque is surrounded by three huge stones, reputed to come from Mecca. The horizontal one was supposedly suspended in air for many centuries, until it lowered itself for fear of injuring the faithful. The Turks constructed a mosque here in 649 C.E., but the present structure was built in 1787. Tell the bus driver you're going to "Tekke" to be dropped off at the turn-off. From there, you'll have to walk 1km. The mosque lies next to the **Larnaca Salt Lake.** In winter, the lake is covered with water and pink flamingos. Legend claims that this body of water was created one day when St. Lazarus was passing through the area. Hungry and thirsty, he asked an old woman for some grapes from her vineyard. She refused, so as punishment for her greed, St. Lazarus turned her vineyard into the salt lake. A quarter of a mile farther west are the excavations of a late-Bronze Age harbor town. The area is fenced off, but you can still get a good view. Discoveries from this site are on display in the fortress in Larnaca. To get to the site from the mosque, cross the ditch, take the dirt road to the right, and turn left at the fork.

The same bus that goes to the mosque continues on to the village of **Kiti** (25 min. from Larnaca), where you can visit the church of **Panagia Angeloktisti** ("built by the angels"). The section of the church containing the stunning mosaics of the baby Jesus flanked by angels Michael and Gabriel was constructed in the sixth century C.E.; the remainder, including the dome, was constructed in the twelfth century on top of the sixth-century basilica. The entrance dates from a fourteenth-century crusader chapel. Note the Frankish coat of arms on the exterior south wall. (Open daily 8am-5pm.)

Forty kilometers from Larnaca and 9km off the main Nicosia-Limassol road is the **Stavrouni Monastery.** According to tradition, the monastery was constructed by the order of St. Helena in 327 B.C.E. on a site called Olympos, which had formerly been occupied by a pagan temple. At the time, Helena, sister of the Roman Emperor Constantine, was returning from Palestine, where she had located the Holy Cross. She presented a fragment to the monastery, but to this day, no one has been able to locate the holy relic; the faithful believe that it is hidden in the monastery and performs miracles. In the summer of 1988, women were forbidden from entering the monastery. Men can visit Monday, Wednesday, Friday, and Sunday, but rumor has it that Stavrovouni will soon close its doors to all visitors. Check at the Larnaca tourist office for information. There are no buses to Stavrovouni, but you can get to the pottery village of Kornes and then walk or hitch up to the peak. A private taxi will cost about C£20.

# Free Famagusta District and Agia Napa Αμμοχωστος και Αγ. νάπα

Fifteen years ago, Agia Napa was a quiet farming and fishing village. Most tourists flocked to Famagusta, 7 miles to the north, letting Agia Napa's ruined monastery and white sandy beaches lie peacefully vacant. But when the Turks occupied Famagusta in 1974, Greek Cyprus lost one of its major resorts, and Agia Napa was developed almost overnight into a tourist center full of luxury hotels, holiday apartment complexes, and overpriced restaurants. Many refugees from Famagusta live in this area now, in order to be as close to their homes as possible.

In the center of Agia Napa are banks, many restaurants, and the **tourist office** (tel. 217 96), at the corner of Kyrou Nerou and Makarios Ave. (Open June-Aug. Mon.-Sat. 8:15am-1:30pm; Mon. and Thurs. also 4-6:15pm; Sept.-May Mon.-Sat. 8:15am-1:45pm; Mon. and Thurs. also 3-5:30pm.) Across from the tourist office is the fourteenth-century **Monastery of Agia Napa,** which was constructed after a miracle-working icon of the Virgin Mary was found at the site. Notice the combination of architectural styles: Following its Byzantine construction, the building was alternately renovated by Venetians, French Crusaders, and nineteenth-century Cypriots. Every Sunday in summer at 8pm, there is Cypriot **folk dancing** in the square near the monastery.

Inexpensive accommodations in the town are difficult to find, especially in summer. In the center of town, **Kamilari Panayiotis** (tel. (037) 219 86) has roomy singles for C£8, doubles from C£10; inquire at the Gold Shoe Store. To the right (with your back to the water), **Michael Antoniou's Jewelry Store** (tel. 210 78) lets doubles for C£10. Farther away from the center, in the north of the town, **Xenis,** at 34 Demokratias St. (tel. 210 86) has comparable furnishings. (Singles C£8. Doubles C£10.) Along the road to Paralimni, **Savvas Apt.** (tel. (037) 211 87) rents very pleasant, clean, new rooms with kitchen facilities. (Studio apartments C£11.) On the west side of town, **Salmary** (tel. (037) 212 06) has many nice flats. (Studios C£11. Two bedrooms C£12.60.) Beachlovers should take to the **campground** (tel. 219 46), which also rents motorbikes for C£2. (C£2 per tent. 25¢ per person. Tent rental C£3.) Three kilometers from town, the campground is very near the beautiful but crowded **Nissi Beach.**

If you're looking for deserted beaches, you'll find them about half way between Larnaca and Agia Napa, past the army base. Better still, and closer to Agia Napa, are the beautiful beaches north and south of **Protaras.** On the Protaras public beach, next to the Flamingo Beach restaurant, is the private **Costas Camping.** If Costas isn't around, pitch a tent at an available spot. (Limited shading, cold showers, and toilets. C£1.50.) You might want to leave your things in Agia Napa, rent a motorbike, and scan the area for a place. There are a number of rooms to let in the area, away from commercial Protaras. On the road from Paralimni, going toward Agia Trias, **Windmills,** 185 Protaras Rd., rents clean doubles off narrow halls with showers for C£10. Going south right before the village of Pernera, **C. Farkonas** (tel. (037) 215 67), by the sign for the Kalamis restaurant, rents doubles with kitchenettes for C£12. Farther south, just after the Sweet Memories Restaurant, you can rent doubles with private bathrooms and kitchenettes for C£12.

Close to Agii Anargyri and 5 miles east of Agia Napa is **Cape Greco.** You'll find no tourists here, no half-built concrete hotels, no *tavernas,* and no sand—just rocky coves falling into the dazzling blue sea. The cape has remained undeveloped because of a military radar installation, which allows James Bond wannabees to enjoy swimming off the rocks beneath two huge radar dishes. Right before Agii Anargyri, between Cape Greco and Victory Bay, is the **Cape Greco Equestrian Center.** (Horses

C£5 per hr.) About 2km north of Paralimni, a stone's throw away from the green line, is the small village of **Dherinia**; there isn't much here, except **Taylor's,** (tel. 221 35) on Sotera Rd., an excellent restaurant that serves delicious, cheap fare. (Open noon-11pm.) Since you can't cross the border into occupied Famagusta, the best alternative is to go to one of the several tourist view points nearby to look at the "ghost" of the town; construction cranes still stand exactly as they did 15 years ago. Try the **Famagusta View Terrace,** a righteous outfit that would never consider mixing politics with business. (Binoculars with 25¢ admission. Drinks 30¢. Open 10am-6pm.)

**Buses** make the 26-mile trip from the Marina Pub in Larnaca to Seferis Sq. in Agia Napa (June-Aug. Mon.-Sat. 10 per day 8:30am-6:30pm; 11 per day returning to Larnaca 6:30am-5pm; Sept.-May Mon.-Sat. 5 per day 9:30am-4:30pm, returning to Larnaca 7:15am-3pm, 60¢, arrive early to get a seat.) Buses also leave the Marina Pub in Larnaca for Paralimni via Protaras (in summer Mon.-Fri. 9 per day 6:30am-6pm; in off-season Mon.-Fri. 8 per day 6:30am-5:30pm, 7 Sat. 6:30am-3pm; 8 per day returning from Paralimni Mon.-Fri. 5:30am-4pm, 7 on Sat. 5:30am-1pm; 50¢.) Monday through Saturday, nine buses per day (9am-6pm) run from Paralimni via Agia Napa to Protaras and back (25¢). Eight buses go directly to Protaras (6:30am-10pm, returning 7am-11pm, 25¢).

# Northern Cyprus

> For currency information, see Turkish Coast and Istanbul chapter.

> Note: Northern Cyprus was not researched in 1988. Prices and hours will have changed.

If you speak with Cypriots living in the southern part of the island, they'll admit sadly that some of the most beautiful parts of their tiny homeland are in the northern 40% of Cyprus, occupied by the Turkish Army since the summer of 1974. Barbed wire, minefields, and 2000 peacekeeping troops partition the country. Tourists (Greeks or those of Greek descent excluded) are usually allowed to cross the border in Nicosia, provided that they return on the same day by 6pm. This prohibition is officially based on the following logic: All but a few of the hotels in the north existing before the 1974 war were owned by Greek Cypriots, so by spending the night in them you are using stolen property and thus breaking Greek Cypriot law. Additionally, the International Hotel Association has recommended that its members and travel agents not cooperate with the Turks in Cyprus. If you don't return, the hassles will be enormous—you might even be forbidden to enter Greece, let alone Greek Cyprus. The Greek Cypriots are in general very understanding and hesitant to make visitors feel unwelcome, but if you violate the curfew you could face arrest and prosecution.

The only place in southern Cyprus where it is possible to cross the border is at the **Ledra Palace Hotel** (now occupied by the United Nations), just west of the city walls in Nicosia. The checkpoint is open Monday through Friday from 8am to 6am, and closed weekends and Islamic holidays. To get to the border from Eleftheria Square, follow the walls of the old city along Stassinos, Homer, Egypt, and Marcos Drakos Avenues; at United Nations Square, take the right fork. The Cypriot border police will record your passport number and confiscate any overnight luggage until you return. The front of the building, pockmarked with bullet holes, sandbagged, and barricaded with barbed wire, is a grim reminder of Cyprus' recent and turbulent past.

Two hundred yards down the road is the Turkish checkpoint, where your passport number will be recorded again. Taxis at the Turkish checkpoint will gladly take you to see Kyrenia or Famagusta, but such transit has been prohibited by the Republic of Cyprus. Thus, a return to the Greek side is placed in jeopardy. Don't purchase any gifts while you're on the Turkish side because you are forbidden to bring anything back, and don't rent a car in Greek Cyprus intending to take it to Turkish Cyprus—the Turks have been known to impound them. If you arrive by boat on the Turkish side of Cyprus, you cannot visit Greek Cyprus. During part of the summer of 1988, the border was closed to all but those with diplomatic status.

United Nations' resolutions have declared that Northern Cyprus remains part of the sovereign territory of the Republic of Cyprus. Indeed, Turkey is the only country that recognizes Turkish sovereignty in that region. Prime Minister Turgut Ozal of Tukey visited Athens in the summer of 1988, a prelude to later talks by President George Vassiliou of the Republic of Cyprus and Rauf Denktash of Northern Cyprus. The two announced that a settlement for reunification will by arranged by June 1, 1989.

**Cyprus Turkish Airlines** has flights from Istanbul or Izmir to Nicosia's Ercan Airport. From Nicosia, flights go daily to Istanbul, and three times per week to Izmir. There are also flights to and from Europe. However, the International Air Traffic Association (IATA) "does not recognize the Ercan" airport as it operates unofficially, and poses safety hazards because of its proximity and shared air space with the airport in Larnaca. You can travel overland as well as by **ferry** to one of the two Mediterranean ports of Taşucu or Mersin. Boats sail from Taşucu to Kyrenia. (In summer daily at 10am; in winter at least 2 per week; 6 hr.) For faster, more costly travel, there is an elusive **hydrofoil.** Other boats sail from the larger port of Mersin to Famagusta. The Friday sailing continues to Lattakia, Syria. This journey is less pleasant than the Taşucu-Kyrenia one, as the boat (and the crowd) is much bigger, as well as being one of the dirtiest vessels in the Mediterranean.

Should you wish to visit Greece afterward, or to enter southern Cyprus through Greece, you'll want a removable visa so officials will not stamp the passport itself. This visa can be obtained at any of the three Turkish Federated State of Cyprus consulates in Turkey: in Ankara at Incirli Sok. 20, Gaziosmanpaşa (tel. 28 05 47); in Istanbul at Büyükdere Cad. 99, Kuğu Is Hani, Kat. 6, Daire 9, Mecidiyeköy (tel. 173 29 90); and in Mersin at Atatürk Cad., Hamidiye Mahallesi, Yilmaz Apt. #3 (tel. 162 28). Most nationalities, however, don't need an advance visa: Simply ask the customs police in Northern Cyprus not to stamp your passport and they will stamp a removable sheet of paper instead.

Northern Cyprus' **telephone code** is 905. The country has its own postal system, and Turkish Cypriot stamps must be used (rates a little better than in mainland Turkey). All mail going to Cyprus should be suffixed with Mersin-10, Turkey. Northern Cyprus uses the Turkish lire as currency, but many people are eager to accept Cypriot pounds, pounds sterling, or U.S. dollars. Trading on the black market is illegal.

Should you need consular help in Northern Cyprus, you're a bit out of luck, because no one but the Turkish themselves recognizes this territory as a "republic." A representative from the British Embassy crosses every weekday from 9am to 1pm, and can be found at the old British High Commission; walk along Osman Paşa Ave., which runs parallel to the Green Line to the west of the old city, and turn left at the army camp into Mehmet Akif Ave.—the building is on your right.

# Nicosia (Lefkoşa)

If you enter Turkish Cyprus from the south, you'll probably feel as if you traveled much farther than 200km. The south and north of Cyprus are quite different; it's like traveling 200km from Europe to Asia. You'll notice a change in the atmosphere as soon as you pass within the walls of Turkish Nicosia: The buildings look a little older and the shops are more cluttered. You'll surely notice the statue of Atatürk and the portraits of him posted throughout the city. Toward the center of the old town, near the city market and the Selimiye Mosque, you may see similarities with the Greek side—the food and the buildings—but you may also be struck by the old-world character of the busy streets, filled with bicyclists and horse-drawn fruit and vegetable wagons.

Across the street from the old British High Commission is Nicosia's **tourist office** (open April-Sept. Mon.-Fri. 8am-2pm; Oct.-March Mon.-Fri. 8am-1pm and 2:30-5pm), but there is a more convenient office in the old city. On the right, you'll pass the small, simple Arabahmet Mosque, built in the early seventeenth century. Up ahead in the distance you'll be able to see the twin minarets of the Selimiye Mosque, continuing in this direction, you'll pass through most of the city's shopping district. **Kyrenia Avenue,** on the left, leads to **Atatürk Square** and its Venetian column, taken from Salamis as a symbol of Venetian rule on the island. This is the main square on the Turkish side of the city, containing a post office, a few travel agencies, and an English bookstore. Shared taxis wait here. The road continuing to Selimiye runs roughly parallel to the Green Line. To your right down any given side street you'll see murals depicting Turkish soldiers in patriotic scenes. For the **police,** dial 713 11; for **first aid** 734 41. Nicosia's **telephone code** is 020.

One block before the Selimiye Mosque you'll pass Asmaalti St., which leads to the **Buyuk Khan** (take the first left) and the **Kumarcilar Khani** (straight ahead), lodgings once used by Anatolian merchants and embodying two of the city's most notable examples of Turkish architecture. The Kumarcilar Khani, the smaller of the two, is open in the morning and serves as a surrogate tourist office (the official one is several kilometers out of town), distributing helpful information on Nicosia and the rest of the Turkish quarter.

The monumental **Selimiye Mosque,** formerly the St. Sophia Cathedral, is decidedly the most impressive building in Turkish Nicosia, with its ribbed vaulted archways, flying buttresses, and ornate carvings. Built between 1208 and 1326 in the French Gothic style, this cathedral was where Cypriot kings were coronated. Converted into a mosque in the sixteenth century under Ottoman rule, it has since deteriorated due to neglect. Look for the map of Cyprus cut into the sandstone beneath the transept. A **covered market,** extremely cheap by Greek standards but expensive by Turkish, can be found next to the mosque. Try *sucuk,* almond candy dipped in boiled grapes.

The **Turkish Cyprus Ethnographic Museum,** *Mevlevi Tekke,* on Kyrenia Ave., contains tombs of important Mevlana dervishes and sheiks as well as a fascinating exhibit of traditional Ottoman dress and artifacts, including silk wedding gowns, swords, turbans, and solemn youngsters peering out of curled sepia prints. (Open in summer Mon. 7:30am-2pm and 3:30-6pm, Tues.-Fri. 7:30am-2pm; in winter Mon.-Fri. 7:30am-2pm. Admission 75¢.) The **Museum of Barbarism,** outside the walls northeast of town, is the grisly Turkish answer to the Museum of National Struggle in Greek Cyprus; the museum is set in the home of a Turkish regiment physician, Major Ilhem, whose wife and children were murdered by EOKA terrorists in 1963. (Open in summer daily 9am-1:30pm and 4:30-6:30pm; in winter 8-11:30am and 2:30-5:30pm. Free.) For information and directions, inquire at the Kumarcilar Khani.

To visit the city's lesser sights (such as the **Mehmet II Library,** the **Sarayonu Mosque,** the **Arabahmet Mosque,** the **Lapidary Museum,** and the **Bedesten Church**), you must ask for a guide at the Kumarcilar Khani. Regular opening times are impractical since there are so few tourists. The guide simply unlocks doors for you, so you pay only the regular 75¢ admission fees.

# Kyrenia (Girne)

Kyrenia may be the most appealing harbor town on the island. The newer part of the city, dominated by the luxury Dome Hotel, is not so memorable, but the old port nearby retains an idyllic setting, with Kyrenia Castle at one end, and unobtrusive cafes and stone buildings surrounding the rest of the harbor.

## Practical Information, Accommodations, and Food

If you come by boat from Taşucu, you can walk up from the picturesque harbor to the main street, **Humiyet Caddesi**, on which lie all the shops, restaurants, and the **bus station**. The **post office** (open in summer Mon. 7:30am-2pm and 3:30pm-6pm, Tues.-Fri. 7:30am-2pm and 4-6pm, Sat. 8:30am-12:30pm) and **telephones** (open Mon.-Fri. 7:30am-9:30pm, Sat.-Sun. 8am-6pm) are 100 yards away from the bus station square, on the main coastal road to the east. Messages in English and advertisements for flats for rent are posted on a tree outside the post office. The **police** are just off the square on the street that leads down the hill to the castle. The **tourist office** (tel. 521 45) is at the other end of town; walk down Humiyet Cad., turn left at the Doroma Hotel, and walk 200 yards up the residential road, Fehmi Erçan Cad. They speak English and supply maps, transportation schedules, and other printed information. (Open May-Aug. Mon 7:30am-6pm, Tues.-Fri. 7:30am-2pm; Sept.-April Mon.-Fri. 8am-5:30pm.) Minibuses go to Nicosia very frequently, as soon as they fill. Every hour, buses go to Güselyurt.

## Sights

The preeminent sight in Kyrenia is the huge medieval **castle** at the harbor's mouth. Built by the Byzantines with material plundered from the ruins of the now nonexistent Roman city, it was fortified by the Lusignans and refortified by the Venetians. In fact, the whole city used to be enclosed by walls extending from the castle to the tower on Humiyet Cad., and to the site of the Greek Archangelos Church and back. These walls have since fallen, but the castle is intact, now housing the interesting Shipwreck Museum. When you enter the castle after going through the tunnel, make a left through another tunnel to the small Byzantine chapel, the only remaining structure from the Byzantine period. Almost all of the present castle dates from the Lusignans, except for the outside Venetian walls and tower. Notice the Lusignan coat of arms above the doorway arch. Opposite the museum (or on the left side of the courtyard if facing the water) are dungeons with deep pits in the center. The scraps from the royal family's dinner were dumped from above as the prisoners attempted to grab at the flying food; their intended and cruel punishment came when they reached too far and fell into the pit. The **Shipwreck Museum** contains the well-preserved skeleton of a Greek merchant vessel that sunk over 2000 years ago. Also exhibited are some of the 400 amphoras that were discovered at the site. Those with pointed-bottoms carried wine, with round-bottoms, oil. (Castle and museum open daily 8am-1pm and 2-5:30pm. Admission $1.50, students 75¢.)

The other sight is the old town itself, a warren of jumbled old buildings, some with picturesque wooden balconies. Directly above the harbor is a modern **Folk Art Museum** in a 300-year old building. (Open Mon.-Fri. 8am-1pm and 2-5:30pm. Admission 75¢.)

## Near Kyrenia

Eight miles from Kyrenia is **St. Hilarion Castle,** the most impressive of the three fortresses situated high in the Kyrenia range—the other two being Buffavento and Kantara. St. Hilarion's namesake was the sixth-century Syrian hermit who spent most of his life living near Gaza and making pilgrimages to monasteries in the area; he left Palestine in search of peace and seclusion and, after some adventures, spent the last five years of his life in a cave in Cyprus. The castle was built by the Byzantines in the tenth century and fortified by the Lusignans in the thirteenth century. For two years, the German Emperor Friedrich II controlled it; it was abandoned as a military fortress by the Venetians. Yet as recently as 1974, the Turkish Army used the castle as an observation post. (Open 8am-6pm.) The castle is accessible by bus or *dolmuş.* Take the St. Hilarion turn-off on the Nicosia-Kyrenia road, 5 miles south of Kyrenia, and then walk or try to catch a lift the remaining 3 miles.

**Bellapais Abbey,** 4 miles southeast of Kyrenia, is an exceptional cluster of buildings in various states of preservation. Built by monks of the Order of St. Augustine in the late twelfth century, the hillside sanctuary commands a view of the surrounding countryside. The fourteenth-century central courtyard with its elegant arcades, the large empty church to the south (closed to visitors), and the nearly flawless refectory on the north side suggest the abbey's prosperity in earlier days. (Open daily 9am-1:30pm and 2:30-6pm. Admission 75¢.) Be sure to ask for the small pamphlet (free) describing the site. Four buses per day go to Bellapais.

# North Coast

The rest of the Cypriot coast stretches westward to the Roman ruins at Vouni and eastward to the wild and sparsely populated Karpas Peninsula. Buses run to the west along the coast as far as Lapta, then turn inland for Güzelyurt. From here, you can catch a *dolmuş* to the villages of Gemikonaği or Lefke. A little longer and sandier is the Altin Kaya Beach, just short of the village of **Alsančak.** You have to pay to get into **Mare Monte Beach,** just outside of Alsančak, but you get umbrellas and immaculate sand. Beyond here the coast becomes rockier and the road soon turns inland.

The town of **Güzelyurt** is a market town lying amid miles and miles of lemon, orange, and tangerine groves. The coastline here isn't of much interest, and is relatively inaccessible, rocky, and quite polluted. The road from here to Gemikonaği is controlled by the military; signs reading *yasak* ("forbidden") are everywhere. Still, you might want to carry on 2km past Gemikonaği to the sites of Soli and Vouni. **Soli** is a completely reconstructed theater upstaged by the great view of the sea. **Vouni** has a Roman pavilion, with mosaic floors second only to those at Paphos. Unfortunately, you have to ask at the police station in Gemikonaği for a pass to allow you to either of these spots.

The road (and the Kyrenia-Famagusta bus) follows the coast to the east for 10km only, and then you're on your own. Occasionally buses run to **Esentepe,** 30km east of Kyrenia on the coast. If you can get there, it's worth it—the coast stretches for mile after uninhabited mile beneath the sharp crags of **Buffavento** and **Five Finger Mountain.** There is a castle at the former, built around the same time as St. Hilarion, but presently in a worse state of repair; it's reached by an arduous one-and-a-half-hour climb, and occupied by the Turkish Army, who may or may not let you in after you've gone to all that trouble. Far less strenuous is the long, sandy beach 19km east of Kyrenia. Unmarked, a road leads down to the water from the main road exactly at the 12 mile milestone erected by the British. Beyond Esentepe, the coast gets even quieter, until you reach the rugged solitude of the **Karpas Peninsula,** where only the odd farmer breaks the timeless silence.

# Famagusta (Magosa) and Salamis

Famagusta has been the most serious commercial casualty of the war in 1974. Once a prosperous city, with a beautiful esplanade stretching for miles in front of hotels and honeysuckle-wreathed villas, it is now a deserted ghost town, fenced in and overgrown with weeds. The old city, habitually the Turkish quarter, still remains, and contains some historical gems. The Roman city of Salamis is nearby, and is well worth a visit. On the whole, though, Famagusta epitomizes the troubles of Cyprus.

If you arrive by boat, you enter the old city along **Liman Yolu Sokak,** which leads up to the main square. Continuing on, you reach **Istiklal Caddesi,** the main shopping street that winds up to the city gate. Outside is the Monument of Victory, where the road forks into three prongs. The right-hand road takes you north along the coast to the beaches, Salamis and Karpas, the center road to the bus station, and the left-hand road to the ferry office at Turk Bankası Ltd. Walking back from the monument, you'll find a road that leads to the right just after the city gate. This used to lead to the new town of Verosha, but now, 500m after passing the **post office** (open Mon. 7:30am-2pm and 3:30-8pm, Tues.-Fri. 7:30am-2pm and 4-6pm, Sat. 8:30am-12:30pm) and **telephone** office, it ends. You'll see only barbed wire, Greek signs, and overgrown weeds at the end of the road. If you enter the old city by the Monument of Victory, the **tourist office** will be on your left. (Open in summer Mon.-Fri. 8am-2pm; in winter Mon.-Fri. 8am-1pm and 2:30-5pm.) For the **police,** dial 653 10, for **first aid** 653 28. The **telephone code** is 36.

The walled city of **Magosa** welcomes you with an old gun chamber at the entrance. Just about everything here is old. There are two old gates to the city: a sea gate and a land gate. Scattered about the town are old churches from the period of Lusignan rule, the most notable of which is **Lula Mustafa Paşa Mosque,** on the main square. A Gothic edifice set absurdly among palm trees, its anomaly is heightened by the tiny minaret sticking up from one of the towers. Built in the fourteenth century as St. Nicholas Cathedral, this was where the Lusignan kings were crowned "Kings of Jerusalem." Today, this is the main mosque of Famagusta. Also impressive, but in worse repair and no longer in use, is the **Sinan Paşa Mosque,** formerly the Church of St. Peter and St. Paul, at the bottom of Istiklal Cad. (Open Mon. 7:30am-2pm and 3:30-6pm, Tues.-Sun. 7:30am-2pm.) At the opposite end of the city facing the sea sits the castle where a certain Moorish captain is said to have wrongly imprisoned his wife Desdemona—a mistake immortalized in Shakespeare's *Othello.* The center was constructed by the Lusignans and remodeled by the Venetians in 1492. Notice the winged lion over the entrance, symbol of the republic of Venice. This castle is closed to the public, but the tourist office may be able to arrange a visit.

About 10km up the coast from Famagusta are the ruins of the Roman city of **Salamis.** Any of the buses stopping on the right-hand prong past the Monument of Victory will take you to the turn-off, less than a kilometer from the ruins. The buses will be labeled "Yeniboğaziçi Tuzla" or "Matluyaka"—the last may take another route, so be sure to ask the driver for Salamis when you get on the bus. These buses come infrequently, so you may want to take a taxi. Though the road is busy, hitching is not that good; back from the site it is far easier.

Easily the most impressive monument is the colossal **gymnasium** and **baths** complex, right on the sea near the ticket stand. The forest of columns, reconstructed in the 1950s, gives some idea of the size of the original building. The group of headless statues found on the site now resides in what used to be the swimming pool. Separated by a wall from the gymnasium are the well-preserved baths. The honeycombed section under the floor gives a view into the heating system of the baths, where fans fed hot air through these ducts. The original **theater** was even larger than the reconstructed one standing today. Walking down the left fork past the theater from the gymnasium, you'll reach the other body of ruins, which are in a greater state of disrepair. Here are the city temple, of which only the foundation remains, and the agora. (Open daily 8am-6pm.)

# TURKEY

US$1 = 1460 Turkish Lira (TL)
CDN$1 = 1211TL
UK£1 = 2467TL
AUS$1 = 1171TL
NZ$1 = 967TL

1000 Turkish Lira (TL) = US$0.68
1000TL = CDN$0.83
1000TL = UK£0.41
1000TL = AUS$0.85
1000TL = NZ$1.03

---

*A Note on Prices*

Due to skyrocketing inflation (a devastating 70% in 1988), Turkish prices have fluctuated dramatically over the past year. In order to give our readers a more accurate estimate of costs and expenditures in Turkey, price listings in this section of the text have been reported in U.S. dollars, a relatively stable currency and one that is easily converted. A dollar sign ($), unless otherwise denoted, signifies U.S. dollars.

---

Alluring and still relatively unspoiled, Turkey rewards the budget traveler with inexpensive accommodations, fine cuisine, and warm hospitality. Tracing the roots of its civilization back over 10,000 years, Turkey has a varied cultural and archeological heritage. Nor should its natural beauty be overlooked. Quiet beaches pop up along the idyllic coasts of three seas. Mountain ranges, peaked with snow, glisten over the crops and herds in Anatolia. English and German are widely spoken in major towns, and a network of tourist offices offers valuable information and help. More and more travelers are beginning to discover the advantages of vacationing here. As such, Turkey's days as an unspoiled treasure may be numbered. In 1988, an anticipated three million visitors flocked to the country. Tourists from all over the world are discovering that Turkey is the true budget traveler's paradise.

Once you leave the major resorts along the coast, the warmth and generosity of the people you meet will astound you. The Turks may shower you with small gifts—cigarettes, cups of tea, freshly picked fruit, or perhaps a small goat—and eagerly inquire about your impressions of Turkey. The first reaction of most Western visitors to this unprecedented hospitality is suspicion, but except for a few hustlers in heavily touristed towns, the geniality is genuine.

The Greek government disapproves of tourists taking advantage of cheaper fares to Greece for easy access to Turkey, and, depending on your sources, you may get confusing information on how to travel between the two countries. But there is no law that prevents you from crossing over, regardless of what tourist authorities may lead you to believe. Many travelers make one-day excursions daily. But check into regulations on longer trips. If you have flown to Greece on a European charter flight, you are required to stay in Greece for your vacation (in other words, you can't take advantage of cheap fares to Greece in order to visit Turkey). *Be certain* to contact your agency for details.

# Planning Your Trip

## Useful Organizations

The **Turkish Cultural and Information Office** can supply general information about travel in Turkey and will send you a travel guide, several maps, and regional brochures. Write to 821 United Nations Plaza, New York, NY 10017 (tel. (212) 687-2194), or 2010 Massachusetts Ave. N.W., Washington, DC 20036 (tel. (202) 429-9844). In Great Britain, 170-173 Piccadilly, London, W/V 9DD (tel. (01) 734 86 81 or 82). Offices are also located in other European nations and Japan.

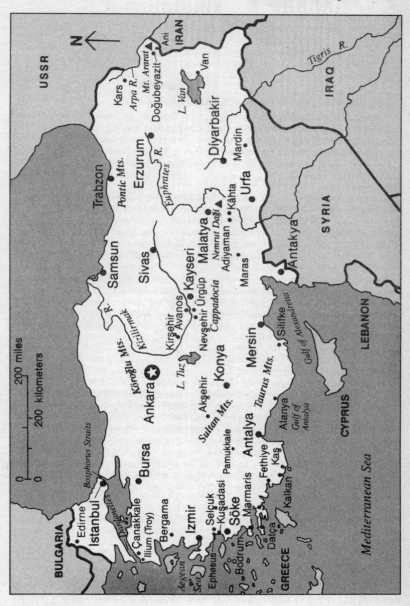

The **Turkish Embassy** in your home country can also provide you with useful information or answer specific questions. In the U.S.: 1606 23rd N.W., Washington, DC 20008 (tel. (202) 387-3200). In Australia, 60 Muggaway, Red Hill ACT 2603. In Great Britain, 43 Belgrave Square, London SWIX 8PA. In Canada, 197 Wurtemburg St., Ottawa, Ont. KIN 8L9. In New Zealand, (Attn: Turkish Honorary Consulate General), P.O. Box 2259, Otahumn, Auckland, 6.

## Documents, Identification, and Insurance

Citizens of the U.S., Canada, Australia, New Zealand, and the U.K. do not need a visa to visit Turkey. Citizens of other nations should check regulations at offices of the Turkish embassy or consulate in their home country. For additional information, refer to Documents and Formalities in the Greece Introduction.

Travelers planning to move on to Bulgaria should obtain a visa before reaching the border; they are available (1-hr. wait) at Yıldız Posta Cad. 15, Gayrettepe, Istanbul (tel. 166 26).

The **International Student Identity Card (ISIC)** and **Youth International Educational Exchange Card (YIEE)** offer reduced entrance fees to some state-run museums and archeological sites. Students should keep in mind that discounts are widely available. Turkish Airlines offers 60% off on European flights and 50% off flights to the Middle East or Asia. (Students no longer receive discounts on domestic flights, however.) Turkish Maritime Lines gives 15% off international lines, 50% off domestic, and 10% off train fares.

Motorists must either carry a "green card" for international insurance or obtain Turkish third-party insurance from any of the insurance agencies at the frontier posts. In case of an accident, the **Turkish Touring and Automobile Association** will carry out necessary repairs and forward the bill to your own country. The head office is at Halaskârgazi Cad. 364, Şişli, Istanbul (tel. 1 467 090). See Insurance in the Greece Introduction for further explanation.

## Customs

Upon entering Turkey, travelers may bring along: one camera and five rolls of film, necessary prescription drugs (bring the prescription), one transistor radio, and no more than 400 cigarettes, 50 cigars, 200g tobacco, 1kg coffee, 1.5g instant coffee, 1kg tea, and five 100cc or seven 70cc bottles of spirits, of which no more than three can be of the same brand. No sharp instruments or firearms of any sort may be brought in, and under *no circumstances* should you bring any illegal drugs into Turkey (see Drugs below). To import animals, such as seeing-eye dogs, you must present a certificate, translated into Turkish by an embassy or consulate, proving that the animal has had a rabies vaccination at least 48 hours before departure.

There is no limit on the amount of foreign currency you may bring into Turkey, but you may not take out more than $1000 worth of Turkish currency. For information on currency exchange, see Money below.

It is absolutely forbidden to export antiques from Turkey, even though shopkeepers may try to tell you otherwise. Make sure that the curious knick-knack you pick up as a souvenir isn't an antique.

## Money

Turkey's inflation rate is high, so expect the prices listed to have increased substantially by 1989. The official currency is the *Turkish lira (TL)*. Coins are divided into 5, 10, 25, and 50 *lira* pieces, and paper currency comes in 10, 20, 50, 100, 500, 1000, 5000, and 10,000 *lira* notes. It is hard to get change for bills of 1000TL or more at museum entrances and cheap restaurants.

Currency can be exchanged almost everywhere, but banks and exchange bureaus offer the best rates: Look for the signs "change/exchange/wechseln." Turkey has 24-hour currency exchanges at border crossings, major airports, and train stations; major tourist areas have places to change money on weekends. Hold on to exchange slips when you convert foreign money into Turkish *lira,* since you may have to present them when you're re-converting your cash. If you take gifts out of Turkey, you will have to prove that they were bought with legally-exchanged foreign currency. If you change dollars into *lira* at Pamukbank, you may change *lira* back into dollars at an airport, railway, or frontier post branch of Pamukbank only if you have your receipt (and if the amount is less than or equal to the amount you originally converted).If you are coming from Greece, exchange your *drachmae* before arriving: The few banks that accept *drachmae* invariably exchange them at an absurd rate.

Istanbul's American Express Bank, across from the Istanbul Hilton, will change large denomination notes ($100, $500) into small notes ($10, $20). (Open Mon.-Fri. 9am-noon and 1:30-4pm.) Iktisat Bank, the official Visa Card representative in Turkey, will give cash *lira* to you; the transaction will later show up on your Visa bill. There are Iktisat banks in Istanbul, Ankara, Izmir, Kuşadası, Mersin, Marmaris, Ürgüp, Kayseri, and Antalya.

Traveler's checks are accepted throughout the touristed parts of Turkey, but they may be exchanged only in banks, large hotels (if you have a reservation), and some stores.

If you need to have money wired to you, have it sent to Istanbul. The sender must have an account in their home country to wire money, which is subsequently deducted from the account and sent to a bank in Turkey. This takes several weeks at least, and you'll probably have to accept all or most in *lira.* Turkish banks may tell you that they have no foreign currency, so you'll have to insist that they do—tell them that you have done this procedure before. Citibank will send money to points in Adana, Ankara, Bursa, Gaziantep, Iskenderun, Istanbul, Izmir, Mersin, Samsun, and Trabzon. For more information, see Sending Money in the Greece Introduction.

## Mail and Telephone

Mail to or from North America usually takes from 10 to 14 days. Post offices (known as PTT) are easily recognized by their yellow signs. Large post offices in major urban areas are open Monday through Saturday from 8am to midnight, Sunday from 9am to 7pm. Smaller post offices share the same hours as other government offices (Mon.-Fri. 8:30am-12:30pm and 1:30-5:30pm). To send mail Poste Restante, write the person's name, "Poste Restante," and "Merkez Postanesi" (Turkish for main post office), and the town's name and postal code. Letters cost a small fee to pick up. Be sure to check under both your first and last name, and have a form of identification handy. Also, specify *Uçak Ile* (airmail) when requesting stamps, and write it on your mail (or ask for aerogrammes). Postage to North America is 17¢ for postcards, 21¢ for letters; to Europe, 12¢ and 15¢, respectively; to Australia and New Zealand, 13¢ and 16¢.

Telephone calls, including international calls, can be placed at the central post office. To use a Turkish phone, you must first purchase *jetonlar* (tokens), which come in three sizes: small tokens (*küçük*) cost 5¢ for local calls; medium tokens (*ortah*) cost 29¢ for inter-city calls; and large tokens (*büyük*) cost 87¢ for international calls. Calls can be made 24 hours from most large PTTs or until 11pm in smaller towns. To avoid a long wait, buy a few *jeton,* quickly place your call, and give out the pay phone number from which you are calling; the caller can then immediately call you back. Pay phone numbers are not posted, but you can ask someone at the post office for it. Specify if your call is "normal," "*acele*" (urgent), or "*yıldırım*" (very urgent). Collect calls to the U.S. cost $3.46 per minute. Telegram charges are roughly 22¢ per word.

## Women Travelers

*In some places I have seen women who put a piece of cloth over their heads to hide their faces, and who*

> *turn their backs or huddle on the ground when a man
> passes by. What is the meaning of this behavior? Gen-
> tlemen, can the mothers and daughters of a civilized
> nation adopt this strange manner, this barbarous pos-
> ture? It is a spectacle that makes the nation an object
> of ridicule. It must be remedied at once.*
> —*Mustafa Kemal Atatürk, First President of the
> Republic of Turkey, 1923-38*

Atatürk's "at once" has not yet arrived for the majority of Turkish women. Especially in small towns, men and women tend to socialize separately, the men at *çay*
shops, and the women at home. Women are on the same legal and political footing
as men in Turkey, but ancient customs fade slowly: Although nothing prevents a
woman from entering a mosque, the force of tradition and an unwritten law decree
that men and women are segregated in all such public places.

Although the Turkish people are warm and hospitable, women should be cautious, especially when traveling alone. Don't hitchhike, and anticipate spending a
little extra for secure accommodations. If you are harassed, the best thing to do
is to scream and run, or say that you are going to the police. A normal fear of the
authorities along with the knowledge that the police usually side with the foreigner
should be enough to deter a would-be assailant.

*Dress modestly.* In the west, avoid tank tops or short shorts; in the east, wear
long skirts, long-sleeved blouses, and a head scarf. Particularly in smaller villages,
you may wish to cover your knees to avoid offending the locals. Carry a headscarf
with you at *all* times. Shorts can be worn in Kuşadası, Bodrum, Marmaris, and
Kaş, the four major resorts—and, of course, around any beach.

## Drugs

*Avoid drugs.* The horror stories of lengthy prison sentences and dealer-informers
are true. Embassies are generally helpless in such cases. The minimum sentence for
possessing even the smallest quantity of illegal drugs in Turkey is 16 months; Turkish law also provides for "guilt by association," which means that those in the company of the person caught are subject to prosecution. The movie *Midnight Express,*
which depicts the horrible experiences of an American imprisoned in Turkey on
drug charges, is based on fact.

# Getting There

You can get to Turkey directly by bus, train, or airplane, or by crossing from
the Greek islands of Samos, Rhodes, Kos, Chios, and Lesvos, or from Cyprus. All
overland traffic from the east must pass through Turkey; boats from Lattakia, Syria
go to Famugusta in Northern Cyprus, from where you can travel to either Taşucu
or Mersin on the eastern stretch of Turkey's south coast.

## From North America

From North America, you can fly to Istanbul and journey from there or arrange
for domestic travel to other regions. In the summer of 1988, fares on the major airlines from the U.S. to Turkey cost approximately $700 round-trip; investigate char-
ter flights for cheaper fares. Remember that if you travel from the U.S. to a major
European city and then travel to Turkey, you may decrease your costs.

## From Europe

**Yugoslavian Airlines (JAT)**, **Romanian Airlines** (Tarom), and **Pakistan Air** all
offer low fares to Istanbul from the U.S. and major European cities, although these
airlines have no offices in the U.S. (Yugoslavian Airlines' departure schedule and

luggage transport capabilities are also unreliable.) **Turkish Airlines'** fares are exorbitant, but a 50% student reduction brings them in line with the budget carriers. THY also has regular service to Turkey from European countries, and offers 60% discounts on its European flights to students under 28 years of age. In addition, **Pan Am** sells a Youth Pass for $600 round-trip. Scan the travel classifieds of newspapers and consult budget travel agents for other airlines.

From points in Europe, **train** travel might be the cheapest alternative, but it certainly isn't the most convenient, since Eurail and InterRail are not valid in Turkey. The Turkish rail system is rivalled only by the Greek as Europe's most antiquated and least efficient. Rail service is provided from Venice, Munich, and Vienna.

You can travel by **boat** from points other than Greece, including Ancona, Italy and Lattakia, Syria. There is also a cruise that travels from Venice to Izmir from June through September (3 days, $170).

## From Greece

**Athens** and Istanbul are connected by Euroways Eurolines bus and by train. If you have a railpass, take the train as far as Alexandroupolis, and ride the bus from there. Beware: The 38-hour ride from Athens will wear out even the most seasoned traveler. The quickest but most expensive option is an Olympic Airways **flight** to Istanbul or other points in Turkey.

If you want to **hitch** to Turkey from Greece, try to make it to Istanbul in one ride from Alexandroupolis or Thessaloniki; there isn't much traffic. You are not permitted to walk across the border. Make sure your driver's car doesn't get stamped in your passport (but rather on some other, disposable piece of paper), or you'll need to produce the car to leave the country. The officials might suspect that you sold it on the black market. If you dare to bring your own car into Turkey, you can drive for three months without a *Carnet de Passage,* although the vehicle will be registered on your passport. If you plan to stay longer, you must apply for a *triptique* at the Turkish Touring and Automobile Club. (See Documents above.)

There is direct **ferry** service between Piraeus and Izmir, but it's cheaper to take a ferry from one of the islands. Travel agents in Athens can help you sort through options.

From **Samos,** one boat travels daily in the summer from Samos Town to Kuşadası and nearby ruins at Ephesus (leaving at 8am, returning at 5pm); three ferries per week also depart from Pythagorion. In the off-season, only half as many boats make the crossing. You must deposit your passport with the travel agency the night before you sail, and you must buy a round-trip ticket (3000dr), even if you don't plan to return to Greece. There is a newly imposed embarkation tax of 1000dr per person, as well as an $8 port tax (paid on board) imposed during embarkation ($16 if you stay overnight). Try to pay in U.S. dollars, since the *drachma* suffers an outrageous exchange rate in Turkey (you will probably pay about $2 more). Port taxes are charged only in Kuşadası, Antalya, Izmir, and Istanbul, so if you're planning to spend time elsewhere in Turkey, it may be worth your while to cross over at another point.

From **Rhodes** in the summer, Monday through Saturday, two boats travel daily to Marmaris; in the off-season, service is reduced to four or five boats per week. Departure times are never fixed until the day before. To purchase tickets, get departure information, and deposit your passport (one day in advance), go to the **Marmaris Shipping Company,** 4 Akti Sahturi St., Rhodes (tel. 233 95 or 242 94), opposite the commercial harbor. (Open 9:30am-noon and 6-8pm.) The trip (2 hr.) costs 4000dr one-way, 7000dr round-trip. The boat returns from Marmaris to Rhodes daily during the summer. In the off-season, at least one boat travels per week, according to demand. Tickets may be purchased from **Yeşil Marmaris Tur** (tel. 15 59) and **Engin Tur** (tel. 10 82).

From the island of **Kos,** travel to Turkey is somewhat problematic. If you didn't take a charter to Greece, you can travel to the Turkish port of Bodrum aboard a Greek boat leaving in the morning, or a Turkish boat leaving in the afternoon. Although the Kos GNTO claims that Greek boats are not allowed to carry tourists to Turkey from Kos, it is worth double-checking. The travel agency requires your passport a day before departure.

You can hop the ferry to Çeşme from the island of **Chios**. It runs once weekly from April 15 to May 1, twice weekly from May 1 to June 15 and the last half of September, six times weekly from June to September 15. The passage lasts 1½ hours and costs 4000dr one way, 5500dr round-trip with open return. Leave your passport with the travel agent one day in advance.

From **Lesvos**, a boat to Ayvalık leaves every Wednesday during April and May, and three or four times per week from May through October (2½ hr.). From **Patmos**, planned excursions go to Ephesus in Turkey (500dr round-trip, 1800dr Turkish port tax, 1500dr for a guided tour of the ruins).

From **Northern Cyprus**, the shortest crossing is from Girne (Kyrenia) to Taşucu (6 hr.). There are two boats, the *Liberty* and the *Ertürk,* leaving on alternate days in the summer. In July and August, there is also expensive **hydrofoil** service. Boats run less frequently in winter, on no set schedule. For information on hydrofoils, call 621 89 in Taşucu. There are also **flights** to Istanbul from Nicosia's Ercan Airport.

# Once There

Shops in Turkey are generally open Monday through Saturday from 9am to 1pm and 2 to 7pm. Government offices are open Monday through Friday from 8:30am to 12:30pm and 1:30 to 5:30pm. Banks are open Monday through Friday from 8:30am to noon and 1:30 to 5pm. Food stores, open bazaars, and pharmacies have longer hours. During the summer, on the Aegean and Mediterranean coasts, government offices and other businesses close during the afternoons.

Museums and archeological sites in Turkey are generally open Tuesday through Sunday from 9am to 5pm. Admission prices range from 4-8¢. At some movies or concerts, students may receive discounts of up to 50%.

Official national **holidays** include New Year's Day (Jan. 1), National Independence Day and Children's Day (April 23), Atatürk's Commemoration and Youth and Sports Day (May 19), Victory Day (Aug. 30), and Republic Day (Oct. 29). Many establishments are closed during religious holidays, which fall on different dates each year (see Festivals below).

## Embassies and Consulates

Embassies in Ankara:

**American:** Atatürk Bul. 110 (tel. 26 54 70).

**Australian:** Nenehatun Cad. 83 (tel. 39 27 50 or 51).

**British:** Şehit Ersan Cad. 46/A (tel. 27 58 03).

**Canadian:** Nenehatun Cad. 75 (tel. 27 58 03).

Consulates in Istanbul:

**American:** Meşrutiyet Cad. 104 (tel. 1 436 200 or 09).

**British:** Tepebaşı. Meşrutiyet Cad. 34 (tel. 1 447 540).

Consulates in Izmir:

**American:** Atatürk Cad. 386 (tel. 13 21 35).

**British:** Necatibey Bulvarı 19/4 (tel. 14 54 70-9).

## Tourist Services

The Turks have tourist offices and tourist police in most major cities and resort areas. Some English is usually spoken and the staff will help you find accommodations. In places without an office, travel agents may serve the same function. Check in the regional sections for addresses and phone numbers.

If you encounter non-threatening difficulties anywhere in Turkey, go to the nearest tourist office before you try the police. The tourist office can advise you whether it is necessary to turn to the authorities for help. Of course, for matters of personal safety, seek out the police.

## Emergencies

If you are in need of **medical care** in Turkey, you can probably find a doctor who speaks English in most major hospitals. In Istanbul, there are several foreign hospitals.

**American Hospital:** Güzelbahçe Sok. Nişantaşı (tel. 1 486 030).

**French Hospital:** "Pasteur" Taşkışla 3, Panglatı (tel. 1 484 756); "La Paix" Büyükdere Cad., Şişli (tel. 1 481 832).

**German Hospital:** Sıracevizler Cad. 100 (tel. 1 435 500).

**Italian Hospital:** Defterdar Yokuşu Cihangir.

## Accommodations, Camping, and Amenities

If you need help finding accommodations, consult the nearest tourist office. Like the GNTO, Turkish officials regulate hotels. See several places before deciding where to stay, as cleanliness varies. Avoid rooms facing the street—nearby cafes and discos often blast music late into the night. Make sure your hotel has water before paying. If traveling in winter, check for heating.

If posted prices seem exorbitant, look disappointed and politely bargain: This is often effective. Nonetheless, inexpensive accommodations are usually plentiful. Budget accommodations average $3-4 per person on the Aegean coast, $1.50-2.50 in the east. In lieu of showers, many Turkish towns have a *hamam* (bathhouse), where you can take a wonderful steam bath for under $1.

Many Turks find Western manners brusque, and proprietors are sometimes offended by backpackers bursting into their hotel and asking the price of a room. Be polite: Say hello (*merhaba,*) inquire about the proprietor's health (*nasılsınız*), and only then ask the price. Being received as a guest, you should treat the proprietor as a host rather than a merchant. You may wish to carry a few packs of American cigarettes (especially Marlboros) with you, since they are a highly valued status symbol and provide an appropriate way of reciprocating favors.

Camping is a cheap alternative, and very popular among Turks, although many official campgrounds still aren't registered with the Ministry of Culture and Tourism. Most places charge $1.50 per person. Official government campsites are open from April or May through October. Freelance camping is illegal but many find it entirely feasible if practiced discreetly. Women should never camp alone.

Always carry toilet paper with you (most places don't have any); other toiletries, including tampons, are cheap and readily available, though they may be more difficult to find in remote towns. Condoms should be brought from home or elsewhere in Europe, as availability is quite unpredictable.

## Getting Around

Travel within Turkey is very inexpensive. **Turkish Airlines** has direct flights once or twice weekly from Istanbul to Trabzon or Van ($50), Diyarbakır or Erzurum ($55), Izmir ($50), and Ankara ($50).

Frequent and cheap **buses** run between all sizeable cities. Private bus lines sometimes offer students a 10% discount (show an ISIC card). You will need to go from booth to booth to piece together a complete schedule; one company will not divulge departure times of competitors. Exchanging your ticket can also be difficult. For long trips, there are always overnight buses; request a window seat in the middle of the bus, away from the driver's radio and behind the overhead window. The two seats in the back of the bus recline nearly horizontally. Every so often, an attendant comes around spritzing cologne water to keep you smelling nice. If you're thirsty, say *"su lütfen;"* you'll be brought a bottle of cold water. For long trips, try the comfortable and quick **Varan Tours** buses. They're slightly more expensive but have bigger seats, air conditioning, bathrooms, and serve *çay* (tea). For frequent runs, you'll have to buy a seat an hour in advance; otherwise, buy the ticket the day before.

Despite low fares (with a 10% student discount), **trains** within Turkey are no bargain. They are extremely slow and follow circuitous routes. First-class gets you a slightly more padded seat and a lot more room—most Turks travel second-class. *Couchettes* are also available. There are no train routes along the western coast.

Extensive **shared taxi** service (*dolmuş*) follows fixed routes between small towns. These are usually vans or minibuses, though occasionally cars are in service as well. They leave as soon as they fill up (*dolma* means stuffed and they're not kidding), and are almost as cheap as buses. Best of all, you can get on and off anywhere you like—salvation for the weary hitchhiker.

**Ferries** do not service the western coast, but a **Turkish Maritime Lines** cruiseship sails from Istanbul to Izmir once weekly year-round, increasing to three times weekly from July through September. A boat also travels from Istanbul to Trabzon; another to Alanya stops at Datça, Marmaris, Kaş, and Alanya, returning via Antalya, Fethiye, Bodrum, Kuşadası, and Izmir. Bigger ports have ship offices; otherwise, just get on the boat and find the purser. The cost of the 11-day cruise buys you food and a bunk in a very crowded dormitory room, or a space on deck if you prefer. Students get 10% discounts on all fares.

**Driving** in Turkey is made somewhat easier by the English road signs. Archeological and historical sites are indicated by yellow signposts. Turks drive on the right side of the road; the speed limit is 50kph (31mph) in cities and 99kph (61mph) on the highways. For some reason, official Turkish tourist literature warns against driving at night. Gas is relatively cheap. Road rescue services are located along the major highways; the head office is in Istanbul (tel. 146 70 90 or 521 65 88). If you get into an accident, you must notify the police to file a report. You can rent cars in major Turkish cities. For details, see the local tourist authorities or travel agents.

If you **hitchhike** in Turkey, you'll invariably catch rides with locals. If you're asked to pay for the ride, offer half of what the trip costs by bus. The hitching signal is a waving hand.

# *Life in Turkey*

## *History and Politics*

Historically, Asia Minor has been a conflation of disparate cultures. An early Hittite nation flourished in Central Anatolia in the third millenium B.C.E., creating a society much like their Eastern neighbors, the Sumerians. The Hittites discovered how to forge iron and developed the Indo-European language that became a root of most European languages. The hegemony of the 15th-century B.C.E. Hittite empire extended over Syria in the east and the Aegean coast in the west. The empire declined during the massive immigration of Greek islanders at the end of the second millenium B.C.E. Phrygians inhabited Central Anatolia while Ionians, Carians, and Dorians settled along the Aegean. The coast was conquered by Cyrus of Persia in the sixth century B.C.E., then by Alexander the Great two centuries later. Great metropoli began to spring up, reaching their zenith of prosperity after the second century B.C.E., when the coastline became the commercial and political core of the Roman province of Asia Minor. Under the rule of the emperor of Constantinople, the coastal ports continued to thrive, constituting an integral part of Byzantium.

The Seljuk Turks, who originally hailed from Mongolia, migrated westward over the course of the first millennium C.E. In the eleventh century C.E., they began to settle in the plains of central Anatolia, the region that eventually became the heartland of their permanent home. With the arrival of the Turks, the ports along the coast began to diminish in importance, as cities in the north and east became the major commercial centers. The advent of the Ottoman dynasty of Sultans several centuries later assured Turkish dominion over the entire Near East.

Mehmet II, an enthusiastic patron of the arts and a great modernizer, shaped the Turkish Empire into a major world power and overpowered Byzantium by marching into Constantinople in 1453. Five years later, he declared newly-named Istanbul the capital of the swelling Ottoman Empire. Under the reign of Süleyman the Magnificent (1520-66), the Empire expanded to include Algeria through North Africa and the Near East to Iraq, around to the Black Sea, and across the Balkan countries. Although the Crusaders maintained a tenuous grip on the southern Aegean coast, they were finally run out of the region in 1522. Subsequent centuries witnessed the decline of the Ottoman Empire. Attempts at modernizing the empire and checking administrative corruption failed. The final blow came immediately after the disastrous alliance of the Empire with Germany in World War I, when the Greeks, independent from Turkey only since 1831, invaded Izmir. Mustafa Kemal, an Ottoman general, began mobilizing his forces and repulsing the Greeks while the powerless Sultan looked on.

On October 29, 1923, the Republic of Turkey was proclaimed, and Mustafa Kemal, now called Atatürk ("Father of the Turks") was elected its first president. This man almost single-handedly carved the Turkish state from the collapsed Ottoman Empire. Equating modernization with rapid Westernization and secularization, he abolished the Caliphate, outlawed Muslim tribunals, and changed the alphabet from Arabic to Roman. Atatürk even forbade the *müezzin* (prayer callers) to sing in the classical Arabic of the Koran, decreeing that they could only be recited in modern Turkish. Naturally, these sweeping measures were met with great resistance from the religious establishment. Since Atatürk's death in 1938, there has been some backlash and a relaxation of his reforms, but the massive propaganda effort by the present government to keep Atatürk's popularity alive is an effective way to generate sympathy and tolerance for its own policies. In 1988, a Turk could go to jail for so much as criticizing Atatürk.

Since World War II, Turkey has been struggling with its two-party system of democracy. Recent governments have faced the task of restraining an explosive situation between Muslim extremists on the right and Marxists on the left. In the late 1970s, terrorist warfare laid siege to Istanbul, and the military stepped in. Along with the political "undesirables," most of the hustlers have been cleared out of the major tourist areas by severe police crackdowns. Martial law has since been repealed: Elections in 1983 ushered in the right-wing party of Prime Minister Özal. The leader of the opposition is still in enforced exile, but his party is no longer outlawed. Turkey is slowly and hesitatingly having another go at democracy.

## The Arts

Turkish art is a product of folk, Islamic, and Western traditions. Architecture is the dominant discipline in terms of three-dimensional forms, subjugating painting and sculpture to its purposes. In fact, until the mid-1800s, calligraphy, miniatures, and decorations were the only formal examples of painting. Music, dance, and theater have become more institutionalized and Westernized in the past 150 years. In 1971, concern over the purity of Turkish culture prompted the government to establish the nation's Ministry of Culture. Turkey's culture and politics have been inextricably intertwined.

Many monuments in Turkey were built during ancient Greek and Roman times; Bursa and Istanbul, however, feature some of the finest examples of Ottoman architecture in the world. The *cami* (mosque) serves as the Muslim center of worship. The older mosques typify the best of Turkish art and architecture. You'll notice two styles: the Oriental, Syrian-influenced buildings, with many columns in the interior supporting a low-ceilinged simple structure; and the grandiose Ottoman mosques, symmetrical, lofty structures with great domes, elaborate tile decoration, and stained glass. Look for the *mihrab* (prayer niche), in the center of the east wall pointing towards Mecca, and the *minbar* (pulpit); these are sometimes lavishly carved, tiled, or otherwise adorned. In larger cities, you may also see a *türbe* (mausoleum) or *medrese* (Koranic school).

## Literature

Herbert Muller's *The Loom of History* traces the fascinating history of Asia Minor from prehistoric times to the twentieth century. Turkey's Hellenistic heritage is discussed in F.E. Peter's *The Harvest of Hellenism*. Homer's *Iliad* is a classic traveling companion for these shores. For years, verse was the only acceptable literary genre in the Middle East; Nâzım Hikmet's *Selected Poems* is one of the best Turkish collections. More contemporary authors include Cevat Şakir Kabaağaç, the famed fisher of Halicarnassus, and Yaşar Kemâl, whose *Memed, My Hawk*, and *The Wind from the Plains* have several times won him nominations for the Nobel Prize. Excellent books on modern Turkey are Bernard Lewis' *The Emergence of Modern Turkey* and Lord Kinross' *Atatürk: The Rebirth of a Nation*. For more scholarly works, try Steven Runcinan's *Byzantine Civilization* or Lord Kinross's *The Ottoman Centuries*, both histories of their respective periods. Mark Twain's *Innocents Abroad* offers glimpses of the Turkish coast as only Samuel Clemmens could.

## Language

You've probably never heard anything quite like the Turkish language. A distant relative of Finnish, Hungarian, and Mongolian, it also has roots in the classical Arabic of the Koran. Try to learn as many Turkish phrases as you can; the Turks will appreciate the effort, and you may reduce the chances of being swindled.

In the major coastal resorts, many languages are spoken; English is always common, and French and especially German can be helpful. Buy a phrase book, such as the Berlitz *Turkish for Travelers* or *Say it in Turkish*, and keep a pen and pad handy for addresses, phrases, and numbers. **Langenscheidt** has an excellent Turkish-English pocket dictionary. Keep in mind that when Turks raise their chins and shut their eyes they mean "no," and when they wave a hand up and down, they mean "come." Placing the palm flat against the chest is a polite way of refusing an offer.

Certain letters and combinations of letters are pronounced differently than they are in English. Turkish is a phonetic language, and all sounds are pronounced. Special vowels, consonants, and combinations include:

| Turkish | English |
|---|---|
| c: | "j" as in john |
| ç: | "ch" as in church |
| ğ: | lengthens the preceding vowel |
| ı: | (no dot on the "i") "u" as in tummy |
| i: | "e" as in me |
| j: | "s" as in leisure |
| ö: | "eu" rhymes with French deux |
| ş: | "sh" as in ship |
| u: | as in too |
| â: | dipthong of ea, or faint ya |
| ü: | "ew" as in dew |
| ay: | "uy" as in buy |
| ey: | "ey" as in obey |
| oy: | "oy" as in boy |
| uy: | "oo-ee" as in Louis |

Some useful phrases include:

| | |
|---|---|
| merhaba (MER-hah-bah): | hello |
| evet: | yes |
| hayır (HIGH-er): | no |
| lütfen (LEWT-fen): | please |
| teşekkürler (tesh-ek-KEWR-ler): | thank you (formal) |
| bir şey değil (bir-shay-DEE-ul): | you're welcome |
| allaha ısmarladık: | good bye (said by guest) |
| güle güle (gew-lay gew-lay): | good bye (said by host) |
| günaydın (gun i-duhn): | good morning |
| iyi akşamlar (ee-ak-sham-LAR): | good evening |
| iyi geceler (ee-geh-jeh-LEHR): | good night |
| peki (PEH-kee): | okay |
| su (SOOH): | water |
| hesap (hay-SAHP): | bill |
| Kaç para? (KACH pah-rah): | How much is it? |
| anlamadım (ahn-LA-mah-dum): | I don't understand |
| Afedersiniz (ahf-feh-DER-si-niz): | Excuse me |
| Nedir adınız? (neh-deer-AHD-in-iz): | What is your name? |
| istiyorum (IS-tee-yor-oom): | I want |
| nerede? (NEH-reh-deh): | Where is |
| lokanta (loh-KAN-tah): | restaurant |
| postane (post-AHN-eh): | post office |
| müze (MEW-zeh): | museum |
| otel (oh-TEL): | hotel |
| yer, oda (yehr, OH-da): | room |
| tuvalet (too-vah-LET): | toilet |
| hava alanı (hah-vah ah-LAHN-ee): | airport |
| otobüs (oh-toh-BOOS): | bus |
| doktor (dohk-TOHR): | doctor |
| bakkal (bahk-KAHL): | grocery |
| eczane (ej-ZAHN-eh): | pharmacy |
| banka (BAHN-kah): | bank |
| polis (poh-LEES): | police |
| sol, sağ (sohl, saa): | left, right |
| Saat kaç? (sah-aht KAHCH): | What time is it? |
| pasaport (pahs-ah-PORT): | passport |
| tren (tren): | train |
| bilet (bih-LET): | ticket |
| burada, orada (BOOR-ah-dah, OHR-ah-dah): | here, there |
| dün (dewn): | yesterday |
| bugün (boo-GEWN): | today |
| yarın (YAHR-un): | tomorrow |
| İngilizçe biliyor musunuz? (in-gih-LEEZ-jeh bihl-ee-OHR moo-soo-nooz): | Do you speak English? |
| Türkçe bilmiyorum (TURK-cheh BIHL-mee-yohr-oom): | I don't speak Turkish. |

The numbers from one to ten are: *bir* (1), *iki* (2), *üç* (3), *dört* (4), *beş* (5), *altı* (6), *yedi* (7), *sekiz* (8), *dokuz* (9), and *on* (10).

The days of the week are: *Pazar* (Sun.), *Pazartesi* (Mon.), *Salı (Tues.)*, *Çarşamba* (Wed.), *Perşembe* (Thurs.), *Cuma* (Fri.), and *Cumartesi* (Sat.).

## Religion

Over 95% of Turks are Muslim, and Islam affects all spheres of life, even in modernized Turkey. Islam was founded by the prophet Muhammed in the seventh century C.E., after he received the revelation that he was the final prophet of God. The faithful worship Allah (God) and follow the scriptures of the Koran (the word of God). Muslims are expected to pray at five specific times during the day, to give a portion of their wealth as alms, to fast during daylight in the holy month of Ramadan, and at least once in a lifetime to make a pilgrimage to Mecca.

Before entering a mosque, Muslims wash themselves and take off their footwear. Foreign visitors should do likewise. Non-Muslims are permitted to visit most mosques, but they may be excluded from some very sacred places. Don't visit a mosque during prayer time, and always dress modestly. Men and women should have their arms and legs covered; women should also cover their heads.

## Traditions

A popular pastime is visiting the Turkish *kahve* (coffeehouses), where people sit, sip coffee or tea, and play *tavla* (backgammon). In Istanbul look for men smoking *nargile* (bubble pipes).

You should go to a *hamam* (Turkish bath) at least once. It has been a custom since medieval times, due to the Islamic emphasis on cleanliness. Men and women use separate bath houses, or use the same place on different days. Enter the bath house, deposit your clothes in a cubicle, don the provided *peştemal* (towel), and proceed to the *göbek taşı* (large heated stone), which produces a sauna-like effect. As you sweat, an attendant will give you a rub-down. Afterwards, take a dip in a cooler pool.

Folk traditions pervade Turkey. Turkish folk music is played mostly on traditional percussion and wind instruments. Each region has its own special folk dance, heroes, and traditional costumes. Some of the most popular dances include the *Kaşık Oyunu* (spoon dance), done from Konya to Silifke, with men and women in colorful garb beating wooden spoons; the *Kılıç Kalkan,* from Bursa, in which men dressed in Ottoman fighting gear act out battles; and the *Zeybek,* an Aegean dance performed to symbolize bravery and heroism. Traditional sports include *Yağlı Güreş* (grease wrestling), *cirit oyunu* (tossing javelins at competitors on horseback), and *deve güreşi* (camel wrestling).

Certain superstitions persist in Turkey. The belief in the evil eye is strong, and many people wear amulets or pieces of Koranic text to ward off evil spirits. In tourist shops, amulets with blue eyes stare up at you from necklaces, pins, and keychains. Note that it is illegal to insult another person in Turkey. Conduct debate civilly or you may find yourself in jail.

### Bargaining

One of the most useful arts to master in Turkey is bargaining. It is best to make larger purchases in Istanbul or Izmir, where the competition keeps prices low. Authentic Turkish carpets and other craftwork, however, should be purchased in other areas, since prices can be twice as high in Istanbul. Don't hesitate to haggle, especially when dealing with smaller establishments. The Turks expect it.

When shopping, take your time. Let the merchant know you've seen the competition—this will give you good bargaining leverage. Be persistent: Decide how much you want to pay and then don't budge. When you first offer your price (start with half the amount you are quoted) and the proprietor makes a face and acts insulted, remember that it's a test of wills. Pout and make your own faces in response. Try gaining their sympathy. Or tell them you saw the same item around the corner for a much lower price. If they tell you to get it there, pretend to head for the other shop. You should head for the door at least three or four times while bargaining; this technique works at hotels as well. The shopkeeper will probably call after you, demanding to know what you are willing to offer. Grab the chance to haggle again and stick to your price.

## Food

Turkish food is generally fresh and painstakingly prepared. Turkey is also one of the few places left in the Mediterranean where eating very cheap still entitles you to sample a great variety of dishes. In restaurants, it's customary to go to the back counter and look around before choosing. You can't normally bargain in restaurants because prices are fixed by municipalities—one exception is fish. Streetside ice cream and drink vendors will usually overcharge tourists; watch how much the Turks are paying, and don't pay any more than that. As far as sanitation goes, tap water in all cities is safe since it is heavily chlorinated. Food is often not so clean, but squeezing lemon juice over your food helps with digestion. If you have problems, yogurt will replace your body's natural bacteria content.

Popular dishes include: *tarhana çorbası,* a tomato-yogurt soup; *cacık,* yogurt with cucumber and garlic; *güveç,* vegetables and spices; *erişteli çorba,* a tomato noodle soup; *balık çorbası,* a hearty, spicy fish stew; *pilav,* rice served with a light sauce; *pilaki,* navy beans in a tomato sauce, often with meat; *mantı,* small ravioli covered with a yogurt and peanut oil sauce, sprinkled with red pepper (a specialty of Bodrum); and *mücver,* a breaded, spiced, and deep-fried zucchini dish (you don't even have to like zucchini to love it). Most famous, however, are *dolma,* stuffed vegetables usually filled with chopped meat, rice, onions, and seasoning. Common varieties include *biber* (peppers); *domates* (tomatoes); and *patlıcan* (eggplant). *Imam bayıldı* is cold eggplant filled with onions, parsley, and tomatoes. Try *çoban salatası,* cucumber and tomato salad, which can be very spicy. *Zeytin* (olives) are available everywhere and taste terrific.

The ubiquitous barbecue joints specialize in *döner kebap,* slices cut from a leg of lamb roasting on a spit, and *şiş kebap,* skewered chunks of lamb. When in Bursa or Istanbul, try *Iskender kebap,* a delicious concoction of lamb, yogurt, pita, and tomato sauce. In the coastal resorts, the favorite is *balık kebap,* or fish kebap, skewered cubes of fish roasted with lemons, tomatoes, and green peppers. Along the Aegean coast, *kalamar* (squid) can be bought for a reasonable price. Along the Mediterranean coast, particularly around Kaş, the best buy is *sokor* fish. Charcoal-broiled sardines wrapped in grape leaves are inexpensive and easily available in August. In September, in Istanbul and along the Black Sea, try *palamut* (the smallest—about the size of mackerel—are the most tender and expensive). In Izmir, try the *trança.* The best place to eat octopus is in Bodrum at the Ahtapot Restaurant. After it is caught, the creature is beaten against a rock hundreds of times (to tenderize it), then skinned and fried, boiled, or cut into a salad.

Be sure to try a *menemen,* a delicious loose omelette with tomatoes and onions. *Pide* is a distant Turkish relative of pizza—flat bread served with your choice of eggs, meat, tomatoes, cheese, or spices. Or try *köfte,* a spicy member of the meatball family—it comes either skewered and roasted or served in a tomato broth, with potatoes and vegetables.

There is an endless selection of confections—*baklava,* flaky pastry jammed with nuts and soaked in honey; *kadayıf,* a shredded-wheat dough filled with nuts and sugar; and *helva,* a sesame seed and honey loaf. Of course, there is always Turkish Delight (*lokum*). Most restaurants also serve some sort of fresh fruit or melon. *Tavuk göğsü* (chicken pudding) or *sütlaç* (rice pudding) are both excellent. The fruit-flavored *dondurma* (ice cream) is also delicious. Most Turks draw out their evening meal interminably (usually 7-11pm). Those with strong stomachs throw down some *rakı,* a licorice-flavored liqueur, and stagger home.

It is difficult to spend a day in Turkey without pausing at a *çay* shop and ordering a glass of *çay* (a light herb tea). You'll also be offered tea at just about any shop you enter. Ironically, *kahve* (Turkish coffee), drunk so widely throughout Greece and the Middle East, is heavily taxed and difficult to procure in Turkey. Nevertheless, you'll soon enjoy voluminous imbibing of tea (grown along the Black Sea coast). For snacking, try *börek* (layers of cheese and light dough). Bottled drinks include *meyve suyu* (fruit drink; try cherry or the ambrosial peach nectar); *meyveli gazoz* (a sweet Turkish soda); *ayran,* a mixture of yogurt and milk; *soda* (soda water); *su* (Turkish designer water); and *maden suyu* (carbonated mineral water). *Bira* (beer) is very popular: *Efes-pilsen* and *Tekelbeyaz* are light, while *Tekel siyah* is dark. Turkey has a sizeable grape crop and all the coastal resorts are well-stocked with domestic wine.

## Climate

In the summer months, the Aegean and Mediterranean coasts are very hot, with average daily temperatures straddling 90°F. Beware of mosquitoes, particularly on the Mediterranean Coast. *Bring repellent.* The swimming season from Bodrum south, and all along the Mediterranean coast, lasts from early May well into October. On the Black Sea coast (Istanbul included), the swimming season is shorter, from June through early September, and fall brings considerable rainfall; winters aren't especially cold, but usually pretty wet and miserable. As you move inland, the climate becomes more drastic; the area around Urfa usually exceeds 100°F in the summer, while the north of Van it stays relatively cool because of the high altitude. In the winter, Urfa is temperate, while most of central and eastern Anatolia is bitterly cold, with heavy snowfalls.

## Festivals

There are numerous holidays and festivals in Turkey, both religious and secular. During the month-long Islamic holiday **Ramadan** (April 6-May 5 in 1989), pious Muslims do not eat, drink, smoke, or travel between dawn and sunset. Only one or two restaurants may be open during the day in the smaller towns and inland. Large celebrations mark the holiday's conclusion, when it becomes practically impossible to get bus and train tickets and hotel rooms. The semi-annual feast of **Bayram** lasts three days.

In the last week of April, the **Spring Festival** is held in Manisa. **May Day,** the feast of spring, marks the beginning of a month of festivities along the coast, the first of these being the **Festival of Ephesus.** A series of theater, music, and folklore festivals are all held in the ruins of ancient Greek theaters. Next come the festivals of Silifke, Marmaris, and Bergama. On June 29, the **Feast Day of St. Peter** is honored at Antakya by ceremonies in the grotto of St. Peter. In August, the one-week **Troy Festival** is held at Çanakkale. On August 15, the **Assumption** is celebrated near Selçuk in the House of the Virgin Mary.

In the off-season, festivities continue. Demre stages a **Santa Claus Festival** December 3-7; the **Whirling Dervishes** of Konya perform December 14-17 during the Mevlânâ Commemorative Ceremonies; some towns hold a camel wrestling contest January 15-16; and the more conventional human grease wrestling contests are held in Edirne May 29-June 6, during the **Kırkpınar Festival.**

# Northwestern Turkey

## Istanbul

Minarets silhouetted against a hazy orange sunset, the clarion cries of the evening call to prayer, the wail of ships' horns, the aromas of fish, charcoal, spice, and rosewater—Istanbul is a feast for the senses. Inconsistently though unmistakably Eastern, this city has been the capital of two far-flung empires, the Byzantine and the Ottoman. Today, it embraces an eclectic culture: Men smoke *nargiles* (water pipes) while their sons listen to transistor radios, and office clerks clad in business suits

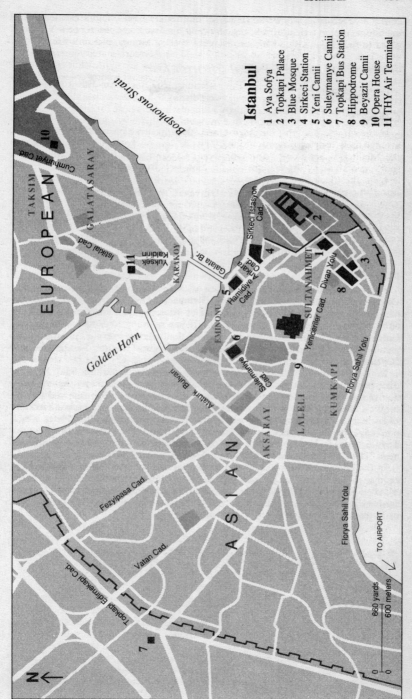

## Istanbul

1 Aya Sofya
2 Topkapi Palace
3 Blue Mosque
4 Sirkeci Station
5 Yeni Camii
6 Suleymanye Camii
7 Topkapi Bus Station
8 Hippodrome
9 Beyazit Camii
10 Opera House
11 THY Air Terminal

share the streets with women wrapped in traditional scarves. Labyrinthine streets
lead to unexpected treasures, vestiges of untold history. From the magical Topkapı
Palace to the elegant Blue Mosque, Istanbul sparks the imagination's fire.

## Orientation and Practical Information

Waterways divide Istanbul into three sections. The **Bosphorus Strait** (Boğaziçi)
separates Asia Minor from Europe, likewise distinguishing Asian Istanbul from European Istanbul. The Asian side, mostly residential, offers little for the tourist. Most
historical sites, markets, mosques, and museums of the older quarters are situated
on the southern bank of the **Golden Horn,** an estuary which splits the European
half of the city. The more modern northern bank contains **Istiklâl Caddesi,** the main
downtown shopping street, and **Cumhuriyet Caddesi,** Istanbul's own Fifth Avenue,
where all the airline offices and expensive hotels are located.

The entire city is broken into small quarters; learn their names quickly—they'll
help on public transportation. Budget travelers converge in **Sultanahmet,** right
across from Aya Sofya. Other important quarters are **Taksim,** home of the airline
offices and the American Express office; **Kumkapı,** a seaside quarter with many restaurants; and **Eminönü,** on the southern end of the Galata Bridge, site of the **Sirkeci
Train Station** and the ferry station for the Bosphorus. The tourist office will provide
you with a free map; as long as you remain near landmarks you won't get lost.

If you come by plane, you'll arrive at either **Yeşilköy Airport** (domestic flights)
or **Atatürk Airport** (international flights), which are connected by a free bus. There
are a few campgrounds and one hotel nearby (see Londra Mocamp, Accommodations). To get into town, take the **Turkish Airlines bus** (tel. 1 433 399), which leaves
from the Domestic Departures Building, stops in Aksaray, and terminates its run
at the THY Airlines Terminal in Şişhane. If you're going to Sultanahmet, you'll
want to get off at Aksaray. From the airport, the bus runs every 30 minutes from
5:30am to noon, and after the arrival of late THY flights (30 min., 54¢). Public bus
#96 and *dolmuş* run into town until 9pm and cost only 15¢. The bus stop is on
the highway in front of International Arrivals, beyond the parking lot.

**Buses** in Istanbul are convenient and cheap. Tickets (12¢, students 6¢) are sold
in advance at kiosks marked "Plantonluk," at larger bus stops (e.g. Eminönü,
Karaköy, Taksim), and at private kiosks marked "Akbank." The people hawking
tickets at bus stops charge an 8¢ premium. (In a pinch, you can usually buy one
from someone on the bus.) Service begins at 6am runs every two to five minutes
on major routes; it becomes increasingly less frequent after dark, and stops around
11pm. The slowest routes pass through the commercial districts around Istiklâl
Caddesi—estimate 30 minutes from Sultanahmet to Taksim. Read the wooden sign
board at the side of the bus or ask the driver if he is headed for a particular quarter.
The sign on a bus going to Sultanahmet will usually include Beyazıt if it's from
the north, or Eminönü coming from the south or west. Buses suffer in Istanbul's
ensnarled traffic, so you may want to walk.

A **dolmuş** (shared taxi), either a minibus or an American beauty from the '40s
or '50s with fins and buffed chrome, is faster than the bus and generally costs 16¢.
*Dolmuş* run on fixed routes, usually between the main bus stops in each quarter
(if you ask they'll let you off en route); sometimes their own stop is nearby.

If you're **hitching** to Asian Turkey or to Europe, take bus #81 from Sultanahmet
to the Londra Mocamp, where you can best find a ride. This and the mocamp outside of Ankara are two of the best places from which to hitch into the Middle East.
Only one major highway, Rte. 100, runs out of Istanbul. To the west, Rte. 100 goes
to Edirne and the rest of the European continent. Route 100 East takes you to the
heart of Anatolia as well as the southern beaches.

**Tourist Information Offices:** In Sultanahmet, on Divan Yolu Cad. at the northern end of
the **Hippodrome,** across from the Sultan Pub (tel. 5 224 903); in Galatasaray (Regional Direc-
torate), 57-B Meşrutiyet Cad., near Galatasaray Sq. and the British Consulate (tel. 1 456
875); in Taksim, the Hilton Hotel Arcade (tel. 1 330 592); in Karaköy Maritime Station (tel.

1 495 776); and in the International Terminal of the airport (tel. 5 737 399). All offices open daily 9am-5pm.

**Budget Travel: Gençtur,** 15 Yerebatan Cad., 3rd floor (tel. 5 265 409 or 5 280 734), right in the center of Sultanahmet. Very helpful. Sells ISICs, distributes free maps, and provides a Poste Restante service. Also organizes Turkish language classes and voluntary workcamps in villages. Open Mon.-Fri. 9am-5:30pm, Sat. 9am-1pm. **Seventur Travel Shop,** 2-C Alemdar Cad. (tel. 5 124 183), next to the Aya Sofya, also sells ISICs and provides a Poste Restante service. The agency is authorized to issue plane and bus tickets; other travel agencies in Sultanahmet may swindle travelers by selling bogus bus tickets. Open Mon.-Sat. 9am-7pm.

**Consulates: U.S.,** 147 Meşrutiyet Cad., Tepebaşı (tel. 1 436 200). **British,** 34 N. Meşrutiyet Cad. (tel. 1 447 540). **Bulgaria,** 15 Yıldızposta Cad., Gayrettepe (tel. 1 662 605). **Iran,** Ankara Cad., Cağaloğlu (tel. 5 120 090). **Iraq,** Teşvikiye Cad., Teşvikiye (tel. 1 605 020). **USSR,** 443 İstiklâl Cad., Tünel (tel. 1 443 587). **Syria,** 3 Silâhtar Cad., Nişantaşı (tel. 1 482 735). **Greece,** 32 Turnacıbaşı, Galasaray (tel. 1 450 596). **Yugoslavia,** 96 Vali Konağı Cad., Nişantaşı (tel. 1 481 004).

**Currency Exchange:** Banks' exchange counters open Mon.-Fri. 8:30am-noon and 1:30-5pm. The bank at the **Karaköy Maritime Station** is open until 6pm on weekdays, and after hours and on weekends whenever a ship arrives. **Imar Bankası,** on Divan Yolu in Sultanahmet (tel. 5 227 309), does not charge commission when cashing traveler's checks. Open Mon.-Sat. 9am-5pm. **Yeşilköy Airport's** exchange booth is open 24 hours, and the exchange booth at **Sirkeci Train Station** opens for each arrival. Remember to keep your receipts; some banks will not change lira back into dollars even with a receipt (see the General Introduction to Turkey).

**American Express:** Hilton Hotel lobby, Cumhuriyet Cad. (tel. 1 329 558). Holds mail but charges US$3 for people without AmEx traveler's checks or credit cards. Open Mon.-Sat. 9am-midnight, Sun. 9am-8pm. Banking services at **Koç American Bank,** 233 Cumhuriyet Cad., across the street from the Hilton and 100m up the hill. Money wired here without a fee if you accept Turkish lira; 1% fee for other currencies. Open Mon.-Fri. 9:30am-12:30pm and 1:30-3pm.

**PTT:** Istanbul has 113 post offices, with the main branch at 25 Yeni Postane Sokak, 2 blocks southwest of Sirkeci Train Station; from Sultanahmet, walk up Yerebatan Cad., turn right at the Iranian Consulate, and follow Ankara Cad. down the hill to the train station—the PTT is signposted on one of the streets off to the left. Stamp, telephone, and telegram services open 24 hours. Crowded around midday; Poste Restante line can take 20 min. If possible, have mail sent to Gençtur's in Sultanahmet, and buy stamps (*pul*) in the postcard stores. Postal rates to the U.S. are 17¢ for cards, 21¢ for letters. All PTTs accept packages; if a customs officer is not present, you will be directed to the **Kadıköy, Beyazıt,** or **Tophane** (on Rıhtım Cad.) offices. The branch just off the western end of Taksim Sq. on Cumhuriyet Cad. is efficient for mailing packages or making long-distance calls. Open Mon.-Fri. 8am-8pm, Sat. 8am-6pm. The **Hilton** will send packages under 1kg. Open Mon.-Sat. 8am-8pm, Sun. 8am-noon.

**Telephones:** Payphones are scattered throughout the city, though few work. Use *küçük jeton* (small tokens) for local calls. All Istanbul numbers have 7 digits; occasionally you see a 6-digit number, but these are prefixed by the single digit intra-city area code. The **area code** for the European side north of the Golden Horn (Taksim, etc.) is 1, the European side south of the Horn (Sultanahmet, etc.) is 5, and Asian Istanbul (Kadıköy) is 3. **International calls** can be made at payphones in the Taksim and Central PTTs using *büyük jeton* (big tokens). Look for the yellow phones marked *Uluslararası* or *Milletlerarası,* which means international. (Calls to the U.S. take 10 *jetons* per min.); throw them in the machine as fast as possible.) **Collect calls** can be made only to the U.S., Canada, England, Italy, Holland, Spain, Sweden, and Japan.

**Airports: Yeşilköy Airport** for domestic flights (tel. 5 737 388), and **Atatürk Airport** for international flights (tel. 5 737 145). Both airports are 30 min. from downtown. **Türk Hava Yolları** ("THY," or Turkish Airlines) offers a 50% reduction to ISIC holders (on international flights only), and a 10% reduction on all flights for families. Call 1 454 208 for information. **Pakistan Air, Yugoslavian Air,** and **Romanian Air** usually sell the cheapest tickets to and from Europe, though service can be spotty. **Pan Am** student fares are even lower.

**Trains: Haydarpaşa Station,** on the Asian side (tel. 3 360 475). Ferries between the station and Karaköy pier #7 run every 30 min. (schedule posted on the pier). The pier is about halfway between the Galata Bridge and the Karaköy tourist office, where all tickets for Asia can be purchased in advance at the TCDD office upstairs. The office accepts couchette reservations for Ankara (should be done 2 days in advance). Europe-bound trains leave from **Sirkeci Station** (tel. 5 270 051), in Eminönü. (Oct.-May daily at 6:15pm; June-Sept. daily at 8:50pm.) To: Sophia ($32); Belgrade ($47); Athens ($34); and Munich ($94). Student discounts for those 26 and under.

**Buses: Topkapı Bus Terminal,** just beyond the city walls on Millet Cad. (the terminal doesn't appear on maps). From Sultanahmet, take any bus with Topkapı written on the side panel (20 min., longer at rush hour). All bus companies have offices at Topkapı, including **Varan Tours** (tel. 1 491 903) and **Pamukkale** (tel. 5 822 934).

**Ferries: Turkish Maritimes Lines,** on the waterfront at Karaköy (tel. 1 444 233), just west of the Haydarpaşa ferry terminal; it's the building with blue awnings marked "Denizcilik Yolları." Pullman to Izmir and Trabzon and points in between (meals not included). Luxury cruises to Venice and Antalya also available.

**English Bookstores: Redhouse Books Kitapevi,** 48 Rızapaşa Yokuşu (tel. 522 39 05); follow Uzun Çarşı from the Örücüler Gate of the Grand Bazaar, and turn right on Rızapaşa Yokuşu. Excellent and eclectic selection of English language books and guidebooks, including *Strolling Through Istanbul* ($19) and *Istanbul: a Brief Guide to the City* ($7.75). Open Mon.-Fri. 9am-6pm. **Aypa Bookstore,** 80 Divan Yolu Cad. (tel. 5 226 225), in Sultanahmet, sells cards, foreign newspapers, and an extensive selection of Turkish phrase books. Open daily 8am-8pm.

**Laundromat: EMEK,** 1 block down Klodfarer Cad. from the Hotel Klodfarer. Expensive (jeans 80¢, shirts 40¢). Open Mon.-Sat. 8am-5pm. Cleaning staff in hotels usually does laundry for less.

**Hospitals: American Hospital,** Admiral Bristol Hastanesi, Nişantaş, Güzelbahçe Sok. (tel. 1 314 050). **German Hospital,** Sıraselviler Cad., Taksim (tel. 1 438 100).

**Police:** Tel. 1 666 666. May not speak English.

**Tourist Police:** In Sultanahmet, Alemdar Karakolu (tel. 5 285 369). Help with stolen goods and any legal problems. Open daily 9am-6pm, phone answered 24 hours.

## Accommodations and Camping

Istanbul's budget accommodations are concentrated in the **Sultanahmet** district. Your hotel will be convenient to historical sights and located in an attractive setting, but you'll also be surrounded by droves of backpackers, isolated from the locals and assaulted by persistent carpet and leather merchants. The police reputedly place undercover agents posing as drug dealers in this area.

Prices in Sultanahmet range from $2.50 for a rooftop, to $5 for a single. Rates go up in July and August. If you're willing to spend a little more, you look at third- and fourth-class hotels in the adjacent **Lâleli** and **Aksaray** districts. West of the **Grand Bazaar** and **Istanbul University,** these two quarters cater to large European tour groups. Less scenic, this area suits travelers who seek quieter and nicer rooms. Singles cost $10-$15.

To get to Lâleli and Aksaray from the airport, take the Turkish Air bus or #96 to Aksaray. Walk along Ordu Caddesi and turn left on Fethibey Caddesi, just after the Lâleli Camii.

To get to Sultanahmet from the airport, take either the airport bus or #96 to Aksaray, and then another public bus (any will do) down Ordu Cad. to Sultanahmet. From the Sirkeci Train Station, take any bus going from Eminönü to Beyazıt. From the Haydarpaşa train station, take the ferry to Karaköy, cross the Galata Bridge, and take any bus going from Eminönü to Beyazıt. The Sultanahmet bus stop faces a large square with Aya Sofya on one side and the Blue Mosque on the other.

**Yücelt Hostel (IYHF),** 6 Caferiye Cad. (tel. 5 136 150), "in the shadow of the Aya Sofya." Clean, crowded rooms. The cafeteria is mediocre and overpriced; the library and Turkish bath are more frill than function. Still, a great place to meet travelers and find out what's going on in Istanbul. Dorm room $4-5 per person, doubles $5.50. Showers included.

**Hotel Anadolu,** 3 Salkım Söğüt Sok. (tel. 5 121 035). Take a right off Yerebatan Cad. Clean and bare. Impressive view of the Aya Sofya. Amiable management. Singles $3, doubles $7, roof $1.50 per person. Showers included.

**Topkapı Hostel,** at Ishakpaşa Cad. and Kutlugün Sok. (tel. 5 272 433). Facing the Topkapı Palace entrance, take a right and walk down the hill. Rooms somewhat cramped. Friendly management and quiet location. Dorm room $4, covered rooftop $3. Showers and breakfast included.

**Hotel Popüler,** at Küçükayasofya Cad. and Yeğen Sok. (tel. 5 274 709), a few blocks south of the Blue Mosque. Well-removed from "hotel row" in Sultanahmet. Small yet clean rooms with portable showers. Tastefully decorated with *kilim,* copper antiques, and straw mats. Appealing lounge with spectacular view of the Bosphorus, cheap beer, and backgammon. Singles $7.50, doubles $15.

**Hotel La Mira,** #28 Fethibey Cad. (tel. 5 262 322), in Lâleli. A few blocks up from Lâleli Camii at the corner of Ağu Yokuşu. Good-sized rooms with clean, private bathrooms. Singles $10, doubles $13-16. Hot showers and breakfast included.

**Sultan Tourist Hostel,** Yerebatan Cad. (tel. 5 207 676). From the Aya Sofya, walk 100m; it's on the left. Small rooms with sink. Singles $7.50. Doubles $9.

**Hotel Bÿükayasofya,** 5 Caferiye Sok. (tel. 5 222 981), just left of the Aya Sofya. Tucked away and partly covered with ivy. A bit grimy. Comfortable lounge. Singles (3 or 4 to a room) $5, doubles $7.50. Hot showers included.

**Londra Mocamp** (tel. 584 01 30), 1km from the airports, along the highway to Istanbul. Stay here if you are stuck at the airport. Facilities include cafeteria, bar, pool, and showers. $1.30 per person. 98¢ per tent. Bungalows for 2 $8.62.

## Food

Istanbul is a gustatory delight. From the sandwich stands in the streets to the elegant seafood restaurants on the Bosphorus, you can expect high quality, great variety, and reasonable prices. While Sultanahmet may be the best place to stay, it is not the best place to eat—you'll do much better in the **Kumkapı** district, south of the Grand Bazaar, or the **Tepebaşı** quarter, near the British consulate. For a quick stand-up lunch, the numerous *kebapçıs* or *köfteci* will easily fill you up for less than $2. Stop at a *büfe* (snack shop) for a grilled cheese and a soft drink for no more than $1. Even a complete meal at a cheaper *lokanta* shouldn't run you more than $3. For a little more you can order grilled seafood at **Sarıyer** or **Rumeli Kavağı**—both a scenic bus (#25 from Eminönü) or ferry ride north along the Bosphorus. Although eating out is so economical, you should shop in one of the open-air fruit markets. Two markets are centrally located: one in Tepebaşı, near the British Consulate, and another in the Mısır (Egyptian) Bazaar, near the New Mosque.

**Tepebaşı: Çiçek Pasajı** ("Flower Passage"), tucked away in the heart of the new city, just north of Istiklâl Cad. on Sahne Sok. (Not to be confused with the restaurant of the same name on Istiklâl Cad.) Cluster of restaurants in a glorified alleyway. Mostly local crowd. Lively, festive atmosphere with Turkish folk musicians. The **Mercan Restaurant,** on the main thoroughfare of the "Flower Passage" is a great place to start the evening. *Midye dolması* (stuffed mussels) and beer $1.50. Open daily 11am-midnight. For late night merry-making, try **Kimene Restaurant,** also on the main thoroughfare. The bland, almost non-existent decor in no way portends the colorful atmosphere. When the *rakı* starts flowing, local musicians begin to serenade restaurant patrons. *Kebap,* salad, and rakı $5. Open daily noon-1am. **Yeni Rejans Restaurant,** #15 Olivo Geçidi (tel. 144 16 10), offers Russian food right in the middle of Istanbul. Walking north on Istiklâl Cad., turn left at #244, and go down a small alleyway—it's next to the Victoria Kebap Restaurant. Founded in 1930, this place is truly an anachronism. Under high ceilings, an elderly waiter clad in a green tuxedo silently shuttles amongst dimly lit tables. The perfect setting for a Le Carré spy novel. Russian dishes include *borscht* (75¢) and *chicken kiev* ($4); also serves Turkish food. Open daily noon-3pm and 7-10pm.

**Sultanahmet:** The restaurants along **Divan Yolu** serve typical but overpriced Turkish cuisine. The cheapest, **Sultanahmet Köftecisi,** at the end of Divan Yolu, across from the tourist office, caters to a local crowd. *Köfte,* salad, bread, and drink $2. Open daily 11am-11pm. For greater variety, try **Vitamin Restaurant,** 16 Divan Yolu (tel. 5 265 086). Dishes include *patlıcan dolması* (stuffed eggplant), *mercimek çorbası* (lentil soup), and *kebap.* Meals $2-4. Open daily 7am-midnight. You shouldn't leave Istanbul without visiting the celebrated **Pudding Shop,** #6 Divan Yolu (tel. 5 222 970), known as "the beginning of the hippie trail" from which '60s wayfarers journeyed east towards Nepal and beyond. The appeal to the Flower Generation seems elusive in the cafeteria-style atmosphere, but the proof is in the pudding. *Sütlaç,* a milk and rice concoction, is especially tasty. They also serve chicken ($1.50), *kebap* ($1), and beer (60¢). Open daily 7am-midnight.

**Kumkapı:** South of the Grand Bazaar, this quarter looks onto the Sea of Marmara. From the Grand Bazaar, cross Divan Yolu and walk down Tiyatro Cad. until you reach Büyük Kömürcü Sok; follow this little street to **Kumkapı Meydanı,** which is lined with many seafood restaurants. Prices vary daily; it all depends on the catch. You might try **Minas Restaurant,** Kumkapı Meydanı (tel. 5 229 646), a friendly family restaurant that caters to a mostly Turkish crowd. *Lüfer* (bluefish), caught daily in the Bosphorus is an Istanbul speciality ($3.75). Open daily 11am-11pm.

**Galata Bridge:** Several seafood restaurants of comparable quality squeeze between car and boat traffic beneath the bridge. Prices vary from $4-10 for a full meal. Not the most relaxing place. If you're not being hounded by restaurant proprietors, you'll be lost in the hordes of pedestrian traffic. Try a fried-mackerel sandwich (30¢) cooked on the fishing boats moored between the Galata Bridge and the ferries.

**Çamlıca:** If you have extra time, make the trek to the Asian side for a great view from Istanbul's tallest hill. At the summit, adjacent to the beautiful park with flower gardens, is a charming restaurant with brass tables and a fireplace. Meals $1-3; snacks available outside for much less. Take the ferry to Üsküdar from Eminönü (16¢) and hop on bus #11, 11A, 11B, 114, 11E, 11M, or 11U. Ask to be let off at Çamlıca. You will have to walk or take a taxi 1.5km to the top of the hill.

# Sights

Istanbul deserves weeks of touring, but three or four days of legwork will acquaint you with an unforgettable array of mosques, churches, and museums. For a scholarly historical background of Istanbul's sights, buy *Strolling Through Istanbul,* by Hilary Sumner-Boyd and John Freely ($20). *Istanbul: A Brief Guide to the City,* by the same authors, is a more compact, readable version ($8). Both are available at Redhouse Kitabevi on Rızapaşa Yokuşu, or Aypa Bookstore on Divan Yolu.

**Aya Sofya,** or The Church of the Holy Wisdom, was built in 532 C.E. by the Emperor Justinian on the site of a pagan temple. It was Constantinople's cathedral for 900 years, then served as a mosque from the 1453 Turkish conquest until 1935, when Atatürk converted it to a museum. The dome was the largest in the world until St. Peter's in Rome was built. Unfortunately, for the next few years scaffolding will fill the church's austere space, and most of the celebrated mosaics have been removed to be incorporated into a new mosaic museum. Admission $2.30. Open Tues.-Sun. 9:30-11:30am and 1-4:30pm.

Sultan Ahmet I built the **Blue Mosque** (Sultanahmet Camii) nearly 1100 years after Aya Sofya's construction, a brazen attempt to do Justinian one better. Many believe he succeeded. The mosque's silhouette is unforgettable, and the deep blue Iznik tiles glorify the interior. Although Islamic religious leaders of the day didn't want the Sultan to exceed the number of minarets at Mecca, he tactfully avoided a religious controversy by providing the money and workers to erect a seventh minaret there. Inside the Blue Mosque you'll notice the iron bars running across the domes. These bars ensure that the whole structure bends in earthquakes—it's withstood 20 so far. You may visit the mosque at any time, but try to avoid noon rituals. English-speaking Turks often loiter around the entrance during the day, eager to give potentially instructive freelance tours. Agree on the fee before the tour.

To your right as you leave the Blue Mosque are the **Carpet** and **Kilim Museums** with carpets and woven *kilim* (prayer rugs) from all over the Moslem world (open Tues.-Sun. 9am-5pm). This is a good place to visit if you are at all interested in picking up a carpet or *kilim* of your own. Keep in mind though that the finer tapestries cost 50-100% more in Istanbul than in the Anatolian provinces. Turkish carpets are made by knotting colored wool or silk around a framework of parallel woolen threads, a process which requires a high degree of manual dexterity and nimbleness. Most are made by young girls between the ages of 6 and 13. With the modernization of Turkey and mandatory schooling for young children, the Turkish government now assumes responsibility for the continuation of this traditional art form.

On the northwest side of the Blue Mosque is the site of the ancient **Byzantine Hippodrome,** where Constantine and Justinian presided over chariot races and circuses. In the Hippodrome stand the **Egyptian Obelisk,** the upper part of an obelisk from the fifteenth century B.C.E. which was brought to Constantinople in 390 C.E., and the **Serpentine Column,** taken from the Temple of Apollo at Delphi. Right near the Serpentine Column is the sixteenth-century **Ibrahim Paşa Palace,** a museum of Turkish and Islamic art featuring tiles, Korans, and an especially fine collection of carpets. The courtyard has a picturesque tea house. (Open Tues.-Sun. 10am-5pm. Admission Tues.-Fri. 40¢, Sat.-Sun. 20¢.)

Walking back to Divan Yolu along Klodfarer Cad. you'll pass a small park opposite the Klodfarer Hotel. Underneath lies the fourth-century C.E. **Binbirdirek Cistern.** Knock on the door of the shack to ask for a flashlight-guided tour (tip the guide about 70¢). This cistern is larger but doesn't compare aesthetically to **Yerebatan Cistern,** by the Aya Sofya, the largest underground resevoir in Istanbul still holding water. Yerebatan contains 336 columns, two of which have reliefs of the mythic figure Medusa. Admission $1.50, free to ISIC holders. Open daily 9am-5pm.

If you return to Divan Yolu and head west, you will come, on your right, to the enormous **Grand Bazaar** (Kapalı Çarşı). The summer invasion of tourists inflates prices as much as 300-400%. Fake or faulty merchandise abounds. Beware of glassy, bright *kayseri*—these shoddy imitations of Persian carpets are worthless. As usual, haggling is a hassle.

On the up side, the Bazaar is a great place to buy soft, supple glove leather jackets in the latest European styles. Bargain persistently for anything, and be stubborn. For that essential purchase, stick to the price you want to pay and then come back to the store a few days in a row with the same offer. If you get ripped off, you should rationalize it as a cultural experience.

The old part of the Bazaar is a jumble of shops selling hookahs, bright baubles, copper filigree shovels, Byzantine-style icons resting on red velvet, ancient Turkish daggers (made in Taiwan), silver flintlock guns with mother-of-pearl handles, silver and gold coins, ceramic pipes, pocket watches perhaps from the era of the sultans, onyx, jade, and plastic miniatures, shoe-shine kits of polished wood and brass, Farsi texts, chess sets, and hand puppets—among other treasures. The gold is mostly 14-carat, and contrary to rumor, it is not cheaper in Turkey. Shopkeepers kill time in the back of the store over a backgammon board, beckoning the passersby "to look, friend, not buy." (Bazaar open Mon.-Sat. 9am-7pm.)

After a long day of haggling at the Grand Bazaar, drop by the **Şark Kahvesi,** at the end of Fesçiler Cad., for a cup of *kahve* (coffee), or a game of backgammon or cards. Coffee 35¢, tea 20¢, and soda 40¢. Open Mon.-Sat. 9am-7pm.

To the west and adjacent to the Grand Bazaar is the smaller **Sahaflar Çarşısı** (used book market). Intriguing old books appear in these shops, as well as hand-illustrated manuscripts, paintings, and a variety of posters at low prices. The market opens up to a shady tea garden, bustling with Turks, tourists, and pigeons. Opposite is the gate to Istanbul University and **Beyazıt Mosque,** Istanbul's oldest standing mosque. To the west stands **The Calligraphy Museum** (Beyazıt Hat Sanatları Müzesi). It houses a collection of *Tuřalar,* or Sultans' monograms, and a notable set of Korans, including one which has been penned on a 4' by 6' parchment. Open Tues.-Sat. 9:30am-4pm. Admission 23¢, 7¢ for ISIC holders.

Follow the walls of the university, to the right, as closely as you can, and turn left when you reach the university's rear grounds. In front of you will be the **Süleymaniye Mosque,** acclaimed by many as the crowning jewel of Sinan, the Empire's greatest architect. Sinan was buried on the grounds of the Süleymaniye by order of Süleyman the Magnificent in the late 1500s. Enter from the south, under an elegant colonnaded gallery, to view the stunning stained-glass windows filtering in the morning light. To the east of the mosque is a majestic courtyard, and to the west is a graveyard, where Süleyman and his wife, Roxelana, lay in *türbe* (tombs) opulently bejewelled with blue *iznik* tiles and, for the Sultan, diamonds. (Tombs open Wed.-Sun. 9:30am-4:30pm.)

Walking back to the Golden Horn from Süleymaniye, you will pass through the noisy jumble of the **market quarter,** where vendors hawk wares amid the clamor of traffic. In the middle of this quarter, only 200m from the Horn, is the unassuming exterior of **Rüstem Paşa Mosque.** The interior of this mosque is almost entirely inlaid with blue *iznik* tiles. Walking towards the Galata Bridge, you'll come to the **Yeni Camii** (New Mosque), with its bright, soaring interior; this "new" mosque was built in the seventeenth century.

The **Mısır Çarşışı** (Egyptian Bazaar), built as part of the Yeni Camii complex, is an authentic alternative to the Grand Bazaar. You may be overwhelmed by the melánge of sights and smells within this covered market: barrels heaping with exotic spices, the aroma of ground coffee wafting through the air, tantalizing desserts drenched in syrup. Don't miss the open courtyard of the bazaar, a wonderful shaded area lined with cafes and *kebapçı.*

From the mid-fifteenth century until the mid-nineteenth century, the **Topkapı Sarayı** was the nerve center of the Ottoman Empire. Both the grandiose façade and the exquisite interior awe even the dispassionate visitor. Since the various museum collections housed in Topkapı are so extensive, it's best to punctuate your tours inside the palace with time spent sunning on the terraces or sitting in the rose gardens. The palace was originally the site of the Ottoman government and the Empire's most exclusive schools, as well as the home of the Sultan and his sizable entourage of wives, eunuchs, and servants. Though the attractions seem endless, don't miss the **first court,** with its huge East Asian porcelain collection; the **Harem;** and the **Treasury,** which houses an inestimable wealth of diamonds, emeralds, gold, and jade, as well as a collection of important religious artifacts. To see the Harem, you must take a guided tour (3 per day in English; open Wed.-Mon. 10am-4pm, 77¢). (Palace grounds open Wed.-Mon. 9:30am-5pm. Admission $3.)

Istanbul's other great museums are down the hill from Topkapı—enter the gate marked "Archeological Museum." Inside you'll find the **Çinili Köşk** (Tiled Pavilion), a little pleasure palace now turned museum. The **Museum of the Ancient Orient** (labeled in English) has an interesting collection of Hittite, Babylonian, Sumerian, Assyrian, and Egyptian artifacts. Among them are a tablet from the Hammurabi Code and older laws, a peace treaty between a Hittite ruler and the Egyptian Pharaoh Ramses II, ancient love poems, and medical prescriptions. The **Archeological Museum** (labeled only in Turkish and French), displays a sizable collection of early Greek, Hellenistic, and Roman marbles and bronzes, including the supposed sarcophagus of Alexander the Great. (All three museums open Tues.-Sun. 9am-5pm. Admission 77¢.) The park on the ramparts of the Topkapı Museum overlooks the Bosphorus and Golden Horn and offers a pleasantly cool respite from Istanbul's sweltering streets. (Open until sunset. Free.) A mandatory stop for Byzantine-art lovers is the impeccably preserved **Kariye Camii** a long way up Fevzipaşa Cad., near the Edirne Gate, best reached by *dolmuş* or bus #39 or 86 from Sultanahmet. Once a Byzantine church, then a mosque, and finally a museum, the building has superb fourteenth-century frescoes and mosaics. The freshness, realism, and expressiveness of this strain of late Byzantine art influenced early Italian painters such as Giotto. (Open daily 9:30am-4:30pm. Admission 19¢.) From here you can see the ruined **Theodosian Land Walls,**which stretch from the Golden Horn to the Sea of Marmara. Originally constructed in the fifth century C.E., the looming ramparts have been surmounted only twice, once by the Crusaders in the thirteenth century, and once by Mehmet the Conqueror in 1453 when the Ottomans captured Constantinople.

For all its modernity, modern Istanbul has some allure for the sightseer. The **Galata Tower,** built by the Emperor Justinian in 528 C.E. and rebuilt in 1348 by the Genoese so they could spy on the old city, still serves its purpose today. The tower was also the take-off site of the first intercontinental flight, executed with a Da Vinci-style hang glider. The view alone is worth the admission. (Open 10am-8pm. Admission 77¢.) Alongside the Bosphorus, **Dolmabahçe Palace** was the home of sultans from the mid-nineteenth century until the end of the Ottoman Empire after World War I. Goose-stepping soldiers guard the royal dock and the memory of Atatürk, who died in the palace at 9:05 (all the clocks stopped at the time). The kitschy French-style architecture exhibits the sultans' eclectic tastes during the decline of their empire. (Open Tues.-Wed. and Fri.-Sun. 9:30am-4pm. Admission $3.) To get to Dolmanbahçe from Sultanahmet, take bus T4.

## Entertainment

Istanbul closes up shop early—few places are open after midnight. Travelers congregate in the restaurants and bars at the foot of Divan Yolu Cad.; a beer costs about 60¢. For a true feel of Istanbul, trek up to the **Çiçek Pasajı** (see Food above) for an evening of piquant food, potent drink, and traditional Turkish music. **Rakı,** a licorice-flavored spirit nicknamed "Lion's Milk," flows quite freely in the many taverns of the "Flower Passage." Alternatively, venture to Lâleli or Beyazıt and spend the evening at a Turkish tea house. **Ali Paşa's Bazaar,** a sixteenth-century courtyard near the entrance to the Grand Bazaar on Divan Yolu Cad., is a great place to have a glass of delicious Turkish tea, meet some locals, and smoke a *nargile* (water pipe). Pipes cost about $1 and will last two or three people all evening. A wad of fresh tobacco sits at the bowl of the pipe, and an attendant walks around replenishing the lumps of red-hot charcoal that are placed on top of the tobacco (open until 11pm).

If the frenzied chaos of Istanbul has begun to fray your nerves, a cruise along the **Bosphorus** may renew your spirit. Boats leave from pier #4 in Eminönü at 10:30am and 1:30pm, and return from the Black Sea in the evening ($2.25). You might consider getting off at a stop and catching the ferry on its way back. While no evening tours of the Bosphorus are available, you might consider riding a ferry to one of Istanbul's northern suburbs on either the European or Asian side of the Bosphorus (16¢). Villages such as **Arnavutköy** and **Bebek** boast numerous seafood restaurants which offer meals at reasonable prices.

If you're yearning to try a **Turkish bath,** the more authentic baths can be found in the nearby cities of Edirne and Bursa. However, Istanbul baths can provide a reprieve for the down and dirty. Avoid the much-publicized **Çağaloğlu Hamamı** in Sultanahmet on Yerebatan Cad. Instead, try the **Mercan Örücüler Hamamı,** #32 Uzun Çarşı Cad., just outside the **Örücüler Kapısı** (Gate) of the Grand Bazaar (tel. 5 279 263). Although somewhat pricey ($2.75 for a self-service bath, an additional $4.60 for a massage), the hot steam, the immaculate chambers, and the dearth of tourists make this a worthwhile deal.

If you've heard about the straight or gay **nightclubs** off Istiklâl Cad., north of the Horn, think twice about going. Many are tacky neon money-vacuums with no one inside except prostitutes who will harrass customers to buy them drinks. The nightclubs north of Taksim Square along Cumhuriyet Cad. are a little more respectable (and safer), but steep first drink prices tend to deter the budget traveler. The extortionate price of attending a **belly-dance** performance will also dismay the budget visitor. Inquire at the tourist office if you're interested; locations change frequently. Sometimes you can find gypsy dancers in small restaurants, accompanied by a few rag-tag musicians; try looking around the Çiçek Pasajı (see Food above). Be prepared to throw the dancer a little money or else she'll never move away from you.

The Istanbul Festival, an international festival in its seventeenth year, unfolds with a flourish in June and July. Performers in 1988 ranged from the Whirling Dervishes of Konya to Joan Baez and Miles Davis (not together). Ask at the tourist office or call 1 604 533 for more information. The **Sound and Light Show** at the Blue Mosque is quite corny but offers a captivating view of the illuminated minarets and domes. (Schedule posted at tourist office. Free.)

## Near Istanbul

**Eyüp,** the fourth most sacred pilgrimage site in the Islamic world after Mecca, Medina, and Jerusalem, houses the fifteenth-century tomb of Eyüp, companion of Muhammed. The Golden Horn ferries depart twice hourly from pier #6 in Eminönü, above the Galata Bridge (in summer 7:35am-7:30pm; off-season 7:35am-6:40pm; 1 hr.; $1.25). Islam has influenced many Turks in Eyüp. You may see young boys costumed regally, brought here by their families; the trip is traditional for Istanbul boys before circumcision. Climb the hill above the cemetery for a view of the Golden Horn.

Another line of ferries goes to the **Princes' Isles,** leaving from pier #5 by the Galata Bridge. They depart hourly starting at 6:50am; the last ferry returns from the isles at midnight (during summer, $1.25). The ferry stops at four of the nine islands of this little suburban archipelago, depositing the weary for a relaxing afternoon. The scenery is beautiful, the towns are not overdeveloped, and best of all, there are no cars. You can tour an island by horse-drawn carriage; be sure to bargain. Some people prefer the quieter atmospheres of **Burgazada** and **Heybeliada,** but **Büyükada,** the largest and most picturesque of the islands, offers the best swimming in the Istanbul area.

# Edirne

In the first century C.E., the Emperor Hadrian, on a tour of the Greek world, founded this city and named it Hadrianopolis. (Hadrian, who traveled more than any other Roman emperor, personally hiked through every Roman territory without imperial regalia or headgear.) The city rose to prominence in 1363 after Sultan Murat I, unable to conquer Constantinople, moved the Ottoman capital to Hadrianopolis and renamed it Edirne. The new capital served as a base for further European conquests.

Edirne's glorious past lives on today. Not only can you admire Sinan the Great's extraordinary mosque, but for a modest price, you can lather up in his *hamam,* **Sokullu Hamamı.** Indeed, Edirne contains the finest examples of Ottoman architecture that remain intact. If you're really lucky, you may be in town for the annual **Kırkpınar Wrestling Tournament** in mid-July.

## Practical Information, Accommodations, and Food

The center of Edirne is **Hürriyet Square** at the intersection of Saraçlar and Tâlâtpasa Cad. On one side of the square is the large Üç Serefeli Mosque.

**Tourist Office:** Hürriyet Sq. (tel. 1 15 18), 1 block from Üç Serefeli Camii along Tâlâtpasa. Very friendly staff of student volunteers. Free maps. Open July-Aug. daily 8am-9pm; Sept.-June Mon.-Sat. 8am-5:30pm, Sun. 9:30am-5:30pm.

**Currency Exchange: Garanti Bankası,** #15 Hürriyet Meydanı, next to the tourist office (tel. 1 37 13). Exchanges AmEx travelers' checks without commission. Open Mon.-Fri. 8:30am-noon and 1:30-5 or 6pm. After regular business hours, go to **Restaurant Zogo** (cash only), across the street from the PTT.

**Transportation:** The main **dolmuş** station in the plaza to the right of the Eski Camii. Fare 12¢ to Kapıkule and the **train station,** which are only a few kilometers from the Bulgarian border. (You can walk across.) Trains run to Istanbul and Bulgaria. *Dolmuş* also take you to the main **bus station.** Buses run about every ½ hr. to Istanbul and cost less. Between Serefeli mosque and the Turkish bath you will find *dolmuş* to the Beyazıt II Mosque.

**Post Office and Telephones:** Saraçlar St., 2 blocks from Hürriyet Sq. Open 24 hours.

For accommodations, try some of the hotels on Maarif Caddesi, just off Hürriyet Sq. The **Konak Hotel** (tel. 1 13 48) offers clean singles for $3, doubles $5.50. The somewhat charming hotel has a large common area and courtyard. One block farther on the left is the **Şato Otel,** a slightly dilapidated wooden building with clean, spartan rooms for $2.70 per person. Although a bit more expensive, check out the **Otel Ami,** 8 Maarif Cad. (tel. 217 82), next to the Konak Hotel. Singles $4, showers (rare in Edirne) $1.20 extra. (The scarcity of showers might propel you to Edirne's inexpensive Turkish baths.)

**Saraçlar Caddesi,** with restaurants right and left, offers the usual selection of Turkish grilled meat and stuffed vegetable dishes. Fried liver is a local specialty, as is *badem ezmesi* (sweet almond paste) for dessert. The menu at **Şark Kebap,** 142 Saraçlar Cad. (tel. 2 17 55), offers a variety of dishes. A full meal including *pilav* (rice) costs less than $2. For a spicy meal, try the *Adana Urfa Kebap* ($1). You can sample *badem ezmesi* at most any dessert shop in the **Ali Paşa Bazaar.** The **Saray Restaurant/Bar** 73 Saraçlar Cad. (tel. 2 05 95), has cheap beer (50¢) and videos.

## Sights

Edirne's mosques display the gamut of Islamic architectural styles. The jewel of the town is **Selimiye Camii** (completed in 1579), another masterpiece of Sinan the Great, the foremost Ottoman architect. This enormous mosque is a study in symmetrical counterpoint, from the main dome that rests on eight columns to the 999 windows that light the interior. Behind the mosque is a museum featuring fez from the Whirling Dervishes and medieval armor and weaponry. (Open Tues.-Sun. 8:30am-noon and 1:30-6pm. Admission 16¢. Free to ISIC holders.) The understated **Eski** (Old) **Camii** (completed in 1414) has Arabic inscriptions painted in black on its walls. Twenty years after the Eski Camii was completed, the Ottomans built the **Üç Şerefeli Camii.** Note the unique plan of its minarets; each contains three interwoven spiral staircases.

The **Beyazıt Camii,** about 5km north of town (take a *dolmuş),* was used in the fifteenth century as a sort of religious hospital; here the Ottomans treated physical and psychological diseases with water, music, and prayers. Mosques can be visited during daylight hours, but try to avoid dawn and sunset services. Scarves for women hang just inside the entrance to each mosque.

Edirne shops converge at three covered markets: The biggest is the **Ali Paşa Bazaar,** designed by Sinan, which runs along the top of Saraçlar Cad. Low prices, superior service, and exemplary architecture make Edirne's Turkish baths better than those in Istanbul. Try either **Sokullu Hamamı,** a sixteenth-century bath beside Üç Şerefeli Camii (open daily 6am-midnight for men, $1.15; 9am-5pm for women; $2.30, $4 extra with massage), or **Tahtakale Hamamı,** 97 Saraçlar Cad. (open 6am-midnight for men, $1.15, $4 for massage; 10am-6pm for women, $2.30 with massage).

In mid-July, Edirne hosts its annual **Kırkpınar Wrestling Tournament,** in which young, brawny men grease up and wrassle the old-fashioned way. The first tournament is said to have been in the early Ottoman period, when two hulks vying for local supremacy wrestled in the fields outside the town. In an unresolvable stalemate, both dropped dead. Every year since, a match has been held to commemorate this most heroic event. Check for the exact dates of this event at any tourist office in Turkey. Tickets can be purchased in Edirne at the **Belediye** (town hall) across from the Eski Camii. The museum behind the Selimiye Camii contains photographs and memorabilia of past contests.

# Bursa

After the Selçuk Empire disintegrated into a handful of fractious kingdoms, Osman, the founder of the Ottoman dynasty, led his tribe to glory by conquering Bursa in 1322. His son, Orhan, decided to make it the capital, though Edirne garnered that distinction 11 years later. Today Bursa has a paradoxical identity as both an industrial center and a wealthy resort area. The greatest attraction lies in the well-preserved Ottoman monuments scattered throughout the city. After touring the sites, you might indulge in one of the many thermal baths in Çekirge (western part of the city). Nestled in the foothills of the verdant Ulu Dağ Mountain, Bursa provides amusement year-round. During winter, skiers schush down **Ulu Dağ,** Turkey's leading ski area.

You can reach Bursa by **express ferry** (be sure to specify express) to Yalova from Eminönü (5 per day, $1.10). Early ferries, leaving at 8:30 or 9am, are crowd beaters. Once in Yalova, hop a *dolmuş* or bus to Bursa ($1). The entire trip takes about 3½ hours. Buses to Bursa from Istanbul depart from Topkapı, traversing the industrial wasteland immediately east of the city. In Bursa, look for the **tourist information booth** in the station (open in summer daily 8am-5pm, sometimes until 7pm). To get to the center of town, take a *dolmuş* marked "Heykel" to Atatürk Cad. From beside the large fountain you can see Ulu Camii, the covered market, and the **main tourist office** (tel. 2 12 359; open July-Aug. daily 8:30am-5:30pm; Sept.-June Mon.-Fri. 8:30am-5:30pm).

## Accommodations, Camping, and Food

If you must stay in the noisy and far-removed bus station area, try **Otel Ozendim** (tel. 1 49 471) directly across from the depot at 135 Garaj Karşısı. Simple, and no frills. (Singles $3. Doubles $4.25. Hot showers 80¢.) You can stay in a central location along Tahtakale Cad., one block uphill and parallel to Atatürk Cad. From the post office, it's the third street on the left. The **Hotel Uğur**, #27 Tahtakale Cad. (tel. 2 11 989), has bright, slightly cramped rooms that look out onto a courtyard. (Doubles $3. No hot water.) **Otel Marmara**, at #3/A (tel. 212 097), is more spacious but otherwise nondescript. (Doubles $4.25.) On the top of Uludağ is **Millıpark Camping** (tel. 452 81); take the cable car here. ($3 per person, $2.25 per tent.)

*Iskender kebap,* an excellent dish with a special sauce of tomatoes, butter, and garlic, is served at restaurants throughout Turkey, but it originated in Bursa. Several restaurants named "Iskender Kebap" specialize in the dish; they are clustered in the area just below and to the left of the Atatürk statue (with your back to the bus station). All prices in this area are about the same, $2.25 for a full meal. **Rodop Izgara Salonu,** 93 Atatürk Cad., across from the Great Mosque (tel. 2 17 863), offers the standard *kebap* meal for $2. If you're really low on dough, check out **Yeşil Çoruh Lokantası** in the open-air market in Tahtakale for a 50¢ meal. Freshness is not guaranteed.

## Sights

The **Ulu Camii** (Great Mosque), built during the reigns of Yıldırım Beyazıt and Mehmet I in the 1400s, has both religious and secular significance. In addition to a beautiful *mihrab* (niche indicating direction of Mecca) and an extraordinary ablution fountain, the mosque houses a carved wooden *minibar* (pulpit), which scholars believe represents an astrological chart. Ulu Camii also gave rise to the Hacivat and Karagöz puppets.

Hacivat and Karagöz were builders who used to entertain other workers with now-famous jokes, skits, and stories. Construction of the Great Mosque was so delayed by the merrymaking that the king had the pair executed. In a fit of remorse the king asked the puppet-maker Şeyh Küşteri to reenact their dialogues; the puppets, made from camel hide, were projected against a light screen like Indonesian shadow puppets. (Ottomans with possessions in India and pirate ships sailing Indonesian waters probably absorbed the puppet craft from Southeast Asia.) To this day, puppet shows with the clever Hacivat and the innocent Karagöz are performed throughout Turkey. By the tomb of Hacivat, Karagöz, and Şeyh Küşteri, a small theater, puts on shows nightly during the **Bursa Festival** in July.

Green was undoubtedly the "in" color of 1421: Look no further than the **Yeşil Camii** (Green Mosque) and **Yeşil Türbe** (Green Mausoleum). Built concurrently, these structures flaunt turquoise and green tiling on their façades and interiors. In the Yeşil Camii, the tiling that symbolizes heaven is best seen from the lavish Sultan's section; ask the custodian for access. Across the way, Yeşil Türbe's striking hue is accentuated by finely carved wooden doors and small stained-glass windows. The **Turkish and Islamic Art Museum** and the **Ethnographic Museum** are nearby. (Mausoleums and museums open Tues.-Sun. 8am-noon and 1-5pm. Admission for museum 16¢.) The **Yeşil Tea Garden,** by the mosque, serves great brew and offers rousing games of *tavla* (backgammon) and a fine view of Bursa. (Open daily 6am-midnight.) Downhill from Çekirge Cad., about half-way to Çekirge, lies **Yeni Kapıca,** a sixteenth-century Turkish bath. Two adjacent baths in mirror image (one for each sex) feature central bathing pools (80¢, $2 with massage). These baths also have private rooms where men and women can bathe together in tubs about the size of a toilet bowl ($2.25).

For that much-wanted arts-and-crafts lesson, witness the silk production for which Bursa is famous. Villagers carry into town burlap sacks filled with silkworm cocoons, which are then boiled, spun, and woven. The brilliantly dyed and patterned material *(ipek)* can be purchased in the **Kapalı Çarşı Bazaar** by the tourist office for $6-12 per square meter, depending on the color, weave, and quality. Bursa knives, highly regarded for their slicing and dicing, are the *ginsu* of Turkey.

To reach the **cable car** station, take a *dolmuş* marked *Teleferik* from the Kafkaf pastry shop on Atatürk Cad., two blocks past the statue. The cable car runs every hour on the hour from 9am to 9pm to the mid-station, and every hour on the half hour from the mid-station to a small town perched on the mountain (2000m). Be prepared for cold temperatures and sudden changes of weather. Good skiing last from late December until mid-March. With a permit you can stalk wild boar in the **Millıpark** (national park) beyond the Uludağ mountains (23¢ entrance fee). Beware of wolves and packs of wild dogs.

### Near Bursa

By taking a 30-kilometer detour from the Yalova-Bursa highway, you can visit **Iznik,** the ancient city of Nicaea. The First Ecumenical Council met here in 325 C.E. Pressured by the Emperor Constantine, the assembly of bishops accepted the Nicaean Creed, which stated that God and Christ were one and the same. Six more Councils convened throughout Asia Minor to resolve debates. The last Council, in 787, returned to Nicaea and met in the church of Aya Sofya.

Iznik is a busy little town still enclosed within its ancient walls. It has a **tourist office** and some cheap rooms above tea houses. Freelance camping (a short hike away) and bungalows ($3 for 2) are also available. Set alongside a huge lake, Iznik offers good swimming and fresh "fish kebaps."

# Aegean Coast

The cat is out of the bag on the Turkish Aegean coast. It's tough to keep crystal clear waters, a sinuous coastline, and 5000 years of history a secret. Even tougher is resisting the allure of the Aegean Coast once you've sampled it. Inexpensive and unspoiled, the Aegean Coast has only recently begun to see the tourism that jaded observers might otherwise expect.

A tourism of sorts started relatively early in this area when the ancient Greeks established ports here. As Alexander the Great and subsequent Hellenist rulers pushed the empire eastward, those ports became the focal points of commerce along the major trade routes of the ancient world. Even as Greek civilization declined, the port cities burgeoned. Today, the extensive Hellenistic ruins at Pergamon, Ephesus, Aphrodisias, and Hierapolis, among others, stand as well-preserved testaments to an illustrius classical past.

Scholarship followed commerce to Asia Minor. Thriving trade with the East in goods and spices led to heightened exposure to other cultures and languages. Western philosophy, mathematics, and science germinated in the blossoming Hellenic civilization—particularly in the teachings of Heraclitus of Ephesus and in the works of Thales, Anaximander, Anaximenes, and Anaxagoras, all scholars in the Ionian school of Miletus. The Apostle Paul's proseletyzing mission sparked the rapid transmission of Christianity that culminated in 323 C.E., when Emperor Constantine converted, the formative event of the Byzantine Empire. Despite the preponderance of Islam, Christian pilgrims continue to converge here to visit the seven churches of Asia Minor, referred to in *Revelations* 2:7: Pergamon, Thyatira, Smyrna, Sardis, Philadelphia, Laodicea, and Ephesus. Ephesus still attracts attention from spiritual leaders, whether in an epistle from Paul or in a papal declaration of 1963 enshrining an allegorical residence of the Virgin Mary.

Although the prosperity of Hellenistic trade has declined, the tourist industry has proved quite lucrative on the Aegean Coast. The regrettable convergence of overdevelopment has been confined to resort towns like Kuşadası and Marmaris. The strand's splendor is complemented by an honest and friendly populace.

The cross-over from Turkey to Greece, although once problematic, no longer poses a great threat to travel plans. No legal barriers prevent tourists from traveling from the Greek islands to Turkey, though complications are sometimes reported. Charter-flight travelers to Greece who venture to Turkey should beware the stringent minimum-stay penalties imposed by the Greek government. Consult your travel agent and the General Introductions to Greece and Turkey before planning such excursions.

# North Coast

Whereas most of the Aegean Coast delights visitors instantly, the northern coast may gratify only the patient, the persevering, or the passionate classicists. If you persist, you may revel in the authenticity of the surroundings and the scarcity of tourists.

## Çanakkale, Gelibolu (Gallipoli), and Truva (Troy)

With comfortable and inexpensive accommodations, Çanakkale is a good base for exploring Gelibolu and Troy. Buses travel frequently here from Bursa (5½ hr., $4.75) and Istanbul (5 hr., $4.75). The town has a few sights of its own: an **archeological museum** with artifacts from Troy (open Tues.-Sun. 10am-5pm), a **fortress**, and vintage World War I cannons commemorating the Gelibolu battle. The **tourist information office** (tel. 1 1 87) located near the ferry station is open Mon.-Fri. 8am-5pm and Sat.-Sun. 8am-8pm.

The Aegean coast's northernmost resort, Çanakkale faces the narrowest point of the Dardanelles. Across the Dardanelles on the European side lies the battlefield of **Gelibolu**, where Australian, New Zealand, and British landing parties suffered a brutal defeat to Turkish forces under Atatürk in 1915. Ferries leave every hour on the hour to Gelibolu (15¢), where you can hire a taxi ($12) to tour the battlefields. Better yet, join a tour organized by **Troyanzac Travel Agency** in Çanakkle, located by the bell tower ($8-12 per person). On April 25, many Australians and New Zealanders make pilgrimages to Gelibolu to honor the dead.

**Truva**, or Troy, is 32km south of Çanakkale. *Dolmuş* and minibuses leave frequently from the bus station. Most budget accommodations can be found in the area surrounding the clocktower. **Hotel Konak** (tel. 1 150), behind the clocktower, has immaculate rooms with private bathrooms and showers. (Singles $3. Doubles $5.25.) Across the street, the **Hotel Kervansaray** has even cheaper rooms. This old-style Turkish home features a charming garden atrium. (Singles $2.30. Doubles $3.80. Hot showers 60¢ extra.)

You will find fresh seafood in restaurants along the **Quay**. Try **Bizim Entellektüel Restaurant** (tel. 43 22) for fresh *lüfer* (bluefish), salad, and a beer ($4). Cheaper meals are available in the many stands behind the Quay. **Yalova Liman Restaurant** (tel. 10 45) sells fried mussels and beer for only $1. The rooftop terrace offers an inspiring view of the Dardanelles. (Open daily 11am-midnight.)

The ruins of ancient Troy are unquestionably the Aegean coast's most overrated tourist attraction. Near the end of the nineteenth century, Heinrich Schliemann, a German-born American millionaire turned amateur archeologist, became convinced that the Homeric myths were not mere fiction. He staked out the most promising location along the Turkish coast and paid local workers to begin excavating. To the astonishment of the academic world he proved his point, thereby laying the strategy for his subsequent discoveries of Mycenae and Leknossos. Although Schliemann found ancient Troy, frankly, there is not a whole lot here. Classicists who can supplement the remains with images of Homeric heroes will probably be stirred by the place. Nine different layers of major epochs have been excavated and dubbed Troy I through Troy IX for easy reference. Troy I dates from 3200 B.C.E., Troy II is the earliest known example of a planned city. Troy VIIIA is believed to be the city of Homer's *Iliad*. (Open in summer 8:30am-8pm; off-season 8:30am-5pm. Admission $1.60.)

## Pergamon

Love and death, philanthropy and theft—Pergamon owes its checkered past to these contrarieties. Its ruins, over 30,000 acres worth, are located on two principal sites: the **Acropolis** looming majestically above the town and the **Asclepion** (medical center) lying in the valley below. The most notable attraction is the mammoth **amphitheater,** capable of seating 10,000 spectators. The Roman emperor Caracalla built the theater after he was healed by the physician Galen, Asclepion's director in Pergamon. Allegedly, no patient ever died here, though many were probably rushed out the back door just before expiring. An impressive portion of the Asclepion stands, including a marble colonnade, healing rooms, and theater. The ruins of a huge gymnasium, a Roman circus, several temples, and the lavishly frescoed **House of Attalus** also lie scattered about. Pergamon's most remarkable pieces, however, have been spirited to foreign quarters. In ancient times, the library of over 200,000 volumes was surpassed only by the library in Alexandria. When its Egyptian rival went up in flames, Mark Antony plundered Pergamon's shelves and presented the collection to his beloved Cleopatra. Most of the **Altar of Zeus,** considered by many to be the exemplary artistic achievement of the Hellenistic era, forms the centerpiece of the Pergamon Museum in East Berlin.

The ruins of Pergamon sit adjacent to the pleasant, modern city of **Bergama,** accessible by **buses** from Çanakkale (4 hr.), Bursa (6½ hr.), and Izmir (2 hr.). Bergama is about halfway between Bodrum and Istanbul, making it a good place to break up the journey for the night. (Bergama-Istanbul 10½ hr.). Try to take a bus that drives into Bergama; most drop you off at the turn-off 7km away; frequent *dolmuş* service into town is available.

From the bus station, take a right onto the main road. The **PTT** here is open 24 hours and in addition to its usual services, will exchange cash at any time. To reach the **tourist office** (tel. 18 62), turn left out of the bus station and walk two blocks—it's on your right. The **telephone code** for Bergama is 54 11.

Accommodations, scarce in Bergama, are nevertheless comfortable and cheap. The most charming hotel is the **Pergamon Pension** (tel. 123 95), a 150-year-old Greek-style mansion with high ceilings and a cool garden. Heading from the bus station, past the PTT, you'll see a fork; bear to the right—the pension is on the left. ($3.80 per person; hot showers included.) The restaurant is also excellent. Just up the main street from the **bus station** in Bergama is the **Park Hotel** (tel. 12 46), popular with backpackers because of its convenient location and clean rooms. (Singles $3.80. Doubles $5.40. Hot shower $1.20 extra.) For that cheap dungeon touch, visit **Akinci Pension** (tel. 15 54). From Pergamon Pension continue farther into town, make your first right, then another right, and finally walk down the narrow winding alley. (Doubles $4.70 include hot showers, but the rooms have no windows).

To reach the Acropolis, follow the main road past the **Byzantine Basilica.** Turn left off the road and walk towards the first ruins, the Lower Agora. Here you'll find a footpath that winds among the ruins to the summit. (Open in summer daily 8:30am-6:30pm; off-season 8:30am-5:30pm. Admission Mon.-Fri. 40¢.) The Asclepion is in another direction—2km from a turn-off to the right, past the bus station, and back out of town to the main coastal road. The **archeological museum** displays artifacts from Pergamon as well as a collection of traditional Turkish crafts. (Admission 40¢. Open daily 8:30am-noon and 1-5:30pm.)

## Izmir

Once ancient Smyrna, Izmir is the only surviving major Hellenistic city in Asia Minor. The diversion of the River Hermus prevented Smyrna's harbor from silting like those of Ephesus and Miletus, and thus the city has continued to be one of the area's main trading ports. Earthquakes, wars, and fires ravaged Izmir over the centuries, leaving very little of the original city intact. Apartment buildings and tree-lined boulevards now cover the old city, making Izmir a pleasant stopover or base for exploring nearby ancient cities.

The **tourist office** (tel. 14 21 47), in the Büyük Efes Hotel on Cumhuriyet Meydanı, provides free maps and friendly assistance. The **bus station** (*otogar garaj*) has connections to most parts of Turkey. For **Çeşme** and other points west, go to the **Konak Terminali.** Get there by taking a *dolmuş* (10 min.) from **Konak Square.** From the bus station, take any bus marked Konak and get off at Montrö Meydanı. Walk up Şenevresbey Bulvarı—the Büyük Efes Hotel is on your left. (Open in summer Mon.-Sat. 8am-8pm, Sun. 9am-5pm; in winter Mon.-Sat. 8:30am-5:30pm.) From Cumhuriyet Meydanı, head down Gazi Osman Paşa Bulvarı (away from the water). About 5 blocks down Gazi Bulvarı is a large circle called 9 (*dokuz*) Eylül Meydun, where the main **dolmuş station** is located. From 9 Eylül Meydanı, take Anafartalar Cad. to the **railway station.** Izmir has an **American Express** office, 2B Nato Arkası Tâlâtpaşa Bulvarı (tel. 21 79 27); a **U.S. Consulate,** 92/3 Atatürk Cad. (tel. 13 13 69); and a **British Consulate,** 49 St. 1442 (tel. 21 17 95).

One should begin a room search from 9 Eylül Meydanı. The **Otel Saray,** 635 Anafartalar Cad. (tel. 13 69 46) is a tranquil oasis graced with a sunny atrium and airy rooms. Three blocks past the railway station, turn right as Anafartalar continues at a 90° angle. The hotel will be on your right ($3.80 per person. Hot shower included.) **Bilen Palas Otel,** 1369 Sok. (tel. 13 92 46), right off 9 Eylül Meydanı, is exceptionally clean. (Doubles $7.70. Cold showers 75¢.) The **Bayburt Oteli,** 1370 Sok. (tel. 12 20 13), with an atrium and rooftop terrace, offers respite from Izmir's heat and noise. Be prepared to dish out some cash to an indifferent management. Turn right (south) off Gazi Bulvarı well before you reach 9 Eylül Meydanı. (Doubles with private showers $11.15.) For less pristine accommodations, try the **Vatan Oteli** at #628 (tel. 13 06 37), which encloses a courtyard. The rooms are small and somewhat grimy. (Doubles $5.40.)

You can find cheap Turkish cuisine all along Anatartalar Cad. Inexpensive seafood restaurants hem in Atatürk Cad. **Cankay Çorba Salonu,** on the corner of Gazi Bulvarı and 1370 Sok, serves an excellent and filling meal for roughly $3. (Open 24 hours.)

The remains of Izmir's **Roman agora,** just south of the clock tower in Konak Sq., warrant a special visit. (Open in summer daily 9am-7pm; off-season 9am-5pm. Admission 32¢, 19¢ with ISIC. Complement this with a trip to the **archeological museum,** with its collection of Roman statues. (Open daily 9am-5:30pm. Admission Mon.-Fri. 32¢.) Above the city at Mt. Pagos is the **Kadifekale,** the "Fortress of Velvet," originally built in the fourth century B.C.E., but restored numerous times by various conquerors. From here you can get a magnificent view of the city. At the end of Anafartalar Cad. is the Izmir **bazaar,** which is less expensive and less kitschy than Istanbul's. (Open Mon.-Sat. 8:30am-7pm.) In late August, Izmir holds a huge international import-export fair in Kültür Park (Cultural Park).

## Sardis

Sardis was the capital of the Lydian kingdom in the seventh and sixth centuries B.C.E. A native Anatolian people, the Lydians embraced Greek culture while contributing significant innovations of their own, including dice, balls, and coinage. Appropriately, Sardis was the home of King Croesus, the richest man in the world. Hoping to prepare for the future, he consulted the oracle at Delphi, which told him that if he crossed the River Halys he would destroy a powerful empire. Eager to fulfill the prophecy, he rushed his troops across the river and was promptly defeated by the Persians.

Sardis can be visited easily from Izmir, or as an ambitious daytrip from Kuşadası. Take one of the frequent **buses** that travels to **Salihli** and ask to be let off at Sardis or Sart (1½ hr.).

From the bus stop, walk 100m and you'll see the reconstructed marble court bath-gymnasium complex. Behind the gymnasium is the synagogue, and alongside, parallel to the highway, are a series of Byzantine shops. It's a 15-minute walk from the highway up the hill to the Temple of Artemis (follow the yellow arrows). Along the way you'll pass an ancient Lydian gold refinery and a dome from a twelfth-century Byzantine basilica built on top of a fifth-century church. (Site open daily 8am-8pm, but don't worry if you come when it's closed—the ruins aren't fenced in.) Admission 32¢ per site.

Alexander the Great commissioned the reconstruction of the **Temple of Artemis**, one of the largest Ionic temples of ancient times. Only a few columns remain, but their scrolled capitals are exquisite. The most interesting structure at Sardis is the recently restored synagogue, a handsome edifice dating from the second century C.E., with elegant mosaic floors. The gymnasium, with its spiral-fluted columns and exquisitely carved façade, is no less impressive.

On the way to or from Sardis, try to make the short detour to the city of **Manisa**. The **archeological museum** houses artifacts from Sardis and its surroundings. (Open Tues.-Sun. 8:30am-5:30pm; off-season 8:30am-5pm. Admission Mon.-Fri. 32¢, Sat.-Sun. 16¢.) Also visit the **Muradiye Camii** nearby, designed by the Ottoman architect Sinan in the sixteenth century. The **Ulu Camii** (Main Mosque) features Corinthian columns pilfered from ancient Roman structures.

## Çeşme

Sit back in a sleepy harbor and ponder a brilliant sunset in Çeşme, a lovely resort one hour west of Izmir. (Minibuses leave frequently from the Konak Terminali.) Next to the bus station is the helpful and friendly **tourist office** (tel. 266 53; open in summer daily 8:30am-7pm; off-season Mon.-Sat. 8:30am-5:30pm). Continuing along the shore you'll find the **PTT** (open 24 hours); Çeşme's **telephone code** is 549.

Çeşme abounds with pensions that charge about $9 for doubles in high season. Look for accommodations along Bağlar Sok., which runs diagonally inland from the tourist office, and along Müftü Sok., which intersects on the left. The cheapest places are **Işık Pansiyon** (tel. 263 05; doubles $7.70) and **Adil Pansiyon** (doubles $6.15).

If you like camping, you've come to the right place. *Dolmuş* travel around the peninsula until 8pm with routes from Çeşme to Ilıca (6km), Altınkum (10km), and south along the beach (5km). You can find campgrounds nearly everywhere, or you can camp freelance.

Nightlife in the area centers around **Ilıca**. Right on the Çeşme-Ilıca highway, **Disco 9** fills up every night in summer, despite its steep cover charge ($3.90). The **Çardak Bar**, an open-air cafe right on the water, is cheaper. From the Ilıca Beach, walk uphill and take a left past the Park Aport Hotel. If languor is what you seek, sip a beer in one of the many cafes lining Çeşme's harbor and watch the sun set behind the Greek island of Chios. If you have the energy, hike up to the **castle**, which was originally built by Ottoman Sultan Beyazıt II in order to spy on Chios, 8 miles away, and now houses a tiny museum. (Open daily in summer 9am-noon and 1-6pm; in winter daily 8:30am-noon and 1-5:30pm. Admission 32¢.) In late June, Çeşme holds an annual international festival that showcases popular European actors and musicians. The performances are broadcast throughout Europe.

From Çeşme it is only an hour by boat to the Greek island of **Chios. Ertürk Ferry-boat,** Cumhuriyet Meydanı 11/A (tel. 267 68), runs boats Tuesday through Sunday from mid-July to mid-September, less frequently in May, June, and October, and once per week on Thursday from November through April ($20 one-way, $25 round-trip, $30 open round-trip).

# Kuşadasi

Kuşadası is an unfortunate paradigm of tourism run wild. Firmly tacked on the itineraries of a half-dozen luxury cruise liners and easily accessible from Samos, the town has become tawdry and expensive. Its popularity, however unfortunate, is deserved—Kuşadası is the best place to base yourself for visits to four of Turkey's most interesting ancient sites: Ephesus, Priene, Miletus, and Didyma. If crowds really bother you, you might consider staying in the much quieter village of Selçuk only 2km from Ephesus and 20km from bustling Kuşadası. To its credit, Kuşadası is by the sea and has a nightlife. Bear with the chaos as long as it takes you to see the nearby sites, then head south or east to discover something better.

## Orientation and Practical Information

Most visitors in Kuşadası arrive by boat. The harbor master, duty-free shop, fish market, passport police, and customs are all in the port area. There is no way around paying the port tax, but it is cheapest in dollars ($7); in other currencies, most notably *drachmae*, it will cost $2.50 more. By bus, Kuşadası is a two-hour ride from Izmir. The bus station is about 1km east of the main port. The tourist office is at the port. Just beyond looms the turreted walls of an ancient Seljuk, *kervansaray* now the **Kervansaray Hotel**, which is a central orientation point. Facing the Kervansaray Hotel, the street to the left running parallel to the sea is **Atatürk Bulvarı;** to the right and up the hill is **Yalı Caddesi.** If you continue up the hill to the end, you'll find many cheap pensions along **Aslanlar Caddesi.** Slightly to the left of Kervansaray Hotel, running perpendicular to the sea, is **Barbaros Hayrettin,** where you'll find the PTT, travel agencies, banks, and tourist shops. At the end of the street is a medieval watchtower, which now serves as a police station. Slightly to the left from here, away from the water, is **Kahramanlar Caddesi,** Kuşadası's less expensive commercial strip. On your left will be the bus station. You can do your grocery shopping on the streets that intersect the watchtower and run parallel to the waterfront.

**Tourist Office:** In the port (tel. 11 03). Each staff member speaks either French, German, or English. Often more than one visit is advisable. Complete listings of accommodations, campgrounds, and bus schedules. Will call and make reservations for you in town or elsewhere. Open April-Nov. daily 7am-8:30pm; Dec.-March Mon.-Fri. 8am-noon and 1:30-5:30pm.

**Currency Exchange:** Banks have booths by the waterfront. Open daily 8am-9pm. The PTT also exchanges cash until 11pm.

**PTT:** Halfway up Teyyare Cad. Services open Mon.-Fri. 8:30am-noon and 1:30-5:30pm, Sat.-Sun. 9am-5pm. Stamps available 24 hours. Telegraph and long-distance **telephones** open 24 hours. **Telephone code:** 6361.

**Buses:** At the back half of the bus station. Buses to Izmir (every ½ hr., $1.20), Denizli (5 per day, $3), and Istanbul (5 per day, $9.25). For buses to Aphrodisias or anywhere to the north, transfer in Selçuk. To Bodrum, Priene, Miletus, or Didyma, you must make connections in Söke.

**Dolmuş:** In the front half of the bus station. Every ½ hr. 7am-8pm to either Ephesus, Selçuk, or Söke—tickets from the appropriate window. Less frequent runs to other neighboring villages, especially Davutlar.

**Ferries:** One-way ferry fares to Samos fixed by the government at a rate 25% higher on the Turkish side, regardless of the agency: $25 one-way, $30 round-trip, $45 open-return round-trip. Port tax to leave Greece $7. Port tax to enter Turkey $10.50. Turkish boats leave in summer daily at 8:30am, returning at 5pm; in off-season, ferries only run 2 or 3 times per week. From Greece, you are only permitted to take a Greek boat. Every Wed. at 3pm, the *Orient Express* leaves Kuşadası for Venice, Italy via Patmos and Katakolon (cheapest cabin—no deck space available—to Venice £265, all meals for the 2½-day journey included).

**Rentals: Toya-Sun Rent-A-Car** (tel. 33 44), 60 Atatürk Bulvarı. Offers the cheapest car rentals. $14 per day, 14¢ per km; unlimited mileage also available at $97 for 2 days. Additional

$3.85 per day for insurance required. Moped rentals most reasonable at **A.G. Tourism and Travel Co.**, 60/4 Atatürk Bulvarı. $10 per day. Prices vary in off-season.

**Bookstore: Kuydaş Kitabevi** at the upper end of Yalı Cad (tel. 20 28). (Sign reads *Haşet.*) Sells newspapers, guidebooks, and stationery. The owner speaks perfect English.

**Hospital (Hastahane):** On the waterfront at the northern edge of town (tel. 10 26).

**Police (Polis):** In the watchtower (tel. 10 22). Headquarters, Hükümet Cad. (tel. 13 82). Tourists should go to the watchtower. English isn't spoken in either station. In an emergency, they'll get a translator for you.

## Accommodations and Camping

Compared to Greece, accommodations here are cheap (although expensive by Turkish standards), and finding a room is rarely a problem. Pensions are least expensive, but they often fill up in high season. The cheaper ones are along Aslanlar Cad.

**Pansiyon Su,** 13 Aslanlar Cad. (tel. 14 53). Walk up Yalı Cad. and make a left—it's 1 block down on the right side. Cheap, clean, and very friendly. Singles $2.30. Shower 40¢.

**Hotel Ada,** 12 Aslanlar Cad. (tel. 23 52). Quite new, clean, and very friendly. Singles $6. Doubles $7.70. Hot showers any time.

**Şafak Pansiyon,** 25 Aslanar Cad. (tel. 17 64), 1 block up from Pension Su. Terrific view of the harbor. Cheap, but stangely aromatic bathrooms. $1.90 per person. Hot showers 40¢.

**Hotel Rose,** Aslanlar Cad. (tel. 11 11). Friendly management. Cozy lounge decorated with *kilim* and Turkish carpets. Bed on covered rooftop $3 per person.

**Orient Pansiyon,** 3 Okurlar Sok. (tel. 28 83), off Barbaros Hayrettin, just before the police tower. This carpet-filled wooden building is perfectly located (you don't have to climb the hill), but the bathrooms smell. Management inhospitable. $3.85 per person. Showers 27¢.

**Istanköy Pansiyon,** 4 Türkmen Mahallesi Ünlü Sok. (tel. 13 28). A 4-story building visible from the municipal "beach." There are usually rooms here when other pensions fill. Doubles $3.70. Free outdoor cold showers.

**Camping: Önder** (tel. 24 13) and **Yat Camping** (tel. 13 33), 2-3km north of town on the Selçuk-Izmir road. Take a Selçuk *dolmuş* or walk. Both have good facilities. At Önder, $3 per tent, bungalows for 3 $9.25. At Yat, $4.30 per tent.

## Food

On the average, prices are slightly higher than in less-touristed areas, but the food is quite good, particularly along **Kahramanlar Caddesi.** You'll have to fork it over at the places along the harbor and on Barbaros Hayrettin, with the exception of **Liman Aile Çay Bahçesi** on the waterfront. Fish in Kuşadası, as in the rest of Turkey, is expensive, but if you're in a group of four or more, order a large one. Liquor is a rip-off when ordered in restaurants.

**Güvercinada Cafeteria,** on Bird Island. A pleasant surprise. Dramatic sunsets (free), cheap beer (60¢), and piping hot *lahmacun* (Turkish pizza) straight from the hearth (40¢). Turkish dancing from 10pm. Open daily 7:30am-3am.

**Kuşadası Çorba Salonu,** 24 Sağlık Cad. Make a left at the police watchtower and walk about 4 blocks—it's on the right side. *Kuzu tandır* (half sheep's head) $1.50, *paça* (sheep's intestines soup) 50¢, *beyin* (sheep's brains with lemon and parsley) 75¢, and other dyed-in-the-wool Turkish cuisine. They also serve spit-roasted lamb and chicken ($2). Open daily 11am-11pm.

**Gamalı Köftecisi,** on Camiiatik Cad. From the police watchtower turn left onto Sağlık Cad; turn right after 2 blocks, then left—it's on the left. Simple Turkish fare for a little less. *Köfte* $1.15, *kebap* with yogurt $1.50. Open daily 11am-11pm.

**Konya Pide Salonu,** 65 Kahramanlar Cad., just past the bus station on the road to Söke. Specializes in *pide,* a relative (many times removed) of pizza. Cheese *pide* with meat or eggs (*peynirli*) 75¢.Open daily 11am-midnight.

## Sights and Entertainment

Connected by a slender causeway, Kuşadası's only substantial tourist attraction is its picturesque namesake, **Bird Island,** a tiny fortified islet graced with cozily cushioned cafes, blessed by a perimeter of excellent rocks from which to swim, and capped with a fine view of the port. Birds, however, are noticeably absent.

The Grand Bazaar and Barbaros Hayrettin are among the most expensive places to shop in the country. Nonetheless, as the merchants will never tire of reminding you, it doesn't cost anything to look and sip a glass of çay. Another favorite occupation among visitors is to spend all day basking on the meager **beaches** that line the coast in either direction. The beach by the yacht harbor, to the right of the port and customs office if facing the water, is crowded and dirty. Better, but not by much, is **Kadınlar Plajı,** the main beach, 3km beyond Bird Island. Taxis run passengers on a collective basis from the taxi stand next to the Kervansaray Hotel. Instead, visit the sandy, clean, uncrowded beaches 20km south of Kuşadası. Take any *dolmuş* marked **Siteler** or **Davutlar** and hop off at any beach. *Dolmuş* leave from the Kuşadası bus station (about every 20 min.).

In addition to its wealth of archeological treasures, the scenic countryside requires attention. **Kalamanki National Park,** known to local Turks as the **Millı Park,** 30km south of Kuşadası, is an unspoiled expanse of woodlands, glistening waterfalls, cliffs, and deserted beaches. *Dolmuş* marked "Millı Park" leave every half hour. *Dolmuş* also leave about four mornings per week for **Güzel Çamlı,** which is a 5-kilometer walk from the park. Since the park is completely uninhabited, hitching tends to be best on weekends, when Turkish families go for picnics. Right before the entrance to the park are three very pleasant beaches.

# Ephesus (Efes)

Dig no further than Ephesus for your wholesale archeological needs. The ruins from the Roman and early Christian era are nowhere as extensive or well-preserved as in this remarkable locale, only 3km from Selçuk and 17km from Kuşadası. Even if you're visiting the Turkish coast for only one day, follow the swarms of tourists who cross over from Samos and make a beeline for the ruins.

## Practical Information and Accommodations

Disregard the large signs at the travel agencies on Samos and in Kuşadası that insist that guided tours of Ephesus are "highly recommended." The tours are expensive ($21 per day) and the guides tend to rush you through the 2000-acre site. Visit on your own instead. Consider procuring a good guidebook to Ephesus in one of Kuşadası's souvenir shops. *Ephesus: The Way It Was,* by Dr. Ü. Önen, is available at the Kuydaş Bookstore in Kuşadası. Each description is accompanied by an artist's sketch of how the site appeared in its heyday ($4.60). Bring a water bottle to the site, since most of the time you'll be wilting in the heat at least 1km from the nearest refreshment stand.

To get to the site, head for the Kuşadası bus station, hop the *dolmuş* to Selçuk, and tell the driver you want to get off at Ephesus. The main entrance, where you pay admission, is 1km away, but the actual ruins start just a few meters from the road to Selçuk. To return to Kuşadası, it is advisable to catch a *dolmuş* from Selçuk, since they're usually full when they pass the turn-off for Ephesus. You should stop in Selçuk anyway to supplement your exploration of Ephesus with a visit to the excellent **Ephesus Museum** (see Selçuk). You might try your luck hitching along the Selçuk-Kuşadası road.

The site at Ephesus is open in summer daily from 8am to 7pm; hours are slightly curtailed in the off-season. Admission is $1.50. Next to the entrance are **toilets** (2¢), a **post office,** a **police station,** and some overpriced restaurants. In the first or second week of May, the annual **Festival of Ephesus** presents drama, music, and folklore events in the ancient theater.

The only accommodation within walking distance is the **Tusan Motel & Camping** (tel. 10 60), 1km toward the Selçuk-Kuşadası road. ($4 per tent.) You can find better accommodations in Selçuk.

## History

The allure of Ephesus is on scale with its illustrious past. As a strategic coastal gateway to the Eastern world, this Ionian refuge grew into the second largest city in the Roman Empire, site of one of the "seven wonders of the ancient world," and a shrine for Christians.

The origins of Ephesus are shrouded in myth. Legend has it that the city was founded in a manner prescribed by the Delphic Oracle, which foretold that the appropriate site would be disclosed by a fish and a wild boar. Eventually, the day came when a fish leapt from the flames over which it was being cooked and set fire to the neighboring brush, startling a wild boar, which was later slaughtered on the spot where the city of Ephesus was built. The city's location had to be changed several times due to the continual recession of the harbor waters. Today, the ruins of the ancient port lie 10km inland from the coast.

There was a reluctance to move, partially due to the Ephesians' desire to remain near the colossal **Temple of Artemis.** This dazzling structure was described by Pausanias as the "most wondrous of the seven ancient wonders" and "the most beautiful work ever created by humankind." The first major structure ever to be built entirely of marble, and the largest edifice in the ancient Greek world, the Temple of Artemis was four times larger than the Parthenon in Athens. Remarkably, this massive monument was built twice. A madman named Erostratus set fire to the temple in 356 B.C.E. on the night of the birth of Alexander the Great. According to legend, Erostratus succeeded only because Artemis was absent, watching over Alexander's birth. Alexander fittingly reconstructed the temple to its original dimensions, and the offerings and donations of hundreds of thousands of pilgrims each year enabled it to grow so wealthy that it became the world's first bank. Today, little remains of the magnificent structure; it was sacked by plundering Goths in the third century C.E., later by the Byzantines (you can see some of the original columns at the Aya Sofya in Istanbul), and more recently by the voracious British School of Archeology. Nonetheless, a great deal remains of the sprawling city that grew up around the temple.

Ephesus reached its zenith under Roman rule when, as capital of the province of Asia, its inhabitants numbered over 250,000, second in population only to Alexandria. Most of the ruins that one sees today date from this period. Saint Paul, recognizing the significance of such a metropolis, arrived in 50 C.E. and converted a small group of Ephesians to the new religion, making Ephesus the spiritual center for the Christian faith in the Roman empire. The city's name provides a title for one of the Epistles of the New Testament (*Ephesians*). Acts xix presents a vivid picture of life in Ephesus during the mid-first century C.E. As the site of the tomb of St. John and the first basilica, Ephesus was among the first cities to attract Christian pilgrims.

To illustrate the transient nature of life, Heraclitus of Ephesus once remarked that one can never step into the same river twice. His wisdom proved all too accurate. As the neighboring river Caÿster emptied into the Aegean, it choked Ephesus harbor with silt, transforming it into marshy swampland. By the sixth century C.E., the recession of the sea had sealed the fate of the city. The swamps became infested with malaria and triggered a tremendous epidemic, resulting in more than 200,000 deaths.

## Sights

If you're not on a guided tour, you will approach the ruins from the road between Kuşadası and Selçuk; your first glimpse of the site will be the remains from the outskirts of the ancient city. The most important of these is the **Vedius Gymnasium,** to your left as you proceed down the road to the main entrance. On the west end of the gymnasium courtyard (the main entrance is at the north end of the site) are public lavatories and a running water source. Farther on, also on your left, you can make out the contours of what must have been an enormous **stadium** (the seats were removed to build the Byzantine city walls). Just before the main entrance are the ruins of the **Double Church** (Church of Councils) where the much-noted Ecumenical Council of Churches met in 431 C.E.

Once you pass through the main entrance, you won't be able to resist charging to the center of the site and looking straight down the **Arcadian Street,** a magnificent and colonnaded marble avenue. Like the present-day tourist drag in Kuşadası, it was lined with shops and extended to the harbor, where visitors disembarked and trading ships docked with cargo from the Far East. The street eventually degenerates into a small marsh, but many of the original columns have survived.

At the far end of the avenue, turn around and admire the marvelous view of the **Grand Theater.** With seating for 24,000, the theater dominates the entire site from an elevated setting, carved into the side of Mt. Pion. The acoustics of the theater are remarkable: Even at a whisper, voices from the stage reach the topmost row. Every April in ancient times, the Ephesians celebrated the Festival of Artemis; 89 golden idols of the goddess were marched with singing and dancing to the Grand Theater where plays were staged. Over the centuries, the theater was gradually enlarged to accommodate the growing population of the city. The top commands a fine panorama of the surrounding valley.

To the left of the theater's exit you'll find the **Commercial Agora**—the main plaza of the city. In the center of the colonnaded spuare stood a huge horologium, a combination sundial and water clock. The four circumscribing rows of majestic Roman columns clearly demarcate the market's original proportions. Running between the agora and the theater is the slightly elevated **Marble Road,** which led all the way to the Temple of Artemis. Peek down one of the small holes in the road for a glimpse of the advanced sewage system. Strewn with a variety of architectural fragments, some with striking bas-reliefs, the road leads past the agora to the **Library of Celsus,** on your right as you face the hillside. Almost entirely reconstructed by Viennese archeologists, its elaborately carved marble facade suggests the dazzling luxury of ancient Ephesus. The Austrians couldn't resist leaving their thumbprint: The beautiful reconstruction is marred by bold inscriptions in the marble interior, in which they assume full credit for the present state of the structure. In its heyday, the library's collection was considered the third most important in the world, surpassed only by those in Alexandria and Pergamon.

Across from the library at the corner of the Marble Road and Curetes St. are the remains of the **brothel** that was dedicated to the love-goddess Aphrodite. Before entering, visitors would wash their feet and offer prayer to the goddess. Business took place by candlelight in the small, windowless side rooms. Also located in the area are a wine cellar, a wine press, some baths, and a row of public toilets. At the end of the brothel, farthest from the Grand Theater, is a sacred pump whose water supposedly made sterile women fertile. Here was found the famous statue of Priapus, the prodigiously-endowed god of sex now displayed in the Ephesus Museum in Selçuk. If you leave the brothel from the water fountain you'll face the **Byzantine Fountain;** its limestone blocks constituted part of a monumental Christian tomb.

Continuing up the hill, the left side of the road is dominated by the imposing ruins of the well-preserved **Temple of Hadrian,** whose intricately carved facade was recently renovated. The marble archway contains friezes depicting the mythical creation of the city of Ephesus; a bust of the goddess Cybele adorns the keystone. Originally an Anatolian fertility goddess, Cybele was revered by the Romans after an oracle correctly predicted that if a statue of the goddess was brought from Asia Minor to Rome, they would conquer Carthage. Beyond the temple and adjoining the rear of the brothel you'll find the **Baths of Scholastikia,** named after a wealthy Christian woman who leveled several important buildings in the fifth century C.E. in order to restore and extend the city's bath complex. Her headless statue still remains *in situ.* Across the street from the Temple of Hadrian begin the yet unearthed

**Terrace Houses** that extend up the hill. They once housed the wealthiest and most prominent families of the city who decorated the interiors with superbly preserved frescoes and mosaics. A visit here merits the extra entrance fee (30¢; closed noon-1:30pm).

Farther up the hill, to your left along Curetes St. after the temple, you'll find the ruins of the exquisite **Fountain of Trajan.** The reconstruction of the fountain consists of various fragments excavated at this location piled piecemeal to simulate the original structure. The statue of the Emperor Trajan that stood before the fountain has been completely destroyed, except for its base. Trajan's two royal feet and a globe symbolized his dominion over the entire world. The series of statue bases that line the following stretch of Curetes St. once displayed the figures and busts of a variety of famous Ephesians.

If you continue from here to the right, you'll come to the scanty remains of **Domitian Square,** the site of the first temple of Ephesus to be dedicated to a Roman emperor. Still farther up, you'll find the equally meager remnants of the State Agora. It was in this corner of town that political affairs were negotiated and resolved—hence the proximity of the small, well-preserved **Odeon,** just across the way, which served as a council chamber and lecture hall. Today, the Sacred Way culminates in an alternative admission booth to the site and a refreshment stand. Farther up the road, outside the main site, lie the surviving fragments of the **East Gymnasium,** which many believe was constructed for women athletes. Only regular taxis run along this road, so you must either hitch or walk back to the main road to catch a *dolmuş* to Kuşadası or Selçuk.

If you make a left after the hill before you reach the main road you'll come to the hokey site of the **Grotto of the Seven Sleepers.** According to Christian tradition, seven men fleeing persecution in the third century C.E. hid out in these caves. When they awoke, one of them went to buy bread and discovered that he and the group had been sleeping for 209 years and that bread prices had risen.

# Selçuk

Selçuk's main claim to fame is its proximity to the ruins of Ephesus, but the village is also home to three important attractions of its own: the Ephesus Archeological Museum, the Basilica of St. John, and the House of the Virgin Mary. What's more, on the second Sunday in January, Selçuk hosts a **camel-wrestling festival,** in which bulls batter each other to the accompaniment of the *davul* drum and the *zurna* flute. Rest assured, the fight is stopped before any harm is done—camels are valuable property. The international **Selçuk-Efes Festival,** held in the first or second week of May, includes art displays, Turkish and foreign folk dancing, and musical performances.

## Orientation and Practical Information

The small village of Selçuk consists of one main road. The bus stop with the bus company offices lies at the intersection between this road and the road to Kuşadası and Ephesus. Across the street is the **tourist office** (tel. 13 28), which provides maps and complete lists of pensions. (Open in summer daily 8:30am-6:30pm; off-season Mon.-Fri. 8:30am-5:30pm). Just behind this office lies the Ephesus Museum, with the best public bathrooms and a place to check your pack. Next door is the **hospital** (tel. 14 07), and across the street is the **bus station,** from which the Kuşadası *dolmuş* leaves. About 250m down the road to Ephesus on the right side are the sparse ruins of the **Temple of Artemis.** If you're on the main road with your back toward Ephesus, make a left to get into town. Four blocks away is the clock tower, and two blocks behind it is the **PTT.** (Open 24 hours.) Banks, restaurants, the police, and the public baths are also located in this area. A few blocks farther back is the **train station** (tel. 10 06). Selçuk's **telephone code** is 5451.

## Accommodations and Food

Since the whole village goes to sleep after sunset, the main reason for staying in Selçuk is to be at the ruins bright and early the next morning. For evening activity, head to Kuşadası, only a short ride away. The cheapest pensions (listed below) cost roughly $3.85 per person.

Pansiyon Öztürk (tel. 19 37), the first left past the clock tower and the next left turn. Very friendly management. Large, immaculate rooms; some with balconies. Private hot showers.

Erol Pansiyon (tel. 32 36), 1 block past the clock tower and another turn—it's 2 or 3 blocks down on the left. Small but clean rooms. Friendly, English-speaking management.

Pansiyon Kırhan (tel. 22 57), behind the museum. Pleasant garden. Charming rooms. Hot showers.

Pansiyon Baykal, right next door to the Ephesus Museum (tel. 19 08). Cheapest rooms, but fairly cramped.

The Seçkin Restaurant (tel. 16 98), 22 Cengiz Topel Cad., 1 block behind the clock tower, serves a great variety of tasty and inexpensive dishes with a complete wine list. (Open 7am-midnight.) Also try the restaurant in the Ak Otel, on the same street as the museum. Although a bit more expensive, you can dine in a lovely garden courtyard.

## Sights

Over a century's worth of excavations are tastefully arranged in the Ephesus Museum. Its most famous pieces are two beautiful statues of Artemis, identified by her multitude of breasts, and the arresting statue of Priapus, the well-equipped deity of sex. Also of note are the fragments from the Temple of Artemis, a fresco portrait of Socrates found at the Terrace Houses, and a fine collection of ancient coins and glass. (Open daily 8:30am-6:30pm. Admission 75¢.)

The fourteenth-century Isabey Mosque provides rare evidence of Seljuk penetration this far west. A portion of the mosque is still used for worship, while the rest contains an impressive array of Ottoman tombstones. The four large granite columns that support the two domes come from the Harbor Baths at Ephesus. Some of the marble used to build the mosque was taken from the nearby remains of the Temple of Artemis. Farther up the hill you'll come to Persecution Gate, a colossus constructed in the sixth or seventh century C.E. from material taken from the stadium at Ephesus. The southernmost entrance to Byzantine Ephesus now serves as the entrance to the basilica and the rooftop site of numerous storks' nests.

Beyond the archway sprawls the Basilica of St. John, which contains the tomb of St. John the Theologian. In the sixth century, Emperor Justinian decided to construct this massive basilica over the grave in place of the small second-century C.E. chapel. St. John's body was originally kept in a room underneath the large dome of the basilica; the dust from this room was supposed to have supernatural healing powers. Today the grave is surrounded by four small marble columns in the center of the site. (Open daily 8:30am-6:30pm. Admission 75¢.)

The road that leads uphill to the right as you face the basilica brings you to Selçuk Castle, a Byzantine citadel with crenelated walls that endow the village skyline with a medieval aura. It looks impressive from the town, but it is just a circular hall with a small, abandoned mosque in the center. Both the hall and the minaret of the mosque afford an excellent view of the countryside, but Ephesus itself is tucked behind Mt. Pion.

Selçuk's most famous attraction is also its least impressive—the scanty remains of the once glorious Temple of Artemis. The second turn-off to the right on the road to Ephesus leads to the temple's original site. The fragments of the great altar and its columns have been shipped to museums in Vienna and London.

Christian and Muslim pilgrims congregate 7km outside of Selçuk at Meryemana, or the House of the Virgin Mary. According to the Bible, the Virgin Mary lived in Ephesus for the latter part of her life. In the early nineteenth century, a devout

German nun who had never set eyes upon Ephesus was said to have seen the house of the Virgin in a vision. She wrote a book discussing the plan and location of the house in detail. After her death, excavations around Ephesus unearthed a first-century C.E. stone cottage that fit her description perfectly. A small chapel was recently built over the site. Mass is held on weekdays at 7:15am and on Sunday at 10:30am. On August 15, the Assumption is celebrated and the Archbishop of Izmir conducts mass. If you visit Ephesus beforehand, exit through the back gate, where you will find taxis waiting to take you 9km to the chapel.

# Priene, Miletus, and Didim (Didyma)

Priene, Miletus, and Didyma lie in a neat row south of Kuşadası, conveniently located for that concentrated dose of ruins. Take some time and perch yourself on the slopes of Mt. Myrale to view Priene, recline in the amphitheater of Miletus, or wait for an epiphany from Apollo at Didyma. With an early start, a modicum of efficiency, and a blessing from Hermes, you may reach all three sites in a daytrip, but you may prefer to explore the ruins in two separate days. It is possible to take a single-day organized tour of all three sites from Kuşadası (or more expensively from Bodrum) for $20 per person, lunch included. Check with the tourist office. Otherwise, you can visit all three sites from Kuşadası through a series of *dolmuş* rides (about $3.50 per person).

For a daytrip, the best strategy is to get out to Didyma first and then work your way back north. Take a *dolmuş* from Kuşadası to **Söke.** Then pick up a second *dolmuş* to Didim, where Didyma is located. To get to Miletus from Didim, you can easily catch a *dolmuş* or hitch a ride to **Akköy;** it's 5km to Miletus. Hitching might be best. From Miletus, you have two choices—either backtrack to Akköy and catch a *dolmuş* to Priene via Söke, or use charm and finagle your way onto one of the many tour buses at the site. You can start at Priene and try to hitch to Miletus and Didyma from the many tourists or flag down a *dolmuş* heading south.

All three sites are open in summer daily from 8:30am to 7:30pm and in the off-season from 8:30am to 5pm. (Admission 75¢.) Priene and Miletus both have cafes, Didyma has two restaurants, and the bus station in Söke has a number of places offering cheap food. If you want to stay close to the ruins, take a dolmuş from Akköy going south to Lake Bafa where there are a number of campsites, or stay in Altınkum Plajı (Beach), just a few kilometers down the road from Didim (see Didyma).

## Priene

Poised spectacularly on the slopes of Mt. Mycale at the foot of a jagged rock cliff, Priene is imbued with an entrancing mystique and a checkered past. Once a major port, it stands out as one of a few surviving examples of a Hellenic metropolis in which the streets were laid out in a grid pattern. Founded by the Carians in the tenth century B.C.E., Priene fell to a group of Greek immigrants with the aid of the Ephesians. Adopted as an Athenian protectorate in 350 B.C.E., it was liberated soon after by Alexander the Great. The town was later dominated by the kings of Pergamon, and finally by the Romans, when during the reign of Augustus it re-attained its glory. As with other coastal cities, Priene declined slowly as alluvial deposits silted its harbor, strangling all commercial activities.

The *dolmuş* drops you off by a cafe and a souvenir shop. To reach the site, follow the road that climbs straight up the slope and forks off to the right of the direct road to Miletus and Didyma. First you'll encounter the massive ancient walls that circumscribe the ruined metropolis, constructed upon a series of terraces along the slope of the mountain. From the main entrance, a path conducts you to what was once the main avenue of ancient Priene. To your left will be the unmistakable **Bouleterion,** or Senate House, a well-preserved and elegant square auditorium. With a seating capacity of 640, the Bouleterion was reserved as a council chamber for the highest elected officials of the community. The interior chamber was adorned with a huge marble altar on which sacrifices were given both at the opening and closing of the sessions. Only the foundation of this altar remains.

Larger congregations convened just up the hill at the **theater,** a handsome structure with a seating capacity of 5000. Encompassed by a grove of pine trees, the theater's intimate, peaceful atmosphere contrasts strikingly with the barren rock face of Mt. Mycale in the background. The front row of the theater retains its five **thrones** of honor carved with their dignified bases in the shape of lions' paws. On the left side of the stage are the remnants of a water-clock that was used to enforce the time limit on political debates and orations.

Further along the upper terrace at the city's highest point, the **Temple of Athena** transports you back to the focal era of Hellenistic architecture. Designed by Pytheos, the architect who designed the Mausoleum of Halicarnassus (one of the ancient world's seven wonders), and financed by Alexander the Great, the temple's front steps and interior floor remain largely intact. Although only the foundation of the great altar remains visible (the rest has been removed to the Istanbul Museum), five fluted columns running the length of the northernmost edge have been resurrected.

Descend from the temple to visit the vast remains of the private houses of Priene, an unusual and well-preserved example of Ionian domestic architecture. The houses were fitted with baths and served by a continuous water supply.

Heading back towards the entrance of the site you'll pass through the spacious **agora,** where a woman could never visit alone; if she did not own a slave, her husband would go for her. Many statues of the gods were discovered in the agora; in the center was a public temple where official ceremonies and sacrifices took place. Across from the agora to the north (the theater is in the north end of the site), is the **Sacred Stoa,** where official city business was announced. Behind this is the **Prytaneum,** the storage vault of the city's sacred flame. Brought to Priene from Athens by the first settlers, the flame was extinguished only when the city was invaded. Upon liberation, the flame would be rekindled from another temple.

To the right of the agora you'll see the third-century B.C.E. **Temple of Olympic Zeus.** At the southern end of the site is the **Gymnasium,** with the names of many young athletes engraved into the walls. On either side of the main hall were small rooms for bathing or exercise.

On a hot day you're sure to find an oasis in the **Şelâle Restaurant.** From an adjacent ancient, moss-covered aqueduct a luscious waterfall cascades into a reflecting pool. What's more, the food is inexpensive and good. Try the *kebap* with yogurt and cucumber salad. The manager will change cash (not checks) and perhaps put you up *gratis* in a storage room by the restaurant. If you have no car, beg a ride to Miletus.

## *Miletus*

Now landlocked by arid plains, Miletus once sat upon a slender tongue of land surrounded by four separate harbors. Prosperous and enviable, the city was destroyed and resettled more than once because of its strategic coastal location. Like its Ionian confederates, the silting of its harbor and waters by neighboring rivers caused the decline of this once sprawling metropolis. For centuries, Miletus stood at the forefront of the major commercial and cultural developments of Western civilization. In the fifth century B.C.E., the Milesian alphabet was adopted as the standard form of Greek writing. Miletus was later the headquarters of the Ionian school of philosophers, which included Thales, Anaximander, and Anaximenes, who helped lay the foundations of mathematics and the natural sciences. The city's leadership, however, eventually faltered in 499 B.C.E., when Miletus headed an unsuccessful Ionian revolt against the Persian army. The Persians retaliated by wiping out the entire population of the city, massacring the men, and selling the women and children into slavery.

The main attraction of the site is the **theater,** clearly visible from the Priene-Didyma highway. Well-preserved, with a seating capacity of over 25,000, the theater dates from Hellenistic times, though most of what is visible is Roman work. It was originally positioned right at the water's edge. Notice the owners' names on some of the front row seats.

During all but the summer months, the remaining portions of Miletus are flooded marshland. To the right of the theater as you enter the site is a Selçuk **Kervansaray** (currently under restoration). Facing the theater, the footpath meandering to your right leads you to the **Faustina Baths** (behind and to the left of the theater), erected by Faustina, wife of the Roman Emperor Marcus Aurelius. To the left (north) of the baths are the **North and South Agoras.** Next to the baths is the **Delphinium,** or Sanctuary of Apollo Delphinius. The temple was first constructed to honor Apollo, who had transformed himself into a dolphin and conducted the Cretans to Miletus. All of the priests of the temple were sailors. The peculiar dome-shaped structure just beyond the baths is the **Mosque of Ilyas Bey.** Although the minaret is now missing, the *mihrab* of this fifteenth-century Islamic shrine is exquisitely decorated. About ½km before the main entrance is a small **archeological museum.** (Open daily 8am-12:30pm and 1:30-5:30pm. Admission 75¢.)

## Didim (Didyma)

Ancient Didyma was the site of a sacred sanctuary dedicated to Apollo and an oracle that brought in most of Didyma's fame and wealth. The first Didyma oracles date from about 600 B.C.E. About 100 years later, the sanctuary was destroyed by the Persians at the same time that they plundered Miletus. The temple lay deserted until Alexander the Great arrived and the dried-up sacred spring began to flow again. The present sanctuary was begun during the second and first centuries B.C.E. and work continued until the second century C.E., but the original plans proved too ambitious and were never brought to fruition.

The **sanctuary** at Didyma ranked as the third largest sacred structure in the ancient Hellenic world after its gargantuan neighbors to the north, the Temple of Artemis at Ephesus and the Temple of Hera on Samos. Since virtually nothing remains of either of the latter two buildings, the sanctuary at Didyma stands alone as the best surviving example of such colossal temple architecture. It was built to last—many of its individual marble slabs weigh over a ton.

Though unfinished, the temple flourished during the Roman period. It attracted pilgrims from all over ancient Greece, and citizens of nearby Miletus and Priene visited regularly during the various annual religious festivals. The sacred road that ran from Miletus to Didyma ended at the gates of the ancient temple, currently the site of souvenir shops and restaurants, and the final stretch was lined on both sides with statues (now in the British Museum). A church was constructed on the site in 385 C.E. after Emperor Theodosius outlawed the solicitation of pagan oracles.

Entering at the main gate, you will pass an enormous Corinthian capital that crowned one of the columns surrounding the temple. You will also notice a charming marble **Persian lion,** and to your right a striking bas-relief of a giant **Medusa head**—a fragment of an ornate frieze that originally ran all around the exterior of the temple. The full magnitude of the temple is only apparent once you climb the 13 steps up the stairway to the main facade. All that remains of the more than 100 gigantic columns are the bases and lower sections. The tapered and fluted shafts of the two restored columns possess a remarkable degree of delicacy despite their proportions (2½m in diameter and nearly 20m high). A third surviving full column remains unfluted, an indication that construction of the temple was never completed. To transport such cumbersome chunks of marble, the Greeks constructed long shafts of stone leading to the temple site, lubricated them with soap, and then slid the building materials over the slippery surface.

In front of the temple is a water source, thought to be the sacred spring that the priestesses tapped when receiving oracles from Apollo. Climb the steps to enter the forecourt. Past two rows of columns, through the **Hall of Twelve Columns** is the **Hall of Two Columns,** where visitors seeking the oracle waited to hear the pronouncements. From here, 22 steps lead down to the **audition,** but visitors were not permitted there; they were forced to wait for their news in the waiting room. Most likely, the visitors arrived in the Hall of the Two Columns through one of the two marble side tunnels. In ancient times, the audition was covered with a wooden roof; today it contains some fragments of the frieze that adorned the uppermost portion of these walls.

In the southeast corner of the courtyard are traces of another **sacred fountain,** as well as the foundations of a **naiskos**—a tiny temple that housed a venerated bronze statue of Apollo. The temple appears to have been erected in about 300 B.C.E. before the larger edifice was begun, and also served as the site of the oracle. Only priests and priestesses of the sanctuary were permitted to enter the naiskos. Those who came to consult the oracle were required to await the delivery of a written message.

The small modern resort of **Didim** nearby offers some inexpensive pensions; the **Orakle Pansiyon** (tel. 15 85), overlooking the temple, is the cheapest ($3.85 per person). Three kilometers south is the resort town **Altınkum.** This place is full of pensions, campsites, and Turkish tourists; if you're allergic to crowds, stay away in summertime. You can also try camping at the **Tuntas Motel** (tel. 10 18), near the *dolmuş* station ($3.85 for 2). To head south from Didim, you must first go north to Akköy. From there, frequent *dolmuş* go to Miletus, or you can catch a bus to Bodrum and beyond.

# Pamukkale (Hierapolis)

Whether as Pamukkale or ancient Hieropolis, this village has been drawing the weary and the curious to its thermal springs for over 23 centuries. The Turkish name—meaning "cotton castle"—refers to the extraordinary surface of the snow-white cliffs, shaped over millenia by the accumulation of calcium deposited by mineral springs. Dripping slowly down the massive mountainside, the water forms multiple semi-circular terraces that spill over into dramatic petrified cascades of stalactites, creating a series of wading pools. The ancient site itself only requires a couple of hours to see in depth, but surely you will want to indulge in an effervescent mineral bath, the kind once renowned throughout Asia Minor for its curative powers.

## Practical Information

Few direct buses run to Pamukkale. However, frequent *dolmuş* and minibuses run back and forth between Pamukkale and the bustling regional capital of Denizli, which has extensive service to all major Turkish cities. Less expensive and less comfortable—except for overnight couchettes—are the direct trains that travel from Izmir and Istanbul to Denizli. *Dolmuş* and minibuses to Pamukkale leave from directly in front of the Denizli bus station—about 100m south and across the street from the train station. Buses run twice hourly between Izmir and Denizli via Selçuk.

The **tourist office** (tel. 133 93) is located at the train station in Denizli. (Open Mon.-Fri. 9am-5pm.) Pamukkale is large enough to have a **PTT** (open daily 8am-midnight) and a **first aid center,** which is located behind the Roman Baths (now a museum). There is also a small **tourist information booth** at the end of the row of curio shops when you enter the main site. (Open daily 8:30am-6pm.) The booth provides maps of both Pamukkale and Denizli. Pamukkale's **telephone code** is 6218.

## Accommodations, Camping, and Food

Finding accommodations in Pamukkale is not difficult since everyone and his brother will hound you for a room. The motels in the tourist complex are all expensive, but the tiny village that lies in the valley beneath the tourist area has many relatively inexpensive rooms. From the wading pools on the cliff's edge, a long road leads down to the village. Try to visit during the week, as many Turks tend to flock to the resort on the weekends. To avoid pension peddlers, you may want to make your base in Denizli (whence you can also visit Aphrodisias). Yet another option is to camp at either **Cam Tur**, on the road to Denizli ($2.30 per person), or the **Beltes, Tusan,** or **Mistur** motels in the tourist complex.

**Halley Pension** (tel. 12 04), in the center of town next to the mosque. Immaculate, quiet, with friendly management. Doubles with shower $6.15.

**Qzcan Hotel** (tel. 11 96), behind the Pizzeria Restaurant. Clean rooms with private bath. Doubles $7.50-11.50.

**Kervansaray Pension** (tel. 12 09), left at the fork down the street from the pizza place. Dinky swimming pool. Mediocre rooms. Doubles in pension (not hotel) $7.50. The owner's brother runs **Aspawa Pension** (tel. 10 94) nearby, which is spotless but has no amenities. Doubles $9.25.

**Gold Star Pansiyon**, right next to the Pizzeria Restaurant. Friendly management. Just a few rooms, a pool, and a smelly bathroom.

The town of Karahayıt (4km north of Pamukkale), site of the Red Springs, has a few cheap pensions. Most rooms have private bathtubs fed by the hot springs that steam up your room. The camping facility at the Red Springs has swimming pools and reasonably clean bathrooms ($2.30 per person).

A convenient place to eat in Pammukale is the **Pizzeria Restaurant** (tel. 12 18), which serves excellent Italian-American-style pizza for $1.50. Stay away from the usual Turkish fare. (Will exchange money also.)

## Sights

Pamukkale will prove particularly appealing if you're missing the comforts of a hot bath. The warm water springs forth oxygen bubbles like an endless supply of overheated soda. Three large motels have sprouted up among the thermal springs and ancient ruins, and on weekends local Turks flock to bathe in the flat, fan-like pools. There are actually two different series of terraces situated on either side of the main highway to Denizli. Elegant, broad, shallow pools, which gradually increase in depth down the slope, are located in front of the Tusan Motel, the one nearest the highway. The deepest, most intricately shaped, and most popular terraces are directly behind the nameless restaurant-cafe facing the main parking lot. You can fully submerge yourself in some of the baths.

Between the motels stand the huge vaulted archways of the **Hierapolis City Baths.** The visible portions of this first-century structure are all that remain of one of Asia Minor's greatest ancient tourist industries. The springs of Hierapolis were particularly popular with vacationing Romans. After an earthquake leveled the spa in 17 C.E., Hierapolis was promptly rebuilt, reaching its heydey during the second and third centuries C.E. The city bath's glossy marble interior has now been converted into a mediocre **archeological museum.** (Open 9am-noon and 1:30-5pm. Admission 75¢.)

Carved into the side of the mountain, the huge **Grand Theater** dominates the vista of Hieropolis. Almost all of the seating area for 25,000 is intact, and the variety of ornately-sculpted decorative elements adorning the façade and stage area are very well preserved. Proceed with caution here since the theater is still under excavation. In front of the theater are the remains of the third-century C.E. **Temple of Apollo.** Behind the temple stands the **Nymphaeum,** or Monumental Fountain. To the right of the fountain (facing the theater) is the famous **Plutonium,** a hole with grating over it that emits poisonous carbonic acid gas which the ancients believed could kill all living creatures except priests. The Turks call it *Cin Deliği* (Devil's Hole). Further to the right you will find a hot-water spring. If you continue on the footpath, you'll reach the sixth-century **Christian basilica.**

Down the road to Karahayit is the north **city gate** on the right. Following this are the ruins of a fifth-century Christian basilica dedicated to St. Philip, martyred here in 80 C.E. Outside the gate is the **Necropolis,** consisting of more than 1200 tombs and sarcophagi. People who wished to be buried here believed that the proximity to the hot springs and vapor-emitting cracks would ease their trip to the Underworld. Up on the hill among the tombs lies the **Martyrium,** an octagonal fifth-century edifice believed to have been erected upon the site where St. Philip was martyred in 80 C.E.

For a different taste of Pamukkale's thermal springs, take a plunge into a sacred fountain, housed within the **Pamukkale Motel** up the hill toward the amphitheater. A dip in this ancient pond, supplied by a neighboring stream with a steady flow of naturally heated mineral water, is like bathing in warm Perrier. The pool is also a paradise for archeology buffs, who can explore the ruins from ancient Hierapolis that are easily visible in the clean water. A swim costs 60¢ per person per hour. (Open daily 9am-6pm.)

You can also visit the technicolor **Red Springs** 3km away at **Karahayıt.** (*Dolmuş* leave frequently from the top of the hill.) An iron source here has created what looks like the result of a chemistry experiment gone wild—different shades of red, orange, and yellow color the water spilling over the hill. Cooler pools for bathing are available at the campground downhill (75¢).

# Aphrodisias

While the ruins of Aphrodisias have been scrutinized for decades, archeologists believe that a great deal remains unexcavated. The highlights of the ruins excavated to date include a beautifully preserved Roman stadium and an equally well-preserved *odeon,* as well as a temple, an *agora,* a palace, and some thermal baths.

Ancient Greeks made pilgrimages here to pay their respects and make requests to Aphrodite. The village evolved into a metropolis when King Attalos III bequeathed Pergamon to the hated Romans, spurring an exodus. A community of artists brought Aphrodisias fame for its sculpture and plastic arts. Crafted from the fine white and bluish-gray marble of nearby quarries, the finest statues in the Roman Empire were often marked with the imprint of the celebrated Aphrodisian school. Aphrodisias was also an important intellectual center of Asia Minor; the great medical scientist Xenocrates lived here. With the rise of Christianity, the temples were converted to churches and the city's name was changed to Stavropolis ("City of the Cross").

Aphrodisias' artistic heritage is evident in the ruins of the city. Drama obviously played an important role as witnessed by the grandiose **theater.** Fantasize about the limelight of antiquity and proceed down the steps to the stage and orchestra pit. Just beyond the theater lie the sparse remains of the **agora.** To your right (with your back to the theater) the **theater baths** recall the hedonistic past of the lustful populace.

The remaining sites lie behind the theater. Once you've walked back to the top, you'll notice a dirt footpath winding down the backside of the hill. From this summit, you can survey the city's layout. The looming structure at the bottom of the hill is **Hadrian's Bath,** equipped with a sauna, frigidarium, and changing rooms. To the right, the **Temple of Aphrodite** marks the site of ancient worship to the goddess. Although only a portion of its 40-column spiral-fluted Corinthian colonnade remains, the temple is still elegant. Dating from the first century C.E., the shrine originally housed a famous statue of Aphrodite that was similar in appearance to the Artemis of Ephesus. So far, only copies of the original have been unearthed. With its extraordinary blue marble stage, the **odeon,** just to the south, was the council chamber for the town's elected officials. The nine columns standing nearby were resurrected as part of a building named by archeologists the **Bishop's Palace,** due to the large number of religious artifacts and statues unearthed on its premises. Some of the original marble floors remain intact.

The pinnacle of a visit to Aphrodisias, however, is the best-preserved ancient **stadium** ever excavated. With a seating capacity of 30,000, even the marble blocks that once marked the starting line for foot races are still in place in the central arena.

Also visit the excellent museum; among its highlights, you'll find larger-than-life statues of Aphrodite and Satyr carrying the child Dionysus. (Open daily 9am-6:30pm. Admission $1.50.)

The ruins can be reached on a daytrip from either Kuşadası (165km) or Pamuk-kale (110km). From Kuşadası, take a *dolmuş* to Selçuk, then a bus to Nazilli, a *dolmuş* to Karacasu, and finally a *dolmuş* to the ruins. There are few direct buses from Selçuk to Aphrodisias. Kuşadası travel agencies offer a hurried package single-day tour to Pamukkale and Aphrodisias for $40 per person.

Transportation to and from Pamukkale is no less of an ordeal. First you must take a *dolmuş* from Pamukkale to Denizli, then a bus to Nazilli. From there, pro-ceed as listed above. Alternatively, you can take a tour with Efes Tourism in Pamuk-kale to Aphrodisias ($30, lunch included).

In Aphrodisias, stay at **Chez Mestan** (tel. 14 30), which also offers a restaurant serving delicious food. (Doubles $11.50 with shower. Camping $1.50 per person.)

# Bodrum

Ensconced in the serpentine coastline of the Bodrum Peninsula, a sun worshiper's paradise brimming with beaches, secluded coves, and uninhabited islands, Bodrum is understandably the favorite retreat of many Turkish jet-setters, intellectuals, art-ists, and wealthy city-dwellers. In fact, Bodrum is probably the most cosmopolitan and liberal town on the Turkish coast. Bodrum is not without historical attraction either—its excellent Crusader castle houses the unique Museum of Underwater Ar-cheology and the scanty remains of the mausoleum of Halicarnassus, one of the seven wonders of the ancient world. Whether you arrive in Bodrum by boat from Kos or by bus from Marmaris or Izmir, you will be awestruck by the panorama of this picturesque resort.

Bodrum was built upon the ancient city of Halicarnassus, a powerful port town and capital of ancient Caria. (The Carians were an indigenous people of Anatolia who lived in this area prior to the Greek invasion.) Halicarnassus was known for its succession of female rulers who became leaders after the deaths of their fathers, husbands, or brothers. One such ruler was Artemesia I, who led a fleet against the Athenians in their war with Persia in 480 B.C.E.; her story is related in the *Persian Wars* by Herodotus, himself a native of Halicarnassus. In 377 B.C.E., the famous Mausolus of Cairo came to power and made Halicarnassus his capital. Under his governance, the city became a mighty port. Mausolus instituted draconian penal and civil codes that called for punishment for minor offenses, such as men having long hair. Work on his tomb began during his reign, and was finally completed in 353 B.C.E. after his death. The tomb provided the etymological roots of the modern word "mausoleum." Later, Alexander the Great, marching across Asia Minor, razed Halicarnassus so it became forever unable to regain its former glory.

## Orientation and Practical Information

Streets in Bodrum are often poorly marked. Orient yourself with respect to the *kale,* the centrally located castle from which most of the town's main streets ema-nate; on either side of the *kale* are long bays. Some of the cheap pensions are along the bank left of the *kale* as you look out to sea, right in the line of fire of 1000-watt disco speakers. Breakwaters almost completely enclose the other port, which forms the older and more picturesque half of the town. Ferries and most yacht cruises depart from this harbor.

The main thoroughfare along the waterfront starts from the castle and runs along the enclosed right harbor: It begins as Karantina Caddesi, becomes Belediye Mey-danı after the mosque, changes to Neyzen Tevfik along most of the harbor, and ends at the marina, **Yat Limanı** (yacht harbor). Going left from the castle, Kasa-phane Caddesi becomes Kumbahçe Mahallesi, then changes to the main commer-cial drag of **Cumhuriyet Caddesi,** and ends by the Halikarnas Hotel as Paşa Tarlası.

Extending back from the castle towards the bus station, **Kale Caddesi** is Bodrum's main shopping strip; it becomes Cevat Şâkir Caddesi, bordering the parking lot of the bus station from where all buses, taxis, and *dolmuş* depart.

**Tourist Office:** In front of the castle (tel. 10 91). Complete accommodations listings and a lousy map. Better maps available at the bookstore—get the one with the peninsula on one side and a town plan on the other. Bus information as well. Leave your baggage here while searching for a room. Open May-Sept. daily 8am-8pm; Oct.-April Mon.-Fri. 8am-noon and 1:30-5pm.

**Travel Agents: Karya Tours,** 6 Dr. Alim Bey Cad. (tel. 17 59), and also at the ferryboat landing (tel. 19 14). Coordinates ferries to Kos and the Datça Peninsula. Tickets might be a little cheaper here. Also organizes daily excursions to: Pamukkale ($34); Ephesus ($32); and Didyma, Miletus, and Priene ($28). Open daily 8am-9:30pm. Also excellent is **Flama Tour,** opposite the yacht marina at Neyzen Tevfik Cad. (tel. 18 42). They have ferry tickets, car rental, and run guided tours in English. Tours to: Ephesus ($30); Iasos ($20); Didyma, Priene, and Miletus ($28); and Caunos ($29).

**PTT:** Cevat Şâkir Cad., 4 blocks from the bus station as you walk towards the harbor. Open 24 hours. Another PTT at the ferry landing. International telephones also next to the castle. In summer, expect to wait in line.

**Telephone Code:** 6141.

**Buses:** Bus companies next to the bus station. Also a Pamukkale office on Belediye Meydanı. Several buses per day to Marmaris, Izmir, and Istanbul. For Kuşadası, take a bus to Söke and then a *dolmuş.*

**Dolmuş:** From the bus station to anywhere on the peninsula. Major destinations such as Torba or Turgut Reis are served every ½ hr. in the summer. In high season, fares double. To Gümbet, outfitted jeeps run from the parking lot as frequently as taxis.

**Ferries:** Tickets sold through any travel agent but sometimes cheaper at Karya Tours. Boats to Kos (June-Aug. daily; May-Sept. 3 per week; $14.60 one-way, $20.40 round-trip). All boats leave at 9am and return at 5pm (1½ hr.). Ferry to Datça Peninsula, 8km from Datça and 80km from Marmaris (June-Aug. daily; $11.50 one-way, $15.40 round-trip).

**Moped Rental: Turquoise Tours,** Atatürk Cad. (tel. 15 07). Mopeds $9.60 per day, $24.60 for 3 days. Bicycles $3.85 per day, $9.60 for 3 days. Also has scuba-diving tours. Open daily 8:30am-8pm.

**Bookstores: Recep E. Cingöz Gazeteler** (tel. 26 30), behind Adilye Mosque on Kale Cad., has a wide selection of guide books, postcards, and newspapers. Open Mon.-Sat. 8am-9pm. You can find *Time* and *Newsweek* magazines beneath the Belediye Mosque. The **Bodrum Public Library** (*Kütüphane*), 65 Cumhuriyet Cad., has a wide selection of English books and allows foreigners to check them out up to 1 week, with a passport as collateral. Open Mon.-Fri. 8am-noon and 1-5pm.

**Hospital:** Turgut Reis Cad. (tel. 10 68), past the ruins of the mausoleum.

**Police:** Next to the castle (tel. 10 04).

## Accommodations and Camping

During the summer, rooms (especially singles) become scarce. Pensions are a better bet than hotels; there are hundreds of them and they're inexpensive for Bodrum at $3.80-4.60 per person. Because rooms are at such a premium, you'll have less luck bargaining here than elsewhere during the summer. Often there are rooms available in private homes. Look for signs that read "Oda Var" or "Boş Oda Var."

**Yenilmez Pansiyon** (tel. 25 20). Look for a sign along Neyzen Tevfik (the road along the right harbor facing the water). Large, airy rooms. Quiet location with pleasant garden. Bathrooms a bit grimy. Doubles $6.15 with hot shower.

**Aşkın Pansiyon,** Uslu Sok. (tel. 14 99). Make a left off Cumhuriyet Cad. before coming to the harbor (you'll see the sign). Good location near the harbor. Quite clean, with hot water. Doubles $9.25.

**Belmi Pansiyon** (tel. 11 32), also off Neyzen Tevfik, 2 blocks closer to the center. Fine location, comfortable rooms. Rooftop terrace with nice view. Doubles $7.70. Hot showers 75¢.

**Şenlik Pansiyon** (tel. 26 92). Reasonably clean rooms and large garden courtyard. Doubles with hot shower $9.25.

**Amca Pansiyon,** on Neyzen Tevfik Cad. (tel. 15 16). Mediocre in all respects. Doubles with shower $9.25.

**Camping:** Grassless, shadeless, and dirty campsites within Bodrum will probably persuade you to camp elsewhere. **Yuvam Camping** (tel. 11 97), 150m inland off Neyzen Tevfik (look for the sign). $1.50 per person with tent, $2.30 per person without tent. Slightly nicer is **Uçar Kamping,** fenced off with barbed wire. $2.30 per person. They also offer some sweltering bungalows named after characters from the television show *Dallas:* "Ceyar," "Suelin," "Babi," "Pemelâ," and "Lusi." Take a left at the south fork. $7.60 per person.

# Food and Entertainment

Bodrum is a gastronomic paradise with restaurants to satisfy every budget. Of course, for the cheapest provisions, stock up at the big fruit and vegetable **markets** every evening, next to the bus station. Along Cumhuriyet Cad. before the harbor, a number of *kebap* salons and stands offer fried mussels, fried intestines, and ice cream. There are a few good, untouristed restaurants on the first street to the left after the bus station (facing the water). The port is famous throughout Turkey for its fish restaurants.

**Sokkalı Ali Doksan Restaurant,** at the beginning of Kale St. and the second left. Located under tented area. The restaurant is unmarked, so ask. Simple Turkish fare but locals swear it's the best deal in town. Don't miss it. Full meal of meat, salad, and drink $2. Open Mon.-Sat. 11am-2:30pm and 7-9:30pm.

**Bodrum Restaurant** (tel. 27 40). Turn left past Adilye Mosque—it's 2 blocks on the right. Recommended for its variety and prices. *Kebap* ranges from $1.25-1.50. Menu changes daily. Open daily 8am-11pm.

**Orhan's No. 7,** 7 Eski Banka Sok., off Kale Cad. in a vine-covered alley that is full of restaurants. Extraodinary seafood, especially octopus, but expect to pay twice as much for a meal. Very popular among Turks. Full meal with drinks $6. Open daily noon-2am.

**Fiesta,** at the beginning of Cumhuriyet Cad. Comfort for homesick Americans. Hamburgers, ham sandwiches, and Coca-Cola at low prices. Most sandwiches 75¢. Open daily 9am-11:30pm.

For nightlife in Bodrum, the **Halicarnassus Disco,** at the end of Cumhuriyet Cad., is the place to go. However, most budget travelers balk at the $15 cover charge, allegedly necessary to recoup the $1.2 million poured into the building of this psuedo-Roman marble theater. (The stage is the dance floor.) Pleasant pubs suffice for just relaxing and listening to music. Most bars are visible from the street and full of tourists. Others, frequented by Turks who make their summer residence in Bodrum, are more discreet. If you can shoulder the $4.50 first-drink charge, visit the **Mavi Bar,** near the end of Cumhuriyet Cad. This popular Turkish hangout features floor cushions, *kilim,* and musicians famous throughout Turkey. For a similar ambience without the high cost, try the back porch of the **Buona Sera Bar,** 75 Cumhuriyet Cad., which has a nice terrace garden. Beer is $1.50, rakı $1.50. (Open 24 hours.)

# Sights

Rising from the azure waters of the harbor is the **Kale,** the well-preserved Crusader castle that epitomizes the daunting features of the medieval fortress. It was constructed by the Order of the Knights of St. John during the fifteenth and sixteenth centuries C.E. on top of the ruins of the ancient acropolis. When they were forced to retreat from the Holy Land in 1291 C.E., the knights relocated their headquarters on the nearby island of Rhodes. An expedition, arriving in Bodrum in 1402 C.E., immediately began construction of the castle, using the last remnants (but no remains) of the mausoleum of Halicarnassus, finally completing it in 1513. The castle towers were built by knights of different nations; four of them are accordingly known as the English, German, French, and Italian towers. In addition, there exists the squat yet handsome **Harbor Tower** and a sinister-looking battlement christened the **Snake Tower.** Despite the castle's immense proportions and extensive crenelated fortifications, only 10 years after its completion the knights were compelled to surrender in 1523, overpowered by Sultan Süleyman the Magnificent and forced to retreat to Malta. The Order survives today as an international health organization.

The castle houses Bodrum's **Museum of Underwater Archeology,** a fascinating collection of ancient shipwreck remains from sites along the surrounding Turkish coastline. The institute, the only one of its kind in the world, is affiliated with Texas A&M University and partially funded by *National Geographic Magazine,* and has been the subject of several documentary films.

A Byzantine chapel in the central courtyard of the castle houses the **Bronze Age Hall,** and contains finds from a 1200 B.C.E. shipwreck, including the ship's lamp, weights, and scrap bronze that was in transit to Cyprus. Huge jars found on board date from 1600 B.C.E., and their artwork strongly suggests the existence of a trade route between Crete and the Asia Minor coast. Scattered in every corner of the museum are thousands of ancient amphoras (large clay vase-shaped jars that held produce such as wine and olive oil), since adopted by the souvenir shops as the tourist symbol of Bodrum. The museum also exhibits *cam* (glassware) recovered from a variety of ancient and medieval wrecks. Other highlights of the museum include a fine collection of Mycenaean pottery (1400-1200 B.C.E.) and several Ottoman cannons originally used to defend the castle. (Open Tues.-Sun. 8:30am-noon and 1-5pm. Admission 75¢.)

The ruins of ancient **Halicarnassus,** site of one of the seven wonders of the ancient world, are Bodrum's better known if less picturesque attraction. Most of the remains were either destroyed or, as in the case of the large monuments and temples, remain buried underneath the modern town of Bodrum. The city walls are visible at points, as are the meager remains of the **theater.** The most famous of the ruins, the **mausoleum,** consisted of a rectangular foundation and stone pedestal upon which the sepulchral chamber rested, surrounded by 36 ionic columns. The mausoleum was covered with a gigantic pyramidal roof, and crowned by a statue of Mausolus driving a chariot drawn by four horses. Towering to a height of 50m, the colossal edifice was clearly visible from long distances at sea. The freize that once adorned the lower pediment was removed first by the Crusaders to decorate their castle, then by the English to the British Museum in London. An authentic plaster copy of it now stands at the site. To get to the mausoleum, follow the signs from Neyzen Tevfik, up Tepecik Hamam Sok., and onto Turgut Reis Cad. (Open Tues.-Sun. 8:30am-noon and 1-5pm. Admission 75¢.)

## *Near Bodrum*

Bodrum's popularity among Turkish tourists stems mainly from its location at the head of the enchanting **Bodrum Peninsula.** After a day of swimming, sunning, and a relaxing dinner, you can return to the nightlife of Bodrum. Don't miss the opportunity to visit the southern beaches by *dolmuş motorları.* These boats leave Bodrum's harbor daily at 9am and return at about 6pm, visiting several otherwise inaccessible beaches.

Most of the tours stop off at Kara Island, the beaches at **Çapa Tatil, Kargı, Bağla,** and **Karaincir,** and the village of **Akyarlar.** Fare is usually between $3.80 and $7.70 per person, depending on the tour. In summer, boats also leave daily from the front of the castle to tranquil **Orak Island** ($30). A less remote and more popular daytrip is the voyage across to **Kara Island,** which offers both beaches and natural springs. Boats leave every two hours from the castle ($3.50 per person round-trip). Departure times are the same to the beach at **Baradakçı,** which has become very popular ($1.50 round-trip). Just 3km outside of Bodrum is **Gümbet Beach,** the most popular sunbathing spot in the area; unfortunately, it is crowded and chaotic. Pensions are expensive here, but **Setaş Camping** (tel. 14 07) may fall within budget range ($3 per person). Because the beach at **Bitez** is narrow, seaside bars have built wooden docks out onto the water, where you can order drinks while you sunbathe. The

beach, around the next large cove from Gümbet, is more peaceful than that at Gümbet but there are no cheap accommodations.

For longer stays on the peninsula, head inland by *dolmuş*. The most accessible
point, **Turgut Reis,** is 18km away from Bodrum. It's a one-dimensional beach-eat-
sleep tourist town, alluring to some because it has the widest beach on the peninsula.
Pensions cost about $3.75 per person.

The most popular spot with Europeans, **Gümüşlük,** at the far western end of the
peninsula, also makes an excellent daytrip from Bodrum. The Turkish name means
"silver-like," from the ancient silver mines that were discovered in the area. Near
the beach lie the ruins of ancient **Myndos,** a fourth-century B.C.E. Carian port impregnable even to Alexander the Great. The site consists of the impressive city wall,
3m thick, and a Roman basilica. The beach here is sandy but quite small. By the
water is **Mindos Pansiyon and Restaurant** (tel. 14 20), which has doubles for $10,
and good seafood at the restaurant. Next door is **Fenerci Motel Restaurant** (tel.
14 20). Try *köpoğlu,* a wonderful concoction of yogurt, eggplant, and potatoes. Doubles $11. Breakfast included. Down the coast, 100m towards Turgut Reis, is **Ali
Baba Camping.** (Sites $1.20 per person.) **Pide Salonu,** at the far right side of the
beach, serves *pide* for 75¢.

**Yalıkavak,** a few kilometers north of Gümüşlük, is similar but not quite as pleasant. The cheapest pension, though far from clean, is above the **Liman Restaurant.**
(Doubles $1.20.) Uncrowded **Gölköy,** on the north coast, seems ideal until you real-
ize there's barely a beach. **Korkmaz Pansiyon** (tel. 14 30) offers spacious and clean
rooms. (Doubles with private bath $13.) Walk down (with the shore on your right)
and turn right at Baba Pension.

You'll probably want to skip the village of Torba, which has turned into a glitsy
vacation resort. **Güvercinlik,** a small harbor town with no beach, lies off the main
road from Bodrum to the north. The spotless **Barka Pansiyon** (tel. 28 50) is the
cheapest in town. (Doubles $12-15. Breakfast included.)

For Turkish students, the most popular way to spend time along the Bodrum
Peninsula is to travel down the so-called **Mavi Yolculuk** ("Blue Voyage") since the
most spectacular stretches of coastline are accessible only by boat. The catch is that
it takes a large group of people (10-12) to make the undertaking financially reasonable ($40-50 per day, varying by month). Also, you must reserve a boat the winter
before (by Feb. or March) and make a down payment. However, don't pass up an
opportunity to be a leach and tag along with an already organized group. Inquire
at travel agencies in Bodrum—just look for the large signs saying *Mavi Yolculuk.*

# *Mediterranean Coast*

Extending east of Marmaris to the Syrian border, Turkey's long Mediterranean
coast offers everything from lively resorts to long expanses of unexplored beaches.
The rugged stretch from Fethiye to Kaş remains unspoiled, while the less scenic
coast between Antalya and Alanya, dubbed the "Turquoise Coast" or the "Turkish
Riviera" by tourist propaganda, draws flocks. Farther east, the coast remains unex-
citing.

During the first and second millennia B.C.E., the area around Fethiye and Kaş
formed the Kingdom of Lycia. Not known for much else, the Lycians placed a heavy
emphasis on burial rites and funerary monuments. Rock tombs are carved into cliff-
sides all along the coast, while almost everywhere you look—in the middle of city
streets, littered around the countryside, and even perched on off-shore islands—you'll see Lycian sarcophagi. The sites of a number of Lycian cities also
punctuate the coast. Most significant among these are the ruins of **Xanthos.**

The best boat connection between the Greek islands and Turkey's Mediterranean
shores is the ferry between Rhodes and **Marmaris,** which leaves daily in summer.
Unfortunately, Marmaris is not among the coastline's typical or attractive resorts.

Allow enough time to explore farther east, and west to the enchanting Datça Peninsula. Distances on the maps are deceiving: Beyond Fethiye, the road winds through mountain terrain and becomes as slow as it is scenic. If you are at all sensitive to motion sickness, reserve seats in advance for the front of the bus and bring your own paper bags. Boats run regularly between Northern (Turkish) Cyprus and the ports of **Taşucu** and **Mersin.** Travel from these ports to the Republic of Cyprus is impossible. Antalya has an international airport with remarkably cheap domestic flights to major Turkish cities (to Istanbul $50). A quick, inexpensive way to get from the Mediterranean coast to Istanbul is a direct bus from Antalya. **Varan Tur** bus company is about 50% more expensive, but for such a lengthy trip, air-conditioning, comfortable seats, a bathroom, and continuous çay are well worth the extra money.

Accommodations along the western segment of the Mediterranean coast are, generally, inexpensive, and excellent seafood restaurants abound. Often in summer, the smaller communities, most notably Kalkan and Kaş, suffer water shortages; in order to ration the supply, the regional government may shut off all water in certain towns from 7am to 6pm. Shut-offs are always announced by local authorities in advance but can last for days.

# Marmaris

Refrain from hasty judgements when evaluating Marmaris, located at the intersection of Turkey's Aegean and Mediterranean coastlines. In summer, Marmaris is crowded with Turkish tourists, but unlike Bodrum, yachters are a minority here (even though the yacht harbor is the most pleasant part of the town). Marmaris' crowded, overdeveloped shoreline and dirty beach are all that most visitors who come via the daily ferry from Rhodes ever see of Turkey, yet some of the most beautiful scenery of the Turkish coastline is only a few hours away. Wooded mountains along the coast and on nearby islands stand as a verdant backdrop to the harbor's deep blue water. You can also travel in the other direction—to Rhodes (see Ferries in Practical Information). Dramatic vistas and secluded beaches in every direction will make you want to linger in Marmaris; catch one of the dolmuş boats that depart every morning for the unspoiled islets.

## Orientation and Practical Information

You're never more than 3 blocks from the sea in Marmaris, one long sprawl of hotels, restaurants, and cafes hugging the shoreline. The most commercialized section of town is just before the fortress, consisting of several blocks of souvenir shops. If you are standing at the tourist information/customs office, the old city and the yacht harbor on your left are the most pleasant parts of Marmaris. Steer away from the the crowded promenade and dirty beach to the right.

**Kordon Caddesi** runs along the main waterfront, becoming **Atatürk Caddesi** at the bend toward the main beach. The shopping bazaar by the fortress consists of **Iskele Sokak** and **Yeni Çarşı.** The latter extends back from the waterfront and eventually becomes **Datça Road** as it leads off up the hill.

**Tourist Office: Kordon Cad.** (tel. 10 35), across from the main ferry dock. They provide maps, suggest excursions, and sometimes help locate a room. English spoken. Open in summer daily 8am-noon and 1-7pm; in off-season Mon.-Fri. 6am-noon and 1-5pm.

**Travel Agencies:** Several along the waterfront, but none is particularly helpful. Tour prices set by the government. Excursions must be arranged on the docks with the skipper.

**Telephone Code:** 6121.

**Bus Station:** Follow the waterfront east to the end, turn inland 1 block, cross the footbridge, and turn left. Buses to Izmir (every hr., $4.60), Istanbul (8 per day, $2.30), Datça (10 per day, $1.50), Fethiye (10 per day $3), and Bodrum (3 per day, $3).

**Ferries:** To Rhodes in summer Mon.-Sat. at 8:30am; in off-season 2-3 per week. Prices set by the government ($20 one-way, $30 same-day round-trip, $40 open round-trip). Passports must be given to the agency the night before departure. Tickets available at any travel agency.

**Hospital:** On Datça Rd. (tel. 10 29).

**Police:** At the corner of Kordon and Fevzi Paşa Cad., below the post office (tel. 14 94). No English spoken; they'll contact the tourist office for a translation.

## Accommodations, Camping, and Food

Most of the reasonable pensions are in the area around the bay and the yacht harbor. You can save money at pensions close to the bus station, outside the harbor; however, you're sure to miss whatever ambience Marmaris posesses if you stay here.

**Kordon Pansiyon,** 8 Kemeraltı Mah. (tel. 47 62). From the post office, walk inland 1 block, turn left and walk 1 more block. Family atmosphere, centrally located. £3.85 per person. Showers included.

**Star Pansiyon,** 28 Ismet Paşa Sok. (tel. 17 77). From the post office, walk 2 blocks inland and turn right. Quite clean, though cramped and a bit noisy. Moderately-priced restaurant below. $3.85 per person. Showers included.

**Yaşar Pansiyon,** across the bridge (tel. 20 77)—the one with "Pansiyon" written in large letters on the 2nd story. Clean rooms with use of kitchen facilities. New rooms and bathrooms upstairs especially nice. $3.25 per person.

**Biricik Pension** (tel. 18 98), behind the old city. From the public fountain (with the mosque to your right) make 2 lefts, 1 right, and follow the signs. Cluttered, haphazardly-built pension. No amenities, little privacy. $3.85 per person.

**Ufuk Pansiyon,** Tepe Mah. Kışayalı Sok. (tel. 14 69), on the road that runs along the bay. Somewhat cramped and dirty and loud, but good location right on the waterfront. $3-3.85 per person.

**Camping:** There are many camping establishments in the area, most of them around the right-hand bay (facing the water). Every 5-10 min. the "İçmeler" *dolmuş* drives around the bay stopping at the campgrounds. **Amazon Camping** (tel. 16 82) charges $2.30 per person, $2.30 per tent.

The better restaurants are scattered throughout the old city, inland from the harbor. For delicious *kebap* and *köfte* (75¢), try **Han Köfte Salonu** (tel. 20 54); from the post office, go ½ block inland and turn right. (Open daily 8am-midnight.) **Ay Yıldız Restaurant** has delicious *adana* (spicy meatballs on a stick) for $1.15. (Open 5am-midnight.) One step up in quality (and price), **Özyalçın Meathouse,** a few doors down from Star Pansiyon, specializes in *kebap* ($1.50). (Open 3pm-midnight.) The restaurants around the yacht harbor serve terrific seafood. The prices are all about the same; expect to pay $5.40 for swordfish or $3 for *kalamar*. For a cheap and tasty snack, try **Mavi Köşe Börekçisi,** next door to the Kordon Pension. Meat or cheese *borek* (filled pastry) costs 45¢.

## Sights

Marmaris itself has little to offer besides a large town beach and a **fortress,** built in 1522 by Süleyman the Magnificent as a military base for his successful campaign against the Crusaders of Rhodes. The alleyways hugging the castle walk form the oldest and most picturesque section of the city. Only 1½km away, **Günnücek National Park** features a small beach and picnic tables set against a forest containing some rare frankincense trees. To reach the park, follow the coastal road past the marina and out of town, across the small wooden footbridge.

The best **beaches** and scenery around Marmaris are accessible only by boat. Lush shrubbery covers the gray rocks of the coast, contrasting beautifully with the blue Bay of Marmaris. Serving the bay, *dolmuş motorları* boats depart from the harbor along Kordon Cad. every morning for a variety of destinations. The drivers are casual about the itineraries. Most boats take the tour that stops at **Paradise Island Beach** and then **Akvaryum,** the Turkish version of an aquarium. You're free to go diving when the boat anchors. The tour then continues to some phosphorous caves and to **Turunç Beach,** across the bay from Marmaris; since electricity was installed in 1979, the beach has become popular with Turkish vacationers. Flanking Turunç to the north and south respectively are **Gölenye Springs,** where the waters reputedly cure intestinal ailments, and the less crowded **Kumlu Beach,** near the scanty remains of an old fortress. Both are convenient by boat. Most of the mouth of the Bay of Marmaris is sealed off by the heavily wooded **Nimara Peninsula,** along the far end of which are the fluorescent phosphorus caves by **Alkoya Point,** another favorite destination for Marmaris' excursion boats. You can sunbathe beneath the mountains at the edge of this fertile valley. Sandwiched between the peninsula and the mainland is the tiny uninhabited island of **Keçi,** which offers a nice view of the surrounding coastline.

# Datça Peninsula

Jutting out from the coastline at Marmaris, the slim Datça Peninsula extends 120km into the sea, a short distance from the Greek island of Symi. Blessed with plenty of fresh water, this jagged spur of land is lush green, and deeply cleaved by stunning blue fjords. The first 50km out of Marmaris are absolutely stupendous, the scenic beauty becoming more awesome with each turn along the brown, mountainous spine of the peninsula. If you're camping, head 30km east of Datça to the extremely well-run **Aktur Camping** (tel. 61 46). Part of a vacation village with a beach, rooms to let, windsurfer rentals, and plenty of tourists, the campsite does allow some privacy amid its pine forest. ($1.50 per person. $1 per tent. 2-person bungalows $46.) The peninsula's **telephone code** is 6145.

The small village of **Datça** lies on the south shore of the peninsula, 80km west of Marmaris. Ten **buses** per day (6am-7pm) run between here and Marmaris. You can also take a boat from Bodrum (in summer only, daily at 9am, sometimes at 5pm also, $11.50). Tickets are available at most travel agencies in Bodrum. The small **tourist office** in Datça can arrange a taxi to Knidos ($23), gives out a creative little blurb on the history of the village, and provides maps. (Open June-Sept. daily 8am-7pm; in winter Mon.-Fri. 8am-noon and 1-5pm.)

## Accommodations and Food

Bloodthirsty mosquitoes invade this paradise each evening. Be sure the pension you stay at is well-equipped with either repellant spray or pellets. From the bus station, walk toward the harbor and make your first left. The **Huzur Pansiyon** (tel. 10 52) lets clean, breezy rooms. ($3.85 per person.) A family atmosphere complements spacious rooms at **Sadık Pansiyon** (tel. 11 96) across from Huzur Pansiyon. ($3.85 per person.) The **Yalı Pension** (tel. 10 59), 20m down the road to Marmaris, has basic, non-descript rooms. ($3.85 per person.) You can freelance camp almost anywhere just outside of town. **Ilıca Camping,** however, has a beach, a restaurant (with late '60s tunes), and bungalows with private bath (bungalows for 2, $7.70; $15.40 for 3). Camping costs $2 per person. The animated owner, Feridun, might take you on a wild boar hunt.

The beachside **Denizatı Restaurant** allows you to escape the crowds and higher prices of the restaurants above the harbor. The food, however, is mediocre. (*Kebap* $1.70, fish $3. Open daily 7am-2am. Disco starts around 10pm.) The **Tavaça Restaurant,** above the harbor, is costlier, but serves excellent seafood dishes. Try to go early to get a seat on the seaside terrace with its priceless view of the harbor. (Fish $5. Open daily 11am-midnight.) For an inexpensive and early breakfast, try **Saray Pastanesi** around the corner from the bus station. They also serve Turkish pastries. (Egg, bread, butter, honey, and tea $1.40. Open daily 7am.)    •

## Knidos

At the tip of the peninsula, **Knidos** was one of the artistic and intellectual centers of the ancient Hellenic world. It was the home of Sostratos, the architect who designed the Pharos lighthouse at Alexandria (one of the "seven wonders of the ancient world"), and of the astronomer Eudoxus, who first calculated the circumference of the earth. The city was renowned in antiquity for its statue of Aphrodite. One of the first female nudes to be sculpted in ancient Greece, the work scandalized Hellenic society, which had until that time confined itself to the naked male form. When the Greeks refused to let the statue remain on their territory, its sculptor Praxiteles offered it to the people of Knidos. Ships would dock here just to view the famous statue housed in the Temple of Aphrodite; a small back door to the temple allowed especially eager visitors to inspect the statue's sensuous behind. Nothing remains of the statue today, but the curves of the ancient metropolis are still discernible.

Once a wealthy port city and one of the original six cities of the Dorian League, Knidos was built in honor of Apollo; the shrine to Apollo that the people of Knidos erected at Delphi is evidence of its prosperity. You can see the two ports on either side of the causeway, as well as the city walls dating from Hellenistic times. Most of the remains are above the east harbor, including two theaters and two temples dedicated to Dionysus and Demeter. Outside this area are two medieval fortresses surrounded by the ancient necropolis of Knidos. The remoteness of the ruins adds to their charm.

Because Knidos is a government-regulated archeological zone, pensions and restaurants are forbidden to operate. There is a small cafe where you can get drinks and a snack. Naturally, there's a good beach out here, but it's tough to reach: 3km before Knidos down a steep hill to a rough and choppy sea.

Best reached by boat from either Marmaris or Bodrum (see Bodrum), Knidos is worth visiting for the breathtaking approach. From Datça, you can proceed to Knidos by jeep, charter boat, *dolmuş*, or thumb. Jeep or taxi costs $23 per carload for the 35-kilometer trip. Boats leave at 9am ($7.70 per person).

# Caunos and Dalyan

On the way to Fethiye you'll pass Lake Köyceğiz, connected to the sea by a river passing through a large swampy area. Along this river are the ruins of the ancient Carian harbor city of Caunos, which, like other ancient coastal cities, has been set back from the water by silting. Tourist officials elsewhere assert that Caunos will soon be as heavily visited as Ephesus. Not only do archeologists turn up new structures each summer, but the natural scenery—mountains, marshes, and greenery—sets this apart from other sites in Turkey. The ruins are accessible only by boat from the nearby town of Dalyan (½ hr., $11.50 round-trip; motorboat fits about 15 people). It is a 10-minute walk up the hill to the ruins. While on the boat, be sure to notice the rock tombs on the cliff above the river. The tombs date from the fourth century B.C.E, though several were re-used during Roman times. Note that the largest one with four columns was never completed.

As you come up the hill in Caunos, look up to see the precariously perched **kale** (castle). From the base of the mountain, you can climb the lofty theater for a panorama of the ruins and distant beach. Facing the theater, the ruins of the **basilica** are on your left. The ancient harbor of Caunos holds the remains of a recently excavated fountain and several temples.

Your boat driver will usually take you to the beach (25 min.), the lake, or the hot springs (both past Dalyan) for an additional $11.50. Make it clear that you want to go to the beach—this beautiful deserted stretch is highly preferable to the swampy, brackish waters of Lake Köyceğiz. It is possible to arrange to camp overnight on the beach and be picked up the next day.

Stretched along a marshy channel, **Dalyan** stays cool in summer but tends to host many mosquitoes. If you choose to stay, you should have no difficulty finding accommodations: It seems like there are more pensions than inhabitants. **Kristal Pansiyon** (tel. 10 49) has extremely friendly management and spotless rooms. ($3 per person.) Make a left down the road that follows the river for the **Sahil Pansiyon** (tel. 11 87), a pleasant establishment located right on the water. ($3 per person. Hot showers and kitchen use included.) At the end of the road (a 15-min. walk) is **Gel-Gör Restaurant Pansiyon** (tel. 10 78), also by the water, with small rooms for $3 per person; the restaurant is excellent as well. The **PTT** is in the center of town. (Open daily 8am-7pm.) Dalyan's **telephone code** is 6116. To reach Dalyan from either Marmaris or Fethiye, take a bus running between the two towns, get off at the town of Ortaca, and take a *dolmuş* from there.

# Fethiye

Most vacationers are in search of something more pristine and picturesque than the tumble of concrete buildings that line the dusty streets in the small, modern port of Fethiye. Telmessos, the ancient Lycian city founded on this spot in the fourth century B.C.E., was known for its astrologists, fortune tellers, and oracles. But the stars crossed in 1958, when the earthquake that leveled Marmaris demolished Fethiye, leaving only the spectacular Necropolis of Telmessos, rock-hewn tombs carved into the cliffs that overlook the city. The modern city was named in memory of the fighter pilot Fethi Bey at the time of the founding of the Turkish Republic.

## Practical Information, Accommodations, and Food

Fethiye is the town closest to Ölü Deniz (14km), one of the Mediterranean's most captivating beaches. **Atatürk Caddesi,** the main avenue running parallel to the harbor, has **banks, pharmacies,** and most of the town's shops. The **tourist office** (tel. 15 27), on the waterfront at the large pier where cruise ships dock, has pension listings and will reserve rooms for you. You can leave your bags at the Tourism Association next door when looking for a room. (Open May-Sept. daily 8am-noon and 1-7pm; Oct.-April Mon.-Fri. 8am-noon and 1-5pm.) The **police** (tel. 10 40), **post office,** and **hospital** (tel. 40 17) are a few blocks east of the tourist office down Atatürk Cad. The **bus station** is at the edge of town on the main road, about 1½ km from the city center. Buses depart to Kalkan and Kaş (12 per day) and Marmaris (10 per day). The *dolmuş* station to Ölü Deniz is behind the PTT. The shop at 19B Fevzi Çakmak Cad. sells English-language newspapers. Fethiye's **telephone code** is 6151.

The town explodes with inexpensive pensions, since supply far exceeds demand, but unless you need to catch an early morning bus or boat, don't spend the night in town.

> **Ülgen Pension,** Cumhuriyet Mah. (tel. 34 91). Follow the signs from the traffic circle or from Atatürk Cad. Clean and friendly. $3.85 per person. Hot showers included.
>
> **Kale Pansiyon,** Cumhuriyet Mah. (tel. 28 69). Signs on Çarşı Cad. lead you up Kale Sok. Beautiful view of the town and the sea. $3 per person. Hot showers included.
>
> **Pınar Pension,** Cumhuriyet Mah. Next door to Kale Pension and identical in every respect. $3.85 per person. Showers 40¢ extra.

**Rafet II,** in a covered alley around the corner from the baths, serves tasty, albeit small, portions. *Trança* (skewered fish) costs $5.40, and is a welcome variation on an old theme. (Open daily 8am-midnight.) For inexpensive *pide,* try **Pizza 74,** near the water, on the traffic circle. (Meat or cheese *pide* 50¢. Open daily 11am-midnight.) Stock up in Fethiye's produce markets to avoid high prices in Ölü Deniz.

## Sights

The road from the north into Fethiye traverses dense pine forests and ascends steep hillsides thick with the sound of crickets and the smell of hot sap. This region was so isolated from the rest of Asia Minor that it insulated Lycian culture. Believed to be the descendants of the pre-Hittite society that lived in Anatolia, the Lycians remained independent until their heroic stand against Cyrus' Persian armies in 545 B.C.E. The tombs of their city, the **Necropolis of Telmessos,** are the most significant vestiges of their culture. The facades of the cliff-hewn tombs resemble Greek temple facades down to the pediments, porticos, and cornices; the tombs themselves are thought to be replicas of Lycian homes. Connected to the road by several flights of steps just off Kaya Cad. (off Atatürk Cad.) is the **Tomb of Amyntas,** which is identified by a fourth-century B.C.E. inscription on the left-hand column. If you climb the approximately 150 steps to the tomb, you'll find a tiny tomb chamber through the opening. You can enter the other tombs as well, though they require a bit of clambering around the rocks. From the necropolis you can see the remains of the **Fethiye Tower,** as well as several of the islands sprinkled about the Bay of Fethiye. Scattered throughout town are a number of sarcophagi. Although most of them date from Roman times, there is an interesting one near the post office that dates from Lycian times. In town, next to the hospital, is an **archeological museum** containing Lycian artifacts from neighboring digs. (Open daily 8am-noon and 1-5pm. Admission 40¢.) Be sure to see the stone inscribed with Aramaic, Greek, and Lycian. One block up from the tourist office and to the right and behind are Fethiye's *hamamlar* (Turkish baths). ($1.50, massage 75¢. Open daily 8am-10pm.)

Fethiye's main beach, **Çaliş,** only 5km to the north, is a relatively uncrowded crescent of sand extending over 3km. From June through September, a little municipal vehicle runs every hour from the harbor, supplemented by *dolmuş* service. Boats run from here to the beaches on the off-shore isle of **Sövalye.** Twelve kilometers farther lie the even less inhabited beaches at **Günlük Bay** and **Katrancı Bay;** either one can be reached by *dolmuş* or by any of the frequent buses to Izmir. **Dirlik Kamp** and **Seketer Kamp** at Çaliş, and **Mokamp Ruzi** at Günlük Bay, have a variety of camping facilities from tent sites to bungalows, including a pension. They are a bit cheaper than the campgrounds at Ölü Deniz (see below). You can camp unofficially at **Katrancı** in the picnic area—a blissful spot surrounded by pines and overlooking a handsome rocky cove.

## Near Fethiye

Excursion **boats** leave the harbor at Fethiye for a variety of destinations. Some provide transport just to nearby beaches for 50¢. The most popular daytrip is the so-called **Twelve Island Tour,** which hops from one to the next of the 12 principal members of the archipelago scattered about the **Bay of Fethiye.** Several of the islands have small beaches, and the boats pause to allow time for swimming and exploration. (Leaves daily 10am-6pm, $15.)

Other popular daytrips include a tour to the historical sites of Xanthos, Letoon, and Patara (see Near Kalkan) for $13 per person (2 per week). There is also a tour to Dalyan and Caunos (3 per day, $13 per person). Inquire about all tours from Fethiye at **Big Tur,** 18 Atatürk Cad. (tel. 34 56; open daily 8am-8pm).

# Ölü Deniz

Posters of the partially enclosed lagoon at Ölü Deniz hang on the walls in almost every Turkish hotel or tourist office. Fourteen kilometers from Fethiye, the spot is a Shangri-La fantasy of endless sandy beach and turquoise water. You won't discover traditional Turkish culture here, but the sun and surf culture thrives. The usual seaside cluster of ice cream stands, souvenir shops, and gaudy restaurants is absent. In their place is a string of well-contained campgrounds, replete with bungalows, hot showers, and cafeterias. Whatever distaste you have for campsites, restaurants, and tourists will fade if you walk along the beach at dawn or dusk, when the scenery claims its full majesty.

The hedonistic ritual is to sun and swim all day (and you can swim 9 months of the year), eat excellent food, and then dance and drink the night away at one of the free discos in some of the campsites; the discos at Derya, Deniz, Sun Kamp, and Moon Disco are open until 2am or 3am.

## Orientation and Practical Information

Even if you're coming from the east, you can most easily reach Ölü Deniz from Fethiye. During the summer, *dolmuş* depart every hour from Atatürk Cad. behind the PTT; they sometimes run as late as 1am. In off-season, *dolmuş* run less often, if at all, but you can always take a shared taxi from the parking lot across from the bus company offices. Agree on a price before the ride. Hitching in summer isn't a bad alternative, especially from Ölü Deniz back into town. From town, you must walk 2km to the turn-off.

The town has **grocery stores** and a **PTT** (by the entrance to the lagoon; open daily 7am-11pm) but little else. You can change money at some of the larger campsites and at the grocery store behind Derya Camping and to the right. Otherwise you must take care of everything else in Fethiye. Ölü Denzi's **telephone code** is 6151.

## Accommodations and Camping

If you stay in Ölü Deniz, you'll probably find yourself in a campsite or bungalow along the beach. Some campsites have bungalow-like buildings that are actually full-fledged motel rooms with furniture and private baths. Taxis are frequently paid to drive prospective customers deep into a campsite, delivering them into the welcoming hands of the proprietors. Insist upon looking around before committing yourself and, of course, don't believe what the employees of one campground tell you about their neighbors. Start from the road and walk to the left (facing the water) to get to most of the recommended places. Listed below are high-season prices; rates should be much lower at other times, and you should be able to bargain easily. The cheapest way to spend the night is on the roof of Deniz Camping or Kum Tur Motel.

**Ölüdeniz Camping** (tel. 12 50), about 300m north from the exit road, past the municipal beach. Don't confuse this with Ölüdeniz Pension on the exit road or Deniz Camping (below). Distant from the center of activity, but set at the edge of the lagoon, with a small beach and plenty of grass. Bathrooms slightly dirty. Also the best place to stay if you don't have a tent. Camping $2.30 per person. 2-person bungalows $6.15.

**Kum Tur Motel** (tel. 14 30), south along the beach almost to the dirt road. No grass. Roof $1.50. Doubles with bath $11.50.

**Deniz Camping** (tel. 16 68), just south of the exit road. Usually crowded, but well-run and centrally located. Roof $1.50. Musty bungalows $11.25. Breakfast included.

## Food

Eating inexpensively at Ölü Deniz is a challenge. Most people eat at the campground cafeterias, where the food is good but overpriced. One hundred meters up the road to Fethiye from the beach, **The Pirate's Inn** serves breakfast and delicious, interesting entrees for cheap prices. (Fish *kebap* $3.85. Prawns $3.85.) You can get good *pide* at Deniz Camping (85¢). The best restaurant for seafood, admittedly a splurge, is at **Han Camping**, just south of the exit road. (Fish *şiş* $3.85.) You can get water at the spring by the military office (past the road to Fethiye before the national park), or buy it bottled.

## Sights

The primary attraction of Ölü Deniz is a mammoth sweep of uncrowded sand that plunges suddenly into sparkling turquoise waters. The beach climaxes at its northwestern tip in the tranquil circle of the **blue lagoon,** from which Ölü Deniz derives both its name and a great deal of its fame. The legend goes that a captain, his son, and Brooke Şhields were fleeing pirate ships in this area. The son told the captain that he knew of a place to hide and directed him towards Ölü Deniz. As they were pulling into the bay, before they could notice the lagoon, the pirates descended upon them. Thinking he had been tricked, the captain murdered his son in a fit of rage, hence creating the name "Ölü Deniz," meaning "dead sea." Brooke, luckily, escaped unblemished.

The area around the lagoon is now a national park that fills with Turkish families in the summer. The waters are surrounded by a band of handsome mountains, with a gentle white sand bar breaking the turquoise surface. Picnic tables and a refreshment stand are nearby. (Admission 25¢ per person.) In the morning, before the heat, you can take the 20-minute walk; later on in the day a *dolmuş* does the circuit. The coastline below the road is magnificent.

Two favorite excursions from Ölü Deniz go to the nearby remains of Greek Christian communities that were compelled to evacuate by the local Muslim population. The larger of the pair is **Kaya,** 10km away and accessible only by a dirt road. Derya Camping offers daily tours to this site and to a waterfall ($15 per person). A group can probably negotiate a cheaper fare by taxi. The more popular destination, tiny **Agia Nikola Island,** has great swimming and a fantastic view of the coast and the remains of a Byzantine basilica. Deniz, Derya, and Sun Camping all organize boat trips (4-5 hr.) for $3. Boats leave daily from the lagoon somewhere between 11am and noon, once a charter group of 10 to 20 is established.

## From Ölü Deniz to Kalkan

Eighty-five kilometers from Ölü Deniz and 22km from Kalkan are the ruins of the ancient Lycian capital of **Xanthos.** Examples of Lycian rock tombs are located at this attractive sight along the former Xanthos River, now called the Eşen. Unwilling to surrender during a revolt against the Persians, the Xanthians gathered all their women, children, and valuables within the city walls, torched it, and fought until their last soldier died. In the second century B.C.E., they fought equally desperately against Rhodes. As a reward for supporting the Romans when they invaded Anatolia, the Xanthians were granted favorable status and their city was fortified. Most of the ruins are from this period except for the sixth-century B.C.E. Lycian **Tomb of the Harpies,** a monolithic column with a funeral chamber on top. This chamber is decorated with a plaster cast of the celebrated frieze depicting the Harpies, mythological winged creatures who could be summoned to destroy invading armies. The original frieze now stands in the British Museum.

As you walk up the dirt path leading to the site, you'll notice the **Roman City Gate** dedicated to Emperor Vespasian, on your left. Farther up the path and also on your left stands the **Roman Theater.** Notice the Tomb of the Harpies and another Lycian tomb at the far end of the theater. From the top of the theater you can see the scanty remains of the **Roman Acropolis** and **Byzantine church.** The theater opens onto the **agora,** at the far end of which stands the **Xanthian Obelisk,** which bears an inscription describing the battles between the Lycians and the Athenians during the Peloponnesian Wars. If you follow the path by the parking lot, you'll pass a **Byzantine basilica;** on the left-hand path is a series of **rock tombs** carved into the hillside, complete with the typical elements of early Greek architecture. The funeral monuments are located near the **amphitheater** and **agora,** both from Roman times.

To get to Xanthos, take any **bus** running between Fethiye and Kalkan or Kaş, and get off at the village of Kınık (Fethiye-Kınık 1½ hr.; Kalkan-Kınık 1 hr.).

Ten kilometers southwest of Xanthos are the ancient ruins of Letoon, which date from the Roman and early Byzantine periods. **Letoon** was a Lycian religious sanctuary, and myth has it that this was the place where the nymph Leto, mother of Zeus' children Artemis and Apollo, fled Hera's wrath. At the site there are three temples each to Leto, Apollo, and Artemis, a memorial function, and a pool. Scholars hope that an inscription found on the Leto Temple in Lycian, Greek, and Aramaic (now in the Fethiye Archeology Museum), will prove as valuable in deciphering Lycian as the Rosetta Stone was in decoding hieroglyphics.

Twenty kilometers farther south (17km west of Kalkan) is the old Lycian port city of **Patara**, once the seat of the Roman governor to Lycia and the site of an oracle to Apollo. Because of silting, the ruins are currently located in a dried-up marsh by the sand dunes and the beach. On the right of the road to the beach, you face the triumphal arch to the city called the **Mettius Modestus Arch,** built in 100 C.E. Surrounding this gate is a **necropolis** with numerous sarcophagi. Five hundred meters before the gate is a large tomb; look across the small ravine and notice the matching tomb tucked into the opposite hill. Walking from the gateway to the sea, you'll pass the ruins of the Roman baths, a Christian basilica, and the **Baths of Vespasian.** To the right (facing the water), you'll come to the **theater,** tucked into a hill of sand. Above this are the remains of another temple. Farther to the right and back from the water is a **granary,** built during the reign of the Emperor Hadrian.

If the ruins at Patara don't float your boat, check out the 18-kilometer-long beach. About 6km down the dirt road from the highway is the new town of Patara, which consists of two excellent pensions, **St. Nikolas Pension** (doubles $7; some with balconies) and **Ali Baba Pension** (doubles with private shower $10.50), and the cheap but dirty **Topaloğlu campground** ($1.50 per tent; bungalow for 2 $4.60). At this point the road forks: The left turn passes the ruins and reaches the main beach after 1.5km; the right fork meanders through olive groves for several kilometers and runs into some immense sand dunes. You can easily walk for 15 minutes and find nobody else around.

At the part of the beach opposite the road you can rent shade makers ($1.15) and purchase cold drinks and sandwiches. Farther back on the road are two restaurants, one of which has bathrooms and showers. You're not allowed to sleep on the beach; those that do hide behind a sand dune so that the night patrol can't see them.

To get to Patara, take any bus going between Fethiye and Kalkan and get off at the turn-off. From there it's 6km to the beach, an easy hitch. Sometimes, *dolmuş* will take you as far as the pensions. A bus goes directly to the beach every morning from Kalkan, and three per morning make the trip from Kaş. It's easier to hitch a ride to the main road when returning and then stop any bus or *dolmuş* going in your direction.

Sorry to debunk the polar propaganda, but this area of Turkey is the real land of **Santa Claus**; he was born right here in Patara in the fourth century. Famous for his annual gift-giving expeditions, he became the Bishop of Myra, and was martyred there. After visiting his birthplace, check out his church and his grave at Myra near the village of Demre. The archeological museum in Antalya houses his relics. Rumor has it that Rudolph drove an antiquated *dolmuş* in this same area.

# Kalkan

Kalkan may be the quintessential Turkish fishing village—an enchanting harbor enclosed by a graceful stone breakwater and surrounded by a huddle of austere stone houses with handsome wooden balconies. Unfortunately, Kalkan is slowly being dogged by Mediterranean coast-style commercialism; the residents of the village realize that they can make far more from shuttling tourists than from fishing. Furthermore, the port is being expanded, a new hotel is being constructed, and quaint little houses are converting to cute boutiques ominously displaying "American Express Cards Welcome" stickers. Recently, some German charter companies established contracts with some of the pensions, making accommodations costlier and tainting the authentic ambience. And there are dogs everywhere.

Kalkan does not have a tourist office. The **PTT** is by the bus stop at the top of the village. (Open daily 7am-11pm.) Kalkan's **telephone code** is 3215.

Rooms in Kalkan are relatively expensive; and there are a few exceptions. By the PTT, the **Yılmaz Pension** (tel. 11 15) is clean but a bit noisy. ($7.70 for 2 or

3 beds and private bath. Roof $2.30 per person.) One block down towards the water, the **Kervan Han Pansiyon** (tel. 10 83) has spartan rooms but a spacious terrace. ($3.80 per person. Terrace $2.30.) Just across the alley is the simple **Cengiz Pansiyon** (tel. 11 96; $3.80 per person). Most restaurants in Kalkan offer all-you-can-eat buffets for the rabidly hungry. Quality varies from place to place and night to night. One of the best deals is the **Köşk Restaurant,** which lays a sumptuous table for $3 per person. Food may also be ordered a la carte for 75¢-$1.50 per dish. Open daily 8am-1am. Strange as it may seem, it's difficult to find fresh fish here in summer. Several bars opened in Kalkan in the past year, most of which are usually empty.

Kalkan is a haberdasher's fairyland. Tailors line the street to the left of the PTT and down to the water. If you can stay a few days, you can get a pair of custommade Turkish-style trousers (the puffy kind). If you're just passing through, you can purchase the same ready-made.

Kalkan proper does not have much to offer in terms of a beach—just a bunch of rocks on the left side of the harbor. Once you pass by this, however, things start looking better. A short climb brings you to a smaller (and usually completely deserted) pebble beach. About 3km along the road to Kaş, a very steep climb beneath a small metal bridge, lies the lovely little sandy beach of **Kaputaş.** The best beaches, however, are back along the coast between Kalkan and Fethiye, especially around Patara.

**Kalkan,** on the main road between Fethiye and Kaş, is serviced by all buses running between the two ports (1½ hr. from Fethiye; ¾ hr. from Kaş). It's fairly easy to hitch a ride between Kalkan and Kaş. The highway between the two cities hugs the coast every inch of the way, with wonderful views of off-shore islands. Before you continue down the coast, though, be sure to do a little star-gazing in Kalkan. According to Herodotus, nearby Halicarnassus is "where the moon and stars are observed nearest in the world."

# Kaş

The amiable fishing village of Kaş, tucked away at the base of a rugged mountain and surrounded on three sides by the Mediterranean, casts an irresistible spell over its visitors. With inexpensive accommodations and restaurants, genuine hospitality, and miles of serpentine coastline, Kaş is one of the coast's most seductive retreats. The road to Kaş winds by calm, glittering inlets dotted with deserted patches of pebble beach. An uninhabited peninsula extends from one side of the town's harbor, curving round to create a calm lagoon edged with rocks, ideal for swimming. You can sip *çay* by the waterfront, explore the mountainous countryside, take a boat trip around the area, visit nearby historical sites, or just seek out a secluded cove and soak up the sun.

## Practical Information

Most of the town's activity centers around the small harbor front along the main street, **Cumhuriyet Caddesi.** At the small waterfront mosque, the street changes its name to Hastane Caddesi and leads down the peninsula, while **Elmaslı Caddesi** branches off to the right and becomes the road to the bus station. By the statue of Atatürk on Cumhuriyet Cad., **Çukurbağlı Caddesi** leads to the PTT. The street going up the hill behind the tourist office is **Uzun Çarşı Caddesi.**

**Tourist Office:** Cumhuriyet Cad. (tel. 12 38). Some staff members speak English. Will refer you to pensions and allow you to leave your bags while you look for a room. Area maps must be purchased at bookstores ($1.15).) Open April 21-Sept. daily 8am-noon and 1-8pm; in off-season Mon.-Sat. 8am-noon and 1-5:30pm.

**Travel Agencies:** Nearly all agencies offer tours to Kekova ($5.75). Tour prices vary slightly, so shop around before you purchase your ticket. Beware of tour packages to other locations (Myra, etc.) that may cancel at the last minute due to insufficient interest. **Andifli Travel** (tel. 19 79), on the waterfront by the mosque, has a tour to the nomadic village of Gömbe

(70km inland), famous for its *kilim* ($13.50, lunch included). **Simena Tourism and Travel Agency**, 7 Uzun Çarşı (tel. 14 16), runs daily trips to nearby attractions and organizes a 3-day "blue voyage" ($110 per person, all meals included). Purchase domestic airline or ferry tickets here; from the Atatürk statue, walk away from the water and make a right up the hill. **Pamfilya Travel and Yachting Agent** (tel. 12 73), on the road uphill with the water on the left of the Atatürk statue, runs excursions and specializes in yacht charters. ($38 per day. Meals included.) Travel to Kastelorizo, offered by local agencies, is neither cheap nor worthwhile, since Greek law prohibits spending the night on a round-trip from Turkey.

**PTT:** Çukurbağı Cad. (tel. 14 36). Open daily 8am-midnight. Telegrams and international telephones open 24 hours. **Telephone code:** 3226.

**Bus Station:** At the end of Elmaslı Cad. Buses to Antalya (every hr., 4½ hr.); Fethiye (2 per hr., 2 hr.); Marmaris (5 per day, 5 hr.); and Izmir (4 per day, 17 hr.).

**Bookstore:** Upstairs at 11 Uzun Çarşı Cad. Good selection of novels and guidebooks in several languages.

**Laundromat:** Antique Pension, down the street from the Kısmet Pension. Wash $3.70.

**Hospital:** Hastane Cad. (tel. 11 85), 500m past the mosque, just before the campground.

**Police:** Tel. 10 24. Continue uphill from the post office and turn left.

## Accommodations and Camping

Kaş' growing popularity is reflected by the diminishing availability and increasing prices of rooms to let. Official pension prices stand at $6.15 per person, $7 with private bath. The pensions listed below post prices that are lower than the municipal rates, except in August.

**Kısmet Pansiyon** (tel. 18 88). Walk up Uzun Çarşı Cad. Turn left at the Lycian tomb. Clean rooms, some with nice views of the harbor. Rooftop lounge has tables, a refrigerator, and a garden canopy. Doubles $7.70. Rooftop beds $1.50.

**Yalı Pension**, Hastane Cad. (tel. 11 32), between the harbor and the ancient theater. Drop a wad of cash for seaside terraces perched above the rocky coastline. Doubles $11.50.

**Mini Pension** (tel. 10 38). Go up Uzun Çarşı Cad., the road behind the tourist office that runs up the hill, then turn left—it's next to the Kısmet Pansiyon. Very clean but small rooms. Pleasant rooftop lounge with a great breeze, plants, and a view of the harbor. Doubles with private bath $11.50.

**Kaptan Pansiyon**, 34 Cumhuriyet Cad. (no tel.) Directly across from the harbor. Clean and spacious, with a family atmosphere. Balconies look out onto the water. Doubles $9.25.

**Camping: Kaş Camping** (tel. 10 50), Hastane Cad., past the theater, on a steep and rocky site. Beautiful location but mediocre facilities. Camping $1.50 per person, with tent $2.30 per person. Bungalows for 2 $6.15.

## Food

The fruit and vegetable **market** is midway between the bus station and the harbor. The local government fixes prices on all food except fish, which can be quite expensive ($5.40-7.70). *Mercan* (red coralfish) and tuna are area specialties. *Dolma*, goulash, and other pre-cooked dishes cost 70¢. *Şiş kebap, köfte,* and other barbecued meat or liver dishes cost $1-1.50.

For breakfast, try the **Noel Baba Pastanesi**, across from the harbor. (Coffee, freshly-squeezed orange juice, and pastry around $1.80.) If you can't swallow more watered-down *Nescafé*, treat yourself to filtered coffee (75¢) at the **Sandwich Shop**, across from the PTT. They usually offer scrumptious pastries (50¢) and sandwiches. (Open daily 9am-9pm.)

**Aslı Restaurant**, the first restaurant in a covered alley across from the harbor on Cumhuriyet Cad. Fill a plate with vegetarian appetizers for $1.50. Entrees include fresh seafood (prices vary daily), *şiş kebap* ($1.50), and chicken ($2.30). Open daily 8am-midnight.

**Eriş Restaurant,** next to the tourist office. Tablecloths, music, fancier atmosphere than the competition, and the largest variety of food. Good *dolma* and desserts. Meals from $5-6 with beer. Open daily 11am-midnight.

**Çınar Kebap Restaurant,** at the corner of Uzun Çarşı, near the tourist office. A good place for a quick meal—though not the best quality. *Kebap* or *adana* $1.50. Open daily 8am-10pm.

## Sights

The main **beach** of Kaş is neither large nor sandy, but it is removed and usually uncrowded. Walk 15 minutes along the dirt road off Hükümet Cad. The rocky shore hinders swimming, but you might try off the rocks to the right of the harbor—just walk past Kaş Sea Tour and up the road. Better swimming, warmer water, and a more intense landscape await you in the opposite direction from Kaş, following Hastane Cad. along the peninsula. On the way you'll pass the photogenic ruins of a lovely little **Hellenistic theater.** The only ancient structure in Kaş nearly intact, it overlooks the sea from a solitary elevated perch, commanding an excellent view of the Greek island of Kastelorizo. Climb to the topmost level to admire the landscape and test the resonating acoustics.

Continuing along the peninsula beyond Kaş Camping, you'll come upon the calmly shimmering waters of the inlet formed by the peninsula. Baked to a warm temperature in summer and stocked with myriad exotic fish, the peaceful lagoon is good for swimming or snorkeling. After the 20-minute walk from town, the road dips to meet the water at an ideal spot for off-shore swimming. Or climb down from the road and pick a spot of your own—but beware of the sea urchins inhabiting the rocks just off-shore and wear shoes. Farther along, the coast is virtually deserted except for a handful of nudists attracted by the extreme privacy (which you have disrupted) of the area. Women should pick a spot carefully: When the local fishing boats discover a woman sunbathing nude, they head back to town and promptly return with a full load of spectators.

If you are interested in more active sightseeing, a trail leads from town up to the summit of the neighboring mountain. The one-hour hike is rewarded by the expansive view of Kaş and the surrounding coast, as well as a variety of impressive **Lycian rock tombs** carved into the jagged rock faces of the neighboring cliffs. Look for the trail that runs approximately underneath the electrical lines.

## Near Kaş

Excursions from Kaş may take you to Lycian and Roman remains, nearby beaches and sea caves, and a Greek island.

The farming community of **Demre,** an hour's bus ride east of Kaş on the road to Antalya, sits on a smooth, fertile plain sandwiched between the mountains and the sea. The town itself is dusty and unattractive, but several interesting sites lie nearby. A few minutes' walk from the bus stop is the **Tomb of St. Nikolas,** housed in a well-preserved fourth-century Byzantine basilica. The saint is better known to Turks as Baba Noel, and to North Americans as Santa Claus. He was buried here in Demre. In 1087, thieves plundered his tomb, escaping to Bari, Italy with his bones and that funny red cap. Today, the burial chapel in the basilica houses his marble **sarcophagus,** intact except for the gaping hole bored by his Italian kidnappers. The entrance to the basilica is covered with faded frescoes of the saints dating from the fourth century. St. Nikolas is pictured in the lower niche immediately to your right as you enter. Each December 6, the saint's birthday is celebrated with a commemorative three-day festival and symposium. (Basilica open daily 8:30am-7pm. Admission 75¢.) In Demre, stay at **Noel Pansiyon** (tel. 23 04), which has clean, decent rooms and friendly management. (Doubles $7.70.)

The ancient remains of **Myra,** 2km inland from Demre, feature some notable **Lycian rock tombs** and the remains of a **Roman theater.** Taxis gladly take you to the site, but walking or hitching is easy. The only pension here is **Likya Pansiyon** (tel. 25 79), with a lovely vine-covered terrace and rooms that look onto the ruins. (Doubles $7.70.) By Demre's harbor is **Andriake** (Çayağzı), where the sandy beach borders more Lycian and Roman ruins.

The headliner around Kaş is the foray to nearby **Kekova,** a partially submerged Lycian city about 2 hours east. You'll visit by boat some Byzantine ruins, Kekova, and two nearby fishing villages, one of which lies under a cliff honeycombed with Lycian tombs and a hill crowned with a half-ruined castle. Both are surrounded by a dozen or so huge Lycian sarcophagi. Notice the tombs leaning on the sides of some of the village homes.

The masses also visit the **Blue Caves,** home of the Mediterranean's only colony of seals. The water's phosphorescence is extraordinary. It is easiest to enter in the mornings before the sea becomes rough. Nearby, 2km after Kalkan, is **Doves Cave,** home to hundreds of wild doves; you can get here only by swimming. Opposite this cave, the wide **Güvercinlik Cave** spouts a cold underwater stream.

You might also head north to the mountain village of **Gömbe,** famous for its *kilim* and trout farms. Choose your fish from one of the pools and watch it being cooked. Tours cost $13.50, but you'd do just as well taking a *dolmuş.*

Though less convenient to Greece, the coast east of Kaş has a great deal to offer. At **Finike,** the road leading inland to Elmalı and Korkuteli passes the Lycian site of **Limyra** (after 12km), where you'll find more **tombs** set into a rock face above a Roman **acropolis.** The resort of **Kemer** is about 80km closer to Antalya, and a nice stop, with miles of fine beaches and some good seafood restaurants.

# Antalya

Poised between jagged mountains and the azure sea, Antalya is a rough but scenic four and a half-hour bus ride from Kaş. You'll probably stay here to visit the nearby Roman cities of Perge, Aspendos, and Side, but Antalya itself is worth a short visit. Less touristed and more Turkish in character than other Mediterranean cities, Antalya allows a visitor to meander through the labyrinthine streets of the **old city,** enjoy a dinner near the harbor, and swim at the beaches to the east and west of the city. The **bus station** is some distance inland. From there, walk down Kâzım Özalp and turn right onto Cumhuriyet Cad. to find the **municipal tourist office** (tel. 152 71), below the Atatürk statue (*Atatürk Heykel*). They provide maps and can help you with accommodations and tours of nearby sites. (Open in summer only Mon.-Fri. 8am-noon and 1:30-5:30pm.) The **main tourist office** (tel. 117 47) is west from here, along Cumhuriyet Cad. (Open in summer daily 8am-7pm; in off-season 8am-6:30pm.) Next door is the **Turkish Airlines Office** (open Mon.-Sat. 8:30am-8pm, Sun. 8:30am-5:30pm), with frequent flights from Antalya to Istanbul ($50), Izmir ($50), and Ankara ($46), as well as to Munich and London (60% student reduction). The airport is 10km away. Buses marked "Hava" leave frequently from the Atatürk statue (60¢). Farther down Cumhuriyet Cad., at the corner of Anafartalar Cad., is Selekler Çarşişi, a mall with clothing stores and the **Ardik Bookstore** (tel. 703 56), which sells English-language newspapers and books. (Open daily 8am-8pm.) A block down Anafartalar on the left you'll find the **PTT.** (Open 24 hours.) Antalya's **telephone code** is 311. About 500m west, you'll find the **Turkish Maritime Lines** office, 40 K. Evren Bulvarı Cad. (tel. 111 20), agents for the *Akdeniz,* which stops in Antalya once per week in summmer and also stops in Istanbul, Dikili, Izmir, Marmaris, Kekova, Alanya, Fethiye, Bodrum, Kuşadası, Izmir, and Istanbul. (From Antalya to Fethiye 9000TL; Bodrum 11,000TL; Izmir 14,000TL; Kuşadası 14,000TL; and Istanbul 20,000TL; 10% student reduction.) The **police** (tel. 283 61) are based at the yacht harbor and speak English. The **hospital's** (Medical University) telephone is 120 54. The government municipality (tel. 115 82) can also help with complaints or problems.

If you're visiting Antalya for any length of time, stay in the old city, southeast of the yacht harbor, with meandering alleys and charming wood and plaster homes from Ottoman times. **Adler Pansiyon** (tel. 178 18), in a beautiful Ottoman house at Barbaros Mah. and Civelek Sok., is located in the heart of the old city. From

Hadrian's Gate, take a right on Imaret Sok. and then a left on Civelek Sok. (Doubles $7.70.) **Tunay Pansiyon** (tel. 246 77) is a little musty, but has clean bathrooms. To get there, descend from the clock tower towards the water. (Doubles $9.25.) The bohemian **Sima Pansiyon,** east on Cumhuriet Cad. and left after Ismet Paşa Cad, offers budget accommodations in dorms ($3) or on the roof ($2.30). There is a row of cheap restaurants in a bustling alleyway at the intersection of Atatürk Cad. and Cumhuriyet Cad. From the bus station, walk to the main road, Kâzım Özalp Cad., and continue 1 block down to the left.

Founded as Attaleia in the second century B.C.E. by King Attalos II of Pergamon, Antalya used to be surrounded by walls built by the Greeks and later fortified by the Byzantines and Seljuks. You can use the **Tower of Hırdırlık,** near the sea and the city park, and the **clock tower** as orientation points. A few blocks behind the clock tower stands **Hadrian's Gate,** built of marble in 130 C.E. to commemorate the visit of Emperor Hadrian. Nearby is the **Kesik Minare** (broken or truncated minaret), which was transformed from a Byzantine church by the Seljuks. The structure was actually built as a Roman temple before it was converted into a three-nave basilica (4th century B.C.E.). To the left of the clock tower is the curious fluted minaret of **Yivli Minare Cami** (Alâeddin Mosque), also converted from a church to a mosque during the Seljuk regime. The **archeological museum's** well-presented exhibits range from pre-historic times to the Turkish Republic. The museum also displays important finds from Perge, Aspendos, and Side. It is located 1km from the town's center, west along Kenan Evren Bul. (Open Tues.-Sun. 9am-noon and 1:30-6pm. Admission 75¢.)

## Near Antalya

The closest beach to Antalya is **Konyaaltı Beach,** just west of the archeological museum. Though campgrounds abound here, the area has become a shanty town of permanent campers, which detracts from its privacy and scenery. From any *dolmuş* stop in town, take *dolmuş* marked "Konyaaltı Liman." Thirteen kilometers in the opposite direction is the sandier, less crowded, and deeper **Lara Beach.** The best campground here is **Uzur Camping.** ($2.70 per tent.) *Dolmuş* leave every 15 to 20 minutes from the central *dolmuş* station on Ali Çetinkaya Cad. (actually the continuation of Cumhuriyet Cad. to the east) for *Lara Plajı* (20 min.). About 8km west of Antalya is a small pebble beach and park at **Ulaş.** Antalya is known for its spectacular **waterfalls** (*Düden*). The upper falls lie 11km to the north, accessible by *dolmuş* (½ hr.); the smaller lower falls are at the sea by Lara Beach.

Thirty-four kilometers northwest of Antalya, the ruins of **Termessos** sit atop a mountain in a dense woodland forest. Because of its impregnable location, Termessos was spared the ravaging of Alexander the Great. The ruins include a **Stoa of Attalos,** a theater, a bouleuterion, a **Temple of Artemis,** and some tombs.

# From Antalya to Alanya

East of Antalya stretches the former Roman province of **Pamphylia.** A guidebook proves very helpful when visiting the ruins: The local publication *Pamphylia: An Archeological Guide* ($3) is more informative and better translated than most. You can take an organized tour of the sites from one of the travel agents ($11.50), or rent a car in Antalya if you are in a large group (around $20 per day, plus mileage). The three principal sites near Antalya—Perge, Aspendos and Side—may be visited in a day-trip, provided you start early. Bring a hat and plenty of water.

## Perge and Aspendos

The residents of **Perge** (16km from Antalya) believed that their city was founded by Greek heroes after the Trojan War, but the city did not earn its place in history until the appearance of Alexander the Great. Initially situated at the Acropolis on the east side of the site, Perge gradually spread to the south, becoming enclosed by walls (still visible) during Hellenistic times. When Alexander the Great swept through Asia Minor, the citizens of Perge prudently sided with him and were spared. Experts believe that Artemis was worshiped here—the temple to her appears on coins from Perge, but has not yet been located. Don't worry about crowding in the **stadium;** there's room for 12,000 people. On the east side under the seats were 30 chambers—10 led spectators to the area, while the remainder were used as shops (notice the shopkeepers' names inscribed on the walls). The long colonnaded avenues are all in good condition and give a vivid sense of what the city was like during its heyday in the second and third centuries. (Site open in summer daily 8am-7pm; in off-season 8am-5:30pm. Admission 75¢.) To get to Perge from Antalya, take a *dolmuş* to Aksu from the central *dolmuş* station, then walk 2km.

Perhaps the most impressive ancient theater in Anatolia graces the ruins of **Aspendos,** 49km from Antalya. Founded by colonists from Argos, Aspendos was built as a river port and naval base. The **theater** (15,000 seats) is one of the best preserved in the world—even the marble covered stage remains almost completely intact. Built in the second century C.E., the theater was covered with a wooden roof, and the five doors in its lower walls were used for the actors' entrances and exits. During Seljuk reign it was converted into a palace and covered with green and blue tiles. The **aqueducts** that brought water from 30-40km away still stand. (Site open in summer daily 8am-7pm; in winter 8am-5:30pm. Admission 75¢.) To get to the turn-off from Antalya, take the Manavgat *dolmuş* 5km past the village of Serik. From the turn-off, the ruins are another 4km; *dolmuş* run infrequently, but taxis are available. It's best to hitch a ride on one of the many tractors.

## Side

Side's ruins are adjacent to the beaches—considering the summer heat, this is a feature not to be overlooked. The name *Side* is derived from the ancient Anatolian word for pomegranate, which symbolized abundance. Like other cities of Pamphylia, Side was colonized by Greeks, in this case from the ancient Aegean coast city of Kimi, in the seventh century B.C.E., but most of the ruins date from Roman times. After suffering constant pillaging by pirates and Arab invaders in the eighth and ninth centuries, Side's inhabitants simply gave up protecting themselves and abandoned the city. The ancient site was first resettled in the 1890s by Turkish refugees from Crete. You may notice a Greek ambience and even hear some of the older people speaking Greek. Today, Side is a favorite vacation spot for people from Ankara, and is thus crowded and touristy.

The **tourist office** (tel. 12 65) is located on the Manavgat road about 1½km out of town. They provide free maps, have accommodations listings and will keep your bags while you look for a room. (Open in summer daily 8am-7pm; in winter Mon.-Fri. 8am-noon and 1:30-5:30pm.) Side's **telephone code** is 3213.

By Turkish standards, accommodations are expensive (doubles $11.50), but quite comfortable. Your best bet is to try the **Kale Pension** (tel. 12 66), the first left off the main drag, then the next left. Clean rooms open onto a lovely foliated terrace. (Doubles $7.70, with private showers $11.50.) The two nicest, **Özden Side Pansiyon** (tel. 11 37; bungalows for 2 $9.25; treehouse terrace $2.75) and **Winter Palas** (tel. 11 97; bungalows for 2 $9.25), contain lounges and lush gardens. Walk downhill on the main drag and turn left at the Jungle Bar. There are numerous campsites on the road from Manavgat to Side. About 200m to the east stretches the best beach in Side (you'll have to walk to the end to avoid the crowds), an ideal place to sack out—you can even roll out a sleeping bag in one of the empty wooden shacks. The outdoor shower at the Nymfeum Disco is convenient.

You'll have no problem finding the ruins, which are well-marked. The Hellenistic walls to the city are large and impressive (1.7m wide, 10m high). When you enter Side, on the left you'll notice the **memorial fountain-Nymphaeum.** The marble facade of the fountain used to depict punishments administered to those who committed sexual sins or sins against the gods. The second-century C.E. theater of Side is impressive and unique; unlike other theaters that were constructed into the hills, this one is built on level ground using arches. It is also the largest in the area, seating 25,000 people, though not as well-preserved as that of Aspendos. Other ruins include two agoras—one with a temple to the Goddess of Tyche (Good Fortune) and a public lavatory at the southwestern corner; the other, the State Agora, with many statues of gods and a central hall for imperial worship. The site is 1½km from the city and can be reached by following the beach to the west. The ancient Roman baths now house a delightful **archeological museum.** Among its treasures are a bust of Hermes from the second century C.E., a sculpture garden of amphorae and sarcophagi, and the Three Graces. (Open in summer daily 8:30-11:45am and 1:30-5:15pm; in off-season Tues.-Sun. only. Admission 75¢.)

A few direct **buses** go daily to Side from Antalya and Alanya; otherwise take one running between Antalya and Alanya (about 1 per hr.) and get off at the turn-off near **Manavgat,** recognizable by its barber-pole minaret. From here it's an easy dolmuş ride to Side (3km). The waterfalls at Manaugat are well worth a stop. There's a fine beach at **Yeşilköy,** about 18km past Side towards Alanya, where the Alarahan River flows into the sea.

# Alanya

Alanya, an hour east of Manavgat, is an unabashed resort town teeming with tourist shops and hotels. Most of the tourists here are either Turkish or German. The town lies at the base of a large promontory, dominated by the walls of the thirteenth-century **Alâeddin Castle,** and flanked on both sides by rather unappealing beaches; better beaches lie farther out along the peninsula. The *otogar* **(bus station)** is somewhat out of town. Usually the bus will stop along the main coastal road after going to the *otogar* (if coming from the west); tell the driver you want to go into Alanya just to be sure. From the main coastal road, walk east (left facing the water) past the **PTT** (open 24 hours), then take the next right into town. Alanya's **telephone code** is 3231. Out towards the dock, you'll find the **tourist information office** (English spoken), which gives out a map of the town. (Open daily 8am-6pm.) Across the street, the small but well-organized **Museum of Alanya** houses a collection of coins and ceramics, old carpets, a bronze statuette of Herakles from the second century C.E., and an elaborate wooden guest room from Alanya.

From the museum, take a left and then the right fork up the hill to **Yayla Palas** (tel. 10 17), a simple place, but very clean and cheap. (2500TL per person. Showers included.) Rooms overlooking the bustling street are noisy until the music stops between midnight and 1am. Also try the **Hotel Ankara Palas,** 18 Müftüler Cad. (tel. 10 14; doubles 5000TL). Inquire at the tourist office about camping; there is no permanent campground in Alanya, so available sites change frequently. The restaurants along the water have atmosphere, but dinners can quickly add up to 2500TL. Less expensive restaurants can be found back in town. A cheap place to breakfast is **Cüce,** on the second parallel road in from the shore.

The historical sites of Alanya (ancient **Korakesion**) are all located on the peninsula. Most of the sites date from the Seljuk period, although the city was also important in Hellenistic times and was used as a refuge by pirates for a time during the Roman period. The present castle, consisting of three walls, was constructed by Seljuk Sultan Alâeddin Keykubat I after he procured Alanya from the Byzantines and converted it into a powerful naval base. The Mecdüddin cistern (reservoir) still delivers rainwater to houses within the inner castle. Facing the eastern side, the **Red Tower,** a five-story octagonal structure, was built in 1225 C.E. to protect Alanya's valuable shipyard. On all sides are holes, through which molten pitch or boiling oil were poured on enemies. The entrance is on the west side.

Just slightly north of the Red Tower is a dockyard where you can rent **boats** to explore the caves and beaches around the peninsula. Beginning in the west by Damlataş Beach is the **Damlataş Cave,** which can also be reached by the road that runs along the beach. This cave is electrically lit and is famous for its curative effect on asthmatic patients. The other caves and small beaches are only accessible by boat.

South of Damlataş Cave are **Kleopatra Beach,** the phosphorus **Blue Caves, Lover's Cave,** and **Pirate's Cave.** Twenty kilometers from Alanya, back towards Antalya, is **Incekum,** with a clean, clear sandy beach surrounded by a pine forest (camping and picnic facilities available). Take a dolmuş to Manavgat and ask to be let off at Incekum. From Alanya, buses run to Antalya every two hours.

Five **buses** per day make the seven-hour trip to Silifke, stopping in Anamur en route. The area east of Alanya is the beautiful ancient land of **Cilicia,** through which migrating peoples and invading armies have passed throughout history. Antony gave this region to Cleopatra as a wedding gift. The Byzantines built many castles and forts here, but they were conquered by the Arabs and Seljuk Turks; the latter finally gained control of the region in 1077 C.E.

## Anamur

If you're traveling east along the coast, break up the trip in Anamur. Set in a plain ringed by the Taurus Mountains, Anamur is one of the most relaxing beach resorts on the coast. It is graced by the Roman city of Anamurium, a medieval castle (*kale*), and miles of sandy beach. From the *garaj,* walk 200m up the hill to the **tourist office** (English spoken), which distributes maps of Anamur and *dolmuş* information. (Open daily 8am-6pm.) Farther up the street on the left is the **PTT.** The *dolmuş* station is 200m up from the tourist office. *Dolmuş* leave for the Kösekbükü caves, 17km away, and for Anamurium, 7km away on the beach. To the right (with your back to the sea), the *dolmuş* leave for Iskele Beach, 3km away. Continuing farther to the right is the Baş *dolmuş* station for rides to the *kale,* 7km away.

Right on the water's edge, the **Kale** at Anamur, a singular example of fortification, is thought to have been constructed by the Romans in the third century C.E. The present structure dates from the Crusades, though it was also used by the Karamak and Ottoman Turks. Twelve kilometers away, also on the beach, is **Anamurium,** an ancient Roman city originally built by the Phoenicians. You can camp at either **Yalı** or **Dragon** campgrounds, on the shore below the town.

## Taşucu and Silifke

The scenic road from Anamur to Taşucu is punctuated with pine forests and cliffs plunging onto sandy beaches. Between Anamur and Taşucu, right before Yanişli and after Sıphalı, is a deserted beach. Eight kilometers south of Taşucu in Boğsak is **Gürbüzler Camping,** on a long strand. Six kilometers closer to Taşucu, but without sand, is **Akçakıl Camping** (tel. 14 51; $3 per person with tent, breakfast and private facilities included; bungalows for 2 $12). There are no buses to Boğsak, so you'll have to hitchhike or take a taxi from Taşucu ($2.50).

**Taşucu** is the beach-front port for larger Silifke, and a recently built concrete tourist town. Stay here only if you plan to catch a ferry to Northern Cyprus. On the waterfront, the **tourist office** (tel. 14 99) distributes maps and ferry information. (Open April-Sept. Mon.-Fri. 8am-noon and 1:30-5:30pm.) Across the street is the **PTT.** (Open daily 8am-noon.) Taşucu's **telephone code** is 7593. Also in the harbor area are the three ferry boat offices. **Liberty Ferryboat** (tel. 17 17 in Taşucu; (581) 549 77 in Girne) has a boat leaving Taşucu for Girne every Monday, Wednesday, and Friday at noon, returning Sunday, Tuesday, and Thursday at 11am. **Ertürk Ferryboat** (tel. 10 33 in Taşucu; (581) 523 08 in Girne) has service on alternate days (Tues., Thurs., and Sun. at 11pm, returning Mon., Wed., and Fri. at 10am). Both boats cost $8 one-way (students $4.50), $11.50 round-trip (students $7), plus a small port tax. You can cut transit time by taking the **hydrofoil** service offered by **Barbaros Kıbrıs Express** (tel. 14 34 in Taşucu; (581) 535 54 in Girne). Hydrofoils depart Monday, Wednesday, and Friday, and cost $16 one-way (students $12), $29 round-trip (students $23). To reach the sandy, crowded **beach** at Taşucu, walk east from the harbor. On the way, if you pass behind Barış Pansiyon, you will find the noisy but clean **Sahil Pansiyon** (tel. 10 52); $3 per person). **Sema Pansiyon** (tel. 12 41), farther east and a block inland, has spacious balconies but won't take groups of men. ($3.50 per person.)

**Silifke,** 10km from Taşucu, is a crowded, dusty town that could be safely by-passed, except if you need its bus connections to points east, west, and inland. Mersin is two hours away. You can also travel to Anamur (3½ hr.), Antalya (9 hr.), and Alanya (7 hr.). **Buses** leave from the station for Mersin every 20 minutes, making stops at the beaches along the way.

With your back to the bus station, the **Museum of Silifke** is 200m to the right. (Open daily 8am-5:30pm. Admission Mon.-Fri. 80¢, Sat.-Sun. 40¢.) If you make a left after walking down from the bus station, you'll come to a hill where the ruins of the city are located. Founded by Seleucus I, General of Alexander the Great and military head of Asia Minor and Syria, Silifke was originally named Seleucia on the Calycadnos. Before being captured by the Ottoman Turks in 1471, the town was successively controlled by the Isaurians, the Arabs, the Byzantines, the Armenians, and the Seljuks. **Silifke Castle,** which offers a hilltop view of the brown town, was constructed in the twelfth century by the Armenians to defend against the Seljuks. Crossing the Göksu River (Calycadnos in ancient times) is a modern stone bridge built atop the one constructed by Roman Emperor Vespasian and his sons.

The best place to stay in Silifke is the **Hotel Akdeniz,** 95 Menderes Cad. (tel. 12 85); walk 1km to the left from the bus station, past a second century C.E. Temple of Jupiter. These clean rooms can be effortlessly bargained down from $4 for doubles, or $6 for doubles with private facilities. The **tourist office** (tel. 11 51), on the side of the river opposite the castle, distributes maps, bus information, and general information sheets, and will help you find accommodations. (English spoken. Open daily 8am-6pm.) On the same side as the castle you'll find the **PTT.** (Open 24 hours.) *Dolmuş* to Taşucu leave across the street from the PTT. Silifke's **telephone code** is 7591.

Three kilometers from Silifke in the village of Meryemlik is the underground **Church of Saint Thecla.** After St. Thecla heard St. Paul preaching in Konya, she decided to convert to Christianity and devote her life to leading others toward a pious life. She moved to a cave in Silifke where she performed various miracles, but was later murdered by robbers. After his conversion to Christianity, Emperor Constantine constructed a basilica over the cave of St. Thecla. Nearby is a second basilica built by Emperor Zeno. Take the *dolmuş* to Taşucu and get off at a small cafe where there is a sign for *Aya Takla;* then walk 1km to the church. (Open daily 8am-5:30pm; if closed, ask around for the *bekçi,* or guard.)

# From Silifke to Mersin

The coast east of Silifke contains several newly built boomtowns that welcome invasions of Turkish tourists every weekend. The beach at Susanoğlu (15-20 min. from Silifke) would be perfect if it weren't so crowded. Nearly identical campsites line the beach here. Farther towards Mersin is **Narlıkuyu.** A subterranean river here dumps cold, fresh water into the sea with such force that it pushes the salt water back; you can sometimes see animals lapping it up. At the water's edge is a Roman bath containing an extremely well-preserved mosaic of the Three Graces.

Two kilometers from the main road are the lovely caves of **Cennet ve Cehennem** (Heaven and Hell). The bus drivers have a nasty habit of dropping you 5km past the turn-off, so insist on having the bus stop at the Narlıkuyu Museum and walk or hitch 3km uphill to the caves. The grandest of the three caves is Heaven; the wishing well cave (in Turkish, Dilek Mağrası) is interesting but ruined by graffiti; and Hell is simply the pits. According to legend, the cave which the Turks call Heaven is where Mother Earth was impregnated by Tartarus and as a result gave birth to Typhon, a grotesque monster with serpents for arms and legs. This great Typhon was then imprisoned in the 120-meter abyss of the Hell cave. You need a lamp (and consequently a guide—they own the lamps) for the first two caves, and can arrange an impromptu tour of all three for only 1000TL after some haggling. The mouth of Heaven is situated at the base of a gorge behind a twelfth-century Armenian chapel. The wet clay path is super slippery and the young boys acting as guides may leave you scrambling in a suffocating envelope of darkness. The descent into the wishing well is a 30-meter plunge down a rusty, winding staircase. Unfortunately, there are no accommodations at the caves, and those in Narlıkuyu start at $5 per person.

The next town towards Mersin is **Akkum Beach.** Try to find a room in a private home (about $2.50), or stay at **Zorlu Pansiyon,** just opposite the beach, with hot water, a balcony view, and rooms with private facilities. ($3 per person.)

At the resort town of **Korykos,** the Castle of Korykos stands on the beach opposite the ruins of **Kız Kalesi** (Maiden Castle), a sea castle situated on an islet offshore. According to legend, a king was told that his daughter would die of a snake bite, so he imprisoned her in this castle out at sea. But someone brought her a basket of figs with the snakes concealed, and the prophecy was fulfilled. The two castles used to be connected by a sea wall, but this no longer exists, so the only way to get to the sea castle is to swim or take one of the small boats that shuttle back and forth. Pensions abound in town, and there are campsites nearby, but they are usually crowded, especially on weekends. Farther toward Mersin in the town of **Kocaha-sanlı** is a beautiful government-run campsite and pine-shaded picnic area. There's plenty of beach here to absorb the crowds.

Thirty kilometers north of Silifke are the ancient ruins of Olba-Diocaesarea and Ura at **Uzuncaburç.** To reach the site, take one of the infrequent *dolmuş* that leave from across from the tourist office in Silifke. Ancient **Olba**("happy city") became famous when Seleucus I, the same man who founded Silifke, constructed what is today the best-preserved **Temple of Zeus** in Asia Minor. For about 100 years, the city was then ruled by priest-kings. When the Romans conquered Olba, they renamed it **Diocaesarea.** The site also includes a theater, an ancient fountain (still used today by locals), and a first-century B.C.E. **Temple to Psyche,** of which five Corinthian marble columns remain. In Byzantine times, the temples were converted into churches and new Byzantine churches were constructed; the remains of two of these lie south of the theater and a third, the **Stephanos Church,** is located 200m from the high tower. Farther east is the city of Ura. Inquire at the tourist office in Silifke for their free guidebook to these sites.

# *Mersin*

Turkey's largest Mediterranean port and gateway to Northern Cyprus, Mersin offers tourists the standard amenities of a large city as well as transportation to, and a consulate of, Northern Cyprus. The **tourist office** (tel. 163 58), staffed by a helpful multilingual crew with maps and brochures of Turkey and Turkish Cyprus, is located by the Turkish Maritime Lines Agency at the harbor. (Open daily 8:30am-5:30pm.) There is another tourist office at the bus station. (Hours vary.) The **PTT** lies ¾km west of the main tourist office. (Open 24 hours.) **THY** offices are located in the concrete arcade by the Big Mosque. The **train station,** 2 blocks in from the harbor near the hospital, services points east to Adana. Intercity **buses** leave from the station 2km north of the downtown area on Zeytinli Bahçe Cad. Municipal buses serve the length of the city along the waterfront and also run from the station to the waterfront. Mersin's **telephone code** is 741.

**Hotel Doğan,** 11 Büyük Hamam Sok. (tel. 217 50), a few blocks inland from the Big Mosque, officially charges $3 for doubles (no showers); bargain. The hotel is across from a *hamam,* or bathhouse. (Men only. Open 5am-10pm. Bath 80¢. Massage 60¢.)

Ferry tickets to Magosa, Northern Cyprus can be purchased at the **Turkish Maritime Lines** across from the tourist office ($18, 10% reduction for students). Ferries depart every Monday, Wednesday, and Friday at 10pm (10 hr.). The Friday ferry continues to Lattakia, Syria ($21, 10% student reduction). If you plan to enter

Greece sometime later, don't let customs officials in Northern Cyprus stamp your passport. You can request that officials stamp a separate sheet of paper that can be detached from your passport upon departure. If these precautions are not taken, Greek customs officials will bar your entry upon seeing Turkish Cypriot stamps on your passport. Policy concerning travel to Northern Cyprus changes frequently, so you should inquire at the **Consulate of Northern Cyprus,** Istiklâl Cad. and 153 Sok., 4th floor (tel. 162 28 or 158 20), in downtown Mersin.

East of Mersin is the city of **Tarsus,** supposedly established by Seth, son of Adam. Tarsus is famous as the birthplace of St. Paul. Most of the ancient city ruins, however, lie hidden beneath the modern city.

# Antakya

Antakya dominates the fertile Turkish province of Hatay, surrounded on two sides by Syria; it was annexed to Turkey by a 1939 plebiscite. Although you'll see shop signs in Arabic, you'll find that most locals speak Turkish as a second language. Hitching to Syria is easiest from here, though bus transportation is more convenient through Gaziantep.

As ancient Antioch, the city played an important role in the Hellenistic and Roman periods. Seleucus, a general under Alexander the Great, founded the city and ruled over much of Asia from here. The population swelled to half a million and Antioch became famous for liberality and frivolity. Later, during Roman rule, the Apostle Peter settled here and gathered the first Christian congregation in a grotto now outside of town. The city's location on the edge of the Roman Empire left it open to conquest by Sassanians, Arabs, Byzantines, and Crusaders. By the time the Turks got hold of it, Antioch's glory had been reduced to ruins. A glance at the crumbling walls along the surrounding mountain ridge will give you an idea of the size of the ancient city, compared to the population of 100,000 living here today.

Antakya's main plaza, Atatürk Meydanı, lies right by the river. Here you'll find the **archeological museum** and the **PTT** (open Mon.-Sat. 7am-10pm). Walk down Atatürk Cad. to Alam Meydanı, where the **tourist office** is located. (Open Mon.-Fri.) Returning to Atatürk Meydanı, cross the bridge and look diagonally to the right to see **Saray Oteli** (tel. 254 37), which has clean rooms with a sink in each. (Doubles $4. Showers 80¢.) If you pass Otel Saray on your left and continue several blocks down Hürriyet Cad., you'll reach **Zümrüt Palas Oteli** (tel. 112 70). It's not as clean but has breezy balconies. ($2 per person.) Along the way, **Restaurant Abdo** offers chicken breasts for only 80¢.

Antakya's **archeological museum** is world-renowned for its superb collection of Roman mosaics. Recovered from the nearby site of Daphne, these mosaics represent the late Roman style adopted by the Byzantines. The museum also displays some interesting Hittite and Assyrian remains. (Open Mon. 1:30-5:30pm, Tues.-Sun. 8:30am-noon and 1:30-5:30pm. Admission Mon.-Fri. $1, Sat.-Sun. 50¢.) **San Pierre Kilesi,** 2km from the center of town, is celebrated as the world's first church. Peter's original congregation coined the word Christianity to describe their new religion. The church is just a small cave with no artwork apart from remnants of floor mosaics and a facade added by the Crusaders. To get there, cross the main bridge and turn left, then follow the road to Reyhanlı. (Open Tues.-Sun. 8am-noon and 1:30-6:30pm. Admission 75¢.) Twenty-one kilometers farther are the nineteenth century B.C.E. ruins of **Açcana,** capital of a small kingdom that was heavily influenced by the Hittites and Assyrians. Little remains of the palace and temple here but a few walls and some steps, but ruins this old are hard to find. *Dolmuş* will drop you off 500m from the site. (Admission 50¢.) Be sure to visit the **market** area, northeast of the main bridge, and the winding alleys of the **old city,** southeast of the bridge. The inhabitants of Antakya frequently picnic around the water cascades at **Harbiye,** 7km south from the east side of the bridge. (*Dolmuş* run the route frequently.) Restaurants offer service at tables that stand in the chilly water; up the hill are several inexpensive pensions.

The **bus station** is located off Hürriyet Cad., which runs south to the main bridge. The most frequent connections are to Gaziantep and Mersin; buses also run to Istanbul and Ankara. If you have a Syrian visa already, you can take a bus directly to Aleppo (*Halep* in Turkish), 100km away ($9). You must exchange US$100 at the border. From Aleppo, you can change buses for other Syrian cities. Daily buses also run to Jordan (*(Ürdün,* $19).

### Near Antakya

Coming from the west you may pass through **Iskenderun,** ancient Alexandria-ad-Issus. This unbearably humid port city has little of note except for its **tourist office** at 49/A Atatürk Bulvarı (tel. (881) 116 20; open Mon.-Fri. 8am-noon and 1:30-5:30pm). The coast south of here is dotted with beaches and several crowded vacation villages. The tourist hordes continue up to **Uluçınar,** also called **Assuz.** The cheapest accommodations here can be found at **Yıldız Pansiyon.** ($3 per person.) To the south, the road separates lush farmland and mountain ridges from a deserted gravel beach.

**Gaziantep,** 200km northeast of Antakya, is a city of 450,000 in the center of Turkey's pistachio-growing region. The city is of little interest to tourists, but is the best connection point to the **Middle East.** Daily buses run to Aleppo ($9), Damascus ($9), Lakkatia ($9), Baghdad ($18), Saudi Arabia ($29), and Jordan ($19). Hitching is easy from here.

# Central Turkey

It's only when you see the austere Anatolian Plateau, with mile after rugged mile of barren moonscape, that you feel you're really in Asia. Asia Minor's earliest settlements sprouted here; Neolithic, Hittite, and Phrygian sites still dot the area. In the eleventh century, the invading Seljuks from the Central Asian steppe formed their capital in Konya, though today Asia Minor is ruled once again from the interior: Ankara, the capital of the Turkish Republic, is surprisingly modern but offers little of interest to the tourist.

# Konya

The oasis now called Konya has attracted settlers since the early Bronze Age. Later, St. Paul favored Konya (then called Iconium) with a visit, transforming the city into a significant Christian center. In the eleventh century, the Seljuk Turks swept through Asia Minor, gaining an awful reputation in the west and paving the way for later Ottoman conquests. They made their capital in Konya and replaced its churches with the greatest mosques of the era, most of which survive today. Konya is also the home of the Mevlâna order of Whirling Dervishes, which wielded great political power from the Seljuk period until 1923, when Atatürk dissolved the order.

Konya is a large and rapidly industrializing city, though it retains a very conservative Islamic character; you'll notice most of the men wearing the traditional Muslim hats called *derviş.* Konya is a good place to pick up Turkish carpets. Most of the sights are in the small city center; get a map from the **tourist office** (tel. 110 74), on Mevlâna Cad., the main street, next to the Mevlâna Tekke. (Open in summer daily 9am-6pm; in off-season 9am-5pm.) The **PTT** on Alâedin Cad. is open 24 hours. Konya's **telephone code** is 331.

*Kilim* (woven rugs) hang in every room at the **Yeşil Bursa Hotel,** 8 Keçeci Sok. (tel. (331) 128 14); head southwest from the Selimiye Mosque. (Doubles $5. Showers

50¢.) You'll find much cleaner rooms at the new **Hotel Tur**, 13 Eş'ârizade Sok. (tel. 198 25), around the corner east of the tourist office. (Doubles $6.) Also try **Hotel Seyran** (tel. 218 90) just behind the Kapı Camii. (Doubles $5.50.) The local specialty is *fırın kebap*, a chunk of oven-roasted lamb; try it at **Meşhur Fırın Kebabi** and **Hacı Şükrü Fırın Kebapi,** both on Uzun Bedestan Cad., a few blocks north of the Kapı Camii. (Lunch only, noon-2pm. $1 per portion.)

You can spot the thirteenth-century **Mevlâna Tekke** by its enameled green tower. Inside the complex, originally a kind of monastery, are the *türbes* of Celâleddin and other dervishes, and an interesting museum exhibiting prayer rugs, musical instruments, elaborately decorated garments, and ancient books. The order's founder, Celâleddin, was initially inspired by a "legion of beings clothed in green mantles," who took him to the heavens to see "strange things of a celestial nature." He then established the order to promote brotherhood among people of all religions and to communicate with God through the ecstatic whirling dance, which induces a meditative trance. The heretical order now performs for tourists between December 12 and 17 (tickets from 50¢). (Tekke open Mon. 3-6pm, Tues.-Sun. 8:30am-6pm. Admission 90¢.) Konya's other major attractions are on or around **Alaadin Tepesi** (Alaadin Hill), several hundred yards up Hükümet Cad. This mound probably contains layers of civilizations reaching back to the Bronze Age. **Alaadin Camii,** near the hilltop, is a very plain, early thirteenth-century mosque in the Syrian Seljuk style. Note the pieces of Roman and Byzantine columns incorporated on the facade, and the interwoven black and white marble that matches that on the **Karatay Medresesi,** below the mosque across the street. Here, the Seljuks studied astrology in the reflection of the night sky off the pool in the main chamber. The Karatay now houses a collection of Seljuk tiles. The double-headed eagles and lions represented on some tiles are ancient Anatolian symbols adopted by the Seljuks, despite the Muslim edict prohibiting the representation of living beings in art. Several blocks south of the hill is the **archeological museum,** which houses interesting Classical and Hellenistic art, with one outstanding piece: a third-century sarcophagus illustrating the labors of Hercules. (Open Tues.-Sun. 8am-noon and 1:30-5:30pm. Admission 70¢.) While you're in Konya, be sure to spend some time wandering in the enchantingly chaotic **market,** between the Aziziye Mosque and the PTT.

Ten buses per day run between Konya and the Mediterranean town of Silifke (5 hr., $3.50), even more frequently between Konya and Ankara (5 hr., $3.50), and 15 times per day to Izmir. Nighttime buses run to and from Istanbul. If you arrive at the bus station during the day, take a mini-bus marked "Mevlâna" to the center; at night, try a conveyance unique to Konya, a three-wheeled cart. Both leave from behind the station. After midnight, you'll have to take a taxi.

## Near Konya

Every half-hour, a municipal bus leaves from Alaadin Cad. for isolated **Sille,** 8km away. Situated in a small valley, the village faces a cliff into which numerous rock dwellings have been carved, though none of them are large. Sille also has a fourth-century church, **Aya Elena Kilisesi,** though its frescoes are much more recent. If it's not open, climb the wall and, if you're thin enough, slip through the bars in the back window. (Open daily until 3:30pm.)

Approximately 160km southeast of Konya is the mountaintop site of **Karadağ,** covered with the crumbling ruins of several churches. The existence of so many churches puzzles scholars, for there is no record of any sizable population here. There's no population now, either, which makes it difficult to reach. First take a bus to Karaman, then a *dolmuş* to Kilbasan; from there, you'll have to hitchhike or take a *dolmuş* ($12) to Karadağ. You might not make it back to Konya in the same day, in which case you can find accommodations in Karaman.

The basis of Turkey's claim to being one of the birthplaces of civilization lies at **Çatalhöyük,** near the town of Çümra, 50km south of Konya on the Silifke road. An advanced Neolithic community, Çatalhöyük vies with Jericho for the title "world's first city." Its famous cave drawings and artifacts have been removed to

Ankara and Holland, and little remains but a few crumbling walls. The tour isn't worth it, but the guidebook on sale at Mevlâna is. Take a bus from the Eski Garage near Pira Paşa Mosque to Çümra (45 min.), then take a taxi the remaining distance ($5 round-trip).

# Ankara

Like Washington, Bonn, or Canberra, Ankara is the capital but not the first city. Its role as capital started when Atatürk based his provisional government here in 1920. When he declared the Turkish Republic in 1923, Atatürk sought to remake the country, beginning with Central Anatolia, and moved the seat of government from Istanbul. A constant rural influx has expanded the city 100-fold since then, bringing the population to 2.5 million people. The city's modernity surprises those arriving from the countryside. Ankara has a handful of historical sights, a tremendous museum, and is a transportation nucleus for travel east and south.

## Orientation and Practical Information

Although it's quicker to travel between Istanbul and Ankara by bus (at least 2 per hr., 7-8 hr., $6-8), overnight trains may be more convenient and comfortable. (The faster *Mavi Tren* departs at 11pm, 9 hr., $8; *Anadolu Ekspresi* departs at 9pm, 11 hr., $5, couchette $8.) Ankara is also connected to Izmir, Konya, Cappadocia, Erzurum, Trabzon, and other Turkish cities, as well as to Iran, Syria, and Jordan.

Try to arrive with a map; skewed streets and unmarked avenues could lead to premature hair loss. **Atatürk Bulvarı**, the main boulevard, halves the city from north to south. From the north, it first passes **Ulus**, the older section of the city and still the business district where most budget accommodations are clustered. The city's central districts, Sıhhiye, Kızılay, and Bakanlıklar, are farther south along Atatürk. **Kızılay** serves as a junction for five avenues. Bus stops are scattered around the square. **Bakanlıklar** literally means ministries; most government buildings are found here. Frequent buses run along the boulevard. Buy tickets from the kiosks found near major bus stops, or bring exact change (15¢).

**Tourist Offices:** Main office at 33 Gazi Kemal Bulvarı (tel. 230 19 11). Take bus #65 from Ulus. There is a more helpful office in Ulus at 4 Istanbul Cad. English spoken and maps provided. Both open in summer Mon.-Fri. 8:30am-5:30pm, Sat. 8:30am-5pm, Sun. 8:30am-2pm; in off-season Mon.-Fri. 8:30am-5:30pm.

**Embassies:** All embassies in Ankara are south of Hürriyet Sq., along Atatürk Bulvarı. **U.S.,** 110 Atatürk Bulvarı (tel. 126 54 70). **Canada,** 75 Nenehatun Cad. (tel. 127 58 03). **U.K.,** 46a Şehit Ersan Cad. (tel. 127 43 10). **Australia,** 83 Nenehatun Cad. (tel. 128 67 15). Travelers from **New Zealand** should contact the British mission. **Bulgaria,** 124 Atatürk Bulvarı (tel. 126 74 55). **Iran,** 10 Tahran Cad. (tel. 127 43 20). **Iraq,** 11 Turan Emeksiz Sok. (tel. 126 61 18). **Jordan,** 18 Dede Korkut Sok. (tel. 139 42 30). **Syria,** 7 Abdullah Cevdet Sok. (tel. 139 45 88). **Northern Cyprus,** 20 Incirli Sok. (tel. 137 95 38).

**American Express:** 7 Cinnah Cad. (tel. 167 73 34). Take bus #13 from across the Ulus post office. Provide emergency cash for cardholders and hold mail. Open Mon.-Fri. 9am-6pm, Sat. 9am-1pm.

**Post Office: PTT,** on Atatürk Bulvarı in Ulus. Open 24 hours; daily 9am-5pm for Poste Restante.

**Telephones:** At the post office. Open 24 hours. Also at the bus and train stations. **Telephone code:** 4.

**Airport:** Buses leave from the **Turkish Airlines** office (tel. 312 49 00) at Hipodrom Cad., next to the train station to the airport, **Esenboğa,** 1½ hr. before domestic and 1¼ hr. before international departures (50¢). Direct flights to: Istanbul (7am-10pm every hr., 1 hr., $45); Adana, Diyarbakır, Erzurum, Izmir, and Trabzon (1 per day, 1 hr., $45); Malatya and Van (4 per week, 2 hr., $40), Gaziantep (5 per week, 1 hr., $45); and Sivan (2 per week, 2 hr., $40). Indirect flights to Antalya and Dalaman (1 per day, 3-4 hr., $45) and Kayseri (1 per week, 3 hr., $35).

**Bus Station:** On Kemal Bulvarı. Take bus #16 to Ulus, where buses begin for destinations throughout Turkey. Frequent departures to Istanbul, Izmir, Konya, Sivas, Erzurum, Adana, Diyarbakır, Van, and Trabzon. Buses also run to Nevşehir and Ürgüp every hr. until 8pm. Daily to Tehran ($25), Baghdad ($28), and Aleppo ($15).

**Hitching:** Ankara is a good place to hitch a ride on a truck either east or west, as it lies on the main Istanbul-Tehran highway. To head east, try the Bayındır Barajı Mocamp, Kayaş (tel. 19 41 61), 15km east of the city. Any bus to Kırıkkale or Yozgat, or a long-distance bus to Samsun, Trabzon, or Erzurum, will get you there. Going west, your best bet is the Kervansaray Susuzköy Mocamp, 22km west of town on the Istanbul highway. Likewise, any buses to Kazam or Kızılcahamam or the Istanbul bus will get you there.

**Bookstores: Tarhan Kitapevi** (tel. 133 67 31), on the northeast side of Hürriyet Sq. A good sample of contemporary Turkish writing in translation. The **American Association Library** (tel. 126 94 99), across from the AmEx office, houses a comprehensive collection of English-language literature. Open Mon.-Fri. 11am-7pm, Sat. 10am-1pm. Closed July 20-Aug. 25.

## Accommodations and Food

Budget accommodations in Ankara aren't plentiful since it's not really a tourist town. The best place to look is in the **Ulus** district, at the north end of Atatürk Bul. Avoid places right on the main road; they're noisy and cater to the clientele of the seamy nightclubs below. First try **Savan Oteli,** 3 Altan Sok. (tel 324 21 13), conveniently located just off Anafartalar Cad. It has a teahouse frequented by Ankarans. (Singles $4.50, with bath $6. Doubles $9, with bath $10.50.) **Beyrut Palas Oteli,** 11 Denizciler Cad. (tel. 310 84 07), is decent, but avoid the skimpy breakfast, and don't park your car here. (Singles $4, with bath $4.50. Doubles $5.50, with bath $6.) For better but more expensive treatment, try the **Efes Oteli,** 12 Denizciler Cad. (tel. 324 32 11; singles with bath $11; doubles with bath $15). The **Paris Oteli,** 14 Denizciler Cad. (tel 324 12 83), has singles with bath for $12, doubles with baths $16. (Laundry facilities. Breakfast $2.) The Efes has a Turkish bath for men only.

The **Yeni Karpıç Restaurant,** in the mall diagonally across from the main post office, is a bit pricey, but delivers quite a meal on the patio. (Steak and mushrooms $3.) **Urfalı Hacı Mehmet,** on Posta Cad., off the Atatürk Bul., serves *döner* (lamb *kebap*)—great for a quick lunch. **Uludağ Kebapçısı** and **Hacı Bey Kebapçısı,** both at the end of Denizciler Cad., make the best *kebap* in Ankara. Uludağ is the classier of the two. As a dessert, try their *kaymaklı ekmek kadayıfı* (thin layers of bread soaked in syrup and topped with cream). If you turn right off Atatürk Bulvarı just after the post office, you'll come to Ankara's big **food market,** where you'll find everything from sugared almonds to live chickens. For beer, music, and a chance to hang out with university students, try **Café Melodi,** in the Batı Sineması building on Atatürk Bulvarı, 1 block north of Esat Cad.

## Sights

Near the southern end of the citadel that dominates Ulus, you'll find the exemplary **Anadolu Medeniyetleri Müzesi** (Museum of Anatolian Civilizations). Take a taxi ($1-3) or walk up the hill past Ulus Meydanı and the equestrian statue of Atatürk, turn right onto Hisarparkı Cad., and right again onto Ipek St. The museum's outstanding prehistoric, Hattian, Hittite, Phrygian, Urartian, Persian, Greek, and Roman collections could alone merit a visit to Ankara. The setting is unique: a restored fifteenth-century Ottoman *han* and *bedesten* (covered bazaar), populated by canaries, houses a collection of artifacts which trace the history of Anatolia from the dawn of time. English-speaking guides and an illustrated catalogue of the museum are available. (Open Tues.-Sun. 8:30am-12:30pm and 1:30-5:30pm. Admission $1.) While in the area, stroll through the **bazaar,** the town-within-a-town inside the citadel walls, and the twelfth-century **Alâeddin Mosque.**

Don't leave Ankara without visiting **Anıt Kabir,** the mausoleum of Atatürk. Its size and the museum of Atatürk's personal effects will give you a sense of Turkey's reverence for its national hero and the cult that later politicians created around him. The site is in a large park west of the tourist office (a 25-min. walk from Kızılay).

Southbound bus #63 on Atatürk Cad. will take you to the southern entrance of the park, where the mausoleum is located. (Open Tues.-Sun. 9am-12:30pm and 1:30-5pm.)

Other sights in Ankara include the **Temple of Augustus,** built in 25 B.C.E. over the site of earlier temples to Cybele, an Anatolian fertility goddess, and to the Phrygian moon god; it was later converted into a Byzantine church. Nearby are the fifteenth-century **Hacı Bayram Mosque,** the **Ethnographic Museum,** the old **Parliament,** and the zoo.

## Near Ankara

If you're headed east from Ankara, the ruins of **Hattuşaş,** the Hittite capital, sprawl about 200km from Ankara, 25km off the highway to Samsun. The first people to smelt iron, the Hittites conquered Anatolia around 2200 B.C.E. and the Assyrian colonists fled to the southeast. United under a central authority at Hattuşaş, the Hittites vied with the Egyptians for control of the fertile lands and trade routes of Mesopotamia. The western Sea People razed Hattuşaş shortly after 1200 B.C.E., but archeologists have unearthed enough of the ruins to provide a fair representation of the city. Visit the small **museum** in the village of **Boğazkale,** next to the site, to get a sense of the area's history. (Open Tues.-Sun. 8:30am-12:30pm and 1:30pm-5:30pm. Admission $1.) Along the 6-km wall encircling Hattuşaş are the **Great Temple, Lion Gate, Sphinx Gate, King's Gate,** and the **Great Citadel.** Stroll through the Great Temple of the Weather God of Hatti and the Sun Goddess of Arinna, where religious ceremonies were held. To enter the chamber, one had to cross a drawbridge over two pools of water. The two sphinxes from the Sphinx Gate are now in Istanbul and Berlin, but don't overlook the 70-meter long postern, built under the southern fortifications and used for surprise attacks. Your admission ticket ($1) is also valid for **Yazılıkaya,** an open-air temple with the entire Hittite pantheon represented in bas-relief. Yazılıkaya lies 2km south of Hattuşaş. For deeper studies, see Ekrem Akurgal's *Ancient Civilizations and Ruins of Turkey* or *The Art of the Hittites.*

To get to Hattuşaş, take a bus to Sungurlu ($2) and then a *dolmuş* to Boğazkale, right next to the site (80¢). *Dolmuş* are less frequent on Sundays. You need at least half a day to walk through the site; the alternative is hiring a taxi from Boğazkale ($6) or Sungurlu ($20). The **Aşıkoğlu Motel** (tel. (4554) 10 04) is conveniently located across from the museum. The restaurant is decent and the rooms are clean, but it lacks hot water. (Singles with bath $3.50. Doubles with bath $6.) There is a small campsite next to the motel.

# Cappadocia

The ancient province of Cappadocia is historically and visually intriguing. Beautifully eroded volcanic formations create a striking landscape of cone-shaped monoliths (fittingly called fairy chimneys in Turkish) clustered in valleys and along ridges. Mt. Erciyes, in nearby Kayseri, once deposited a thick layer of soft volcanic rock here, along with boulders formed of much harder material. Over centuries, the soft rock eroded away, except for the portions sheltered by the hard boulders, which left conical formations underneath. When Christians fleeing Muslim persecution arrived here in the sixth century, they carved houses, churches, and entire cities out of the same rock. The result is an extraordianary blend of natural and built environments, with architecture as marvelous as its surroundings. The central area of the province is defined by the triangle formed by the city of Nevşehir and the smaller towns of Avanos and Ürgüp, about 300km southeast of Ankara.

If you're only here for a day or two, see at least the major sites of Derinkuyu and the Göreme Open-Air Museum. The region contains farming villages, cone-filled valleys, Byzantine chapels, and underground habitations that could occupy a visitor for an entire week. Of the several towns you can stay in, Göreme is especially picturesque. Freelance camping in the rocks is strictly prohibited, but if the Byzantines hid from the Turks this way, so can others. The rock caves stay warm during the cool Cappadocian nights, unlike the rooftop accommodations offered by many pensions.

# Nevşehir

Most buses drop you off in Nevşehir, though some stop in Ürgüp and Avanos as well. In addition to the Ankara bus (4 hr., $3.50), a bus departs every morning for Konya (3 hr., $3), Mersin, and Adana (4 hr., $3.50), and overnight for Izmir (13 hr., $8) and Istanbul (12 hr., $8). Buses to Kayseri and Niğde are frequent (6-7 per day, 1 hr., 80¢). Although Nevşehir is not especially interesting, it is the center of the region's *dolmuş* routes. Go to the **tourist office** (tel. 36 59), 600m down Aksaray Cad. from the bus station—follow the signs. Although the staff lacks enthusiasm and competence, they can help you contact a student guide who can take you to the sites for less than what the travel agencies charge. They'll also provide a map of Nevşehir and the region, showing all *dolmuş* routes and stations. (Open in summer daily 8:30am-noon and 1:30-6pm; in off-season Mon.-Fri. 9:30am-5:30pm.) One *dolmuş* route runs to the underground city of Kaymaklı and Derinkuyu on its way to Niğde. Another goes to Üçhisar, Göreme and the Open-Air Museum, and Ürgüp. A third goes to Avanos. A fourth travels to Aksaray, where you can catch a bus to Konya or the Mediterranean coast. (*Dolmuş* cost 50¢ on these routes.) Municipal **buses** also run nine times per day at regularly scheduled times (check at the tourist office) between Nevşehir and Ürgüp for a cheaper fare than the *dolmuş*. **Guided tours** offered by travel agencies generally cost the same, whether from Nevşehir, Göreme, or Ürgüp ($11 for a 9 hr. tour). Hitching around the triangle is very easy in summer; you can also hire a taxi ($35-45) or private car for the day.

Don't stay in Nevşehir unless you must; check if your early morning bus also stops at Ürgüp (most do). If you're stuck, stay at the **Otel Sunar Palas,** 2 Belediye Cad. (tel. 14 44); follow Aksaray St. and turn right after Akbank. (Singles $2. Doubles $3.) **La Maison du Turc,** uphill from the bus station along the four-lane street, is run by a friendly Francophile. ($3 per person.) The **restaurants** across from the bus station seem to be the best of Nevşehir's culinary offerings. The 24-hour **PTT** is on Atatürk Cad. Nevşehir's **telephone code** is 4851.

Nevşehir and Aksaray are the easiest access points to **Ihlara Valley.** This river gorge once supported a Christian population of 80,000 in its numerous rock dwellings. You can also visit some of the 105 chapels here, with frescoes in the Byzantine and earlier Cappadocian styles. Descending into the valley from the south at the village of Ihlara, you will emerge 14km later at the town of Selime. You can also ascend from the gorge to the main road after 6km, but you'll miss many Byzantine-style chapels. Transportation to Ihlara is irregular so you should first inquire at the tourist office in Nevşehir or Aksaray.

## Kaymaklı and Derinkuyu

These two extensive underground cities are both south of Nevşehir, on the road to Niğde; the first is 20km away, the second 29km. Both are fun places to spend a couple of hours, particularly if you've brought a flashlight or candle and like to imagine yourself as a ninth-century Christian fleeing from the invading Arab marauders. (Don't we all?) Over centuries of persecution, Christians living in neighboring towns bored this intricate tunnel system to escape from their homes directly into the hidden refuge below. The size of Kaymaklı—miles of tunnels, five levels burrowing down hundreds of feet—is boggling; Derinkuyu is almost twice as big, with escape tunnels (now blocked) 5-6km long, and one passage believed to lead back to Kaymaklı. In both cities, the tunnels were built low and narrow to hamper the progress of invaders and twentieth-century tourists. The tunnels are very poorly marked, and you won't have explored extensively until you get lost at least once—just listen for other tourists. Both cities have unexplored tunnels which are out of bounds, and thus tempting, yet there are stories about tourists who never made it back.

In the tunnels, see if you can distingush the kitchens from churches, the bedrooms from stables. Even during the hottest days it's cool and damp down below, so you might want to bring a sweater. Try to plan your return from Derinkuyu by 6pm, from Kaymaklı by 6:30pm; later *dolmuş* are rare. You may be able to hitch with other tourists. (Both sites open daily 8:30am-6:30pm. Admission $1.)

# Göreme

The name Göreme refers to the general area of Göreme Valley, the cluster of churches known as the Göreme Open-Air Museum, and the town of Göreme, sometimes called Avcılar. The last is a small village in the center of Cappadocia; its proximity to the open-air museums of Göreme and Zelve, as well as its many fine and inexpensive pensions, make it a good base. If you want to experience cave-dwelling with the comfort of a hotel, try **Peri's Pansiyon** (tel. 11 36), on the road to the Open-Air Museum, where rooms are in a giant rock cone; those on the lower level (without windows) are cooler and cost less ($3.50 per person). There is also a quaint bar carved into the rock with authentic Cappadocian decoration. Next door, **Paradise Pansiyon** is quite nice, with a terrace good for sipping beer while watching the sunset. (Roof $1. Doubles $8.) The **Köse Pansiyon and Camping** is a friendly traveler's place run by a Turkish man and his affable Scots wife. Camp here ($1 per person), but don't stay in their filthy rooms. Multi-storied **Halil Pansiyon** (tel. 10 30), on the opposite side of town, is carved into a rock cliff. ($4 per person.) A **PTT** just opened in town. Göreme's **telephone code** is 4857.

The most impressive concentration of sights in the region is at the **Göreme Open-Air Museum,** 1km out of Göreme on the Ürgüp road. The churches here are the legacy of Cappadocian Christianity in the Byzantine Empire. St. Basil, who lived in the fourth century, founded one of the first Christian monasteries here, setting down religious tenets that greatly influenced the teachings of St. Benedict and subsequently the Western monastic movement. The monks of Cappadocia built the majority of the churches in Göreme between the fourth and tenth centuries and inhabited the area until the formation of the modern Turkish Republic, when all Anatolian Greeks were exchanged with the Turks living in Greece. The remaining churches are remarkable for their frescoes, which span most of the Byzantine era. The earliest frescoes are simple crosses and Christian symbols, such as the palm tree and the fish, usually done in red and dating from about 400 years after St. Basil's death. For a time thereafter, during the iconoclastic period, all representations were deemed idolatrous. Finally, toward the end of the first millenium, during the "Byzantine Renaissance," sophisticated and beautiful religious portraits became a standard liturgical article. From this period (eleventh to thirteenth centuries) came the most impressive Göreme frescoes, found in the **Barbara Kilise, Elmalı Kilise** (Church of the Apple), **Çarıklı Kilise** (Church of the Sandal), and **Karanlık Kilise** (Dark Church). If you have time, descend into the gorge. To the left, you can wander for several kilometers, passing ancient habitations, cisterns, and farmers tending their small terraced plots—all without seeing a single tourist. The path to the right continues through stunning scenery, emerging near the town of Göreme. At the museum, there is an underground **post office** and **bank,** which charges no commission on traveler's checks. (Both open same hours as the site: daily 8:30am-6pm. Admission $1.50.)

## Near Göreme

The road north from Göreme to Avanos leads past the lesser site of the Christian sanctuary at **Çavuşin** (admission $1) to the much more interesting **Zelve Valley,** a city carved into the pink rock that had to be evacuated in the early '50s due to landslides. Though its frescoes don't compare with those at the Open-Air Museum, its caverns are much more extensive. (Open daily 8am-5:30pm. Admission $1.)

A few kilometers farther, the landscape switches from Dalí and pop surrealism to something reminiscent of Ansel Adams' American Southwest. The potters of **Alvanos** have been throwing the red, iron-rich Cappadocian clay since time immemorial. Stop in at **Galip Körükçü's Cave-Studio** for a thimbleful of wine and a look at his stork-bearing bat and pots. Apart from being a master potter, he keeps an immense "hair collection." Since 1980, more than 10,000 women worldwide let him cut a piece of their hair and attach it to the ceiling in his rock-cut room. (And you thought shag carpets were cool . . . ) Several kilometers north of Avanos is another underground city, **Özkonak,** similar to the other two but not quite as extensive.

## Ürgüp

The town of Ürgüp, 20km east of Nevşehir, is a good base for exploring the area; the three main sights at Göreme and Zelve are easy daytrips from here. A bus runs nine times per day to Nevşehir (40¢); most of the long-distance buses to and from Nevşehir also call here, and there are *dolmuş* and buses (7am-7pm on the hr., $1) to Kayseri for connections to the east. Daily buses go to Mersin and Adana (4 hr., $3.50), Alanya (9 hr., $9), and Marmaris (15 hr., $12).

The Ürgüp **tourist office** is on Kayseri Cad., inside the garden. They provide maps of the region, *dolmuş* and bus schedules, and help arrange tours. (Open April-Sept. daily 8am-8:30pm; Oct.-March Mon.-Fri. 9am-5pm.) Next door is a tiny **archeological museum.** (Open Tues.-Sun. 8:30am-5:30pm. Admission $1.) You can take your choice between Ürgüp's cheap pensions. On the far east side of town, before the stream, is **Güzelgöz Pansiyon** (tel. 10 94). You have to walk through a cornfield to get to the bathroom, but the place is clean and friendly. (Singles $3.50. Doubles $6. $1 per person outdoors.) Ask to see the owner's award plaque; he was invited to Washington, DC in 1963 to receive a government humanitarian award for bringing a mobile library to Cappadocia—on donkeyback. The personable management at **Sarıhan Pansiyon** (tel. 22 64), 200m from the bus station toward the center of Ürgüp, keeps clean rooms. ($3.50 per person.) **Sâkin Pansiyon** (tel. 19 65) is a 1½-kilometer hike down the road to Avanos, but offers spacious, furnished rooms. ($3.50 per person. Hot showers included.) **Seymen Pansiyon,** just before the road to Nevşehir, has comfortable rooms downstairs and a cool sitting room full of local craftwork. ($5 per person. Hot showers and breakfast included.) The **Cappadocia Restaurant** has the usual assortment of stews, soups, and vegetables at a good price.

Cappadocia's wine industry is centered in Ürgüp. The wineries that appear on the map issued by the tourist office welcome visitors and offer tours. They'll let you sample their wine, hoping that you'll buy a bottle—but after visiting all the wineries, you'll already have drunk the equivalent of one.

The tourist agencies at Ürgüp organize a daily tour of the region (5 person-minimum, $7, $11 with a guide). The nine-hour tour is comprehensive, but a little rushed; you may find yourself too frazzled to appreciate anything by the latter half of the day. The tour visits the castles at Üçhisar, the underground city at Kaymaklı, the Göreme Open-Air Museum, and the rock dwellings at Zelve, as well as numerous other "photo stops" (read souvenir stands) along the way. Count on paying about $4 for entrance fees to the sites.

### Near Ürgüp

The village of **Ortahisar** clusters around a tall fortress hewn out of volcanic rock. From the top of the fortress there's a great view of the rock formations and river valleys that spread for miles around. If you hike around the area to the south of Ortahisar, you'll come across scores of abandoned rock dwellings and several rock churches, the best of which have frescoes from the tenth and eleventh centuries, the latest period of religious art represented in Cappadocia. Ortahisar does not lie on the main Nevşehir-Ürgüp bus route, but is only 2km from the main road, along a turn-off some 6km from Ürgüp.

**Üçhisar** is a slightly larger village, built along very similar lines at the foot of a craggy fortress. Because it is on a hill, the town, and to an even greater extent the fortress, command views of the whole Göreme Valley. Üçhisar also has a pleasant and inexpensive pension, the **Maison du Rêve,** on the opposite side of the castle from the town—follow the signs. (Rooms $5 per person. Hot showers and breakfast included.) Occasional *dolmuş* leave from the town square to Nevşehir, but it's much more reliable to walk 1km to the main road and flag down the Nevşehir-Ürgüp bus.

Once capital of the short-lived Kingdom of Cappadocia and later, as Caesarea, of the Roman province of the same name, **Kayseri** today doesn't really seem part of the region. The unremarkable twentieth-century Turkish-modern **bus station** is Kayseri's *raison d'être* for most travelers. You can get here from Ürgüp on a *dolmuş*. Buses run to Samsun, Sivas, Erzurum, Mersin, and Diyarbakır. There are also frequent buses to Ankara and Istanbul, although from Cappadocia you'd be better off going to Nevşehir to travel west. To reach Nemrut Dağı, take a bus from here to Malatya.

# *Eastern Turkey*

As you travel eastward in Turkey, you'll notice the disappearance of English or German stop signs, likewise of the English or Germans. You'll find this expansive region about 30% cheaper than the west and less-touristed, although the landscape and history are no less rich than that of western Anatolia.

Some caveats are in order for travel here, and some myths need to be dispelled. Women will feel comfortable if they follow a few basic rules: Never wear shorts or tight T-shirts. Although this will not deflect amorous stares, it will secure respectful treatment. The best camouflage consists of long skirts, long-sleeved blouses, and head scarves. Appropriate dress will bridge the cultural barrier between you and the Turks. By the same token, men should not wear shorts. If you dress discreetly, you may find yourself invited to weddings and family meals. You must buy toilet paper at a general store since hotels never have it. Tampons are available in cities.

The climate here spans the extremes. Gaziantep, Urfa, Diyarbakır, and Mardin are hot as *cehennem* in summer, with daytime temperatures above 43°C (110°F). Conversely, much of the northeastern end of Turkey is periodically cut off in winter. In January, Kars experiences nighttime temperatues below -30°C (-22°F), and Hakkâri is virtually inaccessible from November through March. As for language barriers, some of the soldiers come from western Anatolia and thus may speak English or German. Tourist offices in the east have been improving in past years as the Turkish government realizes the potential for tourism here. Still, you'll often find that the staff people are there to practice their English and don't know any more than what's written in the tourist brochures. Just about every town large enough to stop in has a bank, but you should still carry dollars and small denominations of traveler's checks.

Less-than-sanitary restaurants and hotels seem to pose the major problem for a traveler in eastern Anatolia. In all circumstances, avoid the cheapest places where you would be vulnerable to numerous diseases. Admittedly, there are cheaper restaurants and hotels than the ones we recommended here, but they are likely to be intolerably dirty. Avoid dishes made with ground meat, such as *köfte* (meatballs) and the suicidal *çiğ köfte* (raw meatballs). Lemon juice is not especially reliable as a disinfectant, and *eşki,* a potion concocted by some restaurants, is useless. Don't try the tap water, especially in the southeast; drink only the nationally distributed bottled water, fruit juice, or soda.

Transportation poses more difficulties. Buses often leave only when they are full, and schedules change according to demand and road conditions. Frequent over-booking results in quarrels; luckily, helpless foreigners are given priority in conflicts. If you get off a bus between two stops, it might be impossible to find another one later. If you plan to hitch, remember that trucks are painfully slow.

The traveler in this area should know something about the Kurds, since published information about the Kurdish population in Turkey is practically prohibited by the government. East of Adıyaman you start to meet many Kurds, and their num-bers grow as you approach the Iranian border. The Kurds are a nation without a state, stretching over eastern Turkey, northern Syria and Iraq, and northern Iran into Afghanistan. They number about 20 million, including many who live in Istan-bul and Europe. For centuries, the Kurds have mounted raids from impenetrable mountain ranges against those who rule them. Centered in the wild Hakkâri region, they now fight to carve out an independent Kurdistan from the territory of five dif-ferent nations. Government figures put the number of arrested dissidents at around 100 per year, but Hakkâri locals estimate that at least another 50 are killed annually in fighting between the village people and the army. The Kurds' political struggle shouldn't affect your travels, but you might want to check on the situation before you go, especially if you're traveling southeast of Van.

The beauty of this region lies in the harsh steppe lands and the jagged peaks of the countryside, and in the experience—for here is something genuinely of another world. Expect to be stared at, but if anything, you'll tire of excessive friendliness rather than malevolence. Traveling in the east can be the climactic episode of your stay in Turkey—for more stimulation, ask around while you're in Istanbul; you'll likely find many people who've gone and will be able to tempt you further with tales of bewitching Armenian churches at Akdamar and Ani, transfixing scenery at Kars and Hakkâri, magical waters of Lake Van, the bizarre heads at Nemrut Daği, and the exquisite palace at Doğubeyazıt.

The Kurds speak a distinct language that combines features of Turkish, Latin, and Farsi; their written language uses mostly Latin characters. The Kurds are friendly and hospitable to foreign travelers, and are thrilled if you can say a few words of Kurdish; however, such linguistic precocity won't impress local Turkish police, since the language is outlawed. A few helpful words are: *saoul* (thank you; same as Turkish); *merhaba* (hello; same as Turkish); *hkatréte* (goodbye, if you are leaving); *ser çevarahati* (goodbye, addressed to the person leaving); *eriy* (yes); *na* (no); *návete çiye* (what is your name?); *véle* (come); and *hére* (go).

# Nemrut Daği

Nemrut Daği (the 'g' is silent) is heavily visited for good reason. Huge funerary statues of the Commagene Empire (the faces alone are 1m high) sit atop the summit of the 2150-meter peak. There are two ways to ascend the mountain; the more com-mon is from the town of **Kahta,** 70km away. Kahta lies on the road between Adıya-man and Diyarbakır.

As you step off the bus, a group of hustlers will beckon you to join their tour. Check their prices, but don't commit yourself until you've shopped around. Good places to find a tour (and people to share the tour with) are the Merhaba Hotel, the Commagene Hotel, the Mezopotamya Hotel (visible from the bus station), and the more expensive motel 500m beyond the Commagene, in the direction of Adıya-man and Malatya. Tours generally cost about $30, or $35 for a route that also takes in **Eski Kale** (the old capital of the Commagene Empire), a Roman bridge over the River Cendere, and a funerary mound of the princesses and queens of the Empire. Minibuses charge the same, regardless of the number of passengers; the maximum is 10. They depart either in the middle of the night to arrive by sunrise, or in the afternoon for the sunset. Bring a sweater as the summit gets chilly at night. But even virgin wool can't protect you against coach tours. The only solution seems to be visiting the sight during the day; you won't miss much if you miss the overemphasized sunrise or sunset. Taxis from Kahta cost slightly less than minibuses, but a maximum of five people can share one. The two-and-a-half-hour trip up the recently paved road is only possible from May through October. If your bus stops in Adıyaman, you might be offered a reasonably priced tour of Nemrut Dağı ($33-40) but it may be difficult to gather a large enough group to go.

The Commagene Empire was founded in the first century B.C.E. by Mithradates, whose son Antiochus ordered the construction of the huge statues. The Commagenes allied themselves with Pompeii, and then became a Roman buffer state of some wealth but little importance. In any case, they left a monument rivaling Rome's finest: colossal statues built at the foot of a tomb 50m high on an almost inaccessible peak. The builders piled tons of crushed rock beside the statues to create the artificial peak. Antiochus is believed to be buried beneath the rubble. The statues represent Commagene gods, hybrids of Hellenistic and Persian deities, and Antiochus and his father.

In Kahta, try the **Merhaba Oteli.** (Roof $1.50. Doubles with private bath $15, non-students $30.) Walk from the bus station into town and look for the sign. **Commagene Pension and Camping** (tel. 10 92), at the turn-off for Nemrut Dağı, has doubles with private bath for $7. ($1 per person. $2 per tent.)

The more adventurous may choose other ways up the mountain. The first is from the small Kurdish village of **Eski Kahta,** 25km closer to the summit. You can get here from Kahta by minibus, but this consumes too much time and money—$1 to Eski Kahta by *dolmuş,* and then $8 per person to rent a guide and horse for the 10- to 12-hour ascent and descent. You must leave Eski Kahta at midnight to reach the summit by sunrise.

A more reasonable journey is from the north via **Malatya,** a large market town. Buses arrive from Kayseri, Ankara (at least 5 per day, 10 hr., $7), Konya, Diyarbakır, Sivan, Mersin, Adana, and Trabzon. *Dolmuş* and city **buses** shuttle between the bus station and city center (10¢). Malatya is also accessible by **plane** from Ankara (4 per week, 1 hr., $40).

Representatives of the Malatya **tourist office** (tel. 177 33) can be found at the *Emniyet Bürosu* (police station) in the bus station. (Open daily 8:30am-noon and 1:30-5:30pm.) They will shepherd you onto their **tour,** which goes up the north side of the mountain through the villages of Tepehan and Büyüköz. The tour leaves at least once per day, returning the next morning, and costs $7 for transportation and $11 for bed, dinner, and breakfast at the **Güneş Motel** next to Mt. Nemrut. The bus winds up a dirt road, through streams and past beautiful scenery, for six hours, ending at a small Kurdish village in a valley below the summit. You may save $5 if you stay at the so-called "mud hut" instead of Güneş Motel, but rooms are scarce. You can also camp on your own (bring a warm sleeping bag) and eat at the restaurant on the opposite side of the monument. You may want to bring some food anyway, as the restaurant's hours are erratic. Be sure to take the same transportation down the mountain that you took coming up. Continuing over the other side of the mountain may sound attractive, but you probably won't find transportation, and you don't want to get stuck hiking at midday in summer.

If you stay in Malatya, try the centrally located **Hotel Asya,** on İnönü Cad. (Singles $3.50. Doubles $6.) **Park Oteli,** on the corner of İnönü Cad. and Atatürk Cad., is similarly agreeable and clean. (Singles $4. Double $6.50.) The **Emniyet Lokantası,** 13 Atatürk Cad., near the main tourist office, costs about 30% more than the bus station fare but serves clean food and has a nice garden in back.

# Urfa

A tourist brochure declares that Urfa (also known as Şanlıurfa—"Glorious Urfa") is famous for its "horses, lentils, and animal fat." The horses and lentils, among thousands of other things, can be found in the corridors of Urfa's bazaar, which is full of craftsmen selling their handiwork. The animal fat you will find in abundance on your plate at any of the town's restaurants. Urfa, 50km from the Syrian border, is also notoriously hot; temperatures can reach 50°C in July. You'll find life much more pleasant if you take the cue from the Turks at midday—either take a nap or sip tea at one of the shady kervansaray in the market area. During winter, the weather is mild.

The history of Urfa starts with the birth of Abraham in a cave at the foot of the citadel. The story goes that King Nemrut of Babylon had been warned that Abraham would lead the populace away from the state religion, so Nemrut built a huge fire into which he planned to cast Abraham. Before Abraham took off, though, the fire turned into a pond of carp whose descendants still swim around in it today. The seventeenth-century **Halil-Rahman Camii** surrounds the sacred pools. The castle and the ancient site opposite the present city suffered a tumultuous history on the frontier between eastern and western civilizations. The former city was conquered in succession by the Persians, Macedonians, Romans (who called it Edessa), Crusaders, Mongols, and Turks.

The **bus station** is about 1km out of town; to get to the center, head toward the castle and take a left through the middle of the cemetery. The **tourist office** (tel. 24 67) is on your right, 20m before the intersection with the town's main road, Sarayönü Cad. The friendly staff can show you photos of the town, offer you an accurate town plan, and arrange tours to Harran. (Office open Mon.-Fri. 7:30am-noon and 1-4:30pm.) Two left turns away is the immaculate **Lâle Oteli**, 11 Kışla Cad. (tel. 16 42), with a refrigerator full of cold water. (Singles $2.50. Doubles $4.) You may find a location between the bazaar and the castle considerably more interesting. The **Park Oteli**, 101 Göl Cad. (tel. 10 95), has a fantastic illuminated view of the religious complex from the terrace. (Singles $2. Doubles $3.50.) Across from the Lâle Oteli is the **Eyvan Restaurant,** one of the few in Urfa that is not beseiged by swarms of flies. The little *pastane* at 131 Sarayönü Cad. serves delicious lasagna-like *börek* for only 200TL. Head south along Sarayönü Cad. to get to the **post office** (open 24 hours) and most of the sights. Urfa's **telephone code** is 8711.

## Near Urfa

The road south from Urfa to the Syrian border passes through **Sultantepe,** an Assyrian archeological site that, though seemingly modest, has provided scholars with much information about Assyrian culture. Thirty-three kilometers from Urfa, a road leads 11km to the left to the village of **Altınbaşak,** site of the ancient town of **Harran.** This odd village, easily recognizable for its beehive-like dwellings, is where Abraham and Lot stopped on their way from Ur to Canaan. Ruins of a castle and a Seljuk/Kurdish mosque stand on the foundations of a Roman university. To get to Harran, you must hire a taxi ($8) or a minibus-*dolmuş* ($9); either will wait for you at the site. The tourist office will help you find people to share the ride. If the office is closed, head south on Sarayönü Cad. and look for the "taxis to Harran" banner on the right.

# Diyarbakir

Diyarbakır's black basalt walls, said to be the largest after the Great Wall of China, once protected a fragile oasis of civilization from the desert of marauding invaders. But like Urfa, its frontier position made it the first target when new empires emerged. Diyarbakır's desert outpost character has been preserved in the black stone alleyways and fortified architecture of the old city, but modernization has made considerable inroads. Parts of the wall have been knocked down, and most of the main streets are lined with cement block buildings.

The extant walls are largely the work of the Seljuks, as is the city's **Ulu Camii** (Great Mosque). A Byzantine cloister surrounds the courtyard here, while the mosque itself is built in the rectangular Syrian style. The minaret also is square, unlike the standard round Ottoman minarets. Across Gazi Cad. is an Ottoman caravanserai, **Hasan Paşa Hanı,** now full of carpet shops. In the general area behind

Ulu Camii is the **bazaar;** farther along you'll find the **Ziya Gökalp Museum.** Ziya Gökalp popularized the Pan-Turkish movement, which sought to unify all the Turkish-language speaking tribes in Asia. This included a vast area encompassing all the Soviet Muslim republics of today and part of Iran, in addition to modern Turkey. Though popular from the turn of the century on, Pan-Turkism was abandoned by Atatürk in an effort to mend relations with the Soviet Union. The museum occupies the house where Gökalp was born and contains examples of Turkish crafts. (Open Tues.-Sun. 8am-noon and 1:30-5pm. Admission 50¢.)

In the southwest part of the city is the Byzantine **Meryem Ana Kilisesi** (Church of the Virgin Mary), rebuilt several times since the fourth century. The writing on the walls and on some of the paintings is Aramaic, the language that Jesus spoke. Aramaic is now only heard in the liturgy of the Syriac Christian Church and in certain Jewish prayers. The man who lives beside the church raises silkworms; you may see their pods in storage on a series of shelves. Southwest of here is a good section of the city wall to climb and walk along. At the other end of the city, close to the Bitlis Gate, is the ancient Byzantine **citadel,** beside which flows the Tigris River. The **archeological museum** is scheduled to reopen in 1989.

The main street, **Izzet Paşa Caddesi,** runs from Bitlis Gate in the east to Mardin Gate in the south. It intersects the road in from the bus station and Urfa Gate at the site of the huge Ulu Camii. Nearby is Gazi Caddesi, where you will find a **post office** and several **banks.** The **bus station** is 3km northwest of town; to Ankara (5 per day, 9 hr., $6), Istanbul (3 per day, 17 hr., $11), Urfa (6 per day, 3 hr., $2), Malatya (5 per day, 4 hr., $3), Van (4 per day, 8 hr., $6), Adana, and Konya. *Dolmuş* also leave for Mardin. A *dolmuş* will take you into town or stop along the way near the **tourist office** on Lise Cad. (tel. 121 73), where you can pick up a map and tourist brochure, both of which will prove invaluable when making your way through this confusing city. (Open daily 8am-noon and 1:30-5:30pm.) The **THY office** (tel. 101 01 or 123 14) is at 1 Paşa Cad., below Demir Otel. There is a daily flight to Ankara (1 hr., $45), connecting to Istanbul (total 4 hr., $57). For an overnight stay, try the **Mehmetoğlu Oteli** (tel. 128 51), centrally located across Atatürk's monument at Dağ Kapı, the northern gate to the city. Don't worry about the lack of hot water, since 40°C would be considered cool in August. (Singles $2, with bath $2.50. Doubles $4, with bath $5.) The **Hotel Şendi,** at Gazi Cad. and Manan Sok. (tel. 231 05), has an air-conditioned lobby and decent rooms. (Doubles $4.) You might be able to sleep on the roof for much less. The spicy food at the restaurants north on Kıbrıs Cad. might blow your sandals off. South on Gazi Cad. at the *dolmuş* station is **Özgür Lokantası.** (Chicken and herbal rice dish 90¢.) Diyarbakır's **telephone code** is 831.

## Near Diyarbakır

You can take an interesting daytrip from Diyarbakır to **Deyrulzafaran Monastery** via Mardin, a desert city 100km to the south. This monastery housed the Syrian patriarch from the fourth century until 1922, when headquarters were moved to Damascus. Now only one monk and a handful of students reside here. The caretaker, who speaks Turkish and Aramaic, will greet you at the gate and guide you through the chapel and a few other rooms. Ask to listen to a service or a lesson so that you can hear Aramaic spoken. When you depart, show your appreciation by saying *towdee* (Aramaic for "thank you"). *Dolmuş* to Mardin depart regularly from Diyarbakır's bus terminal and from the *dolmuş* station on Gazi Cad. ($1.) From Mardin, you can take a taxi 8km to the monastery ($4 round-trip). The last bus to Diyarbakır leaves at 7:30pm. There are a few cheap accommodations in Mardin if you get stuck.

# Lake Van

The waters of Lake Van change shades constantly, spanning the blue-green spectrum and transfixing all who view it. Trapped by volcanic mountains, the lake sits 1720m above sea level, surrounded by thickly cultivated fields, cow herds, and narrow gravel beaches. Reflected in Van's water is the peak of Mount Süphan (4058m), on the northern shore. Camping on the shore allows you to enjoy cool breezes and Van's strange sudsy water—its high sodium carbonate content allows you to wash your clothes in it without soap. As the lake is six times saltier than the Mediterranean and twelve times saltier than the Black Sea, bathers will have little choice but to float.

An especially attractive Armenian church is on the tiny island of **Akdamar,** 40km west of Van off the south coast of the lake. The **Church of the Holy Cross,** built in the tenth century, displays finely sculpted friezes. (Admission $1.) The island itself is perfect for swimming. A boat runs there for $1 round-trip; get there in the morning. Admission to the church is $1. Any bus heading to Van from the west will pass by the island. From Van, you can take a *dolmuş.*

The city of **Van** lies 5km away from the water. The main avenue in Van, **Cumhuriyet Caddesi,** runs north-south. Two other avenues, **Iskele Caddesi** and **Kâzım Karabekir Caddesi** cut Cumhuriyet Cad. perpendicularly on the northern and southern sides of the city, respectively.

From the intersection of Cumhuriyet Cad. and Iskele Cad., you can take a *dolmuş* 4km to the stunning **citadel** and **ancient city.** On the west side of the castle, toward the water, there's a pleasant teahouse with ice cold beer submerged in a stream that runs under the canopy. The owner may let you camp for free nearby. From here you can climb to the castle, which was originally Urartian and later rebuilt by the Seljuks and Ottomans. Take one of several paths that run the length of the castle. The Urartians came from the northeastern steppes to fill the vacuum left by the declining Hittite Empire. Reaching their peak between 900 and 700 B.C.E., they then suffered numerous defeats at the hands of the Assyrians, and finally fell to the Scythians in the sixth century B.C.E. The most extensive collection of Urartian artifacts rests in the museum in Ankara. The small **archeological museum** in Van houses an interesting array of artifacts. (Open daily 8am-noon and 1:30-5:30pm. Admission $1.) The Urartians were conquered by the Armenians, who made Van the capital of one of their several kingdoms. There are still a good number of Armenian buildings, particularly the decorated churches in the area between Van and Kars. The citadel casts its southern shadow over the old city of Van, of which only two mosques and a bath survived World War I.

The attentive **tourist office** (tel. 136 75) is at the south end of the main drag by the traffic circle. (Open in summer daily 8am-noon and 1:30-6:30pm; in off-season 8am-noon and 1:30-5:30pm.) The **PTT** is centrally situated on Cumhuriyet Cad. (Open 24 hours). Van's **telephone code** is 061.

**Tuşba Travel Agency,** on Posta Sokak, off Kâzım Karabekir Cad., offers tours of the area; they're not cheap, but are comprehensive. The simple Akdamar tour costs $4, boat and museum ticket included. For $11, they take you to Hoşap Castle, Citadel of Çavuştepe, Akdamar Island, and Van Castle. A 14-hour tour visits Erciç, Adilcevaz, Ahlat, and Mt. Nemrut ($21). You can also rent a car ($30-40 per day, insurance extra) or a horse ($7 per hr., oats extra).

The **bus station** is 5km outside of town; most companies offer free transportation to and from the city center. Buses run to Diyarbakır (4 per day, 8 hr., $6), Erzurum (4 per day, 7 hr., $5), Ankara via Malatya (3 per day, 18 hr., $12), Istanbul (2 per day, 24 hr., $17), Hakkâri, and Ağrı. There are also buses to Doğubeyazıt via Galdiran. Service is irregular, so ask at the tourist office.

The **tourist office** (tel. 112 41) is across from the tourist office on Cumhuriyet Cad. There are four flights to Ankara per week (1½ hr., $45), with connections to Istanbul ($60) and Izmir ($60). **Ferries** shuttle between Van and Tatvan. Ask for the schedule at the tourist office.

Two blocks west of the PTT, **Kent Oteli** (tel. 125 19) offers clean rooms and hot water on tap. Ask for a room on the third or fourth floor; toilets on the lower floors are visited en masse. (Singles $5.80, with bath $8.10. Doubles $8.50, with bath $10.50.) **Otel Berkardes**, 154 Cumhuriyet Cad. (tel. 111 16), is similar in quality to the Kent, but more conveniently located. (Singles with shower $7. Doubles with shower $9.) There are clean rooms at the **Hotel Aslan**, Sebzehali Civarı (tel. 124 69), and hot water in the evening. (Singles $3.50. Doubles $5.50.) The restaurant at the boat launch for Akdamar will let you camp on their grounds for $1. Six kilometers east (37km west of the city of Van) is the more serene **Cafer Camping**, with a restaurant. ($2.50 per tent. No showers.) You might just want to freelance camp.

### Near Van

Around **Tatvan**, a nondescript spot at the western end of the lake, only two things are worth seeing: the ruins of **Ahlat**, and the crater lake of **Nemrut Gölü**. Ahlat, 38km north of Tatvan, was first populated by the Armenians, and then by a succession of groups until it was abandoned under Ottoman rule 200 years ago. Today, the ghost town on the lakeshore contains ornately carved Seljuk and Ottoman **tombs**. Just to the north of Tatvan, another **Nemrut Dağı** rises 3000m into the sky, this one without any Commagene statues, but with a crater lake at 2400m. The crater is almost 7km in diameter, its north shore formed by stupendous cliffs hundreds of meters high. The view of the Lake Van from the top is magnificent, and you can camp inside the crater by the lake. There is no public transportation, so you must either take a taxi ($4, negotiable) or climb on foot (14km). *Dolmuş* run from Tatvan to the villages of Ahlat and Adilcevaz, where you can get off at Ahlat.

Two hundred kilometers south of Van lies **Hakkâri**. The town itself serves a large military base and is bland, but the bus ride through mountain passes makes the journey worthwhile. Although officials refuse to acknowledge it, this mountain area is home of the Kurdish insurgency, which is comprised of 500-1000 guerillas who clash periodically with Turkish soldiers stationed here. Don't camp or hike around outside a settlement. If you stay in one of Hakkâri's two hotels, you shouldn't have any problems. If you have time, stop off at the village of **Güzelsu**, dominated by the seventeenth-century Ottoman castle of **Hoşap**, which rests on a crag overlooking a river.

# Ağri, Mount Ararat, and Doğubeyazit

If you can't catch one of the few buses that go directly to Doğubeyazıt or if you are coming from Erzurum, you must go through Ağrı. Buses run from Ağrı to Kars, Van, and Erzurum, as well as to Doğubeyazıt. Don't buy a direct ticket from or to Doğubeyazıt from anywhere but Ağrı—though you may save a few cents, you will also have to wait in Ağrı for up to four hours for a connection.

Little **Doğubeyazıt**, which sits at the foot of Ağrı Dağı (Mt. Ararat), wouldn't normally be worthy of attention, but the view and the partially ruined palace of **Ishak Paşa** make it popular among tourists. The palace was built by an eccentric Ottoman feudal lord in the late eighteenth century in what must be the only spot within 100km from which you can't see Mt. Ararat. Check out the harem and the mosque, and note the fine stone carving on the portals. The Urartian fortress across the ravine offers an overpowering view. The palace is a 5-kilometer trek uphill from town, or you can take a *dolmuş*, which runs until noon (20¢). (Palace open Tues.-Sun. 8am-5pm. Admission $1.) Mehmet, the man at the ticket booth, will let you camp near the palace for 50¢.

**Mount Ararat** is 500m taller than Mt. Blanc, and the net height from the plain to the summit is as great as you'll find anywhere outside of the Himalayas. The mountain is also the legendary resting place of Noah's Ark, although none of the expeditions up the slopes has found any evidence of the ark. If you fancy climbing Mt. Ararat, you first need permission from the authorities in Ankara. The best way to get a permit is to contact the Turkish embassy in your home country. Otherwise, send a copy of your passport to İç İşleri Bakanlığı (Ministry of Internal Affairs) in Ankara, and specify the dates you want to climb. Approval theoretically takes two months, but people sometimes wait up to a year. An escort is mandatory. **Trek Travel Agency,** 53 Emniyet Cad. (tel. (0278) 19 81), will hire an escort for you ($40 per day for the 4-day trip); one escort can take a group of up to 10. If you are not an experienced climber, you should consider the agency's more elaborate tours, which include food, horses, tents, an escort, a guide, *dolmuş,* and accommodations in town ($345). You don't have to be an experienced climber to conquer the legendary mountain, but you must be in good shape. Write to Trek Travel, Aydede Cad. 10, Taksim, Istanbul, 80090 Turkey (tel. 155 16 24) for more information. They will also procure your permit.

In Doğubeyazıt, the **Hotel Erzurum** (tel. 17 08), near the end of town on the road to the palace, has clean, comfortable rooms and exceptionally friendly management. (Singles $5. Doubles $8.) Well-kept **Tahran Oteli** (tel. 22 23), is close to the restaurants. (Singles $3.50. Doubles $7.) Along the main street, 50m toward town from the Erzurum Otel, **Dumlupınar Lokantası** serves a variety of freshly prepared meals (80¢). There is a **PTT** (open daily 7am-11pm) and a few banks in town. Doğubeyazıt's **telephone code** is 0278.

# Kars and Ani

Many a traveler has felt dislocated in Kars, an Eastern Anatolian town guarded by Western Anatolian soldiers amidst Russian architecture. The main reason for visiting Kars is to see the medieval Armenian capital of **Ani,** 45km away. Due to its proximity to the Soviet border, you must get permission to visit Ani from the Kars **tourist office** (tel. 23 00) off Faik Bey Cad., just after the Bağ Kur sign. (Open in summer daily 8am-5:30pm; in off-season when they feel like it.) You must then take your permit to the police station, just opposite as you reach Faik Bey Cad., for final approval. In the morning, you might find enough people in front of the tourist office to hire a minibus ($30) or taxi ($16) that will take you to Ani, wait there for two hours, and bring you back to Kars. Or hitch a ride with one of the cars from Kars. A municipal bus runs to the site at 6:30am, returning from Ani at 5pm; other trips between these hours are possible but unpredictable ($25). If you find you have extra time in Kars, visit the beautiful **Fethiye Camii,** once an Armenian church. There is also a small **museum.** Note the intricately carved church doors, and the striking color harmony on the *kilimler* (rugs) and *heybeler* (saddlebags). (Open Tues.-Sun. 8:30am-12:30pm and 1:30-5:30pm. Admission 50¢. The **Ottoman citadel** that dominates the city is part of a military compound but opens to the public on Sundays and Thursdays until 5pm. (Free.) An **Ottoman bridge, baths,** and a tenth-century **Armenian church** are below the citadel. The **Russian buildings** remaining from the Russian occupation of 1878-1920 line Ordu Cad.

Kars is connected to Trabzon, Ankara, Samsun, Istanbul, Izmir, Diyarbakır, and Konya by way of Erzurum (6 per day, 5 hr., $35). Buses also run from Ağrı and Doğubeyazıt via Ağrı or the more scenic road through Iğdır. The scenic nine-hour odyssey from Kars to Hopa, on the Black Sea coast, finishes up at Artvin (4 per day, $6).

If your lungs can stand the dust and you want to stay in Kars, brace yourself. The **Yılmaz Oteli** (tel. 1074), 1 block south of the bus station, might be the best hotel around, but that's not saying a whole lot. (Singles with bath $6. Doubles with bath $9.) The more dismal **Temel Palas Oteli** (tel. 13 76), 1 block west of the bus station, is slightly cheaper. (Singles with bath $5.50. Doubles with bath $8.50.) If you can stand their toilets, try the **Hotel Nur Saray** (tel. 13 64; singles $3; doubles $4.50). The **Hayat Oteli** (tel. 35 86), is surely not the Hyatt. ($2 per person.) Both are on Faik Bey Cad.

For your dining pleasure, the **Grand Manolya,** 42 Atatürk Cad., has a luxurious look, is clean and serves delicious food at reasonable prices (70-90¢). It also has a pastry shop. You'll be presented with cloth napkins at **Modern Şehir Lokantası,** 80 Faik Bey Cad., where the food is good, though slightly more expensive than at *kebap* places. The **Çobanoğlu Kahvesi,** near the Hotel Temel on Kerim Paşa Cad., often features improvisational *âşık* (Turkish string instrument) players; you can sit and listen from 8:30pm to 11:30pm (20¢). The **PTT,** on Ordu Cad., is open 24 hours. Kars' **telephone code** is 0211. A great alternative to any hotel in Kars is the **Hotel Sartur** (tel. (0229) 13 32) in **Sarıkamış,** 60km from Kars on the road to Erzurum. The hotel offers clean, comfortable rooms facing the famous pine forest of Sarıkamış, a working machine, and fine food. All buses going to or coming from Erzurum visit Sarıkamış. Hike 1½km up the hill or take a taxi ($1) to reach the hotel. (Singles with bath $7.50. Doubles with bath $10. Breakfast 80¢.)

The Armenians have maintained their identity here since the seventh century B.C.E., when they replaced the Urartians at Lake Van. When the Romans reached their borders, the Armenian king launched an attack because the foreigners called him the "king" instead of the "king of kings." Needless to say, his forces were decimated. The Armenians converted to Christianity in 300 C.E., 20 years before the Romans. Although considered heretics by other Christians, the Armenians contributed to Byzantine art and architecture, especially during their artistic renaissance in the tenth and eleventh centuries, when the surviving remains of Ani were built. Later, the Armenian Empire fragmented into several kingdoms, which were easy prey for the Seljuk invaders. Twice in this century, the Armenians have taken up arms against the Turks to win their independence, both times with Russian assistance. But the Armenians were a minority in their homeland, and both efforts were quelled by Turkish forces.

The standing Armenian ruins at Ani are a sad reminder of the Armenians' fate. The site is unexcavated; most buildings still stand from the tenth and eleventh centuries. Impressive double walls span the western side of the city, opening up only at the thirteenth-century double gate of **Alp Arslan Kapısı. St. Gregory Church,** on the north side of the ruins, houses the finest frescoes of the area. Note the geometric precision of the figures, which contrasts with the rougher figures of Byzantine art. The tenth-century **Cathedral of Ani** has lost its dome, but note the high ceiling, blind arches, and elegant pillars. Below the cathedral, the **mosque** has a superb view of the inaccessible **Young Girls' Convent.** Kars Cay, the river, also visible from the mosque, marks the Turkish-Soviet border. The top of the minaret offers a panorama of Ani, but don't forget that you are in no man's land, where cameras staring or pointing toward the border are prohibited. Next you come to **Polatoğlu Church.** Its height and conical dome that rests on a drum exemplifies a unique feature of Armenian architecture. Built in 1001 in honor of St. Gregory, **Church of Gagik** represents a rare example of centrally-planned design. (Open daily 8:30am-5:30pm. Admission $2.)

# *Black Sea Coast*

Browsing through the tourist propaganda, you would think that Turkey had only two coasts, the Aegean and the Mediterranean. However, Turkey's longest and least visited coast skirts the Black Sea. Here you'll find industrial cities and fishing villages, which you'll share only with creeping ivy and a few fishing boats pulled up on shore. Cool breezes from Russia provide relief from the summer heat. Heavy rainfall nourishes this region's abundant forests and thickly cultivated farmland, especially east of Trabzon.

The isolation fostered by adjacent mountain ranges inhibited this coast's impact on the ancient world. Trading posts such as Sinop, Trabzon, and Amisus (now Samsun) did, however, become commercial cities, first exporting local products and then profiting from the silk route trade when Arab invasions blocked the southern passage. Excellent Byzantine structures remain around Trabzon. Elsewhere, you'll see an occasional Byzantine castle and several fine Seljuk and Ottoman mosques.

A highway follows the coastline so closely that you can't enjoy much privacy or quiet on most of the beaches. Hitching is easy, though. Unfortunately, most fishing villages have no accommodations since they see few visitors. If you're not prepared to camp, you'll have to sleep in the larger port towns and explore the villages by day. Campgrounds are spaced about every 50km. Freelance camping is easy but you may have to search a while to find an uncultivated piece of turf.

# Amasya

Set like a gem surrounded by mountains and castles, Amasya is often considered part of the Black Sea region, even though it's not on the coast. This is partly due to its similar geography, but mainly because Amasya has been tied historically to the Black Sea. Amasya was the first capital of the Pontus kingdom that broke away from the Seleucids in the third century B.C.E. The Pontic king, Mithradates the Great, conquered most of Asia Minor from his Black Sea base, and might have become another Alexander had his conquests not coincided with the rise of Rome. A generation later, Julius Caesar finished off the kingdom with his famous declaration "I came, I saw, I conquered."

Most buses will drop you off in town, since the **bus station** is 3km away. In a courtyard on the river, the spacious **Konfor Palas Oteli** (tel. 12 60) rents clean rooms with hot water. (Singles $2. Doubles $3.) The **Hotel Aydın**, 86 Mustafa Kemal Cad. (tel. (3781) 24 63), is cheap at $1 per person, but you have to pour water over your head for a shower. **Çiçek Lokantası,** in the center of town by the Atatürk statue, serves cheap Turkish dishes in a friendly atmosphere. Amasya's **telephone code** is 3781.

The bridge across the river traverses a century. The old town on the other side is filled with cobblestone streets and buttressed overhangs. The restored **Hazeranlar Konağı,** now a museum, gives you a look at the furnishings of an Ottoman house. (Open Tues.-Sun. 8:30am-noon and 1:30-6pm. Admission 25¢.) Also ascend to the **castle** and **rock tombs.** Built for early Pontic kings, the tombs reach up to 8m in height and were originally ornamented with marble facades. If you return to Mustafa Kemal Cad. and take a right, you'll first pass **Beyazıt II Mosque,** a double-domed fifteenth-century Ottoman mosque with stained glass windows and geometric masonwork. Farther along is the small **archeological museum.** (Open Tues.-Sun. 8:30am-noon and 12:30-6pm.) In a building in the courtyard, you'll find some poorly preserved mummies from medieval times. Continue farther along Mustafa Kemal Cad. to the **Gök Medrese,** a Seljuk religious school with a huge portal and some coffins.

# Sinop

Sinop occupies a strange position on the isthmus of a bulb-shaped peninsula. This spot endowed the city with two natural harbors, an asset that made it the largest ancient trade center on the Black Sea. Sinop was also the home of Diogenes the Cynic, a Hellenistic philosopher/historian who lived the ascetic life of a *Let's Go* traveler. When Alexander the Great asked him if he desired anything, Diogenes answered that he only wished the sovereign would stand out of his light. Sinop's importance as a port city has declined since ancient times; it now supports an American military base and a small tourist industry. If you're on your way to or from eastern Turkey, you might stop by for a cup of çay and a view from its medieval walls.

Sinop is connected directly with Istanbul; from the east or south you usually must change buses in Samsun. From the **bus station,** head into town along Cumhuriyet Cad. and take a left at the large intersection onto Atatürk Cad. At the end you'll

512     **Turkey**

see the **tourist office** (tel. 19 96) on the right. (Open Mon.-Fri. 9am-5:30pm.) From
here, follow the other side of the castle wall, turn left, and then right onto Orta
Yol, a few blocks later. On the right you'll see the clean but otherwise nondescript
**Karahan Oteli.** ($1 per person.) Fifty meters into town from the bus station is **Hotel
Gülpalas** (tel. 17 37; doubles $3.50; hot showers included). Sinop also has **camping**
facilities on the southern shore, 2km away on both sides of the city. Sinop's **telephone code** is 3761.

Near the tourist office you can ascend the 3-meter thick walls of the Seljuk **castle**
to sense the layout of the city. The **archeological museum** is uphill on Atatürk Cad.
and to the right. (Open daily 8am-noon and 1:30-5:30pm. Admission $4.50.) The
courtyard full of *stelae* and mosaics is more interesting than the museum itself. Here
also is the **Temple of Serapis.** Originating in Sinop, Serapis emerged as one of the
most popular gods of the Hellenistic period. He became an amalgamation of Egyptian and Greek gods that appealed to the recently integrated Mediterranean world.
The overgrown **Balatlar Church** is a thirteenth-century religious compound with
a few surviving frescoes. From the upper end of Atatürk Cad., make a sharp right
turn, and follow the street beside the taxi stand for ¾km. On the way from the
bus station into town, you'll see the Seljuk **Alaadin Camii,** built in the Syrian style
with several domes.

# From Sinop to Trabzon

The road east of Sinop yields nothing interesting until sandy beaches start appear-
ing around Bafra, 100km away. Next you'll pass through the large port city of **Samsun,** a great opportunity to change buses. Buses run to Ankara (6 per day, 8 hr.,
$6), Istanbul (4 per day, 14 hr., $10), Trabzon, Rize, Hopa, Amasya, Sivan, Tokat,
Kayseri, and Adana. Another 100km east is **Ünye,** which has the comfortable
**Çamlile Motel** (tel. (3731) 13 33), right on the beach, 4km west of town. (Singles
with bath $5. Doubles with bath $7. Triples with bath and kitchen $11.) One kilome-
ter further west lies the friendly **Europa Camping** (tel. (3731) 44 47), with a small
beach and restaurant. ($1 per person.)

Between Fatsa and Ordu, black rock cliffs plunge into green water interspersed
with the pleasant villages of **Bolaman, Yazılköy,** and **Caka.** Past Ordu until Tire-
bolu, the coastline reverts back to sand. Twenty-six kilometers west of Trabzon lies
the fishing village of **Mersin. Mersin Turistik Tesisleri** might let you camp for free
near their private beach. Expect to stay up late though, since they often play blaring
live music.

# Trabzon

Trabzon, once exotic Trebizond, has long been the center of culture on the Black
Sea Coast. Though important in the Greek and Roman periods, Trebizond gained
distinction as a capital city when Alexis Comneni fled here after the crusaders
sacked Constantinople in 1204. The dynasty that he founded became the longest
in Greek history; its rulers lived in lavish Byzantine style. The kingdom held out
against the Turks until 1461, even longer than Constantinople, postponing its demise by diplomatically marrying off its daughters, reputedly the most beautiful
women in the world.

Trabzon is now an industrial city of 700,000, but it still retains some older sections
and fantastic historical sights from the Byzantine era. Unfortunately, the great palace was slowly quarried away over the last few centuries. When a Russian archeologist begged the Ottoman governor to save the remains, the governor replied that
he saw no reason to spare the dwelling of this Comneni person who apparently paid
no taxes to the Empire.

Trabzon is a great place to start or end a tour of eastern Turkey. **Buses** run to
Ankara (3 per day, 12 hr., $9), Samsun (3 per day, 6 hr., $4), Istanbul (6 per day,

20 hr., $13), and Hopa (10 per day, 3 hr., $2.50). There is also daily service to Mersin (20 hr., $14), Adana (16 hr., $14), Kayseri (12 hr., $11), Zonguldak (17 hr., $11), and Kars (12 hr., $9). **Turkish Airlines** flies daily to Ankara (1 hr., $45) and Istanbul (2-4 hr., $60). Buses leave from the THY office (tel. 134 46) at Kemerkaya Mahallesi to the airport one and a half hour before departures. There's also a **Turkish Maritime Lines** ship that hugs the Black Sea Coast from Istanbul to Trabzon. It leaves Istanbul every Monday at 5:30pm, stops at Samsun briefly Tuesday evening, and arrives at Trabzon at 8am Wednesday. The return voyage leaves Trabzon at 10pm the same day and arrives at Istanbul at 11am Friday. (Purchase tickets in advance. Armchairs $9. Rooms with bath $11-36.) From the bus station, you'll want to take the shared taxi-*dolmuş* (with a sign in the front window marked *merkez*) to the main square (15¢). Right at the main square is the extremely helpful **tourist office** (tel. 146 59; open in summer daily 8am-7:30pm; in off-season 8am-5:30pm). Trabzon's **telephone code** is 031.

From the tourist office, you'll find some cheap hotels up a little alley to the east, and on Taksim Meydanı, the main square. The small **Benli Palas Oteli** (tel. 117 50), at Iskenderpaşa Mahallesi, has caring management and clean rooms. (Singles $2.50. Doubles $4.) The rooms at **Derya Oteli,** on Taksim Meydanı (tel. 135 05), are comfortable, and there is a washing machine. (Singles $2. Doubles $3.) You can lounge in the tea garden at the **Erzurum Oteli** (tel. 113 62), at Iskenderpaşa Mahallesi. (Singles $2. Doubles $3.50, with bath $5.) Two kilometers past Maçka on the road to Sumela Monastery is the **Coşandere Campground** (tel. (0431) 15 81). A stream flows nearby and you dine on fresh trout at the restaurant. ($2 per tent.) For *döner* and other *kebap* try **Kuğu Restaurant** or **Büryan Restaurant,** both on the square. ($1 a plate.) **Murat Balık ve Köfte,** on the lower end of the square, serves a fresh fish platter for only 90¢.

Near the tourist office, *dolmuş* leave for **Sumela Monastery,** about 55km away, one of Turkey's most spectacular sights ($3.50 round-trip). Maçka Belediyesi (Maçka municipality) operates a bus that leaves at 10pm from the Gömlekçi bus stop across the harbor and returns at 2pm. (1500dr round-trip.) You may instead want to hire a taxi, which will wait for you at the site ($18).

Established in 385 C.E., this cliffside monastery reached its zenith in the late Middle Ages, when it comprised 72 rooms and an immense library. Behind the four-story facade, little remains except the frescoed main chapel. (Admission to park 20¢.) Monastery open daily 8am-6pm. Admission $1.)

Indulge yourself with more Byzantine frescoes at the thirteenth-century **Aya Sofia church,** now a museum. (Open daily 8am-5:30pm. Admission 100TL.) From the lower end of the square, take a *dolmuş* marked *Ayasofia.* Within the walls of the old city is the **Fatih Camii,** once the main basilica of Trebizond. Although it is covered with plaster, you can still see the basilica's layout and a few geometric mosaics.

The oldest extant Christian structure in Trabzon is the tiny seventh-century **St. Anne Church.** Its doorway, though locked, lies beneath a worn Roman relief. Head west from the square on K. Maraş Cad.—it's 3 blocks beyond the main post office. At the top of the hill behind the town is one of Atatürk's villas. Though he stayed here only two nights in his life, the villa is full of photographs and paintings of Atatürk, and attracts many visitors. If you have an extra half-day, you might visit the **Kaymaklı Monastery,** which is in good condition but not as spectacular as Sumela. Inquire at the tourist office for directions.

# East of Trabzon

This segment of coast is the Shangri-La of Turkey. Clouds blanket the cliffs that follow the shoreline, the air hangs moist, and vegetation sprouts from everything. Campers will have a hard time finding an uncultivated spot; the best places to look are along the beach by the highway or along riverbanks. Many locals spend their summers on plateaus and pastureland called *yayla,* also ideal for camping. On the highway, you may pass signs pointing down dirt roads to small villages. Hiking in this area is enjoyable and scenic. (*Dolmuş* also run occasionally.) Your explorations will be rewarded by glimpses of wooden and brick houses and local dress; note in particular the women's red striped scarves that gather at the shoulders.

Just 30km east of Trabzon is the fishing village of **Kalecik,** with a rock overhang on the opposite side of a Byzantine castle where you can camp. Seven kilometers farther east, you can descend the steep hillside to a beach with showers and changing rooms. Look for the sign that reads **"aile plaj."** (Admission 100TL.) Next, you'll pass the large towns of **Of** and **Sürmene;** both have accommodations. One kilometer west of Of is another Byzantine castle, with an adjacent grassy spot suitable for camping. Farther along, **Rize** is the center of the immense Turkish tea industry. It's large like Trabzon, but without any historical sites. Nearby Gayeli and Ardeşen are both dull, but 29km inland from Ardeşen is Ayder, famous for its hot springs. From Ayder you can hike towards **Mt. Kaçkar** (3937m). Take a *dolmus* from Pazar via Camhemçin to **Ayder** (2½ hr., $2). There, the **Hotel Saray** offers simple, clean rooms. (Singles $3. Doubles $4.50.) The **Ayder Hilton.** It has clean rooms and toilets. ($1.50-2 per person. Upper floors less damp.) The hotels don't have showers since they assume that you will be taking a bath at the **hot springs.** (Open 7am-10pm; 9am-5pm for women. Admission 35¢.) Have *şiş-kebap* or *pirzola* (lamb-chops, $1) at the restaurant below Hotel Saray. Don't miss the *Ayder muhlama,* a *fondue* your arteries will love, with the local cheese, butter, and eggs.

The highway continues along the coast for about 60km, finally turning inland at **Hopa.** Near Hopa's bus station is the not-too-clean **Hotel Saray** (tel. (0571) 12 99; $1.50 per person; hot showers included). Buses stop here on the way to and from Kars ($5). From Hopa, you can take a *dolmuş* to **Kemal Paşa,** a small town whose empty gravel beach, tea factory, and mysterious Byzantine church see few visitors. Thirty kilometers northeast from Hopa is the Soviet border. The village of **Sarp** was cut in two when the border was drawn. Relatives can see each other only by special permission, but they have to use the gate east of Kars. Soviet and Turkish authorities have been negotiating to open the Sarp gate for years, to no avail. Presently, you can visit the village, but you have to get a permit from the military station in Hopa and take a taxi to the site ($12). Camping is strictly forbidden. When the gate is opened, perhaps by the spring of 1989, you will be able to continue your trip into the Soviet Union.

# *Artvin*

On the slopes of a moutain south of Hopa, Artvin serves as a base whence you can explore the area's Georgian churches. As all buses continue to Kars or Hopa, they can leave you at the foot of the city by the fifteenth-century castle. Some bus companies operate shuttles to the city, but otherwise you'll have to wait for the bus run by the municipality for the 5-kilometer haul up the hill (15¢). The city center radiates around the statue of Atatürk in front of the *Vilâyet* (city hall).

One block down the hill, **Kültür Palas** offers clean bathrooms and an excellent view of the city and surrounding mountains. (Singles $2. Doubles $3.) The **Kaçkal Oteli** (tel. 33 97), right below the *Vilâyet* has similar quality, hot water, and a washing machine. (Singles $2. Doubles $3.50.) Whether or not you stay at the expensive **Hotel Karahan** (tel. 18 00), down the avenue; it offers some of the best food in eastern Turkey (about $1 per plate). Breakfast here is unbeatable, with unlimited honey, jam, butter, and fresh bread. (Single with bath $15. Doubles with bath $20.) The hotel's owner, Yavuz Karahan, knows the area well and has prepared a pamphlet that explains how to get to various churches scattered around Artvin. Unfortunately, few are easily accessible. To get to the **Church of Dolişhane,** you need to take the *dolmuş* to Çavçat, walk 2km from the junction, and hike about 3km to the village of Hamamlıköy.

Artvin is close to many *yayla* (plateaus) that are visited by the locals in summer or used as pastures. **Bilbilan yaylas,** known for its cold water springs, could be reached by taking a minibus-*dolmus* to Ardanuç (4-5 per day, 80¢) and from there to Bilbilan (irregular service). You can also hitch. **Kafkanör,** another plateau, is about 11km from Artvin. On the last weekend of June, you can witness the annual **Festival of Kafkanör.** Traditional dancers and other shows are staged, but the main events are the **bull fights.** Like camel wrestling in western Anatolia, bulls wrestle with each other. The owner of the winner is rewarded and honored.

**Buses** operated by Artvin Ekspres and As Turism, both at the city center, run to Hopa (6-8 per day, 2 hr., $1.50), Erzurum (5 per day, 4 hr., $4), and Kars (4 per day, 4 hr., $4), connecting to other cities. The **PTT** is also at the center. (Open daily 7am-11pm). Artvin's **telephone code** is 0581.

# INDEX